CLIFTON L. HALL, *George Peabody College for Teachers*

SAMUEL M. HOLTON, *University of North Carolina*

FREDERICK D. KERSHNER, *Teachers College, Columbia University*

WILLIAM W. SAVAGE, *University of South Carolina*

readings in

AMERICAN EDUCATION

William H. Lucio / Editor, *University of California, Los Angeles*

SCOTT, FORESMAN AND COMPANY *CHICAGO · ATLANTA · DALLAS · PALO ALTO · FAIR LAWN, N.J.*

SCOTT, FORESMAN PROFESSIONAL EDUCATION SERIES

L. C. Catalog Card #63-14553

Copyright © 1963 by Scott, Foresman and Company
Printed in the United States of America

to the reader

The broad problems of education and the specific problems of schooling in the United States have long concerned professional educators, lay persons, and private and public agencies. Because the schools of the United States have been so closely allied to the national interests, it is not surprising that when individuals and groups in our society have been dissatisfied with the accomplishments of schooling they have freely criticized educational programs and practices and have demanded change. At times in our national history the schools have been supported vigorously in particular efforts, but at other times they have been given inadequate moral or financial support. In general, however, open dialogs in a free society are salutary; many of the critical assessments of American education have resulted in worth-while changes in school practices.

There is evidence that the widespread examination of the process of education by persons at all levels of our society has been a unifying and beneficial force, committing the majority of citizens to invest in a system of education which has had the general aim of developing citizens of intellectual and social competence. The degree to which this aim has or has not been met has always been the subject of vigorous discussion: the dimensions of this discussion provide the subject matter of this book.

Readings in American Education presents a comprehensive overview of the historical and contemporary forces affecting the development of education in the United States. It does this by means of 161 readings, carefully selected and systematically arranged to illustrate (a) the effects of social, political, economic, and other forces on education in the United States; (b) the ways in which the school systems have responded to these forces; (c) the kinds of educational aims and practices which have been proposed by persons within and without the schools; and (d) the effects of new knowledge on the educational process. The readings express the views of professional educa-

tors, of scholars in various disciplines, and of lay citizens who have given particular attention to the problems of education.

This book represents a consensus of judgment among its authors, who worked together in planning its organization and cooperatively selected appropriate readings on the basis of their own classroom experience. Thus the readings have demonstrated their effectiveness in illustrating significant ideas and events in American education. The headnotes which introduce major topics and individual readings provide a background for the various educational ideas expressed and thus help the reader interpret the content with greater understanding. No particular philosophies, psychologies of education, or educational theories are urged upon the reader.

Since the educational process is a common concern of all segments of our society, the contents of this book should have wide applicability, although prospective teachers, of course, constitute the audience to which it is primarily addressed. The book may be used profitably in several ways: (a) as a basic readings text for introductory courses in the study of education—one which may be read straight through or dipped into as supplemental reading; (b) as a substantive source for advanced students, particularly those at the graduate level, who are concerned with examining important views, trends, and practices in education; (c) as a reference for experienced administrators, supervisors, teachers, and other persons who may wish to gain perspective for interpreting present trends and planning desirable action.

A textbook cannot "teach," but it may serve to focus thought on ideas, propositions, or theories in some systematic fashion. The reader, if he is to learn from *Readings in American Education*, must actively endeavor to determine meaning, interpret data, draw implications, develop hypotheses, and make appropriate predictions.

W. H. L.

contents

In the introductory headnotes, reference numbers to bibliographical notes are given in parentheses; refer to page 564 for the listing. In the readings, footnotes are employed for all references and explanatory notes, except for a few obvious exceptions.

PART ONE

THE PROCESS OF EDUCATION

The vocations usually regarded as professions are theology, law, medicine, and teaching, largely because they require knowledge of some department of learning or science. The first three are easily identifiable, since the prescribed courses of study are designed to lead to the specific function which the student will perform. Not so with the teacher. He may study many bodies of subject matter: English, mathematics, history, science, pedagogy—even law, medicine, and theology. He obtains his degree, but it may not be in education. Then he expects to teach—meaning *what?* Does the profession of education possess aims or purposes which are as clear cut, as sharply defined, as those of the professions of theology, law, and medicine? If it does, the aims are many times curiously difficult to explain.

For the beginning student of education this is very confusing. Since education is not strictly a content field but draws upon ancillary disciplines it has many aims, no one of which dominates as in the case of the other professions. This plurality of aims is one reason why educators emphasize aims, goals, ends, purposes, objectives, or targets. All these terms have the same meaning: namely, the direction which education should take and the help it can offer mankind.

A profession which does not know where it is going or whether it is really valuable to society is unlikely to be very effective or influential. Not to face the fundamental aims of education is dangerous; it may lead the teacher to confuse means with ends. For example, he may come to feel that high examination scores, well-equipped schools, popularity with students, or good attendance records are sufficient aims for the good teacher. If he is to avoid such errors, the neophyte must have a pretty clear idea of what he is trying to do *by means of* equipment, popularity, high achievement scores, and so on; that is, he must understand the *primary* aims of education.

The public has always displayed great interest in education. As Wendell Phillips put it, "Education is the only interest worthy of the deep controlling anxiety of thoughtful men." Others have identified it with democracy, or with the national destiny. On the other hand, the public often has also displayed some degree of suspicion and distrust for education, particularly in times of crises. Thomas Edison called it "repulsive to most children," and productive of "atrophy of the mental facilities"; Henry Adams said, without a trace of humor, "The chief wonder of education is that it does not ruin everybody concerned in it, teachers and taught." In a sense these are reactions against the uncertainty of the aims of schooling as well as reflections of the myth of the "practical man," the frontiersman, who could solve his simple problems of daily living without much formal education.

Such views reflect the observation by John Dewey that education is a constant compromise between school and society. By "school" he meant the professional schoolmen, the educational experts. By "society" he meant the laymen, the ordinary citizens, the parents of school children, the school-board members, all the educational amateurs who comprise the rest of the population. In America we do not surrender education to unrestricted professional control; we take the wishes of the amateur majority very seriously indeed. One view of the resultant interaction which has shaped American educational history has been presented by Theodore Roosevelt:

"Our progress in educational efficiency must come from two sources: from the great natural leader who happens to be an educator, and from the ordinary citizen who to common sense adds some power of vision, and who realizes the relation of school to society. In pedagogy as in every other walk of life great natural leaders are scarce. Therefore the ordinary citizen of vision and common sense must concern himself with the changing problems of the school, and must insist that pedantic tradition does not keep our schools from performing their full public service" (1).

The readings on the process of education have been chosen to present propositions and ideas concerning both school and society. Many have been written by professional educators, others are the work of lay persons, usually writing in a popular vein, in biographies and other types of general writing. The student needs to examine data from all of these sources if he is to grasp the true nature, the authentic flavor, of American education as it exists today.

This section of readings is divided into two parts. The first—"The Aims of Education" (Readings 1-25)—contains nine topics. Notice how wide the disagreement among intelligent people can be, and how few new arguments have appeared in recent times. Note also how certain aims appear special, narrow, and proximate, while others seem general, broad, and ultimate in nature. A mixture of aims is what each of us has, in practice, but we need to know exactly what the ingredients are that have gone into this mixture.

More than we commonly realize, educational aims will determine the shape of the curriculum, the classroom methods employed, and the quality of teachers themselves. The second part of this section—"The Methods of Education" (Readings 26-63)—deals with the means by which the proper aims of education can be realized. Once again one may see the peculiar relationship between school and society in the United States, and the mixture of simplicity and complexity which has gradually taken shape.

THE AIMS OF EDUCATION

Most societies throughout history have provided some kind of education for the young in order that they might better participate in the life of the group. Since the founding of America, socially conscious parents have felt a sense of responsibility to equip their children to live in a changing society. "My poor children, what will become of them?" asked the father of Hansel and Gretel in the old nursery tale. Leaving children in the woods to shift for themselves has never been a satisfactory solution. In primitive and unevenly developed societies parents have been primarily responsible for seeing that children learn the facts and customs of life. This type of apprenticeship training may have been adequate in certain societies, but the divergent and differential requirements of civilized states require more than a "life experience" type of education.

Why does the country need a system of schools and a corps of professionally expert teachers? Could not the whole matter of education still be handled in the home by parents with an infinite saving of public time and money? Aside from the fact that it sometimes seems imperative in present-day society for both parents to find regular employment, formal schooling always has been considered both a necessity and a blessing. Because of the complexity of civilized states, parental example and simple home prescriptions for behavior no longer suffice. History and modern civilization began with the invention of writing, necessary to the storing away of knowledge and experience for future use. Civilization itself, or at least the perpetuation of civilization, depends upon successfully transmitting to the younger generation accumulated knowledge. Instincts and physical traits are transmitted through genetic inheritance, but civilized knowledge is not. Education is cultural inheritance. Without it civilization would collapse in a few decades.

Total human knowledge cannot be passed on to every child. Each generation must select the facts, concepts, and generalizations appropriate to living in the present and foreseeable future. What new knowledge should be added and what old knowledge omitted in order that the younger generation be best prepared to meet the future successfully? E. L. Thorndike noted that the facts of education "are a selection from the changes that go on in the world." But who shall make the selection and on what grounds shall selection be made? In other words, what are the proper aims of education and who should make changes in the curriculum?

The most important aims of education have not changed much over the centuries, although the relative emphasis placed upon these aims has shifted constantly. Educational thinking in any society concerns itself to a greater or lesser extent with the place of the learner, the requirements of the society, and the nature of the subject matter. As one or another of these aspects assumes first place, different aims will be emphasized. The major aims of education, considered in this section, have received varying emphasis from the time of the Greeks to the present day—and we may be sure that the relative emphasis will continue to change in a fast-moving future. Therefore, teachers must be familiar with the sources, the validity, and the consequences of such aims in order to determine what to teach and how to teach it. A knowledge of the aims of education and their appropriate implementation in the classroom reduces dependence upon flashy nostrums or passing fads, many of which are proffered by persons or agencies remote from the school.

The aims of education

DEFINITION OF AIMS

One of the constants in our society has been the demand on the part of lay and professional persons and agencies for explanations of the purposes of education and schooling. Basically, this demand revolves around the need for definition. By constantly defining and redefining educational aims, by striving to grasp the fundamental issues, and by attempting systematically to determine purposes, teachers can accomplish their tasks and answer the inquiries of patrons more effectively.

In the three selections which follow, one by a contemporary philosopher of education, another by a contemporary general philosopher, and the third by a famous philosopher-sociologist of a century ago, three different approaches are presented. Since they are not in agreement, the reader must determine the assumptions, systems of thought, and consequences of these proposals. Their total effect should be to develop a better understanding of the sources for educational aims and the ways to formalize their statement and to determine implications for teaching. From the differing strands of purpose, each teacher should be able to weave a personal justification for his chosen vocation, although he may reconstruct his views many times before his teaching career is over. To memorize a scholarly description of the aims of education is not very useful unless the author's assumptions are assessed, his system is analyzed, and the consequences of the proposals are tested.

1

Harry S. Broudy

DEFINITION AND PHILOSOPHY OF EDUCATION

In his book *Building a Philosophy of Education* Professor Harry S. Broudy of the University of Illinois, a contemporary philosopher of education, introduces the problem of definitions ably and sympathetically. The meanings which he here gives for education are but samples of a number of definitions devised by others before him. Broudy follows his analysis of the constituents of learning with a description of three different kinds of education: (a) *milieu* or *automatic education* which we share with wild animals, (b) *informal unorganized education* through home instruction, books, television, and newspapers, and (c) *formal education* which takes place in organized schools. The section concludes with a definition which emphasizes the deliberate, organized, and systematic view of education.

Are definitions important? Professor Broudy answers both yes and no. Definitions are like spectacles through which one person may perceive a subject more clearly, but which for the eyes of another may be so colored and cloudy that the subject is distorted and seen better with the naked eye alone. The definer has lent you his tailor-made spectacles, so to speak; they helped him greatly, but may not fit your eyes at all. Broudy raises some critical questions: Is a teacher responsible for the failure of one of his pupils to learn? How can he know whether the continued ignorance of this student is due to teacher or learner? This kind of question should be kept in mind in examining further the aims of education and the methods which are the subject of the next section.

Education is something men argue about. Often it is praised; more often it is blamed for what happens to men and nations. The words "ought" and "must" pervade educational discussions giving them an imperative and urgent mood. One feels that something can and should be done—presumably something different from what is being done.

In such a situation there is always the disturbing possibility that the words being used in the argument may not denote (point to) the same activities nor convey the same meanings to the disputants. The word "education," in its long journey through human history, has acquired ballast and barnacles in the form of subordinate and partially allied ideas that now travel along with it as if they were an original part of the keel itself.

The most familiar meaning of the term "education" identifies it with the *process* of instruction and training that goes on in an institution of learning, in a school.

In the last fifty years another meaning has become familiar: that which refers to the art or science or both of carrying on instruction and training. There are departments of "education" at universities and teachers colleges devoted to the study and teaching of "education" in this sense of the word.

These two meanings are fairly clear. Not quite so precise is the meaning of education when it refers to the *result* of training and instruction. We speak of a man having had a good education or not having had a chance to acquire one. We then mean either that he has or has not attended a school or has not attended it long enough. It is not uncommon for us to remark that Peter So-and-So may have gone to college, but it did not give him much of an education; or we may marvel a little at Gregory This-and-That who has never seen the registration office of a college yet behaves like a man of culture and learning.

This little ambiguity, resulting from the fact that the processes of instruction may or may not leave permanent or desirable results, leads to an even cloudier meaning of "education," what Funk and Wagnall's *College Standard Dictionary* calls,

From *Building a Philosophy of Education*, 2nd Edition, by Harry S. Broudy (Englewood Cliffs, N.J.: Prentice-Hall, Inc.), pp. 3-11. Copyright © 1961 by Prentice-Hall, Inc. and reprinted by their permission.

"The systematic development, cultivation of the natural powers, by inculcation, example, etc."

The same dictionary gives "the training of animals" as one of the definitions of "education," but in the discussion it remarks: "We speak of the *teaching, training,* or *discipline,* rather than of the *education* or *tuition* of a dog or a horse." But why this fastidiousness? To teach a horse tricks is certainly to develop his natural powers systematically.

To add to the complexity of meanings, there is the common assertion that the environment is "educative," as when a person is said to have received his education in the school of hard knocks or in prison—an education that is apparently not systematic at all.

All that has been said thus far is intended as a justification for an attempt to fix the meaning of education a little more precisely . . . .

Education as control of learning

Let us then, as a sculptor might, hew away quickly those sections of the stone that obviously will not figure in the final form of the statue. No meaning of the term "education" intends to include any process that cannot be altered by human effort, or one that will take place without any such effort. No meaning of education, for example, envisions giving a man an extra arm or leg, or changing his nervous system or the method of circulating his blood. Nor does one undertake to educate the hurricane, the fog, or the seasons of the year; rather do we hope to educate men to control these events or to adapt to them. In other words, let us exclude from the proper meaning of education those changes in behavior or structure that are caused by maturation and physical accidents.

This leaves us with a vast number of changes in behavior that are due to *learning*. Such changes differ from those that take place in a chemist's test tube or are exemplified by one rock falling on another. No matter how many times a given amount of base and hydrochloric acid meet in the test tube, if the conditions are kept constant, the same thing happens. Neither the base nor the acid nor the test tube *learns* anything. Similarly, no one has been able to teach one rock to "duck" when another rock is about to fall on it. But throw enough rocks at a cat or a dog and they learn, we say, to avoid the missiles. Learning, then, in its most general meaning, is the kind of change that uses the results of previous experience. The dog swerves at the upraised arm of his tormentor *because* of what he has undergone and done previously. If the acid did suddenly change its attitude toward the base, it would never occur to a respectable chemist to believe that this might be due to the experience of the base with the acid on previous occasions.

Learning goes on wherever living tissue can retain its own history for use in subsequent predicaments. Some learnings are conscious; many are not.[1] To the extent that entities do retain their experiences, and to the extent that what is retained shapes subsequent responses, learning is about as avoidable as breathing.

Clearly, therefore, education has something to do with learning. Is it equivalent to it? Is it a division of learning? Or is learning a subdivision of education?

If learning and education are to be taken as equivalent, then we must be willing to call every chance conditioning—many of which occur without our knowledge or anyone else's—education. If, at the age of three, the sight of a tomato coincided with a violent gastric disturbance so that one subsequently hated tomatoes, the hate certainly was the result of learning, but in what sense can it be called the result of education? Only in the sense that a man's education is the sum total of all his learnings. But if we keep in mind that men are disposed to argue about what education ought to be, it should be evident that only that phase of education which is under the control of man is fit for argument. Since all learning is not under the control of man, some of it has to be excluded from any profitable discussion about education—precisely that part which cannot be controlled.

This leaves us with the term "education" as relevant only to that part of learning which in one sense or another is under the control of men, with the degree of control varying according to circumstances. Therefore, we can speak of various kinds of education:

1. *Milieu education.* There is the kind of learning that takes place almost automatically. We have thus learned apparently without any design on anyone's part to walk on sidewalks; to eat certain foods and to avoid others; to live in houses, etc.

These are customary ways of doing things in a particular culture. At one time there may have been a reason for doing them this way rather than that, and there still may be. If economic conditions were appropriate, we would, no doubt, learn to relish rats and grubs.

A society will deliberately try to insure the younger generation's conformity to these folkways and *mores*, but since the process can be trusted to go on more or less automatically as a by-product of ordinary living, the deliberative element is not always apparent. We may call this *milieu education* or education by *social contagion*.

2. *Informal education.* Other learnings are produced with conscious intent, but the producers are interested primarily in activities other than instruction. They may impart knowledge or information (instruction); or they may on occasion exercise the pupil in the formation of a habit (training); but this is not their sole or even their chief business. This is *informal* education. Parents give a great deal of it; employers give some to their apprentices; and the theatre at times to its patrons. When it is said that education does not stop with schooling, and that schooling is often the least important part of education, the intent is to emphasize the importance of informal education.

3. *Formal education.* Finally, there is *formal* education in which the intent to teach or train, or both, is clear and where an institution is designated to devote itself primarily to this task. Schools from the kindergarten through the university are institutions devoted to *formal* education. Churches, when they establish schools, are engaged in *formal* education; some of their other activities may be designed to promote learning, but they are likely to be informal.

The distinction between formal and informal education is important. In the first place, many agencies in our environment do educate. These may produce learnings that reinforce those of the school, interfere with them, or be wholly unrelated to them. For example, the father who preaches the virtues of economic competition may be interfering with a teacher in school who may be preaching the virtues of economic co-operation.

We thus have the problem of co-ordinating diverse educations that Plato tackled head on in the *Republic*. The state, he decided, would censor all poetry, music, and drama. It would control *all* educative enterprises, formal and informal, so that the future guardians would everywhere encounter the same attitudes toward courage, temperance, wisdom, and justice. To label Plato's solution as autocratic, undemocratic, and totalitarian does not provide a better solution to the

---

[1] Psychologists refer, for example, to latent learning and unconscious learning. The public was agitated some years ago by television advertising that utilized subliminal stimuli to persuade the viewer by suggestions he could not consciously perceive.

problem of the relation between formal and informal education.[2] We are still quite helpless in coping with the influence of the movies, comics, magazines, and television on young children.

Another, less important, reason for making the distinction between formal and informal education is the commonly accepted distinction between schooling and learning on one's own, i.e., *self-education*. The belittling of formal schooling is still a popular pastime in our culture, even though this culture is the best customer the schools ever had. But it takes no great psychoanalyst to trace it to an uneasy reverence for schooling. A man with a degree from a well-known university may be a fool and a failure, but we are likely to be surprised if he is either. On the contrary, the self-educated man bears the burden of proof that what he got from his own efforts is as good as the standard brands. When it turns out to be, it is an occasion of so much amazement that we can safely regard it as a rare occurrence. On the whole, however, the distinction is a healthy one. It keeps formal educators from getting stuffy about their results, and it brings home to all of us the possibilities and importance of self-education. Indeed, the differences among schools of educational philosophy can be reduced to their different answers to the question: What sort of formal education is the best guarantee of successful self-education in subsequent years?

In its broadest and most general usage, therefore, *education is the process or product of a deliberate attempt to fashion experience by the direction and control of learning*. Formal education refers to the process as it is carried on in schools.

On this definition it would be inaccurate to speak of an "educative environment" unless one meant that the environment was trying directly or indirectly to teach something to someone. To say that one *learns* from the environment would be true but not enlightening because there is nothing else from which one can learn. It also would make us cautious about such phrases as "learning by or from experience" and for precisely the reason that all learning is from experience and through it.[3]

---

[2] For a defense of Plato see Robert Jordan's chapter, "The Revolt Against Philosophy: The Spell of Popper," in *The Return to Reason*, edited by John Wild. . . .
[3] Everything depends, of course, on the meaning given to "experience." Thus, for Dewey, sticking a finger into a flame is not experience until we perceive the relation between the flame and the pain. *Democracy and Education*, p. 163. In more customary usage, experience refers to everything of which we are aware, i.e., any and all consciousness.

Some practical considerations.   Do definitions of education make any difference in the practice of education? Charles Peirce, the forerunner of modern American Pragmatism, and William James, its most prominent publicist, agreed that definitions which make no difference in practice are for all practical and theoretical purposes the same.

One cannot be sure whether people line up their practice to fit their definitions or *vice versa*. They may fashion their definitions to give what they do a respectable air of theoretical consistency. Yet, granting this possibility, once the definition is framed, it does tend to crystallize and congeal the practice which it justifies, so that further deviation from it is discouraged as not being quite respectable.

In the definition given [above] there was an admitted attempt to restrict the use of the term "education" to the *deliberate* direction of learnings, namely the direction chosen by the teacher, whosoever the teacher in any given situation might be. Obviously this point would not have been stressed if some educators or philosophers of education did not fail to make this distinction. The equating of growth, life, learning, and education by John Dewey,[4] although perhaps not to be taken literally, has persuaded many professional schoolmen that the boundaries between the school and the community should be abolished wherever possible. It has persuaded them, and they have helped to persuade parents, that the duties of home, government, church, and school overlap so much that separation of them is perniciously artificial and naive. It has been the cause of the endless admonitions to public school teachers that their responsibility as teachers extends far beyond the classroom. How far it extends is impossible to say because if all life is education, there is no logical reason for setting the boundaries anywhere this side of the grave.

The proposed definition makes a real distinction between teaching and learning, contrary to a rather widespread mode of speaking. Many educators glibly pronounce the dictum: "If there is no learning, there is no teaching." This is only a way of speaking because no educator really believes it to be true, or if he did he would in all honesty refuse to take most of his salary. There is a difference between successful teaching and unsuccessful teaching, just as there is a difference between successful surgery and unsuccessful surgery. Both good and bad operations are performed by people called surgeons, and fees are collected

---

[4] *Op. cit.*, p. 62.

for the successes and failures indiscriminately. To teach is to try deliberately to promote certain learnings. When other factors intrude to prevent such learnings, the teaching fails. Sometimes the factors are in the teacher; sometimes in the pupil; sometimes in the very air both breathe, but as long as the effort is there, there is teaching.[5]

Oddly enough, those philosophers of education who are most sensitive to the multiplicity of factors that go into deciding whether learning will take place or not are least sensitive to the absurdity of making the teacher responsible for factors over which he has no control. Of course, teachers usually refuse to take such responsibility, but the more sensitive they are morally, the more their consciences bother them for every learning failure. *Mea culpa*, they secretly cry; not a few of the very best teachers leave the field altogether because they have taken what at best is a careless *cliché* to be a moral and pedagogical imperative.

Even if it were true that there is no teaching where there is no learning, the converse—there is no learning if there is no teaching—would be false, and if the morally serious teacher is discouraged by the falsity of the first statement, the morally indifferent teacher takes advantage of the falsity of the second, since learnings do accrue regardless of teaching.

Maintaining the distinction allocates to the teacher a definite area of responsibility. There are procedures that one can rightfully expect he will follow, and there are results that he can conscientiously try to achieve. By limiting his responsibility, we can give a definite meaning to the responsibilities we assign. There is no meaning without limitation, or more colloquially, every-body's business is nobody's business.

Teaching and pupilage are genuinely correlative terms as teaching and learning are not. A teacher when teaching is always teaching a pupil, and pupilage is the state of being taught. Education, as here defined, always implies a teacher-pupil situation. Even in self-education the relation is present, although the distinction is within one person rather than among different personalities. Even in milieu education, in which one generation teaches another, it is not wholly absent.

So there is a practical difference. By our definition, education is restricted to the deliberately undertaken direction of learning. For learnings otherwise produced it takes no credit and no blame, although it does take them into account. Operating on this definition, schoolmen would be less eager to promise to remedy the weaknesses of all social institutions by what they do in the classroom. Taken seriously, this definition tends to distinguish sharply among the roles of the teacher, the citizen, mother, father, or soldier. Opposite tendencies are encouraged by the Experimentalist or Deweyan definition. Definitions of education not only can make a difference, but what is even more important, they do. Is there then any basis for preferring one definition of education to another, or is this a matter of mere words or personal taste?

Here we are venturing into deeper philosophical waters. We are asking whether definitions are conventional (agreements on the usage of words) or real (reflecting the structures of reality itself). I believe, of course, that this definition is to some extent a real definition; that it does follow the articulation of society into different agencies, each having a specific role to play or function to perform. Education is one such institution and has its own primary function. This function differentiates it from other agencies and their roles. . . .

---

[5] For an extended discussion on the linguistic aspects of this point, consult Scheffler, *The Language of Education*, pp. 41 ff.

2

Alfred North Whitehead

THE AIMS OF EDUCATION

One of the most widely known and highly respected general philosophers of the twentieth century is Alfred North Whitehead. Internationally known for his work as a mathematician, philosopher, and educator, he taught first at the College of Science in London and then, from 1924 until 1936, at Harvard University. This selection presents some of Whitehead's sophisticated, insightful reactions on the aims of education. Readers should note that Whitehead had a strong commitment to the British organization of curriculum as it existed circa 1917, a curriculum designed to emphasize a small number of broad subjects intensively studied. The British system was a contrast to the American system, in which American students made choices from numbers of elective subjects. Whitehead's views should be understood in the light of this difference.

Whitehead covers at least four of the aims of education which are also treated in later selections. The vocational, moral, and "cultured gentleman" purposes receive his endorsement; mental discipline or the "training of compartments of the mind" comes off badly. The reader may discover that this essay has a number of contradictions and highly controversial assertions. He should examine Whitehead's propositions with a view toward their critical evaluation.

Two of the phrases used by Whitehead in this essay have become quite famous, and are often quoted. The first is his denunciation of "inert ideas." Here in the United States Henry Adams had made the same point nine years before the publication of Whitehead's essay when he observed, "Nothing in education is so astonishing as the amount of ignorance it accumulates in the form of inert facts." The second of Whitehead's phrases is his eleventh commandment, "You may not divide the seamless coat of learning." The reader should make certain that he really understands the meaning of such concepts by analyzing Whitehead's views of knowledge and learning which form the basis for these maxims.

Culture is activity of thought, and receptiveness to beauty and humane feeling. Scraps of information have nothing to do with it. A merely well-informed man is the most useless bore on God's earth. What we should aim at producing is men who possess both culture and expert knowledge in some special direction. Their expert knowledge will give them the ground to start from, and their culture will lead them as deep as philosophy and as high as art. We have to remember that the valuable intellectual development is self-development, and that it mostly takes place between the ages of sixteen and thirty. As to training, the most important part is given by mothers before the age of twelve. A saying due to Archbishop Temple illustrates my meaning. Surprise was expressed at the success in after-life of a man, who as a boy at Rugby had been somewhat undistinguished. He answered, "It is not what they are at eighteen, it is what they become afterwards that matters."

In training a child to activity of thought, above all things we must beware of what I will call "inert ideas"—that is to say, ideas that are merely received into the mind without being utilised, or tested, or thrown into fresh combinations.

From *The Aims of Education and Other Essays* by Alfred North Whitehead (New York: The Macmillan Co.), pp. 13-26. Copyright 1929 by The Macmillan Company, renewed 1957 by Evelyn Whitehead. Reprinted by permission of the publisher.

In the history of education, the most striking phenomenon is that schools of learning, which at one epoch are alive with a ferment of genius, in a succeeding generation exhibit merely pedantry and routine. The reason is, that they are overladen with inert ideas. Education with inert ideas is not only useless: it is, above all things, harmful—*Corruptio optimi, pessima.* Except at rare intervals of intellectual ferment, education in the past has been radically infected with inert ideas. That is the reason why uneducated clever women, who have seen much of the world, are in middle life so much the most cultured part of the community. They have been saved from this horrible burden of inert ideas. Every intellectual revolution which has ever stirred humanity into greatness has been a passionate protest against inert ideas. Then, alas, with pathetic ignorance of human psychology, it has proceeded by some educational scheme to bind humanity afresh with inert ideas of its own fashioning.

Let us now ask how in our system of education we are to guard against this mental dryrot. We enunciate two educational commandments, "Do not teach too many subjects," and again, "What you teach, teach thoroughly."

The result of teaching small parts of a large number of subjects is the passive reception of disconnected ideas, not illumined with any spark of vitality. Let the main ideas which are introduced into a child's education be few and important, and let them be thrown into every combination possible. The child should make them his own, and should understand their application here and now in the circumstances of his actual life. From the very beginning of his education, the child should experience the joy of discovery. The discovery which he has to make, is that general ideas give an understanding of that stream of events which pours through his life, which is his life. By understanding I mean more than a mere logical analysis, though that is included. I mean "understanding" in the sense in which it is used in the French proverb, "To understand all, is to forgive all." Pedants sneer at an education which is useful. But if education is not useful, what is it? Is it a talent, to be hidden away in a napkin? Of course, education should be useful, whatever your aim in life. It was useful to Saint Augustine and it was useful to Napoleon. It is useful, because understanding is useful.

I pass lightly over that understanding which should be given by the literary side of education. Nor do I wish to be supposed to pronounce on the relative merits of a classical or a modern curriculum. I would only remark that the understanding which we want is an understanding of an insistent present. The only use of a knowledge of the past is to equip us for the present. No more deadly harm can be done to young minds than by depreciation of the present. The present contains all that there is. It is holy ground; for it is the past, and it is the future. At the same time it must be observed that an age is no less past if it existed two hundred years ago than if it existed two thousand years ago. Do not be deceived by the pedantry of dates. The ages of Shakespeare and of Molière are no less past than are the ages of Sophocles and of Virgil. The communion of saints is a great and inspiring assemblage, but it has only one possible hall of meeting, and that is, the present; and the mere lapse of time through which any particular group of saints must travel to reach that meeting-place, makes very little difference.

Passing now to the scientific and logical side of education, we remember that here also ideas which are not utilised are positively harmful. By utilising an idea, I mean relating it to that stream, compounded of sense perceptions, feelings, hopes, desires, and of mental activities adjusting thought to thought, which forms our life. I can imagine a set of beings which might fortify their souls by passively reviewing disconnected ideas. Humanity is not built that way—except perhaps some editors of newspapers.

In scientific training, the first thing to do with an idea is to prove it. But allow me for one moment to extend the meaning of "prove"; I

mean—to prove its worth. Now an idea is not worth much unless the propositions in which it is embodied are true. Accordingly an essential part of the proof of an idea is the proof, either by experiment or by logic, of the truth of the propositions. But it is not essential that this proof of the truth should constitute the first introduction to the idea. After all, its assertion by the authority of respectable teachers is sufficient evidence to begin with. In our first contact with a set of propositions, we commence by appreciating their importance. That is what we all do in after-life. We do not attempt, in the strict sense, to prove or to disprove anything, unless its importance makes it worthy of that honour. These two processes of proof, in the narrow sense, and of appreciation, do not require a rigid separation in time. Both can be proceeded with nearly concurrently. But in so far as either process must have the priority, it should be that of appreciation by use.

Furthermore, we should not endeavour to use propositions in isolation. Emphatically I do not mean, a neat little set of experiments to illustrate Proposition I and then the proof of Proposition I, a neat little set of experiments to illustrate Proposition II and then the proof of Proposition II, and so on to the end of the book. Nothing could be more boring. Interrelated truths are utilised *en bloc*, and the various propositions are employed in any order, and with any reiteration. Choose some important applications of your theoretical subject; and study them concurrently with the systematic theoretical exposition. Keep the theoretical exposition short and simple, but let it be strict and rigid so far as it goes. It should not be too long for it to be easily known with thoroughness and accuracy. The consequences of a plethora of half-digested theoretical knowledge are deplorable. Also the theory should not be muddled up with the practice. The child should have no doubt when it is proving and when it is utilising. My point is that what is proved should be utilised, and that what is utilised should—so far as is practicable—be proved. I am far from asserting that proof and utilisation are the same thing.

At this point of my discourse, I can most directly carry forward my argument in the outward form of a digression. We are only just realising that the art and science of education require a genius and a study of their own; and that this genius and this science are more than a bare knowledge of some branch of science or of literature. This truth was partially perceived in the past generation; and headmasters, somewhat crudely, were apt to supersede learning in their colleagues by requiring left-hand bowling and a taste for football.

But culture is more than cricket, and more than football, and more than extent of knowledge.

Education is the acquisition of the art of the utilisation of knowledge. This is an art very difficult to impart. Whenever a text-book is written of real educational worth, you may be quite certain that some reviewer will say that it will be difficult to teach from it. Of course it will be difficult to teach from it. If it were easy, the book ought to be burned; for it cannot be educational. In education, as elsewhere, the broad primrose path leads to a nasty place. This evil path is represented by a book or a set of lectures which will practically enable the student to learn by heart all the questions likely to be asked at the next external examination. And I may say in passing that no educational system is possible unless every question directly asked of a pupil at any examination is either framed or modified by the actual teacher of that pupil in that subject. The external assessor may report on the curriculum or on the performance of the pupils, but never should be allowed to ask the pupil a question which has not been strictly supervised by the actual teacher, or at least inspired by a long conference with him. There are a few exceptions to this rule, but they are exceptions, and could easily be allowed for under the general rule.

We now return to my previous point, that theoretical ideas should always find important applications within the pupil's curriculum. This is not an easy doctrine to apply, but a very hard one. It contains within itself the problem of keeping knowledge alive, of preventing it from becoming inert, which is the central problem of all education.

The best procedure will depend on several factors, none of which can be neglected, namely, the genius of the teacher, the intellectual type of the pupils, their prospects in life, the opportunities offered by the immediate surroundings of the school, and allied factors of this sort. It is for this reason that the uniform external examination is so deadly. We do not denounce it because we are cranks, and like denouncing established things. We are not so childish. Also, of course, such examinations have their use in testing slackness. Our reason of dislike is very definite and very practical. It kills the best part of culture. When you analyse in the light of experience the central task of education, you find that its successful accomplishment depends on a delicate adjustment of many variable factors. The reason is that we are dealing with human minds, and not with dead matter. The evocation of curiosity, of judgment, of the power of mastering a complicated tangle of circumstances, the use of theory in giving foresight in special cases—all these powers are not to be imparted by a set rule embodied in one schedule of examination subjects.

I appeal to you, as practical teachers. With good discipline, it is always possible to pump into the minds of a class a certain quantity of inert knowledge. You take a text-book and make them learn it. So far, so good. The child then knows how to solve a quadratic equation. But what is the point of teaching a child to solve a quadratic equation? There is a traditional answer to this question. It runs thus: The mind is an instrument, you first sharpen it, and then use it; the acquisition of the power of solving a quadratic equation is part of the process of sharpening the mind. Now there is just enough truth in this answer to have made it live through the ages. But for all its half-truth, it embodies a radical error which bids fair to stifle the genius of the modern world. I do not know who was first responsible for this analogy of the mind to a dead instrument. For aught I know, it may have been one of the seven wise men of Greece, or a committee of the whole lot of them. Whoever was the originator, there can be no doubt of the authority which it has acquired by the continuous approval bestowed upon it by eminent persons. But whatever its weight of authority, whatever the high approval which it can quote, I have no hesitation in denouncing it as one of the most fatal, erroneous, and dangerous conceptions ever introduced into the theory of education. The mind is never passive; it is a perpetual activity, delicate, receptive, responsive to stimulus. You cannot postpone its life until you have sharpened it. Whatever interest attaches to your subject-matter must be evoked here and now; whatever powers you are strengthening in the pupil, must be exercised here and now; whatever possibilities of mental life your teaching should impart, must be exhibited here and now. That is the golden rule of education, and a very difficult rule to follow.

The difficulty is just this: the apprehension of general ideas, intellectual habits of mind, and pleasurable interest in mental achievement can be evoked by no form of words, however accurately adjusted. All practical teachers know that education is a patient process of the mastery of details, minute by minute, hour by hour, day by day. There is no royal road to learning through an airy path of brilliant generalisations. There is a proverb about the difficulty of seeing the wood because of the trees. That difficulty is exactly the point which I am enforcing. The problem of education is to make the pupil see the wood by means of the trees.

The solution which I am urging, is to eradicate the fatal disconnection of subjects which kills the vitality of our modern curriculum. There is only one subject-matter for education, and that is Life in all its manifestations. Instead of this single unity, we offer children—Algebra, from which nothing follows; Geometry, from which nothing follows; Science, from which nothing follows; History, from which nothing follows; a Couple of Languages, never mastered; and lastly, most dreary of all, Literature, represented by plays of Shakespeare, with philological notes and short analyses of plot and character to be in substance committed to memory. Can such a list be said to represent Life, as it is known in the midst of the living of it? The best that can be said of it is, that it is a rapid table of contents which a deity might run over in his mind while he was thinking of creating a world, and had not yet determined how to put it together.

Let us now return to quadratic equations. We still have on hand the unanswered question. Why should children be taught their solution? Unless quadratic equations fit into a connected curriculum, of course there is no reason to teach anything about them. Furthermore, extensive as should be the place of mathematics in a complete culture, I am a little doubtful whether for many types of boys algebraic solutions of quadratic equations do not lie on the specialist side of mathematics. I may here remind you that as yet I have not said anything of the psychology or the content of the specialism, which is so necessary a part of an ideal education. But all that is an evasion of our real question, and I merely state it in order to avoid being misunderstood in my answer.

Quadratic equations are part of algebra, and algebra is the intellectual instrument which has been created for rendering clear the quantitative aspects of the world. There is no getting out of it. Through and through the world is infected with quantity. To talk sense, is to talk in quantities. It is no use saying that the nation is large,— How large? It is no use saying that radium is scarce,—How scarce? You cannot evade quantity. You may fly to poetry and to music, and quantity and number will face you in your rhythms and your octaves. Elegant intellects which despise the theory of quantity, are but half developed. They are more to be pitied than blamed. The scraps of gibberish, which in their school-days were taught to them in the name of algebra, deserve some contempt.

This question of the degeneration of algebra into gibberish, both in word and in fact, affords a pathetic instance of the uselessness of reforming educational schedules without a clear conception of the attributes which you wish to evoke in the living minds of the children. A few years ago there was an outcry that school algebra was in need of reform, but there was a general agreement that graphs would put everything right. So all sorts of things were extruded, and graphs were introduced. So far as I can see, with no sort of idea behind them, but just graphs. Now every examination paper has one or two questions on graphs. Personally, I am an enthusiastic adherent of graphs. But I wonder whether as yet we have gained very much. You cannot put life into any schedule of general education unless you succeed in exhibiting its relation to some essential characteristic of all intelligent or emotional perception. It is a hard saying, but it is true; and I do not see how to make it any easier. In making these little formal alterations you are beaten by the very nature of things. You are pitted against too skilful an adversary, who will see to it that the pea is always under the other thimble.

Reformation must begin at the other end. First, you must make up your mind as to those quantitative aspects of the world which are simple enough to be introduced into general education; then a schedule of algebra should be framed which will about find its exemplification in these applications. We need not fear for our pet graphs, they will be there in plenty when we once begin to treat algebra as a serious means of studying the world. Some of the simplest applications will be found in the quantities which occur in the simplest study of society. The curves of history are more vivid and more informing than the dry catalogues of names and dates which comprise the greater part of that arid school study. What purpose is effected by a catalogue of undistinguished kings and queens? Tom, Dick, or Harry, they are all dead. General resurrections are failures, and are better postponed. The quantitative flux of the forces of modern society is capable of very simple exhibition. Meanwhile, the ideas of the variable, of the function, of rate of change, of equations and their solution, of elimination, are being studied as an abstract science for their own sake. Not, of course, in the pompous phrases with which I am alluding to them, here, but with that iteration of simple special cases proper to teaching.

If this course be followed, the route from Chaucer to the Black Death, from the Black Death to modern Labour troubles, will connect the tales of the mediæval pilgrims with the abstract science of algebra, both yielding diverse aspects of that single theme, Life. I know what most of you are thinking at this point. It is that the exact course which I have sketched out is not the particular one which you would have chosen, or even see how to work. I quite agree. I am not claiming that I could do it myself. But your objection is the precise reason why a common external examination system is fatal to education. The process of exhibiting the applications of knowledge must, for its success, essentially depend on the character of the pupils and the genius of the teacher. Of course I have left out the easiest applications with which most of us are more at home. I mean the quantitative sides of sciences, such as mechanics and physics.

Again, in the same connection we plot the statistics of social phenomena against the time. We then eliminate the time between suitable pairs. We can speculate how far we have exhibited a real causal connection, or how far a mere temporal coincidence. We notice that we might have plotted against the time one set of statistics for one country and another set for another country, and thus, with suitable choice of subjects, have obtained graphs which certainly exhibited mere coincidence. Also other graphs exhibit obvious causal connections. We wonder how to discriminate. And so are drawn on as far as we will.

But in considering this description, I must beg you to remember what I have been insisting on above. In the first place, one train of thought will not suit all groups of children. For example, I should expect that artisan children will want something more concrete and, in a sense, swifter than I have set down here. Perhaps I am wrong, but that is what I should guess. In the second place, I am not contemplating one beautiful lecture stimulating, once and for all, an admiring class. That is not the way in which education proceeds. No; all the time the pupils are hard at work solving examples, drawing graphs, and making experiments, until they have a thorough hold on the whole subject. I am describing the interspersed explanations, the directions which should be given to their thoughts. The pupils have got to be made to feel that they are studying something, and are not merely executing intellectual minuets.

Finally, if you are teaching pupils for some general examination, the problem of sound teaching is greatly complicated. Have you ever noticed the zig-zag moulding round a Norman arch? The ancient work is beautiful, the modern work is hideous. The reason is, that the modern work is done to exact measure, the ancient work is varied according to the idiosyncrasy of the workman. Here it is crowded, and there it is expanded. Now the essence of getting pupils through examinations is to give equal weight to all parts of the schedule. But mankind is naturally specialist. One man sees a whole subject, where another can find only a few detached examples. I know that it seems contradictory to allow for specialism in a curriculum especially designed for a broad culture. Without contradictions the world would be simpler, and perhaps duller. But I am certain that in education wherever you exclude specialism you destroy life.

We now come to the other great branch of a general mathematical education, namely Geometry. The same principles apply. The theoretical part should be clear-cut, rigid, short, and important. Every proposition not absolutely necessary to exhibit the main connection of ideas should be cut out, but the great fundamental ideas should be all there. No omission of concepts, such as those of Similarity and Proportion. We must remember that, owing to the aid rendered by the visual presence of a figure, Geometry is a field of unequalled excellence for the exercise of the deductive faculties of reasoning. Then, of course, there follows Geometrical Drawing, with its training for the hand and eye.

But, like Algebra, Geometry and Geometrical Drawing must be extended beyond the mere circle of geometrical ideas. In an industrial neighbourhood, machinery and workshop practice form the appropriate extension. For example, in the London Polytechnics this has been achieved with conspicuous success. For many secondary schools I suggest that surveying and maps are the natural applications. In particular, plane-table surveying should lead pupils to a vivid apprehension of the immediate application of geometric truths. Simple drawing apparatus, a surveyor's chain, and a surveyor's compass, should enable the pupils to rise from the survey and mensuration of a field to the construction of the map of a small district. The best education is to be found in gaining the utmost information from the simplest apparatus. The provision of elaborate instruments is greatly to be deprecated. To have constructed the map of a small district, to have considered its roads, its contours, its geology, its climate, its relation to other districts, the effects on the status of its inhabitants, will teach more history and geography than any knowledge of Perkin Warbeck or of Behren's Straits. I mean not a nebulous lecture on the subject, but a serious investigation in which the real facts are definitely ascertained by the aid of accurate theoretical knowledge. A typical mathematical problem should be: Survey such and such a field, draw a plan of it to such and such a scale, and find the area. It would be quite a good procedure to impart the necessary geometrical propositions without their proofs. Then, concurrently in the same term, the proofs of the propositions would be learnt while the survey was being made.

Fortunately, the specialist side of education presents an easier problem than does the provision of a general culture. For this there are many reasons. One is that many of the principles of procedure to be observed are the same in both cases, and it is unnecessary to recapitulate. Another reason is that specialist training takes place—or should take place—at a more advanced stage of the pupil's course, and thus there is easier material to work upon. But undoubtedly the chief reason is that the specialist study is normally a study of peculiar interest to the student. He is studying it because, for some reason, he wants to know it. This makes all the difference. The general culture is designed to foster an activity of mind; the specialist course utilises this activity. But it does not do to lay too much stress on these neat antitheses. As we have already seen, in the general course foci of special interest will arise; and similarly in the special study, the external connections of the subject drag thought outwards.

Again, there is not one course of study which merely gives general culture, and another which gives special knowledge. The subjects pursued for the sake of a general education are special subjects specially studied; and, on the other hand, one of the ways of encouraging general mental activity is to foster a special devotion. You may not divide the seamless coat of learning. What education has to impart is an intimate sense for the power of ideas, for the beauty of ideas, and for the structure of ideas, together with a particular body of knowledge which has peculiar reference to the life of the being possessing it.

The appreciation of the structure of ideas is that side of a cultured mind which can only grow under the influence of a special study. I mean that eye for the whole chessboard, for the bearing of one set of ideas on another. Nothing but a special study can give any appreciation for the exact formulation of general ideas, for their relations when formulated, for their service in the comprehension of life. A mind so disciplined should be both more abstract and more concrete. It has been trained in the comprehension of abstract thought and in the analysis of facts.

Finally, there should grow the most austere of all mental qualities; I mean the sense for style. It is an æsthetic sense, based on admiration for the direct attainment of a foreseen end, simply and without waste. Style in art, style in literature, style in science, style in logic, style in practical execution have fundamentally the same æsthetic qualities, namely, attainment and restraint. The love of a subject in itself and for itself, where it is not the sleepy pleasure of pacing a mental quarter-deck, is the love of style as manifested in that study.

Here we are brought back to the position from which we started, the utility of education. Style, in its finest sense, is the last acquirement of the educated mind; it is also the most useful. It pervades the whole being. The administrator with a sense for style hates waste; the engineer with a sense for style economises his material; the artisan with a sense for style prefers good work. Style is the ultimate morality of mind.

But above style, and above knowledge, there is something, a vague shape like fate above the Greek gods. That something is Power. Style is the fashioning of power, the restraining of power. But, after all, the power of attainment of the desired end is fundamental. The first thing is to get there. Do not bother about your style, but solve your problem, justify the ways of God to man, administer your province, or do whatever else is set before you.

Where, then, does style help? In this, with style the end is attained without side issues, without raising undesirable inflammations. With style you attain your end and nothing but your end. With style the effect of your activity is calculable, and foresight is the last gift of gods to men. With style your power is increased, for your mind is not distracted with irrelevancies, and you are more likely to attain your object. Now style is the exclusive privilege of the expert. Whoever heard of the style of an amateur painter, of the style of an amateur poet? Style is always the product of specialist study, the peculiar contribution of specialism to culture.

English education in its present phase suffers from a lack of definite aim, and from an external machinery which kills its vitality. Hitherto in this address I have been considering the aims which should govern education. In this respect England halts between two opinions. It has not decided whether to produce amateurs or experts. The profound change in the world which the nineteenth century has produced is that the growth of knowledge has given foresight. The amateur is essentially a man with appreciation and with immense versatility in mastering a given routine. But he lacks the foresight which comes from special knowledge. The object of this address is to suggest how to produce the expert without loss of the essential virtues of the amateur. The machinery of our secondary education is rigid where it should be yielding, and lax where it should be rigid. Every school is bound on pain of extinction to train its boys for a small set of definite examinations. No headmaster has a free hand to develop his general education or his specialist studies in accordance with the opportunities of his school, which are created by its staff, its environment, its class of boys, and its endowments. I suggest that no system of external tests which aims primarily at examining individual scholars can result in anything but educational waste.

Primarily it is the schools and not the scholars which should be inspected. Each school should grant its own leaving certificates, based on its own curriculum. The standards of these schools should be sampled and corrected. But the first requisite for educational reform is the school as a unit, with its approved curriculum based on its own needs, and evolved by its own staff. If we fail to secure that, we simply fall from one formalism into another, from one dung-hill of inert ideas into another.

In stating that the school is the true educational unit in any national system for the safeguarding of efficiency, I have conceived the alternative system as being the external examination of the individual scholar. But every Scylla is faced by its Charybdis—or, in more homely language, there is a ditch on both sides of the road. It will be equally fatal to education if we fall into the hands of a supervising department which is under the impression that it can divide all schools into two or three rigid categories, each type being forced to adopt a rigid curriculum. When I say that the school is the educational unit, I mean exactly what I say, no larger unit, no smaller unit. Each school must have the claim to be considered in relation to its special circumstances. The classifying of schools for some purposes is necessary. But no absolutely rigid curriculum, not modified

by its own staff, should be permissible. Exactly the same principles apply, with the proper modifications, to universities and to technical colleges.

When one considers in its length and in its breadth the importance of this question of the education of a nation's young, the broken lives, the defeated hopes, the national failures, which result from the frivolous inertia with which it is treated, it is difficult to restrain within oneself a savage rage. In the conditions of modern life the rule is absolute, the race which does not value trained intelligence is doomed. Not all your heroism, not all your social charm, not all your wit, not all your victories on land or at sea, can move back the finger of fate. To-day we maintain ourselves. To-morrow science will have moved forward yet one more step, and there will be no appeal from the judgment which will then be pronounced on the uneducated.

We can be content with no less than the old summary of educational ideal which has been current at any time from the dawn of our civilisation. The essence of education is that it be religious.

Pray, what is religious education?

A religious education is an education which inculcates duty and reverence. Duty arises from our potential control over the course of events. Where attainable knowledge could have changed the issue, ignorance has the guilt of vice. And the foundation of reverence is this perception, that the present holds within itself the complete sum of existence, backwards and forwards, that whole amplitude of time, which is eternity.

3

Herbert Spencer

WHAT KNOWLEDGE IS OF MOST WORTH?

At the close of the nineteenth century Herbert Spencer achieved an outstanding reputation as "the philosopher of the century," "the greatest intellect since Aristotle," the father of modern social science, and the author of Social Darwinism and evolutionism. The noted sociologist F. H. Giddings declared: "I do not hesitate to say that Mr. Spencer should be regarded as the true founder of scientific sociology, and as its greatest constructive thinker" (2). Educators praised the book of four essays from which this selection is taken as a most important piece of educational writing. David Starr Jordan, President of Stanford University, declared that the schoolmen of England and America "were thrown into dismay by Spencer's question [What knowledge is of most worth?] and its implication." From any point of view this is an educational classic.

What Spencer shows here is the intimate—indeed inseparable—relationship between curriculum organization and the aims of education. Can we discover what subjects are of most worth, and therefore should be of first emphasis in the curriculum?, he asks. Then he replies: only if we know the kind of educated person we want to produce. Most authorities would agree that Spencer was chiefly responsible for launching the modern era of curriculum reform.

Spencer presents five categories of education which compare interestingly with those of Whitehead. In effect, Spencer tells us that education must include all five categories, since its true aim is "preparation for complete living." Dewey and the Progressive educators were to say the same thing a half century later. And what knowledge contributes most to all five? Spencer did not hesitate: *science* is of most worth! (To him, this meant both natural science *and* social science.)

. . . Among mental as among bodily acquisitions, the ornamental comes before the useful. Not only in times past, but almost as much in our own era, that knowledge which conduces to personal well-being has been postponed to that which brings applause. In the Greek schools, music, poetry, rhetoric, and a philosophy which, until Socrates taught, had but little bearing upon action, were the dominant subjects; while knowledge aiding the arts of life had a very subordinate place. And in our own universities and schools at the present moment the like antithesis holds. We are guilty of something like a platitude when we say that throughout his after-career a boy, in nine cases out of ten, applies his Latin and Greek to no practical purposes. The remark is trite that in his shop, or his office, in managing his estate or his family, in playing his part as director of a bank or a railway, he is very little aided by this knowledge he took so many years to acquire—so little, that generally the greater part of it drops out of his memory; and if he occasionally vents a Latin quotation, or alludes to some Greek myth, it is less to throw light on the topic in hand than for the sake of effect. If we inquire what is the real motive for giving boys a classical education, we find it to be simply conformity to public opinion. Men dress their children's minds as they do their bodies, in the prevailing fashion. As the Orinoco Indian puts on his paint before leaving his hut, not with a view to any direct benefit, but because he would be ashamed to be seen without it; so, a boy's drilling in Latin and Greek is insisted on, not because of their intrinsic value, but that he may not be disgraced by being found ignorant of them—that he may have "the education of a gentleman"—the badge marking a certain social position, and bringing a consequent respect.

. . . We are none of us content with quietly unfolding our own individualities to the full in all directions; but have a restless craving to impress our individualities upon others, and in some way subordinate them. And this it is which determines the character of our education. Not what knowledge is of most real worth, is the consideration; but what will bring most applause, honour, respect—what will most conduce to social position and influence—what will be most imposing. As, throughout life, not what we are, but what we shall be thought, is the question; so in education, the question is, not the intrinsic value of knowledge, so much as its extrinsic effects on others. And this being our dominant idea, direct utility is scarcely more regarded than by the barbarian when filing his teeth and staining his nails.

If there needs any further evidence of the rude, undeveloped character of our education, we have it in the fact that the comparative worths of different kinds of knowledge have been as yet scarcely even discussed—much less discussed in a methodic way with definite results. Not only is it that no standard of relative values has yet been agreed upon; but the existence of any such standard has not been conceived in any clear manner. And not only is it that the existence of any such standard has not been clearly conceived; but the need for it seems to have been scarcely even felt. Men read books on this topic, and attend lectures on that; decide that their children shall be instructed in these branches of knowledge, and shall not be instructed in those; and all under the guidance of mere custom, or liking, or prejudice; without ever considering the enormous importance of determining in some rational way what things are really most worth learning. . . .

. . . Before devoting years to some subject which fashion or fancy suggests, it is surely wise to

From *Education: Intellectual, Moral and Physical* by Herbert Spencer (New York: D. Appleton and Company, 1860), pp. 2–18, 84–87.

weigh with great care the worth of the results, as compared with the worth of various alternative results which the same years might bring if otherwise applied.

In education, then, this is the question of questions, which it is high time we discussed in some methodic way. The first in importance, though the last to be considered, is the problem—how to decide among the conflicting claims of various subjects on our attention. Before there can be a rational *curriculum*, we must settle which things it most concerns us to know; or, to use a word of Bacon's, now unfortunately obsolete—we must determine the relative value of knowledges.

To this end, a measure of value is the first requisite. And happily, respecting the true measure of value, as expressed in general terms, there can be no dispute. Every one in contending for the worth of any particular order of information, does so by showing its bearing upon some part of life. In reply to the question, "Of what use is it?" the mathematician, linguist, naturalist, or philosopher, explains the way in which his learning beneficially influences action—saves from evil or secures good—conduces to happiness. When the teacher of writing has pointed out how great an aid writing is to success in business—that is, to the obtainment of sustenance—that is, to satisfactory living; he is held to have proved his case. And when the collector of dead facts (say a numismatist) fails to make clear any appreciable effects which these facts can produce on human welfare, he is obliged to admit that they are comparatively valueless. All then, either directly or by implication, appeal to this as the ultimate test.

How to live?—that is the essential question for us. Not how to live in the mere material sense only, but in the widest sense. The general problem which comprehends every special problem is— the right ruling of conduct in all directions under all circumstances. In what way to treat the body; in what way to treat the mind; in what way to manage our affairs; in what way to bring up a family; in what way to behave as a citizen; in what way to utilize all those sources of happiness which nature supplies—how to use all our faculties to the greatest advantage of ourselves and others—how to live completely? And this being the great thing needful for us to learn, is, by consequence, the great thing which education has to teach. To prepare us for complete living is the function which education has to discharge; and the only rational mode of judging of any educational course is, to judge in what degree it discharges such function. . . .

Our first step must obviously be to classify, in the order of their importance, the leading kinds of activity which constitute human life. They may be naturally arranged into:—1. Those activities which directly minister to self-preservation; 2. Those activities which, by securing the necessaries of life, indirectly minister to self-preservation; 3. Those activities which have for their end the rearing and discipline of offspring; 4. Those activities which are involved in the maintenance of proper social and political relations; 5. Those miscellaneous activities which make up the leisure part of life, devoted to the gratification of the tastes and feelings.

That these stand in something like their true order of subordination, it needs no long consideration to show. The actions and precautions by which, from moment to moment, we secure personal safety, must clearly take precedence of all others. Could there be a man, ignorant as an infant of all surrounding objects and movements, or how to guide himself among them, he would pretty certainly lose his life the first time he went into the street: notwithstanding any amount of learning he might have on other matters. And as entire ignorance in all other directions would be less promptly fatal than entire ignorance in this direction, it must be admitted that knowledge immediately conducive to self-preservation is of primary importance.

That next after direct self-preservation comes the indirect self-preservation which consists in acquiring the means of living, none will question. That a man's industrial functions must be considered before his parental ones, is manifest from the fact that, speaking generally, the discharge of the parental functions is made possible only by the previous discharge of the industrial ones. The power of self-maintenance necessarily preceding the power of maintaining offspring, it follows that knowledge needful for self-maintenance has stronger claims than knowledge needful for family welfare—is second in value to none save knowledge needful for immediate self-preservation.

As the family comes before the State in order of time—as the bringing up of children is possible before the State exists, or when it has ceased to be, whereas the State is rendered possible only by the bringing up of children; it follows that the duties of the parent demand closer attention than those of the citizen. Or, to use a further argument— since the goodness of a society ultimately depends on the nature of its citizens; and since the nature of its citizens is more modifiable by early training than by anything else; we must conclude that the welfare of the family underlies the welfare of society. And hence knowledge directly conducing to the first, must take precedence of knowledge directly conducing to the last.

Those various forms of pleasurable occupation which fill up the leisure left by graver occupations —the enjoyments of music, poetry, painting, &c. —manifestly imply a pre-existing society. Not only is a considerable development of them impossible without a long-established social union; but their very subject-matter consists in great part of social sentiments and sympathies. Not only does society supply the conditions to their growth; but also the ideas and sentiments they express. And, consequently, that part of human conduct which constitutes good citizenship is of more moment than that which goes out in accomplishments or exercise of the tastes; and, in education, preparation for the one must rank before preparation for the other.

Such then, we repeat, is something like the rational order of subordination:—That education which prepares for direct self-preservation; that which prepares for indirect self-preservation; that which prepares for parenthood; that which prepares for citizenship; that which prepares for the miscellaneous refinements of life. . . .

Of course the ideal of education is—complete preparation in all these divisions. But failing this ideal, as in our phase of civilization every one must do more or less, the aim should be to maintain *a due proportion* between the degrees of preparation in each. Not exhaustive cultivation in any one, supremely important though it may be—not even an exclusive attention to the two, three, or four divisions of greatest importance; but an attention to all,—greatest where the value is greatest, less where the value is less, least where the value is least. For the average man (not to forget the cases in which peculiar aptitude for some one department of knowledge rightly makes that one the bread-winning occupation)—for the average man, we say, the desideratum is, a training that approaches nearest to perfection in the things which most subserve complete living, and falls more and more below perfection in the things that have more and more remote bearings on complete living. . . .

[To] the question with which we set out— What knowledge is of most worth?—the uniform reply is—Science. This is the verdict on all the counts. For direct self-preservation, or the maintenance of life and health, the all-important knowledge is—Science. For that indirect self-preservation which we call gaining a livelihood, the knowledge of greatest value is—Science. For the due discharge of parental functions, the proper guidance is to be found only in—Science. For that interpretation of national life, past and present, without which the citizen cannot rightly regulate his conduct, the indispensable key is—Science. Alike for the most perfect production and highest enjoyment of art in all its forms, the needful preparation is still—Science. And for purposes of discipline—intellectual, moral, religious—the most efficient study is, once more—Science. The question which at first seemed so perplexed, has become, in the course of our inquiry, comparatively simple. We have not to estimate the degrees of importance of different orders of human activity, and different studies as severally fitting us for them; since we find that the study of Science, in its most comprehensive meaning, is the best preparation for all these orders of activity. We have not to decide between the claims of knowledge of great though conventional value, and knowledge of less though intrinsic value; seeing that the knowledge which we find to be of most value in all other respects, is intrinsically most valuable; its worth is not dependent upon opinion, but is as fixed as is the relation of man to the surrounding world. Necessary and eternal as are its truths, all Science concerns all mankind for all time. Equally at present, and in the remotest future, must it be of incalculable importance for the regulation of their conduct, that men should understand the science of life, physical, mental, and social; and that they should understand all other science as a key to the science of life.

And yet the knowledge which is of such transcendent value is that which, in our age of boasted education, receives the least attention. While this which we call civilization could never have arisen had it not been for science; science forms scarcely an appreciable element in what men consider civilized training. Though to the progress of science we owe it, that millions find support where once there was food only for thousands; yet of these millions but a few thousands pay any respect to that which has made their existence possible. Though this increasing knowledge of the properties and relations of things has not only enabled wandering tribes to grow into populous nations, but has given to the countless members of those populous nations comforts and pleasures which their few naked ancestors never even conceived, or could have believed, yet is this kind of knowledge only now receiving a grudging recognition in our highest educational institutions. To the slowly growing acquaintance with the uniform coexistences and sequences of phenomena—to the establishment of invariable laws, we owe our emancipation from the grossest superstitions. But for science we should be still worshipping fetishes; or, with hecatombs of victims, propitiating diabolical deities. And yet this science, which, in place of the most degrading conceptions of things, has given us some insight into the grandeurs of creation, is written against in our theologies and frowned upon from our pulpits.

Paraphrasing an Eastern fable, we may say that in the family of knowledges, Science is the household drudge, who, in obscurity, hides unrecognised perfections. To her has been committed all the work; by her skill, intelligence, and devotion, have all the conveniences and gratifications been ob-

tained; and while ceaselessly occupied ministering to the rest, she has been kept in the background, that her haughty sisters might flaunt their fripperies in the eyes of the world. The parallel holds yet further. For we are fast coming to the *dénouement,* when the positions will be changed; and while these haughty sisters sink into merited neglect, Science, proclaimed as highest alike in worth and beauty, will reign supreme.

The aims of education

VOCATION

No major aim of education is easier to accept sympathetically than that of preparation for making a living, most of all a better living. The great mass of people have endorsed this function of the schools whole-heartedly, especially since the Civil War. Before that date many still believed that home and on-the-job training would get one ahead in life much faster than anything to be learned from "impractical" and "lazy" schoolteachers. It was a time of high tide for the self-made men who liked to quip, knowingly, "Those who can, do; those who can't, teach." Today, as the descendants of that self-made generation compete almost desperately for admission to the best schools at every level, these derogatory views seem to have lost all meaning.

The vocational aim is one which is regarded with particular seriousness by business and professional men. It stresses the importance of specialization and of useful, worth-while knowledge, readily applied to the material side of life. Today, primary emphasis is still given to it by certain kinds of schools, such as the private business and secretarial schools, the graduate colleges of engineering, medicine, and commerce, and the military academies.

Some oddities about the rise of vocationalism in America deserve mention. Contrary to what one might suppose, organized labor opposed vocational high schools and night classes for many decades, fearing that these might supply employers with cheap, skilled, nonunion labor. Today, no such feeling exists. Another point is that Booker T. Washington, the first important American Negro leader, made his reputation by advocating vocational education at Tuskegee Institute, in emulation of white Progressives. Finally, it was widely believed in the 1880's that "the idea of industrial education comes strangely enough from a semi-barbarous nation. Russia started in a scientific manner to attend to the development of her internal resources [by schools in] Moscow and St. Petersburg" (3). We of the space era are entitled to raise our eyebrows!

The Progressive era in politics was the time when the vocational purpose was taken most seriously. Between 1890 and 1910, manual training, domestic science, and business education increased far more than any other elements in the curriculum; natural science rose very slightly and the classics lost ground. It was the beginning of what E. L. Thorndike termed the "socialization of education."

Naturally, vocationalists did not think of themselves as being narrow or selfish in their aims. Typical was the sentiment expressed in 1901 by a professor of education in England: "The qualities which make the good citizen are precisely those which also make the successful tradesman or manufacturer." It seems likely that the majority of Americans still holds to this belief; no serious teacher can afford to ignore its existence or to deny its continued importance at the present time.

4

S. T. Dutton

THE RELATION OF EDUCATION TO VOCATION

Samuel Train Dutton was Superintendent of Schools in Brookline, Massachusetts, in 1896, when he wrote this address. Later he became Professor of Educational Administration at Teachers College, Columbia University, and an international figure in the field. Dutton, in this article, was acting as a scholarly mouthpiece for the voice of public opinion. He was spelling out a more detailed "why" for the people's feeling that, as the editor of the *Chicago Tribune* stated in 1887: "The aim of the schools . . . should be to equip the pupils with the appliances for making a living. . . ."

Clearly Dutton felt that vocational education was something bigger than manual training, pottery making, leatherwork, basket weaving, or other pre-industrial arts. Antiquated handcrafts would be replaced—not revived—by the vocational movement. Henceforth people should be trained in manufacturing and distribution, the new tasks useful in the industrial, machine age. Vocationalism ought to be modern, progressive, and anticlassical. In fact, one must compare Dutton with Dewey (Reading 19) or Counts (Reading 21) to discover the similarity between the program of late nineteenth century vocationalism and that of the protagonists of twentieth century education. The final paragraphs of Dutton's selection summarize the breadth and implications of which the vocational purpose was capable. To its enthusiastic supporters, vocationalism was the path to Utopia, to realization of the American Dream, not simply a preliminary to earning good wages.

. . . [As] far as schools were concerned, or the artificial means of education, our country in its younger days had little to offer. To read and write and reckon were accomplishments useful in those days. These, therefore, constituted the school curriculum. Considered as mental training, what was obtained in the schools amounted to but little. Education, in its best sense, was acquired on the farm and in the shop, where the mind was ever alert and active, and where the trained hand was its obedient servant. . . .

In order that we may understand how backward education has been in recognizing the social changes accomplished during the present century and the pressing needs occasioned thereby, it is only necessary to recall what we were, how we lived, and how we transacted business one hundred years ago, and then to contemplate our country as we see it to-day, leading the world in almost every phase of industrial and commercial activity. Our development has been unprecedented, so that the world has stood and wondered. By a combination of favoring circumstances our national domain was extended from the Atlantic to the Pacific. All this vast territory has been rapidly settled, and its virgin soil has teemed with fabulous crops of food products. Farmers and mechanics of Europe have flocked thither until some nationalities

From *Journal of Social Science*, 1896, 34:53-62.

are nearly as largely represented here as in the old country. In the mean time the age of machinery has been ushered in. While the West, with her cheaper methods of production, by means of the railroad was filling our markets with corn, wheat, and beef, enterprising men in New England were building mills and factories upon the banks of every river and mountain stream. The vast mineral resources of the country have been discovered and utilized. The railroad, the steamship, the telegraph, and the telephone have made us all neighbors, and have brought us within speaking distance of every part of the globe. Inventive genius has supplied every craft with labor-saving machines, thus disbarring many forms of labor, and compelling many artisans and mechanics to seek new adaptations of their skill.

Because of this revolution in our material affairs, many political and economic problems have arisen, in the settling of which our governmental machinery has been strained to the utmost. Grave moral issues have tested our loyalty and manhood, and have cost us dearly in treasure and in blood.

Now, it is not unusual for the optimistic observer of our national greatness and prosperity, wishing to find causes therefor, to say that it is largely due to our excellent system of public education. There is a certain sense in which this is true. It is more true of the last twenty years of educational effort than of what preceded. As one who believes that teaching and other educational forces constitute the most generic, the most potent, and the most essential thing in the world; as one who believes that our Lord and Master was essentially a teacher, and not a preacher, that he used educational methods in all his work, and gave the stamp of his divine approval to those methods, and that the church of the future is going to use such methods more and more,—I am not the one to disparage or minimize the importance of the work performed by American schools in the past in moralizing, in disciplining, and in instructing the young. I do say, however, that in a certain important sense our nation has become great and influential, not by reason of public education or of college education, but in spite of it. Or, putting it otherwise, there is a sense in which our country has failed of her opportunity, and is behind the spirit of the present age, because our educational machinery from top to bottom has been old-fashioned, poorly constructed, and poorly organized, and has been able to go only at such a low rate of speed that there has always been too little of the finished product and far too much of the raw material. As I review the history of the past fifty years, I can think of no form of

activity that has been so slow in adapting itself to new conditions as has teaching. Go into a typical American house, whether in city or country, and you see something quite different from what was there half a century ago. The food, the dress, the furniture, are quite changed. You will see books and newspapers, and possibly works of art and musical instruments. Go into a modern hospital, and see the perfect appointments for treating the sick and the injured. Follow the physician, and observe that his methods are diametrically opposed to those in vogue a generation ago. Notice the newer conception of what crime is and how it is to be cured or prevented. Consider what the State and the municipality do for public health, safety, and convenience. Surely, the world has moved rapidly; and with it have gone philanthropy and civic progress. Even theology and the administration of justice are endeavoring to keep up with the procession. But, as compared with some of those things mentioned above, education has been slow, inexcusably slow. Many and many a child in New England, when the schools open the present month in this year of our Lord eighteen hundred and ninety-six, will be sent to the same little dingy school-house where his grandfather went before him, will sit upon the same hard seats, will stare at the same bare and dingy walls, and in too many instances, I regret to say, will recite what he has committed to memory from a book much of which means little to him and the learning of which can do him but little good. This is doubtless an extreme picture, but I am assured by persons holding official positions that it is true to fact. Between this condition of things and the best types of the modern schools found in our large towns and cities there are all grades of mediocrity and excellence. But the significant fact is the tenacity with which we have clung to the methods of the pioneer school. It cannot be denied that the three "R's" have reigned supreme until within recent years. To be sure, the course of study was gradually broadened by the introduction of geography and here and there a little history and science. The methods pursued, however, were so abstract and literary that the child was not trained to observe, to appreciate, or to reason. Sound educational theories and some that were even startling, from such thinkers as John Locke, Comenius, Rousseau, Pestalozzi, and Froebel, had been handed down to us; but we were too much occupied in organizing the rapidly increasing masses of children in our towns and cities into so-called graded schools to devote much time to the finer problems of nurture and instruction. The kindergarten was on exhibition here and there as a curiosity; but teachers smiled at it, and few parents wanted it, inasmuch as it did not teach the children to read and cipher. The wonderful possibilities of childhood as regards the development of faculty and the accumulation of the elements of all knowledge as food for the nurture and enrichment of the immortal mind, these were a sealed book to most people; and, while they were apprehended and preached by certain prophets, they made little headway until recently in reforming actual practice.

But this is not all. Not only in a general sense have we been content to tithe mint, anise, and cumin while neglecting the weightier matters' of the law, but we have failed in arranging our educational courses to recognize one of the most vital factors in any civilized society; namely, Vocation. As the home is the unit and the very soul of our social order, as everything that is best and most effective in forming habits and opinions and establishing character centres there, and as it is the birthplace and seat of those pure affections and high aspirations that sweeten and ennoble our mortal life, so, it must be conceded, vocation is its chief corner-stone; or, to use a stronger and a better figure, it is its very heart's blood. Vocation is a good deal more than the opposite of idleness. It is labor dedicated to the highest purposes; to wit, the cherishing of the family and the home. . . .

. . . [Perhaps] the most serious count of all against our educational system [is] that it does not provide such trade instruction as enables the grammar-school graduate to enter at once upon the pursuit of a handicraft. I need not enlarge upon the great and pressing need of trade schools. Social changes have brought the bulk of our population into cities, where every idle and shiftless member of the community is a menace to the public peace and welfare. It is indeed pitiful to see our American young men pleading for the opportunity to work, and yet failing to find employment because their hands are untrained. Not only in the city, but in the country also, there is need of special training. The hard times that our New England farmers are undergoing are not due entirely to the tariff, and certainly not to the lack of silver dollars. The soil has become impoverished, and needs scientific treatment in order to be made to produce bountifully. Farmers in the East can no longer raise corn and wheat at a profit; but, if skilled in the arts of horticulture and if versed in agricultural chemistry, they may find in their own local markets an abundant return for their labors. Why should not agricultural chemistry be taught in our normal schools? Why should not special schools for young farmers be established to foster our great national industry?

Something has been done by private munificence and by industrial corporations in planting trade schools. But the time has come when the State must meet this issue promptly and generously if we are to keep pace with the nations of Europe.

. . . It is an interesting fact that some of the old [guilds] of London, which still preserve their organization and continue their annual banquets, have begun to apply their accumulated wealth to the founding and support of trade schools. Heaven grant that some of the labor unions of this country may be led to dedicate a portion of their energies and means to the advancement of this cause!

In all attempts to develop a system of trade instruction one principle should be the dominant motive and guide; and that is, to emphasize the dignity of vocation, and to elevate and bless the American home. One objection is quite sure to be raised, and I should not be surprised if it were to come from craftsmen themselves, whose boys and girls are sure to be benefited by this movement; and that is the danger of the over-stimulation of industry, of too many craftsmen and of overproduction. There is an effective answer to that argument in the truth that, while there may be overproduction in those things that provide for the bare physical wants of mankind, as food, clothing, and shelter, there never has been nor ever will be overproduction in those finer aesthetic products of handiwork that satisfy the spiritual wants of mankind. Works of art, whether in statuary or in painting, in music or literature, cannot glut the market. Human needs in respect to those things that delight the eye, kindle the emotions, and feed the soul, are infinite. And, when I plead for trade schools, I want to have the art idea predominate. The outside of the house is well enough. Let us provide furnishings for the inner chambers of the soul. Let the future American artisan have that generous feeling, that deep insight, and that delicate artistic touch that shall lift our common life farther and farther away from what is rude and common and barbaric.

Did time permit, I would speak of hopeful indications as seen in the tendencies of common-school education at the present time. Antipater demanded fifty children as hostages from the Spartans. They offered them in their stead a hundred men of distinction. Jean Paul Richter, referring to this in the first chapter of his "Levana," says that "ordinary educators precisely reverse the offering." I am glad that this is not true to-day. Teachers and mothers are coming to know that the possibilities of a child for a good and useful life are largely wrapped up in his earliest years. The enriching and broadening of the school life, as is now being done, the introduction of science, of literature, of art, music, and manual training into every part of the course, are long steps toward that vocational success and happiness which we desire to see. . . .

5

Theodore Roosevelt

THE EMANCIPATION OF EDUCATION

A professional educator like Dr. Dutton (Reading 4) might have misread the popular voice, but not one of our most admired Presidents. According to William Allen White, Theodore Roosevelt "understood his time" better than anyone else in the United States between 1900 and 1920. Roosevelt, a product of classical, nonvocational schooling, was one of the most vigorous supporters of the vocational purpose. For example, he told the American Historical Association, "A utilitarian education should undoubtedly be the foundation of all education."

In the selection which follows, written by Roosevelt from the White House at the height of his fame, he seems to underscore Dutton on important points. School and society were in agreement, at least for a brief moment. Incidentally, one needs to look closely at what Roosevelt, a gifted politician, had to say about the farmer. The President, while defending rural life, let it be known that the schools should provide technical, scientific, semi-industrial agricultural training. Roosevelt showed no hesitation in advocating federal aid to education, on the grounds that only in this fashion could educational opportunity be made available to all.

. . . [We] have to deal now, and will have to deal in the future, with a nation of families on the land; and our system of public education should be so broadened in its scope as to include not merely the traditional cultural studies, excellent and indispensable in their way, but also instruction relative to the farm, the trades and the home. Our immediate purpose is to take the first steps in providing for the ninety-five per cent who are not now trained for a vocation advantages corresponding to those enjoyed by the relatively few who are trained in the professional and technical schools.

Industrial training, training which will fit a girl to do work in the home, which will fit a boy to work in the shop if in a city, to work on a farm if in the country, is the most important of all training, aside from that which develops character; and it is a grave reproach to us as a nation that we have permitted our training to lead the children away from the farm and shop instead of toward them. We should try to provide the many with training in their professions, just as the few, the doctors, the ministers, the lawyers, are trained for their professions. In other words, the school system should be aimed primarily to fit the scholar for actual life rather than for a university. The exceptional individual, of the highest culture and most efficient training possible, is an important asset for the state. He should be encouraged and his development promoted; but this should not be done at the expense of all the other individuals who can do their work best on the farms and in the workshops; it is for the benefit of these individuals that our school system should be primarily shaped.

I thoroly believe that our people approve of the higher education; but I also believe that they are growing more and more to demand a reform in secondary schools which shall fit the ordinary scholar for the actual work of life. Therefore I believe that the national government should take an active part in securing better educational methods, in accordance with some such system as that outlined in the bill introduced in the last Congress

From *Good Housekeeping*, November 12, 1908, 47: 626-627.

by Mr. Davis. It is not my place to speak of the details of such a bill, but in a general way I feel that the nation should, by making appropriations, put a premium upon industrial, and especially agricultural, training in the state schools; the states themselves being required in these schools to contribute what is necessary for the ordinary training, and the expenditures for the national government to be under the supervision of the Department of Agriculture.

Teachers must be trained, or their teaching will not be adequate; and these teachers must then give vocational training to the scholars in the ordinary schools. The nation would simply co-operate with the state or city or town, and what it thus gives would be applied to industrial, technical, agricultural training. The growth in the consolidated rural school, which has in so many instances supplanted the old-time district school, offers the chance to do the best possible service by means of such a system as that outlined above. Where possible, the secondary agricultural schools should be in farm communities rather than in towns, and the training should be of the most practical character and such as will not only fit the scholars to do their part in farm work, but also fit them to enjoy in the fullest degree the pleasures and opportunities of country life. We should do everything that we can to give well-trained leaders to each country community. The United States Department of Agriculture would preserve an intimate relation to all these proposed agricultural high schools, as well as the

branch stations connected with them, for the work that the Department does is steadily becoming of more and more consequence to the farmers.

All this simply means that the Nation ought to co-operate with the state to help the people help themselves thru better educational facilities, the schools being left wholly and directly under the control of the people thru their local authorities, but suggestion and general oversight as well as improvement being supplied by the experts employed by the Nation, so that the children and the young men and girls in the smaller towns and in the country may have the educational facilities now only to be obtained in wealthier communities.

This would merely be putting into effect that cardinal American doctrine of furnishing a reasonable equality of opportunity of education and chance of development to all our children, wherever they live and whatever may be their station in life. Such a federal co-operation in technical education will help in many ways. It will mean much for country life, for the life of the family farm, for the life of those city workers who seek landed homes in the country near the city in which they work. It will mean much along the lines of the great policy of the conservation of the natural resources of our land. Finally, it will mean much to the Nation of the future, because it will represent the effort to give exact justice, and an equal opportunity for development, to each of the boys and girls who in the future are to make up the Nation.

The aims of education

MORAL AND SPIRITUAL VALUES

For hundreds of years, the guidance of youth in morals has, in Western culture, been centered in the church and in the Bible. In countries where church and state are united, as in Spain, the church schools are also the public schools. In countries where church and state are separated, as in the United States, the church schools are private and must compete with a secular system of education. The typical parochial school of the United States, emphasizing moral purposes, is semifree but not compulsory. Our leading parochial school systems are those of the Roman Catholics, the Lutherans, the Seventh Day Adventists, and the more orthodox Jews.

Emphasis on moral values is by no means confined only to church schools. Nearly every public figure of importance in American history has stated that Christian virtues and belief in God should be taught in all branches and at every level of education, the publicly supported schools included. Clergymen, deacons, and loyal church members entered the teaching profession from its earliest beginnings, and only recently have they ceased to dominate it. American support for the free public school system sprang from the Puritan belief that all persons should be educated at least enough to read the Bible.

Gradually the purpose behind moral training has shifted. At first the goal was personal salvation; later, a writer in the early 1900's remarked that "the true purpose of education is to cherish and unfold the seed of immortality already sown within us." Still later, a new emphasis was placed upon high moral character for the sake of social peace and greater human happiness. Most recently, modern social science emphasizes the relativity of ethics and "good moral behavior." Thus the contemporary equivalent of nineteenth century moral indoctrination has become character building and personality development. But the desirable virtues do not seem to have changed much.

6

A. D. Mayo

METHODS OF MORAL INSTRUCTION IN COMMON SCHOOLS

The extract which follows presents the views of a late nineteenth century Protestant clergyman on the responsibility of the common school for moral education, views which are still held by many churchmen in America. Mayo believed that moral education in the public schools must be based upon concepts, principles, and models drawn from the Christian tradition of American society. Though committed to the nonsectarian nature of public education, Mayo would contend that the public school should teach the fundamental principles of Christian morality as these apply to social, economic, and public life in order that we might develop what he would call "virtuous citizens." Virtues such as honesty, truthfulness, justice, and responsibility would be instilled in pupils. The teacher, of course, would have to be a paragon of Christian virtues and his example would be the most powerful single force in developing acceptable Christian behavior in pupils.

One must realize that this pronouncement was made at a time when the understanding of how behavior, attitudes, and beliefs were learned was considered a relatively simple procedure which emphasized precepts, maxims, examples, and inculcation. The problem of teaching value systems in a pluralistic, stratified, and complex society was not yet a subject for intensive study. Yet the overall emphasis in Mayo's statement has a face validity. Responsible thinkers have proposed that moral and spiritual values which offend no group or person either in a religious or psychological sense can be treated in schools. In recent years, members of many faiths have arrived at general agreement on the aims of programs of "moral and spiritual values." Many schools provide curriculum guides outlining ways for teachers to develop moral and spiritual values in pupils. General purposes such as respect for human dignity, perseverance at tasks, responsibility for one's acts, and recognition of the evil of abuses would be examples of the kinds of aims which churchmen accept as applicable to the public schools.

It is clear that the purpose of public education as Mayo saw it was anything but Godless, and the teacher audience of the period received his words with vast enthusiasm. Morality and good citizenship were indistinguishably intermingled anyway, so why not rely upon the former to produce the latter? To what extent modern educational psychology has really departed from this belief is a provocative question.

What is the common school?   We can not understand the real nature of [the] problem of Methods of Moral Instruction until we rid our minds of a huge drift of vague idealism concerning the province of the common school. In our American enthusiasm for popular culture, we are perpetually forgetting that the aim of our common system of state instruction is neither to develop a scholastic class nor to work up our young friend, Jonathan junior, into a seraph. The only ground on which we can take the people's money for public instruction is that the common school is the corner-stone of our national order of Republican society. The common school-house is not a manufactory of scholars or saints, but of good American citizens. George Washington and Abraham Lincoln were not scholars; Ben. Franklin and Andrew Jackson never claimed to be saints; but they were all, in characteristic ways, excellent types of American citizenship. To make good American citizens of American boys and girls, we have the right to do every thing a wise Republican statemanship may dictate. To make scholars, in the university sense, or to develop proselytes to any church, we have no right to appropriate a dollar of the people's money. Scholarship and sanctity alike are to be dealt with in the people's school just in the degree and to the extent that they minister to a lofty and progressive ideal of American citizenship and American character.

Public morals.   So we are brought down, in the common school, from the stupendous obligation of training souls for eternity to the sufficiently arduous undertaking of keeping the United States of America out of hell by educating American children into a virtuous citizenship as that is practically estimated by the people of every Christian country. This implies, of course, the full recognition by the common school of the existence, sovereignty and providence of Almighty God and the duty of all men and of the nation to love, worship and obey God, in all ways within the province of a government that has for ever repudiated the union of state and church. But the great stress in the common school will necessarily come upon the domain of morality. How to make our children unselfish, just, kind, pure, honest, truthful, lovers of all men, able to live in our order of American society resisting its awful temptations and seizing its grand opportunities, becoming such men and women as the Republic can intrust with her future:—this is the task set for the teachers in the American school-room.

Christian morality the foundation of the Republic.   Of course, the morality taught and enforced in the discipline of the common school is the Christian morality as laid down in the four Gospels, according to its best public appreciation in Christian lands. Less than this we have no right to attempt; more than this we can not achieve. We can not teach an ancient Pagan, a Mohammedan or a Chinese ideal of morality in an American school. We can not inculcate there the distinctive fatalistic morality of a materialistic science or an atheistic philosophy. All these types of morality are repugnant to the common sense and common life of the American people, whose whole order of society and ideas of living are the outgrowth of eighteen centuries of a progressive Christianity. The ideal public morality and religion of the people of the United States is the best attainable resumé of the public religion and morality of all the past of Christendom plus the American right to go to the Bible at first hand, think freely and judge conscientiously on all human affairs. In this broad sense, the ideal morality of the American common school-room is not the creed of any sectary or the conceit of any pedant who may teach therein, but the Christian morality as best apprehended by the Nation that establishes the school. This may be called indefinite; but it is as definite as any public ideal can be in a country where every thing finally hinges, not on a scholastic logic, but on the Christianized common sense of a people which, of all races and nations, has shown the best faculty of walking along dizzy places with a "level head."

So the problem before the common-school teacher in America is to hold before the child, by precept and example, in the most practical way, that Christian morality which is essential to high character in a true American man or woman and a good citizen of the United States. . . .

From *NEA Journal of Addresses and Proceedings*, 1872:12-13.

7

PAPAL TEACHINGS

The views of the Roman Catholic Church concerning education are of increasing importance to every member of the teaching profession, regardless of his faith. These views require understanding not only because of the philosophy and educational psychology involved, but also because of the fact that over 4,400,000 children attend Roman Catholic elementary schools and the enrollment in Roman Catholic high schools tops 850,000.

The selection below is compiled of extracts from papal letters spanning the years from 1875 to 1957. These letters from the Popes to various members of the church hierarchy contain a unifying theme regarding the aims of education—an emphasis upon religious education and moral instruction. This emphasis, for many reasons, is deserving of the attention of the future teacher.

Pius IX: Attendance at non-Catholic schools[1]

The first subject it was intended to discuss was the particular method of education of youth proper to these schools. To the Sacred Congregation, this method has appeared intrinsically dangerous and absolutely contrary to Catholicism. Indeed because the special program adopted by these schools excludes all religious instruction, the pupils cannot grasp the elements of the faith, nor are they instructed in the precepts of the Church, and therefore they are deprived of that which is most essential for man to know and without which it is impossible to live in a Christian manner. In these schools the young are trained right from their tender infancy, the age in which, as is well known, the seeds of virtue or vice take firm root. It is, therefore, an enormous evil that from this formative age they should grow up without any sense of religion.

What is more, in the above-mentioned schools which elude the Church's authority, the professors are chosen from all sects without distinction, while on the other hand no measures are taken to impede such pernicious influence as they might exercise on youth, so that they are able to disseminate error and vice amongst the young.

The fact that in these schools, or at least in the majority of them, the adolescents of both sexes are grouped together in the same classrooms to attend lesson, and boys and girls must sit together on the same benches, exposes them to corruption to a certain extent. The result of all this is that youth is unfortunately in danger of losing its faith, while its good morals are threatened.

General principle. If this danger, which borders on perversion, is not averted, these schools cannot be attended with peace of mind. The divine and natural laws themselves proclaim it. This was clearly defined by the Holy Father when on July 14, 1864, he wrote to the Archbishop of Fribourg: "In all places, in every country where this pernicious plan to deprive the Church of its authority over schools is formulated, and worse still, put into effect, with the result that the young will be exposed to the danger of losing their faith, it is the duty of the Church to make every effort not only to take steps to obtain the essential instruction and religious training for youth, but even more so to warn the faithful and to make it clear to them that they cannot frequent such schools which are set up against the Catholic Church."

These words, founded on the natural and divine law, state definitely a general principle, have a universal bearing, and apply to all countries where this injurious method of instructing youth will unfortunately be introduced. . . .

Leo XIII: The free school and the nation[2]

. . . Now, in our times and with the customs prevalent today, when so many and so various are the dangers which, on all sides, threaten the tender age and innocence of children, there is no better plan than to impart knowledge in conjunc-

---

From *Papal Teaching: Education* (Boston: Daughters of St. Paul, 1960), pp. 66-67, 99-100, 202-203, 555-556.
[1] Instructions of the Holy Office to the Bishops of the United States, November 24, 1875.

[2] Letter *Spectata Fides*, November 27, 1885—to the Bishops of England.

tion with education in faith and morals. For this reason, We have said so more than once, We willingly approve of schools of the sort called "free schools," which have been founded by the assistance and generosity of private individuals in France, Belgium, America and in the colonies of the British Empire, and We desire to see them increase and prosper as much as possible, by increased attendance. On Our part, bearing in view the crowded cities here, We have not neglected—with very real concern and at great expense—to provide for many such schools to be placed at the disposal of the children of Rome.

It is in these schools and in virtue of these same schools that We can preserve intact the magnificent heritage which we have received from our forefathers, namely, the integrity of the Catholic faith. By means of these schools the freedom of parents is still assured. Furthermore—and this is something that has been made very necessary, particularly on account of the unbridled licentiousness in thought and action—a noble lineage of citizens is formed for the country, for none is superior to the one who has embraced the Christian faith with conviction from his childhood and has lived it. The sources, and, so to say, the seeds of all the culture that Jesus Christ has divinely brought to the human race, are to be found in the education of children: for, in practice, adult citizens cannot have a moral make-up that is very much different from that received at the time of the child's first education. The pernicious error of those who prefer children to grow without any religious education destroys all the wisdom of our forefathers and threatens the very roots of civil society. This shows you, Venerable Brethren, that fathers of families must not send their children to elementary schools where no religious instruction is given. . . .

---

[3] From "Education of the Redeemed Man," Encycl. *Divini illius Magistri*, December 31, 1929.
[4] From "The Challenge to Christian Education," Letter to the Third International Congress of the World Union of Catholic Teachers, August 5, 1957.

Pius XI: The essence and importance of Christian education[3]

It is . . . as important to make no mistake in education, as it is to make no mistake in the pursuit of the last goal, with which the whole work of education is intimately and necessarily connected. In fact, since education consists essentially in preparing man for what he must be and for what he must do here below, in order to attain the sublime goal for which he was created, it is clear that there can be no true education which is not wholly directed to man's last end, and that in the present order of Providence, since God has revealed Himself to us in the Person of His only-begotten Son, Who alone is "the Way, the Truth and the Life," (a) there can be no ideally perfect education which is not Christian education. . . .

Pius XII: Education in the era of technology[4]

. . . But, in the meantime, mankind has entered the age of technology. Technology is beginning to change the psychic structure of man, but it must not be permitted to change the Catholic ideal of education. Teachers have pointed out correctly that moral and religious education is now of even greater importance than professional education and communication of knowledge; for modern advances make for excessive activism, for a tendency to adapt oneself without responsibility or resistance, and for an undue receptiveness to sense-impressions that is accompanied by a crippling of reflective thought. It is man in the age of technology who stands most in need of that consistent and uniform education based on absolute truth and on God as the center of existence, an education which only Christian faith and the Catholic Church can provide. We must, therefore, continue our traditional ideal of education in these new times. . . .

The aims of education

CITIZENSHIP: NATIONALISM AND PATRIOTISM

The citizenship aim of education is more complex than any other. It is a product of advanced civilization, and therefore less ancient than moral or vocational purpose, especially in its most obvious form of nationalism and patriotism. The idea of educating for citizenship first arose in classical Greece, where Athens and Sparta disagreed over the kind of citizen to be produced. Spartans wanted a citizen-soldier who would be loyal, dedicated, disciplined, and supremely competent in defending the state from military attack. Athenians desired this also, but valued more the skills and duties of the cultured civilian. The dispute still goes on in every great nation, including the United States.

Another issue has been whether citizenship education should concentrate on developing leaders or followers. Plato had assumed that education was for the elite, the "guardians" of the republic, a practice carried on in the British tradition of education for public service. But modern nationalism as expounded by Hegel and Herder stressed education of the "folk," the common people whose patriotic brotherhood makes a nation strong and united. This, however, was an education for followership, succinctly expressed in Lord Nelson's famous message to his seamen at the Battle of Trafalgar: "England expects every man will do his duty."

Public school systems are the product of the modern national state, largely to ensure that such expectations as that of Nelson's England would be met. Previously all schooling had been essentially private. In fact, the public school systems of the United States and Prussia (Germany) are the two oldest in the world today. Where the state controlled the schools directly, it could be reasonably certain that good citizenship and patriotism would be taught to children. As Theodore Roosevelt wrote, "It is an evil thing for any man of education to forget that education should intensify patriotism, and that patriotism must not only be shown by striving to do good to the country from within, but by readiness to uphold its interests and honor, at any cost, when menaced from without."

At its best, the kind of citizenship education envisioned by Roosevelt could create self-respect and pride in country, serving as a true cement of society. At its worst it could promote an ugly chauvinism, a faceless conformity, and a ruthless repression of any ideas which seemed new or controversial. More conservatively, perhaps, there was a well-defined middle ground, familiar to the instructor of citizenship courses, in which only the machinery of citizenship was treated—for example, how and when to vote, political party structure, or the details of bureaucratic organization. Many political scientists say that citizenship cannot be taught in one packaged course; it must suffuse the entire curriculum, and engage the attention of all teachers regardless of their specific academic responsibilities.

8

Noah Webster

EDUCATION AND A FREE GOVERNMENT

Noah Webster is remembered for his dictionaries and his Blue-backed Speller. But he was also the first great figure in American education after the Constitution was adopted, a Constitution of which he was one of the true fathers. In addition, he was a highly successful textbook writer, the first American to make a living from schoolbooks. Webster speaks of himself in the third person in this open letter, for he was the editor-owner of the New York newspaper *Minerva*. The *Institute* that is referred to was simply a textbook in English.

Although Webster was a strong Federalist, many of his views were essentially democratic. In reading this letter one should note the purpose which lay behind his spellers and dictionaries and texts, and his feeling about the people and popular education. Certainly Webster did more than any other single person to change English colonial education into an American education for American citizens. His mark is still on us when we write "plow" and "jail" instead of the British "plough" and "gaol."

How successful was Webster in his effort to remake American education? Twenty-five years later DeWitt Clinton found the schools full of national fervor, making a "real effort to embody the new spirit of American life—independent, self-proud, vocational," but largely thwarted by methods of mechanical rote memorization and catechizing. As often happens, the methods were inappropriate to the objectives sought.

[*New York, July 19, 1796.*]

. . . The personal or political foes of the conductor of the *Minerva* cannot employ their malignity to less purpose than in representing him as an enemy to the poor or to their instruction. In this instance they attack the man who was not only the *first* but the *only* man to devote a large portion of his life to framing a *system of national education* and introducing it among his countrymen. Before the end of the war he began this plan (a plan similar to that which has occupied the time and talents of the National Convention in France) and framed an *Institute* of the language for the express purpose of facilitating the instruction of youth and spreading learning among all classes of people, the poor as well as the rich. In this instance he introduced some geographical account of his own country and a number of patriotic pieces for the express design of detaching the children of the United States from their dependence on foreign countries for books and ideas, and informing them early with a knowledge and love of their own republican government.

As one hundred thousand copies of this work are now sold annually, it is probable more than one third of all the children in the United States are taught from these books. Indeed, they are generally used in schools taught by *American* instructors, by men who feel a partiality for their native country, their laws, government, and prosperity.

The author has, besides, been attentive in particular to the *common laboring people* in the more necessary and useful sciences by annexing to his *Institute* or publishing in some cheap form the most general truths in agriculture, morals, and politics. By annexing abridgments of these useful subjects to a cheap schoolbook, he has thrown them in the way of *poor people*, and this was his express design.

From *Letters of Noah Webster*, Harry F. Warfel, ed. (New York: Library Publishers, 1953), pp. 138-141.

He has, on all suitable occasions, inculcated the use and necessity of diffusing learning among the mass of people and carrying information to every cottage as the *best means* of maintaining a free government. . . .

In his essays, whose pages are devoted to this subject of public instruction, it is said, "education forms the moral character of men, and morals are the basis of government." "A good system of education should be the first article in the code of political regulations, for it is much easier to introduce an effectual system for preserving morals than to correct by penal statutes the ill effects of a bad system. I am so fully persuaded of this that I shall almost adore that great man who shall change our practice and opinions and make it respectable for the first and best men to superintend the education of youth." . . .

In his *Sketches of American Policy*, a pamphlet published in March, 1785, for the express purpose of proposing and urging the establishment of a National Constitution like the present, and which contained the first public proposition of the kind, the following observations occur in page 28: "The institution of schools, particularly in the New England states, where the poorest children are instructed in reading, writing, and arithmetic at the *public expense*, is a *noble regulation calculated to dignify the human species*. This institution is the necessary consequence of the genius of our government; at the same time it forms the firmest security of our liberties. It is scarcely possible to reduce an enlightened people to civil or ecclesiastical tyranny."

It is needless to multiply extracts. A firm persuasion of these truths led the editor of the *Minerva* to devote his *first* and *best* years, and to sacrifice no inconsiderable portion of property, to compile a *national plan* of education. The success, tho' far from being complete, has been *very considerable*—in some states, *ample*.

The United States are in no danger of monarchy or the aristocracy of hereditary estates and offices.

All the force and intrigue of Europe combined could not introduce here either one or the other.

But these states will always be exposed to *anarchy* and *faction*, because these evils approach under the delusive but specious guise of *patriotism*.

Against these dangers our *best security* is *general information*. Were the *poor laboring* people of any large town as well informed as those who have leisure and opportunity to read all that is said on public affairs, faction would be deprived of nine tenths of its force. Opposition to our government would hardly exist in any shape. It is a deep public calamity that so large a portion of citizens are doomed to drudge all their lives in ignorance and continually liable to be misled by designing men, who artfully tell them any tale that will obtain their votes.

Wherever a man has lost the confidence of the well-informed part of citizens, it is an infallible sign he is a *suspicious* character; and if such a man then resorts to the *poor* for *their* votes, he does it because he can more easily *deceive them.*

This is the great vice of free governments. To correct it, knowledge must be diffused among *all classes* of citizens; and when they *understand* public affairs, they will *not do wrong.*

Thus when errors have spread extensively in this country, the best informed people are the first to be undeceived. Hence the strength of the Federal interest among the senator votes of this state.

So important is this truth, in his view, that the conductor of the *Minerva* would cheerfully give a tenth of all his earnings thro life for the education of poor citizens. A proper system for this purpose would doubtless ensure perpetuity to the American Republic, and thus fulfil the first wish of a good patriot. . . .

9

J. L. M. Curry

CITIZENSHIP AND EDUCATION

The idea of educating the citizen for "good followership" could be, and often has been, carried to extremes. Particularly has this been true in time of war, with its accompanying fear of internal subversion. In 1917 the headmaster of Middlesex School in Concord, Massachusetts, declared that "permissive" educational methods were destroying respect for authority, law, and order, and that "educational preparedness . . . means education for service" either as a patriotic, loyal voter or as a disciplined, obedient soldier.

One of the more effective retorts to this kind of argument was penned with biting sarcasm a few years after the close of World War I by that journalistic gadfly Henry Louis Mencken. The aim of such citizenship training, he said, was "to make the pupil a good citizen, which is to say, a citizen differing as little as possible, in positive knowledge and habit of mind, from all other citizens. In other words, it is the mission of the pedagogue, not to make his pupils think, but to make them think *right* . . . his fundamental function in America is to manufacture an endless corps of sound Americans. A sound American is simply one who has put out of his mind all doubts and questionings, and who accepts instantly, and as incontrovertible gospel, the whole body of official doctrine of his day, whatever it may be and no matter how often it may change" (4). One might well ask at this point if Mencken is not contrasting the qualities of a democratic and a totalitarian citizen.

The demand for citizenship education as a protection against dangerous or unpopular ideas has a long history behind it, particularly in autocratic governments. Curry, a sincere and devoted Virginian of the 1880's, is advancing a similar proposal. Was Curry urging educators to adopt "thought control," or merely asking for a return to Hamiltonian-Jeffersonian common sense?

. . . Education should be so conducted as to make good, law-abiding, self-supporting, productive people. This, however, is wider than the theme assigned. My thesis is limited by citizenship, which implies that the citizen requires some general education, and some special education of a civic character. As to the first, without it the functions of citizenship cannot otherwise be safely discharged, or the just expectations of American citizens be realized. Citizenship in a free, representative, constitutional Republic presupposes more general culture and enlightenment than is needed in a less popular government. Suffrage is a mockery unless based on the intelligence of the voter,—on some knowledge of the character, conduct, and creed of the person voted for. Eligibility to office implies a larger measure of knowledge. Jury and other civil duties cannot be well met by ignorant citizens. What a select or privileged class does elsewhere is here devolved without class-discrimination on the mass of adult male citizens.

From *NEA Journal of Addresses and Proceedings,* 1884:4-16.

It is of little use to concede political rights to all unless they can be so far assisted as to qualify for an intelligent and independent exercise of those rights. The character of our Federal and State governments and general manhood suffrage give American schools a new character, and perforce make them *quasi* national institutions. The educated citizen becomes a bulwark of society as he has a stake in public order and welfare. In the absence of general education, who is hopeful of the perpetuity of our institutions; what guaranty against Nihilism and Communism; the vulgar arts of bribery; what security for property, which owes its existence and value to the recognition and fiat of Society? An ignorant and unproductive citizen is full of "communistic dreams about labor and wages,"—cares little for stability or security, and is the ready tool of demagogue and conspirator. If we choose ignorance, we make ignorance the arbiter of our social and national life; for, as one of our profoundest thinkers has tersely said, "we are tethered to the lowest stratum of our population, and must accept their influence on our politics." . . .

The aims of education

CITIZENSHIP: ASSIMILATION AND SOCIAL MOBILITY

Fortunately, citizenship is a great deal more than a matter of civic leadership and patriotic duty. New to the world, and typically American, were two ideas which constituted the essential heart of what made the citizen of this nation feel himself to be different from any other. Both ideas were deeply interwoven into the fabric of the public school system, and quickly saturated the thinking of both pupils and teachers, almost without their being aware of it.

The first idea concerned the nature of the American, this "new man" or new nationality which was springing up in the temperate zone of North America. Usually known as the "melting-pot" concept, it was argued that by the intermingling and amalgamating of old country immigrants a new American species was being created. The common school system was the instrument to weld the diverse elements of the population into a unified social group. Declared President J. H. Smart of the National Education Association in 1881, "I believe that the American school-room is the place in which that wonderful change takes place, by which the children of every land and every tongue, of every religious creed and of every political faith, are transformed by subtle assimilating processes, from aliens and strangers, into a sympathetic membership in the greatest and best political organization the world has even seen." This belief has been almost universal among Americans, though recently challenged by cultural pluralism—a concept which denies that intermarriage and amalgamation of the various immigrant and native-born groups to form a "new man" are desirable. Cultural pluralists prefer a system of private ethnic schools in which the old-country language and culture will be taught to their children, and the ideal of the United States as a mosaic of nationalities.

The second idea concerned the nature of success in life; that is, how best to get ahead economically and socially in the special conditions of American existence. In the last 100 years there has sprung up a deeply ingrained belief in free education as a social ladder to superior salary and status. Poor and under-privileged groups of all kinds—ethnic minorities, immigrants, the economically deprived, slum-dwelling children—all have looked to the schools with hope and faith as the most effective way for them to by-pass inherited status wherever it seemed to block the way to equal social and economic opportunity. For any-one who was ambitious and industrious, education stood out as the great tool by means of which any individual might become prosperous.

10

F. A. Sawyer

THE COMMON SCHOOLS—WHAT THEY CAN DO FOR A STATE

These views of Senator F. A. Sawyer of South Carolina, written in 1870, are representative of the feelings of a large proportion of the nation's population after the Civil War. Sawyer was speaking on the subject of national unity when he uttered his remarks, viewing the schools as an indispensable force in pro-ducing the good citizens who would keep the country strong. To be sure, his views did not reflect those of many people in the South at this trying time in the nation's history; he was frequently looked upon as a carpetbagger from New England.

In these few short paragraphs Sawyer makes clear his belief that a primary aim of American education should be to act as an assimilating and democratizing agency. By offering a ladder to success, the schools would make assimilation extraordinarily attractive and satisfying to all comers. In essence, Sawyer con-tends that education will achieve its citizenship purposes not by talking about civic virtue, but by offering a direct life experience to each student which will make possible his equal participation in one of the best of national brotherhoods.

. . . To one who is acquainted with the people of the states in which the Common School system has been longest established it is obvious that the proportion of the people who are engaged in employments requiring muscular power *only*, is smaller than in other states. Year by year, as the benefits of the schools grow more and more widely diffused, do a larger proportion of the native inhabitants enter the higher departments of productive industry, while the lower forms of labor are performed by foreigners, or those who by parental neglect or other causes have not availed themselves of the privileges afforded by the schools.

A laudable ambition to better their condition takes early possession of the educated sons of the

From *National Teachers' Association*, 1870:203-204.

American farmer, mechanic or laborer. The fathers perhaps had nothing with which to make their way in the world but their sturdy arms and honest hearts. They were compelled to rely upon the lower forms of labor for their support. The sons, more fortunate, have not only inherited their fathers' habits of industry and integrity, but have in the Free Schools acquired a degree of intelligence which will enable them to direct labor of others as well as their own. They become masters where their fathers were servants; architects and master builders where their fathers were carpenters and jour-neymen, engineers and machinists where their fathers were rude blacksmiths; they draw the plans their assistants carry into execution; they conceive the enterprises which employ thousands of unskilled laborers. The free schools have made them an aristocracy of labor, and their places as mere manual laborers are supplied from other lands or by those who have failed to take the full benefit of the education all can now secure in many of our states. Were it not that the children of these uneducated laborers share with those of other classes the blessings of the schools; and thus there is a constant "levelling up" of the elements of society, there might be a reasonable fear that a class of brutal and dangerous men would become the substratum of society in states whose native population has thus assumed a higher and more influential position than is attainable by the crowd of immigrants who rush to our shores. But a society through which is distributed so much and so powerful an influence from Free Schools has an almost infinite power of assimilation. It takes up and uses the material which comes to it from all the world; and will continue so to do, without serious injury to its own constitution, so long as the preponderance of intelligent natives is so decided as it is in most of the states to which these immigrants go. The education of the native citizen neutralizes and corrects the ignorance of large masses of those who have sought in our country refuge from the oppression of other lands and a home where they hope their children may become wiser, richer and happier than it is their lot to be.

I do not share the fears some entertain that ignorance and barbarism from other lands will overwhelm, or seriously endanger the stability of our free institutions. Our territory is immense; our national character is positive and controlling; our powers of absorption and assimilation are something wonderful; the immigrants that come are widely scattered, and under the heat and in the crucible of our national life, the most heterogeneous ingredients are soon fused into the national product of American Republicanism. Therefore I say let the nations pour out their surplus population on our broad fields; their muscle is our wealth; their arms fell our forests; build our railways, dig our canals, spin and weave our cotton, mine our coal and iron: and their children, under the influence of our schools, make Americans of whom they and we are proud. . . .

The aims of education

CITIZENSHIP: DEMOCRACY AND EQUAL OPPORTUNITY

The idea of education as a means of assuring assimilation and social mobility was certainly one which implied equal opportunity for all children to receive a common educational experience. It was undeniably democratic, too. Nevertheless there was a tendency, noticeable in the early decades of the twentieth century, to rate mere access to schooling of greater importance than the quality of what was being taught in the classrooms. The concept of undifferentiated opportunity still persists in the minds of many, for even as recently as 1960, one nationally famous political figure declared: "The purpose of education in a free nation is to provide equality of opportunity."

Earlier types of citizenship education had stressed obligations and services which every citizen owed to the state. Now the emphasis shifted away from duties to the more pleasant topic of privileges. The new citizenship education focused upon rights and services which the state owed to the citizen.

One of the problems of equal opportunity in education was deciding what it meant. To Theodore Roosevelt, democracy in education implied only that "the chance for an elementary education is open to every man and woman." Others soon argued that without a chance for secondary and at least junior-college instruction for all youth, true quantitative equality could not exist. There were, however, many other kinds of equality proposed in addition to the quantitative. For example, equally well-built and well-equipped school buildings for all, whether urban or rural dwelling, white or Negro, were demanded, and equally competent teaching staff as well. There was a campaign for special education which would provide equal access to knowledge for the crippled, the blind, the deaf, the mute, the mentally unstable or retarded, and others requiring special attention. Yet another movement urged curriculum changes, under the rubric of "life adjustment" or "life experience," which would include studies of marriage and the family, adolescent relations, and other social and nonacademic content. In the name of equal opportunity there was even a proposal to offer complete instruction to foreign-speaking groups in their own languages, a far cry indeed from the assimilative, melting-pot brand of equal opportunity expressed by Senator Sawyer so many years earlier.

As democracy in terms of equal opportunity began to exercise real effect upon American educational practice, criticisms arose, and it was pointed out that equal opportunity for the gifted, or high-ability student, was a subject rarely discussed. In Europe there were comments that American education seemed extraordinarily broad, in terms of the number of subjects provided, but correspondingly shallow in qualitative depth. As the movement for equal opportunity expanded, it appeared that the inequality of education actually obtained by American students became greater, not less. Concern was expressed that the citizenship gains were not enough to counterbalance the losses. The issue is still with us and no valid resolution of the conflict has yet been made.

11

David A. Ward

AN EQUAL CHANCE FOR EVERY CHILD

This short statement by a professional school administrator is an excellent example of the affirmative position in the debate over citizenship as equal opportunity which has agitated so many laymen and educators during the last forty years. One should notice carefully the humanitarian spirit of this essay, which probably influenced many more people than did the actual arguments. There was crusader zeal here, and a high moral tone. During the 1920's, equal opportunity was one of the rallying cries of those who were supremely confident of the efficacy of this remedy for current pedagogical problems.

To be sure, the affirmative side tended to beg some important questions, but not deliberately, since there was an honest belief that good intentions, energy, and common sense were what counted most in producing good citizens. After all, equal opportunity was simply a logical extension of Horace Mann's principle of free education for all, was it not? Behind the words of Superintendent Ward one feels the traditional American faith that education can solve all problems. Surely one need only extend it from the 85% who already have it to the remaining 15% in the city slums and in the poor rural areas, to the physically handicapped and to the adult illiterates, to assure a happy and secure society.

Why should not every child have an equal chance for an education? In our democracy, founded upon the principle that all men are created equal, it is logical to expect that every child should have an equal opportunity to prepare for citizenship. No standard lower than that is worthy the aspiration of any teacher or parent. No standard

From *Journal of Education*, June 10, 1929, 109:639-640.

lower than that can be accepted as the fulfillment of the responsibility of government or school officials, yet we are far from the realization of such a standard of education. So long as the school term varies from ten months to six months; so long as conditions vary from modern well-equipped schools to insanitary and unattractive surroundings; so long as the instruction given varies from the most carefully selected material to the simple rudiments with no adaptation to the child; so long as teacher-training requirements vary from sixteen years to seven years, we are not meeting the obligation implied in the declaration of equality which we accept as the basic principle of our civilization.

What does an equal chance mean? Certainly it does not mean uniformity, because all children do not live under similar conditions. Neither are they all endowed with similar abilities and traits. An equal chance means, then, an opportunity for every child to discover and develop under favorable conditions the powers which enable him to meet most effectively the obligations of life. To this opportunity every child in America is entitled.

To attain this ideal situation three conditions are necessary; first, there must be provided school buildings which are sanitary, comfortable and inviting, with adequate equipment for instruction; second, the curriculum must provide for the varying abilities, tendencies and life opportunities of the child; third, the standard of training for teachers must insure to every child a teacher whose ability, vision and skill can apply the curriculum to the needs of the child.

Not only are sanitary and comfortable buildings necessary, but the child should have pleasant and artistic surroundings. School buildings and grounds which are well-planned and well-kept contribute to the development of character as well as to intellectual growth. Too little attention is often given to the appearance of the school. This is especially true of rural schools, many of which are still much below the standard which should be maintained for reasonable opportunities in child development. Fortunately, however, this condition is being rapidly removed.

Inequality of opportunity of a much more serious nature exists in the character of instruction given. When children are provided instruction in academic subjects only and denied the opportunity of studying those subjects which lead directly to the occupations in which they may enter, or when the rigid curriculum requires that all children in a school conform to the same type of instruction, the opportunity of adapting their education to the life which their native abilities would prescribe is lost. The adaptation of courses of study to the needs of the child, however, is being effectively made in many well organized schools. There is great need that facilities be provided throughout the country for meeting this important obligation of the school.

Above every other consideration in importance is the teacher. Not only trained teachers, but teachers with sincere motives, with skill and vision are necessary to utilize the equipment and apply the curriculum to the best advantage of the children. We are still very far from the realization of this condition, and it is probably the most difficult one to attain. . . .

Happily all of the conditions discussed are improving, but they are not improving as rapidly as the resources of the country should warrant. Why do these conditions lag? What is the remedy? The cause is the lack of vision of the taxpaying public and the remedy is adult education. Educators have been engaged in educating children and asking the public for support in their enterprise. We must begin to educate the grown-ups. . . .

12

Edward L. Thorndike

THE DISTRIBUTION OF EDUCATION

For the negative side in the debate over equal opportunity one can hardly do better than this terse, objective comment by E. L. Thorndike, the noted educational psychologist. While the proponents stressed the spirit of crusade for justice, men like Thorndike preferred cold, logical analysis. The reasoning here is so clear, and so neatly anticipates the position of modern "two-track" advocates, that it speaks for itself. The basic question which Thorndike raised was simply this: Is equal education fair to the gifted children who must provide the country with its elite leadership? Today it seems incredible that so little respect was paid to his argument.

The response of Thorndike's opponents was spirited, idealistic, and, at times, question-begging. They announced that their own program was democratic education, while that of Thorndike and his followers was un-American, since it stressed "aristocratic" subjects like mathematics, pure science, and the humanities, and regarded European education with considerable approval. To this I. L. Kandel (Reading 82) and James B. Conant (Reading 83) have replied that selectivity which provides scholarship opportunities to all who are *able*, regardless of family wealth or status, can hardly be called aristocratic.

. . . The general spirit of our country for the past hundred years has been to make great efforts to increase the amount of education but to pay relatively little attention to its distribution. The plea of reformers has been for more education, regardless of who received it. There has been an indiscriminate urge toward more schools, longer school years, and later compulsory-attendance ages. Education of any sort for any person has been recommended as a national investment without much consideration of the differences in safety and income which may attach to the investment in certain boys and girls rather than in others. The mere volume of education has been taken as a measure of idealism, somewhat as the mere volume of gifts to beggars of all sorts used to be taken as a measure of philanthropy and charity.

In so far as any attention has been paid to the question of who were receiving much and who were receiving little education, the general tendency has been to try to equalize the distribution, by aiding backward communities, increasing the number of days schools were in session, delaying the permissible age for leaving school, enforcing attendance laws, and other lines of effort designed to raise the amount for those who were receiving less than others. The doctrine that equalization of education is beneficent, partly by remedying certain definite accidents and injustices and partly by a mysterious power to advance democracy and social justice, has been very popular. Its influence has been potent, not only in the distribution of education so as to give most to those who have least, but also in the efforts of teachers to bring backward pupils up to grade and in the establishment of special classes for the deficient and dull.

It may be doubted whether either the policy of striving for indiscriminate increase in the volume of education or the policy of favoring especially those who would otherwise have very little schooling was ever the best for the general welfare. A very strong argument could have been made at any time in the last half-century for exercising careful discrimination in the distribution of education, the most being given to those who would use it best for the common good. A fairly strong argument could also have been made that those who would use more education best for the common good would be those who already had a great deal of it—for example, promising young students of science, who, with more education, might make discoveries of great benefit to the world, or promising young physicians, clergymen, engineers, and the like, who, with more education, might serve their communities much better. However, so long as there were many children who had only a few years of schooling, each of less than a hundred days, the benevolent doctrine of changing distribution in such a way as to favor the least educated was rarely questioned. The prevention of illiteracy and the extension of education so that every child would have at least a thousand days of schooling seemed a wise as well as a humane policy, even if not in the end the wisest. . . .

Zeal to produce more schooling, that is, to increase the amount of schooling given in our country, has been one of America's fine idealisms. Such zeal should be maintained, but with it there should be equal zeal to distribute this education so that those will have most who can use it best. What evidence we now have indicates that the ablest receive very little more than the least able. . . . The passion for equalization which had a certain nobility when a large percentage of children barely learned to read and write becomes unwise, almost ridiculous, when the question is of spending our resources to keep in school boys of sixteen, or seventeen, or eighteen who would be happier and more useful at work or at play. Our increased resources should be used to aid young men and women whom nature and nurture

From *School Review*, May 1932, 40:337–338, 344–345. Copyright 1932 by The University of Chicago. Reprinted by permission of The University of Chicago Press.

have chosen to profit from schooling.

Doubtless, great ability will often manage to get education outside of schools or to get along without it, but those who can do so much for the world with so little are the very ones who should be given more. In the wars we are incessantly waging against disease, misery, depravity, injustice, and ugliness, we should not provide our best marksmen with the poorest weapons nor ask our bravest to fight with their naked hands.

The aims of education

THE "CULTURED GENTLEMAN"

The belief that producing a cultured gentleman is the true goal of education goes back at least as far as Aristotle and the classical Greeks. It has always been tacitly allied to the leadership training aspect of the citizenship purpose, but with an important difference. All citizenship education is state-centered, while the gentleman is a supreme individualist who values leisure and creativity for his private aesthetic enjoyment. During the later Middle Ages, the cult of chivalrous good manners was added to the gentleman's equipment, together with respect for science, both of which became part of a gentleman's proper education. This emphasis upon good behavior reminds one of the moral aim. However, a true gentleman behaved properly in order to please himself and his friends, not to serve God or to escape hellfire. Thus while the cultured gentleman concept was undeniably aristocratic, it was also profoundly individualistic and humanistic.

For a long time the gentlemanly purpose was unpopular with the overwhelming majority of Americans. Its emphasis upon good manners and appreciation of the fine arts struck them as outrageous snobbery. It appeared to typify foreign—especially English education to the average person. And its insistence that education for leisure was more important than learning how to make an honest living seemed a lazy man's alibi for dodging hard work. Yet the gentlemanly purpose has always been important in American educational circles. The typical gentlemanly purpose schools were the private preparatory schools, many small liberal arts colleges, and—on the feminine side—girls' finishing schools. In addition, social fraternities and sororities have their roots in the same educational purpose. Only a small percentage of the population, however, was directly affected by the preparatory schools, the small colleges, or the fraternities.

Quite another matter was amateur athletics, which for the last century has deeply affected nearly everyone. College and high-school sports were invented at the "gentleman's schools," and wherever practiced carry with them at least lip service to gentlemanly ideals and behavior. Walter Camp, the father of American college football, insisted that the chivalrous virtues learned on the athletic field carried over into the whole of life, and that sports were an invaluable part of good education in nobility of character.

Recently the growth of leisure, caused by shortened hours of work as the industrial revolution advances, has threatened to democratize the gentleman's purpose of education in appreciation of the fine arts. Good music, art, and literature are more popular than they have ever been. With early retirement from business life increasingly common among us, many are taking a new look at Aristotle's dictum that a gentleman's "education is the best provision for old age." The "cultured gentleman" purpose affects more people today than ever before in its history.

13

John Locke

SOME THOUGHTS CONCERNING EDUCATION

Although an Englishman, John Locke has been called "America's philosopher" because the ideas which shaped the Declaration of Independence and the Constitution were borrowed so heavily from his writings. In addition, he is one of the few Englishmen who can be described as a major figure in the history of education. Locke seems to have believed that if only the natural leaders of society were soundly educated as gentlemen, then morality, good citizenship, independent thought, and the reform of society would all quickly follow. He had no love for traditionalism in education, and he thought good teachers supremely important for the learning process. The term "governor," by which Locke meant a teacher or tutor, has gone out of modern usage, though we still encounter the feminine "governess" occasionally.

Surprisingly, Locke set great store by informal, experiential learning of a sort that we would now consider to be extracurricular activity. He agreed with Sir Francis Bacon that "Travel, in the younger sort, is a part of education," and he who travels goes to school. The popularity of shipboard seminars, the growing practice of granting academic credit for supervised summer travel in Europe, the establishment of university campuses abroad—all bear witness to the forethought of John Locke, who expressed these ideas more than 250 years ago.

. . . To form a young gentleman as he should be, 'tis fit his *governor* should himself be well-bred, understanding the ways of carriage and measures of civility in all the variety of persons, times, and places; and keep his pupil, as much as his age requires, constantly to the observation of them. This is an art not to be learnt nor taught by books. Nothing can give it but good company and observation join'd together. The taylor may make his clothes modish, and the dancing-master give fashion to his motions; yet neither of these, tho' they set off well, make a well-bred gentleman: no, tho' he have learning to boot, which, if not well manag'd, makes him more impertinent and intolerable in conversation. Breeding is that which sets a gloss upon all his other good qualities, and renders them useful to him, in procuring him the esteem and good-will of all that he comes near. Without good breeding his other accomplishments make him pass but for proud, conceited, vain, or foolish. . . .

From *The Harvard Classics—English Philosophers of the Seventeenth and Eighteenth Centuries*, ed. Charles W. Eliot, vol. 37 (New York: P. F. Collier & Son, 1910), pp. 76, 81-83, 191-192.

. . . The only fence against the world, is, a thorough knowledge of it, into which a young gentleman should be enter'd by degrees, as he can bear it; and the earlier the better, so he be in safe and skilful hands to guide him. The scene should be gently open'd, and his entrance made step by step, and the dangers pointed out that attend him from the several degrees, tempers, designs, and clubs of men. He should be prepar'd to be shock'd by some, and caress'd by others; warn'd who are like to oppose, who to mislead, who to undermine him, and who to serve him. He should be instructed how to know and distinguish them; where he should let them see, and when dissemble the knowledge of them and their aims and workings. And if he be too forward to venture upon his own strength and skill, the perplexity and trouble of a misadventure now and then, that reaches not his innocence, his health, or reputation, may not be an ill way to teach him more caution.

This, I confess, containing one great part of wisdom, is not the product of some superficial thoughts, or much reading; but the effect of experience and observation in a man who has liv'd in the world with his eyes open, and convers'd with men of all sorts. And therefore I think it of most value to be instill'd into a young man upon all occasions which offer themselves, that when he comes to launch into the deep himself, he may not be like one at sea without a line, compass or sea-chart; but may have some notice beforehand of the rocks and shoals, the currents and quicksands, and know a little how to steer, that he sink not before he get experience. He that thinks not this of more moment to his son, and for which he more needs a governor, than the languages and learned sciences, forgets of how much more use it is to judge right of men, and manage his affairs wisely with them, than to speak *Greek* and *Latin*, or argue in mood and figure; or to have his head fill'd with the abstruse speculations of natural philosophy and metaphysicks; nay, than to be well vers'd in *Greek* and *Roman* writers, though that be much better for a gentleman than to be a good Peripatetick or Cartesian, because those antient authors observ'd and painted mankind well, and give the best light into that kind of knowledge. He that goes into the eastern parts of *Asia*, will find able and acceptable men without any of these; but without virtue, knowledge of the world, and civility, an accomplish'd and valuable man can be found no where.

A great part of the learning now in fashion in the schools of *Europe*, and that goes ordinarily into the round of education, a gentleman may in a good measure be unfurnish'd with, without any great disparagement to himself or prejudice to his affairs. But prudence and good breeding are in all the stations and occurrences of life necessary; and most young men suffer in the want of them, and come rawer and more awkward into the world than they should, for this very reason, because these qualities, which are of all other the most necessary to be taught, and stand most in need of the assistance and help of a teacher, are generally neglected and thought but a slight or no part of a *tutor's* business. *Latin* and learning make all the noise; and the main stress is laid

upon his proficiency in things a great part whereof belong not to a gentleman's calling; which is to have the knowledge of a man of business, a carriage suitable to his rank, and to be eminent and useful in his country, according to his station. Whenever either spare hours from that, or an inclination to perfect himself in some parts of knowledge, which his *tutor* did but just enter him in, set him upon any study, the first rudiments of it, which he learn'd before, will open the way enough for his own industry to carry him as far as his fancy will prompt, or his parts enable him to go. Or, if he thinks it may save his time and pains to be help'd over some difficulties by the hand of a master, he may then take a man that is perfectly well skilled in it, or chuse such an one as he thinks fittest for his purpose. But to initiate his pupil in any part of learning, as far as is necessary for a young man in the ordinary course of his studies, an ordinary skill in the *governor* is enough. Nor is it requisite that he should be a thorough scholar, or possess in perfection all those sciences which 'tis convenient a young gentleman should have a taste of in some general view, or short system. A gentleman that would penetrate deeper must do it by his own genius and industry afterwards: For no body ever went far in knowledge, or became eminent in any of the sciences, by the discipline and constraint of a master. . . .

. . . The last part usually in education is *travel*, which is commonly thought to finish the work, and complete the gentleman. I confess *travel* into foreign countries has great advantages, but the time usually chosen to send young men abroad, is, I think, of all other, that which renders them least capable of reaping those *advantages*. Those which are propos'd, as to the main of them, may be reduced to these two: first, language, secondly, an improvement in wisdom and prudence, by seeing men, and conversing with people of tempers, customs and ways of living, different from one another, and especially from those of his parish and neighbourhood. . . .

14

W. M. Pomeroy

EDUCATED GENTLEMEN

Here is an essay written by an Amherst student in 1860 which shows how thoroughly the gentlemanly purpose had been absorbed by American undergraduates at small, "elite" liberal arts colleges. From such schools and such students came the American college fraternities and the literary clubs. It was they who invented school spirit and the sentimental love for "alma mater." And it was at these Ivy and Little Ivy League schools that intercollegiate football was born, later to be described by one college president as "the emotional center of college life."

It was in Puritan New England that the concept of the "Christian" gentleman emerged. For the gentleman to be also a good Christian helped to take much of the aristocratic curse off the desire to become "cultured." After the gentleman went through one more refinement and became a "muscular Christian" on the football field, what red-blooded American could still resist the appeal of the cultured gentleman aim of education?

Students may well ask themselves to what extent the ideal of the cultured gentleman still persists as a covert or overt objective in American schools. Do justifications for current practices—for example, certain extracurricular activities in secondary schools—stem from Pomeroy's concept of the well-rounded gentleman?

. . . The end of a Collegiate education is, or should be, to make educated gentlemen. Neither of these words alone embraces the idea. The College graduate should be not merely educated, but he should be a gentleman; not only a gentleman but an educated gentleman. Every College sends out yearly, men who are far from being educated. The really educated are comparatively few, even in the limited sense meant by the phrase "a College education." The number of gentlemen we apprehend to be fewer yet, and how many of the newly fledged alumni can make any pretension to the title of educated gentlemen. This is not the fault of the College; the Faculty are not to blame,— at least, but partially. Neither can the "College system" be held amenable. In its general plan it is probably the best that could be devised, and the details surely cannot be held responsible. Where then does the fault lie but with the Students themselves?

We will start with the supposition that all who go to College wish to come out educated gentlemen. Then let us see what are the means used to attain this end. We are perfectly safe in saying that every Student goes to College with the determination to do well, though each may have his own method of explaining this phrase. Every one has some lofty aspirations, some noble desires, some good end in view. At his first entrance he is met by the electioneering for Societies, and at last, to escape the importunities of the electioneers, he "pledges" to some Society. After the Freshmen have been mostly "pledged" they cease to be the lions of the place, and something now takes place in the shape of "Freshman visitation," or

From *University Quarterly*, October 1860, 2:262-272.

something equally barbarous. Perhaps the new comer is dragged out of bed at midnight and compelled to mount the table and make an impromptu speech, or elucidate the "prosody" of Livy, to the great delight of his tormentors and his own intense disgust; or perhaps, while preparing for his next morning's recitation, he is visited by a party of friends(?) who proceed to have a social smoke, without even saying so much as "by your leave, sir." He goes to recitation with the intention of learning all he can; of making a good recitation if possible; in fact, he supposes at this time that he came to College to learn. He does learn many things which he had better left unlearned. He learns that marks, good marks of course, are to be sought after as the *summun bonum.* He learns a way to obtain them too, without much trouble to himself. He learns that the easiest course for himself is to do as he sees others doing, even the so-called best scholars in the class. So he, with the rest, keeps his book open under the seat, and reads the lesson instead of learning it and reciting it. Or, if the lesson be one in the classics, he prepares it by the aid of that demoralizing help, known among Students by the name of "pony." Surely he forgets that no man ever yet rode to honor, knowledge or greatness. . . .

A College course does not do everything for a man. That is not the intention. It merely lays the foundation, and he is to build the superstructure himself. But there are some things which a man might attain in College if he would, and without which he will find himself lamentably deficient, when he gets out into the world. Among other things which might be mentioned, none is of more importance than the ability to converse well. To do this, it is necessary in the first place to have the ideas, and secondly, to be able to express them clearly and elegantly. Americans, and especially educated Americans, are proverbial for want of conversational talent. Good conversational power is justly regarded as one of the distinguishing characteristics of a gentleman, and when we reflect how much a man's influence is increased thereby, it is really wonderful that we let so lamentable a deficiency go uncorrected. Our Students are social enough, they talk enough. The great deficiency lies in the fact that their talk amounts to nothing. A great share is trivial, nonsensical, to say nothing of that which is really profane and vulgar. When they are thrown into society and are expected to take their part in intelligent conversation, whether on literature, art, or the popular religious or political questions of the day, they are made keenly sensible of their humiliating deficiency. While in College, it is not to be expected that Students will mingle very much in general society, but in their intercourse with each other, a vast deal of improvement might be made in this particular. . . .

. . . The demand of the age is for educated gentlemen, much more than for ministers, lawyers or doctors; men who will exert an influence, not only without the assistance of fortune and station, but in spite of them; men whose education is not merely superficial, whose gentlemanly demeanor springs from the kindly impulses of the heart, and is not that which is made to order, at the rooms of any dancing-master; men who are not so fastidious that they cannot labor in common things for the good of humanity, and for whom it is necessary to pray, as did a Methodist minister at a camp-meeting, for a too-delicate brother: "O Lord, we pray Thee, take the polish from Brother Jackson." By adding the word Christian to our title, we shall have that which expresses the highest type, the most exalted form of humanity. He who is in very truth an educated Christian gentleman, is the noblest work of God's creation, and has reached the highest perfection attainable here. He need have no care for his present reputation, no fear for his future destiny. Would that every Student would labor more faithfully, more earnestly for such a desirable consummation; that all would be more "inflamed with the study of learning, and the admiration of virtue; stirred up with high hopes of living to be brave men and worthy patriots, dear to God and famous to all ages."

The aims of education

MENTAL DISCIPLINE

For thousands of years those who live by their wits, whether inside or outside the schools, have insisted that the true aim of education is to produce a keen, quick-thinking mind. Education should provide exercise and discipline for developing mental facility. When we say in modern slang that a student is "really sharp," we mean that his mental abilities have been successfully developed. This aim of education has a special appeal for intellectuals, and goes back to Plato's "philosopher-kings" as well as to the medieval Scholasticism of Abélard and St. Thomas Aquinas. As Richard Hooker said in 1593, "Education and instruction are the means . . . to make our natural faculty of reason better." From the point of view of such great thinkers as these, the great motto of the schools should be "Learn to think!"

The protagonists of mental training placed reason at the summit of educational achievement, rather than good character, earning a living, becoming a good citizen, or familiarity with the arts. They felt that everything could be tested and changed for the better by rigorous employment of the human capacity for thought, if this capacity were highly developed. They were partial to intellectual creativity and originality. Nevertheless they were accused by their opponents of being icy-hearted and lacking in sympathy for the average individuals who comprised nine tenths of the student total on every pedagogical level. Indeed, the advocates of the mental-discipline approach often came perilously close to endorsing education for its own sake rather than as a means to some more important end.

Unlike the aims previously considered, the mental-discipline purpose can claim no special category of schools primarily dedicated to its inculcation. The indicators of its presence are certain special types of programs which express the mind-sharpening emphasis, and may appear in any kind of school. At the elementary or secondary level these are likely to be problem-solving techniques or curricula. In the colleges one may encounter this emphasis in the Great Books program, in the various Problems of American Democracy courses, or in the case method pioneered by the Harvard Graduate School of Business. All too commonly classical studies, once vocational necessities for religious, legal, and medical training, are now justified and defended by their instructors on mental discipline grounds.

15

Henry Ford

KNOWLEDGE AND EDUCATION

Few men have been praised more highly or denounced more vociferously than Henry Ford. During the 1920's he made all Americans car-borne and pushed mass production to extremes so unprecedented that the whole world paid homage to his industrial genius. Yet this same man published outrageous anti-Semitic propaganda and once admitted publicly that he did not know when the War of 1812 was fought! Like nearly all self-made men, he was extremely suspicious of organized education, on grounds which are expressed with blunt sincerity in these pages taken from his autobiography. Ford was speaking as an ordinary member of society, yet he was not far removed from the brilliant Pascal's observation that "too much and too little education hinder the mind."

Many twentieth century businessmen have felt that Henry Ford expressed their general philosophy of life better than any other spokesman. Years after the builder of the "tin lizzie" had died, Alvan A. Duerr restated the Ford conception: "Business is no great believer in utilitarian or so-called vocational training, which, on the whole, has destroyed more educational value than it has promoted. If the college will turn out a trained mind, which means a disciplined mind that can be made to do its job, [and a sound social attitude] . . . business will gladly provide its own vocational training. And the broader the foundation which the college lays, the easier will be the task of business" (5).

An able man is a man who can do things, and his ability to do things is dependent on what he has in him. What he has in him depends on what he started with and what he has done to increase and discipline it.

An educated man is not one whose memory is trained to carry a few dates in history—he is one who can accomplish things. A man who cannot

From *My Life and Work* by Henry Ford in collaboration with Samuel Crowther (New York: Doubleday & Company, 1922), pp. 247-250.

think is not an educated man however many college degrees he may have acquired. Thinking is the hardest work any one can do—which is probably the reason why we have so few thinkers. There are two extremes to be avoided: one is the attitude of contempt toward education, the other is the tragic snobbery of assuming that marching through an educational system is a sure cure for ignorance and mediocrity. You cannot learn in any school what the world is going to do next year, but you can learn some of the things which the world has tried to do in former years, and where it failed and where it succeeded. If education consisted in warning the young student away from some of the false theories on which men have tried to build, so that he may be saved the loss of the time in finding out by bitter experience, its good would be unquestioned. An education which consists of signposts indicating the failure and the fallacies of the past doubtless would be very useful. It is not education just to possess the theories of a lot of professors. Speculation is very interesting, and sometimes profitable, but it is not education. To be learned in science to-day is merely to be aware of a hundred theories that have not been proved. And not to know what those theories are is to be "uneducated," "ignorant," and so forth. If knowledge of guesses is learning, then one may become learned by the simple expedient of making his own guesses. And by the same token he can dub the rest of the world "ignorant" because it does not know what his guesses are. But the best that education can do for a man is to put him in possession of his powers, give him control of the tools with which destiny has endowed him, and teach him how to think. The college renders its best service as an intellectual gymnasium, in which mental muscle is developed and the student strengthened to do what he can. To say, however, that mental gymnastics can be had only in college is not true, as every educator knows. A man's real education begins after he has left school. True education is gained through the discipline of life.

There are many kinds of knowledge, and it depends on what crowd you happen to be in, or how the fashions of the day happen to run, which kind of knowledge is most respected at the moment. There are fashions in knowledge, just as there are in everything else. When some of us were lads, knowledge used to be limited to the Bible. There were certain men in the neighbourhood who knew the Book thoroughly, and they were looked up to and respected. Biblical knowledge was highly valued then. But nowadays it is doubtful whether deep acquaintance with the Bible would be sufficient to win a man a name for learning.

Knowledge, to my mind, is something that in the past somebody knew and left in a form which enables all who will to obtain it. If a man is born with normal human faculties, if he is equipped with enough ability to use the tools which we call "letters" in reading or writing, there is no knowledge within the possession of the race that he cannot have—if he wants it! The only reason why every man does not know everything that the human mind has ever learned is that no one has ever yet found it worth while to know that much. Men satisfy their minds more by finding out things for themselves than by heaping together the things which somebody else has found out. You can go out and gather knowledge all your life, and with all your gathering you will not catch up even with your own times. You may fill your head with all the "facts" of all the ages, and your head may be just an overloaded fact-box when you get through. The point is this: Great piles of knowledge in the head are not the same as mental activity. A man may be very learned and very useless. And then again, a man may be unlearned and very useful.

The object of education is not to fill a man's mind with facts; it is to teach him how to use his mind in thinking. And it often happens that a man can think better if he is not hampered by the knowledge of the past.

It is a very human tendency to think that what mankind does not yet know no one can learn. And yet it must be perfectly clear to everyone that the past learning of mankind cannot be allowed to hinder our future learning. Mankind has not gone so very far when you measure its progress against the knowledge that is yet to be gained—the secrets that are yet to be learned.

One good way to hinder progress is to fill a man's head with all the learning of the past; it makes him feel that because his head is full, there is nothing more to learn. Merely gathering knowledge may become the most useless work a man can do. What can you do to help and heal the world? That is the educational test. If a man can hold up his own end, he counts for one. If he can help ten or a hundred or a thousand other men hold up their ends, he counts for more. He may be quite rusty on many things that inhabit the realm of print, but he is a learned man just the same. When a man is master of his own sphere, whatever it may be, he has won his degree—he has entered the realm of wisdom.

16

Abraham Flexner

A MODERN SCHOOL

Professional educators, especially on the college level, might dismiss Henry Ford as a busybody—in fact, many of them did so. However, they could not treat so lightly the statements of Abraham Flexner, the father of our modern medical schools and one of the most eminent figures in twentieth century education. Flexner is noted for his influential report on medical education which appeared in 1910. The *Flexner Report,* as it is known historically, was concerned with the kind and quality of education provided for the 4500 medical students being graduated annually at the time. Flexner was concerned with the lack of content in medical science provided for American physicians, feeling that medical education gave too much emphasis to aspects of medical practice and neglected the substantive knowledge of medicine. Flexner's analysis of medical education has a counterpart in current proposals for changes in the content of teacher-education programs.

Beyond any doubt, Flexner believed that traditional education was ineffective and that a different type of educational program was called for in order to provide better training of the intellect. This paper was prepared by Flexner in 1916 for a private meeting of the General Education Board, one of the philanthropic predecessors of the Ford Foundation of today. The result of the meeting was a decision to endow the proposed Lincoln School of Teachers College, Columbia University, which quickly became one of the most famous and influential of the early Progressive education showpieces. So in the beginning, outstanding college educators like Flexner, President Charles W. Eliot of Harvard, and President Nicholas Murray Butler of Columbia gave powerful support to the new educational experimentation in the belief that better intellectual development would result. Whether that confidence was justified by subsequent events is a question which the present generation of students of education will have to decide for itself.

. . . I suggest, that, in the first place, a man educated in the modern sense, has mastered the fundamental tools of knowledge: he can read and write; he can spell the words he is in the habit of using; he can express himself clearly orally or in writing; he can figure correctly and with moderate facility within the limits of practical need; he knows something about the globe on which he lives. So far there is no difference between a man educated in the modern sense and a man educated in any other sense.

There is, however, a marked divergence at the next step. The education which we are criticising is overwhelmingly formal and traditional. If objection is made to this or that study on the ground that it is useless or unsuitable, the answer comes that it "trains the mind" or has been valued for centuries. "Training the mind" in the sense in which the claim is thus made for algebra or ancient languages is an assumption none too well founded; traditional esteem is an insufficient offset to present and future uselessness. A man educated in the modern sense will forego the somewhat doubtful mental discipline received from formal studies; he will be contentedly ignorant of things for learning which no better reason than tradition can be assigned. Instead, his education will be obtained from studies that serve real purposes.

From *Occasional Papers, No. 3: A Modern School* by Abraham Flexner (New York: General Education Board, 1916), pp. 8-10.

Its content, spirit and aim will be realistic and genuine, not formal or traditional. Thus, the man educated in the modern sense will be trained to know, to care about and to understand the world he lives in, both the physical world and the social world. A firm grasp of the physical world means the capacity to note and to interpret phenomena; a firm grasp of the social world means a comprehension of and sympathy with current industry, current science and current politics. The extent to which the history and literature of the past are utilized depends, not on what we call the historic value of this or that performance or classic, but on its actual pertinency to genuine need, interest or capacity. In any case, the object in view would be to give children the knowledge they need, and to develop in them the power to handle themselves in our own world. Neither historic nor what are called purely cultural claims would alone be regarded as compelling.

Even the progressive curricula of the present time are far from accepting the principle above formulated. For, though they include things that serve purposes, their eliminations are altogether too timid. They have occasionally dropped, occasionally curtailed, what experience shows to be either unnecessary or hopelessly unsuitable. But they retain the bulk of the traditional course of study, and present it in traditional fashion, because an overwhelming case has not—so it is judged—yet been made against it. If, however, the standpoint which I have urged were adopted, the curriculum would contain only what can be shown to serve a purpose. The burden of proof would be on the subject, not on those who stand ready to eliminate it. If the subject serves a purpose, it is eligible to the curriculum; otherwise not. I need not stop at this juncture to show that "serving a purpose," "useful," "genuine," "realistic," and other descriptive terms are not synonymous with "utilitarian," "materialistic," "commercial," etc., . . .

It follows from the way in which the child is made and from the constitution and appeal of modern society that instruction in objects and in phenomena will at one time or another play a very prominent part in the Modern School. It is, however, clear that mere knowledge of phenomena and mere ability to understand or to produce objects falls short of the ultimate purpose of a liberal education. Such knowledge and such ability indubitably have, as President Eliot's paper pointed out, great value in themselves; and they imply such functioning of the senses as promises a rich fund of observation and experience. But in the end, if the Modern School is to be adequate to the need of modern life, this concrete training must produce sheer intellectual power. Abstract thinking has perhaps never before played so important a part in life as in this materialistic and scientific world of ours—this world of railroads, automobiles, wireless telegraphy, and international relationships. Our problems involve indeed concrete data and present themselves in concrete forms; but, back of the concrete details, lie difficult and involved intellectual processes. Hence the realistic education we propose must eventuate in intellectual power. We must not only cultivate the child's interests, senses, and practical skill, but we must train him to interpret what he thus gets to the end that he may not only be able to perceive and to do, but that he may know in intellectual terms the significance of what he has perceived and done. The Modern School would prove a disappointment, unless greater intellectual power is procurable on the basis of a realistic training than has been procured from a formal education, which is prematurely intellectual and to no slight extent a mere make-believe. . . .

The aims of education

THE REFORM OF SOCIETY

The idea that reforming society is a proper aim of education requires some explanation. In a sense, every aim considered thus far implies that if it were successfully applied in changing human behavior, society would be improved as a direct result. The key word here is *implies*. Other educational purposes had reflected the desires of society; here for the first time we have educators arguing that they should produce new ideas of their own which should be taught to the younger generation in order that social changes might come quickly. No longer would teachers merely carry out the orders of politicians and businessmen; instead they would lead society themselves. Reform was too important to be left in the hands of amateur abolitionists or temperance crusaders; surely professional social-scientist educators were more competent in all such areas.

The reform of society seemed to call for education of the whole man, not merely educating his mind or his hands or providing him with specific prescriptions for behavior on special occasions, as, for example, how to act on election day, or when listening to a concert. Education, said J. F. Clarke, "is the unfolding of the whole human nature. It is growing up in all things to our highest possibilities" (6).

Progressive education and the reform of society through education came to be regarded as interchangeable terms. Although Progressive education included far more than this single purpose, it remains true that neither subject can be easily separated from the other. There was no special type of school devoted to the reform purpose and only a relatively small number of schools could be labeled as "Progressive schools." Progressive education, as a new movement in educational theory and practice, expected to capture or transform *all* schools by the force of its example rather than by a systematic design.

The Progressive education movement came at a time in the twentieth century when it attracted attention around the world for its originality and its thoroughly American character. Yet it was extremely eclectic, borrowing notions from many places—from G. Stanley Hall's child study movement, from Freud's psychology, from the pragmatic philosophy of William James and Dewey, from business vocationalism, from Flexner's mind sharpening, from Rousseau's nature worship, to mention a few examples—without losing its quality of originality.

Reform was taken so seriously by Progressive educators that it often seemed they were trying first to destroy and then to rebuild everything—the curriculum, school administration, and teaching methods. Despite this, they were surprisingly popular. Their very eclecticism gained support from unexpected sources—from businessmen, labor leaders, college intellectuals, and moral spokesmen. They appealed with special force to youth, and its burning desire to change the traditional policies of a "fuddy-duddy" older generation. Within the movement romanticism and scientism battled for control, often becoming inextricably confused in the process. The romantic side showed up in a Progressive interpretation of pansophism (the feeling that everybody can learn all about everything), in its criticisms of the textbook, and in its emphasis on natural child growth. The scientism can be seen in the Progressive conviction that education could be a science founded upon psychology, with new theories and terminology, and that the focus of much of the experimentation should be on method.

Among the internal problems which Progressive education faced, and never answered satisfactorily, was whether it should give priority to the development of individualism or to adjustment to society. Another difficulty was that although the movement was launched with strong support from higher education, its rapid shift to an elementary- and secondary-school focus alienated most of the original college supporters. Finally, the Progressives utterly lacked effective organization or internal unity. The contradiction and discord within the movement grew to the point where the general public gradually became confused, irritated, and at length hostile. Because of the lack of a rigorous system of thought, the movement was subject to many misinterpretations.

Even so, Progressive education was immensely exciting. Some of its ideas and practices will be as permanently useful as the work of Plato, Comenius, or Rousseau. The problem is one of deciding which aspects of Progressive education lacked validity, and which were testable. In the ebb and flow of educational history, almost certainly future generations will again feel the urge to use the schools to reform *their* societies. The rigor with which we examine a prior effort in this direction may help to provide clues to better predict the consequences of any new proposals for reform.

17

W. G. Todd

EDUCATION AND LIFE

The selection below is taken from a baccalaureate sermon delivered by a relatively unknown Unitarian minister, the Reverend W. G. Todd, on July 14, 1875. It was delivered to the graduating class of Derby Academy at Hingham, Massachusetts, a private preparatory school most of whose students expected to enroll at Harvard University. In the sermon one finds evidence of the religious roots of Progressive education, and many clues to explain why it won support from religious liberals concerned with moral uplift.

However, the reform-of-society theme receives less attention here than the emphasis on total education. Readers will be aware of the use of a broad and undefined terminology—educating the "whole man," education as "an unfolding of the whole nature," and even the title of the address, "Education and Life." Throughout, there runs the strong moralistic tone which later in the 1920's characterized the Progressive movement. One is likely to conclude by wondering if the program of the Progressive educators was really so daring and challenging after all. Could it have been merely the efforts of a new generation of teachers to respond to the traditional wishes of society?

. . . All this work, too, which means so much to ourselves as individuals, means just as much to society and the state. The people, not the king, sustain American society. Our culture finds its roots in no royal court, but each man's hearthside upholds the nation's dignity, culture, and morals. To make the nation, we begin at home; to influence public sentiment and make laws, we begin with number one. Where do we vote, and when? Not at the polls alone, nor on election days. We are voting all the time; and in this most vital voting the woman's as well as the man's ballot is counted. It is not the men whom we send to the state house and to Washington who make our laws, but we who have made them before the men were sent. They never act effectively beyond our sentiments; and, when they rise to their greatest heights of moral excellence, it is only the high tide of our sentiments at home. In public sentiment, we make a king, we create a creator, and

he is made out of the books we read, out of the thoughts we think, out of that hour or half hour which the mechanic, merchant, and day-laborer can wrest from the hand of idleness. In our literature we find the expression, "Savior of his country." It has heretofore been applied to one man, and associated with a peculiar emergency. To-day, every intelligent, educated voter is the savior of his country, and the occasion which makes him such is not a peculiar, but a permanent, condition of affairs.

But time will not permit me more than thus briefly to touch upon the broader reference of your lives and your studies. Now, in all this talk about culture, improvement, &c., I may perhaps seem to some of you to have neglected the religious side of the question, and to have placed too much dependence on education alone. Let me, then, say now, in plain language, that all the true and natural religion of which I have any knowledge, that all the true and natural religion which I believe God, and not man, has ordained, is, and always must be, included in the terms "education," "culture," and "growth" as I have been using them. There is no such thing as a genuine religion shut off by itself and outside of these. In this world of God's orderly and formulated thinking, which we call laws of nature, and in this age of scientific thought, which, bowing before these eternal laws in humility, saying, "Not my will, but thine," praying, "Give me truths, for I am weary of these surfaces,"—this age, which is changing the whole aspect of theology, and pushing to the wall man's vain imaginings, man's false supports in morals and thought, there is no room left for that kind of religion which is outside of law, or different from the processes and laws of true education, culture, and growth.

Understand me, however, not as using these terms in any narrow sense. Education is not mere learning, stored in memory, but an unfolding of the whole nature. Culture is not that superficial thing which often bears the name whereby a man plasters things upon his external self as the Indian his paint and gaudy trappings. True culture is of the spirit, is internal and eternal, including the whole man, his faith as well as reason, his worship and devotion as well as thought and investigation.

A man is only educated when this educing process refers to the bringing out or unfolding of his whole nature; and if religion is not in this process, it is not at all. A man is only cultured when he is refined in every part, like gold cast into the furnace; and, as I know of no fire that purifies one part of the gold and not another, so I know of no true culture that refines the head and not the heart, that refines man human-ward and not God-ward. And what is true of these is true of growth also. Religious faith and worship cannot be separated from thought. You gain no knowledge without that faith which is inseparable from the state of mind necessary to its attainment. You gain no single thought, no plane of moral life, no grade of character, no point in development

above you that you do not first admire, worship, and long for. The contest between religion and intellect is like war between a man's hands and his feet. Your hands of faith and aspiration reach up, apprehending and feeling after a round in the ladder of life above you; and, by these, you draw yourself upward and climb to a higher level, raising thereby, step by step, the plane of comprehension and intellect on which your feet stand. The whole work is one effort of one organic whole. The separation of religion and education is also like separating sweetness from the unfolding of the rose. As form, color, and sweetness are different manifestations of the flower's unfolding, so the intellectual, moral, and spiritual are different manifestations of an unfolding in each individual. The intellect is alone incomplete. It is only half. Religion, not morality, is the other half. Religion is not, as sometimes said, the mere aroma of morality, not a mist of sentiment arising from its ebullition; but its inspirer, and, together with the intellect, its creator. If cloud-like, it is, like the clouds of heaven, the creator of the stream, and, together with thought, the creator of that applied power which runs the machinery of human society.

Whatever man may say of the needs of religion as one thing, and the needs of education as another, I simply know they are two names of a single process, and a single journey of life, towards the Mount of God. I simply know one fact,—a fact verified by past and present,—that God is the end, the end of all natural human unfolding and growth. He is hinted in every fact; he is revealed in every law; every cause of existing phenomena points to Him, every principle in life or thought, and every gleam of human beauty or shade of darkness, just as the broken sunbeams of color point to the perfect yet invisible ray of light back of them, and just as those beams of invisible light, still further back, are seen as one central yet omnipresent sun. . . .

18

Thomas Alva Edison

OBSOLETE EDUCATION

These observations of Thomas Alva Edison, the famous inventor, provide a fine example of the views of the period on vocational education and the mind-sharpening concept of learning. The contents of this article illustrate the kind of business social thought which was fertile ground for the ideas of educational reform. Individuals, either as private citizens or in their roles as school board members, further helped the Progressive movement by financial support. Edison's remarks, appearing just before World War I when Dewey's writings were coming into the limelight, aroused wide interest and controversy.

Much of Edison's hostility to the schools was due to his personal experience with them. He had only three months of formal instruction, refusing to return when he overheard his teacher tell an inspector that he was "addled" and not worth keeping in school. Thereafter he was entirely self-taught, relying upon library books and his mother's suggestions. As a result Edison had no love for the educational status quo. He declared that society could progress only if enough people were made dissatisfied with it. He praised the unrest of youth as "a fine thing for the world." Some of his other ideas were to replace textbooks with visual aids, to employ IQ tests and questionnaire (or objective) examinations, and to overhaul existing teaching methods completely. "Life, itself . . . is becoming an advanced institution of learning," he wrote. The pronouncements of well-known figures like Edison lent weight to the emerging educational reforms and raised the question of what kind of education was preferred by the world of business and commerce—traditional or new?

I am frequently asked about our system of education. I say that we have none. Our system is a relic of past ages. It consists of parrot-like repetitions. It is a dull study of twenty-six hieroglyphs.

Groups of hieroglyphs. That is what the young of this present day study. Here is an object. I place it in the hands of a child. I tell him to look at it. If we begin before we have hardened and dried his mind he studies the object with kindling enthusiasm. The mind of the child is naturally active. Why should we make him take his impressions of things through the ear when he may be able to see? The child is a natural born "rubber neck." His curiosity is alert. Give him the chance and he will learn. One glance, if he sees the thing itself, is better than two hours of studying about a thing which he does not see. The child develops through exercise. Give him plenty of exercise for body and brain. The more he works his arm the bigger the muscles; the more the faculties are exercised in a normal way the greater the brain. The folds of the brain grow deeper through observation; they grow fallow from disuse. If we educate too abruptly—if we cram the mind with facts memorized for themselves alone—what comes? Pure atrophy. This matter of education is a big question for the American people. It is of the utmost importance that every faculty should meet its environment. What is the use of crowding the mind with facts which cannot be utilized by the child because the method of their acquisition is distasteful to him?

I like the Montessori method. It teaches through play. It makes learning a pleasure. It follows the natural instincts of the human being. That system of education will succeed which shows to those who learn the actual thing—not the ghost of it. I firmly believe that the moving picture is destined to bear an important part in the education of the future. One may devote pages to the descriptions of the processes of nature to be learned by rote in the schools. Suppose instead that we show to the child the stages of that process of nature—the cocoon itself, the picture of the cocoon unfolding, the butterfly actually emerging. The knowledge which comes from the actual seeing is worth while. The geography which comes from travel is better than the geography of the books; the next thing to travel is following the same scenes through the moving picture.

I am now conducting an educational experiment the results of which I shall announce one of these days. We have two classes, each consisting of twelve pupils under fifteen years of age. One is composed of girls and another of boys. They are being taught from moving pictures, and after seeing the pictures they write the results of their observations. We give them no formulae, no statements; we leave all to their own observation. The faculties are being quickened and stimulated by this method of study, which has in it an element of play as well, while the knowledge obtained is not from mere memorizing. There is much ignorance in the world, mostly from lack

From *The Diary and Sundry Observations of Thomas Alva Edison,* ed. Dagobert Runes (New York: Philosophical Library, 1948), pp. 111-114.

of proper observation. If we had a better system of education we should have hardly any room for "crooks."

The trouble with our way of educating as generally followed is that it does not give elasticity to the mind. It casts the brain into a mould. It insists that the child must accept. It does not encourage original thought or reasoning, and it lays more stress on memory than on observation. The result of accepting unrelated facts fosters conservatism. It breeds fear, and from fear comes ignorance. The seeing of things in the making is what counts. Then the mind can approach the gaining of knowledge without prejudice. Shall we say to the young that they shall merely memorize the observations of others, learn by rote the thoughts of others and, having spent years in the hoarding up of what we call knowledge, begin to think? The exercise in thinking should begin from the earliest years, and it can be directed through bringing the mind in contact with the things that are. What we call conservatism is largely a result of a hard and fast way of teaching, a worship of the twenty-six hieroglyphs, the adoration of symbols, which fosters the creed that nothing can be done which has not been done by our fathers. That is conservatism, which is the greatest foe of progress, for it is well known that it takes from five to seven years for every invention destined for universal use to make its way through the crust of tradition.

19

John Dewey

MY PEDAGOGIC CREED

There are few students of educational thought in the civilized world who have never heard of John Dewey. This famous philosopher taught at the University of Chicago and later at Columbia University, where he became closely associated with Teachers College. In spite of a literary style that at times requires careful interpretation, Dewey was read everywhere with excitement and fascination by those who were discontented with the educational status quo. Certainly it is in the pragmatism and instrumentalism of William James and John Dewey that the philosophical roots of Progressive education are firmly embedded.

The following selection by Dewey is composed of key elements in his "Pedagogic Creed," published in 1897, and is one of Dewey's first pieces of systematic writing on the subject. Many persons consider that this essay was the generating force for the Progressive education movement. One should keep in mind that Dewey was a philosopher, not an educator, and his views are therefore couched in philosophical terms.

What the school is

I believe that the school is primarily a social institution. Education being a social process, the school is simply that form of community life in which all those agencies are concentrated that will be most effective in bringing the child to share in the inherited resources of the race, and to use his own powers for social ends.

I believe that education, therefore, is a process of living and not a preparation for future living.

I believe that the school must represent present life—life as real and vital to the child as that which he carries on in the home, in the neighborhood, or on the playground.

I believe that education which does not occur through forms of life . . . is always a poor substitute for the genuine reality and tends to cramp and to deaden. . . .

The subject-matter of education

I believe that the social life of the child is the basis of concentration, or correlation, in all his

From *School Journal*, January 16, 1897, 54:77-80.

training or growth. The social life gives the unconscious unity and the background of all his efforts and of all his attainments.

I believe that the subject-matter of the school curriculum should mark a gradual differentiation out of the primitive unconscious unity of social life.

I believe that we violate the child's nature and render difficult the best ethical results, by introducing the child too abruptly to a number of special studies, of reading, writing, geography, etc., out of relation to this social life.

I believe, therefore, that the true center of correlation on the school subjects is not science, nor literature, nor history, nor geography, but the child's own social activities.

I believe that education cannot be unified in the study of science, or so called nature study, because apart from human activity, nature itself is not a unity; nature in itself is a number of diverse objects in space and time, and to attempt to make it the center of work by itself, is to introduce a principle of radiation rather than one of concentration.

I believe that literature is the reflex expression and interpretation of social experience; that hence it must follow upon and not precede such experience. It, therefore, cannot be made the basis, although it may be made the summary of unification.

I believe once more that history is of educative value in so far as it presents phases of social life and growth. It must be controlled by reference to social life. When taken simply as history it is thrown into the distant past and becomes dead and inert. Taken as the record of man's social life and progress it becomes full of meaning. I believe, however, that it cannot be so taken excepting as the child is also introduced directly into social life.

I believe accordingly that the primary basis of education is in the child's powers at work along the same general constructive lines as those which have brought civilization into being.

I believe that the only way to make the child conscious of his social heritage is to enable him to perform those fundamental types of activity which make civilization what it is.

I believe, therefore, in the so-called expressive or constructive activities as the center of correlation.

I believe that this gives the standard for the place of cooking, sewing, manual training, etc., in the school.

I believe that they are not special studies which are to be introduced over and above a lot of others in the way of relaxation or relief, or as additional accomplishments. I believe rather that they represent, as types, fundamental forms of social activity; and that it is possible and desirable that the child's introduction into the more formal subjects of the curriculum be through the medium of these activities. . . .

I believe that there is, therefore, no succession of studies in the ideal school curriculum. If education is life, all life has, from the outset, a scientific aspect, an aspect of art and culture, and an aspect of communication. It cannot, therefore, be true that the proper studies for one grade are mere reading and writing, and that at a later grade, reading, or literature, or science, may be introduced. The progress is not in the succession of studies but in the development of new attitudes towards, and new interests in, experience.

I believe finally, that education must be conceived as a continuing reconstruction of experience; that the process and the goal of education are one and the same thing. . . .

The school and social progress

I believe that education is the fundamental method of social progress and reform.

I believe that all reforms which rest simply upon the enactment of law, or the threatening of certain penalties, or upon changes in mechanical or outward arrangements, are transitory and futile.

I believe that education is a regulation of the process of coming to share in the social consciousness; and that the adjustment of individual activity on the basis of this social consciousness is the only sure method of social reconstruction.

I believe that this conception has due regard for both the individualistic and socialistic ideals. It is duly individual because it recognizes the formation of a certain character as the only genuine basis of right living. It is socialistic because it recognizes that this right character is not to be formed by merely individual precept, example, or exhortation, but rather by the influence of a certain form of institutional or community life upon the individual, and that the social organism through the school, as its organ, may determine ethical results.

I believe that in the ideal school we have the reconciliation of the individualistic and the institutional ideals.

I believe that the community's duty to education is, therefore, its paramount moral duty. By law and punishment, by social agitation and discussion, society can regulate and form itself in a more or less haphazard and chance way. But through education society can formulate its own purposes, can organize its own means and resources, and thus shape itself with definiteness and economy in the direction in which it wishes to move.

I believe that when society recognizes the possibilities in this direction, and the obligations which these possibilities impose, it is impossible to conceive of the resources of time, attention, and money which will be put at the disposal of the educator.

I believe that it is the business of every one interested in education to insist upon the school as the primary and most effective interest of social progress and reform in order that society may be awakened to realize what the school stands for, and aroused to the necessity of endowing the educator with sufficient equipment properly to perform his task. . . .

I believe, finally, that the teacher is engaged, not simply in the training of individuals, but in the formation of the proper social life.

I believe that every teacher should realize the dignity of his calling; that he is a social servant set apart for the maintenance of proper social order and the securing of the right social growth.

I believe that in this way the teacher always is the prophet of the true God and the usherer in of the true kingdom of God.

20

THE RELATION OF EDUCATION TO THE WELL-BEING OF STATES

In a sense, the idea that education should aim at the reform of society is older than one might think, for the citizenship purpose of the nation-wide common school system was exceedingly idealistic and broad-ranging. Here, in the lengthy comment prepared by the editor of the *New Englander* on the occasion of Horace Mann's Eleventh Annual Report to the Massachusetts Board of Education, one can see some of the deep citizenship roots of Progressive education.

The editor's belief that education could and should reshape society is evident. To insist that universal education will make a nation wealthy (and eliminate poverty) is startling enough. To go further and say that it will destroy nine tenths of the crime, drunkenness, and immoral behavior to be found in society positively takes one's breath away. Yet our forefathers seem to have accepted such assumptions without much difficulty, and thus the unique American faith in the power of education to solve all problems was born.

The assumption that universal education alone is a sufficient instrument for all social change may be naïve; however, students should be aware that a similar emphasis is being placed upon education in some of the emerging nations in, for example, Africa. The question may be raised: "What social, economic, and political influences must be taken into account in order to design an educational program to serve as an instrument for social change?"

. . . Modern nations have adopted systems of education differing in character, according to the reigning ideas of the people. But all aim to repeat themselves in their posterity by some kind of educational institutions. Whether the mass of the people shall be educated or not, and what shall be the kind of education imparted, depends upon the object which the leading minds of the nation have in view. The early colonies of New England opened the fountains of knowledge to all. The first system of free schools in the history of our race was adopted on these western shores. It was a new measure, a most radical step, an innovation beyond all former innovations. Our fathers reasoned—and nobody now questions the soundness of their logic—that if *all* were trained aright, intellectually and morally, the people would be able to take care of themselves, and save the enormous bill it had always cost the world to be civilly and ecclesiastically governed. They denied

From *New Englander,* April 1848, 6:208-209, 212-213.

that God created a few men with better blood in their veins, on purpose to be the monopolists of all the wealth, and learning, and power of the world. And they acted consistently. The success of their experiment shows their wisdom. Public schools are esteemed among us as necessaries of life, and New England men carry them wherever they go in their migrations: so that they are established, with various modifications, in all the northern and western states of the Union.

Look now at the result of the general education of the people in those states where the school system has been in operation for the longest period? You behold a degree of order, thrift, enterprise, wealth, virtue, and general comfort and happiness, unequaled in any country where the like cause has not been operating. In Massachusetts and Connecticut this cause has been at work for two hundred years; and although we can not say precisely what proportion of influence is to be attributed to the public schools of these states, and what to other influences which have tended to the same results, yet wise men never hesitate to assign them a prominent place among the causes which have made these states so prosperous. The great mass of the people have been so educated in these schools, have acquired such an amount of knowledge, and been subjected to such mental and moral discipline, that their skill and efficiency in all kinds of productive labor, and the facility with which they turn their hands to all sorts of business, are mentioned to their credit throughout the world. They have thus been qualified, beyond any other nation, to be a self-supporting and self-governing people. Whence the contrast between them in respect to character and condition and those states and nations which have no similar system of public education? Whence their wealth? Not the opulence of the few scattered amidst a thousand poor; but the abundance and independence of the masses? the wealth that enables them to sustain their numerous churches, their civil, charitable and literary institutions? to invest millions in public works at home and abroad? to meet the calls of benevolence which come so frequently from the East and the West? to add ornament and luxury to the comfort and competence of tens of thousands of happy homes? Did our ancestors unlade upon these shores the riches of England? Did the mother country, in her maternal kindness, give her daughter a princely dowry? Did it not rather cost us millions to get ourselves safely out of this mother's grasp? Since we can not find the cause in any superior advantages of soil or climate, we must seek the answer in intellectual and moral influences; and of these, none is more fundamental, indispensable and peculiar, and none less unquestionable than our system of primary schools. Each rising generation has received in the family, the school and the church, the moral and mental training that has made the people frugal, temperate, industrious, dexterous in adapting means to ends, provident of the future, and skillful in turning every thing to the best account; which is a sufficient explanation of their unparalleled prosperity. They have gathered wealth from their hard soil, from their granite hills, from their lakes of ice, from every water-fall, more abundant than the golden dust of the fabled Pactolus. They have turned the desert into a garden, the wilderness into a fruitful field, and spread the sails of commerce to every breeze. All this they owe to their common school system; at least as *one* of the necessary conditions. . . .

[The] united testimony of . . . eminent teachers [given in Mann's report] is quite satisfactory, the most so of any evidence that the nature of the subject will admit of. It should satisfy the most skeptical, that if our country could for one generation be supplied with a sufficient body of common school teachers, of the right qualifications, and the attendance of all the children be secured for a succession of years, that it would supersede nine-tenths of all the dishonesty, pauperism and crime of the land, besides augmenting the physical strength and prosperity, the competence and wealth of the people, beyond all comparison in the past history of the world. The question, therefore, whether such a system of instruction is practicable, is one of absorbing interest. Mr. Mann undertakes, in his report, to demonstrate the ability of Massachusetts, (and by parity of reason the ability of other states,) with a school fund which yields per scholar only one-third as much as that of Connecticut, to provide herself with teachers and schools of this high character, and to secure to herself all the advantages of which we have spoken. He maintains that she can do this without feeling the expense; that she would find the outlay a most profitable investment, a lucrative business transaction, such as any sagacious capitalist would be glad to undertake and pay a bonus for the privilege. Indeed the increase of expense for general education would be small, if the public schools were raised to that degree of excellence, which should save to society the burden of supporting private schools for the same branches of instruction. But it is to be taken into the account, when calculating the cost of the proposed measure, how much society is likely to *save* by the consequent diminution of vice and crime; and to *gain* from the greater skill, industry and thrift of the people. The amount of interest thus saved and accumulated, a thousand sources of heavy taxation closed, innumerable sound, intelligent minds actively employed in all branches of industry, and continually developing new materials of convenience and wealth, is incalculable. Only a faint conception of the result can be formed by consulting the statistics of crime, the cost of courts and jails, the loss of property by fraud, theft and arson; or the statistics of vice, as the waste of life and property by intemperance—which would be saved to society by the thorough course of education proposed in this report. The expenses of criminal prosecutions that would be saved to the state by a right education of the people, would more than pay for that education. But a still greater sum would be saved by the prevention of vice; and to all this is to be added the actual gain to society from the more skillful and industrious ap-

plication of the productive forces of the nation. An English statesman remarked, that England *saved* the expense of public schools, at a loss of $50,000,000 annually. The remark has a too just application to our own New England. We owe our salvation to our public schools, and yet suffer them to languish, at the annual sacrifice of millions of dollars. The ambition of the people is rather to live in fine houses, than to rear up a nation of noble men; to hoard or to squander their earnings, rather than appropriate them to the first want of the country, education—to the most money saving of all social expedients—to the most productive of all investments—to universal mental and moral cultivation—the gift to all men of capacity to enjoy the treasures of learning—the elevation of all above mere animal pleasures to the enjoyment of the works of God. . . .

21

George S. Counts

THE RESPONSIBILITY OF THE SCHOOL

That the true aim of education ought to be the reform of society was perhaps most strongly stated by Professor George S. Counts of Teachers College in 1932. His was about as militant a position as a bona fide Progressive educator ever took. In fact, many people were frightened by his proposals, especially if they did not read them. When Counts announced "that the teachers should reach for power is my firm conviction," and urged teachers to throw off their "slave psychology" and work for the good of the masses, people felt cold shivers chase up and down their spines. Were the teachers about to launch a Red Revolution, and establish a dictatorship of the professoriat?

As time passed, it became apparent that this was not the case. Counts was a great disappointment to the radical left. He did travel in Russia, and write books about the Soviet school system, but he was more critical than complimentary. Probably his call to action—it was uttered in 1932 at the depth of a great depression, one should notice—helped the average teacher's sense of pride and self-importance at a critical period in our history. Did he have in mind anything more concrete than an urge to improve moral and spiritual values? To decide, one should carefully compare Counts' proposals with those contained in Readings 17 to 20.

. . . That the existing school is leading the way to a better social order is a thesis which few in-

From *Dare the School Build a New Social Order?* by George S. Counts, pp. 5-7, 28-32, 55-56. Copyright 1932 by George S. Counts. Reprinted by permission of The John Day Company, Inc., publisher.

formed persons would care to defend. Except as it is forced to fight for its own life during times of depression, its course is too serene and untroubled. Only in the rarest of instances does it wage war on behalf of principle or ideal. Almost everywhere it is in the grip of conservative forces and is serving the cause of perpetuating ideas and institutions suited to an age that is gone. But there is one movement above the educational horizon which would seem to show promise of genuine and creative leadership. I refer to the Progressive Education movement. Surely in this union of two of the great faiths of the American people, the faith in progress and the faith in education, we have reason to hope for light and guidance. Here is a movement which would seem to be completely devoted to the promotion of social welfare through education.

Even a casual examination of the program and philosophy of the Progressive schools, however, raises many doubts in the mind. To be sure, these schools have a number of large achievements to their credit. They have focused attention squarely upon the child; they have recognized the fundamental importance of the interest of the learner; they have defended the thesis that activity lies at the root of all true education; they have conceived learning in terms of life situations and growth of character; they have championed the rights of the child as a free personality. Most of this is excellent, but in my judgment it is not enough. It constitutes too narrow a conception of the meaning of education; it brings into the picture but one-half of the landscape.

If an educational movement, or any other movement, calls itself progressive, it must have orientation; it must possess direction. The word itself implies moving forward, and moving forward can have little meaning in the absence of clearly defined purposes. We cannot, like Stephen Leacock's horseman, dash off in all directions at once. Nor should we, like our presidential candidates, evade every disturbing issue and be all things to all men. Also we must beware lest we become so devoted to motion that we neglect the question of direction and be entirely satisfied with movement in circles. Here, I think, we find the fundamental weakness, not only of Progressive Education, but also of American education generally. Like a baby shaking a rattle, we seem to be utterly content with action, provided it is sufficiently vigorous and noisy. In the last analysis a very large part of American educational thought, inquiry, and experimentation is much ado about nothing. And, if we are permitted to push the analogy of the rattle a bit further, our consecration to motion is encouraged and supported in order to keep us out of mischief. At least we know that so long as we thus busy ourselves we shall not incur the serious displeasure of our social elders. . . .

That the teachers should deliberately reach for power and then make the most of their conquest is my firm conviction. To the extent that they are permitted to fashion the curriculum and the procedures of the school they will definitely and positively influence the social attitudes, ideals, and behavior of the coming generation. In doing this they should resort to no subterfuge or false modesty. They should say neither that they are merely teaching the truth nor that they are unwilling to wield power in their own right. The first position is false and the second is a confession of incompetence. It is my observation that the men and women who have affected the course of human events are those who have not hesitated to use the power that has come to them. Representing as they do, not the interests of the moment or of any special class, but rather the common and abiding interests of the people, teachers are under heavy social obligation to protect and further those interests. In this they occupy a relatively unique position in society. Also since the profession should embrace scientists and scholars of the highest rank, as well as teachers working at all levels of the educational system, it has at its disposal, as no other group, the knowledge and wisdom of the ages. It is scarcely thinkable that these men and women would ever act as selfishly or bungle as badly as have the so-called "practical" men of our generation—the politicians, the financiers, the industrialists. If all of these facts are taken into account, instead of shunning power, the profession should rather seek power and then strive to use that power fully and wisely and in the interests of the great masses of the people.

The point should be emphasized that teachers possess no magic secret to power. While their work should give them a certain moral advantage, they must expect to encounter the usual obstacles blocking the road to leadership. They should not be deceived by the pious humbug with which public men commonly flatter the members of the profession. To expect ruling groups or classes to give precedence to teachers on important matters, because of age or sex or sentiment, is to refuse to face realities. It was one of the proverbs of the agrarian order that a spring never rises higher than its source. So the power that teachers exercise in the schools can be no greater than the power they wield in society. Moreover, while organization is necessary, teachers should not think of their problem primarily in terms of organizing and presenting a united front to the world, the flesh, and the devil. In order to be effective they must throw off completely the slave psychology that has dominated the mind of the pedagogue more or less since the days of ancient

Greece. They must be prepared to stand on their own feet and win for their ideas the support of the masses of the people. Education as a force for social regeneration must march hand in hand with the living and creative forces of the social order. In their own lives teachers must bridge the gap between school and society and play some part in the fashioning of those great common purposes which should bind the two together.

This brings us to the question of the kind of imposition in which teachers should engage, if they had the power. Our obligations, I think, grow out of the social situation. We live in troublous times; we live in an age of profound change; we live in an age of revolution. Indeed it is highly doubtful whether man ever lived in a more eventful period than the present. In order to match our epoch we would probably have to go back to the fall of the ancient empires or even to that unrecorded age when men first abandoned the natural arts of hunting and fishing and trapping and began to experiment with agriculture and the settled life. Today we are witnessing the rise of a civilization quite without precedent in human history—a civilization founded on science, technology, and machinery, possessing the most extraordinary power, and rapidly making of the entire world a single great society. Because of forces already released, whether in the field of economics, politics, morals, religion, or art, the old molds are being broken. And the peoples of the earth are everywhere seething with strange ideas and passions. If life were peaceful and quiet and un-

disturbed by great issues, we might with some show of wisdom center our attention on the nature of the child. But with the world as it is, we cannot afford for a single instant to remove our eyes from the social scene or shift our attention from the peculiar needs of the age. . . .

To refuse to face the task of creating a vision of a future America immeasurably more just and noble and beautiful than the America of today is to evade the most crucial, difficult, and important educational task. Until we have assumed this responsibility we are scarcely justified in opposing and mocking the efforts of so-called patriotic societies to introduce into the schools a tradition which, though narrow and unenlightened, nevertheless represents an honest attempt to meet a profound social and educational need. Only when we have fashioned a finer and more authentic vision than they will we be fully justified in our opposition to their efforts. Only then will we have discharged the age-long obligation which the older generation owes to the younger and which no amount of sophistry can obscure. Only through such a legacy of spiritual values will our children be enabled to find their place in the world, be lifted out of the present morass of moral indifference, be liberated from the senseless struggle for material success, and be challenged to high endeavor and achievement. And only thus will we as a people put ourselves on the road to the expression of our peculiar genius and to the making of our special contribution to the cultural heritage of the race.

22

William H. Burnham

THE NORMAL MIND

The theories of Progressive education seemed to be a mass of inconsistencies, as the bewildered layman tried to puzzle them out. On the one hand, there were Dewey and Counts contending that the aim of education was the reform or drastic alteration of society. On the other hand, those whose primary interest was good mental health were claiming that the aim of education was adjustment to the social environment, which meant *not* changing society at all. What could be more contradictory? Who was right? As the application of Freudian ideas to education increased, particularly on the elementary level, these questions were increasingly difficult to answer.

The idea of education for adjustment became immensely popular from 1940 onward. Would it not produce more serenity and less nervousness to get along with the boss rather than to fight him? Would not conformity and togetherness, sharing and teamwork make an individual child or adult happier than resisting the demands of the group?

But those who wished education to reform society were critical of the case for adjustment. What about men like George Washington and Thomas Jefferson who had protested against elements of the age in which they lived? Were they maladjusted? Another question: Was adjustment to the social environment equally important in all societies—democratic or Fascist or Communist or primitive? Was a "contented-slave" mentality the product of education for adjustment? These were some of the questions arising from the aims expressed here by Professor Burnham.

Adjustment

The common aim of education and mental hygiene is adjustment. All are familiar with the idea of development and training as adjustment. We refer to the evolution of the physical organism as adjustment. We think of normal living as adjustment to one's environment, physical and social. We conceive of education as adjustment. Thus Gregory, at a recent meeting of the British Association, referred to education as a deliberate attempt at systematic training in adjustment to one's environment.

Everybody to-day says that education means adjustment. Mental health also means adjustment; and all the forms of mental disorder and the like are now referred to as cases of maladjustment. In all this discussion of adjustment usually there is little that is directly helpful in regard to how children may be trained to make right adjustment and to avoid wrong adjustment or maladjustment, as we call it. . . .

The aim of education

Thus the recognition of the significance of the mental attitudes is the key to the modern psychology of education and society. The aim of education is the development of right attitudes and interests. A liberal education, as President Eliot has pointed out, is a state of mind. Civilization is a state of mind. Peace, for which so many everywhere are working, is a mental attitude. More concretely, in every subject of study and

From *The Normal Mind: An Introduction to Mental Hygiene and the Hygiene of School Instruction* by William H. Burnham (New York: Appleton-Century-Crofts, Inc., 1924), pp. 27-28, 308-309.

every field of education, the important thing is the development of certain attitudes; in hygiene, for example, the attitude of prevention, the attitude of emphasizing positive habits of health, etc.

Of course, it may be said that this is merely a point of view and gives us nothing very definite and concrete. It is really more than a point of view, but even merely as such it is of great importance; for one's point of view determines what one sees, it determines whether one sees clearly or not, it determines whether one sees things in right perspective or not.

The mental attitudes

1. The mental attitudes, permanent interests, and habits of study and of thought acquired in the school are the significant things.

2. The mental attitudes are also important conditions of learning.

3. One of the greatest advances in modern education is the recognition of the great rôle of the mental attitudes and sets of the mind and of the necessity of appeal to these attitudes, making them both the beginning and the basis of instruction and training, and also the aim of education.

4. Attitudes, like conditioned reflexes, are produced in two ways, by repetition and by shock, but usually by the natural repetitions involved in the doing of tasks.

5. The attitudes developed in any subject, and by any task or form of learning, are important for the mental health as well as for education.

6. The conflicting attitudes developed in different situations and in different social groups should be integrated in one general attitude toward life. This seems to be accomplished by some central interest, or great ideal, or the like.

23

John Dewey

WHAT IS PROGRESSIVE EDUCATION?

The name of John Dewey was invoked by every Progressive educator, most of all by those who believed in the reform purpose. The misinterpretations of Dewey were legion and it is interesting to see what Dewey himself thought about the movement in which he had played such a central role, as he looked back on fifty years of its influence.

In the following summing-up, Dewey recognized the growing attacks on Progressive education; they were not without some justification. He did not retreat from his original position, however, merely expressing disappointment that more had not been accomplished. Though he fails to mention the "adjustment" emphasis specifically, he has considerable to say about the importance of education and change. One of his most interesting points is the warning that the revolutionary idea of our day, once it triumphs, is doomed to be the new status quo of tomorrow. Thus much educational change is short-lived and temporary. Did Dewey believe that Progressive education had gone to seed, and was ripe for harvesting by a new educational reform movement? Answers to this question will vary, one may be sure!

. . . In the course of more than half a century of participation in the theory and practice of education, I have witnessed many successes and many failures in what is most popularly known as "progressive education," but is also known as "the new education," "modern education," and so on. These designations are singular but they cover a plurality of different movements which have in common the general objective of improving the educational system but which differ from one another in many specific respects—ideas, principles, policies and programs. The confusion in public discussion of educational problems does not arise from using the term "progressive education" instead of "new education" or vice versa. It arises from using these designations as if they were proper names, denoting a singular entity. This is hardly the place to enter into terminological problems; however, it is in place to point out that I shall use the designations "progressive education" and "the progressive education movement" as common names, that is, as convenient linguistic means of referring to the whole complex of diversified movements and efforts to improve the practice and theory of education.

During the past few years, organized attacks on

From Introduction by John Dewey to *The Use of Resources in Education* by Elsie Ripley Clapp, pp. vii-x. Copyright 1952 by Elsie Ripley Clapp. Reprinted by permission of Harper & Row, Publishers.

the achievements of progressive education have become more extensive and virulent than ever before. The current effort to turn the clock back in education is a real cause for alarm but not for surprise. The educational system is part of the common life and cannot escape suffering the consequences that flow from the conditions prevailing outside the school building. When repressive and reactionary forces are increasing in strength in all our other institutions—economic, social and political—it would be folly to expect the school to get off free.

For the same reason, it is folly to think that the progressive education movement was something thought up and put over by the teachers all by themselves. On the intellectual side, it was part of the wider movement of thought, the inquiries into the nature and problems of growth which constitute the great contribution of the second half of the nineteenth century to the advancement of human knowledge in the biological, psychological and sociological sciences. On the social side, it was part of the widespread effort to liberate individuals and institutions from bondage to repressive modes of life. Without the support of the progressive and enlightening forces in the community, intellectual and social, the teachers of new vision would have been at best like Arnold's Shelley, ineffectual angels, born out of their time, and all their best plans and ideas would have had little or no effect on the educational system.

The most widespread and marked success of the progressive education movement has been in bringing about a significant change in the life-conditions in the classroom. There is a greater awareness of the needs of the growing human being, and the personal relations between teachers and students have been to a noticeable extent humanized and democratized. But the success in these respects is as yet limited; it is largely atmospheric; it hasn't yet really penetrated and permeated the foundations of the educational institution. The older gross manifestations of the method of education by fear and repression—physical, social and intellectual—which was the established norm for the educational system before the progressive education movement began have, generally speaking, been eliminated. But the basic attitudes underlying the gross manifestations have in many areas still to be rooted out. The fundamental authoritarianism of the old education persists in various modified forms. There is a great deal of talk about education being a cooperative enterprise in which teachers and students participate democratically, but there is far more talk about it than the doing of it. To be sure, many teachers, particularly in the kindergarten and elementary schools, take the children into sharing with them to an extent impossible and inconceivable under the old system whose supreme achievement of educational wisdom is enshrined in its maxim: spare the rod and spoil the child.

In the secondary schools and colleges, however, there isn't much sharing on the part of teachers in the needs and concerns of those whom they teach. Of course, the conditions still too largely prevailing in the school—the size of the classes, the load of work, and so on—make it difficult to carry on the educative process in any genuinely cooperative, democratic way. These conditions, however, are not the sole causes for the failures in educational democracy, as is evident from the fact that in "progressive" schools where these deplorable conditions do not exist education as

thoroughgoing sharing is often rather more a theme of discourse in various courses in the curriculum than a practice observable in the conduct of the school. . . .

It should be a commonplace, but unfortunately it is not, that no education—or anything else for that matter—is progressive unless it is making progress. Nothing is more reactionary in its consequences than the effort to live according to the ideas, principles, customs, habits or institutions which at some time in the past represented a change for the better but which in the present constitute factors in the problems confronting us. The fact that a given change was made in order to realize a desirable end in view signifies that the life-conditions before and after are different. In the process of attaining that good, a new situation was created. A new complex of life-conditions was brought into existence presenting its own distinctive characteristics and problems. Blind attachment to what was good for a state of affairs that no longer exists prevents recognition of the needs of the present and blots out of view the desirable ends that those needs should generate. As Emerson puts it, the attained good tends to become the enemy of the better.

New problems cannot be met intelligently by routine application of ideas and principles which were developed in solving different problems. New problems demand for their intelligent solution the projection of new purposes, new ends in view; and new ends necessitate the development of new means and methods. Of course, the "new" is, in all cases, relatively, not absolutely, new. Even though something absolutely new may be desirable, and some may delude themselves into thinking they have something absolutely new, the continuities in culture and experience exclude the possibility of anything having in fact this absolute character. The danger of cutting through all relations and connections inherited from the past is purely chimerical. The real danger is in perpetuating the past under forms that claim to be new but are only disguises of the old. . . .

24

Marie Syrkin

THEORY AND PRACTICE IN THE SCHOOLS

This reading and Reading 25 are examples of the attacks upon Progressive education to which Dewey responded. The first is by Marie Syrkin, a New York City high-school teacher. The second is by Professor Arthur Bestor, a prominent historian and a well-known critic from the university environment. The reader may wish to contrast Miss Syrkin's position with that of Dewey to determine whether she has correctly interpreted Dewey's views.

What Miss Syrkin concerns herself with is the effort to adapt Progressive education from the small, expensive private or experimental schools, in which it had been most successful, to the mass public school system. Her discussion of the reasons why the effort had encountered so many setbacks is illuminating. In addition, Miss Syrkin raises the intriguing question of how much change the adoption of Progressive education had really made in the average student's classroom life. Did real change consist only of talk and slogans? Or could it be found in actual teaching practices? There is one question which may arouse the curiosity of some readers: Was Marie Syrkin really an opponent of Progressive education, after all?

. . . Many of the slogans of modern education have made their way into the conventional public school-room. The doctrine of spontaneous activity, however, is one which public school teachers are more likely to honor than obey. No public school teacher can view calmly the prospect of movable furniture in class-rooms with forty or fifty students. The possibility is appalling. Any person who has ever been immured in one room with the small battalion of children entrusted to a single instructor knows how difficult the mechanics of instruction would become if there took place the "spontaneous" rising and moving about of forty-five instead of fifteen children. The quantitative numerical difference introduces a wholly different qualitative factor. Similarly, the flexible tentative program which is so wisely adjusted to the individual needs of the children of a progressive school would make a bedlam of a huge institution of several thousand.

Differences in size and number present problems that cannot be met by proclaiming the incontestably valuable concepts of modern education. In the physical set-up of the public schools this difference has been appreciated. Even the most modern public schools do not place movable furniture in the class-rooms, except in such specially equipped rooms as art-rooms or laboratories. The obvious handicaps under which the public school works have imposed certain limitations on the physical adaptation of the schools to the theories of modern education, but much of the ideological hypothesis has been adopted, despite the fact that equivalent handicaps obtain in the intellectual sphere.

In the public school, you will also hear about

"interest" versus "effort," child initiative and adequate relation to life's experience. A valiant attempt is made to energize the cumbersome machinery of the public school with the same current that has galvanized the experimental school on the assumption that the mass-school can also be a "free" school. A generation of school teachers has grown up with the idealistic vocabulary of progressive education on its lips.

Certainly, such a view of education and its goals is richer than the earlier one of the school as a place where a recalcitrant child was to be drilled into mechanical obedience and stuffed with prescribed information. Unfortunately, however, these brave dreams assume reality for the most part only in the descriptive literature about our schools and in the speeches of school officials. It is true that in many schools with small classes, chosen teaching personnel and equally chosen student bodies, the brightest principles of modern pedagogy are actually put into practice. There are honor classes with magnificent teaching adapted to individuals, in many of our public schools. By and large, however, the schools have adopted the theory without adequate provision to put the theory into practice. Consequently, they have lost whatever advantage was possessed by the old-fashioned disciplines without gaining the creative power of the new methods. The result is frequently the reverse of what modern pedagogy had intended. The student, instead of becoming a more cultivated individual and a more conscious member of society, becomes weaker rather than stronger.

I do not wish to be understood as saying that the underlying objectives, or even methods, of progressive education cannot be successfully introduced into the public schools. However, to adopt them in theory, without providing the appropriate means for carrying them out, is in some ways more harmful than an honest outright re-

From *Your School, Your Children* by Marie Syrkin, pp. 150-154. Copyright 1944 by L. B. Fischer Publishing Corp. Reprinted by permission of A. A. Wyn, Inc.

fusal to have any truck with new-fangled ways. To pay lip-service to the concept of school as society, and then to cram the students into classes of over forty, where no real opportunity for the development of individual personality exists, is more injurious than if we were to make a realistic survey of conditions and devise measures adapted to the situation that we face. One cannot indefinitely conceal a cynical opportunism in educational practice under the noble idealism of progressive educational theory. The victims in this self-defeating game are the young people of our schools. The fact that the schools represent a great financial outlay to the community only adds to the irony of the situation.

Every really imaginative educational procedure, which presumes to set the unfolding of individual capacity to the maximum as its aim, is predicated on the assumption that the group will be small. In the average class of a public school an inevitable pattern sets in. The teacher has to cover certain ground in the course of her period. For this she needs a routine of procedures and disciplines in the class-room. The only individuals that emerge from a class of forty-five will be a few bright students and a few particularly poor or unruly ones; the remainder constitutes a more or less anonymous mass. The fact that a teacher is able to address each student by name does not mean that she is aware of each one as an individual: this is psychologically impossible. A teacher with 200 to 250 pupils a day

cannot be expected to possess the nervous resources for a genuine consciousness of the shifting array before her. Nor can the students have any real knowledge of each other. The class, which should function as a coherent group, actually consists of little cliques, and the shy, the silent, the self-conscious rarely find occasion for self-expression, except when prodded by the teacher out of her pedagogic obligation to see to it that everyone "recites." This is formal rather than authentic self-expression. Again, one has gone through the motions. One has assimilated the theory that every member of a class is of equal significance and that no undue emphasis should be placed on either the more gifted or the more turbulent, but in reality little opportunity to reach the quiet average boy or girl in the group has been given. Yet, if we think in purely numerical terms, that is precisely the pupil in whose favor the teacher's attention ought to be weighted. It is this child, the unknown quantity, who ought to become known if we really take seriously the fine talk about the development of personality.

One might say that though such a situation is unfortunate as far as the interests of sound pedagogy are concerned, no vital issue is at stake. This is a dangerous error. There is no such thing as an anonymous individual in a democracy. If a student leaves the school with a smattering of information and a deterioration of personality, society is by that much the loser. . . .

25

Arthur E. Bestor

THE VANISHING SENSE OF PURPOSE IN EDUCATION

Useful perspective for the words of Professor Bestor may be found in the estimate of Progressive education penned by Claude Fuess, longtime headmaster of Andover Academy, twenty years earlier (7). Fuess felt that the Progressive movement had shaken pedagogical smugness (which was good), but that it had been more effective in pointing out flaws in traditional education than in providing an effective blueprint for a new education. Dewey he considered obscure, nebulous, and not very helpful for the ordinary teacher. Progressive education had made the schools more flexible and responsive to individual student needs, but it worked best on the elementary level, losing its effectiveness as one moved up the educational ladder.

Fuess suggested two serious weaknesses in Progressive education. First, student freedom without guidance was risky. Progressive schools often succumbed to sentimentality and coddling without realizing what was happening.

Second, the Progressives were poor on correlation, too often producing in the student only "miscellaneous and uncoordinated knowledge." With preadolescents, he concluded, Progressive education had definitely succeeded. For the later high-school stage its success was extremely doubtful.

In a sense, as a critic of existing practice, Arthur Bestor resembles Abraham Flexner (Reading 16). Bestor's points speak for themselves; they may be compared profitably with the earlier Fuess estimate. When the reader has finished this selection, he would do well to ask himself: What are the "well-conceived educational aims" which Bestor demands? Are his proposals any more explicit than those he criticizes? If the reader cannot answer the questions in terms of specific goals, and with concrete facts, then he should probably engage in some thoughtful review.

Americans have unbounded faith in schools, but they seem to distrust the results of schooling. We send, at public expense, an ever-increasing proportion of the population to school and college, yet we are suspicious of the highly educated man who offers to make some return by devoting his special training to the public service. At graduation we are proud to see our sons and daughters march forward in cap and gown, but in the morning newspaper we recognize the very same cap and gown as the cartoonist's accepted symbol for folly and ineffectiveness.

Universal, free, public education is part of the democratic creed, which Americans accept but which they would find it hard to explain in rational terms. It does not appear that many of them seriously expect society to get its money's worth out of the process. We pay our school taxes, but we rarely conceive of ourselves as making thereby an investment in the intellectual advancement of the nation. Our motive seems to be little more than warm-hearted benevolence. We hate to think that any child should be deprived of his fair share of anything so costly, so ornamental, and so well-regarded as education. To put the matter bluntly, we regard schooling as a mere experience, delightful to the recipient but hardly valuable to society. The school or college has become, to our minds, merely a branch of the luxury-purveying trade. Like the club car on a passenger train, it dispenses the amenities of life to persons bound on serious errands elsewhere.

Now, public opinion is not so perverse as to adopt such a view without cause. It is fully aware of the traditional claims of education. It is prepared to believe that knowledge is a good thing both in its own right and for the practical uses to which it can be put. It sees a connection

between good citizenship and the ability to think. What it is skeptical about is the ability of our schools and colleges to impart these qualities of mind to their graduates. Responsibility for this disbelief rests squarely upon the men and women who are professionally engaged in education. They have allowed themselves to become confused about the purposes of education, and they have transmitted that confusion to the public. They have sponsored school and college programs which make no substantial contribution to knowledge or to clear thinking, and which could not conceivably make such a contribution. The public, seeing no point in much of what is done under the name of education, have developed a justifiable skepticism toward education itself. They are willing to keep on playing the game, but they refuse to think of it as much more than a game. . . .

In the last analysis, it is not lack of effort but lack of direction that has resulted in the mediocre showing of our public high schools. Where educational aims have been well conceived, as in many fields of higher education and professional training, the money and the effort that Americans have poured into education have produced unmistakable progress. Seventy-five years ago American public schools were poor, but so too was American training for medicine, for law, and for research in the sciences and arts. All these fields have shared in the great American effort for educational improvement. But how different are the results! Would we be satisfied to hear the dean of a medical school assert merely that doctors today are just as well prepared as when they learned the theory of medicine in a few months of lectures and picked up the practice in the back office of an old-fashioned sawbones?

The difference is not a matter of money. It is a matter of adequate aims. In the sciences, in scholarship, in the learned professions, the men responsible for educational progress have been scholars and scientists in their own right. They

From *Educational Wastelands: The Retreat from Learning in the Public Schools* by Arthur E. Bestor (Urbana: University of Illinois Press, 1953), pp. 1-2, 8, 10-11.

have begun by accepting the traditional aims of their respective disciplines and professions, and they have defined their task as the carrying out of these recognized aims in a manner more effective than ever before. They have deliberately measured their achievement, not in terms of some slight improvement over the past, but in terms of the best that could possibly be done by any man, in any place, at any time. Until public school educationists can learn to think in this same way—until they acquire sufficient intellectual humility to accept the guidance of past experience and of the considered judgment of the modern learned world—no amount of financial support can possibly raise our schools above mediocrity. And mediocrity, given the possibilities which America offers to public education, is nothing else than downright failure. . . .

[My thesis here] is that schools exist to teach *something*, and that this something is the power to think. To assert this, of course, is to assert the importance of good teaching. Professional educationists are fond of beclouding the issue by suggesting that those who believe in disciplined intellectual training deny the importance of good teaching. Nothing could be farther from the truth. It is sheer presumption on their part to pose as the only persons in the academic world with a concern for good teaching. Disciplined intellectual training depends on good teaching, and scholars and scientists in American universities have shown as much genuine concern with good teaching as professors of education, many of whom betray an amazing disregard of its principles in the conduct of their own classes.

The issue in American education today is not drawn between those who believe in scholarship but are indifferent to good teaching, and those who believe in good teaching but are indifferent to scholarship. The issue is drawn between those who believe that good teaching should be directed to sound intellectual ends, and those who are content to dethrone intellectual values and cultivate the techniques of teaching for their own sake, in an intellectual and cultural vacuum.

THE METHODS OF EDUCATION

Not many years ago, during the course of a New York *Herald-Tribune* radio forum on the goals of education, Dean Millicent McIntosh of Barnard College noted the importance of method in teaching. "I submit," said she, "that the actual *content* of a course is not so important as the *method* by which it is presented; that the material of the curriculum is insignificant in comparison with the quality of those who teach." Coming from a person in the world of college arts and science, this was a real tribute to the indispensable role played by good teaching in the educational process. As with an army in a field campaign, so with a school system; the best of plans made by headquarters will fail unless the troops on the firing line are skilled in a methodology appropriate to the overall mission in which they are engaged.

The damage which results from poor teaching has been frequently commented upon by both lay and professional persons. For example, journalist H. L. Mencken reflected his personal experiences when he stated: "I know a good many men of great learning—that is, men born with an extraordinary eagerness and capacity to acquire knowledge. One and all, they tell me they can't recall learning anything of value in school. All that schoolmasters managed to accomplish with them was to test and determine the amount of knowledge that they had already acquired independently . . ." (8). Mencken went on to say that as a boy he had been fascinated by chemistry and physics, but teachers destroyed this natural interest. Physics "was taught so abominably that it immediately became incomprehensible to me, and hence extremely distasteful, and to this day I know nothing about it." In Mencken's case poor teaching literally did more harm than no teaching at all, and shut off a potential learner from a field which he would otherwise have explored independently.

How can the teacher make certain that such an appalling charge as Mencken's is never brought against his own instruction? In essence, any teaching method is simply the successful interaction between *content* and *pupil*. The teacher must select methods which achieve the end of relating content to pupil, and only methods which achieve this are valid. The teacher must acquaint himself with the purposes, application, and validity of different methods of presenting material. To be chained to one type of presentation which does not bring students into *contact* with content or subject matter is an inexcusable reason for inadequate teaching. Further, the selection of method requires the teacher to discover as much as possible about the learning process, so that he can better effect the interaction between content and pupil.

Obtaining a good knowledge of teaching methods probably comes first. Commenting in his down-to-earth fashion upon how quickly students appear to forget most of what they allegedly have learned, Thomas Edison said, "They fail to learn because the methods of teaching are wrong. They forget because the methods of instruction have made them actually dislike knowledge. Learning is not made interesting, and most young people will not acquire information which seems uninteresting." In one way, to "know" the major teaching methods is a simple matter. Although a list of hundreds of so-called methods could readily be made, most of them can be fitted fairly well into one of six categories: (a) the lecture or demonstration method, most common on the senior high school and college level; (b) the recitation method (drill, question-and-answer, tests), most common on the elementary and junior high school level; (c) the discussion method, a group process found at all levels; (d) the problem or problem-solving method, more common on the elementary and secondary levels, though one associates the variant case method with high-level graduate university instruction; (e) the project-activity method, which is largely confined to elementary and secondary schools; (f) teaching aids, not a true method by themselves, but important adjuncts to any method.

Everyone knows that you do not learn to drive an automobile merely by being shown the controls, and it is much the same with teaching methods. One must discover how to use methods appropriate to a task so that they will bring the desired result. At this point simplicity yields to complexity, and the teacher must give thought to the nature of the processes of teaching and learning. Intensive and continuing study of the pupil and his learning behavior when various methods are employed is of critical importance.

Psychology has always been the key to these processes, even before the word *psychology* was well known. When Bronson Alcott praised the growing desire to study "human nature" a century or more ago, he defined it as "the mysterious process by which the human mind accomplishes its great purposes." Today we would call this a neat description of the science of psychology. It is by applying the findings of psychology together with tested experience that systematic teaching methods are developed.

The methods of education

BY WAY OF INTRODUCTION

Readings 26 and 27 are efforts to survey, or introduce, the subject of good teaching method. The first is a historical description of specific methodological fashions, which are linked to the contemporary development of psychology.

The second is an analytical and psychological description of the teaching-learning process. Each approach has its virtues, and to concentrate on one at the expense of the other would leave the young teacher ignorant of new ideas important for his chosen profession. In fact, method is so closely interwoven with aims, process, and content that to wrench them apart almost guarantees distortion.

The relation of method to aim should be clear enough. If one believes in the primary importance of intellectual development, or perhaps the acquisition of vocational skills, he would seem less likely to employ lecture than some variety of problem-solving method. But if one holds that moral character and personality development are most essential, then discussion or activity methods might seem to make particularly good sense.

Method is also related to process, however. As Emerson said, "The secret of education lies in respecting the pupil." First the naturalist educators and then the psychologists insisted that methods which ran contrary to the instinctive desires of children, or ignored the affective feelings of adolescents, were largely doomed to failure. Nor should the natural gifts of the teacher himself be overlooked, for the teaching-learning process will hardly gain effectiveness by forcing the instructor to use methods for which he has scant competence and no liking.

Method relates closely to content and its structure, too. A course in driver education or swimming would seem by the nature of its content to rule out lecture as a principal reliance, whatever the aims or teaching skills of the instructor. A course in trigonometry or integral calculus would seem ill-fitted to the project-activity method; a course on citizenship problems brings to mind problem-solving or at least discussion; a survey of the myriad happenings in the rise of Western or world civilization might call for lectures to simplify and concentrate massive bodies of data.

So complex are these factors that no two teachers are likely to reach optimum effectiveness by teaching in precisely the same manner. The knowledge and study of method enables the teacher to adapt more easily to new teaching situations, but it can never be more than a means to the higher end of effective education. Like Ponce de Leon in search of the fountain of youth, an occasional lay person or professional educator is sure that he has found the only method of teaching which with a little perfecting will solve all our problems. "Fanaticism is the seamy side of enthusiasm," an English pedagogue once observed. Whether good teaching is an art with which a few people are endowed at birth or a scientific skill to be acquired by careful study has long been argued. The reader may also wish to consider the view that teaching may be *both* an art and a science. At any rate there is some agreement that both the gifted and the average teacher can profit from discovering what educational method has to offer him.

26

F. M. Underwood

THE EVOLUTION OF EDUCATIONAL METHOD

In the article which follows, a high-school administrator provides us with a historical summation of the various educational methods employed in American schools up to 1939. Perhaps one should add that very little new in methods of instruction has appeared since Underwood wrote, with the possible exception of the recent findings in automated teaching and computer-based instruction. Readings 61, 62, and 63 give a more detailed discussion of recent findings in automated instruction and their probable effect in the classroom. In this piece Underwood's method is expository and his language simple. Clearly the message is directed at laymen and novices little acquainted with the specialized nomenclature used by professionals in the field.

Nearly every method, teaching technique, and educator mentioned by Underwood will be treated at greater length in the readings which follow. The accuracy of Underwood's strictures is of less importance at this time than the sense of panoramic sweep. After becoming more familiar with each topic, the student may find it worth while to decide for himself how accurate Underwood's final judgment seems from a contemporary point of view.

Let us begin with the early school in this country, of which the "hickory stick" or the "birch rod" has come to be regarded as the symbol. The motive to work was largely compulsion. The "subject matter set out to be learned" was externally imposed on the child. The pupil was to do what he was told, speak when he was spoken to, and ask no questions. The subject matter was organized into "logical" units, arranged from the logically simple to the logically complex. This was a teacher-centric situation. Memorizing was a dominant activity.

The first advance came with the introduction of the Herbartian theory of teaching. This was hailed as a great inspiration, at the time. Relationships between things and events were elaborately "developed" by question and answer, the teacher asking the questions and the pupils answering the questions. "Reproductive" thinking was introduced. The pupils thought the matter through under the guidance of the questions of the teacher. It was a real advance because pupil thinking was stressed. However, the teacher was the most active person in the classroom, and it still was a teacher-centric situation. There was a semi-psychological organization of the subject matter.

Then came the "doctrine of interest." John Dewey and Frank McMurry were outstanding leaders of this movement. The pupil's aroused interest was regarded as fundamentally essential to any high type of learning. The situation changed from a teacher-centric to a pupil-centric one. The "logical" organization of subject matter began to give way to a "psychological" organization.

This led to the "doctrine of motive." "Motivation" became the shibboleth. It was held that the pupil must not only be "attracted" to the subject matter, but he must be *moved to action*.

This theory of interest and motivation finally culminated in the "problem method" and the "project method." The advocates of the problem method said a problematic situation is the only stimulus to thinking, and that a problem to be of use must be a problem *to the child*—one which he considered was worth while to him, and one to which *he desired* a solution. Hence, said they, school work should be organized as problems, real to the pupils. The advocates of the "project method" said it was not sufficient for a pupil to be "attracted" to a thing, and "moved to action"; they said he must also set up a goal or purpose which would guide his action through to the achievement of the goal or purpose. This required pupil initiative, resourcefulness, self-reliance, and self-direction. It placed more responsibility upon the pupil, and changed the role of the teacher from director to guide. It utilized the pupil's purpose as far as possible, and tended to change the curriculum to a series of purposes set up by the pupils, under the guidance of the teacher. Much more freedom was accorded pupils in the classroom, but the attempt was made to hold them responsible for a wise use of their freedom. William H. Kilpatrick was the outstanding leader of this movement.

About this time also the theory of the "socialized recitation" came in. Under this theory, the class was considered a cooperative social group which was to conduct its activities as far as possible on its own initiative. The teacher was in the background and was a sort of consulting expert and counselor. This focused attention on the importance of the socialization of the child as an educational objective, and the socializing value of activities.

There was a movement during this same period to modernize older techniques of teaching. Formerly there had been an over-emphasis on *drill*

From *Educational Method,* February 1939, 18:230-233.

in teaching. It had been too much of a dry repetition, externally imposed, and was used for some purposes for which it was not appropriate. You cannot develop appreciation by a drill technique, neither can you develop thinking by it. In the development of habits and skills, however, the laws of habit formation control our method. A habit is an automatic response to a stimulus. The drill technique of teaching is the appropriate technique in this field. It should be limited to this field, and modernized so that adequate motivation is its first principle. It is then suitable for use in its proper field.

The "exposition" method is appropriate where explanation is the purpose. You cannot expect a pupil to discover for himself everything the race has discovered before him. Many things must be explained to him. "Exposition" is probably the oldest technique of teaching. It was used, along with demonstration, which is a form of exposition, almost exclusively by primitive man—for example, in teaching young boys how to prepare a hide or construct a weapon. It still has a place in our teaching. Where economy of effort is desired, the exposition method is indicated. The use of pictures, still and motion pictures, stereographs, various visual aids to teaching, and the use of school excursions are samples of the "exposition" method of teaching, still appropriate for the realization of some of our teaching purposes. There is a skill involved in this type of work which the teacher needs to master, if it is to be effectively done, from the modern point of view in teaching. Several students made the same remark about a high school teacher of mathematics, who had the reputation of being a great teacher. The remark was, "He always explained everything so clearly that all of us could understand it." In other words, he was a master of the "exposition" technique of teaching. Jesus of Nazareth, in his teaching by parables, and Socrates, in his question-and-answer development of generalizations, exemplified very excellently the "exposition" method.

The theory of the "project method," largely because a number of its advocates desired a new name for the theory, here branched into what has been called "the activity program" and "creative education." There were really no new ideas in these movements except the new names. These new names gave some people who had offered objections to the "project method" an opportunity to climb on the band wagon and join the procession. The advocates of the activity program emphasized the activity of the pupil rather than the purpose behind it. The "creativists" emphasized the pupil as "artist," and the appeal to the originality and individuality of the pupil. The whole project theory, however, still underlies the whole scheme of things. These movements, largely because of the influence of the Gestalt psychology, next adopted the name "large unit" instruction. This merely shifted the emphasis to working on broad activities or problems, involving more complexity and variety of activity. The correlation and integration of all the elements involved received the chief emphasis.

This leads us to a review of this whole development of educational method. We see movements come and go. We see "methods" hailed as panaceas, then fade out of the picture, or into subordinate positions. We hesitate to accept the latest proposal as a panacea and are inclined to choose the valuable features of all acceptable methods and integrate them into what would seem to be a dependable philosophy of educational method.

This brings us to what has been called the "eclectic method." The word "eclectic" is derived from a Greek word meaning "to choose." Under the concept of this method the teacher realizes that he has many purposes to achieve in the education of the child, and he therefore proposes to utilize the most appropriate method for the realization of each of his purposes as it emerges. He finds it absolutely impossible to accomplish the exceedingly wide variety of purposes of teaching by the use of any one method. He finds a place for "drill" (which had been discarded), for the "development" lesson, for the "problem method," for the "project method," "large unit instruction," and "creative education," though these are not his entire stock in trade. He realizes that he must, above all, be a versatile artist, master of a great variety of "techniques" and "methods," if he is to realize to the fullest extent his responsibilities as a teacher. He feels that not all teaching should be done on a "project," "activity," or "creative" basis. He, therefore, will put each of these proposed methods into its proper place in his repertoire and use each where it seems most appropriate. The "assignment" technique, the "study" technique, the "appreciation" technique, the "exposition" technique, and others also find a place. He is concerned with the fine art of teaching as well as the learning process. He studies the techniques of teaching which are present when the highest degree of learning is taking place, and adapts his teaching procedures so as to accomplish the best results. He is ready to adopt or use any technique or any method which produces the desired result. He has a truly "eclectic" attitude toward teaching. Can any less extensive program of method adequately meet the varied needs of the teacher?

27

William H. Burton

BASIC PRINCIPLES IN A GOOD TEACHING-LEARNING SITUATION

Dr. Burton's article provides a striking contrast to Reading 26. Underwood wrote chiefly from experience; Burton presents a summary of the findings from professional literature. Underwood eschewed professional language; Burton makes full use of it. Underwood's analysis is simple and undifferentiated; Burton reduces his subject to detailed outline form, broken up under eight main headings. Actually Burton covers a great deal more ground than does Underwood, and he is obviously more psychologically than classroom oriented.

Since Underwood wrote, there has been a great upsurge of interest in learning theory, which goes far to explain the very different atmosphere which pervades the Burton article. Burton is attempting to provide a list of principles, both from research and from learning theorists, upon which there is some general agreement. Throughout the article Burton attempts to relate what is known about learners to appropriate methods of teaching. Some of the internal references listed by Burton should be profitable sources for further study, particularly if readers wish to delve more deeply into some of the propositions and the meanings of the terms employed.

A simple definition will be adequate for the summary here presented: Learning is a change in the individual, due to the interaction of that individual and his environment, which fills a need and makes him more capable of dealing adequately with his environment. A technical definition satisfactory to leading theorists in the field would be more difficult to state and is not necessary for our purposes.

The effort to summarize principles of learning which underlie desirable teaching situations is seriously complicated by the fact that there are approximately a dozen learning theories available. No one has yet formulated a systematic theory satisfactory in all respects. But many facts about learning are known and accepted. There is also agreement on the place of experimental procedures for the demonstration of facts and principles. Serious differences between the various theories remain regarding the nature of certain facts, the primacy of other facts, and the interpretation of facts. These differences must, of course, affect any statement of basic theory and principle.

The differences between theorists are due in part to differences in basic viewpoint and accepted premises. Sometimes two or more theories deal

with different types of learning problems, different motivations, or other factors, without sufficient attention to, or development of, a systematic theory to cover more ground. Sometimes, even, disagreements will cut across the groupings of theorists so that some in one camp are in agreement with some in the rival camp and in disagreement with their colleagues. These differences cannot, in the present state of knowledge, be shrugged off when we are dealing with efforts at systematic theory. We can, however, get on with a more limited job of setting up a reasonably consistent statement of principles useful in everyday teaching.

Hilgard[1] has reduced the confusion considerably by classifying the ten or a dozen theories into two basic groups which he labels *stimulus-response* (connectionism, conditioning, behaviorism) and *cognitive* (Gestalt, organismic, sign-significate). Some theories do not fit clearly within either group. He goes on to point out that although no single systematic inclusive theory is as yet available, the situation is not as bad as it seems. He avoids premature systematization on the one

From *Phi Delta Kappan,* March 1958, 39:242-248.

[1] Ernest R. Hilgard. *Theories of Learning,* revised edition. New York: Appleton-Century-Crofts, 1955. Chapter 1.

hand, and naive eclecticism on the other, showing that something can be learned from the serious efforts of each group of theorists. In any practical situation, as contrasted with efforts to build a systematic theory, this is a sensible view. Pure theory, an absolute necessity for full understanding, is not available. We therefore accept any facts and principles which have been carefully demonstrated and which aid us in understanding and promoting learning.

. . . [This summary] will follow Hilgard's view and include principles which promise to be useful, regardless of theoretic origin. Every effort will be made, however, to maintain internal consistency in the statement.

Textbooks on learning and on teaching carry, among them, a considerable list of principles of learning basic to good teaching. It may come as something of a shock to the so-called practical schoolman to discover that learning theorists agree on only a limited number of these principles. Two excellent summaries[2] of agreement among theorists are available. The fifteen or so agreed-upon principles are not reproduced here, since they will be included within the various summaries to follow.

I. The general purposes of learning

The overall purposes of learning are relevant to the social order within which they operate. We believe in the democratic way of life with its emphasis on (a) opportunity for the fullest development of the unique capacities of the individual, and (b) a socially oriented group within which the individual may realize his destiny. This means that one goal of learning will be the development of creativity, individual initiative and responsibility, and leadership. The other will be the development of social skills and good human relations. The use of experts and of experimentation will be learned within the democratic social process. An extended list of democratic values could be made. The following brief list may be taken as guides for learning, and particularly for teaching:

1. The dignity and worth of the individual is a primary tenet of Judeo-Christian democracy. Respect for the individual is a corollary.

2. The common good of the group is a social aim of democracy. A proper balance should be maintained between the development of the independent individual and the social individual.

3. Obligations as well as rights are inherent in a democracy. The development of a "democratic conscience" in the individual is necessary to such a society.

4. A flexible functioning of the group with freedom for all to contribute is essential to democracy, and hence to the democratic learning process.

5. The process of group discussion, deliberation, and decision on common problems is the process of democracy. Decisions are based on consensus preferably, or on tentative majority decisions when consensus cannot be achieved. (Detailed principles governing group process are summarized separately later.)

II. General principles of learning[3]

The principles of learning are worded differently by various psychologists. Readers may substitute any wording or listing they prefer for the composite one given here.

1. The learning process is experiencing, doing, reacting, undergoing. The actual pattern to be learned is the chief aim, but a multitude of varied learning activities and outcomes also occur. Active participation by a learner is preferable to the kind of passive reception usually involved in listening to a lecture or watching a motion picture.

2. Responses during the learning process are modified by their consequences.

3. The learning situation is dominated by a purpose or goal set by the learner, or accepted by him, and should lead to socially desirable results. The purposes and goals arise in the life of the learner.

4. The learning situation, to be of maximum value, must be realistic to the learner, meaningful, and take place within a rich and satisfying environment.

5. The learning process occurs through a wide variety of experiences and subject matters which are unified around a core of purpose.

---

[2] Ernest R. Hilgard, *ibid.*, pp. 485-487, and T. R. McConnel, "Reconciliation of Learning Theories," Chapter 7 in *The Psychology of Learning* (Forty-First Yearbook, Part II, National Society for the Study of Education.) Bloomington, Ill.: Public School Publishing Co., 1942.

[3] It is not possible in a short article to cite research background for each principle listed. The two research summaries already noted (Hilgard, and the Forty-First Yearbook, Part II, N.S.S.E.), together with several dozen individual research studies, were consulted. Texts in psychology and in principles of teaching were checked, though these are secondary sources. The two summaries contain bibliographies, Hilgard's alone covering over thirty pages.

6. The learning experience, initiated by need and purpose, is likely to be motivated by its own incompleteness, though extrinsic motives may sometimes be necessary. (See later summary on motivation.)

7. The learner will persist through difficulties, obstacles, and unpleasant situations to the extent that he deems the objectives worth-while.

8. The learning process and achievement are materially affected by the level of aspiration set by the learner. Individuals need practice in setting realistic goals for themselves, goals neither so low as to elicit little effort, nor so high as to fore ordain failure. Realistic goal-setting leads to more satisfactory improvement than unrealistic goal-setting.

9. The learning process and the achievement of results is materially related to individual differences among the learners. The capacity of the learner is a critical factor in deciding what is to be learned and by whom. Brighter pupils can learn things that less bright ones cannot learn; older children can, in general, learn more rapidly than younger ones. (Any decline in adult years depends upon what is being learned.)

10. The learning process proceeds most effectively when the experiences, materials, and desired results are carefully adjusted to the maturity and background of experience of the learner. (See later summary on readiness.)

11. The learning process proceeds best when the learner can see results, has knowledge of his status and progress, when he achieves insight and understanding. That is, information about the nature of a good performance, knowledge of his own mistakes, and knowledge of successful results, aid the learner.

12. The personal history of the learner—for example, his reaction to authority (many other factors might be cited)—may hamper or enhance his ability to learn from a given teacher.

13. Tolerance for failure is best taught through providing a backlog of success that compensates for experienced failure.

14. The learning process proceeds most effectively under that type of instructional guidance which stimulates without dominating or coercing; which provides for successes rather than too many failures; which encourages rather than discourages.

15. The learning process in operation is a functioning unity of several procedures which may be separated arbitrarily for discussion.

16. The learning products are socially useful patterns of action, values, meanings, attitudes, appreciations, abilities, skills. The products are inter-related functionally but may be discussed separately.

17. The learning products accepted by the learners are those which satisfy a need, which are useful and meaningful to the learner.

18. The learning products are incorporated into the learner's personality slowly and gradually in some instances, and with relative rapidity in others. The realness of the conditions under which the learning takes place and the readiness of the learner contribute to integration.

19. The learning products when properly achieved and integrated are complex and adaptable, not simple and static.

20. Transfer to new tasks will be better if, in learning, the learner can discover relationships for himself, and if he has experience during learning of applying the principles within a variety of tasks.

21. There is no substitute for repetitive practice in the over-learning of skills (for instance, the performance of a concert pianist) or in the memorization of unrelated facts that must be automatized.

22. Spaced or distributed recalls are more advantageous in fixing material that is to be long retained.

III. General principles of re-learning[4]

The learning of new social values and behavior is often a matter of re-learning, complicated by the presence of undesirable values and patterns of action.

1. The processes and principles governing the acquisition of socially acceptable learning and of learning detrimental to society are basically alike.

2. Re-education is the achievement of changes in the learner's knowledge, belief, and values.

3. Re-education affects the cognitive structure of the individual, his perception of the physical and social worlds, that is, it changes his knowledge, beliefs, and expectations.

4. Re-education modifies the learner's personal values with respect to group and interpersonal relations.

5. Re-education influences the learner's behavior in social situations.

---

[4] Kurt Lewin and Paul Grabbe, "Conduct, Knowledge, and Acceptance of New Values," *The Journal of Social Issues*, August, 1954, pp. 56-64. Available also in Kenneth Benne and Bozidar Muntyan, *Human Relations in Curriculum Change*. New York: Dryden, 1951, pp. 24-33. See also Kurt Lewin, "Field Theory and Learning," in *The Psychology of Learning*, Forty-First Yearbook, Part II, National Society for the Study of Education, pp. 215-242. The principles here are reworded and rearranged from the original statement.

6. First-hand experience does not guarantee correct concepts; the total learning situation must be conducive to a change in cognition.

7. An individual's perception of the facts and values of a situation affects his behavior.

8. The possession of correct facts in the face of false perceptions does not assure change in inadequate social stereotypes.

9. Inadequate stereotypes are as difficult to obliterate as are incorrect concepts stemming from ignorance and misinformation.

10. Changes in emotional reaction do not necessarily follow acquisition of correct factual information.

11. A change in the "culture of the individual" is equivalent to a change in values, a change in the perception of social relationships, a change in "action-ideology."

    a. Hostility to re-education may stem from loyalty to old values.

    b. The new set of values must be freely chosen and accepted if re-education is to be successful.

12. Emotional acceptance of the new set of values must be a gradual process.

13. The new set of values necessary to change behavior is acquired frequently with belongingness to the group subscribing to the new values. A strong "we feeling" aids in changing values.

(At this point a few other principles might be listed, but they would be repetitions of, or obvious inferences from, general principles of learning.)

IV. Group process and learning

The use of group process obviously facilitates the learning of skills of communication, of participation and cooperation, of discussing evidence and conclusions. Recent research shows that, contrary to some common beliefs, pupils working in pairs or small groups do better in other areas also than when working individually. Results were superior in paragraph writing, solving algebra problems, improving reading ability, as well as in some of the tasks usually thought of as individual.[5]

1. Group process, properly applied, establishes communication and promotes interaction within a group of learners and between groups.

    a. The psycho-physical setting for group activities should enhance effectiveness in sharing information and ideas.

        (1) Books, audio-visual materials, and all other aids to learning should be assembled for the convenience of the learners.

        (2) The meeting places for large and small groups should be arranged to promote freedom of discussion.

        (3) Experts and consultants—resource persons—may be called in for various purposes.

        (4) Direct training in group process helps to facilitate its use.

        (5) Accurate records should be kept of process and results.

    b. Group process should create a social system of channels of communication between any group of learners and other groups, and with the community within which the school is located.

2. Group process should deal with the problems of the learner within the group, problems common to small groups within the class, and with problems of interest to the whole class.

    a. The readiness of the group should determine what type and level of problem and of learning experiences are to be used.

    b. Clarification and definition of purposes and problems, the selection of activities and materials, provision for evaluating progress, should be accomplished through free participatory discussion.

    c. Experts and consultants may aid in clarifying problems, in opening up new ways of solving them.

    d. Experimentation and simple tryout should be utilized.

    e. Evaluation of the process and its achievements, and of the degree of participation should be continuous. This often aids in clarifying or extending purposes, or in discovering new ones.

3. Leadership in group process should foster initiative and interaction as widely as possible for members of the group. Group process provides for wide sharing and changing of leadership in place of fixing authority in one person.

    a. Individuals who participate in a functioning and productive group are likely to develop desirable attitudes, social skills, and understandings.

    b. Leadership is substituted for authority in effective group process.

    c. Authority, when used, is derived from the group and is the authority of the group over itself. Democratic authority may be delegated to any individual or committee to be exercised for the good of the group; it may be revoked when not so used.

4. Group process used for a sufficient time should modify the thinking and behavior of all participating learners.

---

[5] David H. Russell, *Children's Thinking.* New York: Ginn & Co., 1956, pp. 266-267.

a. The individual learns both as an individual and as a group member when he reorganizes his thinking and behavior toward problems which are of group concern.

b. The individual will learn the value of group activity as he participates in extensive continuing opportunity to make decisions.

c. The individual should be accorded respect and will learn many individual behaviors when he presents sincere arguments in disagreement with the majority of the group.

5. Group process used for a sufficient time should develop desirable social skills and human relations, with accompanying ability to effect changes of social value.

a. The learner will see the value of uncoerced consensus and action based on group decision.

b. Changes in persons, with resultant changes in institutions or procedures, may be effected.

V. *Preserving the learner's security*

Distrust, fear, and insecurity are quite normal reactions to change. The abandonment of old and trusted knowledges and values with the acceptance of new values and behavior patterns is a serious matter for learners at all levels. The older the learner the more he has identified with his knowledges and values and the more necessary it is to conduct learning enterprises so that security and mental health are preserved. The need for security, being normal, must be respected by teachers and not sneered at, as we sometimes unhappily see. The general strategy is to begin with the known and to proceed with challenges likely to beget success; to proceed slowly enough that the learner may develop insight and understanding and may achieve appropriate skills for operating new knowledge and values. The discussion here is related to the more remote principles of re-learning set forth in summary No. III earlier.

1. Begin with problems real to the learners involved, but which contain challenge. Dealing with the familiar and with a challenge which is not overwhelming reduces tension.

2. Begin with problems which will likely yield success. Failure on a self-selected problem is not so devastating as is failure on an imposed task.

3. Allow time for development of understanding and for achievement of new skills and behaviors.

4. Develop a strong group feeling, but with full respect for the individuals within the group. (See earlier discussion of group process.)

5. Provide an atmosphere of freedom and spontaneity. An emotional climate free from tensions contributes to confidence and security.

6. Provide support in the form of recognition for contributions, praise for results.

7. Provide assurance that individual learners may contribute freely, may differ with the majority, may suggest new leads. Creative activities when accepted not only aid the learner in achieving results, but contribute to security.

8. Recognize and build upon differences in interests and special abilities within the group. A favorable effect results from aid given to learners in understanding themselves, both their capabilities and limitations, and in understanding their relationship with others and with the group.

9. Adjust the pace carefully to the individuals and the group. Slow acceptance and development are natural.

VI. *The motivation of learning*

1. A motivated learner learns more readily than one who is not motivated. Motives may be general or specific, intrinsic or extrinsic.

2. Motivations which are too intense (especially pain, fear, anxiety) may be accompanied by distracting emotional states and by undesirable learning products.

3. Excessive motivation may be less effective than moderate motivation, especially for certain kinds of tasks.

4. Learning under intrinsic motivation is preferable to learning under extrinsic motivation.

5. Purposes and goals which make sense to a learner, which meet a need, which restore the natural equilibrium of the learner, are effective.

6. Purposes and goals should be geared to the interests, activities, and maturities of the learners.

7. Extrinsic motivations operate as follows:[6]

a. Motivation by reward is generally preferable to motivation by punishment, motivation by success preferable to motivation by failure. Marks, rewards, punishments operate as follows:

(1) Marks, rewards, and punishments not functionally related to the learning situation will beget learning, but it is learning soon lost and accompanied by detrimental concomitant learnings.

---

[6] Learning theorists differ considerably among themselves on these points. The summary here is an effort to give such guidance as is possible lacking a final systematic theory.

(2) The more closely the mark, reward, or punishment used as motive is a natural outcome of the learning process, the better effect it has. Learning is stimulated and undesirable concomitants are at a minimum.

(3) The more clearly the learner sees that the mark, reward, or punishment is an inherent aspect of the learning situation, not artificial and imposed, the better the learning which results.

b. Social motives of competition and rivalry operate as follows:

(1) Routine skills and factual information are readily acquired under these motives without immediate detrimental results.

(2) Certain conversational skills and more general types of thinking may be encouraged, but may have detrimental concomitants.

(3) Creative work—imaginative work generally—is not affected favorably.

(4) Individual mental hygiene and social welfare generally can suffer severely under motives of rivalry and competition. Unhappiness, frustration, and cheating may result with the individual; exploitation, social injustice, and waste may result with the group.

c. The newer social motives of cooperation, recognition by one's fellows, opportunity for participation in planning and decision making, seem to have very beneficial effects upon immediate and later learning. (A considerable revolution in human thinking concerning competition and cooperation, both in world affairs and in individual concerns, is underway. Data are appearing from time to time which should be noted.)

d. Commendation and praise for work well done are excellent incentives. Indiscriminate or undeserved praise has a detrimental effect. Praise is better than condemnation, but the latter is preferable to ignoring the learner's efforts.

e. Success achieved by the learner in adjusting his levels of aspiration to possible achievements is valuable.

f. Goals and levels of aspiration set by the learner's family or social class may be effective, but may also have serious ill effects.

g. Liking for the teacher seems to be a safe incentive with very young learners. With older learners liking must be combined with respect. The teacher's personality should be used sparingly as an incentive, since this type of motivation can invite detrimental concomitants.

h. Sarcasm and ridicule secure only the most undesirable and detrimental learning outcomes.

(Continued use of sarcasm can only result from stupidity on the part of the teacher, or as an outlet for a frustrated personality.)

8. Learning without purpose and learning to do difficult, unpleasant, distasteful tasks under compulsion and coercion does not train the learner to persist with unpleasant learnings in real life. This does not mean that difficulty is to be eliminated from learning experience. Learners will persist through serious difficulties if the objective is deemed worth-while. That is, learning under purpose is the best guarantee of persistence in learning to overcome difficulties.

9. The maintenance of interest (or motivation) is important in learning. This can be done by several means, of which the following are illustrations:

a. Use a variety of learning activities or experiences.

b. Adapt closely to individual differences, especially in group work.

c. Make use of success and recognition by the group.

d. Adapt to levels of maturity and experimental background.

e. As the teacher, manifest sincere enthusiasm.

f. Take stock and re-plan from time to time.

VII. The principle of readiness

1. Readiness is the stage in a learner's development when he can learn easily, effectively, and without emotional disturbance. Readiness is one of the most important factors in adjusting learning opportunities and experiences to the learner.

2. Readiness is not a separate and disparate trait; it is a condition brought about by many factors: the individual's rate of growth or maturing, background of experience, mental capacity, attitudes and interests, oral language development, emotional and social adjustments, health, kinesthetic coordination, and others.

3. Readiness for various types of learning and learning experience appears at different times. There is a succession of readinesses.

4. Readiness cannot be forced in advance of natural growth, but programs of experience which compensate for limited experience, which make up deficiencies in certain of the items listed in (2) above, are useful.

5. Readiness or the lack of it should not be assumed without investigation or tryout of certain activities. Observation of the learner's reaction

to opportunities to learn is the safe guide to determining whether readiness is present or not. . . .

VIII. *Principles of teaching*

A list of principles of teaching would consist of a list of inferences drawn from the principle of learning set forth in the preceding pages. Any reader can derive these principles for himself through inspection of the summaries on learning. Instead of presenting a semi-repetition, there is substituted a listing of the characteristics of the learner himself, paralleled by a listing of the characteristics of a setting for learning which would fit the learner. The statements under "Setting for Learning" are directives for teaching.

THE LEARNER	THE SETTING FOR LEARNING
1. The learner, like all living organisms, is a unitary, integrating whole.	1. The desirable setting for functional learning experiences will provide for natural integration of feeling-doing-thinking.
2. The learner, like any other living organism, seeks always to maintain equilibrium or balance.	2. Desirable learning experiences will provide opportunity for success in meeting needs and solving problems, but will also give constant challenge to go beyond immediate situations.
3. The learner is a goal-seeking organism, pursuing aims to satisfy needs, thus to maintain equilibrium.	3. The desirable setting for learning will be dominated by purposes and goals set up by the learner or learners, either by themselves or with appropriate guidance from the total group, including consultants.
4. The learner is an active, behaving, exploratory individual.	4. The setting must provide freedom to explore, to construct, to question, to differ, to make mistakes: freedom to develop creative contributions. The limits of freedom are democratic controls, rights of others, and good taste.
5. The learner has a pattern and rhythm of growth peculiar to the individual. Notable differences exist between individuals, in speed of learning, energy output, depth of feeling, facility of insight.	5. Widely varied types of learning experiences should be provided, adaptable to levels of maturity, to different rates, interests, abilities, and so forth.
6. The learner brings with him a personality, a set of aims, values, social habits.	6. The purposes and experiences established should arise out of and be continuous with the life of the learner. The family background, and social-class status, as well as the individuality of the learner, must be taken into account.
7. A learner may be quite immature in relation to one set of standards and experiences, and quite mature in relation to another.	7. Learners need sympathetic guidance while building an awareness and personality within their own experiences. They need protection from situations in which they can not yet act intelligently; protection from fears and anxieties; protection sufficient to insure security and status on various levels; plus challenge to grow, to conquer problems, to develop self-reliance. The learner needs guidance from consultants who know and understand the problems of a growing personality; who see learning as a developmental process. Guidance must be free from domination or coercion.

8. The learner is a social animal, if normal, and naturally seeks activities involving other persons.

8. The setting must provide many varied opportunities to work in "we" relationships, developing eventually into self-directed group activity. The whole range of interactive human relationships, the co-operative group process, is essential to the development of mature socialized personality.

The methods of education

TRANSFER OF TRAINING AND THE FORMAL LECTURE

Once upon a time, a number of years ago, there was a boy who was just entering high school and didn't know what courses he should take. He told his father that he thought he would like to take accounting, typing, music appreciation, problems of marriage, contemporary American literature, and driver education because they all seemed practical and useful. His father told him that he should take four years of Latin and mathematics and three years of Greek, because these would teach him to think logically and to develop the habit of hard work, and they would provide skill in puzzling out mysteries. This in turn would develop his confidence and ability in *all* subject areas and for the problems of life. Who was right?

This boy, as you might have guessed, followed his father's advice. Looking back over his career as a mature man, years later, he felt well satisfied. In his sober judgment a habit of hard work was set, the classics helped his liking for and understanding of the nature of the English language, and the scientific method of mathematics he used all his life. However, he did pick up some accounting in night school, and found it highly useful also. He remembered that his friends who did not take classics and mathematics seemed happier in their schoolwork than he, for which he had at the time envied them. But he also knew that he was intensely proud of his high-school education, and he often bragged (in a tactful way, to be sure) about his tough courses. Was he better off than his fellow students, or was he kidding himself?

In essence, our brief case study presents the age-old problem of transfer of training. To what extent does the study of Latin or Greek make one a better citizen? How effective is the study of historical facts in helping one to interpret and predict events? Does training in mathematical reasoning transfer to other problems requiring a similar but not identical skill? In the past it was thought that if the mind was trained in one particular arena, transfer would automatically take place to new and unique situations. Findings from psychological research have raised questions regarding the concept that training in specifics will *automatically* transfer to other situations. Current beliefs on transfer contend that if subject matter is treated in such a way that broad generalizations having wide applicability are learned, and if the methodology of a discipline is understood, then students can apply their learnings to new and recurrent situations. Later sections in this book will present discussions of contemporary views of learning and provide a basis for understanding the problem of transfer of learning.

The lecture method is one of the oldest and most solidly entrenched methods of instruction. It is well suited to, and usually found in, the social studies and some humanities like literature and philosophy. It is not well suited to humanities like foreign language and the fine arts, or to natural science, or to skill subjects like physical education, driver education, or the industrial arts. For a teacher the question is, "Do I think I can present my own subject better by lecture or by some other method?" He must consider also which method best meets the particular needs of his students and recognize that the objectives which he has set will determine the appropriateness of any method.

In general one can say that the higher the level of instruction, the more successful the planned lecture seems to be. College and university classes, where nearly every student has a long attention span, appear to offer the best natural environment for lecturing. No one knows whether the lecture is superior or inferior to other instructional methods, although a great many studies of the process have been made.

28

Frank M. Rich

A FAMOUS FALLACY—"MENTAL DISCIPLINE"

Can learning skills or habits gained in one area of study be transferred successfully to help grasp or gain mastery over another? Do "A's" in Latin mean that the student is more likely to get "A's" in other subjects? The question of transfer of learning (once more commonly called transfer of training) has had a stormy history. At the time Frank M. Rich and Frank Henry Selden had their verbal slugging match, people were disputing whether transfer of training existed at all. Today most accept transfer as a fact, but the old debate continues on the new basis of how important transfer is. The successors of Rich say its importance is slight; the heirs of Selden insist its role is great.

Underlying the transfer-of-learning controversy is a very important issue, i.e., whether the learning gained from a single study or group of studies has only specific values for specific problems, or whether it has general value for the unpredictable problems likely to be encountered in future life situations. If learning cannot be transferred, so Rich argues, then the mind-sharpening purpose is a delusion and a fraud. Worse than that, the whole notion of an education is invalid, for none of the problems studied in school are likely to recur exactly as originally studied.

Rich proclaims that the evidence of research proves that there is no such thing as a trained mind. Selden retorts that if the evidence says anything so palpably absurd, then there is something wrong with the evidence. The Rich selection follows; the Selden article is Reading 29.

One of the costliest fallacies, especially in secondary education, is the theory of mental discipline—the belief that observation, memory or reason, exercised in a school subject like Latin, geometry or chemistry, creates a mental power or training available for use in any situation where observation, memory or reasoning is employed. With scientific measurements of mental traits Thorndike and other psychologists have been able to demonstrate what common sense has always shown—that practice in a given field develops facility in that field and in no other. There

From *Journal of Education*, November 1937, 120:359.

is little if any transfer to other activities. A person who should advocate a course in trap shooting for prospective bookkeepers because trap shooting develops *promptness* and *accuracy* would be considered foolish enough, a victim of mere words, for which there is no corresponding equivalent in the mind. But one who talks of developing any all-around *memory* or *reason* is almost as shallow a victim of words, for such abstract faculties do not exist. Every mind has a million different kinds of memory, one for faces, one for clothes, one for names, one for love letters, each unlike the other. A college-bred gentleman who has memorized the vocabulary of half a dozen languages cannot remember a list of errands, or a dinner order for a table full of people, any better than the illiterate but intelligent stage driver or waiter with no mental discipline but experience. A professor of mathematics, highly trained in logical reasoning in his subject, does not think his way through a balky automobile or a defective plumbing system any better than a clear-headed farmer who has never got beyond the rule of three. The mathematics student may be able to reason out new problems in mathematics through the help of old ones, but in so doing he is not made any more logical about inheritance taxes, higher criticism or learning to sail a boat. The intellectual faculties are not like muscles, to be strengthened by vigorous gymnastic exercise. Outside the actual subject matter that an educated man has studied he is as ignorant and helpless as anybody else of equal native ability. The study of a foreign language, for example, not only fails to increase general mental efficiency and habits of work, it fails to increase general language ability. Studies of the abilities of bilingual children show that one language interferes with the other. Command of two languages is bought at the cost of lessened ability in other fields. (See Huse's "Psychology of Foreign Language Study.")

The "trained mind" is a delusion, a gold brick. We can never get anywhere in education till we set learners to work upon the practical activities that need to be mastered, in a form as nearly as possible like what will eventually be used in the outside world. If the virtue desired here is merely glib talk we should continue to fill up the program with talking, but if anything more serviceable is desired it will have to be learned by practice. The proper aims of school work were well defined some years ago by the National Committee on the Reorganization of Secondary Education. They were listed as the seven cardinal objectives—health, vocation, worthy home membership, wise use of leisure, the fundamental processes (three R's), good citizenship and ethical character. They have been mentioned with approval in most recent books on secondary school education, and each day in the official National Education Week program is dedicated to one of them. Although the replies to a recent questionnaire from 1,228 high school principals showed that 539 or 44 per cent. had not used these principles as the basis of changes in their own schools, and 255 had not even heard of them.

29

Frank Henry Selden

TRANSFER OF LEARNING NOT A MYTH

Some years ago there arrived at one of our large universities a new head of a department who was, and is, nationally known as especially competent in psychology and its application to educational methods. At that time one of the recurring discussions of whether a training in one subject carries over into other subjects was in full swing. For some reason a number of persons from various faculties who were particularly interested in this question were called together and the recently arrived authority gave us a very care-

From *Journal of Education,* April 1938, 121:120-121.

ful and lengthy discussion of the question, going over the mass of accumulated data proving that training in one subject does not carry over into other subjects or result in general development of any mental power.

Then, after all the theory had been given us, he straightened up, looked at us in a very serious manner, and said: "But we know it is not so. Our experience disproves the whole mass of accumulated evidence. There is certainly something the matter with the evidence." There the discussion stopped, but my study of this question did not stop. Since then I have had opportunity to test out this theory in many ways in my own dealings with young people, and advanced students, including those with higher degrees, as well as keeping careful watch of what others have done. The recent article in the Journal of Education by Frank M. Rich on "Famous Fallacies," [Reading 28] in which he discusses this question, recalls some of my experiences and conclusions that may be helpful to others at this time.

In studying this question there are three factors to be considered: First, the methods used in making the test; second, the type of persons used in the test; and third, the material or subject matter used to produce the intellectual change. All the tests so far recorded, so far as I know, have been made by those thoroughly habituated to traditional methods of using the traditional subject matter in the traditional way on ordinary groups of ordinary boys and girls. This being the case, we have no right to form any conclusion as to what might be accomplished. We can only conclude that the traditional subjects taught in the traditional way to the ordinary type of boys and girls in ordinary groups do not result in the development of any general powers or any general improvement of the group as a whole which carries over into other subjects. With this conclusion we may all agree.

The next step would be to see if there is any carry-over with any individual unit in the test. Has there been any carry-over of any mental power by any one of the members of any class in the group? If there has been, then the conclusion must be that when all the factors of the test are properly harmonized there will be a carry-over, and that only because some factor has been imperfect has the test resulted in the general opposite conclusion.

That there has been some carry-over by some of the pupils in all of the tests seems probable from the reports, although in an average of the whole there may appear to be no such development. Another factor which has been overlooked is that of a positive lowering of general ability of some pupils as a result of studying (or pretended studying) of subjects in which they have no interest or a positive dislike. After separating out these two fractions of the groups, we have left another and large fraction—those who "take" whatever the teacher directs, with neither interest nor opposition. It is rank nonsense to suppose that such efforts would lead to any material change in the mentality of these pupils.

From this analysis of the problem our question becomes: Will the use of the proper type of subject matter applied properly to some one individual cause a general awakening of the whole mental capacity or the improving of any other capacity than the one directly under discipline? To this the answer is undeniably that such proper use of school facilities will carry over. This I have many times demonstrated, and it can be demonstrated in any school where there is a teacher who knows how to select the proper subject matter to fit the pupil's needs and teach it as it should be taught.

With proper subject matter properly taught, substantially all that large class of boys and girls now set aside as subnormal can be brought up to average and often superior standards in all the essential subjects. There is abundance of records of actual accomplishments in dealing with such problem pupils which leaves no question regarding this statement. Why is this not being done? Because of the fallacy that we must hold to the general type and purpose of traditional schools because this is the only type those now in control can either administer or teach.

The most famous fallacy of all is that boys and girls were made to fit what teachers happen to want to teach, rather than that the schools ought to take boys and girls as nature provides them and give them the instruction they should have. When this fallacy is fully realized we shall then be ready to recognize a number of other fallacies of secondary importance, such as that we can educate modern boys and girls with subject matter that belongs to a bygone age; that we can teach mathematics as a memory drill and have it develop reasoning power; that committing to memory isolated facts from science to pass an examination makes scientists (or lovers of science) of the memorizer; and that memorizing trade processes in a trade school is fitting for modern industry—a most expensive fallacy.

It is the fallacy of assuming that there can be no carry-over that has led to the nonsense of attempting to force pupils to memorize bits of information from almost every conceivable subject to the injury of young people, the disgust of parents, and bankruptcy of the taxpayers. There are many fallacies in our present administration of public education, but they are not likely to be eliminated, because those in control have been so thoroughly indoctrinated with out-of-date theories by memory drills that they have not developed their general intelligence.

The above mentioned and many other fallacies must be overcome, and we must have a personnel that have minds capable of carrying over into the ever developing new fields of learning before we can have modern schools. When this is done and our schools are brought up to modern standards and each pupil given proper instruction, then we shall find that the carry-over is so great that we can simplify the course of study for each pupil, limit the variety of subject matter, teach it better, show a far greater progress from year to year, eliminate much of the repeating, and do away with substantially all of the troublesome criticism of the schools by parents and taxpayers. We shall then find those who dominate the administration of public and private education making some progress toward more efficient schools, rather than seesawing over how they can force all young people to stay in school all day until they are twenty-one and then continue to attend evenings the remainder of their lives.

30

Norman A. Dubois

TEACHING BY THE LECTURE SYSTEM

For almost two thousand years the lecture has reigned supreme among the various methods of instruction. Until a century ago this method, which is here described by Norman A. Dubois, was regarded with respect and admiration on all sides. Two things brought this state of affairs to an end. One was the rise of large-circulation publishing houses and Carnegie's free public library system. It was no longer possible for lecturers to pretend to original genius, with their sources so easily available to earnest student searchers. The second was the decline of the public lecture system, which in its lyceum and chautauqua heyday had commanded the services of Ralph Waldo Emerson, Mark Twain, John Fiske, Henry Ward Beecher, Susan B. Anthony, and a host of other outstanding figures of the era. At first the public lectures had been serious and educationally useful; by the end of the nineteenth century they had become commercialized, trivial, and often frivolous. Ambrose Bierce defined a public lecturer as "one with his hand in your pocket, his tongue in your ear, and his faith in your patience."

The growing dislike for public lectures carried over to the private lectures of the school system. Some educators, like Harry S. Vaile (Reading 31), wanted to abolish the lecture completely, and a great many other educators came to take the same position. The fight is an old one, and the arguments in use today differ little from those employed by Vaile and Dubois in 1909. Unfortunately, the critics tended to describe a bad lecture with great accuracy, and then assume that no other kind of lecture was possible.

Probably the student would do well to ask himself, as he reads these two selections: Who are the best teachers under whom I have studied, and what methods did they use? Can a lecture be interesting? Have lectures aroused or drowned my curiosity to read more on the subject? What methods of instruction in my experience have stimulated me to new ideas?

. . . In most of our schools, existing conditions make the lecture system by far the best for presenting a science to a class of students. This fact is more especially true in a largely experimental science, such as in chemistry or in physics. As the teaching of chemistry has been the vocation of the writer, what follows will probably apply more

From *Science*, July-December 1909, 30:628-630. Reprinted by permission.

to the teaching of chemistry than to the teaching of any other science. The question then resolves itself into: what is the best method for conducting a lecture course so that its qualities shall be clearness, comprehensiveness, individual completeness and individual broadness? It is not alone sufficient to give a man knowledge. The subject must be presented to him in such a manner as to interest him sufficiently to make him exert himself to learn it. Care must also be taken to show him where he can find the more detailed information. It does not suffice to teach any subject from one point of view. The failure to present a subject broadly turns out narrow men. It is broad men the world demands and these are moulded by viewing a subject from as many different standpoints as possible. For the broadest diffusion of knowledge, men of different years should be given somewhat different standpoints and shown where to find their knowledge somewhat differently. A hard-worn path should not be followed. A lecturer who writes a set of notes which he intends to follow year after year, without revision, soon finds that his intention was unsound. A lecture on almost any portion of a fast-growing science like chemistry needs more or less revision every time it is given. . . .

The lecture itself can not do all the teaching. It should, however, lead, interest and inspire the student. The subject matter should be covered as completely as the time will allow, but not so rapidly that the average student can not grasp it readily. In order that the student should get the most out of a lecture he should be required to read carefully the corresponding pages in the accompanying reference book before the lecture takes place. The references of the pages to be covered at each lecture should be given at the previous lecture. The student should by all means study these pages in conjunction with his notes the same day the lecture is given, and more diligently the parts which were emphasized in the lecture. To interest the student as well as to insure greater clearness, as many typical experiments as possible should be carried out on the lecture table if the course is a complete one. If the course is only a preliminary one these experiments may be wholly or partially omitted. The manner of presenting the experiments has a large influence in communicating inspiration to the students as well as does the personality of the lecturer. To have this inspiring effect in the highest degree the lecturer must above all use good English and so choose his words that the least possible effort on the part of the student is required to comprehend the subject. The experiments must go smoothly. No muddy, half-way experiments should have a place on the lecture table. The man who has the reputation of never having an experiment fail always tries his experiments carefully before the lecture. The giving of experiments with a three-minute preparation nearly always results in few experiments and many failures. This always gives the students less respect for and less confidence in the lecturer, and the qualities which the lecturer should endeavor to have in his lecture, those of interesting and inspiring the students, are lost. . . .

31

Harry S. Vaile

THE LECTURE IN THE CLASSROOM—A PROTEST

The futility of the lecture as a method of class instruction has been demonstrated over and over again by theory and by experience. But tradition is strong. Condemnation has failed to kill the evil and indeed it even flourishes today as luxuriantly as ever. Universities and colleges and even schools of lower grade are following the example of past

From *Educational Review,* April 1909, 37:399-402, 404-405.

generations and are foisting upon their students this same wretched travesty of true teaching. . . .

The printed book has really deprived the information lecture of its excuse for being. Such a lecture is a criminal substitute for the printed page. One of the most unsatisfactory experiences which the writer went thru as a college man, in company with many other sufferers before and after his day, was a lecture course with an instructor who literally dictated from his manuscript as to an amanuensis, reading so slowly that it was easy to obtain a verbatim report in longhand. This procedure did indeed put the student in possession of a manuscript book containing the full text of the lectures, but this is a ridiculously small item of profit to be placed over against the waste of time and effort. Such a reversion to the medieval process of literally "manufacturing" books is absurd, while the human phonograph possest hardly as much personality as a mechanical phonograph, which would have served the purpose just as well. Fortunately such a practise is not common. If the lecturer has more animation than this automaton had, he still merely reads or delivers offhand instalments of his manuscript. He cuts off the flow of words when the bell rings for the end of the class-period, only to open the sluice gate again when the next period arrives, and so on to the end of the course. Doubtless many a reader of these words will feel that any metaphor suggesting moisture and fertility is in painful contrast with the hours of mental aridity and barrenness which his memory brings before him!

Under this never-ceasing flow of words what are the members of the class doing? Leaving out of account the indifferent, who are planning to use the notes of a fellow-student, perhaps in the form of a printed "digest," those who depend upon themselves to get profit out of the course and to prepare for the examination are busily engaged in "taking notes." It is a sound doctrine of psychology that the mind can not entertain two different ideas at the same moment. It may seem to do so but in reality it simply jumps from one to the other, not dwelling long enough upon either to lose its grip on the other. It was facility in this vibratory process of mind that enabled Julius Caesar to dictate those famous six letters simultaneously. Regardless of the fact that the mind's power is thus limited, the note-taker is required to reproduce the substance of the lecture while the lecturer is proceeding, a thing which it is impossible to do with success except in the case of the avowedly dictated lecture. The note-taker can not catch the thought, condense the expression, and write down the words, and at the same time get and keep in mind another idea which follows hard upon the former and is to be treated in its turn in the same way, without damage both to the record which he is making and to his grasp of the idea which he must record next. He may find, in fact, when he gets to the next idea and is ready to put it into words, that he has lost it altogether. So here is a gap in his record, perhaps the omission of a vital point in the development of the lecture. Even if he succeeds in avoiding any serious omissions, his report at best will be disconnected and fragmentary and may contain

more or less serious errors and misunderstandings. If of course he has the time and the sustained determination to write out his report in full while he still has some recollection of what he heard but did not put down in black and white, and has the opportunity of correcting errors and clearing up uncertainties by consulting the lecturer, his report will then be faithful to the general substance of the lecture, but will not be as satisfactory and useful as the original lecture would be if accessible in printed form. So, at the very best, he has only succeeded in doing at a heavy expense of time and effort what the instructor with the aid of the publisher ought to have done for him. Students may take time for this laborious process of "writing up notes" which they could better spend otherwise, but this sacrifice the instructor has no right to demand of them.

There is still another serious charge to be brought against the lecture method. The lecture is not a true pedagogical process because it does not have as its goal the true end of education, namely, the development of the intellectual powers of the student. The chief demand made of him is that he shall put upon paper his hasty impression of the speaker's thought, even if not the speaker's very words. He has at the time no opportunity of questioning his comprehension of the content of the lecture or of bringing it into vital connection with his existing knowledge; in other words, as the Herbartian would say, the lecture method sets at defiance the principle of apperception. Whatever questioning and assimilating of the matter he ever does he must do afterwards upon the meager and unsatisfactory basis of his notes.

Of course it would not be true to say that a lecture course never acts as a stimulus to originality and individuality. But if such is the effect, it is due to the rare quality of the speaker's thought and personality, which exert some part at least of their full power in spite of unfavorable conditions. The contention of this protest is not that the method is everything and the man nothing, but that the teacher's personal influence ought to have opportunity of working freely upon the minds of his students as it can not do under the lecture method; and that, conversely, the student has the moral right to be able to put himself freely and unreservedly in the way of receiving all the inspiration the instructor is capable of giving him. . . .

It must be admitted that there has been a deplorable decline in our country in scholarship and enthusiasm for scholarship. Recently our scholarship has been publicly arraigned by one of our own citizens as inferior to that of Europe and the charge has not been refuted and can not be. It seems reasonable to attribute this decline in large measure to the failure of the present generation of college-bred adults to come into contact in college days with the contagious enthusiasm of real teachers. They have not imbibed respect for culture and the intellectual life. Hence the atmosphere surrounding their children is one of low ideals of education and its worth. The effects of this lowering of ideals are not confined to college or university but appear plainly in the secondary school as well, where teachers who themselves possess high reverence for scholarship have to struggle against a depressing weight of indifference. Of course, other causes have cooperated to create the present low ebb of scholarship, but the deadening character of much of the instruction in college and university is in part responsible. Hence, in the interest of scholarship and culture, it is to be regretted that the mechanical lecture method still prevails in spite of its manifest irrationality and in spite of its demonstrated failure. It has the strength of tradition to support it and therefore it dies hard.

The methods of education

NATURALISM

The word *naturalism* has many meanings—in philosophy, in literature, in theology, and in science. Naturalism in education has a meaning rather different from its significance in other fields. Generally speaking, it means to let nature do the teaching, to allow the child to "grow naturally," to interfere with natural processes of learning as little as possible, to rely upon personal experience as a guide rather than on systematic theories. "Natural" education was a part of the European Romantic Movement, and it shared many of the best-known traits of romanticism. Prominent among these are a belief in the essential goodness of man, a preference for intuitive rather than logical knowledge, a liking for feeling and emotion, a fear that discipline destroys freedom, and a worship of the primitive in all forms but especially in outdoor nature. Romanticism was a marvelous intellectual device for encouraging people to rebel against long-established governments and destroy social restraints. Theories of naturalism served as a basis for the criticisms of traditional or classical education.

The naturalism movement contains some of the greatest names in the history of education, including many of the reformists of the early decades of the twentieth century. Readings 32 to 36 present the case for naturalism in some detail. In this introduction, therefore, it may be helpful to look for a moment at this school of thought through the eyes of one of its greatest critics, Johann Friedrich Herbart, the father of educational psychology.

Herbart attacked Rousseau and naturalism from almost every angle. Education must be scientific and based on psychology, he said, and stress science, discipline, and mental force. Skilled instruction was more important for effective learning than reliance upon nature. Herbart insisted that the teacher must "fill the mind" rather than exercise the muscles and entertain the fancies of children. He concluded that "conventional education seeks to prolong existing evils; 'natural' education means to repeat if possible from the beginning the succession of evils already overcome." Such was the voice of scientific rather than natural education.

Today one can only say that both sides were right and yet both sides were wrong. Without naturalism the schools would be more like prisons. Without Herbart's science they would be more like playgrounds.

32

John Amos Comenius

PRINCIPLES OF INSTRUCTION

John Comenius (1592-1670) has been called "the pioneer of modern educational science" and the man who really initiated the age of educational reform in which we live. His name was really Jan Komensky and he was a devoted Czechoslovakian (Moravian) churchman. During his lifetime Comenius reorganized the Swedish school system, and but for the Puritan Revolution would probably have done the same for England. His writings were translated into a score of languages and have been read all over the world.

The source of Comenius' ideas of reform lay in a curious mixture of religious mysticism and modern science. The idleness of school children, he felt, was often due to the inability of teachers to present a lesson properly. Therefore he urged a host of educational reforms. He favored the use of visual aids (he wrote the first illustrated textbook); a well-organized school system (his proposal has been called the "exact counterpart of the existing American system"; compulsory free education for all without regard to class, sex, or color; and a vocationally useful curriculum. He wrote such works on teaching methods as the one from which this selection has been taken.

Comenius' romanticism caused him to urge a world academy of scientists and a universal organization of knowledge (in the form of an encyclopedia). A world language was to be invented and world peace made a fact through some kind of world government. He was the forerunner of a long line of "natural" educators—Rousseau, Pestalozzi, and, especially, Froebel. In this tradition lie the historical roots of Progressive education. Comenius' psychology was primitive, but in other respects (curriculum, administrative organization, method) he was amazingly modern.

In all the operations of nature development is from within.

For example: in the case of a bird it is not the claws, or the feathers, or the skin that are first formed, but the inner parts; the outer parts are formed later, at the proper season.

Imitation. In the same way the gardener does not insert his graft into the outer bark nor into the outside layer of wood, but making an incision right into the pith, places the graft as far in as it will go.

In this way he makes the joint so firm that the sap cannot escape, but is forced right into the shoot, and uses all its strength in vivifying it.

So too, a tree, that is nourished by the rain of heaven and the moisture of the earth, assimilates its nutriment, not through its outer bark, but through the pores of its inmost parts. On this account the gardener waters, not the branches, but the roots. Animals also convey their food, not to their outer limbs, but to the stomach, which assimilates it and nourishes the whole body. If, therefore, the educator of the young give special attention to the roots of knowledge, the understanding, these will soon impart their vitality to the stem, that is, to the memory, and finally blossoms and fruits, that is to say, a facile use of language and practical capacity will be produced.

Deviation. It is on this point that those teachers fall into error who, instead of thoroughly explaining the subjects of study to the boys under

From *The Great Didactic of John Amos Comenius*, M. W. Keatinge, ed., vol. 2 (London: Adam and Charles Black), pp. 271-275, 280-285, 288-292, 295-396.

their charge, give them endless dictations, and make them learn their lessons off by heart. Even those who wish to explain the subject-matter do not know how to do so, that is to say, do not know how to tend the roots or how to engraft the graft of knowledge. Thus they fatigue their pupils, and resemble a man who uses a club or a mallet, instead of a knife, when he wishes to make an incision in a plant.

Rectification.   It therefore follows
(i) That the scholar should be taught first to understand things, and then to remember them, and that no stress should be laid on the use of speech or pen, till after a training on the first two points.
(ii) That the teacher should know all the methods by which the understanding may be sharpened, and should put them into practice skilfully. . . .

Nature, in its formative processes, begins with the universal and ends with the particular. . . .

Deviation.   From this it follows that it is a mistake to teach the several branches of science in detail before a general outline of the whole realm of knowledge has been placed before the student, and that no one should be instructed in such a way as to become proficient in any one branch of knowledge without thoroughly understanding its relation to all the rest.

It follows also that arts, sciences, and languages are badly taught unless a general notion of the elements be first given. I remember well that, when we began to learn dialectic, rhetoric, and metaphysics, we were, at the very beginning, overburdened with long-winded rules, with commentaries and notes on commentaries, with comparisons of authors and with knotty questions. Latin grammar was taught us with all the exceptions and irregularities; Greek grammar with all its dialects, and we, poor wretches, were so confused that we scarcely understood what it was all about.

Rectification.   The remedy for this want of system is as follows: at the very commencement of their studies, boys should receive instruction in the first principles of general culture, that is to say, the subjects learned should be arranged in such a manner that the studies that come later introduce nothing new, but only expand the elements of knowledge that the boy has already mastered. Just as a tree, even if it live for a hundred

years, puts forth no new branches, but only suffers those that already exist to develope and to spread.

(i) Each language, science, or art must be first taught in its most simple elements, that the student may obtain a general idea of it. (ii) His knowledge may next be developed further by placing rules and examples before him. (iii) Then he may be allowed to learn the subject systematically with the exceptions and irregularities; and (iv), last of all, may be given a commentary, though only where it is absolutely necessary. For he who has thoroughly mastered a subject from the beginning will have little need of a commentary, but will soon be in the position to write one himself. . . .

Nature begins by a careful selection of materials. . . .

Deviation.   It follows from this: (1) That it is best to devote the mind to the pursuit of wisdom while it is still fresh, and before it has acquired the habit of dissipating its strength over a variety of occupations; and that the later the education begins, the harder it will be for it to obtain a hold, because the mind is already occupied by other things. (2) That the result must be bad if a boy be instructed by several teachers at once, since it is scarcely possible for them all to use the same method, and, if they do not, the boy's mind is drawn first in one direction and then in another, and its development is thus hindered. (3) That it shows great lack of judgment if moral instruction be not made the first point when the education of children or of older boys is commenced; since, when they have been taught to control their feelings, they will be the more fit to receive other instruction. Horse-tamers keep a horse under absolute control with an iron bit, and ensure its obedience before they teach it its paces. Rightly does Seneca say: "First learn virtue, and then wisdom, since without virtue it is difficult to learn wisdom." And Cicero says: "Moral philosophy makes the mind fit to receive the seeds of further knowledge."

Rectification.   Therefore
(i) Education should be commenced early.
(ii) The pupil should not have more than one teacher in each subject.
(iii) Before anything else is done, the morals should be rendered harmonious by the master's influence.

Nature prepares its material so that it actually strives to attain the form.

Thus the chicken in the egg, when sufficiently formed, seeks to develope itself still further, moves, and bursts the shell or breaks through it with its beak. After escaping from its prison, it takes pleasure in the warmth and nutriment provided by its mother, opens its beak expectantly and swallows its food greedily. It rejoices to find itself under the open sky, exercises its wings, and, later on, uses them with enjoyment; in a word, it displays a keen desire to fulfil all its natural functions, though throughout the whole process of development it advances step by step.

Imitation. The gardener also must bring it about that the plant, properly provided with moisture and with warmth, take pleasure in its vigorous growth.

Deviation. Therefore, those who drive boys to their studies, do them great harm. For what result can they expect? If a man have no appetite, but yet takes food when urged to do so, the result can only be sickness and vomiting, or at least indigestion and indisposition. On the other hand, if a man be hungry, he is eager to take food, digests it readily, and easily converts it into flesh and blood. Thus Isocrates says: "He who is anxious to learn will also be learned." And Quintilian says: "The acquisition of knowledge depends on the will to learn, and this cannot be forced."

Rectification. Therefore
(i) The desire to know and to learn should be excited in boys in every possible manner.
(ii) The method of instruction should lighten the drudgery of learning, that there may be nothing to hinder the scholars or deter them from making progress with their studies.

The desire to learn is kindled in boys by parents, by masters, by the school, by the subjects of instruction, by the method of teaching, and by the authority of the state.

By parents, if they praise learning and the learned in the presence of their children, or if they encourage them to be industrious by promising them nice books and clothes, or some other pretty thing; if they commend the teachers (especially him to whom they entrust their sons) as much for their friendly feeling towards the pupils as for their skill in teaching (for love and admiration are the feelings most calculated to stimulate a desire for imitation); finally, if, from time to time, they send the child to him with a small present. In this

way they will easily bring it about that the children like their lessons and their teachers, and have confidence in them.

By the teachers, if they are gentle and persuasive, and do not alienate their pupils from them by roughness, but attract them by fatherly sentiments and words; if they commend the studies that they take in hand on account of their excellence, pleasantness, and ease; if they praise the industrious ones from time to time (to the little ones they may give apples, nuts, sugar, etc.); if they call the children to them, privately or in the class, and show them pictures of the things that they must learn, or explain to them optical or geometrical instruments, astronomical globes, and such-like things that are calculated to excite their admiration; or again, if they occasionally give the children some message to carry to their parents. In a word, if they treat their pupils kindly they will easily win their affections, and will bring it about that they prefer going to school to remaining at home.

The school itself should be a pleasant place, and attractive to the eye both within and without. Within, the room should be bright and clean, and its walls should be ornamented by pictures. These should be either portraits of celebrated men, geographical maps, historical plans, or other ornaments. Without, there should be an open place to walk and to play in (for this is absolutely necessary for children . . .), and there should also be a garden attached, into which the scholars may be allowed to go from time to time and where they may feast their eyes on trees, flowers, and plants. If this be done, boys will, in all probability, go to school with as much pleasure as to fairs, where they always hope to see and hear something new.

The subjects of instruction themselves prove attractive to the young, if they are suited to the age of the pupil and are clearly explained; especially if the explanation be relieved by a humorous or at any rate by a less serious tone. For thus the pleasant is combined with the useful.

If the method is to excite a taste for knowledge, it must, in the first place, be natural. For what is natural takes place without compulsion. Water need not be forced to run down a mountain-side. If the dam, or whatever else holds it back, be removed, it flows down at once. It is not necessary to persuade a bird to fly; it does so as soon as the cage is opened. The eye and the ear need no urging to enjoy a fine painting or a beautiful melody that is presented to them. In all these cases it is more often necessary to restrain than to urge on. The requisites of a natural method are evident from the preceding chapter and from the rules that follow.

In the second place, if the scholars are to be interested, care must be taken to make the method palatable, so that everything, no matter how serious, may be placed before them in a familiar and attractive manner; in the form of a dialogue, for instance, by pitting the boys against one another to answer and explain riddling questions, comparisons, and fables. . . .

The civil authorities and the managers of schools can kindle the zeal of the scholars by being present at public performances (such as declarations, disputations, examinations, and promotions), and by praising the industrious ones and giving them small presents (without respect of person).

Nature developes everything from beginnings which, though insignificant in appearance, possess great potential strength. . . .

Terrible deviation. In direct opposition to this principle a terrible mistake is generally made in schools. Most teachers are at pains to place in the earth plants instead of seeds, and trees instead of shoots, since, instead of starting with the fundamental principles, they place before their pupils a chaos of diverse conclusions or the complete texts of authors. And yet it is certain that instruction rests on a very small number of principles, just as the earth is composed of four elements (though in diverse forms); and that from these principles (in accordance with the evident limits of their powers of differentiation) an unlimited number of results can be deduced, just as, in the case of a tree, hundreds of branches, and thousands of leaves, blossoms, and fruits are produced from the original shoot. Oh! may God take pity on our age, and open some man's eyes, that he may see aright the true relations in which things stand to one another, and may impart his knowledge to the rest of mankind. With God's assistance I hope, in my *Synopsis of Christian Wisdom,* to give an earnest of my efforts to do so, in the modest hope that it may be of use to others whom God, in due season, may call to carry on the work.

Rectification. In the meantime we may draw three conclusions:

(i) Every art must be contained in the shortest and most practical rules.

(ii) Each rule must be expressed in the shortest and clearest words.

(iii) Each rule must be accompanied by many examples, in order that the use of the rule may be quite clear when fresh cases arise. . . .

Nature does not hurry, but advances slowly. . . .

Deviation. For the young, therefore, it is torture

(i) If they are compelled to receive six, seven, or eight hours' class instruction daily, and private lessons in addition.

(ii) If they are overburdened with dictations, with exercises, and with the lessons that they have to commit to memory, until nausea and, in some cases, insanity is produced.

If we take a jar with a narrow mouth (for to this we may compare a boy's intellect) and attempt to pour a quantity of water into it violently, instead of allowing it to trickle in drop by drop, what will be the result? Without doubt the greater part of the liquid will flow over the side, and ultimately the jar will contain less than if the operation had taken place gradually. Quite as foolish is the action of those who try to teach their pupils, not as much as they can assimilate, but as much as they themselves wish; for the faculties need to be supported and not to be overburdened, and the teacher, like the physician, is the servant and not the master of nature.

Rectification. The ease and the pleasantness of study will therefore be increased:

(i) If the class instruction be curtailed as much as possible, namely to four hours, and if the same length of time be left for private study.

(ii) If the pupils be forced to memorise as little as possible, that is to say, only the most important things; of the rest they need only grasp the general meaning.

(iii) If everything be arranged to suit the capacity of the pupil, which increases naturally with study and age.

Nature compels nothing to advance that is not driven forward by its own mature strength. . . .

Deviation. Now the faculties of the young are forced:

(i) If boys are compelled to learn things for which their age and capacity are not yet suited.

(ii) If they are made to learn by heart or do things that have not first been thoroughly explained and demonstrated to them.

Rectification. From what has been said, it follows

(i) That nothing should be taught to the young, unless it is not only permitted but actually demanded by their age and mental strength.

(ii) That nothing should be learned by heart that has not been thoroughly grasped by the understanding. Nor should any feat of memory be demanded unless it is absolutely certain that the boy's strength is equal to it.

(iii) That nothing should be set boys to do until its nature has been thoroughly explained to them, and rules and procedures have been given.

Nature assists its operations in every possible manner. . . .

Deviation. It is therefore cruelty on the part of a teacher if he set his pupils work to do without first explaining it to them thoroughly, or showing them how it should be done, and if he do not assist them in their first attempts; or if he allow them to toil hard, and then loses his temper if they do not succeed in their endeavours.

What is this but to torture the young? it is just as if a nurse were to force a child to walk, while it is still afraid to stand on its legs, and beat it when it failed to do so. Nature's teaching is very different, and shows that we ought to have patience with the weak as long as their strength is insufficient.

Rectification. From this it follows:

(i) That no blows should be given for lack of readiness to learn (for, if the pupil do not learn readily, this is the fault of no one but the teacher, who either does not know how to make his pupil receptive of knowledge or does not take the trouble to do so).

(ii) That the subjects that have to be learned by the pupils should be so thoroughly explained to them, that they can understand them as well as they understand their five fingers.

(iii) That, as far as is possible, instruction should be given through the senses, that it may be retained in the memory with less effort.

For example, the sense of hearing should always be conjoined with that of sight, and the tongue should be trained in combination with the hand. The subjects that are taught should not merely be taught orally, and thus appeal to the ear alone, but should be pictorially illustrated, and thus develope the imagination by the help of the eye. Again, the pupils should learn to speak with their mouths and at the same time to express what they

say with their hands, that no study may be proceeded with before what has already been learned is thoroughly impressed on the eyes, the ears, the understanding, and the memory. With this object, it is desirable to represent pictorially, on the walls of the class-room, everything that is treated of in the class, by putting up either precepts and rules or pictures and diagrams illustrative of the subjects taught. If this be done, it is incredible how much it assists a teacher to impress his instruction on the pupils' minds. It is also useful if the scholars learn to write down in their note-books or among their collections of idioms everything that they hear or read, since in this way the imagination is assisted and it is easier to remember them later on.

Nothing is produced by nature of which the practical application is not soon evident.

For example, when a bird is formed it is soon evident that the wings are intended for flying and the legs for running. In the same way every part of a tree has its use, down to the skin and the bloom that surround the fruit.

Therefore

Imitation. The task of the pupil will be made easier, if the master, when he teaches him anything, show him at the same time its practical application in every-day life. This rule must be carefully observed in teaching languages, dialectic, arithmetic, geometry, physics, etc. If it be neglected, the things that you are explaining will seem to be monsters from the new world, and the attitude of the pupil, who is indifferent whether they exist or no, will be one of belief rather than of knowledge. When things are brought under his notice and their use is explained to him, they should be put into his hands that he may assure himself of his knowledge and may derive enjoyment from its application.

Therefore

Those things only should be taught whose application can be easily demonstrated. . . .

Nature produces nothing that is useless. . . .

[Imitation] in schools. In schools therefore

(i) Nothing should be studied, unless it be of undoubted use in this world and in the world to come,—its use in the world to come being the more important (Jerome reminds us that knowledge, that is to be of service to us in heaven, must be acquired on earth).

(ii) If it be necessary to teach the young much that is of value solely in this world (and this cannot be avoided), care must be taken that while a real advantage is gained for our present life, our heavenly welfare be not hindered thereby.

Why then pursue worthless studies? What object is there in learning subjects that are of no use to those who know them and the lack of which is not felt by those who do not know them? subjects, too, which are certain to be forgotten as time passes on and the business of life becomes more engrossing? This short life of ours has more than enough to occupy it, even if we do not waste it on worthless studies. Schools must therefore be organised in such a way that the scholars learn nothing but what is of value. . . .

33

Jean Jacques Rousseau

ON EDUCATION

Though Comenius (Reading 32), a man of the late Middle Ages, was the source for many of the ideas of modern education, it was Rousseau (1712-1778), a man of the French Revolution, who gave tremendous impetus to educational reforms. Somehow he made people feel that educational reform was full of social dynamite and therefore an urgent concern of every citizen. This French-speaking Swiss from Geneva was, in many respects, an unusual individual. As a boy he was accused of being an idler, a liar, and a cheat; as an adult he was a vagabond and developed an acute persecution complex. However, Rousseau's personal behavior had little relation to his social influence, for his writings provided the main philosophic base for the French Revolution and for the upheavals in education which accompanied that tremendous human hurricane.

Rousseau's naturalism is much more obvious than that of Comenius. Man is by nature good—only the environment is bad, said Rousseau the sociologist. Primitive nature and South Sea Island living are innocently virtuous—civilization is corrupt and makes others corrupt, said Rousseau the anthropologist. Reason and logic are less trustworthy than the emotions and intuitive knowledge, said Rousseau the romantic. Religion as taught in the churches should be abolished and replaced by a natural religion enforced by the government, said Rousseau the theologian.

In one of the most famous books in pedagogical literature, *Emile, or Treatise on Education* (1762), Rousseau the educator presented his views. (The volume was ordered burned by the French Government.) *Emile* was a plan for bringing up a child so that he would emerge morally and mentally self-reliant and free. Nature should do the educating, with the least possible artificial help from the teacher. Only after puberty can education be more than play, said Rousseau; haste in learning makes warped minds and damaged bodies. Always the child should learn by experience, not by reading books. There was an exception to prove the rule: "One book . . . which furnishes the happiest treatise of natural education. . . . Aristotle? . . . Pliny? . . . Buffon? No—it is *Robinson Crusoe*." The selection below, if interpreted in the light of the milieu in which it appeared, should help to explain the attractiveness and wide appeal of Rousseau's writings, as well as to better clarify the position taken by a completely naturalistic thinker.

. . . The first tears of young children are requests; if we are not careful, they will soon become commands; they begin by begging our help, they end by making us their slaves. Thus, from their very weakness, whence at first arises the sense of their dependence, there soon follows the notion of domineering and command. This idea, being excited less by their own wants than by our care, is the first evidence of moral effects of which the immediate cause is not due to nature. . . . All vice takes its rise from weakness; an infant is vicious only because he is weak; give him power and you make him good. An all-powerful Being could never do ill. . . .

Do not command your pupil to do anything in the world—absolutely nothing. Do not let him even imagine that you claim any authority over him. Let him know only that he is weak and that you are strong; that from your respective situations he necessarily lies at your mercy; let him learn it, let him know it, let him feel it; let him from the first feel on his proud neck the hard yoke which Nature has imposed on man, the heavy yoke of necessity, a yoke which is fashioned by the nature of things and not by the caprices of men. Let the bridle which constrains him be compulsion, not authority. In case of acts which he ought not to perform, do not forbid him —prevent him, without explanation, without argument. . . . By this method you will make him patient, even-tempered, resigned, and well-behaved, even when he is not indulged in his inclinations: it is our nature to endure patiently the necessity of things but not the unkindness of our fellows. "It is all gone" is an answer in face of which a child never complains if he believes it to be true. After all, there is no middle course; we must either exact nothing or subject him from the first to the most rigid obedience. The very worst education is to keep a child wavering between his own will and yours, to be eternally disputing which shall be master. I had a hundred times rather let him invariably have his own way. . . .

He breaks the windows of his room. Let the wind blow in day and night; do not mind his catching cold. It is better that he should catch

cold than that he should do such silly things. Never complain of the inconvenience which he is causing you; but contrive that he may be the first to feel it. At last you have the windows mended, but without saying anything to him. Should he break them again, you change your method. You say to him very coldly but without anger, "These windows are mine; I had them put there, and I want to make sure that they are not broken." Then you shut him up in a dark room without windows. At the novelty of this proceeding, he will begin to cry and storm; no one listens. Soon he grows tired and changes his tone; he sighs and groans. A servant happens to pass; he asks to be let out. The servant does not make an excuse for not complying, but observes, "I too have windows to protect," and walks away. After the child has remained there some hours, long enough to tire him heartily and make him remember it, someone will suggest his making you a proposal to let him out on condition of his breaking no more windows. . . . You go; you hear his proposal and instantly accept it. "What a good idea! What a pity you did not think of it sooner! We shall both be gainers by it." Without requiring any protestations or confirmation of his promise, you embrace him and take him back at once to his room. . . .

I have said enough to make it clear that I would never have punishment inflicted on children as punishment; it should follow as a natural consequence of their misdeeds. Hence you will never declaim against lying, nor punish them directly for telling untruths; but you will contrive that they feel the ill effects of lying, by not being believed when they speak the truth, and by being accused of acts of which they are innocent in spite of all their protests. . . .

Falsehoods are of two kinds, false statements concerning the past and false promises with regard to the future. . . . [As regards the first] it is the law of obedience which produces the necessity for lying, because obedience is painful and children secretly try to escape it. . . . If you never punish or scold him and never demand anything from him, why should he not tell you all he has done as openly as he tells any of his little companions? . . . [As regards the second] a child can hardly be said to deceive when he makes a promise; for he thinks of nothing but how to escape from some immediate difficulty. If he could escape a whipping or obtain a box of sweets by

From *Rousseau on Education*, R. L. Archer, ed. (New York: Longmans, Green and Company, 1912), pp. 83-84, 96, 103-105, 108-110, 119, 176, 179-180.

promising to throw himself out of window the next day, he would promise on the spot. . . . It follows that children's lies must be attributed to their masters, and that trying to teach them to tell the truth is the same thing as teaching them to tell lies. . . . For my own part, as I give my pupil only practical lessons and had rather see him good than learned, I never try to find out the truth from him for fear lest he should disguise it, and never exact any promise from him for fear lest he should be tempted to break it. . . . If his intractable disposition ever compels me to enter into any agreement with him. I shall take my measures so well that the proposal shall always come from him and not from me; that, when he has once promised, he shall always see a real and immediate interest in keeping his promise; and that, if he ever fails to do so, the ill consequences shall appear to rise naturally from the order and constitution of things and not from the resentment of his tutor. . . .

Mothers take for extraordinary signs the most usual and ordinary tokens, such as vivacity, flashes of humour, playfulness, and a subtle simplicity, which are characteristic of their years and prove that a child is but a child. . . . Treat him therefore according to his age in spite of appearances, and beware of exhausting his strength by an unreasonable desire to see him exert it. . . . Forward children make ordinary men. Nothing is harder than to distinguish between real stupidity and that apparent dulness which is an indication of a strong intellect. . . .

But you are alarmed at seeing a child spend his early years doing nothing. What! Is it nothing to be happy? Dancing, playing, and running about all day—are these nothing? He will never be so busy all his life. [The authority of Plato and Seneca is then quoted.]

The apparent ease with which children learn operates greatly to their prejudice; and, though we fail to notice it, is a plain proof that they learn nothing. The delicate texture of their brains reflects like a mirror every object which is presented to them; but nothing penetrates or is left behind. A child retains the words, but the ideas are reflected back; the hearer may understand, but he himself understands nothing. . . .

I am, however, far from thinking that children are capable of no kind of reasoning. On the contrary, I observe that they reason excellently on matters with which they are acquainted and which concern their present and obvious interest. It is in the extent of their knowledge that we deceive ourselves; we attribute to them knowledge which

they do not possess and set them to reason about things which they cannot understand. We are still further mistaken in wishing to make them attend to considerations which can in no degree affect them, such as their future interest, or their happiness and reputation when they grow to manhood—arguments which, to beings who are devoid of all foresight, signify absolutely nothing. Thus all the studies which are imposed on these poor unfortunates relate to aims entirely foreign to their minds. Judge, then, of the attention which they are likely to bestow on them! . . .

In thus relieving children from all obligations, I free them from their greatest source of misery, namely books. Reading is the scourge of childhood, yet it is usually the only occupation that is given. At twelve years of age Émile will hardly know what a book is. But you will say, "Surely he ought at least to learn to read." Yes, he shall learn to read when reading will be of any use to him; till then, it only serves to disgust him. . . .

Émile has little knowledge, but what he has is truly his own; he knows nothing by halves. Among the few things he knows and knows thoroughly, the most important is that there are many things, of which he is now ignorant, which he may one day know; that there are many more known to others which he will never know; and that there is an infinity of others which no one will ever know. He has an all-round training, not in point of actual knowledge, but in the faculties of acquiring it; an open intelligent outlook, adapted to everything, and, as Montaigne says, if not instructed, at least capable of receiving instruction. It is sufficient for me that he knows how to discover the purpose of his actions and the reason for his opinions. Once again I say, my object is not to furnish his mind with knowledge, but to teach him the method of acquiring it when necessary, to lead him to know its exact value, and to inspire him above all with a love of truth. By this method we make small progress, but we never take a useless step and are never obliged to turn back. . . .

We are born twice; first to exist, then to live; once as to species, afterwards as to sex. Those who consider women as imperfect men are certainly wrong, though outward resemblance favours the opinion. Till puberty there is no apparent difference: face, form, complexion, even voice, are all nearly alike; girls are children, so are boys; the same name serves for creatures so alike. . . .

But man was not born to remain a child for ever. Nature prescribes a time when childhood ends; and this critical period, short though it be, has far-reaching consequences. As the roaring of the sea foretells the coming storm, so is this tempestuous revolution foretold by a murmuring of the passions. A dull heaving warns us of the approach of danger. A change of disposition, frequent outbreaks of passion, and a constant agitation of mind make the pupil almost impossible to control. He becomes deaf to the voice that used to tame him; like a lion in his fury, he disdains his guide, he refuses to be led. . . .

The second birth has come; now is man truly born to live and "nothing human is strange to him." Hitherto our care has been child's play; now it is serious earnest. The time when ordinary education ends is the time when ours must begin . . . .

34

Delia A. Lathrop

OBJECT LESSONS: THEIR VALUE AND PLACE

Modern educational reform was carried on further by the work of Johann Heinrich Pestalozzi (1746-1827), a German-speaking Swiss from Zurich and a professional school teacher. As a youth Pestalozzi had been a dreamer, a poor student who hated the dreary details of exact knowledge. Throughout his life he was incapable in business affairs. When he discovered Rousseau's exhortation to go back to nature, Pestalozzi enthusiastically burned all his books, vowed he would never read another, and turned farmer. A few years later, however, he had opened a school for destitute children which became world famous.

The naturalism of Pestalozzi was less doctrinaire than that of Rousseau, but very strong. He believed that training the intuition and the senses was the basis of true education, which should develop the whole nature of man. The pupil should learn by doing, by self-activity; work was more important than words in the schoolroom. Maximum freedom of the learner was a cardinal principle, with the student analyzing his own experiences. *Object teaching*, briefly described in this selection, was one of his key teaching methods.

Pestalozzian influence was probably stronger in the United States than in any other large country, especially on the elementary level. The Oswego Movement was really a Pestalozzian movement, and teachers trained at the famous Oswego Normal School of E. A. Sheldon in the late nineteenth century spread the new object lessons all over the country. Naturalistic thinking about education was an inevitable accompaniment.

. . . What is an object lesson? It is a conversational lesson in which an object or its representation is studied by the pupils in the use of their various senses, under the guidance of the teacher. Such a lesson is given, *primarily*, for the purpose of encouraging children to investigate for themselves, and, *secondarily*, for the knowledge of the facts to be discovered—i. e., first, for discipline; second, for instruction.

Allow me to call your attention to some points in this definition.

1. *An object or its representation is present for study*. Some one inquires, "Would you never give a lesson upon an object not present? I answer, rarely, and only when the members of the class

From *NEA Addresses and Journal of Proceedings*, 1870:49-58.

have such familiarity with it as that their conception of the thing shall be to them as real an object of study as the object itself. Such conditions would almost never be met. A leading object of these lessons being to cultivate accurate observation, they should be so given as to allow the exercise of this power under the supervision of the teacher.

2. *It is conversational.* Children must not only be encouraged to see, but be allowed to tell what they see, or soon they will cease to look. There is so much delight in telling, that half the world will search long and laboriously for something to tell, for the one reward of communicating it to the other half when found. This desire is innate, and its gratification necessary to the world's progress. Only conversational lessons afford children this stimulus to effort.

3. *It is under the guidance of the teacher.* She should hold the children to a point herself determines; only thus will she be able to make her work methodical. Each lesson should have a beginning, a progression, and a conclusion, containing a summary of events concisely stated—a confused and aimless talk is not worthy the name—and reference should be had in this summary to the order of importance and dependence of the facts observed. So each lesson becomes complete in itself. This does not mean that it is exhaustive. No teacher is under obligations to tell the whole truth to her pupils. Children are not competent to learn everything in regard to any object. It requires great skill in the teacher to select such facts for them as are adapted to their mental condition, and can be attached at most points to those already in possession. By a proper arrangement of these facts they become a clearly defined unit in the educational building, yet hold fixed and necessary relations to every other unit of the structure and to the structure itself. For each lesson should be given with reference to other lessons, oral or otherwise, so that by association it may be fastened in its place, and be made in its turn serviceable as a basis upon which to build future knowledge.

Having stated what I understand by an object lesson, I propose to consider, the value of such lessons. [Miss Lathrop's discussion of the advantages of object lessons is summarized below.]

1. As before said, one of the important ends they are adapted to secure is *the culture of the observation* [training the child to be carefully observant].

2. *Object lessons cultivate ease and exactness of expression* [by means of the discussion of the object].

3. *Object lessons lead children into fields of inquiry to which their attention might not otherwise be called* [thus stimulating their imagination and intellectual curiosity].

4. *Object lessons afford variety in school work* [with a resultant rise in student interest in the classroom].

5. *Object lessons, in the lower grades, prepare for books, and in the higher they supplement them.* [In other words, they motivate the child to want to read, and to appreciate the relationship between printed symbols and living reality.]

6. Again, object lessons supply *the elements from which science must be constructed* [giving the child a glimpse of the vast realm of knowledge and creating an insatiable desire for learning].

7. *Object lessons cultivate the judgment and understanding of pupils* [by making them think for themselves].

8. *Object lessons afford an opportunity for a unification of knowledges* [or, as we would say today, for integration of facts and an increase in total understanding].

I have not yet referred to the value of object lessons to teachers themselves. This I regard as a consideration of no mean importance. The mass of lower grade teachers have no necessity for intellectual effort in the performance of their daily duties, and the consequence is not only no intellectual growth, but actual retrogression. Every teacher holding such a position should hail with real delight any necessity for investigation and study. The giving of object lessons makes such a necessity and brings an abundant reward for the effort in increased knowledge and a quickening of the intellect. And then the ability to talk extempore to a class in such a manner as to rivet their attention, is no mean accomplishment. The power so to control a school of fifty children as to have each one perfectly interested, perfectly free from uncomfortable restraint, ready to talk if there is anything to say, and to listen attentively to the teacher if she desire it, is an accomplishment to be coveted by every teacher. The tact necessary to lead to the apprehension of truth without telling it; to guide children without carrying them; to use all their own knowledge in leading them to the unknown beyond them—this is the perfection of the teaching art. Toward all this the giving of object lessons pushes the teacher. If she does not attain perfection, she is driven by a constant impulse in that direction. Necessity is the goad of progress to us as to others, for we are subject to all the human infirmities, indolence not excepted.

35

Friedrich Froebel

THE EDUCATION OF HUMAN NATURE

The next great figure to appear in educational naturalism was the German Friedrich Froebel (1782-1852), founder of the kindergarten. Like Rousseau and Pestalozzi before him, Froebel had been neglected as a child. After failing as a forester, an accountant, and an architect, Froebel turned to education, where he at once succeeded. By the 1830's he was specializing in infant education; by the 1840's he had invented the kindergarten.

Froebel's views were directly shaped by reading Comenius, Rousseau, and Pestalozzi, from each of whom he borrowed extensively. However, he disliked Pestalozzi's object lessons and vocational instruction as being too mechanical and insufficiently spiritual, and he wanted even more activity. In addition, Froebel was a great nationalist who opposed education in the home, preferring external schools and vigorous training for citizenship. He regarded man as a "divine, human, and natural being." Obviously the child also possessed a divine nature which should be developed progressively by education.

The ideas which are sampled in this selection were brought to the United States by workers interested in kindergarten education, and they spread rapidly through elementary education circles. Thoroughly child-centered, moralistic, and romantic, Froebel was well attuned to the late Victorian age.

An eternal law pervades and governs all things. The basis of this all-controlling law is an all pervading, living, self-conscious and therefore eternal Unity. This Unity is God. God is the source of all things. Each thing exists only because the divine spirit lives in it and this divine spirit is its essence. The destiny of every thing is to reveal its essence, that is, the divine spirit dwelling in it. It is the special function of man as an intelligent and rational being to realize his essence fully and clearly, to exercise, practise, and reveal the divine spirit in him, freely and consciously in his own life.

The Theory of Education is the body of doctrine derived by thoughtful men from insight into this law, as a guidance in the apprehension and attainment of man's true calling.

The Art of Education is the free application of this knowledge and insight to the development of rational beings and their training towards the fulfillment of their destiny.

The Purpose of Education is the realization of a faithful, pure, inviolate, and therefore holy, life.

Education, then, must develop the divine spirit in man and make him conscious of it, so that his life may become a free expression of that spirit.

Education, in other words, should lead man to a clear knowledge of himself, to peace with nature, to unity with God.

The divine essence of things is recognized by its manifestations. But although all education, all instruction, all teaching, all free life, attaches itself to these manifestations of men and things, and through them acts upon the inner spirit, yet education must not draw conclusions concerning the spirit directly from the manifestations. The nature of things is such that in some ways inferences should be drawn negatively.

Failure in applying this truth—that is drawing conclusions concerning the essence directly from its manifestations—is the chief reason for the many mistakes of life and education. Hence it is of the utmost importance that parents and teachers should familiarize themselves with the application of it in its smallest details. This would secure a clearness, certainty, and serenity, in the relations between parents and children, pupils and teachers, which are now sought in vain. For the child who

From *Froebel's Chief Writings on Education*, S. S. F. Fletcher and J. Welton, trans. (London: Edward Arnold Ltd., 1912), pp. 31-35, 40-41, 44-45, 49-51, 62.

outwardly appears to be good is often not good inwardly; that is, he does not desire the good deliberately, nor from love, esteem, and recognition, of it. On the other hand, the churlish, stubborn, self-willed, child, who outwardly appears to be naughty, has frequently within himself the most active, eager and vigorous desire for the good; while the absent-minded boy is often following a fixed thought which makes him disregard everything around him.

Hence the fundamental principles of education, instruction, and teaching, should be passive and protective, not directive and interfering.

We give room and time to young plants and animals, well knowing that then they will develop and grow according to the laws inherent in them. We do not interfere, because we know that this would disturb their healthy development. But the young child is treated as wax or clay which can be moulded into any form. Why does man, wandering through gardens and fields, meadows and groves, fail to open his mind, and refuse to listen to the lesson which nature silently teaches? See how the weed, growing amid obstacles and restraints, scarcely gives a hint that it obeys an inner law. Then look at it growing in the open field, and see what conformity to law it shows, what harmonious life in all its parts. So children who appear sickly and constrained because their parents have forced upon them in their tender years a form and calling opposed to their nature, might under natural conditions develop with beauty, uniformity, and harmony. . . .

. . . [Education] must be passive and protective rather than directive, otherwise the free and conscious revelation of the divine spirit in man—which is the free development of the human race—is lost. But this development is the final aim of all education and life, for it is the ultimate destiny of man.

It follows that purely directive education should not begin until self-consciousness is attained; for only then is the essential nature of the individual evident. Hence, before the origin and kind of the defect of the primitive healthy nature in any pupil become manifest, all that can be done is to place him in an environment so adapted to him that it will make clear both to himself and to others the consequences of his actions, and at the same time afford the fewest opportunities for the exercise of his evil tendencies.

Nevertheless, the eternal spiritual ideal speaks with absolute and relentless authority when he to whom it addresses itself either sees the reason of the command or accepts it with simple and childlike faith. In all good education, in all real instruction, all true teaching, then, necessity should evoke freedom, law should induce self-determination, external compulsion should develop internal free will, outer hatred should beget inner love. But all education, instruction, and teaching, fail whenever hatred gives birth to hatred, law to deceit and crime, compulsion to slavery; when oppression degrades the oppressed, and severity leads to deceit and obstinacy. To avoid this, and to attain its opposite, all directive education must be adapted to the child's nature. This is attained when it expresses an immutable law and excludes all caprice. So all true education, teaching, and instruction, must always be two-sided. It must give and take, unite and divide, be directive and adaptable, active and passive, definite and flexible, firm and yielding. So it is with the pupil. . . .

Not in religious training only but in every aspect of training it is most important that the child's development be recognized as a steady evolution of stage from stage. Most disastrous is it to act on the opposite theory—to divide the very marrow of life by marking sharp contrasts and setting definite limits between stage and stage, and so losing sight of the ever-present identity of the inner essence in all the relations in life. In actual life the stages—infant, child, boy or girl, youth or maiden, man or woman, old man or matron—show an unbroken transition. Nowhere do they appear as separate and distinct. Most harmful is it to disregard this—to look upon the child or the boy as so wholly different from the youth or the man that their common human nature is acknowledged but dimly in thought or speech, and scarcely at all in act. Yet this is commonly done. The boy fails to remember that he was once a child and that the child will in time be a boy; similarly the youth ignores the bonds between himself and the boy. Worst of all, the grown man no longer finds in himself his own early stages of development, but speaks of the child, the boy, and the youth, as beings unlike himself in nature, capacities, and tendencies. This dividing up of life into contrasted stages is due to a lack of observation of one's own development, beginning in early years and ever becoming more precise. It originates more evils than can be enumerated. . . .

To sum up: man is in the child; the unity of humanity is inherent in childhood; so it follows that all that the man shall ever be or do exists in germ in him as an infant. So if we would train him aright, so as to develop both his individuality and his common human nature, we must from the first see him both as a particular human being and as in essential relations to his surroundings. But the unity of his inner life finds many and diverse manifestations, which appear successively in time. So it is in diverse particular experiences that the child learns to know both the world as related to himself and his own inner life as related to the world. Hence it follows that his powers and tendencies, the activities of his senses and limbs, should be developed in order, each as it appears in his life.

[The] first stage of childhood is of the greatest importance, because in it the child first begins to comprehend the nature of his surroundings. It matters much whether this outer world appear to him as noble or as ignoble; whether as a mere instrument of selfish gratification or as having a high and spiritual function; whether as pure or as impure; whether as ennobling or as debasing—in a word whether he grasp its true nature or see all in false and distorted relations. . . .

[Parents] and family should regard contact with nature as one of the chief moving forces of the life of the child, and should make it as full and rich as possible. And the best means is play, for at first play is the child's natural life.

Play, then, is the highest expression of human development in childhood, for it alone is the free expression of what is in the child's soul. It is the purest and most spiritual product of the child, and at the same time it is a type and copy of human life at all stages and in all relations. So it induces joy, freedom, contentment, inner and outer repose, peace with all the world. From it flows all good. A child who plays vigorously, freely, and quietly, and who persists till he is thoroughly tired, will of a certainty grow into a capable and quietly persistent man, ready to sacrifice his own present ease when a higher good for himself or for others demands it. Can childhood ever show more beautiful than in a child so absorbed in play that sleep has overcome him unawares?

Childhood's play is not mere sport; it is full of meaning and of serious import. Cherish and encourage it, then, O parents! For to one who has insight into human nature, the trend of the whole future life of the child is revealed in his freely chosen play. . . .

O Parents! let us see that our children get what is wanting in ourselves. Let that creative, life-giving, force which we lack be transfused from their lives into ours. Let us learn from our children; let us heed the gentle monitions of their lives, the tacit demands of their minds. Let us live for our children. Then will their lives bring us peace and joy, then shall we ourselves begin to grow into wisdom.

36

A. P. Drucker

THE SOCIAL VALUE OF THE MONTESSORI SYSTEM

The last member of the naturalistic quintet, Maria Montessori (1870-1952), appeared in the twentieth century. The first woman medical graduate in Italy, she developed unusually effective methods of teaching mental defectives, so much so that children of "idiot" classification passed the standard examination for reading and writing competence set by the state. Feeling that her techniques might be equally helpful for normal children, she established infant schools in the slums of Rome. These *Case dei Bambini* quickly became world famous. By the time of her death in 1952, Dr. Montessori had organized school systems and research institutes in Italy, Spain, England, India, and the Netherlands.

The Montessori system stressed two elements. One was sense training, by means of wood blocks, fitted pegs, spools of thread, and the like, to develop muscular control. The other was freedom of the child. This meant for the child free movement in the classroom, free discipline via self-training and self-control *à la Rousseau,* and for the teacher observation and correction of pupil activity on an individual basis rather than by conventional group control. Dr. Montessori disliked student immobility in the classroom, likening the children to "butterflies transfixed with a pin."

In America, Dr. Montessori was overshadowed by the similar and contemporary pedagogical experiments of Progressive education. Unlike the early figures of naturalism, she was thoroughly conversant with psychology and medical science. She symbolizes the fact that today permissiveness in education rests upon much more solid ground than the sole authority of the great names of the past—Comenius, Rousseau, Pestalozzi, Froebel.

. . . [The] Montessori system, more than any other, is adapted to the poor and dependent. All its teaching and activity is directly applicable to the every-day life of the children. Stress is laid first and foremost upon the two great tenets of social efficiency—self-help and service. Not only are the little ones taught to take care of themselves, but they learn to be helpful to others. Muscular and sensory development have been the ground work of every previous educational system; but never have they been effected through such practical activities as those which we see these little ones engaged in—fastening their garments, lacing their tiny shoes, plaiting their hair, sweeping and dusting the room, putting playthings neatly away, setting the table and deftly serving the school repast to the other children. They are trained in helpfulness and courtesy toward one another. Plants and animal pets committed to their care and protection instil in them the duty of kindliness and the sense of responsibility. In short, every feat of little hands and minds has been thought out by this great woman, with an eye to "the socialized home of the future, living, provident, kindly; educator and comforter."

Perhaps the distinguishing feature of the Montessori method is the peculiar system of discipline in these schools. As it is not so much the acquiring of knowledge that is sought in the Montessori schools as the developing and training of character, the discipline is based upon the perfect freedom of the children to do what they please and when they please. Through freedom the children are taught self-control and respect for

others. It is brought home to them that liberty is not license and freedom not abandonment. For there are two rules observed which keep the little ones within bounds: First, no one may deface or spoil anything. Secondly, no one may use his or her freedom to do aught that would hurt others. In practice, therefore, the apparent freedom of the Montessori schoolroom resolves itself into either doing the work of the day or not doing it. Either playing or not. A child may practice the exercise of the day, sleep, read, or be idle—as he chooses. The teacher remains in the background, helping only where her help is asked, but ever observing and studying the children. And still no child is ever found idle, owing, first of all to the general spirit of industriousness in the schools, and secondly, to the attractiveness of the exercises and the materials. Everything is done in playful mood, and happiness is the atmosphere of the room. Thus the children all unconsciously grow, develop, and learn the great lesson of how to live. Past achievement impels endeavor to achieve new skill and so the desire for activity is engendered not by an extraneous compelling force, but from within. The child learns the joys of achievement; he becomes self-reliant; he tastes the sweetness of helping others; he learns the duty of service and usefulness. He learns to work and play without injuring or disturbing his neighbor. In the concluding words of Madame Montessori, "Directed by an intelligent teacher, who watches over their physical development as well as over their intellectual and moral progress, the children . . . arrive at a splendid physical development, and in addition to this, there unfolds within them, in all its perfection, the soul, which distinguishes the human being."

From *Journal of Criminal Law and Criminology* (Northwestern University School of Law), Vol. 4, No. 5, 1914, 778. Reprinted by special permission.

The methods of education

PSYCHOLOGY IN EDUCATION

The immense importance of psychology in modern education has been mentioned already. It has been said of psychology that it has a "long past, but a short history." In other words, people have always wondered how the mind works, and what it is made of, but not in a scientifically organized fashion. When the word was first used, it signified the study of spirits and ghosts; later it designated knowledge of the human soul; only about a century ago did it acquire its present common meaning—the study and prediction of human behavior.

Modern psychology came to the United States toward the close of the nineteenth century, where it was immediately applied to education by such figures as William James, G. Stanley Hall, and E. L. Thorndike. Although Johann Herbart is certainly the true father of modern educational psychology, in the United States that role was played by E. L. Thorndike, who wrote the first textbook in educational psychology in 1903 and helped launch the *Journal of Educational Psychology* in 1910. Four brands of general psychology have been particularly influential in education: (a) the genetic psychology of Galton and Binet, from which educational testing is chiefly derived; (b) the behaviorism of Watson, with its emphasis upon conditioned reflexes; (c) the abnormal psychology of Freud, stressing mental health, sex drives, and the role of emotional and irrational forces in behavior; and (d) Gestalt psychology, which asserted that man learns by patterns, in sudden flashes of total comprehension rather than by the gradual accumulation of tiny facts.

Psychology has been applied to a number of special fields. For example, in medicine it has produced psychiatry; in business it has revolutionized personnel management, placement, and advertising; in the military it has provided sharp measures of human performance for the training and placement of large numbers of persons. But only in education, or at least pedagogy, has it come to dominate an entire field. Educational psychology provides the scientific base for (a) the nature of subject matter and curriculum reform, (b) educational counseling and guidance, (c) the study of individual differences, which is closely associated with the testing movement, and (d) the nature of the learning process in children, adolescents, and adults, with its immense significance for the understanding of what constitutes good teaching.

In the area of educational testing and measurement, psychology has produced the IQ test and the objective examination, plus a host of other objectivized tests useful in admission policies and in class assignment. In the area of teaching and learning the psychologists have devoted ever-increasing efforts to the study of the process. Though much of the research has been carried on in laboratory situations, in recent years the findings from psychology are more and more frequently being tested in school situations.

37

Arthur P. Coladarci

THE RELEVANCY OF EDUCATIONAL PSYCHOLOGY

Here Professor Coladarci of Stanford University makes a simple and straightforward case for the usefulness of educational psychology to the average teacher. He warns that the subject is not a magic talisman to cure all teaching problems, nor does it claim dictatorial infallibility in analyzing instructional method. Principles of learning are not to be considered as prescriptions to be applied indiscriminately. The teacher must first determine *what* learning is desired and then apply appropriate learning procedures. In essence, adaptation, not adoption, should govern; appropriate learning principles are determined in the laboratory of the classroom in terms of purposes and the terminal outcomes desired of pupils.

It may seem odd, at first glance, that educational psychology should require any such justification as the one presented here. However, the experts in a field of knowledge are often most reticent to suggest useful application of its insights to other areas. Professor Coladarci tells us that educational psychology is essentially a habit of thinking, a pattern of approach to individual teaching problems. This is a useful concept, though not easily and quickly comprehended.

The relevancy of an applied area depends in part upon the definition of the process, institution, or event to which it is applied. The contribution that can be made by *educational* psychology is partially a function of the particular meaning invested in "education." This statement is not merely the usual innocuous preface to an extended discussion. Indeed, it is our major thesis. Too many teachers and administrators have thought of educational psychology as consisting only of an ordered catalogue of educational prescriptions, which, together with those provided by the other foundational fields in education, "tell" the teacher "how to teach" and the administrator "how to administer." The fallacy lies not only in the much too complimentary respect for the status of our knowledge in these areas but, more fundamentally, in the conception of education as a collection of successful recipes—the teacher or administrator is a person who has been armed with a bag-of-tricks into which he reaches for a decision regarding any given specific professional problem. Although this unfortunate orientation becomes an increasingly less frequent one, it still exists and may be partially attributable to the turn-of-the-century efforts to make education "scientific" by attempting to make it merely more *factual* (1).[1]

If one, however, thinks of the nature of the educator's role in another way, educational psychology, and education generally, become more powerful, exciting and rigorous. The conception we have in mind can be described by beginning with a rather coarse but generally acceptable definition of the educator's role: to help the learner change his behavior in specified desirable directions. Although the definition is too ambiguous

for detailed analysis, it serves to point out the two basic factors involved: a *process* ("behavior change") and a *criterion* ("specified desirable directions"). Suppose that the educator has clearly specified what he means by "desirable" behavior changes in the form of operationally stated educational goals (2). It appears, now, that the focal task for the teacher is to so interact with his pupils, and to so arrange the conditions and materials, that these pupils will change in the hoped-for ways. Put in these terms, the teacher's task can be seen as one of manipulating the learning situation in such a way that the *predicted* behavior changes actually do occur. If, at this point, the educational psychologist could say that we now know which manipulations will produce the desired changes, no problem would exist—we have only to apply the correct recipe. However, educational psychology cannot do this. Any particular combination of teacher-pupil-class-group-community-available materials, etc., is somewhat different from any other combination. There is no general prescription that can be considered to be clearly valid for particular cases. The teacher, then, *must be an active, continuous inquirer into the validity of his own procedures.* As Corey puts it:

"Most of the study of what should be kept in the schools and what should go and what should be added must be done in hundreds of thousands of classrooms and thousands of American communities. The studies must be understood by those who may have to change the way they do things as a result of the studies. Our schools cannot keep up with the life they are supposed to sustain and improve unless teachers, pupils, supervisors, administrators, and school patrons continuously examine what they are doing. Singly and in groups, they must use their imagination creatively and constructively to identify the practices that must be changed to meet the needs and

From *Educational Leadership*, May 1956, 13:489–492.
[1] [Numbers in parentheses refer to the references at the end of this reading.]

demands of modern life, courageously to try out those practices that give better promise, and methodically and systematically gather evidence to test their worth" (3).

At the risk of belaboring the point, let us put it in somewhat different form before considering the relevancy of educational psychology. The educator's decisions about methods, materials and curricular procedures should be thought of as *hypotheses* regarding the way in which the desired behavior changes can be brought about. These hypotheses must be *tested* continuously by inquiring into the degree to which the predicted behavior changes actually occurred. This view has been referred to elsewhere by the writer (4) as "teaching behavior defined as the-testing-of-hypotheses behavior." The crucial element is *tentativeness;* ideas and decisions about method and curriculum are to be held hypothetically, continuously tested, and continuously revised if necessary.

Given this conception of the educator's role, how can educational psychology be brought to bear on it in helpful ways? The contribution can be broken down into two related categories. First, educational psychology, as a body of information and an arena of research activity, can help in the generation of the educational hypotheses. Intelligent hypotheses are not chosen randomly nor are they found full-blown. An intelligent hypothesizer thinks along the lines of the following model: *"On the basis of the best information now available to me, I* hypothesize that this procedure will produce this result." To translate this into the context of education, we might say, for instance: *"On the basis of what I now know* about individual differences and the reading process, I hypothesize that this kind of grouping-for-reading will lead to the kind of pupil progress in reading that I would like to bring about."

Educational psychology, as a source of information, contributes to the "on-the-basis-of-what-I-now-know" portion of the statement. It helps provide information on which to base hypotheses for particular purposes and particular children. The teacher or administrator who takes this point seriously will understand that one cannot merely "take a course in educational psychology," but that he must constantly keep informed about those developments in this area that are most relevant to his particular educational responsibilities. The reader may also note that this conception of the interaction between educational psychology and the teacher means that every teacher can *contribute to* educational psychology in the process of testing his hypotheses.

A second kind of contribution which educational psychology can make is that of helping teachers and administrators to acquire the attitudes and skills necessary to intelligent hypothesizing and the testing of hypotheses. Limitations of space preclude an explication of this. Generally, what is involved is learning such skills as how to interpret data intelligently, how to observe accurately, how to avoid common logical fallacies in making inferences, how to make adequate decisions regarding what data should be gathered, ways in which data can be gathered and recorded, etc.

Both of these contributions . . . are shared by [other fields] . . . In the writer's view, this is the *raison d'être* of any field that purports to be "foundational" in professional education. Educational psychology, of course, has many additional and somewhat unique values for the educator. We have chosen to overlook those in this discussion since they are covered comprehensively and in detail in the available published literature. Those who are interested are invited to examine the published reports of a committee organized by the Executive Committee of the National Society of College Teachers of Education. The first report (5) discussed the ways in which educational psychology relates to curriculum development; the second (6) considers the nature of educational psychology and its general place in teacher education; the third (7) gives detailed attention to the ways in which specific areas of educational psychology can be helpful to the prospective teacher; the last report (8) describes present practices and developments in the teaching of educational psychology.

It is appropriate, in this case, that the final comment should be cautionary as well as benedictory. The writer has stated his position as though there are no responsible competing alternatives to it. Any dogmatic flavor in the statement is more a consequence of brevity than of intent. Many persons will hold that such a conception of education as we have presented here is both impractical and not valuable. Our response would be that the orientation is at least practical in the sense that many, many educators have learned to behave as inquirers; the orientation appears to be valuable in that where one finds such an educator he usually finds him to be valued by his colleagues, ego-involved in his profession, and able to criticize his procedures rationally. In short, such educators do exist and they appear to make the profession a better one by their membership in it.

References

1. B. Othanel Smith. "Science of Education," in W. S. Monroe (editor), *Encyclopedia of Educational Research,* Macmillan, 1950. p. 1145-52.

2. Robert M. W. Travers. *Educational Measurement.* Macmillan, 1955. p. 19-36.

3. Stephen M. Corey. *Action Research to Improve School Practices.* Bureau of Publications, Teachers College, Columbia University, 1953. p. viii.

4. Arthur P. Coladarci. "Are Educational Researchers Prepared to Do Meaningful Research."

California Journal of Educational Research. 1954, 5, 3-6.

5. "The Psychological Basis of the Modern Curriculum," *Journal of Educational Psychology.* 1948, 39, 129-69.

6. "Educational Psychology in the Education of Teachers," *Journal of Educational Psychology.* 1949, 40, 257-94.

7. "Educational Psychology for Teachers," *Journal of Educational Psychology.* 1950, 41, 321-72.

8. "Current Practices and Innovations in the Teaching of Educational Psychology," *Journal of Educational Psychology.* 1952, 43, 1-30.

38

Harold E. Jones

THE EDUCATIONAL PSYCHOLOGY OF PERSONS

If Professor Coladarci (Reading 37) makes the case for the usefulness of educational psychology in layman's language, then Professor Jones makes the case rather differently and in professional terminology. He too is interested in the value of his discipline for the society to which we all collectively belong though he also outlines the implications of his field for the individual teacher. Jones is presenting arguments for the general value of educational psychology and appeals to teachers to apply more systematic procedures in their work in the classroom. He also notes that the educational psychologist has a responsibility to acquaint teachers with better methods of accomplishing the teaching-learning task. A different quality of light may be shed by examining some of the specific uses of educational psychology as presented in the other articles in this section. Students would find it worth while to consult one or more current texts in educational psychology in order to grasp some of the dimensions of the field and to discover the concerns of educational psychologists (9).

In his discussion of recent trends in educational psychology, Professor Jones gives useful additional clues to the matter of "relevancy." Seemingly, psychologists are as deeply involved in the dispute over individualism versus groupism, and as uncertain which should have priority, as are the rest of us.

If we are sometimes perplexed as to the field covered by educational psychology, we can look back to a time when it had very definite boundaries. A quarter century ago it was bounded on the east by Thorndike and on the west by Judd. For all to see, its Principia were in Judd's vigor-

From *Journal of Educational Psychology,* December 1946, 37:513-526.

ous writings and in Thorndike's three volumes, which spread before the fascinated student a feast of wisdom about original nature, learning, and individual differences. It is no accident that for many years, following this lead, the subject-matter of educational psychology was drawn very largely from two allied branches: differential psychology and the experimental psychology of learning. For two decades the great preponderance of new research dealt either with aptitudes and attainments, or with studies of verbal learning or of classroom techniques for imparting specific knowledges and skills.

But science, which Vannevar Bush has described as the endless frontier, cannot be static and still remain science. Even though the individual student may sometimes be as stationary as the bottom man on a totem pole, educational psychology as a whole moves forward not only within the field to which it was originally devoted, but also into new topical areas. These newer topics are closely associated with development psychology, with social psychology and personality.

It would be a mistake to regard such changes as an about-face, a denial of former goals, or a conversion to a new faith. There have, to be sure, been over-reactions against earlier fields of interest; there have been crusading attempts to devalue measurement and scientific experiment, and to elevate the 'whole child' into a position of awe and mystery. The advocates of children's needs, of the child-centered school, or of self-expression or self-activity have sometimes carried these reasonable concepts into a sphere of hallellujah which seems foreign to the more sober purposes of science.

But these are phenomena of exploit, marked by emotional rejection or affirmation and by a kind of enthusiastic confusionism. We are concerned here not with the squeaks in the machinery, but with the more lasting products of its operation. To use an organic rather than a mechanical analogy, we may say that educational psychology, like other sciences, has been subject to growth, with aspects both of differentiation and of integration . . . the differentiation of new problems and methods, going beyond our initial preoccupation with individual differences and learning, and the integration of new with earlier achievements.

These growth changes are organically appropriate. We may also call them logical, for we would all concede that the purpose of educational psychology is to assist in the process of education, and this process obviously entails not merely technical learning, not merely the mental ability and educational readiness to learn, but also the personal motivation to learn, the control of maladjustive interferences with learning, and the personal traits which make possible the use of learning in socially desirable ways.

From earlier years we can point to many solid accomplishments which bear on the efficient classification of school children, on techniques of learning and teaching, on the measurements of

skills and the prediction of readiness to acquire skills. But it is now realized more clearly than before that this is not enough, for we are more concerned with the implications of the fact that 'persons' go to school, not just an equipment for learning, not just memories, minds or intellects.

The person in the educational process

There is, of course, no lack of evidence as to the importance of the person in the educational process. Some of this evidence has been summarized by Gordon Allport in his illuminating discussion of "The Ego in Contemporary Psychology." (1)[1] Allport points out the rôle of ego involvement, or what we might more simply term the personal stake, in learning, memory, judgment, attitudes, and beliefs. An example is the relationship between learning and the affective tone of the material learned. It is common knowledge that pleasantly toned materials are in general easier to learn than those which are affectively neutral. Unpleasantly toned materials on the other hand may be either easy or hard to learn. They are likely to be hard if the unpleasantness carries an ego reference, if it involves the learner as a person and leads to a feeling of personal uneasiness, infringement or guilt.

Thus, although we can predict for groups, we cannot safely predict for individuals the relative difficulty of things to be learned. We must take into account not only the average difficulty value of the material, but also the learner as a person. Although this seems too obvious to be stressed, Allport observes that in the Yearbook on Learning (15) which the National Society for the Study of Education published only four years ago, "One searches its four hundred sixty-three pages in vain for any mention of the ego, and almost in vain for any recognition of interest. True, one finds occasional remarks to the effect that 'the teacher who neglects the simple but powerful word of praise does so at her pedagogical peril,' but the potential significance of such remarks for learning theory seems lost to view." (2, p. 465).

The personal factors which exert their powerful rôle in learning are also—it should be unnecessary to say—to be found in every aspect of teacher-pupil relationship and in every aspect of educational psychology bearing upon such rela-

---

[1] [Numbers in parentheses refer to the references at the end of this reading.]

tionships. This leads us to the further point, on which we are now (in principle) mostly agreed, that education is concerned not only with the acquisition of subject-matter and the personal factors which may influence this, but also in a direct way with personal maturing, personal and social adjustment, and preparation for community membership.

Growth trends in educational psychology

To observe the actual trend with regard to some of these topics, I have made a rough classification of the research reports in the *Psychological Abstracts,* including all of those which seemed to be conceived with reference to the psychology of education, whether they were in that section of the *Abstracts* or were noted in cross-reference. Account was taken only of empirical studies, not including discussions, summaries or announcements, without data, of a new test or rating scale.

Of these research reports in 1929, approximately forty-five per cent dealt with aptitudes, prognosis or achievement. Only six per cent dealt with personality . . . in terms of a broad concern with personal characteristics, including non-intellectual traits, or in terms of a concern with social relationships, motivation, or adjustment. Ten years later, in the last year before the war, fourteen per cent dealt with personality, and in a more recent count, for the present year, this has increased to twenty-two per cent, while studies of educational achievement and prognosis have diminished slightly.

Thus we seem to have some indication of a trend, and this is also shown by our textbooks in educational psychology, although sometimes in less marked form, for textbooks often have a cultural lag of several years behind scientific practice. Starch's *Educational Psychology,* (21) perhaps the best in the field in 1919, contained practically nothing about personality or child development. This is also true of Pintner's, (16) appearing ten years later. Jordan (11) in his third edition, published in 1942, makes the observation that "most of the desirable outcomes of all education are encompassed in the one of a well-balanced personality—it is the problem of educational psychology to bring about this end." About thirteen per cent of Jordan's volume appears to deal with personality, about ten per cent with interests and motivation, about eight per cent more with growth, and the remainder with topics of more classical repute.

But we also have examples, in very good circulation, of texts which show a somewhat more marked change of emphasis. Gates' *Psychology for Students of Education,* (6) in its first, 1922, edition contained about fifteen per cent of what might be termed child development materials . . . growth, personality, children's interests and attitudes, emotional and social development. In the 1930 edition this had grown to thirty per cent, and by 1942, in an edition by Gates and collaborators, (7) to forty-five per cent. Similarly, Pressey's *Psychology and the New Education* (17, 18) contained in 1933 about thirty per cent of child development materials, and in 1944, forty-five per cent.

Limitations in current trends

Thus it is apparent that many teachers in training are today learning much more about non-intellectual aspects of behavior than was the case a few years ago. But we should not neglect to observe that even those studies which emphasize an interest in personality do not necessarily illustrate a concern with persons as individuals. They are more likely to deal with personality traits in the abstract, and with the analysis of trait relationships. Often they exhibit a preoccupation with applying the techniques of measurement to elusive and complex variables, such as 'neurotic tendency' or 'dominance' or 'introversion.' When, in this manner, a well defined and significant personality characteristic is reliably and validly measured we can only feel gratification at the successful extension of scientific method. But too often what we find is a mere numeralization, to use Kantor's phrase, with the neglect of essential features because they are not numeralizable.[2]

When the educational psychologist does speak of persons, in what context does he use this term? Usually, it appears, in a context of sampling. Not persons as having individual personalities, not cases with case histories, but statistical cases, units to be assembled into distributions, tallied in correlation plots, or punched into IBM cards. All of these are useful operations, no doubt foreshadowed as necessary when man began to learn to count. But perhaps it would be better to speak of the units of these operations not as cases,

---

[2] Kantor adds (what should be more obvious to us now than twenty years ago, because there are so many examples of it) that to numeralize or quantify badly conceived variables "can only lead to results which are increasingly precise in their misguidance." (12, p. 44).

persons, or individuals, but as nonentities, for the person with whom the mass measurer deals is usually a nonentity in every respect except for one or two or half a dozen measured variables. Possibly it is with this in mind that the individuals in a sample are represented as X_1, X_2, etc., for each is genuinely unknown. The struggle for statistical respectability may not be a struggle to know more about them, but rather a conscientious attempt to increase the N by adding more nonentities to the sampling aggregate.

Scientific hazards

I do not wish to imply that this is in itself an unsatisfactory situation. On the contrary, it may be quite satisfactory providing we recognize the principle of scientific growth and are prepared to work with trends rather than against them. The textbook writer who marches ahead of the trend (a rare and perhaps non-existent individual) would find himself in the position of displacing well-established, scientifically grounded materials in favor of more dilute outpourings of a newer psychology. It is freely admitted that much of what is now written in the name of personality and child development is scientifically, shall we say, immature. I hope this adjective will be taken in a friendly spirit and not, as someone has said, as a bone of condescension.

One recalls a discussion by James Marshall (13) entitled "Plato, Buddha, and President Hutchins," in which he presents the problem of neurotic scholarship: the neurotic scholar being one who sees daring in an asterisk and finds immortal security in a footnote. We would not substitute this conception of careful research, or re-research, for more genuinely adventurous enterprise, but we are justified in looking most judicially through our bifocals at studies which have 'purposes' and 'techniques' too far out of balance.

Gardner Murphy (14) has described the danger to any science whose methods are developed entirely in advance of its problems, so that the experimenter sees only those phases of a problem for which a method is already at hand. The danger is one of congealing research into a few self-limiting sectors. But there is also a danger, which is by far more to be regarded in the study of personality, of letting our purposes and aspirations so far outrun our techniques that we become complacent in the use of intuition and of other primitive ways of knowing, and neglectful of verifying the things we think we know.

If this is the case, the question may be raised as to whether educational psychology, in becoming more personalistic, may not be in danger of losing or weakening its standards as a science. In considering this question, it is necessary to distinguish between research functions and teaching functions. We must also distinguish between scientific method applied in the interest of science, and scientific method applied in the interest of education or guidance.

Allport has been our most eloquent American advocate of the view that since "every mental function is imbedded in a personal life," and since "each personality is a law unto itself," the primary goal of the psychology of personality must be to understand the individual forms of mental life. (1, Ch. 20). The comparison of one person with another in respect to their common traits is considered to be only a secondary goal.

Idiographic research of this nature, directed at "understanding some particular event in nature or society," or the unique individual case, is contrasted with nomothetic studies which are directly concerned only with universal phenomena and general laws. Now, the uniqueness of the individual personality, and the influence of unique personal factors upon every aspect of the educational process, are general principles. But the way in which these personal factors operate in any given case, as distinguished from any other case, is a specific matter—important for guidance, for education, but not a prime preoccupation for the scientist. Skaggs has observed that if we carry Allport's doctrine to its extreme there would be as many psychologies as there are individuals. "Whenever a new baby is born a new psychology would have to be written. When it died it would be put aside as of no further interest because this was a unique person." (20, p. 237).

And yet the teacher, as well as the therapist, must study persons as individuals because the art of teaching as well as of therapy demands individual understanding and individual treatment. In studying persons, we have a choice of relatively more scientific and relatively less scientific methods. The former, we would agree, involve the appropriate use of systematic and standardized techniques of assessment. They involve predictions from these assessments, on the basis of statistical probability. The less scientific approaches consist of interpretation in which data, more or less explicitly known, are combined in what may be called clinical inferences. What is the nature of these inferences as used by the counsellor or teacher? If we speak of them as representing intuition, or clinical insight, or Verstehen, or emphatic or sympathetic understanding, are we describing a process which is qualitatively different from scientific logic—a process shared by clinicians, insightful teachers, poker players, and other artists in human relationships, but not by scientific workers?

Sarbin has noted that these interpretative processes can be described in one of two ways: "Either they are statistical predictions, made in an informal, subjective, and uncontrolled way, or else they are purely verbal manipulations, unverifiable, and akin to magic." (19, p. 214) In the former case, they represent an early step in scientific procedure, or perhaps we should say a pre-scientific method which we must all practice when we wish to take account of factors which are not precisely measured or not explicitly formulated, and of relationships and probabilities which are guessed at or 'hunched' at but not exactly known. In the latter case, however, in which Sarbin describes inferences as akin to magic, the procedure is anti-scientific and belongs in the addled region of lore, primitive intuition, and superstition.

The case study as a training device

If it is the task of the teacher to know something about his pupils as persons, then it is also the task of the educational psychologist to acquaint the teacher with the best methods for doing this . . . with methods for measuring abilities, for observing behavior, for interviewing, and for synthesizing these and other approaches. The individual case study is an indispensable aid in this area of instruction. Whether or not it is in itself a contribution to science, we can agree that it is a contribution to teacher-training.

During the past five or six years a number of case reports[3] have been published for this purpose, and to an increasing extent textbooks now draw upon case studies in order to present concrete examples of individual behavior in life situations. In its proper sphere as an educational device, the case study offers an important supplement to our standard textbooks, and should (to offer one opinion) make up from a quarter to a half of the reading assignments in educational psychology. A serious limitation in this material lies in the small number of cases that can be represented; the more thorough they become, the smaller the number, with the likelihood of special selections which express the bias of individual writers. We must guard particularly against

selections which appeal to the clinician's fascination with pathology, but which may not reflect the samples of behavior and behavior dynamics ordinarily encountered by teachers.

Field methods

The further point must now be made that teachers should learn to study persons not merely through the eyes of psychologists who write case studies, but through their own eyes. In many institutions students have little opportunity to acquire, through field experience, techniques of case study. Practice-teaching of subject-matter is demanded, but not practice in learning about and understanding children.

This major weakness in training teachers was one of the principal concerns of the Teacher Education Commission, of which I had the privilege of being a member, and which has recently finished a nation-wide coöperative program directed toward the location of problems in teacher-training and the development of methods for dealing with these problems. One part of this program involved the establishment of the Child Development Collaboration Center at the University of Chicago, where teachers in training, teachers, and professional consultants could work together in conferences, study groups, and workshops, making use of materials which have been assembled from various child research centers. Another part of our Commission's program was in the development of methods of child study which could be practiced by teachers in training. An example of this is presented in some detail in the book published by the Commission, *Helping Teachers to Understand Children* (5).

In one of the school systems coöperating with the Commission, an intensive program was carried on for several years, beginning with a meeting of a group of teachers with a psychologist. The teachers were asked to present problems for discussion. Their problems were of this nature: "What would you do with a child who steals?" "How would you handle lazy children?" "What are the ways to stop so much inattention?" Such questions, typical of what psychologists are often asked by worried and overworked teachers, suggest a failure to understand the relation between behavior and a pupil's earlier experiences, his developmental status, his aspirations. They suggest that teachers are primarily concerned not with understanding behavior, but with obtaining ready-made techniques for controlling and disciplining pupils. The comment seems justified that "Perhaps the most disconcerting thing about

---

[3] See, for example, references 3 and 10.

these questions was that the teachers seemed to expect answers to them . . . " (5, p. 2), in terms of standard general procedures which would be applicable to any child showing the problem mentioned. This demand of teachers for authoritative prescriptions in managing children is probably related to the fact, as Burling has pointed out, that the classroom teacher is 'officially' placed in a position to wield authority. "She is backed by the state law and the attendance officer and behind them is the State Reform School. It takes a person with a very deeply rooted respect for personality not to succumb to the temptation of this position and to use authority in inappropriate situations." (4, p. 159). If we think of this, as Burling has suggested, as an occupational hazard of teachers, we need to take special steps in teacher selection and in teacher-training to avoid overdevelopment of the drive to dominate, rather than of the drive to understand.

These comments are not offered in a spirit of unsympathetic criticism of teachers. If they are deficient in understanding children, or lacking in a psychological approach to behavior problems, must we not attribute these shortcomings in large part to our own failure, as educators of teachers, to give them an effective orientation toward children?

In the particular school system just mentioned, cumulative records had been maintained, for a number of years, containing descriptions of individual children. As a first step in a program of in-service training, the teachers decided to make a study of these records, in consultation with a representative of the Commission. The result of this study was the realization that these records, although cumulative and often voluminous, contained very little objective information about any child. As a rule, they set forth general impressions, without specific evidence. Moreover, these impressions were heavily weighted with value judgments—appraisals of behavior as good or bad, as attractive or disagreeable. If the child's family was mentioned, it was likely to be in terms of social standing, with little or no information about psychological factors. A good deal was said about the child's achievement, his success or failure as a scholar, but very little of a definite nature about his characteristics as a person.

It was then decided to undertake a coöperative child study program. Study groups were set up, which worked together in collecting developmental records and observational data, and which discussed these records with the Commission's consultant. From the teachers' own evaluation of this program, after a three-year period, it was quite apparent that they had gained new attitudes and new ways of thinking about children. They were more alert to motivational factors in family relationships, and to interpersonal relationships in the classroom. They were more aware of the nature and significance of individual differences, not merely in abilities but also in aspirations, not merely in mental growth but also in physical and physiological maturing. "The impact of the culture, enlisting the influences of social status upon developing personalities became better understood. The school itself became seen as an arena of important social interaction among children." (5, p. 399).

Such changes could hardly occur without some corresponding changes in teaching methods and in the emotional climate of the classroom. Teachers came to rely less upon threats and admonition, and more upon ingenuity in developing coöperative procedures. Less time was needed for discipline, more time was free for understanding and working with the individual. The implications of this extend, of course, to the curriculum and also to school administration, for it is idle to expect progress in teacher-child relationships if these are submerged in large classes. The educational situation represented by Mark Hopkins at one end of a log is no longer within our present scheme of things. The delicate balance of teacher and pupil on opposite ends of the log is replaced by the concept of a teacher pulling a load—a teaching load, composed, it would seem, of an inert aggregate of pupil units in average daily attendance.

A proposal for undergraduate and graduate training

The brief account that I have just given is of a program of in-service training designed to combat this concept and to make up, in some respects, for deficiencies in the pre-service education of teachers. The deficiencies are to a large extent a matter of curricular inertia, due to the preservation of vested interests in course programs. The most important vested interest, in this connection, is the standard beginning course in educational psychology. We think it is a good course; in a study by Jensen, from the testimony of three thousand students educational psychology was regarded as the most valuable part of their program. (8) Since this course was established some thirty or forty years ago, we have witnessed the rise of new courses: in child development and in personality. Each of these is now busily engaged in setting up its own vested interest, with its own secure spot in the catalogue, its own textbooks, its own personnel.

I have no quarrel with any of these parts of the curriculum, except this: that they are parts, not too well integrated, and that the individual child they discuss is rarely treated in an integrated way as a person. The question has been raised before, and I think this is an appropriate place to raise it again, as to whether our teaching would not be more effective if we were to organize these separate courses into a more unified program. This is already being done in some places, but not as yet generally. Such a program would inevitably give greater attention to persons, to the physical, physiological and social factors in the development of persons, and to field work in the observation of behavior. It would prepare for later more specialized work, in the psychological laboratory on the one hand, or in individual case study or guidance on the other. There are implications here also for the research work of advanced students.

Some years ago, Yerkes, reporting on the Yale Anthropoid Station, proudly announced that the Station then possessed fourteen chimpanzees which were born in captivity and whose life histories were known. For biological inquiry, this life history was regarded as the distinctive resource of the Yale station. Yerkes went on to state: "Within a few years there will not—or at least need not—be an individual in the colony whose ancestry, birth date, developmental and experimental history are not matters of reliable record and steadily increasing value." (22)

I once proposed that every leading department of psychology should have as part of its equipment a well-organized cumulative record upon a sample of children studied from infancy. (9) A student who has a year or two years to devote to a dissertation might then be working with a known sample of cases, and upon a problem bearing a significant relation to other problems of development. The problem might be normative, experimental, clinical, or represent a combination of methods. If longitudinal records are valuable, perhaps for many purposes indispensable, in the study of chimpanzees, should we not also enter a claim for their importance in normal human psychology and especially in educational psychology—not merely for research in child institutes, but more widely for the training and research of graduate students in psychology and education.

Through such a course of study we might expect to develop a generation of students who are more at home with the biological and other disciplines which coöperatively study development, and who are also more at home with the individual child as a person.

References

1. Allport, G. W. *Personality: a psychological interpretation.* New York: Holt, 1937. Pp. 588.
2. ————. The ego in contemporary psychology. *Psychol. Rev.,* 1943, 50, 451-478.
3. Blos, P. *The adolescent personality.* New York: Appleton-Century, 1941. Pp. 517.
4. Burling, T. "Psychiatry and education" in *Psychiatry and the war.* Springfield, Ill.: C. C. Thomas 1943. Pp. 595.
5. Commission on Teacher Education. *Helping teachers to understand children.* Washington, D.C.: Am. Council on Educ., 1945. Pp. 468.
6. Gates, A. I. *Psychology for students of education.* New York: Macmillan, 1930. Pp. 612.
7. ————, Jersild, A. T., McConnell, T. R., and Challman, R. C. *Psychology for students of education.* New York: Macmillan, 1942. Pp. 805.
8. Jensen, H. T. "Three thousand students evaluate an education course." *The Educ. Forum,* 1943, 7, 127-132.
9. Jones, H. E. *The growth study as a psychological method.* Soc. for Res. in Child Development. Nat. Res. Council, Washington, D.C., 1935. Pp. 7.
10. ————. *Development in adolescence.* New York: Appleton-Century, 1943. Pp. 166.
11. Jordan, A. M. *Educational psychology.* New York: Holt, 1942. Pp. 597.
12. Kantor, J. R. "Current trends in psychological theory." *Psychol. Bull.,* 1941, 39, 29-65.
13. Marshall, J. "Plato, Buddha, and President Hutchins." *Harpers magazine,* 1941, 183, 27-35.
14. Murphy, G. "The research task of social psychology." *J. of Soc. Psychol.* 1939, 10, 107-120.
15. National Society for the Study of Education. *The psychology of learning.* Forty-first Yearbook, Pt. 2. Bloomington, Ill.: Publ. School Pub. Co., 1942. Pp. 502.
16. Pintner, R. *Educational psychology.* New York: Holt, 1929. Pp. 378.
17. Pressey, S. L. *Psychology and the new education.* New York: Harper, 1933. Pp. 594.
18. Pressey, S. L. and Robinson, F. P. *Psychology and the new education.* New York: Harper, 1944. Pp. 654.
19. Sarbin, T. R. "The logic of prediction in psychology." *Psychol. Rev.,* 1944, 51, 210-228.
20. Skaggs, E. B. "Personalistic psychology as a science." *Psychol. Rev.,* 1945, 52, 234-238.
21. Starch, D. *Educational psychology.* New York: Macmillan, 1919. Pp. 473.
22. Yerkes, R. M. "Yale laboratories of primate biology, incorporated." *Science,* 1935, 82, 618-620.

39

George S. Hubbell

EXAMINATIONS—WHY AND HOW

Examinations are much older than psychology, at least in the written essay and oral question-and-answer forms. This article by a college professor of English literature provides much useful information for both teacher and student, regardless of their special subject area. Professor Hubbell makes two points, among many others, which may deserve special emphasis. He stresses quite rightly that examinations should be regarded primarily as teaching devices, and only secondarily as grade-determining conveniences. He might well have devoted even more time to his warning that examinations must be related to local student folklore and psychology. Whenever students believe, whether rightly or wrongly, that an examination is unfair, that it is unreasonably hard or unreasonably easy, that it will be graded with favoritism or not graded at all, the examination loses its effectiveness. Nowhere in the routine of education is honesty, openness, and rapport with students so necessary as in examinations.

I ask myself these two questions: What are my examinations for? By what particular provisions are they equipped to accomplish their purpose?

Without looking the matter up in any textbook of education, but treating it as a special concern in my own instruction, I recognize the following aims for examinations:

1. They should furnish an incentive to study and review.

2. They should require students to assume points of view and to attempt plans of classification for which other work of the course does not provide.

3. They should require a selection of the essential and the relevant, a judicious use of memory.

4. They should give to all students equally an opportunity for expression, helping to make study more than passive learning.

5. They may enable students to develop a widely valuable technique for meeting similar formal tests.

6. They help a teacher to decide which students excel.

The above list is carefully devised with respect to its omissions and evasions. For example, I do not value examinations as a means of discovering what a student knows. Except incidentally, perhaps it is unimportant, especially at the end of a course, that a teacher should measure the extent of knowledge in his class. Nor do I think it of great consequence to learn a student's opinions and reactions. In fact, it is not what an instructor finds out but what the student gains that most matters.[1]

And now comes the nub of this discussion. What sort of examination will best serve these purposes? I shall consider the question briefly in regard to each function in turn . . . .

1. In order that the prospect of examinations may induce intelligent study and review, an instructor must encourage or assume some sort of morale among his students. For this purpose, both the fear of failure and the desire for preference, underlying motives which commonly induce students to study, are likely to develop unwholesome, irrelevant, and disturbing emotional currents. Such fears and ambitions smack of the primitive childish mind which a college student is trying to outgrow. And they suggest the untamed motivation of the barbarian mind which culture seeks to

From *English Journal*, June 1931, 20:502-506. Reprinted with the permission of the National Council of Teachers of English.

[1] Tests for the express purpose of revealing probable ignorance or faulty reasoning are often useful, but they seem to work best at the beginning of an hour, when the ignorance uncovered may be immediately attended to. The papers may be collected after five or ten minutes, and the answers may be read aloud by the instructor for general criticism by the class. It is not necessary to tell who wrote the various answers. This is a teaching device, valuable to the students by its revelation of their need for instruction, to the teacher by its indication of what instruction is needed. But a test deliberately set to reveal ignorance seems an unfair basis for grading.

modify. Rather, the enlightened inquisitiveness which Matthew Arnold extols, and, less directly, the desire sometime to build as well as to discover, are the motives to which a college instructor must appeal. And he must make it clear that the examination will actually call out and display the achievements to which such motives prompt. If information spreads that special preparation is not actually necessary or particularly helpful, then the examination will probably fail in this important function.

2. The order in which a class studies successive aspects of a subject generally implies some particular classification of the material. And a classification, especially when thus ready-made, conditions perspective and sometimes leads to false evaluations. Yet for a class to follow out many classifications is only to court confusion. Near the end of the course, however, several approaches may be suggested, which an individual student can then follow through independently. This independence, possible to any considerable extent only when most of the material has already been covered once, really constitutes one of the most valuable advantages of reclassification. For the best, perhaps in a certain sense the only, education is self-education.

3. An examination will probably not promote the use of sound judgment unless the questions are carefully adapted for the purpose. Some teachers favor putting as little as possible into the test questions. They expect the student to use his judgment in defining, selecting, organizing, and presenting material in his answer. The difficulty in this method is that in effect it encourages the substitution of impromptu good sense for foresighted discretion in preparing. Students like to find out in advance whether the questions will be "general or specific." If they will be general, probably a rather scattered knowledge will furnish material enough to fill out a somewhat attenuated discussion. Such a test rarely proves an incentive to careful preparation. For preparation gives a student no great advantage over the alert among his lazy classmates, nor does it contribute much to the improvement of the answers he himself can write. Thus if his teacher should put on the board the single word "Whitman," and give him twenty minutes to show what he can do, he is likely to find abundance of knowledge and ideas only an embarrassment. The lazy classmate, with only a few tag-ends of information and just one or two unsubtle generalizations, can, if astute, write nearly as good a paper. At least the lazy one will not be hampered by sad disproportion between a little time and a great wealth of matter to express. Nor are clever snap judgments in

themselves laudable. They are, indeed, the bane of contemporary thinking.

The program is so to put each question that those who have not mastered certain essential material will find no scope for an effective parade of their little knowledge, and yet to avoid throwing the test as a prize to mere memorizers, perhaps defective in judgment and imagination. This problem must, I feel certain, be solved in the questions, not in the reading of the answers. Teachers often entertain the delusion that they can discriminate among answers, no matter how general the topics assigned, but of course they cannot do it. Surely I need not point out the mountain of evidence now available on that subject. The firm confidence which some still feel in their ability to distinguish a B answer from a C answer might seem amusing, were it not stupid or pathetic. Answers are there or not there. Being there, they may prove right or wrong, full or incomplete, straight or garbled; they are, in fact, subject to an infinite variety of classifications, not one of which offers any certain clue to a grade. One must know just about what answer a particular question requires. So the papers may be consistently scored according to a fixed standard. The rank of the students in the class group may then follow the score, and the grade may accord with the rank. But the rank and the grade are less indicative than the score. The interval between that score and a possible perfect or maximum score means "so much to go." It is the challenge to achievement, the desirable substitute for envious emulation, or aspiration to honors.

4. Three cautions are necessary in giving students the opportunity to express themselves: (*a*) They must understand that their expression is subject to the laws of evidence: it must be competent in the material, relevant and reasonable, unprejudiced, honest, adequate, clear. (*b*) The questions must be framed to make possible such answers. (*c*) Corrections must check both unwarranted generalizations and unimaginative transmission of mere facts. Some teachers have a horror of literalness; others cannot abide suave or enthusiastic gushing. One should discourage both, and set up instead a spirit of solid but imaginative constructiveness.

5. Why do some students go through college and graduate school without ever learning how to take an examination? That many do, every college teacher knows. In fact, even faculty members have testified that they themselves learned the art only after their student days. Yet the technique is simple: (*a*) mastery of facts and rehearsal of generalizations in advance, (*b*) apportioning of available time among the questions, (*c*) giving

of complete essentials before discussion and expansion under each question, (*d*) reservation of ample time for revision and filling out of doubtful points. The principal mistakes most common among students are three in number: (*a*) preparation too late for thoroughness but just right for weariness, (*b*) unsystematic arrangement that obscures correctness and completeness even if they are present, (*c*) careless mistakes due to lack of adequate revision.

Undoubtedly students are warned and advised in these matters. But they do not practice what they are told. It helps, however, especially in the lower division, if a teacher will make clear during the entire course what part examinations and tests arc expected to play in the work, just what should be done in review and preparation, and in what way questions should be answered. Then on the examination paper great gain may be realized by proper planning and wording of the questions. It may take weeks to make out a single examination.

6. Since grades must be given, a teacher does well to base them chiefly upon examinations of various sorts rather than upon recitations or prepared papers. Pythagoras was wise to interpose an opaque curtain between his students and himself; on both sides it prevented confusion of matter with manner. Recitations refract everything by intrusive emotions. It is impossible by recitations alone to judge fairly the relative attainments of students. Essays, term papers, or written reports offer a good medium for teaching and learning. But it is impossible, generally, to rank such work with assurance. It is as difficult to grade as an examination made up of general questions.

In fine, the necessity for grades is our principal difficulty. Who cares whether Smith is a fraction of a point better than Jones, in Professor Brown's opinion? Smith will be interested to find that he has improved in what he knows or can do; he may profit by discovering what are his shortcomings. But as for his standing relative to that of Jones, comparisons are odious. To finish at the head of his class should be small comfort to this Smith if he realizes that he has learned little or nothing. Examinations offer greatest value, therefore, when they indicate sharply and broadly what is mastered and what is not. . . .

40

Mrs. A. C. Martin

WHAT SHALL WE ATTEMPT IN ELEMENTARY SCHOOLS?

Students may be mildly surprised to discover that *nobody* likes examinations. Here we find one experienced teacher proposing, in an address to the National Education Association, that examinations be abolished completely, at least on the elementary level, for reasons which seem respectable enough. One should note that the date of this appeal, 1874, makes it certain that the essay examination is what Mrs. Martin is protesting against.

Just after World War I, psychologists came forth with what they called "new-type" (objective) examinations which soon spread throughout the American school system. In 1920 Professor William McCall declared in an article in the *Journal of Educational Research* (10) that objective tests of the true-and-false type would be fairer to students, more comprehensive in coverage, and "make examinations a real pleasure instead of an onerous task to both teacher and pupils." He predicted that the traditional essay examination would never disappear altogether, but that the new objective type was psychologically sounder and soon would be generally accepted. Today objective tests are being widely used and—perhaps proving that they are a vital part of American education—being widely criticized.

. . . when I pronounce the kind of work required in the Examinations, as now practiced in the Elementary schools throughout the country, to be the one great reason why our methods are

From *NEA Addresses and Journal of Proceedings*, 1874:278-279.

so mechanical and wooden,—the barrier which keeps us to this narrow path of study, and prevents us from escaping from the tread-mill into which we have been driven. As I have complained [earlier in the speech] of the mass of geographical detail—the reiteration of the rules of syntax—the year-in and year-out plodding at arbitrary processes in Arithmetic—the dead drag upon the memory by which all this is accomplished,—how many of you have said to yourselves, "It may be true, but in no other way can the pupils be made ready for the Examinations."

Just what part committees, superintendents and teachers have taken respectively in the argument (doubtless to most of them an unconscious one) which has settled the matter, I am not able to distinguish; but the course of it seems to be, in brief, as follows: Examinations are a means of education, universal, indispensable; but only certain things, taught in certain ways, can be made to show at an Examination,—can be brought into court as it were; therefore we have bound ourselves in bonds (that have proved of iron) to teach only these things in these ways.

So in answer to any criticism, the Grammar School teachers would say to me, "Our method is the result of years of experience. We must prepare these scholars for these Examinations, and we find that nothing but this very repeating and re-repeating will do it. They learn South America this year; but if they don't do it again next year, it will be forgotten. So long as committees set Examinations, and we and our work must stand or fall by them, so long must we keep on as we are, plodding,—wearisome and irrational though it may be."

My reply to such a protest is this question: Is it an Utopian vision, an impossible dream, to propose as a remedy for the inadequateness, the narrowness of our Elementary Schools, the doing away with the whole system of Examinations, as we now understand them?

I admit that they are useful in their place—for certain ends indispensable; but that place is not an Elementary School; those ends are not the training of children. The idea of them, first and last, belongs to modes of thought and study wholly remote from childhood. In an evil hour, it was imported from its place in college work to our Elementary Schools. The college, receiving its students from many different sources, must set some standard to which all must conform, in order that all may begin to work together; hence the need of an examination, and also the need of preparing those who intend to pass it by similar ones in the upper schools. But in Elementary

Schools no such need exists. The children in a city or town are all under one head. The superintendent knows, or ought to know, what is their work, and under what influences they are, as they move from class to class. The teacher, if she be fit for her place, is more competent than any one else to say who shall be promoted; and one day each month devoted by committees to watching the regular work of a school will test it better than the strictest half-yearly Examinations.

After all our pains to set tasks that can be tested by "Examinations," how difficult it is to do justice, either to scholar or teacher, an audience like this knows better than I.

But the chief objection to our Examinations in Elementary Schools comes not so much from their insufficiency as a test, but . . . hinted, from the very nature of childhood itself. In the upper schools and the college, the student is learning to divide his knowledge into accurate and inaccurate, and to judge of it; he is fitting himself to meet crises in life, to which he must summon for instant use all his power and all his acquirements. In such a work the stated Examinations are no doubt a necessary, a valuable help. The want of such a training is one of the losses which the pupil who leaves school at fourteen must suffer. What he gets of that training he must get for himself in the experience of life, but any attempt to give it to him before his mind is mature enough for it, is as foolish as to expect the manly strength of forty from the beardless boy.

If a child's mind is growing naturally and freely, it appropriates a thousand things, of which it could give no account next year or next month even, but which all go to make it full and strong at last, and without which it will be but a meagre starveling. To a fresh, bright boy or girl, wisely guided, but neither cramped nor forced, the fair, sweet to-day is the outcome of many fair, sweet yesterdays; but it would be the idlest nonsense to set them to answer what went to make them so. To do to-day's work rightly, not to prepare for some future ordeal, is the only possible standard in the teaching of children. What that daily work makes their minds, not what they have acquired, is what will tell on the future man or woman.

Not until the child is capable of self-activity— that is, of working upon his own mind—and is conscious of the power, is there either justice or sense in applying a system which secures its end by Examinations. I think we hardly realize how late the power of spontaneous reflection or reasoning is developed in a child, because most persons will mistake the child's following such a process in another for his own original work. . . .

41

Mary E. Reene

IF NOT TESTING—WHAT?

Not all educators were enamored of the new psychology and its unique testing methods. Some, like Miss Reene, although they might prefer no examinations at all, realized that such an outcome was extremely unlikely. As long as parents insisted upon some form of grades, and regarded with suspicion the complicated informal evaluations with which some school systems attempted to replace conventional methods, examinations of a demonstrably objective nature were sure to flourish.

Nevertheless a substantial element among educators of the 1930's began to attack objective examinations as a major obstacle to the test-free classroom. One educator of the time denounced the objective examination as "a mere memory quiz," nerve-wracking, and based on trickery. He observed that students shaped their plans of study upon past examinations, not on what the professor talked about, for "after emphasizing great principles [in class] the test is made on minute facts. . . . Perhaps the worst form of quiz is the true and false test. It has been called the lazy teacher's test. . . ." Such was the disillusionment expressed after two decades' acquaintance with the objective tests which had been expected to do so much "to make examinations a real pleasure." Nevertheless Miss Reene's question, "If not testing—what?," has yet to be answered convincingly.

To test or not to test, that is the question at present agitating an important part of the educational world. Educators of national repute have aligned themselves in opposing groups, and while the issue rages and the leaders dispute, the rank and file either unthinkingly follow traditional policies or grope in the shadows of indecision, looking for guidance.

With the emphasis on the factual material in the separate subject course of the traditional school, objective tests found a place and the movement flourished. Narrow educational aims, limited range in subject matter, formal textbook assignments were all features which made this type of test entirely adequate. They were short cuts to discover what the children did not know. Some opportunity to exercise judgment and discrimination was provided in the "best answer" or "ranking answer" type but, for the most part, they were purely "Yes-No" tests on factual matter. They were based on the textbooks and on

material which seemed important to the teachers. Examinations could be conducted with the minimum of thought and effort. The interest and accomplishment of the children were sacrificed on the altar of efficiency. As these tests grew in favor, the essay type of examination fell into disrepute. Blue pencil and midnight oil went with them and there were few to mourn their passing.

At the same time, but quite apart from the testing movement, was an even more significant educational development—one centering around activity. This started in different parts of the country, slowly developed but gradually gained so much momentum that it influenced education nationally and even internationally. This new type of education shifted the emphasis from subject matter to the child, stressed a different sort of content, and set up new objectives. The watchword of the new school was experience—"learning by doing." Experiments, construction, excursions, interviews, creative expression became important parts of its program. Textbooks were no longer the only sources of information. Uniform accomplish-

From *Educational Method,* May 1936, 15:403-406.

ment was no longer desirable. Lock-step education was outlawed. Child interest determined the course and learning could no longer be pigeon-holed under separate headings. Units of work which cut across subject matter lines developed; ". . . the raw material of the world and life, the accumulation of ideas and tradition incorporated in the written word"[1] became the material.

With this widening of the scope of education, memorization of all the facts was both undesirable and impossible. Emphasis was now placed on individual reaction and such involved abstractions as attitudes, loyalties, appreciations. The objective tests were entirely inadequate. The very outcomes which the new school was stressing were impossible to test.

From out of the past, the essay tests were resurrected. Educators began to see learning possibilities in assembling material for written expression, in thinking through problems, in planning systematic organization, in explaining causes, in describing events, in comparing and contrasting the present with the past, and in tracing movements. With this type of examination, children could show growth in their selection of material, in critical judgment, in original thinking, and could, to some extent, reveal their attitudes, enthusiasms, and convictions.

Despite these worthy features, the more progressive and courageous educators were ready to eliminate all thought of examinations and testing. They believed that all the desirable features of the written essay could be retained but could be divorced from the unpleasant association with examinations, and could become learning rather than testing exercises.

"What knowledge is of most worth?" is sometimes difficult to decide. If it is collecting and remembering factual material, then testing has its place in the educational program. That certain factual material is necessary in the interest of scholarship is conceded, but there has been too great emphasis upon it in the past. Earl Rugg[2] concludes, from Osburn's study of fifty-six thousand final examination questions in history, that eighty-six per cent were seeking to list only two aims: to discipline the memory and to teach the power to organize facts. In the past and even today, in the minds of the majority, fact-gathering is education. People fail to realize that real assimilation takes place when education is the result of experience, of problem-solving, of creative endeavor, and when depth of understanding

involves emotional reaction. Education is not alone what an individual knows, but what he feels. That Keats confused the names of two Spanish adventurers in his great poem is not too significant. What is important for Keats and all his readers is that he could vision the discovery of the Pacific, that he could recreate the scene and sense the wonder of that awestruck group "silent upon a peak in Darien."

The objectionable features of marks and grades always go hand in hand with tests and examinations. The competitive motive, so prevalent in the society of today, is introduced into the schools with all its undesirable consequences, and competition becomes the most important factor in school work. Interest in learning for its own sake, coöperative enterprises, the sharing of experiences cease to exist when external incentives dominate. Even the teacher exaggerates the importance of examinations and focuses her attention on passing grades. She loses her sense of proportion and stresses points which loom large in official examinations or standardized tests although otherwise of no great consequence. She loses sight of the fact that education is only important when it fosters individual growth, encourages group coöperation, interprets environment, stimulates imagination, provides opportunity for creative impulses, and leads to wider interests.

Another very real objection to tests and examinations is the physical and mental strain attendant upon preparing for them. This feature is too well known for further comment, but an additional and accompanying evil is the undesirable practice of cramming, often regarded all too lightly. Not only does cramming outrage the very idea of true scholarship, but it has a more serious consequence —it develops slovenly, ineffective study habits and no real learning results.

Despite all the evil features, tests and examinations still persist and are an important part of school life. The question arises: "Has testing any place in the educational program of today?" The intelligence tests, when rightly interpreted, are of inestimable value for adjusting pupil load; the diagnostic tests, in the more formal subjects, reveal individual needs and make for greater teaching efficiency; the informal tests, with the material for solving at hand, have excellent learning possibilities when used as study exercises. When testing aids teaching, it has a legitimate place in the educational scheme. . . .

---

[1] Beard, Charles A., *A Charter for the Social Sciences*, p. 16.

[2] Rugg, Earl, *Historical Outlook*, December, 1927, p. 372.

42

H. L. Mencken

EDUCATION

Is good teaching an art or a science? Is it an ability with which one is born, or is it a skill which can be acquired readily through formal instruction? Psychology with its exploration of learning theory seemed to say that good teaching was a skill which could be learned, given certain basic thresholds of individual ability. H. L. Mencken, who seldom agreed with anybody, violently denied this. In so doing he expressed with much accuracy the deep-seated suspicion of method felt by the conservative mass of people.

One must pierce through the sarcastic surface of Mencken's indictment of educational psychology, which he called "a grotesque compound of false premises and illogical conclusions," in order to discover his definition of good teaching. Of course he considered it an art rather than a science. The two bases of good teaching are effective communication, which is the ability to make students understand and enjoy ideas unfamiliar to them, and sincere enthusiasm for one's own subject. Teaching method should be simple, Mencken thought, something which a child could grasp; this led him to defend the use of the birch rod and the factual drill. Fortunately, one is not required to accept Mencken's teaching tools along with his argument that good teaching is in some respects an art.

. . . A couple of days spent examining the literature of the New Thought in pedagogy are enough to make the judicious weep. Its aim seems to be to reduce the whole teaching process to a sort of automatic reaction, to discover some master formula that will not only take the place of competence and resourcefulness in the teacher but that will also create an artificial receptivity in the child. The merciless application of this formula (which changes every four days) now seems to be the chief end and aim of pedagogy. Teaching becomes a thing in itself, separable from and superior to the thing taught. Its mastery is a special business, a transcendental art and mystery, to be acquired in the laboratory. A teacher well grounded in this mystery, and hence privy to every detail of the new technic (which changes, of course, with the formula), can teach anything to any child, just as a sound dentist can pull any tooth out of any jaw.

All this, I need not point out, is in sharp contrast to the old theory of teaching. By that theory mere technic was simplified and subordinated. All that it demanded of the teacher told off to teach, say, geography, was that he master the facts in the geography book and provide himself with a stout rattan. Thus equipped, he was ready for a test of his natural pedagogical genius. First he exposed the facts in the book, then he gilded them with whatever appearance of interest and importance he could conjure up, and then he tested the extent of their transference to the minds of his pupils. Those pupils who had ingested them got apples; those who had failed got fanned with the rattan. Followed the second round, and the same test again, with a second noting of results. And then the third, and fourth, and the fifth, and so on until the last and least pupil had been stuffed to his subnormal and perhaps moronic brim.

I was myself grounded in the underlying delusions of what is called knowledge by this austere process, and despite the eloquence of those who support newer ideas, I lean heavily in favor of it, and regret to hear that it is no more. It was crude, it was rough, and it was often not a little cruel, but it at least had two capital advantages over all the systems that have succeeded it. In the

From *Prejudices, Third Series* by H. L. Mencken, pp. 239-242. Copyright 1922, 1949 by Alfred A. Knopf, Inc., and reprinted by their permission.

first place, its machinery was simple; even the stupidest child could understand it; it hooked up cause and effect with the utmost clarity. And in the second place, it tested the teacher as and how he ought to be tested—that is, for his actual capacity to teach, not for his mere technical virtuosity. There was, in fact, no technic for him to master, and hence none for him to hide behind. He could not conceal a hopeless inability to impart knowledge beneath a correct professional method.

That ability to impart knowledge, it seems to me, has very little to do with technical method. It may operate at full function without any technical method at all, and contrariwise, the most elaborate of technical methods, whether out of Switzerland, Italy or Gary, Ind., cannot make it operate when it is not actually present. And what does it consist of? It consists, first, of a natural talent for dealing with children, for getting into their minds, for putting things in a way that they can comprehend. And it consists, secondly, of a deep belief in the interest and importance of the thing taught, a concern about it amounting to a sort of passion. A man who knows a subject thoroughly, a man so soaked in it that he eats it, sleeps it and dreams it—this man can always teach it with success, no matter how little he knows of technical pedagogy. That is because there is enthusiasm in him, and because enthusiasm is almost as contagious as fear or the barber's itch. An enthusiast is willing to go to any trouble to impart the glad news bubbling within him. He thinks that it is important and valuable for him to know; given the slightest glow of interest in a pupil to start with, he will fan that glow to a flame. No hollow formalism cripples him and slows him down. He drags his best pupils along as fast as they can go, and he is so full of the thing that he never tires of expounding its elements to the dullest. . . .

43

Amos Bronson Alcott

SPIRIT AND METHODS

Bronson Alcott, the father of author Louisa May Alcott, has been described as "the most transcendental of the Transcendentalists." Certainly he was one of America's first gifted teachers. In his schools he introduced organized play, single-student desks, singing, dancing, parent-teacher clubs, and beautified school surroundings; and he abolished corporal punishment. Partly for his educational radicalism and partly for his personal idiosyncrasy (he was, for example, a vegetarian who would eat only "aspiring vegetables," which grew *upward* rather than *downward*), he received the reward of dismissal and failure.

Nevertheless Alcott was an immensely effective teacher, a kind of American Pestalozzi. Here we find him on the side of good teaching as an art, a spirit, and an instinct. One should especially note his belief in individual "style" in teaching, and his significant statement, "We watch results rather than processes." Current studies in automated teaching which stress systematic learning programs and precise assessment of results would support this view of Alcott's. There is, indeed, much content for the twentieth century student to mull over in these nineteenth century words.

I have good encouragement . . . in finding the teachers devoted to their duties and successful.

At my monthly visits I have sought to inspire them rather with confidence in their chosen ways than

From *Essays on Education (1830-1862) by Amos Bronson Alcott*, Walter Harding, ed. (Gainesville, Florida: Scholars' Facsimiles & Reprints, 1960), pp. 153-154.

to interfere by counter suggestions of my own, believing that here in this matter of teaching the following out each of her tendencies and views would best subserve the common interest. Teaching is a personal influence, for the most part, and operating as a spirit unsuspected at the moment. I have wished to divine the secret source of success attained by any, and do justice to this; it seemed most becoming to regard any blemishes as of secondary account in the light of the acknowledged deserts. We require of each what she has to give, no more; not that this measure or method, this study or that, should be the one preferred by us. We watch results rather than processes.

Does the teacher awaken thought, strengthen the mind, kindle the affections, call the conscience, the common sense, into lively and controlling activity, so promoting the love of study, the practice of the virtues; habits that shall accompany the children outwards into life? The memory is thus best cared for, the ends of study answered, the debt of teacher to parents, of parents to children, and so the State's bounty is best bestowed.

Nor shall we hold all amenable equally to the ideal standards. Let us judge each by her own, and hold her fast by its demands. Each is to be judged by temperament, training, opportunities, experiences; the due allowance being made for all under the circumstances. The motive is the main-spring of the rest. A teacher entering her school for any reward other than the love of teaching, shall not claim the praises deservedly due to devotion and genius. Most of our teachers are young women, seeking, some of them perhaps with mixed motives, the earning of a livelihood, yet doing good individually as must every lover of children; and sure of her recompense, since she who loves her work finds the best reward in the doing, and is thus twice paid. What comes from the heart finds the heart, and is approved by it for services readily rendered.

Teaching is an instinct of the heart; and with young children particularly. It needs kindly sensibilities, simple feelings and sincere; love abounding. Young women are better suited to the work, and more excellent than most men. This interest is essential in all, for admirable as one's qualities may be in other respects, and surpassing her gifts, the secret touch of sympathy is the sole spring of success. The heart is the leader and prompter. No amount of learning avails without it. . . .

44

Aldous Huxley

THE DANGERS OF GOOD TEACHING

In this short selection Aldous Huxley utters a word of warning to the successful teacher, the person who is full of pride in his success with student audiences. There is a danger in being too skillful, he suggests. When does a class become sheer entertainment and pleasure, a "regular circus," instead of a learning experience? When does a lecture give so many precut answers that no further words or reading seem necessary, at least to pass the final examination? A good lecture may be the result of one man's wide reading, contemplation, and insight— but if students merely memorize his conclusions, has anyone but the teacher-lecturer really learned much? Such are the dangers of teaching which fails to account for learning in the student rather than in the teacher. More than anyone else, good teachers should be constantly aware of the effect of their teaching.

. . . [Teachers] may be, and frequently are, charming, intelligent, and persuasive. They may put things well; they may speak in a way that will

From *Proper Studies* by Aldous Huxley (London: Chatto and Windus, 1927), pp. 112-113.

command attention and awake emotion and enthusiasm; they may have a power of making difficulties seem easy. The child will listen to such teachers and will greatly appreciate them—particularly if he has an examination to pass in the near future. But the more accomplished a teacher is in the art of lecturing or coaching, the worse he is as an educator. Working on the old-fashioned system, the clever teacher (deplorable paradox!) does almost more harm than the stupid one. For the clever schoolmaster makes things too easy for his pupils; he relieves them of the necessity of finding out things for themselves. By dint of brilliant teaching he succeeds in almost eliminating the learning process. He knows how to fill his pupils with ready-made knowledge, which they inevitably forget (since it is not *their* knowl-

edge and cost them nothing to acquire) as soon as the examination for which it was required is safely passed. The stupid teacher, on the other hand, may be so completely intolerable that the child will perhaps be driven, despairingly and in mere self-defence, to educate himself; in which case the incompetent shepherd will have done, all unwittingly, a great service to his charge, by forcing him into a rebellious intellectual independence.

The methods of education

PROBLEM, PROJECT, AND GROUP DISCUSSION

College intellectuals are prone to look down upon "mere methods" of teaching as too simple and shallow for academic respectability. College students preparing to teach, on the other hand, are likely to feel that methods of instruction are more necessary for their personal success than any amount of pure theory of education or psychology. The Progressive educators were realistic enough to devote a large proportion of their efforts to the improvement of classroom methods, for almost the first time in two thousand years.

Of course, old roots for the new twentieth century methods do exist. Discussion is as old as Socrates; problems in laboratory science go back to the Renaissance; the naturalistic educators had preached the virtues of learning by self-instruction via personal experience. But except for the Pestalozzian object lessons so popular in the late nineteenth century schools, nobody had worked out concrete teaching procedures which could seriously challenge the old-time schoolroom routine. The Progressive educators *did* work out such new methods, those which we are about to examine. And in most school systems of the country today, the new methods have made life in the classroom immensely different from what our grandparents remember.

The three methods—problem, project, and group discussion—resemble one another and are in fact closely related. In Readings 45 to 56 they are discussed roughly in the order of their appearance. The *problem* method can be considered the oldest and the group-discussion method is clearly the youngest. The problem method gained easiest and widest acceptance, and stressed the individual quality of learning experience. The *project* method as advocated by Professor Kilpatrick shifted its attention from the individual to the group. From the 1920's it dominated elementary and much of secondary education practice. *Group-discussion* emphases are comparatively recent, being associated with the rise of social psychology and the ideas of Kurt Lewin during the past two decades.

The first three readings exemplify aspects of the problem method. Note that subject matter is the most important consideration in this case, with student activity having only incidental value. Next come four selections on the project method. On the surface, problems and projects would seem to be pretty much alike, but the readings should give a much clearer understanding of how the project put student activity in first place as an educational objective, with mastery of subject matter as a secondary consideration. The vastly increasing antagonism, as project replaced problem, becomes less mysterious.

Five articles on types of group discussion conclude this section. Here one can see the extent of certain influences toward reducing the emphasis on individual mastery of subject matter. One should remember that the protagonists of group dynamics have not yet conquered their opposition to the extent that the proponents of problem and project methods did earlier.

45

William B. Owen

THE PROBLEM METHOD

Here is probably the first adequate explanation of the problem method ever published. Professor Owen, impressed with the seriousness of his message, has gone to great pains to be simple in language and logical in presentation. He appeals for support to pragmatist philosophers, to psychologists, to natural scientists, and to businessmen. The problem method, it was thought, would make the study of subject matter resemble real-life situations more than ever before.

Supporters of the problem method believed that they were merely advocating the application of the tried and true scientific method to the entire curriculum. What had been confined formerly to the chemistry and physics laboratories would now move into every classroom. Learning would be *real*, because the method was so real. But can a social situation be put into a test tube and analyzed as effectively as a sample of baking powder or iron oxide? We have now had forty years of problem-solving instruction. Are citizens today better able to solve problems in private and public life than were their ancestors?

Educational thought is subject to frequent shifts of emphasis. Now it is the curriculum that is criticized. Again it is the method of teaching that receives chief attention. All at once we are discussing the organization and administration of the schools. These shifts are unsettling. Just as one has his own system worked out, he has to square himself with the new demand. No teacher wishes to be behind the times. Everyone is ambitious to know and use the latest and best in theory and practice. Professional pride and the desire for professional advancement conspire to keep one alert and moving. In spite of popular tradition, the modern teacher neither is nor is permitted to be stationary, conservative; education is in a flux. Change is everywhere dominant. It is hard to keep one's feet on the ground. Even the direction is lost sight of. Some one is always arising to challenge every effort and to dispute every result. It is a wonder that anyone retains his courage and confidence.

All this, however, is but evidence of growth. The past three decades in American education have wrought wonderful changes. The whole conception of what education is has been broadened and defined. All tradition has been subjected to scrutiny and examination. Nothing has been allowed to escape. A new theoretical basis has been laid for our practice. New aims, new standards, new methods, new values have been stated. Progress in all related sciences has compelled progress here. New concepts, new technique, new terminology have been introduced. Education has gained the right to be classed as a profession.

This change and growth has begun to reveal certain definite and discernible tendencies. Fundamental lines of development are giving stability and meaning to the process. Social life, for example, is accepted as the test of value of any curriculum or method. The method of testing processes by their results has been carried over

From *Chicago Schools Journal*, December, 1918. Published at Chicago Teachers College; reprinted by permission.

into this realm. The school is an institution designed to insure social continuity and social progress. There is a vast deal to be done in the way of embodying the new points of view in concrete form. But the method of experiment is relied on to give us this result. We are confident, not that we have achieved finality, but that we have arrived at a method of progress.

In the midst of all this change, we draw back when a new organization, a new method is proposed. We have seen too many devices have their day. We are suspicious of panaceas. We have learned only to unlearn too many educational slogans. The doctrine of interest, the Gary system, the theory of concentration, the doctrine of correlation, where are they? Is it strange that the teacher becomes blasé, suspicious, conservative, and contemptuous? Storm-tossed, with the earth and sky mingled together, our greatest need would seem to be stability and a guiding star.

Just now we are asked to accord hospitality to another newcomer, the Problem Method, or the Problem-Project Method, if you please. We shall have to take account of it, whether we will or no. Just how seriously we should consider it, we have a right to inquire. Perhaps we can assure ourselves of the right answer by an examination of its scientific credentials. Where did it come from, how does it happen to be here, what claims does it make, on what are its claims based? This article will attempt to answer some of these questions. No effort will be made to expound the method either in outline or in detail. It will be sufficient to trace it to its origin in certain scientific and practical tendencies of the day. Perhaps we can then judge how much likelihood there is that it has come to stay, as much as anything really stays.

The Problem Method, or Problem-Project Method, is the formulation for educational use and application of results gained in five fields of thought and activity. These are: (1) Modern Philosophy, (2) Modern Logic, (3) Modern Psychology, (4) Modern Science, (5) Modern Industry. These fields overlap, of course, but it is aside from the purpose of this article to trace their mutual relations and interdependence. Corresponding to these five sources, we find five outstanding moments, factors, elements, as you will, that form the basic structure of the method. These are: (1) the philosophy of experience, (2) the logic of purpose, (3) the psychology of the act, (4) the method of science, (5) the process of industry. Let us consider each briefly. They may seem formidable garbed in their technical terminology, but they are really very simple. If only we can make them seem so!

1. *The philosophy of experience.* The term experience in philosophy and education is fundamental. It cannot be defined. We all know what it is. It is the all-inclusive term for all that we are aware of. It applies to the whole or to any part of the content of our lives. A sensation, a thought, a feeling, a resolve, an ideal, a wish, a hope, a party, a battle, a football game, a map, anything and everything that we know of we classify as experience. The experience philosophy takes the point of view that the most effective control of life is to be had from the control of the inner life, *i. e.*, experience. It thus takes radical issue with the behavioristic school that would ignore, if not deny, the inner life, and would seek the control of life from the study of outward behavior. Perhaps it would be truer to say that the experience philosophy includes both the inner and the outer under the concept of experience. For education, two positions taken by this philosophy are fundamental. The first is that *experience can be controlled.* We have control of anything when we can wield it to accomplish our purposes. We can control our experience so as to bring about desired results in our experience. We can direct our present experience so as to bring a future experience that we foresee. This is all rather abstract, but still clear and simple. By having the experience of planting a seed under certain conditions we can have later the experience of seeing the plant, the flower, the fruit. Education is the enlargement and control of experience.

There are two kinds of experience: (1) direct experience and (2) indirect experience. Direct experience is produced by the object or situation being present to stimulate us. We have direct experience of a battle when we are in it. We have direct experience of an orange tree when we see, touch, handle the tree and fruit. Indirect experience is produced by communication. We read about a battle and try to imagine ourselves there. We study about the orange tree, see pictures of it, buy the fruit, and construct an image of it. But the object or the situation is not present to the senses. Indirect experience approximates direct experience. It is like it in quality but differs in degree and completeness. We read about the Parthenon, see pictures of it, compare it with other monuments, but there is an added sense of reality when we actually behold it. The relation of direct and indirect experience is this: *Indirect experience is possible to us only as direct experience has given us the elements of the communicated experience.* I can understand the geography of Africa, which I have never seen, only to the degree that my direct experience has made me able to understand and image a tropical climate, a sandy waste, wild animals, dark-skinned men, and the like. *Indirect experience is valuable to us only as what is communicated enables us to enlarge and control our direct experience.* We read that phosphate rock will restore soil. We purchase and use it in a worn-out field. We receive a great increase. Indirect or borrowed experience has controlled our action but has resulted in an enlarged and direct experience. The second fundamental position is that *experience is social.* The individual has it. It is peculiar to him. But it is social at the same time. It is gained in coöperation and communication with others. Others are a part of his experience. They make it possible. They join with him to create it. Others have elsewhere and at other times had and handed over to him their experience in word, institution, custom, invention, and the like. Coöperation and communication are the social activities resulting in the enlargement and control of individual experience. Education should consciously carry on these activities so as to maintain the continuity of individual experience. The classroom group provides the opportunity. The socialized recitation is this social process made into a conscious method of instruction.

2. *The logic of purpose.* The second fundamental moment or factor in the problem method is the standpoint of modern logic. The essence of this position is that thought should be studied as a function rather than as a structure. It asks what thought does. It inquires under what conditions it arises, how it goes on, what results it produces. Our older books on method were built on the inherited structural logic that goes back to Aristotle. They laid great stress on induction, deduction, reasoning, questioning, defining and the like. Functional logic emphasizes the fact that thinking takes place in the presence of a problem. It describes how the mind proceeds to solve this problem. The problem forces the forming of a purpose. Thinking seeks the realizing of this purpose by forming a plan and trying it out. If it succeeds, the problem is solved, the purpose is accomplished, the plan is proved true. This functional logic, it may be said, is but the refined exposition of the method of modern science, particularly biological science. Aristotle's logic was based on the scientific procedure and results of the century preceding him. Modern logic is based on the scientific procedure and results of the last century. For education the vital point is that problem, purpose, and thinking are seen to be indissolubly linked. No problem, no purpose, no thinking. Add that problem, purpose, and thinking belong to experience, not to behavior, and that all three involve social coöperation and the

connection of the second fundamental moment with the first becomes at once apparent.

3. *The psychology of the act.* The third fundamental moment in the problem method is the psychology of action. This psychology is based on the anatomy of the nervous system. This nervous system consists of a series of five elements—sense organ, sensory nerve, brain, motor nerve, muscle. A complete act involves all five. Reflex and instinctive acts do not require thinking. Habitual acts may dispense with thinking. New situations, however, cannot be met by reflex, instinctive, or habitual reactions. The new problem requires thought for its solution. The brain suspends the activity of the series of the five elements until the right action is thought out. Once thought out, the series is restored and the act follows. If the right result follows, the problem is solved. But it takes a complete act to get a complete experience. Only the complete experience can test the value of the thought. That is why we "learn by doing." The problem, therefore, calls for a new form of action and thinking is the means of establishing this new form of action. Modern functional logic and modern biological psychology coincide in their emphasis on the relation of problem, purpose, and thought.

4. *The method of science.* The fourth moment in the problem method is the method of modern science. As indicated above, this procedure has furnished the basis of modern logic. But the scientist is not studying logic. He is solving problems. These problems are objective. They are practical, arising in the field of industry; or theoretical, arising in the prosecution of research. The method of procedure has been learned by experiment. Experiment always starts with a problem. It may be a problem to the student, as in high-school physics, or a problem to the world of science, as the isolation of an ion. The success of the scientific procedure or method has dictated the method of instruction in the sciences. Therefore we have the laboratory. The problem method is established in science instruction. Only recently have the teachers of science recognized that in the earlier years the pupil's problem was the starting point for the teaching of elementary science. This is the step forward taken by the movement in general science. The example of the sciences, therefore, has contributed practically to the theory and practice of the problem method. It might not be too much to say that science has been the chief source of the movement.

5. *The processes of industry.* The fifth moment in the problem method has been contributed by industrial processes. Industry, that is, manufacturing, the trades, the domestic arts, agriculture

and the like, have definite practical problems to solve and definite purposes to accomplish. The problems and purposes are clear and tangible. The schools have learned how to imitate industry. The manual training shops, the cooking laboratories, state their curricula in the form of problems. The pupils make a chair, a table, a gas engine; they print a pamphlet; they make bread, bake potatoes, can peaches; they design and make a dress. The problem and the purpose of the activity are definite and clear. The procedure is learned as a means to an end. The solution has the practical, objective test of the result obtained.

The problem method is, then, no mere device. It is not a new formula of success. It is an effort to make available for school procedure the results of modern philosophy, modern logic, modern psychology, modern science, and modern industry where they coincide in making the problem the starting point for purposeful activity, for thinking. It attempts to make school procedure tally with the theoretical and practical procedure of the world. It aims thus to connect the school with life.

46

Max R. Goodson

PROBLEM-SOLVING IN THE ELEMENTARY SCHOOL

Professor Goodson's article gives a clue to the popularity of the problem-solving method in discussing how it can be used with the youngest child as easily as with the college senior.

Earlier in his article the author gives a detailed example of a problem on the fourth-grade level, involving a trip to a newspaper plant. The emphasis is not upon the nature of newspapers, but upon the human relationships of those in the group and upon the problem-solving process itself. Teamwork is important: "For children to solve problems, a team relationship among them that embraces the necessary competencies for making the changes by problem-solving needs to be developed." And again: "Without group development, children frequently never become emotionally emancipated from their blind acceptance of the authority-role of the teacher."

In the thirty years which had elapsed since the problem method was initially suggested, thirty years studded by problems courses in nearly every conceivable subject area, gradually the focus had shifted from "facts" to process. It had shifted also from vocational, citizenship, or other purposes to intellectual development. In fact, we may well ask whether the problems method of Owen and the problems method of Goodson were really the same method at all.

. . . Traditionally, the elementary school had the limited function of teaching such skills as reading and arithmetic, and of transmitting elementary information. This function was founded on the assumptions that the elementary school should prepare for either life or the high school and that the best preparation was made through the narrow areas suggested above. Problem-solving was considered a higher mental process. Therefore, it appeared to require a maturity above that reached by children in the elementary school grades. This kind of conceiving of the function of education in the elementary school is sharply criticized today in both theory and practice. . . .

There are two reasons why problem-solving is important to children. The first has to do with the character of our society. The second is related to the process by which children can grow into the kind of maturity required by our times.

Ours is clearly an adaptive society. Changes in the industrial-technological side come very readily and have accumulated at an astonishing

From *Progressive Education*, March 1950, 27:147.

rate. Science has been the chief impetus. Science, applied to such problems as the production of food, machines, power, and the use of the scientific method in solving biological problems of plant and animal breeding and of medicine, has altered conditions of life very materially. These alterations have had deep repercussions upon economic, political, and social institutions. Adaptations in these institutions involve human-relation changes that, up to and including the present, have been destined in our society to come more slowly.

Clearly, our type of society requires a creative and problem-solving approach by people. Patterns of thinking and acting that have gone before are not sufficient to the requirements of an adaptive society. Children are marginal people in the sense that they have not internalized the old patterns. They do not have an investment in tradition. Nevertheless, they very quickly make their ad-

justment to social conditions by adopting the ways of their parents and other adults *unless* the elementary school uses a problem-solving approach. This is true because the rudiments of maturity are founded in the young years of the elementary school. If the disposition for using a problem-solving approach—the approach of science—is to be acquired, its cultivation must start early and continue through the entire period of formal education. If delayed, the habit-system of the child becomes overlaid with the old and obsolete patterns of culture. Then adjustment becomes more difficult and intelligent choice-making—thinking through problems and acting upon the best intelligence as a way of meeting human situations—faces great odds. Therefore, it is of the greatest importance that problem-solving become one of the basic functions of the elementary school.

47

PROBLEM-SOLVING REMEDIATION

This editorial from *School Review*, written at approximately the same time as Reading 46, goes a long way toward explaining why so many teachers grew disillusioned with problem-solving. There had always been failures, of course, but usually by comparatively small margins, and there never were many of them. With problem-solving, the gap which separated "pass" from "fail" was tremendous, and as much as half a class might find a solution beyond its powers. Little wonder that so many teachers faltered and then turned in other directions.

The four steps in formalized problem-solving were: (a) state the problem clearly; (b) gather data and propose several solutions; (c) critically evaluate these solutions; and (d) after comparison select the best solution and verify it. If many students could not master even the first of these steps, then the future of problem-solving in the total curriculum was far from bright.

In our teaching and testing, we give greatest emphasis to the products of thought—the answers and solutions that students give to the problems presented to them. Little attention is given to the processes of thought—the ways in which students think about problems, the considerations used to make one choice rather than another, and the feelings and emotions which accompany an attack

on a problem. Although, in practice, the emphasis is on the products of thought, there is little doubt that most teachers regard the development of sound habits of thinking as an important objective of education. We place so much stress on the products of thought because they are easier to observe, because we believe that they are good indices of the kinds of thinking being done, and because we have so little time in which to study the processes of thinking of our students.

Although we may be unable to justify use of the time and energy required to study the processes of thinking of all students, it would be

From *School Review*, October 1948, 56:436-438. Copyright 1948 by The University of Chicago. Reprinted by permission of The University of Chicago Press.

desirable to make such investigations for atypical students. There is some evidence that attempts to change the habits of thinking of failing students can be quite successful and that such changes are reflected in improved products, as measured by examination scores.

In an unpublished Master's thesis ("Experimental Studies in Problem-solving of College Students," Department of Psychology, University of Chicago, 1946), Lois Jean Broder describes an experimental technique for improving the processes of thinking, and consequently the products, of failing students. This study, which involved more than sixty students, showed the technique to be very effective in bringing a high proportion of the students up to an acceptable level of academic performance.

Since Miss Broder was attempting to study mental processes rather than products, it was necessary to secure some criteria of what constituted good or desirable kinds of thinking. For this purpose she interviewed a number of students who consistently received marks of A or B on the comprehensive or other examinations taken during their career in the College of the University of Chicago. She presented these students with selected problems from the various tests and had them "think aloud" as they attacked these problems. A careful and complete record was made of the kinds of thinking revealed in this situation. These she considered to be the "model" methods of attacking the examination problems.

The failing students were then interviewed under similar conditions. The records of the problem-solving of the failing students and the successful students were compared for the major differences in the methods of attack. These differences were classified under four major headings: understanding the nature of the problem, understanding the ideas contained in the problem, general approach to the solution of problems, and attitudes involved in the problem-solving.

Understanding the nature of the problem. The "model" students appeared to have a much better definition of the problems that they were to attack than had the failing students. The former were able to find a point at which to start attacking the problem and had little difficulty in determining just what the problem was all about. In contrast, the unsuccessful students frequently misunderstood the directions for the problem or quickly forgot what they were expected to do. Frequently the unsuccessful students so altered the problem as to make it completely different

from the problem originally posed. In many instances the unsuccessful students' difficulties arose from careless reading.

Understanding the ideas contained in the problem. A major difference between the two groups was found in the ability to bring relevant knowledge to bear on the problem. Although it was quite clear in many cases that the unsuccessful students had all the information necessary for solving the problem, they appeared to be unable to use the information effectively. Many of the unsuccessful students were apparently unable to understand and attack a problem unless it was presented in a form similar to that in which they had originally encountered the material in textbooks, lectures, and discussions.

General approach to the solution of problems. The major difference in this area was a very active and systematic attack on the problem by the model students as contrasted with what seemed to be an almost aimless drifting through the problem by the failing students. The latter group had little control over the problem, and they were often unable to attack it directly or to break large problems into subproblems which could be attacked separately. Frequently the failing students mechanically re-read the problem many times until something struck a familiar note.

The failing students appeared to solve problems on the basis of impressions and feelings about which solutions were correct. They selected answers and then tried to justify them. All too frequently the justification had little or no relevance to the solution that they had chosen. The groups also differed in attention to important details, the failing students being relatively careless.

Attitudes involved in the problem-solving. Many of the unsuccessful students took the attitude that either one "knows" the answer to a problem at once or that nothing can be done about it. That is, they did not believe that reasoning or extensive working with a problem was of any value. If a problem looked to be at all complex or difficult, they gave up quickly. Again, there was a difference between the two groups in the frequency with which they introduced personal considerations into their problem-solving. The unsuccessful students had difficulty in attacking problems with any degree of objectivity and persisted in selecting solutions which agreed with their own values and desires rather than those which satisfied the conditions set by the problem. . . .

48

William H. Kilpatrick

THE PROJECT METHOD

Next to John Dewey, the name of William Heard Kilpatrick of Teachers College, Columbia University, is probably the most famous in the annals of Progressive education. This article introducing the project method helped put him on the road to national and international eminence. Kilpatrick never claimed to have invented the term or the method. Both were first employed around 1900 in manual-training courses from which they quickly spread to agriculture and home economics courses. Kilpatrick's contribution lay in suggesting that the project method could be usefully employed for instruction in every subject area of the entire curriculum.

Teachers eagerly took up the new idea, often in conjunction with the less radical problem method. By 1940 there were many varieties of projects, among them (a) material projects, in which the students made something tangible like a bookrack; (b) learning projects, where a skill was acquired; (c) intellectual or problem projects, in which the purpose was gaining factual information; (d) aesthetic projects, in which the student learned to enjoy and appreciate the fine arts; and (e) study projects, which were simply term papers. In all such projects there was an increasing tendency toward pupil planning and "activity," especially outside-the-classroom activity.

The project method aroused heated and bitter disputes. In part this was due to Kilpatrick's spiritual, moralistic, emotional language and his tendency to be dogmatic in his value judgments, so different from the cautious and practical tone of Reading 45. Some of Kilpatrick's newly invented words confused people. Nevertheless the method spread rapidly in the elementary and secondary schools. We live today in the final phase of a half century of controversy over the project.

The word 'project' is perhaps the latest arrival to knock for admittance at the door of educational terminology. Shall we admit the stranger? Not wisely until two preliminary questions have first been answered in the affirmative: First, is there behind the proposed term and waiting even now to be christened a valid notion or concept which promises to render appreciable service in educational thinking? Second, if we grant the foregoing, does the term 'project' fitly designate the waiting concept? Because the question as to the concept and its worth is so much more significant than any matter of mere names, this discussion will deal almost exclusively with the first of the two inquiries. It is indeed entirely possible that some

From *Teachers College Record,* September 1918, 19:319-321, 323, 334-335.

other term, as 'purposeful act', for example, would call attention to a more important element in the concept, and, if so, might prove superior as a term to the word 'project'. At the outset it is probably wise to caution the reader against expecting any great amount of novelty in the idea here presented. The metaphor of christening is not to be taken too seriously; the concept to be considered is not in fact newly born. Not a few readers will be disappointed that after all so little new is presented.

. . . In attacking with successive classes in educational theory the problem of method, I had felt increasingly the need of unifying more completely a number of important related aspects of the educative process. I began to hope for some one concept which might serve this end. Such a concept, if found, must, so I thought, emphasize the factor of action, preferably wholehearted vigorous activity. It must at the same time provide a place for the adequate utilization of the laws of learning, and no less for the essential elements of the ethical quality of conduct. The last named looks of course to the social situation as well as to the individual attitude. Along with these should go, as it seemed, the important generalization that education is life—so easy to say and so hard to delimit. Could now all of these be contemplated under one workable notion? If yes, a great gain. In proportion as such a unifying concept could be found in like proportion would the work of presenting educational theory be facilitated; in like proportion should be the rapid spread of a better practice.

But could this unifying idea be found? Here was in fact the age-old problem of effective logical organization. My whole philosophic outlook had made me suspicious of so-called 'fundamental principles'. Was there yet another way of attaining unity? I do not mean to say that I asked these questions, either in these words or in this order. Rather is this a retrospective ordering of the more important outcomes. As the desired unification lay specifically in the field of method, might not some typical unit of concrete procedure supply the need—some unit of conduct that should be, as it were, a sample of life, a fair sample of the worthy life and consequently of education? As these questionings rose more definitely to mind, there came increasingly a belief—corroborated on many sides—that the unifying idea I sought was to be found in the conception of wholehearted purposeful activity proceeding in a social environment, or more briefly, in the unit element of such activity, the hearty purposeful act.

It is to this purposeful act with the emphasis on the word purpose that I myself apply the term 'project'. I did not invent the term nor did I start it on its educational career. Indeed, I do not know how long it has already been in use. I did, however, consciously appropriate the word to designate the typical unit of the worthy life described above. Others who were using the term seemed to me either to use it in a mechanical and partial sense or to be intending in a general way what I tried to define more exactly. The purpose of this article is to attempt to clarify the concept underlying the term as much as it is to defend the claim of the concept to a place in our educational thinking. The actual terminology with which to designate the concept is, as was said before, to my mind a matter of relatively small moment. If, however, we think of a project as a pro-ject, something pro-jected, the reason for its adoption may better appear. . . .

As the purposeful act is . . . the typical unit of the worthy life in a democratic society, so also should it be made the typical unit of school procedure. We of America have for years increasingly desired that education be considered as life itself and not as a mere preparation for later living. The conception before us promises a definite step toward the attainment of this end. If the purposeful act be in reality the typical unit of the worthy life, then it follows that to base education on purposeful acts is exactly to identify the process of education with worthy living itself. The two become then the same. All the arguments for placing education on a life basis seem, to me at any rate, to concur in support of this thesis. On this basis education has become life. And if the purposeful act thus makes of education life itself, could we reasoning in advance expect to find a better preparation for later life than practice in living now? We have heard of old that "we learn to do by doing," and much wisdom resides in the saying. If the worthy life of the coming day is to consist of well-chosen purposeful acts, what preparation for that time could promise more than practice now, under discriminating guidance, in forming and executing worthy purposes? To this end must the child have within rather large limits the opportunity to purpose. For the issues of his act he must—in like limits—be held accountable. That the child may properly progress, the total situation—all the factors of life, including comrades—speaking, if need be through the teacher, must make clear its selective judgment upon what he does, approving the better, rejecting the worse. . . . [Education] based on the purposeful act prepares best for life while at the same time it constitutes the present worthy life itself. . . .

In conclusion, then, we may say that the child is naturally active, especially along social lines. Heretofore a régime of coercion has only too often reduced our schools to aimless dawdling and our pupils to selfish individualists. Some in reaction have resorted to foolish humoring of childish whims. The contention of this paper is that wholehearted purposeful activity in a social situation as the typical unit of school procedure is the best guarantee of the utilization of the child's native capacities now too frequently wasted. Under proper guidance purpose means efficiency, not only in reaching the projected end of the activity immediately at hand, but even more in securing from the activity the learning which it potentially contains. Learning of all kinds and in its all desirable ramifications best proceeds in proportion as wholeheartedness of purpose is present. With the child naturally social and with the skillful teacher to stimulate and guide his purposing, we can especially expect that kind of learning we call character building.

The necessary reconstruction consequent upon these considerations offers a most alluring 'project' to the teacher who but dares to purpose.

49

Walter F. Fogg

PROJECT VS. SUBJECT: A CRITICAL REVIEW

The battle over the project method saw teachers divide at first into two opposing factions. The Progressives favored projects and an activity program; the conservatives took a stand for older modes of instruction and a subject-matter or "content" program. Gradually there arose a third and intermediate group, calling themselves liberals. These liberals were convinced, to use Walter Fogg's words, "that neither the project nor the subject method of education is exclusive of the other. All projects of necessity involve content, and all mastery of content involves some kind of activity."

Walter Fogg was a secondary-school teacher from Scarsdale, New York, who recognized that even for a middle-ground liberal who could see virtues in each alternative, it was necessary to lean at least slightly in one direction or the other. Consequently, Fogg's personal preference is stated in the last sentence of this selection.

. . . [There seem to be] at least the following serious objections in the activity program: It involves, to begin with, a philosophical dilemma hard to escape, for the less control that is exercised by the teacher the more does learning become random and haphazard. Recognizing this, the progressives now recommend more control. But with more control comes less freedom of expression. Now this is true also of a content course, but with this difference—the advocate of the content curriculum recognizes this fact and willingly sacrifices freedom as a relatively unimportant consideration. Not so the progressive. Freedom of action is the very cornerstone of his philosophy. Thus, to be at all practical, the progressive teacher must "stack the cards"; and exactly to the degree that he does this he becomes, at the same time, less progressive.

Secondly, the activity program is too complicated to administer surely. It requires a genius in every classroom. There simply are not enough of these to go around. Furthermore, even if we admit its value for primary stages of education, it certainly is not economical for the higher levels, where the mastery of word symbols and other

tools of learning makes activity less necessary and a greater use of verbalism more direct.

The third objection is that the activity program emphasizes the development of the individual at the expense of the social being. Now we need individualism, but look around you in any group of adults the products of the content school and see if there is any lack of it. There never will be any lack of it. Differences in environments and inheritances will always assure that. What we need sorely is education for social living—adjustment not primarily to ourselves but to the people and things around us.

The fourth objection to the project or activity program is the danger that the project which was intended as a means to an end may become the end itself. Granted that, if the project is expertly conceived and expertly executed, this danger will not materialize, too often the delicate adjustment needed to assure success is lacking, and when a project fails the waste involved is enormous.

As opposed to these disadvantages of the activity program, what advantages does the content method afford?

First, it is, by its very nature, more simple and more concrete. Its age, far from being a weakness,

From *School and Society*, March 2, 1940, 51:277-278.

is one of its strongest assets, for it has in it the benefits of years of tradition and experiment. Its goals are more immediate and tangible, and therefore more measurable. Its road to learning may not offer many scenic wonders, but it is unmistakably marked and it is straight.

Second, it is relatively simple to administer and much better suited to the democratic concept of education, which invariably implies education for large numbers. All the successes we know of that have been claimed for the activity program have been in relatively wealthy communities and with selected groups.

Third, it is a better preparation for adult life, since it is avowedly organized on this basis rather than on the basis of the unfolding of the individual in response to felt needs in childhood. By the same token, it serves society better, since it aims at the development of the social being, rather than the individualist. Now, this does not imply totalitarianism at all, for to avoid this we have only to see to it that the content taught includes conflicting points of view. Indeed the content program has one recommendation usually claimed by its opponents: namely, it is a closer approximation of life itself. It does not dodge the

necessity, occasionally faced by every one, for doing an unpleasant task against his inclinations. The standards of the activity program are set by the individual for himself. This is a luxury that few of us can afford in a world where so many standards are set for us.

Finally, the objection that a content or discovery program can not be creative does not seem to us at all valid. The mere acquisition of facts certainly is not creative, but what creation could there be without facts? Do we really create anything in the complete sense of the word? Do we not rather create by discovering new patterns into which to put old things? And in another sense, does not the acquisition of a learned response "create" a different and therefore new personality? Certainly, if we do not quibble over terms, the discovery of something that we did not know before—even though it may have had antecedent existence—is to all practical purposes equivalent to creation.

In closing we should [affirm] that none of the above objections is all black nor all white. The prevailing tone is grey. But when there must be an emphasis on either the activity or the content we feel that it should be toward the latter.

50

J. L. Meriam

"ACTIVITIES" IN THE SCHOOL CURRICULUM

While Fogg (Reading 49) was a middle-of-the-road liberal, Professor Junius L. Meriam of U.C.L.A. was a bona-fide Progressive educator. Many of the Progressives themselves had begun to take alarm, as projects grew more bizarre and the claims for them more sweeping. Those critics inside the Progressive camp had a fine spokesman in Meriam.

There are two of Meriam's points which need underlining. One was his fear that project method and "activities" were turning into the same thing, although Meriam did not believe they needed to do so. The other was his feeling that pseudoproblems were crowding out genuine problems in the average project. This in turn pointed up how difficult it was to decide just which projects or activities were really practical examples of adult life experience.

Meriam was particularly alarmed because of his conviction that such tendencies, if not reversed, would kill the whole Progressive education movement. Indeed, Samuel Tenenbaum claimed that Kilpatrick, who saw this trend developing just before World War II, quietly dissociated himself from the movement (11).

. . . 1. The project method grossly abuses the beautiful purposing in children. It is wrong to deceive children into accomplishing the teacher's purpose, e.g., learn to read the hornbook by allowing them to follow their own purpose, e.g., eating the gingerbread.

2. The project method is responsible for "soft pedagogy." It is an injustice to children to sugarcoat their school experiences. Life should be rich and enjoyable, but the discipline of effort is an essential part.

3. The project method reverses relative values. Appreciating the service which the grocery store renders to the household is worth more than knowing the product of eight times nine. Frankness concludes that doing is more valuable than knowing. But this project method subordinates the activities of life to mere means of learning about life.

4. The project method perpetuates an obsolete curriculum. So long as this method is effective in the teaching-learning process, just so long are school officials content with the learnings of the past rather than concerned with the activities of current life.

In earlier years, prior to about 1930, the terms project and project method were greatly confused. Even Kilpatrick's excellent concept of project as a purposeful act has been generally used as synonymous with that of the method of motivation by projects. Similarly in recent years, since about 1930, the terms activities, units of work, social studies, etc., have been used quite indiscriminately to refer to acts in normal life and to school methods in the teaching-learning process. Obviously great divergence is to be found as to what constitutes an activity, as used in courses of study formulated independently by schools over a wide geographical area. My examination of . . . 8,833 unit topics collected since 1932, supplementing [an] earlier study, reveals a very evident confusion and also suggests a basis for clarification. Both confusion and clarification follow experiences with the project and project method. . . . [School] practices have continued on much the same policy for the past quarter of a century though the terms used have changed from projects to activities. . . .

By way of summary as to the current—almost universal—use of the activity program, . . . analysis of activity units reveals that its dominant function is the motivation of studies not of pri-

mary concern to children; that the nature of these activities is centered upon the physical and social movements of the children themselves. This conclusion is supported by the grade placement of these activities. The following items will illustrate:

In the traditional school Africa is seldom, if ever, studied below the fifth grade. That country is too foreign for children less than ten years old. But this study reveals pupils in the third grade— only eight years old—studying (?) Africa; at least they make grass houses, said to be in imitation of those of African tribes.

Similarly, the airplane is studied (?) by pupils in kindergarten, first, second, and third grades as frequently as by pupils in the upper grades. It may be readily recognized that this modern instrument brings a thrill to such little children, but surely this instrument for travel and for deadly war combat is far too complicated as a school subject for children five to nine years old.

This study reveals that the post office as a school topic is found in the first and second grades six times as frequently as in all the other grades. Six- and seven-year-old children do thrill over licking postage stamps and opening envelopes— especially at Christmas and Valentine seasons. But sane judgment denies that such activity constitutes a study of our postal service.

Primitive life (this is ancient history or anthropology) appears twice as frequently in the first three grades as in the four upper grades. Teachers "kid themselves" in their fake study of cavemen by having their six- to eight-year-old pupils dig little holes in the wet sand, or of the mound builders by making crude sod houses in the school yard. This is a travesty on life and harks close to tragedy in school.

I strongly advocate *an* activity program for our schools, both elementary and secondary. But I wish to register my opposition to the activity procedures evidenced in these eight thousand and more activity units. Professor Bagley's criticism in 1931 is even more appropriate today: our schools are "playing at the work of education." This playing with our education will continue so long as our schools are committed to the fondling and petting of our pupils rather than to disciplining them in real effort. This trifling with our school work will continue so long as teachers and curriculum makers insist upon a curriculum of the three R's—abstractions from real life, and then resort to activity units in real life as a means of motivating the teaching-learning process. Our so-called "progressive education" is in serious danger of tremendous reverses, essentially because our school officials and educational theorists lack

From *Teachers College Record,* April 1943, 44:513-514, 517-518.

the logic and the courage to be really progressive by way of positively helping our pupils cope more adequately with the demands of current life in place of acquiring the conventional learnings of the traditional school.

The 8,833 activity units emphasize, almost unanimously, a curriculum of the three R's motivated by the physical and social activities of children. This popular policy of learning by doing is most dangerous and pernicious—a concept of activity too narrow and superficial to last long. Doing through learning is far more vital. This suggests a plausible activity program for our schools—a curriculum taken directly from the life and surroundings of children and expressed in terms of their activities and those environments conducive to activity. The three-R skills are valuable tools, efficiently acquired incidentally. Far more fundamental than the so-called fundamentals in school are the activities in normal life.

51

Fred T. Weisbruch

GLORIFYING THE HIGH SCHOOL PROJECT

The two preceding critiques (Readings 49 and 50) were written by friends of the project method. To appreciate this fully, one must read an attack by an avowed enemy from the conservative camp. Such a person was Fred Weisbruch, a high-school science teacher from St. Louis, Missouri. As a scientist, Weisbruch approved of the problem method, but projects were anathema to him. As he saw it, the project idea was merely a device to make problem-solving easy by removing any real problem from the intellectual operation, giving it a new name, and going through some empty, problem-solving motions.

Does the activity device really work in arousing student interest or in teaching more effectively? Does it really prepare students for life? These were hard, basic questions, and most project advocates considered them unfair. It hardly seems safe, however, to leave them unanswered.

. . . It is possible today for a high school student to spend four years in a system, which by an ingenious arrangement of courses, permits him to exercise the very minimum of his talents and guarantees him no return on the investment. Regardless of what course he follows, he will certainly engage in a multitude of activities, some of them not even distantly related to education. Most of these activities have been thought up by his teachers over a period of many years, until they have become almost an integral part of the educational system. Today, these same teachers will tell you that these activities are necessary because the students cannot do without them. In most cases the student has been convinced that he not only needs them but loves them.

Among these activities one which is outstanding because of its utter futility as a means of

From *School Science and Mathematics,* June 1949, 49:438-439, 442-444.

instruction, is the so-called "project activity." By exercising it to its fullest extent a none too promising high school student can, by diligent application of a pair of willing hands and sharp tools, emerge at the end of four years, a none too promising graduate, to become a less than promising college freshman. To him, this limerick could be aptly dedicated.

> There was a young student named O'Hare
> Whose IQ was just passing fair.
> He cut and he pasted,
> 'Til four years were wasted,
> And departed none the worse for the wear.

I refer to the "project" or "scrap-book" student who has been conditioned to do things rather than learn things—who is trained to visualize through pictures what he cannot grasp through mental effort. In using the word "project," I do not wish to condemn all such types of activity which may, in their proper place, prove of some value to the student. Nor do I wish to confine the criticism to such projects alone but to all such forms of activity which are rapidly becoming a substitute for any form of serious mental effort. It is the present day trend to confuse external activity with the learning process which is at fault. It is this trend which is to be deplored and the influence which such thinking has had on both the high school curriculum and the pattern followed by some of our science textbooks.

From the first let me define the meaning of this particular form of activity and point out some of the classifications. A project can be lightly defined as a carefully outlined, over-emphasized activity which, if the student never heard about it, would be just as well. It consists, in its primitive form, of buying an expensive scrap book and then filling it with unrelated and often ill-suited cut-outs from pictorial magazines. This is the lowest form or, "Oh Mother, see what I have done" type of project. Fortunately, either the lack of initiative on the part of the teacher or the limited imagination of the student has confined this phase of the project activity to the lower grades and the freshman year of high school. Then there is the in-between or "Well, boys and girls, what shall we do today" type of project, which goes on to the more complicated and presumably more skillful task of building things. This is a third dimensional field and requires both manual dexterity and a set of steady nerves. Projects of this kind are exhibited in school room cabinets on open-house night and take the form of block houses (see *Robinson Crusoe*), ship models (see *Treasure Island*) and plaster of Paris models of various undefined and unrecognizable objects. The usual remark heard at these exhibits, interspersed between the ahs and ohs of fond parents is, "What's it supposed to be?"

Finally we have the upper level of activity which is dignified with the name of "science project." These projects result from the fertile imagination of the science teacher; for science is a fruitful field for projects of every description. As a rule they are not received with too much enthusiasm because by this time Junior begins to suspect why he is in school and is frankly bored by the whole business. Projects of this type combine most of the talents required for the first and second variety. The completed project eventually finds its way into Junior Achievement groups, Science Fairs and Science Club exhibits, where suitable awards are given. . . .

We can create giants but we insist upon turning out mental pigmies under the preconceived idea that students are not able to grasp even the most

fundamental concept of a scientific truth. Is it logical therefore, to substitute something which is not true for the truth which we believe they cannot digest? Today we face the apparent paradox of a civilization which is showing an increasing interest in all the fields of science and a student population which is progressively dropping off in science enrollment. If the fault does not lie with science teachers and those who administer the policies of the high school, then wherein does the fault lie? Possibly we have watered down the science course until the student no longer has any desire for something which to him has lost its usefulness. In seeking scientific truth and in our attempts to impart it to the student, however discouraging this may become, it is the duty of the science teacher to seek it doggedly and perseveringly, without taking time out from the essential objectives in order to stray into the remote byways of projects and pageants.

It is time that science teachers come back to the fold and re-examine their objectives, re-specify their aims and re-define the meaning of education in science. I often wonder if some teachers are feeding their students on project activities because these externals are demanded by the student or because the teachers want them or need them since they give a false sense of progress —a visual accomplishment which they can hold up for all to see. We should among other things, re-examine our sense of values. Does the science course help to prepare for leadership—a leadership with a deep spiritual realization that science is to serve humanity and the individual through unselfishness, sacrifice and devotion? Certainly the opportunities are many of bringing a student to a sense of these spiritual values through science education. The youth of today are crying for leadership and we who can give it to them through the medium of a science course are reaching them plaster of Paris models instead of bread.

I believe that our high school science courses can be re-established in their rightful place in the curriculum if corrective measures are taken to improve both the quality of teaching and the subject matter of the courses. This can be done by re-examining and re-evaluating the objectives of the science course. The first objective should be to impart an understanding and appreciation of the simple laws and principles of science and should be arrived at through diligent pursuit of the meaning and function of these laws in our modern civilization. But first it will be necessary for the science teacher to convince himself that a student is capable of attaining this end. Evidently we must remove the false idea that a subject must be made easy in order to be attractive to the students. Certainly a great deal of basic training is necessary, both in study habits and in mental discipline, in order to raise the level of student attainment so that he can master these fundamental subjects. The opposite trend, that of lowering the standards of the course, or sugar-coating it with non-essentials is quite evident today. The result is that we are shaping our science courses to fit the lowest degree of attainment rather than insisting that the student be raised to the level of requirement of the science course. The latter is the line of least resistance but unfortunately the trend is progressive and it is hard to understand where the downward course will stop.

Lastly, the science laboratory, if it is going to be effective at all must be the focal point for resolving some of the difficulties encountered in the lecture room. Again the objectives of the course must be clearly stated and rigidly adhered to. For otherwise the laboratory becomes just another place to continue a series of disorganized thought processes begun with the textbook and the lecture period.

It is unfortunate that the tendency to emasculate the subject matter for the easy assimulation of the mediocre student has become so prominent in the laboratory practice. What an excellent opportunity the laboratory offers for clear thinking and scientific reasoning; for instilling the fundamentals of the scientific method and for forming sound habits of observation and deduction. What a waste of effort and of opportunity if it were to degenerate into a workshop for projects and pageants.

52

Charles S. Pendleton

THE SOCIALIZED RECITATION

The contemporary group-discussion concept or method has had at least two important precursors. One was modern athleticism, with such immensely popular team sports as football. In 1922 an English authority was claiming that "the group game is of vital importance in education." A second was the socialized recitation, which suddenly appeared on the teaching scene just after World War I. Together with activity-centered problems and projects, it was a favorite of the early Progressive educators.

The socialized recitation tried to transform dreary classroom exhibitions of memory into a lively exchange of information, and thus to utilize discussion as a learning procedure. From the beginning it emphasized attitude formation and character building ahead of content mastery and was especially recommended for courses in citizenship. Its opponents called it dangerously radical. Today we can see that the socialized recitation was not only harmless politically, but that it was an early forerunner of the shift to group methods.

. . . The socialized recitation is not a modified recitation, or any recitation at all, in the conventional sense, but a substitute for the recitation as a classroom procedure. Further, it goes beyond the classroom and becomes an attitude of the school. It is essentially not a concrete, specific method, but rather a point of view. It does not necessarily mean this or that particular procedure. But it nearly always does mean the prevalence in the typical classroom of seven conditions. Let us consider these in detail.

In a socialized school every pupil develops and exercises initiative. He must have a self-starter. He must have self-dependence. He must be an individual as well as a member of a cooperating group. He must be able to use his peculiar powers to help the group, and he must on occasion be able to subordinate himself to the common effort and the common good. There is a tremendous education here in personal effectiveness—in executive power, if you please—the sort of thing that commands the greatest prizes in the real world beyond. A large part of this kind of development, so invaluable in a true education, comes only indirectly from the teacher, tho he is always conscious of it and always back of it. He sets the

From *NEA Addresses and Proceedings,* 1920:417-418.

conditions; and the boys and girls, living a normal life tho at high tension, react upon and educate each other.

There is a far-reaching endeavor to make the school as much as possible like the real world. The typical old kind of school resembles nothing there closely, except the penitentiary. Its pupils go forth, so far as the school predetermines it, into a strange environment. The socialized school, however, in ideals, in conduct, and in subject-matter, endeavors to be an understudy for American citizenship and the fullest realization of the opportunities of life. It teaches facts; but Americanism, it holds, is less a matter of informational knowledge than of habits of conduct. The attitudes and predilections to action which will serve best adults in the business and play of our adult life are specifically ingrained into the fabric of the school. Education aims to serve society directly.

It must be granted, no doubt, that the socialized recitation has shortcomings and limitation. Some of these may be overcome as we experiment; others may not be. It seems, for instance, to be much better suited to good teachers than to poor teachers—to enable the former to teach better but the latter to shirk work and to relax or lose utterly what little grip on their classes they otherwise have. It seems to get better results from excellent and good pupils than from the inherently dull. It is apparently less well adapted to the opening lessons on a subject of a phase than to carrying forward and amplifying work already begun. It consumes, in general, more time per unit of subject-matter than the recitation system; the question is whether the results are commensurate. It is full of pitfalls for teachers weak in "discipline." It brings many unhappy moments to teachers poor in scholarship or deficient in general information; such may steer adroitly past the Scylla and Charybdis perils of a ten-page lesson, carefully crammed and personally conducted thru a recitation period; but will go surely upon the rocks or into the depths during a socialized hour. These are only a few of the difficulties the idea presents.

53

S. R. Slavson

GROUP EDUCATION FOR A DEMOCRACY

As problem, project, and socialized recitation methods began to fade, their former supporters turned to group-discussion techniques based upon group-learning theory. Professor Slavson tells us in this article, for instance, that after having taught activity programs for "many years" he finally recognized that it was the group situation which had done his students more good than the activity itself. "The function [or proper aim] of the school in a democracy, therefore, is to supply opportunities for activity in a group setting."

Theoretical sociologists like Slavson relied heavily upon Freudian doctrines of mental health and Kurt Lewin's social psychology of human interrelatedness and group dynamics. They warned against "overemphasizing the intellect" on the grounds that intellectual learnings are secondary to social learnings. In other words, the social aspects of learning (which have sometimes been called "togetherness") were more to be desired than individual brilliance and unconventional behavior.

. . . As educators, we must ask ourselves the question: Are we localizing our educational process too much? Are we overemphasizing the intellectual achievement at the expense of more essential experiences that lay the foundations for wholesome social adjustment and therefore also wholesome character structure? Are we, through our eagerness to pass on informational material, depriving children and youth of group and activity experiences that are essential to them and therefore [contributing] to personality maladjustment? Are we, through our didactic emphasis upon subject-matter knowledge, preventing the development of the capacity to navigate in a complicated social environment in a way that would retain

From *Journal of Educational Sociology*, December 1939, 13:232-235.

personal integrity and bring about social advantage?

The answer to all these questions lies in the introduction of the group process to the classroom. It is not possible in so brief a paper to give the extensive implications of these queries. Surely, as one reads the rich literature dealing with education, sociological problems, and democracy—especially in the light of developments in Europe—one must become fully cognizant of the value of education as a social experience. But, in addition to social adjustment, the group provides intellectual learnings as well. The present writer has had opportunities for considerable experimentation in group learning both among children and adults. In a skillfully set environment, free activity leads to subject-matter learnings. Children, and adults as well, under free conditions gather into small groups on the basis of common interests or personal likes. They enter into a dynamic intellectual interstimulation. They ask questions of one another; they challenge; they explain; they look up material together; they argue; they agree; they disagree. These and other forms in which intellectual activity is both stimulated and tolerated are evolved as a result of free active group life in an educative setting.

It seems to me that even progressive educators have for years made the mistake of assuming that creative activity alone develops personality and trains character. As we read the literature of progressive education, we become aware of this emphasis. Creative expression is the watchword and the major objective. But, as I look back at many years as a progressive classroom and activities teacher, I am becoming more and more aware of the fact that it was not the activities themselves that were of such importance, but rather the fact that these activities were free *in a group situation*. To my mind, this latter fact is the outstanding element in the very evident physical and mental development of our pupils. The praise and recognition that these children gave one another; the cooperative experiences in common interests; the feeling of responsibility toward the teachers, the class setting, and the school were, as I see it now, much more important than the fact of having produced beautiful paintings, impressive clay modeling, fine scientific reports, or plays. The situation of being accepted, of integrating with other people, or receiving respect, consideration, and freedom from an adult were much more permanent influences than the satisfaction of the so-called creative expression. It seems to me that the concept of activity, as it applies to education, must be viewed more widely than is generally the case. Educative activity occurs on five differ-

ent levels. To be sure, these coalesce, overlap, and frequently are simultaneous. They are motor, emotional, aesthetic, intellectual, and social activity. One might say that all the preceding phases of educative activity culminate or are unified in the last—the social activity—which acts as a stimulant and instigator to the others. Supposing we supplied possibilities for all types of motor and aesthetic activity to a child completely isolated from others. His personality would still remain undeveloped and he would be unfit for group living. However, a child placed in a free activity group would be stimulated into the various avenues of expression along all the other lines, and thus his education would be assured. The richer the environment to which the group is exposed, in terms of opportunities for occupations and learnings, the richer would the group's stimulation upon each member also be.

The function of the school in a democracy therefore is to supply opportunities for activity in a group setting. In this type of education, the role of the teacher is that of a person who sets situations for activity and for personal interaction. Group living in the school must be evolving as it is everywhere else in a free society. Group life is part and parcel of the democratic plan of life. Hence, in a school, as well, the evolving element of group living must be carefully planned. As the child grows older and becomes more ready for participation and for initiating more types of activity, it is necessary that the teacher supply possibilities for him. The capacity range for group living for very young children may be limited to the orderliness of the classroom. As they grow older, these children can participate in maintaining order and decorum in the entire school. The school must also become a factor in the neighborhood life. By means of councils, and associations, the matter of playgrounds, housing, political and social problems come under purview. Pupils should become aware of and increasingly take part in philanthropic, charitable, and patriotic movements. In other words, the school must aim to create an *articulate community*. If education is to serve democracy as it should, vital interest in community and national life must be aroused among pupils at school. They must see and function in an ever expanding area and in ever evolving interests, to encompass international and world affairs. All this, of course, cannot be done without planning, discussing, studying, reading, reporting, and taking action. This is the cycle in which group learning occurs; out of which grow those attributes and attitudes which are essential to desirable character, wholesome personality, and social responsibility and real democracy.

54

James M. Laing & Paul F. Munger

THE GROUP PROCESS CONCEPT

In this neatly structured statement by Principal Laing and Professor Munger we see the theorizing of Slavson treated in practical terms. To be sure, the authors seem to have appropriated the problems method virtually unaltered, as one may see by comparing their ideas with those presented in earlier selections. And there is a surprising amount of faith placed in the educational power of such mechanical factors as name cards, seating, coffee drinking, and smoking.

Of primary importance is the authors' assertion that ideas which result from group discussion are superior to those produced by the individual unaided mind. This is what George Orwell termed "group-think," and businessmen call "brainstorming." In a sense it is the "bull session" of the fraternity house or college dormitory, dignified and glorified. In this connection perhaps one should ponder the statement of Arnold Toynbee in his twelve-volume *Study of History:* "As far as we know at present, only single minds can think thoughts and express them. . . . There have never been such things as collective thinking and collective writing. . . . Any document that purports to be the product of a committee will prove—if it makes any genuine contribution to knowledge and understanding to be the unacknowledged work of some single anonymous draftsman" (12). However, we must also recognize that a group can propose plans, work out individual assignments, and allow individual thought, yet be a team operation for certain aspects of a problem.

Like many another educational innovation, group process has been scoffed at, laughed at, and intellectually spat upon. It has been characterized as an artifice of the incompetent teacher who is "short" on factual information and lacking in instructional know-how. It has been generalized as scholastically profitless and a sure-fire method of wasting time.

Group process is not a new educational tool, nor is it one that can stand alone without the help of other techniques. It is supplementary and supportive. When well used, it is a process fundamental to the well-established guidance concept that the most lasting solution to a problem is one that has been worked through by the person to whom the problem *is* a problem.

Few business ventures under our present competitive system of enterprise have proved successful without a co-operative involvement of a number of people. The motivational "trigger" varies from situation to situation, but a combination of effort is a primary requirement for business success.

Every college campus has a student union, and included in the facilities it makes available for students is a lounging room where informal groups can gather for project planning of one type or another. A recognition of this kind of student need by those who build student unions gives support to a number of current studies which indicate that the most lasting concepts have grown out of group situations where there is free interaction.

What is group process?

Group process is any face-to-face interaction in which there is problem solving and co-operative functioning involving more than two persons. In a group process an individual can participate in social planning and control. He can feel that his efforts will not be submerged and lost by forces too great for him to cope with as an individual.

Group process is not a number of clever devices or tricks by which a few individuals seek to manage others in order to gain their own ends. On the contrary, it is a means by which the resources of several individuals are mobilized into a solid pattern of agreement on common goals and

From *Education*, December 1959, 80:231-234. Copyright © 1959 by The Bobbs-Merrill Company, Inc.

by which effective action is directed to the attainment of these goals.

Group process is a method of democratic socialization by which the initiative of the individual and the right of the individual to sustain ideas which others may be unwilling to accept or support is maintained. In group process there is a mutual respect for the ideas of all members of the group. There is also the belief that supportive ideas of many have a greater potential for productivity than the ideas of an individual. To be effective, all the members of the group should present their ideas on the issue under consideration. When the multitude of ideas presented to the group are pieced together and discussed, the resulting concept can be truly characterized as the brain child of all.

One might liken group process to a number of jungle natives seated cross-legged around the bare framework of a canoe. One holds out a piece of bark covering, and, if it seems to be sound, it is allowed to become a part of the boat. When a member of the group offers a piece which is of inferior quality it is rejected. As the pieces of bark are accepted and fitted into place around the frame, the boat takes shape. Finally, when the last piece is in place the project is truly group constructed. The quality is superior to a boat constructed by an individual because each part has had to withstand the test of group analysis.

Preparation is necessary

Effective group work requires special preparation which is not essential for other types of problem-solving situations. The first step in setting the stage for effective group process is to provide opportunity for those involved to know each other better. If they do not know each other with some degree of intimacy before their work begins, members of a group must take the time to develop such a relationship. To the uninitiated this relationship development might seem to be of little importance. It can well be the most difficult step, because it is time consuming and adds the element of frustration to those steeped in the tradition of the individualistic approach to problem-solving.

There are many ways in which the "getting acquainted" process can be implemented. A few of the more common can be cited as follows. Initially each person in the group should give his name and tell something about himself. This gives a general orientation to the group composition. The simple device of having each person put his full name in large letters on a card that can easily be seen by all during discussion has its place in setting the stage. The importance of

this simple device can best be explained by recalling the difficulty in conversation when one member cannot remember the name of another member of the group or is not certain that the name he recalls is the correct one. It may mean that he is unable to concentrate on the problem under discussion because he is concentrating on name recall. This is likely to lessen the freedom with which he interacts in group participation.

The seating of group participants so that they face each other in some type of informal pattern makes it possible to see and interpret facial expressions as well as hear what is said. There are few things less likely to produce a free flow of discussion than the back-of-the-head view of the person to whom one directs his remarks.

Some type of "tension dispeller," such as coffee or smoking, has much to do with the freedom of the discussion setting. An acceptant atmosphere is another factor in establishing a proper setting for the function of group process. If group members do not respect and accept each other's feelings, none of them is free to express himself seriously on an issue.

Problem must be solved

The success of any group process situation requires a definite problem to be solved, with each member of the group committed to the solution of that problem. The interest of group members may grow as group participation brings out the varied facets of the problem. Group loyalty should be so developed that individuals with a lesser degree of concern for the problem are willing to explore with others in an effort to increase interest. Groups that are formed to work upon broad general problems should be allowed, after thorough discussion, to select the specific aspects upon which the majority wish to work. They should be allowed to set up the priorities for dealing with each problem.

The four steps necessary for utilizing group process in an effective manner are: (1) setting the goals; (2) selecting the procedure; (3) executing the plan; and (4) evaluating process and product.

Setting the goals

Individuals who plan future action alone are not likely to establish specific objectives, because they feel insecure. In a group the individual has an opportunity to test a suggested goal on a number of individuals who will have a share in its execution. The responsibility for success or failure is spread among many, but the success potential is enhanced because the less acceptable goals have not passed the test of group sifting. Traditionally, in group situations, the task or goal is determined from outside the membership of the group. Too often the efficiency of an aggressive status leader results in pushing through a predetermined program. When the group establishes goals, a technique is provided whereby the group working co-operatively can control the design of its own endeavor.

Selecting the procedure

How the ends are to be achieved is also a matter of consensus, gained through a thorough sifting of all points of view. Decisions are group decisions, approved and sanctioned by all. There is no set pattern of procedure by which goals are attained. The pattern of procedure must be tailored to fit the situation which gave rise to the goals set by the group. After the group has developed several procedural steps of an action sequence, it must select those steps which offer the greatest success potential in carrying out the group's goals. This involves group decision as to how to accomplish each step and who should do what. In arriving at a decision regarding both of these questions the group acts co-operatively. The decision as to final plans for action should be the result of a careful study by the group of the probable outcomes.

Executing the plan

Both group discussion and group planning may assist in clarifying issues and in bringing about motivation in the desired direction. Motivation alone, however, does not lead to change. It is necessary to transform motivation into concrete goals and to translate these goals into actions which carry the group beyond discussion and planning to the actual completion of the work.

The old cliche, "The proof of the pudding is in the eating," is most apropos to group process. If the work of the group is to bring about change in behavior, the plan and procedure upon which it has agreed must be carried into action. Unlike the traditional committee report which so often is filed and allowed to "die" from disuse, group process prescribes that some form of group action shall translate the verbal into tangible and material reality. The "action research" concept lends itself to the execution of the group process plan. It involves the active participation of all who have had a part in goal-setting and in activating the problem-solving process.

Evaluating process and product

A plan effectively carried to completion always results in some significant change of behavior or in some concrete manifestation of the effort of the group. It is the obligation of the group to view its work objectively and to pass judgment upon its value. The function of social inter-action is not to endorse efforts of the group but to evaluate its work. In essence, the group looks back over what it has done and tries to find out how well it has performed. Although group evaluation draws conclusions regarding the effectiveness of total performance, it is a continuous process extending from the analysis of the problem to the concluding act of the project.

Evaluation sessions at the conclusion of each group meeting tend to crystallize the thinking that has taken place and to select the ideas which are pertinent to the problem.

One evaluative device is to select group members to observe the group in action and to help the total group evaluate its own efforts. These individuals serve to keep members from straying too far from the purpose of finding a solution to the problem.

The group should keep an account of the development of its experiences. These records should be periodically reviewed so that no good ideas are overlooked.

After the problem-solving action has been completed a post-analysis should be initiated. This results in summary, conclusions, and recommendation for further group process activities.

55

Maynard C. Waltz

LEARNING BY GROUP DISCUSSION

Whether the group be directed and planned in advance, or "nondirective" and spontaneous in its actions, the core of the group approach was two-way discussion rather than one-way lecture or conventional recitation methods. In this older, less professionally sophisticated argument by a New England high-school teacher in behalf of more discussion in every classroom, there is a great deal that is of immediate value to the nonspecialized teacher.

Perhaps one should pause here to reflect that "group discussion" can mean very different things. In its simplest form it represents an informal and comparatively spontaneous interlude to the monotony of even the best-planned teacher presentation. At its most highly developed stage it is a theory and practice for total, or at least basic, instruction throughout the entire curriculum.

Group discussion is one of the best aids to learning that we have. By group discussion I mean oral participation by the members of the unit in the solving of real problems. By learning, I mean a gradually acquired change in behavior which is more or less permanent and which better enables the child to adapt himself to his environment. In learning through discussion the members of the class may present facts that have been gathered pertaining to the problem and then arrive at a conclusion or they may individually present their solutions and then defend them. The class or group as a whole, with the teacher as guide, acts as the final judge of the case. Such discussion will complete the learning cycle of stimulation, assimilation and reaction. Without it the learner will neither know what he knows nor will it be fully his own. . . .

Group work . . . provides for learning by allowing students to plan for attacking a problem which they themselves have suggested, to report on individual research work, to clarify their own ideas, to make judgments, to share experiences, and finally to analyze, abstract, compare and generalize data. These activities enable the timid students to develop confidence, foster attitudes of open mindedness and suspended judgment, offer an opportunity for leadership development, encourage group co-operation and social harmony, teach critical thinking and the ability to express logical thoughts in good English. Such discussion should help pupils to think, for the solution of similar problems will in most cases naturally follow Dewey's five logically distinct factors in reflective thinking which are[1]: (1) felt difficulty; (2) its location and definition; (3) suggestions towards possible solutions; (4) development of these suggestions by reasoning; (5) further experiment to test the usefulness of the conclusions reached.

I believe that group discussion will help us to make use of the following principles which the latest experimental evidence on learning supports:—

1. Mere repetition increases the possibility of learning, but does not guarantee learning. In order to learn through repetition, the subject must know the meaning of what he is repeating, why he is repeating it, and when he will arrive at a known goal.

2. Explanation and diagnosis are helpful in learning.

3. Discrimination is a big factor in learning.

4. The efficiency of recall is increased by recitation.

5. A definite contrast between the right and the wrong assists in motivated learning.

6. Children working in groups make fewer mistakes than those working singly.

7. Competition increases learning.

8. Praise and blame may be helpful in learning.

9. A set task or problem is the best kind of motivation.

10. Interest and the intention to learn are fundamental factors in learning.

11. There is a close connection between the amount of meaning which the material to be learned has for the learner and the time required for mastery.

There are certain dangers in the discussion method which should be mentioned. In the first place, there is the danger that the class will become too formal, and degenerate into a detailed teacher-question and pupil-answer recitation. The spirit of the group must be friendly and most of the questions and information must come from the class. In the second place, there is the danger that the opinions of a few loquacious ones will be emphasized at the expense of fact and that the majority will take a minor part in the work. In the third place, time may be spent on irrelevant phases of the topic. In the fourth place, the advance work may not naturally grow out of the review. Finally there may be no conclusion, summary or check, which causes the pupils to close the period with the feeling that they have acquired a complex mass of heterogeneous material, but no definite information which they can use later.

From *Journal of Education*, June 19, 1933, 116:312-313.
[1] John Dewey: "How We Think" (1910), page 72.

The teacher may avoid some of these dangers by calling attention to the important points, by correlating the review and the advance, by encouraging pertinent discussion and questioning during the presentation of a report, by encouraging an expression of honest opinion, by giving outside help, by insisting that all sides be presented fairly and demanding frequent written as well as oral summaries.

It seems to me that regardless of whether you believe in the trial and error, gestält, conditioned reflex or Tolman's sign-gestält-expectation theories of learning you can devote a great deal of time to class discussion with excellent results, for it can be most readily adapted to those principles in any of these theories which you have reason to believe are correct.

Class discussion is only one of several excellent methods of teaching and consequently should not be used to the exclusion of the others. My point is that we should use more group discussion in our teaching.

56
Leighton H. Johnson

ABUSES OF GROUP DISCUSSION

One of the best and most succinct critiques of the group-discussion method was penned by Leighton Johnson of San Francisco State College. His analysis centers upon the key issue of whether individual growth is helped more than it is hindered by group emphases. In the background ring echoes of the raging debate among modern intellectuals over individualism or collectivism as the nation's best hope.

Certain foes of the group emphasis have denounced its tendency to elevate intuition and shared emotions above logic and independence of mind. The language of Lewin's group dynamics has been called "cultism" by others. In your opinion which side in the debate over group methods of instruction seems most rational?

. . . [Enthusiastic] and zealous promoters of group discussion frequently made it something complex, involved, and even esoteric where it had been a natural and simple thing before. This kind of enthusiasm has resulted frequently in extremes which represent not good use, but abuse, of the method of group discussion.

The source of much abuse was the fundamental mistake of exalting the group to such a status that it completely overshadowed the individuals who composed it. The group was regarded as an entity far greater than the sum of its parts. The notion that group opinion was preferable to individual opinion became axiomatic and unquestioned among dedicated proponents of these views. They talked about the spirit of the group and the behavior of the group, as though these characteristics were quite different from the spirit and behavior of the individuals involved. A point of view well stated by Franklyn Haiman was easily and frequently overlooked: "Although it is true that individuals may behave quite differently under group conditions—such as those of a lynch mob—than they would singly, nonetheless it is still the individual who is doing the behaving." The expression "group thinking" was freely employed with little or no consideration of what it might connote. The elevation of the status, rights, and welfare of the group over the status, rights, and welfare of individual personalities within the group did not bother zealous advocates of group process. They apparently failed to realize that this preferential attitude toward the group, and the consequent de-emphasis of the standing of individuals, is the basic tenet of collectivism and the fundamental assumption underlying collectivist thinking.

Closely related to this attitude toward the status of the group over that of the individuals in it is the point of view which insists that decisions and actions of the group be based on complete agreement. Alert thinkers have warned us about increasing tendencies toward conformity in our social institutions. The plea to obtain complete agreement in discussions would seem to constitute an extreme manifestation of such tendencies. The

From *School and Society*, November 1957, 85:324-326.

compulsion to obtain perfect consensus has been pushed to an extent where it is increasingly recognized as a major abuse of group discussion. Those who urge the necessity of securing complete agreement in the group overlook the fact that common opinion may often be wrong and that new insights and fresh ideas often develop in individuals and minorities before they are acceptable to the majority. This is not an objection to consensus which is fairly arrived at and a desirable outcome of deliberation. It is an objection to that insistence on consensus which stifles unusual and imaginative thinking. The exhortation to achieve full consensus may lead to general agreement on trivia, platitudes, truisms, and mediocrity; and the discriminate thought, the unique observation, the new idea, and the promising suggestion are easily disregarded. Some who habitually stress the principle of complete consensus can be quite ruthless in quashing unusual ideas. They overlook or underestimate a democratic tradition of long standing which values the minority report and the dissenting opinion. What the minority members of a legislative committee or the dissenting judges of a higher court of law have to say on controversial issues has been generally respected in democratic governments. Abusers of group discussion who dispose of unwelcome ideas by submerging them under calls for consensus may accomplish more than they realize in subduing unusual and promising thinking in an age which cries out for it.

Preoccupation with process in group discussion has fostered other abuses. At times more attention is given to process and procedure employed by the group than to substantive findings or recommendations that are developed. Many educators are familiar with this typical situation: A long meeting has been devoted to the exploration of a complex problem. At the end of the meeting, a "process observer" or "process recorder" delivers a report or analysis of the way the group has conducted its business, and this report is longer, and perhaps more closely attended, than the report of findings, conclusions, and recommendations. This would seem to be putting form before substance and secondary before primary objectives.

Such overemphasis on process is the basis for a poor kind of rationalization, for when the group has accomplished nothing of importance in line with its ostensible purpose, it can justify the expenditure of time and effort on the grounds of alleged growth in group thinking and group sophistication.

In addition to this handy excuse for unsatisfactory progress, there is another outcome of preoccupation with process that should be noted. Overconcern for group process and group behavior may stimulate curious neurotic tendencies in some individuals. Thus, at the end of a discussion period, the process expert may chide the group for departing from accepted principles of group dynamics, and immediately persons in the group will take these sins upon themselves. They recite the particular wrongs they have done and, with an almost masochistic satisfaction, agree that these errors have impeded the best progress of the group. This procedure is so reminiscent of typical discipline techniques among totalitarians that one wonders about its propriety in a supposedly democratic setting. This concern for group acceptance, in an age of widespread anxiety, leads to a desire for approbation completely out of proportion to the jeopardy in which individual integrity is placed.

The need for self-determination and self-direction in discussion groups has been emphasized in recent years. There is little argument against the proposition that, in a democratic discussion, it is desirable for the participants to have some say in outlining the work of the discussion group, its procedures, and the topics it will consider. Likewise, members of a discussion group should be able to depart from, or modify, previously set tasks when this seems wise. In past situations, when many educational meetings were so predetermined that the participants had little leeway in which to do original thinking as they made their way over the course laid out for them, this emphasis on greater self-determination for discussion groups was much needed. Indeed, in some educational gatherings it continues to be much needed today. But in many cases the reaction against planning and organization led to abuses such as unreasonable lack of plans and failure to follow any consistent or continuing attack on important issues. The usual inefficiency and ineffectiveness of unplanned, undirected, irresponsible talking is obvious. A less apparent abuse is often overlooked. This is the opportunity which is provided in unstructured, extremely flexible meetings for the manipulators, the salesmen, and the representatives of special interests. Such people are quick and skillful in swinging irresponsible discussions onto their particular interests and concerns. Again we are reminded of opportunities coveted by totalitarians. It is ironic but true that, as with many concerns of free people, pushing desirable reforms to extremes can lead to decidedly undemocratic abuses.

How often are new ideas silenced in educational meetings by those who demand concrete, tangible, so-called "practical" thinking? This abuse of ending theoretical, speculative inquiry suggests a preoccupation with ideas which are simple, familiar, and uninspiring, as opposed to thoughts which are complex, abstract, and provocative. The first mode of thinking has been overemphasized, perhaps, in American educational thought; the second is the time-honored practice of intelligent and philosophic minds.

There never has been any doubt that good group discussion is useful in the education and social advancement of a democracy. Earnest consideration of challenging issues in a face-to-face situation is a particularly appropriate procedure in a free society. It would seem most important, therefore, that educators and all citizens exercise continual care that group discussion be carried on as a thoroughly democratic course of action. Without due care, group discussion can suffer at the hands of the overzealous and shortsighted, and a procedure long cherished for its rewarding returns will lose value as it is increasingly abused.

The methods of education

THE TOOLS FOR TEACHING

First of all, one should be quite certain that he really knows what a teaching aid is. A *teaching aid,* or tool, is something used by the teacher. A *learning aid,* or tool, is something used by the student. There is a real difference. The main kinds of teaching aids are books, audio-visual resources, machines, and what we might loosely call "supplies." Learning aids include all these things plus many more—the teacher himself, the school environment, commercial newspapers and other mass media, the student's parents and friends, in fact the whole environment in which the student lives.

Are some teaching tools, especially teaching machines and television, truly an aid to the teacher or in reality a threat to his job? This is a question very close to the heart of the young person about to enter the teaching profession. For the first time in history, teachers are really beginning to understand how laboring men have felt when faced with unemployment because new machinery was now performing their old tasks. Will technological unemployment develop as the use of mechanized teaching increases? Will teaching machines rob the teacher of his central place in the classroom and reduce him to merely grading and recording tests constructed by outside experts? Will his professional status decline to that of a tutor, a clerk, an office worker?

No one knows for sure. The past record is comforting, however, as Readings 58 and 63 spell out in some detail. There have been many predictions that the inexpensive book, the monitorial system, radio, and films would make teachers superfluous, or at least greatly reduce their number. Each time the prophets have been mistaken, and the fears of those intelligent enough to understand the threat have been groundless. On the positive side, the effect of many of the new instruments has been to direct the attention of teachers to better ways of presenting materials and to more systematic ways of structuring content.

57

Jerome S. Bruner

AIDS TO TEACHING

One of the most influential and widely read books in recent years, so far as professional educators are concerned, is *The Process of Education,* written by the Harvard psychologist and public-opinion expert Jerome Bruner. The extract below is his chapter on teaching aids. Bruner separates these devices into four categories based on intended purpose rather than external form, which is unusual.

Like most prominent figures in education circles, Bruner tends to reject the idea that teaching aids can threaten a teacher seriously, even though the integrated teaching film which he describes at some length would seem to preëmpt most, if not all, of the teacher's classroom time. He would prefer us to think about the level at which specific teaching aids would be most effective—elementary, secondary, or college.

Students would profit by reading Bruner's entire book, particularly in connection with the article by Philip H. Phenix (Reading 127), since both authors are analyzing the structure of knowledge from a relatively new point of view. It will be of interest to the student to compare the re-interpretations of knowledge or content presented by Bruner and Phenix with Comenius' view of "universal knowledge" or pansophy (Reading 32).

There has been a great deal of discussion in recent years about the devices that can be employed to aid in the teaching process. These devices are of many kinds. Some of them are designed to present material to the student of a kind that would not be available to him in his ordinary school experience. Films, TV, microphotographic film, film strips, sound recordings, and the like are among the devices ordinarily employed in such work. Books also serve in this role. These are the tools by which the student is given vicarious though "direct" experience of events. It does not serve much to dismiss such materials as "merely for enrichment," since it is obvious that such enrichment is one of the principal objectives of education. Let us call these *devices for vicarious experience.*

A second type of teaching aid has the function of helping the student to grasp the underlying structure of a phenomenon—to sense the genotype behind the phenotype, to use terms from genetics. The well wrought laboratory experiment or demonstration is the classic aid in such activity. A closer look at our efforts to get students to grasp structure indicates that there are many other devices and exercises that have the same function. The effort to give visible embodiment to ideas in mathematics is of the same order as the laboratory work. The Stern blocks, Cuisenaire rods, and Dienes blocks, as well as the demonstrations of Piaget and Inhelder mentioned earlier, have the

same function. So too do certain kinds of charts and representations, either in animated or still form. Models, such as a model of the molecule or an idealized model of the respiratory system, serve a comparable function. Needless to say, films and television as well as adroitly illustrated books can be adjuncts to the effort at producing clarity and concrete embodiment.

But there are other, more subtle devices that can be and are being used to lead the student to a sense of the conceptual structure of things he observes. Perhaps the best way to characterize them is to call them "sequential programs." There are certain orders of presentation of materials and ideas in any subject that are more likely than others to lead the student to the main idea. The courses being devised by the University of Illinois Committee on School Mathematics, the School Mathematics Study Group, the Physical Science Study Committee, and others are excellent instances of the well conceived sequence designed to lead the student to an understanding of basic ideas and structures.

The whole range of aids from the laboratory exercise through the mathematical blocks to the programmed sequence we shall, for convenience, speak of as *model devices.*

Closely related to these are what might be called *dramatizing devices.* The historical novel that is true in spirit to its subject, the nature film that dramatizes the struggle of a species in its habitat, the exemplification of an experiment executed by a dramatic personality, exposure to greatness in government by a documentary on the life and service of a Winston Churchill—all these can have the dramatic effect of leading the student to identify more closely with a phenome-

From *The Process of Education* by Jerome Bruner (Cambridge, Mass.: Harvard University Press), pp. 81-92. Copyright 1960 by The President and Fellows of Harvard College. Reprinted by permission of the publishers.

non or an idea. Undoubtedly, this "aid" in teaching can best be exemplified by the drama-creating personality of a teacher. But there are many additional dramatic aids upon which teachers can and do call—and one wonders whether they are called upon often enough.

Finally, the past decade has witnessed the emergence of various *automatizing devices,* teaching machines, to aid in teaching. While such devices vary quite widely, they have certain features in common. The machine presents a carefully programmed order of problems or exercises to the student, one step at a time. The student responds selectively in one form or another to the alternatives presented in a problem or exercise. The machine then responds immediately, indicating whether the response was or was not correct. If a correct response is made, the machine moves to the next problem. The progression in difficulty from problem to problem is usually quite gradual in order to keep the student from the discouragement of excessive failure.

What one teaches and how one teaches it with the aid of such devices depends upon the skill and wisdom that goes into the construction of a program of problems. The art of programming a machine is, of course, an extension of the art of teaching. To date, most of the programming has been intuitive and has been entrusted to a teacher of known reputation. It has been remarked by teachers who have written tapes for teaching machines that the exercise has the effect of making one highly conscious of the sequence in which one presents problems and of the aims of the sequence —whether, for example, one is trying to get children to memorize material or use material cumulatively in doing progressively more difficult problems.

Perhaps the technically most interesting features of such automatic devices are that they can take some of the load of teaching off the teacher's shoulders, and, perhaps more important, that the machine can provide immediate correction or feedback to the student while he is in the act of learning. It is still far too early to evaluate the eventual use of such devices, and it is highly unfortunate that there have been such exaggerated claims made by both proponents and opponents. Clearly, the machine is not going to replace the teacher—indeed, it may create a demand for more and better teachers if the more onerous part of teaching can be relegated to automatic devices. Nor does it seem likely that machines will have the effect of dehumanizing learning any more than books dehumanize learning. A program for a teaching machine is as personal as a book: it can

be laced with humor or be grimly dull, can either be a playful activity or be tediously like a close-order drill.

In sum, then, there exist devices to aid the teacher in extending the student's range of experience, in helping him to understand the underlying structure of the material he is learning, and in dramatizing the significance of what he is learning. There are also devices now being developed that can take some of the load of teaching from the teacher's shoulders. How these aids and devices should be used in concert as a system of aids is, of course, the interesting problem.

The matter of "integration" is nicely illustrated in a report on the teaching films used by the Physical Science Study Committee. "Until quite recently, most educational films were enrichment films, designed primarily to introduce phenomena or experiences that would otherwise be unavailable inside the classroom. Such films are necessarily self-contained, since the producer is ignorant of what his audience has previously learned or what it will go on to learn; he can neither build upon the student's immediate past nor lay the groundwork for his immediate future. In the last few years, another kind of educational film, stimulated to a large extent by television, has made its appearance. These films present the entire substance of a course, and are designed to minimize the need for a teacher. Clearly, it is possible to make extremely useful films in either of these forms, and such films have indeed been made." Stephen White, who has had a major part in producing the films used in the high school physics course prepared by the PSSC, then goes on to say in his report on the film work of that group, "Every film produced by the PSSC must meet two conditions. It must (1) further the presentation of the PSSC course as a whole, and (2) set the tone and level of the course. For the PSSC film is part of a complex that includes also the text, the laboratory, the classroom, the student, and the teacher."

White describes some of the problems of making the film fit. "The film must fit into this complex and never disrupt it. Obviously, this principle imposes serious restrictions on the producer. The most important of these for the PSSC films lies in the relation between the film and the laboratory. Only at his peril may the producer include in a film experiments which the student should and could do in the laboratory. Occasionally such an experiment will be included because it is essential to the logical development of the film's theme, in which case it is done briefly and allusively. More often, it is considered desirable to repeat on film, with more sophisticated apparatus, an experiment that is suitable for the school laboratory; in such cases the film is made in a manner which indicates clearly that it should be shown *after* the student has done the lab work, and the teacher is strongly urged to defer it until that time."

Other elements in the complex must also be taken into account. "Other restrictions on the film require it to follow the logical development, the spirit, and the vocabulary (where it exists) of the text. Finally, the film must always respect the position of the teacher; it must leave for him those activities which are necessary for him if he is to retain the respect of his class. All these are negative, but the film makes positive contributions to the complex as well. It serves the classroom by directing attention to those aspects of the subject which will best stimulate classroom discussion. Thus, the PSSC film on 'Work and Mechanical Energy' deliberately calls attention to the temperature rise in a nail on which work is being done, and thus opens discussion of thermal energy, which the class will meet next. And the film, wherever possible, serves the individual student directly by suggesting work he himself can carry on outside the school; it is for this reason that many PSSC films contain sophisticated experiments performed with simple apparatus."

The writer discusses a second function performed by the integrated teaching film: "The second condition that every film must meet—that of setting level and tone—may well be the most important contribution that the film medium can make. By directing attention to the important questions and the important problems, the film can help assure that all the great mass of fact and concept and theory and application that constitute any field of knowledge will fall into a coherent pattern in which the more important aspects will be clearly differentiated from the trivial. This is most difficult to achieve with the printed word; on film it can be accomplished at times with a gesture. Beyond meeting these two conditions, PSSC attempts in each film to make other substantial contributions to the learning process. Each film shows a real scientist in action, presenting him not as a disembodied intellect but as a normal, active, occasionally fallible human being, dealing rigorously and respectfully with real problems and deriving not only satisfaction but at times excitement from the intellectual pursuit in which he is engaged. It is in this implicit fashion that the films attempt to elucidate the nature of scientists and of the scientific life. . . . The films are scrupulously honest. Experiments that are seen on the screen were carefully performed and are accurately reported. The temptation to use the legerdemain inherent in film processes has been steadily resisted, and in those rare cases where it is used to produce a desirable effect, the student is told explicitly how it is used and why."

The task of the PSSC—the creation of a single high school course in physics—was a specialized one, and the particular problems of the course may not relate to all forms of curriculum construction. Yet there is always a question as to the purpose of any particular device—be it a film of paramecia or a slide projection of a graph or a television show on the Hoover Dam. *The devices themselves cannot dictate their purpose.* Unbridled enthusiasm for audio-visual aids or for teaching machines as panaceas overlooks the paramount importance of what one is trying to accomplish. A perpetual feast of the best teaching films in the world, unrelated to other techniques of teaching, could produce bench-bound passivity. Limiting instruction to a steady diet of classroom recitation supported only by traditional and middling textbooks can make lively subjects dull for the student. The objectives of a curriculum and the balanced means for attaining it should be the guide.

A discussion of teaching aids may seem like an unusual context in which to consider the teacher's role in teaching. Yet, withal, the teacher constitutes the principal aid in the teaching process as it is practiced in our schools. What can be said of the teacher's role in teaching?

It takes no elaborate research to know that communicating knowledge depends in enormous measure upon one's mastery of the knowledge to be communicated. That much is obvious enough —whether the teacher uses other aids or not. It is also quite plain from recent surveys that many primary and secondary school teachers are not, in the view of various official bodies, sufficiently well trained initially to teach their subject. It is also the case that, with the present high turnover in the teaching profession, even relatively well prepared teachers do not have sufficient opportunity to learn their subjects in that special way that comes from teaching it. For teaching is a superb way of learning. There is a beautiful story about a distinguished college teacher of physics. He reports introducing an advanced class to the quantum theory: "I went through it once and looked up only to find the class full of blank faces—they had obviously not understood. I went through it a second time and they still did not understand it. And so I went through it a third time, and that time *I* understood it."

There are certain measures that must be taken to improve the quality of teachers, steps that have been proposed many times and that need no elaboration here. Better recruitment and the possibility of better selection, better substantive education in teacher training institutions, on-the-job training of younger teachers by more experienced ones, in-service and summer institutes, closed-circuit television to continue the education of teachers, improvement in teachers' salaries—all of these must obviously be pursued as objectives. But equally important is the upgrading of the prestige of the teaching profession. This upgrading will depend upon the degree to which we in America are serious about educational reform and the degree to which efforts are made to improve not only the facilities and salaries available to teachers but the support they can count on from the community and from our universities.

One special matter concerning the teacher as communicator of knowledge must be mentioned: the training and qualifications of the elementary-school teachers. . . . [The] training of children concretely and intuitively in logical operations that will later be taught more formally in upper primary and secondary school requires special training, and it is not clear what the most effective form of training is. Special emphasis should very likely be given to such work—research on how to train teachers for such teaching along with research on the actual teaching of younger pupils.

The teacher is not only a communicator but a model. Somebody who does not see anything beautiful or powerful about mathematics is not likely to ignite others with a sense of the intrinsic excitement of the subject. A teacher who will not or cannot give play to his own intuitiveness is not likely to be effective in encouraging intuition in his students. To be so insecure that he dares not be caught in a mistake does not make a teacher a likely model of daring. If the teacher will not risk a shaky hypothesis, why should the student?

To communicate knowledge and to provide a model of competence, the teacher must be free to teach and to learn. We have not been sufficiently mindful of the ways in which such freedom can be achieved. Notably, we have been neglectful of the uses to which educated parents can be put. Various schools have experimented successfully with plans that use parents for the semiprofessional tasks that keep teachers pinned down. Parents can certainly help in supervising study halls, in grading routine quizzes, in preparing laboratory materials, and in the dozens of routine operations necessary in a school. The

effect would be to free the teacher for teaching and study. If the teacher is also learning, teaching takes on a new quality.

The teacher is also an immediately personal symbol of the educational process, a figure with whom students can identify and compare themselves. Who is not able to recall the impact of some particular teacher—an enthusiast, a devotee of a point of view, a disciplinarian whose ardor came from love of a subject, a playful but serious mind? There are many images, and they are precious. Alas, there are also destructive images: the teachers who sapped confidence, the dream killers, and the rest of the cabinet of horrors.

Whitehead once remarked that education should involve an exposure to greatness. Many of us have been fortunate. But there is no simple plan for attracting greatness to the teaching profession. Emphasis on excellence is still the slow but likely way. Might it not be the case, however, that television and film might expand the range of identification figures—models of greatness—within the special limits imposed by one-way communication? We know relatively little about effective identification figures for children at different ages and in different circumstances. Are Olympian models the only ones or the best ones for engaging a child's sense of competence or greatness? Perhaps promising high school students as guest teachers from time to time would do better? They might also lure more talent into teaching.

In sum, then, the teacher's task as communicator, model, and identification figure can be supported by a wise use of a variety of devices that expand experience, clarify it, and give it personal significance. There need be no conflict between the teacher and the aids to teaching. There will be no conflict if the development of aids takes into account the aims and the requirements of teaching. The film or television show as gimmick, the television system without substance or style in its programs, the pictographically vivid portrayal of the trivial—these will help neither the teacher nor the student. Problems of quality in a curriculum cannot be dodged by the purchase of sixteen-millimeter projection equipment. The National Defense Education Act provides considerable sums of money for the development of audio-visual aids. The intelligent use of that money and of other resources now available will depend upon how well we are able to integrate the technique of the film maker or the program producer with the technique and wisdom of the skillful teacher.

58

Foster McMurray & Lee J. Cronbach

THE CONTROVERSIAL PAST AND PRESENT OF THE TEXT

Few teachers would deny that today, and for centuries past, our principal teaching aid has been the textbook. Here McMurray and Cronbach review the troubled career of the textbook since its first appearance. As one surveys the familiar names of educational naturalism, the feeling emerges that textbook and teaching changes are inextricably entangled with one another.

"Textbooks" used in today's classrooms may include novels, essays, newspapers; they may include the *Federalist Papers,* the Constitution, a volume of poetry, a census abstract, an encyclopedia. Are these really textbooks? What would the critics of textbooks have to say about them?

Socrates, holding forth in the market place of Athens, evidently taught his disciples without the aid of written texts; and so, apparently, has every culture educated its young, except for the Chinese and the modern Western world. Textbooks have, however, played a major part in the Western education of the last 500 years. The libraries of Alexandria and of the medieval monasteries were the spores of the Renaissance. The printing press put the works of Aristotle and Copernicus in every center of learning.

Now the student could absorb the new thought and the old directly from an authoritative text, rather than having to rely on the memory of his teacher. Indeed, before the advent of printing, the teacher could have gained *his* knowledge only by hearsay from some other teacher or from a brief look at a precious but inaccurate manuscript during a continental tour long years before. The printing press served as a pump for the Renaissance, flooding with new ideas the fields where knowledge was growing. As universities flourished and as lower schools came into being, each teacher who had gained his own knowledge from books came to regard his task as one of familiarizing his students with the content of the most important known works, or "texts."

Five centuries have brought fundamental changes in educational outlook. Education is no longer an exclusive service to a learned class. Where it was once a mark of "quality," education has become, at least in America, a household necessity. Education has turned from the formal and classical to a more utilitarian program, seeking to equip the student for responsible citizenship and self-support. Education has taken increasing responsibility for the person's whole development rather than for his training in basic disciplines alone. But regardless of these changes, the textbook has remained a principal instrument of education. It is because the old traditions, and thus the place of the textbook, have been challenged by new aims in education that present study of the text is necessary. Present-day criticism of the text arises largely because many writers contend that in its present form or perhaps in its essential nature the printed text is unsuited to the new aims of education.

The text and the social reformer

Criticism of textbook conservatism. Doctrines critical of the text are no novelty, dating back at least to Rousseau. There is indeed a remarkable correspondence between his statements and those of contemporaries. W. H. Kilpatrick writes as follows: "If we, to save a student's time, furnish him with the final orderly statement of our expert thinking so that he simply 'learns' this or simply 'learns and understands' it, we shall very likely prevent him from building an adequate knowledge of the region or matter at hand."[1] This might well be an echo of Rousseau: "Our first teachers of philosophy are our feet, our hands, and our eyes.

From *Text Materials in Modern Education,* Lee J. Cronbach, ed. (Urbana: University of Illinois Press, 1955), pp. 9-27.

[1] William H. Kilpatrick, *Remaking the Curriculum,* p. 92. New York: Newsom & Co., 1936.

To substitute books for all these is not to teach us to reason, but to teach us to use the reason of others; it is to teach us to believe much and never to know anything."[2]

Rousseau believed man to be an inherently noble and virtuous being, who had been degraded by social institutions into an evil state. Rousseau urged that children be freed to build a more suitable culture afresh from nature. The child could learn whatever nature presented by direct experience. Thus, he could rediscover whatever knowledge he needed to guide his life. Rousseau went so far as to recommend that children be forbidden to read books until they reached adolescence, lest their freshness of view and creative outlook be dimmed.

Essentially, Rousseau assumed that there is freedom in ignorance, that having concepts set before one necessarily blinds one to alternative interpretations. Mumford makes clear why this position is unsound:

"Before every attempt to describe the world of life and time there stands an unspoken prologue: human history itself. Without that prologue, the rest of the play would be an unintelligible buzz and blur. Neither history nor nature is given directly in contemporary experience, except in snatches that would be meaningless if they were not part of a long sequence of interpretations to which man has given his days and years . . . . What we know of the world comes to us mainly by interpretation, not by direct experience; and the very vehicle of interpretation itself is a product of that which must be explained: it implies man's organs and physiological aptitudes, his feelings and curiosities and sensibilities, his organized social relations and his means for transmitting and perfecting that unique agent of interpretation, language."[3]

It should be noted that Rousseau and his followers did not object to texts as an educational device because they thought texts ineffective. Their objection was at root a matter of social principle. With the highest motivation they sought to free the present from the liabilities of the past. They desired to change society. Those who are trying to avoid what they regard as the errors of a past generation speak in affinity with those who talked then of building a new order, of reconstructing society. It seems inevitable that a desire to escape the limitations created by the past causes some writers to try to forget the past altogether. The text is always a means of carrying forward into the future whatever insights, customs, and techniques have been found serviceable in the past. In fact, it can be nothing else. The text is conservative, because it conserves the past; therefore, it can be an anathema to a revolutionary philosophy. Sometimes the reformer fears that we cannot think *of* the past, without thinking *like* the past.

In proposing to abandon the text and similar methods of education, Rousseau wished to build a man who is freed from the limitations of growing up in an imperfect culture. Anthropological studies show, however, that even the "savages" of the South Sea Islands have developed a culture of their own. We now know that the very act of imbibing mother's milk is a socializing experience which ingrains certain cultural tendencies. There is no hope of insulating the learner from the culture in which, for better or for worse, he finds himself. The problem, then, seems to become this: how to make more and more of his culture useful to the learner.

Texts as a liberalizing influence.   The text is a device for helping the child fit into his culture, but culture need not be passed on unedited, good and bad aspects alike. In fact, the nature of the text itself, as we shall see, demands that its maker be highly selective in the material he presents. The textmaker is a gatekeeper who lets us have the knowledge he considers of most value. Therefore the text can actually serve as a vehicle for social reform. Orwell's "Big Brother" and all the other dictators, immediately upon seizing power, set about revising the schoolbooks of the nation in order to plant "proper" thoughts in the heads of the young. The revised schoolbooks stress those parts of the cultural past—race purity, for example—which support the new state doctrine; they suppress, nullify, or ignore traditions which are inimical to the state. American occupation forces in Germany and Japan have also sought to use the text for social reform. They have sought to reverse the trend of thinking in those nations by developing new texts which emphasize stories and traditions to teach children to take responsibility for their own government.

In a different way, a most striking example of social change through printed materials followed Luther's doctrine that every person should read the Bible for himself rather than depend upon others' interpretations. The Bible was translated and carried into every home. People who learned to read and think for themselves went on to create new nations and new systems of government.

[2] J. J. Rousseau, *Émile,* p. 90. Translated by W. H. Payne. New York: Appleton, 1896.
[3] Lewis Mumford, *The Conduct of Life,* p. 25. New York: Harcourt, Brace, & Co., 1951.

Reforms in educational method have frequently been presented through textbooks. When the texts became popular, the new doctrines they represented were accepted also. In the seventeenth century, Johann Amos Comenius set out to promote the visionary educational aim of ultimate universal knowledge for everyone. He invented new teaching methods and designed new sorts of textbooks to demonstrate them. As he went throughout Europe attempting to win converts to his new ideals, he encountered only indifference. To his dismay, however, he found that his hearers, though they denied his ideals, had an almost indecent eagerness to use his improved textbooks and methods. In the eighteenth century, Basedow disseminated a new set of methodological reforms in a textbook which came to be called, after Comenius' most successful text, the *orbis pictus* of the eighteenth century. Again, in the nineteenth century, America eagerly adopted the reforms of Pestalozzi, which had first been introduced through several textbooks organized on Pestalozzian principles. It was only later that these ideas became known as a body of educational theory. Historically it is clear that the text is a means by which education can be led in new directions, and it seems incongruous that present specialists in education should look upon the text with disfavor as unduly conservative.

Rather than being unduly conservative, proper texts can be a modernizing influence. This is well illustrated in the current concern of the National Science Foundation and national scientific organizations with the need to keep texts up to the minute. According to Director Alan Waterman of the Foundation, "good textbooks are vital to the progress of science, especially in those fast-developing sciences at the frontiers of knowledge."[4] Many present-day texts are open to severe criticism, he says. "One group of scientists has indicated to the Foundation that only at the most advanced graduate level are the new and far-reaching ideas in mathematics introduced into the curriculum. Few of the elementary courses and elementary texts show any change as a result of these new concepts." Here is severe criticism directed at the conservatism of texts, but the argument is not that it is in the nature of texts to be conservative; on the contrary, the scientists are unhappy because they think texts can and should be fully contemporary in spirit and content. It is of interest to note that the Foundation is currently supporting a study of physiology textbooks to achieve this aim.

Perhaps unconscious attitudes of educators have motivated controversy about texts. Margaret Mead observes the division between teachers devoted to classics and teachers whose outlook is dominated by the ideals of progress. As she sees it, each expresses in his teaching his own style of life. The person who has grown up contentedly in a setting largely directed by tradition and ritual, achieving satisfying status almost as a natural heritage of his kind, is ready to show children his stable world and to emphasize the goodness of the past. Such a teacher may even be opposed to innovation and experimentation, like the Navajo priest who would find it sacrilege to try a better technique for the rain-dance. In contrast, the teacher who in childhood was inoculated with the virus of "getting ahead" and rising above the level of his parents is dedicated to change and shuns traditional behavior as a form of stagnation. His style is expressed in the maxim: "You never know whether it will work unless you try it." The one educator, facing back to something rewarding and wanting youth to share his satisfactions, cannot sympathize with the other, who focuses on the delightfully unpredictable future and wants to stir children to an ambition to make their own revolutions.[5] Mead's sketch, oversimple though it is, seems to describe much of what goes on between specialists in subject-matter fields and proponents of new ideas in education. Such biases would account for some of the differences in opinion regarding textbook education and experimental education.

Though "modernists" attack the textbook, it would appear that the textbook might actually serve in the modernists' behalf if modern educational doctrine were to be embodied in new text materials. So far, no "great" text has appeared to incorporate the new ideas in educational method. The lack of a great modern textbook raises the question whether there is something in modern educational doctrines which is incompatible with the use of textbooks. Possibly these new ideas and beliefs about education are hostile to textbooks. There are indeed some elements in modern doctrine which would support anti-text sentiment, but more often than not hostility to the text has grown from misinterpretations of key ideas.

Before turning attention directly upon this history of modern theory and its misapplication, we

[4] Alan T. Waterman, "America's Stake in Pure Science," *The Wiley Bulletin*, XXXVI, No. 1 (Spring, 1953), 1, 3, and 4.

[5] Margaret Mead, *The School in American Culture*, p. 48. Cambridge, Massachusetts: Harvard University Press, 1951.

shall look at certain developments of the early twentieth century which showed concern for, rather than opposition to, texts.

Measurement, research, and the 1931 yearbook

The so-called scientific movement in education exercised a profound influence in the first part of this century. After it was discovered about 1900 that numerical calculations of pupil performance of school tasks were a clinching makeweight in arguments regarding educational practice, investigators ranged the length and breadth of the curriculum, measuring the effectiveness or ineffectiveness of the procedures used. These studies demonstrated undeniable failures of the curricula. Increasing numbers of investigators gathered data on one educational shortcoming and another, and this led to critical studies of the text as one of many aspects of education.

During this period "measurement" was king. The textbook was judged by a score card not unlike the card used in selecting a prize cow. Certain characteristics of the text were singled out for inspection, scoring weights were assigned on each characteristic, and the summary score was used to decide whether the text should be adopted. Taking the score card at face value involved faulty assumptions: for example, that one of the textbooks was better than the others, no matter what the school or the teaching methods into which the others would fit. Typography was given disproportionate emphasis in judging effectiveness.

Score cards came under criticism, but not before they were widely used. In 150 cities investigated late in the 1920's, 84 superintendents used a score card to select texts; only 27 superintendents considered score cards to be of no value; the other 39 superintendents were noncommittal on the use of them.[6] The score cards constituted an important form of pressure on text authors and publishers. But at no time were they connected with opposition to texts per se.

Investigations into the comparative effectiveness of the various methods of teaching reading, arithmetic, and other subjects had marked influence on text production and also on advertising. Whenever evidence implied that one pattern of organization produced measurably greater learning than older methods, the text which was organized in such a pattern held a considerable advantage over its competitors. Schools were readily persuaded to change from one text to another when such evidence could be offered. This was a distinct departure from the practice of a century earlier, when Webster and McGuffey were used uninterruptedly for two generations. Now, when studies were made of the success of pupils in classes taught by some of the "progressive" doctrines, especially those doctrines which advocated building a new curriculum for each class, such evidence became a source of attack upon texts qua texts. The more conservative educators, however, never disputed whether texts were desirable. Their concern was with improving their form and content.

The Textbook in American Education, a yearbook published in 1931 by a distinguished committee headed by J. B. Edmonson,[7] came as a climax to numerous studies made under the influence of Thorndike and Bagley. *The Textbook in American Education* was in one sense a consolidation of all then known about the text. It was much like our own volume in intention, except that the writers in 1931 seemed to see the knowledge of their time as relatively final, whereas we seek chiefly to raise questions. The eighteen chapters indicate the problems which aroused interest at that time; there is a chapter each on typography, cost, and marketing methods, but one (and only one) on the textbook and the method of teaching. Philosophical issues surrounding the textbook were to these writers a minor consideration compared to the host of issues that could be mowed down by factual investigation.

A particularly interesting chapter of the yearbook describes the feelings of publishing houses regarding the criticisms and demands on the texts of that era. One complaint today, valid or not, is that publishers cannot plan books because educational theory is constantly shifting. In 1931 the irritant was not a shift from one educational doctrine to another but only a proposed shift from one sequence of topics in geography to another, or some other change in details. In 1931 the educators asked the simple question, "What pattern do we use to get this subject across?" They were not aroused by the vaster doctrinal issues as to why and how pupils are being educated.[8] One publisher lamented "the tendency of influential persons in the field of education to be guided entirely by theory and by experiments conducted in more or less artificial situations." This spokesman said that the publishers accept opinions de-

---

[6] J. B. Edmonson and others, *The Textbook in American Education*, p. 148. Thirtieth yearbook of the National Society for the Study of Education, part II. Bloomington, Illinois: Public School Publishing Co., 1931.

[7] *Ibid.*
[8] *Ibid.*, pp. 176-77.

rived from educational research when they agree with common sense, but never otherwise.[9] Since common sense is often a restatement of tradition, whether right or wrong, it is possible that this attitude has blocked some improvements which might otherwise have been made in text materials during the past generation.

Another extract from the cross-sectional year-book will further indicate the flavor of educational thinking two decades ago. The textbooks published by state governments were beginning to disappear, as part of a trend toward locally written courses of study. This trend also allowed different textbooks to be used in different schools of a state, and so permitted greater flexibility. Said the eminent Dean E. P. Cubberley in one passage:

"The disadvantages of uniformity in school textbooks (from school to school) become even more marked when we pass from the elementary school to the junior and the senior high schools. Both these types of schools are new and rapidly changing institutions, where method and particular content count for less, and the knowledge and personality of the teacher count for more, than in the case of the elementary school. . . . Teachers trained by different methods, teachers teaching different types of classes and students, and teachers in small rural high schools and in large city high schools, all have different textbook needs."[10]

In his next paragraph Cubberley defined "improved textbooks" as those which "represent real advances in content or in the organization of subject matter."[11] No doubt his opinion of what constitutes textbook improvement reflected the feeling of conservatives like William C. Bagley. Nevertheless, the newer educational doctrines had become so widespread that Bagley's chapter, "The Textbook and Methods of Teaching," treated the way in which new teaching methods were likely to change the traditional use of the textbook. Bagley made these statements, even though he had little sympathy with the new educational doctrine:

"There is a general impression that the textbook very largely dominates classroom instruction in American schools. This impression remains in spite of the wide and increasing vogue of an educational theory which lays a minimum of emphasis upon the systematic mastery of knowledge and a maximum of emphasis upon the all-round growth and development of the individual, especially through meeting and solving the problems that arise in the course of his daily life. With the increasing acceptance of this theory, one would expect a lessening of the time given to the study and recitation of textbook materials and an increasing prevalence of activities, projects, laboratory work, and the like. In the mastery of such items of knowledge and skill as are still regarded as essential, one would expect that assignments and recitations based on textbook materials would by this time be giving place to one or another of the various types of self-instruction; and in subjects of instruction that lend themselves to group study and discussion, one would expect the class exercise to take with increasing frequency the form of the socialized recitation."[12]

A working definition of the text

Before considering the various "progressive" viewpoints regarding text materials, we should make clear the definition of texts employed by our own committee. Our committee has directed its work to the study of "text materials." The concept of the text has broadened greatly since the day of Noah Webster. Once there was no doubt that the text in any school would be a hardbound book to be followed by the teacher in regular order from front to end. In recent years, however, text*books* have been supplemented by a variety of other text materials. Workbooks were introduced to aid teaching of the study-and-recite type. Pamphlets (each constituting a text for a single unit), books of readings, laboratory manuals, and many other printed communications are used in place of or alongside the old sort of text. Sound motion pictures, recordings, wall charts, and other such devices are also fulfilling the functions of text materials.

In order to concentrate effectively, the present committee has restricted its interest to printed text materials of the sort which can be placed in the hands of every pupil. This permits us to side-step the problem of classroom films and problems of school libraries. Our definition does leave us as much interested in pamphlets and other novel sorts of texts which permit flexibility in curricula as in the conventional type of book. Indeed, one of the many questions that interests the committee is whether any of these newer forms of printed

[9] *Ibid.*, p. 177.
[10] Ellwood P. Cubberley, "The State Publication of Textbooks," in J. B. Edmonson and others, *op. cit.*, pp. 240-41.
[11] *Ibid.*, p. 241.

[12] William C. Bagley, "The Textbook and Methods of Teaching," in J. B. Edmonson and others, *op. cit.*, p. 7.

materials can make a major contribution to the American schools, possibly even replacing the conventional text*book* for some purposes. It will be obvious, however, that most previous research has been done on the bound, organized book, and this evidence must shape much of our thought. What distinguishes conventional textbooks from other published materials? If we examine what it has meant in the past to use a textbook, we might arrive at the following generalization.

The textbook is a textbook by virtue of the principles which control its selective organization of subject matter. (1) The materials must hang together in some way, and coherence is usually achieved in terms of an organized discipline. (Thus a text is a text in grammar, geology, geography, or some other "subject.") (2) Not all the information which exists in any one discipline can be presented in the text. Therefore, the writer seeks to incorporate the essentials; that is, to define basic concepts, statements, principles, and to explain and illustrate their application. (3) The text is usually written for immature learners. Therefore, the discipline must be simplified to whatever degree fits the intended learner. It is understood that texts written for more advanced learners will later present the same discipline with more precision. (4) Typically, the text is organized as a course of study, so that chapters are to be studied in sequence. Later chapters presuppose an acquaintance with earlier chapters.

Text materials having this character were suited to traditional schooling. If there is a genuine difference between traditional and modern schooling, then certain of the characteristics which made textbooks satisfactory for older schools make the same books unsatisfactory for newer schools. Deduction alone will not tell us *which* characteristics are no longer appropriate. We must examine specific doctrines as they have developed within our century to determine this.

Dissatisfaction of early progressivists with the traditional text

An impression has continued into the present day, shared alike by traditionalist and progressive, that reliance on a textbook is incompatible with modern educational doctrine. There must be a measure of truth in this impression, but just how much we can determine only by examining recent developments in education. We need to know how much of the opposition to the text inheres in the logic of modern doctrines and how much is a by-product of emotional reaction against every-

thing associated with traditional education. Two observations point to the need for such examination. (1) Our schools purchase and use more textbooks than ever before, in spite of the anti-text bias; this suggests that educators are finding texts compatible with their present ideas. And (2) we find that the fashionable doctrines of today differ from the doctrines of early progressivism. Possibly, therefore, the educator should seek new attitudes and new theories regarding the use of text materials. When John Dewey and his adherents led in the development of the doctrines of progressive education a generation ago, they little questioned the value of knowledge to the pupil. They proposed that the student learn more, rather than less, of the knowledge which the traditional school had attempted to transmit through the traditional textbook. ". . . We expect to get *more* subject matter, better thoroughness and organization, and *besides* to build better minds, richer and finer interests, finer personality adjustments, and better moral character." (italics ours)[13] As the learner in this program matured, he would perforce learn increasingly from printed materials organized in disciplines, much as he had been expected to learn in the traditional school. Thus, after pointing out that the first step in teaching method is to find "the material for learning within experience (of the learner)," Dewey says: "The next step is the progressive development of what is already experienced (by the learner) into a fuller and richer and also more organized form, a form that gradually approximates that in which subject matter is presented to the skilled, mature person."[14]

Early progressivism was therefore not an attempt to discard the intellectual part of our cultural heritage. Neither was it an attempt to free the scholar from the need to consult and read printed materials. It was in part a reform in aims: the progressive wanted to use the intellectual aspects of the cultural heritage, but he wanted to select from it and modify it, not be buried by it. The progressive reform was largely a reform in methods. These were the reforms that led to severe criticism of the textbook as then known.

The new methods were trying to develop learning on the basis of personal experience. To learn from thinking about experience required that the learner try to solve problems which were genuine to him. He had to solve his own problems rather than problems artificially constructed for him. It was argued that the only way for the learner to

---

[13] Kilpatrick, *op. cit.*, pp. 59-60.
[14] John Dewey, *Experience and Education*, p. 87. New York: MacMillan Co., 1938.

obtain problems of this sort was to engage him in vital activities wherein he would pursue personally held goals. Our readers are probably familiar enough with the general aspects of the *activity* school that no further description is needed here. It is important, however, to think about the inadequacies of the traditional text for problem-solving as Dewey defined it.

When a text is used as a course of study, self-enclosed, entire in itself, only chance matches the problems of the text with the personal problems of the student. For the purposes of progressive learning by personal experience, the selection and treatment of teaching materials is dictated by the demands of the student. But the traditional text is logically organized and is designed to fit a mass market. This material cannot be printed in some other order which would fit more closely the requirements of each individual pupil. This was one criticism of the text. A second criticism was that writers tended to oversimplify the subject they presented. The immature learner often came away with false understandings and verbalisms. The third criticism was that the text frequently presented its material in such a way as to enshrine its subject matter. It endowed it with a finished perfection and an unchangeable rightness, with a character of final truth that might stifle further examination on the part of the student. Having learned a polished statement of truth, the student would then tend not to readjust or qualify it as he acquired new experience. A fourth of the faults that made the preorganized text unsuited to the teaching by problem-solving was that it did not teach the student to select materials. The traditional textbook was intended to be accepted in its entirety. In the progressive conception of problem-solving, the pupil should learn to select and reject materials from culture. Reference materials would serve better because they have to be selected; the pupil would have to decide whether they could help him in reaching a solution to his problem. The textbook writer, however, performs whatever selection and rejection is needed, and the student has only to learn what the writer puts before him. If learning is supposed to help people solve the problems of their lives, the progressives would argue that they must learn in connection with the problems of their lives. If the learner sees the text as an arbitrarily imposed study requirement, he does not discover that its content really helps him in living. Thus teaching in school becomes a useless formality.

These arguments were so clear that they might have led to the adoption of a new type of text. The problem-solving method of education would have replaced the textbook with collections of reference materials—books, periodicals, pamphlets, etc. From this collection the learners would locate the information their problems required. The teacher would then face a new problem: how to effectively present ideas and information when they are not organized into a text. Furthermore, how and when could a transition be made from a random sampling of various kinds of useful knowledge to the study of knowledge within a discipline? For, as Dewey emphasized, the logical systems and meanings—the disciplines—which organize the resources of a culture are essential to the full understanding in any field.

The return to subject matter

These further stages in a sophisticated program of education for problem-solving never appeared. Instead, early progressivism came to be replaced by an increasing concern about course content. This new concern is clearly represented in two popular contemporary doctrines, "life adjustment" education and "social reconstructionism." Advocates of these doctrines are trying to develop curricula which will promote the learning of certain attitudes, skills, and kinds of knowledge which the proponents believe to have special importance.

Proposals under the name of life adjustment would draw topics for study from a list of problems both personal and social which are known to be recurrent in our society. A unit of study would be constructed for each problem, and each unit would be placed in a planned sequence or course of study. The student would have placed before him selected source materials dealing with the unit. This would be as much a preplanned, preorganized course of study as any other type of subject curriculum. The unit would constitute the core of the school program. The special interests and needs of individual pupils would be met by additional courses, and some of these might be traditional courses in subjects. The social reconstructionist program resembles the program based on problems of life adjustment, save that its emphasis is upon the study of social, rather than personal, problems.

Neither of these programs is like the earlier problem-solving education proposed by Dewey. They employ a prearranged collection of text materials. In Dewey's proposed new method the student could not have followed a prearranged collection of materials. When students worked on their own problems, each one brought his unique curriculum and text with him. The organization of content came from the learning process, and the school provided relevant reference materials to help the pupil interpret and learn from his experience. The other programs find materials for learning not necessarily within the experience of the learner but in "standard" social and personal experience. The difference is that the progressives proposed a new method for teaching problem-solving as a *general* tool, whereas the new proposal was designed to modify and adapt the subject matter to the study of particular important problems. In this emphasis on subject matter the two contemporary doctrines of life adjustment and social reconstructionism are more traditional than early progressivism.

Many characteristics of the traditional textbook are therefore appropriate for use even under the most recent educational doctrines. For if a program of study can be preplanned, the materials preselected and preorganized, then the teacher and student should be able to use a textbook. We should note further that under the most extreme pupil-centered educational program it is still conceivable that organized texts can be used . . . .

The life adjustment program would have to alter texts in one major respect. Materials of learning have been organized around subjects or disciplines. The reform doctrines suggest that the material be organized around life problems. Thereby, the textbook would lose the start-to-finish logical organization that characterizes traditional textbooks.

Even though textbooks could logically be accepted in the curriculum most widely advocated today, the bias against textbooks continues. Possibly educators do not realize the extent to which the contemporary curriculum concepts differ from those of the early progressives. Individual educators accept a collection of ideas and slogans which mix the contributions of early, intermediate, and late progressivism. These jumbled combinations lead to the erroneous but widely held conviction that learning from a textbook is inconsistent with "modern education."

Concepts of learning opposed to the text

The psychologists, among whom Dewey was one, have suggested two aspects of learning which raise questions about the use of the text. These writers discuss possibilities of learning from experience and creative learning, or learning by creative discovery. These views were considered in Dewey's early proposal regarding problem-solving, but they have not been carefully considered in the new doctrines such as life adjustment and social reconstructionism.

Learning from experience. "If one attempts to formulate the philosophy of education implicit in the practices of the newer education, we may, I think, discover certain common principles amid the variety of progressive schools now existing. To imposition from above is opposed expression and cultivation of individuality; to external discipline is opposed free activity; to learning from texts and teachers, learning through experience. . . ."[15]

It is regrettable that some statements, such as this one by Dewey, are interpreted literally. Some educators have thought that Dewey meant that learning from a book is not a way of learning through experience. Dewey could not have meant to say that the text has no place in the "newer" education; to read a book is undoubtedly an experience. We should therefore inquire what Dewey and those educators who attempted to follow him might have meant when they set learning from books in contrast to learning from other experience.

Two related theses which are true to some degree state the possible inadequacy of experience derived from books. (1) A learner can interpret a symbol in books only by projecting his own experience into it. The learner cannot give meaning to what he cannot connect with his own experience, to what he cannot "realize." How can we groundlings, for instance, no matter what we read, know what it feels like to fly a jet plane faster than sound? (2) The learner does not adopt an idea and use it in making further interpretations unless he goes beyond mere reading of it. It is only when he tries to use its meanings in real activities that he finds it functional and really learns it.

These statements do make a legitimate complaint against the way in which text materials have often been used. The teacher and the textbook writer may presuppose that the learner has a background which he simply does not have. Classroom activities ought to help provide the learner with the necessary background for understanding a symbolic communication. If the book is studied as a collection of words, apart from corresponding overt physical activities, the student loses an important type of experience. It is also true that in the traditional school the learner has frequently found little resemblance between the world about which he reads and the one in which he lives. The course content is remote, or it speaks of nearby events in abstract ways that have no significance to him. Then the content of

[15] *Ibid.*, p. 5.

learning is meaningful to the learner only because it helps him satisfy the requirements of the school, and he never thinks to use it outside the school. In overt activities the student could use what he learns from books and thus make his reading a deeper kind of experience.

Sound criticism this, but it gives neither grounds for discarding texts nor support to the confused idea that learning from books is not a part of learning from experience. The attention of both the theorist and educator should be directed to the problem of how the learner can better use the experience of others to enrich his own store of knowledge and experience and thus become a better problem-solver.

Creative learning, or learning by discovery. "Learning is increasingly seen as creative of its own subject matter, not simply an acquisition of what was already there."[16]

This belief has contributed to the sentiment against textbooks, for it suggests to some that the textbook simply passes on the ideas of the past and thereby stifles the independent thinking and latent creativity of young people. There is some measure of justice in this feeling. It cannot be denied, as we have pointed out before, that some textbooks have been written so as to suggest that the content is endowed with an unquestionable perfection. To what extent this criticism applies to current textbooks can be determined only by investigation.

One should be cautious in criticizing the text for having an authoritative tone. Many textbooks, especially in science, *are* authoritative presentations of the most reliable and most rigorous knowledge in our culture. What is meant, then, when it is said that learning is a creative act? What do we mean when we encourage the learner to criticize rather than passively accept knowledge? Does this suggestion mean that the learner should develop his ideas by himself, using none of the resources of his culture? As we have seen, this would be an eminently Rousseauean position, and an impossible one. It violates our whole knowledge of the nature of civilization and its value. Some educators seem to believe that one cannot learn from communication with others. They could not hold such views deliberately, yet only this sort of belief could support a bias against ever using text materials in education.

Considered further, perhaps the phrase "creative learning" implies that culture can limit, as well as facilitate, the process of thinking. This

would not lead us to reject the textbook as a resource in education, but it might suggest that we use it only in the most appropriate ways. An attempt to avoid excessive reliance on cultural traditions is especially found in art education. The customary technique is to permit the child to work in his own way, with a minimum of aid from models. It is felt that the child who becomes unduly aware of models will be unable to express himself, first because he will become excessively concerned with mechanics, and second because he will feel inadequate when he compares his own work with the models. In geometry a comparable technique would encourage the pupil to experiment with squares and triangles to see what principles he could intuitively discover. He probably will not discover anything unknown to Euclid, but he will gain a sense of the reasonableness of the discipline and a feeling that he can master geometry beyond a *memoriter* level.

This idea of creative learning makes new demands on the text. It implies that a premature organization of knowledge may make learning formalistic to the student. If he had learned to experiment with perspective for himself, he would understand it. If a text is his first introduction to perspective, he may be able to criticize perspective according to rule, without feeling the adequacy of a drawing or recognizing the merit of experimental or exotic art. To develop an undue respect for formalized knowledge may preclude mature creativity which goes beyond that knowledge. The learner should develop a respect for present principles as well as confidence and work methods which permit him to develop additional principles. He can acquire this if he has experience in creation throughout his entire training in an area.

Therefore, the textbook should be supplemented by, or make provision for, creative opportunities. Even in the most creative arts no one has proposed that the artist should be trained by being kept forever isolated from the discoveries of others. It is only proposed that the experience of others should be made known to him gradually and tentatively, so as not to let convention bind his thinking. The text inhibits creation when it advocates "the one best way"; it encourages creation when it organizes past experience so that the learner can grasp its values and limitations.

The phrase "creative learning" is also employed in another way: Effective problem-solving is creative. Any student is being creative when he works out the best course of action to take in solving a problem. This type of independently creative thinking deals with a specific, unique situation. One can only solve specific problems by using

---

[16] Kilpatrick, *op. cit.,* p. 18.

knowledge about the stable properties of people, objects, and relationships. The learner who is trying to solve a problem which has historic roots cannot "create" the history of his problem. He must learn it as it exists. If he fails to find out what others have stated about his situation, he is being unintelligent. Communication with others teaches about the characteristics of the world. The more one acquires of that knowledge, the better able he is to solve his particular problems. A careful assessment of the value of knowledge in creative learning must lead the educator to more, not less, reliance upon the textbook as a medium of instruction.

The doctrine of learning by creative discovery contends that the learner can only acquire an idea through his own insight. The Gestalt psychologists argue that learning is a process of sudden insights or reorganizations.[17] Philosophers assert that ideas are noncommunicable. An idea may or may not be an idea when it is communicated to a second person, depending upon whether that second person can use it in his thinking. The receptor, not the communicator, determines whether a communication becomes an idea; unless the receptor can enmesh the new symbols with the ideas he already has, they never become an idea for him.

These views do not, however, oppose the use of the text. Insight is the process of reorganizing and reinterpreting materials which the learner encounters. The textbook could supply suitable materials for use in this reorganization. The learner must discover for himself what the world means; but the textbook can help him in arriving at his interpretation. The questions raised in the name of "creative learning" are questions as to the best way to use text materials in school.

---

[17] George Katona, *Organizing and Memorizing*. New York: Columbia University Press, 1940. Max Wertheimer, *Productive Thinking*. New York: Harper & Bros., 1945.

Evaluation of criticisms

This [reading] has examined the opposition to the text. Dissatisfaction with the textbook because it is conservative does not provide a reason for discarding it. It would be unrealistic and detrimental to discard what the past has learned. Even a reconstructionist trying to build a better society can learn from the experience of the past. The related doctrine that one should learn by his own discovery is similarly rejected if it is taken to mean that each child must create a new culture for himself. Most of the opposition to the textbook has been critical of particular methods of textbook education and therefore offers no final judgment that the textbook should be eliminated. Each of the criticisms, no matter what its origin, points toward modifications of the text and its use, not to its abolition.

Of all the opposition to the text, only the program originally espoused by Dewey, in which learning was to rise from the daily experience of the child, is incompatible with major reliance on the preorganized textbook. Even in an activity program the defect of the text lies in its preorganization rather than in the fact that printed materials are unsuitable for instruction.

What text materials are like and how they are used are determined by the way schools are organized and operating. When proposals are made for changing the schools, old ideas and new ideas are combined in some way to arrive at an actual method of teaching. In the recent past, a tendency wholly to disparage the text was a by-product of attempts to modify and improve the curriculum. But the fact that there is bias against the text even when use of the text is consistent with the philosophical proposals of the attackers indicates that we have not learned how to prepare and use text materials. . . .

59

James B. Palmer

IN DEFENSE OF TEXTBOOKS

How can teachers make the best use of textbooks? How can one determine which textbook is best to use in a given course? These questions are in part answered here by an established editor and publisher of books, a man who earlier in his career was a high-school biology teacher, a secondary-school supervisor, and then a college professor of education. Here at last is a topic which every student may scrutinize with the critical eye of his own experience!

An increasing amount of criticism is being lodged against textbooks. On some occasions, the attack reaches the point where one is stimulated to ask for a reconsideration, a general stock taking, in order to determine just what the fundamental purpose of textbooks may be. "Attack" is not too strong a word, because the professional zeal of theorists often leads to exaggerated statements or a disproportionate emphasis upon exceptional situations. Perhaps such statements are necessary since conventional practices and lackadaisical ways of thinking require quite a jolt if they are to be improved or set aside. But the elements in the situation are too often distorted, and at times the basic difficulties are not brought to light. Such a state of affairs might be deplorable, were it not for the fact that the destructive criticism is ordinarily made in good spirit and undue criticism is perhaps more wholesome than none.

First of all, what do we mean by the term "textbook"? A textbook is merely a book adapted to the purposes of learning. There is no set form. The varieties are many. Some textbooks are little more than books of texts, that is, mere points of departure for the learner or for the teacher. Many textbooks used to be of this type. Others, such as foreign-language texts, are convenient collections of readings with suitable helps, such as exercises and vocabularies. Others, such as histories, may be well-balanced narratives, precisely like the lectures that a teacher would deliver, if he were teaching by the lecture method alone. Still others, such as science books, are comprehensive treatments of the subject matter, including explanations of important concepts and suggestions for investigation and further study. These characteristics and others indicate the forms or combination of forms that are now prevalent.

Let us point out the obvious, namely, that textbooks should not be the whole course of instruction. If instruction in schools is to be vital, it must be interlaced with the life of children in and out of schools. Books are only means to an end, at most, guides to the understanding of realities. The more of personal experience, of oral and written expressions, of visual aids, and of printed materials other than texts that can be included in school work, the better for all concerned. Such procedures may constitute the entire program in some courses, a large portion of it in many other courses, but only a limited amount of it in some others, depending upon the purpose of the instruction and upon the circumstances that are inherent in our program of mass education.

There is little reason to attempt to defend the abuse of textbooks, if indeed any defense be possible. Explanations are easily found in unfortunate situations, but after all, they are explanations, not justifications. Such transgressions as an inordinate amount of memoriter learning, a spoon-feeding of so many lines of a particular book each day, or a non-thinking, mechanical consideration of the materials in the textbook are generally due to poor teaching or to arduous conditions. Serious shortcomings of the teaching procedures or of the learning situations cannot be made up entirely by any books now available, but examples might be given to show that the use of good books has reduced the handicaps that children would have suffered otherwise.

What, then, is the place of the textbook in instruction? We can say that a good textbook provides a rounded conception of the subject, in terms that pupils can understand, and that the content is organized in such a way as to be conducive to better teaching. Furthermore, good textbooks are systematic. They present in relief the basic principles and fundamental relationships which should be understood by the children. Textbooks serve, therefore, as the basal reference in a course of study, a core around which source material may be gathered and activities arranged. Presumably the textbook is a device to be used to advantage, not a panacea for educational ills. The unenlightened use of any device leads to inadequate or unfortunate results. But in the hands of a capable teacher, a certain increased efficiency of instruction may be obtained. The fact that there are unsatisfactory textbooks is beside the point. If all textbooks could be shown to be unsatisfactory in some degree, that fact would also be beside the point. The new textbooks are as good as the best teachers know how to make them, for it is the teachers who write the textbooks. In addition, it is ex-teachers chiefly who edit and publish them. Imperfections and perfections in textbooks reflect no more on the textbooks than the quality of instruction by other methods reflects on those methods.

Dissatisfaction with the textbook is a wholesome condition, if it leads to an improvement in this

From *Harvard Educational Review*, October 1937, 7:430-433.

universal aid to learning. Many advances have already been made; others are in the offing. Worthy of special note are the enrichment of content; the emphasis upon increased adaptation to pupils' mentality, their background of experience, educational status, and reading ability; the vast improvement in visual aids in the books; the abundance of suggestive helps for teaching and learning; and the realization by authors, publishers, teachers, and pupils, that the book is not the subject, but rather one well-ordered presentation of the content for the purpose of enhancing learning. There is reason to expect additional advances as authors become more proficient in their work. Certainly the alert staffs of publishing houses will continue to take advantage of new processes and better devices in printing and making books.

Are we, in truth, likely to discard the textbook? For example, can a new subject, like physical science, make much headway in the rank and file of secondary schools without a well-organized treatment of this recombination of material in book form? Or, where would the average pupil, in the average school, under the average teacher, obtain from a year's study of world history a basic understanding of the story of civilization, if there were no books that could be used as textbooks (or basal reference books) in the course? Such examples affect the schools not only as they are, but as they are to be. Textbooks are essentially a practical device. What is needed is better books used more effectively.

Tirades against the abuse of textbooks are in good order. School procedures always tend to become overformalized to the point where the requisite vitality in the program is squeezed out. Moreover, prohibiting the use of textbooks in order to force teachers to find other resources or to catch up new combinations of content and procedure, may have some point in situations where the authorities can afford to engage in expensive experimentation. Considerable evidence at hand indicates, however, that the ideas of innovating, experimental schools and the fresh material accumulated in their programs may best reach the rank and file of classrooms through new and improved textbooks or similar aids to instruction. There is plenty of need for the milder form of experimentation in average school situations, but ordinarily it must deal with minor improvements in the content and in the procedure. Such refinements are easier to attain if the best of the products of experimental schools is used as a base. The busy teacher, eager to develop his charges to their fullest capacity, realizes the need of all sorts of assistance, particularly the well-planned, richly equipped, durably bound materials that the ablest educators have prepared for the purpose. They demand them ever increasingly; they use them ever more effectively. When the evidence is all in, is there anything more important than to supply better teachers with better books?

60

Gilbert Seldes

TELEVISION AND EDUCATION

Educational television, both of the broadcast and the closed-circuit variety, has received an immense amount of attention. Everyone agrees that it is important, but just *how* important has not been decided. Here a respected journalist and critic of the entertainment arts focuses upon the competition between educational and commercial television for control of the medium. He accepts it as a fact that a student can pass a course examination just as effectively by watching television courses in his own home as by spending the same amount of time in the classroom, indeed an immensely important fact if true.

Since Seldes wrote, educational television has undergone change, most of it being in the rapid improvement of technology. Still unanswered is the qualitative question of whether images, voices, and music on a screen have any clear-cut advantage over direct personal instruction.

. . . The value of television as an instrument of direct teaching has been demonstrated. Experiments using control groups have been made: the same lectures have been given, notably in a Canadian experiment, in the classroom, by radio and over television. The television students showed up at least as well as, and often better than, the others in comprehension and, tested again later, in retention. The Pittsburgh educational station put on a series of courses for students who had failed in an examination and nearly three-fourths of those who took the make-up exams passed them. There have been other experiments, and while the evidence is not conclusive, no negative evidence has yet been adduced.

Little is now known about the value of regular transmissions, after school hours, of programs centering on the curriculum. The "fact" at our disposal comes from simple experience: such programs are in direct competition with the entertainment programs transmitted at the same time, many of them produced specifically for children. And the existence of such competitive programs provides the background for speculation, since no facts exist, on the value of the educational television station as a cultural rather than a directly educational agent. For if television for education is to be considered in the context of our social life as a whole, the anti-cultural potential of commercial television must also be examined.

A closer look at direct educational broadcasting is needed. By the end of this year, twenty-five TV stations will be in operation. Many of them are incorporated into the educational systems of their States—Alabama, for instance, has a network of three stations created and supported by the State. Others have come into existence through local community effort, as in St. Louis, where the initial enthusiasm flagged after a few years of great promise. The only station on the Atlantic coast between the Canadian border and Miami is WGBH-TV, a creation of The Lowell Institute which had previously combined a dozen cultural institutions centering on Boston into a Broadcasting Council, beginning with an FM radio station; the colleges, museums and musical organizations involved contribute to the support of the station and the deficit has been made up by the parent Institute. The station in Pittsburgh supported itself for one year, to the extent of two-thirds of its operating expenses, by selling its monthly bulletin to its listeners (about 100,000 of them paid two dollars each, knowing it to be a contribution to operating costs).

One significant element in the history of educational stations is a technical one. Commercial broadcasting occurs almost entirely in that portion of the spectrum known as the Very High Frequency band and most receivers, of the 35 million now in use, are adjusted to these frequencies only. Most of the frequencies available to educational stations are, however, Ultra Highs. Their programs cannot be received unless a converter (costing about $30 at present) is attached to the VHF set. The successful educational stations are chiefly those which have been fortunate enough to get a VHF license. (At the time the allocations were made it was expected that all television would eventually move into the UHF band. In that area more stations can be accommodated, but the Federal Communications Commission lethargically permitted the growth of the restricted VHF system to such a point that a complete change-over now seems improbable.)

The above refers, of course, to public broadcasting. Closed-circuit use of television, by which classrooms are linked to the central studio and the signal does not go out on the air, is unaffected by frequencies. It has been widely used and is the system now undergoing the severest test—a 5-year project in a single county in Maryland. In other experiments, as in Pittsburgh and St. Louis, various techniques have been tried: the most important one will eventually give us the data we now lack for deciding whether the presence of a teacher in the classroom, while a broadcast is going on, is an essential element. In St. Louis it was found that "students in large-group television classes (100 to 150 pupils, without a teacher in attendance) in 9th grade English composition and 9th grade general science showed a degree of achievement at least equal to that of control classes, taught in the conventional manner." In Pittsburgh, the classes were of normal size and a teacher was present; progress was in some cases more and in some less than that of the control group. (It should be remembered that the control group was taught by long-tested methods, the experimental group by methods totally new to the teachers as well as to the students.) Other methods include a combination of television and correspondence courses (first-year algebra in Nebraska) and the broadcasting of the first half of a regular seminar, the members of which remained in the studio for further discussion after the program went off the air (WGBH in collaboration with Harvard—a public not a closed-circuit program).

From *Confluence*, 1957, 6:169-175.

One other factor should be mentioned: the Educational Television and Radio Center established by the Ford Foundation. Taking an almost timid view of its functions, the Center acts as an exchange or booking agent for educational stations and also commissions educational stations and other producing organizations to make educational films. In the latter capacity it is semi-creative, in the former it makes available to the "educational network" kinescope-films of programs put on by the member stations. The opportunity to experiment in the techniques of television education, to establish a genuine workshop in method, to study the basic problems and correct the errors of stations which have to provide immediate programs, has however not been grasped. In the spring of 1957, the Center cooperated with the National Broadcasting Company in the preparation of a series of programs which the network fed, over its coaxial cable, to educational stations and also used on some of its own outlets. The programs were not uniformly impressive. They did, however, serve to illuminate many of the problems of educational television. . . .

61

Donald Cook

PROGRAMED LEARNING: A REVOLUTION IN INSTRUCTION

Automation is not confined to factories and clerical offices. Its shadow falls darkly over the classroom as well. Here Dr. Cook, Director of Programming for Basic Systems, Inc., explains how these teaching machines will be servants, not masters, of the teacher.

Experts like Cook greatly prefer "programed learning" to the less accurate phrase "teaching machines." Their attitude toward teaching springs from psychology and science rather than from tradition or subject matter. They expect to change some textbooks and some study procedures, not teaching in the classroom.

The work of scholars is transforming the world with increasing rapidity, but the transmission of learning itself has not changed appreciably for such a long time that educated people themselves may be surprised at the possibility of radically altering the teaching process. Since the introduction of movable type in the 15th century, the many developments relevant to education—the power press, typesetting devices, and the more recent proliferation of "audio-visual" inventions—have all been refinements of the basic principle of the storage and presentation of information. But the behavior of the student—the nature and course of his contact with that information—has for better or for worse remained the province of the individual instructor. For books, films, and records are passive agents, which make no pro-vision for the active engagement of the student, and their uncritical use under the pressures of mass education may at times dilute the process of learning.

New approaches

But within the last six years a new development has occurred whose effects are now gathering increasing momentum. The development is based upon a fundamental modification in methods of instruction, which takes account of the findings and methods of modern experimental psychology and is aimed directly at the interaction of the learner's behavior with the subject-matter of the course. The basis for this new approach—let us call it *programed learning*—was set down by Harvard's experimental psychologist B. F. Skinner, in a paper entitled "The Science of Learning and the Art of Teaching," published in the *Harvard Educational Review* (Spring, 1954). This paper

From *Graduate Faculties Newsletter,* Columbia University, November 1960.

undertakes three tasks: to analyze the conditions under which effective learning occurs, to sketch a method of curriculum design which would take advantage of these conditions, and to describe the technical means by which such a curriculum could be put to use.

Everything we know about the nature of learning suggests the importance of the following conditions: (1) the active participation of the students must be enlisted at each step along the way; (2) the material must be arranged and presented in a rational and cumulative sequence; (3) swift and effective tutorial appraisal must reply to each step the student masters.

Problems and programs

The principles, stated informally and without the technical documentation of research, are hardly more than a re-phrasing of the precepts of Comenius, whose *Didactica Magna* was published in the 17th Century. Yet how rarely are they approximated! Mark Hopkins at one end of a log and a student at the other is still perhaps the closest approximation to such ideal conditions. The usual classroom, in which the teacher is responsible for say thirty students, is hardly suited to their realization. By an iron law, the greater the attempt to engage the behavior of the students through tests and exercises, the more time must be spent in the drudgery of correcting papers. At its very best, the time lapse between a student's effort and the teacher's confirmation or correction is still too long for maximal effect. Teaching in groups leads to compromises in presentation, group standards, bargaining relations with students, and the other ailments so familiar to student and teacher alike.

Skinner's solution is, in a word, to automate education. Instruction takes place through a program, in which the student participates in the following instructional cycle: (1) he *reads a small unit* of information (exposition, definition, or example) which calls for a response on his part— by way of answer to a question; (2) he *composes a response*—for example, by filling in a blank or labeling a diagram; (3) he is *informed of the correct answer* while the relevant material and his answers are still in view; (4) he then advances the program to the next step.

Gadgets and devices

Such a method can be closely approximated by an ordered series of index cards whose front frame carries the instructional material and question, and whose reverse frame carries the answer. Instead of a text, the student works through a stack of cards. In fact, Skinner, and by now many others, have built a variety of mechanical devices to present the program, and these have several advantages. (These devices have been given many names; among them are: self-instructors, self-tutors, learning cyclers, and—the most widespread term, and also the one which has horrified the most people—teaching machines). Such devices, which can be simply built and are about the size of a portable phonograph, have several windows and a handle, and house the instructional program on a long paper roll. The student reads the single exposed frame, writes his answer on the movable paper through an open window, then advances the program. The correct answer appears to view. In some models, the student's response moves under a window so that it cannot be altered. Certain other specialized models will not advance the program if the answer is wrong, while others, yet more specialized, shunt the student into special remedial programs if the answer is wrong. In many versions of the machine, an automatic tally is kept of right and wrong answers.

It is an ironic characteristic of the American temperament that it exhibits uncritical fascination with the very gadgets which horrify its sensibilities, and for a time it seemed as if there were to be more types of "teaching machine" available—including commercial models—than usable programs. But the program is, of course, the thing; and the observer of programing research and development over the past several years has seen a number of extraordinary implications gradually take shape. In order of decreasing obviousness, they may be put somewhat as follows:

Programed learning *does* provide immediate return for the student at each step of the way. He knows where he stands at all times, and quickly enough for the appraisal to affect the behavior that produced it—rather than being merely a "mark" to boast about or haggle over.

The complete instructional cycle—material, question, answer, appraisal—can take place dozens or even *a hundred or more times an hour*, in a process in which teaching and testing are blended into one seamless process. The teacher, freed from drudgery, can turn attention to the worthier functions of discussion, conference, preceptorial —and on a more individualized basis.

The student proceeds at his own best rate. The dull student goes more slowly, with lessened shame or anxiety, while the bright student is not held back. An objective criterion—mastery of the program—is again applicable to all, for each to attain in his own time. If a student is ill, he does not fall behind; and if he moves from one school to another, he takes his program with him.

The possibilities so far listed were envisaged as long ago as 1924 by the psychologist S. L. Pressey, who built and experimented with the first automatic testing machines, which would, he added—almost as an afterthought—"teach informational and drill material more efficiently, in certain respects, than 'the human machine.'" Perhaps due to the emphasis on testing (as well as other reasons), neither Pressey nor the world saw some further implications which have become clear more recently. Let us continue:

What about mistakes? If they are recorded on the program, a teacher can inspect his record before a conference with the student, and thus *know* what the difficulty is in each particular case. Initiative in the teaching relation is thus returned to the teacher, who need not probe at random to discover the student's difficulty.

If a given section of a program generates errors in many students, *there is something wrong with the program.* It can be corrected by rewriting the frames or inserting additional frames to "thin out" the material. Thus the very device which provides feedback to the student, also provides feedback to the instructor. Perhaps the most exciting implication of programed learning is its effect on the product of education—knowledge itself. *For the first time a means is available to produce permanent records of behavior in interaction with instruction and, it is clear, a repository of instructional culture will rapidly develop.* Open to modification on a trial and error basis, with "storage" of the results of these variations, the evolution of programs will be extremely swift. The prospect opens up that as knowledge grows, instructional methods will develop apace. Such records will constitute a library for the educator, both of his own subject matter and of the cultural process of its communication. Exposed to instructional achievement in his field, and aware of a medium for its communication, he will be motivated to contribute variations and improvements. The sophisticated mastery of educational skills may take a great leap upwards.

If programing can evolve into a powerful technique, one of the specific consequences may be that a student can work through a program to mastery with a minimum of errors—in the limiting case, none. To proclaim such an ideal is disturbing to many, especially if their own education has been hard won, but it is a possibility with several points to recommend it. Studies of many kinds have shown that the best students are also the most rapid learners, make the fewest mistakes, and retain their skills the most securely. Apparently mistakes and suffering are not now at the heart of effective education. It must be emphasized that a possible science of programing only *begins* with a specification of the material to be learned. Programing entails not only "breaking material into small steps," but also applying principles of behavior to the design of the sequence of steps. We want to make sure that the student eventually makes the right response for the right reasons—has not learned by rote, will not misapply general rules, and so on—but the process of building this effective repertoire represents an untouched frontier. Early research in this area has already uncovered a number of exciting leads, and they are of interest not merely to program technicians. The step-by-step analysis of the process of dialectical development which grows out of constructing 10,000 frames for a one-semester course may be of interest to philosophers as well. . . .

From all this a number of issues emerge which may appear novel, but are all of long-standing interest.

The possibilities

There is no doubt that programed learning is effective. It breaks open the bottleneck of the student-teacher ratio which is of such critical dimensions in education today. Traditional humanists express concern which seems to blend the prophecy that "it won't work" with the fear that it will. Nobody expects teachers to be replaced, yet there is uncertainty as to how their roles may be altered in the new situation. The evidence so far is that effective programing makes for *more* creative students, and the teacher may rightly suspect that his status-giving control over his subject may be challenged. The sober evaluation of the limits and optimal conditions governing the place of programed learning awaits careful research.

Certainly a revolution is taking place in the relation between the *creation* of learning and its *dissemination* to "consumers." It is conceivable that more efficient methods of dissemination may allow a natural hierarchy of function to reestablish itself, with beneficial results in all quarters of the educational enterprise—knowing, discovering, teaching, and learning.

62

Lawrence M. Stolurow

TEACHING MACHINES AND EDUCATION

Here Professor Stolurow offers us a kind of science-fiction peek into the schools of the future, as the educational engineers of automation technology imagine them. Automated study halls, pocket-size homework, and identification plates are among the more striking possibilities. One thing which seems to have receded into the background is the personal impact of the teacher upon the individual student.

Left unanswered are some perplexing questions. Will teaching-machine exercises really interest pupils? Will they be considered dreary catechisms or fascinating puzzle-games by the student of tomorrow? And again, are teaching machines equally useful and stimulating for both slow and fast learners? The testing of various theories in the laboratory of the classroom may help to resolve these important issues.

Teaching machines appear to be here to stay. They have many important implications for the future of education, some related to the teaching process and the teacher, others to the school as an organization (including its personnel and physical facilities), still others to the effects upon students.

Teaching

Teaching machines may eventually provide the basic data for a new theory of teaching, the missing counterpart of the theory of learning. It is anticipated that the machine, as a controlling device, will serve to eliminate the effects of extraneous variables and permit the identification of basic variables and their interrelationships. In effect, the teaching machine is an educational laboratory. It can do for education what physics, chemistry, and psychology laboratories, for example, have done for their areas. The variables of interest can be manipulated in a rigorous way, conditions can be standardized, etc. The machine can provide information about methods of teaching free of uncontrolled variations due to differ-

ences among teachers. Once the basic variables in the instructional process are identified, they can be studied in relation to social and personality factors.

The teaching machine seems to be a major breakthrough in education comparable to the book, radio, and television. Its potentiality needs to be explored and efficient and effective means devised for making it available. It can maintain the optimum conditions of communication and control considered essential in modern learning theory. Although mass media communicate effectively, they do not control; they are "open loop" systems. This means that for rapid modification of the learner's behavior systems they lack the critical feedback ingredient. The teaching machine, on the other hand, is a closed loop system which does provide feedback.

Skinner (1954) indicated that one of the most serious criticisms of today's classrooms is the relative infrequency of reinforcement. Many students, he points out, are dependent upon one teacher for knowledge of results; consequently, the total number of opportunities for the teacher to reinforce knowledge is quite limited. One of the places where these inefficiencies reveal themselves most dramatically is in so-called drill subjects like arithmetic; children typically fail to learn arithmetic quickly and never do achieve a high level of confidence in their knowledge and/or skill (Skinner, 1954). Skinner also points out that with current methods of instruction the symbols

From *Teaching by Machine* by Lawrence M. Stolurow. Cooperative Research Monograph No. 6 (Washington, D.C.: U. S. Department of Health, Education, and Welfare, 1961), pp. 145-150.

of mathematics have become standard emotion-provoking stimuli. The teacher is usually no happier about this than the student and is inclined to avoid the drill subjects to talk about material of greater inherent interest. Skinner asks why the classroom should be less automated than the family kitchen.

Fry (1959) has reinforced the statements of Skinner and has pointed out some of the prime difficulties of current teaching aids such as motion pictures. Neither the rate of presentation nor the amount of repetition is varied to suit the individual's needs; they are not adaptive. Particularly since these devices are used with groups they also must be too slow for the fast student and too fast for the slow one. Fry agrees with Skinner that the teacher has been outmoded as a device for rewarding the learner, but in his view there is no danger of the teacher's being replaced by teaching machines, for although some subjects might be taught better by machine than by a live teacher, there are other subjects which the classroom teacher can present much more effectively.

Fry points out the implications of teaching machines for progressive education. The machine not only substitutes reward for punishment as a main incentive, but it also requires student participation and elicits mental activity. The machine is exceedingly versatile; the program can be designed to fit the most rigid requirements of the conservative educator who stresses "mental discipline"; it can be either factual or thought provoking; it can include logic or rote drill.

Fry also indicates the implications which teaching machines have for objective research in education. They allow for more convenient investigation of method problems at different stages of the development of the programs. Furthermore, the data collected tend to be freer of the variations produced by different teachers, and thus a more precise check on the effectiveness of the variables can be obtained.

Blyth (1960) has pointed out an additional contribution of the teaching machine as a means of achieving more adequately than possible heretofore the democratic ideal in education. The machine has equal patience for fast and slow learners. It responds in the same way to the poor and the rich, to all races, creeds, and religious groups. Furthermore, with mass production techniques, it could extend education to illiterates and outlying groups who otherwise might not have the benefit of education. While increasing the efficiency of instruction it could also make it more economical.

Teacher

As early as 1926 Pressey pointed out that education was at present the most inefficiently carried on of any large-scale undertaking in this country (p. 376). This, in his view, was due largely to a cultural barrier which prohibits the application of modern technology to the teacher's problems. Conservatism in the profession and the fact that teachers were relatively cheap were said to be contributing factors. In his view the introduction of automation devices would free the teacher for ". . . her most important work, her developing in her pupils fine enthusiasms, clear thinking and high ideals" (p. 376). In a later paper Pressey, (1932, p. 672) points out that labor saving is not only legitimate in education but it also may become an economic necessity. Since education is a large-scale industry, it should use quantity production methods. By this he did not mean the mechanization of education but rather the freeing of the teacher from clerical duties and drudgeries to enable him to give his students more adequate guidance in learning.

Teaching machines are not devices for eliminating the teacher (e.g., Barlow, 1960); rather they are a way of implementing his instruction and of multiplying its effectiveness. They take some of the drudgery out of the teacher's job; for while the teacher is still the responsible planner of the learner's instruction, he is no longer tied to the specific detail of instruction and drill. This routine aspect of his job can now be carried out by machine. The machine, in this way, allows the human teacher to plan and determine individual needs (e.g., Blyth, 1960; Skinner, 1954; Stolurow, 1960 a and b). He can develop new and more efficient methods of instruction and can keep the content of the course up to date. He can plan programs to meet individual needs and spend more time getting to know his students and his subject matter.

School

Ramo (1957) has probably been the most imaginative in conjecturing about the impact of teaching machines on the future of education with respect to its physical plant and management procedures. In the school of the future, as Ramo sees it, the child would possess a "charge-a-plate" identification unit which would be inserted in a machine to identify him and to locate his records throughout his educational development. The typical schoolday would consist of a number of periods spent, as now, in rooms with other students and a teacher; however, some periods would be spent with the machine. The machines might or might not be attended by a human operator, depending upon the particular needs of the student or the inadequacy of the machines. Even in the classroom learning situation, which would involve not only a human teacher but also motion pictures and television, there would be programed questions which would require the student to respond by pushing various keys (e.g., Carpenter *et al,* 1950). In this way a student would always be an active participating learner rather than a passive receiver of information and with a machine would be constantly in touch with the teacher.

When the student is alone in front of a machine-tutor he is equipped with controls that permit him to see animated films and other aids which should contribute to his learning. In such an ideal situation, he is completely on his own and can pace the material at whatever rate he chooses. In this situation, as in the classroom of the future, he is constantly required to respond to questions. The machine is prepared to take a principle and go over it from time to time, with altered presentation and additional detail, as required, and even possibly to switch to alternative methods of presentation, all available in its library upon request. Ramo envisions all of this to be backed up by a whole new industry.

Staff.   With respect to school personnel, this revolution in education would mean that high school teaching staffs would include educational analysts, specializing in various subjects, who would review student records on an individual basis. They would be constantly seeking to discover problems and needs for special attention through direct contact with teacher and pupil. They would diagnose information and difficulties and make recommendations for improvement. Thus the school would become partially transformed into a guidance center with a minimum of routine assigned to the teaching staff. The staff member, as a consequence, would be elevated to the role of thinker and planner, using his highest intelligence and skills. Teachers would provide the essential educational functions. Ramo envisions a new type of educational specialist, the "teaching engineer," an engineer concerned with educational process and with the design of machines as well as with the design and programing of instructional materials, a person for whom knowledge of computer operation and programing would be essential.

With respect to the school changes, Fry (1959) indicates that an automated studyhall or library is likely to be an important part of the school of the future, just as the chemistry laboratory, the machine shop, etc., are important components of today's schools. The student would be likely to carry home a small machine, at least a punchboard, to do his homework since it is a convenient pocket size and more effective for teaching. The textbook might be different, too, perhaps a programed text, cut-back page programed book with separate answer sheets, or a scrambled textbook ("Tutor Text").

Student.   The student of the future is hard to imagine. Since the industrial revolution, man seems to have learned to live with and derive benefit and pleasure from a wide assortment of machines; the need to learn to use different types of machines seems to be accelerating. A new profession, that of the human engineer, has developed to meet the challenges of this need. It is the human engineer's job to work with the hardware engineer at the design stage so as to make the demands upon the operator and the maintenance personnel minimal; thus machines are not designed to require three arms, or eyes in the back of one's head. Similarly, the teaching machine will be designed to be used by students. The demands made upon the student will be minimal and determined by educational objectives, e.g., the need to learn to write.

If machines are widely used, the student may learn to study by himself and to play and work with others; thus an important separation will be achieved. After all, what symphony was written by a group? What scientific theory was the product of a group? While groups have a very important place and students need to learn to get along with others, one might ask whether this should be done in the same setting as the learning of mathematics, chemistry, etc. Might it not be better for the student to study alone and to use what he has learned in a group setting?

Fad or fixture

Many educators wonder whether these machines are just an educational fad. The answer to this question is obviously a matter of opinion and not one of fact, since evidence will have to be accumulated for several years to come. Certain facts argue for the possibility that teaching machines might be more of a fixture than a fad. Not all mediums of education are equivalent; the machine has certain advantages over a book. It is the most controlled of all teaching conditions; and it is designed, when properly accomplished, to take the learner from a state of lack of knowledge to full knowledge in such a way as to suit his individual needs. A conventional textbook does not always do this. In fact in serving several purposes, or masters, it must compromise each to satisfy all. The book is efficient for storing and making conveniently available large amounts of information; it has primarily a storage function and an access function. While it can be prepared so as to perform a fairly efficient teaching function as well, doing this appears to make less efficient use of space, and the result is a bulky and cumbersome device; then it is no longer performing the storage and access functions so efficiently. The teaching machine, on the other hand, serves a single purpose: teaching.

Most mass media suffer from their failure to make specific cues and responses clear (display function). In their typical format they do not require overt response; this is associated with the deficiency of eliminating the feedback loop, which informs the learner of his own progress. The teaching machine, on the other hand, displays one item of information at a time and makes salient the critical cues. Also, if the learner fails to understand a point, he can repeat it before going on. The machine also requires or makes almost mandatory some form of response before correct answers are supplied. With a teaching machine, the learner is in control, in that his responses determine what he does next within the preplanned limits of the program; thus there is feedback and adjustment of the learning situation to the needs of the individual.

Not all media are equivalent for educational purposes; they are designed to serve many functions besides that of education. The teaching machine, on the other hand, is designed specifically to teach. It introduces controlled communication, which the other available media do not.

Thus it appears to be a potential fixture in the education system and not just a fad. Its problems are those attendant upon anything new; it takes time to learn how to derive maximum benefit from its use with minimum difficulty in programing.

References

Barlow, J. A. Project Tutor. *Psychological Reports*, 6:15-20, 1960.

Blyth, J. W. Teaching Machines and Human Beings. Paper presented at the 1959 annual meeting of American Council of Education, *The Educational Record*, 1960.

Carpenter, C. R., *et al. The Classroom Communicator*. Special Devices Center, Office of Naval Research, Port Washington, Long Island, N.Y., Technical Report SDC 269-7-14. October 1950.

Fry, E. B. Teaching Machines: The Coming Automation. *The Phi Delta Kappan*, 41:28-31, October 1959.

Pressey, S. L. A Simple Apparatus Which Gives Tests and Scores—and Teaches. *School and Society*, 23:373-376, 1926.

Pressey, S. L. A Third and Fourth Contribution Toward the Coming "Industrial Revolution" in Education. *School and Society*, 36:668-672, 1932.

Ramo, S. A. New Technique of Education. Institute of Radio Engineers Transaction on Education, E-1, 37-42 1958; also published in *Engineering and Science Monthly*, 21:17-22, October 1957.

Skinner, B. F. Science of Learning and the Art of Teaching. *Harvard Educational Review*, 24:86-97, 1954.

Stolurow, L. M. Teaching Machines and Special Education. *Educational and Psychological Measurement*, 20:429-448, 1960. (a)

Stolurow, L. M. Automation in Special Education. *Exceptional Child*, 27:78-83, 1960. (b)

63

George F. Kneller

A CRITICAL ANALYSIS OF TECHNOLOGY IN EDUCATION

There is an almost instinctive suspicion of machines deeply ingrained in most of us, which comes easily to the surface. As long ago as 1879 the editor of the *New Englander* wrote: "Modern education has made immense progress in its methods and appliances. . . . The perils to which it is exposed proceed from an excessive faith in method and machinery, and in what is called the science of teaching, to the neglect and dishonor of that skill which can give teaching efficiency and success."

The remarks of Professor Kneller of U.C.L.A. reflect the position of a critical analyst, and they are especially interesting for teachers. His implication that programed learning requires memorization and penalizes creative reflection is extremely important, as is his charge that automated teaching is a standardizing rather than an individualizing force. What are the proper aims of education, we must ask ourselves, and how well does programed learning fit in with them?

Whether we like it or not, automated teaching is here to stay. Merely to oppose it is futile. Education must mirror the age it strives to improve. It cannot isolate itself from automation any more than from other social or economic changes. For automated teaching is one more consequence of the application of technology to human life. The question to be asked is not, "Do we accept automation," but "How much of it and under what conditions?"

Wise technology will certainly improve standards of teaching. It will encourage teachers to be more precise in their presentation and force them to distinguish more carefully between objective fact and personal opinion. I am less hopeful that it will lighten the load of repetitive work and so free the teacher for more creative tasks, as we so often hear, for servicing and looking after the machine is likely to entail its own kind of drudgery. I like the machine's capacity for correcting errors immediately and its promise to standardize levels of achievement but not at the risk of destroying individual eccentricity. I like the fact that it tests the student continuously instead of examining him at widely spaced intervals, although I fear that too much of this type of reinforcement will develop a limited kind of memory.

On the other hand, as I have stated elsewhere,[1] I have very definite reservations about the scope of the Skinnerian machine, about the amount and kind of instruction it can usefully undertake. Let me recapitulate briefly. In the first place, Skinner claims that, because there is a constant interchange between machine and learner, the effect of his machine upon the student "is surprisingly like that of a private tutor." But whatever the similarities between a tutor and a machine, the differences are far greater. The tutor can inspire his pupil through all the resources of his per-

sonality. He can encourage his pupil in widely flexible ways. A machine can only be the occasion of inspiration, whenever the pupil succeeds in his efforts. How often a child will work, not for knowledge as such, but for the knowledge he discerns through the impress of his teacher's personality. Many a child learns simply out of his affection for his teacher. What kind of affection does a child have for a machine? You reply, perhaps, that machines may one day become the vehicles of their designers' personalities, in the way that books reflect the minds of their authors. But, however valuable the book, it will not substitute for anyone who can bring life to learning. If a machine is a tutor, then anything from, with, or through which a student learns is likewise a tutor.

Skinner states that, "Mistakes, if made, result in no social disapproval or ridicule from others." Certainly, there are advantages to be gained in working apart from the group. But in a class of 30 students, all of whom are working individually with a machine, the performance of each of them will eventually become known to others in the class, and social interaction will simply be delayed. Even so, social disapproval is something that the pupil had better get used to early in life. If mistakes can be made without social disapproval, they might either tend to lead to social irresponsibility or logically result in some sort of self-flagellation, which would be just as unfortunate. As psychologists certainly know, it is better for most individuals to suffer in the company of others —"misery loves company"—than to suffer alone.

Skinner has also claimed on behalf of his machines that, in order to understand something, a child must be able to either repeat it or else act "appropriately" when the same variables are represented. Notice here the behaviorist assumption that the interior life of the individual must be externalized into observable actions. But what criterion of understanding is mere repetition? How easy it is to repeat a formula and yet barely comprehend it. Again, let us suppose the pupil disagrees with the information he is supposed to

An unpublished paper presented by George F. Kneller before the American Psychological Association, New York, September 1, 1961.
[1] *School Review,* Summer 1962.

repeat. What, then, becomes the "right" answer? The machine tends to force a learner into an unreal dilemma—to be either for or against. A real teacher would be alive to shades of meaning. So, conceivably, might the super-human machine of the future, but not the ones we have now.

Does the child really understand if he acts "appropriately"? It is true that "appropriate" action in response to similar stimuli is one criterion of understanding. But it is not the only one, nor is it exhaustive. The essence of genuine understanding lies in the ability to "transfer" what one knows to a variety of situations other than the original. I truly understand something when I have related it to the rest of my knowledge and can apply it to novel problems as they arise. This wider and more profound awareness of a thing's significance lies beyond the power of machines adequately to measure, for their standards of measurement are essentially quantitative.

The machine quantifies and depersonalizes what is qualitative and personal. It functions best with ideas that are precise and easy to define. Yet knowledge itself is not made of such stuff; it suggests images, stirs associations, and awakens a host of uncertain feelings. The human imagination is not a computer; it throws up ideas in the raw. Creative knowledge requires an aura of imprecision and undefinable suggestion; it is not bound by the limits of the discursive intellect; it cannot be accumulated item by item, in the manner suited to a machine. It must include insight, an intuitive "feel" for things, a perception of similar patterns in diverse phenomena. To learn is not simply to "respond to the world" but to "interrogate reality," to question data, and actively to create one's own picture of the universe.

Studies by Jenkins and Russell[2] on the psychological structure of our language suggest that we as a society are becoming more homogeneous in our verbal habits. This is of great help to the use of technology in education. But J. P. Guilford[3] and others assert that problem-solving is facilitated by originality in word association. Our language habits are also becoming less abstract and more concrete. Could it be that our schools unknowingly are standardizing verbal behavior? "This trend toward uniformity and concreteness in the United States," says Howard Kendler, "is responsible for what appears to be a tendency for the great scientific discoveries of recent decades to be made by foreigners."[4] The great problem technological types of instruction have to face, therefore, is how to preserve and enhance individual creativity and at the same time maintain efficiency in mass education.

But I would like to extend the area of discussion to something far more crucial. Compared to the huge servomechanisms of commerce and industry, the teaching machine is a bagatelle. We all know that many such mechanisms today are making important decisions. Who programs the data on which these decisions are based? What presuppositions do they reflect? What values are enmeshed among the facts, subtly transforming them? The modern corporation is a hierarchical power structure, administered by "line and staff," in which crucial decisions, taken at the top, are executed at successive levels by organization men who subordinate themselves in act and thought to the demands of the corporation. Do we not also observe the same creeping conformism in the echelons of "big government"? We see in our society an ever growing centralization of power which is little by little eroding the right of the individual to dissent. Is it likely that the programers of education will be able to resist this trend?

It would be the height of optimism to expect that educators themselves will control the content that is fed into educational machines. When has public education ever determined political policy? What social values have the schools ever directly established? In fact, as teachers' oaths so eloquently attest, the schools are used mostly to perpetuate the existing order, rarely to rebel against it. At first our programers may rest content with universal scientific knowledge, innocuous information, and knowledge at a low level of differentiation. But why should they stop there? We may be sure that, as these machines evolve toward an ever greater refinement and comprehensiveness, their potential for indoctrination will not remain unused. Preferences will be sunk into facts like steel into concrete. Students will absorb values and attitudes simultaneously with data. We know that machines standardize. We know that they could be used, step by step, to swing every individual into line. We know that their purpose is to instruct each pupil in a complete course of study precisely as the programer has specified. Since they are experts at rewarding progress, or so their advocates claim, how can the pupil help being pleased when he has satisfied the machine?

---

[2] J. J. Jenkins and W. A. Russell, *A Comparative Study of Word Association Norms.* Technical Report No. 22, ONR Contract No. 8onr-66216, University of Minnesota, 1958.

[3] J. P. Guilford, "Creativity," *American Psychologist,* 5 (1950), 444-454.

---

[4] Howard H. Kendler, "Teaching Machines and Psychological Theory," in Eugene Galanter, ed., *Automatic Teaching.* New York: Wiley, 1959, p. 183.

Remember the classic understatement of Norbert Wiener: "There is a much greater tendency for the person to conform to the machine than the machine to conform to the person."

If we seek exact responses and reward those who conform to the demands of the machine, we are likely to snuff out the precision spark of revolt that is necessary to healthy growth and creativity. We shall *literally* have mechanized learning. (We may, of course, produce the opposite reaction, complete noncooperation and juvenile Luddites.) This danger is the more serious when, as Wiener tells us, the programing of machines is being itself programed (machines are programing machines) and thus we are getting machines which are more remote from the people who control them than ever before. Could any machine teach the healthy civil disobedience that has brought reform after reform to this country?

We need also to be concerned about values. The more visionary of our experts on educational machines predict that we shall actually be able to teach and test for values, as indeed, we are now teaching logic by way of machines. But logic is not axiology, and such a hope could only mean that we would have, or should have, *norms* of values. Just how specific are the value norms, or even value alternatives, in American democratic education? If they exist, they lie on a very general level of acceptance and are hardly subject to the kind of precise, objective discrimination that would be necessary for advanced programing. Other technologists presage the day when educational diagnosis can take place, much as with a motor car engine. But this would imply that we have in education a sort of mechanistic situation that can be scientifically or technologically analyzed, and determined; or that education itself were largely a science capable of exact measurement, when the fact of the matter is that education of its very nature has little that is accurately measurable or scientific about it.

This does not mean that teaching machines should not be used in matters involving human values. Machines may very well help us specify our values more clearly without necessarily assuming they must be normative. They may help us find more scientific data which will lead to a more objective assessment of the tasks of education. In short, machines may compel us to concentrate more on factor analyses of content that is to be programed, in order to reduce unnecessary or obstructive variability. Finally, machines may help us sort out many complex quantitative arrangements that keep the human mind from getting on with the central problem to be examined.

I suggest that those who tinker with educational machines should look a little further into the kind of future which their own actions are preparing. The premature application of machines to education is mined with pitfalls. A narrow behaviorism in theory can lead only to narrowness in practice. For every mechanist such as Skinner we need an idealist like Rogers, for every technologist a moralist, for every well-adjusted person another with abrasive edges. In this country the enormous, at times well-nigh monolithic, pressure of public opinion, leaves us particularly susceptible to collective emotions, to mass hysteria. Spellbound masses invite self-destruction. Let oratory blaze. Let subtle propaganda fire the adult, formulate the child. And we shall not be too intelligent to stampede.

Of course, I am well aware that the power and potentiality of thinking machines have been exaggerated; and Wiener, for one, engages in convenient ellipses in his cybernetic theories. He has admitted his unfamiliarity with the social sciences and depends too much on analogical reasoning. That the anatomical structure of the central nervous system is demonstrably like the wiring diagram of a digital computer is undeniable. But to accept this fact as sufficient explanation in itself is to imply that machines *behave* like human beings, and this of course is an illusion. In the first place, the original analogy is physically a poor one; it is somewhat crude. It can be used only for mechanically operational purposes. In other words, it is crudely imitative of, rather than synonymous with, certain measurable aspects of cerebral structure and behavior. We readily admit that conceivably there is nothing that the human brain can do that eventually the machine will not do. By the same token, we must agree that there is nothing the machine can do that the human brain cannot do, even though it may take the brain much longer. In short, the machine will perform only those kinds of tricks that the brain can actually teach it to perform. Hence, any comparison between human minds and electronic brains must logically break down at certain points where strategic decisions have to be made or unexpected foci established. The automatic devices of computers may well respond to the operations of symbolic logic, and neurological models may well be said to think, feel, desire, mean, believe or judge something. But there is an irreducible residue in the mind of the person who programs the machine that consists of the acceptance or rejection of such abstract personal entities as assertion, belief, interpretation, reflection and everything else that guides the machine's miraculous feats of behavior.

But even if we should be hospitable to cybernetic notions, there are biologists who would seem to reject them. C. J. Herrick tells us that man's psychophysical makeup is organically so complex and unpredictable that only the element of freedom of choice is a constant. Inherent in the structure of man is what Herrick calls "intentional self-determination," the greatest characteristic of which is the "free and creative feature of mentation."[5] The human brain is best at handling the unsuspected and unpredictable. Man's choices and hence responses have an unprecedented range and variety. Even a scientist, remarks Frank H. Knight, "cannot by scientific method predict *his own* behavior in investigation." His natural reactions and creations amply demonstrate that he is by no means a stimulus-bound animal. He is even capable of transcending his biological makeup and cultural milieu if he so wills! The ineluctable fact is that man is born free. He is biologically synonymous with freedom. He is, if he so wills, and can get away with it, the chief determinant of all his actions.

It follows that the machine's powers at introspection will never become greater than analogous human powers, except, perhaps, through accidental connections, and even here, the introspection which the machine might provide would always be subject to assessment by humans, hence corrected or rejected. But humans have a great deal of difficulty measuring introspection or making predictions about it.[6] Accurately to program reliable elements of introspection would therefore require a lot more positive data than we have at present. It is only because the computer's physical structure can be known in its every detail from point of origin of its behavior to a final conclusion that we can make predictions about its capacity for introspection. We may of course be able to learn much thereby about human introspection. However, when that day arrives, the word will have lost its meaning or have radically changed it. The whole realm of intuition, subjectivity, and anything else which cannot now be measured accurately or technically would come to an end. In its place we would conceivably build a world of men which accounted for his characteristics as an information-processing system. This would become the next stage of development in the behavioral sciences; so that where as of now we are having difficulty measuring the imponderables about human behavior, we may eventually succeed in bringing about a kind of behavior—an information processing kind of behavior—in mankind that would indeed be measurable and predictable all right but probably terribly monotonous and regrettably depersonalizing.

Yet to the casual eye perhaps the most obvious objection to the widespread use of machines at this juncture is a purely practical one, the inability of teachers to keep them repaired. How often in the average class does an audio-visual program work without a hitch, without guffaws and cheers at the expense of the embarrassed teacher? If past experience has anything to teach, it is that the machines will fail because, ironically enough, they will not always work. They will constantly need repair. Students will forever try to outwit them or throw them out of gear. We shall either have to keep an engineer on the staff or else turn out teachers who are likewise engineers. How many teachers are mechanically minded? The teacher will be released from drill only to be shackled in turn to a box of tricks. He will spend precious time repairing his machines, greasing them, adjusting their parts, supervising students who use them, covering them with dust cloths, locking them up for the night, and providing the business office with periodical inventories of all the machines, tools, and gadgets in his possession. By all means use machines, but let us use them selectively.

One final word of warning to all who have capitulated to the machine. I heard tell the other day of a teacher who had just spent two hours visiting an IBM exhibition of automatic machines and on his way down in the elevator an attractive woman screamed. It appears that a young man had pinched her. The teacher could not help but shout aloud in glee: "Thank heaven there are some things left that still have the personal touch!" If there is no one left on earth to otherwise guarantee this sacred fact, rest assured that the philosophers will be glad to fulfill their duty!

---

[5] C. J. Herrick, *George Ellett Coghill*. University of Chicago Press, 1949, pp. 201 ff.

[6] See Herbert A. Simon and Allen Newell, "Models: Their Uses and Limitations," in Leonard D. White, ed., *The State of the Social Sciences*. University of Chicago Press, 1956, pp. 66-83.

PART TWO

THE ROLE AND STATUS OF AMERICAN EDUCATION

Generally speaking, a society supports its schools for the purpose of furthering its own particular goals and social philosophy. One way to assess the role and status of education in any society, therefore, is to determine what social forces have or have not been accounted for in the program of the schools. Historically, there has been considerable variance from country to country—and, over a period of time, within individual countries—in the overall philosophy and purpose of education. In some societies, school programs have seemed to reflect the special aims of particular social classes or political groups. During the Hitler regime in Germany, for example, the purpose and direction of the schools were almost wholly determined by the socio-political aims of the Nazi party.

Systems of education often differ significantly even among neighboring countries that seem to have much in common—witness, for example, the differences between our system and that of Canada. Every educational system is the product of a particular people living at a particular time in a particular place, and it quite naturally reflects the goals and philosophy of the society of which it is a part. Thus, it is unreasonable to expect that a system effective in one country can successfully be *adopted*, wholly and without modification, by another country with different traditions and different aims. It is always possible, on the other hand, that particular aspects of any country's educational system can appropriately and profitably be *adapted* to the differing needs of another society.

In the United States, the role played by the schools has reflected the aims of our citizens and the ever-changing social, political, and economic forces at work in our society. Early in our history, American schools, tending to imitate those of Europe, were designed to satisfy the aims of particular segments of the new society and therefore were limited in purpose and function. As Edwards and Richey have pointed out, "the colonists who established homes along the shores of Virginia and New England during the opening years of the seventeenth century did what colonists usually do under similar circumstances: they transplanted to the new environment the old institutions with which they were familiar in the homeland" (1). Such imitation did not continue, however; a process of adaptation rather than adoption took place, characterized by a spirit of open-mindedness and a willingness to accept educational innovations. American society differed in many aspects from the homelands of the colonists, and a system of education developed which uniquely reflected both the social forces operating in this country and the expressed wishes of the majority of citizens for universal free public education.

Despite the national unity of the American people, despite their many common beliefs and values and social interests, the United States is basically a pluralistic society which accords high respect to diversity of ideas and behavior. Its people are of many different races, religious beliefs, social classes, occupational groups, and ethnic backgrounds and they reside in many different geographic and climatic regions. Its states have differing historical backgrounds and economic conditions. Such heterogeneity has been a source of pride and even of strength; a zeal for uniformity has never been one of our national weaknesses.

On the other hand, the many political, economic, social, and geographic differences found in the United States make the problems of providing an adequate educational system for all citizens particularly complex. No thoughtful person would solve these problems by proposing changes that would eliminate our heterogeneity and create the drab uniformity and lack of freedom found in a typical dictatorship. The complexity of our educational problems represents a challenge to be accepted and solved within the framework of the political and economic principles that have made this country great.

The readings in Part Two contribute to an understanding of the social, political, and economic forces affecting the public schools of the United States. They also provide some insight into the systems of education in other countries, for purposes of comparison and contrast with our own system. Finally, they provide at least a partial picture of American education as it is now and of the challenges that it must meet in the immediate future. They do not minimize our weaknesses and mistakes but provide the basis for a frank assessment of our educational problems and of the strides we have taken to solve them.

Students interested in investigating further the effects of various social forces on education and schooling may wish to examine local sources of information in their own state. Such sources include: (a) publications of state departments of education and of various legislative committees on education; (b) current reports on education by associations of teachers, taxpayers, and other interested parties; and (c) interviews with teachers, principals, school-board members, social workers, juvenile authorities, and teachers of the behavioral sciences. For information on comparative education, students will find it profitable to consult published materials (2), including UNESCO reports, and to talk with visitors and students from foreign countries.

SOCIAL FORCES AND EDUCATION

One of the more difficult problems for students of education to understand is the nature of the social forces which affect the purposes and functions of schools in the United States. The topic is a complex one, and only general considerations can be essayed in this introduction (3).

Changes in public education have resulted both from formal legislation and from the informal influences of individuals and groups. The voices of private citizens and lay organizations are frequently raised in attempts to constrain the functions of schooling to explicit ends or to expand these functions to include new and different tasks. Formal and informal influences may overlap when particular demands of special groups or agencies are embedded in legal enactments.

While the views of some lay groups are concerned with provincial and limited views of the purposes of schooling, other lay groups have provided hypotheses and proposals which have proved valid when tested in schools. The problem which has constantly faced those responsible for decisions in schools has been to determine the relative worth of proposals in the light of current and future social requirements, selecting those which facilitate and rejecting those which hinder the school in achieving its mission. Attempts to account for social demands have sometimes resulted in decisions based more on affective feelings than on cognitive thought. An inability to formalize a statement of the explicit mission of schools has been one of the difficulties in deciding which social demands should be accepted for implementation in the schools. Since the public schools have long been viewed as the property of all the people, all patrons have considered that they have the right to express themselves.

In addition to the influence of individuals and groups, other more massive and powerful forces have sometimes been directly or indirectly influential in decisions affecting the kind and quality of education in the United States. Such forces include increased earning power and shorter working hours, new frontiers of science and their implications for peace and war, and the uncertainties of living in a time of constant international tension. The school is a social agency which reflects, often with startling clarity, the character of the society which supports it.

Social changes reflecting the ideological and physical struggles for national survival in the United States and elsewhere have brought public demands for new kinds of emphases in schools. Depending upon the nature of the social stimulus, these demands have ranged from altering the content of the curriculum to more rigorous discipline and higher standards of pupil achievement and performance. The educational climate reflects the nation's state of mind. Contrast the emphasis upon more human-relations teaching in post-World-War-II schools, at a time when the world had had enough of "man's inhumanity to man," with the sudden emphasis upon more rigorous education following the first space exploits of the USSR.

Another social force, the increase in population, particularly in the last decade, has resulted in demands for more schools and for more extended periods of schooling. Concurrently, new and expanding occupational fields have required the schools to provide programs to develop new kinds of professional, technical, and vocational skills. The increasing numbers of students in school mean new or expanded educational programs, new facilities, and more teachers.

These requirements pose serious financial problems for schools, which compete with other social agencies for tax support.

Many influences, both public and private, which have required the attention of schools have had worth-while results. For it has been the interest of individuals and groups and the recognition of the forces of social change that have enabled Americans to maintain a climate of open discussion about the problems of schooling. Foreign observers have considered the continued dialogue about education one of the strengths of our system. In a pluralistic society, social forces which are recognized, evaluated, and accounted for in educational decisions can be a source of strength. When segments of a society are constrained, or abrogate their right of participation in matters of educational concern, a sickly status quo may result. Similarly, when the more massive social forces exemplified by new knowledge, exploding population, or regional illiteracy are not given cognizance in educational planning, then the existence of schools may be threatened. By their very nature, schools must account for changes in knowledge and serve as instruments to improve the state of man. The rational and systematic assessment of social forces and appropriate recognition of them in schooling are critical functions in an open society.

64

Robert J. Havighurst & Bernice L. Neugarten

SOCIAL STRUCTURE IN AMERICA

It has been stated that one of the purposes of schools in the United States is to prepare children to be effective adults and useful citizens. The achievement of this purpose, however, is more complex than it appears. Children vary greatly in their abilities and aptitudes. Important also is the fact that the United States is composed of different ethnic, religious, racial, and regional groups. Within these groups are different social classes, with different values, different purposes in seeking an education, and different social, economic, and personal needs.

Schools in a pluralistic society must have programs of instruction that will provide for the differential abilities of all children who attend them. Therefore, there must be various curricula within a single school. Teachers must understand not only the social classes of which they themselves are a part but also the other social classes from which come some of the children whom they teach. Finally, the programs and activities of schools within the same school district or system must vary according to the groups and social classes they serve in their neighborhoods or communities. The description of social classes and schools in the following selection emphasizes these demands on our schools.

The society in which American children grow up is highly diversified and complex. It consists of many different groups of people, with charac-teristically different ways of life. The children, the schools, and the teachers reflect this diversity, as can be seen in the following descriptions of three fifth-grade classrooms:

Miss Johnson stood in the hallway beside the door of her fifth-grade classroom in Center School

From *Society and Education* by Robert J. Havighurst and Bernice L. Neugarten, pp. 1-11, 19-24, 26-28. Copyright 1957 by Allyn and Bacon, Inc., Boston. Reprinted by permission of the publisher.

in Homeville as the boys and girls marched in. She closed the door, then walked to her desk in front of the room, where she took out her attendance record and checked off the names of the children as they came from the coat room. They stood and repeated in unison the pledge of allegiance to the flag which was mounted in the corner by the geography globe. Then they took out their arithmetic books and began to work the problems she had listed on the blackboard.

She knew her class pretty well, by now, two months after the beginning of school. They came from all over Homeville, these fifth-graders, after spending the first four grades in neighborhood schools. Center School had all the children of Homeville from the 5th to the 8th grades.

How different they were, she thought. They came from 30 different families, at least eight churches, and several nationalities. However, they all spoke English, though the little boy whose family had just moved to town from a Missouri farm had not been easy to understand, at first; and Stephen Stenius, the Lithuanian boy whose parents had been brought over from a displaced persons camp in Europe by the local Lutheran church, had just a trace of a foreign accent that made his speech seem more careful and correct than that of the local children.

As she walked up and down the rows of seats, Miss Johnson stopped occasionally to help someone who was having difficulty. She leaned over to see what Bob Wilson had written on his paper, and she noticed his dirty hands. His hands were always grimy, she thought, and she must remind him at recess time to wash them—but not now, because he would have an excuse to go to the washroom and leave his work behind. He was the third Wilson child she had taught, and they had all been slow pupils. Still, she thought, they could probably read and calculate better than their father, who worked on the crew that cleaned the streets. Then she moved over to Carmelita, the Mexican girl whose father worked on the railroad section gang. The little girl flashed a quick smile at her and showed her work. She obediently corrected a mistake and started on another problem. Carmelita was a dutiful child, but passive and rather slow except when the class had a program for Halloween. Then Carmelita was a star, with her gay colored clothes, her sparkling black eyes, and her clear, true voice.

The first one to finish with the lesson was Sidney, the Jewish boy whose father ran the Army store. Sidney had told Miss Johnson that he was going to be a doctor when he grew up, and he worked hard in school.

Patricia Morgan raised her hand and asked for help on a problem in long division. It was a pleasure to help Patricia. With her steady grey eyes and clear blonde skin and hair, Miss Johnson thought she was the most attractive child in the room. In another three or four years the girl would be sent to a private school in the east, and then to Vassar, where her mother had graduated. Patricia's father was a doctor, and her mother was the daughter of the bank president. Her grandfather had been one of the first settlers in the county and had acquired a thousand acres of the best corn land to start the biggest fortune in Homeville. Patricia was just an average scholar, but she worked steadily, and her mother had told the teacher that she was not to be favored over the other children.

The pupils were all different, certainly, but they all shared the common life of the school, and they shared Miss Johnson, their teacher.

Miss Bond was seated at her desk in a corner of the room as her fifth-graders came in from the schoolgrounds. They went first to the coatroom to hang up their coats and then to their seats, or they gathered in little groups, talking to one another. School would not start for another two or three minutes. Looking out the window Miss Bond could see other children arriving, many of them in automobiles driven by their mothers, with occasionally a child coming in a long black Cadillac driven by a chauffeur wearing a dark cap. Other children walked from nearby houses.

She rose to pull the drapery across one window where the morning sun bore in too directly. Outside the window the grounds were landscaped. The children played in the large field on the other side of the building. Now the last boy sauntered in, and the class was slowly getting to work, most of them sitting at their desks grouped in one half of the room, while a few were sitting at worktables using reference books. It was a large, light, airy room, with green blackboards and green-colored bulletin boards on which brightly colored posters were mounted. The fluorescent lights were not needed this morning, but it was cool, and the floor was comfortably warmed by inlaid heating coils.

Forest Park School was a show place, and Miss Bond felt fortunate to be able to work in such a fine building, in the finest suburb of the metropolis. For five years now she had taught in this school, after ten years at Homeville. She was an excellent teacher, for the best of teachers were employed at Forest Park and then only after they had shown their quality elsewhere. She had fewer pupils than she had had in Homeville, and the school had much better equipment with which to work.

The children were all at work now, most of them on arithmetic, though one small group worked at a table getting together a report about the first Thanksgiving. They were a good-looking lot, clean and sweet-smelling; as though, Miss Bond thought, they had come out of lavender-scented bedclothes. There was Estelle Woodford, taking charge of the committee, acting just like her mother who was President of the Garden Club and who had been PTA president last year. Tommy Beauregard raised his hand to ask for help. He was a plodder, certainly not one of the stars in the class, but he kept at his work. She knew that he would work hard through high school and then through Princeton, and then probably work up into the management of the industrial machinery company of which his father was president and principal stockholder.

Helen Fischer sat in a corner, studying from a sixth-grade arithmetic book. She had finished the fifth-grade book and was going ahead on her own. The girl was too much on her own, thought Miss Bond, as she looked at Helen's slender back and black hair. Dr. Fischer was a psychiatrist who had just bought a big house and moved his family out from the city. Neither the girl nor her mother seemed to have made friends yet, as far as Miss Bond could tell from her observations of the children at play and the mothers at PTA meetings. She would like to help Helen get on more friendly terms with the other children but she hardly knew how to go about it. If this had been Homeville, she would have spoken to some of the mothers and suggested that they invite Helen to their daughters' parties. But in Forest Park she did not know how to do this. She supposed the little girls had parties, but she knew nothing about them. She had thought of speaking to Mrs. Fairbairn, her PTA room mother, but Mrs. Fairbairn seemed so occupied with her own plans for the year's activities and so sure of how Miss Bond should fit into them that the teacher felt there was no room for her to make suggestions about the welfare of Helen Fischer.

Her relations with the mothers were different from what she had known in Homeville. She felt that she had an accepted place with Forest Park mothers, and a respected place, but that she should not step out of it. Only twice had she been in the home of any of her pupils—and then on the occasion of a tea to plan a school program. On these occasions she had been uncertain about what kind of dress to wear, and whether to wear gloves, and she had been uncomfortable. The women spoke of the Eastern colleges they had

attended, and Miss Bond was afraid they would ask her where she had gone to college. Suddenly the state teachers college which had meant so much to her had become something to keep quiet about.

There was only one pupil who reminded her even faintly of her own childhood. That was Anna Metzger, whose father had a bakery shop in the small shopping center of the town and who lived with his family in a flat above the store. Miss Bond's father had owned a small grocery store in a small town. Anna was indeed as much of a teacher's pet as Miss Bond would ever allow herself, and the teacher was pleased when the girl showed attachment to her by bringing little gifts and occasionally something good to eat from the bakery. Anna had friends among the children, for she was good-natured and friendly and quick at games. But Miss Bond wondered whether Anna would be accepted into the clubs and the social life of the younger set of Forest Park when she reached high school age.

Mrs. Gordon stood at the girls' entrance to the grimy, red-brick school seeing that the girls formed an orderly line ready to march in when the buzzer sounded. She heard a scuffle behind her and a big eighth-grade girl landed on the ground beside her. "Damn you!" the girl shouted, and then looking up at Mrs. Gordon she said, "Teacher, they pushed me."

"Get back in line," said Mrs. Gordon. "How can we make the little children behave when you big girls act like that?" By this time the lines were moving into the building. Mrs. Gordon followed them in and up to her own fifth-grade room on the third floor. There was a lot of noise coming through the open door but it died down as she strode into the room, and with a strong alto voice said, "Good morning, boys and girls."

"Good morning, teacher," several of them answered, and smiled as she smiled at them.

"Ray, will you please open the window?" Mrs. Gordon asked, and a big boy raised a window. She had to do this every morning, for the smell was very strong during the first few minutes. There were children in her class who were sewed into their long underwear about this time of the year, and might not get a bath until Christmas. Two boys wore pieces of stocking on their close-cut heads, covering a shiny ointment used to treat ringworm.

Forty boys and girls stood beside forty desks in five rows, and, placing their hands over their hearts, they repeated the pledge of allegiance to the flag, "and to the Republic, for which it stands." Mrs. Gordon liked this ceremony. It was a symbol of unity in a variegated group which she sometimes called her "United Nations." About half of the youngsters were Negroes, mostly very dark-skinned, but some light brown and yellow, barely distinguishable from several Mexicans in the class. There were four Puerto Ricans whose fathers recently had come to work in the foundries of the city. Several children with Polish names and three or four with Scotch names, who spoke a hill-billy English from Kentucky, were the only blondes in the room. There were also several Italians and two Chinese.

Mrs. Gordon had been in the John T. Mc-Manus School in the Canalport district of Metropolis for 15 years. Previously she had taught in two schools which were known among teachers as "better schools," because the children came from families of professional men and business men and lived in better houses. Most teachers liked these other schools, but Mrs. Gordon had not liked either the children or the parents in those schools. The children had been argumentative with her—they would quote their fathers or mothers, or bring to school something they had read that didn't agree with her statements. As for the parents, she thought they were always criticizing. They found fault with everything and everyone from the Superintendent of Schools down to the janitor. The PTA was always organizing in-service training programs on such matters as race relations and remedial reading and putting pressure on the teachers to attend these meetings. So when she heard of a vacancy in the McManus school, where there was a principal who was known as a "good one to work under," Mrs. Gordon had applied for the transfer.

The John T. McManus School had been tutor to thirteen thousand children during its 75 years of existence. About half the children had been pupils for the full eight years, while the others stayed shorter terms. At first the bulk of them were children of Irish immigrants. Then the Irish moved out of Canalport to better houses further from the factories of the neighborhood, and the Bohemians and Hungarians moved in. Their children were followed by Italian and Polish children, and since World War II these families were moving out, and Negroes, Mexicans, and Puerto Ricans were coming in. The McManus school had some distinguished graduates, including three state senators and the present Sheriff. At present it had the best eighth-grade basketball team in the city.

Mrs. Gordon knew all these things, and was proud of them. Her own two children had gone to school in the "good" residential district where she and her husband lived, and they were now in college. Having raised her own children, she never had any doubts about her ability to handle other people's children. She ruled them firmly. The children felt that she was a fair teacher, although a strict one, and many of them in later years looked back to their year with her in the fifth grade as the year they "learned how to work," and they thanked her for it.

There were all types of children in her room, Mrs. Gordon thought. Of course, most of them were slow and lazy about learning, like their parents. They would drop out of school as soon as they reached the age of 16. But she could teach them a little more than their parents knew. There were a few bad ones. She was keeping her eyes on John Washington, a tough, over-age Negro boy with a sullen expression. One day he had been annoying the boy sitting in front of him, and the boy had turned his head sharply and rammed it into Washington's open knife. The gash in his cheek had required five stitches. The principal had warned the Washington boy that if he ever came to school with a knife again he would be sent to the special school for delinquent boys. Mrs. Gordon knew that McManus had graduated some hoodlums and thieves as well as three state senators, and she regarded it as her job to reduce delinquency by firm control of her pupils.

There were a few children in her room who would make good—maybe even in a big way, Mrs. Gordon thought. There was Maria, the Puerto Rican girl who had the looks and possibly the talent to become a great dancer. Mrs. Gordon personally took Maria to the settlement house in the neighborhood and asked the Director to place the girl in a dance group. She told Maria's mother that the girl had talent and must be kept in school until she had learned enough English and enough manners to be accepted by the people she would have to work with if she became a dancer. There was also David Widder, the Negro boy who scored the highest in the class on an intelligence test. He was a good reader and good at arithmetic, and she thought he might become a scientist or a doctor. She told him this, and she told it to his father and mother whom she summoned to school. She told them about Donald Matthews, the highest ranking boy in her first class at McManus, also a Negro, who had just won a fellowship for graduate work in chemistry at the State University.

Mrs. Gordon knew that the great majority of her pupils would grow up to be hard-working, respectable people, and from her they needed patient teaching and firm handling.

In these three classrooms we see through their teachers' eyes something of a cross section of the children of America. These children come from widely varying backgrounds; in their appearance and behavior, they reflect the fact that America is made up of many different social groups, each with its own way of life. These children will come to school with different attitudes; they will learn differently; and they will use education differently in their lives.

These three teachers teach in very different kinds of schools. Miss Johnson teaches in a school in a small Midwest city, where, in the same classroom, there are children coming from all parts of town and from a fairly wide range of social backgrounds. Miss Bond in her exclusive suburb has, by comparison, a homogeneous group. Almost all her children come from "good" homes where great importance is placed upon the quality of education and preparation for college. Mrs. Cordon, teaching in what is often called a "slum" school, also has a fairly homogeneous group in terms of socioeconomic characteristics, although it is a group quite different from Miss Bond's.

These three teachers, all of them good teachers, will have quite different teaching experiences and will derive different kinds of satisfactions from their work. This is true not only because they are teaching children from different social groups, but because they themselves have come from somewhat different social backgrounds and are different in personality and in their attitudes toward children.

Social structure

A social group consists of people who share certain common ways of behaving and believing. This is why they are a group rather than just an accidental collection of people. When a number of people share certain ways of behaving and believing, they are said to possess and to share a *culture*.

Culture and subcultures.   By a culture, we refer to the patterns and products of learned behavior: the etiquette, language, food habits, religious and moral beliefs, systems of knowledge, attitudes, and values; as well as the material things and artifacts produced—the technology—of a group of people. By culture, we refer, in short, to the patterned way of life of a society. (The term society refers to the persons who share a given culture, and to the network of relationships that exists among the members of the group.

A human society does not exist apart from a culture.)

Culture is a human production, and man differs from animals because he creates culture, and because he transmits what he has learned and what he has created from one generation to the next.

A complex society such as modern American society has both an over-all culture, a way of life shared by all Americans; and a set of subcultures, ways of life that differ from one subgroup to another. Whenever a smaller group of people within a society have certain ways of behavior, certain attitudes and beliefs, that constitute a variant of the over-all culture, we say they have a subculture of their own. For example, nearly all Americans share a common language, use the same systems of money, weights, and measures, dress somewhat alike, and have certain political principles in common. These ways of life, shared by nearly all Americans, make up the American culture. At the same time, within the American culture, there are a number of subcultures that are characteristic of subgroups of Americans. There are subgroups based upon ethnic or nationality factors—German, Polish, English. There are subgroups based upon racial factors—Negro, Chinese, white. There are various religious groups, each with their somewhat different beliefs and attitudes. There are differences between rural and urban groups, between groups living in the North and South, in New England or the Midwest.

The people of a certain subculture share certain common practices, beliefs, or attitudes that are not held by other American groups. For instance, an Italian group may have certain special foods and methods of cooking; a Baptist group, certain religious practices; and a Southern group, certain speech habits. Any and all of these mark off the groups as subcultures of the common American culture.

Social classes.   While ethnic, racial, religious, and regional subgroups exist, there is another type of social grouping that cross-cuts all the others and which refers to *social class* groups. Thus, there are middle-class (as well as upper- and lower-class) Catholics, Protestants, Jews, German-Americans, Italian-Americans, Negroes, and whites.

In every American community there are groups of people who recognize themselves as being similar in many ways. They live in the same kind of dwellings, have similar eating habits, dress in pretty much the same ways, have rather similar tastes in furniture, literature, and recreation, and have about the same amount of education. Even though they may come from different ethnic and religious backgrounds, when two members of such a group meet and start a conversation they soon find that they have much in common. Such a group is called a *social class*. It consists of people who mingle together freely, have rather similar social habits and values, and whose young people tend to intermarry.

Social class membership.   One of the tests of membership in a social class is that of social intercourse, actual or potential. The members of a social class tend to belong to the same social organizations, to entertain one another in their homes. If they live in different cities, or in different parts of a big city, they may not actually associate with one another; yet if they meet as strangers they soon recognize a good deal of similarity in their ways of life.

Sometimes subcultural differences based upon ethnic or religious factors effectively separate members of a given social class. For example, intermarriage between Jew and Catholic is rare, even at the same social class level; and social visiting and entertaining is not common between lower-middle-class Methodists and lower-middle-class Italian-Americans. Yet, even in those instances in which there are barriers to social intercourse, members of a given social class share a common subculture. In many respects, lower-class Negroes and whites are more alike in their way of life than lower-class and middle-class Negroes; in the same way, middle-class Protestants and Catholics are more alike than lower-class and middle-class Protestants.

The social-class hierarchy.   The various social groups that are found in America are organized into one functioning society, a society with an intricate pattern of interrelationships between groups, but one in which an over-all structure exists. This organization or structure can best be described in terms of social classes and the hierarchy of social classes.

The members of a given social class recognize more or less clearly that their class occupies a position on a social scale. The position may be at the top, near the middle, or at the bottom. It is not that one class is better than another in a moral sense, but that some classes have more economic and political power and more social prestige than other classes.

All societies, large or small, primitive or modern, show this phenomenon of rank: some people who are the leaders and people of high prestige occupy positions at the top; others occupy intermediate positions, with less prestige than those at the top; and still others are at the bottom

of the social scale. This is true regardless of the political form of government. A democracy has rank; so does an absolute monarchy; so also does a communist society such as the Soviet Union. While the king and the nobility are at the top in a monarchy, in the Soviet Union the top people are the leaders of the Communist Party and the high government and military officials. In a democracy the people at the top are those who have earned or inherited economic power or social prestige.

Social classes in America.   Some people, when they first become acquainted with the idea of social class, tend to deny their existence in America because they feel that they are undemocratic. Yet all of us in America are aware that differences in social rank exist in any community; we discuss these differences frankly, whether or not we use the term "social class" in describing them. The reader can refer to his own community and will recognize at once that there are certain people in it who are considered "the best families" or "the elite," others who are "the leaders" or "pillars of the community," others who are "just nice, respectable people" or "the working people," still others who are "poor, but honest" or "good people, but nobody," and still others who are "bottom of the heap." We Americans speak of people who have "gone a long way up," or "climbed the social ladder," or of people who have "dropped a notch." We speak, too, of marrying "above" or "below" one's own position and of having made "good" or "poor" marriages.

Whatever the terms used in a particular group, such expressions refer clearly to a social organization characterized by different levels of rank and prestige. This organization or structure in our society is a recognized reality and a part of our everyday living.[1]

To repeat, all modern societies, whether they are democratic, autocratic, or totalitarian, have social classes. In a democracy, the social classes

---

[1] Novelists as well as social scientists have been interested in the structure of our society and have written stories about it. Sinclair Lewis, in *Babbitt,* describes the efforts of George Babbitt to move from upper-middle-class to upper-class status. In Christopher Morley's book, *Kitty Foyle,* the heroine is in love with an upper-class man but does not marry him because the social distance between them is too great. Another example is John Marquand who is a close observer of social class phenomena, especially at the upper levels. In his novel, *Point of No Return,* he presents a social class picture of a New England town, and good-humoredly brings a social anthropologist into the story to make the social class factors in the story more explicit.

have equal political rights and there is substantial movement of people from one class to another—movement that we call *social mobility*. The democratic ideal of equality of opportunity means, in our society, opportunity to rise in the social scale. It does not, however, deny the fact that the scale exists. . . .

Cultures of the social classes

Having delineated the outlines of the social structure that characterizes America, the social scientist inquires further into the differences in way of life between social classes. In other words, seeing that people group themselves into different classes is only the first part of understanding how the society is organized and how people relate to one another. How do the groups differ in behavior, in beliefs and attitudes, in values? In other words, what is the subculture that characterizes each of the social class groups?

In describing the cultures of the various social classes we will make use of the five-class structure that has been found to be characteristic of the small and medium-sized American cities. The following descriptions are only brief, thumbnail sketches, but they should suffice to point out the most salient differences in the styles of life between social class groups.

These descriptions are taken from the published studies of social structure already mentioned. They apply to the majority of people in a given social class, but not to every person in the class. There are exceptional people who have the major socioeconomic characteristics of a social class but who do not follow its way of life in all respects.

Upper class. Upper-class people generally have wealth in the family, and usually have had a tradition of family wealth for several generations. A few upper-class people may themselves have little money, but may be the respected cousins and nieces and nephews of formerly wealthy and high-status families. Upper-class people belong to certain exclusive social clubs. They belong to the boards of directors of art museums, symphony and opera associations, and of Ivy League colleges. They tend to support charitable organizations, chambers of commerce, the higher status churches, and the Republican Party (in the North); but their support is usually silent (the power behind the throne) and they leave the offices in these organizations to be filled by upper-middle-class people. Upper-class people are likely to be interested in history and biography, and to be well versed in the traditions of their own families.

Their houses, gardens, summer places, automobiles, and clothes are thought to be in the "best taste" and are not flamboyant or conspicuous (except possibly for the newcomers to the upper class, who have not yet learned to avoid ostentation). Upper-class people usually belong to the Protestant Episcopal Church, to the Presbyterian or Congregational (as in Midwest), or to the Unitarian or Congregational (as in New England). Relatively few belong to Catholic or Jewish churches.

In the eyes of upper-class people, education is a matter of proper rearing, and formal schooling is no more important in this connection than are other aspects of training the young to fill their adult roles properly. Training for an occupation is not of primary importance, since the children will inherit high status and cannot go any higher by occupational success. Nevertheless, the occupation must be of the "right" type for the upper class. Girls are likely to study French, art, music, and literature, rather than a vocation such as home economics, journalism, or teaching. The boys may go into business or into one of the higher status professions, such as architecture, medicine, law, and (infrequently) the ministry in an upper status denomination. Boys and girls generally attend private schools and the high status Ivy League colleges or selective women's colleges.

Some of the parents of the children in Miss Bond's class in Forest Park are in the upper class. Living in an exclusive suburb, they may send their children to the public school, at least for the first few years. If they live in smaller cities without private schools, they may send their children to the local public schools until they are old enough, at 12 or 14, to go away from home to a private school.

Upper-middle class. About half of the adult members of this class have climbed to their present status from lower beginnings. Hence this class seems to be made up largely of active, ambitious people. The men are energetic about their jobs as business executives and professional men; the women are energetic at their activities of homemaking, club work, PTA, and civic organizations. The members of this class do not have aristocratic family tradition, but are often interested in building up such traditions. "We do not care about our ancestors," they say, "It isn't *who* you are, but *what* you are." The great bulk of leadership positions in civic, business, and professional organizations are held by upper-middle-class people: for example, Rotary and Kiwanis Clubs, the League of Women Voters, the Chamber of Commerce, the Medical Society, the Ministerial Association, and the Bar Association.

Their houses are medium to large in size, neat and well kept, usually have a flower garden or lawn that is cared for by the family, and a recreation room or a wood-working shop in the basement. When the children are young this type of family will employ a full-time domestic servant if possible, but increasingly the housework is being done by the lady of the house with the help of a cleaning woman once or twice a week.

The upper-middle-class family is conscious of the importance of money. It may be a quite wealthy family, with money earned in the present generation; more usually the income is "adequate," enough to pay for a comfortable home, a new automobile every three or four years, a fair-sized insurance and pension plan, college education for the children, with some left over for modest investment in stocks and bonds.

Most such families take a summer vacation of three weeks or longer and sometimes a winter vacation also. They are likely to travel on vacation by automobile, to go to a summer cottage on a lake, or to go abroad. They patronize the theater and the symphony concerts, and they read such periodicals as *Harper's Magazine,* the *Atlantic Monthly,* and the *New Yorker.*

Almost every family is affiliated with a church, and the active church leaders come mainly from this class. The favored churches are Presbyterian, Congregational-Christian, Methodist, Baptist (in the Middle West) and Unitarian (in New England). There are also numerous Roman Catholic, Lutheran, and Jewish upper-middle-class people. Nearly all of the members of this class are native-born Americans, and most of them have native-born parents and grandparents.

Education is extremely important to people in this group. Many of them have risen into this class through professional careers, and they feel that it is almost essential that their children secure a college degree if they are to maintain upper-middle status in the next generation. The children generally go to public schools, and then to the State University or to privately supported liberal arts colleges.

The new and exclusive suburbs of the big cities are populated largely by upper-middle-class people. They are, for instance, most of the parents of Miss Bond's Forest Park school. They live also in "good" residential sections of Homeville and every other town or city, small or large. (Miss Johnson has several upper-middle-class children in her Center School class, but Mrs. Gordon left this group behind when she transferred to the McManus school in a slum neighborhood.)

Lower-middle class. This large group is often called "the common man" group by those above them in the social scale. They in turn look down on the upper-lower-class people and call them "the common man." Their houses are usually comfortably furnished and well kept, but small to medium in size and located in areas nearer "the wrong part of town." Occasionally a young doctor or teacher coming into a new community will buy a house in a lower-middle-class area and his older associates will shake their heads and say, "He made a mistake to buy in that area."

Being white-collar clerical and sales workers, factory foremen, such members of labor's aristocracy as railroad engineers, railroad conductors, and photo-engravers, or small building and electrical and plumbing contractors, people in this class are proud of their economic independence. Most farm owners who operate their own farms are also in this class.

The members of this group travel widely in this country by automobile, but almost never go abroad, as do people in the classes above them. They make up the bulk of members of fraternal organizations such as the American Legion; their wives are active in the women's auxiliaries. They are fairly active in the PTA, and they furnish the bulk of membership in the Protestant and Catholic Churches. They also furnish the lay leadership of some churches, especially the Baptist, the Lutheran, and in many places the Methodist churches. Many lower-middle-class people are Catholics, and some are Jews. This class has in it appreciable numbers who are children or grandchildren of immigrants.

For most lower-middle-class people, a high school education is important, and a third of their children go to college. They regard schooling as essential for good jobs, and they expect their children to be obedient pupils. (Some of the hardest-working and brightest pupils in Miss Johnson's room in Homeville are lower-middle-class, and she likes to work with them. They are seldom discipline problems.)

Upper-lower class. The "respectable working people," the skilled and unskilled, the "blue-collar" (as compared to the "white-collar") workers, make up the upper-lower class. This is usually the most numerous class in a community that is self-contained and is not a satellite or suburb of a large city. These people live "across the tracks" or "on the wrong side of town." Their houses are small, though often well kept, and sometimes have additions built by the owner in his spare time. Most of the women expect to work in a factory, retail store, or office when they are not tied down at home by children.

This group contains a large fraction of people whose parents were immigrants—such as Italians, Poles, Bohemians, Japanese. They are often Catholics, but there are also considerable numbers in the fundamentalist Protestant denominations such as the Assembly of God, the Pentecostal, and Holiness churches. Often, they are also members of the Baptist and Methodist churches and, in the big cities, there are large numbers of Jews in this class. However, a considerable minority of this group are not church members, and some of them are hostile to churches.

People of this class spend most of their money as it is earned. Their only major type of investment is in a home. They may buy furniture, television sets, and major appliances "on time." If they own life insurance, they pay premiums by the week, and not quarterly or semiannually, as upper-middle-class people do. They seldom have savings of much magnitude and are dependent in their old age almost entirely on Social Security or Old Age Assistance payments.

Most people in this group do not belong to civic associations, but a few belong to fraternal organizations, and most of the men belong to labor unions. Their leisure time is spent mainly at home, watching TV or listening to the radio, working in the vegetable garden, and "fixing up" the house.

Education is not especially important for the members of this group, though most of them expect their children to go further in school than they have gone. No more than 5 or 10 per cent of their children go to college. There is very little reading in their homes; they buy almost no books and only a few magazines or newspapers. Such reading matter as they do have is usually of the "pulp" or "comic" variety. (Miss Johnson has a large number of children of this class, as does Mrs. Gordon.)

Lower-lower class. All the rest of the society look down on the lower-lower class, and call them by a variety of names: "Yellowhammers," "Okies," "Arkies," "people that live like animals," "trash," and so forth. It is generally believed that most of the delinquency, crime, and sexual promiscuity is found in this class. While this is true in over-all terms, yet there are a considerable number of respectable people classified as lower-lower because of their poverty.

Members of this class are likely to be passive and fatalistic about their status, though occasionally they all argue that they are "just as good as anybody else." They accept the poorest hous-

ing, and the most menial and irregular jobs. Sometimes their families are very large and cannot be supported on the wages of an unskilled worker, thus requiring aid from public or private agencies. Whenever divorce or desertion breaks up a family the woman is likely to have to secure government Aid for Dependent Children to support herself and her children.

Lower-lower-class people may be divided into two groups. There are those who have been at the bottom of the heap for several generations and seem destined to stay there, except for an occasional mobile son or daughter who climbs up and then out of the family's sight. There is also the newest immigrant group who are doing the heavy work of our industrial society while they are learning American ways of life, but who will eventually move up the social scale. The lower-lowers include (in addition to people with English, Scotch, Irish, German, and Swedish names who have fallen to the bottom of the social scale) many immigrants, some children of immigrants, and now many Negroes, Mexicans, and Puerto Ricans.

Some lower-lowers are members of fundamentalist Protestant churches, some are Catholics, but many are unattached to any church. They seldom belong to formal organizations, except occasionally to a labor union.

Many lower-lowers are transient, moving about in search of work or to avoid the sheriff. This class has a high proportion of unattached men and boys, who travel about in search of work and adventure. The migratory farm laborers of the country come largely from this class.

The children of lower-lower-class families produce a large share of "problem" children in the schools: the slow learners, the truants, the aggressive, and the delinquent. (Mrs. Gordon has taught many of these children at the McManus school, and Miss Johnson knows them, too.) This groups draws a good deal of attention from the educational authorities. In city school systems, some are placed in "ungraded" rooms or "opportunity classes" for slow learners. Some get considerable help from remedial reading specialists, counselors, and truant officers. In small towns, where there are fewer specialized school services, teachers may give such children little attention, except to keep them out of mischief. Nevertheless, a child from such a family is, occasionally, a real "find," with ability and interest in school; and teachers are usually alert to help such a child. . . .

Socioeconomic characteristics of the social classes

The preceding descriptions have dealt mainly with the common ways of behaving and believing, the habits and values, of the several social classes. People can be located on the social class scale by comparing their habits and values with these descriptions. People can also be located on the social scale by noting who their friends are and with whom they associate.

It should be clear, from what has been said thus far, that social class differences are broader in nature and more inclusive than socioeconomic differences. To reiterate, social classes as we have been describing them, are based upon factors of social participation, with members of a given class feeling "at home" and on an equal basis with members of the same class, but with the absence of such feelings between members of different classes. At the same time, members of the same class share a common culture or a common way of life—including not only similarities in the amount of income and type of job, but also in such matters as etiquette, dress, speech, attitudes toward education, civic responsibility, religious participation, and so on.

It is nevertheless true that socioeconomic factors are highly correlated with social class placement. Although there are many individual exceptions, upper-class people are generally the most wealthy, and lower-class people, the least wealthy; upper-status people are engaged in one set of occupations and lower-status people in another; middle-class people live in bigger and more comfortable houses than do lower-class people; and upper- and middle-class people have more education than do lower-class people.

An index of social class position. Since there is a close relationship between socioeconomic factors and social class placement, an expedient method of *estimating* a person's social class position is to utilize socioeconomic facts about him, such as his occupation, his income, or his education. Such socioeconomic characteristics can each be converted into a rating scale, and a person can be given a rating on each of them. For example, in dealing with occupations, physicians will be given a higher rating than plumbers, corporation executives a higher rating than factory foremen. Similarly, in dealing with education, graduation from college is given a higher rating than graduation from high school. In estimating a person's social class position, his combined ratings on several socioeconomic characteristics give a more accurate estimate than his rating on any one characteristic alone. As a consequence, several socioeconomic ratings are combined into what has been called an "Index of Status Characteristics" (ISC) (Warner, Meeker, and Eells [*Social Class in*

America. Chicago: Science Research Associates], 1949).

The most widely used index of social characteristics is one made by adding the ratings from several of the following socioeconomic scales:

Type of occupation

Type of house lived in (size, condition, style of architecture)

Area of community lived in (rated on the basis of residential desirability)

Amount of income

Source of income (whether from inherited wealth, profits, salary, wages, or charity)

Amount of education

Generally three or four of these ratings are combined into a single composite rating, and divisions or cut-off points on the composite scale are made to define the range which fits each of the various social classes.

Because the use of an ISC is a relatively convenient and quick method of estimating social class position, it is widely used by social scientists in studies of modern communities.

To illustrate the use of the Index of Status Characteristics, let us examine the social status of Mrs. Gordon, the fifth-grade teacher in the McManus school.

Mrs. Gordon's occupation is rated 3 on a scale where 1 is high and 7 is low. Her husband, a radio engineer, has a rating of 2, and since a wife usually takes the status of her husband, she will be assigned his occupational rating. They live in a seven-room apartment in a three-story building of 1925 vintage, a building of twenty apartments built around an open court. The janitor keeps flowers growing and grass carefully tended in the court. The apartments are at least partially redecorated every year. The rating for this type of dwelling is 3. Their apartment is in a "good" area of the city, but not by any means the best. The rating for this area, based on the judgment of real-estate men and on the consensus of people who know the city, is 3. Mr. and Mrs. Gordon both get a salary as their principal source of income. This is rated 4, a step above "wages," rated 5, and a step below "profits, fees, or commissions" which is rated 3. (The higher ratings of 1 and 2 go to people who live on income from inherited wealth or income from wealth accumulated during the present generation.) Mr. and Mrs. Gordon together earn $13,000 a year, which places them in the category rated 2. Mr. and Mrs. Gordon have both graduated from college, which gives them a rating of 1 on amount of education.

Their score on the Index of Status Characteristics is 15, obtained as follows:

Occupation	2	Source of income	4
House-type	3	Amount of income	2
Area lived in	3	Amount of education	1

The possible range on this particular scale is from 6 to 42. From several community studies it has been found that an ISC between 6 and 10 usually indicates upper-class status, while a score from 11 to 18 indicates upper-middle status. Thus when an ISC score is used to estimate their social status the Gordons fall in the center of the upper-middle class. . . .

65

Wilbur B. Brookover

SOCIAL CONTROL OF EDUCATION

We have already pointed out that the American schools have the responsibility of serving many different groups and social classes. If the United States is to survive in a world where approximately 95 of every 100 people are not Americans—and where many of those 95 are actively or potentially hostile to this country—then all our children must receive the best possible education in terms of their individual needs and abilities. Is American education meeting this challenge?

In the following selection Wilbur B. Brookover, an eminent sociologist, indicates that public education at the present time tends to emphasize the needs of the groups and classes represented on local school boards, because of the control these boards exercise over administrators and teachers. (The author refers to the teacher as "she." This conventional use of feminine pronouns in statements about teachers tends to hide the fact that one of every four teachers in America's schools is a man. In high schools, the percentage of men is much greater.) Dr. Brookover indicates, furthermore, that what is taught is often controlled by the most powerful groups in a community or state. The dangers of narrow provincialism, of special groups determining *what* shall be taught and to *whom* in a complex and heterogeneous society, deserve careful thought.

In its broadest sense social control refers to any action on the part of one person which determines the action of another.[1] Since the behavior of human beings always develops in interaction with others, all behavior is, in a real sense, controlled by these contacts. Much of the behavior of any person is influenced by the actions and expectations of others. As these are internalized, they become the person's own norms of behavior, and hence a controlling force. This is an important consideration in the analysis of the control of the school because the process by which its teachers and administrators are selected involves an understanding of their dominant values and beliefs.

More narrowly, social control refers to the external determination of the individual's actions by others who have the power or influence to do so. Sometimes such control is presumed to cause the person to act in ways divergent from his own norms. This external control, of course, is exerted by some person or group possessed of power, which may take the form either of physical force or the use of symbolic means to bring about the

From *A Sociology of Education* by Wilbur B. Brookover (New York: American Book Company, 1955), pp. 60-71.

[1] There are several books and sections of books which will help the reader to obtain a more complete understanding of this whole topic. Among these are E. A. Ross, *Social Control*, New York: Macmillan, 1901; F. E. Lumley, *The Means of Social Control*, New York: Appleton-Century-Crofts, 1925; and J. S. Roucek, *et al.*, *Social Control*, New York: Van Nostrand, 1947. Kimball Young, *Sociology*, New York: American Book, 2nd ed., 1949, Chaps. 29 and 31, gives a good brief discussion.

prescribed or expected action. In American society, as in others, interaction is largely on the symbolic level, and most control is verbally administered through symbols that anticipate some type of pleasant or unpleasant consequences. The anticipation of rewards and punishments from those in power is a real part of the life of the school teacher or administrator in any American community. Even though physical force is seldom used to direct the behavior of those in charge of the educational program, the system of control is none the less real.

External control of education

Many Americans, imbued with the faith that education can change the social order, assume that the schools are independent agencies. As such they are presumed to function without regard to the other parts of society. This is far from a valid assumption, since no part of a social system is free of the norms and system of power in this way. Education is no exception. This is particularly clear in light of the knowledge that the school system in America was created by the churches, the state, and other community organizations. However, the power to control the public schools in the community may not be directly given to the agencies which took part in their establishment. It is important to learn by whom they are controlled, for what ends, and by what means.

Sources of control

Direct control of the educational system rests with the teachers and administrators of the schools. The day-to-day decisions regarding the educational process are made by the teachers. Within the range of accepted activities, the teacher is not only permitted, but also expected to exert authority over the conduct of the children. When teachers are faced with decisions for which there are no clearly understood norms, consultation with the administrator is the common practice. Such consultation is frequently a means of transferring the responsibility for making the decision to the administrator. This protects the teacher from the criticism of those who have the power to force compliance with their wishes. Teachers frequently make decisions concerning some children, but not others. The child whose parents have no power may be the object of decisions that, with few exceptions, are made by the teacher without prior consultation. In contrast, the children of families known to have positions of power in the community may be immune to the teacher's control, and in many cases to that of the principal or superintendent as well. If the teacher is doubtful of her immunity to outside power, she is more likely to seek the administrator's protection than to make the decision without consultation.

Administrators usually have greater latitude in the exercise of control. This differential probably derives from their better understanding of what can and cannot be done without arousing the external sources of power rather than from any difference in the range of permissiveness. This superior understanding of the limits of their control has caused many school principals to be severely criticized by their teachers. Not infrequently, teachers make decisions concerning students before consulting the principal and later fear that the powers of the community will disapprove of the action. Faced with this possibility, the teacher wants the principal to support her decision. If doing so is likely to threaten his position, the administrator may ask the teacher to face the aroused patron without his support. In such a situation the teacher's hostility is almost certain to be directed against the administrator.

If the democratic processes were to function ideally, one might expect the ultimate control of the educational system to rest with the majority of the people of all classes. Generally the political structure provides for a vote by certain eligible citizens to select school board members or other officials who, in turn, select board members. Rarely does a high proportion of the population participate in any election involving school policies. While this abstention frequently gives the teacher greater freedom from external control, at the same time it permits special interest groups to exert pressure on the school board and school staff. Occasionally an entire community becomes aroused by a crisis in a school program. At such times genuine majority opinion may be so expressed that educational policy may be said to be determined by the bulk of the citizens. Such decisions are rare and are usually followed by a return to power of the special interest groups.

An understanding of the actual control of the schools depends upon analysis both of the community power structure and of the personnel of school boards. As to the former, there has been no adequate study; but a description of the behavior of school boards tells us much of the groups in direct control.

Until the last three-quarters of a century or so, no formal schooling, beyond the few years necessary for a mastery of reading, writing, and a little arithmetic, was considered necessary except for the elite, who were expected to enter professional occupations. Only the higher-status citizens showed any great interest in education at that time. They therefore determined school policy without interference. This tradition has continued in some strength to the present time. All of the studies now available indicate that the members of school boards are drawn almost exclusively from professional and business groups in the towns and cities, and from the higher-status farm groups in strictly rural areas.[2]

This is evident, too, in the class identification of the members of the school boards in three towns studied by Warner and his associates. In one community all five board members were classified as upper-middle class; in the second community, three were upper-middle and two were lower-upper; in the third community, six were in middle-class and two in upper-class categories.[3] It is clear that the school boards in these communities were dominated by the upper-middle and upper-class groups. Consequently they are predominantly professional, business, or other white-collar persons. The manual workers and other lower-status groups are not proportionately represented, although in most cases they have the privilege of voting for board members.

Such school boards might, and often do, operate the schools in the interests of the majority of the people, which, in most communities, would be lower-status groups. Yet, if there are differences in goals, the desires of the groups with whom board members are identified are likely to take precedence over those of the lower-status groups. Furthermore, it must be recognized that the board members do not act independently in the making of educational decisions. It is, therefore, important to know who may influence the board members. There is no adequate evidence on which to base an answer to this question, but in broad scope it is known that churches, veterans' organizations, real estate groups, chambers of commerce, and other business and professional organizations frequently put pressure on the school authorities. Pressure is also exerted by the laboring people, but not so often and not so strong.[4]

In addition to the organized pressure which may be brought to bear on the school board members or teachers, there are frequently even more significant informal channels of influence. This is illustrated by the report of a Midwestern school trustee to the writer. When asked with whom he liked to talk before making up his mind about some school questions, he revealed the names of two men. One of these was a retired school principal who had lived in the community for many years; the other was a relatively high-status man who was influential in the councils of the dominant political party. This school trustee seldom made a decision without consulting these men. On many occasions, of course, he would have made decisions which would have had their support anyway, but he felt the need of being assured of their backing before he acted.

There is real need for an extensive study of both the frequency with which such informal channels of influence operate and of the interests or groups which such educational opinion-leaders represent. We can only assume from studies in other areas of behavior that the school board members are unlikely to seek the opinions of persons of lower status than their own.

Aims of control

[The authors have noted elsewhere] that many Americans expect the educational system to solve many social problems and to increase the opportunities for social mobility. It seems unlikely that school boards, composed of higher-status people and influenced as they apparently are by persons with similar interests, would knowingly initiate an educational program which would result in major changes in the class structure. In this respect the school boards and their associates in control are desirous of maintaining the *status quo*. They are either in satisfactory positions or sufficiently near to such positions that the class structure is not oppressive to them.

In other areas the agencies of school control are likely to seek those ends agreeable to the status and occupational groups with which they are identified. The professionals want their own children to receive the type of academic training that will prepare them for higher levels of college and professional training. Controlling groups may have no well-established opinion concerning the training of children who are not likely to seek

[2] For further detail on the composition of school boards see: George S. Counts, "The Social Composition of School Boards," *University of Chicago Supplementary Educational Monographs, No. 33,* 1937, and Harold Hand, "Who Runs Our School Boards?" *The American Teacher,* Vol. 23, 1939.
[3] W. L. Warner, Robert Havighurst, and Martin Loeb, *Who Shall Be Educated?* New York: Harper & Bros., 1944.

[4] For further discussion of this point, see Mark Starr, *Labor Looks at Education,* Cambridge, Mass.: Harvard University Press, 1946.

higher education. In this case the demand for academic training will be most salient for them. The business-management interests among the controlling group will have similar desires for their own children. For the children of working-class families, however, they may have more definite ideas. Generally businessmen want these children to receive a type of training that will make them efficient and tractable workmen in their offices, stores, and factories. Along with this, such school boards would like to have the children of working-class parents well indoctrinated with the businessman's point of view in regard to the capitalistic system and the relations of management and labor.[5]

Most of the organized pressure groups effective in controlling the schools desire the same ends as those represented by the board members. Veterans' groups and other "patriotic" organizations may, however, place more emphasis on the particular brand of Americanism which they represent. The American Legion through its Americanism Commission has been particularly active in exerting pressure on the schools to teach those things that are believed to result in the Legion's concept of American behavior.[6] The churches, with various interpretations of ethics and values, have always exerted effective pressure to see that the schools teach the values they espouse. Church groups frequently represent different social-class groups, but in most cases those embracing the values of the dominant group in the community are most effective in controlling the school program. In general, except for times when the general public becomes aroused, the wishes of the higher-status white-collar groups take precedence in the educational program.

Means of control

Perhaps the most effective means of controlling the school is through selection and dismissal of teachers, and through informal pressures. School boards and their supporting groups have not hesitated to refuse employment to teachers who, regardless of other qualifications, were believed to present ideas or materials which would stimulate youth to think, or to do, anything likely to upset

the *status quo*. This is illustrated by the case of Mr. R who had taught for many years in a Midwestern town.

Mr. R had the reputation of being a good teacher, although he was relatively liberal in his views on certain social issues. On one occasion the daughter of one of the leading industrialists reported to her father a statement that he was purported to have made about some of the inequalities in the American economic system. Without investigating the accuracy of the report, the industrialist demanded that the school board dismiss the teacher. This the board was prepared to do, but the board members decided to have an open meeting in which the views of the citizens could be heard before proceeding with the dismissal. The charges of the industrialist were presented and various persons supported them. Before voting, however, another influential person spoke in Mr. R's defense. His comments were to the effect that Mr. R was a member of a highly respected family and had served the community for many years. The spokesman also reported that he had obtained from Mr. R a promise to refrain from making any statements that would not be approved. On the strength of this promise the board voted to continue Mr. R's employment.

Although Mr. R was not dismissed, as he would have been without the support of influential friends, he was effectively throttled in his teaching. Furthermore, it is very likely that the superintendent and the board of education will exercise extreme care in the selection of new teachers to prevent the reoccurrence of such a situation. The history of teacher tenure in innumerable American communities provides similar cases. Under the latent threat of dismissal, every teacher knows that there are certain subjects he must avoid or of which he must be so cautious that he is ineffective.

Informal pressures are frequently exerted on the teachers by such means as gossip about their ideas or behavior, comments conveyed by the children of powerful patrons, recognition or ostracism, and many others. The case of Mr. J is more obvious, but it still illustrates the pressure exerted by one of the elite of the community in which he taught.

A few years ago arrangements had been made by the officials of a teachers' association for the Town Meeting of the Air to be broadcast from its annual meeting. A week before the meeting it was learned that the topic of the Town Meeting concerned communists in labor unions and

[5] See Starr, *op. cit.*, and Frank Sparks, "What Management Wants from Our Schools," *Studies in Higher Education,* Lafayette, Ind.: Purdue University, 1944, pp. 22-26.
[6] See H. L. Chaillaux, "The American Legion's Interest in Education," *The Annals of the American Academy of Political and Social Science,* Vol. 182, 1935, pp. 116-119.

that one of the speakers was a well-known Communist Party member. Mr. A, a leading citizen and businessman of the locality, immediately wired the governor of the state asking him to intercede to prevent the Town Meeting and specifically to prevent this Communist from appearing before the assembled teachers of the area.

Mr. J, a high-school teacher, had served for a year on the Association's Executive Committee which planned to serve as a welcoming committee for the Town Meeting speakers. Shortly after Mr. A's protest to the governor had been made public, Mr. J publicly stated that he would not greet the Town Meeting speakers and that he did not approve of bringing unionism into the schools.

Mr. J's statement clearly indicates that he dared not support the program, which he had previously helped to arrange, after the elite of his community had registered its disapproval. No doubt this incident renewed in many other teachers an awareness of the need to maintain the *status quo* in the social system. A teacher's failure to bow to such pressure frequently means dismissal.

A second method often used by the power group to control the nature of the educational program is the restriction of tax funds for the school. Many administrators of schools which provide only the traditional academic program designed for higher-status children would like to enrich the program to serve the needs of other groups. Such a program requires larger budgets. Industrial interests and other heavy taxpayers frequently oppose such programs. Through propaganda and other influence on the school board, these groups are often able to restrict the school program.[7]

Budget limitation is very often associated with a propaganda campaign against a school program that includes all the "expensive frills." Such campaigns are sponsored by special interest and the higher-income groups who control, or at least have influence through, informal channels and mass communication media such as newspapers and radio stations. Their support of traditional education in the "fundamentals" finds a favorable response among many persons whose children's welfare would be much better served by a broader, but perhaps more expensive school program.

"The New York State Chamber of Commerce in 1939 adopted a report to the effect that the state should pay only for enough education 'to kill illiteracy.' 'The state,' it said, 'must endeavor to carry all the youngsters up to that point, but beyond that point youngsters will do better if they have to put up a real fight to go on, and beyond that point, it is a fair question whether the State should bear all expenses or whether parents amply able to educate their own youngsters should pay for it.'"[8] This appeal to the traditional values of individual initiative may have some effect on the opinions of those desiring something from the schools that the Chamber of Commerce did not wish. If so the schools are less likely to be encouraged to spend any money on programs to give the lower-status youth any higher-class values.

The National Association of Manufacturers, The American Legion, The American Medical Association, private utilities companies, and many other organizations as well as the Chamber of Commerce have carried on nation-wide campaigns to provide the teachers with "acceptable" teaching material and to influence the content of textbooks.[9] These campaigns sometimes take the form of essays or speech contests in which the material to be discussed is sharply defined by the sponsoring agency. The indoctrinational aspects of such contests are illustrated by the following case known to the author.

The school which Martha was attending cooperated with a high-status women's organization which was sponsoring an essay contest on great American women. The teacher encouraged Martha, who was one of her brighter students, to enter the contest even though she came from a working-class family. Martha chose to write an essay on the life of Eleanor Roosevelt. When the representative of the women's organization called at the school to discuss the better essays with the teacher and their authors, the teacher presented Martha's as one of the best. The lady was quite incensed and reprimanded Martha with the comment, "Why should you write about her? She is not a great woman." Martha's essay received no further consideration in the contest.

Although the means may be subtle, the ends desired by the controlling groups in the society are constantly being placed before the teachers.

[7] See F. T. Rope, *Opinion Conflict and School Support, Teachers College Contributions to Education,* No. 838, New York: Columbia University, 1941, for an excellent analysis of the program of this sort in one American community.

[8] The Institute of Propaganda Analysis, "Propaganda Over Our Schools," *Propaganda Analysis, 4,* February, 1941. The major portion of this is quoted from the *Monthly Bulletin,* Chamber of Commerce of New York, Nov. 1939.

[9] See Institute of Propaganda Analysis, *op. cit.,* and F. E. Lumley, *The Propaganda Menace,* New York: Century, 1933, pp. 301-329, for analyses of some such campaigns to influence the curriculum content.

Internalized attitudes of teachers

The analysis of the external pressure on the teachers of American schools makes it almost unnecessary to mention that teachers' own attitudes and values also play a role in the determination of the educational program. Much of the discussion of external controls might leave the impression that all teachers were constantly struggling to resist the powers seeking to determine educational policy. Although there are some teachers who feel the yoke of control, many have so completely internalized the desires and beliefs of the controlling group that these attitudes are clearly their own. This seemingly results from three major processes: (1) the selection of persons who hold such values, sentiments, and beliefs; (2) interaction and identification with people in the schools who hold such values and beliefs; and (3) the desire for the security, status, and approval which those in control are in a position to give.

We know all too little of the attitudes, values, and beliefs of people who enter the teaching profession. . . . [It] is impossible to say at this time whether the behavior of teachers is the result of selection of teaching personnel or of the social forces that operate upon them after entering the school. Evidence from one study indicates that college students of education are slightly more liberal concerning the employment of members of minority groups in the schools than are experienced teachers and board members. There is also evidence indicating that teachers are slightly more liberal on some issues than members of school boards, but when the data in this study are examined, one is impressed with the similarity between teachers and their employers.[10] If these are typical of other attitudes, prospective teachers may be somewhat more liberal than school board members, but the difference in beliefs is relatively slight. This is true also of differences between prospective teachers and experienced ones. It is possible that these last differences may be accounted for by the selection of the more conservative of the prospective teachers.

Although liberal persons may be chosen for teaching positions in some cases, our limited evidence suggests that the teaching profession as a whole is conservative in its social attitudes. In general, new teachers move in a circle of friends and acquaintances from the teaching field and/or from positions allied with education. As the new teachers come to identify themselves with other teachers, they assume the role of the teacher, and no doubt internalize the attitudes and beliefs of the group with which they most frequently interact. New teachers who rebel are more likely to be unhappy in their work and to arouse the suspicions of those in control. They are, therefore, not likely to last long.

The third factor which may affect the internalized attitudes of the teaching profession is the desire for status in the community. Available evidence[11] indicates that the majority of teachers come from lower middle-class families. By becoming teachers they acquire somewhat higher status, although they are seldom accepted as full members of the higher-status groups. Their success in achieving such social positions is, in part, dependent on the internalization of the values and beliefs of the group toward which they aspire. In their striving for acceptance in higher-status positions in society, they frequently come to favor the values and beliefs of the people who control the educational system. This is particularly true in many cases because their tenure, as well as their social status, is dependent on the acceptance and teaching of such values.

There is still much to be learned about the control of the American educational system and the ends which those in control desire the schools to serve. Apparently control is more likely to rest in groups relatively conservative in regard to social change. Both the school staff and those who have power over the teachers and administrators are inclined to place high value on the culture and social structure approved by persons satisfied with the society and their positions in it.

---

[10] Florence Greenhoe, *Community Contacts and Participation of Teachers*, Washington, D.C.: American Council on Public Affairs, 1941, pp. 31-37.

[11] Greenhoe, *op. cit.*, pp. 8-14; W. L. Warner, Robert Havighurst, and M. L. Loeb, *Who Shall Be Educated?* New York: Harper & Bros., 1944; W. L. Warner, et al., *Democracy in Jonesville*, New York: Harper & Bros., 1949; and A. B. Hollingshead, *Elmtown's Youth*, New York: John Wiley & Sons, 1949.

THE SCHOOL AND OTHER SOCIAL INFLUENCES

The school is but one of the agencies of society which influence the education of the young. Though the school exists to serve the needs of a changing society, the precise purposes of schooling have not been formally defined, at least not on a national level. Problems concerning the proper relationship between schooling and other educative forces have long been evident. In part, problems have arisen from the failure to differentiate *schooling* from *education*. If, for example, clear distinctions are not made between *schooling* as a function concerned with limited and explicit learning opportunities and *education* as the sum total of *all* learning contacts, then it is understandable why conflicts concerning the overall purposes of education have arisen. Many forces are at work to make this a difficult problem to solve: Lucio and McNeil point out that "Much of the conflict . . . derives from efforts of some pressure groups to extend the functions of the school, while others seek the restriction of functions to tasks which are not likely to be performed by any other agency" (4).

Even more specifically, no clear-cut boundaries have been formulated between the educational responsibilities of three primary social agencies—the school, the church, and the family. Has it been decided that only the school should deal with intellectual development, only the church with the moral and religious, and only the family with the affective and social? The difficulties of drawing the lines suggest the range of problems involved, not only in the relationships among these agencies, but in the influence of the numerous other forces impinging upon the program of education.

In addition to the content of the educational program of each of the agencies, there is also a problem of the methods employed. What is to be the role of indoctrination in the teaching procedures used by the home, the church, and the school? What happens when scientific method as taught at school conflicts with beliefs accepted on faith in the church or in the home?

The school not only shares responsibilities with other agencies such as the home and the church; it has more direct responsibility to the society itself. One aspect of this responsibility is teaching respect for the laws of the society. To what extent is the existence of juvenile delinquency in the society a problem of the schools of the society? Is there evidence that the schools sometimes contribute to the development of delinquency? Is there evidence that the schools could be used to reduce the incidence of delinquency in the society?

Discussion of the relationship of the school to the society is incomplete without some consideration of the "peer culture" in which the student is to be found. Much that is taught by the primary educational agencies is filtered through the mesh of acceptance by one's peers. How can the "gang" be so molded as to reinforce those learnings which seem socially acceptable?

The school and other social influences

THE SCHOOL AND THE CHURCH

Consideration of the relationship of the school, as an agency of the state, and the church has several different dimensions. In the first place, there are certain values which all of the agencies of a democratic society hold in common with the religious groups represented in our churches. It may be presumed that both state and church are concerned with the teaching of values such as respect for human dignity, recognition of abuses and evils, and facing facts and consequences. In the second place, religion has held so important a place in the development of our culture that an understanding of that cultural heritage and of the institution of religion is important to an understanding of the society. Thus, the school as an agent of the state has, in some fashion, considered the nature of religion. In the third place, both the Constitution and the principle of democratic respect for the individual's freedom of conscience make it imperative that the public school not be used to indoctrinate the individual in a particular religious belief. The critical problem is to determine the degree and kind of religious emphases to be accounted for in schools. Readings 66 to 71 attempt to deal with one or another of these dimensions.

66

William H. Kilpatrick

RELIGION IN EDUCATION: THE ISSUES

Over one hundred years ago a battle was waged to free the public schools from sectarian influences, with the result that public schools have remained nonsectarian ever since. However, the issue of religion in schools still concerns segments of the American public, and students of education need to understand the problem in its historical perspective in order that the reasons for persistence of the problem will be clear. Decisions on this issue may well affect the course of American education for decades to come.

An analysis of the religion-in-education problem was made by a leader of the Progressive education movement, Professor William H. Kilpatrick. In this article Professor Kilpatrick demonstrates the concern of the Progressive movement for the dignity of the individual and for his freedom from the coercion of the state in arriving at his fundamental beliefs. The Progressive education movement was also concerned with the possible divisiveness of a system of parochial schools which might tend to maintain sharp lines of cleavage within the society itself based on differences of religious belief and practice. The questions and possible responses which different groups might make to them, listed by Kilpatrick at the end of his article, are capsule statements of problems still of concern today.

My task as assigned by the editor is to "set forth the issues within this whole area of religion in education." . . . [The] aim here will be to "set forth"—differentiate, make clear, and relate —the several issues involved, but not to discuss their merits.

Few if any matters before the American people cut any deeper into contending issues both as historically oriented and as currently held. And few problems are accordingly more complex. Because of this complexity an adequate analysis is not easy. The treatment here adopted is three-fold: (i) to choose a simpler instance from among the various issues involved and subject this to a

preliminary try-out treatment in such way as to bring out a sample portrayal of the values felt to be at stake by the various opposed parties; (ii) to consider the differing meanings given by the opposed groups to certain important conceptions; and finally (iii) to present a list of significant issues which emerge from the study of the problem of religion in education.

A sample issue

The sample issue chosen for try-out treatment is the fairly widespread public school practice of singing Christian Christmas carols in spite of the fact that the school is public and includes

From *Progressive Education,* 1949, 26:98–102.

non-Christian children among its pupils. It happens that the writer has recently been called upon by a responsible group of citizens to discuss publicly this very issue.

Concerning this practice of carol singing three questions present themselves, the three overlapping more or less and each presenting a distribution of answer attitudes.

1. Is this practice of carol singing desirable from a religious point of view?

In answer we have a scale of response attitudes varying from a strong *yes* at one end on down to zero and then rising up to a strong *no* at the other end. Those with the strong *yes* may historically be deeply rooted in America or they may be fairly recent comers to these shores. If deeply rooted, they may never have had any other thought than that America is in origin, and in fact of population, a Christian country. If newcomers, they may feel strongest their loyalty to their church. Both such groups probably wish the public school to bring up all children in the Christian tradition. If some pupils come from anti-Christian or non-Christian homes, these zealous ones will probably feel that somehow such unfortunate children do not adequately represent America and, at any rate, it won't hurt them to take this slight part in a "real" religious program.

Down toward zero on the scale, but still on the positive side, there will be certain Christian-bred teachers who are relatively indifferent to the religious argument, but feel that Christmas carols are a desirable part of the culture and that the general Christmas interest will make the children willing to learn and sing them. Those who oppose this carol singing divide into two groups. First are the Jews and certain non-Christians who prefer not to have their children taught, in this seeming authoritative fashion, these Christian songs. Second are certain thoughtful citizens, both non-religious and some earnest and zealous Christians such as Baptists and Quakers, who openly oppose and reject any intermingling of church and state in the public school. These feel that to subject the Jews to this embarrassing situation is a direct denial of ethics and democracy as well as a violation of the proper separation of church and state.

2. The second question develops from the first: Will a proper democracy and sensitive ethics be willing to embarrass Jewish or other non-Christian pupils of the public school by such practices as singing Christian carols or reciting the Lord's prayer?

In answer we again find a scale. At one end comes a strong *no*; democracy and ethics alike oppose such practices. Lower down in the scale and on the *yes* side are those who identify democracy with majority rule and, being in the majority, are relatively insensitive to the feelings of groups other than their own.

3. The third question relates explicitly to the legal aspect of the problem: Is it legally permissible for the public school to engage in such specific Christian practices as singing Christian Christmas carols?

And here again we find an answer scale, varying from a strong *no* through zero to a definite *yes*. On the *no* side are many who feel that the *obiter dicta* of the Everson and McCollum decisions of the Supreme Court show that a majority of the Court count that "the prohibition [of the 1st amendment as broadened by the 14th] broadly forbids state support, financial or other, of religion in any wise, form, or degree" (Mr. Justice Rutledge). Others, on the *yes* side, attack the McCollum decision as going entirely too far and count themselves meanwhile legally free to teach the singing of such carols.

These three points of view serve to give us some notion of how the American people divide on the general question. We next dig a little deeper into the differences.

Meanings involved in the issues

The opposed groups in this matter of teaching religion in the school understand certain crucial terms in such different ways that to understand and evaluate the opposed positions we have to understand the differing meanings given by them to these terms. Six terms seem to demand this special treatment: religion, religious freedom, secularism, spiritual, democracy, teaching.

1. *Religion.* The strongly different understandings of what religion is enter definitely into the active issues here under consideration. The nature of religious authority is perhaps the chief factor in dispute. We again find a scale and can easily distinguish on it seven different positions.

(1) At one end stand those who believe that an infinite, omniscient, omnipotent personal God has made the head of their church His vicar on earth, giving to him "the mandate and the right to teach with authority . . . in matters of faith and morals." When the head of this church has in proper manner made a decision regarding any doctrine, "this is in itself complete, absolute, and final proof of the truth of this doctrine."

(2) Lower down in the scale are those who believe in this same infinite God but hold that His word to man is the Bible, these counting this to be the infallible and inerrant word of God. It then

becomes the duty of men to study this book to learn their duty.

(3) Further down the scale scattered along are various "modernistic" positions as to the extent of man's available knowledge regarding the will of God. The disciplines of "higher criticism," "comparative religion," and modern science acting together have for these groups put the authority of theology and belief in religious doctrine much more on a par with what man can by inductive study find out for himself. Possibly at this point belongs John Locke's statement: "He that takes away reason to make way for revelation puts out the eye of both." An adverse critic (J. B. Bury) says of this general position that "during the last three hundred years, reason has been slowly but steadily destroying Christian mythology and exposing the pretentions of supernatural revelation."

(4) Perhaps overlapping with the position just preceding and leading definitely to the succeeding position, we find position (4) which defines religion as "the quest for the values of the ideal life, involving three phases: the ideal, the practices for attaining the values of the ideal, and the theology or world view relating the quest to the environing universe." It is the term "theology" in this definition which joins position (4) with position (3). The term "world view" if taken alone would perhaps unite position (4) with position (5).

(5) This position leaves no place for the supernatural, but still recognizes an essential aspect of life which may well be called religious: "Any activity, pursued in behalf of an ideal end against obstacles and in spite of threats of personal loss, because of conviction of its general and enduring value, is religious in quality."

(6) Further down from supernatural authority, possibly below zero in attitude toward religion, stands the assertion: "A deep belief in a personal deity destroys all deep belief in the unconquerable personality of man."

(7) Finally comes the definite anti-religious statement of Karl Marx that religion is the opiate of the people.

So much for the various understandings of what religion means.

2. *Religious Freedom.* From the differing conceptions of religion and religious authority discussed above there follow at once different conceptions of a proper religious freedom.

In the first of these seven conceptions of religious authority we find proponents saying that their church, "convinced through its divine prerogatives of being the only true church, must demand the right of freedom for herself alone." In some countries, however, they "will be obliged to ask full religious freedom for all, resigned at being forced to cohabitate where they alone should rightfully be allowed to live." In other words, "such a right [to religious freedom] can only be possessed by truth, and never by error."

James Madison's statement of the opposed position assumes that no one has as yet found a way of learning about religion except by reason:

"We hold it for a fundamental and undeniable truth, "that Religion or the duty which we owe to our Creator and the Manner of discharging it, can be directed only by reason and conviction, not by force or violence." (*Va. Decl. Rights,* Art: 16) The Religion then of every man must be left to the conviction and conscience of every man; and it is the right of every man to exercise it as these may dictate. This right is in its nature an unalienable right."

3. *Secularism.* Dictionary (1947): "The view that public education and other matters of civil policy should be conducted without the introduction of a religious element."

From certain people who uphold the first definition of religion given above comes this statement: "The failure to center life in God is secularism, which . . . is the most deadly menace to our Christian and American way of living."

A group expressing the second definition of religion supports the general position just quoted with these words: "An acceptance of basic religious truths is the foundation for spiritual growth, and the motivation for moral conduct."

By contrast, many holding to the 3rd, 4th, and 5th definitions of religion as given above would accept the dictionary definition of secularism as just given, and affirm not only that such a secularism is no menace but that it is the only proper work of the public school. In keeping with this attitude and in anticipation of the discussion on "spiritual," a recent educational yearbook, *The Public Schools and Spiritual Values,* asserts "both the logical possibility and the practical potential adequacy of the public school to teach such spiritual values as": "moral insight, integrity of thought and act; equal regard for human personality wherever found; faith in the free play of intelligence both to guide study and direct action, and, finally, those further values of refined thought and feeling requisite to bring life to its finest quality." And they propose to do this "on the basis of human reason and experience and without necessary recourse to religious authority."

4. *Spiritual.* Webster gives nine senses in which the term spiritual is used. Of these the 2nd and

3rd together give one definition, and the 4th and 5th similarly give another.

"2. Of or pertaining to the intellectual and higher endowments of the mind . . . also highly refined in thought and feeling

"3. Of or pertaining to the moral feelings or states of the soul, as distinguished from external actions. . . .

[That these 2nd and 3rd senses precede the 4th and 5th is apparently no other than historic priority of usage.]

"4. Of or pertaining to the soul or its affections as influenced by the divine spirit. . . .

"5. Of or pertaining to sacred things or the church. . . ."

It is natural then that the 1st and 2nd definitions of religion as given earlier would incline rather to the 4th and 5th meanings of the term spiritual; while the 4th and 5th definitions of religion would tend to use the 2nd and 3rd meanings of spiritual.

5. *Democracy.* This term (excluding the Communistic propaganda use of it) tends to be used in two senses: one as a kind of government, government by the people; the other includes government by the people but goes beyond and deeper than government to stress the spirit of ethics and the Golden Rule which should, but may not, predominate in majority rule.

It is the second sense of democracy which seems especially to demand that the dominant Christian group consider, for example, the minority groups, both religious and non-religious, before it demands Bible reading, the Lord's prayer, Christmas carols, and the like in public schools.

6. *Teaching* looks to two quite different types of character according as it stresses (i) obedient acceptance by the learner of what the teacher wishes to inculcate or whether (ii) it stresses the upbuilding of self-directing character, the ability and disposition to consider the total situation, including the rights and feelings of all others involved, before deciding to act.

One of the justices in the McCollum case said of position (1) in religion: it "does not leave the individual to pick up religion by chance. It relies on early and indelible indoctrination." Emperor Francis of Austria (c. 1882) illustrated the same ideal of teaching from a political point of view: "Obedient subjects are more desirable than enlightened citizens." Herbert Spencer favored the second type of teaching: "The aim of your discipline should be to produce a *self-governing* being; not to produce a being *to be governed by others.*" A later educator develops the same thought:

"Children in school must be allowed freedom . . . to develop active qualities of initiative, independence and resourcefulness, before the abuses and failures of democracy will disappear."

Statement of issues

Following all the foregoing, we are now ready to present a list of the issues which seem to be most significantly involved in the problem of religion in education. The chief interest is of course the disputed area of religion in the public school. It appears wise to present the issues in connection with certain questions which lead naturally to the issues.

Q. 1: Is religion to be given an essential place in education? The answer to this question raises acutely the problem of what meaning to give to the terms *religion* and *teaching* as discussed above.

Groups (1) and (2) of religion will in general answer *yes* to this question, meaning to teach their authoritative creeds by indoctrination. In their own privately controlled schools religious teaching will permeate all else. In connection with the public school, released time will be sought for a special period of indoctrination.

Group (3) will likewise answer *yes* to Q. 1, but will not in general expect other than Sunday school or released time teaching; and this position will move away from plain indoctrination toward the second type of teaching.

Groups (4) and (5) will be largely indifferent as to whether the term *religious* be applied to the teaching they support. And both will urgently demand teaching in behalf of social and moral ideals, using the second type of teaching.

Group (6) possibly, and group (7) certainly, will oppose the teaching of anything customarily called religion. But each group will wish to teach its own social and moral ideals, group (6) by the second type of teaching, group (7) by indoctrination.

Out of this multiform answer there emerges the following complex issue:

Issue 1: What does religion mean? What differing kinds of teaching of religion do the several meanings of religion respectively favor? What shall be done about it all?

The next question splits into two according as we, first, ignore (for the sake of this discussion) the legal possibility that the Supreme Court has settled the question and, second, accept that the McCollum decision rules out from the public school all teaching of religion.

Q. 2: Disregarding the legal aspect, is it *otherwise right* for the public school to teach religion as such and (a) require all to take it or (b) permit non-conforming parents to have their children excused or (c) apportion school funds to any religious group wishing to set up its own school?

As to option (a), we may rule it out of consideration. The world in general, and America in particular, has progressed too far from an established church to permit this option. Some have proposed that the public school teach the common elements underlying all religious outlooks (including the non-religious); but since to call this religion would provoke strong antagonism from the active religions the plan need not be considered. It is not teaching religion *as such.*

Option (b) was perhaps sufficiently discussed under question 2 of a sample issue, but it seems wise to present here the specific issue:

Issue 2: Does, or does not, the spirit of democracy require that the public school avoid acts which formally separate the pupils of one religious group from the rest?

Option (c) of Q. 2 leads directly to a very important issue not thus far herein discussed:

Issue 3: Do we wish the segmentation of our population by religion, as in Quebec? and with probable resulting political parties or blocs as in Belgium and the Netherlands?

If Q. 2 (a) be answered in the negative, then two related issues emerge:

Issue 4: If the school is to inculcate nothing of religion, does this forbid such practices as Bible reading (as worship), the Lord's prayer, and the singing of Christian Christmas carols?

Issue 5: Can the school practice any of these Christian religious observances without improperly disregarding the rights and feelings of all non-Christians thereby concerned?

This issue in part repeats Issue 2, but it seems wise to repeat it in this more explicit setting.

Q. 3: Supposing that the McCollum decision does forbid any public school support of religion in guise, form, or degree, what shall the opponents of the decision do? This question leads directly to a further issue:

Issue 6: Shall effort be made to amend the Constitution so as to permit the appropriation of public money for teaching religion?

There appear signs that the movement so to act is already under way.

Q. 4: How is character built? How shall those character traits be taught that are required for good individual and group living?

This question, understood in the light of the discussion of the terms religion, secularism, spiritual, and teaching, leads at once to two further issues:

Issue 7: Is supernatural religion necessary to the effective teaching of the character traits required for good individual and social living?

Issue 8: Is the public school guilty of attack on religion if it acts on the basis of the answer *no* to Issue 7?

Three final issues complete the list.

Issue 9: Is higher education justified in considering whether religion is not now properly in process of remaking in the light of increasing knowledge?

Issue 10: Is the public school justified in teaching, on its merits, a conception of morality and spirituality which follows from Issue 9?

Issue 11: Are the students in high school and college to be encouraged to criticize in class the various systems of religion with their consequent effects on civilization in order to find out what they should themselves believe?

67

VALUES

The teacher should be able to identify the common values which seem basic to both democracy and our Judeo-Christian heritage. These common values appear implicitly or explicitly in the Constitution and its Bill of Rights and in the Bible and the creeds of the major religious groups.

The Educational Policies Commission, which prepared the 1951 report from which this selection is taken, is a commission of the National Education Association; the statement thus represents an official position of the organized teaching profession. The report was authorized during the 1948 meeting of the National Association and published in 1951. The position of the NEA has remained firm since this statement was made. Readers may compare this 1951 report with related recent statements by other agencies and individuals to determine if there are new or reinterpreted versions of moral and spiritual values to be given consideration. Among the references recommended are the following: (a) "National Goals in Education," Chapter 3 of *Goals for Americans* (comprising the Report of the President's Commission on National Goals), Columbia University: The American Assembly. Published by Prentice-Hall, 1960, and (b) *The Pursuit of Excellence* (The "Rockefeller Report" on Education), Garden City, New York: Doubleday and Co., 1958.

It is often alleged that the American people, unlike the people of dictatorships, lack a clear vision of the values on which their society rests. Whether or not this generalization is true, it is important to ask whether a substantial agreement exists among the people of the United States concerning the moral and spiritual values by which they should live and which they wish to see embodied in the character and conduct of their children.

Such a scheme of values can hardly be discovered by any amount of study of the external facts of American life. Like all other societies, the United States falls short of achieving its highest moral and spiritual ideals. In spite of relapses and variations in practice, however, there is a generally accepted body of values which the American people tend to use as a compass for finding their way through political, social, economic, and personal issues.

The American people are agreed on certain values

The codification of the values of American society has been attempted before by many individuals and groups, including this Commission. If our society were a completely static one, such reformulations would presumably be unnecessary. The desired characteristics of our society could be written down somewhere, once and for all, and then referred to as occasion arose. Such a procedure, however, is repugnant to the dynamic nature of American society. The Commission does not, therefore, suppose that by enumerating the following values it will achieve either originality, completeness, or finality. Rather, this analysis is offered to help clarify the moral and spiritual values upon which the American people as a whole have agreed to manage their individual lives and their corporate activities, including their public schools.

Many of these values find political expression in the Constitution and Bill of Rights. Although

From *Moral and Spiritual Values in the Public Schools*, Educational Policies Commission (Washington: National Education Association, 1951), pp. 17–34.

these declarations are not couched in terms of rituals or other religious forms, the major religious groups can discover in their respective Bibles and creeds many statements which support them.

1. Human personality—the basic value. Among the values here proposed, the first is fundamental to all that follow. The basic moral and spiritual value in American life is the supreme importance of the individual personality.

The inherent worth of every human being is basic in the teachings of Christianity and of many other great religions. The individual personality can acquire a capacity for moral judgments and a sense of moral responsibility. This doctrine sharply challenges every form of oppression. It implies that each human being should have every possible opportunity to achieve by his own efforts a feeling of security and competence in dealing with the problems arising in daily life. It implies also that self-realization cannot be fully achieved without social relationships based on moral and spiritual values.

In educational terms, this value requires a school system which, by making freely available the common heritage of human association and human culture, opens to every child the opportunity to grow to his full physical, intellectual, moral, and spiritual stature. It favors those plans of school organization and instruction which recognize and meet the varying needs and aspirations of individuals. By exploring and acknowledging the capacities of each child, education seeks to develop all his creative powers, to encourage him to feel that he can do things of value, that he belongs, and that he is wanted. It discourages every tendency toward despotism. It assigns no superior moral status, but rather a more definite moral responsibility, to the strong and the able. It endeavors to arouse in each individual a profound sense of self-respect and personal integrity.

2. Moral responsibility. If the individual personality is supreme, each person should feel responsible for the consequences of his own conduct.

Moral responsibility and self-discipline are marks of maturity. The young child often craves adult direction. If, however, parents and teachers protect a child unduly from the difficulties of decision-making and the consequences of those decisions, his childish pattern of dependency may continue into adulthood. While everyone, at times, needs the advice of parent, friend, teacher, physician, or clergyman, one who is unequal to the problems with which life confronts him is dependent on the thinking of others and will blame them for the outcome of his own conduct. He may let the formalized codes of political, social, or religious institutions substitute for his own sense of moral responsibility, leaning heavily on those institutions which tell him what to believe and what to do. For him, the defeats of life, far from strengthening his character for future encounters, only build habits of evasion and self-pity. Such habits cripple the personality development of the individual, prevent his achievement of the responsible citizenship required by the democratic ideal, and distort values.

Good schools, then, will help children and youth to grow up. During childhood, a judicious balance between protective authority, on the one hand, and delegation of responsibility, on the other hand, can sustain the necessary sense of security while inducing growth toward mature personal integrity. Toward the end of adolescence, the individual should have acquired a large measure of self-reliance tempered by social conscience. He will see that the supremacy of the individual personality means both self-confidence and responsibility to treat every other person with respect and consideration. In maturity, then, self-discipline will be sustained by an inner hardihood that enables one to deal firmly with himself and gently with others.

3. *Institutions as the servants of men.* If the individual personality is supreme, institutional arrangements are the servants of mankind.

Domestic, cultural, and political institutions are not in themselves suitable objects of veneration, except insofar as they contribute to the moral and spiritual values of human life. The family as an institution contributes to social stability, and provides protection for the young. A family which is linked by affection rather than merely by authority affords a training ground for wholesome human relations. Similarly, schools and other institutions justify their existence as they contribute to the growth, happiness, and well-being of individuals. Governments, too, as stated by the Declaration of Independence, are instituted among men to promote their inalienable rights. Social institutions, then, are means of serving people. They are never more important than people. Man was not made for the Sabbath. While institutions

should not be changed for trivial or transitory reasons, they should be subject to adjustments according to the needs and values of the individuals who function in them.

That social institutions resist change is well known. One of the major functions of education is to encourage a continuing appraisal of the suitability of existing institutions to the current and prospective needs of the people. Of course, the schools of a totalitarian state are powerless to perform a function of this kind. In our country, however, the schools neglect a proper duty if they fail to provide the knowledge, skill, and attitudes whereby public intelligence can function wisely to keep social institutions in line with moral and spiritual values. The schools should, indeed, go further to develop in all young people a strong sense of responsibility for community well-being and a willingness to devote themselves unselfishly to it.

4. *Common consent.* If the individual personality is supreme, mutual consent is better than violence.

Voluntary cooperation, contrary to the idea of survival of the fittest, is essential to all forms of life. According to the American system of values, no partisan interest is authorized to overreach the popular will. This does not mean the repudiation of force under any and all circumstances. Force, tempered by humanity, regulated by law, and safeguarded by justice, must restrain those who reject the methods of peace. The principle that group decisions should be made and enforced by common consent applies in all relationships of life. The principle is the same whether the group is 150 million citizens, or a thousand members of a student body, or three men planning a fishing trip.

This element of the American system of values calls for an educational program which gives many opportunities for friendly cooperation. It does not imply a lawless or chaotic school. It does require that, within limits set by degrees of maturity, the reasons for established controls be made clear to those who are subject to them; that controls be imposed only when necessary to the well-being of the group; and that their administration be tempered by due regard for the imperfections of human nature and for the rights of both minorities and majorities. In proportion as it makes use of discussion, compromise, negotiation, and voting, a society requires public enlightenment. It is well that all citizens receive the franchise, better that they may vote without fear, and still better that they shall actually use this civic privilege. But there is one achievement even higher. That is the exercise of the franchise by citizens who are informed and humane with respect to the issues involved. The men who established our government foresaw the relation of education to the social order which they were forging in the fires of revolution and public debate. They looked upon education in both knowledge and ideals as a guarantee that the nation so conceived might endure.

5. *Devotion to truth.* If the individual personality is supreme, the human mind should be liberated by access to information and opinion.

Custom and complacency have deprived us of a sharp awareness of the morality of intellectual freedom. Yet, in terms of human history, the rights of a man to speak his mind, to worship according to conscience and training, and to have access to knowledge and divergent opinions are recent achievements. Today these rights are denied to a large proportion of the people of the earth. The totalitarian strategy of deception makes it especially necessary that respect for truth be more fully understood, more keenly appreciated, and more consistently applied. The perversion of liberty to destroy all liberties, the misuse of discussion to sabotage action, the attempt to exercise censorship and thought-control, and the surrender to rule by a mob or by a tyrant are threats to this aspect of our moral values. When a man can be punished for speaking his mind, he is tempted to say what is safe and not necessarily what his convictions direct. Thus, when intellectual freedom is denied, men who might otherwise maintain integrity may turn to deceit and hypocrisy.

The public schools should provide young people with experience in the processes of seeking truth, of comparing opinions, and of appealing to reason on controverted questions. Mastery of this kind of intellectual honesty is a difficult task. It is not achieved by allowing children to do as they please. Just as the school cultivates hostility toward the arbitrary use of power, so it must also cultivate loyalty to the methods of rational discussion and deliberation. The school should not countenance capricious misuse of the intellectual freedoms. While it encourages frank appraisal of institutions, practices, governments, and public officials, it should insist that this process be guided by canons of truth and decency.

6. *Respect for excellence.* If the individual personality is supreme, excellence in mind, character, and creative ability should be fostered.

Every man is entitled to equal rights before the civil law; every man should be governed equally by moral standards. Yet men also differ greatly in qualities of mind and spirit. Although "all men are created equal," as truthfully and eloquently stated in the Declaration of Independence, it would be folly to deny that people as we find them differ greatly. Our society, more than any other, should prize every kind of genuine worth, provided only that superiority is not falsely attributed to individuals because of their wealth or ancestry or other accidental circumstance. The common welfare depends to a considerable degree on the extent to which we lift into positions of power and trust our most gifted and upright representatives. It is at least as great a denial of human dignity to thwart the development of those possessed of superior qualities as it is to withhold from others their full opportunity for growth.

In terms of education this value means a careful inventory of all the useful abilities of all young people. It means emphasis on the necessity of selecting leaders and representatives in terms of their probity and good judgment. It means teaching the individual's responsibility for recognizing and placing in posts of leadership persons of the highest talent, training, and virtue. It means that the highly gifted as well as the average or handicapped students need individual attention. The school should stimulate and recognize the achievement of excellence in every sphere of life, in skilled production, in social and civic leadership, in literary and artistic creativity, in scientific insight, in technological ingenuity, in social sensitivity, in physical health and stamina, and in personal integrity.

7. *Moral equality.* If the individual personality is supreme, all persons should be judged by the same moral standards.

There is no more clearly defined element in the American system of values than the profound conviction that no man has a moral and inborn right to injure, persecute, dominate, or exploit others. It is recognized as a mark of virtue by all the great religions that one should treat other people as one would wish himself to be treated.[1] Thomas Jefferson gave political emphasis in his first inaugural to "equal and exact justice to all men, of whatever State or persuasion, religious or political." The American character is typically marked by an earnest search for justice and fair

---

[1] *Christianity*—"As you would that men should do to you, do you also to them." *Buddhism*—"Minister to friends and families by treating them as one treats himself." *Confucianism*—"What you do not like when done to yourself, do not do to others." *Hinduism*—"Let no man do to another what would be repugnant to himself." *Judaism*—"Thou shalt love thy neighbor as thyself."

play and by a quick hostility toward obsequious-ness and arrogance alike.

In terms of the life of the school, this value calls for a fraternal and friendly spirit, with conditions of equality, sympathy, and helpfulness established everywhere. It calls for the repudiation of discriminations based upon family, race, nationality, religion, or economic status. Whatever differences exist among individuals should be regarded by the school, not as the basis for the formation of clannish, secret, or mutually hostile groups, but rather as a means to enrich the common life. A spirit should be developed which is keenly resentful of all injustice, ruthlessness, special privilege, denial of opportunity, persecution, and servility. The positive ideals of a domestic society of equal opportunity, and of a world society of free peoples living under a regime of peace and fair play, should be raised before the young. School experience should reinforce these ideals.

8. Brotherhood.   If the individual personality is supreme, the concept of brotherhood should take precedence over selfish interests.

We seek to develop a self-reliant and industrious body of citizens, each of whom will earnestly strive to provide through his own efforts for the comfort and well-being of himself and those dependent upon him. Nevertheless, the care of those among us who may be prevented from doing this by a fault not their own—by ignorance, or feebleness, or lack of opportunity, or other misfortune—is an inescapable moral responsibility of all citizens. Whether by individual action, or through voluntary cooperation, or from the public purse, this responsibility must be met. Brotherhood leads to a broad and expanding humanitarianism, a sympathetic concern for the distress of other people. Our ideal is the good Samaritan, rather than the man who asked whether he must be his brother's keeper. The rise of industrial civilization has made inevitable an increasing measure of cooperative activity for the protection of the unfortunate. Brotherhood, moreover, implies more than material assistance; it means a willingness not only to share with the needy but also to attack the causes of want and suffering.

For these reasons, the public school should be regarded as an agency for increasing the learner's usefulness to the entire society as well as a road to individual success. Such a school, while it moderates the egoistic tendencies and strengthens the social and cooperative impulses, will also insist that each individual learn to accept individual responsibility. Such a school will be consistent in fostering participation in a variety of humane and constructive community activities and at the same time applauding and encouraging every effort to achieve self-reliance and self-respect.

9. The pursuit of happiness.   If the individual personality is supreme, each person should have the greatest possible opportunity for the pursuit of happiness, provided only that such activities do not substantially interfere with the similar opportunities of others.

"The pursuit of happiness" is a ringing phrase in the Declaration of Independence. But what is happiness? Surely not excitement, exuberance, material comforts alone. Temporary pleasures provide relief from boredom and responsibilities. But happiness is surely more than a mere summary of such pleasures. Although happiness is conditioned by material elements such as shelter, food, and clothing, the importance of such factors diminishes once adequacy is achieved. Although happiness may be elusive in grinding poverty, neither can it be bought with great wealth. Lasting happiness is derived largely from deep personal resources and from the affection and respect of others. The cultivation of such happiness may demand deferment of present pleasures for larger and deeper satisfactions in the future. It may require effort and sacrifice. Thus, the pursuit of happiness must be guided toward long-range goals.

The schools, therefore, should give a large place to those types of experience that satisfy spiritual needs and inspire the noblest achievement. This is particularly true of the various forms of creative expression, including art, literature, music, and all other ways through which beauty in its varied forms has been added to the social and cultural inheritance. It is the function of the schools to help every person to find and use the keys that unlock these riches. In addition, the discipline of the young should make clear, at promising opportunities, that in foregoing a momentary pleasure one may often develop resources of mind and spirit which will in the future bring a more complete happiness. Since happiness depends in no small part on social acceptance, cliques or tensions in school that alienate some students from the group should be discouraged.

10. Spiritual enrichment.   If the individual personality is supreme each person should be offered the emotional and spiritual experiences which transcend the materialistic aspects of life.

Moral values have consequences chiefly in social relationships. Spiritual values, however, take effect mainly in terms of inner emotions and sentiments. The entire outlook of many people is deeply affected by these spiritual feelings. Spiritual values arise from many sources—from the creative artistic expressions of the human spirit, from the noble monuments of architecture, from the impact of great religious pageantry and time-honored ritual, from the memory of heroic men and women who have nobly served humanity, from contemplation of the stars or of a blade of grass, from simple ceremonies of thankfulness or of grief, from the smile of a well-loved companion, from poetry and music, from sincere religious experience and faith. The well-meaning, high-minded individual who lacks such experiences remains an incomplete person. Beyond reasoned moral conviction and efficient social action, there is the inner life of the spirit which gives warmth and drive to dispassionate precepts of morality.

From whatever source derived, spiritual values and appropriate experiences to develop them are a major concern of all good schools. Although the public schools are estopped from teaching any of the denominational creeds, they have their responsibilities toward religion, as is pointed out later. [See Reading 68 for a discussion of this section.] Many other channels remain open for developing spiritual values. A good school will extend full recognition to the arts as means for expressing and evoking the inner life of the spirit. The school itself will be a place of beauty and refinement. The level of esthetic appreciation will be lifted. The best heritage of the human spirit in music, poetry, and the arts will be open to all. Creative abilities will be sought out and fostered. In the teaching of science, mathematics, and social studies, opportunities for spiritual enrichment will be created and used. Above all, the life of the school community will itself be an ennobling and elevating experience.

Values are interrelated

The values identified in this chapter have been separated merely for purposes of analysis. From the same school experience and at the same time, a child may grow in his sense of moral responsibility, develop habits of self-discipline, gain insight into the idea that institutions are the tools of man, and enhance his appreciation of the moral equality of his playmates. The high-school boy who speaks up at a staff meeting of the school newspaper to urge that a classmate from a minority group be invited to serve as sports editor may be exemplifying simultaneously the values of moral equality, respect for excellence, human brotherhood, intellectual freedom, and opportunity for the pursuit of happiness.

Conflicts in values must be resolved

Life demands a continuing series of moral decisions. Broadly speaking, these choices are of two general kinds.

The first type of decision is perhaps the most common and is certainly the easiest. It involves a decision to act upon, or to ignore, acknowledged moral and spiritual values. In such a case it is easy to see what "ought" to be done. The voice of conscience is clear enough, however great may be the moral fortitude required to execute its verdict.

The second type of moral decision is far more difficult. It plagues us when acknowledged values conflict. How shall we act when the harsh circumstances of life offer only a choice between undesirable alternatives? What, for example, shall we do in a situation where the values of equality and respect for excellence conflict? Or when the value of brotherhood collides with the value of common consent? In such situations, reflection and ingenuity may sometimes suggest a plan of action to satisfy both of the conflicting values. But, when no such reconciliation can be found, the choice of a course of action can be made only in terms of the anticipated consequences—whether they are temporary or lasting, whether they affect many people or few. Out of some such moral calculus emerges a judgment as to which course of action, all things considered, is the ethical imperative.

Agreement on acceptable behavior is general

The values stated earlier . . . call not only for assent but also for action. When these values find expression in the life of an individual, everyone recognizes that person as being worthy of emulation and admiration. An individual who accepts these basic values would be considerate of others. He would avoid arrogance. He would respect social customs and institutions in proportion as they satisfied the needs of human beings. He would seek to apply cooperative methods to the solution of group problems. He would want force to be regulated by law, applied with justice, and moderated by compassion. He would make a consistent effort to discover the truth about problems that might be presented to him for decision as an individual or as a citizen. He would claim and use his birthright of intellectual freedom; intellectual honesty would characterize his thoughts and his words. The achievement of excellence by others would evoke from him not envy but gratitude. Resenting both special privileges and denials of opportunity, he would not accept the former for himself nor impose the latter upon others.

Through the character of an individual who accepts these values runs the iron thread of personal integrity. He would reject all deceit and chicanery as an imposition upon others and a degradation of himself. He would be a man who could be trusted to speak the truth, to act with vigor in removing unwholesome community influences, to keep his word, to abide by lawful decisions, and to play the game of life according to rules which the acceptance of these values imposes equally upon all. A clear and compelling sense of civic duty would lead him to act energetically and unselfishly for the well-being of the community.

American democracy cannot select any system of religious faith as the sole basis for the values to which all Americans subscribe. Nevertheless these moral and spiritual values themselves command, with minor exceptions, the allegiance of all thoughtful Americans. It is not surprising that this should be so, for each of us has been surrounded from birth by an invisible network of values which guide and direct his life. However we may disagree on religious creeds, we can agree on moral and spiritual values. For that reason, we can usually agree in turn upon what constitutes good conduct in a particular situation. The fact that we can agree to judge behavior in terms of common values and at the same time agree to differ with respect to the religious interpretation of the source of these values is an asset and achievement of no mean importance. Whatever may be our shortcomings in actual conduct, there is no doubt that the American people, as a whole, approve such traits as honesty, truthfulness, integrity, compassion, cooperativeness, and reliability—and disapprove their opposites. The reason that one set of traits is approved and another rejected is that a scheme of values has been developed throughout American life which, with minor exceptions, is accepted by all as a yardstick against which human conduct can be appropriately measured.

It is worth while to reaffirm such values. For values refine the methods and lift the goals of living far above materialistic or even merely humanitarian levels. Although assent to these values may be dictated by reason, their driving power is generated in large part by the spiritual and emotional loyalties which they create in the hearts of mankind.

68

THE PUBLIC SCHOOLS AND RELIGION

In this statement by the Committee on Religion and Education of the American Council on Education in 1953, the nature of the problem of teaching *about* religion without teaching *religion* is clearly recognized. Nevertheless it is logically argued that religion should be studied as an integral part of the American heritage.

Public education in the United States is committed by federal and state law to the general principle that sectarian religious instruction must be excluded from the curriculum. This does not mean, however, that the problem of what to do about religion in the public schools has been solved. On the contrary, there is no clear-cut understanding of what the schools should or should not do in this field.

Some people think that the schools should leave religion completely to organized religious groups and to the home. They fear that any consideration of religion in the school will result in dangerous divisions in the community because of the emotional factors with which religion is surrounded; or they believe that the public school in a democratic society cannot handle religion without violating the religious liberty of minority groups.

Many people, however, are convinced that the public school's program of general education becomes distorted and impoverished when all religious references are excluded. They fear that neglect of religion will undermine the very foundations of individual and social morality. In their

From *The Function of the Public Schools in Dealing with Religion*, American Council on Education (Washington: National Education Association, 1953), pp. 1-7.

opinion the Founding Fathers did not intend to exclude religion from the schools when they restrained Congress from any move toward an "establishment of religion."

In actual practice one finds many activities which are not consistent with the assumption that religion has been excluded from the public school program. For example, Bible reading is required in some states and permitted in others. The observance of certain religious holidays, such as Christmas, is characterized in nearly all schools by the use of religious subject matter, music, and religious ceremonies. Some schools, particularly those in communities which are nearly homogeneous from a religious standpoint, go much further than this in the encouragement of participation in religion by the pupils of the school.

A few schools are beginning to experiment with the factual study of religion in order that pupils may understand its role in history and in the development of values and standards in our society.

What to do about religion in the public schools is a persistent and vital problem. It will not be solved by drifting. We urge that this problem be studied carefully, with appropriate experimentation in different communities that are willing to undertake it. The solution will have far-reaching effects on the future unity and soundness of American society.

In 1947 the Committee on Religion and Education issued our first report, *The Relation of Religion to Public Education: The Basic Principles,*[1] in which we attempted to define the problem and to state the principles on which the practice of the public schools should be based. In the light of intervening developments we would perhaps modify our position in certain respects, but in general we still subscribe to the major principles which were stated at that time. Relevant conclusions from that report may be restated as follows:

1. The problem is to find a way in public education to give due recognition to the place of religion in the culture and in the convictions of our people while at the same time safeguarding the separation of church and state.

2. The separation of American public education from church control was not intended to exclude all study of religion from the school program.

3. Teaching a common core of religious beliefs in the public schools is not a satisfactory solution.

4. Teaching "moral and spiritual values" cannot be regarded as an adequate substitute for an appropriate consideration of religion in the school program.

5. Teaching which opposes or denies religion is as much a violation of religious liberty as teaching which advocates or supports any particular religious belief.

6. Introducing factual study of religion will not commit the public schools to any particular religious belief.

7. The role of the school in the study of religion is distinct from, though complementary to, the role of the church.

8. The public school should stimulate the young toward a vigorous, personal reaction to the challenge of religion.

9. The public school should assist youth to have an intelligent understanding of the historical and contemporary role of religion in human affairs.

The mounting concern over the appropriate place to be given religion in public education is evidenced by the many books, articles, and other pronouncements published in the past decade, particularly since our 1947 report. Two recent policy statements of educational leaders will serve to illustrate this concern.

The Educational Policies Commission of the National Education Association of the United States and of the American Association of School Administrators published its report on *Moral and Spiritual Values in the Public Schools*[2] in 1951. [Reading 67 is an excerpt from this report.] The commission maintains that the public schools, in discharging their responsibility for the development of the moral and spiritual values which the American people desire their children to hold, can and should teach *about* religion.

There are differences in opinion among both educational and religious leaders about the adequacy of the commission's statement, particularly regarding its treatment of sanctions for values and ways in which it proposes that schools should deal with religion. This emphasizes the complexity and importance of the problem. We think, however, this report by one of the most influential educational groups in the United States is highly significant both because of the position taken and particularly because it indicates the increasing awareness on the part of educators that public schools must find appropriate methods of dealing with religion.

Although a detailed critical analysis of this document might serve to refine our committee's position on the broad problem of the relationship of religion to public education, it would be somewhat irrelevant to the immediate task of reducing our committee's 1947 position to practical

[1] Washington: American Council on Education.

[2] Washington: National Education Association.

specifics, as suggested by the purpose of the exploratory study. The following extracts will illustrate the position taken by the commission.

The commission says,

". . . when a point about religious opinion or religious practices arises in a classroom discussion the teacher will not brush it aside with a statement that he is not allowed to discuss this matter in the public school. There can be no doubt that the American democracy is grounded in a religious tradition. While religion may not be the only source of democratic moral and spiritual values, it is surely one of the important sources. For this objective reason, if for no other, an attitude of respect toward religion should prevail in the schools. . . ."

Further on, the commission states,

"A democratic society grants to every citizen the right to believe as his conscience and training dictate. The public schools can and should stress the meaning of this right to their students. Properly applied, this privilege means not only freedom of belief, but respect for the beliefs of others. . . . In declaring that the public schools should not teach religion, we wish to be entirely clear that teaching against religion is equally intolerant and intolerable. The teacher of science, for example, who tells young people that religious faith is to be condemned because it is "unscientific" is taking an unprofessional advantage of their immaturity as well as exhibiting his own. . . ."

Under the heading "The Public School Can and Should Teach about Religion" the commission says,

"The public schools can teach objectively *about* religion without advocating or teaching any religious creed. To omit from the classroom all references to religion and the institutions of religion is to neglect an important part of American life. Knowledge about religion is essential for a full understanding of our culture, literature, art, history, and current affairs. That religious beliefs are controversial is not an adequate reason for excluding teaching about religion from the public schools. . . ."

The second policy statement to which we wish to call particular attention was published in the spring of 1952 by the superintendents of schools of cities in the United States and Canada with population over 200,000 under the title *An Educational Platform for the Public Schools: Some*

Phases of Instructional Policy.[3] It is our understanding that this statement is the result of discussions held during the past several years and that it is considered tentative and therefore subject to revision in the light of further study and discussion. An extract indicates the concern of this group of educational leaders with the place of religion in the development of moral and spiritual values.

The superintendents say,

". . . History reveals the belief of the American people in God. The public schools reflect this belief in high degree. We approach the basic ethical values of life through the concepts of the Fatherhood of God and the Brotherhood of Man. . . . Religious freedom and the separation of church and state are also basic in the American tradition. No government agency (including the public schools) can have any supervision, control, or jurisdiction over religion. The teaching of religion is definitely a responsibility of the home and the church. But it is a proper function of the public schools to support and reinforce the home and the church in discharging this important responsibility. The public schools are not Godless and are not materialistic. They are not sectarian. The public schools recognize the essential place of religion in the American way of life, but they cannot endorse, nor can they favor, any particular religion or religious system.

"Moral, ethical, and spiritual values are an essential element of the public school program; the schools emphasize these values and also teach the role of religion in the development of the culture. . . ."

Our position with respect to the problem under study may be briefly summarized as follows:

The public school is limited, as the private institution is not, in its treatment of religion. The constitutions, statutes, and interpretations thereof in the forty-eight states, and the decisions of the Supreme Court of the United States, make it illegal for the public school to teach religion in the sense of the attempt to inculcate sectarian religious beliefs. Even if agreement could be reached among the religiously minded on a "common core" or set of basic propositions common to and acceptable to Roman Catholics, Protestants, and Jews, there would remain the nonreligious groups in the community who would maintain that their rights were violated by any attempt to inculcate general propositions embodying religious beliefs.

[3] Chicago, Ill.: Educational Division, Field Enterprises, Inc.

On the other hand, to be silent about religion may be, in effect, to make the public school an antireligious factor in the community. Silence creates the impression in the minds of the young that religion is unimportant and has nothing to contribute to the solution of the perennial and ultimate problems of human life. This negative consequence is all the more striking in a period when society is asking the public school to assume more and more responsibility for dealing with the cultural problems of growth and development.

Therefore, it is vitally important that the public school deal with religion. There are many ways in which this may be and indeed is being done. Some are good; others, in our judgment, may be dangerous to a greater or lesser degree. All public schools, however, can provide for the factual study of religion both as an important factor in the historical and contemporary development of our culture and as a source of values and insight for great numbers of people in finding the answers to persistent personal problems of living. Religion can, and in our judgment should, be studied in the same way as the economic and political institutions and principles of our country should be studied—not as something on which the American public school must settle all arguments and say the last word, but as something which is so much a part of the American heritage and so relevant to contemporary values that it cannot be ignored.

69

E. C. Bolmeier

LEGALITY AND PROPRIETY OF RELIGIOUS INSTRUCTION IN THE PUBLIC SCHOOLS

On June 17, 1963, the Supreme Court ruled that states and local governments may not require Bible reading or recitation of the Lord's Prayer as religious exercises in public schools. This ruling was based on the religious provision of the First Amendment to the Constitution: "Congress shall make no law respecting an establishment of religion or prohibiting the free exercise thereof," which was extended to the states by the Fourteenth Amendment. The decision settled cases arising from opposition to such activity as required by a state statute in Pennsylvania and by a school board ruling in Baltimore. The Court said in part: "The place of religion in our society is an exalted one, achieved through a long tradition of reliance on the home, the church, and the inviolable citadel of the individual heart and mind. We have come to recognize through bitter experience that it is not within the power of government to invade that citadel, whether its purpose or effect be to aid or oppose, to advance or retard. In the relationship between man and religion, the state is firmly committed to a position of neutrality. Though the application of that rule requires interpretation of a delicate sort, the rule itself is clearly and concisely stated in the words of the First Amendment."

This followed the Court's ruling of June, 1962, in the case of *Engel v. Vitale*, against the recitation in New York public schools of a prayer composed by the State Board of Regents. The Court then held that while the use of such a prayer would not constitute establishment of one religion, "government in this country, be it state or federal, is without power to prescribe by law any particular form of prayer which is to be used as an official prayer in carrying on any program of governmentally sponsored religious activity."

Although these decisions aroused much comment at the time they were handed down, the Court was not defining new issues. Such questions have arisen many times in the last seventy years. In this selection E. C. Bolmeier, an expert in the field of school law, analyzes the legal status of religious instruction and stresses a distinction between the teaching of moral and spiritual values and the inculcation of sectarian beliefs. In addition to treating the overall question of religious instruction in public schools, the author summarizes judicial interpretations on a number of important court cases concerned with Bible reading in schools, the distribution of sectarian literature in schools, and released time for religious instruction. This article should help teachers understand the judicial limitations placed upon the teaching of religion in schools as well as help clarify the ways in which moral and spiritual values may still be encompassed by the teacher.

Religious instruction in the public schools constitutes one of our most significant, controversial, and unsolved educational problems. For over a century now, the pendulum of religious emphasis in the public-school curriculum has been swinging back and forth. Sometimes, in some places, the pendulum has swung so far as to collide with constitutional guarantees of religious freedom. Other times it has moved so far in the opposite direction as to leave a curriculum that is totally barren of spiritual influence or inspiration.

The problem has been aggravated by a growing divergence of professional and lay opinions regarding the proper place of religious instruction in the public schools. Too often these opinions are based upon prejudices, suspicions, and ignorance. It is high time that school personnel and patrons resolve their conflicting attitudes on this serious issue. A general policy should be formulated whereby school administrators and teachers could perform their professional duties with the assurance that their acts are not only legal but also beneficial to all pupils regardless of church affiliation or religious beliefs.

In the formulation of a policy regarding religious instruction in the public schools, such questions as the following should be considered. (1) What is the background of religious instruction in the public schools? (2) What legal principles have evolved through judicial interpretations of religious instruction in the public schools? (3) What is the proper application of the legal principles on religious instruction in the public schools?

Development of secularization

The most prominent characteristic of our early schools was the predominance of the religious purpose in instruction. The early colonial schools were established for the very purpose of religious training. The sole purpose of the elementary school was to enable the child to read the Catechism and the Bible, and to "know the will of the Heavenly Father." The earliest secondary schools were established to insure a supply of learned ministers.

Unity of the religious purpose in the early colonial school was natural and feasible. Each colonial settlement was compact in area and homogeneous with respect to religious belief. The community which resembled a "religious republic" represented a single religious faith. Consequently there was no clashing as to the nature of religious instruction to be provided.

The monopoly of a single-sect in the colony, however, was short-lived, as evidenced by the early enactment of legislation providing for freedom of religious worship. As secular interests began to compete with religious thought, the character of the schools began to change.

The changing character was accelerated by a shift of emphasis to the needs of the State and to industrial, civic, and national needs. This change is known as the "secularization of American education." Many thought then, as many think now, that the secularization of public education was a fatal national mistake.

Bitter opposition followed the secular movement, and the cry was raised that "the public schools are godless schools." Nevertheless the movement spread rapidly, with two main factors contributing to the change. First, the conviction that the life of the Republic demanded an educated and intelligent citizenry, which required general education for all in the common schools controlled by the State. Second, the great diversity of religious beliefs necessitated tolerance and religious freedom through a consideration of the rights of minorities.

The justification of the secular change of our schools is stated most succinctly by Cubberley, renowned educational historian: "The secularization of education with us must not be regarded either as a deliberate or a wanton violation of the rights of the Church, but rather as an unavoidable incident connected with the coming to

From *Educational Forum,* May 1956, 20:473-482.

self-consciousness and self-government of a great people."

Despite vigorous opposition, secularization of the American schools soon won legal sanction. Statutory and constitutional provisions supporting the movement became widespread. Now virtually every state constitution contains provisions for the separation of Church and State.

Although the majority of these state constitutional provisions are designed to prohibit the division of school funds for sectarian purposes, many others refer specifically to religious instruction in the public schools. At least ten state constitutions prohibit "sectarian instruction or influence" in the public schools. Moreover, the First Amendment and the Fourteenth Amendment to the federal Constitution have been interpreted frequently as having similar restrictions.

Within the limitations of the federal and state constitutions—and sometimes in contradiction to them—there are also many statutory provisions regarding religious activities in the public schools. The most significant of these relate to the use of the Bible.

The statutes frequently specify—sometimes in vague terms—the manner in which the Bible is or is not to be used. Twenty-seven states have no law dealing with the use of the Bible in public schools. Of the twenty-one states which do have laws regarding the matter, four of them prohibit the use of the Bible in the public schools; five permit such use; and the other twelve states prescribe Bible reading in the public schools. Moreover, the Bible is read in a large number of schools in many states where the statutes are silent on the subject. Of the twelve states requiring Bible-reading, five of them stipulate that no comments be made with regard to the readings.

Due to the wide variation of laws and practices regarding religious activities in the public schools, there are no clear-cut policies on the problem. It is no wonder then that school administrators and teachers are groping about it in the attempt to reconcile what is proper and what is legal. Many promote religious activities in the public schools, hoping that their practices are legal, or, if not, that they will not be challenged by court action.

As a matter of fact, many of the public-school practices in connection with religious activities and influences have been the subject of litigation. Consequently, it is the interpretations of the state courts and the United States Supreme Court to which we must turn for the most authoritative answers as to the legal limits of secularization and sectarianism in the public schools.

Judicial interpretations

The court decisions of cases involving religious influence in the public schools present an interesting and significant account of secular trends and limitations.

Without attempting to analyze or even enumerate all the applicable cases tried in the courts, several leading cases may be cited which indicate (1) judicial prohibition of Bible-reading in the public schools, (2) judicial confirmation of Bible-reading in the public schools, (3) judicial repudiation of distributing sectarian literature in the public schools, and (4) judicial discrimination of plans releasing pupils for religious instruction.

Prohibition of Bible-reading. An early Wisconsin case, *Weiss v. District Board of Education,* 44 N. W. 967 (Wis.) (1890), arose on a petition to compel the reading of the Bible in the public schools. Without going into detail on this case, the court ignored the petition—holding that the state constitution forbade the practice. Now there is nothing electrifying about this case. It is cited merely because it was one of the earliest cases in point, and that it establishes the legal principle that, within the limitations of the federal Constitution, the respective state constitutions determine what religious instruction may or may not be provided in the public schools.

That principle was sustained in an Illinois case, *People v. Board of Education,* 92 N. E. 251 (Ill.) (1910), in which the court held that the First Amendment to the federal Constitution left the states free to enact such laws as they might deem proper with respect to religion, restrained only by limitations of the respective state constitutions, but that the reading of the Bible, the singing of hymns and the repeating of the Lord's Prayer were in violation of the provisions of the constitution of the State of Illinois.

The court, in another case, *Herold v. Parish Board,* 68 So. 116 (La.) (1915), ruled that the reading of the Bible, including the Old and New Testaments, in the public schools was a preference given to Christians and a discrimination made against Jews, and therefore was a violation of the constitution of the State of Louisiana.

A case, *State v. Weedman,* 226 N. W. 348 (S.D.) (1929), arose in South Dakota in which the court did not exactly declare Bible-reading in the public schools to be unconstitutional, but it did refer adversely to the practice in discussing the case. The Supreme Court of South Dakota ordered a mandamus to compel the school board to readmit a number of Catholic children who had refused to attend the opening exercises in which passages from the King James version were read, and to permit them to be absent during such readings thereafter.

Confirmation of Bible-reading. For every case in which a court ruled Bible-reading in the public schools as unconstitutional, there have been many more cases in which the practice has been judicially approved. With the decision of a case, *Lewis v. Board of Education*, 285 N. Y. S. 164 (1935), in New York, in 1935, it appeared that the issue was settled conclusively. In that case the usual charge was made that the Bible is a sectarian book and its use in the public schools violates constitutional provisions. In denying the allegation the court said:

"In no sense does the practice of reading from the Scriptures destroy or weaken or affect the cleavage between church and state; the practice does not bridge or conjoin the two. . . . It is not maintained that dogmatic religion is being foisted upon any pupil. No special creed or sect or tenet is favored."

In 1951, however, litigation on the subject was resumed in New Jersey, *Doremus v. Board of Education*, 75 A. (2d) 880 (N.J.) (1951). A statute in question provided that at least "five verses taken from that portion of the Holy Bible known as the Old Testament shall be read, or caused to be read, without comment, in each public-school classroom. . . ."

In challenging the constitutionality of the statute the following line of reasoning was presented:

"The principle of the separation of the church and state is established in the constitution of the United States, namely the first and fourteenth amendments which prohibit the intermingling of religious and secular education in the public schools; the reading of the Bible and the reciting of the Lord's Prayer in the public schools are religious services, religious exercises and religious instruction; they are themselves in aid of one or more religions and in preference of one religion or another; and therefore those acts are contrary to the named constitutional provisions."

The Supreme Court of New Jersey disagreed with the above allegation. The court's opinion not only upheld the constitutionality of the disputed statute but commented on its appropriateness and timeliness in the following notable words:

"While it is necessary that there be a separation between church and state, it is not necessary that the state should be stripped of religious sentiment. It may be a tragic experience for this country and for the conception of life, liberty and the pursuit of happiness if our people lose their religious feeling and are left to live their lives without faith. . . . We are at a crucial hour in which it may behoove our people to conserve all of the elements which have made our land what it is. . . ."

The case, *Doremus v. Board of Education*, 342 U.S. 429 (1952), was appealed to the United States Supreme Court where, on March 3, 1952, it was dismissed for want of jurisdiction.

Thus we note that there is a preponderance of jurisdiction validating Bible-reading in the public schools, particularly where it is not contradictory with state laws, and where two conditions are met: (1) the teacher must not comment on passages read; and (2) pupils who disapprove may not be required to participate in the Bible-reading exercises.

Distribution of sectarian literature. According to judicial opinion, the instructional use of sectarian literature in the public schools is in conflict with provisions of the United States Constitution and certain state constitutions. Consequently other less direct methods of using the public schools for sectarian indoctrination, are sometimes employed—or at least attempted.

Among such practices as have been the cause for litigation is the distribution of sectarian literature to pupils. A case, *Miller v. Cooper*, 244 P. (2d) 520 (N.M.) (1952), in which it was charged that the defendants were using the public schools as a medium for the dissemination of religious pamphlets is illustrative. Evidence in the case revealed that the pamphlets were published by a certain Protestant Church. Although the teachers did not hand them to the pupils or instruct that they be taken or read, it was found that the pamphlets were kept in plain sight in a school room and were available to the pupils and the supply was evidently replenished from time to time. In ruling the practice unconstitutional, the New Mexico Supreme Court declared: "We condemned such practice in *Zellers v. Huff*, and condemn it here. . . ."

A more publicized case, *Tudor v. Board of Education*, 100 A. (2d) 857 (N.J.) (1953), arose recently in New Jersey, where at the request of Gideons International, the school board adopted a resolution permitting the distribution of Bibles to pupils. Even though the resolution stipulated that the Bible would be given only to pupils who requested them and whose parents indicated in writing that they desired their children to have the Bibles, it met with opposition by Catholics and Jews. A Jewish parent charged sectarianism because the Bible in question was the King James version. The court agreed that the Bible was sectarian and that its distribution was a violation of both the federal and New Jersey Constitutions.

On appeal, the case, *Tudor v. Board of Education*, 75 Sup. Ct. 25 (1954), was carried to the United States Supreme Court, but was returned October, 1954, with the refusal to reopen the case.

On the basis of the two cases cited it may be inferred that the courts will not permit the use of the "school machinery" for promoting sectarian interests or influences—even by indirect means.

Discrimination of plans for "released time." A more litigious technique of using the "school machinery" for promoting the interests of sectarian instruction is to release pupils from regular school activities and school time to pursue religious education in the various faiths to which they or their parents subscribe.

This so-called "released-time" program has been conducted in many public-school systems, with or without statutory regulation. Like other instances of intermingling public-school and religious activities it has brought forth many protests and challenges of constitutional violation. The courts have found some of the practices legal, and others illegal, depending upon the degree to which the "school machinery" was being capitalized upon, and upon other rather discriminatory factors.

In the first case, *Stein v. Brown*, 211 N. Y. S. 822 (1925), dealing with the released-time issue, a New York court held that the furnishing of cards for a released-time plan of religious education violated constitutional provisions which prohibited the use of public funds or property to aid denominational schools. The court concluded that "religious instruction belongs to the parents of the children and the churches and religious organizations of the country. It should be given outside of the public schools and outside of school hours."

An opposite decision was rendered just two years later in another New York case, *People v. Graves*, 219 N. Y. S. 187 (1927). The court upheld the legality of the released-time issue here because the cards upon which parents of pupils were to indicate their written consent to the outside religious instruction of their children were furnished by agencies other than the school authorities. In the earlier case such cards were printed by the pupils.

Almost two decades later another released-time case, *People v. Board of Education*, 68 N. E. (2d) 305 (Ill.) (1946), reached the state courts. This time a writ of mandamus sought to compel the Board of Education of the City of Chicago to "immediately revoke, cancel, and appeal" the state board's action authorizing the superintendent of schools to excuse public-school children, at the requests of their parents, for an hour each week, before the end of the regular school period, for the purpose of attending religious education classes at places outside of the school activities or property. The court conceded that "the board of education should not help sustain or support any school controlled by a church or sectarian denomination or aid any church or sectarian purpose," but refused the petition because the court did "not deem it the duty of a school board to be hostile or antagonistic to religion or churches, nor should it interfere with the free exercise and enjoyment of religious freedom."

While the released-time controversy was litigated in Illinois, it was ruled in a California case, *Gordon v. Board of Education of City of Los Angeles*, 178 P. (2d) 488 (Cal.) (1947), that "a statute providing that pupils with written consent of parents may be excused from school to participate in religious instruction does not violate that provision of the state constitution guaranteeing free exercise and enjoyment of religious worship."

It was at this time that another case, *McCollum v. Board of Education*, 68 N. E. (2d) 305 (Ill.) (1946), was developing which was to have nationwide repercussions. The school board of Champaign, Illinois, permitted religious instruction in the public schools under a released-time arrangement, whereby pupils whose parents signed "request cards" were permitted to attend religious-instruction classes conducted during regular school hours in a school building by outside teachers furnished by a religious council representing various faiths, subject to the approval and supervision of the superintendent of schools. Attendance records were kept and reported to the school authorities in the same way as for other classes. Pupils not attending the religious-instruction classes were required to continue their regular secular studies.

Even though a trial court, and, later the Supreme Court of Illinois, found the Champaign arrangement valid, the United States Supreme Court ruled that it was unconstitutional on the grounds that (1) tax-supported property was used for religious instruction, and (2) the compulsory school attendance regulation was capitalized upon to aid the religious classes. *McCollum v. Board of Education*, 333 U.S. 203 (1948) [see Reading 93].

Not dismayed by the decision of the United States Supreme Court, the public schools of New York City devised a program of released time, patterned somewhat differently from the one in Champaign. Nevertheless it was litigated promptly, *Zorach v. Clauson,* 100 N. E. (2d) 463 (N.Y.) (1951), with the charge that the school served as "a crutch" on which the churches leaned for support of their religious training.

The New York court did not agree with the allegation, and justified its decision upholding the program on the grounds that, in the New York City program there was neither supervision nor approval of religious teachers and no solicitation of pupils or distribution of cards. The religious instruction had to be outside the school building and grounds. There could be no announcement of any kind in the public schools relative to the program, and no comment by any principal or teachers on the attendance or nonattendance of any pupil.

As was anticipated, the state court's decision was appealed to the United States Supreme Court where on April 28, 1962, it was affirmed. *Zorach v. Clauson,* 72 S. Ct. 679 (1952). It is significant to note, however, that three of the nine judges dissented vigorously.

Under present jurisdiction, therefore, released-time from the public schools for religious instruction is legal. As in the case of Bible-reading, however, the practice is sanctioned judicially only under very limited circumstances.

Application of legal principles in religious instruction

An objective view on the legality of religious instruction in the public schools, in the light of constitutional and statutory provisions and the judicial interpretations placed upon those provisions, indicates convincingly that such instruction is indeed limited. In fact any instruction or related activity in the public schools which smacks of sectarian influences is illegal. Any activity which aids one or more religious sects, or prefers one religious doctrine or another is out—legally.

Now under these limited conditions, what may the school official or teacher do which will be most beneficial to the pupil from a spiritual point of view? Outside of doing nothing at all, three general courses are open, each of which has its obstacles, and each of which has its supporters. One course is to provide and promote religious activities in accordance with one's personal or church beliefs, irrespective of the law. Another procedure is to emphasize the religious activities just as far as possible within legal limits regardless of relative benefits which may accrue. The other alternative is to concentrate on a school program which stresses moral and spiritual values, for which there would likely be no legal restraint.

Violating the law. As the evidence has indicated, various practices of providing religious instruction in the public schools have been held illegal by the federal and state courts. Many more practices, if adjudicated, would be declared illegal. School systems in virtually every state violate in some way the legal principles concerning religious instruction in the public schools.

Some school authorities violate the law *unknowingly* because of their ignorance on the subject. No school administrator or teacher is to be exonerated on such grounds. A qualified school administrator or teacher should be familiar with the legal aspects of his profession. Every reputable institution of higher learning will stress, in its pre-service training, the illegality of sectarianism in the public-school program. There is also an abundance of professional literature dealing with the subject. For the school administrator or teacher who still is in doubt as to the application of the laws in his own state, reliable opinions and suggestions may be gotten by request from the state superintendent's or attorney general's office. Such precautions would avoid much needless and costly litigation.

School authorities who violate the law *knowingly,* with the rationalization that their personal or denominational views on religious influences in the public schools must take priority over those stipulated in the laws and as interpreted by the courts, are still more to blame. It is startling to observe that some persons holding responsible church or school positions, fall into this category.

An incident was related recently where a young lady who was in her first year of teaching experience became perplexed and worried as to the legal and proper emphasis of religious instruction in her classes. She sought advice from her father who was a superintendent of schools. The young teacher's correspondence with her father went something like this: "Dear daddy, I have been attempting to explain to my pupils certain passages of the Bible in accordance with the training I received at home and in our church. Now from what I have heard and read I am afraid I have been violating the law. Please advise me what to do." In essence the father's reply was: "Dear daughter, you have been violating the law—keep on violating the law."

It is an unfortunate reflection on the school which provides in its program activities which are in contradiction to existing laws. Of all places where respect for and obedience to the laws should be taught by exemplification, or otherwise, it is the school.

Crowding legal limits in religious influences. Much credit is due the school administrator or teacher who injects as much religious atmosphere into the public-school classroom as is possible without including sectarianism or any other religious aspect prohibited by law. It is an honorable attempt to do that which is both legal and proper.

Over-emphasis of the religious motive always extended to the very limits of legal boundaries, however, may not always be proper—or at least profitable. That is, the efforts of providing certain religious activities in the public school may not be justified by the spiritual returns to the pupils. For example, permission or prescription to read, without comment, several verses of the Scriptures from the Bible may not be worth the effort. While some contend that daily scripture reading will tend to counteract the apparent godlessness now existing, others believe that perfunctory reading of the Bible under compulsory circumstances may dull rather than stimulate spiritual qualities.

Possible over-emphasis was exemplified in a Northern state where the writer was serving as a superintendent of schools some years ago. A candidate for the office of state superintendent of education promised the voters that if she were elected to the position, she would try to bring back to the schoolroom the religious atmosphere which was lost in a period of over-secularization. In her ardent attempt to fulfill her campaign promises, this good lady succeeded in having enacted into legislation a bill which would require a printed and framed copy of the Ten Commandments to be hung in every classroom throughout the state.

It is well-remembered how finally a large crate of the framed Commandments arrived at our school. Detailed regulations were included as to where and at what height they should be hung, to be in view by the pupils when leaving the classroom. The reactions of the teachers were passive; those of the pupils were more so. It cannot be recalled that anyone stopped to read—less heed—them as he hurried out to participate in the recess activities.

That, however, was not the end of the Commandment affair. Later, at a PTA meeting in one of the classrooms, an observing adult noticed that the Commandments were listed in the order preferred by one church denomination in the community but contrary to the order preferred by another denomination. The controversial discussion which followed can well be imagined. For a while it looked as though some of the Commandments would be violated right there. Fortunately the incident did not reach the state of litigation. There has, however, been litigation on matters just as trivial, where attempts have been made to develop a religious environment in the public schools.

The real danger in stressing the more superficial aspects of religious instruction in the public schools is that they may be considered as adequate for a program of moral and spiritual development. It would be unfortunate to promote a program of religious instruction which creates and agitates denominational differences and animosities, in lieu of a broader and more effective program of moral and spiritual values divorced from all sectarian influences.

Stressing moral and spiritual values. Stressing moral and spiritual values in the curriculum does not necessarily preclude friendly relations between religion and public education. In fact, it is both legal and proper for the public school to teach about religion, and to point out that religion is an important element of American life. This can and should be done, however, without the injection of sectarianism or indoctrination of specific religious beliefs.

A curriculum conceived in terms of moral and spiritual values will strive to improve and develop human personality, moral responsibility, devotion of truth, respect for excellence, moral equality, brotherhood, the pursuit of happiness, and spiritual enrichment for every school pupil.

It is extremely doubtful that such objectives would be achieved by sectarian practices which have been the subject of litigation even if they were legal.

Moral and spiritual growth cannot be accomplished adequately by conducting religious exercises for a brief period of the school day. Neither can it be achieved in a single course, even though it is a course in Bible. This full potentiality of moral and spiritual development requires constant stress wherever possible and feasible for the entire school day in every single class and other activity carried on in the school—and outside of the school, too.

A British philosopher and theologian is quoted as relating that:

"Not long ago I met one of our great school masters—a veteran in that high service. 'Where in your time-table do you teach religion?' I asked him. 'We teach it all day long,' he answered. 'We teach it in arithmetic, by accuracy. We teach it in language, by learning to say what we mean—"yea, yea and nay, nay!" We teach it in history, by humanity. We teach it in geography, by breadth of mind. We teach it in handicraft, by thoroughness. We teach it in astronomy, by reverence. We teach it on the playground, by fair play. We teach it by kindness to animals, by courtesy to servants, by good manners to one another, and by truthfulness in all things. We teach it by showing the children that we, their elders, are their friends and not their enemies.'

"—Finally he added a remark that struck me— 'I do not want religion' he said, 'brought into this school from outside. What we have of it we grow ourselves.' "

It is generally conceded that the teaching of moral and spiritual values can be accomplished most effectively through exemplification. Therefore, the selection of the teachers, under whose influences the pupils develop, is a most important consideration.

A teacher who possesses a good moral character and manifests it in all relations, with all pupils, at all times is the answer to moral and spiritual growth. Call it religious instruction if you will; but it is needed urgently in our public schools today. And, moreover, there is no court in the land which would disapprove.

70

Henry H. Hill

PUBLIC SCHOOLS MUST BE SECULAR

Dr. Hill has wielded an important influence on educational thought, both as chairman of the Educational Policies Commission of the National Education Association and as president of the George Peabody College for Teachers. In this article he contends that a secular school system is important in a democratic and pluralistic society, for such a system enables children of all faiths to mingle freely. He also points out those social restrictions which may be involved in the development of parochial schools; yet he defends, of course, the right of the church or parents to send their children to such schools. On this latter point, Dr. Hill's views are supported by the courts, which have ruled that children are not required to attend public schools, but may enroll in any educational institution which meets acceptable academic standards. The following article was taken from an official report of the Educational Policies Commission of the National Education Association and thus represents a policy statement of that organization.

I feel I must begin by pointing out the danger, in the years ahead, of bitter and disruptive religious divisions and quarrels in America. Such divisions are common in Germany, for example, where religion and politics are frequently identical in the life of the community, where preachers and priests are supported by taxes, and where substantially all schools are confessional and under control either of the Catholic or the Protestant churches. Citizens so divided find it hard to get along together, much less with other nations. What is a local disturbance can in such a case become an international threat. So far we have avoided this particular kind of bitterness in the United States because we remain essentially secu-

From *Atlantic Monthly,* October 1952, 190:75-77.

lar in our political party organization. We do not support our churches by taxes. Being a Republican or a Democrat carries with it as yet little intimation of a man's religion or lack of it. Nearly 90 per cent of all our children attend the public schools, which are secular and not denominational.

There is now in some quarters a demand that the public schools teach religion. Whose religion? What creed or ritual? However much we may like the plan of teaching that religion common to all recognized religions in the United States, the religious leaders have not produced such a text. Nor are they likely to do so. In both Protestant and Catholic bodies there are leaders who insist that truth cannot tolerate error. It seems to be "my truth, your error." These same leaders do not favor or practice interfaith understanding for this and other reasons.

In the opinion of thoughtful observers religion itself cannot be taught in our public schools. If one religious group will not permit the King James version of the Bible to be read and another will not permit the Douay version, can we expect further excursions into purely religious matters?

When, then, by statute or by public opinion or controversy, the public schools are stopped from teaching religion—we do not here discuss released time and other possible compromises of value which affect a minor fraction of the children—they may be and are occasionally referred to as godless. This charge is misleading or else there is some peculiar religious alchemy which takes place en route between church and school.

As a former superintendent of public schools in Arkansas, Kentucky, and Pennsylvania it has been, over a period of thirty years, my privilege and duty to recommend to boards of education the appointment of some hundreds of teachers. Without a single exception they have been members of a recognized church—Protestant, Catholic, or Jewish. If we may identify church membership with goodness—and surely most of the good people are in the churches; if we may identify membership in any church or synagogue with godliness as contrasted with godlessness, then how and at what moment do good and perhaps godly teachers become godless as they step from the churches and homes to their posts of duty in the public schools? Are all places of assembly or work—the stores, factories, courts, farms, trains, and market places—to be regarded as godless because in them man does not, through ritual or formal act, worship God or study or recite the dogma of his church? Are the Mohammedans to be regarded as godlier than Christians if they practice their religious devotions daily seven times, stopping their immediate duties at a given time or signal?

To ask these questions is to invite the thesis in which I happen to believe. The good or godly teacher has a quality—let us call it moral and spiritual values—which will "rub off" on her associates wherever she is. Is not this thesis acknowledged in the suspicion—unfounded for the most part—with which denominations sometimes regard teachers who belong to other denominations? The essential question is: Can and will this teacher teach by example and precept and through the daily life of the school those abiding values in which all religions believe? If there be no values to rub off, then indeed we should worry.

On rare occasions I have heard what seems to me the irresponsible assertion that our public schools are "as Stalin would have them." I do not believe Stalin would be likely to select Protestants and Catholics and Jews as teachers.

The word "secular" is sometimes substituted for "godless." There is being read into this word, which has been used to designate civil as separated from religious affairs, the pejorative idea that secular is evil.

What else can schools open to all American children be except nondenominational? They must remain secular unless we change those underlying concepts and practices which have to date made and kept America relatively free from the religious quarrels, wars, and intolerances which drove many of our forefathers, fettered by oppressors, to escape to America. Are we willing, as members of church groups, to insist that the homes and churches handle matters of religious beliefs and that the public schools deal with common moral and spiritual values?

Let me state candidly my own position. It involves divided allegiance, as is only right and proper. As a Presbyterian I have the responsibility to see that Presbyterian religious values are taught to Presbyterian children. This I believe may be done and has been done by the church through Sunday school and vacation schools and in other ways, leaving the public schools to provide those relatively noncontroversial values and learnings necessary to American citizenship.

As a citizen I have the responsibility of supporting and defending and improving the public schools where in any now conceivable future the great majority of all children will be educated for peace or war.

As an individual I have the responsibility to do what I can to build intercultural understanding and to work constructively for good will and tolerance among all faiths. I have both the freedom and the responsibility to take my stand in behalf of those values and practices in which I believe.

I agree with President James B. Conant, former chairman of the Educational Policies Commission, that both private and denominational schools have a constitutional right to exist. Further, I think both private and public schools provide each other stimuli to better performance. Without specific knowledge I assume the American Catholic schools are in some ways the best Catholic schools in the world, and I would infer that the challenge of good public schools has helped produce this. In a similar way public schools are sometimes challenged by the best practices of private and parochial schools.

The right to do something and the wisdom of doing it are not identical. Lutherans, Catholics, Methodists, Baptists, Episcopalians, and Congregationalists, for example, have the right to establish their own schools from nursery school through the graduate school, or, speaking more practically, for the twelve grades prior to college. Yet I would regret to see the day come when the last Lutheran, Catholic, Presbyterian, Methodist, Baptist, Episcopalian, and Congregationalist disappeared from the public schools. Since it is estimated that 90 per cent of all who attend private and parochial schools are Catholics, I shall be more specific and say I would regret to see the last Catholic child depart from the public schools. There are perhaps four million, or roughly half, who attend public schools now.

It has been my personal experience to know and like many members of other faiths. How do we know them, and hence like them, if we do not associate with them? If, for example, all the eight or nine million Catholic children and youth should go through twelve years divorced in their daily school life from all association with those of other faiths, would we not be taking a step towards the German pattern? Suppose then—to follow the argument further—that all other denominations of substantial size should do the same thing. Would we not, wittingly or unwittingly, have jerked the rug of common integrating experiences out from under our young citizens? Would we not have laid a possible foundation for the spread of the necessary religious diversity to other facets of public life at a time when we need unity in facing a hostile world of Communists?

It is important that parents who exercise their right to provide education for their children through private schools should understand and support the public schools from whence have come, and will continue to come, 80 to 90 per cent of all our armed forces. It is important that parents who exercise their right of choice to provide religious education for their children through schools established to perpetuate their creeds should understand and respect the views of the majority of American citizens, who believe religious education should be cared for by the home and church. It is important that those of us who believe wholeheartedly in the public schools should understand and respect the legitimate rights of other Americans to support other schools. It is, we believe, our privilege to call to the attention of all American citizens what the full and complete exercise of these rights would mean in creating all over again those old religious and class bitternesses so prominent in much of Europe's history.

To guard against increasing tensions between public schools on the one hand and private and parochial schools on the other, there should be a united effort on the part of religious leaders to provide common agreements and sanctions for moral and spiritual values to be taught in the public schools. It is dangerously easy and appallingly irresponsible to voice hurtful and sweeping criticism against the public schools for the very conditions which divergent religions have in part produced. We need not dodge our disagreements, but we may speak quietly and fairly and responsibly, putting the welfare of our great American nation ahead of the complete and ultimate exercise of all our own personal or religious rights. Both churches and state will be served by this.

Perhaps you have read E. M. Forster's *Two Cheers for Democracy*. He gives one cheer for the variety of life and therefore the better opportunity for more individuals to live richer lives. He gives another cheer for criticism—that is, the possibility of free criticism which exists in full measure only in a democracy. Mr. Forster fails to give a third cheer because he thinks democracy deserves only two cheers.

My third cheer is for public education, its unique contribution to a classless society and to a freedom and tolerance largely unknown among countries with class education systems, and for the educational options offered the American people.

I am *for* public education. I am *not* anti-Catholic, anti-private school, or anti-religious, any more than I am anti-chocolate ice cream because I select vanilla. Three cheers for our democracy, our republic, if you prefer, our representative form of government, and for the options which make us free.

71

Virgil M. Rogers

ARE THE PUBLIC SCHOOLS "GODLESS"?

There should be a clear distinction between "secular" schools and "Godless" schools. Dr. Rogers describes how the nature of religious instruction makes it inappropriate for use with the "quasi-captive audiences of children in the public schools." He goes on to say that the principles underlying the public school system do not in any way conflict with the Judeo-Christian ethic. Thus he sees no particular grounds for conflict between subject-matter areas in the democratic public school as the basis for moral behavior and the concepts developed in the church or synagogue as the basis for spiritual behavior. Rogers contrasts the nature of early American society, where groups were relatively homogeneous with regard to religious beliefs, and our present-day pluralistic society, in which every conceivable faith is represented. He points out that the homogeneity which characterized the schools of earlier days "is gone forever." Rogers notes that religious heterogeneity alone, aside from any other consideration, would be sufficient reason to maintain nonsectarian schools.

To public school educators one of the most heartening documents of recent times is the 30-page pamphlet *The Church and the Public Schools,* an "official statement" published by the Presbyterian Board of Christian Education with the approval of the 169th General Assembly of the Presbyterian Church, U.S.A. They have grown so accustomed to pressures from groups wanting to introduce their particular brands of religion into the public schools, so inured to the round of applause any popular speaker has been able to count on by reference to educators' having "taken God out of the classroom," that to read this carefully studied argument and note its straightforward recommendations is to feel that they no longer walk alone; that even at this long last the all-important American concept of separation of church and state may yet be saved.

Because Christianity has long been the major religion in the United States, the one associated with the country's beginnings, the greatest pressures have naturally come from Christian groups. The counterpressures have come from the minority religious groups, which have felt that their children had the right to attend school without suffering offense, even by implication, because of the faith of their fathers. There have been counterpressures also from those who think that their right not to "believe" must be protected, that there is a vast difference between a faith which might seek to draw all men to itself by quality in daily living and a faith which would impose itself upon more or less captive children.

Surely the professions that are dedicated to the common good cannot, for the very work's sake, afford misunderstandings of one another's sincere efforts. Thus when the Presbyterians in their pamphlet issue a challenge for educators and religious leaders "to establish a system of intercommunication," that challenge, I believe, should immediately be accepted. In that spirit I should like here to present a few aspects of the public school situation which may not be obvious to many who are wholeheartedly involved with organizational religion.

The American concept of separation of church and state is, I believe, the supreme protector of all our individual freedoms. Most spectacularly is this the case with religious freedom. The specific ancient evils which built to the point of intolerability out of which this great concept was born have long since become unimaginable to us, so that our present danger is that we may allow ourselves to drift all unthinking into the sort of climate in which those ancient evils are revived.

But, comes one recurring question, why should people object to Bible instruction today when there was no objection in the public schools of our fore-

From *Educational Forum,* May 1958, 22:435-439.

fathers? Better than any other question could, this one brings into relief the differences between our nation as it is today and as it was a century ago, when Horace Mann was making his annual reports on all phases of education to the state of Massachusetts. Now many of us have neighbors who are practically commuters between the United States and Asia or the Near East. And when almost any discussion group on world affairs turns up one or two Indians or Pakistanis who voice objections to "Christian imperialism," one knows with conviction that the homogeneity which characterized the population of our nation's earlier days is gone forever.

The population which the nation's earliest public schools served had no obvious occasion to question whether the Bible might properly be taught for religious purposes. "Religion" meant the Bible, including the New Testament. Now, however, more than 250 religious sects are represented in public school enrollments. I have personally known as many as 22 affiliations in a single classroom. Each adherent feels his belief to be "true," else he should not be affiliated.

Shall the Koran be taught in these schools? The Book of Mormon? *Science and Health?* Shall the schools use the Old Testament, to which Judaism subscribes, or the New Testament, on which Christianity is largely based? And shall this New Testament be the King James Version or one of the more recent Protestant versions, even though only the Douay Version is permissible for Roman Catholic students? Educators are constantly encountering people who think of the public schools as the "Protestant schools" in spite of the fact that approximately half of all Roman Catholic children in this country attend them.

It is incontrovertibly true that American communities of the past century and their educators were not sufficiently alert to the shifting from a comfortably homogenous society to one of varying religious loyalties. In that failure to recognize and make provision for differences lies one of the reasons for the growth of the Roman Catholic parochial school system in this country. Abundant testimony to this fact is to be found in the history of public education in the state of New York. The right of the parochial system to exist must be owned and defended, but it is well also to keep in mind that a major result of the irresponsible inveighing against the "godless public schools" and the demands for "religion in the schools" is bound to be the strengthening of that parochial system.

For the public schools are not the "Protestant schools." They are the schools provided by government for "all the children of all the people" by virtue of common citizenship in the United States of America. As such they and they alone are to be financed from the public treasury.

They must of course be *secular*. There is nothing sinister and unclean about that word. It is not to say "godless," "anti-religious," "in league with evil," but merely "secular"—like the courts or the presidency. Jesus' own recognition of the validity of certain separations was expressed in His words, "Render unto Caesar the things that be Caesar's." Thus the American public schools must be secular. It is my reasoned conviction that the day this secularism ceases, our cherished heritage of freedom is on its way out, no matter what names we pin on the pitiful skeleton that remains.

But, some will argue at this point, it is not still true that God has been taken out of the classroom? This is, I know, a worrisome point to many sincere people. May I with equal sincerity question whether such a statement might not be imputing extravagant powers to educators and boards of education? How is that which "before Abraham was" to be thus easily exorcised?

Is it not a combination of two old tricky businesses that causes so much of the trouble at this point? One is the ancient conflict between the letter, which killeth, and the spirit, which giveth life; the other is the perennial problem of concept and definition. That "God is spirit" (Moffatt translation) is for many of us today as difficult a concept as it was when the Gospel of John was written. Is it not a sad commentary on the effectiveness of the churches' teaching that so few of their members ever get beyond the externalization of their particular brand of religion? Thus accustomed to labels, many cannot recognize their creed when they meet its embodiment unlabeled. This fact has a peculiar irony with reference to Christianity, since much of its Founder's teaching concerned itself with discrepancies between label and actuality. ("Which now of these three, thinkest thou, was neighbor unto him who fell among the thieves?")

Labels aside, a pretty good case can be made out for the public schools as the most nearly complete embodiment of the Christian ideal existing in our society today. That ideal is, as I understand it, set forth in the "new commandment": "that ye love one another." Throughout the years this ideal has not noticeably been furthered by divisive warring to establish the particular verbalizations of some particular fragment of creed. Today's youth are as a rule alert to the point of cynicism when it comes to recognizing gaps between verbal preachment and social practice. It is part of the business of education to inculcate the habit of searching for meanings beneath verbal surfaces. The most cursory scanning of any magazine's advertisement pages will show how necessary this is on the level of material products. It is education's obligation to carry that habit of careful search for meanings on into the realm of ideas.

Some educators and many religious leaders were shocked at the findings of Hartshorne and May's *Studies in Deceit* (Macmillan, 1928) that there was not necessarily any correlation between verbalizing of moral sentiments and putting these to practice in daily life among students. Specifically, it was found that students with records of faithful attendance at Sunday school were no less prone than the unattending to cheat in the classroom. Such a program as Ernest Ligon's for character education is based on awareness of the fact that it is practice and not verbalization which makes for moral character. Merely to teach children to repeat the admonition that they love one another is by no means to bring that love into action.

What is it to love a person? Is it not to respect him as a person, and to be willing to put effort into helping him find his way into the more abundant life which comes from entering into a creative relationship with the universe? This is the philosophy underlying modern public school education, however short practice sometimes falls of the goal. There are of course theological ways of stating such aims. Psychology asks that the school seek the child's "integration." The teacher may say merely that she wants to help him "find himself." Jesus said, according to the beautiful King James translation, ". . . if therefore thine eye be single, thy whole body shall be full of light."

Many—ministers and rabbis, church members and the unchurched—have deplored the Christian churches' shortcomings in living up to their creed in the matter of race relations. Yet all this time the public schools have been suffering little children to come unto them—black, brown, yellow, red, white, and mixed. Such exceptions as we are all aware of have not been the doing of the school people themselves. It is in the schools that the great immeasurables have been fostered—the raised level of self-respect through participation in school music and athletic programs, achievement of creditable scholastic standing, holding of school offices, and above all perhaps the experience of understanding by a sympathetic teacher. The usual thing here is that children shall be known by their fruits, not by their coloring.

Never has one of my own three children had a Negro Sunday school teacher; two of them, however, were taught in public junior high by an excellently qualified Negro. Never, except on self-consciously set up "visiting" occasions, have they sat in Sunday school beside Negro seekers after God; yet they have shared many a school classroom. At public school camp one term my son's bunkmate was a Negro—"and, boy, is he nice!" was the postcard comment.

Of late the churches have undertaken some very laudable projects on behalf of the migrant worker. But the public schools have been aware of him for a long time. They have known all along that he wasn't a bum because they knew his children. Only last April the Golden Reel award in the education division of the film festival sponsored in New York by the Film Council of America was awarded to the National Education Association's centennial film, *A Desk for Billie*. This is the true story of Billie Davis, child of a migrant family, who found that everywhere she went in America the school's doors were open to her, there was a teacher eager to help her and a "desk of her own."

The American public schools are predicated on the principle of the brotherhood of man (though some of their patrons continue to object to it). The natural inference from such a predication is the fatherhood of God. Any citizen is free to make this inference, as he must be to reject it. The churches, on the other hand, proceed from the premise of the fatherhood of God though often these words are not made flesh in the practical terms of the brotherhood of man.

It must be concluded that the churches and the schools have separate functions, and that the churches' ends are not to be achieved by their being permitted by the state to instruct quasi-captive audiences of children in the schools. Yet it must be apparent to any close observer who is not blinded by a need for labeling that no principle underlying the American public school system is in conflict at any point with the Judeo-Christian ethic. As church and synagogue perform their true function they will, I am sure, find in many children and young people what might be called a "first foundation" which these youth have been helped to build in the public schools. Billie Davis, for example, is now by profession a writer of religious literature. Often—and surprisingly, considering a child's environment both inside and outside the home—they will find him respecting honesty, searching for truth, and knowing who his brothers are.

The school and other social influences

THE SCHOOL AND THE FAMILY

In many areas of education it is difficult to make a clear-cut distinction between the responsibility of the family and that of the community operating through the school. In the first place, it is necessary to decide which types of instruction are to be offered by the home and which by the school. In the second place, the differing capabilities of different families must be considered. And finally, the constantly changing patterns of family life in a dynamic society require a continual re-evaluation of the school's role and of the need for family-life education.

Discussion of school and family relationships suggests a basic concern about the proper relationship between the professional teacher and the parent. Is the teacher responsible to the individual parent or is he responsible to all parents who support the schools? Should the teacher concern himself primarily with the welfare of the child or should he respond to the wishes of the parent? Under what circumstances—if any—should the teacher consult the family regarding the instructional process or content?

72

Ruth Kotinsky & Arno Bellack

THE RESPONSIBILITY OF THE SCHOOL

Two outstanding authorities in curriculum construction indicate here the immense problem of deciding the nature of the school program. The school educates the child; but one may well ask why his upbringing is sometimes considered to be the sole prerogative of the schools. The child is the product of a number of experiences, many of which fall properly outside the limits of the classroom, the playground, and the library. Thus, as these authors point out, close cooperation among the school, the family, and other social agencies is essential.

The health of the nation is not yet what it could and should be. "Let the schools get busy!" The divorce rate is high. "There is something wrong with the schools!" Citizens are too frequently apathetic about issues affecting the common welfare. "Civic education is *the* major responsibility of education in a democracy!" Vocational competence is less than employers would like to find ready-made. "What are we paying school taxes for?" Time off the job is on the increase, and commercial interests sometimes stoop to exploit it, sometimes seduce into debauchery and viciousness. "And I thought the worthy use of leisure time was one of the major objectives of modern-day schooling!" The ethics of our people must be raised to higher levels of decency and imbued with more refined values. "The schools ought to do something about it!"

"The schools are the bulwark of democracy!"

"The Empire was built on the playing field of Eton!"

Thus one line of vituperation.

Then another, just as insistent, if less loudly voiced:

From *High School Journal*, October 1951, 35:21-26.

"Why are school people getting concerned about out-of-school youth? That's our territory! We're the ones who know about young people on the loose." "How can the schools think they are in a position to do anything about the health needs of children? Only doctors are equipped to administer health funds and programs." "They think they're trying to run a recreation program down there at Public School XYZ, but they don't even have a trained director!" And so on and so on.

Let the schools do it. Only don't let the schools encroach on our territory. Only let us get into the schools because our cause is good, and should reach every child, and, after all, all the children are in the schools.

It is indeed a confused and confusing picture, composed of many elements, and pointing in a major way to the need for clearer definition of function on the part of all the institutions, services, and professions that bear upon the lives of children and adolescents.

The schools themselves, their history in this country, and the history of educational thought in part account for the hyperbole of expectation expressed about the results and comprehensive efficacy of their endeavors, and for the all-inclusiveness of the functions they frequently strive to perform on the child's behalf. The struggle to provide free public education for all the children was not easily won; universally available access to the acquisition of certain knowledges and skills was seen as the broad avenue on which all the young could walk to better jobs, better pay, increased social status, and consequently to all the good things of life. Moreover, as educational thought then ran, information in and of itself, equally and widely available, would assure all that was required for an alert and conscientious citizenry. Knowledge and skill, disseminated to all through the public school, could open the doors of Utopia.

Then came the reconstruction in educational theory that took the stress off knowledges and skills and called urgent attention to the indisputable fact that the teacher deals with the whole child. In order to achieve the goals that were once sought through the imparting of knowledges and skills—health, citizenship, worthy use of leisure, and all the rest—the teacher must see the child not as a "mind" or an "intellect," but as a living organism in which the physical, the emotional, and the intellectual are inextricable, and may perhaps best be regarded as but slightly differentiable manifestations of the living whole. What is more, the human organism is social in nature, so that the social environment, too, must be taken into consideration in the interpretation of his thought, feeling, behaving, and the way in which they are formed.

None of this served to make definitive the function of the school—either the goals that are specific to it, or the peculiar and particular contribution that it has to make to the achievement of these goals. In the old days its contribution was clear: the development of knowledges and skills, and these could be said to have constituted its more proximate goals as well, for it was assumed that once they were acquired, all personal and social benefits followed inevitably. Now that it is recognized that knowledges and skills are but attributes of a person, and to be effective must be attributes of an effective person, where does the school come in?

The answer has tended to be: "Everywhere, because the school must deal with the whole child in his social environment." Logical as this is, it gives rise to a number of difficulties, not the least of which is the problem of curriculum construction (going all good places with a whole person in a total social environment lends little guideline for selection). Moreover, such universality of goal and lack of defined, differentiated contribution lay the school open not only to all the charges noted above, as though it were solely responsible for every kind of social problem, but also to the clamorings of those who look upon its pupils as captives of a sort, by law immured where one can surely get at them—with immunization shots, or anything else that is good for them and which they may otherwise escape.

This is not to say that health services in the schools are not good things. But are immunization shots in and of themselves educational? Or are they given exclusively in order that the school-age child shall not lose time out of his schoolroom endeavors? Clearly the answer to both questions is *no*. Freedom from communicable disease is a good in itself, without regard to interruption of schooling, and the immunization shots, mechanically administered, at best contribute nothing that is educational in value, and at worst may do damage to the developing personality with which education is now so vitally concerned.

No matter how whole the child with whom the schools deal—and there can be no escaping this wholeness—the fact remains that the school is primarily responsible for his education, for example, and not primarily responsible for his health. A healthy child or man may still be uneducated, and an educated one may still not be entirely well—even if his education has been of a kind to sensitize him to the importance of health, provide him with certain basic understandings in relation to it, and make him aware of the role and earmarks of the reliable expert. The teacher does not diagnose cardiac disease, and the doctor does not lead the child through those experiences by which he acquires the skills of communication (not that the skills of communication are the whole of the teacher's job, any more than cardiac disease is the whole of the doctor's, but the point remains).

The need to state such truisms bespeaks the confusion out of which the various professions have not yet found their way since the concept of the whole child has borne in upon them. It is not only in school that the child—or adult, for that matter—is whole. He is whole also when the doctor sees him, and the social worker, and the recreationist, and religious leader. It is in his very nature not to be fractionable. And gradually all the professions that deal with him are attempting to take account of this wholeness. The doctor is leaving off his exclusive concern with disease and its cure, and is coming to take more and more responsibility for health—which can be defined only in terms of the functioning person, emotional and social, as well as physical. Gradually, too, he is coming to recognize that in health or illness, the patient is having experience of considerable moment when he is in contact with members of the medical profession, and he is attempting to find ways to make that experience more and more comfortable, reassuring, participating, independence producing—in brief, in the best sense of the term, educational in nature!

So concern for the whole child is not the exclusive prerogative of the school; fortunately, the hospital, the social agency, the playground, all the places where children are gathered together are coming more and more to share in this concern. The school has perhaps greater difficulty than some other children's services in defining its role in relation to this wholeness because of the more explicit recognition among educators that the whole of experience is educational in nature—or at least, that there is no experience from which the individual does not learn, whether what he learns stimulates growth or stunts it. This recognition must give rise to great rejoicing among educators when they see a wider dissemination of practice in relation to the wholeness of the personality in the home and among the members of all professional groups that serve children and adolescents; it should not give rise to the notion that, since all experience is learning experience, and the school's business is learning, all the experience of the child should be the school's primary responsibility, or to another notion, that there is no distinction between the function of the school

and that of the home, say, or of any other institution that bears on the life of the young.

First, it must be recognized that the school cannot control all the child's significant experience if it would. When all is said and done, it has been calculated that from birth to the age of eighteen, if the child has been in regular school attendance from the age of six, he has spent something less than seventeen percent of his waking hours under school auspices. Furthermore, the intensity of the meaning of the school experience varies from child to child, and this will probably always remain so, even after schools in general have come closer to providing experiences meaningful to all—there will always be some to whom school is pivotal, and some to whom it is scarcely even peripheral, and many all along the wide range between.

Moreover, it gives one pause to read the criteria in the life history devised for sorting the democratically minded from the Nazi-minded in the Prisoner of War Camps at the conclusion of World War II: of the six criteria developed, only one was germane to the school, and that had more to do with personal relationships than with any other aspect of school life.[1] If a prisoner of war had, during his adolescence, developed a personal devotion to a teacher—and it might be some other adult, not a teacher—who had strong democratic leanings, he himself was somewhat more likely to follow along in the same direction. But four of the criteria had to do with feelings and relationships in the home, and the sixth had to do with breadth of experience—like travel and reading—and the capacity to respond positively to its stimuli. This study was perhaps too initial, and based on too few cases, to be taken as definitive. Still it is a straw in the wind that whispers a basic question: is it the schools alone that support democracy, or a democratic culture that supports a democratic school—a culture to which the school undoubtedly makes its contribution, but to which, by the nature of cultures, the school cannot in and of itself give basic form and dedications?

The wholeness of the child, the fact that he is affected for good or for ill by all his experiences, wherever encountered, and, most important of all, the intimation that the democratic personality is the outgrowth of a sum total of a variety of strategic experiences in the home, school and elsewhere, do, taken together, provide a great common base of inquiry and endeavor on the part of all institutions and professions that constitute any significant part of the child's experience.

---

[1] Levy, David, "Anti-Nazis-Criteria of Differentiation" *Psychiatry* (Vol. XI, No. 2) May, 1948.

These considerations do not, however, abrogate the special contributions which each has to make to the propitiousness of that experience taken as a whole. All share the same more ultimate goal: a competent, effective personality, giving much to life, and getting much from living, functioning well in a democratic order. But each has its own angle of approach, each its role to play, each its own very special more proximate goals.

Were this not so, we should be in for something of a return to the primitive, with ministration to the mind, body, and soul, and initiation into social roles and mores, all entrusted to the same personnel. Whereas now, so much is known about the ways of the body, let us say, that no one man can master the growing knowledge in the course of a lifetime; and the problem becomes by so much more difficult when the body is seen as functioning in response to the inner drives imbedded in it and the outer environment, not only physical but social. What can be said of knowledge about the body can be repeated with only slight variation for knowledge about learning, or social response, or the emotional concomitants of living.

Those who are versed in one have much to contribute to those who are versed in the others if the more ultimate goals of all are to be more fully realized; there is much call for collaborative work and mutual enrichment among professional workers concerned with the child. But unless each has a distinctive oar, always more astutely and knowledgeably contrived for its special purpose, there can be no mutual exchange and cultivation, but only reiteration of the great common denominators. Thus it behooves the school, the health service, the social service, the home, and all the others, each not only to work with all the others, but also to seek to define ever more clearly its own special role and particular goals in the great common endeavor.

73

Philip W. L. Cox & Blaine E. Mercer

FAMILY AND NEIGHBORHOOD

This reading discusses the universal and yet unique aspects of the American family as a social and educational institution. Recognizing that no family lives completely apart from the community, the authors stress the relationship of the family to neighborhood influences. They also dwell upon the importance of social class and status roles. This article points out that although much is still to be learned about human adjustment, a stable society must rest upon a basis of stable homes and neighborhoods. Thus the teacher must know the dynamics of social and cultural change if he is to understand how family experiences of his students are related to their actions with peers and adults outside their families.

The family as a universal institution

One of the institutions common to all mankind is the family. It varies greatly in specific form and function from one society to another and even from one group to another within the same society, but it exists in some variation everywhere and among all people. The dependence of the infant on the protection and nurture of older persons assures very intimate associations of the child with parents and, usually, with siblings during his early, most formative years.

Both biological adaptation and social learning take place in the young child from hour to hour. His learning is chiefly by trial and success or error, but his biological equipment is such that these successes and errors are largely functions of his intimate relationship with older associates.

Babies differ by nature in spontaneous bodily movement (mobility) and in emotional expression (temperament). Their patterns of interaction with

From *Education in Democracy* by Philip W. L. Cox and Blaine E. Mercer, pp. 62-73. Copyright © 1961 by McGraw-Hill Book Company, Inc. Reprinted by permission.

other human beings and with material objects, as well as with their physiographic environments, are learned through practice. Habits of adjustment (which appear about the fourth month) are, therefore, products of learning, but biologically inherited predispositions determine in considerable degree which habits will be learned and which rejected.

In a relatively homogeneous society, the sum total of interactions results in behavior patterns that are more alike than unlike because the social environment to which individual children must adjust is similar. The student of the social foundations of education deals with personality traits which are common to all normal persons just as he does with any other facts of human development.

Nevertheless, the specialist in this field is usually peculiarly cautious where such generalizations are concerned. Two reservations are in order. First, he is keenly aware that some patterns which are almost universal in one society may be unusual or nonexistent in another; consequently, they must be treated with reference to social conditioning in the family and the community rather than to biological equipment. Second, in common with modern psychologists, he is skeptical of any specific cause-and-effect relationship that might be inferred from the relating of feelings to behavior.[1]

Innate capacities are widely agreed to be less potent drives to human conduct for the great preponderance of men than are the social customs that condition the individual. "Men spring from culture."[2] These reservations do not mean the denial of the universality of certain equipment or the reality of the driving effect of emotion. They do mean that biological inheritances are frequently less important than culture in determining individual and group attitudes and conduct. The student of personality formation finds a major concern, therefore, in drives which have to do with the way men relate to one another, whether these drives spring primarily from the inherent nature of the person or the customs and taboos of the social group.

Approached in this way, the questions of what comes first in time and in importance, nature or nurture, and of the actuality of three, a hundred, or no inherited patterns of behavior become academic. Fear, anger, sex feelings, and other emotions are realities, and to understand personality is to understand the characteristics, the causes, and the effects of their varied manifestations in the social environments where they occur. *Effects are further causes*—there is a chain reaction. Each type of manifestation is to be evaluated in terms of its probable influence on individual and, for the educator, on social welfare.[3]

The American home

The family, functionally and structurally, is the most important conditioner of the child's personality. The infant comes into the world with relatively few inherited behavior patterns and with a great capacity for variety in adaptation to his environment. The acculturation process in the family depends upon the plasticity of the child.

It is almost inevitable that there should be considerable conformation of the baby's habits and attitudes to the family's functional requirements. Feeding, sleeping, dressing, comforting, and all other aspects of infant care involve human beings and their natural and acquired traits. Some of these traits relate to voice, skills, gestures, moods, and standards of hygiene, noise, orderliness, and other behavior characteristics.

There is, of course, great diversity in these matters, not only among different homes, but also within any home from one time and occasion to another. In most American families, home regimen and domestic values are not inherited en bloc from ancestral customs and standards. Home life is itself plastic, reflecting not only the frequently unlike mores of parents and other adults, but also the many other factors that arise in the modern society. Among these factors are various technological gadgets in the home (such as nursing-bottle warmers, thermostatic controls, portable telephones, cooking timers, and plastic toys and containers) and also the influence of individuals and agencies concerned with child welfare. At one time, child specialists and agencies recommend early habit formation and impersonality in child care. A few years later, they advo-

---

[1] Cf. Clyde B. Moore and William E. Cole, *Sociology in Educational Practice*, Houghton Mifflin Company, Boston, 1952, pp. 57-78.

[2] Leonard W. Doob, *Social Psychology*, Henry Holt and Company, Inc., New York, 1952, p. 46.

[3] For more detailed and comprehensive treatment of original nature and social conditionings, see Gordon W. Allport, *Personality: A Psychological Interpretation*, Henry Holt and Company, Inc., New York, 1937, Charles Horton Cooley, *Human Nature and the Social Order*, Charles Scribner's Sons, New York, 1902, John Dewey, *Human Nature and Conduct*, Henry Holt and Company, Inc., New York, 1922, Clyde Kluckhohn and Henry A. Murray (eds.), *Personality in Nature, Society, and Culture*, 2d ed., Alfred A. Knopf, Inc., New York, 1954, and L. P. Thorpe, *Psychological Foundations of Personality*, McGraw-Hill Book Company, Inc., New York, 1938.

cate flexibility of schedule, postponement of some aspects of training, and much mothering (fondling, singing, talking) by adults.[4]

Nevertheless, these variations are but deflections of the stream of acculturation by which most children learn the conventional practices and standards of American life (for example, eating at table, sleeping in a bed, control of elimination, cleanliness, dress, and forms of address). And the child's nervous and organic system responds to this inculcation of culture in such ways that his personality emerges as a pattern of habits, adjustments, standards, and beliefs. This pattern is, for good or for ill, not fixed in childhood or even in adulthood; but it does underlie the feeling of "fitness" or "unfitness" by which many later experiences and standards are judged.

Growing up is an age-old and very complex business for the human being, endlessly varied as the individual experience is. The regimen of child-care institutions, however intentionally and intelligently organized and administered, has not been so successful as home rearing has been. Despite the frustration, disharmony, punishment and reward according to whim, and the frequently unhygienic conditions of home life, somehow the child who grows up in his home is more likely to survive as a reasonably normal individual than one brought up in a child-care institution.[5] There are subtleties in the relationships and mutual adjustments of the child-parent-sibling complex that seem almost to defy analysis.[6] These subtleties are parts of the social inheritance, through which responsiveness, security, adventure, and recognition are sought and found, hour by hour and day by day. Ego shapes itself in a world it never made but which it in part accepts and in part rejects progressively, experimentally, selectively, and continually.

Interrelations of family and neighborhood

Neighborhood influences. What has been said regarding family life is, in greater or less degree, true of the neighborhood. Of course, the relatively homogeneous neighborhood, where most families have similar customs, values, antagonisms, and

fears, reinforces the individual family's patterns more strongly than does the more heterogeneous neighborhood. But whether a neighborhood is fragmented or unified in any and all respects, other than nearness of residences, it affects people's attitudes and behavior. Propinquity to play areas, gang hangouts, churches, and police stations, for example, deserves serious attention in the study of forces which stabilize or disorganize family life.

No neighborhood exists in a social vacuum. Generally, indeed, the standards and behavior of the cohesive neighborhood are more varied and responsive to the patterns of the general community culture than those of any one family are likely to be. Even if all residents are Negroes rather than whites, Orthodox Jews rather than Protestants, or middle-class rather than lower-class, they share many interests and experiences with residents of other neighborhoods. Many of them see the same movies and television programs, follow the same comic characters in the same newspapers, root for the same athletes, are confronted with the same advertising displays, are allured by the same factions, and are appealed to by the same political devices.[7]

Moreover, the same individualistic impulses and urges that make growing children respond by a mixture of acceptance and rejection to the standards and practices of home life, characterize their maturation as members of local groups. The neighborhood usually provides the early out-of-home environment wherein the adaptation mechanisms are developed in contrast to those patterns learned in the family circle. Here, the family patterns are modified, avoided, or vigorously asserted. Experience is often a tough school, with frustration, deprivation, and physical pain exacted as the price for gaining status in one's age group. In extreme cases, indeed, the experience compels the child to lead a double life or, more accurately, multiple lives.

He may be timid, but compensate for it by "acting tough" or "covering up." He may be a gentle, cooperative brother and yet belong to a destructive callous gang. He may be a devout "Christian" and yet hate all who are not recognized as members of his own groups. He may be a bitter rebel in his own home, and yet a docile member of his team, class, or "set." He may be meticulously honest under one set of conditions but a liar and thief under another set.

---

[4] Cf. Martha Wolfenstein, "Trends in Infant Care," *American Journal of Orthopsychiatry*, vol. 33, pp. 120-130, 1953.

[5] James H. S. Bossard, *The Sociology of Child Development*, Harper & Brothers, New York, 1954, pp. 51-72. See, also, René Spitz, "Hospitalism," in *The Psychoanalytic Study of the Child*, vol. I, International Universities Press, New York, 1945.

[6] Bossard, *op. cit.*, pp. 91-118.

---

[7] Although the neighborhood exemplifies the local community, it is the intensified *process of communication* due to propinquity that must be emphasized. Neighborhood and family mediate between the community's values and behavior and those of individuals.

Family and neighborhood influences not clearly distinguished.   The dilemmas related to conflicting and evanescent selves are exceedingly complex and often lead to frustration. Both the family and the neighborhood are human environments into which practically all children are introduced for development. They provide the face-to-face relationships that serve as a nexus between infancy and maturation.

The means by which acculturation is fostered provide one way of distinguishing family processes from those of neighborhoods. Means characteristic of the family are sibling- and parent-child relationships, sleeping, eating, and dressing customs, expressions of affection, scolding, and rewarding. Processes of the neighborhood are those connected with church, school, gang, team, corner gossip groups, play field, movie theater, parties, and excursions. Obviously, there is much interpenetration between family life and neighborhood life. Older brothers and sisters, and sometimes parents, may participate in the same neighborhood institutions and practices as does the individual child who is striving for his own adjustment.

As has already been pointed out, moreover, both family and neighborhood absorb many of the values and stereotypes that are "American." The climate of opinion, in so far as it fosters attention to personal appearance, social and economic rivalry, self-assertion, and voluntary conformity to language, dress, and other behavior patterns, controls in large degree the standards that are exalted in the home and the neighborhood.

Even within families and relatively homogeneous neighborhoods, the inevitable conflicts between the values and the practices approved by adults (many of which are likely to be accepted by children as standard patterns) often have serious repercussions on group unity, loyalty, and authority. In the American melting pot, the potent instruments of communication penetrate almost irresistibly the ego ideals of young and old.

Variety of family and neighborhood acculturation processes.   If the individual child were standardized in native equipment and early experience, it might be possible to classify the processes and effects of family and neighborhood upon his development. Of course, this is not the case. The securities and insecurities of childhood, the fears and frustrations, the affectional experiences and the successes, the early or late development of abilities to walk, speak, and read, and the successive states of health of any individual are too numerous and varied for it to be possible to make other than very crude categories of environmental settings or of types of personality development.

Nevertheless, such classifications aid in understanding the ways in which primary group processes condition the mental, emotional, and physical growth of the individual. It should be kept in mind that there are some important constants in these interpersonal processes: the helplessness and consequent dependence of the young child; the plasticity of the human infant and his potential for conditioning and learning; the mores that exalt obedience, affection, kindliness, parental authority, individualism, and conformity; and the moral drive of habits and standards built into the individual mind of childhood, chiefly by parents and their substitutes.

The varied, and often elusive, effects of family and neighborhood influences on the development of the individual personality are further complicated by the patterns of mobility in the United States. Transiency of residence in a neighborhood is one form of mobility. Identification of self with a coterie not confined to the home community is another form of mobility. School attendance and membership in youth-serving organizations selectively enlarge the neighborhood experiences of boys and girls and constitute still another form.

The efforts of the larger community's constructive social agencies (such as governments, churches, and welfare agencies) are necessarily adapted to the conditions and trends of family and neighborhood life. There are two major reasons for this. In the first place, the effects of their homes and neighborhoods on young people determine in large part the occasions and opportunities for these agencies to function. In the second place, the success of the methods available to meliorative agencies depends on the primary groups' understanding of, and support for, their ends and efforts.

Significant motivations conditioning family and neighborhood

In the modern world, no family lives to itself. Its internal relationships and practices merge with the social organization and the general style of life which characterize the community. The family in a depressed neighborhood adapts itself to slum facilities, standards, and emotionalized attitudes; its members may accept or reject, but they cannot ignore, their neighbors' ways of life. The same holds true for families in other types of residential areas. Children who grow up in one type of social and economic environment are in varying degrees products of their neighborhoods as well as of their families.

Most of the social-class characteristics identified by recent sociological investigators are products of such adaptations. They are the result of the interactions of individuals and groups in the context of the customs and value systems of their neighborhoods. The personality outcomes, though individually unique, are similar enough to justify classification. And the advantages are not all with middle- and upper-class neighborhoods.[8] The lower-class environment, in general, favors "more gratification and easier outlet for children's organically based drives"—rage expressions, aggressive behavior, and sex expressions. The middle-class neighborhood mores restrict physical aggressions to patterned forms, either rule-controlled contests or subtleties of posture or gesture. Overt sex expression and fist fighting are discountenanced and so overcontrolled that children's personality problems focus about aggression and sex. Compensations and sublimations for these repressions take many forms, among them initiative and skill in social and economic competition, ambition for class prestige, and fear, anxiety, and guilt about sexual and crass physical behavior.[9]

Among the small[10] and rather esoteric upper class, "good form" in manners, taste, and accomplishments outweighs overtly expressed competitive ambitions. Family pride and class awareness, subtly transmitted, make for dependency on parental approval. Upper-class neighborhoods tend to be coteries or cliques, self-sufficient and mildly individualistic, influential in artistic and intellectual affairs, but somewhat outside the stream of the dynamic social life of the community. Boys and girls are frequently trained and educated separately, especially during adolescence. Engaging in competitive behavior which is obviously for self-advantage is "not done"; etiquette, "honor," and discretion are mandatory.

Numerous sociological researches have shown that, while social-class membership has especially important ramifications in the lives of children and youth of the lower and middle classes, as compared to the upper class, it is, nonetheless, important in the lives of all three. Although the findings of research on child training, as it is influenced by social class, are somewhat conflicting,[11] there can hardly be doubt of the general significance of class to the life ways of American young people. Irregular employment in a slum area makes hunger, cold, and sickness experiences to be dreaded and compensated for. Hence, the neighborhood tolerates acts and attitudes that shock the prudent and responsible bourgeoisie. Children running loose, violence and disorder in the crowded homes, recourse to orgies, predatory gangs, cleavages and segmental prejudices, narrow loyalties to leaders and institutions, all these complicated and inconsistent phenomena have survival values within some neighborhood frames of reference. Where and under what conditions one develops and adapts determines what his personality will be far more truly than the reverse.

Many questions that are matters for individual decision in the middle-class neighborhood are economically resolved among the poor. Woman's place is more likely to be where she can help stave off hunger and cold. Children more frequently must care for themselves and for their younger brothers and sisters if there is to be any care at all. The sacredness of private property is little esteemed among the propertyless. Law-enforcement officers are often resented as representative of middle-class standards that seem to have little application to slum neighborhoods. This attitude is accentuated among immigrant groups who retain a fear of governmental supervision.

[8] Allison Davis and Robert J. Havighurst, *Father of the Man*, Houghton Mifflin Company, Boston, 1947, pp. 17-29.

[9] *Ibid.*, pp. 24-25.

[10] W. L. Warner and P. S. Lunt report that, in Yankee City, the upper-upper class contained 1.4 per cent, and the lower-upper class 1.6 per cent, of the population. *The Social Life of a Modern Community*, Yale University Press, New Haven, Conn., 1941. "Five per cent of the respondents in a Gallup poll said they were upper-class. George Gallup and Saul F. Rae, *The Pulse of Democracy*, Simon and Schuster, Inc., New York, 1940, p. 169. Similarly, Richard Centers found that 5 per cent of a cross section of American males categorized themselves as "upper-class." *The Psychology of Social Classes*, Princeton University Press, Princeton, N.J., 1949, p. 77.

[11] Studies of Chicago and Boston families, while revealing some disagreements, showed a much clearer relationship between social-class and child-rearing practices (for example, greater severity with respect to toilet training among lower- than among middle-class families and more freedom of movement for children among the middle-class families) than indicated by other studies in New Haven, San Francisco, and Eugene, Ore. See Allison Davis and Robert J. Havighurst, "Social Class and Color Differences in Child-rearing," *American Sociological Review*, vol. 11, no. 6, pp. 697-710, 1946. Robert R. Sears and others, *Patterns of Child Rearing*, Row, Peterson and Company, Evanston, Ill., 1957, Martha Sturm White, "Social Class, Child Rearing Practices, and Child Behavior," *American Sociological Review*, vol. 22, no. 12, pp. 704-71, 1957. George Psathas, "Ethnicity, Social Class, and Adolescent Independence for Parental Control," *American Sociological Review*, vol. 22, no. 8, pp. 415-423, 1957, and Richard A. Littman, Robert C. A. Moore, and John Pierce-Jones, "Social Class Differences in Child Rearing: A Third Community for Comparison with Chicago and Newton," *American Sociological Review*, vol. 22, no. 12, pp. 694-704, 1957.

Status and role as determinants of choice. An urge for self-expression is an attribute of every human being. Indeed, several selves generally characterize an individual, one being dominant in one situation, another in a different circumstance. An aggressive star on the athletic field may become a gracious host in the evening. One selects the role that he will assay in the light of his estimate of his capacities, his "audience's" supposed receptivity, and some ego ideal that he hopes to achieve. Success in fulfilling his chosen role, he expects, will in degree bring recognition by whatever "audience" he courts.

The "audiences" which are valued vary for different individuals and for the same individuals at different times and in different settings. The often-heard generalization that the individual tends to be group-satisfied must be cautiously applied. The specific group settings to which he responds are ephemeral and varied. On occasion, the dominant group influence may be that of a coterie (a gang, clique, an ethnic or religious segment). At another time or in another mood, group satisfaction may be sought somewhat imaginatively and vicariously in a group ideal, myth, or stereotype (behavior believed becoming for a Baptist, a musician, or a spaceship pilot).

To be sure, all the varied forms of approval which the individual seeks are conditioned by his culture and so, in a broad sense, group satisfactions are implicit. Roles and statuses that arouse individual enthusiasm in a slum quarter are likely to be different from those that stimulate members of an upper-class neighborhood. In neither case, however, is there uniformity for all persons in the neighborhood.

The concept of the special potency of the peer group in influencing an individual's attitudes, beliefs, and behavior is fruitful in that it properly emphasizes a somewhat specific in-group acceptance and toleration. But here, too, caution is needed, for the individual usually belongs to several peer groups, the members of each of which may be superiors or inferiors in other settings. Football peers are not necessarily social-class peers or musical peers.

Irrational authority of group and institutional figures. Habitual behavior and its accompanying attitudes are generally unreasoned, though they may be reasonable or, at least, amenable to rationalization. They are adopted and practiced because conformity to the ways of the family, neighborhood, and other groups with which the individual identifies himself maximizes security. "Right" and "wrong," "fitting" and "unfitting," "loyal" and "disloyal" are terms of great moral significance. But they reflect the essentially irrational authority of the mores. Affection, approval, and hence security within family and other primary associations require at least some compliance with the standards accepted by the groups. Failure to conform is met with disapproval, perhaps by punishment; certainly it results in social isolation, at least temporarily.

The moral structures of the family, the gang, the athletic team, and ethnic, religious, and occupational groups are not altogether compatible. So each person learns to differentiate among the "right" and "fitting" behaviors and the "wrong" and "unfitting" ones for each occasion. To tell the truth, for example, is moral in general. In specific situations, however, withholding the truth or even lying to protect one's fellows is morally approved; in such cases, loyalty supersedes honesty, becomes "more moral." Moral development, then, comes out of the subtle process of compromising and resolving the conflicting, irrational elements of the moral structure the individual necessarily obtains from his social experience.

Irrational and incompatible as these complex adjustments are, they are of prime importance. Throughout history, the family and its immediately associated groups have been universal conditioners of individual personality patterns. The subtleties of human adjustment to the ways of life of parents, siblings, and neighbors are neither clearly nor completely understood. It is known only that stable home and neighborhood conditions are necessary for the preservation of the texture of stable societies.

The conflicting currents of rapid social and cultural change often disorganize long-established family and neighborhood patterns and so sacrifice something of their stabilizing influence. The effects of these disorganizing forces are, however, ambivalent. Outmoded in-group prejudices and narrow loyalties may help the individual in identifying with his childhood and parochial peer groups, but they are likely to unfit him for membership in the broader community which is characterized by diversity of association and outlook. Nevertheless, family and neighborhood conditionings are so potent that social changes are likely to be insignificant unless they affect, or find support in, these primary groups. Hence, the efforts of reformers, merchandisers, social workers, and educators are likely to fail if they do not gain the cooperation of families and neighbors.

The interpenetration of broader social movements and organizations and of local communities has gone so far in the modern world that some authorities believe it is almost necessary to initiate reforms in family and community patterns before attempting to interpret them as general social norms.

Ideas crystallized in national and world organizations are in many cases hatched and nourished in numerous small communities. Some totalifarian states have quite successfully used the concept of planting germinal ideas in small communities so that they may "catch fire" and appear later in national concepts. The Russian rulers may still be pondering why the Ukrainian farmers have not wholeheartedly taken over the notions of collectivized agriculture injected into their centuries-old way of life, which is characterized by a closely knit family-neighborhood-community structure. Some effort has been made, of course, to identify the collective farm with the historic *mir* (village) in the minds of peasants. In Nazi Germany, slogans and rituals were effectively related to warmly remembered village ceremonials and traditions. The father concept and the authoritarian patterns of German family life are reflected in the words patriotism and fatherland; the priest and the monarch are "father figures." The term "fireside talks," popularized by President Roosevelt in the 1930s, was analogous to the family council.

Most successful state reforms have come through the local channels first. Historic examples of this sequence are those of the Gracchi brothers of Rome, the Napoleonic Code in France, the socialization of Mexico, and the breakdown of the sharecropping system in the Deep South. The degree of success of the reforms has depended largely upon the amount of interpenetration existing among the local communities involved.

National policies, if they are to become permanent and basic to the life of the people, must have their roots in local community organization. Open forums and town halls are still necessary and basic to the "jelling" of concepts due to become national issues.[12]

---

[12] Recent communications research indicates the importance of group memberships and communication in the acceptance or rejection of messages which come to an individual via the mass media. Group norms and the patterns of person-to-person communication (especially through "opinion leaders") suggest the importance and potentials of public forums in a democracy. Cf. Elihu Katz and Paul F. Lazarsfeld, *Personal Influence: The Roles Played by People in the Flow of Mass Communications*, Free Press, Glencoe, Ill., 1955, pp. 130ff., 331-332.

74

Hilda Taba

CHANGES IN FAMILY LIFE AND THE HIGH SCHOOL PROGRAM

One dimension of the problem of school and family relationships is the constantly changing character of family life. The extent to which the schools should help the child understand the family must be thoughtfully considered, as must the significance of family changes as they concern the program of the school itself. The high-school program, for example, should make provision for meeting the needs of the adolescent whose sense of values has become different from that of his predecessors.

The literature dealing with cultural changes leave no doubt that changes in the family as a social institution have a profound effect on the development of individuals. Both anthropologists and psychologists reiterate the fact that the family is the nexus in the shaping of personality and character and the most potent influence in inducting young people into the culture. This fact remains even when combined with an awareness that the changes in the family are not independent of the changes in culture generally and that both the causes of these two types of changes and the consequences flowing from them cannot be separated.

However, this brief article must confine itself to the impact of the changes in the family. These might be viewed in several clusters, as follows:

From *High School Journal*, May 1959, 42:302-306.

The urbanization of the family is one factor. This reduces the space for the family unit, hence also the size of the unit. It furthermore is both an expression of and the cause of the disappearance of the family as a common economic enterprise. The old-fashioned family, to which we still find nostalgic references, shared in common the responsibility for making a living for the family. This productive center, therefore, also furnished a realistic setting for inducting the young into such sturdy virtues as responsibility for common welfare, thrift and cooperation. The modern family has no such resort. Not only are the family members separated in work but specialized in what they do. Even the leisure pursuits are specialized by age. We find thus the modern urban family member pursuing a separate career in work as well as in leisure. This leaves the family unity dependent on the somewhat fragile ties of affection and personal relations, both pursued in a fairly limited interpersonal contact.

The increasing mobility is another factor. It is said that in California seven out of ten families change houses every year. Scores of families move from one end of the United States to another. This mobility dislocates neighborhood ties, dissolves the extended family structure, dissolves the fabric of mutual friendships. The parents of these mobile families face their children alone, without the supportive structure of the extended family and the neighborhood. In more permanent communities with stable population the principles, rules of conduct and standards of the primary family were transmitted in a texture in which whatever one family stood for was more frequently supported by the extended family and a growing child or an adolescent was, in effect, under consistent supervision all the time. His behavior was responded to and judged wherever he was and by the same standards. In urban communities and in those composed of mobile families, this is not likely to be the case. A child, and especially an adolescent, faces a variety of standards and values in his contacts and spends a large portion of his days anonymously, not known by any adult.

In other words, the urban, mobile family pattern creates a social distance between the generations, and therefore weakens the capacity of the family to transmit values, codes of behavior and attitudes. This is not necessarily because parents are of lesser stature than was Grandfather Schwalm who took his grandson by the hand and not only taught him how to thresh wheat but also a good deal about the sturdy values by which to live, but the situation which made it possible for him to be an effective model for his grandson no longer exists.

To this social distance between generations we need to add the psychological distance which increases with the acceleration of social change. The codes of conduct, the things to talk about, and even the language shift enough with each generation to impede communication in the already shortened periods of contact.

An additional difficulty, only partly caused by the above condition, is the hesitancy, the ambivalence and outright confusion or conflict about the roles of family members: about the roles of parents as parents, the role of women. Parents no longer are sure what it means to be good parents; they are unsure about their authority as persons as well as about the authority of their values and standards. Woman's role more and more combines that of a homemaker with that of earning a living or pursuing a career. This ambiguity further weakens the impact of the family unit on children.[1]

Finally, as high schools approach a hundred percent attendance of the high school age group, they begin to number among their students the children from a type of family who formerly did not darken the high school doors: students whose families do not support the motivation to learn and to strive, who themselves have neither the background nor orientation to value education, at least not in the shape in which it is offered in high schools, namely a program developed primarily for another type of adolescent. While this factor does not represent a change in family structure, it is a change in families who send their children to school.

What does this suggest for high school programs?

The American public as well as the American schools have always expected the schools to deal with any problems of the society. Historically they stepped into any gap or difficulty that was created by a change in society. They undertook acculturation of the large number of immigrants. Today they are asked to do something about prevention of delinquency, about the rising divorce rate, about the high number of accidents on the highways, and even about the Sputnik. The problems emerging from the diminishing power of

---

[1] For further analysis of these factors see: Nelson Foote and Leonard S. Cotrell, Jr.: *Identity and Interpersonal Competence*. University of Chicago Press. 1955. Pp. 20-29.

the family to provide appropriate socialization of children and adolescents is no exception. It is evident that the high school needs to assume a heavier role in filling in the gap in value education and in inducting the adolescents into constructive membership in our culture than was necessary formerly.

As one considers the efforts to meet the impact of the changing family, two main directions stand out. One lies in the direct attack on improving family relations. This is exemplified by an effort to introduce courses on family, family relations and sex education into high school programs. These efforts operate on the assumption that the role of the high school is to restore family life to its former status and to restore family unity by a greater literacy about the nature of the family as a social force, and about the quality of interpersonal relations and the roles of family members. In view of the fact that unity in the modern family largely depends on the quality of interpersonal ties, which are no longer supported by the soil of a common enterprise, anything that can be done to improve the interpersonal competency is to the good. However, there is a question regarding the potency of factual information and a somewhat didactic direct teaching in restoring the feelings, attitudes and concepts which the life patterns fail to support.

Another, and perhaps a more realistic, line of thought is to analyze the gaps in value education left by the diminishing role of the family. What are the added tasks in character education, in education for the core values of the culture? What sensitivities and feelings are likely to be uncultivated? What ambiguities and insecurities need to be dealt with?

This line of thought leads not to new courses but to reconsideration of the current program and to retooling it for this new task. One possibility seems to lie in the programs of literature and of writing. Is it necessary that these be governed solely by the criteria of literacy about literary forms and types of composition? Would it not be possible to address the reading and analysis of literature to the task of extending sensitivity and identification with the basic values of our culture, including the values of the family? Could not writing be addressed to expression and exploration of feelings, of roles in the family as well as in other clusters of interpersonal relationships? The high schools participating in the intergroup education project experimented with such patterns and found them not too impractical. For example, in one Negro high school in which it was found that the patterns of family

and community life both developed a low level of ego-ideal, and a limited conception of ways of spending leisure time or of type of human relations to be expected of family life, stress was put on harnessing reading of literature and writing to extending sensitivities in these areas and possibly adding to the nature of the loyalties and beliefs the students held.[2]

Another possibility lies in a more conscious use and a wiser programming of the adolescent group life in school. It is scarcely necessary to point out the fact that peer group association is a potent force in building character and value orientation.[3] While contemporary adolescents are prone not to listen to the older generation, be it parents or teachers, they are extremely sensitive to peer opinion and respond with conformity to peer group atmosphere. Yet, as one considers the value systems of current adolescent peer groups, one finds them devoid of any value orientation, if not outright egocentric and antisocial. Studies of group life and activities in high school indicate that the students most in need of orientation into American culture, because of handicaps in family background, are least likely to be participants in high school activities, let alone share in the leadership and responsibility for these activities.[4] The activities themselves are so routinized and ritualized that they leave the value orientation untouched and even support, inadvertently, inappropriate and undesirable values, such as snobbishness and exclusiveness. Students with a deviate background, either because of their social class origin or personality, are outright excluded. In other words, the high school program has not paid too much attention to the value aspects of the process of socializing adolescents and simply does not socialize the deviates and, especially, not the lower class student. The secondary school is as yet untouched by the developments which took place in the first half of the century and which influenced the elementary program. The program building in secondary schools has still to face the task of its role in facing some of the consequences of social change, including that of the change in the style of family life.

---

[2] See Hilda Taba, *School Culture*. ACE. Chapter I; Hilda Taba and Deborah Elkins: *With Focus on Human Relations*, ACE, Washington, D.C., 1950, Chapter III; Hilda Taba, Elizabeth Wall Brady, and John Robinson: *Intergroup Education in Public Schools*, ACE, Washington, D.C., 1952.

[3] See Robert J. Havighurst and Hilda Taba: *Adolescent Personality and Character*. John Wiley, New York, 1949.

[4] Hilda Taba: *School Culture*. ACE. Washington, D.C., 1955. Chapter II and V.

75

Robert J. Havighurst

ADOLESCENCE AND THE POSTPONEMENT OF ADULTHOOD

An important problem in the relationship of the family to the education of the child is that of transition from childhood to adulthood, or the period of "social adolescence," as it is called in this article. Professor Havighurst analyzes the difficulties of this period, particularly those related to changing cultural attitudes toward marriage. Of great interest is his reconsideration of some earlier attitudes toward marriage for college students. He also notes the special problems of the 8 to 10 per cent of young people who, failing in school and failing at work, are most likely to become delinquent. He goes on to suggest the need for more help from the school in order to overcome the problems of young people, whom he divides into three groups according to their experience of moving into adulthood.

Adolescence, the transition from childhood to adulthood, consists of a biological constant and a cultural variable.

The biological constant is the period of puberty, from about twelve to sixteen years of age, when the boy or the girl develops into the biologically adult male or female. The timing of puberty varies little under changing conditions of diet and race. It does vary among individuals, presumably because of hereditary differences.

The cultural variable is remarkably varied. In one society, marriage may come close to the end of puberty, at fifteen or sixteen years of age, and the boy may move into the girl's home. There the young couple gradually learn to become responsible parents and workers. For them adolescence may last another five or ten years, being completed when they move into a house of their own. In another society, marriage for a man may not come until he is in his thirties and has an established livelihood and a house for his bride, who is usually much younger. In this case adolescence closes with a late marriage, after the man has spent fifteen or twenty years to become self-supporting.

Marriage does not necessarily mark the end of adolescence. Self-support and the establishment of a separate home are surer signs of the beginning of adulthood. Marriage is a truer mark of

the ending of adolescence for girls than for boys. But in societies where girls are married as children, some other event is a better indicator of adulthood.

In contemporary America marriage is often one of the events of adolescence rather than the end of adolescence. In contemporary America the most useful social definition of the end of adolescence is that of self-support. The most useful psychological definition is that of the establishment or achievement of a sense of personal identity.

In a complex modern society such as that of the United States there is a great deal of variety in the ending of adolescence and the beginning of adulthood—variety between social classes and even among individuals of the same social class. There is also a rapid change in this phenomenon. In the United States the rate of change is more rapid and the problems are more visible and more pressing than in most other societies.

Since 1900 there has been a general tendency toward the postponement of adulthood. This tendency is part of the massive movement of modern society toward industrialization and urbanization and is the cause of some of the major maladjustments in modern society, including the disease of juvenile delinquency. These maladjustments are found all over the world wherever urbanization and industrialization are in progress.

Young people can be divided into three groups according to their experience of moving into adulthood. These three groups existed in 1900, as they do now, but in different proportions.

From *School Review*, Spring 1960, 58:52-62. Copyright 1960 by The University of Chicago. Reprinted by permission of The University of Chicago Press. This article is based on a lecture given on October 27, 1959, at the Institute for Religious and Social Studies in New York City.

The first group is made up of those who follow a long course of educational training before they become self-supporting. These are the young people who take a four-year college course, at least, and perhaps further graduate or professional training. Since 1900 this group has increased from 4 per cent to 22 per cent of all young men and from one per cent to 12 per cent of young women.

The second group is made up of those who normally take adult roles of self-support at about age eighteen to twenty. The young people in this group complete secondary school and then go to work at steady and satisfactory jobs. Their numbers have risen from 10 or 15 per cent of an age group in 1900 to 50 to 70 per cent today.

The third group is made up of young people who normally are self-supporting and fill adult roles at sixteen to eighteen years of age. They attend school until age fourteen or sixteen, then go to work or get married, seeking to fill adult roles as soon as possible. In 1900 this group made up about 80 per cent of young people. Many of them lived on farms. Today they make up about 20 to 30 per cent of youth. Relatively few of them live on farms.

Under the conditions prevailing in 1900 the first group had a rather long period of social adolescence; for the second group there was a three- to five-year transition period that led rather smoothly into adult roles; for the third group there was little postponement of adulthood beyond the biological end of puberty.

In all societies with a complex division of labor there has been a group of young people who followed a long trail from puberty into adulthood. During the interlude they prepared themselves for the more complex adult positions, which carried high status. Whether they attended the university or learned their work in an apprenticeship in a law office or a business office, they had a long road to follow.

Today this group gets more formal education than before. Larger proportions are going beyond four years of college into graduate schools or professional schools, which keep them in a student role until they are twenty-five or even thirty years old.

The principal change in this group since 1900 is its great increase in numbers. It now includes a fifth of the young men and about a tenth of the young women. This increase in numbers is dictated by the mounting demand of modern society for people with technical training.

Postponement of adulthood puts these young people in a favored economic position. Most of them come from middle-class families that have taught them to postpone immediate pleasures for greater future satisfaction. They see this pattern in their own parents and identify with it. They have learned the art of sublimation of their impulses. The Kinsey studies show that these young people seek direct sex outlets later and less frequently than young people with less education and with working-class expectations. Until recently they postponed marriage until they were ready to take up an adult work role.

But a considerable number of these young people are now marrying in their early twenties. This means that for this group marriage is a part of adolescence and not the beginning of adulthood. This is probably a useful adaptation to adjust the disparity between biological and cultural realities.

For the young women who marry young men while the latter are still in the stage of social adolescence, the situation is on the whole acceptable. The wife becomes an adult before her husband, by taking responsibility for a home and often by having children. For her this is more satisfactory than prolonging her adolescence by taking jobs that are only makeshifts for her. To follow this course would mean continuing the adolescent dating pattern of her teens, while she waited for her future husband to finish his training.

Thus the dilemma of postponed adulthood is being solved by this growing group of young people, through some combination of sublimation of biological urges with a redefinition of the place and function of marriage in the life cycle.

This account of the causes and results of delayed adulthood for a particular segment of youth may quite rightly be criticized as optimistic. Readers may point out that it is written from a sociological point of view and omits psychological and dynamic consequences that may be damaging to the individual. It is important to ask what the postponement of adulthood does to self-esteem and self-direction, which are essential characteristics of the autonomous person.

In a provocative little book called *The Vanishing Adolescent*, Edgar Friedenberg argues that today the major developmental task of adolescence —the task of self-definition, or achievement of identity—is poorly achieved because adults, and especially secondary-school teachers, do not treat adolescents properly. He says, "Adolescence is the period during which a young person learns who he is, and what he really feels. It is the time during which he differentiates himself from his culture, though on the culture's terms. It is the age at which, by becoming a person in his own right, he becomes capable of deeply felt relationships to other individuals perceived clearly as such."[1] At the close of his book he says, "I believe that adolescence, as a developmental process, is becoming obsolete. The kind of personal integration which results from conflict between a growing human being and his society is no longer the mode of maturity our society cultivates."[2]

This argument has much to recommend it, and I shall refer to it in the discussion of the youth of the third group, whose adulthood is blocked. But for the young people in the first group, who have such a long period of adolescence, I doubt that conflict between the youth and his society is necessary for the achievement of self-definition or of self-esteem.

This task is probably most difficult in a changing and fluid society, where *achieved* status is more important than *ascribed* status. In the society of today the individual with good potential and good education has to choose between an almost bewildering variety of possible vocational identities, knowing that he must not only choose but also work hard to achieve the identity after he chooses it. Shall he become a teacher? A lawyer? A doctor? An engineer? If he decides to become an engineer, what kind? And shall he plan to remain a "real" engineer or shall he use his training as a base for going into business management? If he decides to become a physician, what specialty shall he train for? And shall he go into practice, research, or teaching?

Society has declined to tell him what to do. It is up to him to make the decision. The fact that he has a long period of university and post-graduate training or training on the job may make his identity more stable and more permanent than it would be if he had to make a decision at the age of twenty. The process may be long drawn out, and the young person may have to cope with some feelings of uncertainty and insecurity, but as a result he may become a person with a complex and stable identity that is well adapted to modern society.

The second and largest group at present consists mainly of those who complete secondary school and then go to work. This group also includes a few who quit school a year or so before high-school graduation to take a job and a few others who start college but drop out by the end of the first year.

This group makes a gradual entry into adult roles between the ages of seventeen and twenty.

They regard high-school graduation as a necessary step toward the kind of job they want. Their high-school dating leads them rather smoothly toward marriage; more than half of the girls in this group are married by the age of twenty, and more than half of the boys are married by the age of twenty-three. For this group marriage marks the end of adolescence.

About 50 per cent of boys and about 70 per cent of girls are in this group as they grow up.

They are the modal group in a modern urban society. Their social adolescence extends from three to five years beyond their biological adolescence and seems to involve relatively little strain for them.

A three- to five-year postponement of adulthood is easily tolerated as long as the young person is taking steps that surely lead to it, such steps as high-school graduation, apprenticeship to a trade, a steady job with promotion, engagement to be married.

In a modern complex society this type of progress to adulthood would seem to be the easiest, although it is gained perhaps at the expense of individuality, drive, and other upper-middle-class virtues.

In 1900 this group was much smaller than it is today—about 15 per cent of boys and 10 per cent of girls at that time.

The third group consists of boys and girls who find the path to adulthood blocked and experience great difficulty in achieving responsible adulthood. In this group lies most of the social pathology of youth today. It is made up of about 30 per cent of the boys and 20 per cent of girls.

These boys and girls generally drop out of school at the age of fifteen or sixteen after a history of failure, frustration, and frequently of bad behavior. Maladjusted to school, many of them are also maladjusted to work and family life, and make little or no progress toward responsible adulthood during the next few years.

Although at present they form a pathological group, in 1900 and during the preceding century they were the average group, with relatively good adjustment. In 1900 this group made up 80 per cent of boys and some 90 per cent of girls. They reached the end of elementary school at age fourteen or fifteen and then went to work, mainly on farms and in homes. Some of the boys became apprenticed to learn a trade. More than half of all boys lived on farms at that time. Those who did not go to the city with a definite vocational objective remained on the farm and became self-supporting farm workers by the time they were sixteen or seventeen.

[1] Edgar Z. Friedenberg, *The Vanishing Adolescent* (Boston: Beacon Press, 1959), p. 9.
[2] *Ibid.*, p. 133.

The adult work role came just as early as these boys were physically ready for it, and marriage came along at that time or a few years later. Girls of this group worked in their own homes or in other people's homes, learning the role of homemaker, and they married in their late teens or early twenties.

For this group in 1900 there was a direct transition from puberty to adult work and marriage roles. The shift was so visible that no young person could doubt where he was and whither he was going, even if he was so unusual as to be five or seven years in the process.

This group has grown much smaller, having lost most of its members to the second group, that group of young people who finish high school and then go to work. It has become a maladjusted group; the young people in it find the pathway to adulthood blocked.

At about seventh or eighth grade the members of this group begin to have trouble in school. They have been slow, dull students. They have known failure. Coming from the wrong side of the tracks, they have known discrimination in social life. They realize that school will be no easy pathway to adulthood for them, as it is for most of their schoolmates.

When they reach the legal school-leaving age, they drop out of school. By this time many of them have a police record for minor delinquency. Others have become apathetic and intimidated, and have lost confidence in themselves.

At this point, at the age of fifteen or sixteen, they are no longer children, but they cannot find their way into adulthood through high school. About two-thirds of them are fortunate enough to break into an adult role by successful work or successful marriage. Those who succeed follow the pattern that was common for this group in 1900 but is difficult for them today. They go to work on the farm or in an unskilled occupation, and they make good at it. By the age of eighteen or nineteen they are well established in a work role which has low social status but is nevertheless an adequate adult role. The girls are likely to be married by this age.

My colleagues and I have been studying this group whose pathway to adulthood is blocked in school. We find that, of some 25 per cent of young people who are in this group, about two-thirds find a quick and fairly satisfactory way to adult roles through work and early marriage. They do so in spite of the difficulty young people under the age of eighteen have getting work in our society. Practically every member of this successful group has a family that has given adequate affection, security, and discipline.

The 8 or 10 per cent who drop out of school and then do not find a way to adulthood through work are indeed the failures of our society. Juvenile delinquency is heavily concentrated in this group. In nearly every case families are inadequate and have not provided their children with a base of character on which to build.

When the boys in this failing group get work, they generally prove to be untrustworthy, or aggressive and hostile, and cannot hold a job for any length of time. Nor are they successful if they enter military service. If they are not rejected on the ground of mental or personal incompetence, they are likely to be let out of the service after a few unsatisfactory months.

A remarkably high proportion of the girls who drop out of high school get married almost at once. In our study of a cohort of youth growing up in a midwestern city, we found that sixty-seven out of a total of 230 girls dropped out before high-school graduation. Forty-five of them were married by the age of seventeen; eighteen at age seventeen; twenty-one at age sixteen; and six under sixteen years of age. Some of these marriages show signs of being successful. These girls have been able to achieve an adult role after failing in school. Other marriages are already clear failures, leaving the girls with only a pathetic and useless symbol of adulthood.

This tragic group of 8 or 10 per cent of our youth, who are not able to grow up through the school, through work, or through marriage, suffer not so much from postponement of adulthood as from a set of roadblocks that may prevent them from ever achieving adulthood. They will never achieve self-definition or identity. They have had their share and more than their share of conflict with teachers, parents, and policemen. Whether they are apathetic and fearful, or hostile and delinquent, they have been defeated.

Any conclusion about the present condition of youth must be based on an affirmation of values. The following seem most relevant:

1. There is value in a productive adult life as a worker, parent, and citizen. Adulthood should be started fairly early in life, but age twenty-five or thirty is not too late for a person who will lead a complex life. A high proportion of young people will live to be sixty-five or seventy, and will have a forty-year adult career, even if they start as late as twenty-five or thirty.

2. There is value in a self-directed and self-defined life. In a complex modern society a person with high ability is likely to require time to establish his identity and to prepare himself to fill the roles he defines for himself.

3. There is value in adolescence as well as in adulthood. For many young people a long, slow adolescence is a period of great happiness. In an economy of abundance there is no great social need for young people to cut short their adolescence in order to contribute to the economy.

4. There is value in growth toward adulthood. No one can be satisfied with stagnation during adolescence. Young people need assurance that they are growing up, even though growth is slow and complex.

5. There is value in physical sexual fulfilment, and this value is found most fully within marriage. Consequently marriage may very well be a part of adolescence rather than a mark of its termination for young people who need a long time to prepare for roles other than the family roles.

The following conclusions flow from the application of these values to the present-day situation of youth in the United States.

Educational preparation may be profitably accelerated for the small group who will need three or more years of study in a graduate or professional school. These young people might well enter college a year early or do work of college level in secondary school, to save time for their later education.

Marriage should be approved at age twenty to twenty-five for those young people who will need to study until age twenty-five to thirty. However, many of these young people can successfully sublimate their biological impulses and enrich their adolescent life and their adult life thereby.

The great majority of youth, who today complete secondary school and then go to work, suffer no difficulties because of the postponement of social adulthood for three to five years after they achieve biological adulthood. This period of growth into adulthood seems appropriate to them personally and desirable from the point of view of the welfare of society. During the period of adolescence educators and religious leaders should seek to help the members of this group become more self-directed, more clear about their place and their goals in life.

There is a group of some 8 to 10 per cent of youth, more boys than girls, who find the pathway to adulthood blocked. They are failures in school and failures in the world of juvenile work. Some of the girls marry early but do not make a success of marriage. This group represents a serious social problem for modern society. Juvenile delinquency is heavily concentrated in this group. School and society must somehow find a way to open the pathway to growth for them. The ordinary school and even the special school for maladjusted youth have failed to find the solution. The families of these boys and girls have failed them. This is a problem that requires radical efforts for its solution.

76

Lee O. Garber

MARRIAGE "NO CAUSE" FOR BARRING HIGH SCHOOL STUDENTS

Should high-school students marry? If they do marry, should they be allowed to stay in school? Because young people are now marrying at an earlier age than before, this problem has become a vital one. It may surprise you to learn that courts have ruled upon the desirability of school attendance by boys and girls who have married. Everyone knows that acute social problems result from such early marriage, since there is a high divorce rate in this age group. Nevertheless, the arguments for universal education apply to those who are married as well as to those who are not. Indeed, their need for an education (both for their own welfare and for that of society) is perhaps greater. In this article an important authority in school law points out the nature of the legal right of the married student to remain in school.

What authority does a board of education have to enact rules and regulations concerning married students? A reading of the statutes is seldom rewarding as few, if any, states have enacted specific legislation covering the matter. Therefore, any legal guidance available will have its source in the common, or decisional, law.

Surprisingly enough, there has been little litigation in this field. The question first came before the courts a number of years ago as the result of board rules barring students who marry from continuing to attend public schools. When the legality of such rules was questioned, the courts of both Kansas and Mississippi held that school boards were without authority to enact rules that made it impossible for married students to continue their education at public expense.[1]

A few years later a different sort of case came before the courts in Louisiana. Here it was held that a young girl of compulsory school age could not be convicted of truancy for failing to attend school following her marriage.[2] The court reasoned that marriage emancipates a minor female and releases her from attendance.

Then, about two years ago, another case involving the legality of a school board rule relating to married students was questioned in Tennessee.[3] Here, the board, alarmed at the number of marriages taking place among high school students and their possible effect on the general well-being of the school, enacted a rule that any student who married during a school term would be automatically expelled for the remainder of that term. The court, taking judicial cognizance of the rulings in the Kansas and Mississippi cases previously mentioned, ruled that while a school board may not provide permanent expulsion for students who marry, it may bar them from attendance for a reasonable length of time, if it believes this is necessary for the well-being of the school.

Aside from the cases just mentioned, there appears to have been no such litigation in the higher courts until recently, when the court of civil appeals of Texas held that a board rule restricting married students from participating in extracurricular activities was reasonable and, therefore, enforcible.[4]

In this case, one Jerry Kissick brought an action seeking an injunction to restrain a board of education from enforcing a rule providing that "married students or previously married students be restricted wholly to classroom work; that they be barred from participating in athletics or other exhibitions, and that they not be permitted to hold class office or other positions of honor. Academic honors such as valedictorian and salutatorian are excepted."

The plaintiff was a resident of the district and a student in its schools. During the 1958 season he was a letterman on the football team. While only 16 years old, he was married (March 1959) to a girl who was 15. As a result, he was barred from participating in football because of the board rule. He stated that he planned to continue on the team during his remaining years in high school and that he was looking forward "to an athletic scholarship and college."

Specifically, the plaintiff contended the rule was invalid and unenforcible. He contended it violated public policy because it penalized marriage. The court rejected this contention. In so doing, it agreed that "it is . . . the policy of the law to look with favor upon marriage and to seek in all lawful ways to uphold this most important of social institutions," but it noted that this "principle however is referable to those of lawful age (male, 21; female, 18)." With respect to those under age, it stated that the legislative policy, as reflected in the statutes, was different, and noted that they revealed "a public policy . . . unfavorable to and in outright discouragement of 'underage applicants' for matrimony."

The plaintiff also contended that, since the board rule was enacted following the date of his marriage, it was inapplicable to him because it was retroactive in its effect. The court noted that "the question here posed is of whether the playing of football, coupled with an athletic scholarship potential, is such a scholastic right as entitles one to [the] protection" of a constitutional provision prohibiting the enactment of legislation of a retroactive character. Quoting from an earlier Texas case, it stated that the provision in question applies only where the "application of the law would take away or impair vested rights acquired under existing law." Therefore, because plaintiff's right "must be classed as contingent or expectant in contrast to a vested right, which is an *immediate fixed right* of present or future enjoyment," the court again overruled the plaintiff's contention.

The court also noted that the plaintiff's constitutional right to attend the school in question and participate in its functions was subject to such reasonable rules and regulations as the board might adopt. With respect to the board rule

From *The Nation's Schools,* August 1960, 66:66, 92. Copyright 1960 by The Modern Hospital Publishing Co., Inc., Chicago. Reprinted by permission.
[1] Nutt *v.* Board of Education, 128 Kan. 507, 278 P. 1065; McLeod *v.* State, 154 Miss. 468, 122 So. 737.
[2] In re State in Interest of Goodwin, 214 La. 1062, 39 So. (2d) 731.
[3] State *v.* Marion County Board of Education, 302 S.W. (2d) 57 (Tenn.). For a detailed explanation of this case see: The Nation's Schools, 61:63, 64 (April) 1958.
[4] Kissick *v.* Garland Independent School District, 330 S.W. (2d) 708 (Tex.) (reported Dec. 18, 1959).

here challenged, the court held it was reasonable and stated that "courts will not interfere in such matters unless a clear abuse of power and discretion is made to appear."

Court favors board

Finally, with respect to the plaintiff's contention that the resolution in question was "arbitrary, capricious, discriminatory, unreasonable and void," the court again ruled in favor of the board saying: "Undoubtedly . . . [the regulation] had a direct relationship to objectives sought to be accomplished by school authorities—that of discouraging the marriage of teen-age students." In support of its position, the court relied heavily on the Tennessee decision in which it was held that a board rule barring married students from attending school for the remainder of the term following their marriage was reasonable and enforcible.

This case is significant because it adds a little more to our understanding of the authority of a school board to take action that has the effect of discouraging teen-age marriages. It serves as a precedent for holding that while married students may not be barred from attending school, they may be barred from participating in extracurricular activities. Whether the courts of other states will follow this rule remains to be seen. They need not, but, in the absence of any statute to the contrary, it is believed that most, if not all, will.

The school and other social influences

THE SCHOOL AND THE PEER GROUP

Closely related to the educational effect of the family is the influence of the peer group—the customs, standards of behavior, and moral values held in common by a group of boys and girls. Fads of language usage, cults of behavior, ways of dressing, reactions to adults are all illustrations of peer-group codes. Actually, it is difficult to separate arbitrarily the influences of family and peer group. Many bewildered parents have found—sometimes with dismay—that much is learned in the peer group over which the family has little real control.

Fortunately, in most instances the effect of the peer group upon its members is not harmful; in many cases it wields an effective positive influence. The school is in a strategic position here, because it can sometimes help mold the attitudes and mores of the peer group. It has the opportunity of providing activities, of discussing standards, of shaping attitudes. Since the peer group offers most opportunity for the practice of socialization, the school can accomplish much in projecting its standards through the group to the individual.

77

Theodore Bienenstok

THE PEER CULTURE OF YOUTH AND THE SCHOOL

This author analyzes the nature of the peer culture and points out many of the distinguishing characteristics of different age groups. Peer groups, he states, present a powerful force which can be used by the schools in fostering "socially desirable habits, attitudes, and relations." Just exactly how this can be done is a challenge to the teacher, who must understand first the complexity of peer relationships. However, more and more schools are recognizing the need to capitalize upon peer-group interests without compromising the mission of schooling and guidance workers or community agencies, and students themselves are developing programs which meet the informal needs of youth. The reader will do well to consult some of the recent literature on the problem (5) to see the effective methods which have been employed to meet this problem.

Inevitably, all who care for children come to realize that youth lives in a world of its own. Here in groups of their age-mates, boys and girls tend to create a body of customs, standards of behavior and moral values that constitute a distinctive culture. The requirements of this sub-adult peer culture exert a growing pressure upon the child as he progresses toward maturity. In fact, a satisfactory adjustment to his group of contemporaries and their demands is one of the major tasks in the child's social development. It is therefore essential that the teacher understand the nature of peer groups, so that their potential value for education may be capitalized, and some of their disadvantageous effects counteracted.

Role of peer culture in transition from childhood to adulthood

The formative influence of the peer culture can best be understood if considered in connection with the difficult transition from childhood to adulthood. Conditioned to one set of behavior patterns in childhood, the individual must revise his conduct from almost all points of view as he assumes the role of an adult. Growing up means that new patterns of behavior must be learned, and new adjustments made, in activities, interests and habits.

All societies are faced with the problem of this change and regulate it in various ways. Some try to assure a continuity of conditioning by allowing the child to put into practice forms of behavior essentially the same as those upon which he will rely as an adult, but graded to his physical and mental capacity. Other societies which expect, as we do, basically different conduct from a child than from an adult, try to minimize the strain of this change. Either they give new duties and prestige to age groups of young people at each stage of development, or they mark the passage from childhood to adulthood by publicly ritualized steps, the meaning of which is clearly understood and accepted by both the youth and his elders.

In contrast to this, in modern societies of the Western world, while it is expected that young people will become emancipated from parental control and will make their own way in the world, the exact time, manner and meaning of such emancipation remains uncertain, and a subject of dispute and recrimination. Only grudgingly and with reluctance does modern society accord status to growing-up boys and girls. In some situations they are treated like adults and are asked to show maturity of conduct and a sense of responsibility. In other situations they are treated like children incapable of taking responsibility or of making even simple judgments.

Confused about their role and function in society, and lacking a definite place in the scheme of things, young people turn to their own peers, or equals, for guidance, protection and support. The peer culture thus created helps to carry them over the adolescent period of strain and stress. In close personal relations with their contemporaries they can satisfy their needs for security, for belonging, and for status, while gradually trying to free themselves from dependence upon their families.

Peer culture in childhood

As soon as a child begins to play with other children, he ceases to be a member solely of a family group and enters the society of his peers. In the early years of elementary school, of course, parental influences are still predominant, but little by little the standards of age-mates come to the fore. Actions and opinions of play associates increasingly occupy the child's attention, and there is a growing desire for identification with the peer group.

A major factor fostering this tendency today is the impact upon children of mass media of communication. Radio and television programs, comics and movies transmit to the child the values and rules of behavior prevalent in his peer culture. Mass media tell him what other children eat, wear and read, what interests they have, and what particular slang they use in intimate communication. They create for him a picture of what boyhood and girlhood are like in the culture. Well-known personalities of comics and movies such as Superman, Hopalong Cassidy, Bugs Bunny and a host of others, suggest to a child ideas and images of things and activities which he may share with other children of his age. All this lore

From *Educational Forum*, November 1953, 18:313-319.

is further spread throughout the peer group by way of continuous exchange on playgrounds and in school.

The direction received by a child from his contemporaries and from mass media extends even to the norms of parental behavior. What children of a given age should be allowed to do, how they should be brought up by their parents, how much spending-money they should receive can be learned from these two sources of authority. And such information may be, and actually often is, used successfully by the child to oppose parental commands and prohibitions and to influence parental action.

Character of peer grouping in preadolescence

The importance of the peer group increases greatly in the preadolescent period. In contrast to the earlier stage of development, when contacts and associations with age-mates were organized and directed by adults, youngsters now spontaneously seek to form "gangs" and "cliques" removed from adult supervision.

Segregation by sex, which is characteristic of this period, goes together with a differentiation of roles and values along sex lines. Boys disapprove of girls, unless they are nearly like boys. Games and plays are assigned to one sex or the other. Crossing of sex lines is subject to ridicule, when done by boys; it requires a change of behavior, language and appearance, when attempted by girls. Lines of inclusion and exclusion are drawn sharply. Conformity to group norms is enforced by boys through "razzing," raillery and ostracism—quite often in fist fights or other types of physical aggression. Girls assure conformity primarily by the method of exclusion.

The effect of peer groups on preadolescent boys

Play groups of preadolescent boys often tend to develop a rather closely knit organization, with a more or less formal leadership. These so-called "gangs" perform a vital function in the process of socialization. In collective undertakings conducted by the peer group, boys learn and practice the social virtues of cooperation, self-sacrifice and loyalty to the group, while outdoor activities such as roaming neighborhoods and streets, camping out, playing Indians and cowboys, cops and robbers, offer many opportunities for the exercise of daring, resourcefulness, self-reliance and initiative. The free life led by the "gang" satisfies the boys' deep desire for adventure, excitement and novelty.

The very fact that all these experiences are taking place in an atmosphere of intimate fellowship and freedom from adult supervision apparently makes them more effective in molding character and personality than the conventional training in a classroom situation.

Due to the rising desire for independence from adult pressure, "gangs" are more thoroughly enjoyed if they are somewhat on the "subversive" side in terms of adult standards. This does not mean that generally accepted social norms are totally rejected, but only that some adult-fashioned values are abrogated or prohibited by the preadolescent peer code of behavior. Thus, studying too much may expose one to the suspicion of being a sissy, while paying strict obedience to the wishes of adults may be looked upon with disfavor by the peer group. Even in a not too delinquent "gang," a child may be expected to lie in order to protect a pal from punishment, and sometimes stealing may be encouraged—either for fun or to display one's courage.

"Cliques" of preadolescent girls

Organized "gangs" composed entirely of girls are very rare. Girls are more inclined to form smaller "cliques" of friends, which are strongly exclusive and normally have little formal organization or leadership. On the whole, information regarding such "cliques" is scanty. Apparently there is no system of mutual obligations between members in such groups and little, if any, deep-seated loyalty to the group. Girls, being more carefully supervised than boys, tend also toward more conventional patterns of behavior and interests.

Change of grouping in adolescence

In adolescence a change takes place in the pattern of juvenile groupings. Social activities in company with the opposite sex become the focus of interest, and this in turn leads to the breaking up of one-sex groups of boys or girls into a two-sex pattern of "dating." There is some evidence suggesting that at present this change occurs even as early as the sixth or seventh grade level; though boys, maturing more slowly than girls, may show little inclination for such activities and are almost pushed into them by dancing classes organized in schools.

The "dating" pattern

A "dating" relationship is highly patterned by norms of peer culture. "Dating" starts as an invitation by a boy to a girl for an evening's public entertainment. Food and drink to be consumed on this occasion, place and type of entertainment are to be proposed by the boy; clothes to be worn and favors to be accorded by the girl to her escort are clearly prescribed or understood in advance. On the whole, "dating" is largely dominated by the quest for thrill and is regarded mostly as an amusement, but frequently it develops into serious courtship. In those cases where partners are emotionally uninvolved, the elements of competition and building of prestige play an important role. Boys and girls evaluate each other as desirable "dates" in accordance with a rating of popularity assigned by the peer group. On the other hand, a person's status and prestige will be greatly influenced by the rating of the person with whom he or she dates. Under these conditions, rivalry and competition for desirable "dates" is keen, and this in turn introduces a good deal of suspicion and antagonism into the "dating" relationship. The anxiety accompanying the competitive process of being accepted in "dating," and the associated standards of desirability—phrased in terms of good clothes, physical appearance, "smooth" manners and ability to entertain and dance well—bring to a number of young people strong feelings of humiliation, frustration and failure.

Demand for conformity in peer culture

Peer culture is essentially intolerant of deviation. It demands almost complete conformity to the dominant concerns and standards of the group. Except for those who have already won high prestige in the group, only slight leeway is given for individual variation from the accepted pattern. There seems to be a distinct tendency on the part of contemporaries to suppress any idiosyncratic qualities among themselves. Any claim to independent judgment, taste, personal behavior or opinion must be surrendered. "He thinks he is big," or "He thinks he is somebody" are often heard in the peer groups. The fear, even among the very young, of standing out in any direction, combined with the fantasy enjoyment of such achievement, is illustrated by the following interview reported by Wolfe and Fiske in "Children Talk About Comics":

"A. I like Superman better than others, because they can't do everything Superman can do. Batman can't fly and that is very important.
Q. Would you like to be able to fly?
A. I would like to be able to fly if everybody else did, but otherwise I would be kind of conspicuous."[1]

Since norms of peer culture cover so many aspects of personal and social life of young people, strenuous efforts are made to appear and behave like the group and to do what the group does. This is not an easy task, however. Standards of behavior and qualifications for status in the peer group undergo many changes between childhood and maturity.

Values promoted by peer culture

The limited number of studies at present available shedding light on children's and youth's value systems seem to indicate that the most admired qualities in the preadolescent boys are competence and leadership in group games, fearlessness and daring. To win the approval of the peer group it is better to be aggressive, boisterous and not too tidy, than to be submissive, extremely reserved or too clean. Boys who are enthusiastic, happy, fun-loving and "good sports" are preferred to those who are sulky, shy and timid, impudent, and hard to get along with. Interestingly enough, many characteristics which constitute a problem for the teacher, such as restlessness, talkativeness and attention-getting, are often associated in preadolescence with traits highly admired by the peer group.

In adolescence the value system of boys still places great stress on physical prowess, skill in athletics and self assertiveness, but in this period such qualities as ease and poise, personableness and grooming (all particularly effective with the opposite sex) become equally important.

For girls the problem of adjustment to the changing values of the peer culture is more difficult than for boys. In preadolescence it is desirable to be friendly, pretty, tidy and quietly gracious. Enthusiasm, good humor and docility are also approved of. On the other hand, aggressive and boisterous behavior is disapproved of strongly by girls. A partial reversal of values occurs in adolescence. The "ladylike" design for status among peers is replaced by new patterns. One constellation is a somewhat aggressive, buoyant "good fellowship" with both boys and girls, in which dominating tendencies, previously frowned upon, now become desirable. Another constellation

---

[1] Communications Research 1948-1949, edited by Lazarsfeld, Paul and Stanton, Frank. New York: Harper, 1949. pp. 26-27.

of traits, this one particularly attractive to boys, but not always appreciated by other girls, is the "glamor" type of a well-groomed, attractive, self-possessed and sophisticated personality.

There is at present little indication as to how certain intellectual, volitional and emotional qualities, such as imagination, aesthetic sensitivity, creativeness, etc., are rated by the peer group. What is known about the peer culture suggests that it favors the normal as against the unusual personality, the attractive as against the outstanding, the likeable and pleasant as against the strong-willed and independent. Since participation in group life is expected, while withdrawal on any grounds arouses suspicion and is an offense in the eyes of the peers, sociability appears to rank higher than individuality. In this situation, not a few youngsters whose personality characteristics and conduct go beyond the tolerance level of the peer group are likely to suffer social neglect and isolation.

Parents' and teachers' attitudes toward peer culture

The difficulties confronting youth in trying to meet the exacting demands of the peer culture are intensified by the failure of adults to understand the complexity of this adolescent problem. Attitudes of parents toward the peer group and its culture alternate between approval and alarm. Parents want their children to be popular and accepted by other children, and they show the keenest interest in the way the child manages his peer relations. Many parents tend even to regard the success of their children in the peer group as a true measure of their own success in the parental role. Along with this, however, goes a certain anxiety that some of the apparently irresponsible "good time" activities of youth may lead them to forsake the more serious interests, and the obligations to do satisfactory work in school.

There are also other reasons why peer culture is likely to result in conflicts between parent and child. While parents often urge the adolescent to stand on his own feet, to assume greater responsibility for his actions and to demonstrate his independence, they become irritated when in seeking self-direction a child defies parental authority, or turns away from parental ideas, beliefs, and sometimes ways of living, to gain acceptance by his peer group. Furthermore, some parents are at a loss to understand the vacillating behavior of the rebellious child who, while he takes most of his cues from his peers, will still at times seek parental advice, protection and reassurance. Finally, many parents, bewildered by new ideas on how to bring up children, and confused by the incongruity of their own habits and beliefs in a rapidly changing society, are too often apt to be intolerant of changing attitudes and standards in their offspring.

Teachers, also, fail frequently to grasp the complexity of peer relations. Sociometric studies have shown that teachers tend to confuse the social adjustment between children with the social adjustment between children and adults. It was found that children most liked in class by teachers are not always highly regarded by their peers, while pupils teachers prefer least are often popular with their peers. Indicative of the lack of orientation in peer values is the known fact that teachers' judgments of the social adjustment of pupils show a declining accuracy from kindergarten to the seventh grade.

Educational implications of peer culture

The implications of the material just presented confirm the desirability and soundness of many accepted educational practices such as school assemblies, student councils, social clubs, social parties, etc. All of these activities offer opportunities for children to gain acceptance and status in the peer group. If anything, such activities should be more widely spread and regarded as an integral part of the school curriculum and not as extra.

But in dealing with peer groups it is worth remembering that they are not an unmixed blessing, for they carry potentialities for both good and bad influence. The school will do well to use the powerful group forces in fostering among young boys and girls socially desirable habits, attitudes and relations. Yet, at the same time, the school has the responsibility to counteract the ill effects of complete submission to peer pressure, whenever independent judgment, conduct and action on the part of an individual child is warranted.

Experience of various schools has shown that peer groups can be effectively used in combatting juvenile delinquency. Similarly it was found that codes of behavior cooperatively drawn up by parents, faculty members and teen-agers are faithfully observed by the boys and girls when such norms become accepted as peer group standards. It is perhaps not too far-fetched to assume, for instance, that the pressure of peer groups could be mobilized against irresponsible driving of cars.

Some states are already making extensive use of student school-bus drivers with highly satisfactory results. As reported, these student drivers have maintained an enviable safety record.

Peer groups frequently tend to favor aggressive, shocking and irresponsible behavior. Turning a corner in a car on two wheels, or staying out late at night, or being impudent to parents and teachers is often a required practice. Yet these same peer groups, once they have accepted different standards, will with equal success teach boys and girls habits of responsible and socially desirable conduct.

The challenge to the teachers, then, is to recognize the power of the peer group over its members and to harness that power for educationally useful purposes. At times this may require injecting new and more desirable values into the peer culture. But if this attempt is successful, forceful pressures stemming from the peer group will support educational efforts to change the behavior of individual boys and girls.

78

Margaret Mead

ARE WE SQUEEZING OUT ADOLESCENCE?

A prominent anthropologist comments on some of the problems raised by shifting social patterns, which seem to her to be accelerating the earlier assumption of adult responsibility by young people, who might better profit from a prolonged adolescence. This article might well be compared with the one by Professor Havighurst (Reading 75), who seems to view some of the same phenomena in a different light.

A human baby can learn to speak Bantu or English, French or Iroquois; to adjust to a world organized on the principles of higher mathematics! Man is born with the capacity to acquire any knowledge that his forefathers have gained. Thus each generation can devote its beginning years to learning what past generations took much longer to work out—and can go ahead from there. To absorb this knowledge man needs the long learning period of childhood and youth, and this long childhood is one of the main reasons why he has been able to advance so rapidly.

What a society does with this learning period is a decisive element in determining not only the level of its culture but its survival in a socially competitive world. How fast are its children to be made to grow up? Is the most precocious child to set the pace and all the rest to be spurred ahead because of this high standard? Or is the slowest to set the pace—as was true among the Samoans,

where all the children had to wait until the slowest had learned enough and where precocity was the greatest sin? Or is the standard to be set by the average pulling all the more precocious children back and dragging the slowest along?

Do we have to be so unimaginative as to insist on any one of these three equally dull solutions? The question becomes particularly important when we look at adolescence. What are we doing with this period in which there is such a very wide spread in young people's readiness to use their bodies and their minds and their emotions in the same way that their age mates do?

The very phrase *age mate* becomes a kind of absurdity in junior high school, where tiny youngsters several years away from puberty are classified with well-developed girls who look almost ready to be the mothers of another generation. Some of these youngsters have scintillating intelligence and the bodies of children. Others are still childish in mind though mature in body. Yet all are pushed into a common mold, pushed ahead to match not the highest intellectual development but the most precocious physical development.

From *National Parent-Teacher* (The PTA Magazine), September 1960, 55:4-6. Reprinted by permission of author and publisher.

This means, among other things, that in our junior high schools the pace is set by the girls, as it has been ever since the children entered first grade. Little girls are more docile and more verbal than boys, more anxious to please, and because these are qualities that our schools reward, the girls appear to excel the boys. If the schools would place as high a value on some other qualities—originality, creativity, stubborn individuality of style, refusal merely to conform to please—the boys, recent investigations show, would come out better. Docility, verbal compliance, and the wish to please don't go very well with originality. So from the start our grade schools expect girls to set standards in schoolwork, standards of orderliness, accuracy, legibility in handwriting, and proper outlining, with a B following an A and a II following a I. The boys, for the most part, simply remove themselves from this world. They play games, think about cars, follow the major leagues. Meanwhile the girls forge ahead.

Then comes junior high school, which accentuates the differences in each sex and between the sexes because it is limited to the years of greatest disparity in growth. By this time the girls are, on the average, two years ahead of the boys in their physical development. Some of them are already buxom young maidens who in an earlier period of history would have been betrothed or perhaps married. The boys, on the other hand, are not only further behind the girls than before but incredibly diverse in size and shape, from Tom Thumbs to those tall, thin creatures whom Australians call "a long drink of water." Or they may be inordinately fat.

Hardly any of the boys have a sufficient internal stirring of approaching manhood to turn them spontaneously in the direction of the girls. Girls appear to them as alien creatures—too big, too demanding, too sure. Left to themselves, the boys would pull the girls' pony tails or pelt them with snowballs, or ignore them altogether. Once in a while a boy might defend a smaller girl and thus begin to think about protecting his own and other boys' sisters, a habit which has almost disappeared in the United States. But most junior high school boys would have nothing to do with girls their own age.

Neither would the more mature junior high school girl be attracted by the reluctant, fumbling dance steps of her boy classmates. She would much prefer older boys, much older, even college "men."

In most human societies, unlike our own, this difference in pace is respected. Small boys and girls are not required to compete with each other in a school established essentially for girls, where girls get used to being ahead and boys to falling behind. The young adolescents of both sexes need time to learn, to grow, to get accustomed to their changing bodies and changing impulses, and to begin to become persons in their own right.

The more primitive the society, the shorter the learning period has been. The children of hunting peoples like the Eskimo or the Australian aborigines had to become expert in adult skills very early, and as soon as they were physically mature they married. But one of the first signs of an advancing civilization is the lengthened learning period of adolescence, which postpones the time of adult responsibility.

But this used to be true only of the privileged classes—children of the wealthy or the nobility or those special children of the poor who showed such outstanding ability that they were permitted a precious breathing spell for learning. The children of peasants and fishermen and poor people in cities were still permitted a very brief interval between childhood and adulthood. Sex and marriage came early for them, and once married they had no more time to develop or learn. Girls became mothers at fifteen and were old and tired at thirty, worn out by the cares of early motherhood.

In the United States today, however, the common man lives as kings once lived. More energy is available to cool his food than could once have been provided by a thousand slaves carrying blocks of snow from the mountains to cool the bath or the banquet of a monarch. The house of the common man has luxuries no ancient palace could afford—heating and lighting, foods from all over the earth, new and wonderful materials. In that house news of the world is brought to him, and from it messages are sent, both with astounding rapidity. Without leaving his own easy chair he has gained an extensive knowledge of what is going on in the world.

As we have produced these and other marvels of well-being for human life, we have thought also that we are giving our children something no children have ever had before. We offer them, combined, the onetime advantages of the highly privileged with the new possibilities of an industrialized country. Not only do we educate the children of the rich or the future elite, but everyone. First came elementary education for all, then high school education for all—a goal undreamed of two short centuries ago.

But we are in serious danger of falling short of our ideal, however much we may appear to have reached it when we see the hordes of bright-faced youngsters pouring out of our impressively beautiful school buildings. For something is wrong. The symptoms have been enumerated too often to need more than mention here: the increase in juvenile delinquency and crime, the number of young people whom we permanently stigmatize as failures, the waste of talent, low academic standards, the high drop-out rate. These are the obvious deficits of an educational system that has become too impersonal and too standardized to take account of the individual child whose first failure, if caught in time, need not lead to retardation, truancy, and delinquency.

Just as severe a price is being paid by the children who make high grades, have an admirable record in extracurricular affairs, and have good chances at higher education of many sorts. Along with their conformity to the school's demands goes conformity to another kind of demand, one begun in the junior high school—that they be adult beyond their years. Boys are expected to begin to go through the motions of courtship long before they are physically or emotionally ready for an interest in girls.

Once the sons of the privileged classes were left free, in these precious years, to study, read, play, experiment, climb mountains, fish, hunt, sail boats, explore the world of the mind and of the soul, dream dreams, pledge themselves to impossible causes, and dedicate their lives to great deeds. Now that we are all, in a material way, so privileged, we have failed our young people. At a time when their minds are attuned to aspiration and achievement we have not given them a chance either to aspire or to achieve. For the stimulating and exciting challenge of friendship with members of their own sex, we have substituted "going steady." Mothers report that this makes the boy "much more serious about his work," not recognizing that such seriousness, though it leads to good grades, early career choice, and early adulthood, cuts the boy off from the searching, exploring, and experimenting which will some day result in real maturity.

From first grade on we have trapped our boys in a female-modeled environment, in which the kind of lessons girls do well are the kind of lessons everybody does. Later we insist on keeping children of the same age together, which means that the more mature girl dominates the scene. Both boys and girls, therefore, are denied a real adolescence and forced instead into premature adult activity. Rich and privileged as no nation has ever been, do we have any reason to push our children into such premature adulthood, as if they lived in a country where the majority of the people still do not know where tomorrow's meal will come from?

This sorry situation has come upon us gradually, as high schools broadened after World War I to include all sorts of children, many of whom would not go to college, and as the separation of children by age became more and more rigorous. The junior high school seemed a good idea—a way of introducing young people by degrees to the different structure of high school. But it was invented without due regard to what we already knew about the tremendous discrepancy between boys and girls of junior high school age. Nor have we reckoned with the ever growing pressure toward precocity, toward becoming adult before one really became adolescent. Long pants and lipstick and nail polish and dating have crept down into the grades, and social, not intellectual, preparation is emphasized in the junior high school.

The fruits of all this are bitter: lowered educational standards, a world that is much harder for boys than for girls (although it is from our boys that most of our scientists and leaders will come), short-circuited careers, low levels of aspiration, the tremendous hostility of men toward women, and the uneasy contempt of women for men.

None of it can be changed overnight. But there are things that every responsible community can do. First, it should urge a different kind of emphasis in elementary school, so that the special abilities of boys will be recognized more and their greater waywardness and variability penalized less. Second, there should be a determined effort to reduce social activities at the junior high school level, to encourage solitary pastimes, and to promote separate activities for boys and girls (all of which are discouraged today by parents and teachers alike). Third, adolescent social affairs should cut across high school and college lines. Then maturing girls can meet older boys who are ready, physically and emotionally, for the pressures of dating. Fourth, there should be a serious exploration of the advantages of growing up slowly. The long days of adolescence will never return—those days in which both boys and girls have their last leisure to search their souls and to try, without commitment, the many possible roles they may take in the world.

We complain today that our young adults are narrow, selfishly interested only in the security of their own families, without horizons and without dedication, although they are good, hard-working husbands and wives, fathers and mothers. One explanation is that we turn them into potential husbands and fathers, wives and mothers far too soon. We stunt their moral and intellectual growth as it was once stunted by the narrowness of a primitive culture or the narrow horizons of poverty. But for us there is no such excuse.

The school and other social influences

THE SCHOOL AND JUVENILE DELINQUENCY

Discussion of the relationship of the school to other agencies leads to discussion of the relationship of the school to the law. As an agent of the state, the school is obviously concerned with teaching respect for the laws of the state. There is some evidence also, however, that it exerts its influence in more subtle ways. Potential delinquency, for example, may be detected among students in the school population before the problem becomes serious. There is even evidence to suggest that some delinquency may be caused by the action of the school, or at least might be avoided by a more effective school program.

In considering the appropriate limits to the school's program, one point of view suggests that the school has certain residual responsibilities for the welfare of the student who may find little support from his church, from his family, or from his peer group. It seems foolhardy for the state, operating through the school, to neglect its citizens when it will be the state, operating through its prisons and welfare agencies, which later must attempt to remedy its own neglect.

79

John E. Owen

HOW DELINQUENT ARE OUR JUVENILES?

In this article a British sociologist analyzes the nature and extent of the problem of juvenile delinquency. Perspective on this problem is needed if we are to propose a role for the public school in combating it. This selection was written in 1956, at about the time the problem became acute. Thus it has a certain historical interest, particularly if it is compared with more recent data. For example, has the number of narcotic addicts increased? What, if anything, has been proposed or done about violence in "comics," in television, in movies?

How extensive is the serious misbehavior of American youth? What are its causes, and what efforts are being made to correct it?

That the problem is widespread and disturbing, no informed observer can deny, even when allowances are made for sensationalism and the perennial alarmists. Statistics require careful interpretation, if for no other reasons than the different reporting systems and legal definitions of delinquency in the forty-eight states, but many signs point to a marked rise in youthful crime over the last ten years, with a considerable increase over the pre-1939 figures. Almost everybody has

a theory as to the causes of this particular problem and could with equal facility prescribe a remedy. Professional workers in the field, with a greater knowledge of the ramifications of personality growth and environmental conditioning, are less confident. Nevertheless, certain factors and influences do appear to have a positive relationship to the total situation. As is the case with nearly all our national problems, we are at an advantage today in having far more valid and accurate knowledge than did our predecessors in less complex eras.

Very high birth rates during World War II have produced an increased teen-age population. According to a recent nationwide investigation

From *Educational Forum*, January 1957, 21:203-206.

by a U.S. Senate Subcommittee, one million children came into conflict with the law in 1953. Thefts and acts of mischief accounted for most of their offenses. Approximately one child in a hundred reaches the courts every year, but this figure includes many neglected and dependent juveniles who fall under court jurisdiction, and overlooks both the undetected offender and the child who is treated by social workers and other unofficial agencies. The ratio of lawbreakers to the *total* juvenile population is very small, and there are many communities where juvenile delinquency is, for all practical purposes, nonexistent. But in many cities the more serious type of misconduct, including sex offenses and drug addiction, has given decided reason for alarm. Vandalism, which causes half a million dollars' damage in the schools of New York City alone, is also on the increase. Boy delinquents appear to outnumber girls by four to one.

One disturbing feature is a rise in youthful addiction to drugs, particularly heroin and marijuana. Exact figures are not available, but witnesses before the Senate Subcommittee estimated that the national total of teen-age narcotics users is at least 25,000. Further testimony placed the New York City figure at 7,500, and it was stated that no fewer than 8% of children coming before the juvenile courts of Los Angeles County had had contact with narcotics. A Chicago survey revealed 5,000 known addicts, one-third or more of them being under 21.

This particular problem, like delinquency generally, is confined mainly to urban areas, concentrated especially in their slum sections. California and the Pacific Coast are reported to have an alarming and highly profitable drug traffic, some of it originating in nearby Mexico, though heroin's chief source is Red China. Many authorities on this particular problem, including government officials, believe that Communist China deliberately promotes the illegal importation and use of narcotics into the United States as a means of weakening the country. The U.S. Federal Narcotics Bureau has estimated that one in every 3,000 persons now takes drugs, as compared with one in 10,000 in 1945 and a far lower ratio in the 1920s. There have been many demands recently for more stringent control, increased border and port patrols, heavier punishments (even including the death penalty) for violators, and medical help to their victims. President Eisenhower has appointed five Cabinet members to a special committee to study the problem.

Sociologists and youth workers are agreed that there is no one cause for these conditions. Leading magistrates, judges, probation officers, and police officials have pointed to a general and growing disregard for authority, weak home and school discipline, sensational and salacious "comics," over-emphasis upon crime and violence in films, radio, and television programs, undermanned and underpaid probation staffs, inadequate individual treatment to offenders, too few institutions for rehabilitation, lack of police and judges specifically trained to deal with youth, and excessive leniency on the part of juvenile courts. Many "repeaters" are released on probation, and by the time a young man gets into court, he may already have had earlier contact with the police and juvenile agencies and showed some tendency for crime. Other relevant factors include the illegal sale of liquor to minors, and the fact that many mothers are employed outside the home.

The incidence of Negro offenders is disproportionately high in terms of their small ratio (10%) to the total population. But the records tend to exaggerate the Negro's *actual* criminal conduct, and have to be interpreted in the light of environmental influences, such as economic handicaps, an unstable family situation, unequal access to decent housing, relative discrimination in the courts, and meager recreational facilities. It is also necessary to consider the disorganizing effects of migration to the North and wartime experiences, together with the difficulty of many Negroes in adjusting to norms established and enforced by white society.

Many social scientists have pointed to the dislocations and aftermath of the war. Adolescents today were born in a period of economic depression, they grew up during the abnormal years of international hostilities, and they lived through the uneasy peace, followed by Korea and the present tension. An impending draft and the strained world situation make it impossible to feel any security regarding higher education, or plans for marriage or a career. The resulting tensions serve to incite a youthful philosophy of sensate and immediate pleasure-seeking. The conflict of norms in our heterogeneous national culture, between, for example, the Puritanism that stems from colonial New England and the greater lawlessness of the western frontier tradition, is another factor that cannot be ignored.

Dr. Robert Lindner, well-known Baltimore psychiatrist, maintained that youth has abandoned solitude and individuality in favor of pack-running and predatory assembly. A similar diagnosis, centering around "mass-man" and insecurity through loss of identity, is found in David Riesman's *Lonely Crowd*. Although organized religion is outwardly flourishing, the direct influence of its current theological pre-occupations upon social conditions is problematical. And in practice, one or two hours a week in Sunday School appears relatively indecisive in counteracting the moral climate prevailing during the week.

Notwithstanding, there are signs of progress. In the first place, we are as a nation very much aware of the problem, and awareness is always the first stage toward a solution. At the local, state, and national level it is becoming realized that action must be taken. President Eisenhower's message on the State of the Union early in 1955 proposed federal legislation to assist the states in coping with the problem. In many cities and towns a new co-operation is in evidence between churches, schools, parents, recreational centers, police, and juvenile courts, producing a "community strategy" by pooling all constructive resources. Many clergymen work on citizens' committees and regard their churches as community centers to give attractive and practical programs for youth. Curfews have been enforced in some localities, action has been taken against unwholesome comic-books, and this particular industry has drawn up a code of ethics and a plan for self-regulation.

The very gravity of the problem and the attendant publicity it has received have acted as a spur in many communities. Social workers and child guidance clinics are re-orienting their programs to meet the needs of disturbed adolescents. Youth workers are urging a greater parental vigilance and sympathetic guidance for teen-agers.

A certain amount of irrational behavior is an almost inevitable outcome of a period of profound social and cultural change. Apart from the widespread insecurity inherent in the temper of the age, the decay of the neighborhood as a close-knit "way of life," and the almost convulsive changes in our society in the last 50 years are very pertinent factors that render juvenile misbehavior and living today very different from that of their elders. Our increased mobility by virtue of a shifting labor market, the weakening of old controls, rapid urbanization, and the effect of the automobile upon social behavior are coercive realities in the current scene. Dr. Grace Sloan Overton, a nationally-known counsellor with long experience in handling the problems of youth, maintains that young people today are not bad or immoral but are *confused,* and hence parents and teachers must learn to find a common meeting-ground with them while living in an age which in many respects has no counterpart in American history.

The fact remains that the vast majority of young people are law-abiding in their behavior and attitudes. In the meantime, countless individuals and organizations are striving to identify, salvage, and rehabilitate the maladjusted minority. That they have to do so may seem ground for despair. That they *are* doing so is ground for hope.

80

William C. Kvaraceus & Walter B. Miller

COMMON MISCONCEPTIONS AND DELINQUENCY

Some of the findings of the National Education Association project on juvenile delinquency, of which Dr. Kvaraceus was the director, are presented here (6). The authors point out the clear relationship between the problem of social class and our view of delinquency, indicating that behavior that is considered maladjusted from the point of view of middle class standards may seem perfectly reasonable from the point of view of the child or peer group involved. In order to understand delinquency it is important first to understand the differences which exist among social classes.

Most people have very definite opinions on delinquency, which usually purport to go directly to the "cause" or "cure" with one deft stroke. Unfortunately, the problems of norm-violating behavior are not so simple; otherwise, delinquency would have long since ceased to be a major topic of national concern.

. . . [The] delinquent and delinquency . . . function as a hostility target for some segments of the community. Perhaps its continuance as such a target is closely bound up with various myths, half-truths, antidotes, and nostrums that have grown up around its "cause" and "cure." In fact, some of the myths of delinquency are changing with the times and are becoming more sophisticated. Witness the current emphasis on "emotional disturbances," where before discussion centered around "lack of recreation" and "slum areas." Once some unitary factor was assigned as "cause"; now "multiple causation" is glibly cited. For some, the term "unhealthy" has replaced the term "immoral" as a primary deprecatory epithet, but the evaluative overtones remain the same.

It will be necessary in the following sections to explore some of the ideas which are misleading or incorrect but which still, like legends, persist in the folklore surrounding delinquency. Although there may be an element of truth in some of these notions, they are open to serious challenge as absolute or categorical statements concerning the nature and sources of delinquency. Some may contain half-truths which have been falsified through overgeneralization and indiscriminate application. Moreover, many misconceptions have resulted from translating the information obtained from a small and frequently biased sample into universal conclusions and prescriptions.

False dichotomy.   All youngsters cannot be filed conveniently into two major categories of "delinquent" and "nondelinquent." Norm-violating behavior exists on a continuum. Most people break a rule or regulation at one time or another, some people more often than others. Some of these violations are minor and infrequent; others represent more serious behavior and may become habitual. But one delinquent act does not necessarily make a delinquent.

Delinquency as maladjustment.   From the point of view of the delinquent, most delinquent behavior is purposive and adjustive. From the vantage point of middle-class norms and status, such behavior is frequently seen as a maladaptation. But in looking at this same behavior from the child's point of view, one can see that the child frequently uses it as means of adapting or adjusting in accordance with his essential frame of reference. Occasionally, he may even be solving a serious problem, which has long been confronting him, in the best and only way he knows how —through his delinquency. Delinquent "malbe-

havior" is usually "adjustive behavior," and only from the outsider's point of view does the child seem "maladjusted."

Delinquency: a pseudodiagnostic rubric.   Merely to dub a boy or girl "delinquent" is not to explain anything about his behavior, for the term "delinquent" does not represent a useful diagnostic concept. Series of norm-violating behaviors, which run counter to legal codes and which are engaged in by youngsters, are only symptomatic of something else in the personal make-up of the individual, in his home and family, or in his cultural milieu.

Working-mother myth.   Many people point to the working mother as a major cause of delinquency. This is predicated on the concept of the intact middle-class family in which the mother stays home to rear her children and does not accept employment outside the home lest she neglect her young. The mother-child axis as the basic determinant of behavior and personality is largely a concept that stems from an overly heavy emphasis on certain elements in psychoanalytic theory at the expense of other very important factors. This is not to deny the importance of the mother-child relationship at various points in the child's life . . . .

Current studies on the negative effects of working mothers on their children are far from conclusive. The working mother will not suffice as a simple, neat causal explanation of delinquency. Moreover, the working mother has a very different meaning and effect in the middle-class home than in the lower-class family.

"Broken" home.   Causative pronouncements and inferences concerning the broken home and delinquency are popular and, seemingly, timeless. Although the "broken" home explanation, like the "working-mother" concept, has some utility, more precise definitions of broken homes are required and the precise effects these have in different milieus need to be determined. There is, for example, always the question of the psychologically broken home, even though both parents are living together. There is the question of a lower-class culture pattern in which separation is a standard or an acceptable style and, thus, a broken home has a different connotation in this frame of reference than in others. There is also the need to describe the specific type of household system and then relate this type to the manner in which it is accepted by the youngster. Then, too, there is the question of the impact of the physically broken home on the first four or five years of the child's

From *Delinquent Behavior: Culture and the Individual* by William C. Kvaraceus and Walter B. Miller (Washington: National Education Association, 1959), pp. 32-41.

life, as against the impact of breaks that may occur later in life. Finally, there is the problem created by the physically and psychologically broken home when the child comes before the law and disposition is made in such a manner that the legal agency itself decides to break up the family. And there is readily available evidence that a child with two parents to back him up is more likely to get a break in court and to be treated as a problem child who should be helped by a nearby clinic; but if the home lacks the nuclear design[1] so prominent in middle-class culture, the child is more than likely sent off to a state institution.

Studies on causes of delinquency that are based on court and institution cases carry the heavy built-in bias of the broken home because of this screening process, in which a youngster from an intact home generally goes back home or to the clinic and the youngster from a broken home goes to an institution. Consequently, these studies can be frequently misleading.

Labeling a child a potential delinquent simply because he comes from a broken home or explaining away his behavior on this basis is an ever-present danger. Putting all the blame at the door of the broken home is a neat, but too easy, a way out. Too often it becomes a respectable, though tricky, way of psychologically dismissing the youngster who is difficult to diagnose and who needs help that can not be easily prescribed.

Mental retardation myth.   "Delinquents have a lower IQ" is a common statement for which there is little scientific support. It appears even less valid when nonverbal and "culture-fair" tests are used. It is true that many lower-class children may score lower on "intelligence tests" than middle-class children, but the kind of "intelligence" measured frequently involves intellectual capacities especially emphasized in middle-class life—verbal fluency, reading comprehension, and substantive knowledge derived from conventional middle-class interests. However, even these differences tend to fade as more effective and sensitive instruments are devised and as more representative samples of the delinquent population are compared to nondelinquents from the same milieu. Many delinquents turn out to be extremely bright when they are viewed within the context of their own milieu.

Playground myth.   There is a highly organized school of thought which says, "Give the boy a place to play and he won't get into trouble" and

"A community with many playgrounds is a community with little delinquency." Several research projects have indicated that there is no direct or discernible relationship between the usual recreation program and delinquency rates. Unquestionably, however, a particular type of recreation program that is carefully planned and administered under certain auspices, direction, and leadership —*if coordinated with other efforts*—can effectively redirect or channel energies away from illegal activity into organized athletics and other leisure-time pursuits.

A special problem is presented by the "rotten apple" or "sinner" who traditionally won't even try the standard groups, partly because he won't be accepted and partly because he would rather join other "rotten apples" or others more willing and ready to decay. A major problem, always to be faced, is how such a youngster can be involved in constructive leisure programs.

Bad companions and evil gang leader.   Parents in both lower and middle classes frequently cite the "bad companion" as the source of their youngster's delinquency. The only difficulty here is that the parents of the alleged "bad boy" make the same claim, but of others in the group. There is also the problem of "the gang" which is labeled "bad" but whose members seldom do much more than hang around street corners or find the back way into a theater, a bowling alley, or a variety store. In many ways, this gang plays a constructive role in the socializing process for any youngster from any class.

The stereotype of the juvenile gang generally includes the idea of one overpowering evil-doer and a group of weak, or sheeplike, followers. This stereotype is often tied to preventive myth which says, "If one can get to the leader, then the gang can be reached and straightened out." This kind of "Little Caesar" leadership does exist, of course, but in the typically organized gang there are usually at least three or four leaders. Depending on the particular situation, one or another member assumes primacy and makes the basic definitions but only after a great deal of interaction and discussion in which almost all members take part. The mythical figure of one evil, powerful leader "manipulating all those weak and spineless kids" does not correspond to the facts and can be classified as less than a half-truth.

Physical attributes and heredity.   Contrary to many opinions, delinquents are as healthy, if not healthier, than their nondelinquent contemporaries. A theory which has maintained its hold on the public mind is that one can recognize a delin-

---

[1] An intact household centering around two child-rearing adults.

quent by facial or body characteristics. This has little basis in fact; for example, the highly organized gang member must generally be strong, physically skillful, and mentally alert.

The "bad-seed" explanation for delinquency and crime, once so popular among researchers concerned with the blood lines of the Jukes, Kallikaks, Nams and Zeros, never seems to fade away. Updated versions of this thesis continue to appear, generally in the company of modified and modernized adaptations of the Lombrosian tradition. For example, certain differences in physical constitution have been identified recently and related, presumably, to delinquency and nondelinquency. It is true that strength, athletic prowess, and toughness, which center around body constitution, all play a very important and functional role in the concerns of lower-class street-corner society. Here psychological concepts of self and of others based on physical traits in a certain social milieu may generate, though only indirectly, a tendency toward norm-violating behavior. There is little solid evidence for any close or direct tie-in of norm-violating behavior and hereditary components. Nevertheless, it is likely that hereditary-biological types will continue to furnish the simplest explanation of all for delinquency and always within an aura of "scientific method." Those who want a handy explanation for delinquency can always invoke the ancestors, particularly the not-so-dear departed. But, as a matter of fact, there should be less concern with the seed and more concern with the soil and the sun which so nurture and develop these youngsters that they are enabled to accept and pattern themselves after those persons in the home, neighborhood, and community who exemplify norm-violating behavior.

The deteriorated neighborhood and slums. Research has pointed out that slum clearance in itself is not an answer to delinquency. Hot and cold water, central heating, and fresh paint, in and of themselves, neither relate to nor automatically reduce delinquency. Attention should be directed to the inhabitants, to their relationships and culture, not to the number of rooms and the brick and mortar of their residences.

Idle hands. The hue and cry—like that raised for "recreation"—for change in child labor laws to allow the 14- to 17-year-olds to gain employment appears unrealistic when evidence which clearly indicates that there is little room or opportunity for them in the present labor market is taken into consideration. As a preventive, "keeping youth busy," whether through compulsory ed-

ucation, drafting for service in the armed forces, providing fun through recreation, or early employment, can, at best, only temporarily postpone behavior that is symptomatic of more deep-seated or culturally oriented factors. Youngsters need opportunity for meaningful school-work-play activity in the maturation process. Moreover, they are quick to detect artificial "busy work" as against vital and genuine activity-experiences. Merely "keeping idle hands occupied" touches only surface symptoms and overlooks underlying factors known to generate norm-violating behavior patterns.

Curfew and legislation. "Let's change the law" is often heard as a cure for juvenile delinquency. There is no question that enlightened legislation provides the legal definitions of approved and protective cultural practices in our own and other countries. Nevertheless, a legislative measure will not serve as an antidote for cultural and psychological forces that tend to create norm-violating behaviors; these forces must be understood and offset through carefully planned preventive and control efforts based on valid research.

There is no demonstrated relationship between "curfews" and delinquency reduction. Reliance on some quick legislative "gimmick" will not insure any long-term success in delinquency prevention or control. Carefully thought out legislation can enable the community to support and conduct more promising programs of aid for the delinquent at the local and state level. But good legislation alone is only enabling; it is not curative.

Punishment as an antidote. Frequent appeals for a resort to severe tactics in an effort to manage the norm-violating behavior of youngsters are heard in every community. Greater reliance on the birch rod, the night stick, and the woodshed is a perennial recommendation for a simple and straightforward solution to the "delinquency foolishness." Although some delinquents may be impervious to this technique and thus suffer no great harm, others may be only further confused and confounded by harsh punitive and retaliatory methods. Delinquents, as well as nondelinquents, need fair but firm treatment when they step out of bounds. They must also learn the natural consequences of their actions and that they will have to assume responsibility for them. There are effective uses of various types of punishment that may be invoked with the delinquent. However, to overlook causative factors and to capitulate to the punishment routine will neither prevent nor control further expressions of norm-violating behavior.

Delinquency as aberrant or deviating behavior. Delinquency is frequently regarded as a form of deviant behavior. Such a concept assumes the existence of a unitary system of institutional norms. But there are many institutional systems and, hence, many norms. The norms of the dominant middle class serve as the main vantage point (or disadvantage point) for interested and concerned lay and professional workers. Prevalent forms of norm-violating behavior, seen through this window, may appear to be distortion or aberrancy; but if viewed, for example, in terms of lower-class street-corner society, the delinquency may appear as conduct that yields status and prestige—as illustrated by attitudes toward car theft and early sex experience in certain neighborhoods. . . .

81

William Van Til

COMBATING JUVENILE DELINQUENCY THROUGH SCHOOLS

There are ways in which the program of the school may be used to lessen the impact of juvenile delinquency. In this article some of these methods are explained. The author points out that one of the critical aspects of such programs is to be found in public understanding of the need for the school's participation: a program of education to combat delinquency can be only as good as the citizenry will let it—or make it—be. The optimum cooperation of the community is desirable in all phases of education; it is vital in solving the problem of juvenile delinquency.

With the rise in juvenile delinquency, the medicine men are once again prescribing their favorite panacea. For prevention and cure of delinquency, we are advised to "get tough," "go back to the woodshed," "apply the nightstick." A feature article urges, "Let's Get Tough with Delinquents." A religious personality tells his television audience that juvenile delinquency has increased in direct ratio to the decline of razor strops and woodsheds. A letter to the New York *Times* from a former official of the Department of Correction of New York City states "that the presence and application of the nightstick by police against young hoodlums will act as a deterrent to delinquency."[1] A metropolitan newspaper editorializes, "A stout strap vigorously used at home can often do more good than repeated summonses to adolescent courts. It can and should also be used on parents themselves when obviously needed to drive home plain parental duty."[2]

More sensible advice comes from Benjamin Fine, education editor of the New York *Times,* in *1,000,000 Delinquents.* Though Fine is fully aware of the increase in juvenile delinquency, he refuses to surrender to hysteria and adopt the woodshed panacea. His study recognizes that the average increase in juvenile delinquency cases was 45% between 1948 and 1953; more children came before the children's courts in 1953 than in any previous year (435,000); Attorney General Brownell predicted before an NEA convention recently that there was every sign that there would soon be 1,000,000 children annually in trouble serious enough to cause their arrest. Fine writes, "The [woodshed] attitude . . . at its worst and most dangerous, is emotion (in the objectionable sense), reactive rather than thoughtful. It represents the type of identity thinking that we share with the lower animals. Teen-age purse-snatcher

From *Educational Leadership*, March 1956, 362-367. This article also appears in *The Making of a Modern Educator* by William Van Til (Bobbs-Merrill, 1961), pp. 204-211.
[1] Letter to the Editor, "Curbing Delinquency: Judicious Whack with Policeman's Nightstick Is Advocated." New York *Times,* November 25, 1955.

[2] Quoted by Benjamin Fine, *1,000,000 Delinquents.* Yonkers-on-Hudson, New York: World Book Company, 1955. p. 132.

with slip-knife-evil-crime-fear-HATE! Hit him over the head! Lock him up! Punish him! Don't care if we kill him! . . . The woodshed technique may be valuable or even necessary in some few instances. But to advocate it, as some do, as a general philosophy, will do considerably more harm than good. . . . There is no evidence that severe punishment of itself given to children or their parents has any effect whatsoever in curbing juvenile delinquency. Conversely it is difficult to measure its ill effects."[3]

Dr. Leonard W. Mayo, chairman of the National Mid-Century Committee, has pointed out that it takes more than just a strapping to cure delinquency. Corporal punishment may merely harden the delinquent in his belief that he is alone in the world and that he has been deserted. Potential and actual juvenile delinquents need understanding more than flogging.

Naturally, the advocates of the return to the woodshed are among the severest critics of modern programs of education. Their editorial spokesmen satirically deride "the bleeding hearts who say education is the answer." A favorite whipping boy is "progressive education." So it is good to hear one of America's great deans of education, Ernest O. Melby, respond: "In a democratic society, the only effective discipline in the long run is self-discipline. It was self-discipline that the progressive school sought to teach and in its best form actually did teach successfully. In some substantial degree practice in self-discipline has found its way into a large proportion of American schools and to the degree that it has been adopted it is a prevention of juvenile delinquency. Unfortunately not nearly as many schools as one might hope for have adopted such disciplinary practices. Therefore, to whatever degree education is responsible for juvenile delinquency, it is the persistence of the 'old school' with its failure to meet the needs of children that is more to blame than the adoption of the newer procedures."[4]

Justine Wise Polier, for two decades a justice in New York City's Domestic Relations Court, has noted an interesting similarity between the drives of the get-tough spokesmen and those who attack modern schools. "It is not surprising that those who would indulge their desire to get tough with children and punish parents are those who scorn the long and tedious process of education and are also among the vanguard of those who

are attacking our schools today. In these attacks one finds the same drive to secure conformity and docility through force (sometimes euphemistically called discipline); the same drive to control from the outside; and the same lack of faith in the possibilities of education to help children and adults alike learn self control and their responsibilities and rights in a democratic society."[5]

The woodshed panacea is at best debatable even when conceived only as an emergency measure to curb and control a slum area which has temporarily gotten out of hand. But as a national proposal for the prevention and cure of juvenile delinquency, it is tragically misguided. Juvenile delinquency is complex, multiply caused and multiply prevented. Many of society's agencies must team up to contribute to prevention and control of delinquency.

The good modern school is one among several agencies which can contribute to prevention and cure of juvenile delinquency. Actually and potentially, it is a far more effective agency than the return to the woodshed. This is no sentimental claim; instead, it is based on what we know of the nature of the delinquent.

Good schools with modern programs are needed for all children. But they are particularly needed for the present or the potential delinquent. According to research well-summarized by Kvaraceus,[6] the life of the delinquent is more likely than that of the non-delinquent to be characterized by:

Living in slum areas
Overcrowded, poorly furnished and badly kept homes
Poverty and deprivation
Bad home conditions
No family recreation
Parents less interested in his future
Home characterized by quarrelling, rejection and indifference
Discipline, if not completely lacking, depending heavily on physical punishment
Less mental ability
Ten points lower than non-delinquents on IQ scales
Instability
Resentment of authority
Emotional conflicts

[3] *Ibid.* p. 135, 138, 142.
[4] Ernest O. Melby, "Five Fallacies About Modern Education." *New York Times Magazine,* November 27, 1955. p. 36.

[5] Justine Wise Polier, "The Back-to-the-Woodshed Trend." *Child Study* XXXI (Summer 1954) 3. p. 16.
[6] William C. Kvaraceus, *The Community and the Delinquent.* Yonkers-on-Hudson, New York: World Book Company, 1954. Chapter 4.

Inclination to look for adventure away from
  home
Disliking school
Lacking career plans
Doing poorly in school
Receiving low grades
Failing to be promoted
Behaving badly
Escaping through truancy.

The delinquent reacts to his inner problems
with outward aggressive behavior in a society
which finds his conduct bothersome and contrary
to how life should be lived.

Good schools and adequate support

There are two central questions in regard to
the school's contribution to prevention and control of delinquency. "What kind of school does
America need?" "Will America support the kind
of school it needs?" This article will deal primarily
with the first question.

How can a school help the potential or actual
delinquent to live democratically as a worthy
citizen?

The modern school can create an atmosphere
in which democracy has a chance to thrive. This
is an atmosphere of acceptance, belongingness,
affection, being wanted. Delinquents definitely
need such an atmosphere. Delinquents are short
on acceptance and understanding. They do not
find it in their homes. Too often they find it
only in the anti-social behavior of their gang.
They will not find it in an inadequate school
where coldness, suspicion, and tension are in
the very air, and where rigidity and unnecessary
restrictions rule.

A modern school can build democratic citizenship through giving children a chance to take
part. Youngsters learn teamwork through working
in groups with others, through speaking out
frankly in discussions, through taking part in
extracurricular activities such as athletics, band,
clubs. To help the active and adventurous delinquent, the modern school stressing participation
is preferable to the inadequate school where the
children sit passively while the teacher tells them
exactly what to do, and exactly how to do it.

If America is to have citizens fit for a democracy,
rather than personalities like the cowed slaves of
Communism, America needs modern schools which
work toward the self-discipline which is characteristic of the democratic man. Obviously, controls are
necessary and they exist in a good modern school.
But, when possible, the student takes part in

setting the rules. Good schools have student councils and governments. Steadily the good teacher,
like the good parent, expands the limits of freedom, the area of self-discipline. The inadequate
school which struggles to keep the lid on through
autocratic discipline engages in bitter eternal warfare with the increasingly rebellious delinquent.

A good modern school can contribute to democratic living through a program which develops
a wide range of interests. Potential delinquents
need outlets for activity, for expression, for adventure. They need to come in contact with a
widening world. The inadequate school which
attempts to fill all free hours of potentially
delinquent youngsters with extra and increased
homework rather than attempts to develop self-
propelling, enduring interests, is on a dead-end
road.

If we are to build better school programs to
contribute to the fight against delinquency, we
need schools with modern programs geared to
individuals.

A good modern school has a curriculum which
includes varied offerings. The program includes
vocational education, work experience, remedial
instruction such as remedial reading. It includes
twentieth century offerings like general science,
general mathematics, industrial subjects, home
economics, physical education and agriculture—
subjects which scarcely existed in 1900. Many
classes in a modern school help people to come
to grips with their personal and social problems.
A program of varied offerings gives the delinquent a better chance to get something out of
school.

We must not forget that the typical delinquent
is a slower learner than others. He needs remedial
help. He also needs vocational education and work
experience. But only 20% of all high school students have work experience or training for work.
Eighty per cent graduate or leave school without
work experience or training for work.

The formal classical curriculum of abstract
bodies of knowledge has little meaning for the
delinquent. Formal college entrance programs
have no relationship to his life. Only 20% of all
children entering school continue education beyond high school. Eighty per cent must be prepared for self-support by age 18. Two out of three
high school graduates enter the labor force. Only
one in three continues education. However capable the college scholars a school produces, it
is an inadequate school if it requires an inappropriate curriculum for most of its youngsters,
including potential or present juvenile delinquents.

A modern school provides for the individual
student abundant opportunities for guidance.

Guidance comes best through both specialized guidance personnel and through classroom teachers themselves. In a good school records are kept. Systematic testing supplies background. Case studies are made. A delinquent needs somebody who will listen. If the guidance personnel also can turn to specialized services when needed, great possibilities for social betterment through the schools open up. To point out that the juvenile delinquent in particular needs guidance and allied help is to emphasize the obvious. An inadequate school, which has no guidance facilities, loses its great opportunity to help the delinquent. Experts say that one counselor is needed for every 250 pupils. But only 20% of schools in America have counselors. Of these there is only one counselor to 525 pupils. In one study, for 6½ million children there were 6,780 counselors or one counselor to a thousand children. We need four times as many counselors.

A good school does its best to see that everyone has some success in the things that an individual is able to do, rather than penalized for failing to succeed in things which by sheer biological make-up the individual is unable to do. The delinquent needs success, not endlessly repeated failure. In an inadequate school, he fails again and again. Low in ability, he is expected to read at the same rate and with equal understanding as the better equipped students. He becomes the conspicuous class "boob." Repeated failure contributes to drop-outs.

All too many of our children drop out before completing high school. There are now a million 14-17 year olds out of school. More than 300,000 of them are unemployed. Half of these unemployed are seeking jobs, the other half are not seeking and often are drifting. Sixty-one per cent of the children between 14 and 17 who appear in juvenile court are out of school drop-outs. The chances of court appearances are about one in four for school drop-outs and only one in 50 for those enrolled. To fight delinquency, we need more good modern schools which have holding power, not inadequate schools which lose many students through drop-outs.

The school can also acquaint all of the youngsters within its reach with the pressing social realities of their times.

Specifically, schools can develop programs of family education, helping all boys and girls to understand the problems and potentialities of the American family. Poor family living makes a great deal of difference in the creation of delinquents. Young people can study the total problems of recreation that they, today as young people and tomorrow as adults, can increasingly improve recreational opportunities for all, including potential delinquents.

Many good modern schools also help young people to look directly at their problems of personal living. They learn to understand themselves, their relationships with other boys and girls; understand racial and nationality backgrounds; the problems of delinquency itself. This is a type of group guidance which develops greater self insight. It is a mental health program which becomes part of the regular content of the classroom.

But these activities will not be engaged in by an inadequate school which conceives its instruction to have nothing to do with the actual ongoing life of a young person in society.

In answering the question, "What kind of school does America need if we are to prevent and control juvenile delinquency?" emphasis has been placed on a good school with a modern curriculum.

Obviously the school has still other contributions. For instance the school plant should be used by young and old outside of school hours. Early identification of potential delinquents and consequent handling and referral are of high importance. The development of parent education can be a great help. Above all, the school's efforts should be part of a total planned all-community attack by coordinated agencies.

"Will America support the kind of school it needs?" Who could close without pointing out the crucial importance of this question? For two things are urgently needed: public understanding and financial support.

School men can develop the kind of modern school described here only if the people, to whom the schools belong, understand its necessity. If the citizenry demands good schools with a modern program of education to meet the challenge of delinquency, good education will prevail. If, instead, the citizenry permits or even demands inadequate practices, these will prevail with unfortunate results.

The schools cannot do their jobs without financial support. In America today we are desperately short on teachers. We are even shorter on good teachers who understand children. Our insufficient classrooms are overcrowded. Our classes are too large for individualization. We haven't space for all of the children of the American people. We now have 7½ million 14 to 17 year olds. In 1960 we will have 9½ million. In 1965 we will have 12 million. We haven't the funds to set up sufficient special services. We haven't the money to make inadequate schools into good modern schools.

Federal aid to education is among our hopes.

COMPARATIVE EDUCATION: A GROWING FORCE

We have already noted that different cultures require different kinds of education. Nevertheless, there are important similarities between cultures and hence between their patterns of education. Recent years have seen a renewed emphasis in America and elsewhere on the study of the educational programs of other nations, a field of study called comparative education. There has also been a tendency on the part of some Americans to express concern over the important differences between American and European schools, particularly at the secondary level. Some of those who were concerned seemed more aware of the academic traditions of the schools under consideration than of the political and social implications of a school system for a nation. That an aristocratic pattern of education is not appropriate for a democratic nation seems not to need elaboration. That it is possible to provide for many segments of the population in a single comprehensive school would seem so well established as to require little additional proof. Nevertheless the vigor of the assault necessitates consideration of the problem.

Comparative education: a growing force

THE COMPARISON OF AMERICAN AND EUROPEAN SCHOOL SYSTEMS

Because of the historical interdependence of America and Western Europe, there are many basic similarities between their school systems. But there are also important differences. In a sense, the school system of any nation evolves as the one most appropriate to that particular culture. This integral relationship between a nation's culture and its schools explains why the vast social changes occurring all over the world require continual analysis and reanalysis of education. Comparative studies are important in assessing the ways in which various nations meet new demands and thus in providing applicable generalizations for use by other nations.

82

I. L. Kandel

THE STUDY OF COMPARATIVE EDUCATION

Since World War II there has been a renewed interest in comparative education. This interest has been stimulated by a number of factors: (a) the rise of new nations and new educational systems; (b) increased exchange of persons between countries; (c) the active participation in world-wide educational efforts by such agencies as UNESCO and educational foundations; and (d) the aid programs of several nations. All of these activities have contributed to the need to study the social milieu of education. Further, many of the new countries of the world, particularly in Africa, have considered the area of comparative studies important in helping them to plan their own educational systems. Thus comparative education has become a rediscovered instrument for analysis and programing of education.

For approximately thirty years Professor Kandel of Teachers College, Columbia University, has been the leading American authority on the study of comparative education. In this article he points out the justification for such study and some of its pitfalls. As you read the selection you will come to understand that concepts other than "education" and "school system" are involved in comparative education. A knowledge of the culture, the history, and the ideals of any nation must precede discussion of its educational system.

The study of comparative education involves more than the study of systems of education from the point of view of their organization and administration, their curricula and methods of instruction, the participation of the public, the status of teachers, and so on. Like the study of the history of education, comparative education seeks to discover underlying causes to explain why the educational systems of different countries differ from each other, what are their motivating aims and purposes, what their sources are, and what general principles may emerge. For the present it is difficult to compare standards of attainment in the schools of different countries and even in such a matter as literacy the standards that are used to define and measure it may vary from country to country. Attention was directed shortly after World War II to the question of equivalences but little progress has been made.

The difficulty of assessing and comparing standards does not, however, militate against the comparison of the ideas and principles that underlie different educational systems. A comparison can be made of the effects upon such systems of political theories, of available economic resources, and of the culture patterns, as well as of the philosophical principles upon which they are based. A distinction should be made between (1) descriptive accounts of individual systems of education or "foreign school systems" (Auslandspädagogik), each account written by a different writer, and (2) comparative education (Vergleichende Pädagogik) in which the educational systems of several countries are discussed by one writer from a single dominating point of view, resulting in a work in which a genuine comparison is consistently maintained. The term "international education" which is sometimes used as a synonym for "comparative education" is meaningless, since the term has an entirely different connotation and is (or should be) concerned with the development of certain intellectual and emotional attitudes through instruction in the schools and may only impinge on the character of an educational system very indirectly.

International co-operation in education for the exchange of ideas, for stimulating the study of the same problems in different countries with different culture patterns, and for the promotion of similar human aims in education is not only possible but desirable. One of the best examples of such co-operation, before UNESCO was established, was the international inquiry into examinations sponsored by the International Institute of Teachers College, Columbia University, and conducted from 1931 to 1938. A number of European countries and the United States co-operated in this venture. Important results were reached in each country but the threat of war brought the study to an end.

Such international ventures, however, are not the same as the study of comparative education. Like descriptive articles in yearbooks and other publications, they may provide the material and content for comparative study, which aims at discovering underlying ideas and purposes which can, like the history of education, contribute to the enrichment and enlargement of one's own point of view and to a philosophical foundation for education, if only to show that other influences than the traditionally pedagogical and psychological play an important part in determining the character of an educational system.

It is obvious from these general statements that the educational system of one country cannot be transferred to another, since the study of comparative education is directed to discovering how a national system of education is rooted in its culture. Nowhere has this principle been more clearly stated than in the lines of Robert Bridges:

"Since each group as it rose was determin'd apart
By conditions of life which none other could share,
By climate, language, and historic traditions."

From *Educational Forum*, November 1955, 20:5-15.

This principle may even be carried further to indicate that certain differences may exist within a national culture and that local environments must be taken into consideration in planning an educational system. The emphasis on *Heimatkunde, étude du milieu,* local or regional studies, and the community school all have their justification in differences in local cultural environments from which a start must be made.

Attempts to introduce the educational system of one country to another have always ended in failure because it sprang from and was adapted to a different cultural environment. This has been true of British education in India and other parts of the Empire, of American education in the Philippines and Puerto Rico as reported in surveys conducted by Paul Monroe and his colleagues in the twenties, and of the educational systems of suzerain countries in their attempts to advance the assimilation of their colonies to the mother country. Only the future will prove whether the influences of the occupying powers will have a lasting effect on the educational system of Germany and Japan. Education must be adapted to and grow out of the cultural environment of the people to be educated. Just as the process of educating children must start from the immediate environment in which they live, so a national system of education becomes something alien, something artificial unless it is related to and rooted in the national culture in the broadest sense of the term; this is the essence of *Bodenständigkeit* emphasized in the educational theory of the Weimar Republic.

In a lecture delivered at the beginning of the present century Sir Michael Sadler made the following statement: "In studying foreign systems of education we should not forget that the things outside the schools matter ever more than the things inside the schools, and govern and interpret the things inside. . . . A national system of education is a living thing, the outcome of forgotten struggles and difficulties and 'of battles long ago.' . . . The practical value of studying in a right spirit and with scholarly accuracy the working of foreign systems of education is that it will result in our being better fitted to study and understand our own."

On the general principle that a national system of education reflects the culture pattern of a nation and that a universal system of education is impossible Sadler had already been anticipated, though in different terms, by Wilhelm Dilthey in his essay, *Über die Möglichkeit einer allgemeingültigen pädagogischen Wissenschaft* (1888). Dilthey stressed the historical, cultural, and social forces that determine the character of an educational system and militate against the development of a universal system of education. Emile Durkheim, whose approach to education was sociological, also stressed the determining influences on education of a people's culture patterns when he delivered his inaugural address on *Pédagogie et Sociologie* at the Sorbonne in 1902.

So far as philosophies of education are concerned their study is not excluded from the field of comparative education but in the main as they have a direct impact and exercise a formative influence upon the actual practices of educational systems. A great deal is written, of course, in the realm of pure theory of education which may not affect educational practice. It would be an interesting exercise to compare such theories but for the present the study of comparative education is concerned with educational systems as going concerns.

Educational systems cannot be transferred from one cultural environment to another, but ideas and principles can be studied, modified and fruitfully adapted to suit new conditions. The whole history of education is the history of the cross-fertilization of ideas. Roman education was transformed through the influence of Greek theories and practices. Jewish and Arabic philosophy and learning exercised a potent influence on medieval Christian thought. The Renaissance, starting in Italy with the revival of the humanities, changed the character of secondary education in particular in the countries of Western Europe, while the Reformation stimulated the provision of elementary education in European countries and in some American colonies. Later the Prussian elementary school served as a pattern for the promotion of elementary education in France and the United States in the first third of the 19th century. The world owes a great deal to Froebel's idea of the kindergarten, to the spread of Herbart's theory and methods, to Maria Montessori's work for young children, to the philosophies of Kerschensteiner, Dewey, Ferrière, and Decroly which extended far beyond the boundaries of their country of origin. Finally, the United States has contributed to the development of a science of education through the elaboration of objective tests and measurements, although they were first suggested in France and England. The American ideal of providing equality of educational opportunities has stimulated efforts in the same direction in other countries as an inherent aspect of the ideal of democracy, even though the American solution of one high school for all is not universally accepted. These examples chosen from what could be a more extensive list, do not mean that a uniform system of education will be established throughout the world, but only that just as science exercises a worldwide influence, so too in education ideas and theories can transcend national boundaries and affect progress through what can be learned from other educational systems. But it has been pointed out that even in a field as objective as science, the methods of solving problems tend to be affected by the national character which conditions the scientist.

Each nation has or aims to have the educational system that suits its needs and the first aim of every educational system is to reproduce the type. In one of the early Special Reports on Educational Subjects, published at the beginning of the century, Sadler in discussing this question pointed out that what a nation wants and expects from education is indicated by the questions they are likely to ask about an individual. The German would ask "What does he know?"; the Frenchman, "What diploma or certificate does he hold?"; the Englishman, "What kind of a fellow is he?" and the American, "What can he do?" Each of these questions reflects the aims of an educational system. And while fundamental changes have taken place since Sadler wrote, questions such as these are still pertinent.

It is important, therefore, in studying the educational system of a nation to devote considerable attention to its social, political, and economic organization and its cultural background. Take, for example, the recent development of the nursery school. There may be psychological arguments for it—that the period of infancy is the most crucial period in the development of the human being. In its origin, however, the creation of nursery schools by the McMillan sisters can be traced to the social situation and the changing conditions of the home and of the status of women. Later the further recognition of the place of the nursery school has been due to a desire to give all children an equal start in life in healthy and happy surroundings and to conserve the manpower of the nation in view of the smaller size of families. In the United States the slow development of nursery schools is due to two factors—the smaller number of children in the family and the entrance of an increasing number of women into wage-earning occupations—but these schools were introduced first as centres for the psychological study of the growth of children. In Nazi Germany there was and in Soviet Russia there is still another reason for the earlier start in schooling—to begin the conditioning process as early as possible.

The rise of the nursery school, like the development of public elementary education, is a result of the industrialization of society. So too the raising of the school age is due in part to a desire to extend equality of educational opportunities and to provide a longer educational preparation for the complex problems of life today. In large part it is due also to the fact that the more advanced industrialized nations can dispense with the labor of young persons. On the other hand, it will be found that where the national economy is still mainly agricultural, the highest percentage of illiteracy prevails, e.g., the Balkan countries, Italy, Egypt, Latin America, China and India, as well as the larger areas of what are known as underdeveloped societies.

In general it may be taken for granted that as the influence of social institutions which have in the past performed useful educational functions declines, they are gradually assigned to the schools, e.g., early childhood education, new subjects of instruction such as domestic economy and manual training, vocational training, adult education, etc.

In the history of education the church has been the strongest force in education. For over a thousand years schools were either provided by or under the supervision of the church. Following the Reformation and on the principle of *cujus regio, ejus religio,* the state entered into partnership with the church and each state asserted the right to determine the particular religious denomination to be tolerated within its borders and consequently asserted the right to control education together with the relevant church authorities. As nations gradually developed into national self-consciousness, the church was gradually subordinated to the social, political, and economic interests of the state. The dominant aim in education was no longer religious but political and national, determined in each country by the political character of the state and administered by secular authorities. Nevertheless, the problem of religious instruction in the schools has nowhere been satisfactorily settled; it was crucial in the debates on the Education Bill in England during the war; it has created a serious obstacle to the reform of education in France; it has been a source of difficulty in the postwar reorganization of education in the states of Western Germany; and it has been seriously debated and has led to court actions in the United States in the last fifteen years.

The relation between politics and education is not new. That relationship had already been recognized by Plato and Aristotle. When Plato undertook in *The Republic* to discuss the just state, his work became one of the outstanding treatises on education. The guardians of the state were to devote special attention to education and rearing. "For if by a good education they (the citizens) be made reasonable men, they will readily see through all these questions" which are fundamental to the stability of the state. In the *Laws* Plato made the Minister of the Education of Youth the most important of all the state officials. In the same vein Aristotle wrote in the *Politics* "Of all things that I have mentioned that which contributes most to the permanence of states is the adaptation of education to the form of government." In the *Ethics* Aristotle stated that "We laid it down that the end of politics is the highest good, and there is nothing that this science takes so much pains with as producing a certain character in the citizens, that is, making them good and able to do fine things." The idea was repeated by Montesquieu who wrote in *l'Esprit des Lois* that "the laws of education ought to be in relation to the principles of government."

It was not until the end of the 18th century, when the national state began to emerge, that these principles were adopted as the basis for the creation of national systems of education. Thus the General Constitution of Prussia laid it down in 1794 that "Schools and universities are state institutions charged with the instruction of youth in useful information and scientific knowledge. Such institutions may be founded only with the knowledge and consent of the state."

In 1808 Napoleon issued a decree to the same effect that "No school, no establishment of instruction whatsoever may be set up outside the Imperial University and without the authorization of its head." This decree was based on the principle defined by Napoleon three years earlier: "Of all political questions that (of education) is perhaps the most important. There cannot be a firmly established political state unless there is a teaching body with definitely recognised principles. If the child is not taught from infancy that he ought to be a republican or a monarchist, a Catholic or a freethinker, the state will not constitute a nation; it will rest on uncertain and shifting foundations, and it will be constantly exposed to disorder and change."

These principles may be contrasted with the educational aim defined by George Washington in his Farewell Address (1796): "Promote then as an object of primary importance, institutions for the general diffusion of knowledge. In proportion as the structure of government gives force to public opinion it is essential that public opinion should be enlightened." This principle was repeated by every public figure in the United States from Washington's day to the present and may be found in *Expressions on Education by Builders of Amer-*

ican Democracy (1941). His principles are permanent even though they may at times be forgotten by self-constituted patriots.

In England the provision of schools by the State was long resisted because it was feared that they would be used to control the mind. Of all the arguments against a state system of education the strongest was that of John Stuart Mill in his essay *On Liberty* (1859), where he wrote: "That the whole or any large part of the education of the people should be in state hands, I go as far as anyone in deprecating. All that has been said of the importance of individuality of character, and diversity in opinions and modes of conduct, involves, as of the same unspeakable importance, diversity of education. A general state education is a mere contrivance for moulding people to be exactly like one another; and as this mould in which it casts them is that which pleases the predominant power in the government, whether this be a monarch, a priesthood, an aristocracy, or the majority of the existing generation; in proportion as it is efficient and successful, it establishes a despotism over the mind, leading by natural tendency to one over the body. An education established and controlled by the state should only exist, if it exist at all, as one among many competing experiments, carried on for the purpose of example and stimulus, to keep the others up to a certain standard of excellence." Neither the Board of Education nor its successor, the Ministry of Education, prescribes the curriculum but exercises leadership through its inspectors and the publication of suggestions. While uniformity is not insisted upon or expected and while freedom is granted to the teachers, they are expected to show a corresponding responsibility in its use.

It may then be taken as an axiom that "As is the state, so is the school." Under one of the principles (the authoritarian or totalitarian) the state comes first and the function of the school is to mould the individual to a particular pattern desired by the state—"to be in the right line" in Soviet Russia, the equivalent of *Gleichschaltung* in Nazi Germany. Under the other principle (the democratic or liberal) the function of the school is to develop each individual to his fullest capacity as an intelligent citizen who will have a part in determining the character of the state. Many of the differences between national systems of education may be traced back to the differences in the political nature of the state. The explanation of many other aspects of education—centralized or local administration and their relations, types of control and inspection, prescription of curricula and methods or freedom, the preparation of teachers, standards and examinations and the participation of the public—can be found most generally, but not always in the political aims of the state. The reservation "not always" is added because there are democracies with systems which are highly centralized because of the demographic conditions.

The last thirty years have seen changes in education which have resulted from political changes. In Germany there have been four different types of education—Imperial, republican, Nazi, and now possibly democratic. In Soviet Russia, after some fifteen years of experimentation of all kinds, education must be "In the right line" like every other aspect of communist life and culture; the latest aim is indicated in the title of the translation by George S. Counts and Nucia P. Lodge of a Russian treatise on pedagogy: "I want to be like Stalin." In Nazi Germany the whole aim of education was to co-ordinate everybody and produce uniformity of mind, for the remark of a Nazi henchman wrote, "Since Hitler came into power no German has any private life except when he is asleep. As soon as he awakes, he is a soldier of Hitler," applies equally to the citizen of any of the Communist states. In Fascist Italy the guiding principles were "Nothing against the state; everything for the state; nothing outside the state" and "Il Duce is always right." In Japan a Bureau of Thought Control was established to prevent students in particular from "harboring dangerous thoughts."

The totalitarian state controls every aspect of education and culture. Control, however, need not always be determined by political ends. The pre-war system of education of France was under authoritarian bureaucratic control, partly through fear of external aggression, partly as a heritage from Napoleon, and partly through a desire to maintain the standards of French culture. In the period between the two wars the French teachers demanded greater freedom to adapt education to the local environment. A slight modification of authoritarian control is now under way and greater freedom is being allowed to teachers.

There is another form of authoritarianism which cannot be explained in any of these ways—political or cultural. This form arises from a slow and imperceptible entrenchment of bureaucracy and was found in New Zealand and the Australian States. Centralization and control of education were developed at a time when the population was sparsely scattered and local government had not yet emerged. The only way to provide schools was by the central government. Changes are beginning to be introduced. This is not yet true, however, in the Latin American countries

where control of education is normally in the hands of a central authority.

In contrast to the totalitarian and authoritarian systems stands the administration of education in the liberal, democratic states, particularly England and the United States; the emphasis has always been on decentralization with greater participation on the part of the public locally. In both countries efficiency has to some degree been checked through fear of central control. In both countries it has now been realized in the interests of making the ideal of equality of educational opportunity a reality, the controls, national or state authority must participate to a greater degree than in the past in providing these conditions under which the fullest educational opportunities are made available to every boy and girl irrespective of accident of place of residence and family circumstances, but without seeking to prescribe either the content or the methods of instruction. This has been the intent of the Education Act, 1944, and of the proposals for Federal aid for education in the United States. In both countries it is definitely recognized that the advancement of education depends not upon dictation and control by a central authority but upon an alert public opinion. In both countries the principle has been accepted that larger areas of administration must be established not only in order to ensure adequate local support for education but also to promote what Sir Michael Sadler described as "variety within a national framework." As President Wilson once wrote, such a system not only demands intelligence but elicits intelligence. A close-knit organization of education may be efficient in its operation, but it militates against local initiative on the part of teachers and public, and is an obstacle to progress.

There is, however, another reason for encouraging and maintaining the interest of the public in its educational concerns. That reason is that opportunities are provided to keep the public informed when new ideas are being introduced in the schools. For there is always the danger of opposition to innovations which comes from those adults whose education has been different. Today there is still another justification arising from the fact that the expenditure of funds for education must be greatly increased and without a public that understands that such expenditure is necessary for the well-being of the individual and for material welfare, plans for reform may easily fail. There has never been a period in the history of education when so many changes have been proposed requiring the intelligent support of the public. Because of the tradition of the dual system of education—one for the masses in elementary schools and another for a minority in secondary schools, there are sections of society in many European countries which feel that opportunities for secondary education are not "for the likes of them or their children." There are also other groups so strongly influenced by the tradition of the academic type of secondary education that they tend to look upon other types, better adapted to the capacities and needs of pupils, as inferior substitutes. Here a lesson, which has already been learned in England, can be learned from the United States, of the variety of methods and devices that have been adopted to secure public interest and support for education.

Up to this point there have been discussed the relations between the political character of the state and education, the impact of which results in important differences between educational systems of different countries. There are of course other methods of approach. If the social has not been mentioned, it is because it is inherently part of the political and culture pattern. And yet the existence of social and economic stratification must be taken into account, since a program of developing equality of educational opportunities based on ability inevitably means not only free education but also a system of maintenance grants. But differentiation of educational opportunities depends not only upon individual differences of ability but also upon the recognition of a nation's economic and technical needs. Education is a social investment in human beings and education brings dividends not only in the wellbeing of the individual but also in the welfare and progress of society.

There is still another factor besides the political which makes for such differences, even where the political theory and practice may be similar. This is the concept of nationalism. That education cannot avoid being rooted in national culture has already been emphasized—language, history, geography, mores or ways of behavior, all those aspects of life or culture patterns which make for common loyalties and a sense of membership in the political group called a nation. The first aim in any system of education from the primitive to the modern is to reproduce the type, or to induct the younger generation into membership of the society in which they are to live.

Inevitable as this approach is, it has created a problem as nationalism became militant and aggressive resulting in a tendency to look upon other nations as inferior or as hostile, to look for differences rather than the elements common to all human beings. Sir Ernest Barker once defined a nation as "the house of thought which men have made that their minds may dwell there to-

gether." Even from the point of view of ideas and culture it can be shown that such a house cannot be detached, that the bricks of which it has been built have been the results of the labors of men in all ages of history, of all nations, and of all races of mankind. The particular architecture of the house of thought has been determined by the national character or mentality developed by the tradition of the group as it develops common objects of allegiance. Señor Madariaga has defined national character or mentality as "the shape, the scent, and the color" of the actions and ways of thinking of members of the same nation, of their qualities and their defects. National character is a cultural not a physiological or racial phenomenon.

Still another definition of a nation which has more clearly influenced educational practices may be mentioned. Discussing the meaning of a nation Renan wrote: "What constitutes a nation is not speaking the same tongue or belonging to the same ethnic group, but having accomplished great things in common in the past and the wish to accomplish them in the future." Unfortunately in the subject which has been most widely used for purposes of nationalistic indoctrination—history —the things accomplished in the past are always associated with the glories of the battlefield and of conquest and the things to be accomplished in the future are to redress defeat, regain lost territory, or to make further conquests. The heroes of the child in school are the heroes of the battlefield. The heroes who have enriched mankind with ideas and ideals are ignored. The Constitution of UNESCO opens with the statement that "Since wars begin in the minds of men, it is in the minds of men that the defences of peace must be constructed"; it would be more accurate to say that "wars are put into the minds of children while still in school." On the whole a definition of a nation which more correctly diagnoses what ails the world is that of Huxley and Haddon in *We Europeans*: "A nation has been cynically but not inaptly defined as a group of people held together by a common error as to their origin and a common aversion to their neighbors."

The study of comparative education is thus concerned with discovering the impact of such a concept of nationalism on education. Today it is more concerned with this question than ever before. The issue at present is to discover whether nationalism and internationalism are compatible with each other. Comparative education can study the educational systems of different nations objectively. It is not its function to criticize political ideologies but to show their effect upon systems of education. But it can make an important contribution by emphasizing the evil effects of the wrong kind of nationalism in the light of history and its effects on the welfare of human beings.

The importance of this issue has been recognised in the Constitution of UNESCO in the declaration, "That the ignorance of each other's ways and lives has been a common cause, throughout the history of mankind, of that suspicion and mistrust between the peoples of the world through which their differences have too often broken into war." To promote better understanding between nations UNESCO has undertaken as one of its activities to promote studies of nationalism and internationalism with three aims in view:

"1. To bring to light the distinctive character of the various national cultures and national ideals.

2. To help in stimulating the sympathy and respect of the nations for each other's ideals and aspirations and appreciation of national problems.

3. To study and recommend for action possible measures which can bring the nations into closer cooperation, while maintaining fullest respect for their cultures and ideals."

There is no better statement than this of the aims of the study of comparative education, for while it recognizes and safeguards the existence of national cultures and systems of education, it looks to reconciling their conflicting interests. This field of investigation has sought to promote an understanding of educational systems in the light of their culture, their political structure, and their national aims. For it is through education that the hopes, aspirations and problems of a nation can be understood.

83

James B. Conant

AN AMERICAN LOOKS AT EUROPEAN EDUCATION

As High Commissioner to Germany and a former president of Harvard University, Dr. Conant is well informed about the distinctions in purpose of American and European schools. His studies of the American high school and investigations of teacher education have brought him into close contact with the essential character of American schooling. His judgments are highly rational and reflect careful thought. Notice the objective way in which he approaches the comparison of American and European education. Impressed by the similarities as well as the differences, he here issues a word of caution to those Americans inclined to belittle the American school.

History shows that, except under conditions of duress brought about by external forces, schools and colleges have developed gradually in different parts of the world in response to a variety of different conditions. They are a product of the society they serve, and they also influence the future of this society. Reformers who have sought to change education have had to be content with minor alterations or else have had to devote a lifetime to their task.

It is clear that various educational devices have in the past been outmoded by social changes. The

From *The High School in a New Era*, Francis S. Chase and Harold A. Anderson, eds., pp. 20–30. Copyright © 1958 by The University of Chicago. Reprinted by permission of The University of Chicago Press.

situation of Oxford and Cambridge during the first two-thirds of the nineteenth century is a case in point. For two generations many leaders of public opinion argued for the need of either establishing modern universities in England or reforming the two ancient seats of learning. Eventually both courses of action were followed; the modification of Oxford and Cambridge by successive royal commissions was so radical as to constitute the equivalent of a series of drastic biological mutations. By the end of the century English universities were once again well adapted to the tasks at hand.

To one interested in comparative education, it is fascinating to see how, today, many nations are struggling to solve the basic problems connected with their educational systems. To a student of comparative education, many questions about education in different countries are questions almost without meaning. Asking whether European schools are better than schools in the United States is like asking a comparative anatomist whether a whale is a better mammal than an elephant.

The comparative anatomist is interested in examining the similarities and differences to be found in animal or plant organs which carry out the same function; he is very cautious, however, about proclaiming the virtues of a device found in one particular species over a device for a similar purpose found in another. Of course the anatomist knows that mammals are modified only slowly by changes in environment; unlike schools or colleges, no man-made decisions will radically alter the structure of the functioning organism he is examining.

Some will argue that this vitiates my analogy; they may claim that the essence of human organizations lies in the fact that conscious acts of men and women can change them, and, as history shows, overnight if need be. "But wait a moment," the student of the comparative anatomy of schools will say, "not overnight surely, except at the point of a bayonet or in our time under the shadow of armored vehicles and tanks." And such changes, he will argue, are the equivalent of pathological alterations.

Education for the professions

First, I should like to examine in particular the way the future members of the professions are recruited, selected, and educated in certain European nations and the United States.

For a number of professions one phase of professional education—the final stage, so to speak—is essentially identical in all countries. There is little to be gained by noting the minor differences to be found in various nations. This is true of medicine, of engineering, and of the natural sciences; it is likewise true, to a lesser degree, of certain areas within the social sciences and the humanities. It is possible to pass judgment on the work of the medical faculty of a university, for example, almost without taking into account the traditions of the institutions or its surroundings. Considering the training of a medical man only from the standpoint of professional competency, it would not be too difficult to classify all the medical schools of Europe and America into groups according to their degree of excellence. The same would apply to the training of engineers and research scientists.

It is not so much professional education as the education provided *prior* to professional studies that varies from nation to nation. This is particularly true if one directs attention to the way the future members of the professions are recruited and selected. Nowhere on the European continent will one find the equivalent of the American four-year liberal arts college. The European youth, unlike his American contemporary, passes directly from a university-preparatory school to professional training.

Americans find it difficult to imagine an educational system without a college; Europeans find it hard to imagine what sort of an institution an American college can be. And the task of explaining the situation in the United States to a German, for example, is not made easier by the fact that there are more than fifteen hundred four-year colleges in our country (some, part of a university; some, not); their curriculums and criteria for admission and graduation vary enormously. The one thing they have in common is the right to award a Bachelor's degree—an academic symbol derived from the Middle Ages which has completely disappeared in German-speaking nations, though not in France.

One sometimes hears it said that the characteristic feature of American education is the proportion of our youth attending a university. So phrased, this is a completely misleading statement. What is characteristic is the very large proportion of our youth from eighteen to twenty years of age who are engaged in full-time studies; the fraction is something like a quarter to a third. In Great Britain, France, Germany, and Switzerland not more than a tenth of the youth are so engaged. Equally characteristic are the figures for school attendance at the age sixteen to seventeen. In America more than 75 per cent of those of this age are in school full-time; in European countries and Great Britain the corresponding figure is less than 20 per cent. Some Europeans have said that only a rich nation could afford to keep so many of its youth in school so long. But with the increase in automation, it is a question whether the withdrawal of a considerable fraction of youth from the labor force is a luxury. The type of training needed in the distributive industries more and more requires considerable "book learning."

At all events, when we consider the proportion of youth engaged in *professional* studies, the position of the United States is not so different from that of the rest of the world. Perhaps it is fair to compare the proportion of young men enrolled in the first year of a university in Europe or Great Britain to the proportion in the United States entering engineering, law, and medical schools and starting in the graduate schools of arts and sciences. Taking the figures for young men, the proportion in the United States seems to be something like 6 per cent; surprisingly small, many would say. But what is equally surprising is that similar figures represent the situation in all nations for which I have seen statistics. Therefore one could say that the proportion of youth studying *professionally* in a university is about the same in the United States as in other nations. What *is* different between America and Europe is the method by which this very small percentage is selected and educated prior to engaging in professional studies.

Selection of students for pre-professional study

Today, unlike the situation of a hundred years ago, the education of members of the professions (particularly natural scientists and engineers) is a concern of statesmen; public opinion has an interest in hearing the answers to such questions as the following: Are we training enough professional people? Are we including in our education for the professions a large fraction of those who have the requisite ability, or are we overlooking many with high potentialities?

In a totalitarian state these questions lead directly to a control of the entire educational process; the capable are to be sorted out and educated for the different professions according to the nation's need for these professions. This is essentially the directive of the Party Executive Committee to those in charge of schools and universities in the Soviet Zone of Germany. In a free country the political situation is, thank God, very different, not only because of the impossibility of government's ordering youth into different educational channels but because of the freedom of parents to express their desires to school authorities and, if need be, to politicians.

National concern with the number and quality of scientists and engineers is clearly a result of the last phases of the Industrial Revolution, which started two hundred years ago. Parental concern with education as a way by which a son may better himself economically and socially is a consequence of the spread of that spirit of democracy of which Tocqueville wrote more than a century ago. It has taken time for the equalitarian doctrines of the French Revolution reinforced by American notions to affect European education; but there is no doubt that the problem of selecting future university students is becoming more, rather than less, difficult in England and a number of European states. The question of

social prestige is becoming involved, as it has been involved with us in America for at least fifty years.

Let me give a few concrete examples. During the Second World War the British Parliament made certain changes in the English system of tax-supported schools. Among the objectives which the new legislation sought to achieve was the widening of opportunity for children of the less well to do; another was an elimination of the great difference in prestige that in the past had characterized one type of tax-supported school as compared with another. The traditional view of the content of a school program was, however, not modified. A long course was held to be necessary; and selection of those capable of entering those schools which provided this course was to be made at the age of eleven to twelve.

From the point of view of a parent with a low income and a talented child, the new arrangement must appear to be better than the old. But parents of medium income view the altered situation highly critically. In the past, the "grammar schools" had provided excellent roads to the universities open to those who could afford to pay a moderate fee. (For well-to-do families the usual road to the university is provided by the famous "public schools.") The new regulations abolished the fees and made the admission of *all* children subject to a competitive examination. And to make matters worse, so some parents have said, a new type of examination is employed—so-called psychological tests that has no apparent relation to school work! As a result the whole subject of selection at age eleven-plus is a topic of heated discussion among educators and laymen.

In one county in England the experiment is being made of abolishing the examination in two selected geographic areas and sending all children from eleven to fifteen to one school and then providing grammar-school places for those whose parents are willing to keep them in school until at least sixteen. Presumably ability to handle the work in the grammar school will be the determining factor in deciding who goes on to the university. The article in the London *Observer* reviewing the experiment carries the heading "Eleven-plus Condemned." This caption corresponds to the sentiment expressed in a number of articles and letters to the editor that have been appearing in British journals and papers in the last few years.

On the European continent, too, difficulties have arisen in regard to the process of selecting those who are to attend the Gymnasium in preparation for a university education. Each one of eleven states in the Federal Republic of Germany has complete authority in educational matters; so too have the twenty-five cantons in Switzerland (with a few exceptions). A comparison of the roads to the university in each of these states is interesting; it shows how different local conditions have modified to a certain degree the European pattern. The points at issue are often the exact length of the pre-university school course and the methods by which pupils are selected for the special pre-university schools.

The parental pressure varies greatly from place to place and reflects differences in tradition and economic circumstances. Sometimes the selection can be made solely on the basis of advice given by teachers and accepted by parents. Sometimes examinations are required in order to decide who should start on the road to the professions. If so, parental protests frequently arise. In one German state I heard a mother complaining that the entrance tests for the Gymnasium were so foolish and arbitrary that many of her friends could not get their children admitted; as a consequence the parents were pressed into the expense of sending them to private schools. In France, where the road to the professions has been studded with stiff competitive examinations, anguish over the selection process has been particularly acute. The entrance examinations for the pre-university schools (lycées) have just been abolished, and the program in these schools lightened. Selection of the pupils who head for the university is now to be made on the basis of the primary-school record. In Switzerland the psychological effect on the child of failure in the pre-university school (in some cantons a half to two-thirds drop out) is giving concern to the school authorities.

In several German states, parents have brought suit against the government because a child had been barred from a pre-university school. The matter has even become a political issue. It is not the method of selection but the length of the pre-university school course that is in controversy. If the course is nine years, then selection must be made at the age of ten to eleven; this was the usual pattern in Germany, I judge, some years ago. But in the postwar years in some states the pre-university course was shortened, and the time of selection correspondingly postponed.

The arguments in favor of keeping all the children together in one school as long as possible are familiar to Americans; an additional (and for Europeans more weighty) argument for a shorter pre-university period of schooling is that it may be easier to select those suited for university work at twelve or thirteen rather than ten or eleven. The abbreviated course has been attacked, how-ever, on the grounds that nine years is necessary if the pupil is to master the subjects required for later university work (particularly Latin). The differences of opinion on the matter seem to run along the usual lines of political cleavage in both Germany and Switzerland; in general, the moderate right favors the longer course, the moderate left the shorter.

In one state election in Germany the issue was of major importance. This is hard for Americans to understand, since the difference of opinion appears to be relatively slight and the educational question involved touches the schooling of not more than a fifth of the children. It is interesting to us as evidence of the intimate connection between school problems and sociological questions.

Requirements for admission to university studies

From what I have already reported, it is clear that the age at which selection is made and the time it is made is intimately associated with the content of the pre-university course of study. And here we meet the second major difference between the road to the professions in Europe and in the United States. In Europe the state determines the requirements which must be satisfactorily fulfilled in order to obtain, on finishing school, the necessary credentials which will enable the holder to enter a university. In Germany and Switzerland, for example, the certificate which a youth obtains after passing a set of final examinations in the last school year is an admission ticket to *any* university. The absence of any such uniform requirements in America astonishes and perplexes the European observer of our chaotic system.

Though each state in the Federal Republic of Germany is autonomous, the standards throughout are essentially the same. Certain variations in the subjects on which a student is examined are permitted, but one may say that the essential subjects are languages and mathematics. In the classical Gymnasium (in Germany called the humanistic school), Latin and Greek are obligatory; in most of the others, Latin and at least one modern foreign language; in a few schools, exposure to a heavy dose of modern languages, mathematics, and natural science is considered a substitute for Latin. A European university is *not* an American college, and language instruction is not one of its functions; scientists, lawyers, medical men, economists, and historians, therefore, have no opportunity for studying any language after they leave school. With this in mind, one realizes why a long school course is believed necessary for future university students. The central position occupied in the curriculums of pre-university schools by foreign languages is a reflection of the role played by both tradition and geography in educational matters. As far as future professional men are concerned, Europeans are convinced that the traditional education in languages, literature, mathematics, and European history comprises the best general education.

For the 75 or 80 per cent who have no ambition or no opportunity to head for a university, formal full-time education ends at fourteen or fifteen; further educational development in part-time courses will depend on the occupation of the young man or woman in question. The apprentice system together with continuation schools takes care of industrial workers, it may be said. For apprentices with special mechanical aptitude, technical schools are available. For the 10 per cent or so who must drop out of the pre-university schools, some special type of education with more emphasis on practical business affairs is needed. This the European would grant, but the idea of a general education for a large proportion of adolescents aged sixteen to twenty-one is unheard of on the continent of Europe.

American and European general education contrasted

"How is it at the end of the road?" one may ask. Are those Europeans who complete the hard journey and arrive at a university and later become professional men (some 6 per cent of the young men) better educated than the corresponding Americans? This is the type of question a student of comparative education refuses to answer; for so much depends on your standard of judgment, on what basis you evaluate the non-professional knowledge, ability, and attitude of a professional man or woman.

One thing is certain: the average American medical man, lawyer, chemist, physicist, or engineer has acquired a quite different store of general knowledge from that of his European counterpart. If command of foreign languages is the test of a well-educated man or woman, relatively few Americans can claim to be well educated. If knowledge of European literature and art is taken as a measure, there again the average American professional man will fail in comparison with the Europeans. European pre-university education is in essence literary education; American college education can rarely be so described.

On the other hand, every American in school and in college will have sampled at least a bit of some of the social sciences. Indeed perhaps the majority of those whom we are here considering will have acquired a considerable knowledge of economics and political science; a large proportion will have studied psychology and sociology. With rare exceptions these disciplines are only available to a European in a university; and while the student enrolled under the law faculty may find time to listen to some lectures in these fields, the medical man and the natural scientist will not.

In other words, those Americans who complete at least three years of a four-year liberal arts college course will have had a kind of academic experience unknown on the continent of Europe. (A possible exception to this statement is the education provided for the future teachers in the pre-university schools who are educated in the famous École Normale in Paris and in the philosophical faculties of the German universities.)

But it is not only the content of the program which characterizes the American college. The whole atmosphere is different from either a European school or a European university. There is far more freedom for the student than in a school, of course, and there is far more personal instruction of the student by the professor than is possible in a university of the European type with its relatively small staff in proportion to the size of the student body. The American student is ready to express an opinion to anyone; discussion is encouraged at every turn. Student activities ranging from dramatics through debating and journalism stimulate student independence; there is no parallel to these expressions of student initiative in Europe. All of which, of course, reflects what Americans have come to believe are important aspects of college education.

Indeed one can sum up the comparison I have been making by saying that the leading citizens of Europe and the United States have quite different aims in mind when they talk about education as apart from professional training. And the difference reflects the different social histories on the two sides of the Atlantic.

Impact of social change on education

As a first approximation, one may say that Europe adjusted its education to modern times nearly a hundred years ago. A period of rapid educational change on the Continent took place in the middle of the nineteenth century; this reflected the first impact of industrialization. The pattern thus established has persisted to the present with relatively few changes; it is obviously intimately associated with the apprentice system of training industrial workers and a relative lack of geographic and social mobility. It also reflects the powerful influence of the university faculties which were well intrenched when the educational changes were in progress, particularly the influence of the professors of the classics.

During the period of change in the United States in which we are still living, traditional academic forces have played a far less important role. But such social factors as the raising of the school-leaving age in the United States and the near disappearance of the European apprentice system were of more importance in determining the shape of the new educational system which is now emerging.

I have written "emerging" because it is clear that in this country we are still in process of adapting our schools, colleges, and universities to the current needs of our society (and trying to adapt to future needs as well). In England, too, a process of change has been, and still is, at work. In the nations of Western Europe, on the other hand (with the exception of Scandinavia), few alterations in the systems have been made in the last fifty years; though there are many educational problems similar to our own and England's, a period of reform has not yet begun.

An American observer cannot help wondering if such a period is not considerably overdue.

It may well be that the more immediate political and social issues in France and the urgent task of reconstruction in post-war Germany have merely pushed aside consideration of educational changes. I seem to detect signs of dissatisfaction in the Federal Republic of Germany which may be the prelude to important actions. In parts of Switzerland the road to the professions is being resurveyed. In France a few important changes have just been made, and a bill providing for a drastic alteration in the French system has been introduced into parliament by the minister of education.

We here in the United States are still engaged in remaking our educational roads; the nature of the task varies considerably from state to state, from community to community. Pedagogic devices and plans for the organization of schools and universities are not always transferable across state lines; they are almost never exportable to foreign countries. But nonetheless the exchange of ideas and blueprints is always helpful because it stimulates and arouses discussion.

We may watch with interest, therefore, the new developments in those Western nations from which came originally our cultural traditions and our ideas about education. The free nations of the world in planning for their youth, as in many other matters, must be in constant communication; for, however diverse their methods, their fundamental aims remain the same: the preservation and extension of personal freedom.

84

William Marshall French

AMERICAN AND EUROPEAN SECONDARY EDUCATION

This article, by a prominent author in the field of secondary education, presents provocatively some of the important issues which become apparent from a comparison of American and European secondary education, and concludes with a number of specific suggestions for improving the high-school program. Dr. French assumes that the function of schooling is primarily intellectual development, and his proposals are consistent with this view. His emphasis on the importance of comparative studies is noteworthy, and the final questions he asks regarding the purpose of schooling reflect the views of many other educational analysts: "*What* shall we teach? *Whom* shall we teach? *Who* shall teach? *How* shall we teach? *For what ends* shall we teach?" These are critical questions which the reader may well keep in mind throughout the reading of this book. The answers given to these questions will, in essence, determine one's view of education and schooling.

Never since American secondary education had its beginnings in Boston in 1834 has there been so much discussion of its strengths and short-comings as at present. From relative indifference the American public has turned to a vital interest in this institution—so much so, indeed, that news-papers and lay magazines are filled with criticisms of and prescriptions for the high school. Even a retired admiral has felt the urge to propose a panacea. Unfortunately, many of these lay critics and reformers know very little about the American secondary school. And those who make compari-sons with secondary institutions abroad not in-frequently know even less about education in other countries. Here a little knowledge of compar-ative education can be a dangerous thing. And making generalizations about American and Euro-pean secondary education upon the basis of ob-serving the performance of a limited number of graduates is equally dangerous. One is reminded of the little boy who wrote, in his third grade essay about Indians: "Indians always walk in single file; at least, the only one I ever saw, did."

A comparison of American and European sec-ondary education might well shed light upon some of our contemporary problems, but much more depth and breadth in the comparison should be sought than is usually the case.

We speak of the American secondary school as if it were a single institution, of a single type. Actually, there is no such creature as a typical secondary school in America, for our decentral-ized system of education, our peculiar traditions and sociological factors have resulted in our hav-ing a wide range of institutions all under the umbrella of "secondary schools." Let us exam-ine the diversity. We have public secondary schools, which enroll approximately 90% of the students in secondary education, and private ("in-dependent") and parochial institutions which enroll the remaining 10%. In each category, we have a wide range in size of schools. The public schools have the largest range in size, from schools of less than ten to schools of more than 5000 pupils. The average enrollment is approximately 200. The author once made a trip half way across Nebraska to give the commencement address to a graduating class. The platform was occupied by the superintendent, the chairman of the board of education, the pastor who gave the invocation and benediction, the speaker and the graduating class. And altogether only five chairs were needed. The whole town turned out for the gala occasion,

for this was the first time in three years that there had been a graduation. The solitary graduate was president, vice president, secretary, treasurer, sa-lutatorian and valedictorian of the class. In fact, he was the class. The superintendent taught all the high school subjects and his wife taught the whole elementary school. Their apartment was in the basement of the school building. In con-trast to this little school, we have huge educational factories which operate more or less on the assem-bly line basis, with more than 1000 graduates a year.

There is just as much variety in the various curricula offered. Some schools are so small that they can offer only a very small number of stand-ard, traditional courses. Often these are given by teachers who have inadequate background in the subjects taught. This is particularly true in those states which do not require at least 18 hours of college preparation in the subject taught. And 18 hours is a pathetically small amount. In Penn-sylvania, for example, one can obtain a college provisional certificate, valid for three years, to teach science upon the basis of 18 semester hours of credit spread over chemistry, physics and bi-ology (both botany and zoology). This certificate is made permanent upon the completion of three years of "satisfactory" teaching and six additional semester hours of work, which is not necessarily in the sciences. It should be borne in mind that some states issue general licenses covering all high school subject fields, and that even in states that now restrict licenses to fields in which special preparation is made, there are still many teachers who obtained such general licenses years ago. The writer, for instance, holds permanent certi-fication to teach any high school subject in New York and in Michigan. Presumably he could legally meet classes in home economics, Latin, physics and chemistry, if he could find a school foolish enough to engage him to teach these subjects.

At the other end of the scale is the large, cos-mopolitan high school with nearly as many sub-jects offered as the five-and-ten has variety of merchandise. In these schools, much guidance is necessary to fit the student into a proper cur-riculum. Few constants are required of all stu-dents, and so great a variety of courses is offered that a diploma carries little guarantee that the various holders have had any common curricular background.

When one surveys all the subjects taught by all the secondary schools, one literally opens a Pan-dora's box. The United States Office of Education reported, in 1950, that thirteen major study fields were offered, and that these thirteen fields were broken down into 274 specific subject titles. Not all these subjects were offered even in the largest schools, of course; and some were offered in very few. For instance, only 185 students studied calculus; 227, first year Greek, in only four states; six, fourth year Greek; 320 Portuguese, and 172, Norse.

Though the typical secondary school in the United States is coeducational, we have secondary schools for boys and secondary schools for girls, in all three types of institutions—public, private and parochial.

Some of the secondary schools are rural, some in small cities, and some in urban areas. In some states, there persists a segregation on a racial basis. Some of the buildings are so inadequate that students go to school in shifts; in other places, the high school dominates the landscape of the countryside as did the cathedral and the castle in ages past. We must conclude, then, that secondary education in America possesses great variety.

In spite of all these differences, however, there are also many similarities among these schools. Though there are important differences, we must remember that a student can transfer from private to parochial to public school with a minimum of difficulty and with little, if any, loss of academic credit. Likewise, one can move from any section of the country to any other and soon find his place in a new secondary school in his new community.

The similarities of these schools result from their springing from a common tradition, from their usage of standard textbooks which have national circulation, from the fact that the teachers come principally from liberal arts colleges or teachers colleges, from the standardizing work of the state departments of education and the great regional accrediting agencies. Despite the diversity of kind, size, control and clientele, these other factors have done much to make our secondary schools remarkably alike.

The fact that we have a common culture in the United States adds to the likeness of our schools. Though we are a people of diverse races, colors, creeds, cultures and national origins, we are all subject, to a large degree, to pressures which tend to blunt the cultural differences. The fact that children of recent immigrants become "Americanized" in a short time demonstrates that cultural differences tend to disappear or to remain only as vestigial elements. The third generation of an immigrant background frequently knows not the language of its grandparents.

Between America and Europe, there is a difference of opinion of what constitutes a secondary education. Even in America, there is not wholehearted agreement. Europeans and tradition-minded Americans regard secondary education as the educational experiences, usually during adolescence, which follow and are built upon the completion of a sound program of elementary education. They regard secondary education as high-caliber learning of "respectable" subject matter in the liberal arts—languages, both native and foreign, both modern and classical; mathematics, science and history. Indeed, in Europe, the secondary school is *the* liberal arts institution, and the graduate is expected to have completed his liberal and general education, for he goes to the university immediately for his specialized or professional education.

Under this traditional definition, the kind and degree of education is emphasized. Rigidly interpreted, an adolescent who has not mastered sufficiently the fundamentals of elementary education and who is not now engaged in the serious pursuit of the liberal arts would not be considered to be enrolled in a secondary school. If he were in a technical, non-academic or life-adjustment type of program, his education would be held to be post-elementary, not secondary.

A newer (though not necessarily better) point of view regarding the definition of secondary education has crept upon us in the United States. Espoused by those who hold that any subject is of [as] much value as any other subject, that it is a terrible crime against childhood and adolescence to retard a pupil, that every child (irrespective of his interests, abilities, aptitudes or gumption) ought to progress orderly through the school a grade per year until he has achieved a high school diploma after twelve years of sitting, that in a democracy every child must have the reward and that it is essentially undemocratic to deny a secondary education even to our intellectually lame, halt and blind—espoused by all these people, the newer conception of secondary education is that secondary education is the schooling of all adolescents who have reached a certain chronological age, usually twelve years. The emphasis is upon the *age* of the pupil, not upon the *subjects* he has mastered or is now studying.

In America, then, under this second definition, the life-adjustment program advocated by Prosser Douglass and a host of others must be regarded as worthy of inclusion in the secondary school. By the same token, those who adhere to the more traditional definition (Bestor, Lynd, Mortimer Smith) would reject much of what the high schools teach as being unworthy of a secondary school.

Here is the crux of the difficulty in American secondary education. Obviously our definition of secondary education and our philosophy of secondary education which grows out of this definition will determine, to a large extent, what we do in the American high school. Parenthetically, the writer would like to suggest that much of our contemporary confusion in American secondary education is due to the fact that we do not, as a people, have a consistent philosophy of education. We have many different philosophies clamoring for recognition, and until we have made a choice among them or have worked out a synthesis among them, we shall hardly know *what* to teach, *how* to teach or *whom* to teach, and we manifestly will not know *for what ends* we teach.[1]

Perhaps out of the present wide-spread public discussion of secondary education will evolve a certain consensus as to the purposes of the American high school.

Whatever may be its shortcomings in quality, the quantitive aspect of the American secondary school is phenomenal. From 1890 when only 6.7% of all persons between the ages of 14 and 17 were enrolled, we have advanced to an enrollment of 84.5% of persons between those ages. In contrast with the European concept, our secondary school has long since ceased to be an exclusive institution for the education of an elite. Rather, it is a logical upward extension of the common school. We cannot here develop in sufficient detail all the sociological factors which have enabled us to pile up this quantitative record, but it is impressive when we recall that perhaps half of the world's present population (estimated at 2,500,-000,000) is illiterate.

Among the factors which have committed America to secondary education for all are these: humanitarianism, our high standard of living and economic surplus which has enabled us to support our adolescents in leisure, the sense that democracy depends upon a wide extension of education beyond the elementary level, the large share of local control over the school program, the extreme desire of each generation to have its children endowed with advantages beyond its own reach, restriction of child labor and a profound national faith in education—perhaps too naïve a faith.

Until recent years, the Europeans knew exactly what they meant by secondary education. Secondary education was a system of schooling reserved for the intellectual and social elite, with some opportunity extended through charity or public grants for adolescents of exceptional ability from the lower social and economic classes to lift themselves by their bootstraps into this more favored element of society.

The European secondary schools were greatly influenced by the educational traditions established in the Renaissance. Since so much of the best thoughts of the most learned and accomplished masters of antiquity and even Renaissance society was written in Greek and Latin, naturally the Renaissance secondary schools emphasized a study of these ancient languages. The very names of European secondary schools reflect this indebtedness to antiquity. *Gymnasium,* the German name for the classical secondary school, comes from the Greek institution where young Greeks took their physical exercise naked and then engaged in philosophical discussions after the exercise period. (Perhaps the highest type of locker-room conversation ever known to the race of man.) The French *lycee* is named for the Lyceum, where Aristotle taught. The English and Early American *academy* is named for the place where Plato taught. Variations of these names, transposed into other European states, reflect the classical traditions of European secondary education.

As long as Europe held close to its classical background, and as long as the peasants and bourgeoisie could be held down, the classical secondary school was triumphant in Western Europe. To a large extent, it still is, for it has a powerful tradition and a proved record of intellectual achievement. Furthermore, we are led to believe that European society accords more prestige to the intellectual than does American culture. The writer recalls that his European students, fresh from the Netherlands, Poland and Czechoslovakia, clicked their heels and bowed in his presence; in fact, it took them some months to become so Americanized as to wave and shout "Hi!"

The spirit of democracy, let loose by World War I and World War II, partly breached the wall of the traditional European concept of secondary education. Under the Weimar Republic, the establishment of the *Grundschule,* a three-year elementary school for all classes, was a sign of the new thought. In Britain, the insistence was heard that the hitherto-deprived classes must have an opportunity at secondary schooling, either through public (in the American sense) council schools or through admission to the traditional public (i.e., private) schools by grants in aid. In France, there was a clamor for *l'ecole unique;* that is, a common school. At present, Britain is experimenting with a cosmopolitan secondary school not too different from the typical urban

---

[1]The writer discusses this point more in detail in his *American Secondary Education* (Odyssey Press, New York, 1957), particularly in a chapter entitled "A Philosophy of Secondary Education."

American high school which offers several curricula.

While an American can rejoice at the extension of secondary schooling to European boys and girls to whom it would have been denied in past generations, we might well be tempted to warn the Europeans that there are dangers in the concept that every adolescent should be in secondary school. We should, at the same time, recognize that many Europeans are not satisfied with their rather highly restrictive system and are moving closer to American practice.

Education for all is a great American ideal. Perhaps, as a slogan carved in granite over an entrance to the Pennsylvania State Education Building indicates, it is America's greatest contribution to civilization. It expresses the idealism, the optimism and the nobility of American democracy. It is a marvelous concept. But some of us who have lived and taught through the last three decades have reservations and, in our more perplexed and despondent moments, wonder sometimes whether this may not be too naïve a faith— a faith motivated by the best intentions and the noblest purposes, but a faith that loses touch with the reality of human nature. We sometimes wonder if we may not have drunk too deeply of the heady wines bottled by Condorcet who ardently espoused the concept of the indefinite perfectibility of man.

Certainly we have enrolled in our high schools this year many young people who are not achieving, even within the most generous and sympathetic evaluation, anywhere near enough to justify their idleness or the expense to the community and state. This sad condition is due to one of two facts: They do not want what the school offers or we do not offer what they want. There may be another factor: They may just want nothing that a school could conceivably offer them.

We may have great sympathy with those pupils of limited ability who try hard and do not have a real measure of demonstrable success. It is harder to be sympathetic with those who have ability and do not use it. To promote the latter and eventually to give them diplomas compounds laziness and teaches the dishonesty of a reward without effort. Admittedly, in the unique experiment of attempting, for the first time in the history of civilization, to make a high school education available to all youth, we have made mistakes. Let us not be ashamed of these errors and let us not apologize too abjectly for them. But let us not continue making them and concealing them. The recently reported action of certain Canadian high schools and at least one Massachusetts school

in dismissing persons of ability who did not perform should be watched with interest. Perhaps the time has come for us to declare that the opportunity for secondary education shall be open to all but that pupils will be dismissed when the point of diminishing returns sets in.

The school is more than a custodial agency. As long as a pupil learns anything that is of value to him and to society, he should be retained, but we ought not to retain non-performers just to keep them off the labor market or to exercise our humanitarianism. Just as Captain John Smith is supposed to have said "Those who don't work, don't eat," we might well say "Those who don't learn, don't stay." Revision of compulsory attendance laws and child labor laws may be necessary.

Society has no right to expect the school to be primarily a custodial institution, with baby sitting as its objective. If there must be custodial institutions, let us set them up outside the high school or let us build a system of national deep freezes to store our surplus non-learners until they pass the compulsory school age. We have a precedent in the storage of surplus butter and cheese in the caves of Kansas and in the payment of federal subsidies to farmers not to produce agricultural products.

A nation which has been relatively complacent regarding its secondary education became most alert when Sputnik I and Sputnik II began orbiting around the earth. We were reminded by countless newspaper and television commentators that the Russian secondary school student has a longer and more extensive background in mathematics and the sciences than the American counterpart. The fact that 40% of our secondary schools offer little or no science was reported in such a way as to imply that 40% of American high school students received little or no instruction in these fields. Two facts were not mentioned: first, these 40% of American high schools are small institutions which enroll proportionately few students; second, the Russian secondary school is a selective and competitive institution, whereas the American school enrolls almost all youths of high school age.

We must recognize, however, that many boys and girls who could study science and mathematics with profit are lulled into a false sense of security by being permitted to take "snap courses" and watered-down "life-adjustment" programs. When psychological studies appeared to blast the foundations of mental discipline and transfer of training, some educators concluded that all subjects were of equal importance, and neglected what were long considered to be the fundamental constants of the school program.

There is a present danger that we may irrationally swing to the other extreme of the pendulum and insist upon a rigorous exposure to a strong program of mathematics and science for all adolescents. Such procedure could be little less than tragic for we do not now have a sufficient supply of competent teachers in these fields to teach all the more than ten million pupils now in our secondary schools. When Mrs. Wiggs' children brought guests home, she stretched the soup by putting water into it, but it would be precarious to water down our teachers of mathematics and science by suddenly retreading teachers of other subjects. Having once been taught French by a retreaded teacher of German, the writer is dubious about the quality of teaching that would result.

Undoubtedly, a higher percentage of our students could profitably study mathematics and science, but we would scarcely care to have repeated here some of the shoddy teaching that characterized Russian teaching in the 1930's, as revealed by emigre writers in *Soviet Education*.[2]

At the risk of alienating some of his fellow professors of education who have drunk deeply and perhaps unwisely of the wines of progressivism and at the risk of being accused of going to bed with Bestor, the writer ventures to suggest that the time has come to restore to the American high school a greater degree of intellectual content, at least for students of average and superior ability. Homogeneous grouping in academic subjects seems indicated. Students who can perform well must be expected to do so. Essay writing must again be cultivated, and the objective examination, whose chief merit is a quick get-away for the teacher, must be reduced to its proper subordinate place.

At the same time, the remarkable progress we have made in understanding the less academic pupil and in inducting him into as much of our culture as he can take must be preserved. Contrary to the traditional European practice, we must teach more than the intellectual aristocracy.

A fundamental presupposition is the idea that we must teach our society that intellectualism must not be suspect and that academic excellence should be encouraged and rewarded at least as much as excellence in other fields—athletics and social adjustment, for example. Unfortunately, the tone of our society and of our schools is such that some students try not to excel lest they be considered maladjusted and "squares."

Firm standards but not the ruthless elimination of those who have academic difficulties is a prescription. A colleague of the writer, Dr. Hagen Staack, has called to his attention something which he has never seen in print and something which is pertinent here. Of the sixty leading Nazis who surrounded Hitler, very few were university graduates. Most of them, like Hitler himself, had been educated enough to despise the lower classes but not enough to be acceptable by the established ruling class. They were frustrated semi-intellectuals who felt a deep resentment against those who had succeeded in the *Gymnasium* and university. Too rigid an elimination of pupils from American secondary schools and colleges might well promote social unrest in our republic, for it is psychologically defensible to strike out, even blindly, if one feels unjustly treated. On the other hand, there is no justification to water-down the content for the superior students to match the pace of plodders, and there is no justification in forcing a pseudo-education upon those who will not or cannot profit from it.

Comparative education is a most valuable study in the preparation of teachers. Traditionally, some comparative education was formerly included in the undergraduate preparation of teachers, usually in a course in the history of education. Unfortunately, we have become so obsessed with the psychological aspects of education and with pragmatic "how to do it" courses that we have neglected the historical and comparative aspects. Without the perspective of history and philosophy, many of our present high school teachers become so engrossed in their day-to-day procedures that they never attempt to build a personal philosophy of education. An intensive study of our historical development and a comparison of our educational traditions and present procedures with those in other leading nations would undoubtedly be a rewarding experience. Even secondary school administrators might well lift their eyes from the sale of bus tickets, from the wrangling of the local interscholastic league and even from the inventory of audio-visual aids to consider the principal functions of the secondary school. They might well ponder these questions: *What* shall we teach? *Whom* shall we teach? *Who* shall teach? *How* shall we teach? *For what ends* shall we teach? A study of American secondary education in comparison and contrast with European philosophies and procedures would be helpful in the development of a perspective. It might make us more perceptive in working out a program of American secondary education for the remainder of our century.

---

[2] *Soviet Education*, edited by George L. Kline. Routledge and Kegan Paul, Ltd., London. 1957.

Comparative education: a growing force

AN APPRAISAL OF PROBLEMS IN COMPARATIVE EDUCATION

Perhaps one of the most fruitful approaches in considering other systems of education is to identify a particular problem in our own system and then to discover whether the same problem exists in some other system and whether a solution for us is suggested by the way it is handled elsewhere. In this manner Readings 85 and 86 have investigated the development of talent and the decision as to what kind of further education may be appropriate. These articles are valuable not only for their factual content but as models of the methodological approach to the problems of comparative education. Both selections are concerned with analyzing the history and structure of education and utilize contrastive analyses in reaching conclusions.

85

James B. Conant

DEVELOPMENT OF TALENT IN EUROPE AND THE UNITED STATES

In this address Dr. Conant points out rather succinctly that the concern of the American educational system is so totally different from that of secondary and higher education in Europe as to make any real imitation of one by the other quite difficult. It is his opinion that in the area of citizenship education "we do a far better job . . . than any other nation in the world." As a competent scientist, Conant separates his recital of facts from his personal viewpoint. By setting forth his proposals and propositions in a reasoned, direct manner and avoiding emotional or hortatory appeals, he leaves the reader in a better position to draw conclusions from the data.

I am well aware that the use of the word "talent" is a bit old-fashioned and not in accord with modern scientific usage. The words "aptitude" and "ability" I recognize are much more current in psychological circles.

I am further aware that those who have studied this whole problem can easily show that any concept such as I am going to use this evening is a vast oversimplification; that no talent or aptitude is simple, but is composed of a number of different factors. But let me go directly to the subject which I have chosen to discuss.

From *North Central Association Quarterly*, Vol. XXXIV, No. 4, April 1960, 265-272. This address was delivered at a meeting of the Commission on Secondary Schools in Chicago, April 23, 1959.

First, I shall remind you of the structure of education in Europe and in the United States. I am speaking of the free nations of Europe, of course; I am going to leave the Soviet Union and its satellites out of account. I will tell you frankly that I think we have heard too much about Russian education.

I am going to talk primarily about Germany, which I know best—Free Germany—and Switzerland; but what I have to say I think would not be very different if one brought into account France and Italy and perhaps the Scandinavian countries, too.

In Continental free nations the educational system is so set up that many families and many children make a tremendously important choice at age approximately eleven. Something like 20 percent of an age group are selected and enrolled in what I will call pre-university schools. They are selected, of course, from only those who apply —an important point which I shall refer to later.

Those who do not apply, or who are not selected for these pre-university schools, go to work at fourteen. The rest of their education for two years is in what we would call a continuation school. There is an intermediate school in certain of the German states and certain Swiss cantons, but this is roughly the situation.

This is quite different from our system of education, which in most states goes to sixteen, seventeen, or eighteen years of age. The university structure is vastly different, too.

One day, when I was in Bonn as High Commissioner, I had the privilege of entertaining a distinguished American. He said, "Could you tell me what is the best liberal arts college in Germany?"

I said, "I am sorry, but there is no such thing anywhere on the continent of Europe."

I don't think he believed me, but I was telling the truth. A liberal arts college is nonexistent on the continent of Europe. The universities are essentially a collection of professional schools— law, medicine, science, theology, and engineering, though in Germany the engineering and some of the sciences are in a separate type. These institutions enroll something like 7 percent of youths of college age; whereas, a larger proportion of our young people go to private schools than would be true in Germany or Switzerland. Perhaps 10 percent or so go to our private schools, for the most part church-connected institutions. I think you would all agree that we could cite a great diversity in our tax-supported schools— a tremendous diversity as compared to Europe. It was easy for me to sum up the European situation in a few sentences. It would take all night to go through, in corresponding detail, what is going on here in the United States.

This diversity has impressed me greatly; and among the many things that I think the average citizen is unaware of, and is therefore apt to be mistaken about in his judgment of American tax-supported education, is the fact that he does not know of the diversity to which I have just alluded. This diversity might be of several types.

In the first place, is the diversity we don't like. It is the diversity we speak of when we mention a good school or a poor school, a school totally inadequately financed or one that is almost, perhaps, adequately financed. The kind of diversity we would hope gradually to reduce—to eliminate, if you will—through more financial support and better administrative decisions, and better recruiting of teachers, too.

The second kind of diversity—experimentation —is a virtue of our system, with its local control and its thousands and thousands of school boards throughout the United States. Surely we will all agree that through diversified experimentation we have made great progress in the last fifty years in solving some of the problems that have confronted the administrators and the teachers in our tax-supported schools.

A third sort of diversity—and this I find the layman so little aware of—is that which comes from the dissimilarity of communities which the schools are serving, particularly the high schools, in which I have been most concerned. The difference between a high-income residential area, for example, outside of a large city is a case in point. I can think of one in the East where 90 percent of the families insist on their boys and girls entering college. Sometimes, at least, they are very specific in their ambitions in regard to a particular college—more specific than the ability of the boy or girl will sometimes warrant. This situation presents problems to the administrator.

The contrast between that community and one in low-income sections of a large city is tremendous. I am sure you all know so well that what would be a good high school in one community would be a poor high school in another. This fact, I think, is very often overlooked by the critics of American public education.

But quite apart from this difference, you then have another based on a number of factors. From my point of view, I would like to discuss, first of all, the difference in size.

I am impressed by the fact that there are some 17,000 high schools with graduating classes of less than 100, which enroll something like one-third of the students of high school age. My point of view, from what I have seen and heard, is that such schools have great difficulty providing for the development of the students' talents except at exorbitant expense.

Then, too, 4,000 high schools take care of two-thirds of the students who are in tax-supported secondary schools. They in turn might perhaps be arranged in two categories: first, what I like to call the "widely comprehensive high school," which is offering a great variety of elective programs, including those supported by Smith-Hughes money, which provide vocational courses particularly for boys; and second, the limited comprehensive high school—limited because the community is not interested in having any of its children take vocational work even in the eleventh and twelfth grades. Therefore, this would be the high-income suburban type, with the families all having strong collegiate ambitions. Thus, such a high school is different from the widely comprehensive institution because it is serving a different kind of community.

A school may be limited in its comprehensiveness also by state laws or by the city situation. I am thinking of the vocational, separate tax-supported schools which one finds in large cities, for the most part, scattered throughout the United States; such as in Connecticut, Massachusetts, and Wisconsin. In those three states, because of the way in which the Smith-Hughes money is administered, one can say that there are both vocational tax-supported high schools and limited comprehensive high schools.

Then, in a few cities in the East, the selective academic high school exists of which the Bronx High School of Science is perhaps the most talked about in recent years; but the Boston Latin School is surely the oldest.

Another way of looking at the problem is to see how the students divide between these schools. The following are rough estimates.

That one-third are found in the small high schools seems clear. Of the two-thirds in the other schools (I am talking about tax-supported schools), it would appear that something like one-half, about one-third of the total, are in what I call the widely comprehensive high schools, and the other in schools which are limited in their comprehensiveness either by state laws or by being in large cities or suburban communities which are not interested in vocational work.

Something like 10 percent of the population seems to live in those communities, including New York City, where a selective academic high school is available for those who want it. I think we can neglect that purpose, however, and speak in general, as I shall, of the development of talents in the comprehensive high school, limited or otherwise, as contrasted to the development of the academic talents in the European situation.

I have already spoken about the diversity of our colleges and our universities and their wide coverage as compared to the universities of Europe—community colleges, state universities, private and public, many of different sorts offering a great variety of programs.

So much for the general framework of the two systems.

What are the talents that I have in mind? I am going to name six. You may have a very different list but, for the purposes of the evening, bear with me as I briefly run through how it seems to me they are handled on the two sides of the Atlantic Ocean.

First of all, if you will, is a talent for dealing with people—leadership—give it many names. It is a group of talents, I suppose, but of first importance in a democracy; second, athletic talent; third, musical talent; fourth, artistic talent; fifth, what I shall call manipulative talent; and sixth, academic talent.

Frankly, in Europe at the taxpayers' expense and in the formal school system, practically nothing is done to develop the first four: the talent for getting on with people, athletic talent, musical talent, and artistic talent. Only the last two, the manipulative and the academic, would be considered by most Europeans as falling within the scope of their educational system.

On the contrary, in the United States we have seen a tremendous movement toward developing all four talents to which I have just referred. The talent for dealing with people is so general and so difficult to define that I would speak of it in the general terms of what we accomplish or attempt to accomplish by courses in the social studies, by our organization of the school, by extracurricular activities in part, and by school government and organization.

If you will allow me to let this situation merge with education for citizenship, I think I can make a positive statement that any foreign observer who tries really to find out what is going on in our tax-supported schools will come to the conclusion that we do a far better job in this respect, including education for citizenship, than any other nation in the world.

The Germans, I found, were not very enthusiastic about some features of our system, but both in Germany and in Switzerland I was asked time and again, "What do you do about education for citizenship? We know it is good. We would like to imitate it if we could."

I suppose the diversity in regard to the development of athletic talent is less than in almost any other. I have this feeling about athletic talent, however: It is the one about which you can talk to a layman realistically and with understanding.

This, I submit, is not without value. Sometimes when I try to get across certain points I use the analogy of athletic talent, for almost without exception the layman, including the parent, recognizes that athletic skill, the final result, involves both identifying somebody with natural talent and securing a good coach to develop it; sometimes, however, there is the feeling that a teacher ought to be able to develop academic skills quite irrespective of the natural endowment of the child.

I now turn to the musical and artistic talent. I don't have to tell you what has been done in this country and in this century to develop this gift.

But here I am sure you will agree that one could find the greatest diversity. I could name school systems in which not much more is being done than in the European schools; but I could name others in which a great deal is being done at taxpayers' expense for avocational ends and almost on a professional level, too, though in some cases private funds are also involved.

The European would say, "Oh, that has nothing to do with the state. That is entirely private, and requires special time and special money. If they want to develop their musical and artistic talents, let them."

I think in no respect is the European situation more different than in its disregard for the development of the musical and artistic capabilities of its students in contrast with the United States.

Now I come to manipulative talent, which when developed leads to skills of a competent craftsman or technician and, in certain cases, although they must be developed in a different way, to those of a surgeon, a painter, or a chemist. It is a funny thing that we make these distinctions about manipulative talent and place them in different parts of our educational system.

We hear some people say that scientists have no manipulative talents. I used to be a professor of chemistry, and I remember well a doctoral student who was working with me. Everything went wrong. Every piece of apparatus broke. Finally he said, "I don't know what is the matter. I don't have any luck. The bottom has dropped out of this beaker again." I replied, "I would advise you to drop chemistry. Nobody wants to hire an unlucky chemist."

But I am talking about the kind of manipulative talent that is not associated directly with the sciences or the medical or the artistic professions; that is, the potential that is developed in the skills of the competent workman and the technician.

In Europe this would be recognized as part of the educational system. Indeed, both in Switzerland and in Germany they would say that a great deal of their industrial success is based upon an educational system for developing the manipulative talents, but quite apart from the academic.

In Europe when a boy graduates and leaves the common school at age fourteen, he goes to work. If he is interested in becoming a skilled workman, his first job will be as an apprentice in one of the schools of the great industrial plants. If you go to the Ruhr, for example, and visit any of their big industries, they will show you with great pride their school, and you will see boys of fourteen starting to spend most of their time developing manual skills.

In addition, the state provides continuation instruction in related subjects and, to some extent (but at a modicum), in the development of an understanding of the history and the significance of the country.

And then, in both Germany and Switzerland, after an apprentice has completed the foregoing training and has had a few years' experience as a skilled workman, he may take certain examinations which involve some knowledge of mathematics. This mathematics, however, is nothing like that required for university admission. Having passed these examinations, the workman is enrolled at age eighteen or twenty in a technicum, or engineering school, for a year or two at government expense. The technicum requires much less mathematics and science than engineering. Through this method they develop and train the people who will be the foremen within the plants.

We see here a whole system. But it does not approximate the vocational basis for the industrial arts in our widely conceived comprehensive high schools, or in tax-supported vocational schools.

Finally, we come to academic talent. The development of academic talent in Europe is what people are thinking about when they praise the European schools. There are roughly three types of these schools. I shall refer to them as pre-university schools for easy identification.

In Germany and in Switzerland (German-speaking and French-speaking Switzerland, too) first is the Gymnasium in which instruction for eight or nine years is based on Latin, Greek (and the possibility of a third language, which would be, of course, a modern language), mathematics, science, and some history. Of course, the development of a knowledge of the literature and composition of the domestic tongue would be included also.

The second type would drop Greek and substitute a modern foreign language.

The third type would drop both Latin and Greek and offer two or possibly three modern foreign languages, with a little more emphasis on science and mathematics than in the other two types.

A very heated argument is going on in both Germany and Switzerland—and I believe in France, to some extent—as to which of these three types is preferable. Actually, in terms of the numbers I have seen, the more popular is the type with Latin but no Greek; the third type, however, which could be called scientific and modern language, is growing in both popularity and importance.

Those who cling to the classical tradition represented by Greek and Latin feel this is a radical step backwards; and you can start a very good argument in many European circles about the relative advantages of the three types of pre-university schools.

Whichever type it is, selection is rigorous; not more than 20 percent of an age group can enter. The course is stiff, and there is a lot of competition, many examinations, much homework, and from one-half to two-thirds drop out. One sometimes gets the impression that all with academic talents are automatically drawn into these schools, whereas those without such ability are excluded.

This is far from being the case. In Europe, far more than in the United States, family tradition plays an enormous rôle. Therefore, there will be great numbers of families in every German state and in every Swiss canton that would never think of trying to have a son or daughter enroll in one of these pre-university schools, however bright they might be.

I talked to the minister-president of one of the large German states, a Social Democratic state ever since the start of the Federal Republic. He said sadly, "You know, we have done all we could in this state to make education cheap, to make it available to everybody, but I must confess we have had no luck in getting our universities really to enroll any large number of the sons of the peasants or of the workers."

The reason was quite clear. Those families just never would think of trying to get their children enrolled in these pre-university schools, although they were free and run at state expense.

How is the selection made? Knowing some of the problems of American education in regard to deciding who will enter what types of institution and who will not and who will elect what subject, I took a particular interest in both of these problems when I was in Germany, and also when I visited Switzerland two years ago. In Germany, selection varies from town to town and from state to state; and in Switzerland, almost from canton to canton, too. Sometimes it is based upon teacher evaluation, sometimes upon written examinations, but never as far as I am aware, upon psychological tests. Aptitude tests have hardly reached the Continent as yet.

I was talking to a very capable administrator in one of the Swiss cantons about this problem. Since boys and girls go to separate schools, as they do in Germany, and since there are the three types I have spoken of, six schools are involved with selection. They all pick out their students at about age eleven. After he had explained their process, I said, "Don't you have any problem with the parents? Aren't there some parents in this canton who are anxious to have their boys and girls enroll in these schools, and yet you don't feel they have the ability to profit from it?"

"Oh yes," he said, "we do. We have really quite a lot of trouble there."

"Couldn't they make trouble for you politically in the canton election?"

"Yes, you are quite right, they could. The problem is getting worse each year."

"What do you do about it?"

"Well, I'll tell you. We get the parents of that group together in the spring, before we make the selection, and we tell them about these schools, and we point out to them that they are very, very difficult indeed, that it is a great deal of hard work, that half to two-thirds will fail, and the students who fail might have great psychological difficulties because they have to transfer back into the common school; or, if beyond fourteen, they can't go to school at all except privately. And then we say to them, 'After all, this school just prepares for the university, and it is very difficult. Unless you are awfully sure your boy or girl is able to do it, why try it? It's just a road to a university.' We tell them that, after all, the university prepares for the professions, and there is no money really in that."

"Well," I said, "does it work?"

"Oh yes," he said, "it works very well. We are very successful in keeping the pressure down."

"Don't you miss some good students in that way? Aren't there some families that ought to be persuaded to have their children apply?"

He looked at me in amazement and said, "But you don't want all the bright boys and girls to go to a university, do you? Don't you want them in other kinds of work, too?"

I felt like saying, "In the United States we would say, 'Yes, we do want them all in the university, and maybe that is one difference between Europe and the United States.'"

I might have added, "I have met some people in Switzerland, too, who are deeply worried as to whether all their potential talent, particularly in science and engineering, was developing as it should," but I let it go.

Perhaps, if I had been accurate, I would have said to him, "We in the United States are interested in and concerned about having all the potential university students receive a university education." In this regard I think there has been a change in mood; and to this change I attribute some of the misunderstanding between the citizens, on the one hand, and those who are operating and teaching in our public schools, on the other. To this change I also ascribe some of the unfair and intemperate criticisms of our publicly-supported schools.

If I remember rightly, back in the 1930's the great public concern—and the people who expressed it were leaders of public education—was with education for citizenship, for establishing a continuing basis for a free society, for understanding the American way of life. With Nazism rampant in Germany and Fascism in Italy and Communism winning converts in Free France, people were concerned with the education of all youth as future American citizens.

Then came World War II with its overriding priorities. Another concern burst forth in which scientists, engineers, mathematical people with aptitudes, were important for winning in the shortest possible time. And now, a mood, increasing since the end of World War II, recognizes the grim struggle we are in with the Soviet Union, and that we live in a deeply divided world marked by atomic weapons and intercontinental missiles. As a consequence people are anxious to an unprecedented degree about whether or not all the potential academic talent is being found and developed. But I don't have to tell *you*. Your own project on discovering and guiding superior and talented students illustrates your own concern with this new mood.

In summary, let me make a few points about developing academic talents in our schools.

First of all, talents should be developed before leaving high school—all of them that I have referred to. If they are not, it is too late in terms of the national interest.

Second, it is quite out of the question to do what a few laymen would suggest, namely, to develop the academic talents through a required curriculum. One of the unfortunate by-products of sputnik is the contention that everybody should be required to study mathematics or foreign language for four years. I don't have to tell this audience that this is utter nonsense. Furthermore, these talents cannot be developed by a required curriculum even for the able, academically talented students. Again I don't have to tell you how impossible that would be.

But I do believe—and here some of you may disagree with me—that because of the national interest, which is quite different from what it was in the 1930's, nationwide those who have academic talents should be urged to develop them to the full while they are in school, and then go on to college.

As for mathematics and languages, I believe that those who have the potentialities for both should study them in high school; otherwise, many doors will later be closed—and I am not referring to college or university admission, which is quite a separate matter. I submit that there is a great

deal of evidence that in every school there is a certain fraction who can do both, and many others who have the talent to do one or the other.

I have visited widely comprehensive high schools where a good share of the academically talented students in four years elected eighteen or twenty courses with homework; and a good deal of homework certainly is required by the program I am recommending.

In addition to studying four years of one foreign language and four years of mathematics I think they should study three years of science, four years of English (which ought to be required of all), and three or four years of social studies, too.

So much for my own personal prejudice on this subject.

If I were to try to sum up the great difference between European and American tax-supported education, I would say the difference is that the Europeans are committed to developing only two talents, and those quite extensively—the manipulative talent by one road (and very largely who will follow that road is determined by family tradition, something approaching a caste system, if you will), and the academic talent by another; that is, through the pre-university school.

In the United States we have developed a system of schools which in many communities, but not all, are concerned with developing a great range of capabilities, each according to his own talents.

These two big differences, it seems to me, go fundamentally to the present controversy over the structure of American public education and what should be done about it. I believe that it is possible to develop in one school the variety of talents characteristic of any student body and to do justice to them all.

I know there are many people who disagree with me. They would say, "Unless you isolate, as they do in Europe, those with the potential academic talents, and concentrate on them, you cannot do justice to them." I disagree. I could name schools which give evidence to the contrary.

I believe that no radical change is required in the basic pattern of American tax-supported education, both elementary and secondary, to make it satisfactory even in this divided world with all the threats and problems that we have with the Soviet Union.

Sometimes I have met well-intentioned, interested parents or laymen who would say, "Seriously, now, don't you think we ought to import the European system?" These people, of course, have heard only of the European pre-university school. Sometimes they have thought that, of course, their own children would be automatically enrolled in these schools, but never about the selective feature or the fact that one-half to two-thirds of the enrolees fail.

Sometimes, just for the fun of it, I would say, "Let's see what it would take to Europeanize American tax-supported education—indeed, American education altogether.

"In the first place, you would have to eliminate all the four-year liberal arts colleges—over 1,000 of them. That would be quite a job. Secondly, you would have to change profoundly the undergraduate curricula in many universities. All the practical work and all the things corresponding to liberal education would be eliminated, and you would turn your universities into professional schools.

"The third thing you would have to do would be to have uniform standards of admission; whereas, there is only one in a European country. Then you would have to change the laws affecting the employment of youth." This I underline to lay audiences.

"You would have not only to change the laws affecting the employment of youth, but also the attitude of management and labor unions, and revert to the situation in 1900 when a boy or girl could get a job, and many did, at age thirteen or fourteen.

"Then, of course, you would have to eliminate all the school boards—abolish all of them—and put the control of the schools in somebody's hands at the state capital who would determine not only the details of the curriculum but who would recruit and hire the teachers and assign them to specific schools in specific towns, without anybody in town having anything to say about it.

"You would also have to provide part-time education—continuation schools—for most of the potential citizens over fourteen years of age.

"But, more important than that, you would have to reverse the whole thinking of the American people. You would have to give up this idea of the importance of local responsibility and local pride in the schools. You also would have to change your attitude toward two concepts which, formulated as ideals, have guided so many generations. I refer to equality of opportunity and equality of status of all forms of honest labor."

Now, frankly, anybody who wants to undertake seriously to bring about any one of those changes is welcome to the job! In my opinion he wouldn't get to first base, nor should he; for I am convinced that we can make every one of those 4,000 high schools as satisfactory as the best in the United States. We can do it provided that the citizens in each community understand the problem, support the schools, and that you and your colleagues in turn will strive with the members of the community to work out the problems school by school. This will take cooperative effort, both among you and with the universities as well. . . .

86

Philip E. Vernon

SECONDARY SCHOOL EDUCATION AND SELECTION IN ENGLAND

In this article an Englishman discusses the effects of the examination system used in England to determine which students will be permitted or encouraged to go to secondary schools. It is of interest that this particular feature of the English system (which a few Americans would have us emulate) is under attack by some Englishmen. Vernon presents a particularly concise description of the English system of education besides pointing out some of its strengths and shortcomings. The "discussion" section of his article contains some interesting conclusions and implications for American education. For example, he reports that "performance on intelligence, as well as achievement, tests tends to be raised by attendance at the better grammar schools and to drop relatively, or fail to increase so rapidly, in the less stimulating modern schools." Do we have counterparts of this problem in America? What is being done in your state to raise the quality of elementary and secondary schools? Vernon's article will provoke other similar questions applicable to American education.

How should we organise our secondary education so as to ensure that pupils in their 'teens will get the kind of schooling which most fully develops their intellectual potentialities? Every civilized country has its own answer to this question, and most of them appear to be very doubtful whether they have yet found the right answer. The system in England is about as different as it could be from that in the United States, and I am going to describe it, not with any intention of advocating its adoption elsewhere (though it does have its strengths as well as its weaknesses), but rather because such a description may help American educators to see some of their own problems in a fresh light.

To understand the English system we must view it historically. A century ago the only advanced education was provided by the so-called public boarding schools (Eton, Winchester, etc.) and the Foundation grammar schools—an education centered round the Classics, whose object was to train men for the universities and the Church. Apart from a few poor scholars, only the sons of the wealthy upper and middle classes could attend these schools. For the vast masses, education was a charity provided by the Churches and other voluntary bodies; indeed the provision of schooling by the State was violently opposed until the reforms of 1870 and 1902. Under the monitorial system, huge classes were taught at minimum cost and with a minimum of trained staff. The curriculum was confined almost wholly to the 3 R's, together with moral instruction which emphasized the virtues of hard work and of keeping to one's proper station in life.

Naturally the picture has changed a great deal since the introduction of universal, compulsory schooling from 5 to 12, later 14, and now 15 years. But the hierarchical structure of independent schools, state-maintained grammar schools, technical and secondary modern schools—closely linked with the social class structure—is still very pronounced.

The independent schools charge high fees; entry is by competitive examinations at 14 (sometimes 11), and the pupils mostly come from private preparatory schools, where the classical languages are taught. They usually stay on till 18 or 19 and enter the universities, and the staff are all university graduates (preferably Oxford or Cambridge), who have *not* undergone any teacher training. Most professional and upper business class parents feel that they are losing face if they cannot send their children to one of these schools, and a "public" or independent-school ed-

ucation is still a considerable asset in admission to higher executive posts, including civil service administration and Army, Navy or Air Force commissions. In addition there are a number of minor private schools patronised by the parents who dislike the State school system but who cannot afford public school fees, or whose children are not clever enough to gain admission to the more reputable grammar schools. In all something like ten per cent of those receiving full-time education between 11 and 18 are attending independent schools of one kind or another, and they still supply nearly half the university populations of Oxford and Cambridge and a major proportion of the upper professional and business classes.

Next in the hierarchy come the State-supported grammar schools, run by the Local Education Authorities, entry to which depends on passing the notorious "11 plus examination." (In fact the examination is taken in the junior schools by the 10½-11½ year age group.) These schools were set up after the 1902 Act of Parliament, but have grown very irregularly so that in some counties and cities only 9 or 10 per cent, in others 40 per cent, or even, in Wales, 69 per cent of the school population gain entry, the overall figure for the country averaging about 20 per cent. At first these followed the same academic curriculum as their prototypes, albeit only a tiny proportion of their pupils reached the universities, and the great majority left at 16 or 17 years. But modern languages soon displaced the previously dominant classics, and science courses by now occupy as many pupils in grammar and independent schools as Arts or humanistic courses. The curriculum is quite broad up till 15 or 16, but then the minority who stay on into the sixth form and (usually) enter universities can specialize on biological or physical sciences, mathematics, modern or classical languages, etc., the choice being governed largely by parents' wishes and the school's advice.

These schools have such high prestige because a grammar school education is almost essential for university entrance and for the professions, and indeed for teaching, nursing and most higher clerical jobs. Their staffs consist of university graduates who have had one year's training in a university education department. The great majority of middle-class parents regard it as a social disgrace if their children fail to gain a place in any grammar school; and a majority of upper working-class parents likewise refuse to regard any education not given in a grammar school as "secondary." Prior to the 1944 Education Act (the Butler Act), children who failed the admission

From *Educational Forum*, March 1957, 21:261-269.

examination could usually gain entry by paying very moderate fees. But now that all State education is free, this loophole is blocked and at least 50 per cent of the population are competing for schools which will only take 20 per cent. Note too that the middle-class parents, who are the most vocal and the most likely to pass on complaints and criticisms to the press and to Members of Parliament, are put on the same footing as the working classes, unless they can afford private or independent school fees. Hence the tremendous pressure on their children to "pass the 11 plus," and the current controversies over secondary school selection.

Technical, commercial and art schools cover only some three per cent of the 11 (or 13) to 16 year population, again with wide variations in different areas. Entry is also competitive, and the parents of very bright children *can* choose to send them there—if available; but for the most part they get the next slice of the ability range, after the grammar schools have had the pick. However, the climate of public opinion is changing, with the realisation of the country's need for more technologists and technicians, and we may expect the numbers, and the prestige, of such schools to rise in the next few years. But the bias against vocational education is still strong, although it is obvious that the humanistic or scientific curricula of the grammar schools are far too academic for the majority of their pupils. (Actually far fewer than the 20 per cent who enter complete the full grammar school course. About one third leave at 15 to 16 without passing any examination, and another third at 16 to 17 with only moderate successes in a few subjects. There can be little doubt that many of these would have been better suited by a more vocationally biased education.) Fortunately there is considerable provision of technical education for 15 or 16 to 19 year olds after leaving school in Further Education Centres, in Technical Colleges, and within industry itself.

We are left now with roughly three-quarters of the population who fail to gain entry to any of these selective schools. "Higher Grade" schools for supplementing the purely elementary education provided by the Church and State schools began in the 1890's, and from 1902 onwards these developed as senior or central schools in populous areas. However a considerable proportion of children, especially in rural areas, stayed on in the elementary schools till leaving age. Some of these senior schools undertook excellent experimental programs among their older pupils, but the majority merely provided a dull continuation of the elementary curriculum to keep the children busy till they went to work at 14. With the passing of the 1944 Act, such schools have been rechristened "secondary modern" schools, and pupils stay on till 15. In intention there was to be parity of esteem between these and other secondary schools—grammar or technical, and allocation to one or other of them was to be based purely on "age, ability and aptitude." But in practice the modern schools still suffer from the stigma of cheap education for the poor, and—as their pupils are predominantly lower working-class— both middle and upper working-class parents tend to despise them. Many of them have admirable modern buildings and equipment, but others are still housed in the worst kind of "slum" school. Early in this century most of their teachers had themselves left school at 16 to 17 and many were untrained, except on the job. By now they have almost all had a 2 to 3 year training college course since leaving school at 17 to 18. But the fact that very few have university degrees contributes further to their poor prestige. It is by no means impossible for the brighter modern pupils to gain transfers to technical or grammar schools or, after leaving, to work up and achieve a university degree or other distinction. But not more than about two per cent succeed in doing so and thus, in effect, failure at 11 plus does mean limitation to a "manual" rather than a "white-collar" job. Being untrammeled by external examination requirements, some modern schools develop broad and attractive curricula with technical, commercial, artistic, agricultural or other biases. But in far too many the pupils come from homes unconcerned about, or opposed to, education. They have been dubbed failures, are bored and rebellious, and the school does little to stimulate their interest.

Selection procedure at eleven plus

Since each Local Authority administers the procedure for admission to its own secondary schools, there are considerable variations. However the majority employ standardised objective tests of verbal intelligence, English and Arithmetic, new versions of these being constructed annually for the purpose by Moray House and other testing organizations. The three standard scores (loosely referred to as I.Q.s, E.Q.s and A.Q.s) are totalled, and entry to grammar school depends mainly on amassing a combined quotient of 340 and over— the figure being adjusted in accordance with the number of places available. Some Authorities prefer the more traditional type of English and Arithmetic examinations, including an essay, despite the subjectivity involved in marking thousands of these papers; and still others substitute gradings or rank orders of attainment supplied by the junior school teachers. It is generally realised that age allowances must be incorporated in these measures in order to give the youngest children in a year's age group an equal chance with the oldest. However, decisions are rarely based on objective test scores or examination marks alone; clearly those scoring 340 are negligibly superior to those scoring 339. Hence a border-zone group consisting of five per cent or so scoring above, and five per cent below, the borderline usually receive more detailed individual consideration. Junior school reports are studied, or the children may be given additional tests, or interviewed by a panel of teachers, or by the staff of the grammar school concerned.

So important is the examination to children's careers, and so widely criticised by teachers as well as by disgruntled parents, politicians and the press, that it has been the topic of a tremendous volume of research. When the results are compared with pupils' achievements 1, 2, and even up to 5 years later in the secondary schools, the efficiency of predictions given by a typical battery of tests, examinations and estimates is remarkably high—probably higher than that of any other public examination that has been investigated. Correlation coefficient of +0.85 and even +0.90 are habitually obtained. Nevertheless even these figures admit of some 10 per cent of incorrect decisions. If 20 per cent enter the grammar schools, 5 (that is one quarter) are likely to turn out unsatisfactorily, and 5 of those relegated to modern schools (that is 6 per cent) could have surpassed them, had they been given the chance. The already mentioned fact that a small proportion of modern pupils transfer in subsequent years, or gain outstanding success by other avenues, is often held to prove that selection is thoroughly inaccurate and unjust. But surely we would expect many children to change as their interests and abilities develop with age, and as their schools and homes stimulate, or inhibit, their intellectual growth. The surprizing thing is rather how accurate selection is for the great majority.

Of the various selection instruments, junior school teachers' estimates tend to be the most valid of all, provided they are scaled or standardised against some uniform test or tests in order to bring the widely varying standards of different schools to a common level. Intelligence tests generally head the list of the objective measures, and the more conventional English and Arithmetic examinations do at least as well as,

if not better than, the new-type objective tests, if care is taken to reduce unreliability of marking. Even the English essay can make a valid contribution to prediction, particularly if more than one essay is marked by more than one marker. With such a very wide range of ability, the marking of essays reaches much more acceptable levels of reliability than is commonly reported in investigations of selected secondary school or university student compositions. Though the interview itself is, of course, very untrustworthy, the additional procedures used with border-zone cases, when carefully controlled, do add to the accuracy of predictions based on tests or examinations alone. These conclusions are stated rather dogmatically; but the full evidence on these and many other points concerned with the assessment of 11 year olds is summarised in a recent report by the British Psychological Society—*Psychological Aspects of Secondary School Selection.*[1]

Apart from its efficiency or inefficiency as a diagnostic instrument, the selection examination has numerous harmful consequences, which lead many psychologists, teachers and other thoughtful people to wish to abolish it, if only some alternative mode of secondary school organization could be found. Inevitably the schools coach for it, and tend to regard the numbers of passes gained as an indication of their success. The better teachers hold out against this, but poorer ones may spend most of the last two years in the junior school training children to cross out and underline, or to do arithmetic at speed. "Intelligence" often becomes a subject on the timetable although, as shown in an earlier article,[2] such coaching produces only limited gains and certainly does not improve all-round intelligence. Other subjects, more valuable to the general educational and personality development of 10-year children, get crowded out; even the writing of English is omitted if the examination contains no essay. A further undesirable tendency in larger schools is the streaming of children soon after entry from the infant schools at 7 years into classes thought likely to pass or fail "the 11 plus." The former are pushed on, and the latter naturally tend to drop behind and so to lose any chance they had of improving in relative ability later. In effect, then, a selection process which is going to affect children's whole educational and vocational careers may take place as early as 7 years.

---

[1] London: Methuen, 1957.
[2] Practice and Coaching Effects in Intelligence Tests. *Educational Forum*, 1954, Vol. 18, pp. 269-280.

Even when schools refuse to succumb to the 11-plus drive, it is hardly possible to control the parents. From far too early an age they give coaching themselves, or send children to outside tutors on Saturdays. Many publishers supply plotted courses or books of specimen questions; coaching agencies even advertize in *The Children's Newspaper*. Though sensible parents try to avoid imposing strain on their children, it is difficult not to infect them with their own anxiety about the outcome. Expensive rewards (such as bicycles) are commonly offered for passing; and on the fatal day, magic charms are often worn, and "Good Luck" cards received from friends and relatives. Fortunately young children are considerably more resilient than some psychologists suppose; and a careful survey of child guidance clinic cases has shown that strain caused by selection very rarely operates as a contributory factor in maladjustment, and then usually only among children who were already unstable. Experiments too have failed to demonstrate any marked effect of the emotional atmosphere on test scores. The reliability coefficient of a typical battery of tests approximates $+0.98$, though even this figure allows of some inconsistencies; in other words, some children who score above the borderline on one day would be below it a week later, or vice versa. It is for such reasons that, if we must have selection, psychologists tend to favour the use of teachers' estimates and school records, as having much less harmful repercussions on the school and the home. But at the same time, accuracy of prediction and fairness would be seriously impaired if all standardised tests or written papers were eliminated.

Discussion

This is a formidable indictment. Moreover there is a further fundamental dilemma which a selective system cannot solve, even when its validity is high as I have claimed above. Probably not much more than ten per cent or so of the adolescent population is really fitted by talent, home and school upbringing, and interests to profit from an advanced academic type of education, to go on to university courses and to careers which require this intellectual training. The majority, even of above average and average pupils, would be better suited by a more practically-oriented curriculum. The present selection procedure certainly enables us to cream off most of this 10 per cent, but we should have to go considerably lower in the scale of ability at 11 years than we do already to be sure of catching almost all of them.

(Even among pupils with average intelligence and attainments quotients of 100, one per cent might be expected to succeed in an academic course, given the opportunity.) And to do this would mean taking into the grammar school still more than at present who are quite unsuited to the kind of education it offers.

The non-English critic will naturally ask why we cling to this antiquated system, and there are plenty of English critics too who attack both selection and the grammar schools. As I have tried to show, the reasons are partly historical: the independent schools and the state-provided modern schools are legacies of the past, and the Local Authority grammar and technical schools represent attempts to adapt this system to the needs of a more democratic and technological age. Any change must be gradual if it is to win public acceptance: the staff, the buildings, the administrative system, and the parents cannot be converted to a more logical reorganization overnight. Secondly we have seen that class prejudice plays a large part. The predominantly conservative middle and upper-working classes, who most value good education, do not like their children mixing, especially during the adolescent years, with lower working-class children. The selection system allows them to preserve their values and mores in the grammar and independent schools. At the same time it allows some degree of social mobility, since it assimilates quite large numbers of the brightest and most responsible lower-class children who do gain entrance at 11-plus. But the middle-class bitterly oppose any move which would further increase class-mixing. The Trades Unions and the Labour party naturally take the opposite viewpoint, and advocate the comprehensive school—somewhat along American lines—both because it would obviate the need for selection and would help to break down class barriers.

Under these circumstances, it is only too easy for any arguments put forward by educationists or psychologists in favour of, or against, the present system to consist of rationalizations, based on unconscious prejudices. Nevertheless there is probably some truth in the claim that streaming by ability, which segregates the brighter children in schools with high intellectual traditions and ideals, and teaches them in smaller classes with better-qualified teachers, does help to bring on these pupils more rapidly. It is commonly stated that English grammar school products, on entry to university, are two years ahead of their American counterparts—that is intellectually; their relative social immaturity is also admitted. In my own case, for example—which is quite typical for one educated in independent schools—

I was taught Latin from 7 and Greek from 10 to 16, Algebra from 8 and Calculus from 14, and specialised almost exclusively on Mathematics, Physics and Chemistry from 16 to 21. But comparisons between the graduates of different countries are almost impossible to check, both because such different proportions reach the universities (only some 3 per cent in England), and because gains in academic achievement may be offset by losses in other, less easily measurable, qualities. Equally it is likely to be true that a slower pace, with less stress on homework and examinations, suits the majority of average and duller secondary pupils, though at the same time this means that any "late developers"—(and they do exist, though more rarely than parents suppose)—may get caught in the system and never have the chance to show their true merits. We have experimental proof that performance on intelligence, as well as achievement, tests tends to be raised by attendance at the better grammar schools and to drop relatively, or fail to increase so rapidly, in the less stimulating modern schools. It is this 'stereotyping effect' of the kind of schooling received which seems to constitute the major defect of selection at such an early age as 11 or even 7 years. Greater flexibility, or ease of transfer up or down, can of course be attained when all pupils attend a common school. Yet at the same time the tremendous value of the intellectual atmosphere, the cultural traditions and the character training provided by the selective schools should not be lightly discarded.

There is no space here to discuss the broader problems of streaming, whether it makes the dull depressed and the bright conceited, whether it is undemocratic, and so on. There are many arguments, and few facts; and it is well to recall Hartshorne and May's finding that in general the school has far less effect on pupils' social and moral attitudes than do the home and other out-of-school influences. In England as in other countries the organization of secondary schooling largely reflects the class-structure and attitudes of the parents, and reforms will not be effected by mere logical theorizing.

Criticisms may well be directed against another important feature of the English system, namely its 'uni-dimensionality.' With the minor exception of the technical and commercial schools, it seems to be assumed that pupils can only be differentiated in respect of their *general* educational capacity, not for ability along different lines. Here too the evidence is complex and controversial; yet both the results of follow-up experiments and factor-analytic researches seem to support this position. We find, for example, that tests of mechanical, spatial or other technical aptitudes, though of some value in extreme cases, are far less useful at 11 years than general intelligence and attainments tests in predicting success at subsequent technical courses. Tests of interests are being tried experimentally, with some promising results. But there can be no doubt that our selection system produces greater accuracy of placement in courses at different *levels* than would any system which tries to predict *types* at the same level. The system does not, of course, preclude cross-classification within the secondary schools for different subjects. Pupils are commonly regrouped for mathematics, foreign languages, etc. As they get older, also, the differentiation of aptitude and interest naturally becomes more clear-cut, hence our (possibly undue degree of) specialization from about 16 on for those who reach the more advanced levels. Yet here too English, as well as foreign, critics are aware of the defects of a rigid interpretation of 'liberal' education, and realise that many advantages may be claimed for a system which allows for a wider choice of subjects, and which aims to guide pupils according to their individual bents.

THE CONTROL AND SUPPORT OF PUBLIC EDUCATION

In purposes, organization, and administration, public education in the United States differs greatly from most systems of education in other countries of the world. There is no national system of schools, nor is there an explicit national educational policy or curriculum. Essentially, public education is controlled by national, state, and local legal requirements. But despite the fact that education in the United States is not the responsibility of any one agency, there is considerable uniformity in organization and general program.

Though the control and support of education are vested in many national, state, and local agencies, these agencies intermesh to determine the kind and quality of education provided. Nationally, the federal government offers assistance to states in financing special programs (e.g., vocational education and programs under the National Defense Education Act) and requires that certain standards be met in these programs. Specific curriculum content, textbook selection, and the means of financing the schools are determined within each state rather than by any central or federal agency. The uniformity which results is due primarily to nation-wide agreement on the question of what constitutes effective educational practices, to the application of regional and national accreditation standards, and to judicial interpretations of the Constitution concerning the rights and privileges of American citizens.

Though local boards of education, in general, are responsible for selecting teachers, the individual states set the standards for certification. State departments of education, as agencies of state boards of education, are usually responsible for setting the broad outlines of curriculum and for determining the textbooks to be used. Within the requirements set forth by the states, local boards of education have considerable autonomy to determine content, to choose appropriate teaching methods, and to select teaching materials.

At an informal and extralegal level numerous agencies, research centers, and foundations have influenced educational programs by suggesting new teaching procedures and materials growing out of their research and study. Professional "codes of ethics" are developed by national and state teachers' organizations in the several states, and these organizations often engage directly in the affairs of school districts to examine violations of professional standards or to appraise personnel practices. Teachers' organizations have long taken an active part in supporting appropriate legislation both at a national and state level. In recent years, regional and national accrediting associations have increasingly influenced public and private education. Accreditation associations, usually supported by contributions of member institutions, are generally composed of professional persons representing many areas of education. These associations have taken the responsibility of assessing the extent to which schools meet certain criteria of excellence. The criteria used to assess individual schools have usually been developed by representative professional committees and study groups. Professional accreditation teams are appointed by the associations to accomplish on-the-site school evaluations, and these reports are then analyzed by a committee of a particular accreditation association. Following this, schools are either accredited for a specific period of time, given suggestions for improvement for a later review, or refused accreditation. The application of accreditation criteria, particularly at secondary and higher levels, has served as a powerful professional force to upgrade the quality of education. Since the standards applied by accreditation associations have affected schools both regionally and nationally, these associations have also contributed to establishing a degree of national uniformity in schools.

Thus it can be seen that the control and support of public education reside in a matrix of many forces, agencies, and institutions, all of which operate so as to achieve some degree of uniformity. In a sense, the kind of school organization which has developed in the United States reflects the pluralistic nature of our society—achieving uniformity in diversity. However, questions have been raised about the way in which our system operates, questions often centering on the point that our public education lacks national definition and singleness of control. Because of the organizational structure of our system, many problems have arisen throughout our history, some of which have been resolved informally and others by the courts. It is interesting to note how many of these issues have been settled in a salutary manner despite the range of differences that seems to exist among those concerned with American education. It is reasonable to suggest that flexibility of control has enabled American schools to meet many emergent demands more successfully than would have been possible in a more structured or rigid system. But since new and yet unknown demands will require new kinds of action, many drastic changes may be necessary for the control and support of public schools. Certainly as larger and larger school systems develop, as more demands are made upon the schools, and as more institutions compete for financial support, there will be various pressures toward unifying or otherwise modifying the system of education.

With this brief overview in mind, students can achieve some understanding of the problems which have confronted schools in the arena of control and support by carefully analyzing the readings which follow. These readings are concerned with various statements by the courts on the control of education and some of the decisions which have been rendered on issues critical to the status of the public schools. In reading the selections in this section the student may wish to give some thought to these questions: What forces are now affecting the control and support of public education? What outcomes may be predicted from the effect of these forces?

87

Ward G. Reeder

SCHOOL CONTROL AND ORGANIZATION

The theory, processes, and problems of administration in business, industry, government, and other organizations have long been a subject of study. Not only has a considerable body of research and literature been produced relating to administration in these fields, but organizational practices have also been changed. In the past few decades increased attention has been given to the study of educational administration, and many major changes have occurred in schools as a result of the systematic analysis of educational administration.

Some of the factors which have brought about the better definition of educational administration include the following: (a) education has become a "big business" in the United States because it involves large financial expenditures and has become a complex enterprise requiring systematic management; (b) the trend in public education is increasingly toward larger administrative units, since the small school unit (stereotyped by the "little red schoolhouse"), which had few management problems, has all but disappeared in favor of consolidated units; (c) larger numbers of students than ever in our history are now in school and are staying in school for a longer period of time; (d) new vocational and professional fields, many of them nonexistent at the turn of the century, have come into being, all requiring efforts to develop curriculum, to provide teaching facilities, and to supervise teaching; (e) teaching staffs have increased and their functions have been differentiated, with administrative functions once performed by teachers now residing elsewhere; (f) special services have grown rapidly, adding to the complexity of school organization; and (g) the functions related to financial and public information, school plant construction, staffing, and staff evaluation have all greatly expanded, necessitating the need for some type of administrative coordination.

These factors have required trained and experienced administrative staffs, just as they have in other organizations, in order more accurately to define goals and determine outcomes, to centralize and unify decisions, to fix the responsibility and accountability delegated by state and local boards of education, and to better manage the internal affairs of schools.

Ward G. Reeder here presents a concise description of the structure, functions, and practices characteristic of American school administration. It is a valuable introduction to the complex nature of the American system of public education; to the manner in which it is organized and administered in the various states; to the relationships existing between state and federal educational agencies; and to the historical development of some of the agencies and administrative positions.

General policies of school control

American versus foreign policies in school control. In no other country do the schools belong to the people as much as in the United States; and in no other country is the administration of the schools as close to the people. Whereas in other countries school management is in the main a governmental affair concerning which the public does not have much voice, in the United States the public controls the schools through such means as the periodic election of school boards and the frequent voting of school revenues. Our people have always opposed giving up any of this prerogative.

As a rule, the administration of the school systems of foreign countries is more highly centralized than in the United States. In most foreign countries, school affairs are a division of the central government, are financed largely or wholly by the central government, and are directed by a minister of education or a secretary of education; moreover, there is complete or great uniformity in school procedures in the various communities of those countries. From the point of view of finance, control, organization, and administration, therefore, the school systems of most foreign countries may be called *national*.

Whereas in most foreign countries there is only one school system, in the United States there is a separate school system for each state and each

territory; thus, there are in the United States state school systems and territorial school systems. Each of these school systems is sovereign and each determines its own destiny; there is no federal control of schools as there is in most foreign countries, nor at present is there federal financial support for general education as there is in most foreign countries. From the point of view of finance, control, organization, and administration there is no American system of schools in the sense that there is an English, a French, a German, or a Japanese system of schools.[1]

Our state and territorial systems of schools are, however, more similar than dissimilar. Although they differ much in detail, in their fundamentals they are somewhat similar. They have, for example, somewhat similar forms of organization, somewhat similar means of financial support, and somewhat similar curriculums. Unquestionably, the domination of a common ideal, namely, *that every individual shall have a certain quantum of education, and may have it at public expense,* has been the chief factor in causing large similarity in our school systems. Guided by this common ideal, our school systems have become increasingly similar through the long-time operation of experimentation and imitation. This experimentation and imitation have proceeded somewhat as follows: a certain community or state has adopted a given policy, has demonstrated the merit of that policy, and before many years

From *The Fundamentals of Public School Administration* by Ward G. Reeder, pp. 36-60. Copyright 1958 by The Macmillan Company and reprinted with their permission.

[1] Since World War 2 the school systems of some foreign countries, especially that of Japan, have become more like ours.

have elapsed other communities of other states —perhaps all of them—have adopted the essential features of that same policy. It is this common educational ideal and this similarity in the essential elements of the American state and territorial school systems which residents of foreign countries and our own citizens have in mind when they speak of the American system of education, or when they call this system a national school system.

Explanations for our policy of school control. Contrary to the practice of most foreign countries, there has never been much, if any, federal control of schools in the United States; there has not been much federal control of schools, because there has not been much federal support of schools. Education was not mentioned in either the Articles of Confederation adopted in 1781 or in the Constitution of the United States adopted in 1788; apparently these frameworks of government assumed, at least by silence, that the job of education was to be left to the states. Moreover, the tenth amendment to the United States Constitution, ratified by the states in 1791, affirmed that "the powers not delegated to the United States by the Constitution, nor prohibited by it to the States, are reserved to the States respectively, or to the people."[2] What are the explanations for the failure of our lawmaking forefathers to make provision for a federal organization, administration, support, and control of schools? The following explanations may be given:

1. The thirteen original colonies which joined hands to form the United States had begun colonial systems of education long before the adoption of the federal Constitution. Moreover, these colonial systems represented various educational traditions and beliefs which the several colonies were interested in maintaining, and which they were afraid that they could not continue under federal control of education.

2. There were many urgent problems of the new federal government, without undertaking those of education. Besides, because society was then less complex than today, education was less necessary; moreover, the home, the church, and

other private agencies were then much more potent factors in education than they are today, and their efforts made a formal educational agency, such as the school, less necessary.

3. Our forefathers were skeptical of making a central government too strong. They desired to maintain a proper balance of power between the federal government and the state governments. They preferred strong state governments rather than a strong federal government. There was not much feeling of nationalism in those days; each colony in the early days was a nation, and did not have much traffic with the other colonies.

Comparative merits of state and national control of schools. Although education in the United States has historically been under the control of the states and of the local communities, and although there appears to have been fairly general satisfaction with such control, arguments are frequently presented for federal control of schools. For federal control, such as most foreign countries have, it is argued that such control would beget greater pedagogical and financial efficiency. It is further argued that in state and local control of schools, funds are frequently wasted both through the adoption of poor policies and through the loose administration of excellent policies; the protagonists of federal control of schools affirm that much of this waste would be eliminated through federal control. For federal control of schools it is also argued that through it, educational opportunities and school tax burdens would be equalized among the various states, whereas state and local control of schools begets large inequalities in such opportunities and in tax burdens.

The arguments just stated for federal control of schools are attacked, however, by the proponents of state and local control. It is argued that state and local control enables the states and the local communities to meet their individual needs, whereas federal control might result in a national bureaucracy and in a national uniformity which would neglect the educational needs of the various states and of the various communities within the states. It is argued, too, that state and local control more readily permits educational experimentation, the results of which may become immediately known to, and adopted by, other states and other communities.

Federal control of schools is not likely to come, so long as the states maintain efficient school systems and finance them without too much federal aid. It, however, is likely to come, as it probably should come, if the states fail to meet their

[2] In view of this amendment, it may be properly questioned whether, without a change in the Constitution, the federal government could legally assume control of education. It is believed, however, that such control would be legal; at any rate, the federal government financed and controlled the educational programs of all the CCC projects, and this practice would seem to be an ample test of the legality of federal control of education.

obligations to their children. For anyone to advocate federal aid without any federal control, is perhaps to advocate nonsense; a certain amount of federal control has always followed federal aid, and, as the present writer believes, a certain amount of it should; but that has always been a much-debated question.

Federal interest in education.   Although education was not mentioned in the Articles of Confederation or in the Constitution of the United States, and although there has not been much federal control of education in the United States, the federal government has always been interested in education. The presidents of the United States and other leaders in the life of the nation have almost universally expressed their faith and their interest in education.[3] For example, George Washington said in his Farewell Address on September 17, 1796:

"Promote, then, as an object of primary importance, institutions for the general diffusion of knowledge. In proportion as the structure of a government gives force to the public opinion, it is essential that public opinion should be enlightened."

It is not merely with sympathetic sentiments and with kind words that the federal government has shown its interest in education. That interest has been shown in at least two material ways. In the first place, the federal government has granted millions of acres of land and hundreds of millions of dollars to the states for the financial support of education.[4] . . . In the second place, the interest of the federal government in education has been demonstrated through the creation of many bureaus, offices, and departments which are wholly or partly educational.

The chief educational agency of the federal government is the United States Office of Education. In 1866 the National Association of State and City School Superintendents (now the American Association of School Administrators) went on record as favoring a federal bureau of education. This organization was supported in its request by many other organizations and by numerous private citizens. A bill providing for such a

department was introduced in Congress in 1866 by James A. Garfield, at that time a member of Congress, and later to become President of the United States. That bill was enacted into law on March 2, 1867; it read as follows:

"Be it enacted, by the Senate and House of Representatives of the United States of America in Congress assembled. That there shall be established, at the city of Washington, a department of education, for the purpose of collecting such statistics and facts as shall show the condition and progress of education in the several States and Territories, and of diffusing such information respecting the organization and management of schools and school systems, and methods of teaching, as shall aid the people of the United States in the establishment and maintenance of efficient school systems, and otherwise promote the cause of education throughout the country."

39th Congress, 2d Session—1867.
(14 Stat. L., p. 434.)

In 1869 the Department of Education, which was created by the law of 1867, was replaced by the Office of Education and made a division of the Department of the Interior. In 1870 the office was renamed the Bureau of Education, and this title was retained until 1929 when the title of Office of Education was restored. In 1939 the Office of Education was transferred from the Department of the Interior to the newly created Federal Security Agency. It is now a division of the Federal Department of Health, Education, and Welfare, and its secretary is a member of the President's Cabinet. The ranking official of the office has always held the title of commissioner of education. Although the commissioner has always been appointed by the President on a semipolitical basis, practically all of the commissioners have been outstanding educators and through their leadership powers have done much to promote the development of good schools throughout the United States.

The aims of the Office of Education, as outlined in the statutes of 1867 creating the office, have been closely followed. The general function of the office has been to stimulate the development of education, not to control or administer it. The chief work of the office has been to collect and to disseminate information on education. The office now diffuses educational information through (1) its many publications consisting of reports of special studies, of a magazine called *School Life*, of the biennial survey of education, and of other educational works; (2) conferences of educational and of lay leaders, these conferences

---

[3] For a selected list of such statements the interested reader is referred to "Expressions on Education by American Statesmen and Publicists," *U. S. Bureau of Education, Bulletin,* 1913, No. 28.

[4] This policy was begun by the federal government as early as 1785, when lot 16 in each congressional township in the Northwest Territory was set aside for the support of schools.

being called by the commissioner of education or by members of his staff; (3) correspondence; and (4) addresses by the commissioner of education and by his staff members. The statistical reports of the office are recognized as the most complete and accurate reports on education of any country, in spite of the fact that the office does not have the legal power to require state and local officials to provide the information on which the reports are based. During recent years, the office has conducted, at the request of local and state governing boards, many surveys of local and state educational systems and of colleges and universities. It has also been given the duty of supervising the distribution and the expenditure of funds for vocational education and for other educational purposes.

A large part of the service of the Office of Education is provided gratis, and any of the service may be procured at actual cost. For example, many of the publications of the office may be obtained free, while those not free may be obtained at actual cost; any of these may be procured from the Superintendent of Documents, Government Printing Office, Washington, D. C. For the use of its staff and of any citizen of the United States, the office maintains what is probably the most complete library on education in the world. Among its numerous services the library staff has prepared bibliographies on many educational topics, and will upon request, so far as its time and its resources permit, prepare other educational bibliographies; such service is available to any school official or school employee or other citizen, usually free of charge.

Many of our citizens believe that the federal government has not shown sufficient interest and participation in education. Further interest and participation in education on the part of the federal government have been advocated from time to time along three lines: (1) a federal department of education, having a secretary of education coordinate with the other federal departments such as the Department of State, the Department of Commerce, and the Department of Agriculture,[5] (2) federal aid to general education as is now given to certain phases of special education, such as vocational education; and (3) the establishment of a national university.

Each of these proposals has had numerous and influential advocates, and most sessions of Congress during recent years have seen bills introduced looking toward placing one or more of the proposals into legislation. None of the bills, however, has yet been enacted into law. The proposal for a national university has been made since the days of George Washington, who made provision in his will for such an institution. This recommendation has been repeated by many succeeding Presidents, but no action has been taken, probably because of the development of many public and many private universities of national reputation. The need for a national university grows less and less as the years roll by.

Although many earlier proposals had been made for a Department of Education and for a federal subsidy for general education,[5] these two proposals became particularly noticeable about the time of the close of World War I in 1919. That war gave education one of the greatest stimuli it has ever received. On the credit side of the educational ledger, that war demonstrated that education enabled our soldiers to make greater progress than they could have made without education; for example, it was found that by far the majority of the men who won commissions in the training camps as officers were college graduates. On the debit side of the ledger, that war recorded the fact that one fourth of the soldiers—and they, it should be noted, were the flower of American manhood, between the ages of twenty and thirty—who responded to the draft were unable to read an English newspaper and to write a letter. The draft also showed that approximately 29 per cent of the draftees could not be accepted for general military service because of physical incompetency. Moreover, it was found that the soldiers who came from certain states, especially the states which had not developed efficient school systems, had much larger percentages of illiteracy and of physical disability than the soldiers who came from other states. These were disconcerting facts, and they stood out as a loud criticism of our state school systems for their not having discovered and corrected these handicaps of our citizenry. Then it was that education came to be more and more looked upon as not a state problem alone, but as a problem in which the federal government must become more and more interested, especially financially, if its welfare and its safety were to be assured. This need for greater federal interest in education was made even more clear by World War 2. Of 18 million men examined for military service during World War 2, one in every twelve was found to be illiterate, semi-illiterate, or mentally deficient.

_____

[5] Recent proposals have been made for a federal board of education to be appointed by the President of the United States, the board in turn to appoint the commissioner of education. Of course, we now have a federal department of Health, Education, and Welfare which has a secretary who is a member of the President's cabinet.

Since 1918, every session of Congress has seen at least one bill introduced for the establishment of a separate federal department of education with a secretary of education in the President's Cabinet.[6] These bills have also provided for a large subsidy to the states for general education. As yet, none of these bills, except those for vocational education, education in critical defense areas, and school lunches, has been enacted into law.

The advocates of these proposals argue that education does not have sufficient prestige at present in the federal government. They point out that in the federal government, education does not rank much higher than such interests as the dairy industry, the plant industry, and entomology. They argue that a separate department of education headed by a secretary of education would make education more articulate. They argue further that education vitally affects the welfare and the progress of the whole nation, and that, in consequence, the federal government should take a larger interest in financing and in otherwise promoting education.

Contrariwise, the opponents of such legislation point out the danger of bureaucracy in any federal control of education. They fear a pauperization of the states and the local districts and an encroachment upon the American ideals of liberty and individuality; they affirm that a federal department of education and a federal subsidy for education would tend to remove the control of the schools from the hands of the people and to place it in the hands of federal officials who would be in a position to regiment the education and the lives of the people. They fear also that placing a secretary of education in the Cabinet would throw education into the maelstrom of "politics" on a national scale.

State versus local control of education

Evolution of state control of education. One of the outstanding changing conceptions of education by the people of the United States has been concerning the relative responsibility of the state and of the local community for education. In the early days the local communities were in complete control of education, and the colonial and the state constitutions and statutes were silent on education. In those days the local communities could provide schools or not provide them as they chose; or if they provided them, they could provide any kind—efficient or inefficient.

It is to the credit of the American people's faith in education that many communities provided truly public schools before there were state laws requiring such action. Schools were often established as soon as the settlers had established their homes; the home came first, then the church, and next the school. In Massachusetts, for example, the first permanent settlement was made in 1620, and schools which were truly public were established there by certain communities as early as 1635.

Notwithstanding the avid and widespread interest of the early settlers in education, it was soon found that leaving to each community the decision of whether schools should be established resulted in a few communities not establishing them. Consequently, the state legislatures deemed it advisable to enact legislation for the universal establishment, the organization, and the support of schools. Massachusetts, for example, as early as 1647, enacted a law which required each community having 50 or more "householders" (families) to establish an elementary school, and each community having 100 or more "householders" to establish a grammar school in addition to an elementary school. Even before the law of 1647, Massachusetts had enacted in 1642 a law which required parents to see that their children were taught to read. The law of 1642, however, placed the educational obligation wholly upon the parent and did not require the establishment of a school, whereas the law of 1647 placed the educational obligation largely upon the community and required the establishment of a school.

The Massachusetts laws of 1642 and 1647 were the genesis of state control of education; they were the beginning of compulsory education.[7] Since that time, hundreds of other laws have been enacted in each of the states to provide for the establishment, the organization, the supervision, and the financial support of schools; in fact, there is today scarcely a feature of the schools upon which the state laws are silent. Moreover, all the present state constitutions have a pronouncement on the importance of education and on the place of the state in education; many of these pronouncements follow closely the language of the famous Ordinance of 1787, which declared that "Religion, morality, and knowledge being necessary to good government and the happiness of mankind, schools and the means of education shall be forever encouraged."

---

[6] See footnote 5.

[7] Compulsory school attendance, though, did not come until 1852, Massachusetts being the first state to enact such a law.

Education as a state function.   From the earliest days the conviction has been growing among the people that the state must be responsible for seeing that its citizens have a certain quantum of education. That the state has accepted this responsibility is shown by the state constitutions, the hundreds of school statutes in each state, and the dozens of decisions of local, state, and federal courts. In brief, education has come to be almost universally regarded as a state function.[8] The assumption of educational control by the state is not fortuitous; state control has come because of the early and the ever-growing belief of the people that education is the buttress of a democratic government and cannot, therefore, be left entirely to the whims of any individual or of any community. In a good government the people cannot be permitted to remain ignorant, although some of them might be content with that status; this is especially true in a democracy.

It is true that for the administration of the schools, the state has delegated most of its functions to counties, cities, towns, villages, townships, and other local school districts. These powers and duties have been delegated by the legislatures, which are the supreme lawmaking bodies in state government. If a state wishes to increase or to decrease the powers and duties which it has delegated to local school officials, it may do so through changing its laws. These laws are merely a reflection of the changing beliefs of the people. Local school officials and school employees are, therefore, merely agents of the state for carrying out the educational dictates of the state; if they are also responsible to the people of the local community, it is only because the state has delegated to the people of the local community a certain amount of the responsibility for education.

Desirable limitations of state control of education.[9]   From the beginning the tendency has been for the state to assume larger control of education. In brief, as the years have rolled by, local communities have given to state government more and more of the control of education. This control has advanced proportionally as the amount of state financial aid for schools has increased. Perhaps it would be more accurate to say that such responsibility has been taken from local communities by state government, because local communities have not given up willingly their educational prerogatives. Much as it has been opposed, the drift has been toward centralization; and, as would be expected, there is a larger amount of state control of education in the older states, that is, the eastern states, than in the newer states of the other sections of the United States.

What are desirable limits of state control of schools? On one hand, there are many persons who believe that state control of schools has already gone far enough in the typical state; in fact, some believe that it has gone too far. They maintain that the state control of schools, which is now exercised in a certain degree in all states, is tending to stifle community interest and initiative, and that it often fails to keep in mind the needs of local communities; they claim that through its power to control education, and especially through its power to determine what shall be taught, the state is likely to try to regiment its citizens by indoctrinating them with only one point of view.[10]

On the other hand, there are many persons who believe that state control of schools in the typical state has not gone far enough. They point out that many communities are ignorant and selfish and would become a cancer upon the state, if they were not thwarted. They contend that schools will be more efficient when the state legislatures enact more stringent laws to determine most educational standards, policies, and procedures of local communities.

The problem is, therefore, that of reconciling in proper balance the two American ideals of (1) individuality and (2) social co-operation. In fact, this problem has existed since the beginning of our government. The problem can never be solved in any democratic government by a program which veers too far either to the left or to the right.

Probably the best type of school control—and this is the ideal toward which practice seems to be striving—would be for the state to establish minimum standards, especially in the more fundamental aspects of an educational program, which every community in the state would be expected and helped by the state to meet. When the minimum standards have been established, prudence would dictate that the local community be permitted to exercise its initiative in experimenting and in exceeding those standards. Good procedure demands, therefore, that each community be given ample freedom of action, but that it be expected

---

[8] Many of our citizens believe that education is the function of the home and the church, rather than of the state; this belief has caused the establishment of many private schools, especially church schools.

[9] An elaboration of the views and facts here stated may be found in *The Structure and Administration of Education in American Democracy,* Educational Policies Commission, 1938, pp. 81-88.

---

[10] This result has been seen in the totalitarian governments of many foreign countries.

to be conscious of its responsibilities to the state in exercising its freedom. In any event, since education is so important for the individual and for society, the state should make sure that no pupil, because of his residence, race, religion, poverty, or other vicissitude of fortune, is denied his educational patrimony; the realization of this ideal will require much more state control of education than is found in the typical state today. This control will be expressed in standards which local school districts must meet.

State control of private effort in education[11]

Evolution of private effort in education. The first schools established in the United States were private, and in many of the colonial and state governments private school enrollment exceeded public school enrollment for several decades. Since the universal establishment of public schools and the improving of those schools, the percentage of the total population enrolled in public schools has been increasing and the percentage enrolled in private schools has been decreasing. This tendency has been noticed particularly during recent decades, and especially in the secondary schools and in the colleges and the universities. The percentage of all elementary school pupils now enrolled in private schools is approximately 13, the percentage of all secondary school pupils now enrolled in private schools is approximately 10; and the percentage of all college students enrolled in private institutions is approximately 49. Public schools don't charge tuition, whereas private schools do, which explains the percentage decrease in private school enrollment during recent years when per pupil costs have increased tremendously.

What are the motives which have impelled millions of parents to send their children to private schools where they usually must pay tuition at the same time as they must pay taxes to support the public schools? Two motives stand out: first, there has been the belief on the part of many parents that the private school is better than the public school—at least that it can better meet the needs of their children; second, there has been the desire, especially in the case of the church schools, to give the child instruction in religion, which cannot now be given legally in a public school.[12]

Amount of state control of private effort in education. With few exceptions, the historic policy of the state legislatures has been to encourage private effort in education. Seldom has legislation been enacted which would discourage private effort. In the early days, not only was there an entire absence of state supervision and state control of private schools, but such schools were frequently supported largely by public money. Shortly after the opening of the nineteenth century, however, the policy of giving public funds for the support of private schools began to be questioned, and it was not long until the legislatures of practically all the states enacted statutes prohibiting the use of public funds for the support of private schools. Moreover, as new constitutions were adopted or as old ones were amended, most of the states wrote into them a section which prohibited the use of public money for the support of private schools.[13]

Coincident with the enactment of legislation prohibiting the expenditure of public funds for the financing of private schools came legislation which established certain state standards and state inspection of private as well as of public schools. At present, such standards and inspection extend from almost nothing in some states to a large amount in other states.

Although they are easily in the minority, some of our fellow citizens believe that for the state merely to control private schools does not go far enough. They would abolish private schools, because they believe such schools are snobbish and do not provide equality of educational opportunity. In brief, they believe that all children should be required to attend the public schools. This belief became sufficiently strong in one state (Oregon) in 1922 to obtain the enactment of a law which would have abolished all private schools for children below the age of sixteen. The law, however, was declared unconstitutional by the United States Supreme Court in 1925. [See Reading 90.] . . .

State organization for education

The beginnings of such organization. Earlier . . . it was stated that education has from almost

---

[11] As used here, the term "private schools" includes church schools. Most private schools in the United States are church schools.

[12] Hundreds of public schools now make provision for the pupils who desire to go to their respective churches, during a certain period, to receive religious instruction. Many also make provision for giving instruction in the Bible in connection with the English courses.

[13] A few states have enacted laws which provide free textbooks, health services, and transportation for private school pupils, the same as for public school pupils. The courts have declared such aid legal, because it is given to the pupils and not to the school.

the earliest days been regarded as a state function; this is demonstrated by state statutes, state constitutions, and decisions of the courts. It was not until 1784, however, that a state established machinery for the general supervision and control of education. This first legislation was enacted by the state of New York when it created the so-called "university" with its Board of Regents, and gave this phantom institution (probably of French origin) and its governing board jurisdiction over the colleges and the academies of the state. The University of the State of New York which was created by the Act of 1784 was not, however, in the commonly accepted sense a university at all; it was rather a state board of education and has remained so throughout its history.

Not only was New York the first state to establish a state board of education, but it was the first state to make provision for a chief state school official. In 1812 the New York legislature enacted a law which provided for the appointment of a "state superintendent of common schools." Gideon Hawley was appointed on January 14, 1813, to this office, and thus became the first chief state school official in the United States, and he became the first school superintendent, state or local.

How are we to account for the long delay in establishing the state board of education and the chief state school official, which today are considered so necessary that the latter is found in every state and the former in practically every state? At least two retarding influences stand out. First, the early theory of individual and community rights met with popular approval. To our forefathers any centralization of power and authority smacked of autocracy; and to autocracy our forefathers were unalterably opposed. Second, the idea of the close association of the church and the state was prevalent and was difficult to eradicate from the minds of the people. These two influences made for decentralization in school organization down to almost the middle of the nineteenth century, and they kept even the beginnings of state supervision of schools from appearing until the opening of the nineteenth century.

The state board of education. The second state[14] to establish a state board of education was Massachusetts, in 1837. Connecticut followed in 1838. Since those dates, practically all states have created such boards with general educational

functions. The few remaining states have state boards of education, but with restricted functions, such as administering the vocational-education laws[15] or administering all or some of the state institutions of higher learning. A fullfledged state board of education is recommended for each state for the following reasons:

1. It is more representative of the interests of all the people than a single individual is. It obtains different points of view. It is more democratic. It is closer to the people.

2. The chief state school official and his assistants are more likely selected on the basis of merit by a board of education than under other methods of selection. Subject to legislative enactments, the board determines educational policies, directs the chief state school official in executing the policies, and keeps him and his staff in office as long as their services are satisfactory. In brief, it helps to remove the state department of education from the cloud of "politics."

3. It has greater prestige with the legislature, the governor, and local school officials than a single individual has. It gives the public greater confidence in the management of its schools.

4. It gives greater stability and continuity to state educational policies. School progress throughout the state is best served when policies and programs can be planned with complete confidence that they will not suddenly be cast into the discard by each new chief state school official.

The general function of the state boards of education varies from that of merely advising the state commissioner of education, as is the case in Massachusetts, to large control of the educational system in the other states. The state Board of Regents, which is the state board of education in the state of New York, has greater powers and duties than the board of any other state. The tendency has been to give the state board of education increased functions, and at present, in most states, it has general supervision over elementary and secondary school education in the state; this function is exercised with the help of the chief state school official and his assistants.

In most states, there is still a two-headed state organization for education, consisting of a state board of education usually appointed by some state agency, on one hand, and a chief state school official elected by the people, on the other hand. The evils inherent in such a two-headed organization have been mitigated in most states

---

[14] Since the New York Board of Regents, established in 1784, had control for several decades only over colleges and academies, the honor of having the first fullfledged state board of education is sometimes given to Massachusetts.

[15] The federal vocational-education law, enacted in 1917, required every state wishing federal aid for vocational education to have some kind of board for the administration of such aid.

by making the chief state school official an ex officio member and an ex officio officer of the state board; the tendency has been to make him the chief executive officer or employee of the state board. Frequently, however, the state board of education is responsible to a different authority than the chief state school official, and this has often led to friction between the two heads.

The number of members on state boards of education ranges from three to twenty-three with seven or nine members being the usual number. The members are selected in one of the following manners: appointment by the governor, appointment by the chief state school official (Wyoming only), appointment by conventions of local school boards, election by popular vote at a regular or a special election, ex officio membership, or by a combination of two or more of the plans just mentioned. As a rule, the members are selected at large, that is, to represent the whole state and not a particular section of the state; as a rule, no legal qualifications are prescribed for the board members except "residence within the state"; with few exceptions, the members serve without pay. The legal term of office ranges from one year to twelve years; the average term in practice is approximately five years.

The tendency in best practice is toward having a state board of education with seven or nine members, all of whom are appointed by the governor or elected by the people. The term of office should be the same number of years as the number of members on the board; one member should retire each year. The members should serve without pay. Their expenses incurred for board meetings should be paid and the number of meetings each year might be limited to ten or twelve. Most features of the office, together with all powers and duties, should be prescribed by statute rather than by state constitution. Constitutions should be regarded as frameworks of government and should not be cluttered with details, especially with details that are apt to need changing frequently.

The state department of education.   Every state has a state department of education, which is composed of the chief state school official and his staff. The title which has been most frequently used in designating the chief state school official is superintendent of public instruction; this title is now found in approximately two-thirds of the states, chiefly western and southern. The next most frequently used title has usually been commissioner of education, which is now found in a few states, chiefly eastern.[16]

The office of chief state school official should be the head and the heart of the school system of the state. It should encourage, supervise, and direct the development of the whole school system of the state from the kindergarten through the university. It should bring every worthy educational endeavor in the state within its vitalizing influence. Unfortunately, this ideal is not always realized; it is not realized, because the legislation pertaining to the office is archaic in many respects. Like Topsy, the office in most states has "just growed," and the growing-up period has been fairly short, dating back only to 1812, the date of its first establishment in New York.

The chief handicap under which the office now labors results from the method of selecting the incumbent of the office. Approximately two-thirds of the states still elect the chief state school official by popular vote, and practically all of these still elect him on a partisan ticket. The remaining states permit either the governor or the state board of education to select him. Popular election may be adversely criticized on the following bases: (1) it establishes residence restrictions for its candidates; (2) it results in a low and static salary; (3) it begets a short tenure for the holder of the office; and (4) perhaps, worst of all, it subjects the selection of the person best qualified for the office to the vicissitudes of "politics." The chief state school official should be an expert in school administration, and the people should delegate the responsibility of selecting him to some such group of their representatives as the state board of education.

There are many other handicaps under which the office of chief state school official still labors. Most of these handicaps are the result of constitutions which were adopted many years ago, and have become petrified and difficult to change. This petrification of the forms of the office has been especially the result of those state constitutions which, as a rule, not only mandate the legislature to create and maintain the office, but prescribe many of its important features. Approximately two-thirds of the states now explicitly provide for the office in their constitutions, and most of these constitutions prescribe certain of the features of the office. Among the features frequently thus prescribed are the title of the office, the manner of selecting the incumbent of the office, the eligibility requirements for the incumbent of the office, the term of office, the salary, the relation of the office to the state board

---

[16] An up-to-date list of the occupants of this office, together with their official titles, can be found in *Educational Directory,* which is published annually by the U. S. Office of Education, Washington, D. C.

of education, and many of the powers and duties of the office. Such features have become petrified over a long period of years and have frequently been unable to give way expeditiously to new and better practices. It is not fortuitous that the more modern state departments of education are found in the eastern states, which as a rule do not prescribe in their constitutions any of the features of the office; those states have left entirely to the legislatures the establishing of such features.

To have the best leadership from the state department of education will require the most favorable conditions pertaining to the office of chief state school official, because the chief state school official makes the department of education principally what it is. Such favorable conditions would be somewhat as follows: The chief state school official should be appointed by the state board of education without regard to his residence, his "politics," or any other extraneous factor; in brief, he should be appointed wholly on the basis of his ability to direct the state's system of education. He should be paid a salary commensurate with his ability and the importance of his office, and such salary should be determined by the state board of education. The term of office should be indefinite, or of a sufficient number of years to make possible the development of a constructive educational program. Under the general control, supervision, and direction of the state board of education, which should appoint him, the chief state school official should be the executive head of the state school system. For the prompt and efficient performance of its work, the office should be given an adequate and a competent staff, and the members of this staff should be selected and paid wholly on the basis of their ability and their accomplishments. They should be selected by the state board of education upon the nomination of the chief state school official. All the recommendations just made are feasible, because the practices on which they are based have been in successful operation in several states for many years.

Local organization for education

Local school-administrative units.[17] Although the state is the legal unit for the control of schools, most of the actual administration of the schools has been delegated by the state to subdivisions of the state; these subdivisions are known as school districts. With the exception of a few decades at their beginning, the school districts have generally been autonomous. As a rule, school districts are entirely independent, fiscally and otherwise, from other governmental agencies. This separation was decided upon by the legislatures, because of the belief that the schools should have protection from the changing fortunes of partisan politics which frequently prevail in the administration of other phases of government. For the reason just given, this separation is still favored by practically all professional educators. But the separation is vigorously opposed by practically all authorities in political science; they believe that the separation is in the long run unwholesome both for the schools and for the other phases of government.

Within the United States, there are now approximately 50,000 school districts, and these districts are governed by approximately 220,000 school-board members. The absurdities in present organization will be immediately glimpsed from the fact that some states still have more school-board members than school employees. There are numerous types of school districts; in fact, each state usually has several types. The districts vary in size from the small rural district, employing only one teacher and enrolling only a few pupils, to the large city and county school systems, employing thousands of teachers and enrolling more than a million pupils. The districts are known by various names, such as county, city, common school, graded, town, township, consolidated, central, community, joint union graded, union high, township high, and county high. The average size of the school districts ranges from a few square miles in some states to 2055 square miles in Utah. The number of school districts in a state ranges from fifteen in Delaware to several thousand in a few other states. In the New England states, the town is usually the school-administrative unit; in the western states the township or a modification of the township is usually the school-administrative unit; in the southern states the county is usually the school-administrative unit.

The tendency in both theory and practice is toward a larger unit for school administration, especially for the rural schools. Every year sees the demise of hundreds of school districts through their merger with other school dis-

---

[17] The *school-administrative unit* should not be confused with the *school-attendance unit*. The territory within which pupils attending a certain school reside is known as a school-attendance unit or school-attendance area. Many school-administrative units

---

contain more than one school, hence more than one school-attendance unit.

tricts;[18] the number of school districts in the United States has decreased by more than half since 1942. Every year, moreover, sees powers and duties subtracted from small administrative units and given to an intermediate unit, which is usually called the county; this tendency has been accelerated recently by the large increase in state aid for schools, and by state laws stimulating the study of local school districts.

Forward-looking educators and laymen are agreed that the greatest handicap to rural school efficiency and progress today is the small units under which rural schools are organized and administered. Moreover, they are agreed that these small administrative units are a chief explanation for the lag in rural school administration compared with city school administration. Such units are a remnant of the horse and buggy days, and in the whole nation they result annually in a waste of millions of dollars in school administration. In only the southern states and in a few others are rational school districts in the rural sections found. In most states of the North and of the West, perhaps at least two-thirds of the school districts should be merged with others. Research and theory have not yet demonstrated what the size of the unit for the administration of rural schools should be, although the county is frequently suggested as the most desirable unit. It is apparent, though, that because of the differences in topography, in distance, and in population density the county may be too large in certain instances and too small in others. In general, the size of the school-administrative unit, whether rural or urban, should meet the following criteria:

1. The unit should be sufficiently large to permit the organization of a complete system of elementary and secondary schools and an adult-education program on an efficient financial and pedagogical basis.[19] For the larger centers of population, provision should also be made for the organization of a system of junior colleges and terminal vocational schools.

2. It should be sufficiently large to make provision for an adequate school-administrative and supervisory personnel.

3. It should not be so large in territory or in population that the people would lose interest

in the schools. The administration of the schools should be kept close to the people.

The local board of education. The schools of each school district in the United States are governed by a group of persons known variously as the board of education, the school board, the school committee, the board of school directors, or the board of school trustees. Such controlling boards represent the people of the school district in the administration of the schools; but, since education is a state function, these boards represent the people of the whole state as well as the people of the local school district.

As would be expected, the features pertaining to the office of school-board member are not the same in every state. There are, however, many common veins running through the school board practices of the various states, and the tendency is for those practices to become more similar. The following tendencies are noted: (1) popular election, on a non-partisan ticket, of the holders of the office; (2) a longer and an overlapping term of office, for example, from three to five years; (3) a smaller number of members, for example, between five and nine; and (4) no salary, except perhaps a small per diem, with a limitation on the number of days a year to ten or twelve. . . .

The local superintendent of schools. Since its beginning in Providence, Rhode Island, in 1836, the superintendency of schools has become almost universal. Every school system, except the very small ones, employs a superintendent. The school systems which do not employ superintendents are almost always rural, and these usually have the supervision of a county superintendent. With the exception of county superintendents, who are still frequently elected on a political basis, the tendency everywhere is to elect superintendents on the basis of their administrative and technical competence. . . .

Other local school-administrative personnel. In all, except the very small school systems, other school-administrative and supervisory employees are usually found. Attached to the office of the superintendent of schools, depending on the size and the type of school system, are such administrative and supervisory employees as the business manager of schools (usually called an assistant superintendent of schools) and his staff, and assistant superintendents in charge of various other activities of the school system. In charge of each local school is usually found a principal. . . .

---

[18] The merger or consolidation of school districts should not be confused with the merger or consolidation of schools. . . .

[19] Small school-administrative units are usually characterized by small, and frequently inefficient, schools; large school-administrative units, on the contrary, are usually characterized by larger and more efficient schools.

88

Newton Edwards

THE SCHOOL AND THE STATE

We have already seen the extent to which public education is a function and responsibility of each of the states, and noted that while the federal and local governments have important roles, they are secondary to those of the state governments. Dr. Newton Edwards, an authority on the legal aspects of education, has summarized the role of the federal government, the states, and the local boards of education. His article is a cogent summary of the critical importance of schools in American society. Readers will find in this article a clear delineation of the overall historical antecedents for our policies of federal, state, and local control, together with descriptions of state controls over private schooling and the functions of administration at the various levels of the educational system. The following selection constitutes part of the opening chapter of Edwards' widely used book on American school law.

Students interested in the further study of educational administration may wish to examine Reeder's text (from which Reading 87 was taken) and others (7) in order to gain a better understanding of one of the important vocations within education.

The public school in legal theory

The courts have been called upon repeatedly to define the function of the public school in organized society. Whatever vagaries may have been entertained by educational reformers or others, the courts have been forced by necessity to formulate a theory of education based upon what they deem to be fundamental principles of public policy. In legal theory the public school is a state institution.[1] Public education is not merely a function of government; it is of government. Power to maintain a system of public schools is an attribute of government in much the same sense as is the police power, or the power to administer justice, or to maintain military forces, or to tax.[2] The state finds its right to tax for the maintenance of a system of public schools in its duty to promote the public welfare, the good order and peace of society.[3] The function of the public school, in legal theory at least, is not to confer benefits upon the individual as such;[4] the school exists as a state institution because the very existence of civil society demands it. The education of youth is a matter of such vital importance to the democratic state and to the public weal that the state may do much, may go very far indeed, by way of limiting the control of the parent over the education of his child.[5] The state cannot, to be sure, prohibit private schools altogether,[6] but it can prohibit

From *The Courts and the Public Schools* by Newton Edwards, pp. 1-8. Copyright 1933 by The University of Chicago. Reprinted by permission of The University of Chicago Press.

[1] *City of Louisville* v. *Commonwealth*, 134 Ky. 488, 121 S.W. 411; *Bissell* v. *Davison*, 65 Conn. 183, 32 Atl. 348, 29 L.R.A. 251; *Leeper* v. *State*, 103 Tenn. 500, 53 S.W. 962, 48 L.R.A. 167; *State* v. *Meador*, 284 S.W. (Tenn.) 890; *State* v. *Haworth*, 122 Ind. 462, 23 N.E. 946, 7 L.R.A. 240.

[2] *City of Louisville* v. *Commonwealth*, 134 Ky. 488, 121 S.W. 411; *Leeper* v. *State*, 103 Tenn. 500, 53 S.W. 962, 48 L.R.A. 167; *City of Edina* v. *School District of City of Edina*, 305 Mo. 452, 267 S.W. 112.

[3] *Bissell* v. *Davison*, 65 Conn. 183, 32 Atl. 348, 29 L.R.A. 251; *Leeper* v. *State*, 103 Tenn. 500, 53 S.W. 962, 48 L.R.A. 167; *Scown* v. *Czarnecki*, 264 Ill. 305; *Fogg* v. *Board of Education*, 76 N.H. 296, 82 Atl. 173, 37 L.R.A. (N.S.) 1110, Ann. Cas. 1912C 758.

[4] *Bissell* v. *Davison*, 65 Conn. 183, 32 Atl. 348, 29 L.R.A. 251; *Scown* v. *Czarnecki*, 264 Ill. 305; *Fogg* v. *Board of Education*, 76 N.H. 296, 82 Atl. 173, 37 L.R.A. (N.S.) 1110, Ann. Cas. 1912C 758.

[5] *Meyer* v. *State of Nebraska*, 262 U.S. 390, 43 S. Ct. 625, 67 L. Ed. 1042, 29 A.L.R. 1446.

[6] *Pierce* v. *Society of the Sisters of the Holy Names of Jesus and Mary*, 268 U.S. 510, 45 S. Ct. 571, 69 L. Ed. 1070, 39 A.L.R. 468.

the teaching of doctrines which challenge the existence of the state and the well-being of society.[7] It may, moreover, require that children be educated in schools which meet substantially the same standards as the state requires of its own schools.[8]

The relation of the public school to the state is clearly defined by a case[9] decided by the Court of Appeals of Kentucky. By an act of the legislature of Kentucky the minimum tax levy for school purposes in cities of the first class was fixed at thirty-six cents on the one hundred dollars' valuation. The Board of Education of Louisville presented to the city council their budget which required a levy of at least the amount provided for by statute. The council refused to make the levy, contending that the statute in question violated the following provision of the state constitution: "The General Assembly shall not impose taxes for the purpose of any county, city, town or other municipal corporation, but may by general laws confer upon the proper authorities thereof respectively power to assess and collect such taxes." In issuing a writ of mandamus which required the council to levy the tax, the court said in part:

"If the maintenance of a public school is a purely municipal purpose, then the section would seem to be conclusive of the matter. But education is not a subject pertaining alone, or pertaining essentially, to a municipal corporation. Whilst public education in this country is now deemed a public duty in every state, and since before the first federation was regarded as a proper public enterprise, it has never been looked upon as being at all a matter of local concern only. On the contrary, it is regarded as an essential to the preservation of liberty—as forming one of the first duties of a democratic government. The place assigned it in the deliberate judgment of the American people is scarcely second to any. If it is essentially a prerogative of sovereignty to raise troops in time of war, it is equally so to prepare each generation of youth to discharge the duties of citizenship in time of peace and war. Upon preparation of the younger generations for civic duties depends the perpetuity of this government. Power to levy taxes is an essential attribute of sovereignty. That is so because the necessity of conducting the government requires that money be raised for the purpose by some sort of taxation. So is the power to educate the youth of the state, to fit them so that the state may prosper; else the taxes raised could scarcely meet demands made upon a government in these times. Whilst the power named is older in point of adoption as a legal maxim, the other is modernly found to be of no less importance. It may be doubted if the state could strip itself of either quality of its sovereignty. Certainly it will not be deemed to have attempted it upon language open to debate."

The reasoning in the foregoing case is supported by a decision rendered by the Supreme Court of Tennessee. The legislature of that state passed an act which prescribed uniform textbooks for the schools throughout the state. A commission was to select the books to be used and to let contracts to the lowest bidder for supplying the books adopted. In sustaining the constitutionality of the act, the court identified the maintenance of a system of public schools with the exercise of the police power of the state. It was said by the court:

"It is immaterial whether we consider this act as deriving validity from the police power of the state or the public character of the schools. It is evident that the basic principle of it is the power of the legislature to subserve the general welfare by prohibiting certain contracts, and throwing around others restrictions tending to promote the general welfare, and protect the citizen from oppression, fraud, and wrong. That the state may establish a uniform series of books to be taught in the schools, which it provides and controls, seems to be a proposition as evident as that it may provide a uniform system of schools, which we take it is not now an open question. . . .

"We are of the opinion that the legislature, under the constitutional provision, may as well establish a uniform system of schools and a uniform administration of them, as it may establish a uniform system of criminal laws and of courts to execute them. The object of the criminal law is, by punishment, to deter others from the commission of crimes, and thus preserve the peace, morals, good order, and well-being of society; and the object of the public-school system is to prevent crime, by educating the people, and thus, by providing and securing a higher state of intelligence and morals, conserve the peace, good order, and well-being of society. The prevention of crime, and preservation of good order and peace, is the highest exercise of the police power

---

[7] *People* v. *American Socialist Society*, 195 N.Y.S. 801, 202 App. Div. 640.
[8] *Wright* v. *State*, 21 Okla. Cr. 430, 209 Pac. 179.
[9] *City of Louisville* v. *Commonwealth*, 134 Ky. 488, 121 S.W. 411.

of the state, whether done by punishing offenders or educating the children."[10]

The relation of the school to the individual on the one hand and to organized society on the other has been clearly stated by the Supreme Court of Illinois in the following language:

"The public school system of the State was not established and has not been maintained as a charity or from philanthropic motives. The first legislative expression in regard to schools in Illinois was in the ordinance of 1787, which declares that 'religion, morality and knowledge being necessary to good government and the happiness of mankind, schools and the means of education shall forever be encouraged.' This declaration grew, not out of philanthropic motives, but out of a consideration of the essentials of good government. The conduct and maintenance of schools by school directors, school trustees and boards of education is no less an 'exercise of the functions vested in those charged with the conduct of government,' is no less a part of 'the science and art of government,' and deals no less with the 'organization, regulation and administration of a State' in its internal affairs, than the construction and maintenance of roads by the commissioners of highways; the conduct and maintenance of the charitable institutions of the State by the board of administration; the inspection of factories, and the enforcement of the laws for the protection of workmen and in regard to the employment of women and children, by the factory inspectors; the performance of the industrial board of the duties imposed upon it by law, and the performance of many other duties by public officials which, however beneficial to individuals, are not undertaken from philanthropic or charitable motives, but for the protection, safety and welfare of the citizens of the State in the interest of good government."[11]

Similarly, it was said by the Supreme Court of New Hampshire:

"The primary purpose of the maintenance of the common school system is the promotion of the general intelligence of the people constituting the body politic and thereby to increase the usefulness and efficiency of the citizens, upon which the government of society depends. Free schooling furnished by the state is not so much a right granted to pupils as a duty imposed upon them for the public good. If they do not voluntarily attend the schools provided for them, they may be compelled to do so. While most people regard the public schools as the means of great personal advantage to the pupils, the fact is too often overlooked that they are governmental means of protecting the state from the consequences of an ignorant and incompetent citizenship."[12]

The state legislature and educational policy

State policy finds expression through the medium of constitutional provisions and statutory enactments. In education, as in all other matters of government, the federal and state constitutions are the fundamental law. The principle is well established, however, that the state legislature, subject to constitutional restrictions, has authority to pass any act of a legislative nature which may in its opinion seem wise.[13] While the legislature may be said to exercise delegated authority, it is authority delegated generally and not specifically. The very act of creating a legislative branch of government confers upon it all powers of a legislative nature except such as are expressly withheld. Thus it has been said by Chief Justice Denio, speaking for the Court of Appeals of New York:[14] "The people, in framing the constitution, committed to the legislature the whole law making power of the state, which they did not expressly or impliedly withhold. Plenary power in the legislature for all purposes of civil government is the rule." It follows that it is for those who challenge the constitutionality of a statute to show that it is forbidden.[15] The Congress of the United States must find constitutional authority for all its acts; a state legislature, on the other hand, may pass any act not expressly or impliedly forbidden by fundamental law.[16]

From what has been said, it is obvious that, subject to constitutional limitations, the state legislature has plenary power with respect to matters of educational policy. In the absence of

[10] *Leeper* v. *State,* 103 Tenn. 500, 53 S.W. 962, 48 L.R.A. 167.
[11] *Scown* v. *Czarnecki,* 264 Ill. 305.

[12] *Fogg* v. *Board of Education,* 76 N.H. 296, 82 Atl. 173, 37 L.R.A. (N.S.) 1110, Ann. Cas. 1912C 758.
[13] *Fletcher* v. *Peck,* 6 Cranch (U.S.) 128, 3 L. Ed. 162; *Sill* v. *Village of Corning,* 15 N.Y. 297; *Commonwealth* v. *Hartman,* 17 Pa. St. 118; *State Female Normal School* v. *Auditors,* 79 Va. 233; *State* v. *Haworth,* 122 Ind. 462, 23 N.E. 946, 7 L.R.A. 240; *State* v. *Meador,* 284 S.W. (Tenn.) 890.
[14] *People* v. *Draper,* 15 N.Y. 532.
[15] *People* v. *Draper,* 15 N.Y. 532.
[16] *Commonwealth* v. *Hartman,* 17 Pa. St. 118.

constitutional prohibitions, the ends to be attained and the means to be employed are wholly subject to legislative determination. The legislature may determine the types of schools to be established throughout the state,[17] the means of their support,[18] the organs of their administration,[19] the content of their curricula,[20] and the qualifications of their teachers. Moreover, all these matters may be determined with or without regard to the wishes of the localities, for in education the state is the unit and there are no local rights except such as are safeguarded by the constitution.

The case of *Commonwealth* v. *Hartman*[21] illustrates the application of the principles of law stated in the preceding paragraphs. In 1848 the legislature of Pennsylvania passed an act which provided for the establishment of free schools for all the children of the state between the ages of five and twenty-one. The constitution provided that the legislature should establish schools throughout the state in such manner that the poor might be taught gratis. The act was challenged on the ground that the constitution did not authorize the establishment of a system of schools free to all. In holding that the mandate to establish schools free for the poor was a minimum and not a maximum grant of power, the court reasoned as follows:

"It is to be remembered that the rule of interpretation for the state constitution differs totally from that which is applicable to the constitution of the United States. The latter instrument must have a strict construction; the former a liberal one. Congress can pass no laws but those which the constitution authorizes either expressly or by clear implication; while the Assembly has jurisdiction of all subjects on which its legislation is not prohibited. . . . In applying this principle to the present case, it is enough to say that there is no syllable in the constitution which forbids the legislature to provide for a system of general education in any way which they, in their own wisdom, may think best."

The Supreme Court of Indiana, in the leading case of *State* v. *Haworth*,[22] expresses clearly and forcibly the authority of the state legislature to determine state educational policy. The issue involved was the constitutionality of a statute which required township trustees to distribute textbooks selected by the state board of education. The statute was assailed on the ground that it violated the right of local self-government. After pointing out that the right of local self-government could in no case be exercised except in matters of purely local concern, the court continued:

"Essentially and intrinsically the schools in which are educated and trained the children who are to become the rulers of the commonwealth are matters of State, and not of local jurisdiction. In such matters, the State is the unit, and the Legislature the source of power. The authority over schools and school affairs is not necessarily a distributive one to be exercised by local instrumentalities; but, on the contrary, it is a central power residing in the Legislature of the State. It is for the law-making power to determine whether the authority shall be exercised by a State board of education, or distributed to county, township, or city organizations throughout the State. . . .

"As the power over schools is a legislative one, it is not exhausted by exercise. The Legislature having tried one plan is not precluded from trying another. It has a complete choice of methods, and may change its plans as often as it deems necessary or expedient. . . . It is clear, therefore, that even if it were true, that the Legislature had uniformly intrusted the management of school affairs to local organizations, it would not authorize the conclusion that it might not change the system."

Since education is a function of the state, school officers are state officers. Consequently, they may be selected in any manner that the legislature may determine. They may be elected by the people, be appointed by the courts,[23] or be selected by any other agencies which policy may dictate. Moreover, it is not necessary that school officers reside in the district where they hold office. Such was the conclusion reached by the Supreme Court

[17] *State* v. *Freeman*, 61 Kan. 90, 58 Pac. 959, 47 L.R.A. 67; *State Female Normal School* v. *Auditors*, 79 Va. 233; *In re Kindergarten Schools*, 18 Colo. 234, 32 Pac. 422, 19 L.R.A. 469.
[18] *State* v. *Meador*, 284 S.W. (Tenn.) 890; *Miller* v. *Korns*, 107 Ohio St. 287, 140 N.E. 773; *Sawyer* v. *Gilmore*, 109 Me. 169, 83 Atl. 673; *Miller* v. *Childers*, 107 Okla. 57, 238 Pac. 204.
[19] *State* v. *Hine*, 59 Conn. 50, 21 Atl. 1024, 10 L.R.A. 83; *State* v. *Haworth*, 122 Ind. 462, 23 N.E. 946, 7 L.R.A. 240.
[20] *State* v. *Haworth*, 122 Ind. 462, 23 N.E. 946, 7 L.R.A. 240; *Associated Schools of Independent District No. 63* v. *School District No. 83*, 122 Minn. 254, 142 N.W. 325, 47 L.R.A. (N.S.) 200.
[21] *Commonwealth* v. *Hartman*, 17 Pa. St. 118.

[22] *State* v. *Haworth*, 122 Ind. 462, 23 N.E. 946, 7 L.R.A. 240.
[23] *Minsinger* v. *Rau*, 236 Pa. St. 327, 84 Atl. 902, Ann. Cas. 1913E 1324.

of Errors of Connecticut in a decision rendered in 1890. An act of the legislature provided that the secretary of the state board of education should be ex officio a member of the school committee of certain towns and districts of the state. In sustaining the act the court made the following significant statement:

"If the reasoning and the conclusions arrived at in the former part of this opinion are right, then towns in Connecticut have no inherent right to elect school committees and never had. In the absence of constitutional restriction we think the legislature may provide that school committees, whether of a town or a district or society, may be composed of any persons and chosen in any manner that it may prescribe."[24]

One other case may be cited to illustrate the freedom of the legislature in determining methods of school support. The legislature of Tennessee passed an act which required the county court of each county to provide funds for the maintenance of a four-year high school in the

county. The act was challenged on the ground that it violated the right of local self-government. In holding otherwise, the court said:

"The public school system is a matter of state, and not local, concern, and the establishment, maintenance, and control of the public schools is a legislative function. To promote the public schools, the state, through the Legislature, may levy taxes directly, or the state, having, as it does, full control over its agencies, the counties, may authorize them to levy a tax, or may by statute require them to levy a tax for the establishment and maintenance of public schools. . . .

"The exercise of the taxing power to promote a system of public schools for all the counties does not infringe upon the right of local self-government, because a public school system, like a highway system, a penal system, or a matter of public health is not of purely local, but of state, concern. The state is a unit, and the Legislature is the state's source of legislative power, from which flows the mandate of the state."[25] . . .

[24] *State* v. *Hine*, 59 Conn. 50, 21 Atl. 1024, 10 L.R.A. 83.

[25] *State* v. *Meador*, 284 S.W. (Tenn.) 890.

89

THE KALAMAZOO DECISION

Any thorough discussion of the evolution of American public education includes reference to the "Kalamazoo Case," decided in the Supreme Court of Michigan in 1874. The court was confronted with a number of critical questions, such as: To what extent can schools be provided for at the expense of the taxpayers? What positions can be established and supported in a school system through the use of tax funds? The scope and nature of American education for many years was to be affected by answers to such questions.

The court's decision in the Kalamazoo case established the principle that tax money could be used to provide free public high schools as well as elementary schools and that personnel (such as superintendents) could be employed to administer the comprehensive system of public education desired by taxpayers. Furthermore, the high schools were permitted to offer instruction in any branch of knowledge deemed necessary in the education of high-school pupils.

The bill in this case is filed to restrain the collection of such portion of the school taxes

assessed against complainants for the year 1872, as have been voted for the support of the high school in that village, and for the payment of the salary of the superintendent. While, nominally, this is the end sought to be attained by

Stuart et al. v. *School District No. 1 of the Village of Kalamazoo*, 30 Michigan 69 (1874).

the bill, the real purpose of the suit is wider and vastly more comprehensive than this brief statement would indicate, inasmuch as it seeks a judicial determination of the right of school authorities, in what are called union school districts of the state, to levy taxes upon the general public for the support of what in this state are known as high schools, and to make free by such taxation the instruction of children in other languages than the English. The bill is, consequently, of no small interest to all the people of the state; and to a large number of very flourishing schools, it is of the very highest interest, as their prosperity and usefulness, in a large degree, depend upon the method in which they are supported, so that a blow at this method seems a blow at the schools themselves. The suit, however, is not to be regarded as a blow purposely aimed at the schools. It can never be unimportant to know that taxation, even for the most useful or indispensable purposes, is warranted by the strict letter of the law; and whoever doubts its being so in any particular case, may well be justified by his doubts in asking a legal investigation, that, if errors or defects in the law are found to exist, there may be a review of the subject in legislation, and the whole matter be settled on legal grounds, in such manner and on such principles as the public will may indicate, and as the legislature may prescribe. . . .

The more general question which the record presents we shall endeavor to state in our own language, but so as to make it stand out distinctly as a naked question of law, disconnected from all considerations of policy or expediency; in which light alone are we at liberty to consider it. It is, as we understand it, that there is no authority in this state to make the high schools free by taxation levied on the people at large. The argument is that while there may be no constitutional provision expressly prohibiting such taxation, the general course of legislation in the state and the general understanding of the people have been such as to require us to regard the instruction in the classics and in living modern languages in these schools as in the nature not of practical and therefore necessary instruction for the benefit of the people at large, but rather as accomplishments for the few, to be sought after in the main by those best able to pay for them, and to be paid for by those who seek them, and not by general tax. And not only has this been the general state policy, but this higher learning of itself, when supplied by the state, is so far a matter of private concern to those who receive it that the courts ought to declare it incompetent to supply it wholly at the public expense. This is in substance, as we understand it, the position of the complainants in this suit.

When this doctrine was broached to us, we must confess to no little surprise that the legislation and policy of our state were appealed to against the right of the state to furnish a liberal education to the youth of the state in schools brought within the reach of all classes. We supposed it had always been understood in this state that education, not merely in the rudiments, but in an enlarged sense, was regarded as an important practical advantage to be supplied at their option to rich and poor alike, and not as something pertaining merely to culture and accomplishment to be brought as such within the reach of those whose accumulated wealth enabled them to pay for it. As this, however, is now so seriously disputed, it may be necessary, perhaps, to take a brief survey of the legislation and general course, not only of the state, but of the antecedent territory, on the subject.

It is not disputed that the dissemination of knowledge by means of schools has been a prominent object from the first, and we allude to the provision of the ordinance of 1787 on that subject, and to the donation of lands by congress for the purpose, only as preliminary to what we may have to say regarding the action of the territorial authorities in the premises. Those authorities accepted in the most liberal spirit the requirement of the ordinance that "schools and the means of education shall forever be encouraged," and endeavored to make early provision therefor on a scale which shows they were fully up to the most advanced ideas that then prevailed on the subject. . . .

. . . In 1827 the educational system was supplemented by "an act for the establishment of common schools," which is also worthy of special attention and reflection, as indicating what was understood at that day by the common schools which were proposed to be established.

The first section of that act provided "that every township within this territory, containing fifty families or householders, shall be provided with a good schoolmaster or schoolmasters, of good morals, to teach children to read and write, and to instruct them in the English or French language, as well as in arithmetic, orthography, and decent behavior, for such term of time as shall be equivalent to six months for one school in each year. And every township containing one hundred families or householders, shall be provided with such schoolmaster or teacher, for such term of time, as shall be equivalent to twelve months for one school in each year. And every township containing one hundred and fifty families or householders shall be provided with such schoolmaster or teacher for such term of time as shall be equivalent to six months in each year, and shall, in addition thereto, be provided with a schoolmaster or teacher, as above described, to instruct children in the English language for such term of time as shall be equivalent to twelve months for one school in each year. And every township containing two hundred families or householders shall be provided with a grammar schoolmaster, of good morals, *well instructed in the Latin, French and English languages,* and shall, in addition thereto, be provided with a schoolmaster or teacher, as above described, to instruct children in the English language, for such term of time as shall be equivalent to twelve months for each of said schools in each year." And the townships respectively were required under a heavy penalty, to be levied in case of default on the inhabitants generally, to keep and maintain the schools so provided for: *Code of 1827, p. 448; Territorial Laws, Vol. 2, p. 472.*

Here, then, was a general law, which, under the name of common schools, required not only schools for elementary instruction, but also grammar schools to be maintained. The qualifications required in teachers of grammar schools were such as to leave it open to no doubt that grammar schools in the sense understood in England and the Eastern States were intended, in which instruction in the classics should be given, as well as in such higher branches of learning as would not usually be taught in the schools of lowest grade. How is it possible, then, to say, as the exigencies of complainants' case require them to do, that the term common or primary schools, as made use of in our legislation, has a known and definite meaning which limits it to the ordinary district schools, and that consequently the legislative authority to levy taxes for the primary schools cannot be held to embrace taxation for the schools supported by village and city districts in which a higher grade of learning is imparted.

It is probable that this act, like that of 1817, was found in advance of the demands of the people of the territory, or of their ability to support high schools, and it was repealed in 1833, and another passed which did not expressly require the establishment or support of schools of secondary grade, but which provided only for school directors, who must maintain a district school at least three months in each year: *Code of 1833, p. 129.* The act contains no express limitations upon their powers, but it is not impor-

tant now to consider whether or not they extended to the establishment of grammar schools as district schools, where, in their judgment, they might be required. Such schools would certainly not be out of harmony with any territorial policy that as yet had been developed or indicated.

Thus stood the law when the constitution of 1835 was adopted. The article on education in that instrument contained the following provisions:

"2. The legislature shall encourage by all suitable means the promotion of intellectual, scientifical and agricultural improvement. The proceeds of all lands that have been, or hereafter may be, granted by the United States to this state for the support of schools, which shall hereafter be sold or disposed of, shall be and remain a perpetual fund, the interest of which, together with the rents of all such unsold lands, shall be inviolably appropriated to the support of schools throughout the state.

"3. The legislature shall provide for a system of common schools, by which a school shall be kept up and supported in each school district at least three months in every year; and any school district neglecting to keep up and support such a school may be deprived of its equal proportion of the interest of the public fund."

The fifth section provided for the support of the university, "with such branches as the public convenience may hereafter demand for the promotion of literature, the arts and sciences," etc. Two things are specially noticeable in these provisions: *first,* that they contemplated provision by the state for a complete system of instruction, beginning with that of the primary school and ending with that of the university; *second,* that while the legislature was required to make provision for district schools for at least three months in each year, no restriction was imposed upon its power to establish schools intermediate the common district school and the university, and we find nothing to indicate an intent to limit their discretion as to the class or grade of schools to which the proceeds of school lands might be devoted, or as to the range of studies or grade of instruction which might be provided for in the district schools.

In the very first executive message after the constitution went into effect, the governor, in view of the fact that "our institutions have leveled the artificial distinctions existing in the societies of other countries, and have left open to every one the avenues to distinction and honor," admonished the legislature that it was their "imperious duty to secure to the state a general diffusion of knowledge," and that "this can in no wise be so certainly effected as by the perfect organization of a uniform and liberal system of common schools." Their "attention was therefore called to the effectuation of a perfect school system, open to all classes, as the surest basis of public happiness and prosperity." In his second message he repeated his admonitions, advising that provision be made for ample compensation to teachers, that those of the highest character, both moral and intellectual, might be secured, and urging that the "youth be taught the first principles in morals, in science, and in government, commencing their studies in the primary schools, elevating its grades as you approach the district seminary, and continue its progress till you arrive at the university." This message indicated no plan, but referred the legislature to the report of the superintendent, who would recommend a general system.

The system reported by superintendent Pierce contemplated a university, with branches in different parts of the state as preparatory schools, and district schools. This is the parent of our present system, and though its author did not find the legislature prepared to accept all his views, the result has demonstrated that he was only a few years in advance of his generation, and that the changes in our school system which have since been adopted have been in the direction of the views which he then held and urged upon the public. And an examination of his official report for 1837 will show that the free schools he then favored were schools which taught something more than the rudiments of a common education; which were to give to the poor the advantages of the rich, and enable both alike to obtain within the state an education broad and liberal, as well as practical.

It would be instructive to make liberal extracts from this report did time and space permit. The superintendent would have teachers thoroughly trained, and he would have the great object of common schools "to furnish good instruction in all the elementary and common branches of knowledge, for all classes of community, *as good, indeed, for the poorest boy of the state as the rich man can furnish for his children with all his wealth.*" The context shows that he had the systems of Prussia and of New England in view, and that he proposed by a free school system to fit the children of the poor as well as of the rich for the highest spheres of activity and influence.

It might also be useful in this connection to show that the Prussian system and that "of the

Puritans," of which he speaks in such terms of praise, resemble in their main features, so far as bringing within the reach of all a regular gradation of schools is concerned, the system of public instruction as it prevails in this state to-day. But it is not necessary for the purposes of the present case to enter upon this subject. It must suffice to say that the law of 1827, which provided for grammar schools as a grade of common schools, was adopted from laws which from a very early period had been in existence in Massachusetts, and which in like manner, under heavy penalties, compelled the support of these grammar schools in every considerable town: See *Mass. Laws, 1789, p. 39;* compare *General Stat., 1860, p. 215 § 2. . . .*

It now becomes important to see whether the constitutional convention and the people, in 1850, did any thing to undo what previously had been accomplished towards furnishing high schools as a part of the primary school system. The convention certainly did nothing to that end. On the contrary, they demonstrated in the most unmistakable manner that they cherished no such desire or purpose. The article on education as originally reported, while providing for free schools to be kept in each district at least three months in every year, added that "the English language and no other shall be taught in such schools." Attention was called to this provision, and it was amended so as to read that instruction should be "conducted in the English language." The reason for the change was fully given, that as it was reported it might be understood to prohibit the teaching of other languages than the English in the primary schools; a result that was not desired. Judge Whipple stated in the convention that, in the section from which he came, French and German were taught, and "it is a most valuable improvement of the common school system." The late superintendent Pierce said that in some schools Latin was taught, and that he himself had taught Latin in a common school. He would not adopt any provision by which any knowledge would be excluded. "All that we ought to do is this: we should say the legislature shall establish primary schools." This, in his opinion, would give full power, and the details could be left to legislation: See *Debates of the Convention, 269, 549.*

The instrument submitted by the convention to the people and adopted by them provided for the establishment of free schools in every school district for at least three months in each year, and for the university. By the aid of these we have every reason to believe the people expected a complete collegiate education might be obtained. The branches of the university had ceased to exist; the university had no preparatory department, and it must either have been understood that young men were to be prepared for the university in the common schools, or else that they should go abroad for the purpose, or be prepared in private schools. Private schools adapted to the purpose were almost unknown in the state, and comparatively a very few persons were at that time of sufficient pecuniary ability to educate their children abroad. The inference seems irresistible that the people expected the tendency towards the establishment of high schools in the primary school districts would continue until every locality capable of supporting one was supplied. And this inference is strengthened by the fact that a considerable number of our union schools date their establishment from the year 1850 and the two or three years following.

If these facts do not demonstrate clearly and conclusively a general state policy, beginning in 1817 and continuing until after the adoption of the present constitution, in the direction of free schools in which education, and at their option the elements of classical education, might be brought within the reach of all the children of the state, then, as it seems to us, nothing can demonstrate it. We might follow the subject further, and show that the subsequent legislation has all concurred with this policy, but it would be a waste of time and labor. We content ourselves with the statement that neither in our state policy, in our constitution, or in our laws, do we find the primary school districts restricted in the branches of knowledge which their officers may cause to be taught, or the grade of instruction that may be given, if their voters consent in regular form to bear the expense and raise the taxes for the purpose. . . .

90

THE OREGON DECISION

The various states have the right—and nearly all of them exercise it—to require children of school age to attend school unless they are physically or mentally incapable of profiting by the instruction offered. Does this right include also the authority to require children to attend *public* schools?

In 1922, the state of Oregon enacted a law that would have required all children between the ages of eight and sixteen to attend public schools. As might have been expected, this statute was challenged by private and parochial schools. A suit was instituted that reached the Supreme Court of the United States in 1925. In its decision the Court declared that a state could require children to attend school and could regulate and supervise private schools and examine the qualifications of their personnel. It could not, however, require parents to place their children in public schools if they desired to enroll them in adequate private or parochial schools. Thus the "Oregon Case" clarified a major question in the states' effort to require that all children be educated.

The force of this decision had considerable effect on the growth of private education. According to the 1960 census, 13.6 per cent of all school children in America, approximately five and one half million, were attending private and parochial schools.

These appeals are from decrees, based upon undenied allegations, which granted preliminary orders restraining appellants from threatening or attempting to enforce the Compulsory Education Act adopted November 7, 1922, under the initiative provision of her Constitution by the voters of Oregon. Jud. Code, § 266. They present the same points of law; there are no controverted questions of fact. Rights said to be guaranteed

Pierce v. *Society of Sisters,* 268 U.S. 510 (1925).

by the federal Constitution were specially set up, and appropriate prayers asked for their protection.

The challenged Act, effective September 1, 1926, requires every parent, guardian or other person having control or charge or custody of a child between eight and sixteen years to send him "to a public school for the period of time a public school shall be held during the current year" in the district where the child resides; and failure so to do is declared a misdemeanor. There are exemptions—not specially important here—for children who are not normal, or who have completed the eighth grade, or who reside at considerable distances from any public school, or whose parents or guardians hold special permits from the County Superintendent. The manifest purpose is to compel general attendance at public schools by normal children, between eight and sixteen, who have not completed the eighth grade. And without doubt enforcement of the statute would seriously impair, perhaps destroy, the profitable features of appellees' business and greatly diminish the value of their property.

Appellee, the Society of Sisters, is an Oregon corporation, organized in 1880, with power to care for orphans, educate and instruct the youth, establish and maintain academies or schools, and acquire necessary real and personal property. It has long devoted its property and effort to the secular and religious education and care of children, and has acquired the valuable good will of many parents and guardians. It conducts interdependent primary and high schools and junior colleges, and maintains orphanages for the custody and control of children between eight and sixteen. In its primary schools many children between those ages are taught the subjects usually pursued in Oregon public schools during the first eight years. Systematic religious instruction and moral training according to the tenets of the Roman Catholic Church are also regularly provided. All courses of study, both temporal and religious, contemplate continuity of training under appellee's charge; the primary schools are essential to the system and the most profitable. It owns valuable buildings, especially constructed and equipped for school purposes. The business is remunerative—the annual income from primary schools exceeds thirty thousand dollars—and the successful conduct of this requires long time contracts with teachers and parents. The Compulsory Education Act of 1922 has already caused the withdrawal from its schools of children who would otherwise continue, and their income has steadily declined. The appellants,

public officers, have proclaimed their purpose strictly to enforce the statute.

After setting out the above facts the Society's bill alleges that the enactment conflicts with the right of parents to choose schools where their children will receive appropriate mental and religious training, the right of the child to influence the parents' choice of a school, the right of schools and teachers therein to engage in a useful business or profession, and is accordingly repugnant to the Constitution and void. And, further, that unless enforcement of the measure is enjoined the corporation's business and property will suffer irreparable injury. . . .

No question is raised concerning the power of the State reasonably to regulate all schools, to inspect, supervise and examine them, their teachers and pupils; to require that all children of proper age attend some school, that teachers shall be of good moral character and patriotic disposition, that certain studies plainly essential to good citizenship must be taught, and that nothing be taught which is manifestly inimical to the public welfare.

The inevitable practical result of enforcing the Act under consideration would be destruction of appellees' primary schools, and perhaps all other private primary schools for normal children within the State of Oregon. These parties are engaged in a kind of undertaking not inherently harmful, but long regarded as useful and meritorious. Certainly there is nothing in the present records to indicate that they have failed to discharge their obligations to patrons, students or the State. And there are no peculiar circumstances or present emergencies which demand extraordinary measures relative to primary education.

Under the doctrine of *Meyer* v. *Nebraska*, 262 U.S. 390, we think it entirely plain that the Act of 1922 unreasonably interferes with the liberty of parents and guardians to direct the upbringing and education of children under their control. As often heretofore pointed out, rights guaranteed by the Constitution may not be abridged by legislation which has no reasonable relation to some purpose within the competency of the State. The fundamental theory of liberty upon which all governments in this Union repose excludes any general power of the State to standardize its children by forcing them to accept instruction from public teachers only. The child is not the mere creature of the State; those who nurture him and direct his destiny have the right, coupled with the high duty, to recognize and prepare him for additional obligations. . . .

[Decree affirmed.]

91

COCHRAN V. LOUISIANA STATE BOARD OF EDUCATION

A basic principle of American government involves, as often stated, the "separation of church and state." Public funds, for example, are not appropriated by states to build and maintain schools operated by churches and religious sects. Nevertheless, if a state provides free textbooks for children in the public schools, can it provide them for pupils in parochial and private schools?

In 1928 Louisiana made available funds to supply textbooks for the children of the state. Its supreme court ruled that the law permitted the state to furnish the books not only to children in public schools but also to those in private and parochial schools. It reasoned that the books benefited the pupils rather than the schools they attended. This position was upheld by the United States Supreme Court in 1930 in this historic decision.

The appellants, as citizens and taxpayers of the State of Louisiana, brought this suit to restrain the State Board of Education and other state officials from expending any part of the severance tax fund in purchasing school books and in supplying them free of cost to the school children of the State, under Acts No. 100 and No. 143 of 1928, upon the ground that the legislation violated specified provisions of the constitution of the State and also section 4 of Article IV and the Fourteenth Amendment of the Federal Constitution. The Supreme Court of the State affirmed the judgment of the trial court, which refused to issue an injunction. 168 La. 1030.

Act No. 100 of 1928 provided that the severance tax fund of the State, after allowing funds and appropriations as required by the state constitution, should be devoted "first, to supplying school books to the school children of the State." The Board of Education was directed to provide "school books for school children free of cost to such children." Act No. 143 of 1928 made appropriations in accordance with the above provisions.

The Supreme Court of the State, following its decision in *Borden* v. *Louisiana State Board of Education*, 168 La. 1005, held that these acts were not repugnant to either the state or the Federal Constitution.

No substantial Federal question is presented under section 4 of Article IV of the Federal Constitution guaranteeing to every State a republican form of government, as questions aris-

ing under this provision are political, not judicial, in character. *State of Ohio ex rel. Bryant* v. *Akron Metropolitan Park District, ante,* p. 74, and cases there cited.

The contention of the appellant under the Fourteenth Amendment is that taxation for the purchase of school books constituted a taking of private property for a private purpose. *Loan Association* v. *Topeka,* 20 Wall. 655. The purpose is said to be to aid private, religious, sectarian, and other schools not embraced in the public educational system of the State by furnishing text-books free to the children attending such private schools. The operation and effect of the legislation in question were described by the Supreme Court of the State as follows (168 La., p. 1020):

"One may scan the acts in vain to ascertain where any money is appropriated for the purchase of school books for the use of any church, private, sectarian or even public school. The appropriations were made for the specific purpose of purchasing school books for the use of the school children of the state, free of cost to them. It was for their benefit and the resulting benefit to the state that the appropriations were made. True, these children attend some school, public or private, the latter, sectarian or non-sectarian, and that the books are to be furnished them for their use, free of cost, whichever they attend. The schools, however, are not the beneficiaries of these appropriations. They obtain nothing from them, nor are they relieved of a single obligation, because of them. The school children and the state alone are the beneficiaries. It is

Cochran v. Louisiana State Board of Education, 281 U.S. 370 (1930).

also true that the sectarian schools, which some of the children attend, instruct their pupils in religion, and books are used for that purpose, but one may search diligently the acts, though without result, in an effort to find anything to the effect that it is the purpose of the state to furnish religious books for the use of such children. . . . What the statutes contemplate is that the same books that are furnished children attending public schools shall be furnished children attending private schools. This is the only practical way of interpreting and executing the statutes, and this is what the state board of education is doing. Among these books, naturally, none is to be expected, adapted to religious instruction."

The Court also stated, although the point is not of importance in relation to the Federal question, that it was "only the use of the books that is granted to the children, or, in other words, the books are lent to them."

Viewing the statute as having the effect thus attributed to it, we can not doubt that the taxing power of the State is exerted for a public purpose. The legislation does not segregate private schools, or their pupils, as its beneficiaries or attempt to interfere with any matters of exclusively private concern. Its interest is education, broadly; its method, comprehensive. Individual interests are aided only as the common interest is safeguarded.

Judgment affirmed.

92

EVERSON V. BOARD OF EDUCATION OF THE TOWNSHIP OF EWING

The question raised in Louisiana concerning the use of public funds for the purchase of textbooks for children in private and parochial schools had a counterpart in New Jersey, where the issue was the use of public money to transport children to private and parochial schools. Under provisions of a state law, the board of education in Ewing, New Jersey, provided free transportation to children attending either public or parochial schools. A taxpayer challenged this procedure. After the Ewing school board was upheld by the Court of Errors and Appeals of New Jersey, the case was appealed to the United States Supreme Court, which in 1947 also upheld the school board's policy. The Court ruled again that the provision of free textbooks or free transportation to pupils benefited the children rather than the schools they attended. Therefore, it decreed, there was no violation of any principle of the separation of church and state.

Because the decision contains a rather extensive statement of the Court's position with regard to church-state relationships in education, it has been mentioned frequently in recent years by high government officials and others in their discussions of what financial assistance, if any, the federal government can give to private and parochial schools.

A New Jersey statute authorizes its local school districts to make rules and contracts for the transportation of children to and from schools. The appellee, a township board of education, acting pursuant to this statute authorized reimbursement to parents of money expended by them for the bus transportation of their children

on regular busses operated by the public transportation system. Part of this money was for the payment of transportation of some children in the community to Catholic parochial schools. . . .

The appellant, in his capacity as a district taxpayer, filed suit in a State court challenging the right of the Board to reimburse parents of parochial school students. He contended that the statute and the resolution passed pursuant to it

---

Everson v. *Board of Education of the Township of Ewing,* 330 U.S. 1 (1947).

violated both the State and the Federal Constitutions. . . .

The only contention here is that the State statute and the resolution, in so far as they authorized reimbursement to parents of children attending parochial schools, violate the Federal Constitution in these two respects, which to some extent, overlap. First. They authorize the State to take by taxation the private property of some and bestow it upon others, to be used for their own private purposes. This, it is alleged violates the due process clause of the Fourteenth Amendment. Second. The statute and the resolution forced inhabitants to pay taxes to help support and maintain schools which are dedicated to, and which regularly teach, the Catholic Faith. This is alleged to be a use of State power to support church schools contrary to the prohibition of the First Amendment which the Fourteenth Amendment made applicable to the states. . . .

Insofar as the second phase of the due process argument may differ from the first, it is by suggesting that taxation for transportation of children to church schools constitutes support of a religion by the State. But if the law is invalid for this reason, it is because it violates the First Amendment's prohibition against the establishment of religion by law. This is the exact question raised by appellant's second contention, to consideration of which we now turn.

Second. The New Jersey statute is challenged as a "law respecting an establishment of religion." The First Amendment, as made applicable to the states by the Fourteenth, commands that a state "shall make no law respecting an establishment of religion, or prohibiting the free exercise thereof." These words of the First Amendment reflected in the minds of early Americans a vivid mental picture of conditions and practices which they fervently wished to stamp out in order to preserve liberty for themselves and for their posterity. Doubtless their goal has not been entirely reached; but so far has the Nation moved toward it that the expression "law respecting an establishment of religion," probably does not so vividly remind present-day Americans of the evils, fears, and political problems that caused that expression to be written into our Bill of Rights. Whether this New Jersey law is one respecting the "establishment of religion" requires an understanding of the meaning of that language, particularly with respect to the imposition of taxes. Once again, therefore, it is not inappropriate briefly to review the background and environment of the period in which that constitutional language was fashioned and adopted. . . .

This Court has previously recognized that the provisions of the First Amendment, in the drafting and adoption of which Madison and Jefferson played such leading roles, had the same objective and were intended to provide the same protection against governmental intrusion on religious liberty as the Virginia statute. Reynolds v. United States, supra, 98 U.S. at page 164, [etc.]. Prior to the adoption of the Fourteenth Amendment, the First Amendment did not apply as a restraint against the states. Most of them did soon provide similar constitutional protections for religious liberty. But some states persisted for about half a century in imposing restraints upon the free exercise of religion and in discriminating against particular religious groups. In recent years, so far as the provision against the establishment of a religion is concerned, the question has most frequently arisen in connection with proposed state aid to church schools and efforts to carry on religious teachings in the public schools in accordance with the tenets of a particular sect. Some churches have either sought or accepted state financial support for their schools. Here again the efforts to obtain state aid or acceptance of it have not been limited to any one particular faith. The state courts, in the main, have remained faithful to the language of their own constitutional provisions designed to protect religious freedom and to separate religions and governments. Their decisions, however, show the difficulty in drawing the line between tax legislation which provides funds for the welfare of the general public and that which is designed to support institutions which teach religion.

The meaning and scope of the First Amendment, preventing establishment of religion or prohibiting the free exercise thereof, in the light of its history and the evils it was designed forever to suppress, have been several times elaborated by the decisions of this Court prior to the application of the First Amendment to the states by the Fourteenth. The broad meaning given the Amendment by these earlier cases has been accepted by this Court in its decisions concerning an individual's religious freedom rendered since the Fourteenth Amendment was interpreted to make the prohibitions of the First applicable to state action abridging religious freedom. There is every reason to give the same application and broad interpretation to the "establishment of religion" clause. The interrelation of these complementary clauses was well summarized in a statement of the Court of Appeals of South Carolina, quoted with approval by this Court, in Watson v. Jones, 13 Wall. 679: "The structure of our government has, for the preservation of civil liberty, rescued the temporal institutions from religious interference. On the other hand, it has secured religious liberty from the invasions of the civil authority."

The "establishment of religion" clause of the First Amendment means at least this: Neither a state nor the Federal Government can set up a church. Neither can pass laws which aid one religion, aid all religions, or prefer one religion over another. Neither can force nor influence a person to go to or to remain away from church against his will or force him to profess a belief or disbelief in any religion. No person can be punished for entertaining or professing religious beliefs or disbeliefs, for church attendance or non-attendance. No tax in any amount, large or small, can be levied to support any religious activities or institutions, whatever they may be called, or whatever form they may adopt to teach or practice religion. Neither a state nor the Federal Government can, openly or secretly, participate in the affairs of any religious organizations or groups and vice versa. In the words of Jefferson, the clause against establishment of religion by law was intended to erect "a wall of separation between Church and State." Reynolds v. United States, supra, 98 U.S. at page 164.

We must consider the New Jersey statute in accordance with the foregoing limitations imposed by the First Amendment. But we must not strike that state statute down if it is within the state's constitutional power even though it approaches the verge of that power. New Jersey cannot consistently with the "establishment of religion" clause of the First Amendment contribute tax-raised funds to the support of an institution which teaches the tenets and faith of any church. On the other hand, other language of the amendment commands that New Jersey cannot hamper its citizens in the free exercise of their own religion. Consequently, it cannot exclude individual Catholics, Lutherans, Mohammedans, Baptists, Jews, Methodists, Non-believers, Presbyterians, or the members of any other faith, *because of their faith, or lack of it,* from receiving the benefits of public welfare legislation. While we do not mean to intimate that a state could not provide transportation only to children attending public schools, we must be careful, in protecting the citizens of New Jersey against state-established churches, to be sure that we do not inadvertently prohibit New Jersey from extending its general State law benefits to all its citizens without regard to their religious belief.

Measured by these standards, we cannot say that the First Amendment prohibits New Jersey from spending tax-raised funds to pay the bus fares of parochial school pupils as a part of a general program under which it pays the fares of pupils attending public and other schools. It is undoubtedly true that children are helped to get to church schools. There is even a possibility that some of the children might not be sent to the church schools if the parents were compelled to pay their children's bus fares out of their own pockets when transportation to a public school would have been paid for by the State. The same possibility exists where the state requires a local transit company to provide reduced fares to school children including those attending parochial schools, or where a municipally owned transportation system undertakes to carry all school children free of charge. Moreover, state-paid policemen, detailed to protect children going to and from church schools from the very real hazards of traffic, would serve much the same purpose and accomplish much the same result as state provisions intended to guarantee free transportation of a kind which the state deems to be best for the school children's welfare. And parents might refuse to risk their children to the serious danger of traffic accidents going to and from parochial schools, the approaches to which were not protected by policemen. Similarly, parents might be reluctant to permit their children to attend schools which the state had cut off from such general government services as ordinary police and fire protection, connections for sewage disposal, public highways and sidewalks. Of course, cutting off church schools from these services, so separate and so indisputably marked off from the religious function, would make it far more difficult for the schools to operate. But such is obviously not the purpose of the First Amendment. That Amendment requires the state to be a neutral in its relations with groups of religious believers and non-believers; it does not require the state to be their adversary. State power is no more to be used so as to handicap religions, than it is to favor them.

This Court has said that parents may, in the discharge of their duty under state compulsory education laws, send their children to a religious rather than a public school if the school meets the secular educational requirements which the state has power to impose. See Pierce v. Society of Sisters, 268 U.S. 510. It appears that these parochial schools meet New Jersey's requirements. The State contributes no money to the schools. It does not support them. Its legislation, as applied, does no more than provide a general program to help parents get their children, regardless of their religion, safely and expeditiously to and from accredited schools.

The First Amendment has erected a wall between church and state. That wall must be kept high and impregnable. We could not approve the slightest breach. New Jersey has not breached it here.

Affirmed.

93

McCOLLUM V. BOARD OF EDUCATION OF SCHOOL DISTRICT NO. 71

The "McCollum Case," as it is usually called, deals with a different aspect of the separation of church and state in the field of public education. Here the question was whether or not public school facilities could be used for religious instruction even under a "released-time" arrangement. (The question of released time for religious instruction *off* the school premises was not the issue; this is held to be perfectly legal.)

Such an arrangement had been made in the public schools of Champaign, Illinois. A parent, Mrs. McCollum, brought suit against the local school board, declaring that the plan was unconstitutional. She finally lost her suit in the Illinois Supreme Court. In an appeal to the United States Supreme Court in 1948, however, she won her case. The Court declared that "released-time" religious instruction in the public schools violated the First and Fourteenth Amendments of the Constitution.

At the time that the Supreme Court announced its decision, more than two million children in various sections of the United States were enrolled in "released-time" programs in the public schools.

This case relates to the power of a state to utilize its tax-supported public school system in aid of religious instruction insofar as that power may be restricted by the First and Fourteenth Amendments to the Federal Constitution.

The appellant, Vashti McCollum, began this action for mandamus against the Champaign Board of Education in the Circuit Court of Champaign County, Illinois. Her asserted interest was that of a resident and taxpayer of Champaign and of a parent whose child was then enrolled in the Champaign public schools. Illinois has a compulsory education law which, with exceptions, requires parents to send their children, aged seven to sixteen, to its tax-supported public schools where the children are to remain in attendance during the hours when the schools are regularly in session. Parents who violate this law commit a misdemeanor punishable by fine unless the children attend private or parochial schools which meet educational standards fixed

by the State. District boards of education are given general supervisory powers over the use of the public school buildings within the school districts.

Appellant's petition for mandamus alleged that religious teachers, employed by private religious groups, were permitted to come weekly into the school buildings during the regular hours set apart for secular teaching, and then and there for a period of thirty minutes substitute their religious teaching for the secular education provided under the compulsory education law. The petitioner charged that this joint public-school religious-group program violated the First and Fourteenth Amendments to the United States Constitution. . . .

Although there are disputes between the parties as to various inferences that may or may not properly be drawn from the evidence concerning the religious program, the following facts are shown by the record without dispute. In 1940 interested members of the Jewish, Roman Catholic, and a few of the Protestant faiths formed a voluntary association called the Champaign Council on Religious Education. They obtained permission from the Board of Education to offer

McCollum v. *Board of Education of School District No. 71, Champaign County, Illinois*, 333 U.S. 203 (1948).

classes in religious instruction to public school pupils in grades four to nine inclusive. Classes were made up of pupils whose parents signed printed cards requesting that their children be permitted to attend; they were held weekly, thirty minutes for the lower grades, forty-five minutes for the higher. The council employed the religious teachers at no expense to the school authorities, but the instructors were subject to the approval and supervision of the superintendent of schools. The classes were taught in three separate religious groups by Protestant teachers, Catholic priests, and a Jewish rabbi, although for the past several years there have apparently been no classes instructed in the Jewish religion. Classes were conducted in the regular classrooms of the school building. Students who did not choose to take the religious instruction were not released from public school duties; they were required to leave their classrooms and go to some other place in the school building for pursuit of their secular studies. On the other hand, students who were released from secular study for the religious instructions were required to be present at the religious classes. Reports of their presence or absence were to be made to their secular teachers.

The foregoing facts, without reference to others that appear in the record, show the use of tax-supported property for religious instruction and the close cooperation between the school authorities and the religious council in promoting religious education. The operation of the state's compulsory education system thus assists and is integrated with the program of religious instruction carried on by separate religious sects. Pupils compelled by law to go to school for secular education are released in part from their legal duty upon the condition that they attend the religious classes. This is beyond all question a utilization of the tax-established and tax-supported public school system to aid religious groups to spread their faith. And it falls squarely under the ban of the First Amendment (made applicable to the States by the Fourteenth) as we interpreted it in Everson v. Board of Education, 330 U.S. 1, 67 S.Ct. 504. There we said: "Neither a state nor the Federal Government can set up a church. Neither can pass laws which aid one religion, aid all religions, or prefer one religion over another. Neither can force nor influence a person to go to or to remain away from church against his will or force him to profess a belief or disbelief in any religion. No person can be punished for entertaining or professing religious beliefs or disbeliefs, for church attendance or nonattendance. No tax in any amount, large or small,

can be levied to support any religious activities or institutions, whatever they may be called, or whatever form they may adopt to teach or practice religion. Neither a state nor the Federal Government can, openly or secretly, participate in the affairs of any religious organizations or groups, and vice versa. In the words of Jefferson, the clause against establishment of religion by law was intended to erect 'a wall of separation between Church and State.'" The majority in the Everson case, and the minority as shown by quotations from the dissenting views agreed that the First Amendment's language, properly interpreted, had erected a wall of separation between Church and State. They disagreed as to the facts shown by the record and as to the proper application of the First Amendment's language to those facts.

Recognizing that the Illinois program is barred by the First and Fourteenth Amendments if we adhere to the views expressed both by the majority and the minority in the Everson case, counsel for the respondents challenge those views as dicta and urge that we reconsider and repudiate them. They argue that historically the First Amendment was intended to forbid only government preference of one religion over another, not an impartial governmental assistance of all religions. In addition they ask that we distinguish or overrule our holding in the Everson case that the Fourteenth Amendment made the "establishment of religion" clause of the First Amendment applicable as a prohibition against the States. After giving full consideration to the arguments presented we are unable to accept either of these contentions.

To hold that a state cannot consistently with the First and Fourteenth Amendments utilize its public school system to aid any or all religious faiths or sects in the dissemination of their doctrines and ideals does not, as counsel urge, manifest a governmental hostility to religious or religious teachings. A manifestation of such hostility would be at war with our national tradition as embodied in the First Amendment's guaranty of the free exercise of religion. For the First Amendment rests upon the premise that both religion and government can best work to achieve their lofty aims if each is left free from the other within its respective sphere. Or, as we said in the Everson case, the First Amendment has erected a wall between Church and State which must be kept high and impregnable.

Here not only are the state's tax-supported public school buildings used for the dissemination of religious doctrines. The State also affords sectarian groups an invaluable aid in that it helps to provide pupils for their religious classes through use of the state's compulsory public school machinery. This is not separation of Church and State.

The cause is reversed and remanded to the State Supreme Court for proceedings not inconsistent with this opinion.

94

BROWN V. BOARD OF EDUCATION OF TOPEKA

Despite the fact that public education is a function and responsibility of a state, can the state segregate pupils in the various public schools on the basis of race? Prior to 1954, the assumption was made that state laws requiring or permitting racial segregation in public schools were constitutional provided the schools for each race were equal in facilities and quality. Such an assumption was based on the "separate-but-equal" provisions of the famous case of *Plessy v. Ferguson,* decided by the Supreme Court of the United States in 1896. By 1954, however, cases had reached the Court from Delaware, Kansas, South Carolina, and Virginia which again questioned the constitutionality of segregation.

In its decision of 1954, quoted below, the Supreme Court declared that "separate but equal schools" were not, in fact, equal and that racial segregation in public schools was unconstitutional. In another ruling, made on May 31, 1955, the Court decreed that all states with segregated schools must proceed with "all deliberate speed" in desegregating them.

Opponents of the Court's decision have criticized it as one made on the basis of sociology and psychology rather than on the basis of interpretation of constitutional law. Regardless of this criticism, however, the decision is now the law of the country. Furthermore, in 1958, the Court declared that "state support of segregated schools through any arrangement, management, funds, or property cannot be squared with the [Fourteenth] Amendment's command that no State shall deny any person within its jurisdiction the equal protection of the laws" (8).

These cases come to us from the States of Kansas, South Carolina, Virginia, and Delaware. They are premised on different facts and different local conditions, but a common legal question justifies their consideration together in this consolidated opinion.

In each of the cases, minors of the Negro race, through their legal representatives, seek the aid of the courts in obtaining admission to the public schools of their community on a nonsegregated basis. In each instance, they have been denied admission to schools attended by white children under laws requiring or permitting segregation according to race. This segregation was alleged to deprive the plaintiffs of the equal protection of the laws under the Fourteenth Amendment. In each of the cases other than the Delaware

case, a three-judge federal district court denied relief to the plaintiffs on the so-called "separate but equal" doctrine announced by this Court in Plessy v. Ferguson, 163 U. S. 537. Under that doctrine, equality of treatment is accorded when the races are provided substantially equal facilities, even though these facilities be separate. In the Delaware case, the Supreme Court of Delaware adhered to that doctrine, but ordered that the plaintiffs be admitted to the white schools because of their superiority to the Negro schools.

The plaintiffs contend that segregated public schools are not "equal" and cannot be made "equal," and that hence they are deprived of the equal protection of the laws. Because of the obvious importance of the question presented, the Court took jurisdiction. Argument was heard in the 1952 Term, and reargument was heard this Term on certain questions propounded by the Court.

Brown v. *Board of Education of Topeka,* 347 U.S. 483 (1954).

Reargument was largely devoted to the circumstances surrounding the adoption of the Fourteenth Amendment in 1868. It covered exhaustively consideration of the Amendment in Congress, ratification by the states, then existing practices in racial segregation, and the views of proponents and opponents of the Amendment. This discussion and our own investigation convince us that, although these sources cast some light, it is not enough to resolve the problem with which we are faced. At best, they are inconclusive. The most avid proponents of the post-War Amendments undoubtedly intended them to remove all legal distinctions among "all persons born or naturalized in the United States." Their opponents, just as certainly, were antagonistic to both the letter and the spirit of the Amendments and wished them to have the most limited effect. What others in Congress and the state legislatures had in mind cannot be determined with any degree of certainty.

An additional reason for the inconclusive nature of the Amendment's history, with respect to segregated schools, is the status of public education at that time. In the South, the movement toward free common schools, supported by general taxation, had not yet taken hold. Education of white children was largely in the hands of private groups. Education of Negroes was almost nonexistent, and practically all of the race were illiterate. In fact, any education of Negroes was forbidden by law in some states. Today, in contrast, many Negroes have achieved outstanding success in the arts and sciences as well as in the business and professional world. It is true that public education had already advanced further in the North, but the effect of the Amendment on Northern States was generally ignored in the congressional debates. Even in the North, the conditions of public education did not approximate those existing today. The curriculum was usually rudimentary; ungraded schools were common in rural areas; the school term was but three months a year in many states; and compulsory school attendance was virtually unknown. As a consequence, it is not surprising that there should be so little in the history of the Fourteenth Amendment relating to its intended effect on public education.

In the first cases in this Court construing the Fourteenth Amendment, decided shortly after its adoption, the Court interpreted it as proscribing all state-imposed discriminations against the Negro race. The doctrine of "separate but equal" did not make its appearance in this Court until 1896 in the case of Plessy v. Ferguson, supra, involving not education but transportation. American courts have since labored with the doctrine for over half a century. In this Court, there have been six cases involving the "separate but equal" doctrine in the field of public education. In Cumming v. Board of Education of Richmond County, 175 U. S. 528, and Gong Lum v. Rice, 275 U. S. 78, the validity of the doctrine itself was not challenged. In more recent cases, all on the graduate school level, inequality was found in that specific benefits enjoyed by white students were denied to Negro students of the same educational qualifications. State of Missouri ex rel. Gaines v. Canada, 305 U. S. 337; Sipuel v. Board of Regents of University of Oklahoma, 332 U. S. 631; Sweatt v. Painter, 339 U. S. 629; McLaurin v. Oklahoma State Regents, 339 U. S. 637. In none of these cases was it necessary to reexamine the doctrine to grant relief to the Negro plaintiff. And in Sweatt v. Painter, supra, the Court expressly reserved decision on the question whether Plessy v. Ferguson should be held inapplicable to public education.

In the instant cases, that question is directly presented. Here, unlike Sweatt v. Painter, there are findings below that the Negro and white schools involved have been equalized, or are being equalized, with respect to buildings, curricula, qualifications and salaries of teachers, and other "tangible" factors. Our decision, therefore, cannot turn on merely a comparison of these tangible factors in the Negro and white schools involved in each of the cases. We must look instead to the effect of segregation itself on public education.

In approaching this problem, we cannot turn the clock back to 1868 when the Amendment was adopted, or even to 1896 when Plessy v. Ferguson was written. We must consider public education in the light of its full development and its present place in American life throughout the Nation. Only in this way can it be determined if segregation in public schools deprives these plaintiffs of the equal protection of the laws.

Today, education is perhaps the most important function of state and local governments. Compulsory school attendance laws and the great expenditures for education both demonstrate our recognition of the importance of education to our democratic society. It is required in the performance of our most basic public responsibilities, even service in the armed forces. It is the very foundation of good citizenship. Today it is a principal instrument in awakening the child to cultural values, in preparing him for later professional training, and in helping him to adjust normally to his environment. In these days, it is doubtful that any child may reasonably be expected to succeed in life if he is denied the opportunity of an education. Such an opportunity, where the state has undertaken to provide it, is a right which must be made available to all on equal terms.

We come then to the question presented: Does segregation of children in public schools solely on the basis of race, even though the physical facilities and other "tangible" factors may be equal, deprive the children of the minority group of equal educational opportunities? We believe that it does.

In Sweatt v. Painter, supra [339 U. S. 629, 70 S.Ct. 850], in finding that a segregated law school for Negroes could not provide them equal educational opportunities, this Court relied in large part on "those qualities which are incapable of objective measurement but which make for greatness in a law school." In McLaurin v. Oklahoma State Regents, supra [339 U. S. 637, 70 S.Ct. 853], the Court, in requiring that a Negro admitted to a white graduate school be treated like all other students, again resorted to intangible considerations: ". . . his ability to study, to engage in discussions and exchange views with other students, and, in general, to learn his profession." Such considerations apply with added force to children in grade and high schools. To separate them from others of similar age and qualifications solely because of their race generates a feeling of inferiority as to their status in the community that may affect their hearts and minds in a way unlikely ever to be undone. The effect of this separation on their educational opportunities was well stated by a finding in the Kansas case by a court which nevertheless felt compelled to rule against the Negro plaintiffs:

"Segregation of white and colored children in public schools has a detrimental effect upon the colored children. The impact is greater when it has the sanction of the law; for the policy of separating the races is usually interpreted as denoting the inferiority of the Negro group. A sense of inferiority affects the motivation of a child to learn. Segregation with the sanction of law, therefore, has a tendency to retard the educational and mental development of Negro children and to deprive them of some of the benefits they would receive in a racially integrated school system."

Whatever may have been the extent of psychological knowledge at the time of Plessy v. Ferguson, this finding is amply supported by modern authority. Any language in Plessy v. Ferguson contrary to this finding is rejected.

We conclude that in the field of public education the doctrine of "separate but equal" has no place. Separate educational facilities are inherently unequal. Therefore, we hold that the plaintiffs and others similarly situated for whom the actions have been brought are, by reason of the segregation complained of, deprived of the equal protection of the laws guaranteed by the Fourteenth Amendment. This disposition make unnecessary any discussion whether such segregation also violates the Due Process Clause of the Fourteenth Amendment.

Because these are class actions, because of the wide applicability of this decision, and because of the great variety of local conditions, the formulation of decrees in these cases presents problems of considerable complexity. On reargument, the consideration of appropriate relief was necessarily subordinated to the primary question —the constitutionality of segregation in public education. We have now announced that such segregation is a denial of the equal protection of the laws. In order that we may have the full assistance of the parties in formulating decrees, the cases will be restored to the docket, and the parties are requested to present further argument. . . . The Attorney General of the United States is again invited to participate. The Attorneys General of the states requiring or permitting segregation in public education will also be permitted to appear as *amici curiae* upon request to do so by September 15, 1954, and submission of briefs by October 1, 1954.

It is so ordered.

95

Sam M. Lambert

THE CASE FOR FEDERAL SUPPORT OF EDUCATION

The federal government provides vast sums of money for certain programs in the public schools of the various states. Nevertheless, the bulk of the cost of public education is borne by the states and the communities within them.

Can the state and local governments, particularly the less wealthy ones, raise sufficient funds through their systems of taxation to provide adequate public schools? Or must the federal government assume a much larger share of the cost in order that every American child can have an education of at least a certain minimum quality?

The National Education Association, America's largest educational organization, believes that state and local systems of taxation cannot provide adequate public schools in most states and that there must be major increases in federal assistance to the elementary and secondary schools in the various states. In this statement the Association not only presents the case for federal assistance but also reviews the current status of public education.

On the credit side

The people of this country can point with pride to the many accomplishments in public education in the past two or three decades. All in all we have come a long way.

From eighth-graders to eleventh-graders. The one achievement that impresses me most is the fact that in just 19 years, from April 1940 to March 1959, we have moved the median years of education completed by adults 25 years of age and over from 8.4 years to 10.6 years. Nineteen years ago we were a nation of eighth-graders; today we are a nation half way through the high-school sophomore year. Despite all the grumbling about spelling and reading over the past decade, I doubt that there is a nation on earth as well educated.

In addition to the many direct personal benefits to the recipients of this additional education, no one should overlook the economic impact on the nation's economy. We are rapidly reaching the point where we will be a nation of high-school graduates. In fact, this level has already been achieved by the typical (median) person in the 25-to-29-year age group.

I wonder if you know that the typical male high-school graduate can be expected to earn over his lifetime (from age 25 to death) $71,868 more than the typical male elementary-school graduate. For the 8,658,000[1] male adults in this country in 1958 with only eight years of schooling, high-school graduation would mean a difference in lifetime income of a total of $622 billion.

It might be well to add that federal taxes on the difference in incomes would probably amount to several billions more in revenue each year.

Consolidation. A second achievement of considerable merit is the progress made toward consolidation of districts and schools. In the past 11 years we have reduced the number of school districts in this country from 83,614 in 1949-50 to 37,153 in 1960-61,[2] or 56 percent. In the past 10 years, we have been eliminating districts at the rate of 4600 annually.

Along with the consolidation of school districts has come the elimination of thousands and thousands of one-room schools. Between 1948 and 1959, the number of one-room schools in this country dropped from 75,000 to 24,000.[3]

Most educators believe these changes are resulting in more and better education for America's children and youth. Many citizens, however, labor under the misconception that school consolidation saves money. Actually it does not. Almost always the larger district spends more money than the districts it replaced. These larger districts, however, provide a broader program which was economically impossible in the small district. Experience has proved that the changes

From *The Case for Federal Support of Education* by Sam M. Lambert (Washington: National Education Association, 1961), pp. 3-22.
[1] U. S. Department of Commerce, Bureau of the Census. *Income of Families and Persons in the United States: 1958.* Current Population Reports, Consumer Income, Series P-60, No. 33. Washington, D. C.: the Bureau, January 15, 1960. Table 26, p. 38.

[2] U. S. Department of Health, Education, and Welfare, Office of Education. "Statistical Summary of Education: 1955-56." *Biennial Survey of Education in the United States—1954-56.* Washington, D. C.: Superintendent of Documents, Government Printing Office, 1959. Chapter 1, Table 14, p. 28. National Education Association, Research Division. *Estimates of School Statistics, 1960-61.* Research Report 1960-R15. Washington, D. C.: the Association, December 1960. Table 1, p. 19.
[3] Gaumnitz, Walter H., and Blose, David T. *The One-Teacher School—Its Mid-century Status.* U. S. Office of Education, Federal Security Agency, Circular 318. Washington, D. C.: Superintendent of Documents, Government Printing Office, 1950. p. 19. National Education Association, Research Division. *One-Teacher Schools Today.* Research Monograph 1960-M1. Washington, D. C.: the Association, June 1960. p. 12.

result in getting more and better education for our money.

More money. In this list of major achievements we cannot overlook the magnificent display of effort on the part of the American people to finance this rapidly expanding enterprise. The investment in public elementary and secondary schools has increased from $5.8 billion 10 years ago to an estimated $15.3 billion in 1959-60,[4] an increase of about 164 percent. Even in constant dollars of 1959-60 prices, the increase was 78 percent, from $8.6 billion in 1949-50 to $15.3 billion in 1959-60. Expense per pupil in average daily attendance increased 83 percent in current dollars and 24 percent in constant prices.

The problem of constructing enough buildings has been staggering, but the people have increased their annual investment in capital outlay and interest from $1.1 billion in 1950 to $3.3 billion in 1960,[5] an increase of 200 percent.

In the past 10 years, we have constructed an estimated total of 594,000 new classrooms,[6] sufficient space to provide a brand new room for every teacher employed at the end of World War I. I doubt that any major public or private enterprise in modern times has ever expanded its physical plant as rapidly.

On the debit side

Drop-out rate. On the other hand, whatever optimism we may have about progress in public education is tempered by the fact that less than 60 percent of our fifth-grade boys and girls stay in school through high school. Out of every 3 reaching the ninth grade, 1 fails to get his high-school diploma.[7] A total of 929,000, or 17 percent, of the 16- and 17-year-old civilians were not enrolled in any school in the fall of 1959.[8]

These facts raise many questions about the adequacy of today's public elementary and secondary schools. Is the guidance program really adequate? Is the curriculum or program of studies broad enough to meet the present needs of America's children and youth? Is the quality of teachers and teaching equal to the demands of a rapidly changing society?

The obvious answer to these questions is No. A 33-percent drop-out rate in the high-school grades is far too high. No one should assume that these 33 percent who quit in the eighth, ninth, tenth, eleventh, and twelfth grades are incapable of learning and thus not worth educating. Some may be, but not 3 to 4 in every 10.

Failure on mental tests. In nearly all the arguments for federal support of education someone drags in the rate of failure on the Armed Forces mental test. However, since the mental requirements for draftees have been raised in recent years because of higher levels of skills required by technological developments in modern warfare, it might be well to consider these figures again. All men called for induction receive an examination which determines their acceptability for active service. In 1959, approximately 25 percent of our young men who took the mental test given to Selective Service registrants did not pass it. The percentage was as high as 62 percent in one state and 50 percent or more in two others. In 10 states, 1 in every 3 registrants failed the mental test in 1959. These rates represent only draftees.[9] Some have raised a question as to whether there is a national interest in education. These figures indicate that if there isn't a national interest in education, there certainly should be.

Voting. Another entry on the debit side of the public education ledger is the failure of American citizens to exercise one of the first and most simple privileges and responsibilities of American citizenship—voting for the people who govern them. I am sure that all of you have seen

[4] U. S. Department of Health, Education, and Welfare, Office of Education. "Statistical Summary of Education: 1955-56." *Biennial Survey of Education in the United States—1954-56.* Washington, D. C.: Superintendent of Documents, Government Printing Office, 1959. Table 13, p. 25. National Education Association, Research Division. *Estimates of School Statistics, 1960-61.* Research Report 1960-R15. Washington, D. C.: the Association, December 1960. Table 12, p. 30.

[5] *Ibid.*

[6] U. S. Department of Health, Education, and Welfare, Office of Education.

[7] U. S. Department of Health, Education, and Welfare, Office of Education. "Statistical Summary of Education: 1955-56." *Biennial Survey of Education in the United States—1954-56.* Washington, D. C.: Superintendent of Documents, Government Printing Office, 1959. Table 6, p. 13.

[8] U. S. Department of Commerce, Bureau of the Census. *School Enrollment: October 1959.* Current Population Reports, Population Characteristics, Series P-20, No. 101. Washington, D. C.: the Bureau, May 22, 1960. Table 2, p. 8.

[9] U. S. Department of the Army, Office of the Surgeon General. "Preinduction and Induction Examination Results, 1959." *Health of the Army* 15: 1-10; February 1960.

the record of voting in the last Presidential election, but I wonder if you have thought about your public schools in connection with this voting record. Over one-third of the people of voting age did not vote in the Presidential election of 1960, and this record was one of the best in the history of the United States. This raises a question about the adequacy of the program of American history and the other social studies.

Unemployment. One of the major problems on the political scene at present is that of unemployment, and unemployment is a frequent bedfellow of inadequate levels of education. Those of you who know the coal fields of West Virginia and the southwestern part of Virginia know that most of those who have been unemployed for months and even years are those whose education stopped at the fifth, sixth, seventh, and eighth grades. The high-school graduates in these areas have proved more flexible and have tended to move to other jobs. The superintendent of one county school system in West Virginia that has two high schools recently told me that not one single person who had graduated from his high schools in the past three years was still in the county. . . .

One by one the inadequacies in breadth and scope of the knowledge and skills the schools are teaching command the public's attention. The controversies not infrequently reach this Congress in the form of a proposed program to do something about them immediately. It does no good to blast the schools today for inadequacies in the preparation of former public-school pupils, although it may help to strengthen the curriculum for pupils now in school. These are the ones who will be in the manpower pool one to 12 or 16 years hence. These are the only ones the schools can do anything for. There is truly a need across the nation now to offer the kind of education in the public schools which will be needed during the next generation. I regret to say that, to date, despite our substantial progress there is a strong tendency to set the curriculum and investment at levels of hindsight rather than foresight.

The 1960's—a decade of trouble

Certain opponents of any type of federal support for education have been trying to convey the idea to the American people that we are over the hump in necessary school expansion. Statements, such as "The rate of increase in the 1950's will decrease in the 1960's" leave little

room for comfort when the facts are examined carefully. Regardless of what anyone says, enrollments are still going up, and each year in the 1960's we will have more students in school than ever before.

Further increases in enrollment. Let's examine the facts. In the decade of the 1950's, the enrollment in the elementary and secondary schools increased 11 million. In the 1960's enrollment will go up another 8.1 million.[10] In fact, the enrollment will continue to increase at the rate of about 1.1 million each year through 1964-65, which is about the same annual increase as we have experienced over the past 10 years. The increase after 1964-65 should begin to drop to about 600,000 per year and continue at this level throughout the last half of this decade. The drop in the enrollment increase which is so comforting to some people is still five years off.

And we are not very certain about the drop in the last half of the coming decade; these children have not been born, much less counted. Furthermore, retention of more of the drop-outs and expansion of the kindergarten grade could result in a far higher increase than that now expected in the 1960's.

On the assumption that we expect only 8.1 million more in the present decade, as compared with 11 million more in the last decade, the cost increase will still not follow the ratio of 8 to 11 because a much larger proportion of the 8.1 million than of the 11.0 million will be in high-school grades where the average cost per pupil is 1.3 to 1.5 times as high. Enrollment in grades 9 through 12 increased only 2.6 million in the 1950's, but will increase 4.0 million in the 1960's. It is likely that the enrollment increase in this decade will prove more expensive than the increase in the past decade.

Classroom teachers. In 1958-59, classroom teachers employed in public schools totaled 1.3 million. According to the U. S. Office of Education, we will be employing 1.7 million by 1968-69 (these figures are for 48 states and the District of Columbia).[11] This means that in this 10-year

[10] U. S. Department of Health, Education, and Welfare, Office of Education. *Projected Enrollments in Full-Time Public and Nonpublic Elementary and Secondary Day Schools Assuming Continuation of 1955-57 Birth Rates, 50 States and D. C.: School Years 1958-59 to 1969-70.* Washington, D. C.: the Office, August 24, 1960. p. 1.

[11] U. S. Department of Health, Education, and Welfare, Office of Education. *National Goals in the Staffing and Construction of Public Elementary and*

period the number of teaching positions will increase by 400,000. If we include supervisors, principals, and other instructional personnel, the need will be even larger.

The figures above, however, show only part of the picture. To replace those leaving their positions in the decade just mentioned, we will find it necessary to recruit and employ 1.6 million teachers in this decade, more than the total instructional staff of public schools today. In addition, to take care of growing enrollment we will need 400,000 new teachers.[12] The new demand for classroom teachers is expected to average 200,000 a year.[13]

This presents a tremendous challenge considering the fact that at present colleges are producing only 129,000 teachers each year, of whom only 95,000, or 73 percent, can be expected to actually go into teaching positions.[14] The only hope of getting qualified personnel is to bring back to teaching the hundreds of thousands who trained for teaching but never taught or who have left teaching for some other calling. A second possibility would be to persuade more of the students going to college to select teaching as a profession.

I would like to digress for a minute to mention the problem of emergency teachers, teachers who do not meet the regular licensing requirements of the various states. You may be interested to know that we now have more emergency teachers on the payroll than we had in 1950-51 (93,917 vs. 75,079).[15] It is estimated that these teachers, half of whom do not have college degrees, are teaching approximately 2.5 million pupils each day. Certification standards differ from state to state. Also, many states in recent years have upgraded their standards for full certification.

The only way we can make a dent in the supply problem in the next 10 years is to reduce the turnover rate among teachers or to find some way of recruiting many more teachers than we have in the past.

In some of the states, teacher turnover is a staggering problem. For example, during the past six years, between 1954-55 and 1959-60, 9183 teachers quit their jobs in West Virginia. This state has had an average teaching force during this period of 15,000. This means recruiting and orienting to their jobs about three-fifths of all teachers in West Virginia every six years. And the situation is becoming worse. In the first year of this six-year sequence, 1954-55, 1114 quit their jobs. In 1956-57 a total of 1422 quit; in 1958-59, 1462; in 1959-60, 1824.[16] It might be well to mention that six years ago West Virginia's average teacher's salary was $2975.[17] In 1959-60, it was only $3825.[18]

Competing for talented manpower. One of the really difficult tasks of the current decade is to get salaries up to the point where the public schools can really compete for talented manpower. Almost everyone is in favor of paying teachers more, but we part ways when we begin to talk about who's going to pay the bill. Any realistic discussion of teachers' salaries should be based on the kinds of persons teachers really are. The American people, including many political leaders, still hold false stereotypes of teachers. This affects decisions on pay scales.

The typical teacher in the United States is no longer a sweet young thing in her early twenties who lives with her mother and father at no cost to herself. She is not a person with only two years of college training. Her working day is not a 6-hour arrangement, and she doesn't always have a 3-month vacation, even without pay.

This typical teacher in the American public school is both mature and well-educated. This person is about 43 years of age, has gone to college 4.7 years, and has taught school for 13 years.[19] One summer in three this teacher goes back to college at his or her own expense. During the school year this teacher averages a 45-to-50-

Secondary Schools, 1959-1969. Washington, D. C.: the Office, April 1960. Table 2, p. 16.
[12] *Ibid.,* Table 4, p. 23.
[13] President's Commission on National Goals. *Goals for Americans.* New York: American Assembly, Columbia University, 1960. p. 82.
[14] National Education Association, Research Division. *Teacher Supply and Demand in Public Schools, 1960.* Research Report 1960-R7. Washington, D. C.: the Association, April 1960. p. 23.
[15] National Education Association, Research Division. *Estimates of School Statistics, 1960-61.* Research Report 1960-R15. Washington, D. C.: the Association, December 1960. p. 12.

[16] West Virginia Education Association. *Teacher Turnover Continues To Be Critical.* Charleston: the Association, November 1960. 3 p.
[17] National Education Association, Research Division. *Advance Estimates of Public Elementary and Secondary Schools for the School Year 1954-55.* Washington, D. C.: the Association, November 1954. Table 7, p. 17.
[18] National Education Association, Research Division. *Estimates of School Statistics, 1960-61.* Research Report 1960-R15. Washington, D. C.: the Association, December 1960. Table 8, p. 26.
[19] National Education Association, Research Division. "The Status of the American Public-School Teacher." *Research Bulletin* 35: 43, 44, 46; February 1957.

hour week in teaching, grading papers, and planning work for the days ahead.[20] With this much college training and experience, and at an age when the worker should be getting somewhere, the typical teacher's salary is likely to be $5200.

Despite the improvement in salaries in recent years, we are not as well off in recruiting able people for teaching as we were in the 1920's, 1930's, and the 1940's. As teachers' salaries have gone up, so have salaries of other occupations which tend to attract potential teachers. Let's take a look at salaries for teaching where 46 percent have four years and 35 percent have five or more years of college training. How does teaching compare with the other professions? The latest comparable figures we have are for 1958 and these are from the U. S. Bureau of the Census.

The average earnings of physicians, lawyers, and dentists was $13,457. The average for engineers was $9647. The composite average for 17 professions requiring college graduation was $9439. The comparable figure for public-school teachers the same year was $4827.[21]

Persons in other professions not only start out with higher earnings, they are much farther ahead after 10 years on the job. Men engineers just out of college, for example, start at an average of $6120; accountants at $5352; sales personnel at $5280;[22] but teachers at only $3900.[23]

After 10 years the engineer is making 67 percent more than when he started; the accountant, 82 percent; the sales worker, 86 percent.[24] After 10 years of work in the classroom, the typical teacher's salary has gone up only 49 percent.[25]

In the years to come, it is going to become more and more difficult to recruit high-level college graduates at the salaries now paid. The U. S. Department of Labor has released some figures which have an interesting bearing on this point. These figures deal with the peculiar shape of the manpower supply during the decade of the 1960's.

According to the Department of Labor reports, the labor force of the United States will increase about 13.5 million workers during the 1960's. But let's look for a moment at the kinds of people who will make up this new labor supply. Approximately 47 percent, or about 1 in 2, will be youngsters under 24 years of age; 41 percent will be 45 years of age and older. This totals 88 percent of the new supply of labor in the next decade.[26]

As you well know, we get very few teachers from this top age bracket, and the number of beginners under 24 is getting smaller every year. Teachers simply do not start teaching as young as they used to. They stay in college longer, and the women are getting married and having children before they enter teaching.

Here are some other interesting facts on this increase in the labor supply during the next decade. Only 13 percent of these additional workers will be 25 to 34 years of age, and this is the group from which we have been getting the majority of our beginning teachers.

Believe it or not, there will be a decline in the number of workers 35 to 44 years of age. This is another important group for teaching, since the median age of teachers falls within this age bracket.

Thus, according to the Department of Labor, the low birth rates of the 1930's have given a sort of hourglass configuration to our population. We will have big increases at the bottom and at the top and a constriction in the middle. We are going to run into an increasing demand for a diminishing supply of certain kinds of workers. Business and industry are also going to be recruiting from the same group we are after. They will be employing more mature educated women to augment the short supply of experienced men. If teachers' salaries could be about doubled in the next four years, we would have an average salary of $10,750; this would be only about three-fourths of what the average in 17 other professional occupations will be by 1965. About the only hope we have of reaching this average is through a third partner in financing education.

In my estimation, the problem of manpower in education, and I am talking about high-level manpower, is more crucial than that of buildings. I think most of us would agree that in our search for quality education, about 90 percent of all the quality we have ever had or ever will have comes through quality manpower.

[20] National Education Association, Research Division. "Teaching Load in 1950." *Research Bulletin* 29: 14; February 1951.

[21] Computed by the NEA Research Division from figures collected by the U. S. Bureau of the Census and reported in: National Education Association, Research Division. *Economic Status of Teachers in 1959-60.* Research Report 1960-R8. Washington, D. C.: the Association, May 1960. 50 p.

[22] Endicott, Frank S. *Trends in the Employment of College and University Graduates in Business and Industries—1961.* Evanston, Ill.: Northwestern University, 1961. p. 5.

[23] Based on NEA Research Division salary surveys and state minimum salary laws.

[24] Endicott, Frank S., *op. cit.*, p. 5-6.

[25] Based on NEA Research Division salary surveys.

[26] U. S. Department of Labor. *Manpower—Challenge of the 1960s.* Supplementary Statistics. Washington, D. C.: the Department, 1960. p. 9.

Teachers' salaries. . . . [T]eachers' salaries vary widely both from state to state and within states. In a handful of the very wealthy districts, a teacher today can earn as much as $10,000 per year. At the other extreme, one of the border states still pays a few teachers as little as $1350 per year. In fact, several hundred teachers in this one state are in salary categories ranging from $1350 to $1899 per year. I am sure there are even lower salaries in one or two other states. The state minimum salary schedule in one state has several classes that begin at less than $1200.

Most people believe we need more men in the teaching profession. Although men tend to enter teaching in rather substantial numbers, many fail to stay in teaching. This claim was verified a few years ago in a nationwide study involving a sample of almost 6000 teachers. The average experience of women in teaching was 6 or 7 years higher than that of men.[27]

In 1959, two researchers at Columbia University completed a very revealing comparison between men who stay in teaching and those who leave teaching for other kinds of work. This study was based on 10,000 men who had been tested during World War II for Air Force cadet training and who could be contacted in civilian life. Within the group 658 men were identified as school teachers, college teachers, principals, or superintendents in 1955. A few years later these teachers were queried again. Some of these men were teaching in 1959 and some had gone into other occupations. All these men had been 18 to 26 years of age when they entered the Air Force in 1943. In 1959, their ages ranged from 34 to 42. The median income of those who had left classroom teaching was more than 25 percent higher than those who had remained in teaching. Only one teacher in 247 had a monthly income of $800. Of the former teachers, 20 percent had incomes this high. When college teachers were compared with the former college teachers, similar differences were found. Former college teachers were averaging 25 percent higher incomes than those who had returned to this field of work.[28]

The important point here is not that these men earn more money by leaving teaching positions, but the fact that on the whole those who left were a more able group than those who stayed. The battery of tests administered by the Air Force showed that those who left teaching were significantly superior to those who stayed in teaching in such important areas as reading comprehension, arithmetic reasoning, and mathematics.

If we want to call a spade a spade, I think we might as well admit that for many years now we have been capitalizing on the fact that teaching, even at low salaries, could attract an adequate supply of well-educated women. Many other fields have not been open to them.

This situation is changing very rapidly. In 1900, 75 percent of all the women in professional occupations were in teaching; in 1950 only 43 percent of them were in teaching.[29] We no longer have a monopoly on the supply of well-educated women. The situation is becoming more competitive year after year. It is also important to realize that in the other professions the gap between the earnings of men and women is narrowing.

In this metropolitan area, secretaries four years out of high school now earn an average of $4600 a year—a figure which tops the salaries for beginning teachers with bachelor's degrees all but in one district in this area. There is no comparison between the responsibility levels of the teacher and those of the secretary. The secretary typically has one boss. The teacher has 30 or more demanding children and twice that many parents to satisfy, in addition to the principals and supervisors on the school staff. The first year of teaching is probably the most difficult one a teacher experiences. It is of no consolation to her that had she taken a secretarial course in high school and gone to work after high-school graduation instead of going to college, she probably would be better off financially. A beginning teacher can earn $4800 in only one school district in this area. Five of the seven school districts in the area start beginning teachers at $4500.[30]

The most important thing that can be said about the manpower problem in education, however, is

[27] National Education Association, Research Division. "The Status of the American Public-School Teacher." *Research Bulletin* 35: 16; February 1957.
[28] Thorndike, Robert L., and Hagen, Elizabeth. "Men Teachers and Ex-Teachers: Some Attitudes and Traits." *Teachers College Record* 62: 306-16; January 1961.
[29] Kaplan, David L., and Casey, M. Claire. *Occupational Trends in the United States, 1900 to 1950.* Working Paper No. 5. Washington, D. C.: U. S. Department of Commerce, Bureau of the Census, 1958.
[30] National Education Association, Research Division. *Teachers' and Principals' 1960-61 Salary Schedules in D. C. Metropolitan Area.* Research Memo 1960-33. Washington, D. C.: October 1960.

this: For the schools of the future we are going to need, and should demand, teachers of far greater ability than we have been getting in the past decade. In the years since World War II, we have been employing just about anyone who could get a degree from just about any college. I think you know this as well as I do.

How are we going to get more persons from the upper half or upper third of the supply of well-educated manpower? By raising standards and salaries. Very soon we must begin to think very seriously about making the master's degree the basic requirement for elementary- as well as secondary-school teachers. If it took four years of college education to teach the children of the 1930's, it is certainly logical to say that it should take five years of preparation to teach the children of the 1960's. Many schools are finding that the scientifically oriented youth is way ahead of many teachers in mastery of the things he is interested in. Knowledge and techniques are changing rapidly. We need the kind of staff which can meet the educational needs of the decades to come.

But we are not going to get such manpower at an average of $5215 per year—not when we are thinking of five or six instead of four years of college preparation, a median age of 43, and an experience level of 13 years. It will take starting salaries of $5000 to $6000 and an average of at least $10,000 to compete for this superior manpower, and about the only hope of reaching such a level is through substantial help from the federal government.

Housing needs. Another perplexing problem of the 1960's is how to build the classrooms which are needed now and which will be required for the 8.1 million more pupils, one-half of whom are going to be in the secondary grades. Each of these secondary-school classrooms is going to be far more expensive to construct and equip than its counterpart in the elementary school.

For the past five years we have been building classrooms at the average rate of slightly less than 70,000 per year. This probably is an all-time record in school construction but, in effect, we have been running fast in order to stand still. Until last year we were cutting away at the backlog of need at the rate of 8000 to 10,000 rooms per year. It appears now that we are headed in the other direction. In the fall of 1959 the shortage was reported at 135,200 rooms; this fall the shortage is reported at 142,100 rooms. This shortage takes on added meaning when we

hear that the number of pupils in excess of normal capacity of buildings is almost 2 million and that 685,000 are on curtailed or half-day sessions.[31] I am sure the Office of Education will provide further information on our progress and lack of progress in school housing.

But before leaving the point, I want to get into the record some figures we have collected on the present size of elementary-school classes. If there is any place in the educational ladder where classes should be small, it is in the elementary schools.

Every other year we ask a sample from the total of 3631 urban school districts to report the sizes of all their elementary-school classes. In the last such study,[32] in the fall of 1959, 1496 districts were asked to submit information, and 1193, or 80 percent, did so. This is what we found about overcrowding in the elementary schools of communities with populations of 2500 or more.

1. About 50 percent of all the pupils in these schools were in classes containing more than 30 pupils each; about 16 percent were in classes of 35 or more.

2. The median size of elementary classes in cities containing 500,000 or more persons was 33.

3. A total of 13,242 classes in the urban districts contained 40 or more pupils each. In these classes we had enrolled a total of 560,038 pupils.

4. 523 elementary-school classrooms contained 50 or more pupils each; 317 of these contained 55 or more pupils.

There has been much debate over the definition of *needed classroom.* It is difficult to establish any standard pattern for reporting additional classrooms needed. On the other hand, the numbers in classes can be counted, and 35, 40, 45, 50, and 55 pupils per class certainly indicates the need for another room.

Variation in classroom needs. School construction needs are not uniformly distributed throughout the nation. Nor do all school districts within a state have similar construction problems. Some areas, because of the nature of their population, have sufficient or even excess classroom facilities for the children they serve, while others, in rapidly expanding localities, are finding it more and more difficult to keep up with the increase in

[31] U. S. Department of Health, Education, and Welfare, Office of Education, news release, January 19, 1961.
[32] National Education Association, Research Division. *Class Size in Urban Elementary Schools, 1959-60.* Research Report 1960-R10. Washington, D. C.: the Association, June 1960. 24 p.

school population. Moreover, some areas have made valiant attempts, by voting special bond issues, to construct facilities as they were needed; in others, formidable constitutional barriers and lack of taxable wealth have made it impossible to keep pace with the growing needs.

As a result of these factors, money appropriated for school construction, in areas where construction is not really needed, would serve no useful purpose.

Data on classroom construction recently received by the U. S. Office of Education from the chief state school officers clearly illustrate this great variance in classroom needs. For example, in the fall of 1960, Indiana had 984,000 pupils; Florida, 979,000; and Georgia, 932,000. All had just under 1 million pupils each. However, when we look at the classroom shortage reported by these three states, we see that the need varies greatly. Indiana reported a need for only 1321 classrooms, but Florida, a need for 4744 classrooms, and Georgia, 3714.[33]

Tennessee and Kentucky, which share a common border, also offer a vivid illustration of the variation in need for classrooms. Tennessee, with 795,000 enrolled in the fall of 1960, reported a need for only 2984 classrooms, while its sister state, Kentucky, with 177,000 fewer students reported a need for 8906 classrooms. Moreover, Tennessee reported 1726 classrooms scheduled for completion during 1960-61, while Kentucky reported only 1331.

. . . [A] small proportion of our elementary-school children still go to one-room schools. Nevertheless, we still have 23,700 of these schools providing the education for nearly 400,000 boys and girls. These young Americans are as important as any of the others; yet some of their buildings are a disgrace to this country. Almost 1 in 20 of these buildings is over 90 years old; two-thirds still lack inside plumbing; most of them are poorly equipped and struggling against great odds to provide a decent atmosphere for school children.[34]

In my opinion, all this debate over the number of classrooms needed is mostly academic. About half were built in the past 10 years, and many of these are crowded. Little is known about the other half except that they are mostly more than 30 years old.

One only has to look around as he walks down the street of most of the cities and towns of the United States. He can see for himself that the need for building schools is still critical.

School drop-outs.   Another problem that is going to cause serious trouble in the decade ahead is the large number of youth quitting school before high-school graduation. Despite the present emphasis on programs for the talented, within a few years the schools are going to be on the receiving end of a lot of criticism over our failure to provide a program suitable for the under-achiever, the retarded, the youth of below-average intelligence. These, by the way, are the characteristics of the majority of those who fail to finish high school. Many come from families who cannot give them any help.

To give you a little better understanding of this problem, let me describe some of the side effects of this problem which have many serious economic and social implications. As you know, the big bulge in enrollment is now moving out of the elementary school into and through the high school. At present we are losing approximately one-third of our youth between the ninth grade and high-school graduation. If this rate continues, the one-third who *will quit* will greatly outnumber the 50 to 60 percent we were losing a few decades ago. It is estimated that within the next 10 years, 7½ million youths will quit school before completing the twelfth grade.[35]

Specialists in the labor field tell us that these youngsters who quit school do not make very good workers. They have no skill to market, they are too young and immature to appreciate a job and stick to it, and they can't demand a wage that will support a reasonable standard of living. All this adds up to the most disgruntled, disillusioned, and unsatisfactory group of workers in America. In addition, more and more of them are having a difficult time finding any kind of employment. The unemployment rate among those failing to finish high school is almost double that of those who do finish, and 3.5 times the rate of those who have had some college education.[36]

The problem is already serious, but it is going to become far more serious in the decade ahead unless we act now. The number of jobs available to unskilled persons is decreasing year after

---

[33] U. S. Department of Health, Education, and Welfare, Office of Education, *op. cit.*

[34] National Education Association, Research Division. *One-Teacher Schools Today.* Research Monograph 1960-M1. Washington, D. C.: the Association, June 1960. 75 p.

[35] U. S. Department of Labor. *Manpower Challenge of the 1960s.* Washington, D. C.: the Department, 1960. p. 16.

[36] *Ibid.*, p. 17.

year, but the number of people to fill them is increasing rapidly. *In a few years there will be nothing for many thousands of them to do.* Before long, these boys and girls will constitute an almost impossible burden on the resources of welfare, relief, and unemployment agencies and on the juvenile courts. To further illustrate the seriousness of this problem, I want to point out that in 1950 we had only 8.4 million persons in the critical 14-to-17-year-age bracket. By 1970 we will have 15.9 million in this group, or almost twice as many. In 1950 we had only 8.9 million in the 18-to-21-year-old group; by 1970 we will have 14.6 million and by 1975, 16.3 million.

In the long run it may be cheaper to educate these boys and girls than to support the costs of the side effects. The type of education which will help to solve the problem, however, is likely to prove expensive: smaller classes in elementary schools, special classes and schools at the high-school level, more counseling, broader and more adequate programs, and specially trained teachers. . . .

An increasing and moving population. Another very important and dramatic problem . . . is the plight of the major metropolitan areas of the United States. The problems they face in education are staggering. These areas are already in serious financial trouble, but the present problems are small compared with what they are going to be in the next two or three decades.

Recently Earle L. Rauber, Vice President and Director of Research of the Atlanta Federal Reserve Bank, pointed out some very interesting facts about the growth of our population. He said the population of the United States in 1975 will be about 222 million, a growth of 70 million in the 25 years since 1950. If present trends continue, this increase will be distributed so as to create the maximum of problems:

"At present, 85 percent of the increase in population is going into the 168 metropolitan areas defined by the Census. If this trend continues, the metropolitan population of this country will grow by some 60 million between 1950 and 1975. Do you have any idea of what this increase means? It means that it will increase by the equivalent of another 1950 New York-northern New Jersey area; another Boston area; another Philadelphia; a Washington; a Baltimore; a Buffalo; a Pittsburgh; a Cleveland; a Chicago; a Detroit; a St. Louis; a Minneapolis-St. Paul; a Los Angeles and a San Francisco area. In addition, there will remain 15 million to be spread among the smaller metropolitan areas. Indeed, if present

trends continue, 71 percent of the increase in the metropolitan population will go precisely into the fourteen areas just mentioned."[37]

Dr. George C. Smith, Vice President and Economist of the F. W. Dodge Corporation, quoted in the same article, described the problem of our growing population in even more dramatic terms. He said that it will be necessary to build a "second United States" within the next 40 years.

"Every house, every building, every factory, every tool, every machine, every facility of every sort will have to be duplicated by then, besides maintaining those we already have at their present efficiency. Why? For the simple reason that in forty years two persons will be living in this country for every one living here now."[38]

I regret that Dr. Smith did not include in his list another teacher, another classroom, another school bus, another textbook for every one we have today. This will also be true.

Neither of these authorities singled out the unique problems of the existing urban centers of the great metropolitan areas. In the past 10 years, the 20 cities that are now the largest increased only 3.3 percent in population, while their suburban fringes increased 56 percent. But while the total population in the big central cities was increasing only 3.3 percent, their school enrollments went up 22.4 percent.

Research and development. . . . According to the former Commissioner of Education, Lawrence G. Derthick: "Research in education has been meager, however, contrasted to other fields. It has been estimated that less than one tenth of one per cent of the more than 20 billion dollars a year spent in this country on education goes into research."[39]

We cannot hope to improve our schools unless funds for research go into the budgets of state education departments and school districts. If we are to educate pupils now in school better than the generations which have passed through school, expenditures for research have a high priority

[37] Rauber, Earle L. "Walking the Dog." *The Genie in the Bottle: A Contemporary View of America's Postwar Economy.* Atlanta: Federal Reserve Bank of Atlanta, November 1960. p. 43.
[38] *Ibid.*
[39] Derthick, Lawrence G. "Dimensions for Progress." *Annals of the American Academy of Political and Social Science* 325: 84; September 1959.

along with funds for teachers' salaries and facilities.

Financing public schools in the 1960's

As I pointed out earlier in my testimony, the investment in public schools increased from $5.8 billion in fiscal 1950 to $15.3 billion in fiscal 1960, and this was a remarkable achievement. Now let us look for a minute at what schools are likely to cost us in 1970. At the present rate of growth and expansion the annual outlay for public schools will probably reach $30 billion by 1970. The costs could be considerably more, but several responsible groups, including President Eisenhower's Commission on National Goals, have estimated that costs by the end of this decade should be at least double their present level.[40]

The recent President's Goals Commission reinforced the recommendations of the 1955 White House Conference which also recommended a doubling of expenditures.[41] Projections of growth in gross national product indicated that a portion of the increase in school cost can be expected to be offset by growth in the economy. However, few people believe that the necessary expansion in school investment can be made without increasing the share the schools require of our total expenditures.

Not many people in this country fully realize what a tremendous load this $30 billion is going to be on local and state revenue programs. Ten years from now public elementary and secondary schools will be costing two-thirds as much as national defense is costing now.[42] In another decade these schools will be requiring almost as much revenue as all state and local services, including education, cost in 1959.

Possibilities of the general property tax.

Can the old reliable property tax continue to carry over half of this additional load? Can a tax geared to the productivity of an agricultural economy cope with the needs of an exploding urban and industrial society? The present levels of property taxes are high.

I wonder if you know that property tax collections in 1959 amounted to $130 per capita in California and New Jersey, and a whopping $133 in Massachusetts. In 1959, property taxes exceeded $100 per capita in 15 states.[43] They are going higher all the time.

Let's look at property taxes another way. In 1959 the people of South Dakota were paying out in property taxes $6.82 of each $100 of personal income; in Montana, property taxes amounted to $6.41 per $100 of personal income; in North Dakota, the figure was $6.09; and in Kansas, $5.99.[44] Property taxes for the country as a whole now amount to almost 4 percent of personal income payments.

Those who have studied the problem can see trouble ahead in some sections of the country. Increased resistance to further property tax increases is bound to come in New England and the Midwest.

Possibilities of additional state revenue.

In recent years the states have been carrying about 40 percent of the cost of public schools.[45] I wonder if we can look to 1970 and predict whether the growing variety of state taxes can continue to carry two-fifths of the cost of public elementary and secondary schools.

Where local taxes are low, state taxes are usually correspondingly high. This is not always true, but if you will examine the levels of state and local taxes, you will find a large degree of inverse relationship.

In 1959, state taxes in the state of Washington amounted to $148 per capita, in Delaware $149, and in Hawaii $170. Even in the low-income state of Louisiana, state taxes amounted to $137 per capita. In the fiscal year 1959, state taxes amounted to over $100 per capita in 15 states. The national average in '59 was $91 per capita.[46]

Let's look at these state taxes in relation to ability to pay. When related to income payments, the levels of state taxes have more meaning. These taxes in 1959 amounted to $8.64 per $100

[40] President's Commission on National Goals. *Goals for Americans.* New York: The American Assembly, Columbia University, 1960. p. 7.
[41] White House Conference on Education. *A Report to the President.* Washington, D. C.: Superintendent of Documents, Government Printing Office, April 1956.
[42] Executive Office of the President, Bureau of the Budget. *Budget of the United States Government, 1961.* Special Analysis G.

[43] U. S. Department of Commerce, Bureau of the Census. *Governmental Finances in 1959.* G-GF59-No. 2. Washington, D. C.: the Bureau, September 30, 1960. p. 26.
[44] *Ibid.*, p. 25, 37.
[45] National Education Association, Research Division. *Estimates of School Statistics, 1960-61.* Research Report 1960-R15. Washington, D. C.: the Association, December 1960. p. 28.
[46] U. S. Department of Commerce, Bureau of the Census. *Compendium of State Government Finances in 1959.* Washington, D. C.: Superintendent of Documents, Government Printing Office, 1960. p. 49-50.

of personal income in Hawaii. In the states of Louisiana and Mississippi, state taxes amounted to $8.37 and $7.24 per $100 of personal income. For the country as a whole, these taxes required 4.2 percent of our personal income payments.[47] And don't forget these figures are for fiscal '59; they have gone up since then. . . .

Let me digress for a minute to show you what happened between fiscal '59 and '60. In the fiscal year 1960, state tax collections totaled $18 billion, up 14 percent over 1959. This rise of $2.2 billion in the past year is more than twice the rise from fiscal '58 to fiscal '59. It is also double the average annual increase over the past decade. At least five states increased their state tax collections by 20 percent or more between fiscal '59 and '60. These include Ohio, up 21 percent; South Carolina, up 21 percent; Utah, up 24 percent; New York, up 24 percent; and Arizona, up 27 percent.[48] Early reports of collections during this fiscal year indicate that collections to date in many states are disappointing primarily because of the effects of the recession.[49]

Local and state taxes combined. Since the support of public education is a co-operative enterprise largely of local and state governments, the only way to make sense out of this picture is to put all state and local taxes together and see how the over-all problem looks.

Here are some interesting statistics: State and local taxes combined for the year 1959 amounted to $265 per capita in California, $253 in New York, and $245 in Nevada. We now have 13 states where the combined state and local tax load amounts to over $200 per person in the population. In addition to the three mentioned are Colorado, Connecticut, Kansas, Massachusetts, Minnesota, Montana, Oregon, Vermont, Washington, and Wyoming.[50]

We should also take a look at this combined tax load in relation to income payments, since income is the source from which taxes are paid. The total load is heaviest in South Dakota, where state and local taxes in 1959 amounted to $12.28 per $100 of personal income. Other states where state and local taxes amounted to over 10 percent of personal income include North Dakota, $12.01 per $100 of income; Vermont, $11.31; Louisiana, $11.24; Montana, $10.90; Kansas, $10.68; Mississippi, $10.57; Minnesota, $10,32; and Wyoming, $10.10.[51] . . .

Many of us have been so concerned about the high level of federal taxation that we have missed what has been happening in the past few years at the state and local levels. *State and local tax revenues combined doubled between the years 1950 and 1958, and the total has gone much higher since 1958.* If you take a close look at state and local tax collections per $100 of personal income, you will realize that they are beginning to look more like the bite of the federal income tax than like that of the traditionally modest state and local taxes.

Of course, this does not mean that some states could not do more, but all of them will have to do a great deal more, even with increased federal assistance, to meet the growing demands of public education.

I think we should note in passing that some of the states putting forth the greatest overall tax effort at state and local levels still have the most inadequate schools in the country.

A few months ago we received a research report from the Tax Foundation that surprised all of us. I think it will surprise you, too. It showed calculations of the average tax burden by level of family income. It showed the impact of all taxes, of federal taxes, and of local and state taxes combined. The federal tax burden, as a percent of family income, went up as the family income increased, but the opposite was true of the state-local tax burden.

For example, the federal tax burden on a family income of $1454 was 15.7 percent; on an income of $8160, it was 17.2 percent. However, the state-local tax burden on a family income of $1454 was 12.6 percent, but on an income of $8160 it was only 8.5 percent. The total impact of federal, state, and local taxation is regressive until we reach incomes running into five figures. For example, the total tax burden on a family income of $1454 was 28.3 percent, but on an income of $8160 it was only 25.7 percent.

The important point in this story is that state and local taxes have become more steeply re-

[47] Computed by the NEA Research Division on the basis of: U. S. Department of Commerce, Bureau of the Census. *Compendium of State Government Finances in 1959.* G-SF59-No. 2. Washington, D. C.: Superintendent of Documents, Government Printing Office, 1960. p. 11. Office of Business Economics. *Survey of Current Business* 40: 17; August 1960.

[48] U. S. Department of Commerce, Bureau of the Census. *State Tax Collections, 1960.* G-SF60-No. 3. Washington, D. C.: the Bureau, August 26, 1960.

[49] Burnham, Daniel M. "States' Squeeze: Recession Reduces Tax Revenue, Lifts Outlays; Higher Levies Likely." *Wall Street Journal,* December 14, 1960, p. 1.

[50] U. S. Department of Commerce, Bureau of the Census. *Governmental Finances in 1959,* op. cit., p. 26.

[51] Tax revenue in relation to personal income was computed by the NEA Research Division.

gressive than federal taxes have been progressive. The result is that the total tax burden (including social insurance taxes) is regressive on family incomes up to those of five digits. Even if we exclude social insurance taxes from the over-all tax burden, the total tax burden on a family income under $2000 is as large percentagewise as on an income of $8000 to $10,000.

What are the elements in this regressiveness of the present state-local tax structure that are throwing the total tax structure into such a peculiar pattern? One item is the general property tax, the mainstay of school support. This is one

of the most regressive of all taxes. This tax hits incomes under $2000 almost three times as hard, percentagewise, as it does the incomes of $15,000 and over. Of course, the sales and excise taxes are also regressive, but they are not as steeply regressive as the property tax.

These conditions, it seems to me, fully justify the use of the federal tax structure for meeting part of the increasing cost of education. It is very difficult to see how we are going to absorb all the additional cost of education over the current decade in a state-local tax system that is already steeply regressive and likely to become more so in the years ahead.

96

THE ROLE OF THE FEDERAL GOVERNMENT IN SCHOOL FINANCE

The National Education Association believes that the federal government should assume extensive financial responsibility for the public schools in the various states. There are also groups and individuals, however, who vigorously oppose any increase in federal funds for public education. Generally, their position is based on the beliefs (a) that the federal government already is confronted with large debts and cannot afford further support of education, and/or (b) that increases in federal expenditures for education will increase federal control of the curriculum and administration of the public schools. Other groups, most of them with a religious affiliation, also oppose additional federal support of education unless similar support is provided to parochial and private schools.

At some point between the positions described above is that of the Committee for Economic Development, a national organization composed of two hundred business leaders and educators. Essentially, the Committee believes, as indicated by its 1959 statement quoted below, that all children in the United States are entitled to a certain minimum quality of education regardless of the states in which they live. In view of the fact that some states lack the funds to provide this minimum level, they should receive financial assistance from the federal government. Under this plan states with adequate resources would not receive federal aid.

The question of the role of the Federal government in school finance has been heatedly debated in the postwar years. Persons earnestly devoted to the improvement of education are to be found on each side of this issue.

The Federal government has participated in the support of public elementary and secondary schools since the land grants of 1785 and 1787. The largest Federal programs at present are those for school lunches and for construction and operation of schools in "Federally affected" districts.

The latter provide payments, regarded as in lieu of taxes, to districts with large numbers of children whose parents are employed on tax-exempt Federal property.

Most other Federal programs are for the promotion of some specific educational purpose—such as vocational education, or the teaching

From *Paying for Better Schools* (New York: Committee for Economic Development, 1959), pp. 31-34, 39-47.

of science, mathematics, and modern foreign languages for which support is provided by the National Defense Education Act of 1958.

The proposals for additional Federal support that are now being most discussed, however, are not intended to promote a particular type of education or educational program but to provide general support of education—although they may restrict the use of funds to some specific object of expenditure, such as construction or teachers' salaries. Proposed support may be in the form of grants or loans to the states or of tax rebates. The proposed allocation among the states may be proportional to school-age population, enrollment, Federal income tax collections, or some other standard. Some proposals would vary aid inversely with income levels; others would penalize states devoting a less-than-average proportion of personal income to education. All these proposals aim either at a higher level of school support, or at lower state and local taxes than would be forthcoming in their absence, or at some of each.

Proponents of general Federal assistance stress that we live in one society, not 50, and we have a national government created to preserve the unity of the society and serve the interests of all of its members. Educational opportunity for all children is essential to the purposes for which the national government exists. It is required for the national defense. The citizens and taxpayers of each state have a responsibility to share in the provision of education for the children of every state. The boundaries of a school district or state set essentially arbitrary limits to the responsibility of citizens to support the education of children within the society. The national interest in, and national responsibility for, schools mean that the Federal government *should* share substantially in school support.

It is further maintained that the states and localities *cannot* finance the increase in school expenditures that the national interest and the welfare of the population require. This increase is claimed to be very large, sometimes estimated at 50 to 60 per cent of present expenditures aside from the cost of rising enrollments, mainly to increase teachers' salaries and to reduce the number of students per teacher. While the revenues of the Federal government rise with the growth of the economy, and at an even faster rate, the revenues of states and localities rise slower than the national income. Additional state and local revenues for schools must come largely from higher tax rates, at a time when other urgent

state and local functions are also clamoring for more funds. Even though it is true that the entire national income lies within the borders of the several states, economic competition among the states keeps each from moving forward energetically to tax the income within its borders. None can get taxes too far out of line with its neighbors, for fear of retarding its own economic development, so all advance together at an inadequate rate.

Finally it is maintained that the states and localities *will not* improve education even as rapidly as they can. The present condition of our schools shows this. To awaken 50 state governments, to say nothing of 45,000 school districts to the need will take a long time—more time than we have. Moreover, in many cases the structure of state governments resting on outdated constitutions and controlled by legislatures that underrepresent urban areas, makes them unresponsive to the desires of their citizens for better schools.

Opponents of any additional Federal aid consider any further encroachment by the Federal Government on the responsibilities of the states and localities undesirable. They believe that the recent record of the public schools in obtaining greatly increased financial support to hire teachers, raise salaries, and build schools during a difficult period of sharp expansion of enrollments, viewed against a long-term record of rising school support, speak strongly in favor of continuing to rely on the traditional sources of school finance. Insofar as the deficiencies of public education stem from financial limitations, and many do not, the proper approach to improvement is greater citizen participation to obtain support for school programs, the reorganization of school districts into sound units accompanied by their release from undue restrictions on taxation and borrowing, and properly conceived state foundation programs. Progress in these directions is in fact being made, and it would not be accelerated by Federal grants. Teachers' salaries have already been greatly increased, and the full effects upon the teacher supply have not yet been felt. Insofar as further pay increases prove necessary, they can be financed from existing sources.

Opponents also suggest that with Federal tax rates now very high, the argument that Federal revenue sources are superior to those of state and local governments has lost its force. Any important relief from state and local taxation involves large sums, and corresponding increases in Federal taxation. With Federal income taxes already high and sharply progressive, substantial additional Federal revenue could be obtained only from taxes with a broad base. Higher rates in the first bracket of the personal income tax (or lower exemptions) or else sales taxes would probably be required. But sales and income taxes are also the main revenue sources open to state governments, and the states may well shoulder most of the burden of increased tax requirements. There does not appear to be a great deal to choose between increased state taxes and increased Federal taxes.

Opponents of additional Federal aid also weigh more heavily than its supporters the prospect that general Federal financial support may mean Federal intervention in school affairs and the seriousness of this development if it should occur.

The majority of this Committee agrees that further extension of the scope of Federal government activities in the field of elementary and secondary education is undesirable. We find that in most of the country additional Federal school support is unnecessary. Hence we oppose Federal grants to support schools throughout the country. However, we also find that some parts of the nation cannot, with any probable allocation of their own resources, support their schools at a level that meets the nation's requirements. Although we are reluctant to see further expansion of the Federal role in education, we conclude that to secure adequate schools throughout the country it is necessary for the Federal government to supplement school finances in the states where incomes are lowest. The following section discusses the need for such support and describes a program to meet this need.

A program for Federal support in the low-income states

There is a strong national interest in the provision of good schools throughout the nation. Each of us, however, wherever he may live, and the nation as a whole, is vitally affected by the quality of education provided to all the children of the country. At the same time there is a strong national interest in a decentralized school system, implying decentralization of major financial responsibility. This decentralization is a guarantee against monolithic political influence over the schools and makes the school system resistant to demagoguery. Moreover it maintains a close connection between parents and the education of their children, and facilitates adaptation of school programs to local needs. On the whole, the de-

centralized system not only has been consistent with good schools but also has contributed greatly to the quality of public education.

The national interest in good schools everywhere and the national interest in a decentralized school system are not irreconcilable. The combination of these two interests calls for the assumption of an important but limited responsibility by the Federal government. This is a residual responsibility. It is to provide support to the extent necessary in situations where the decentralized system cannot provide good schools. And this support should be reserved for cases where the deficiency is clear.

The clear and present need is for Federal financial assistance to the states that have extremely low personal incomes relative to the number of schoolchildren.

The quality of school systems, as we have stressed, cannot be judged exclusively by the resources available to them. Nor is it possible to identify differences in the resources available to the schools precisely with differences in dollar expenditures, since there are also regional differences in the general level of prices and climatic conditions. But schools where expenditures are very low clearly are not, in general, providing an education comparable to that obtained elsewhere. Price differences appear to be fairly small and neither they nor climatic conditions explain much of the inter-state differences in school expenditures.[1]

Present expenditures in a number of states are so low as to demand improvement. Exactly how low is too low is a question not subject to clear-cut answer. But eighty per cent of the national average based on current expenditure per pupil in average daily attendance is, we suggest, a reasonable standard, below which school expenditures should be considered unacceptably low. We arrive at this figure after considering geographic differences in wages and living costs.

Eleven states fell below this 80% floor in 1957-58—most of them far below it. The facts are shown in the table [See next page].

---

[1] States with the lowest expenditures per pupil also have the lowest teachers' salaries. Teachers' salaries in these states are significantly farther below the national average than are earnings in other occupations and differentials in other occupations themselves reflect in part differences in ability. Low teachers' salaries do not permit these states to provide good education at low cost; on the contrary, low financial capacity forces these states to be content with the teachers they can hire at low salaries.

These eleven states had 22 per cent of the nation's public school enrollment. The standards affecting more than one fifth of the nation's school-children cannot be dismissed as unimportant.

The size of the increase in present expenditures that would be required to reach the 80% level (shown in the last column of the table below) leads us to conclude that in most cases the sums required are not likely to be forthcoming from sources within these states.

Mississippi, Arkansas, South Carolina, North Carolina, and Georgia already devote much higher proportions of their personal income to public schools than the country as a whole, despite their low incomes per capita, and would need to increase present expenditures by 26 to 63 per cent.

While the present effort of the other states is not so impressive, low school expenditures in Alabama, Tennessee, Kentucky and West Virginia clearly are due mainly to low income rather than to a below-average ratio of school support to income.

These nine states, at least, have little prospect of closing the gap by increased local support. The low position of their school expenditures is not likely to be corrected automatically in any reasonably short period of time by elimination of the factors primarily responsible for it—low per capita income and many children.

The goal of raising to acceptable levels the resources devoted to public education in states where expenditures now are markedly deficient can be largely achieved by a moderate annual expenditure of Federal funds—provided that the program is directed strictly to the equalization objective. We cannot propose that the Federal government simply provide each state with the amount, if any, required to raise existing expenditure levels to the desired minimum standard. This would penalize states now making the greatest financial effort to support schools and reward states making the least effort. It would eliminate the incentive to increase local support of schools.

We do propose a Federal program that avoids these defects. It is a program designed to aid education in states with personal income per student in average daily attendance in public schools that is below 80 per cent of the national average. For each student in average daily attendance this program would pay such states an amount equal to the product of (1) the amount by which its personal income per student in average daily attendance falls short of 80 per cent of the national average and (2) the national ratio of current school expenditures to personal income.

For example, personal income per student in average daily attendance in the nation as a whole was $11,446. Eighty per cent of this was $9,157. In Mississippi, personal income per student in average daily attendance was only $4,893. Subtracting $4,893 from $9,157 gives $4,264. In the nation as a whole, current school expenditures equalled 2.83 per cent of personal income. For each student in average daily attendance Mississippi would get 2.83 per cent of $4,264, or $121. With 444,200 students, Mississippi would thus receive a total grant of $54 million.

Such a program would permit any state to reach the 80 per cent level in current expenditures by devoting the same proportion of its residents' income to current school expenditure as the nation as a whole. And they could do better by providing more. The formula makes no allowance for the fact that even the same pro-

State	Current Expense Per Pupil in Average Daily Attendance as % of U.S. Average (1957-58)	Percentage Increase in Current Expenditures Required to Reach 80% of the National Average
Mississippi	49	63
Alabama	52	53
Arkansas	60	33
Tennessee	60	33
Kentucky	61	31
South Carolina	61	30
North Carolina	63	28
Georgia	63	26
West Virginia	67	19
Virginia	71	13
Maine	71	13

portion of income devoted to education implies a greater effort by a poor than by a rich state.

The total cost of such a program, if it had been in effect in the 1957-58 school year and if all eligible states had satisfied the two conditions set forth below, would have been $544 million. This payment would have been divided among the 19 states in which income per schoolchild was less than 80 per cent of the national average [See column 2 of the table below].[2]

The nation has a right to assurance that recipient states make a reasonable financial effort

[2]The distribution shown is based on figures for average daily attendance computed from estimates of the National Education Association and should be considered as only approximate.

to support schools from their own resources. Grants should be made only to states that provide current school revenues from state and local sources equal to at least the same proportion of their personal income as does the nation as a whole. In 1957-58, fifteen of the nineteen eligible states exceeded this requirement, all but one by a wide margin. The other four states would have needed to provide a total of $51 million more from their own resources to qualify. Since the national percentage of income devoted to school support may be expected to rise, the minimum effort required of recipient states by this provision will be an increasing one.

The program should also guarantee against the substitution of Federal for local funds in

COST AND IMPLICATIONS[1] OF FEDERAL EQUALIZATION GRANTS
(based on 1956-58 income differentials and 1957-58 expenditures)

State[2]	Personal Income per Pupil as % of U.S. Average (1)	Grants ($ millions) (2)	EXPENSES PER PUPIL AS % OF U.S. AVERAGE	
			Actual (3)	With Support Programs (4)
Mississippi	43	54	49	86
Arkansas	49	37	60	91
South Carolina	49	50	61	92
Georgia	49	95	63	94
North Carolina	54	81	63	88
Alabama	54	55	52	84
New Mexico	60	13	115	134
Tennessee	61	43	60	84
West Virginia	62	24	67	85
Utah	65	10	86	101
Oklahoma	65	25	81	97
Kentucky	67	22	61	78
Idaho	69	5	80	92
North Dakota	72	3	94	102
Louisiana	73	13	98	105
South Dakota	74	2	101	107
Virginia	75	12	71	83
Hawaii	79	[3]	82	83
Vermont	79	[3]	86	87
Maine	80	none	71	71

Total   544

[1]Assumes the provision of additional state and local funds, totaling $51 million, required to qualify for Federal grants in five states; that there would be no other change in school support from existing sources; and that the additional funds would be used entirely for current expenses.
[2]Table includes all states with either personal income per student in average daily attendance, or current school expenditures per student in average daily attendance, below 80 per cent of the corresponding national figure.
[3]Less than $500,000.

the support of education. The evidence presented earlier shows a strong popular urge to bring schools at least up to standards of adequacy typical of the country at large. For this reason, even without a special provision, it is unlikely that the benefits of Federal grants would be offset in any significant degree by a lessening of financial support from within the states. However, as a further assurance against this possibility (in addition to the requirement as a condition of aid for continued matching of the national average effort), a provision should be included to eliminate grants to any state if its per-pupil current school revenues from state and local sources should fall below their level at the time the program is introduced.

Grants should be eliminated under these provisions only after a state is notified and given time to meet the conditions of the program. We do not anticipate that it would become necessary, in fact, to withhold funds for failure to meet the specified conditions. . . .

Several aspects of our proposal, and certain additional implications, may now be noted.

1. There must not be, and the purposes of the proposal do not necessitate, any Federal controls or conditions over education whatsoever associated with the proposed grants. It is only necessary to require that funds received actually be spent for public education, and conformance with regulations to be established by the Office of Education for uniform reporting of average daily attendance and school finance.[3] We stress in the strongest possible terms that the program should include no Federal requirement for "loyalty oaths," and no control of subject matter, teaching methods, teacher qualifications, or any other aspects of the educational process.

2. Our formula utilizes current expenditures rather than total expenditures in the calculation of the amounts to be paid under the proposed program. However, an effective school program requires a proper balance between capital plant and current expenditures. The most efficient use of funds requires that states be free to use Federal grants for either purpose. A requirement controlling use of Federal funds as between current and capital outlay would in any event be largely futile since a state could readily circumvent it by an offsetting shift in the allocation of its own funds.

3. The geographic distribution of low-income states is such that most of the payments under

the proposed program would go to states that until recently maintained segregated school systems, and some of which still do so. The object of equalization grants is to improve the financial support of public schools where it is inadequate, not to affect state policy with respect to segregation or integration. If legislation is necessary or desirable to supplement enforcement of constitutional provisions by the courts, it should be considered separately on its own merits. Under the proposed program funds would be allocated only for pupils in attendance in public schools, and only for use in support of public education.

4. State and local financial planning requires that the approximate amount of Federal grants to a state be foreseeable and that the amount not fluctuate greatly from year to year. On the other hand, it is desirable that payments adjust to changing requirements without long delay. Any legislation adopted must be permanent. Allocations must be based on a formula that determines the dollar amount of payments. They cannot be based on some percentage allocation of an annual appropriation that varies in amount from year to year for the convenience of the Federal budget or with the whim of legislators. It is desirable to base allocations on average personal income during the preceding two or three years in order to minimize any irregular fluctuations and make the amount of aid more foreseeable a year or two in advance. No similar averaging is necessary for average daily attendance, which is not much subject to irregular fluctuations.[4] The formula proposed will automatically adjust allocations, with a short time lag, as the need for equalization aid changes with shifting patterns of per capita income or school attendance.

5. Of the nineteen states that would receive payments under our proposal, all but three are among the states that have already reorganized school districts by compulsory state law, or through compulsory joint state and county action under strong state authority.[5] This is an assurance that there would be little waste of Federal funds resulting from over-decentralization of school districts. However, consideration might be given to some provision for a minimum Federal standard to encourage more efficient school districting, applicable after an appropriate period as a condition for Federal grants.

---

[3]No special reporting requirement with respect to income is necessary since personal income data required by the formula are compiled by the U.S. Department of Commerce, Office of Business Economics.

[4]Although we use average daily attendance in the description of our proposal, average daily membership (the average number enrolled during the year) would be at least equally appropriate. Comprehensive data on this basis are not presently available.

[5]Or, in the case of Hawaii, inherited a single school system from the territorial government.

6. The national figure for current expenditure per pupil in average daily attendance that is used in the formula should be net of payments under this program. The formula leaves grants under other Federal programs undisturbed.

7. In states where per-pupil expenditure is below 80 per cent of the national average, the deficiency in available funds is invariably absorbed in part by classes of above-average size and in part by below-average teachers' salaries. In most of the states where teachers' salaries are very low, they are not so far below the national average as total expenditures per pupil. Given the existing relationships between teachers' salaries and per-pupil expenditures, it is likely that the result of the proposed program would be to raise the average teachers' salary in all states receiving grants to at least 80 per cent of the national average. We consider the raising of teachers' salaries where they are substandard to be an important objective of the proposed program. But it requires no special mention in the formula.

8. The costs of this program would tend to increase for some time as enrollments and per-pupil expenditures rise. However, the increase over the next decade or so is unlikely to be more than in proportion to national current school expenditures, and probably would be a little less, because income per public schoolchild in the low-income states may rise more than corresponding national figures. A check of past experience shows that if such a program had been in effect from 1953-54 to 1957-58, aid payments would have increased by a slightly smaller percentage than total current expenses for public schools. We use $600 million as a round estimate of the annual cost of the program if it is introduced in the near future, somewhat above the $544 million calculated for 1957-58. Over the longer run, raising schools in the low-income states much closer to the standards prevailing elsewhere should itself be a powerful force operating to narrow differentials in productivity and incomes. This would automatically reduce, and perhaps ultimately eliminate, Federal grants under the proposed formula.

These statements presuppose, of course, that there would be no change in the terms of the program. But the proposed program provides an adequate, perhaps even a generous, degree of equalization support. We do not think greater assistance can be justified on equalization grounds.

Our proposal is intended to enable reasonably adequate support for education, as measured against standards prevailing in the rest of the country, to be provided in those states that have relatively small economic ability to support schools. We propose this program in the interest of the entire nation and of the residents of all sections of the country, as well as for its benefit to the children directly concerned. The majority of this Committee believes that it merits support from the entire country on these grounds. We are convinced that the expenditure required will contribute more to the welfare of the country than many existing Federal expenditures, some of which, as we have pointed out elsewhere, could well be cut.[6] But if the program implies higher taxes, these will be well justified by the anticipated benefits. . . .

---

[6] *The Budget and Economic Growth*, CED, 1959.

PART THREE

THE STRUCTURE OF THE AMERICAN SCHOOL SYSTEM

Any study of American public education must include careful consideration of the organization and curriculum of the school itself. Indeed, discussions of the aims, philosophy, role, and status of education are pertinent only when they apply to the existing school system (1).

The school system in the United States, consisting of a series of steps—an educational ladder—from elementary school upward, is the result of both tradition and planned change. The early colonists quite naturally brought with them European ideas about education. Their strong religious beliefs also influenced the type of education they desired for their children. The pattern of American education gradually changed as it became evident that the traditional European education was not suited to a rapidly growing new country with a heterogeneous population. Many of the changes which reflected a break with the European classical tradition were bitterly contested, but nevertheless a unique pattern of American education developed.

The early schools in the United States—ungraded, with small enrollments, limited to a curriculum of a few subjects, and open to students of any age—were highly individualized in that they made provision for varying rates of pupil progress. The first elementary schooling was provided in dame schools in which the rudiments of reading and spelling were taught and in writing schools which emphasized writing and reckoning. Later, the common schools extended the primary-school curriculum, including more advanced work in the three R's. At the secondary level, the Latin grammar schools served as college-preparatory schools and, like the existing colleges, emphasized a religious-classical curriculum. They were supplanted by the private academies and later by the public high schools. In the early primary schools and secondary schools, and even in the colleges, each teacher was in effect manager of his own "school," or at least a separate division of one, and taught all subjects to all pupils.

The pattern of a graded system gradually took form within the common schools. As enrollments increased, it became difficult for one teacher to teach all subjects to pupils of varying age and ability. In response to increasing demands by local communities for better supervision of schools and for a more unified system, larger schools with separate classrooms were built, simple instructional plans were developed, and the graded system became more firmly established. The addition of new subjects led to the placement of content at various predetermined levels and to specialization in teacher assignments. By 1900 most northern states had installed a graded system of schooling, and this pattern of organization eventually spread throughout the country. In spite of the universal adoption of the graded system, its validity has often been questioned and various plans for a modified reorganization or even a drastic revision of the graded structure have been proposed and tried out in schools. Even today, the pattern of American education is not static.

To what extent have the organization and practices of our school system grown out of a systematic philosophy—or philosophies—of education? The historian of American education is sometimes haunted by the possibility that statements of philosophy and purpose are used as mere rationalizations for procedures which have evolved independently. Evidence for this may be found in the tendency to introduce a subject into the curriculum for a specific purpose and then retain it long after the purpose has been lost, and in the tendency to justify practices by appealing to a philosophical position to which those practices have no logical relation. Readers interested in discovering the extent to which educational practices are *logically* dependent upon an educational philosophy (particularly, the validity of the claims that the practices of Progressive education exemplified Dewey's philosophy of education) will find a provocative discussion in Hobert W. Burns' "The Citizen of Education: Fact, Fiction and Forecast" (2).

Though a national definition of objectives has never been accomplished, there is a distinctive and reasonably constant pattern in the organization of American public education. Considerable agreement has been reached about the nature of the curriculum itself and about the activities and services to be rendered by school personnel. It is sometimes intriguing to see how many of the same practices will be justified by differing philosophies of education.

Whatever the defense or criticism of American public education may be, many aspects of its pattern of organization remain remarkably stable and constant. To some observers of the educational scene, this is an indication of the bulkiness of large social institutions, of the cultural lag between suggested reform and the actualization of the reform. To others it is an indication that social institutions evolve as a result of the real needs of the society and not at the whim of the propagandist. The two points of view may not really be at odds with each other. The professional educator may play a part in directing the evolution of the school, but the speed of this evolution is probably determined by more basic forces operating in the society—forces that may be economic, political, or technological. The existing structure of American education and the kind and quality of schooling may be affected by such current ideas and forces as: (a) the need for new kinds of excellence in education, (b) demands for persons capable of meeting new social requirements, (c) the expansion of knowledge and the need to "package" such knowledge for use in schools, (d) the application of automation in industry and in schools, and (e) new findings from the behavioral sciences concerning individual and group reactions.

THE EDUCATIONAL LADDER

One of the distinctive characteristics of American education is its arrangement into a sequential pattern. Unlike the former American pattern and that now followed in some other parts of the world, the same children attend the elementary school, the secondary school, and then the college. No group or class of children is limited to an elementary education while another is permitted to go on to secondary schools. All levels of education are provided at public expense, though the kindergarten program lags in this respect in some sections of the country. There is a serious attempt at articulating the curricula of the differing levels of education.

It seems important for the student to look almost simultaneously at the whole sweep of American education. Only in this way can he accurately judge the extent to which it makes adequate provision for filling the needs of American society.

The traditions of American education have been such that, until recently, the institution with the least prestige was the elementary school and that with the highest, the college. In our early history the tendency was to regard the program of the elementary school as terminal or primarily one of preparation for the secondary school; the program of the secondary school as one of preparation for the college; and sometimes that of the college as merely preparatory for graduate and professional work. Most of the educational philosophers of the early twentieth century have insisted, however, that each level of the school should provide the best program possible for its own group of students and that the matter of preparation for the next level is only of secondary concern.

There is an increasing demand, nevertheless, for a longer and more continuous program of schooling. The growing numbers of junior colleges and the expanded adult and extension programs are responses to this demand. In fact, in some states more persons are enrolled in extension programs in any one year than are enrolled in all the colleges and universities of the state. Some of the factors which have contributed to the demands for a more lengthy and better articulated schooling include increased recognition of the economic value of extended education, rigorous demands for advanced training in the vocations, and, concomitantly, decreased employment possibilities for the poorly educated.

The educational ladder

THE ELEMENTARY SCHOOL

The roots of public education as we know it today in the United States are in the history of the elementary school. Briefly, the elementary school grew out of the Reformation in Europe and was nurtured in America by the desire of the early settlers to have their children able to read the Bible. The elementary school was firmly established in the period of Jacksonian democracy, and it was revitalized by the various reforms during the early twentieth century. Today, it represents the school most clearly designed to provide for the wide range of needs of all American children. Elementary schools are one of the segments of the system which have attracted attention abroad, particularly among newly emerging nations desirous of developing a program of common, universal schooling. Since World War II elementary education has been undergoing many changes, some of which include: (a) the development of ungraded schools; (b) the expansion of curriculum to include such subjects as foreign languages; (c) the teaching of some subjects, such as mathematics, in earlier grades, with new content and new procedures; (d) the study of critical and creative thinking in young children; (e) the use of programed learning materials and automated teaching devices; and (f) the increased emphasis on higher academic standards for elementary teachers, with some states requiring an additional year of training beyond the bachelor's degree.

97

Horace Mann

THE GROUND OF THE FREE SCHOOL SYSTEM

The annual reports made by Horace Mann to the Massachusetts State Board of Education, widely quoted both in Massachusetts and outside the state, contributed greatly to the development of the office of state superintendent throughout the country. Mann's eloquent style and his appeal to patriotic pride are particularly notable. His view of a system of common (elementary) schools as the bulwark of democratic citizenship is illustrative of the shift from a religious to a political aim for education during the period between 1632 and 1846.

The Pilgrim Fathers amid all their privations and dangers conceived the magnificent idea, not only of a universal, but of a free education for the whole people. To find the time and the means to reduce this grand conception to practice, they stinted themselves, amid all their poverty, to a still scantier pittance; amid all their toils, they imposed upon themselves still more burdensome labors; and, amid all their perils, they braved still greater dangers. Two divine ideas filled their great hearts,—their duty to God and to posterity. For the one they built the church, for the other they opened the school. Religion and knowledge, —two attributes of the same glorious and eternal truth, and that truth the only one on which immortal or mortal happiness can be securely founded!

It is impossible for us adequately to conceive the boldness of the measure which aimed at universal education through the establishment of free

schools. As a fact, it had no precedent in the world's history; and, as a theory, it could have been refuted and silenced by a more formidable array of argument and experience than was ever marshalled against any other institution of human origin. But time has ratified its soundness. Two centuries of successful operation now proclaim it to be as wise as it was courageous, and as beneficent as it was disinterested. Every community in the civilized world awards it the meed of praise; and states at home and nations abroad, in the order of their intelligence, are copying the bright example. What we call the enlightened nations of Christendom are approaching, by slow degrees, to the moral elevation which our ancestors reached at a single bound. . . .

The alleged ground upon which the founders of our free-school system proceeded when adopting it did not embrace the whole argument by which it may be defended and sustained. Their insight was better than their reason. They assumed a ground, indeed, satisfactory and convincing to Protestants; but at that time only a small portion of Christendom was Protestant, and even now only a minority of it is so. The very ground

From *Old South Leaflets* V, No. 109, 1846, pp. 177-180 (Tenth Annual Report to Massachusetts State Board of Education).

on which our free schools were founded, therefore, if it were the only one, would have been a reason with more than half of Christendom for their immediate abolition.

In later times, and since the achievement of American independence, the universal and ever-repeated argument in favor of free schools has been that the general intelligence which they are capable of diffusing, and which can be imparted by no other human instrumentality, is indispensable to the continuance of a republican government. This argument, it is obvious, assumes, as a *postulatum*, the superiority of a republican over all other forms of government; and, as a people, we religiously believe in the soundness both of the assumption and of the argument founded upon it. But, if this be all, then a sincere monarchist, or a defender of arbitrary power, or a believer in the divine right of kings, would oppose free schools for the identical reasons we offer in their behalf. . . .

Again, the expediency of free schools is sometimes advocated on grounds of political economy. An educated people is always a more industrious and productive people. Intelligence is a primary ingredient in the wealth of nations. . . . The moralist, too, takes up the argument of the economist. He demonstrates that vice and crime are not only prodigals and spendthrifts of their own, but defrauders and plunderers of the means of others, that they would seize upon all the gains of honest industry and exhaust the bounties of Heaven itself without satiating their rapacity; and that often in the history of the world whole generations might have been trained to industry and virtue by the wealth which one enemy to his race has destroyed.

And yet, notwithstanding these views have been presented a thousand times with irrefutable logic, and with a divine eloquence of truth which it would seem that nothing but combined stolidity and depravity could resist, there is not at the present time, [1846] with the exception of the States of New England and a few small communities elsewhere, a country or a state in Christendom which maintains a system of free schools for the education of its children. . . .

I believe in the existence of a great, immortal, immutable principle of natural law, or natural ethics,—a principle antecedent to all human institutions, and incapable of being abrogated by any ordinance of man,—a principle of divine origin, clearly legible in the ways of Providence as those ways are manifested in the order of nature and in the history of the race, which proves the *absolute right* to an education of every human being that comes into the world, and which, of course, proves the correlative duty of every government to see that the means of that education are provided for all. . . .

98

J. Murray Lee

ELEMENTARY EDUCATION: 1985

An expert in the curriculum of the elementary school here projects into the future what seems to be current thinking on the nature of buildings, staff, organization, and curriculum. Comparison of the objectives of Mann (Reading 97) with those implied here by Lee reveals a continuing concern for the universal quality of the program, with perhaps a differing perception of the dimensions to be considered.

What will the elementary school be like 25 years from today? Perhaps it will help us to look back at the elementary school of 25 years ago—1935. The testing movement of the 20's had a firm impact. Individual differences were being given consideration. Unit teaching was utilized in the better elementary schools. Considerable effort was being expended to provide a more flexible day for the elementary school pupil. Significant implications from research in child development were being given consideration in curriculum planning. In some areas educational radio was making its contribution to the schools.

From *Educational Leadership*, May 1960, 17:475-479.

Today, after 25 years, many of these trends have grown into maturity, with educational television replacing radio. Perhaps the greatest advances have been in media and materials which are available in the elementary school. Texts have been greatly improved, supplementary books and educational films have increased markedly both in number and quality. Tapes and recordings have served many uses. In addition, improvement in school buildings, some increase in the training of teachers, and elimination of many small districts have had an influence on the elementary school program.

Suppose we could look 25 years into the future. We are in a period of rapidly accelerating change. It seems safe to predict that the changes during the next 25 years will be more rapid and of greater significance than the changes of the past 25. We are clearly moving into a period of greater concern. Public interest in education is high, more money is available for research, the challenges of the future are pressing. The atmosphere thus developed for change will undoubtedly accelerate change.

Buildings

The elementary school building for tomorrow will be a one-story structure accommodating between 500 and 1000. There will be many specialized facilities which are not available in the ordinary schools of today. Special rooms will include a health and psychological center, a library, a cafeteria, a gymnasium which may be a multi-purpose room with showers, conference rooms for use of teachers and parents, and outdoor areas. There will be access to a swimming pool. Between two classrooms there will be a work laboratory equipped for construction, science experiments, and even perhaps with individual booths for use of tape equipment, and automatic teaching machines. Each classroom will be equipped with a television set, tape recorder, record player, and typewriters. Each desk will have its own pencil sharpener. In many areas of the United States the school will be air conditioned as well as heated.

Staff

There will be a full-time supervising principal, a school secretary, and secretaries for every four to six elementary teachers.

Each classroom teacher will have a master's degree. He will also have an area of specializa-

tion, such as social studies, arithmetic, science, measurement, child development, and the other areas needed in the elementary school. Each teacher then, in turn, will serve as a resource person when his area of specialization is of concern to the faculty. The kindergarten teacher will teach half a day. She will have special training in individual testing, and in interviewing parents. She will use the afternoon for individual testing, home visitations, and for conducting child-study programs with the parents of the school.

The greatest change in consultant services available will be in the psychological area. There will be a child psychologist for every 2000 pupils. The case load will then be such that the psychologist may work effectively with individual pupils, teachers, and parents. The recognition that the ages five through twelve are of utmost importance in emotional development, second only to the age range birth to five, will thus be implemented by providing the necessary expert help at this age. Other consultants will include the commonly available ones of nurse, speech correctionist, art and music consultants, and elementary supervisor. Special education facilities will continue to be provided, with more attention being given to children with emotional problems. Adequate medical and dental services will be made available where these can not be provided for by the home.

Each school will have a full-time librarian with a clerical assistant who is in charge of all types of instructional materials. A physical education teacher will be available. He will be able to diagnose the physical and muscular development of children to a much greater extent than is possible today. He will also provide a more intensive, individualized program of muscular development in relation to each child's particular needs.

The probability is that new patterns of utilizing staff will be developed. At times the teacher may be working with much larger groups than at present, at other times with small groups or with individuals. Proposals for effective use of staff time should be carefully evaluated in terms of the effects of the new program on children. There has been too strong a tendency in many schools in the past to jump on attractive bandwagons. With the research techniques available today, the seductive glitter of the new should be carefully evaluated.

While a library with a full-time librarian is the heart of some elementary schools today, it will be taken for granted in the schools of tomorrow. It will include books classified by reading level, pamphlets, picture files, record and transcription collections, science and arithmetic equipment, slides, filmstrips, tape collections including TV tape, films, museum-type materials, conference room, listening booths, transparency collections, professional materials for teachers, and files of community resources, including human resources. There will be adequate clerical help for the librarian.

Connected with the library will be a large individualized instruction room. The room will contain listening booths for the use of master or individualized tapes, and a whole series of teaching machines. Children will be assigned to the room for group or individual help. The tapes will provide assistance in teaching foreign language, music, phonics, in speech correction, and undoubtedly in other ways including perhaps giving a committee the opportunity to hear an outstanding leader from a country they are studying. Then there will be a large number of specific lessons, programmed for the teaching machine.

Often, when the teacher has diagnosed the specific difficulty of a child, certain lessons will be prescribed for helping the child with his difficulties. Also, in this room there will be larger booths containing a modified television set. Electronic tape, which promises to be one of the most versatile audio-visual resources of the future, can be placed in the television set for individual or committee viewing. The same tapes can be used for home study with all television sets equipped to handle tapes. The person in charge of such a room would not have to be a certified teacher, but he would be one who could locate materials and operate the machines.

Organization

There will be considerable experimentation with various patterns of organization. The great need is to have such experimentation carefully evaluated. In the primary grades a teacher undoubtedly will continue with his class for a two-year period. This will mean that children will have the opportunity to mature during a span of the present first and second grade without the usual pressures on the first grade teacher. The same plan may be followed during the third and fourth grades. The intermediate grades seem to offer more opportunity for a variety of plans of organization than do the primary grades. Basic to any plan will be a consideration of the best available experiences for boys and girls in all areas, rather than in one limited area, such as reading. Our lock-step graded system may have disappeared as have half grades in the past 25 years. With additional clerical help available to teachers, there will be opportunities to develop

better instructional materials, better evaluative materials, more detailed cumulative records and to conduct better parent-teacher conferences.

Curriculum

In general, the elementary curriculum will have greater flexibility and at the same time, in certain areas, more uniformity. The uniformity will come from television which will bring to the classroom many learnings the teacher would find difficult, if not impossible, to supply. Television will also release the teacher for more individualized instruction.

Social studies is one area in which television undoubtedly will be most effective. There will be a great deal more research identifying concepts, understandings, and misconceptions which students have in a given area. The broad areas for each level will be carefully selected. The important concepts which children can understand and which can be made meaningful will be utilized in planning. Such planning will, of necessity, involve the school personnel in the area served by the television program. The unique contribution which television can make will be made in programs telecast two or three times a week. Comprehensive study guides will be prepared on an area basis which will include references, suggested experiences, and visual and auditory materials. The teacher will have time available then to work with individuals and groups. There are implications in this situation for the establishment of a new type of state-supported curriculum planning staff on a level between present state departments of education and local school systems.

Reading programs will include much more individualized reading. In the first grade this individualization will be accomplished through students' drawing pictures, and telling the teacher or clerk about the picture. This will be recorded on a dictaphone or tape and transcribed by the clerk, for the child's own reading. Throughout the primary grades much greater use will be made of the child's own stories as a basis for reading, for typing them will be relatively easy. Obviously, such a program needs to be handled by a teacher who is thoroughly familiar with the developmental skills in reading and can supplement these with group or individual instruction. In some cases, this instruction may be handled partially by the teaching machine.

More attention will be given to physical and motor development, for the physical education teacher will be an expert in this area. Specific provision will be made for muscular development for all children with specific help on individual cases. School camping and exchange visits both in and out of the country will become much more common.

Programs will be developed that will provide the non-verbal child with feelings of success. Such programs will be greatly accelerated with the provisions for proper psychological counseling of emotional problems. Breakthroughs in biochemistry may develop techniques of medication which will greatly assist children with learning or emotional problems.

Research

In all areas research will help us with the selection of important concepts, avoid duplication and omission of significant generalizations, and obtain a better understanding of what children already know through pre-testing of concepts. Integration of subject fields will increase, but this integration will be carefully planned rather than incidental. For instance, increased emphasis on concepts of physical and mental health will be developed in social studies by careful analysis and allocation of concepts and experiences. New materials and methods will be available for enriching programs for gifted children which will really challenge their learning abilities.

More attention will be given to the development of critical thinking, problem solving, and creative thinking. One of our current difficulties is that so much of our elementary curriculum consists of materials to be learned by the student. In 1985 we will be approaching learning of important content through techniques requiring comparison and evaluation, anticipation of probable outcomes, and creative questions such as, "If this development had taken place, what would have happened?" The approach will be to develop more openmindedness and questioning on the part of the student rather than a mastery of certain specific procedures.

Creative experiences for children will become increasingly effective. We will improve our understanding of how to encourage creative expression in art. Opportunities for developing appreciation of music and literature will increase as additional materials are made available in recordings and in television tapes. More media in all the creative areas will be utilized. Such developments will become increasingly important as leisure time increases due to automation.

Many elementary children will learn a second language taught through television, tapes and recordings, texts, and reading materials. Mathematics and science will undergo rather marked

changes. Basic ideas and principles will be taught earlier by utilizing techniques of discovery through experimentation. Typing will be a skill universally taught.

In-service programs

Due to the introduction of new content and teaching procedures, there will be an emphasis in in-service programs on familiarizing teachers with the necessary content. Much of this work will be presented over television to teachers of an entire area. Such programs will then be followed up in local schools, utilizing their own leadership. Every staff member will have the responsibility of helping to keep the staff up-to-date on experimentation in one of the various areas. More professional materials will be available in each school. Included will be material to strengthen the subject-matter backgrounds of teachers in new or reorganized content.

Parents

There will be more child study groups, again utilizing TV and supplemented by the skills of the kindergarten teacher. Parents will be used as resource leaders and to help where possible in various phases of the school program. Not only will parent-teacher conferences be universal, but many will be held over a Phonovision. Consultants will be available to work with parents of children having special problems, including emotional difficulties.

Many of these seemingly visionary ideas are operating in one or more school systems throughout the United States. The rapidity with which they will become common practice depends on the willingness of school systems and teacher education programs to intensify their experimentation and research, upon increased support for public education, and upon the creative use of the products of technology which appear in the offing.

Faced with many implications for change we should never lose sight that proposals need to be evaluated in terms of helping teachers to contribute to the development of the minds and hearts of boys and girls. Our children of tomorrow may quite literally have more worlds to conquer than have the children of 1960.

P.S. Certain problems will undoubtedly prove too complex for solution, even by automation, such as: dogs following boys to school, missing handkerchiefs and the one lost overshoe.

99

Robert H. Anderson

UNGRADED PRIMARY CLASSES—
AN ADMINISTRATIVE CONTRIBUTION TO MENTAL HEALTH

One of the most vexing problems of elementary school organization and administration is that of student placement in a grade level. A recent and apparently productive proposal for solving the problem is the "ungraded" school. Readers should note that what is proposed here is not a return to the one-room "little red schoolhouse" but rather a reinterpretation of the whole question of whether individual development may be best cared for outside the arbitrary and (historically) accidental grade-level system. Dr. Anderson's discussion of the inherent merits of such a program and the difficulties of putting it into effect throws light on the nature of the elementary school itself.

There has always been a very close relationship between a child's success in school and his mental health and well-being. The many salutary aspects of successful accomplishment contribute directly to a child's sense of personal worth, self-confidence, and continued motivation to reach desirable goals. Conversely, notable lack of success is usually frustrating, embarrassing, and negative in its impact upon the child's developing personality. For these and related reasons, the profession has become increasingly concerned about children's school success and the various administrative and instructional arrangements which influence each child's progress in the various stages of his school career.

In our American society, the public schools are organized in terms of an agrarian economy, with classes operating from September to May or June. Because of the large numbers of children being instructed, the graded school came into prominence at or about the time of the Civil War, and this device became so well entrenched in practice and in law that the phrase "graded school" has come into popular usage as equivalent to "public elementary school." Although the invention of the graded system made it infinitely more simple to organize the educational program, it also created many problems which we have spent much of the past half century attempting to solve. Before graded schools came into being, the progress of pupils in elementary schools was

basically a continuous and individual proposition: when a child finished his work at one level, he went on automatically to the next. The chronological age of a child was less important from this organizational point of view than his mental age. In the graded school, the children were grouped each September on the basis of chronological age limits which were usually defined in law, with "promotion" and "failure" as devices for adjusting the grade placement of pupils who were either behind or ahead of the typical defined schedule.

Yet September, the opening month of school, is only one of twelve months in which children are born each year. In any given group of so-called "six-year-olds" entering first grade in the month of September there will inevitably be some children who are within a few weeks or months of becoming seven and also some children who are not yet six. Especially in view of the inconsistencies in birth-date deadlines legally established in the various states, every class group has a great range in maturity levels. Especially those children born in the period between September and February might very well find themselves either the youngest or the oldest in their class, depending upon the laws which prevail in the state or community. Adding to this the fáct that many children are either more or less mature than other children born in the same month, it becomes obvious that each class has a very wide range of abilities indeed! Therefore, because the children vary greatly both in their

From *Understanding the Child,* June 1955, 24:66-72.

chronological age and their native academic potentiality, the idea of a "grade norm" is only a very rough index at best; and the likelihood of any given group of children starting and ending at the same places each year is entirely remote.

As a result, we have over the years been faced with the severely difficult problem of assigning children each June to an appropriate grade level in September. This has created both headaches and heartaches, not only for the child himself but for the parents, teachers, and administrators who are concerned with that child's welfare. That about one out of every five children who start first grade faces the possibility of a non-promotion within the next few years is a startling and sobering fact which reveals the enormity of the problem.

Searches for a solution

A number of procedures and policies have been devised to meet the serious problem of non-promotion. In the early part of the century, especially in the larger cities, semi-annual promotions became prominent as a means of insuring more homogeneous groupings and providing more flexibility in promotion and failure arrangements. Yet from the beginning the mid-year arrangement became difficult to administer, was not popular with parents of children in the February class, and was unworkable in smaller school neighborhoods which could not maintain adequate class sizes on the split-year arrangement.

A variety of means for making more suitable provision for individual differences have over the past fifteen or twenty years helped to soften the dividing line between grade levels. The so-called "continuous promotion policy" has received widespread acceptance, although few educators need be reminded that continuous promotion is not a thoroughly popular or acceptable arrangement. Mid-year promotions have therefore become far less popular, and except for certain of the largest cities . . . the idea of mid-year classes has been virtually abandoned in America. In these big cities, where administrative changes are more difficult, the mid-year arrangement remains not by preference of educators but largely because of the difficulty of making a change; and presumably the mid-year promotion plan will eventually be abandoned even in these last strongholds.

The rise in both quality and number of public kindergarten programs has had a beneficial effect on the success of children in the early primary grades. Coupled with various schemes which have been developed for "transition primary classes"

and the like, ways have been found for helping young children to make a smoother entry to first grade work and to achieve success when they are finally placed in the relatively formal activities of the first several grades. Furthermore, there has been a heartening and desirable tendency throughout the country to tighten up entrance age requirements, with more and more communities requiring the children to have had their fifth or sixth birthday earlier than the traditional January 1 before they may be admitted to kindergarten or to first grade.

Yet, despite these administrative arrangements and the greater flexibility of instructional programs, it remains true that thousands of children each June are considered unready for promotion to the next grade level and the spectre of failure still haunts thousands of American homes not only in June but in the apprehensive months which precede the "Great Decision."

The ungraded primary school

As a group of students who worked with Helen Heffernan has commented, "non-promotion is devastating to the personality of children. It deadens initiative, paralyzes the will to achieve, destroys the sense of security and acceptance in the family circle, and promotes truancy and delinquency."[1] For the child who gets off to a slow start, for whatever reason, it would therefore be extremely helpful to have some device other than non-promotion for regulating the child's progress. Similarly, the child who gets off to an unusually good start encounters many significant problems when the school resorts to "skip promotions" or "grade acceleration" as a device for moving him on to a more challenging level of work. For both the slow and the fast learner, therefore, the graded school arrangement has severe limitations.

One of the most heartening developments in American elementary education in the past fifteen years has been the ungraded primary school plan. Rather than being a new invention, this administrative mechanism is actually a throw-back to the original ungraded school arrangement which preceded the system in use for the past century. In the setting of modern education, of course, it has a number of different characteristics and is actually something "new" on the educational horizon. The simple logic of ungraded primary classes and the educational flexibility which such

[1]"What Research Says about Nonpromotions," *California Journal of Elementary Education.* 21 (August, 1952), 44.

classes provide make it all the more puzzling that so few communities have adopted this plan.

What is it?

An ungraded primary school is simply a plan whereby children beyond kindergarten age and below the fourth grade level are grouped together in classes which have no grade level designation. In the words of Florence Kelly of Milwaukee, where the ungraded primary school has had its largest application, it is a "plan whereby children of similar chronological age and social emotional maturity are kept together when administratively possible.[2] The administrative labels, "first grade," "second grade," and "third grade" are eliminated in such an arrangement, and the three year course of study preceding the fourth grade becomes a more flexible program with fewer time limitations and fewer crisis points at which difficult judgements or decisions about pupil promotion must be made. The typical child who enters an ungraded primary class following his "promotion" from the kindergarten simply enters a classroom with no label except "primary." For the next three (or more or less, depending upon his maturity and progress) years, he continues to live and work in a classroom which has no label except the word "primary." He continues to do the same kind of lessons, presumably at the same rate of speed, that he would encounter if he were enrolled in a typical first or second or third grade class; the difference, however, is largely in the fact that his teacher has no grade level expectations against which to pace herself and her only obligation is to keep the youngsters moving along as fast as they are capable of moving. In June, when the children take home their final progress reports, no mention is made of a grade assignment for the ensuing year and the parent is simply advised that the child will continue in primary school and pick up in September where he has left off at this point in June.

Although it is particularly helpful if the same teacher can work with each group of children for several consecutive years, this is not necessarily an inherent feature of ungraded primary schools.

For the average or typical child, whose progress corresponds approximately to the levels of difficulty which have been defined throughout the coun-

try for first grade, second grade, and third grade, an ungraded primary school has relatively few direct advantages. Such children will normally complete the first reader by the end of the first year in primary, the second grade work by the end of the second year, and third grade work by the end of the third year in the program. Since most of these children would receive passing grades and be promoted anyway, it can truthfully be said that the ungraded primary contributes little to their own mental hygiene or to their educational welfare as individuals. However, when we come to consider the child who progresses more slowly and the occasional and rare child who progresses very rapidly, we see more clearly the tremendous merits of an ungraded structure. Let us consider, first, the child who is less mature.

The child who (by virtue of younger chronological age, less social and emotional readiness, or intellectual limitations) gets off to a slow start in September of his first year in the ungraded primary school will very likely have completed considerably less than the "normal" program of first grade work by the ensuing June. Traditionally, in a graded school, the teacher faces the difficult problem in June of passing the youngster into a grade for which he is not prepared or failing him and thus requiring him to re-experience many of the lessons he has already successfully completed. If the retardation is less severe, the choice becomes more difficult. In either case, passing or failing the child, the teacher will be conscience-stricken and the child will face either the crushing frustration of failure or the artificial but short-lived elation of a false success. The following September, the teacher who works with a child who has failed finds it very difficult to avoid repeating work the child already knows; and the teacher who receives students with marginal passing grades also finds it inconvenient and difficult to arrange special help and appropriate activities at a first grade level when the majority of her class is organized on a second grade basis. Since grade standards are everywhere, including in the teacher's mind, neither condition is conducive to an ideal learning situation and the problem of what to do when June comes around remains a vexing and disturbing one to all concerned.

The ungraded primary school does not *necessarily* reduce the prospects of a retarded child's losing a year of schooling; but it certainly minimizes (and often eliminates entirely) the frustration and embarrassment which the loss of a year usually causes in a graded program. A child who cannot successfully complete the expected volume of work in an ungraded primary school continues in the ungraded structure for a fourth

[2]Florence C. Kelly, "Can Promotion Practices Give Security to Children?" *The Primary School*, Bulletin No. 61 of the Association of Childhood Education International. Washington, D. C.: The Association, 1952. P. 31.

year (if this is socially as well as educationally desirable in the judgement of the total school staff). Because of the absence of grade labels, however, and since this retardation takes place gradually and almost imperceptibly within the "intra-class groupings" that are used, the failure itself is often disguised and the child sees no artificial or repetitious break in the sequence of his learning experiences. Because they are not trained or encouraged in these early years to pay much attention to grade labels and the general question of promotion, all of the children automatically pay less attention to eventual grade placement of themselves and their classmates than they ordinarily would.

Milwaukee, Wisconsin deserves major credit for being the only large city with a significant and successful ungraded primary school plan. The basic elements of this plan were adopted by the new school system in Park Forest, Illinois, where the author was Superintendent between 1949 and 1954. Whereas Milwaukee is still on the mid-year admissions basis, Park Forest is on a yearly promotional basis. At this point, after six years of successful operation, it seems possible to make certain assertions concerning the significant merits of the Park Forest plan. To begin with, it is acknowledged that the ungraded primary plan has not always been understood by parents, children, and teachers; and the unwanted phrases—"first grade," "second grade," "third grade"—still appear in conversations and in official discussions. Nonetheless, the plan has received increasing support each year and at this point a substantial proportion of children and parents have accepted the elimination of the old grade labels.

Park Forest's experience clearly demonstrates that ungraded primary arrangements cannot be successful unless the classroom teachers understand and accept the philosophy which underlies ungraded primary programs and detach themselves from the time-worn habit of teachers who are professionally wedded to a particular grade level. In general, it has been easier for younger and more recently trained teachers to think of themselves as "primary teachers" than for older teachers who have taught first, second, or third grade and who tend to think and feel in terms of grade-level expectations. Many teachers found it hard to believe they were not being required in June to send home a report indicating passing or failure. Many found themselves instinctively turning to page 1 of the second or third grade books in September, just as they found themselves instinctively aiming at the last pages of those books by the last week of school in June.

A few had qualms about continuing with the same group of children over a period of more than one year, although this situation improved as the years went by and some of their colleagues had strikingly successful experiences working continuously with the same group.

In the Park Forest plan considerable flexibility of groupings is possible because each school is quite large and has at least two or three sections of each "grade" level. A child's progress is measured primarily by his progress in reading, and a modified plan of homogeneous grouping based upon reading progress has proved to be a very workable arrangement. Children who fall below the progress level of other children in the same class are transferred to another primary teacher whose middle reading group is working at the level for which that child is prepared. Assigning the child to a middle group, by the way, insures that he can remain in that same teacher's classroom should he spurt ahead or should he drop further behind as the year moves along. Transfers of children between class groups have less stigma to them because the transfers are from primary group to primary group, rather than from third grade to second grade (or equivalent transfer).

Incomplete records over a six-year period indicate that a surprisingly low percentage of children have actually required a fourth year of primary school, a situation which is attributable in large measure to the flexibility of the program and to the more humane arrangement which it provides for youngsters who get off to a slow start despite relatively good ability. In fact, a phenomenon has been observed in Park Forest which might well be true throughout the country: children whose first-year progress was so slow that they would normally have been failed in a first grade set-up, often "catch fire" in their second or third years and make such excellent progress that they are ready for fourth grade a year sooner than their first year's work seemed to indicate. In fact, the percentage of four-year primary pupils appears unofficially at this point to be in the neighborhood of five or six percent; this is in contrast with the fourteen to twenty percent failures pattern which is common throughout the country. The administrators and teachers in Park Forest are convinced that the administrative flexibility of the ungraded primary school is a major explanation for this low percentage of "fourth year cases." Furthermore, they believe that the children who have required a fourth year have been relatively unaware of their "failure" and they and their parents have been able to accept this arrangement with much less emotional upset and difficulty than if they had failed in a typical or graded school.

The number of children who have managed to complete ungraded primary school programs in two years is insignificant by comparison, although again it is felt that the ungraded arrangement was a far superior method for permitting these children to "advance" to a higher grade. In the few recorded cases, these youngsters completed every lesson within the three year program without skipping or missing anything in the foundation years. Only those children who were physically, emotionally, and socially mature were permitted to move rapidly through the ungraded primary program; other bright children who were intellectually capable of advancing to a higher grade, but whose physical, social or emotional needs would be better met by remaining with their age mates, were given enriched programs and more difficult assignments within the primary school.

Why not everywhere?

In view of the remarkable success of ungraded primary classes in Milwaukee, Park Forest, and about a dozen other places throughout the country, it seems strange that so few school systems are switching to this scheme. Although these pioneering communities have discovered that much thought must be given to parent and to community relations, they have learned that parents are less affectionately attached to grade level designations than is generally supposed. Parents, sometimes even more than teachers, seem ready to accept and to promote educational practices which increase the school's capacity for meeting the individual needs of children. The philosophy which underlies ungraded primary schools has a healthy effect upon teachers' attitudes and practices, as well as upon parents' expectations of pupil progress. But most important, it gives the youngster himself a more desirable and hygienic point of view with respect to his own school progress in the early years.

Some critics have mistakenly branded ungraded primaries as wildly progressive and devoid of standards. Nothing could be further from the truth. In fact, the educational program remains exactly the same except that the *timing* is more flexible and realistic. For the largest percentage of children, there are few perceptible differences between a graded and an ungraded primary school; the chief beneficiaries are those youngsters who are exceptionally mature and capable, on the one hand, or those who get off to a slow start for a variety of reasons. Tension, frustration, and humiliation, embarrassment, boredom—these are some of the problems of children which can be reduced if communities have the courage and the foresight to abolish the outworn scheme of labeled grades at the primary level.

What are we waiting for?

The educational ladder

THE JUNIOR HIGH SCHOOL

The pattern of American public education as we now know it developed in the period between 1893 and 1918. The public high school became the dominant American secondary school, the junior college began its current phase of development, and the junior high school was devised as a rung in the educational ladder. The extent of the development and acceptance of the junior high school is shown by the fact that almost half the students in grades seven through nine are enrolled in junior high schools. Seventy-five per cent of the junior high schools are housed in separate buildings. The American public has supported the junior high school by providing facilities, services, and materials which are equal in quality to those in other segments of our system. To some observers of the educational scene, the junior high school is the most typically American segment of our school system. It, of all our schools, reflects most clearly the fresh design of the educational philosopher rather than the renovation of an older institution, and it is now recognized as a firm fixture of our educational framework. It is worth noting that educators from other countries have increasingly expressed interest in adapting the junior high school to their own systems.

100

Esther J. Swenson

ISSUES CONCERNING ARTICULATION BETWEEN
ELEMENTARY AND SECONDARY SCHOOLS

One of the leaders in elementary education here points out the problems in meshing the traditional program of the high school with that of the elementary school. This problem of articulation is perhaps a primary reason for the existence of the junior high school. There is, however, an unfortunate tendency for specialists in both elementary and secondary education to place too much stress on the transitional aspect of the junior high school. It seems more reasonable to say that the justification for the existence of *any* level of education is to make adequate provision for the educational needs of students of a particular age, not simply to fill the time between two other stages. The philosophy of the junior high school is closely akin to that of the elementary school, but frequently it is staffed and organized like the high school.

John Dewey once said, "All organization is nothing but getting things into connection with one another, so that they work easily, flexibly and fully." That, also, is what articulation is—getting the learner's school experiences "into connection with one another, so that they work easily, flexibly, and fully." This coherence, this continuity of experience should be our concern from day to day, from grade to grade within the same school unit, and from one school unit to another. Our concern here is primarily with articulation from the elementary to the secondary school.

What are the basic issues which we must consider if the problem of articulation is to be solved? After reviewing the available literature on the subject, consulting by mail with several other persons, and giving considerable thought to the question, I have arrived at a classification of basic issues into four categories.

Objectives of education

First, we will never solve the articulation problem except in relation to the position we take regarding the objectives of education at different school levels.

Are the objectives of education at the elementary and secondary levels the same or are they different? In what ways, if at all, are they the same? In what ways, if at all, are they different?

From *High School Journal*, May 1955, 38:281-288.

You who are parents, why do you send your children to school? What do you expect them to get out of school attendance? Teachers, what are you trying to accomplish with and for your pupils? How different are the goals of elementary and secondary education?

Some people say that attainment of skill in reading, writing, and arithmetic belongs to the elementary school. Surely in the elementary school we want children to acquire skill in the use of language. We want them to grow steadily in their understanding of what they hear and read. We want them to grow steadily in their ability to express their own thoughts correctly, clearly, and effectively when they speak and write those thoughts for others to receive.

But when should these important skills and abilities in the use of language be finally achieved? At what point in a child's education should he have "arrived" at his optimum development so that his learning and our teaching of language skills may be terminated? Let me answer with another question: Who of us even now—after 16 or 20 years of schooling—has learned to handle the skills of language with the maximum understanding and performance of which he is capable?

Yes, development of language skills is a legitimate objective for elementary schools, but it belongs as well among secondary school and collegiate objectives.

Now let us take another objective of education which most of us want for young America—development of power in critical thinking. Surely this must belong to the secondary or the collegiate levels of schooling! You have heard it said that if the next lower school (elementary or secondary, as the case may be) would only teach pupils the so-called "basic skills," we in the higher schools (secondary or collegiate, again as the case may be) will teach them to think. Have younger children no problems to solve? Have they no need for original thinking? Have they no creative power? Suppose we *could* limit their elementary school learnings to acceptance of other people's ideas. Suppose we *could* prevent them from thinking for themselves. What sort of preparation would that be for sudden demands for critical thinking as the portals of the next higher school swing open? Will they not need some already acquired experience in facing and solving problems? (If nothing else, they will have plenty of critical thinking to do if they are to meet these articulation problems we adults have set in their paths.)

My questions are not very subtle. The desired answers are quite obviously, and quite intentionally, implied. Lest there be any misunderstanding, let me say directly that the fundamental objectives of education, such as development of basic skills, development of critical thinking, development of character and good citizenship, are objectives for all of education from the cradle to the grave. Differences appear only as we break down the broad, inclusive objectives in terms of types and degrees and levels of attainment within each.

Because we are speaking here of articulation, I am emphasizing here the common objectives of education in elementary and secondary schools. The first basic issue, then, has two parts: (1) How can elementary and secondary school faculties (with their supervisors and administrators) arrive at some agreements on objectives they hold in common? (2) How can they learn to work together toward the attainment of those common objectives?

Growth and development

A second set of basic issues concerning articulation revolve around what we know about child growth, development, and learning. Is physical, mental, social, and emotional development typified by continuity or by sharp cleavages and stages? Are the basic principles of learning the same or different for children and adolescents? Should individual differences among children be considered and carefully dealt with at certain levels and minimized or ignored at other levels of education?

It is no contradiction to say that human growth, development, and learning are typified by both continuity and variation. In the life of every boy and girl continuity of development is apparent; one phase of development leads to another. Irregularities may occur but the continuity of advancement toward maturity need not be lost because of those irregularities—need not be lost, that is, if his teachers understand the developmental process and the particular pupil and his problems.

For each learner in our schools we want continuous development to a level of performance and maturity commensurate with his potentialities. But this can never be achieved unless we accept along with it the fact of individuality. I do not refer here to a passive sort of acceptance of the generalization that all children are different and should be treated accordingly. I am speaking of the need for an active program of doing something about it.

Here we touch upon one of the "sore points" in American education. We have before us in many 12-year school systems a paradox. As the children grow older, as they progress from one grade level to the next, they become *more* and *more* different but we do *less* and *less* about the differences!

We wish it weren't so! We turn our backs on the evidence and pretend that the evidence does not exist.

To expect children to become more and more alike as they progress through our schools is unrealistic. It isn't true. It never will be true. Are we facing this issue? Do you find more and more evidence of adaptations of instruction to individual differences in pupil ability as you go from the first grade to the sixth? Or from the elementary school to the high school? Do you find more and more grouping of children to meet individual needs and abilities? Do you find more and more differentiation of assignments? Do you find more and more careful evaluation of pupil progress in terms of individual abilities? If you do, you must be looking at a most unusual school system!

And what of the basic principles of how people learn? Are elementary and secondary pupils basically different in how they learn? Is readiness a concept which applies only to first graders, or do all learners need a certain readiness—mental, physical, experiential—for every learning experience? Are the older and younger learners any different in the extent to which they are aided or hindered in learning by the presence or absence of rich and meaningful context for learning whatever is to be learned? Is it only with the younger pupils that we need to provide much concrete experience to lead to fundamental abstract ideas? Is it only with the elementary school child that evaluation of learning must be continuous to be most effective?

Is motivation of learning essential at all levels of learning and for all levels of maturity? Or can it be ignored for older pupils? (It can be ignored, certainly, but with dire consequences.)

The fundamental principles of learning and the fundamental principles and the techniques of good teaching are the same at all ages. Why don't we get together on them?

This is our second basic consideration: How can teachers, administrators, and educational workers at all levels get together in their study of the facts of human growth, development, and learning? How can they plan together for the continuous application of their findings in the lives of pupils who cannot stay, as do teachers, at one school level but must traverse the whole course from the beginning to whatever point is for them the end?

Continuity of experience

Our third set of issues grows out of the first two sets. In the light of our decisions regarding educational objectives and regarding child growth, development and learning, what sort of curriculum should be planned to provide the optimum continuity in every child's school experiences as he goes through our elementary and secondary schools? What curricular content should be provided for all pupils? What should be provided for some but not for others? How should the curriculum be organized so as to result in continuity of experience for each learner?

My favorite definition of curriculum is that curriculum is "what the students learn." The real curriculum, the curriculum which has taken effect, the curriculum which will make a difference in the lives of the learners is that part of the hypothetical curriculum which they have learned so that it becomes a part of them. The effective curriculum is not written in a book or a course of study; it is written in the changed behavior of those who learn.

Teaching children and teaching subject matter have been uselessly contrasted. Some people have even indicated that in the elementary school we teach children and in the secondary school we teach content. This is nonsense! There need be no separation here. At any age and at any level of learning we teach content to learners. We teach children study skills and history and attitudes. We cannot teach children without teaching them something. We cannot teach anything except to a learner. Content is taught only when it becomes part of the learner.

What does all this have to do with articulation? A great deal! The effective curriculum of elementary and secondary schools alike is not an arrangement of unrelated layers of curricular content like a Dagwood sandwich, layer superimposed on unrelated layer. If that is what we are providing for our pupils, we have indeed set before them indigestible fare.

Teachers at all levels should have a common understanding of the whole school program. The more each teacher knows about the curriculum which precedes and follows that part taught at a given level, the better are the pupil's chances of a smooth transition from one level to the next.

This takes time, you say, and teachers are overburdened already. Yes, this takes time. It takes precious time, too, to reteach what has already been taught. It *saves* time for the pupil and for the next teacher if a sound foundation is laid for later learnings. It *saves* time if later learnings can be neatly built upon what precedes. It *saves* time for an earlier teacher to know what will and what will not contribute to later essential learnings.

The building of common understandings about curriculum among teachers at different school levels is a basis for improved articulation. This common understanding is being built in some school systems through curriculum study and revision by teachers from different levels, through discussions and demonstrations, through sharing of materials, and in many other ways. Are you doing this in your system?

Training programs

If we were all agreed on the necessity for cooperative study by elementary and secondary school teachers of educational objectives, of pupil development and learning, and of the sequence and organization of curricular content, we could not escape a fourth set of questions to be faced—questions concerning the professional education of teaching personnel. If school people are to deal wisely with the problems of articulating the school program for their pupils, how should they themselves be educated? How can they gain the requisite understanding and competence to deal with issues of the types we have been discussing? Wherein should the education of elementary and secondary teachers be alike and wherein should it be different? How also can teachers already in the profession be helped to face and help solve these problems of articulation?

These questions, like the preceding sets of questions, have so many angles and implications that it is hardly possible to treat them adequately; yet they cannot fairly be omitted. Teacher education institutions must become increasingly aware of needs for better development of common understandings in child psychology, learning, curriculum, and philosophy of education among students who plan to work in elementary and secondary schools. They need to vary programs of teacher training wherein real variations are essential.

School administrators and supervisors need to set up such an atmosphere of cooperative work and study in a school system as is conducive to increased understanding, increased tolerance, increased sharing, and increased activity among the teachers at different school levels to improve Johnnie's and Susie's chances of getting their separate learnings "into connection with one another, so that they work easily, flexibly, and fully."

Accreditation

In all the preceding discussion of issues concerning articulation you have probably noticed the rather obvious omission of any mention of accreditation. The omission is intentional. I do not consider accreditation to be one of the fundamental or crucial issues bearing on the improvement of articulation between elementary and secondary schools. I can easily conceive of a 12-year school system operating in well articulated fashion *with* accreditation at both elementary and secondary levels; but I can also conceive of a 12-year school system operating in well articulated fashion *without* accreditation. In other words, it is not to my mind an essential consideration. In contrast, I *cannot* conceive of a school system providing a well articulated program of continuous learning experiences for its pupils without cooperative consideration and study of educational objectives, child development and learning, and curricular offerings.

To accredit or not to accredit may well become an issue, but it is not a basic issue upon which better articulation rests. I see it, rather, as playing two other roles with respect to articulation between elementary and secondary schools. Sometimes it is the occasion or the situation which precipitates consideration of articulation. The secondary school in Jonesville is seeking accreditation by the Southern Association of Colleges and Secondary Schools. Accompanying study and evaluation of the curriculum of the elementary "feeder" schools seems advisable; or financial expenditures made to bring a secondary school up to standard create undesirable competition for funds; or the secondary school evaluation committee points out the sources of certain pupil characteristics in their elementary school experiences. Yes, accreditation may easily be the precipitating situation which calls our attention to need for better articulation between the two levels.

Sometimes accreditation is nominated to play another role in relation to articulation. It is sometimes suggested as a ready-made answer to problems of articulation between elementary and secondary schools. We are told that accreditation of elementary schools along with secondary schools would eliminate the existing barriers to smooth pupil progress from one to the other. As I see it, the reliability of such a prediction is yet to be established and would depend upon many other factors such as the type of evaluation process and sources of inarticulation in the particular school system. Perhaps the experiments now under way in qualitative evaluation of total school systems (under a committee of this association) will prove more effective in strengthening articulation within the 12-year program than formal accreditation in and of itself could do.

Accreditation is only one of the many procedures or techniques which may be considered *after*—not before—the careful study of a given school's articulation problems in the light of basic issues. A technique or solution cannot stand alone and be successful. A technique, no matter how good, is best used in the light of the purposes for which it was devised.

In the "20's" and "30's" American education thought it had the answer to smoother articulation between elementary and secondary schools —the junior high school. But here we are in the middle of the "50's" with thousands of junior high schools and hundreds of thousands of junior high school age pupils for whom the old barriers still exist. The junior high school is not a complete failure; neither is it a complete success. It could have been more of a success as an aid to smooth progress of boys and girls through our schools *if* we had remembered that complex human problems like those of achieving continuity of educative experience are not solved by administrative edict or by moving children from one building to another. They are solved as we study the basic issues involved and as we choose various solutions to fit the facts at hand and the goals to be achieved.

Summary

Let me reiterate the basic issues with regard to improving articulation between elementary and secondary schools. I have maintained that we can hope to provide a reasonable degree of continuity of educative experience for the children in our schools *only* in so far as everyone concerned will really delve into the study of these questions: (1) What are the common objectives of education throughout the 12-year school, and how can we all make our best contribution to the realization of those objectives for our pupils? (2) What are the fundamental principles of child development and learning which apply at all levels, and how must we operate to utilize those principles in our teaching and guidance of pupils? (3) What do all teachers need to know about the 12-year curriculum to guarantee appropriate continuity and sequence of pupil experience? (4) What can be done in pre-service and in-service situations to help teachers and administrators achieve the understandings implied in the three preceding questions?

It is comparatively simple to state these questions. To answer them is extremely difficult. Solving our articulation problems may not take Churchill's "blood, sweat and tears" (at least, not the first); but it will surely take much study, real understanding, and cooperative planning by all concerned.

101

John H. Lounsbury

HOW THE JUNIOR HIGH SCHOOL CAME TO BE

A professor who has devoted a great deal of study to the junior high school here describes in clear language its historical development. He points out that while the junior high school may not have proved to be quite everything that some people hoped, it has nevertheless been—and will probably continue to be— remarkably successful.

When Indianola Junior High School of Columbus, Ohio, opened in September of 1909, it was the first school to be specifically called a junior high school. Now, 51 years later, there are 5000 schools labeled junior high schools. Another 3000 are called senior high schools. Today, less than 6000 schools remain as traditional four-year high schools in 8-4 systems. The reorganized secondary schools, that is those that deviate from a four-year high school following an eight-year elementary school, now make up 76 percent of the 24,000 secondary schools and enroll 82 percent of the eleven million secondary pupils.[1]

The movement to reorganize secondary education has certainly come a long way since Charles W. Eliot first suggested the possibility of reorganization in 1888. Between that date and 1909-1910, the reorganization movement was confined primarily to the talking stage. Then the appearance of a number of new intermediate institutions moved reorganization into the experimental stage. During the 1920's the junior high school and its partners in the reorganization movement were rapidly growing educational innovations. In the 1930's the junior high school, the senior high school, and the combination junior-senior high school became accepted members of the American school family. By the close of the 1950's the separate junior high school, followed by the separate senior high school, had become the predominant pattern of secondary school organization in the United States. Together these institutions enrolled 50 percent of the secondary school population.

The movement centering around the junior high school, though already quite successful, is still a relatively young movement. Yet the span of this intermediate institution's existence is long enough so that the history of the junior high school movement can be viewed with reasonable objectivity. And it is appropriate to give some attention to the institution's historical development, for our understanding of the present and our vision for the future are incomplete without a knowledge of how and why the junior high school came to be.

From *Educational Leadership*, December 1960, 18: 145-147, 198.
[1]The figures given are 1959 estimates based on preliminary data as reported by the United States Office of Education in the May 1960 issue of *School Life*, p. 10-12.

Multiple causes

As might be expected, a number of causes underlie the development and expansion of the junior high school movement. Things are seldom as simple as they seem at first glance. The glib quick answer of a pseudo-expert satisfies only those who know less. A scholar sees deeper, notes interrelationships, and only hesitantly draws conclusions. With reservation then, the factors which have helped to bring about the tremendous growth of the American junior high school can be considered.

"What is the present after all, but a growth out of the past?" asked Walt Whitman. His question with its built-in answer was well stated, for institutions and major events never spring up independent of time and place. They evolve from and are shaped by the on-going society. The junior high school is a prime example, for it truly grew out of the times and has continued to shift with the times. The whole history of the junior high school movement is closely paralleled to the social economic and political developments of the half-century which encompasses its life. The reader may be expecting some more spectacular statements regarding how the junior high came to be, but that is really the essence of it. The junior high school was initiated, developed and grew because a variety of factors, all of which related to the times, and existing educational theory and practice, supported it in one way or another.

The junior high school did not grow simply because college presidents in the 1890's wanted secondary schools to speed up and improve college preparation. Nor did the junior high school develop because several national committees issued influential reports which supported reorganization proposals in the period 1892 to 1918. The junior high school did not grow because educators were seeking a solution to the appallingly high rate of drop-outs and retardation as revealed by the pioneer studies of Ayers, Strayer and Thorndike. The junior high school did not come about simply because many educators were levying criticisms on the existing system with its all-too-evident ills and shortcomings. Nor did the junior high school start because psychologists, like G. Stanley Hall, supported special institutions as being better able to cope with the "new beings" early adolescents were thought to be.

The junior high school did not grow because educators aspired to put into practice more completely new understandings of individual differences which the psychologists were clarifying through their research in the 1910's. The junior high school did not grow simply because it afford-ed an outlet for the strong reaction against traditional education led by noted educational philosophers. The junior high school was not caused by the fact that the growing masses of immigrants and urban dwellers required a more extensive type of citizenship education. The junior high school was not created because the many who never reached the later years of high school needed vocational training. The junior high school did not come to its current position because it was a good solution to the school building shortage caused by World War I and again by World War II.

No, the junior high school did not develop, grow, and achieve its present status because of any *one* of the enumerated factors; rather, it grew because of *all* of them. The credit for the junior high school cannot be given to Eliot, Thorndike, Hall, or any other individual. Nor can the growth of the junior high school be written off simply because reorganization provided administrators with an expediency solution to the schoolhouse shortage problem. Many were the individuals who contributed to the development of the junior high school and many were the conditions which supported its growth. It was the interaction of the many conditions and factors which caused the successful growth of the movement.

In some instances, even the champions of the junior high school movement came from different philosophical camps. College men advocated reorganization for economy of time. Public school leaders were concerned over better meeting immediate needs and saw the junior high school as a means of doing this. Board of education members may have seen reorganization as an economy move, while teachers may have supported reorganization because it would bring about new and improved special facilities such as science laboratories.

A dominant factor, however, has undergirded the successful development of the junior high school movement over the long haul. This has been the desire of educators to provide an appropriate educational program for early adolescents. Such a desire was both an original impetus and a continuing concern. While certainly not denying the assistance of other factors in the development of junior high school education, we may note that the support of some of these factors has not been sustained. For instance, the original reason for reorganization, economy of time, was the movement's first fatality. The drop-out problem which motivated many early efforts to reorganize has largely been resolved at the junior high school level. The assistance which the junior high school received from the guidance movement is now given to other schools as well. But the attempt to provide an effective educational program based on the nature of young adolescents remains as the basic theme song of the junior high school movement.

Chronological coincidences

"Nine-tenths of wisdom," said Teddy Roosevelt, "is being wise in time." And while we cannot credit an institution, such as the junior high school, with wisdom, this statement may point up an important reason for the successful development of the American junior high school. Accidentally, coincidentally, and in some cases by design, the junior high school seems to have been wise in time. Its growth seems to have been assisted by many chronological coincidences. The way a variety of developments worked together to the advantage of the reorganization movement is at least a partial explanation for the notable success which the movement has enjoyed.

What if G. Stanley Hall had published his volumes on adolescence in 1925 instead of 1905? What if the school building shortage caused by World War I had come *before* the series of committee reports dealing with reorganization rather than *after?* What if the drop-out studies had been made in the 1880's rather than in 1907-1911? What if the movement to chart individual differences had come about before any mention of reorganization had been made? A number of similar questions might be posed, and probably would be equally difficult to answer with confidence. They are, perhaps, purely academic, yet they serve to point up how important the chronological convergence of numerous factors was to the growth and development of the junior high school.

In summary, many factors worked together to cause the inauguration and early success of the crusade to reorganize secondary education. The original impetus for reorganization came from the colleges and was concerned with economy of time and with college preparation. Discussions about reorganization then began to broaden their base. Proposals for reorganization became linked with other school problems, such as the high rate of elimination and retardation. From psychology came further justification. The culture provided fertile soil for the seeds of reorganization whether planted by college presidents, by public school administrators, by psychologists, or by professional educators. So the movement to reorganize secondary education, coming at a propitious time, prospered.

The junior high school may not have been all that many hoped it would be. It may never have proved itself on some counts, yet it has achieved marked success in its relatively brief history. Many new educational practices and ideas have been tested in the junior high school. More experimentation is in the offing, as glimpses of the future are beginning to come into clearer focus. The junior high school story is then an unfinished one; but its success to date augurs well for the future.

102

William T. Gruhn

DISTINGUISHING CHARACTERISTICS OF THE JUNIOR HIGH SCHOOL

In many respects, the distinguishing characteristics of an institution are what justify its existence. Professor Gruhn, one of the leading authorities on the junior-high-school program, here examines the junior high school with this proposition in mind. In reading this selection, the student should remember that when the unique qualities of an educational institution are emphasized, the basic qualities it shares with all good educational agencies may seem to be overlooked.

Early emphasis on administrative practices

The junior high school from the very beginning has had certain characteristics which distinguish it from other types of elementary and secondary schools. Through the years, however, these charac-

From *High School Journal*, December 1956, 40:82-87.

teristics have not always been the same. In the early history of the junior high school these characteristics tended to emphasize administrative practices rather than curriculum and program.

For instance, the junior high school originally was thought of as a three-year school, including grades 7, 8, and 9. In much of the South, where the eleven-year school system prevailed, grades 6, 7, and 8 were the usual junior high school grades. There was much deviation, however, from this practice. There have always been many two-year junior high schools in the United States, and particularly in the West, some four-year junior high schools. Even so, the junior high school has generally been considered to be a three-year school.

Departmentalization was also associated with the early junior high schools. In fact, next to grade organization, departmentalization has been its most distinct administrative characteristic. In some early junior high schools this was the only feature which distinguished it from other types of schools. Even today an elementary school principal may be heard to remark, "We have organized grades 7 and 8 as a junior high school. You see, these grades are departmentalized."

There are several other administrative practices which prevailed in the early junior high schools. They include particularly homogeneous grouping and promotion by subjects. These practices, like departmentalization, were so closely associated with the junior high school that they were considered to be an essential feature of this type of school organization.

Characteristics are changing

The suggestion that the early junior high schools tended to emphasize certain administrative practices should not be misunderstood. Many of them also introduced new subjects into the curriculum, such as industrial arts, home economics, music, art, and general science. It is certainly true, however, that the administrative characteristics were so generally accepted that they seemed to dominate the thinking of junior high school administrators and teachers. Even today any change in these administrative practices is considered by some to be a violation of the basic philosophy of the junior high school.

In the last decade or two much change has taken place in the thinking concerning the basic features of a junior high school. Though we still recognize the importance of administrative practices, today we give much more emphasis to the child and to the type of program which best meets his needs. We believe today that the curriculum, the guidance activities, the methods of teaching, and the extraclass activities are the things that are important. Administrative practices are important only to the extent that they contribute to the development of an educational program which meets the needs of young adolescents.

As a result of this new emphasis in our thinking, some junior high school educators have become quite critical of the effectiveness of the early administrative practices. Departmentalization is being modified by the introduction of core programs; homogeneous grouping is being limited to specific purposes rather than being the general practice in a school; and promotion based on the needs and interests of the individual child is replacing a more regimented policy of promotion by subjects. Let us look briefly, therefore, at some of the features which more clearly distinguish the junior high school of today.

Emphasis on pupil needs

The most prominent characteristic of the junior high school today is the emphasis that is given in the program to meet the needs of early adolescents. Actually, this thinking is not new. If one studies the early literature on the reorganization of the 8-4 plan, one is impressed with the fact that educators believed that some type of 6-6 organization would provide a better educational program for young adolescents than the 8-4 plan. However, in the early junior high schools so much attention was given to administrative practices that pupils needs were somewhat neglected. A renewed emphasis on developing a program designed especially to meet the needs of early adolescents has recently become the most pronounced characteristic of the junior high school.

What such a program is like is not completely clear, partly because our understanding of early adolescents is still somewhat limited. There are certain pupil needs, however, that we know should be met in a junior high school program. For instance, the child at this age is undergoing certain changes in his social relationships. His circle of friends is beginning to extend beyond the immediate neighborhood. Furthermore, the boy-girl relationships for most pupils change considerably between the sixth and the tenth grade. This is further complicated by the fact that girls mature earlier than boys, and therefore at an earlier age have a social interest in boys as boys. The junior high school needs to provide activities to help pupils meet effectively these new social relationships.

There are also certain physical and health needs that are peculiar to the junior high school years. These are not confined to problems of sexual development alone. For instance, posture problems may become particularly pronounced during early adolescence. The matter of personal cleanliness also is rather different among early adolescents from either younger or older children. Then, too, there is the desire, especially among boys, for vigorous physical activity with emphasis on contact sports. The educational program in the junior high school should provide for such peculiar physical and health needs among growing adolescents.

The social and physical needs of young adolescents are only two that should be recognized in the junior high school program. There are also some emotional changes in children that should receive consideration. At no place in the child's school experience is it more important for him to live in an atmosphere that is free from emotional tensions. The color of the rooms, the harshness of bells, the formality of school discipline, the nature of examinations, the policy concerning marks and report cards, and the relationships between teachers and pupils all have a bearing on creating or relieving emotional tensions.

The need for gaining experience in directing their own affairs, the need for satisfying the creative desires of pupils, and the need for continuing instruction in the fundamentals as a basis for further learning also should have consideration in the planning of any educational program for early adolescents. A program of education which satisfies these needs of children should therefore possess the first characteristic of a modern program of junior high school education; namely, that it meets the needs of early adolescents.

Exploration through all the program

A second characteristic of the junior high school today is that exploratory experiences for pupils are provided in all subjects and in all extraclass activities, rather than being limited to one or two so-called try-out courses. In the early junior high schools it was usually assumed that, in each grade, there would be a basic program of instruction in the fundamental skills and knowledge, but that a period or two a day would be set aside for exploratory courses. It is doubtful that the early leaders in junior high

school education intended that it should be this way. Nevertheless, that became the practice in most schools.

Today we believe that every educational activity—whether it be in language arts, social studies, industrial arts, mathematics, or on the athletic fields—should give the child an opportunity to explore his talents and interests. In other words there should be no exploratory courses as such. Rather, all courses and activities should have exploration of pupil talents and interests as one of their purposes.

Exploration in the various subjects will not come about through mere chance. Provision for it needs to be carefully made by teachers and pupils together. The methods of teaching employed, rather than the content of the courses, should have particular emphasis in providing exploratory opportunities. In every classroom there should be as much flexibility as possible, with pupils participating in the planning of learning activities, assuming much responsibility for carrying on those activities, and having much choice in the particular activities in which they would like to engage.

Flexibility in teaching methods is, obviously, achieved more easily in some subjects than in others. In the mathematics class, choices by the pupils may be somewhat limited. But in literature, industrial arts, crafts, home economics, and general science, many opportunities may be offered for pupils to pursue activities that satisfy individual interests and talents. A flexible rather than a regimented approach to teaching is therefore essential if exploratory opportunities are to be provided through all subjects and activities in the junior high school program.

Individualized teaching in all classes

From the very beginning, meeting individual differences was an important function of the junior high school. It was achieved, if at all, through such administrative practices as homogeneous grouping, "multiple-track" curricula, promotion by subjects, and differentiated marks. In recent years we have come to believe that there is only one way to individualize instruction; namely, to become well acquainted with the backgrounds, the abilities, and the interests of individual pupils, and then to work with them as individuals in every learning situation. This emphasis on meeting individual differences through the study of children and the teaching of them as individuals has become one of the pronounced characteristics of the junior high school today.

This point of view has been implemented in practice in a number of ways. For instance, there is less emphasis on homogeneous grouping, and more on methods of teaching that make it possible to work with individual pupils regardless of the approach to grouping that is employed. Schools that employ some type of core curriculum provide an excellent example of this approach. In these schools teachers have fewer pupils for a longer period of time each day. They become better acquainted with their pupils and have more opportunity to work with them in small groups or as individuals.

Certain approaches in teaching methods also are helpful in individualizing instruction. Flexible courses of study, pupil participation in planning learning activities, and a variety of instructional materials make it easier to meet the needs of individual pupils. Much still needs to be done to help teachers develop skill in working effectively with individual children. However, much attention is now being given to teaching methods appropriate for individualized teaching, as compared with administrative practices alone. Therefore this can be considered to be a prominent characteristic of a modern junior high school program.

Developing a school community

More than ever before we recognize that the junior high school should be more than a place where pupils go from class to class and room to room. It should be a community where young adolescents spend three productive and happy years of their lives. Their friends are there, that is where for the present they are doing basic work, and it is the center of much of their social and cultural life. They should participate in the life of the school community, they owe it their loyalty, and they should leave it a better community than when they entered. A recognition of the importance of the junior high school as a community for young adolescents is a fourth characteristic of a modern junior high school program.

It is not easy to suggest how a school might become a satisfactory community for young adolescents. We do know that the initiative must be taken by the principal and the faculty. They must recognize that the pupils, under competent supervision, have a significant contribution to make to the traditions, the administration, the activities, and the program of the school. The potentialities of the pupils need to be developed and directed so that they may contribute to the development of an effective school community.

Conclusion

The four characteristics which have been presented in the preceding discussion are not the only ones that distinguish the junior high school from other types of school organization. Nevertheless, they are the ones which stand out most prominently in those schools which are attempting to develop forward-looking programs. Principals, teachers, parents, and pupils who are engaged in modifying the program of their school would do well to direct their attention to practices which implement these characteristics.

The educational ladder

THE SENIOR HIGH SCHOOL

Unlike the junior high school, the senior high school goes back in its tradition—and, indeed, in many aspects of its program—to the humanistic schools set up during the Renaissance for the teaching of Greek and Latin. Essentially, the tradition of secondary education is an aristocratic one, but the demands of American life have been for something appropriate to all of the children of all of the people. One problem of twentieth century American educators has been to adapt this long-established institution to present-day needs.

Though efforts to develop a comprehensive high school, indigenous to America, have achieved remarkable results, many problems still exist. Studies have pointed out, for example, that many high schools are too small to provide a varied and individualized program of quality: specifically, 70 per cent of the nation's high schools have been judged too small to provide adequate instructional facilities. In order to remedy such conditions, it has been proposed that a four-year high school have a minimum of 300 pupils, with 75 pupils in each age group, and 12 full-time teachers. A major task facing the various states is to eliminate the small high school by district reorganization. Conant (3) recommended such reorganization and proposed that there should be at least 100 students in every high-school graduating class. Problems of the high school other than size include financing the varied offerings of the comprehensive high school, regardless of size, recruiting competent teachers, and defining precisely the mission and tasks of the comprehensive high school of the future.

103

Benjamin Franklin

PROPOSALS RELATING TO THE EDUCATION OF YOUTH IN PENNSYLVANIA

This document is interesting not only because the school which resulted from it became one of the first Academies, but because Franklin's suggestion seems even more appropriate to the organization of the modern high school than to the secondary schools of its day. Of particular interest is the pragmatic suggestion that, since (even in those days!) there was more to be taught than could be covered adequately, the schools should concentrate upon those things that would be *most* useful and *most* ornamental.

Advertisement to the reader

It has long been regretted as a Misfortune to the Youth of this Province, that we have no Academy, in which they might receive the Accomplishments of a regular Education. The following Paper of Hints towards forming a Plan for that Purpose, is so far approv'd by some publick-spirited Gentlemen, to whom it has been privately communicated, that they have directed a Number of Copies to be made by the Press, and properly distributed, in order to obtain the Sentiments and Advice of Men of Learning, Understanding, and Experience in these Matters; and have determined to use their Interest and best Endeavours, to have the scheme, when compleated, carried gradually into Execution; in which they have Reason to believe they shall have the hearty Concurrence and Assistance of many who are Wellwishers to their Country. Those who incline to favour the Design with their Advice, either as to the Parts of Learning to be taught, the Order of Study, the Method of Teaching, the Economy of the School, or any other Matter of Importance to the Success of the Undertaking, are desired to communicate their Sentiments as soon as may be, by Letter directed to B. Franklin, *Printer,* in Philadelphia.

Proposals, &c.

The good Education of Youth has been esteemed by wise Men in all Ages, as the surest Foundation of the Happiness both of private Families and of Common-wealths. Almost all Governments have therefore made it a principal Object of their Attention, to establish and endow with proper Revenues, such Seminaries of Learning, as might supply the succeeding Age with Men qualified to serve the Publick with Honour to themselves, and to their Country.

Many of the first Settlers of these Provinces, were Men who had received a good Education in *Europe,* and to their Wisdom and good Manage-

From *Readings in American Educational History,* Edgar W. Knight and Clifton Hall, eds. (New York: Appleton-Century-Crofts, Inc., 1951), pp. 74-80.

ment we owe much of our present Prosperity. But their Hands were full, and they could not do all Things. The present Race are not thought to be generally of equal Ability: For though the *American* Youth are allow'd not to want Capacity; yet the best Capacities require Cultivation, it being truly with them, as with the best Ground, which unless well tilled and sowed with profitable Seed, produces only ranker Weeds.

That we may obtain the Advantages arising from an Increase of Knowledge, and prevent as much as may be the mischievous Consequences that would attend a general Ignorance among us, the following *Hints* are offered towards forming a Plan for the Education of the Youth of *Pennsylvania*, viz.

It is propos'd,

That some Persons of Leisure and publick Spirit, apply for a Charter, by which they may be incorporated, with Power to erect an Academy for the Education of Youth, to govern the same, provide Masters, make Rules, receive Donations, purchase Lands, &c. and to add to their Number, from Time to Time such other Persons as they shall judge suitable.

That the Members of the Corporation make it their pleasure, and in some Degree their Business, to visit the Academy often, encourage and countenance the Youth, countenance and assist the Masters, and by all Means in their Power advance the Usefulness and Reputation of the Design; that they look on the Students as in some Sort their Children, treat them with Familiarity and Affection, and when they have behav'd well, and gone through their Studies, and are to enter the World, zealously unite, and make all the Interest that can be made to establish them, whether in Business, Offices, Marriages, or any other Thing for their Advantage, preferably to all other Persons whatsoever even of equal Merit.

And if Men may, and frequently do, catch such a Taste for cultivating Flowers, for Planting, Grafting, Inoculating, and the like, as to despise all other Amusements for their Sake, why may not we expect they should acquire a Relish for that *more useful* Culture of young Minds. *Thompson says,*

'Tis Joy to see the human Blossoms blow,
When infant Reason grows apace, and calls
For the kind Hand of an assiduous Care;
Delightful Task! to rear the tender Thought,
To teach the young Idea how to shoot,
To pour the fresh Instruction o'er the Mind,
To breathe th' enliv'ning Spirit, and to fix
The generous Purpose in the glowing Breast.

That a House be provided for the Academy, if not in the Town, not many Miles from it; the Situation high and dry, and if it may be, not far from a River, having a Garden, Orchard, Meadow, and a Field or two.

That the House be furnished with a Library (if in the Country, if in the Town, the Town Libraries may serve) with Maps of all Countries, Globes, some mathematical Instruments, an Apparatus for Experiments in Natural Philosophy, and for Mechanics; Prints, of all Kinds, Prospects, Buildings, Machines, Ec.

That the Rector be a Man of good Understanding, good Morals, diligent and patient; learn'd in the Languages and Sciences, and a correct pure Speaker and Writer of the *English* Tongue; to have such Tutors under him as shall be necessary.

That the boarding Scholars diet together, plainly, temperately, and frugally.

That to keep them in Health, and to strengthen and render active their Bodies, they be frequently exercis'd in Running, Leaping, Wrestling, and Swimming, Ec.

That they have peculiar Habits to distinguish them from other Youth, if the Academy be in or near the Town; for this, among other Reasons, that their Behaviour may be the better observed.

As to their Studies, it would be well if they could be taught *every thing* that is useful, and *every thing* that is ornamental; But Art is long, and their Time is short. It is therefore propos'd that they learn those Things that are likely to be *most useful* and *most ornamental*. Regard being had to the several Professions for which they are intended.

All should be taught to write a *fair Hand*, and swift, as that is useful to All. And with it may be learnt something of *Drawing*, by Imitation of Prints, and some of the first Principles of Perspective.

Arithmetick, Accounts, and some of the first Principles of *Geometry* and *Astronomy*.

The *English* Language might be taught by Grammar; in which some of our best Writers, as *Tillotson, Addison, Pope, Algernoon Sidney, Cato's* Letters, &c. should be Classicks: The *Stiles* principally to be cultivated, being the *clear* and the *concise*. Reading should also be taught, and pronouncing, properly, distinctly, emphatically; not with an even Tone, which *under-does*, nor a theatrical, which *over-does* Nature.

To form their Stile, they should be put on Writing Letters to each other, making Abstracts of what they read; or writing the same Things in their own Words; telling or writing Stories lately read, in their own Expressions. All to be revis'd and corrected by the Tutor, who should give his Reasons, explain the Force and Import of Words, &c.

To form their Pronunciation, they may be put on making Declamations, repeating Speeches, delivering Orations, &c. The Tutor assisting at the Rehearsals, teaching, advising, correcting their Accent, &c.

But if History be made a constant Part of their Reading, such as the Translations of the *Greek* and *Roman* Historians, and the modern Histories of antient *Greece* and *Rome*, &c. may not almost all Kinds of useful Knowledge be that Way introduc'd to Advantage, and with Pleasure to the Student? As Geography, by reading with Maps, and being required to point out the Places *where* the greatest Actions were done, to give their old and New Names, with the Bounds, Situation, Extent of the Countries concern'd, &c.

Chronology, by the Help of *Helvicus* or some other Writer of the Kind, who will enable them to tell *when* those Events happened; what Princes were Contemporaries, what States or famous Men flourish'd about that Time, &c. The several principal Epochas to be first well fix'd in their Memories.

Antient Customs, religious and civil, being frequently mentioned in History, will give Occasion for explaining them; in which the Prints of Medals, Basso Relievo's, and antient Monuments will greatly assist.

Morality, by descanting and making continual Observations on the Causes of the Rise or Fall of any Man's Character, Fortune, Power, &c. mention'd in History; the Advantages of Temperance, Order, Frugality, Industry, Perseverance, &c. &c. Indeed the general natural Tendency of Reading good History, must be, to fix in the Minds of Youth deep Impressions of the Beauty and Usefulness of Virtue of all Kinds, Publick Spirit, Fortitude, &c.

History will show the wonderful Effects of Oratory, in governing, turning and leading great Bodies of Mankind, Armies, Cities, Nations. When the Minds of Youth are struck with Admiration at this, then is the Time to give them the Principles of that Art, which they will study with Taste and Application. Then they may be made acquainted with the best Models among the Antients, their Beauties being particularly pointed out to them. Modern Political Oratory being chiefly performed by the Pen and Press, its Advantages over the Antient in some Respects are to be shown; as that its Effects are more extensive, more lasting, &c.

History will also afford frequent Opportunities of showing the Necessity of a *Publick Religion*,

from its Usefulness to the Publick; the Advantage of a Religious Character among private Persons; the Mischiefs of Superstition, &c. and the Excellency of the Christian Religion above all others antient or modern.

History will also give Occasion to expatiate on the Advantage of Civil Orders and Constitutions, how Men and their Properties are protected by joining in Societies and establishing Government; their Industry encouraged and rewarded, Arts invented, and Life made more comfortable: The Advantages of *Liberty*, Mischiefs of *Licentiousness*, Benefits arising from good Laws and a due Execution of Justice, &c. Thus may the first Principles of sound *Politicks* be fix'd in the Minds of Youth.

On *Historical* Occasions, Questions of Right and Wrong, Justice and Injustice, will naturally arise, and may be put to Youth, which they may debate in Conversation and in Writing. When they ardently desire Victory, for the Sake of the Praise attending it, they will begin to feel the Want, and be sensible of the Use of *Logic*, or the Art of Reasoning to *discover* Truth, and of Arguing to *defend* it, and *convince* Adversaries. This would be the Time to acquaint them with the Principles of that Art. *Grotius*, *Puffendorff*, and some other Writers of the same Kind, may be used on these Occasions to decide their Disputes. Public Disputes warm the Imagination, whet the Industry, and strengthen the natural Abilities.

When Youth are told, that the Great Men whose Lives and Actions they read in History, spoke two of the best Languages that ever were, the most expressive, copious, beautiful; and that the finest Writings, the most correct Compositions, the most perfect Productions of Human Wit and Wisdom, are in those Languages, which have endured Ages, and will endure while there are Men; that no Translation can do them Justice, or give the Pleasure found in Reading the Originals; that those Languages contain all Science; that one of them is become almost universal, being the Language of Learned Men in all Countries; that to understand them is a distinguishing Ornament, &c. they may be thereby made desirous of learning those Languages, and their Industry sharpen'd in the Acquisition of them. All intended for Divinity should be taught the *Latin* and *Greek*; for Physick, the *Latin*, *Greek* and *French*; for Law, the *Latin* and *French*; Merchants, the *French*, *German*, and *Spanish*: And though all should not be compell'd to learn *Latin*, *Greek*, or the modern foreign Languages; yet none that have an ardent Desire to learn them should be refused; their *English*, Arithmetick, and other Studies absolutely necessary, being at the same Time not neglected.

If the new *Universal History* were also read, it would give a *connected* Idea of human Affairs, so far as it goes, which should be follow'd by the best modern Histories, particularly of our Mother Country; then of these Colonies; which should be accompanied with Observations on their Rise, Encrease, Use to *Great-Britain*, Encouragements, Discouragements, &c. the Means to make them flourish, secure their Liberties, &c.

With the History of Men, Times and Nations, should be read at proper Hours or Days, some of the best *Histories of Nature*, which would not only be delightful to Youth, and furnish them with Matter for their Letters, &c. as well as other History; but afterwards of great Use to them, whether they are Merchants, Handicrafts, or Divines; enabling the first the better to understand many Commodities, Drugs, &c. the second to improve his Trade or Handicraft by new Mixtures, Materials, &c. and the last to adorn his Discourses by beautiful Comparisons, and strengthen them by new Proofs of Divine Providence. The Conversation of all will be improved by it, as Occasions frequently occur of making Natural Observations, which are instructive, agreeable, and entertaining in almost all Companies. *Natural History* will also afford Opportunities of introducing many Observations, relating to the Preservation of Health, which may be afterwards of great Use. *Arbuthnot* on Air and *Aliment, Sanctorius* on Perspiration, *Lemery* on Foods, and some others, may now be read, and a very little Explanation will make them sufficiently intelligible to Youth.

While they are reading Natural History, might not a little *Gardening, Planting, Grafting, Inocu-*

lating, &c. be taught and practised; and now and then Excursions made to the neighbouring Plantations of the best Farmers, their Methods observ'd and reason'd upon for the Information of Youth. The Improvement of Agriculture being useful to all, and Skill in it no Disparagement to any.

The History of *Commerce*, of the Invention of Arts, Rise of Manufactures, Progress of Trade, Change of its Seats, with the Reasons, Causes, &c. may also be made entertaining to Youth, and will be useful to all. And this, with the Accounts in other History of the prodigious Force and Effect of Engines and Machines used in War, will naturally introduce a Desire to be instructed in *Mechanicks*, and to be inform'd of the Principles of that Art by which weak Men perform such Wonders, Labour is sav'd, Manufacture expedited, &c. &c. This will be the Time to show them Prints of antient and modern Machines, to explain them, to let them be copied, and to give Lectures in Mechanical Philosophy.

With the whole should be constantly inculcated and cultivated, that *Benignity of Mind*, which shows itself in *searching for* and *seizing* every Opportunity *to serve* and *to oblige;* and is the Foundation of what is called Good Breeding; highly useful to the Possessor, and most agreeable to all.

The Idea of what is *true Merit*, should also be often presented to Youth, explain'd and impress'd on their Minds, as consisting in an *Inclination* join'd with an *Ability* to serve Mankind, one's Country, Friends and Family; which *Ability* is (with the Blessing of God) to be acquir'd or greatly encreas'd by *true Learning;* and should indeed be the great *Aim* and *End* of all Learning.

104

Henry Steele Commager

A HISTORIAN LOOKS AT THE AMERICAN HIGH SCHOOL

In this article a prominent historian examines some of the stages in the history of secondary education and makes suggestions for the future—suggestions which are especially interesting because they represent the views of an academic scholar on the field of professional education.

It is not chance that the prodigious issue of racial equality should have come to a boil in a

case called *Brown* v. *Board of Education* [Reading 94] and that it should have boiled over, as it were, in Little Rock High School. Even the most ardent critic of the Supreme Court would not take issue with the obiter dicta of the Brown case:

"Today education is perhaps the most important function of the state and local governments. Compulsory school attendance laws and the great expenditures for education both demonstrate our recognition of the importance of education in our democratic society. It is required in the performance of our most basic public responsibilities. . . . It is the very foundation of good citizenship. Today it is a principal instrument in awakening the child to cultural values, in preparing him for later professional training, and in helping him to adjust normally to his environment. In these days it is doubtful that any child may reasonably be expected to succeed in life if he is denied the opportunity of an education" [347 U.S. at 493].

This argument, with its brief but comprehensive references to the relation of education to citizenship, culture, special skills, and social adjustment, is an echo of a long series of statements, proclamations, and arguments that began in the 1630's and have re-echoed down the corridors of our history. It takes us back to the justification of the School Act of 1642, "that learning which may be profitable to the commonwealth," and the Act of 1647, "that learning may not be buried in the graves of our fathers in the church and commonwealth," and the commitment to education, not for narrow religious, but for broad commonwealth, purposes throughout the history of the Bay Colony. It found expression, particularly, in the Revolutionary generation: no body of nation-makers were ever so conscious of the role that education should play as were the American Founding Fathers. Thus Jefferson's proposal for "a system of education which shall reach every description of citizen from the richest to the poorest"; thus the provision of the Northwest Ordinance that "religion, morality and knowledge being necessary to good government and the happiness of mankind, schools and the means of education shall be forever encouraged." Thus the ardent Noah Webster's argument: "In our American Republic where government is in the hands of the people, knowledge should be universally diffused by means of schools. Of such consequence is it to society that the people who make laws should

be well informed that I conceive no Legislature can be justified in neglecting proper establishments for this purpose."

Characteristic features of American schools

The characteristic features of the American educational system emerged early and were in large part the product, or the accident, of circumstances and of environment. By the time the high school made its appearance on the educational landscape, the pattern was pretty well fixed: pluralism, or local rather than centralized control of education; secularism, or separation from religious control; a general or liberal rather than a vocational education; and an education of the general populace rather than of the elite.

If we can, formally, date elementary education from the Massachusetts Act of 1642, we can date the high school from the Massachusetts Law of 1827 (leave aside that both laws were ineffective for a long time). Thus the formal advent of the high school came late in our educational system. In fact, it came a good deal later than these dates would indicate, for not until 1864 did New York State require the maintenance of high schools, and as late as 1890 there were only 2,526 public high schools in the entire nation (this in a population of 63 million).

Yet recent as is the high school on the American educational scene, it is, by comparison with the scene abroad, almost a venerable institution. To be sure, there had been schools called "high" in England as early as the fourteenth century (in Exeter, for example, in 1313), and our own earliest high schools took their name from the high schools of Edinburgh and Glasgow. These were not high schools in our meaning of the word, merely the principal school, and it is true that not until well into the twentieth century did any European country provide an effective system of free public secondary education for all who desired it. (Thus at the beginning of this century, only 109,000 pupils attended the secondary schools of Britain, and not until 1907 was provision made for secondary education for those unable to pay the ordinary fees.) Only since the second World War has Britain begun to provide for its 14-18 year-olds as adequately as the United States did sixty or seventy years ago. And what is true of Britain is true of all continental countries, except possibly Holland, Switzerland, and the Scandinavian nations.

The American high school, then, was the pioneer—the pioneer not only in time but in

From *The High School in a New Era* by Francis S. Chase and Harold A. Anderson, pp. 3-19. Copyright 1958 by The University of Chicago. Reprinted by permission of The University of Chicago Press.

program as well—and if older European nations do not borrow heavily from our experience, many of the new nations outside Europe do. In the comprehensive high school, in the single curriculum for all, in the amalgamation of preparation for college and for work; in the emphasis on student government and student activities; in coeducation; in the openness of the curriculum and of the whole academic course (the easy, almost unconscious merging into college); in the emphasis on doing in the processes of learning —in all these and other things the American high school has been a pioneer.

It is the most hackneyed of observations that schools are a function of society, but we should keep in mind that, as American society differed profoundly from European in the eighteenth and early nineteenth centuries, the functions imposed upon schools differed profoundly from those which older societies imposed upon their schools. The story is familiar, and I need not rehearse it: how, especially in the nineteenth century, we required our schools to train citizens competent to govern themselves (a requirement not urgent in the Old World), to absorb and Americanize millions of newcomers from the Old World and elsewhere, to encourage and strengthen national unity, and to teach the habits and practices of democracy and equality and religious tolerance.

Achievements of the American schools

Looking back on the American experience in the perspective of a century or so (about the time we have been at the job of comprehensive education), we cannot, I think, but be dazzled that we have managed so well in so short a time. If we look only to the educational achievement, we see that we have provided more education to a larger portion of society than did any other country in history; we have built a magnificent physical plant and equipped it with educational apparatus, for example, gymnasiums and school libraries; we have supplied more than one million teachers (and who will deny that they are better prepared for their jobs than were the teachers of a half-century or a century ago?). If emphasis seems to be laid too heavily on quantity, may we not add that, qualitatively, the products of the American school system compared favorably with the products of German or French school systems both in competence and in judgment in the great crisis of the World War and its aftermath?

As schools are commonly blamed for the failings or inadequacies of society, perhaps it is not wholly unfair to give them some credit for the larger successes and achievements. After all, Americans, the products of our educational system, succeeded in a great many things which involve intelligence and judgment. They established a nation and held it together, expanding thirteen to forty-eight states with less difficulty than England had with Ireland alone in the same period. They made democracy work reasonably well and did not gratify the expectations of those who were so sure that a majority would inevitably exercise tyranny over minorities. They elected mediocre presidents, but never a wicked or a dangerous one. They never yielded to a military dictator. They settled all their problems, but one, by compromise and concession instead of by violence (and perhaps that one could not be solved by compromise). They adjusted themselves speedily to their responsibilities as a world power. These are not accomplishments that can be confidently traced to the educational system, but it would be absurd to deny that the schools contributed to them.

Not only do our schools deserve some credit for these accomplishments; they deserve some credit for the things they have avoided. Much of our history is, in a sense, an achievement in avoidance—nationalism without "nationalizmus," world power without imperialism, majority rule without majority tyranny, capitalism without class warfare, and so on. The schools, too, have somehow managed to avoid many of the dangers that might have worked irreparable harm to our social or intellectual fabric.

The schools began in New England as exponents of a particular religion but avoided religious fanaticism or too intimate a dependence on the church even in the Colonial period. Since that time, public schools have had no religious dependence, and even private schools have been tolerant. Recollect that as late as the 1860's a Catholic could not attend Oxford or Cambridge Universities and that even Leslie Stephen severed his connection with Cambridge because he could not subscribe to the Thirty-nine Articles. Though the schools are divorced from the church and from formal religion, there has been no failure to inculcate morality.

Though required to take all comers, mass education has not meant a vulgarization of culture or a serious watering-down of the intellectual content of learning. If the American high school does not do as good a job in formal education as the English public school, the French lycée, and the German gymnasium, it is part of an educational process which eventually goes as high as does any other system in the world.

Though the tasks that confronted Americans—and that appealed for educational support—have been intensely practical, there has not been an overemphasis on vocational education in the American system. There has not been a rejection of humanism, or even of classical education, as was threatened by some of the enthusiasts of the Revolutionary period.

Though few societies displayed greater differences and divisions than did the American, our schools have not accentuated, but have mitigated, these differences educationally. We have not separated our students between the many who are called and the few who are chosen, as is still the practice in almost all European countries.

Though upon the schools was placed heavy responsibility for encouraging national unity and inculcating pride in the history and traditions of the nation, the schools were not instruments of chauvinism, nor did they ever, except in the prewar South, allow themselves to become instruments of the state.

It is important that we keep in mind that the school has never been a merely passive agent in the process of serving the needs of our society. Indeed, as a result of the peculiar circumstances of American life, schools have played a somewhat more important role here than elsewhere in setting standards and in creating social patterns: first, because almost from the beginnings of our national history, education has been a secular religion; second, because the schools furnished perhaps the largest and the most familiar framework of experience to a heterogeneous and fluctuating population, and the tendency was strong to adjust to the school; and, third, because in the nineteenth and much of the twentieth century the school, by giving each generation of young a better education than their parents had enjoyed, set standards, as it were, for the parents and persuaded the adult world to yield to those standards and adjust to those demands. In most societies of the Old World (as in more primitive societies), each generation tends to have about the same educational experience as did the preceding generation: children of those who have not gone to secondary school do not themselves go to secondary school; children of those who have not gone to a university do not ordinarily go to the university. But in our society it has almost always been the other way around. In our country, in the game of "schoolmanship," the young know all the plays and have their elders at a disadvantage. This is one of the explanations of that habit which Europeans find so difficult to understand—the grown-ups' habit of yielding to the standards, the demands, the expectations,

of their children and conforming to the notions brought home from school.

The demands of a new era

Now our entire educational system, but especially our high schools, have entered, or are in process of entering, a new era—an era which demands new things of the school and which requires new things from the school. It is to no point to intone the old litanies. The schools are called upon to play a role closer, perhaps, to that imagined for the academies and colleges in the eighteenth century than to that which they did play in the nineteenth. What are the considerations and conditions which require a rethinking of the functions of our schools?

First, our schools are, in a sense, the victims of their own success. If they are not precisely buried beneath the ruins of their own triumph, they are conditioned and committed by their achievements. Most of what we may call the non-academic functions of the schools in the nineteenth and early twentieth centuries have been performed: to give unity to a heterogeneous population, to create a sense of belonging to, to inculcate democracy and equality. These are never ending problems, and I do not suggest that they are wholly solved: witness the problem which New York City faces with its Puerto Rican school children, or the South with its Negro population. But can it not be said that schools have already formulated solutions to these problems, that their application rests with society?

This suggests a second consideration, one which has not, I think, been adequately assimilated by educators: that the school no longer bears the heavy responsibilities in the non-academic realm that it did in the nineteenth century, that it now shares with many other agencies responsibility for non-academic educational activities, and that it is in a better position to devote its attention to what we may call academic functions than ever before. Schools do not need to educate parents through their children, as they once did; and the parents themselves not only are more sophisticated but have more leisure time for their own responsibilities and duties than they had in the nineteenth century. Most important, scores of other agencies are now doing what the school did in the nineteenth century: the press, radio, television, movies, organizations like the Boy Scouts and Girl Scouts, the churches in their enlarged social functions, and others.

Indeed insofar as schools are agents of social development as well as instruments of society, they have a duty to resist, rather than to yield to, community pressures. Because schools are a function of society, a great many educators think it the primary duty of the schools—and especially the high school, which here occupies a crucial position—to "adapt" the young to the society in which they are to live. Needless to say, if each generation of young is merely fitted to the existing order of things, we shall end up with a Byzantine, not a Western, civilization. A dynamic society cannot stay dynamic if the existing order fixes the standards to which all must conform and into which all must be fitted.

Schools are a part of society, but they should not be a complete mirror of society. They should offer not a repetition of experience but a challenge to, and an extension of, experience. They are not a tranquilizer but a conscience for society. Yet at a time when schools are in a better position to emancipate themselves from community pressures than ever before and when the necessity of challenge and experimentation is perhaps stronger than ever before, our schools seem to make a fetish of adaptation and conformity.

When almost every agency proclaims the merits of "private enterprise," the schools, all too often, weakly yield to pressures from filiopietistic or business organizations to beat the academic drum for private enterprise. When almost everybody reads *Reader's Digest* and *Life* and *Look* and *Newsweek* anyway and the young can be trusted to see them outside the schoolroom, students read these magazines in the schoolroom or the school library, rather than less popular and less readily available magazines which they may otherwise never come to know. When the discussion of current affairs commands the daily press, the radio, television, and most conversation at home, the schools, instead of diverting the young to a contemplation of the affairs of Greece and Rome or of medieval England, meekly concentrate on current affairs. At a time when society is perhaps overly concerned with material things—with business and industry, with roads and automobiles— when things are in the saddle and ride mankind, the schools, too, emphasize the practical and the material rather than the intellectual or the aesthetic.

At a time when almost all the institutions of society are in a conspiracy to suppress individuality and heterodoxy and eccentricity and to produce organization men and women, the schools, too, put the hobbyhorse away in the basement and organize group games, emphasize at every point (but nowhere more than in the high school) the virtues of conformity and adaptability in order to produce organization boys and girls. When society hangs breathless on the prowess of a Lew Burdette or a Walt Kowalczyk, schools, too, celebrate competitive sports. When the climate of nationalism is pervasive and almost stifling and a hundred agencies proclaim, day and night, the superiority of everything American to everything non-American, the schools, instead of encouraging the young to challenge old shibboleths and to develop broader and more spiritual loyalties, tend to join in the parade of ostentatious patriotism. When it is regarded as good manners, almost everywhere, to avoid controversy and blur all differences of opinion, schools, instead of preparing the young for a world of controversy, tend to discourage sharp differences of opinion and meaningful discussion in order to achieve general agreement and contentment.

Third, in this connection it is appropriate to observe that, whatever difficulties schools may have in getting enough money for their needs, they no longer have the elementary task of winning or enlisting community support to their very existence that they had in many communities in the nineteenth century and need not make convulsive efforts to win that support. Everybody takes for granted, now, the necessity of free public education through the high school; everybody takes for granted the desirability of adequate classrooms, libraries, laboratories, playing fields, and so on. Yet in one notorious realm our schools are still engaged in enlisting community interest and support on an elementary level and with crude techniques. I refer, of course, to the emphasis on competitive athletics. I know that sports have other functions than that of exciting community interest, namely, to teach fair play, to provide physical training to all, to furnish a healthy outlet for the competitive spirit, to provide areas in which success and prestige are independent of wealth or family.

But these purposes have been achieved, or are no longer urgent, or are rather frustrated by our current emphasis on sports than advanced by it. A system where a handful of boys devote most of their energy to football while five thousand students sit in stands and watch them, is not designed to provide sound bodies to go with sound minds. A system where victory counts for more than the game is not conducive to encouraging standards of fair play (and I think those standards have gone steadily down in the last quarter-century). Neither wealth nor family insure prestige in our schools today, and the alternative of the playing field is by no means as important as it was. As for the safety valve of competition, our need is rather to restore competition in the classroom and to discourage it on the playing field and elsewhere.

The most dangerous feature of the development of competitive sports in the high school remains: its relation to community interest and support. Instead of being a device whereby the community is persuaded to take an interest in the high school, football and basketball have become, in all too many communities, devices whereby the high school entertains or profits the community. More and more, the athletic tail is wagging the academic dog. More and more, young men who are protected by law from exploitation in the labor market and who would never be allowed to work at night, are exploited even at night for the convenience, the entertainment, or the profit of adults. We would not expect or permit our high-school daughters to entertain the community in a night club or a burlesque show; there is no reason why we should permit our high-school sons to entertain the community by what are, in effect, burlesque performances on the playing field.

Not only do our athletic malpractices—born of sound policy in the nineteenth century—do grave harm to the young by denying to *some* appropriate participation in sports, by fostering unsound standards of sportsmanship, and by distracting attention from more serious academic affairs; but they do grave harm to the whole institution of education. For they constitute, at the high-school and the college level, an acknowledgment on the part of the academic community that interest in, and support for, education is to be won, not on its own merits, but by extraneous means. They constitute a gratuitous and unworthy confession that public support (or alumni support) to education cannot be expected except from appeals on wholly irrelevant grounds.

The amelioration of our current, and vulgar, overemphasis on competitive sports in the high school is drastic but relatively simple. Take away the dollar sign. Do away with paid coaches, and the pressure for victory will abate. Do away with travel expenses, and teams will stay home (where they belong) and schools develop intramural sports. Do away with paid admission, and dependence of "other" sports on basketball and football will disappear. Do away with athletic scholarships or scholarship aid (this is largely but not exclusively a problem of the college), and teams will lose as many games as they win, which will be all to the good. If this seems like a revolutionary program, may I suggest that it is the current American practice that is revolutionary. What I propose is, in effect, a return to the old

and tested practices of nineteenth-century England and America and present-day England. It was a calamity that Harvard and Columbia did not follow the example of the University of Chicago in abandonment of intercollegiate football. It will be a calamity if high schools generally do not take to heart the logic of the University of Chicago decision on their own academic level!

Fourth, just as we have not fully assimilated the fact that schools now have community support and that they do not need to use the playing fields as they did a generation ago, so we have not assimilated the fact that the problem of what we may roughly call Americanization has likewise been solved. In the nineteenth and early twentieth century—up to 1914, in fact—when our schools were confronted with the children of immigrants and of freedmen having no knowledge of American history or institutions, and when the problem of creating a harmonious society out of heterogeneous racial and religious elements was a pressing one, the schools were properly required to, and did, take on large responsibilities here. That problem is no longer acute; indeed we may question whether it still exists in any serious sense. Yet just at a time when we have achieved a larger degree of unity than we knew in the nineteenth century; at a time when there are scores of other media to inculcate a knowledge of, and pride in, America; at a time when perhaps the greatest need is to understand other countries and other cultures—at just this time, high schools everywhere concentrate heavily on the teaching of American history, civics, and literature! Not only this, but, all too often, emphasis on the study of things American has wrong motives and wrong objectives. The motives are chauvinistic; the objectives, parochial. The young do not need more nationalism, but less. They do not need less study of Greece and Rome, of Britain, of Canada and South America, and of France, but more. The young do not need to be confirmed in their instinctive belief that fifty years of American literature is worth a cycle of English or French, nor do they need to have their enthusiasm for something called vaguely "the American system" whipped up artificially. There is no reason to suppose that the compulsory study of American history in the elementary school and again in the high school necessarily makes good citizens. And we might keep in mind the sobering fact that the great men who won our independence and laid the foundations for our Republic—Washington, Jefferson, Adams, Hamilton, Madison, Mason, and others—were trained on the histories of Greece and Rome.

Fifth, I doubt that educators have adjusted themselves to the significance of the most elementary educational statistics. In 1890, when our population was 63,000,000, our college population was 157,000. Since then, the population has increased almost threefold; the college and university population, some 20 times! Add to this the fact that something like 25,000,000 Americans participate in some adult-education programs, and the conclusion is inescapable that the high school is no longer our educational terminal. Within a single generation a revolution has occurred: the college today occupies pretty much the place which the high school occupied in 1912.

Of course, in a general way, we all know what is happening, but we still use the high schools as if they were, in a sense, our last chance. An ever increasing number of our young people will have three or four years in which to learn many of the things that high schools now try to inculcate. They are not under such heavy pressure as they were to learn manners and social dancing, to learn typewriting and driving, to enjoy competitive sports and adult social life, to learn the other non-academic subjects to which the schools gave, and give, their attention. Some of these things they can be expected to learn in college. Some they can be expected to learn from the many other agencies now engaged in assuring that the young are well adjusted. Now that most adults enjoy a 35- or 40-hour work week and now that labor-saving devices have shortened the hours devoted to housework, perhaps even parents can resume their traditional tasks of teaching their young some of the things they should know! It is a paradox that, just when technology has made it possible for parents to spend far more of their time in training their children than ever before, they should foist so much responsibility upon schools. There is more justification for using the crucial high-school years for training the mind than there was in the nineteenth or early twentieth century and less justification for not doing so.

There is an additional argument here for concentration on academic activities, and even on rather traditional academic interests. On the one hand, modern technology and automation have simplified the purely mechanical tasks of industry to the point where any reasonably intelligent young man or woman can learn what he needs to know in a week or so. On the other hand, the demands of the professions are so large and elaborate that, more and more, the professional schools prefer that the young learn special skills in college or in the professional school rather than in the high school. Industry, business, col-lege, and professional schools unite in urging the desirability of thorough training in elementary skills in the high schools of today and tomorrow, and the key word here is "thorough."

Sixth, it is possible that abandonment of many of the extra-curriculum activities of the high school and a concentration on academic activities might hasten one badly needed change: the reduction by one year, or more, of the time ordinarily devoted to preparation for college or for industry or business. It was (characteristically) an American, John Fiske, who hit upon the important social law of the prolongation of infancy as one of the human habits that explains not only civilization but morality. Americans have, perhaps, carried the practice to excess. A rich nation can doubtless afford, financially, the prolongation of childhood and youth well into the twenties, but a sensible people will not permit the growing waste of years and of talents involved in our current educational practices.

It is (need I remind you?) an illusion that life is growing longer. It is, to be sure, growing longer at one end (for those who survive), but there is little evidence that the span of years available for work or for public service has lengthened appreciably since the eighteenth century. Men live longer but retire in their sixties. On the other hand, instead of plunging into their profession or into public service at twenty, they are not ready until they are thirty. The doctor, the lawyer, the school administrator, the psychiatrist, the scholar, the statesman—these are rarely able, in our system, to get under way until they are thirtyish. All of us are familiar with the growing habit of turning preparation for a career into a career and of regarding a writer, a scholar, or a statesman who is only forty as something of an infant prodigy!

We are, in a sense, prisoners of the nineteenth-century habit of thinking of education in terms of twelve years. I need not remind my readers that there is nothing sacred about twelve years, whether divided into eight and four or into six and three and three. Nor, for that matter, is there anything sacred about the additional four years we customarily devote to the university. Other societies have not allowed themselves to become bemused by this chronological arrangement and have not suffered for their independence. There is every reason now for speeding up the educational process and getting young men and women into production as rapidly as possible. Military service exacts one or two years of the lives of our young men; the demands of professional training are ever more time-consuming; the nation desperately needs the talents and the energy of the young; the costs that society has to pay for maintaining the young in school are immense; the young themselves, in revolt against the prolongation of infancy, are marrying and rearing families in their early twenties. How much longer can we go on accepting four years as the norm for secondary education?

As the high school is released, or releases itself, from responsibility for many of the extraneous duties placed upon it in the nineteenth century, it can devote more time to academic duties. As teachers are better trained, students better prepared, and new techniques for speeding up the teaching and learning processes developed and applied, the high schools may well be expected to do in three years, perhaps less, what they now do in four.

I suspect that, if they did, students who now go on to college would enter with more enthusiasm for learning than they now have and that many young persons who now find it necessary to go to work at eighteen would be able to enjoy one or two years of college—and maybe find the experience so delightful that they would somehow manage to stay on! I know that general conclusions cannot be drawn from special cases, but it is at least interesting that Jefferson graduated from William and Mary at nineteen, Gouverneur Morris from King's at sixteen, and Jay from King's at nineteen; Hancock from Harvard at seventeen; Samuel Adams from Harvard at eighteen; Emerson from Harvard at eighteen and Charles W. Eliot at nineteen, while the first president of the University of Chicago, William Rainey Harper, graduated from Muskingum College at sixteen and received his Ph.D. from Yale when he was nineteen!

Need for redirection

Educators, then, must emancipate themselves from the notion that they are to reflect, rather than guide, the interests of society; that they must cater to community prejudices as well as to community interests; that they are somehow bound by the educational mechanics of the past. They should emancipate themselves, too, from one psychotic fear whose roots go back into the Old World—the fear of becoming financially involved with the national government.

The relation of the national government to education is a large and complex subject, and I cannot more than touch on it. For reasons familiar to all of us, our schools were, from the beginning, controlled by district, town, and state rather than by the nation. This was, and is, all to the good, for local control made it impossible

for any government or any party to use the schools of the nation as a political instrument. We have assumed that local and state, or private, control cannot be retained if the national government helps foot the bill. This assumption is both illogical and pernicious. It is illogical because it flies in the face of our experience with national support to state universities and to agricultural experiment stations, and national support to a whole series of scholarly, scientific, and artistic enterprises, such as the Library of Congress, the National Archives, the National Gallery of Art, the U.S. Geological Survey, the Coast and Geodetic Survey, the Bureau of Standards, the Smithsonian Institution, and others—all of them largely dependent on federal money but happily free from federal control of their substantive activities. It is pernicious because it inevitably condemns large groups of our children—those who reside in poor states—to an education inferior to that enjoyed by children in rich states. Nor is this a matter that concerns the states alone. The vote of a badly educated young man or woman counts just as much as the vote of a well-educated young man or woman; both alike vote for congressmen and for President and therefore decide national questions of concern to everyone.

Fear of political interference in education is deep-seated and understandable. But so far as the record shows, the national government has not been more guilty than have local or state governments of interference with intellectual freedom; it has been less guilty. The task of educators is not to bewail the inadequacy of local funds and fight to the death against the threat of federal appropriations which may carry with them improper controls. Their task is to find whatever money is necessary to do the job of education as it should be done and to educate legislators and administrators, local and national alike, to the perils of improper interference. There is no evidence that this cannot be done. It has been done in Britain, in Denmark, in Sweden, in Holland, and elsewhere. It has not even been tried in our country, and it is time that American educators abandoned the unmanly practice of scaring themselves with bugaboos of national politics and addressed themselves to the task of educating and civilizing the political processes.

One final suggestion. In the generation after 1830 a large number of American educators—notably, Horace Mann, Henry Barnard, Calvin Stowe—streamed over to Germany and France to study educational practices there. They came home to apply the lessons that they had learned to conditions in this country, particularly to elementary education. Again, in the period from

1880 to 1900, American educators turned to Europe, this time to study higher education, and again they brought back much of value—and some things of little value. Today we have, I think, much to learn about secondary education, especially from the Scandinavian countries and from Switzerland and Holland—countries with democratic education systems closer to ours than are the systems of Britain or Germany or France, and countries, too, with social institutions much like ours. Perhaps some future Mann or Barnard, some future Eliot or Gilman, will bring to secondary education, as these did for the elementary and the advanced levels, the benefit of relevant European experience.

Writing in the 1830's, when Horace Mann and Henry Barnard, Thaddeus Stevens and John D. Pierce, Mary Lyon and Catherine Beecher were just beginning their great work and the high school was still an experiment, Alexis de Tocqueville said: "In that land the great experiment was to be made by civilized man, of the attempt to construct society upon a new basis, and it was there, for the first time, that theories hitherto unknown, or deemed impracticable, were to exhibit a spectacle for which the world had not been prepared by the history of the past."

And at almost the same time Horace Mann, commenting on the Old Deluder Satan Law of the Bay Colony, observed: "As a matter of *fact* it had no precedent in world history, and as a *theory* it could have been refuted and silenced by a more formidable array of argument and experience than was ever marshaled against any other institution of human origin. But time has ratified its soundness."

We, too, can say that time has ratified the soundness of the American experiment in mass education, even to our own time, and that nations whose leaders a century ago had only contempt for that experiment imitate it today. The experiment was successful because the men and the women who launched it and guided it consulted their hopes and not their fears. It was successful because they and their successors gambled on the intelligence and the virtue of the people. It was successful because, in the light of conditions which obtained in the nineteenth century, they were bold, generous, and imaginative.

As the high school enters a new era—an era in which most of its graduates will go on to advanced education, and an era in which its products will be citizens of the most influential of world powers—we should make sure that it is not too timid to challenge its own society, that it is not too conservative to break with its own habits, that it is not too wanting in faith to have confidence in the integrity of its own government.

105

Dorothy McCuskey & John Klousia

WHAT'S RIGHT WITH THE AMERICAN HIGH SCHOOL

Two professional students of secondary education here analyze the strengths and weaknesses of American secondary education. Their article is in answer to the recent criticisms of some laymen, who have attracted considerable attention in pointing out what's *wrong* with the American high school.

The main thing that's right with the American Public high school is that it exists. Don't laugh; this first sentence is not a commonplace. The American public high school, established as a legal part of the American school structure in 1874, has existed as a significant social institution only since the turn of the century, when 519,251 students or 7% of the age group were enrolled. In the historical moment of merely sixty years it has grown to a colossus enrolling about 7 million pupils, ages 14 to 17, or 70 to 80% of the potential age group. Its size alone does not make it significant, unless that size is the symbol of real service to American democracy.

The American common school system, a free upward school path with no artificial barriers extending from the kindergarten through the university, has been named as one of the genuinely creative contributions to world social institutions. The implications of the development of atomic power, either for total destruction or as an unlimited source of energy to bring abundance for all, are revolutionary, but in a sense, no more revolutionary than the idea that all human beings are valuable and that social progress lies in the freedom of each individual to develop to his maximum potentiality. This dream, tested in the laboratory of the young United States, is today one of the major goals of the peoples of the world. Conservative democracies such as England, young democracies such as India, and countries barely out from colonial domination are alike turning to the American comprehensive high school as the kind of institution through which their people can realize their aspirations. This school, inheriting the intellectual traditions of Europe, as well as the practical emphasis of the American academy, has become a unique instrument of democracy.

In evaluating the American high school, then, it must first be looked at for what it is—an institution open to all the children of all the people. Our task of judging the high school is complicated by the fact that the strengths of the school are inseparable from its weaknesses. Our schools have been so open that they have indeed attracted those who would rather sit than work; our compulsory attendance laws have kept in school the scoffers and the delinquents as well as the scholars. Differences in reading ability range from fifth to fifteenth grades; abilities from dull to genius. Some of these youngsters have little interest in cultural studies and many do not have the ability to master abstract concepts. Our schools have attempted to meet the needs of all, for these children of ours have at least two things in common—they are all, or almost all, citizens of our country, and they all have "gifts." Teachers of our high schools have been attempting, not to teach gifted children, but "to help each child find and develop his gifts," to borrow a phrase from a recent pamphlet.[1]

Mary Antin looks at the open school with the eyes of a European. In *The Promised Land* she tells how, on her second day in this country, a neighbor girl from across the alley came to take her to school. "This child who had never seen us until yesterday, who could not pronounce our names, who was not much better dressed than we, was able to offer us the freedom of the schools of Boston! No application made, no questions asked, no examinations, rulings, exclusions, no machinations, no fees. The doors stood open for every one of us."[2] We take these

things for granted, but the rest of the world does not.

The thousands of tiny high schools enrolling less than one hundred pupils do not at first glance look like one of the strengths of the American high school system. Their offerings have been narrow, their resources few, and their teachers spread thin. And yet, these schools too have made major contributions because they brought further education close to pupils, because teachers and pupils were close together. Many an artist and statesman has enriched American life because of the open door of a small high school and the encouragement of individual teachers.

Let us look back then, at what our high schools appear to have contributed in the short space of our national life. As Henry Steele Commager points out in a Life editorial, October 16, 1950, their first task was "to provide an enlightened citizenry in order that self-government might work." Our people have made self-government work. They have made honesty in public office the accepted ideal; they have never yielded to a dictator; they have survived with amazing resiliency the impact of mass media, often controlled by special interests; and they have been sensitive to attacks on freedom. These statements are basically true, we think, in spite of historically momentary and spotty lapses. Our people have learned government by consensus and by compromise, except in one national crisis prior to the general establishment of public secondary schools. The power of the American people has many times been exercised unwisely, but no one, especially our elected officials, has any doubt about where the real power lies. A free people must be an educated people, and we owe our freedom to educational opportunity beyond the elementary level.

The second big task of our schools was to create national unity. One is amazed that the "more perfect union" of 1789 was even attempted, and still more amazed that that union survived the mass waves of immigration and the sectional, geographical differences that the later years provided. Was it luck or the high social improvisation of American democracy which produced the high school at the time of our great mass immigrations of non-English speaking peoples? One after the other, groups such as the Irish, the Italians, Poles, Orientals, and now the Puerto Ricans have come in great waves. Each group came at the bottom of our social ladder; each has in this people-centered country, reached out for the open doors of education, and each has contributed leadership to our national life. True, our society today exhibits prejudices and discrimi-

---

From *High School Journal*, April 1958, 41:298-302.
[1]Association for Childhood Education International, *All Children Have Gifts*, 1957.
[2]Mary Antin, *The Promised Land*. Boston and New York: Houghton Mifflin Company, 1940, 186.

nations toward various ethnic, racial and religious groups among us, but surely these are less because we went to school with our grocer and our bus driver as well as with our surgeon and our lawyer.

Here again, an overemphasis on athletics is an undoubted weakness in most high schools, but oddly enough, even this weakness adds partly to the picture of strength, for the athletic field is one laboratory where acclaim for accomplishment is almost wholly divorced from color or the ancestry of one's parents. This openness in our schools is being gradually realized in increasing openness of vocational opportunity.

Historically, then, we owe much to our high schools. But historical success alone will not justify any social institution. How well do our high schools serve the needs of today, and the future? To meet the widely varied needs of their students, most high schools have developed many different curricula and combinations of curricula. In addition to their common function of preparing young people as citizens, they attempt to prepare them for higher education and for careers at various levels of skill in business, manufacturing and agriculture. In addition, many schools have guidance counselors whose function is to help young people with their problems of growing into maturity, and with making wise choices of educational programs and vocations. How effective are these efforts?

The sharpest critics of today charge that the "omnibus" high school is failing to prepare students adequately for college.[3] They would have us return to the philosophy at the turn of the century and accept as our major task the preparation of a select group for college. Strangely enough, we can offer more proof of doing a commendable job here than the ideal of the critic, namely, the private school. The 1953 test scores[4] of private and public high school seniors who took the College Entrance Examinations Board tests revealed that the public school students received the higher mean scores on 7 of the 9 tests given. On three tests the differences were negligible; but in the two areas, physics and mathematics, where the public high school is supposed to be falling short in this age of atomic energy and sputnik, the public high school showed marked superiority.

Studies completed at Yale, Harvard, and Princeton substantiate the fine performance the public high school is doing in preparing for college. The records of the Phi Beta Kappa headquarters give further proof of this accomplishment. At Harvard, Yale and Colgate a greater proportion of public than private school graduates were initiated into the society, even though more students had prepared in private schools.

An example of the large comprehensive high school achieving a remarkable record for its work is George Washington High of San Francisco.[5] For five consecutive years it has received the Award of Merit Scholarship Certificate from the University of California for the highest grade point average by its graduates in the University. One remarkable aspect of this record is that the school is a melting pot of races and nationalities. It consists of Scandinavians, Chinese, Irish, Polish, French, Negro, Japanese, German and Greek. The religious division is one-third Protestant, one-third Catholic, and one-third Jewish. From this high school representing all racial and socioeconomic levels, over 70% go on to college with outstanding success.

From defending our high schools as to their preparation for college bound students we move to the more difficult task of determining their effectiveness for that 80% of the student body who do not go on to college. This includes the group that are placed in vocational curricula or sent out to work under a selective educational program. We can point to certain social and economic advantages on the high school diploma and to social values of continued holding power of the American high school. While a high school education for their children has become the ambition of parents of all economic classes, the greatest per cent of drop-outs from our present day school is from the lower level of academic ability and lower economic classes.

Many of the non-academically oriented students choose the vocational curricula. Follow-up studies on students in these fields show that 50 to 70% of the students tend to find work in the specialty for which they were trained and are better satisfied with their jobs.[6] The economic advantages of high school training was shown by higher initial pay and also higher wages five years later.

[3]Rear Adm. H. G. Rickover, USN, "The Education of Our Talented Children." An address given at the Seventh Institute of the Thomas Alva Edison Foundation, November 20, 1956, published by the Thomas Alva Edison Foundation, Inc., February, 1957.
[4]For details, see David Irvamato, "Don't Sneer at Public Education," *N. E. A. Journal*, 47: 117-18, Feb., 1958.

[5]Francis V. Rummel, "How He Makes Scholarship Popular," *National Parent Teacher*, 52: 8-9, March, 1958.
[6]*Research in Industrial Education,* Summaries of Studies 1930-1955. U. S. Department of Health, Education and Welfare, Vocational Division Bulletin No. 264, 99-112.

With the advent of automation more specialized training even beyond the high school will undoubtedly result. 1957 marked the turning point at which the "white collar" workers exceeded in number the "blue collar" workers. Technicians are needed in medicine, industry, and service. The growth of the community college terminal program is an educational reflection of this economic need.

If we can agree that the American high school is a social "invention" that grew out of and satisfies a basic value of democracy—faith in the power of educated people to make wise decisions, then our way is clear. Effective high schools have always been sensitive to social need and our broad curricula are evidence of the ability of the high school to change in response to that need. Our high schools will change; they will improve their teaching where needed. They will achieve and maintain balance in their curricula as they keep their sights firmly placed on the goals of education for all American youth.

The educational ladder

THE JUNIOR COLLEGE AND THE COMMUNITY COLLEGE

The junior college and the community college began an important phase of development at the beginning of the twentieth century. Like the junior high school, which came into being about the same time, they represented an attempt to meet newly apparent educational needs that were not being successfully met by existing institutions. One need the junior college was designed to fill, for example, was that for less costly and more diversified learning opportunities for large numbers of high-school graduates, particularly those who for one reason or another would live at home during their college work. Designed both for students who desired a two-year terminal course and those who intended later to attend four-year colleges, the junior college would provide educational services not otherwise available in local communities.

Among the features of the junior college which observers (4) have considered to be unique are the following: (a) the comprehensive and adaptable character of its program; (b) its accessibility to students who might otherwise not be able to continue their education; (c) the adaptability of its program to local or regional social, personal, and vocational needs; and (d) the extent of the services it provides for both regular and part-time students and for students of all ages, intellectual abilities, and vocational aims.

106

Herold C. Hunt

PROBLEMS OF ARTICULATION BETWEEN HIGH SCHOOL AND COLLEGE

Much of the justification of the junior college was based on the failure of the senior college to provide for better articulation of its program with that of the secondary school. This in turn was perhaps the result of the tendency to assume that it was the secondary school and not the college which should make the adjustment. Part of the controversy was over whether the main function of the secondary school was to provide a preparatory program for those students who would attend college, or to provide a terminal program for those who would not. This article serves to catalog some of the ways in which articulation can be achieved.

With understandable nostalgia, when one looks back at his own college experience, he thinks of college as a quiet, peaceful way of life, apart from the main stream, untouched by the changes and increasing tempo of "the outside world." By extension, one regards college teaching today as a continuation of what one remembers. At the same time, those in education at the high school level think of themselves as being in the deepest, swiftest part of the turbulent current. They can cite changes glibly that have altered the composition of the student body, restructured the educational program, and complicated all problems.

They point to their increased high school population with its resulting problems and adjustments. They cite the problems arising because they must prepare their young people for a wider variety of occupational opportunities and a greater number of life activities, for added leisure, for higher civic responsibilities, and for more difficult value judgments. Because the greater high school population broadens the intellectual base of the student body, the curriculum program must offer growth opportunities of a wider intellectual range. This also poses problems.

Often those concerned primarily with high school education feel that these changes and problems are exclusively theirs, but a quick glance at some college statistics will show comparable changes in the college picture. From 1900 to 1950, while the population of the United States doubled, the total higher education enrollment increased more than *ten* times. In 1950, omitting the entire group of veterans—some of whom would have been in college even without G.I. benefits—the higher education enrollment had increased *seven* times over the 1900 figure.

In the fifty years while the total college enrollment multiplied 11.2 times, the holding power of the colleges was increasing even more. The number of bachelors' degrees multiplied by 15.8; masters' degrees by 36.8, and doctors' degrees by 18. During the same period the number of institutions increased by 89.5%.[1]

Many factors have led to this remarkable increase in college attendance and graduate study.

The increase in population has demanded an increase in the number of professional workers. Increased specialization requires advanced training for many occupations which were unheard of earlier in the century. The rise in the accepted level of "common school" education has as a corollary that more individuals will seek an education above that level.

As a result, problems of educational population growth are college problems as well as high school problems, and college curriculum problems parallel high school curriculum problems. Since it is recognized that intelligence levels have not increased eleven times since 1900, it may be assumed that colleges are now, like the high schools, serving a larger segment of the total population, with a wider range of intellectual ability, a greater variety of interests, intellectual and non-intellectual, a greater fluctuation of aspiration level, and a greater range of value judgments and purpose in enrolling in college. These changes have altered articulation between high school and college since the college population is no longer highly selective.

Other changes in the college scene, attendant upon the increase in enrollment, have further altered the articulation problems from the point of view of the high school. One of these is the change in the practical economics of going to college. Although tuition and other costs reflect the general rise in the cost of living, college is no longer the preserve of the well-to-do, or the college town resident. Opportunities for college students to work part time have increased, and colleges have assumed more responsibility for helping needy students find such employment. The number of tax-supported, self-help, or low-cost colleges has increased. The number of scholarships has increased and is more effectively reported.

In 1936, with 674 institutions reporting, 66,708 scholarships and 5,797 fellowships were available with a total value of over eleven million dollars. In 1950, with 1,198 institutions reporting, 141,554 scholarships and 15,369 fellowships were available with a total value of over forty-one million dollars. Between 1936 and 1950, the number of institutions reporting nearly doubled while the number of grants reported more than doubled. Since it is not known how many unreported scholarships were available in 1936, one is not justified

From *Educational Forum,* March 1954, 18:281-285.
[1]*Statistics of Higher Education: Faculty, Students, and Degrees, 1949-50.* Federal Security Agency, 1952, pp. 1-7.

in declaring that the number of grants doubled, but it is within reason to maintain that twice as much information about scholarships was a matter of record in 1950.[2]

Problems of articulation have also been affected by the changes in college entrance requirements. Each year, some colleges join the ranks of those who admit students by examination rather than by rigid course requirements. The unit requirements in other instances have been liberalized. This trend away from specific requirements appears to be continuing.

The college curriculum, too, reflects the changes in the social and industrial structure. Mentioned earlier were the "new" occupations which require college training. There are today in the United States more than 22,000 separate and classifiable occupations. Most of these, it is true, require no college education for entry or success, but each year an increasing number of them do. Many occupations known as "semi-professions" have professional societies which devote their energies to "upgrading" their occupations through higher educational requirements. Nursing, physical therapy, and occupational therapy are three such examples. Landscape architecture, librarianship, transportation, and veterinarians are others. This trend—in business and industry at the management level as well as in the professions and semi-professions—has altered the college educational structure.

The high school's problem can be viewed in true perspective only in relation to the realities of college life. For too many years high schools and colleges failed to communicate with each other. Happily they can and do now sit down together to discuss their mutual problems. For too many years it seemed that high schools and colleges looked at the educational field through opposite ends of the telescope, each, of course, believing that it was the other fellow who had the glass upside down. One is reminded of the old parlor game called "Walk the Plank," in which a string was laid on the rug and then walked along with the aid of a pair of opera classes held upside down. The object of the game was to walk the plank without stepping off, a very difficult trick under the conditions. Seen through the wrong end of the glass, the string appeared to be far, very far away; the walker staggered and tottered and all but fell off the rug under the string. The wrong end of the glass gives the viewer a

disembodied feeling; the field is distant and distorted, and the figure in it, microscopic and unreal. It makes an hilarious game but sad business.

The net result of the changes—increased opportunity, economic assistance and attendance, liberalized entrance requirements and curriculum, the upgrading activities of vocations, and the pressures of the social order—means added responsibilities for the high schools.

For now the high schools must provide the basic preparation for college through good teaching to a greater number of aspiring high school students even as they provide for the wide range of individual differences. What is more, they must provide better guidance for the young people also. In this sense, the high schools have posed for themselves new problems in the solution of old ones. These problems are again mutual ones, calling for continued communication between the high schools and colleges, but also imposing internal responsibilities upon each.

Primarily the problem for the high school now is to provide its students with more guidance—with sufficient information and enough counseling assistance so that they can make the best choices for themselves from the greatly enlarged opportunities which are available to them. It is a simple matter to choose a necktie when there are but two or three patterns and colors, and one can draw the same comparison when the choice is more important.

A few basic premises should be made clear lest one seem to compartmentalize. First, guidance is not advising; it is not directing a choice; it is not leading or piloting or taking someone by the hand and guiding him to a goal, however worthy. Guidance comprises all the efforts of the school to help young people make their own best choices and decisions on the basis of information about themselves and their opportunities. It is the program by which the school hopes to increase the self-direction of each individual.

Second, educational choices are bound up with occupational choices and vice versa; but more than that, both are bound up with an individual's choice of a way of life. Both educational and occupational experiences help to determine the total life experience, the social group, the mode of thinking, and the value judgments. Living is "all of a piece," and one choice affects other choices.

Third, there is no date or time at which one can expect all young people to make their decisions. Maturity is a relative thing; growth is continuous and determined by the individual's own rate. It is no more possible for each freshman

[2]*Scholarships and Fellowships,* Bulletin 1951, No. 10, Federal Security Agency, 1951, p. 1.

in high school to know whether or not he will go to college than it is possible for an individual at fourteen to be able to say that he will marry at twenty. Economic changes that may enter each child's life are not alone to be considered but the child's own growth process.

These three basic assumptions in themselves contain most of the problems of articulation from the point of view of the high school.

When does an information program turn into recruitment? How can the high school provide its students with facts about growing occupations and valuable college opportunities and yet protect its students from persuasive personnel scouts or admissions officers? The matter of recruitment is a serious one to guidance workers, for recruitment and guidance are mutually exclusive. Yet colleges, businesses, and professions—including teaching—quite openly recruit.

Disinterestedness is part of the professional stock-in-trade of the counselor. Disinterestedness requires him to evaluate opportunities for each student as an individual. It may be one's private opinion that experience in the proper college will benefit every youngster but one must eschew that opinion if he is to serve as a wise counselor.

A related problem for the high school is to assemble as much information about further educational opportunities as possible. Catalogs and tours of accessible campuses help in this as do reports from former students, visits from college representatives, movies, and college glamour books. Nevertheless the problem of assembling and disseminating the information remains one of the most difficult assignments. The schools experiment constantly with informational programs and fortunately as a result, the cafeteria-style college day is fast disappearing.

Try as one may to bring information to the students which will help them make long range plans, there will always be some students who arrive at high school graduation with a new and sudden urge to go to college. The natural growth process of some will be responsible; with others, a change in economic status will be responsible. The "late bloomers" pose a special responsibility.

Focusing attention on wise selection of a specific college has both extensive and intensive aspects. Suffice it to say that the counselor's first responsibility is to present the bases of choice. These can be carried on to some extent by group methods, but in the last analysis everyone needs to talk his personal situation over with a creative listener.

It is not enough to find that college-bound students have made a college choice. The student needs to know what that particular college has to offer him, what kind of experience he can expect there, and what it will expect of him. Discussions about fraternities and sororities, dormitory life, college finances, group living, self-discipline and self-reliance are also necessary in an orientation program.

All these are needs of young people—awareness, information, decision, and finally knowledgeableness concerning their new situations. They are needs which the school must help meet through its overall guidance program.

Then there are administrative problems of articulation from the high school point of view. It is to be hoped that the forms used for college requests for information will eventually be uniform or nearly so. The multiple transcript problem also must be solved. As things are now, students request not one or two transcripts to be sent to colleges but four, five or six. This is in part because they are unable to make up their minds, but it is also because until the last minute often students do not know whether they will be accepted.

One further administrative detail needs attention, scholarship applications. Deadlines for filing, lack of full publicity, and requirements all pose problems for counselors.

High schools have no way of knowing when their students do enroll in college and little information about their success once enrolled. A few colleges report freshman grades to high schools, but very few. Colleges would help themselves and help the high schools greatly if they would send a postcard telling the high school which of its students have enrolled. It would help further if the colleges would report the students' progress. Short of a vast and expensive follow-up of all graduates, the high school is helpless to get this information.

Again, what is needed is increased communication. Once the high school knows where its graduates are enrolled, it can share the burden of follow-up to improve its part in the articulation program between high school and college.

Americans believe wholeheartedly in the effectiveness of cooperation and in the value of communication in solving mutual problems. They believe in the natural ability of individuals to make wise choices given sufficient information and adequate opportunity. The whole educational program rests on the belief that for each one there is a satisfying, useful life. The high schools are committed by conviction to their part in an articulation program with colleges which will bring about such a life for each college-bound graduate.

107

Howard A. Campion

THE ROLE OF THE JUNIOR COLLEGE IN HIGHER EDUCATION

Ever since the junior college became recognized as a distinctive institution, there has been an effort to relate it to the rest of higher education. Because the four-year college has tended to have greater academic and social prestige than the two-year college, there has been an accelerating tendency to convert junior colleges into four-year institutions. In many instances this pressure has come from the clientele and staff of the junior colleges themselves rather than from any outside source. Many people, however, consider this trend an unfortunate abandonment of an opportunity to provide a distinctive educational service.

The junior college is a relatively new institution in the development of American education. This institution, like other organisms, had a period of infancy which roughly coincided with the first two decades of the twentieth century. It certainly had a period of adolescence with all the troubles, pimples, and uncertainties of that age! More recently its growth might be likened to the dynamic development of youth, which brings the discovery of new vision, new goals, and fearlessness in attacking the problems of becoming mature.

Is the junior college now an adult? Has it reached the age of accomplishment and at the same time developed the power of self-evaluation? Has it attained and is it entitled to a place of respect and security in the community of educational institutions? Has it proven an ability to meet more effectively some of the challenges of higher education than other types of schools with longer histories and richer traditions?

The answer to these questions is being given today by the *number* of such institutions that have come into being in recent years, and by the quality of the work they are turning out. The nation as a whole today boasts 700 junior colleges, some privately or independently sponsored, many supported in whole or part by public funds. Texas has 46 such colleges, New York 43; Michigan 19; California 66; Illinois 29; Washington 11; Wisconsin 36; etc. The number increases almost daily, two new ones having been authorized by citizens of local districts in California since the beginning of this calendar year. The formation and development of this type of institution is being urged not alone by local citizens, but with

the blessing of the four-year colleges and universities, and with the support of business, industry, labor and service clubs, community organizations, and churches. Such popularity must be deserved—why?

First a look at the purposes and stated functions of a junior college. Typical of "purpose" statements is that of the California Junior College Association which is reproduced in a State Bulletin of February 1958. In this publication Eldorado Junior College is cited as a typical community college of today·

"1. Eldorado Junior College is committed to the democratic way of life.

"2. Eldorado Junior College recognizes the individual as having the highest possible value.

"3. Eldorado Junior College is committed to the policy of granting to the individual the maximum amount of freedom, personal initiative, and adventure consistent with equal opportunities on the part of his fellows.

"4. Eldorado Junior College is committed to the policy of providing for all high school graduates and for all other adults the type of educational opportunity they need and that which the law permits the college to provide."[1]

Purposes

"1. *College Transfer Education* (lower division). Eldorado Junior College provides lower-

From *College and University*, Summer 1960, 35:426-434.
[1]California Public Junior Colleges; California State Department of Education. Sacramento, February 1958.

division college work for those students who plan to continue their education beyond that offered by the college. This education shall be broad enough to include the lower-division requirements in the liberal arts, in business, in science, in engineering, and in other preprofessional fields.

"2. *Vocational Terminal Education.* Eldorado Junior College provides vocational training to those students whose period of formal education will end when they complete junior college. This training is designed as a one- or two-year program to help students develop occupational competencies and the personal qualities essential to wholesome living.

"3. *General Education.* It is intended that every Eldorado Junior College student shall have opportunity to get an education which will prepare him to function effectively as a member of his family, his community, his state, his nation, and his world.

"4. *Guidance.* It is a specific responsibility of Eldorado Junior College to assist its students to 'find themselves.' A program of guidance is provided so that every student may discover his aptitudes, choose a life work, and prepare for the successful pursuit of the life work he chooses.

"5. *Adult Education.* Eldorado Junior College co-operates with the high schools and other public institutions in providing instruction and cultural activities to assist in meeting the educational needs of many adults living in the community. The program of education includes a wide variety of offerings intended to serve these purposes. The courses range from the simplest instruction in reading and writing through advanced technical courses that adults require as they meet their daily problems as citizens, as homemakers, as wage earners, and as individuals in society."[2]

To the above list of purposes many junior colleges add the following:

6. *Remedial* and *"maintenance"* education for those who, through their own fault or because of fortuitous circumstances, have failed to attain a scholastic record that will admit them to a four-year college or university.

7. Serve as a *cultural center* for the community by providing lectures, concerts, forums and dramatic performances.

Characteristics of the Junior College

1. *Legally* a part of the public school system (at least in 15 states) but *educationally* a part of higher education.

2. It is *local* in control and orientation and

therefore more responsive to community needs and desires.

3. It is the only *"open door"* remaining in the scheme of higher education.[3] For many youths it provides "another chance" to secure education on the higher level.

4. The Junior College is not an attic on the high school nor a basement of the university. Jesse Bogue said "this institution is neither the upward extension of secondary education nor the arm of the senior institution, nor the tail of a four-year college. It is an institution that sprang native to American soil from the growing need to furnish advanced education to an increasing proportion of our population."[4]

5. The program of a typical junior college is *flexible* and *diversified* to meet the needs of people of widely varying interests and abilities and serve a rapidly changing economic society.

The Master Plan Survey of California higher education (1959-60) has just been completed and has already been partly implemented by legislative action at a special session that adjourned on April 15th. This survey was conducted by a team of eight: two each from the University of California, the State Colleges, the Junior Colleges, and the Independent Colleges. Dr. Arthur Coons, President of Occidental College, was appointed chairman of the team and co-ordinated the studies made by the team and special depth studies carried on by six subcommittees. The following recommendations were made by the survey team and have been under debate in the legislature for the past month.

I. Structure, function, and co-ordination

Functions of the three systems of public-supported higher education are defined as follows:

Junior Colleges would continue to be locally governed with minimum standards set up by the State Board of Education. Courses would include freshman and sophomore college classes, vocational-technical courses leading to employment, and general courses leading to the two-year degree.

State Colleges would instruct in the liberal arts and sciences, in teacher education and in professions and applied fields which require more than two years' work. They would award undergraduate degrees, through the master's. In addition, the State Colleges might award doctoral

---

[2]*Ibid.*, p. 3.

[3]Burton R. Clark, *The Open Door College.* New York: McGraw-Hill, 1960.
[4]Jesse P. Bogue, *The Community College.* New York: McGraw-Hill, 1950.

degrees in co-operation with the University of California. The State Colleges could also perform limited research.

The University of California would instruct in liberal arts and sciences, the professions, and exclusively in dentistry, law, medicine, veterinary medicine, and graduate architecture. It would continue to be the primary state-supported research agency. The University would have sole authority to award the doctoral degree, but could agree to grant certain joint degrees with the State Colleges.

This section of the Master Plan also recommended the creation of a *State College System* with its own chief executive officer and its own Board of Trustees. The latter would be a 21-man board. Five would be ex officio (the Governor, Lieutenant Governor, Speaker of the House, State Superintendent of Public Instruction, and the Chief Executive Officer of the State College system); and 16 members would be appointed by the Governor. It would be somewhat comparable to the present Board of Regents of the University.

In addition, a 12-member *Co-ordinating Agency* would be created to advise the Governor, the Legislature and the three systems of publicly-supported higher education on matters of finance, program development, and new campuses. This Co-ordinating Agency would consist of three members of The Regents, three members of the new State College Trustees, three Junior College representatives, and three representatives of the private institutions.

II. Distribution of lower division students

It was recommended that freshman and sophomore students in both the University of California and in the State Colleges (now about 51 per cent of the student body) be reduced 10 per cent by 1975. This reduction is expected to channel some 50,000 additional lower division students to the Junior Colleges in the next fifteen years.

III. Selection and retention of students

It was recommended that the University of California, the State Colleges, and the Junior Colleges make studies to tighten and standardize admissions requirements. A suggested formula: that the University of California in the future admit the top 12½ per cent of high school graduates and the state colleges admit only the top 33 per cent of high school graduates.

IV. Institutional capacities and area needs

Recommended in this section were (1) standards for the utilization of classrooms and laboratories; (2) enrollment limitations according to type of institution, and (3) areas for development of future campuses. One point of interest: the three University of California campuses now in the planning state—San Diego, Orange County, and the South Central Coast area—should be started no later than 1962 and completed "without delay." New State Colleges were recommended for San Bernardino County and Southwest Los Angeles. Twenty-two new Junior Colleges were proposed, with seven additional areas designated as probably warranting junior college service by 1975, or a total of 29 new institutions to be added to the existing list of 64. (As noted above, two of the proposed new junior colleges have already been authorized by the voters of local districts.)

The public junior colleges of California have been accorded a full partnership in the tripartite system of public higher education, and if all recommendations are carried out they will grow from a 1960 full-time student enrollment of 100,000 to an enrollment in 1975 of 300,000 full-time students. The enrollment in extended day classes will probably experience an even greater expansion! Can these local institutions triple their capacities in fifteen years, and maintain a quality of educational opportunities equal to that of the past?

Because of this recommended diversion to Junior Colleges and the larger capital outlay and operating load resulting to Junior College districts, it was recommended that the present average of 30 per cent of State support to Junior Colleges be increased by 1975 to 45 per cent, and that the Legislature devise a plan for distributing construction funds through grants or loans or both, as determined by growth.

To help utilize independent institutions' facilities to a larger degree, if students choose to do so, it has recommended an increase in the number and maximum amount of each grant under the present California Scholarship Commission program and adding a room and board grant for those who financially need it.

The Master Plan has made recommendations on utilization of physical plants, standard use of classrooms, laboratories, etc., and space requirements for various functions; and it has recommended greater use of facilities—evenings, Saturdays, and in the summer periods.

It has established enrollment ranges to be observed for existing institutions under described and defined circumstances:

376 The Educational Ladder

a. In Junior Colleges from a minimum of 400 to a maximum of 6,000 except in certain densely populated areas; optimum size 3,500.
b. In State Colleges from 3,000 to 20,000.
c. In University campuses from 5,000 to 27,500.

It has recommended that no new campuses of State Colleges and University be established unless and until adequate Junior College facilities are already established in the area; and such new campuses when established should be upper division and graduate only until the local areas accept the same general kind of burden that the 58 Junior College districts now established have accepted. In other words, no free rides on the State for those areas that have held back in establishing Junior Colleges.

In commenting upon the plan as presented to the State Legislature, Clark Kerr, President of the University of California, made the following statement:

"The Master Plan will enable us to preserve the best features of the historic tripartite system of public higher education in this State. Moreover, it will increase the spirit of understanding among the segments which make up this system.

"The Plan will allow fuller use of state college facilities for graduate work and research, while maintaining the University's leadership and responsibility in these areas. It will make available to every college-age youth in California the maximum opportunity to achieve the best education appropriate to his abilities and interests. It will increase the opportunity of the junior colleges to serve the State, and to work even more closely with the state colleges and the University.

"It will give the state colleges a system of government parallel to that of the University through a Board of Trustees similar to the University's Board of Regents. It will also provide an advisory co-ordinating body composed of representatives of all segments of higher education, public and private.

"The Master Plan is, in short, a milestone in the history of California higher education. When fully implemented, it will work to the benefit of all parts of higher education in the State, and to the advantage of the people of California whom they serve."

Regardless of how rapidly the recommendations of the Master Plan Survey are implemented by the legislature, the findings of this study will most certainly influence the pattern of higher education in California in the years immediately ahead. Some of the problems for junior colleges

that remained unsolved may concern other states and might become the basis of study by the American Association of Collegiate Registrars and Admissions Officers:

1. Will the junior colleges be forced by increasing enrollment to adopt restrictive admission requirements? Will the "selection" of students for this type of college tend to destroy the "open door" policy, and if so where will certain American youth find their opportunity for further education? If this should happen, America may have to invent still another and different kind of post-high school institution.

2. What about retention? If the open door policy is preserved may we expect to find among the many who enter junior college, a few who will not or cannot profit by the offerings of the school? No college, public or private, can justify the expense of retaining "riders." Should not the junior colleges develop a uniform policy of probation which will recognize the importance of their exploratory function by giving those who fail in first attempts an opportunity to try at least one other field of study, but at the same time take steps to prevent the continuous and indefinite enrollment of the malingerer?

3. What will be the effect of heavy overloads on the already hard-pressed junior college in the area of curriculum planning? Will the higher cost of terminal, vocational, semiprofessional and technical courses tend to favor the less expensive regular academic curricula and transfer programs? This could be one of the most serious threats to the democratic character of this American institution which came into being in answer to community needs for a school that would serve all of the educational needs of all of the people.

4. How will the increasing load on our junior colleges affect our pupil personnel policies? Our guidance programs? Our "grading" and "credit" concepts? Our methods of recognizing accomplishment through diplomas, degrees, transfer credits, honors, scholarships?

5. What is the significance of the movement to drop the "junior" from the name of these colleges? Is this good, or does it indicate an ambition to become full-fledged four-year colleges? Or is it on the other hand that in carrying out one of the colleges' most important functions, terminal education, the junior college is not "junior" to any "senior" educational agency?

6. Of course one of the most pressing problems is, and probably will be, that of adequately financing a broad diversified program. As numbers and costs increase where will the money come from if the open door is to be kept open? Can we abandon the hope of keeping the school free of

tuition, and thus available to rich and poor alike? If the institution is to be a "local" project can the local citizens stand further increase in their already high taxes on real property (homes)? With the increased competition from public universities and four-year colleges for support from state funds, how much more aid may the local junior colleges expect from that source?

7. How can the junior college best aid in developing the technicians this economy so desperately needs? The technician represents an area of skill and knowledge that lies between that of the skilled tradesman on one hand and the engineer on the other. The training of these technicians is not a high school job. From an economic standpoint it should not be necessary to fill such jobs with graduate engineers and scientists and yet that is what is happening. The ability to carry on the many tasks in this category can be developed in one or two years of post-high school specialized training, and it therefore becomes a challenge to the two-year college.

And these jobs *are* important in our present way of life. An officer at Vandenburg Missile Base who had recently been transferred there from Cape Canaveral said recently that most of the missile failures which have been so widely publicized and which have been embarrassing to the nation, have been due not to the failure of the scientists and engineers to properly design the rockets, but to the lack of technicians who can build and assemble and service them with accuracy and skill.

8. The junior college in all of its activities must attain a balance that represents its position between secondary education and professional education. In today's Americana the word MIX has a definition far more significant than that given by Webster. In our defense program, our recipe for peace, it is the careful blend of men and ma-

chines. In our educational program we must also seek the right "mix" or blend of men and machines. We must find the right mix of vocational and transfer students; the right balance of scholastic ability and subject mastery in our faculties; the best allocation of upper and lower division students; of the superior and lesser endowed. In pupil personnel work the mix of human and machine elements will be important. How much of our job can be done by machines? How much by blanks, forms, transcripts, and statistical reports? Much, it is true; but as in industry and in the military our greatest accomplishments will always come through human judgment, man's unique ability to capitalize on opportunity, make decisions, offer sound advice and guidance of a personal quality; and something which machines lack, man's ability to *care about the results.*

Here then is a real job for the junior college. It involves recruiting, testing for aptitude, and educational planning for those who possess a potential for this type of work—guidance. It involves planning a program that will prepare the proper persons for this field of employment—curriculum development. It involves a plan that will give status to technical work as a career—evaluation and recognition.

There is more to be said about the junior college but this is enough to indicate that this new institution (none existed in 1900) is here, and here to stay. It will play an increasingly important role in our scheme of higher education in the next decade, and will aid in assuring this country that the maximum human potential will be discovered and developed to the advantage of our social, economic, military, and individual welfare. It will keep the door open for the development of ability of whatever kind. It will, we hope, live up to the expectations of its sponsors and glorify its American birthright.

The educational ladder

THE FOUR-YEAR COLLEGE

While the traditions of the university go back to the Middle Ages, the four-year liberal arts college represents an American development within the university. The proportion of youth in college has increased steadily within the present century and promises to continue increasing at least as rapidly as provision can be made for more students; the pressures to attend college are strong and varied. Despite their popularity, however, the four-year colleges have frequently failed to meet the needs and expectations of students, parents, and the general public, and there is growing concern as to whether the program or the techniques of these institutions are generally appropriate to the needs of society.

Yet over the years the four-year college has grown in influence and is generally considered along with the university system as a capstone of higher education.

108

Ordway Tead

HIGHER EDUCATION: FOR WHOM AND FOR WHAT

A provocative speaker and writer here analyzes some of the problems and pressures being felt by the colleges of today and discusses the basis for determining who should be educated and what should be the nature of the educational outcome. He emphasizes the value of the liberal arts and of a "life-centered" approach to education.

One of the purposes of any consideration of the role of the college is surely to hold the mirror up to going policy and practice, to confront sins of omission and commission, to clarify and refresh high purpose, and to arrive at new insights about desirable directions and methods.

We are not heard in higher education for our much speaking, even though some of us may speak much. We are profited by having our complacency disturbed, by having questions asked which challenge accepted views and practices, and by the proffer of appealing ideas capable of some adaptation within our several institutions. Shared deliberation on education is not for corroboration of the current, but for the confrontation of the conceivable.

My premise here is that liberal education is practical education in the long-run view, and that this assumption throws light on the questions: for whom are colleges designed and what are they intended to do?

I affirm also as a premise my great faith in the indispensable mission of college education, both retrospectively, currently and prospectively considered. We may not do all we should or do it as well as we should. But if one asks—what would American life be like in all its multiform operational activities for which rational thought and effort, superior abilities, disciplined intelligence, scientific and engineering training, and informed, directive capacity are indispensable, if we had no college graduates to staff the many key positions—one quickly realizes the necessity

of college and university education in our kind of large-scale technological culture. The questions posed by my title presumably take all this for granted and center attention on whether we have gone far enough as a society in assuring a college education to a sufficient fraction of those, both young men and young women, of from 17 to 23 or 24 years of age, who must presently staff these thousands of necessary posts. This implies also that they have the ability and willingness to occupy positions as responsible followers no less than as leaders in our employments and avocations. Hence my first topic—who should go to college?

Who should go to college?

A generation ago this problem did not present undue and confusing complexities, either to colleges or to the community. This is no longer true. And it is essential to see this question in perspective if any defensible answer is to be offered for the foreseeable future. For there is a clear national trend here which needs statement in its historic setting.

Our elementary schools were originally private and restricted. Today, they are universal, public, and attendance is required of virtually all children.

Our present high schools were originally private academies designed for the selected few to prepare them for the small number of colleges then extant. Today's high schools cover the country, are publicly supported and include around 80% of our population in this age group. And with the present rate of extension of high school facilities, it appears that well over 90% of those

From *Educational Forum*, January 1955, 19:133-149. The Thorne Lecture, Hofstra College, March 2, 1954.

of high school age will at least be entering high school within the next few years.

A similar pattern is observable in the growth of the American college. It too started as exclusively private with attention centered primarily upon education of young men for the major professions, especially the ministry. Only many years later did we see the gradual extension of public state universities; then, after 1862, came land-grant colleges with specific aims in the direction of training for agricultural and mechanical pursuits. And finally beginning slowly in 1890, there has come the growth of two-year institutions beyond the high school, called junior colleges or, under public auspices, frequently now referred to as community colleges.

The increase of enrollments in this over-all college and university picture has been little short of breath-taking. As of 1953-54, a little over 2¼ million students are participating in higher education; and careful forecasts as to the insistent and qualified demand for college entrance in the next ten years place this figure at anywhere from 3 million to 4 million in the 1960's.[1]

The increasing pressure for and expectation of the opportunity to go to college are due to the following important reasons: the larger number who now complete high school; the larger number who are stirred with the desire to go to college; the experience of tens of thousands of veterans under the G.I. Bill of Rights in securing a free college education which raised the sights of their families and friends as to the possible values of going to college; the unprecedented increase in the post-war birth rate to a point where in a few years the high school populations will inevitably provide much larger numbers ambitious and fully qualified for some college education; the progressively higher wage and salary levels making it practical for more and more families to entertain this expectancy as economically possible for their children.

As to why this heartening desire for more education should constitute a problem, I am here not giving consideration to such staggering difficulties as the inadequacy of plant facilities in existing colleges, nor to the insufficiency of the supply of qualified teachers, nor to the financial ways and means which will assure college enrollment for able students from the bottom income brackets. These are all fundamental and crucial issues.

The problem upon which I shall center attention is the *qualitative* one. In the first place, authoritative studies have indicated that at least 40% and perhaps nearly 50% of our young people have the requisite intellectual capacity—namely, an I.Q. of 105 or over, to profit from at least two years of college work. And presumably one third in this age group would qualify to complete four years. The percentage figure of present college enrollment of young people is around 26 per cent of the age group of 18 to 21 years.

Again, the testimony is conclusive that in recent years there have been as many young people of equal capacity with those enrolled, who are *not* in college for a combination of reasons.

A further disconcerting fact is that at present approximately one-half of the young people who enter high school never stay to graduate. And equally shocking is the fact that in the national average, only one-half of those who enter college remain to get their degrees.

This last situation is profoundly serious in ways that reflect far more upon the educational institutions than they do upon the students who leave school. My contention, supported by much evidence, is that one of the primary reasons for such large withdrawals is that students—both in high school and in college—fail to find that the subject matter offered for study is in their view and experience relevant or valuable as helping them to know themselves and to get assistance as to their effective place in the world outside. At both these levels, taking our country as a whole, educational programs are not believed by many young people to be significant for any kind of progress or "success" in life for them on any terms.

Other reasons for leaving should, of course, be noted. There are frequently economic motives of necessary family or personal support pressing students to withdraw. And there is the subtle but important fact that, especially in the low income brackets and in areas where high schools are inferior or geographically remote, there may be no tradition, potential expectation or stimulated family or individual desire (even for students of top ability) to aspire to a college education.

Further potential enrollments will mean an even greater unevenness than at present in re-

---

[1]See among others, with their own added bibliographical references, *Who Should Go to College?* by Byron S. Hollinshead, Columbia University Press, New York, 1952; *Equalizing Educational Opportunities Beyond the Secondary School*, by Ordway Tead, Harvard University Press, 1947; Section II, *Higher Education for American Democracy*, for U.S. President's Commission on Higher Education, Harper & Brothers, 1947; Report rendered by Dr. Ronald B. Thompson, Registrar, Ohio State University, Columbus, Ohio, prepared for the American Association of College Registrars and Admissions Officers, entitled "College Age Population Trends: 1940-1970," 1953.

spect to the content and quality of secondary school preparation viewed nationally, with which students will seek to enter college. There is the added fact that with widened expectancy or availability of socially justified college entrance, there will increasingly be on the campus not only young people with a relatively high capacity to verbalize and conceptualize, but also those with mechanical, scientific, engineering and artistic aptitudes, as well as those with vigorous extrovert characteristics manifested often in a predominant interest in various forms of human relations, including the extra-curricular programs all the way from athletics to class politics. There is the further factor of a widened spread in the cultural backgrounds of the homes from which students are coming. And the implication of all this already is, and will increasingly be, that the present *conventional* college curriculum as typically taught will surely *not* enlist the interest and the sense of need of more than a relatively small fraction of such a variegated student body.

There has also to be clearer recognition of the variety of motives and aspirations prompting the students of today and tomorrow to go to college. Along with the traditional motives of those wanting to get a fuller education for nurture and potential fulfillment, there are those motivated by ambition for economic advancement, for making the right social contacts, for assuring their entrance to professional schools for reasons partly selfish and partly social. In short, any imputed singleness of purpose for college attendance as we used to think of it, is unrealistic. An acute problem is therefore the adaptation of the college's curricular offerings to varied individual purposes, to varied intellectual levels, and most importantly to a wide spread of aptitudes, interests and potential vocational skills.

I should refer next to one point which has been raised by a number of critics but as to which I find myself not at all alarmed. I allude to the view of those who, drawing an analogy with the plight of the university graduates in Germany prior to World War II, are fearful that we may be in danger of educating too many too much. They doubt that there will be enough vocational opportunities at "high" levels with an accompanying possible higher standard of living for graduates; and they conclude that this disparity of expectation and actuality will create a body of educated but disaffected and frustrated persons having to work at callings using less than their full abilities.

I am reasonably sure that the answer to this fear is that the whole expanding, dynamic character of our technological economy is such that

it is hard to conceive of too many people too well educated to staff the critical posts. Furthermore, it is a false view that the purpose of college education which students and society generally should primarily entertain is economic advancement, rather than the capacity to live a fuller and a more fruitful existence as individual, as parent, and as citizen. In other words, given the rightful equalitarian assumptions of a democratic society, plus the increasing birthrate, plus the need for trained intelligence in more and more occupations, plus the desirable, enriched cultural sensitivity of more and more people, this objection is a bogey. It is a feeble alibi for failing to face up to the total situation which realistically the colleges confront.

The central issue is not a misconceived equalitarian sentiment on the part of those of us who are said to be carried away by our democratic convictions. It is rather an academic lag which is slow to face the facts of the greater potential for more college education of many more selected students once their several kinds of ability are identified, are challenged, and are ministered to in a variety of educationally effective ways.

It is not practicable here to spell out a complete program for offsetting this combination of untoward conditions. But some of the outstanding features of corrective effort should be noted. The program has to start with certain secondary school changes. The arousing of improved motivation for study and increased desire to attend college is one which has to receive its primary attention at the secondary school level. This will involve a much more competent high school program than is now typical, of guidance and counsel for each individual student. It will require an improvement in the educational standards of the high schools in numerous states where they are now below par. It will require a program far more generous than any yet being pushed of liberal provisions for state scholarships on a basis of need for those secondary school students who qualify for and wish to, but cannot afford to go to college, and for Federal scholarships if individual state provisions cannot be made sufficient for the need. It should further mean that more and more high schools will be so organized as to satisfy the designation of being *comprehensive high schools* in which there is a reasonable balance between semi-vocational studies and general liberal studies in the subjects now characterized as the "academic" or college preparatory curriculum. This raises the whole question, also, as to whether the over-all intellectual and personality potentialities of the high school student are to constitute the basis for determining college eligibility. I am convinced that we are all at present far too much fouled up in the arithmetic of credits and not enough concerned about the total promise of college applicants.

A further approach, as to which I find myself in substantial agreement with former President Conant of Harvard, is the desirability both of increasing the number of two-year colleges and allowing them to be effectively terminal for some, while readily providing for others transfer into the third and fourth college years. However, as this approach gains the momentum which I am sure it inevitably will, there must be assurance that the programs of two-year colleges are including enough provocative and relevant general education making its contribution to citizenship, personality development, human relations and emotional maturity, so that the student leaving college at the end of his second year will be entering life with some genuine competence to handle himself as an individual and as a citizen who will make his best social contribution; and so that he will have been stirred with the desire to continue through the years with some broad program of adult education.

This corrective program has also to be confronted at the college level by invoking the following features: First, and of major importance, there has to be eager acceptance by all responsible for the conduct of our colleges of the democratic conviction that *all* the young people of some specified and agreed intellectual caliber not only should have the right to, but the readily available opportunity to go to college for at least two years. We should all agree—professionals, citizens generally, and parents—that the present situation is one of conspicuous and indefensible waste of the maximum talents and contributions of too many young people who are for the above stated reasons precluded today from going to college, or who are not remaining to complete their courses of instruction.

If in individual colleges we who are in responsible posts say in response to this democratic aspiration that our institutions are already as large as they should be or as we desire them to be, or that the danger of creating even larger mass education units especially in our state universities is great, or that we do not see where the financial resources will come from either to enlarge present institutions public and private, or to create needed new ones, the answer would seem to be that at this point we confront a problem beyond the competence of individual institutions to resolve. And our society therefore requires the shaping of policies through some disinterested and over-all national agency, perhaps

a temporary ad hoc commission reporting to the President and the Congress, which will bring home to our citizenry the enormity of this problem on the national level, and point out that a solution may well be beyond the possible present responsibility and competence of trustee and alumni bodies of individual institutions to arrive at.[2]

What I have in mind here is the emphatic documentation of a situation of acute need in a way that would supply ammunition to the President, the Congress and state legislatures as to desirable legislation. It would, of course, be essential that any such legislation, presumably for grants for capital purposes, for scholarships and for other necessary assistance, would be planned and provided in such ways as to assure a complete absence of Federal interference with the processes of education itself.

A second important point is the need for a fresh scrutiny of college admission policies toward a lessening of stress on the arithmetic of secondary school credits. Joined closely with this is the need from the outset of college entrance and throughout the two or four year period, of a more personalized, consecutive academic guidance program, which will help students to find their way into and through such courses of study as will be congenial to their capacities and interests, and helpful to them in ways which will assure their remaining for a graduation which they will find rewarding to their ultimate effectiveness as adults. This implies also, of course, a total student guidance program on *all* phases of individual adjustment and subsequent employment.

The fourth responsibility for the colleges is a fresh scrutiny of the methods of teaching, the quality of teachers, and the offerings of subjects available for study in the first two college years. I shall not here elaborate upon the point that there is too much indifferent and ineffectual teaching in the first two college years. We have by no means addressed ourselves adequately to the use of modern psychological findings as to how students may be brought to learn, and to want to learn, what true learning actually is, and how real learning can assuredly result.[3] All too often,

---

[2] See in this connection the excellent pamphlet published by the American Council on Education (1954) *A Call For Action to Meet the Impending Increase in College and University Enrollment.*

[3] There is a growing literature on this important subject. In my own book, *College Teaching and College Learning,* Yale University Press, 1949, I have not only discussed this subject but offered an extended bibliography of other relevant volumes. A new quarterly has recently been initiated at the Oregon State Teachers College, Corvallis, Oregon, entitled *Improving College*

with our failure to use the best teaching methods in the critical early college years, students are likely to find themselves being constantly lectured at rather than *actively involved* in some experimental sharing of subject matter, the relevance of which for them is being made clearly manifest.

An added requirement is that the teachers assigned to the first two college years should be the best, the most mature, and most dynamic available in each department. Also with a fostering of cooperative professorial attitudes, the introductory work can gradually be brought to be regarded by them as equally if not more important than their senior seminars. But this assumes, of course, that those teachers who are eager to focus on good teaching, are rewarded for good teaching in salaries and rank and themselves regard this as the major commitment of a *dedicated* teacher. A most significant and practical program in this direction which has come to my attention is the annual award given to a conspicuously good teacher each year at Carnegie Institute of Technology along with which goes recognition in salaries and promotion to others selected because of unusually high teaching attainments.

As to the subjects and courses to be available in the first two years, we have made notable progress in a number of outstanding institutions in the provision of a general studies program,—in the natural sciences, social sciences and humanities,—in ways designed to quicken interest, pose significant problems and challenge the students to further study of those problems as the college work progresses. Many of the best programs in general education have already been well described in a growing body of published literature.[4]

Pedagogically, this new look at instructional programs is stressing the active participation of the student, the personalizing of the instruction through small sections, the introduction of some type of laboratory or field work or of alternated study-work programs in designated periods away from the campus. Not all the questions of method about general education programs have been answered; but experience is conclusive that this approach is proving much more evocative, self-propulsive and exciting to students in the first two college years than the older curricula ever did.

Nor can we ignore the problem of the adequate challenging of the intellectually superior student who should not be allowed to be satisfied with those lesser or different standards of attainment which may necessarily have to be held for the more average students. Honors courses, tutorial or preceptorial provisions, majors with rigorous standards of achievement, supervised reading periods and extended senior theses,—these are some of the ways in which we can more and more in all colleges assure that the best students will do their best.

At the other end of the intellectual scale, there is, I venture, a kind of unconscious snobbery on the part of all of us in education who claim some degree of superiority in verbalizing and conceptualizing talents. With us ability to use words and a good education come close to being synonymous. It is, of course, those with this approach who are largely responsible for the programs of present higher education. We all seem reluctant to recognize that there are other gifts, perhaps more directly possessed or apprehended or perceived, but good and useful gifts, which—and here is the key point of a fruitful new outlook—can be improved by education, if only the education can be freshly conceived as heightening perceptive powers of awareness and reality not necessarily reducible to verbal facility and not eventuating solely in conceptualizing skill. It is probable, for example, that the creative and performing arts supply a clue to a kind of education for immediacy of apprehension, which has equal and complementary value to education in verbal felicity and ability to reach reasoned conclusions. I wonder, quite seriously in this connection, whether any college teacher ever asked the athletic coach *how* he trains his less intellectually able but ranking student players. If something of this outlook of greater instructional flexibility is valid, I submit that as the colleges of tomorrow enroll more of the less intellectualistic individuals, their education will surely have to embrace efforts different from the purposes and methods with which we have had such long and loving familiarity.

One final general observation needs to be made. If colleges are *necessarily* and *rightfully* to broaden their instructional program in order that it may become vital for the less endowed, for those well endowed with other than conceptualizing aptitudes, and for the many who mature late mentally, it becomes essential that teachers increasingly strike the note that all college experience is in reality but a *beginning* of the student's needful education; and therefore the desire to *continue to learn* has to become central as one

and University Teaching. Its several issues to date constitute a helpful resource.
[4]A splendid over-all view of this problem may be found in *Accent On Teaching: Experiment in Education,* edited by Sidney J. French, Harper & Brothers, 1954, this being a symposium report by the Committee on General Education of the Association for Higher Education (NEA).

of the reiterated objectives with all students. And the further educational consequence will have to be a continuously strengthened program under various auspices of an adult education which ministers to the total needs of our society beyond the present offerings which seem too heavily slanted toward hobbies or refresher courses for vocational advancement.

College education for what?

The question in the second part of my title was infrequently raised as a major problem up to the time when the total tensions of the second World War, including problems of the draft or of some form of universal military service, became a reality. The changing character and size of our college populations necessarily entail a searching re-examination of purpose, objective and direction.

I by no means always agree with former Chancellor Hutchins of the University of Chicago. But on one score it seems to me that he, among others, has reiterated a valid point, namely that the purpose of the American college is not completely clear in any widely accepted way, is confused, and is infrequently well-articulated. While the following paragraph from his most recent book, *University of Utopia*,[5] may seem exaggerated and oversimplified, it embodies an essential kernel of truth. He says:

"Civilization is the deliberate pursuit of the common ideal. Education is the deliberate attempt to form men in terms of an ideal. It is the attempt of a society to produce the type of man that it wants. How does it determine the type of man that it wants? If it does not know the type of man that it wants, how does it judge the educational efforts it makes? It may be said that the type of man a society wants is the product of many historical and psychological factors and that whatever philosophy enters into the formation of its vision of man is simply a rationalization of this largely unconscious product. But, even if this were so, we know that in every society there is some vision of man, his nature and his destiny, elaborated by philosophers living and dead, which interacts with the traditional view of the type of man desired and which amounts to a criticism of the tradition and the practices of the educational system. Education without a philosophy of education, that is, a coherent statement of the aims and possibilities of education, is impossible."

Dr. Hutchins continues relevantly to our present condition and pressing budgetary needs, as follows:

"The claim upon the financial resources of the country that a university can legitimately make rests on the same ground. Public bodies or private persons who have money to dispense must be asked to do so not on the promise that the university will produce a lot of people in their image but on the assurance that the university will do its best to carry on the independent thought and criticism that the country requires and to turn out graduates who are capable of independent thought and criticism, graduates, that is, who are committed to the fullest development of their highest powers and who can do their part as responsible citizens of a democratic state. . . . A university that is not controversial is not a university. A civilization in which there is not a continuous controversy about important issues, speculative and practical, is on the way to totalitarianism and death."[6]

Those are brave words and they need to be courageously taken to heart. They do not, however, offer us more than a general view as to what the college is purposively about and how it should work to attain its goals.

I see no point in the recital of excerpts from the numerous and often splendidly formulated statements of individual college objectives which have in recent years poured forth from a goodly number of faculties in a mood of encouraging self-examination. Moreover, the more difficult problem lies in the translation of these objectives into operational terms which give promise of marked improvement in the quality of the graduates. It will perhaps be more helpful if we make several more generalized characterizations regarding ways of stating college purposes, indicating as they may both agreements and diversities, yet looking toward some common denominators from which improved programming may derive.

I regret to acknowledge, however, that I shall in the following statement about objectives not be able to discuss a number of vital points which merit inclusion, not to say important emphasis. I refer to such problems as effective citizenship education at the college level; consideration of instruction in political and cultural problems in a global view; the difficulties of scientific education for general students; and the necessary balancing of liberal and vocational claims in the individual college program.

[5]University of Chicago Press, 1954, p. 52.

[6]Idem, pp. 88, 91.

All of these, I shall assume, do or should stem from a common base which says that the educational purpose must look at once at the growth of each individual student and at the claims, tensions and possibilities of our society. There has to be a realization of the virtually complete interdependence and interaction of individual and society in the forwarding of nurture, growth, and responsible freedom for the individual. I shall assume that what society should want from each individual can be reconciled and harmonized with what each individual at his best can be educated to want for himself.

There is, first, the familiar view that college education should be in considerable measure culture-centered. It is charged to conserve the American cultural heritage, to interpret it in its present setting, to stimulate students to accept, to criticize and to extend the realizing of this heritage—in other words to become committed to a responsible regard for the further potentialities of our culture.

Another familiar statement is that colleges are concerned to purvey knowledge, develop intellectual capacity, increase ability to exercise personal power in socially channeled ways, and to enable graduates to achieve amicable, cooperative relations with their fellow men. The singling out of intellectual capacity alone as the college purpose in the way that many utterances of Dr. Hutchins can be interpreted, seems to me erroneously oversimplified. It is impossible to separate intellectual development from concern about physical, moral and spiritual growth. One may heartily agree with Hutchins "that every man and every free citizen needs a liberal education" and yet not conceive it possible to narrow this to its purely rationalistic aspects.

A further interesting expression bearing on the philosophy of education is found in the following paragraph, even though its labored vocabulary invites translation. Professor Richard D. Mosier of the University of California concludes a recent article on "The Crisis in Education" as follows:[7]

"The conception of *reason as the logic of experience*, if it were allied with the conceptions of the aim of education as an *axiological* problem, the method of education as an *epistemological* problem, and the content of education as an *ontological* problem, would go a long way toward resolving the conflicts that form the underlying philosophic foundation of the current crisis in education."

My own rendition of the above would be that college education has to recognize and cultivate the capacity to reason, a process embracing at once its problem solving effort, the criticizing and evaluating of experience, and the ability of imaginative mental rehearsing of or overt experimenting with the possible ways out of confronted difficulties. Along with this has to be stressed the purpose of clarifying standards as to what is valuable, together with identification of the valuable in different departments of living. Also included is some awareness by teacher and student of how we may come to know, of what we can know, and of that in human experience, beyond the tests of science, which involves commitment to certain great and enduring truths and beliefs, or faith. Finally, there is requisite some consideration of the realities as to our own being, the grounds or foundations of Being, and the enrichment of awareness of what we sense as the natural and beyond that the self-transcendent in experience, out from which the learner should be stirred to a heightened sense of responsible dedication. In short, higher education has to advance the qualities of rationality, of evaluative and appreciative capacity, of affection for one's fellow, and of willingness to assume responsibility for personally and socially creative conduct in a community upon which he is dependent and in which he has a real but limited freedom or independence.

There is, again, a point of view often referred to as the functional view with which, among others, the name of Dr. W. W. Charters is associated, especially in his advisory work with Stephens College in Missouri. In this approach, the typical life functions which each individual has to confront are those of being a citizen, a worker, a family member, a leisure-time person, and an individual soul in its inescapable aloneness. And the educational program is therefore to be shaped so that the student is enabled to function more effectively in each of these five areas in which life requires his participation. There is, moreover, no reason why this functional view cannot be in some measure interwoven with other concepts of college purposes. But in any case it is important that these functions be viewed educationally in an intellectually rigorous way that gets beyond purely practical methods, toward a probing in the direction of first principles and philosophic justifications.

One other approach to the problem of objectives which I shall briefly characterize is at once my own expression and the conviction also of a growing number of others who are now raising similar questions. What, in short, are we deeply

[7]See *Educational Theory*, October 1953, p. 346.

about in carrying on colleges? Why do we make so little effort to confront explicitly in college the problems and issues which bedevil us in the numerous areas of life itself? Why do we not more fully face *head on* the tension and conflicts of the human spirit today and of the society and culture in which we live? Why do our colleges not address themselves *more directly* to the central concerns of human bewilderment and aspiration? Why do we not ask ourselves more insistently what *are* the major life needs and possible enduring satisfactions[8] of our students, and how are they to be more assuredly ministered to? Why not acknowledge frankly that education of the mind can be dangerous unless the purpose of cultivating moral responsibility and individual commitment to truth-seeking, excellence and righteousness, is also kept ascendant?

Take as an illuminating approach to the kind of life issues which require direct confronting the six polarities or dichotomies to which Professor Huston Smith of Washington University, St. Louis, has called attention in an as yet unpublished report on curricular reorganization now being studied by his faculty colleagues.[9] He reminds us of the following areas of stress which plague us with uncertainties, both in the realm of thought and in practical affairs, personal and social. Indeed, as to these we are bound to ask ourselves to what extent our colleges even pretend to clarify some helpful outlook upon them. These opposed views concern:

   absolutism versus relativism
   objectivity versus commitment
   authority versus freedom
   egoism versus altruism
   the state (and all other large corporate organizations) versus the individual
   the secular versus the sacred

I believe that under these several conceptual frames subsume many of the basic confusions of our day,—confusions which glorify the relative, make a virtue of moral neutrality, minimize our vigilance as to the need for freedom, misconstrue the deeper meanings of selfhood and of solicitude for others, oppose the state to the welfare of the individual; and preoccupy us with secular and material values to the ignoring of the sacred.

It will be said, of course, that certain of these six polarities are likely to be considered in one or another course in political science or philosophy. It will also be said that in listing these six

areas of tensions I depart from the usual course subjects and that we have to have something to study "about" beyond such broad concepts as these. My point about all this would be that *of course* we have to study some subject matter and that *of course* content has to be tough and rigorous. And, most important, that the only fruitful way of studying the most profound issues is by an interdisciplinary attack.

But the further and still unanswered point is that if the basic issues relevant to our living are not identified and confronted by every student in *some* college instruction with some illumination as to possible reconciliations of opposites or possible new integrations, when and where will the student ever confront reflectively those exigent and spiritually disturbing tensions? Also, if there is to come, as there has to, a more consistent and persistent effort at interdisciplinary courses in general education, it is problems of this kind which have inevitably to be introduced. Indeed, within the frame of the familiar water-tight compartments now too typical of college instruction, there can always properly be recognition by the teacher not only of primary but also of supplementary purposes and broad, humane insights which should enrich every course in every subject.

A final noble testimony to that liberality which is the over-arching college purpose is expressed by Karl Jaspers in these words: "We humans need education in critical thought and comprehension, we need the world of history and philosophy if we are to become competent to form independent judgments. The whole population must be raised to a higher level in a continually intensified educational process; it must be brought from half knowledge to whole knowledge, from the contingent thinking of the moment to methodical thinking, in which everyone can lift himself out of dogmatism into freedom. This is the hope for the evolution of the majority, that in its decisions and resolutions by vote it will consciously and deliberately choose that which is better."[10]

I have deliberately refrained from offering a simple answer to the question as to what colleges are for. Indeed, the present diversity of expressed college objectives is itself a stimulating and encouraging evidence of vitality. However, the general approaches and outlooks suggested by this discussion do perhaps require a concluding section as to the ways and means of implementing the probable outcomes of any reexamination of the purposes of a college.

---

[8]See McEwen, W. P., *Enduring Satisfaction,* Philosophical Library, New York, 1949.
[9]To be published in the spring of 1955 under the title *Basic Issues in Higher Education,* Harper & Brothers.

[10]See his *The Origin and Goal of History,* Yale University Press, 1953, p. 168.

Implementation

On this score I shall place first emphasis upon the central role of the college teacher. He is no longer to be only the dispenser of facts and knowledge. He is no longer merely *telling*. He has to be the guide, counselor and friend, pointing each student to the ways and means by which he can himself become a willing, eager, self-propulsive learner of what he is helped to discover to be needful for himself and deeply satisfying for his fullfillment and social creativity. Beyond being a walking bibliography, the teacher has to have phosphorescence, intellectual glamour, moral dedication and some insight into the things of the spirit. I realize full well that there are not enough good college teachers to go around. But I also realize and believe that American college leaders have to rise up in active affirmative and virtually missionary zeal to proclaim first, that we are not attracting the best minds and the warmest personalities into teaching; and, second, that even if we were, the usual process of attaining a Ph.D. is all too often in grave danger of killing the incipient spark of intellectual and spiritual spontaneity which is the teacher's priceless asset. There will be no ultimate improvement in the college teaching situation without a virtual revolution in the way in which young people are selected and prepared for the high vocation of being a college teacher. And in this process the importance first of an operational grasp of the fundamentals of the learning process and, second, of guided apprentice experience in teaching actual college classes has to be recognized as indispensable.

I venture, also, that in the colleges of the future the broad orientation of instruction is not to be "subject-centered" or "student-centered" in the limited sense in which those phrases are often used. It is no mere rhetoric to affirm that instruction has to be increasingly *life-centered* in the profound sense of confronting great living issues. It has to be life-centered with great enhancement both in the instructional appeal to students and in the gain in their capacity to attack life. And this they will achieve through the utilization of any one of a number of fresh and vigorously pursued methods of approach.

There is, for example, on this score of fresh approaches to subject matter, one avenue through the explication of a selection of great and influential concepts. I refer to study which would focus on constellations of ideas which surround the words democracy, leadership, justice, personal power, selfhood, the state, science and similar basic concepts. I have been interested to see that

in a recent address Dr. Alvin Eurich agrees with me about the probable fruitfulness of this approach.

There is the approach through the study of "persistent issues" as exemplified in contemporary society. This is already being utilized in a number of institutions.

There is, again, the approach through a sampling of carefully selected "representative and significant problems"—in history, the social sciences, philosophy, political science and the natural sciences.

I emphasize that such approaches to newly oriented, significant subject matter would for instructional effectiveness all have to be interdisciplinary in character, drawing upon insights and knowledge from a variety of fields.

Two further points merit highlighting in conclusion. I refer to the new importance having to be assumed by the humanities in the college of tomorrow; and some understanding of what is meant by a freshly conceived recognition of the relations of a purified religious outlook to higher education.

E. E. Cummings, in his recent Harvard lectures, quotes Rilke as follows: "Works of art are of an infinite loneliness and with nothing would be so little reached as with criticism. Only love can grasp and fairly judge them." And to this quotation, Cummings adds the following: "In my proud and humble opinion, these two sentences are worth all the *soi-disant* criticism of the arts which has ever existed or will ever exist."[11] This may be exaggeration, but it should remind us that the philological and linguistic approaches to the study of the literary humanities is horrendously deficient and bleak. One is reminded in this connection of the imprecations which Bernard Shaw called down upon any teacher who might subject his plays to analysis in the manner in which all too many teachers have analysed and desiccated the sublimities of Shakespeare's plays. These comments are warnings against a continuation of unimaginative outlooks in too much present soulless and visionless teaching of the humanities.

It is important to make the vigorous affirmation that the humanities supply the eloquent open sesame for fulfilling the purposes of value affirmation which are central to the mission of the liberal college. The anguished, aspiring, prophetic voices of mankind have their articulation and their communicative power in the utterances of the great books and the other great art ex-

[11]See Adams, J. Donald in *New York Times Book Review Section*, February 14, 1954.

pressions as globally evoked throughout history. And I use the words "great books" in a more inclusive sense than that employed by the cult which centers attention on the study of a too restricted list of classic volumes. We have to reconceive radically the function and the methods of the study of the humanities to assure that they speak vitally and on eternal issues to which today's students eagerly seek answers. It is in these studies that the visions of human greatness are suggested. For the essential contribution of the humanities is to illuminate and reaffirm the great human ideals of beauty, freedom, justice, mercy, loving kindness, truth-seeking and the centrality of the spiritual in the life of man. This contribution has also to interpret to students as nothing else can the meaning and the human impact of guilt, sin, suffering, tragedy, death, destructive hate and redemptive love. The humanities have to tell us, as Karl Jaspers[12] says, that "tragedy is not enough" in our philosophy of life. They have to tell us, as Paul Tillich[13] puts it, that the "courage to be" is, when once possessed, a releasing power of tremendous force in its ultimate assertion of the human outreach toward the Source of our being.

There is, indeed, a sense in which a lively awareness of what the humanities have to say in their historic perspective comes close to being a disclosure of that aspect of human experience which we are entitled to identify as religious. And my concluding point is as to whether our growing sense of the reality of high religion, beyond dogmas, doctrines and denominations, may not lead us on to seeing that exclusion of a religious awareness from education is indefensible and prevents these two great areas of thought, insight and action from cross-fertilizing as fully and helpfully as they properly should. Why, quite simply, is not all education at once an intellectual, moral and *sacred* enterprise? Is not every effort to fulfill the individual and to make his society contributory to that fulfillment a sanctified or *sacred* as well as humane effort?

I am not ignoring obvious issues of the separation of church and state, of possible state support for church-related schools, nor the issue of what, if any, kind of instruction about religion is acceptable in colleges which are not church-related. It rather seems to me that beyond the legal phases, it is not only possible but essential to approach this concern more profoundly in relation to human needs as viewed in historic and universal context.

I find a possible approach here if we ask dispassionately what are the modes, moods, or component elements which the religious spirit embodies when the sacred is being realized and awareness of a transcendent relation of humanity to that beyond itself is striving to find human expression. I suggest (out of the thought of many beside myself) that we find a number of such widely agreed components. The following are needful as aspects or attributes of high religion:

(1) participation in individual action, performance and *accomplishment,* in which *creativity* and growth are dominant purposes;

(2) recognition that continuous *change* characterizes all life in a disturbing but inevitable flux and novelty;

(3) acknowledgment of human *dependence* on powers beyond ourselves which are by no means completely identifiable or definable;

(4) recognition of lawfulness, form and *order* to be somewhat apprehended through present knowledge and by persistent continuous study of the interrelations of man with the rest of the cosmos;

(5) appreciation of the stirring and heartening *beauty* to be found in the cosmos and in works created by men;

(6) recognition of the reciprocal interdependence of individual fulfillment and an awareness of membership and *belonging* in an ever widening *community* of love and fraternal regard;

(7) recognition that the appraising of what is valuable, of what has Godlike *value,* is deep in our natures as a continuing imperative upon us;

(8) recognition that in our individual *aloneness* we seek to transcend our little selves by meditation, contemplation and otherwise, in order to be at one with a larger whole which partakes of the *holy*—or, as the old phrase has it, the search "to be alone with the Alone." Finally, I propose,

(9) recognition that there is for each individual a genuine if limited *freedom* of choice, together with an ever-present reality of *redemptive love* proffered freely, if inexplicably, to all who sense that in their freedom they have fallen short or fallen away from their own highest commitments.

I ask that you note the key words here. They are: creativity, change, dependence, rational order and lawfulness, knowledge, beauty, community membership, value, aloneness, meditation, freedom, redemptive love.

In appropriate, reasonable, loving and committed combinations expressed in concrete experiences, these components qualitatively pursued

[12]See his volume, *Tragedy Is not Enough,* Beacon Press, Boston, 1952.
[13]See his volume, *The Courage to Be,* Yale University Press, New Haven, 1952.

characterize the religious way of life. These several words identify natural and universal experiences. And an individual life that comprehends within itself experiences consciously possessed of these attributes at a devoted, high level of quality is *sharing religious experience.* Individual motives and actions may thus come to have a kind of sanctity. The individual when his conduct is possessed of such qualities is participating in experience which transcends the secular or the perfunctory. He shares an immanent naturalism combined, when the individual's awareness is most deeply felt, with an ecstatic upward transcendence of the human toward the divine or sacred. It is largely thus that there comes to pass the individual realization of the eternal and unutterable mystery of man in God and of God in man. And this insight of religion (always capable of being extended by education) can be for our day the advance intimation of a renewal of the human spirit in purpose and direction which promises to the committed an unrealized power for good.

I am suggesting, in short, that it becomes increasingly possible for college teachers to accept a modern, intellectual and spiritual outlook and devotion beyond positivism or scientific humanism. To the extent that teachers may already have religious affiliations, these will be enriched and deepened. And to the extent that they have no such affiliations, it becomes rationally defensible and desirable for them to become sensitive to the possible fusion of education with a high religious attitude and faith.

In summary, I have been affirming the necessity that a greatly enlarged fraction of qualified young people should have the benefit of a college education. I have said that as this occurs it will be necessary that there be appropriate modifications and diversifications in the content and methods of instruction supplied to students with differing aptitudes and interests.

I have reaffirmed the crucial value of the liberal arts to be transmitted through the approaches today characterized as general education; and with a reinterpretation of the humanities as central in assuring that they become the vehicle for imparting the vision of man's spiritual greatness and freedom.

I have also indicated that the college's purpose of forwarding individual growth for social responsibility and creativity requires changes in our methods of educating teachers; requires the far wider use by teachers of new psychological insights into the learning process. And it requires the dedicated and essentially moral and sanctified outlook on the part of more and more teachers which will enrich their scholarship and their personalities, and thus assure that pervading their instruction is a winsomeness of appeal and a spiritual relevance which students will find increasingly irresistible.

109

Samuel M. Holton

THE EMERGING PATTERN OF COLLEGIATE EDUCATION

The college program is here analyzed in terms of the extent to which it helps students achieve greater maturity. The author concludes that if the colleges are to deal successfully with this important challenge, their program must be carefully redesigned with this in mind.

Like Topsy the older patterns of collegiate education in this country and in Europe have "jest growed." Their traditions go back to the medieval cathedral and the Greek city-state. Their selective philosophy is borrowed from a class conscious Europe. Their teaching techniques were taken from the German universities of forty-five years ago. Their curriculums have been pieced together from the debris of many now discarded theories of education.

It seems clear that these institutions are not representative of the best which their philosophers, sociologists, and psychologists could design. These thinkers are generally agreed that the American college should prepare students to live

From *Educational Forum,* January 1953, 17:203-213.

better lives as adults. Is the program which is offered really likely to produce more mature adults? Can the majority of our colleges say that their students have become more mature than if they had not attended college? A few thoughtful college leaders say no and are doing something about it.

It is not easy to define what constitutes maturity and mature living, for mature living has many facets. It is made up of such things as mature thinking, social maturity, physical maturity, and moral and emotional maturity. It is these which are necessary for the improvement of American democracy.

The mature thinker is willing to consider alternatives. He is familiar with the nature of evidence. He possesses an open mind with regard to questions related to any phase of living or existence. He is free of bigotry. He recognizes the tentative nature of conclusions based on incomplete evidence.

Many college trained adults are little more mature as thinkers than if they had not attended college. Are they less willing to accept rumors about public officials unsupported by adequate evidence? Will they not accept, and even preach, the superiority of one social, religious, or racial group over another? Are they willing to discuss dispassionately their religious or political beliefs in a spirit of honest inquiry? Are they not willing to wage and accept political campaigns based on deliberate misrepresentation, bigotry, and unsupported charges of disloyalty? Have they not become excited over the radio play describing an invasion from Mars? Will they not brand as "communistic" or "radical" political or religious beliefs with which they disagree?

Social maturity, to take another example, involves an understanding of other people. It involves a certain flexibility of interest. It includes an awareness of social custom. It includes ability to mix with other people of different occupations without a display of tenseness. It involves skill in maintaining pleasant relationships with different types of people. It involves skill in a variety of social activities such as conversation and recreational games.

This is perhaps the phase of maturity which the traditional college is best developing. Nevertheless many of the better students of the colleges become social misfits as adults. They have lost their interest in social problems in their absorption with some academic pursuit. They are content to withdraw from society to the protection of the University campus, the artists colony, or the professional clique. They prefer to live in the exclusive residential settlements. They are impatient with the trivial talk of the mechanic or grocer. They profess an ineptness in business transactions. Their children are encouraged to play only with others of their kind. They partake only grudgingly in the civic and religious activities of their communities. They express the viewpoint that expansion of educational or cultural opportunities would unfit too many people for the menial tasks of the society.

Physical maturity would seem to come almost automatically—regardless of what the college might do. Nevertheless maturity of attitudes and habits with regard to the use of our bodies is seldom seen. Few college graduates have even reached desirable stages of physical strength and skill. College graduates fail to practice generally recognized rules of health. They overeat. They exercise immoderately or not at all. They suffer from nervous breakdowns. They die of heart and kidney diseases brought on by poor physical habits.

Emotional maturity involves an understanding of the nature of emotion. It requires rational consideration of problems arising from emotional drives. The emotionally mature person is likely to be well adjusted to the problems of living.

College trained people seem little more able to understand and control their emotional impulses than others. They are perhaps more likely to become despondent and commit suicide. They find it necessary to resort to divorce to solve other emotional problems. They suffer from stomach ulcers and other "nervous" disorders. They develop artistic temperaments. They become domineering over their children and acquaintances. They are hypochondriacs.

If it is the responsibility of the college to provide for the mature development of each of the students with whom it works, then we may evaluate each of the procedures of the college in terms of what it contributes to the development of mature adults. While it is not easy to define or recognize all of the major phases and facets of maturity, we should be able to recognize some of them and to design a program which will assist in their development.

Institutions are limited in achieving their highest functions by the people or materials with which they work, by the surroundings in which the work is carried on, and by the understanding which the leadership has of its functions. The American college is no exception.

American college students, faculties and plants are good. The student has been selected by the high school. Free public education sends to higher institutions those whose backgrounds have been most favorable for social and educational development. They are in general a young, ambitious, idealistic, well-mannered group. Their four years in college are a period of transition from home to independent living. Here they will develop their own scale of values, and in the new environment the social, economic, and moral values of the home will be questioned.

Like the students the members of college faculties constitute a select group. The college professor has been chosen from what were considered the best of the preceding ranks of students. The grouping of mature scholars within a faculty provides stimulation for each of them. Libraries and laboratories assist in this teacher growth. Social status is high and working conditions are pleasant. Freedom of thought and speech are quite real.

College plants worth hundreds of millions of dollars also contribute to the promise of the college. Most of them are designed to be independent of the usual distractions of the city. Relaxation in a congenial atmosphere is encouraged by tree-shaded lawns. Beauty is stressed and often achieved. Libraries containing thousands of books make the cultural heritage available. Laboratories and classrooms are designed to meet many needs. Dining and living facilities are frequently attractive and comfortable. Space is provided for recreation and physical exercise for both students and faculty members.

With good students, faculties, and plants much may be expected of the American college. Where it falls short of its potentialities, the blame lies in the organization and administration of these assets.

The major emphases in the average college program reveal the degree of understanding of the function of the college on the part of those responsible for its organization and administration. These emphases, the product of accumulated concern for the mechanics of mass education and lack of conscious design, suggest poor understanding of how maturity may be developed. The mechanics have become so cumbersome that they seem almost to have destroyed the possibilities inherent in good students, able faculties, and handsome plants.

The development of mental maturity, for example, has become subordinate to the accumulation of course credit gained in fifteen to twenty hours a week of class attendance. A college diploma is earned mechanically by collecting such credit. Mechanically, failure in course work is followed by dismissal or late graduation. Mechan-

ically, the school year starts with registration lines and closes with final examinations. Tardiness to class is a serious fault. Absence draws the attention of deans. Conscientious work is rewarded by excuse from the necessity of class attendance. The mechanics of keeping school obscures the development of mental maturity.

Several colleges have sought relief from restrictions placed by emphasis on class attendance. Harvard was one of the first to allow students free election of their courses. Chicago has provided for students to stand examinations which will exempt them from class attendance. Hiram College, in Ohio, has materially reduced the number of different classes which a student will attend at any one time. The English universities have never stressed class attendance to the degree that it has been stressed in America and there has been a tendency in some of the American colleges to attempt to modify the English tutorial system for American use. Experimental programs at Berea and Black Mountain have removed much of the mechanical emphasis on course credits. Miami is deemphasizing class attendance. Nevertheless in spite of demonstrated success in most of these experiments American colleges continue to place much of their faith in course credits as a necessary adjunct to the development of mental maturity.

With the emphasis which is usually placed on class attendance, one would expect the class procedure to be very effective. Such confidence would be misplaced. The most frequently used teaching device is the lecture. This is likely to be dull and monotonous. Some lecturers are of course artists and showmen, but they are in the minority. Lecturing as a teaching device is reinforced by grades and examinations. The final mark gets primary student and faculty attention. As a result the student is likely to study only to earn the mark, ignoring the deeper values of the subject. It becomes more important to memorize than to understand. Mental maturity is largely ignored.

Educational research has shown that grades and examinations are poor measures of understanding. They serve primarily to hide the inadequacies of the lecture system. Without the quiz the lecture might be recognized as a failure.

A second portion of the program concerned with the development of mental maturity is the science laboratory. It is sometimes argued that the purpose of the lab is to develop an appreciation of scientific method. The essential part of scientific method, however, is freedom of inquiry —use of a logical approach to solve a real problem. The college laboratory is generally lacking in such freedom, particularly at the elementary levels. The typical experiment is "performed" by following the directions of a laboratory manual to find the answers already reported in the text. The answer is known in advance, and so is the procedure. Success is determined not through the development of a scientific method, but through the manipulation of apparatus and figures. Even as a demonstration of points covered in the lecture more vivid and less amateurish techniques are available.

The unpublicized work of such science departments as the Botany Department at Duke University, where laboratory manuals and textbooks have been largely dispensed with and the laboratory time used frankly for whatever type of activity which seems appropriate to the material being studied, is hopeful modification of weak practice.

Mental maturity comes most surely in conditions which provide close contact with mature teachers and a chance to wrestle with real problems. Many of the smaller colleges and some of the larger such as Harvard and Yale have had some success in providing such contact by utilizing dining and living facilities. In the latter institutions smaller campus living units have been set up under the direction of mature members of the staff. In these units group discussions and counseling have been encouraged. The idea is a fruitful one. It is perhaps unfortunate that it has been largely superimposed on the more rigidly formal emphasis on class attendance rather than substituted for it.

It is difficult to imagine a Socrates or a Christ in the frequently impersonal setting of most of our colleges. Large dormitories, large classes, long lunch lines almost inevitably imply impersonal contact between student and teacher. There is little opportunity for the understanding and respect which results from close acquaintance between student and teacher. The German pattern which we have accepted is foreign to the kind of mental maturity which we desire to develop.

Maturity of thought cannot be divorced from the intimate details of living. The American college will achieve more when it sets up the kind of environment in which maturity can be developed through example and practice.

Closely related to the idea that mental maturity can be gained through lectures, quizzes, and "labs" is the emphasis placed by college leadership on academic standards. There seems to be an assumption that learning must be painful. When techniques and procedures in the college program become obviously of little value they are then said to be good for the discipline involved. The student who is unable, or unwilling, to submit to such a program of discipline is eliminated. When we remember that the freshman was, himself, selected from a much larger population, we have reason to question this process of continued selection. Should education be primarily concerned with selection? Is education in a democratic society for those least in need of it?

Emphasis in the college on standards is not an unconscious one. Each academic year brings reference in faculty meetings and student publications to the importance of high standards. The idea seems to be that the prestige of the college or faculty is determined by the difficulty of its courses. The school that fails a large number of its students is said to have "higher standards" than the one that does not. It might be more reasonable to assume the reverse. The school which provides a program for each of its students and thus continues their education might be the better school.

If the function of the school is to select, then it should be judged on how well it selects. If the function of the school is to assist the student to attain maturity, then it should be judged on the basis of how much maturity he attains. So long as we insist on judging the school on the basis of only the student who is graduated we encourage the selection of those who already know much of what the school wishes to teach. If we are really interested in the development of maturity, our standards must be set in terms of how much more maturity each of the students who is admitted to the school has achieved by the time he leaves the school. All students entering, not just those who are selected to receive the diploma, are the responsibility of the American college.

Some of our junior colleges have recognized more clearly their responsibility to all of their students than four year colleges attached to large universities. This has been particularly true of the public junior colleges in California.

While the processes of the college for developing mental maturity are centered around lectures, quizzes, and standards, the development of social maturity is, in the colleges for men at least, less highly organized. For less than half of the student body of many of our colleges, the social fraternity is the vehicle for the direction of the social education of the student. Its importance is out of proportion to its actual membership.

In some schools fraternities have been banned or rendered relatively ineffective. For those who belong stress is on membership in a small and closely knit group. The stated ideals of the group are generally quite commendable. The fact remains that as expensive adjuncts to college education fraternities put an emphasis on social selection which is unwholesome. Membership becomes sometimes more important than any other phase of student life. The unsupervised program of the fraternity does not justify such confidence on the part of the student. Furthermore failure to be selected brings grief to many worthy students.

The existence of the fraternity may indicate a need within the college for intimate units of social grouping and perhaps even for better provision for community living. These needs should be met for all students as a part of the regular framework of the college itself.

Princeton, among the larger American colleges, has taken significant steps in the direction of providing for the social life of its entire student body rather than merely for the socially select. There dining clubs under competent sponsorship form a very important part of the undergraduate life of every student. The resulting attitudes are quite enviable.

A second type of provision for the social maturity of the student is through student directed activities. Among the activities which might be listed in this connection are the political organizations, culminating in some form of student government; the student newspaper, and other student publications; the glee club, and other musical organizations; the dramatic groups, and organizations dealing with public speaking; and various organizations sponsoring other types of social activity. It is this phase of the college program which alumni tend to list as the most educational. Nevertheless, it is a small portion of the student body which actively takes part. Like the rest of the college program, it tends to provide the best education for those least in need of it.

A third, but relatively insignificant part of the college program for the development of social and mental maturity, is the sponsorship by the college of public lectures and concerts. In general, students take little part in this portion of the college program. It is the college faculty and community which attends and benefits most from such activity.

Yale uses its smaller living units to stimulate greater interest in such informal cultural-social activity with a great deal of success. There each of the ten "colleges" of approximately four hundred students has its own widely attended series of lectures and programs managed by student leaders.

The need for developing physical maturity is imperfectly recognized in the American college in its emphasis on athletics. This program as it now exists in the colleges assumes three forms: the varsity or intercollegiate team sport, intramural sports, and the formal physical education program. A large part of the capital outlay of some institutions is in gymnasia, swimming pools, tennis courts, and stadia. A few of them can boast golf courses and riding stables. In some schools the director of the program of physical education and athletics is a more highly paid official than the president.

Of the three phases of athletic activity the varsity program generally gets the big share of attention. Its place in providing for physical maturity seems rather obscure. For about two months football provides entertainment and spectator recreation for the student body, alumni, faculty, and the general community. In some communities basketball and baseball serve the same function. Other activities such as tennis, track, and swimming seem to be of interest primarily to the participants.

The number of students actually participating in all of the varsity sports is relatively small. The more spectacular of the sports do provide a basis for continued contact with the alumni. They bring in revenue to the school program, generally expended on other varsity sports. They serve to advertise the school. In the process they create in the popular mind a false impression as to the purpose of the college. (Perhaps the gravest criticism of institutional ethics is on the question of the eligibility of football players.) Even if participation in team sports may be of value, the extreme expenditure of time and energy required by the varsity sports renders the rest of the educational program practically valueless to the player in the regular season.

Some school officials have seriously questioned whether it was the responsibility of public and private institutions to sponsor commercial recreation in the name of education. The University of Chicago is one of several schools which have found that varsity athletics were not a useful part of their program for the development of physical maturity and have dropped them from their program. Others have taken rather careful steps to prevent the varsity program from hampering the rest of the educational program. Serious students of the public high school are recognizing the influence of college professionalization on practice at the secondary level.

Some critics of varsity athletics have hailed the intramural program as the answer. Certainly more students can take part. Certainly less stress is placed on long hours of practice. Here, it is felt by some, athletics assumes its place as a part of a balanced program of education in living. In few schools is the intramural program really popular. Those which have the largest programs find it necessary to stimulate student interest through offering elaborate trophies, through building up campus rivalries, or through requiring participation. Group pressure is placed on the individual member of fraternity or dormitory units to take part, even though he may feel some other activity to be more profitable.

Whether as social and educational activity intramural sports are worth the time expended is questionable. They are valuable in so far as they provide fellowship and recreation. The great majority of the sports stressed will not be used after the completion of the college program.

The formal physical education class is sometimes said to be the "real" educational activity of the college dealing with the physical needs of the student. Many colleges require at least two years of participation in this program. Proponents claim three purposes: the teaching of basic athletic skills and recreational activities, provision for "proper physical development," and provision for systematic exercises. It seems doubtful that large numbers of students continue to use the skills taught as basic. Nor has it been shown, despite many studies, that significant gains have been made in the status of health of students participating in the physical education program. The fact that the college does not require participation in the program by upper class and graduate students seems to indicate doubt on the part of officials as to the need for systematic exercise.

Some schools, including the University of North Carolina, have set up physical education clinics which attempt to determine the physical needs of entering students and to provide at least in extreme cases suitable corrective attention. This represents at least consideration of the importance of developing physical maturity in the student by starting from an understanding of his particular needs.

The amount of emphasis placed on moral and emotional development varies considerably from one college to another. There is at the present time not one but several different patterns of emphasis. Each pattern represents a different conception as to the function of the college in this phase of maturity.

At the beginning of the century the daily chapel service was an important part of student life in most American colleges. It served as an opportunity to discuss moral, religious, and emotional problems which lent themselves to group attention. This practice has been abandoned gradually for various reasons: the complexity of the daily schedule, increase in the size of student bodies which made such gatherings less feasible, resistance on the part of students who objected to the "preaching" which was likely to take place, and realization on the part of faculty and administration that the areas dealt with required individual rather than group attention. Where the services were primarily religious it was felt that attendance should be voluntary.

Most schools of any size now attempt to provide for moral and emotional development through what is referred to as guidance. The emphasis is usually restricted to dealing with "problems" rather than with providing systematic assistance to all students. Where counselors are assigned for all students they usually are more concerned with problems of scheduling course work than with assisting students in emotional or moral development.

Some of the Eastern schools try to take advantage of the presence of graduate students and young faculty members to provide more counselors than are generally available in other colleges. This has been really successful where the counselor was readily available in a natural relationship, preferably as a regular member of a dormitory or dining group.

The average American college attempts to make some provision for the development of its students in each of the major areas of maturity: physical, mental, social, and emotional. Its program for maturity is centered around class attendance, with its lectures and laboratory procedures; around selective standards; around a poorly supervised social life; around the athletic program; around student activities; around a variety of formal and informal activities labeled "Guidance"; and to a very slight degree around such things as lectures and concerts. The degree of maturity to be achieved from such emphases is being questioned. Slowly colleges are evolving a new program.

The leaders of some of our colleges are coming to recognize that the maturity of students in all phases of living cannot be provided by assembly line procedures. They are coming to recognize that education must become highly personalized.

Best thought seems to suggest a simple living unit of from thirty to fifty people. The fellowship now available only in the fraternity house would become available for the entire student body. The emphasis would be taken from the expensive and glamorous "weekend" characteristic of many modern campuses and placed on a more maturely directed practice of daily living.

Since the teachers would share in the life of the smaller community, personal guidance would become readily available. The fifteen minute conference with an impersonal official which is now the more frequent contact between faculty or administration and the students would be replaced by longer, more informal contacts. Many of the things which affect the maturity of the student would come to the attention of the counselor with whom he was living.

In such a school formal class procedures could be relegated to the background. Lectures of general interest to several different groups of students might be attended as at present and then used as a basis for further analysis within the living unit. Basic courses needed for the maturity of practically all students should be given on an individual or small group basis within the unit itself. More highly specialized courses might be given as at present, primarily on the third and fourth year levels, but should be recognized as secondary to the life in the campus unit itself.

The small living unit on the college campus would give as much experience in the art of wholesome living as possible. Students and teachers would work and plan together. Problems in group ethics and behavior could be dealt with rationally. The economics of operating the living establishment could become a part of the educational program. There would be a better basis for determining which members of the group were not profiting from the experiences offered. No student would "flunk out" for failure on academic courses, but would stay in school or leave on the basis of his ability to profit from continuing in school. When he left, the student might be given a formal statement of the things which he had done in school, not a relatively meaningless college diploma.

Some important activities could not easily be carried on within the small living unit. These could be retained as a part of the college-wide program and stressed in proportion to their apparent worth in developing student maturity. Grades, examinations, and course credits would become less important when the adult adviser was in a position to tell as to whether a student was profiting from the work he was doing. Increased maturity could become the criterion for judging the student's success. With a reduction in mechanization of the educational process such paraphernalia as marks and records would become less important.

While social, mental, and emotional maturity could be provided better through the introduction of small closely knit living units, similar changes might assist in the development of physical maturity. Emphasis on the type of physical education which concentrates primarily on exhibitionism could be replaced by a new or at least neglected concept of physical education pursued primarily either for recreation or for the development of increased maturity in understanding and use of the body.

Physical education as a formal class activity would be discarded in favor of a highly individualized clinical procedure. The physical needs of a student would be determined and he would be shown how those needs might be met. The student who needed to develop greater physical stamina through proper diet might have such a diet prescribed. The student who had not learned the value of regular exercise might be taught it. The student who needed some type of corrective exercise might be given it. Recreational facilities and instruction in their use might be provided for all.

The stress in the emerging college will be on clinical determination of needs and careful planning to meet them. Freshmen will be assigned to living units on the basis of their apparent abilities and interests. It will be the duty of advisers to assist them to determine their educational needs and to find in the college the facilities for meeting them. The entire process will devolve around consideration of how well each student is progressing in his development toward more mature adulthood. If a student does not know how to get along with people then his adviser will help him to determine why and what may be done about it. If he does not have a sufficient background of information on which to build a personal philosophy then an attempt will be made to provide it. If he is interested in music, he may be given an opportunity to study it. If he knows little of art and literature, he will be led to enjoy them.

Only when a program is consciously designed to allow all students to achieve greater maturity can we expect the American college to serve that function. This requires that those in positions of authority recognize the problem. Where leadership is chosen on the basis of administrative experience rather than on the basis of philosophical understanding of the function of democratic education, we will change very slowly from our present weak practice. Where the leaders have vision we are making progress.

The educational ladder

ADULT EDUCATION

Partly because of the feeling that education must be a lifelong process, not one confined to a certain age level, and partly because of the tremendous changes which have taken place and are continuing to take place in American society, there is a strong argument for more formal attention to what is referred to as adult education. Whether adult education is to be an extension of the activities of some other segment of the educational ladder or an institution in its own right, it is increasingly apparent that more and more provision must be made for education beyond the level of the traditional schools.

110

Ambrose Caliver

THE NATIONAL CONCERN FOR ADULT EDUCATION

The growing necessity for a broad program of adult education is set forth in this article by the chief of the Adult Education Section of the U.S. Office of Education. The author examines the guiding role that existing institutions and organizations must play in this undertaking.

Adult education offers such potent remedy for some of the ills of society, and such valuable aid to the individual for self-fulfillment and social adjustment, that it should be the concern of everyone. In fact, the changes characteristic of modern life make adult education a *must*. Accelerated by science and technology, these changes have made an impact on the individual and society that we can no longer view with indifference. We can no longer meet our current problems by educating only our children and youth; nor can we expect to prepare even our children and youth in the traditional sense for all the problems they will face when they become adults.

Many changes are under way that require the education of adults, but some are particularly demanding:

Our population is growing fast. By 1975, estimates say, it will reach 225 million—55 million more than we have now.

Our population is becoming more mobile, thanks to rapid developments in transportation and communication.

Our population is getting older. Medical science and better health measures are extending our lives.

Our expanding economy demands a larger and more highly qualified work force.

Tremendous advance in the production of power is resulting in speed, complexity, and bigness. This change lies at the root of nearly all other changes and transcends them all in importance. Man took most of history to advance from muscle power to horsepower, to waterpower, and then to steam, gas, and electric power. But within the past two decades he has come into possession of nuclear energy, which surpasses the earlier powers so far that there is hardly a basis of comparison.

Implications of these changes for adult education lie in their impact on the individual in every aspect of his life—as a worker, as a citizen, as a member of a family, and as a *person seeking self-fulfillment*. They become more evident in the light of trends that have developed concurrently with the changes already mentioned: Urbanization, increased leisure time, occupational changes, rising standards of living, changing character of home and family life, increase in chronic disease

From *School Life*, April 1957, 39:5-6, 10-12.

and mental illness, a "shrinking" of the world, and a change in our sense of values.

When we intelligently and honestly appraise the current scene, we see that we cannot keep abreast of the times, nor be prepared for the demands of the future, except through adult education. The needs to be met, the problems to be solved, and the opportunities to be grasped will not wait. The knowledge, skills, and understandings required in this brave—or fearful—ever-changing world must be acquired by adults *today*. It is no longer an issue whether adults *can* learn: that they can and will has been scientifically proved. Rather, the matters that concern us are these: That man's intellectual, social, and moral advancement has not kept pace with his material advancement; and that education can be a powerful aid in correcting the lag.

Most of the changes in our world are caused by forces so deep below the surface of ordinary daily experience that they are not easily discernible. Adult education can aid in identifying, describing, and explaining these forces, relating them to the day-to-day activities of citizens in such a manner that the people will understand the effects of these forces upon themselves and see how they in turn may adjust and give direction to the forces.

Another contribution that adult education can make is to restore to the individual some of the qualities he had as a child but too often has lost in the process of his growing up—the qualities of curiosity, interest, zest, self-confidence, imagination, and creativity. Certain adult education programs are developing in people the knowledge, skills, and attitudes that go far in helping them to recapture these qualities, and to accept and act upon the principles of lifelong learning, not only for their own improvement but for the national welfare. Such programs need to be multiplied and extended.

Adult education can help the Nation make full and effective use of its human resources. Even though it has been spotty and limited, adult education has already demonstrated its worth in helping to meet manpower requirements—in military and civil defense, in our national economy, and in our social and cultural life.

These demonstrations suggest the potentialities in adult education for meeting both the short-range and long-range needs of our dynamic civilization. But these potentialities cannot be fully achieved until adult education is accepted as an integral part of our regular educational programs, which in the past have been largely devoted to children and youth. Those who say that we can-

not afford the expense should remember that no nation is so poor, nor is any nation so rich, that it can justifiably neglect the education of its people.

Although many millions are now engaged in formal adult education activities, we have hardly begun to avail ourselves of our opportunities.

Not only can every citizen profit in one way or another from adult education, but some groups in the population offer a special challenge. To these, adult education is obligated to make a special contribution.

One of these groups is the undereducated. We concede that we require more and more education to live effectively in our rapidly advancing world; yet we have more than 60 million adults who have not finished high school, 44 million who have not finished the ninth grade, and nearly 10 million who are functionally illiterate.

We can better appreciate the economic significance of these figures when we realize that our modern world of work, based more and more on automation, is becoming increasingly inhospitable to the undereducated. The Department of Labor estimates that within 10 years we will have 15 million adults who are unemployable because they are inadequately trained.

Another group is our older people. During the last 50 years the lifespan in the United States has been lengthened by nearly 20 years; the general population has doubled, but the number of persons aged 45 to 64 has tripled, and the number of those who are at least 65 has quadrupled. For these older persons, adult education can do more than contribute to comforts, health, satisfactions, and happiness: it can also utilize competencies and refurbish latent talents and creative powers.

A third group worthy of particular attention is the young adults. In many respects they are the most neglected group, yet they stand in the greatest need of help. In 1950 we had 34⅓ million young men and women 15-29 years old. During the next decade, it is estimated, the number of 18-to-24-year-olds will increase by about 5 million, and the greatest increase to the labor force will be 2.7 million in the 14-to-24-year group. What these numbers imply for adult education is obvious.

Many of those young people have just left, or will soon leave, the sheltered life of the school and are plunging into the whirl of the workaday world. Others have left the protection—or lack of protection—of their parental homes to set up homes of their own. Sooner or later most of the young men will do their stint in the military forces. Still others, unable to find a job, or a mate, or a faith, may become drifters, even delinquents.

All of them stand between two worlds—one which they think they are glad to leave, the other which they approach with hesitancy and fear—and for most of them the first has ill prepared them for the second. Yet they are the persons who will perpetuate the race and rear the children, who will be our future workers, citizens, and leaders. They need knowledge, skills, understanding, and ideals, and they need them *now*.

It must not be assumed that the adult-education programs and activities now in operation are neither recognized nor appreciated. They are. Were it not for them we would be in a far worse plight than we are. A great number and variety of agencies are engaged in adult education—public and private schools, colleges and universities, professional groups, voluntary agencies, industry, labor, and agricultural groups, philanthropic foundations, government, and religious and civic groups—and the number of programs they conduct runs into the thousands.

Many of these programs are excellent, some are moderately good, still others range from mediocre to poor. Underlying them is a great variety of philosophies, principles, and policies, and an even greater variety of design and practice.

In the heterogeneity of adult education programs are seen both their strength and their weakness. Some people believe that heterogeneity reflects a good thing—the tailoring of programs to suit individual needs. Others think that it makes for confusion, waste, and lack of purpose. Still others believe that the multiplicity of agencies under many different auspices results in duplication of effort, unwholesome competition, and lack of coordination.

Whatever the deficiencies, we must live with this heterogeneity and multiplicity in organizations, programs, and efforts because these are in the tradition of America and stem from the genius of our people. Moreover, they stem from the very heterogeneity of the needs adult education is designed to meet.

But it is not in the best interest of either adult education or the Nation that we continue to tolerate deficiencies and difficulties that can be remedied or removed. It is therefore incumbent upon us to clear away the roadblocks that are preventing adult education from traveling with the speed, efficiency, and effectiveness that the times demand.

Clearing the road is not alone the concern of the professional adult educators, the teachers and lay leaders in the field, or of any single organization or group of organizations, public or private. It is the concern of all, and of each, that adult education prepare for the tasks that lie ahead; that it make itself ready to assist in meeting the needs of individuals and the Nation during the next half, or at least the next quarter, of this century.

All the agencies have some obligations in common in this matter; but certain ones, because of their very nature, have particular obligations.

For example, it would hardly be questioned that it is the responsibility of institutions of higher learning to be especially concerned with research into the various facets of adult education, and with the preparation of teachers and leaders.

That so few of these institutions are now engaged in such activities should be a matter of national concern. Because so many public school teachers are involved in various programs and activities of adult education, because the habits of continuous learning and the qualities conducive to these habits can best be cultivated in childhood and youth, and because a good elementary and secondary school program depends mostly on the education and enlightenment of the adults in a community, it seems essential that prospective and inservice teachers be given an opportunity to learn about the need for adult education and the principles underlying it.

Professional associations, voluntary organizations, and certain lay groups, because of their unique position and peculiar role in our social and cultural advancement, have their own major contributions to make. One of these, it seems, is to help interpret the implications of scientific and technological progress for the average citizen, and to create a climate conducive to adult education in the communities and in the Nation as a whole. These organizations may also be helpful to governments in developing and maintaining a sensitivity to the education needs of their adult citizens, and in translating that sensitivity into public action.

The major responsibility of the public schools and certain other agencies that conduct programs of adult education is so obvious that it will not be discussed here. Suffice it to say that the qualifications and dedication of the personnel and leaders of these agencies should be of such high order that the best and latest in the theory and practice of adult education may find through them a ready channel of communication to the ultimate consumer—the average citizen and adult learner—who is the *raison d'etre* for all our concern.

Another challenge to adult education lies in the ample evidence all about us that many of our citizens do not yet have a penetrating understanding of the principles underlying American institutions, purposes, and ideals as they are exemplified in our system of free enterprise, our public school system, our practices stemming from the Bill of Rights and our belief in the worth and dignity of every individual. Many adults have yet to feel the stimulation that comes from seeing the application of these principles in everyday life. These are matters that all Americans should understand and feel, particularly as they apply in the realm of human relations. And to the extent that they do not understand, they weaken our national effort to demonstrate the efficacy of our leadership in the free world, and pose a threat to our way of life at home.

The average American citizen needs also a clearer and better understanding of the world situation and his country's part in it. This need President Eisenhower emphasized in his recent inaugural address—

"Now this is our home—yet this is not the whole of our world. For our world is where our full destiny lies—with men, of all peoples and all nations who are free or would be free . . .

"We recognize and accept our own deep involvement in the destiny of men everywhere."

Giving this world outlook to those who are to make decisions is an adult education responsibility of the first order. That it be given speedily is of national concern, a concern that the President voiced when he added—

"And for them—and so for us—this is no time of ease or of rest."

Time is of the essence!

To meet this need we cannot rely upon the education of children and youth alone. The changes are too swift and demanding. The quickest, the surest, and the most effective way of meeting it is through a comprehensive program of adult education, designed specifically for this purpose and executed with intelligence and boldness.

Another need, one that especially concerns the individual, has four facets that offer challenges to adult education:

To help the individual to remedy the defects and fill the gaps in his earlier schooling.

To show him how to function effectively in his various roles and to adjust and contribute to a rapidly changing world.

To help him understand and adjust to the changes that automatically occur in him as he grows older.

To develop in him the desire, the knowledge, the skills, and the attitudes for lifelong learning and continued self-improvement and self-fulfillment.

One of the greatest needs that adult education can help to meet is the need for wide diffusion of the knowledge, methods, and spirit underlying the advances that have given us the new world. This must take place before we can begin to understand and accept what the technological and scientific advances mean for a genuine improvement in our living.

Here adult education has a special obligation to those persons who have completed their formal schooling. Discharging that obligation requires better communication and cooperation between our creative thinkers and the rest of us, so that we can translate the results of science and technology into the thought, language, and behavior of the average citizen. It is important to the national interest that we quickly find ways of using the gifts of science and technology to improve the quality of our lives. To do so, we must depend heavily on the various types and forms of adult education.

The problem of health illustrates well another challenge to adult education. Many of the illnesses of modern man are psychosomatic. Certain chronic and organic ailments that today are rapidly increasing are related to the mind and the emotions. Other diseases and physical ailments are related to nutritional habits and the use of leisure time. All of this adds up to the fact that much of the poor health afflicting many of us is behavioral.

Just to mention this fact is to indicate the responsibility of adult education. By providing individuals with opportunities to learn the facts of health and to develop habits and attitudes conducive to health, adult education can help to alleviate some physical ailments and to prevent others. Authorities tell us that an important aspect of today's diseases, in contrast to those of the past, is that their detection and treatment rely more heavily on the individual and his own behavior, more on ideas than on drugs, more on education and guidance of the individual and the community than on direction and prescription from experts. It is this very circumstance that presents such a challenge to adult education.

We also have needs within the field of adult education itself. We need a better articulation between adult education and the other areas of education. We need to improve the quality of teaching and supervision; to develop programs, materials, and methods that are better suited to the interests and experiences of adults. The several groups and agencies conducting programs need to do more cooperating and coordinating; they need to work together to clarify and agree on terms, definitions, and policies. The various workers need to communicate more with each other.

These needs, although relatively simple, are highly essential. Moreover, they are of national concern and must be approached with the same intelligence, highmindedness, and dedication as all the others.

Overarching them all, however, is the need for a complete and fundamental educational reorientation. In the face of the cataclysmic changes we have been discussing, such an orientation is necessary if adult education is to be conceived in its proper context. It will require some people to revise their ideas about the nature and purposes of education, as well as about organization, administration, and financing of education. Especially will it require many to take a new approach to instructional materials and methods, to learning and the learner.

If we are to meet the challenge posed by the prospects of the last half of this century, we must be as imaginative, as creative, and as bold as the scientists and engineers have been in creating the world that presents this challenge. Timid, weak, and limited approaches will not suffice. Reshuffling the old ideas and doing a good job of educational housekeeping will not suffice. More attention to enrollments and class-attendance reports, to budgets, units, credits, diplomas, degrees, and standards—important as these are—will not suffice. In fact, these things alone will have no significance in the long run, except in relation to the reorientation that is so overwhelmingly needed.

If the many needs are to be met, each program should have the benefit of an overall synthesizing, coordinating, and guiding agency—not necessarily administrative—which is sufficiently removed from the sphere of competition, tension, and vested interest to enlist the confidence of all concerned. It should operate from a high level and in the interest of all the people. It should have authority, but should exercise it in a disinterested and neutral manner. It must have an overview of the whole field, with its sights high and its horizon wide. It must be guided by a broad philosophy, practical idealism, and deep insight. And it must be motivated by interest in and dedication to the total community welfare.

Wherever programs are operating without the services of such an agency, it is the obligation of the citizens to explore the possibilities of revamping an existing agency for that purpose, or to create a new one.

On local and State levels, the public school systems might meet the need, or at least take steps to initiate such an agency. As the educational arm of government, they are the servants of all the people and hence have an obligation to exercise a concern in the public interest.

On the regional level, several school systems and/or universities might take the lead in their service areas.

On the national level, the Office of Education seems to have a clear responsibility: to work in cooperation with other Federal agencies and national organizations.

Those who say that this is too ambitious and comprehensive an undertaking should direct their attention to the discovery and development of nuclear energy, to the plans for greater use of automation in our economic system, and to the worldwide plans for the Geophysical Year. These projects and activities were brought to successful fruition only through cooperation and coordination by many different individuals and agencies and through articulation, synthesis, and integration of many different processes, all on a broad and long-term scale. It took vision, patience, and determination.

The goals of adult education greatly transcend in importance the goals of the projects just referred to. In fact, unless we achieve the long-range goals for adult education, achievements in these other spheres will eventually be nullified.

It is of national concern that the people of America become aware of the trends that make adult education more necessary today than ever before . . . appreciative of what and how adult education can contribute to the solution of many of our most important and urgent problems . . . sensitive to the ways in which adult education can give us deeper insights into the meaning of life and the relatedness of its various parts . . . and understanding of adult education as an aid in reconciling the conflict between material and human progress and values.

These goals are of such concern to the well-being of all our citizens, and to the maintenance and advancement of our way of life that it is the obligation of local, State, and Federal governments to give the people every possible and appropriate assistance in developing and using, to the optimum, all the available resources in the achievement of those goals.

THE CHARACTER OF THE CURRICULUM

Undoubtedly the way in which the educational system is constructed has a great deal to do with the effectiveness of our schools. Yet organizational factors must always take second place to the curriculum itself. There is good reason for this: administration and organization merely adjust and service the various parts of the educational machine, while curriculum determines how and for what purpose that machine is used. The word *curriculum* is usually defined as the whole body of courses offered in a school system. It is derived from a Latin word meaning "race course," a point which any modern student can appreciate.

Unlike medical, legal, or other specialized advanced institutions, the elementary and secondary schools find themselves in a position where they must constantly defend their curricular practices. Everyone is an expert on the curriculum of the common school because everyone has been in school, an experience which invariably seems to leave vivid memories. For this reason the public-school teacher can never take the social usefulness of his subject for granted in the way that college professors often do. If he is to convince the many doubting Thomases of his community that he and his school are really doing the job they ought to be doing, then he must understand the curriculum thoroughly.

The seventeen selections which follow may be grouped into five rough categories. Readings 111 to 114 deal with aspects of the *subject-matter curriculum,* and the dissatisfaction with it which so many different people have so often expressed. Readings 115 to 117 are concerned with the *core curriculum,* by means of which the Progressive educators proposed to integrate subject matter. The article by Donald Oliver (Reading 118) deals with a third alternative, the *unit concept* (a teaching procedure advanced by Professor H. C. Morrison). Next come five treatments of the *activity* curriculum (Readings 119 to 123), a curriculum theory which represents the high-water mark of Progressive curricular reform efforts. Readings 124 to 127 might be combined under the heading *Whither the Curriculum?*—for they express various facets of the dislike for certain curricular reforms, a dislike which has risen to a crescendo since the end of World War II.

There are many other forms of curriculum, but for the beginning student the selected divisions presented in this section should serve to introduce a complex subject by acquainting him with the dimensions and focal issues of the twentieth century curriculum controversy.

111

Carleton Washburne

THE CASE FOR SUBJECTS IN THE CURRICULUM

Ever since formal education began, the curriculum has been organized around subjects. What this means in personal terms is that we study special areas of knowledge, one at a time, and that some of us prepare to teach one such special area to the students of tomorrow. In broad theoretical terms it means that we subdivide knowledge into logical segments, which in combination should cover the main fields of human knowledge. There has always been controversy about which subjects are most important (see Reading 3), but not until Progressive education arrived on the scene did anyone question whether choice of subject matter should determine curriculum structure and change.

The Progressive leaders *did* question subject matter, and they forced their opponents (those who were in colleges of education came to be called "Essentialists") into a formal defense of what had previously seemed too obvious to require defending. Progressives argued that the promotion and direction of individual growth and development were the primary purposes of organized education, and that the curriculum should be organized psychologically to achieve this purpose. Essentialists retorted that transmitting the skills and fundamental knowledge upon which modern civilization is based was the primary purpose of education, and that the curriculum should be organized logically to make the task of mastering this essential knowledge as simple as possible. The article below attempts to reconcile these two viewpoints. How successfully the author accomplishes this purpose is for the reader to judge.

The traditional breaking up of the curriculum into subjects, each of which was kept in a water-tight compartment, unrelated to the others and unrelated to the child's life, has resulted in a natural and wholesome reaction. This reaction has led to "activities programs," "project method," and "integration."

Like most reactions, this one has swung to the opposite extreme. It is supposed that one center of interest must be the basis for all of the child's work, and that it is a violation of sound psychology and of the child's rights, to have a period in the day set aside for arithmetic and another period for spelling. I remember visiting a school that boasted of its "centers of interest." In one grade the "center of interest" for the month was fish. There the history had to do with the history of fishing; the geography, with fisheries; the reading was all on fish and fisher folk; the compositions were on the same subject; the spelling words were chosen from this field; even the arithmetic problems all dealt with the price and weight and quantities of fish. This story may sound fishy, but I assure you it is true.

More intelligent attempts at integration use some one activity—sometimes a chance activity resulting from the interest of a child—on which the whole class can center. As the children carry this activity or project forward, the teacher sees to it that they do not avoid any arithmetical, literary, artistic, or other implications—in fact she often drags in these implications by the heels. When she doesn't, she guiltily smuggles in an arithmetic period or a spelling period and says nothing about it.

A complete interrelation of all things a child studies is unimportant and unnecessary. Life itself is full of separate, unrelated activities. We adults go to a movie or a dance. We read a book, attend a luncheon or dinner. We go to a concert or a baseball game. We do certain jobs that are parts of our vocation. We find no disintegration of our lives as a result of our divergent and diverse activities. On the contrary, the variety adds zest to living.

What is really important is that each thing we teach the child be integrated with his own life and his experience. It must fulfill some need; it must give expression to some impulse; it must contribute to some thinking. It must, in short, have significance. But the significance of one thing may be quite different from that of another, and no harm whatever is done by variety of experience, provided that the separation is between one subject and another, and not a separation between the subject and the child.

In mastering a skill, readiness and ripeness are necessary. Any test shows a wide divergence between the slowest and the fastest child in a class—the range is usually at least four years. To assume that one center of interest, one project, is going to result in learning processes that fit equally children of widely disparate stages of maturity is to ignore the facts.

In mastering a skill certain technics need practice, and the amount of practice needed varies with individuals. If all children in a class are

From *NEA Journal*, January 1937, 26:5.

trying to master the same technic at the same time with the same amount of drill, even tho it has been "motivated" by a project or "integrated" with the other subjects in a center of interest, the children are deprived of their right to wait until they are ripe before being required to try to master a topic. The psychology of learning is ignored.

In mastering knowledge, a certain order and organization are needed. So, too, are certain foundations. To give a bit of knowledge here and a bit of knowledge there, because they happen to be related to a project or a center of interest, is to fail in the orderly development that characterizes the thinking of an educated person.

It is manifestly absurd to suppose it contrary to sound education to be systematic and orderly, to suppose that thoroness is the antithesis of good learning. Yet the time has come when a person almost has to apologize for a kind of education that develops a subject in an orderly, systematic manner.

The answer does not lie in a reversion to the old compartmentalization of the curriculum, but neither does it lie in an attempt at complete correlation and the kind of "integration" which assumes that all subjects must be integrated with each other and with some center of interest or grow out of some one activity.

The solution lies in having a basic course required of each child as he reaches the right stage of development, and including in that course only those items which really function or can be made to function in the experience and training of the child. Each of these things—call them subjects if you wish—should be taught in relation to the child's life and interests. They should be taught when the child is ready to use them thru having his interest aroused and when he has reached the mental age found by research to be most suitable to the learning of a given topic. And in doing this, the school may well use a number of the old categories—arithmetic is, after all, quite different from social science, and spelling is not related to creativeness and initiative.

On the other hand, any balanced educational program must provide a rich background of experience and activities. It must provide, thru electives and thru opportunities in connection with common enterprises or activities, a chance for each child to find and follow his own special interests and abilities; a chance for him to use originality, creativeness and initiative; and most decidedly opportunities for him to work cooperatively with his fellows and to develop a sound social consciousness. These are basic parts of his education. But so, too, is the mastery of those fundamental skills and that body of common knowledge which are essential to living in an organized society.

112

Noah Webster

COMMENTS ON EDUCATION

These extracts from the letters of Noah Webster, America's first great educator, reflect the fact that the old subject-matter curriculum was anything but rigid and changeless. It was under ceaseless attack, and curriculum experts were constantly involved in making reluctant concessions to the demands of critics. To be sure, the changes sought were nearly all of one kind—to add another subject to the curriculum so that students might be better informed about important new areas of knowledge. This pressure for change is not a thing of the past; today we hear demands that such new subjects as demography, social psychology, and cybernetics be added to the secondary-school curriculum.

Webster, himself an educational reformer in his younger days, was by the late 1830's alarmed over this constant tinkering with the curriculum. The objections which he raised are still live issues among contemporary educators. Webster was a publisher, not a teacher, and he had no interest in defending the pedagogical status quo. Rather he argues from the point of view of the students and the public.

New Haven, February 27, 1841.

Dear Sir,

I have seen in the *Hampshire Gazette* a series of remarks on the subject of establishing an institution in Hampshire County for a thorough education in the languages and useful sciences. Whether such an institution is wanted or not, I shall not inquire. If it is, perhaps some improvements in the academies already existing in the county might supersede the necessity of another. It appears to me that in general our citizens are too much disposed to *multiply* seminaries of learning rather than to *improve* the course of studies in those which now exist.

In my view the prevailing errors in this country are the hurrying of pupils too much in their studies and the imposing too much labor upon young minds by teaching them too many things. The great difference between the classical attainments of scholars in England and Germany and in this country arises chiefly from those errors. Neither in Latin, Greek, nor English are our youth thoroughly instructed in the initiatory studies. They obtain a superficial knowledge of the rudiments of language, and are then urged forward prematurely to higher studies, and, in many cases, to studies of sciences which they can never want; for which they have no use, either as citizens or Christians. In this way many children spend time in learning that which can not be useful to them in their occupations for procuring subsistence, while they neglect to learn what they want every day.

We have among us men of visionary views, who seem to suppose that education in literature and the sciences will cure all our public evils. In this they are most wofully mistaken. Our public evils are not to be cured by the improvement of the *head* but by the reformation of the *heart*. Christ and his apostles never attempted to reform mankind by philosophy.

This hurrying plan of education is adapted to make superficial scholars. Accurate scholarship is not to be gained by leaping over the first elements, but by taking step by step and, as Locke has remarked, *by learning one thing at a time.*

I have been struck with surprise to see how men engaged in promoting education mistake the laws of the human mind. It is this mistake which has originated the scheme of teaching *spelling* and *definitions* at the same time. This scheme can be executed only in familiar words: it can

not be extended to abstract terms or words of multifarious meaning without leaving error or defect in knowledge.

I once saw objections made to the reading lessons in Webster's *Spelling Book* amounting to this: that these lessons consist of short and detached sentences having no connection as in continuous discourse. True: but this is one of their principal excellences. Such sentences are best adapted to the capacities of children of four, five, and six years of age. They are learned with ease and remembered; whereas a long continuous discourse would be read, but forgotten. A book of rudiments is not intended to teach long lessons on any subject; it is to teach words and familiar truth. It is this brevity, which constitutes the great value of *proverbs* and *maxims*, of which Solomon has given a sublime example. The same may be said of our popular proverbs, many of which contain important truth in a nutshell. These being short and easily committed to memory are learned and repeated by our yeomanry from generation to generation. But the sentiments or truths which they contain in continuous discourse would never be learned and repeated at all. It is surprising that men who superintend instruction should make such mistakes in estimating the powers of the human mind.

Since I have mentioned Webster's *Spelling Book*, I would remark further that a great part of the *lessons for reading* consist of definitions expressed in correct language. I doubt whether there is a book extant which conveys so much valuable truth in the like compass. This truth is learned by the process of learning to read.

I wish to see our systems of education improved, but I wish to see *more practical* and *less theoretical* instruction. . . .

October 30, 1837.

. . . The common people have no occasion for one half the studies or sciences proposed; and the time given to them would be wasted on the greatest part of the children. Besides, I think it doubtful whether most parents would or could spare their children's time for such studies. Boys who are to be farmers and mechanics must put their muscles into exercise at an early age, that is, at eight or nine years old; or they will fail of the strength and firmness requisite for manual labor. If boys are to attend to books only till they are fourteen or sixteen years old, if they are not averse to study, they will contract such a fondness for books that they will not readily leave them for work; nor have the habit of loving work, which is essential to steady perseverance in labor and, of course, to success.

From *Letters of Noah Webster*, Harry R. Warfel, ed. (New York: Library Publishers, 1953), pp. 507, 518–520.

Besides, the schemes of education proposed will encourage that indisposition to labor and foster the disrelish or contempt of it which now manifest themselves in all parts of our country. All young persons seem desirous to *get above* manual labor and be *gentlemen,* whether they have property or not, or, at least, to seek a living in some occupation more genteel than farming and mechanical employment. This disposition is already an evil, and if too much encouraged will fill the country with idlers who have a smattering of learning, just enough to inflate their vanity without furnishing them with ability to be useful. . . .

113

Charles W. Eliot

THE NEW EDUCATION

One of the most far-reaching changes in the history of the American educational curriculum was sponsored a century ago by the young president of Harvard, Charles W. Eliot. This was the famous "elective system." It was the direct result of the curriculum changes which had upset Noah Webster. So many new courses of study had been added to the college curriculum that no student could possibly take more than a fraction of them in four years. Which courses were of most worth? And should these essential courses be required of all students? As this selection demonstrates, Eliot agreed with Herbert Spencer (Reading 3) that science courses were of most worth. Nevertheless, he declared that except for English grammar and literature the choice (or election) of courses should be left entirely to the individual student.

This pattern was quickly adopted by nearly all American colleges and high schools of any size, but it soon became obvious that the elective system had serious weaknesses. Professor W. C. Bagley, in a study conducted in 1908, found that most high-school students chose courses because they were easy to pass, not because of the educational values which they recognized in the subject itself. Critics of the times began to ask if the proper aims of education were being turned into a mockery by the elective system.

. . . The American people are fighting the wilderness, physical and moral, on the one hand, and on the other are struggling to work out the awful problem of self-government. For this fight they must be trained and armed. No thoughtful American in active life reaches manhood without painfully realizing the deficiencies and shortcomings of his own early training. He knows how ignorance balks and competition overwhelms, but he knows also the greatness of the material prizes to be won. He is anxious to have his boys better equipped for the American man's life than he himself was. It is useless to commend to him the good old ways, the established methods. He has a decided opinion that there are or ought to be better ways. He will not believe that the same methods which trained some boys well for the life of fifty or one hundred years ago are applicable to his son; for the reason, that the kind of man which he wants his son to make did not exist in all the world fifty years ago. So without any clear idea of what a practical education is, but still with some tolerably distinct notion of what it is not, he asks, "How can I give my boy a practical education?" . . .

We wish to review the recent experience of this country in the attempt to organize a system of education based chiefly upon the pure and applied sciences, the living European languages, and mathematics, instead of upon Greek, Latin, and mathematics, as in the established college

From *The Atlantic Monthly,* February 1869, 23:203-205, March 1869, 23:366-367.

system. The history of education is full of still-born theories; the literature of the subject is largely made up of theorizing; whoever reads it much will turn with infinite relief to the lessons of experience. But it should be observed that it is experience in mass, the experience of institutions, the experience of a generation, and not individual experience, which is of value. To have been a schoolmaster or college professor thirty years only too often makes a man an unsafe witness in matters of education: there are flanges on his mental wheels which will only fit one gauge. On the other hand, it must be acknowledged that conservatism is never more respectable than in education, for nowhere are the risks of change greater. Our survey of the institutions which represent the new education in this country will be absolutely impersonal; the merits of different systems are to be discussed, not the characters or qualifications of the men who have invented, or worked under, these systems. This limitation of the discussion is judicious, from all points of view; for in no country is so little attention paid by parents and students to the reputation of teachers for genius and deep learning as in our own. Faradays, Rumfords, and Cuviers would get very few pupils here, if their teachers were unmethodical and objectless,—if, in short, they taught under a bad general system. Spasmodic and ill-directed genius cannot compete in the American community with methodical, careful teaching by less inspired men. This American instinct seems, on the whole, to be a sagacious one. Nevertheless, it is only when genius warms and invigorates a wise and well-administered system, that the best conditions are attained. . . .

But now some one may ask, To what good end all [the] discourse about the improvement of technical education? Are not Americans already the most ingenious people on the earth? Have we not invented mowers, and sewing-machines, and the best printing-presses? Are we not doing countless things by machinery which other people do by hand? Is there really any need of instructing Americans in the application of science to the arts? The answers to these incredulous suggestions are not far to seek. In the first place, it is emphatically true that Americans have invented a large number of labor-saving machines of the greatest value. They are powerfully incited to this sort of invention by the dearness of labor in this country. Secondly, this same scarcity of laborers, and the consequent abundance of work for all willing hands, enable an American to pursue the precarious rewards of invention, perhaps for years, with the certainty that if, after

all, he wins no prize in the lottery, he can readily find some steady employment to keep his old age from absolute want. But if a European once falls out of the ranks of industry, he has infinite trouble, in case he fails in his adventures, to recover any standing room whatever in society. An American may do with impunity, and without real wrong perhaps, what a European could only do in the spirit of the most reckless gambler or in the confidence of inspired genius. Freedom, and the newness and breadth of the land, explain this favored condition of the American. But it is to be noticed that the chief American successes in invention are of one sort,—machinery and mechanical appliances. In other departments of invention, which require greater knowledge, we are obviously borrowers, rather than lenders. How many millions of dollars are sunk every few years in mining enterprises, through sheer ignorance? Freiberg and Swansea have to be called upon to smelt American ores. The best managers of American print-works receive patterns of the latest French designs by every steamer. The aniline colors are not American discoveries. There are hardly twenty miles of good road, in the European sense, in the whole United States. The various chemical industries are chiefly foreign. American ingenuity has been of more limited range than is commonly imagined. Not a few reputed American inventions are really of European origin. But, however this may be, we may zealously endeavor to strengthen the scientific professions in this country without being a whit less proud of the undisputed achievements of American ingenuity. It is not a question of promoting fertility of invention by improving technical education. Inventors are a law unto themselves. What the country needs is a steady supply of men well trained in recognized principles of science and art, and well informed about established practice. We need engineers who thoroughly understand what is already known at home and abroad about mining, road and bridge building, railways, canals, waterpowers, and steam machinery; architects who have thoroughly studied their art; builders who can at least construct buildings which will not fall down; chemists and metallurgists who know what the world has done and is doing in the chemical arts, and in the extraction and working of metals; manufacturers who appreciate what science and technical skill can do for the works which they superintend.

Americans must not sit down contented with their position among the industrial nations. We have inherited civil liberty, social mobility, and immense native resources. The advantages we thus hold over the European nations are inestimable. The question is, not how much our freedom can do for us unaided, but how much we can help freedom by judicious education. We appreciate better than we did ten years ago that true progress in this country means progress for the world. In organizing the new education, we do not labor for ourselves alone. Freedom will be glorified in her works.

114

Heywood Broun

BEYOND THE THREE R'S

In his day, Heywood Broun was one of the nation's most respected newspaper columnists. His specialties, oddly enough, were the fields of dramatic criticism and organized labor. In this selection he writes as a labor spokesman, and his complaint is that the existing subject-matter curriculum is prejudiced against labor.

A comparison of Broun with Eliot (Reading 113) and Webster (Reading 112) will show that their approaches are virtually identical. Each seeks to reform the curriculum by changing the subject-matter emphasis. Webster speaks for an American majority of farmers and merchants, Eliot for the new America of businessmen and technologists, Broun for the industrial wage-laborer. But each man accepts the primacy of logically organized subject matter in the curriculum.

. . . Everybody in America remembers periods of abundance in our national life which were also periods of panic and great suffering. People have starved while fruit and produce rotted in the fields or freight yards. Prices were so low that it was not worth any man's time to move them. The problem of distribution can't be wiped out of the picture.

However, if it is true that labor costs tend to fall below subsistence levels on account of the competition between those who are too young to have acquired experience and those whose skill begins to slacken, then it would seem the part of common sense to keep some of these competitors out of the market. Naturally there should be an effective child-labor law to keep the very young from underbidding their elders. But there must be something on the positive side as well. You cannot keep young men and women idle even for the sake of preserving jobs for those in the group above forty-five years of age. The answer lies in a vast extension of public education. And I think that in addition to extending facilities there should be a change in the general nature of the curriculum. I have an interesting letter along these lines from Dr. Duncan M. Chalmers:

From *The New Republic*, June 1, 1938, 95:100-101.

"It is about time for laboring groups to begin a concerted attack on our educational institutions. There is no reason why labor should be taken in by cries of the necessities of maintaining the purity of academic pursuits. The only people who gain by such a stand are those who have no intention of seeing labor obtain a real measure of economic democracy. An educational policy that has no rapport with social actualities is a menace to security and a bulwark of reaction. It is inexcusable that recent discoveries in physics, chemistry and biology should remain laboratory curiosities until such a time as some private concern sees a profit in their application. Most of these advances are the result of collective research and can only be socially useful when applied for a collective purpose.

Our public schools with their meager technical and scientific culture turn out only unskilled or semi-skilled workers when we consider the comparative complexity of our means of production. This is not a necessary state of affairs. A more adequate scientific culture can be developed and made available to the average boy and girl. A social structure headed by a few clever people and without the intelligent coöperation of the average man or woman is a forerunner of tyranny and destruction. As things stand now, both labor leaders and political leaders in this country are at the mercy of technicians whose own training invokes no recognition of their social responsibilities. Millikan, Compton and other great scientific names are rarely associated with social reforms and collective benefits. The "applied" scientists on the TVA, technicians of the USPH Service, geneticists, biochemists, animal experimenters *et al.* in federal, state and coöperative institutions are the genuine foundation architects of a better social order. Their work has much to gain when closely allied with laboring groups; but their work is futile when tied to a profit economy."

It may be argued of course that if we are suffering from technological unemployment an increase in efficiency may leave us even worse off than before. But obviously the slack would have to be taken up not only by the shorter working life. It is not fantastic to see the possibility of a society in which the average man remains in the formative stage of training until he is twenty-five and then slips off the harness at forty-five. Naturally certain indispensable persons of high talent would go on beyond this period. But the rest would be in the reserve corps.

Moreover, while we are rearranging curricula, I would go even farther than Dr. Chalmers. The study of the liberal arts might well undergo revision in a democratic scheme of education. The fight against the dead languages is being won. Today the student can get by with small Latin and less Greek. That is just as well, for the insistence on such subjects tended to create a Mandarin class. Naturally classical scholarship should not perish from the earth, but it can safely be entrusted to specialists and volunteers.

What concerns me is the study of living languages and particularly English in our secondary schools and colleges. If I speak bitterly of the time I was forced to spend with "Silas Marner," I will undoubtedly be told that much progress

has been made since the days when I was a scholar—if indeed the name applies. But the foundation of instruction in English still depends upon the forced perusal of a certain number of required books. I hold that the average man would have far more fervor for Shakespeare if he met him up an alley rather than in a classroom.

To my mind the fundamental essential in the study of English should be training to enable the pupil to read a newspaper intelligently. This instruction should give the pupil the ability to read between the lines and also make himself acquainted with the invisible footnotes which lie at the bottom of many columns printed in our daily press. If the newspapers of America fall very far short of keeping all channels of information clear, the fault lies largely with the reader. He is not critical enough by half. Sometimes he has a vague uneasy feeling that he is being fooled and done in, but he is not expert enough to put his finger on the trouble. When we have developed a public which demands more complete coverage and an increase in impartial reporting, those demands must and will be met.

Again it seems to me that many phases of the science of economics by which we live or die are taught not at all in high school and only indifferently in the colleges. All of us are concerned with the problem of trade unionism. It touches those who belong to unions and those who do not. It is a subject which comes up in our daily life constantly in a score of forms. And these are not problems which can be solved by any rule of thumb.

Orators urge us, and quite properly I believe, to work for the more abundant life in the United States. But we will not get very far along that road unless we know the precise nature of our objectives and how they may be attained. Education must be modeled to meet the requirements of the common man. Labor should not forever be crucified upon a curriculum.

115

Joseph S. Butterweck

CORE CURRICULUM—THE IDEAL

The rumblings of dissatisfaction with the "crowded curriculum" which had resulted from the elective system were intensified between 1900 and 1914 by the ideas of John Dewey and the rise of Progressive education. Discontent exploded after World War I in the form of two related proposals for curricular reform. On the college level it was the survey-course movement, designed to replace the large number of departmental introductory courses with a few broad interdepartmental survey courses. On the elementary and secondary levels it was a core curriculum, whose distinctive feature was a two- to four-hour course, required of all students, providing a core of "common learnings."

"Core" was a word which every teacher had to comprehend during the 1920's and 1930's. This was no easy matter, for "core" meant so many different things to so many different people that a vast amount of confusion developed. Since one group of core supporters expected it to give students a broader and better knowledge of subject matter, while another saw it as a device to destroy both subject-matter divisions and subject-matter emphases, the confusion should not be surprising. Professor Butterweck here presents a lucid description of the thinking of three important groups which carried the core curriculum to many successes in the United States.

Words are merely symbols whereby one conveys meaning to others. But when a word assumes a variety of meanings it conveys nothing but confusion. This is the state in which we find the terms "Core" and "Core Curriculum" today.

With one group of educators the word "core" is used synonymously with "minimum essentials." It means those courses or that subject matter to which everyone should be exposed at a particular grade level.

To a second and rather large group it means giving one teacher the responsibility to teach two or more of the commonly accepted areas of knowledge. To this group core is largely an administrative device to insure greater concern for the growth and development of the pupil.

A third group, small in number, views core as a means of helping pupils gain experience in areas of living which provide wholesome growth opportunities at their stage of development. To this group core is the kernel around which experience revolves; it becomes the *raison d'être* for the subject matter to be selected, the skills to be developed, the understandings to be acquired. To this group core is a method of learning.

Let us briefly analyze these three concepts of core to note their psychological and philosophical implications.

1. *Core as minimum essentials for general education.* What is the subject matter that should be taught to every twelve-year-old or seventh grader? Is it certain rules in English usage? Certain classics that are supposed to represent the best in literature? Certain mathematical skills? Certain knowledge of the science of one's environment or the social-civic problems of contemporary life?

These questions were answered in the negative long before the term core came into use as a curriculum device. The idea that a common body of knowledge can be found that is a *sine qua non* for any individual at any age in any environment runs counter to that psychology of adjustment that experimentation has taught us to be valid.

Any concept of core, therefore, that consists of a fixed body of knowledge to be acquired at a particular age must be eliminated as a basis for the organization of a secondary-school curriculum.

2. *Core as an administrative device.* The idea of a self-contained class unit is traditionally the property of the elementary school. It was only for a short period that departmentalization crept into the intermediate grades, at a time when the efficient teaching of a fixed body of subject matter challenged the educator. That period passed when we recognized the child rather than subject matter as the center of the school's concern.

It is but natural, therefore, that the idea of the self-contained class should be accepted as an essential step in the solution of the curriculum problem in the secondary school, particularly in view of the fact that the secondary school is now embracing the philosophy of education on which the elementary school has based its curriculum revision.

But does it follow that similarity of philosophy must be associated with similar implementation of the philosophy? Is control of a class by one teacher necessary to safeguard the integrity of the pupil? Is there not virtue in a pupil's contact with the personality of several teachers, provided that there is a consistency of treatment by them? Does not much of the education of the adolescent grow out of his adjustment to a variety of adult per-

From *School and Society*, October 4, 1952, 76:213-215.

sonalities, each contributing a kind of enthusiasm, a type of conformity, a quality of sympathy, a form of autocracy—all contributing to the development of a social resourcefulness of quality which helps adults make adjustments to the several problems of living in a complex society? How can he acquire these characteristics if his adjustment demands in school are straight line to one adult personality?

Another shortcoming arises out of this self-contained, class-controlled-by-one-teacher philosophy. Pupils are different in interest, in ability, in personality. Teachers are just as different in interest, in ability, and in personality. While one teacher may be a wholesome stimulation to a given pupil, that same teacher may be "poison" to another pupil. One teacher, because of his interest in, enthusiasm for, and ability to guide the pupil's learning in the field of literature, brings out the best in a pupil with special aptitude in literary activities. A budding writer or literary critic or an intelligent consumer of the arts may be found through such a teacher.

Likewise, the teacher, who is a lover of nature, to whom the birds, the trees, the butterflies, or the September skies are objects of intimate communion and who can impart this enthusiasm to others, will find an appreciative audience among younger adolescents. But such a teacher may have little concern about the social implications of the subject of his interests. In the role of a social-studies teacher he would have little of himself to give; he would be just another teacher; but as a stimulator of interest in nature he is a genius.

Shall we deprive our pupils of these unique teacher personalities in order to gain the advantages of the self-contained, single-teacher class?

3. *Core as an experience center.* Modern philosophy of education buttressed by an organismic psychology of learning dictates that that learning is most valuable which clusters around and emanates from a single purpose accepted by the learner as important to him at the moment. This central purpose may be a problem to be solved or it may be something to be created—a material object, an idea, or a work of art.

Those who promote the concept of core that we designate herein as "an administrative device" frequently accept this point of view of curriculum construction. They assume that this concept of learning emerges readily when one teacher is responsible for a class. But in so doing they lose sight of the sparsity of creative intelligence in the human race. Or perhaps we ought to say that the method we use in educating teachers tends to neutralize such creative intelligence as was supplied by nature. . . .

The American concept of democracy is moving from that of competition to that of co-operation. Gradually the techniques used to educate our children and youth are assuming the co-operation rather than the competition pattern.

Unfortunately, our higher education is generally lagging behind in this respect. The competitive examination, the fact-cramming and "regurgitating" lecture method, the fractionalized nonfunctional curriculum are all too common in higher education in our schools of education as well as in our liberal arts colleges.

Students too frequently are attracted to teaching as a profession because they succeeded in this type of "ivory-tower" living rather than because they have acquired the attitude and skills essential to help youth develop the abilities essential for success in a democratic society.

The greatest problem confronting public-school administrators today is, therefore, one of inservice education of teachers, that of reorienting the teacher from the competitive fact-learning concept of learning to that of co-operative planning and functional living, to what today is being referred to as a life-adjustment curriculum.

Teachers whose education in secondary school and college was devoid of learning through experience cannot adjust themselves readily to an experience-centered curriculum. They need much help to reorient their own way of life. Left to their own resources they are likely to fail or to revert to what they know through their own school experience—the lecture or telling type of learning or the teacher-controlled question and answer recitation.

The group-dynamics movement is, however, making us aware of the fact that there is more professional potential in a small group working as a unit than there is in each member of the group working individually. Schools which have used small groups of teachers co-operatively responsible for the growth and development of groups of pupils—the school-within-a-school concept—have discovered that the experience curriculum is more likely to emerge than if these teachers worked individually either in their subject-matter areas or in a self-contained core situation.

Teachers must live what they expect of their pupils. The group dynamics involved in the co-operative enterprise among pupils applies equally well to teachers. To work co-operatively there must be an agreed-upon common objective; this objective must be definite, tangible, and possible of attainment; it must be the core around which activity revolves and from which the sustenance emanates that gives the activity vitality. For the teachers this is the growth and development of a group of pupils. . . .

The ideal core curriculum has six characteristics:

1. Experience rather than a definite body of subject matter to be acquired must be its *raison d'être*.

2. The ability of the pupil to control a constantly expanding phase of life's problems must be the basis for measuring its success.

3. The maximum use of the school's resources (particularly the varying teacher personalities) must be the administration's ideal for organization.

4. Consistency in the values to be imposed upon or exacted from pupils must emerge from the co-operative pooling of the individual values of the several teacher personalities.

5. The individual pupil's self-realization in a social setting must be the ultimate objective sought.

6. All of those areas of life from which the problems of adult living arise must become the matrix out of which pupil experiences emerge.

All of this means that, if the school is to be society's agent to insure its constant progress toward the democratic ideal, it must enable its youth to taste dynamically of those phases of life which are real to youth and to taste of them in such a manner that it will gain a gradual identification with the world whose destiny it will be directing in adulthood.

116

Allan Abbott

A FABLE

Although Teachers College, Columbia University, has often been regarded as the home of Progressive education, Progressive views have not been the only ones expressed by the faculty. Indeed, there have been times when critics of Progressive education actually seemed more numerous than its defenders. One such critic was Professor Allan Abbott, chairman of the Department of English. In his fable it is easy to detect the subject-matter curriculum, the specialized teacher, the elective system, and the integrated core curriculum. Another parody in a similar vein is *The Saber-Tooth Curriculum* by J. Abner Peddiwell (pseud.) and Several Tequila Daisies (5).

Similar to the criticism of the "core" were the comments directed at the survey course. For example, the editor of the *New Republic* pronounced survey courses to be thin and superficial, a "mental soft drink." An artist declared, "To me United States education is like a puddle in the road—very broad but only two inches deep." It was, indeed, an interesting time in which to be a curriculum expert.

There was once a well-ordered though conservative Zoo. It had a Lion House and a Monkey House; it had a Turtle Pond and a Seal Pond; it had a Bear Den and a Wolf Den; it had a Buffalo Run and a Gazelle Run; in fact it had all the Things that a well-ordered and conservative Zoo always has. And it had well-trained Men to do all the things that should be done—men trained to Feed the Lions and men trained to Feed the Snakes; men to Drive the Camels and men to Herd the Buffalo; men to explore the Earth for new Animals and men to write Learned Books about them at Home. At the Gate, you could, according to your tastes, buy anything from a Picture Postcard of the Giraffe to a Treatise on the Freudian Complexes of the Gorilla. And every Sunday and Holiday Daddies would bring their Children to smell the Tiger and ride the Elephant, to checkle at the Bears and grimace at the Monkeys, and do all the things that Children do in a well-ordered conservative Zoo.

From *Teachers College Record,* April 1934, 35:600.

One day, a Frontier Thinker visited the Zoo. "Dear, dear," said the Frontier Thinker, "This will never do; this Zoo is sadly Out of Date. It is over Compartmentalized—the Frontier is not at all like This. You must take down all these Artificial Barriers; the Children will learn much faster under the free Stimulation of Realistic and highly Socialized Surroundings. There will be Activity leading to further Activity, a Felt Need, Problem-Solving, and Rapid Evolution of a New Social Order."

"But," ventured one of the trained Keepers, "how about my Gazelles, that we brought with so much Trouble and Expense from Africa?"

"Gazelles?" said the Frontier Thinker, "Five years from now there will be no Gazelles."

So they took down the Barriers, and Integrated the Zoo. And immediately the man who knew how to Feed Snakes was trying to Pitchfork the Tiger, and the man who knew how to Tame the Tiger was being chased by the Herd of Buffalo, and the man who knew how to Lasso the Buffalo was hiding in the Microscope House, and the man who knew how to use the Microscopes was trying to Save the Babies, and there was plenty of Activity for all, until the Police came with Machine Guns.

The Frontier Thinker was right. In Less than Five Years—in fact, before Nightfall, there were no Gazelles. For that matter, there were no Lions; there were no Children; there was even no Frontier Thinker.

117

John W. Tibbetts

CRISIS IN THE CORE CURRICULUM

The core curriculum is no longer new, and at present it is not expanding. How much influence has the "core" really exerted? One study in 1948 reported that 3.5 per cent of American high schools had true core programs, while 6.6 per cent used some modification of the core idea. However, figures of this sort can be very misleading. Teachers everywhere were forced by the challenge of the core idea to take a new look at their subjects and to stress the interrelatedness of knowledge in their presentations. How many of the other 93 to 96 per cent of our schools made curricular or methodological changes to avoid shifting to the "core" we shall never know, but it must have been a very large number.

In this article a secondary-school teacher summarizes some of the most common objections to the core curriculum as a concrete program rather than as a general theory. To these objections might be added the lack of materials to teach "core" courses, and a conflict with the ability-grouping principle; other factors are discussed by Grace Wright in *Core Curriculum Development: Problems and Practices* (Washington, D.C.: Office of Education, 1952). Not the least of the obstacles to the core-curriculum movement was the competition offered by other, newer curriculum proposals.

Not many years ago, as educational history goes, a daring new curriculum was proposed, based on the principle that no one learning area was isolated from another and that certain ones, in particular, had extremely high degrees of correlation. This curriculum was named "core," derived from the belief that there existed a general core of knowledge around which most subject areas are developed.

The need for this different type of curriculum was supported by the pronouncements of psychologists and philosophers. As early as the end of the eighteenth century, Johann Friedrich Her-

From *The Clearing House*, February 1959, 33:345-347.

bart demanded "unity" in the learning experience. A half century earlier, Jean Jacques Rousseau proposed an educational program based on real life problem solving. In the nineteenth century, Charles de Garmo and Charles McMurry introduced correlation into the system. Later, John Dewey's emphasis on unity in education gave rise to the development of the unit in learning which eventually broadened into the core curriculum.

A brief glance at the development of the core program in the last fifty years would look something like this: in 1910 a number of junior high schools gave impetus to the development of the core by introducing "broad courses." In 1918 the Commission for Reorganization of Secondary Education recognized that "unification" and "specialization" were supplementary roles of secondary education. Eight years later the National Society for the Study of Education indicated the necessity for grouping subjects. The movement toward a definite core experiment was further accelerated by the emphasis on a "wholeness of learning" recognized by the Gestalt psychologists.

In 1928, the now famous Eight Year Study was launched. It is unnecessary at this point to enter into a description of an already well-documented and widely discussed experiment in which thirty schools installed a new type of curriculum in the fashion of correlation or core. It is sufficient to note here that it was during this study that the core curriculum came into being as a movement of considerable importance.

The core programs have met with considerable success. Despite a lack of any conclusive research to show their superiority, the graduates of schools (both high school and elementary) have, in most instances, met with general success in their educational pursuits.

However, in the curriculums of many current core programs throughout the country, there is a startling tendency toward a weakness which has long been fatal to educational curriculums: that of resisting the forces of growth and change. This is especially true in the light of current attacks on educational programs' not now fitting into the "solid" and "traditional" blocks of science, mathematics, languages, and the like. Despite the hysteria accompanying these cries against educational "frills," many educational leaders who are victims of this public pressure are, for the first time in many complacent years, really looking at their programs with a critical eye. The wake of this inspection can be beneficial—or disastrous.

Any curriculum which is to keep from becoming static and stagnant *must* constantly make itself available to scrutiny and revision—to improvement and modernization. How will the core curricu-lums withstand the scrutiny of modern America and the space era? In how many school systems has the original core framework become the "sacred cow" of its founders and fellow worshipers? In approaching the vulnerability of some of these programs, we need to note their strengths and weaknesses and to ask ourselves if they (and indeed any curriculum) are cognizant of their own bastilles.

One continuing criticism of the core program has been that colleges do not generally have programs which prepare students to become effective teachers of the "core." What have our core leaders done or are they doing to study and rectify this situation?

Many cores have been criticized because they have forced teachers who are prepared in such areas as physical education to become teachers of the core—oftentimes without adequate insight by the administrators into the effects upon both the teachers and their students. (This problem is, of course, not peculiar to the core program.)

In some schools, the core program has become an area of creeping intrusions. This is especially true in many "modified core" programs, which combine only two or three subject areas in larger blocks of time. Is it justifiable, because this longer block of time exists, to use the core for *all* homeroom and routine form-completion activities?

How carefully have the core programs considered teacher load and effectiveness of teaching? In some instances odd-hour blocking of time has required as many as five separate daily preparations by teachers. For example, in a two-hour block core program which is fitted into a five-period day, the teacher may have one advanced core class in English and social studies and one core class for slow learners, with the fifth hour of a totally different nature, such as mathematics or science. This means that each day two separate social studies preparations, two separate English preparations, and a math or science preparation must be made. In schools having such programs, this situation could be improved by merely changing to a six-period day, utilizing shorter periods. The teacher could then teach three core classes with two at the same level, thereby cutting the preparations from five to a maximum of three.

These are but a few examples of inadequacies that exist in many of our core programs throughout the nation. These inadequacies might well receive closer consideration by administrative and teacher groups.

I believe that the core curriculum has much to offer. It is a program which can adjust dynamically and effectively to the demands of this or future civilizations. It provides opportunity for the exploration of problems, development of related skills, sound psychological group relations, concerted and long-range surveys, and opportunities for discussive and research techniques; all of which are essential—especially in our technological world, where developments in human relations and in technology must go hand in hand if we are to survive as a nation and world.

The crisis in the core is this: Will core programs, with their great potential for tomorrow's world, permit themselves to be discarded by public and educational opinion due to lack of administrative concern, preparation of qualified teachers, and static organization? If this crisis is to be averted, there must be a concerted effort by those who have experienced the successes of the core and who believe in its possibilities. This effort must overcome the sacred aura which has, all too frequently, negated this dynamic curriculum to a form of static traditionalism.

118

Donald W. Oliver

THE UNIT CONCEPT IN SOCIAL STUDIES: A RE-EXAMINATION

The unit concept, which was applied to all parts of the curriculum, furnished stiff competition for the "core" during the 1930's. The leading protagonist of the unit method of teaching was a Dartmouth graduate, Henry C. Morrison, who was the New Hampshire Superintendent of Schools and later Professor of Education at the University of Chicago. His original ideas were based on observations of high-school students in the North Atlantic states and perfected in his work with students in the Middle West.

Morrison urged the organization of all curriculum materials into learning units. A learning unit might be an experience (a term preferred by Progressives) or a body of subject matter (a concept preferred by traditionalists). Modern teaching methods and devices were to be employed within the learning unit according to a mastery formula. Learning units differed from lesson plans in being much larger and in being based on educational psychology and theory. Although the unit concept has few active supporters today, it continues to be influential, as Professor Oliver points out in this article. In a remarkably broad range of subject fields, large units have replaced small units as the basic plan of organization for conventional survey courses.

In educational circles, the assignment-recitation method of teaching needs little introduction: it is a read-recite method. The teacher assigns students a certain number of pages in the textbook on one day. The next day the teacher tests the students' knowledge of the material by oral recitation. The method is associated with a strong emphasis on day-to-day memorizing of isolated facts.

During the first quarter of this century, a growing lack of faith in the assignment-recitation method spurred an intensive search for new teaching procedures. Several approaches were worked out, which their inventors called "unit" methods. The methods were very much alike. All of them, for example, set forth a series of steps or phases that teacher and student were to follow. In preparing a unit, a teacher was to draw up a statement of understandings to be attained. The statement was to be followed by an overview of the subject, which was to be used to motivate the students. Next, the teacher outlined the content to be assimilated and drew up descriptions of student activities. Finally, the unit provided for evaluation (3).[1]

From *School Review*, Summer 1958, 66:204-205, 209-210, 215-217. Copyright 1958 by The University of Chicago. Reprinted by permission of The University of Chicago Press.

[1] [Numbers in parentheses refer to the references at the end of this reading.]

Articles on unit methods that appeared in professional journals assumed that the unit approach—however that approach happened to be defined—is more conducive to student learning than the traditional assignment-recitation method. This assumption became the subject of much speculation, qualification, testimony, and empirical research, most of it in search of confirming evidence.

The history and the meaning of the unit concept deserve to be re-examined. A new appraisal at this time should certainly be of considerable importance to educators, if only to illustrate how a concept may insinuate itself into the vocabulary of a profession, even though efforts at careful definition and validation fail.

Henry Morrison is often credited with originating the unit method, though most of the ideas in his major work may be found in the writings of earlier thinkers. Much of Morrison's thinking can be traced back directly to the Herbartians—at least to De Garmo (1), who attempted to interpret and apply Herbart's ideas to American education. The Herbartians believed that thinking proceeds through a series of predictable phases to a given product of learning. From natural thought phases, steps of instruction were inferred. These steps, it was claimed, accomplish five tasks essential in learning. Through these steps the student clarifies the perceptions he already has; he acquires new perceptions; he recognizes the relationship between the new perceptions and the old; he classifies, generalizes, and integrates perceptions into a total cognitive system, and he applies the new knowledge as a working part of his conscious life. . . .

Like his predecessors who designed unit methods, Morrison proposed a systematic approach to the teaching process. His approach includes five phases—exploration, presentation, assimilation, organization, and recitation—each of which must be successfully completed to attain an objective. These five phases, he notes, are "not an application of the Herbartian five steps" (2: 256). The exploratory step assesses what the students already know, provokes interest in the unit, and gives the teacher clues to the most meaningful way to present the unit. In the second step, presentation, the "teacher approaches the task of imparting . . . the understanding which is the unit" (2: 267). In the third step, "the classroom is organized as a study-room in which day after day the pupils carry on the process of study which constitutes the assimilation stage in the learning of a unit" (2: 281). During the assimilation stage the teacher tries to assess student progress by objective tests and by discussion or "rapport" testing. The objective tests used call for the application, not merely the recall, of factual material. In the fourth phase—the organization phase—the "problem is now to gather up the argument of the unit in outline form, with the essential supporting facts. Once more, the organization is focused upon the central understanding and not upon the assimilative material" (2: 325). In recitation, the fifth and last step, the pupils re-present the unit. Morrison carefully distinguishes this step from the traditional daily recitation. Instead of reciting isolated bits of information for the teacher's benefit, the students present to the class a more generalized kind of knowledge that they really understand.

If we accept Morrison's definition of adaptation and the use of this concept as a basic objective in education, the gross features of his systematic approach to teaching almost inevitably follow. In the first place, the important cognitive changes implied in "adaptation" require time. Morrison says one of his units may take several weeks (2: 256). Second, the unit must be based on a single understanding or insight rather than on the organization of related material into meaningful wholes. Third, a distinction must be made between assimilation of material as an end in education and assimilation as a means to a basic change in cognitive outlook.

Morrison's five steps are clearly related to his idea of how learning takes place. His explanation of the learning cycle in terms of stimulus, assimilation, and reaction is very close to Dewey's analysis of thinking. Morrison conceives of this cycle as a universal principle in problem-solving. He states that the "cycle is apparently the process through which all adjustments to environment at the level of human consciousness are made" (2: 162). . . .

The conclusions reached by experimenters and reviewers of experimental research on the social-studies unit in high school warrant at least one generalization. When factual retention is the outcome measured, unit methods, as defined in various experiments, give no striking evidence of superiority over other teaching methods. This finding perhaps should have punctured the inflated claims made for the unit method by early proponents; actually it did not. In fact, the majority of vocal curriculum-makers continue to expound the values of the unit twenty years after the issue might be considered dead.

. . . Although educators do not agree on what a unit is, they continue to use the term. Is it possible that this concept, which has no precise meaning, can still be useful to educators concerned with teaching procedures?

The positive feeling that many curriculum experts have toward the unit raises a second question. Their feelings are based on the assumption that the unit describes a teaching procedure that is superior to other procedures. Evidence indicates that this belief is not necessarily well founded. Research on the subject is inconclusive. Is it appropriate for educators to act on an assumption surrounded by so much confusion and supported by so little evidence?

Nor is more evidence forthcoming. Although educators and other applied social scientists are showing more and more concern for guiding and changing the thinking process, the literature reflects fewer and fewer attempts to define carefully and validate experimentally teaching procedures designed to bring about such changes. Is there any reason why an observable teaching procedure cannot be subjected to empirical validation?

Our closing questions raise a basic issue: Isn't the unit really a vessel? Isn't the unit like the physician's black bag? Aren't the size and texture trivial compared with the instruments and medicines inside? Are we lost in discussions of structure, when in the end it is the content that really counts?

References

1. Charles De Garmo, *Herbart and the Herbartians.* New York: Charles Scribner's Sons, 1896.

2. Henry C. Morrison, *The Practice of Teaching in the Secondary School.* Chicago: University of Chicago Press, 1931 (revised).

3. B. Othanel Smith, William O. Stanley, and J. Harlan Shores, *Fundamentals of Curriculum Development,* p. 578. Yonkers, New York: World Book Co., 1950.

119

Laurence S. Flaum

THE ACTIVITY HIGH SCHOOL

The spirit, purposes, and methods of the activity curriculum are outlined here by Professor Laurence Flaum, one of its most earnest supporters. The loss of vigor among the supporters of the core curriculum late in the thirties can be traced in large measure to the secession of the Progressive element. This group had never liked the core emphasis upon required common learnings of a subject-matter nature. They saw education as a psychological process, in which students should plan their own program, much like Eliot's elective system on the college level. The activity method would abolish subjects in favor of normal life activities grouped into types. If the key to learning was psychology, then, as Progressive curriculum pioneer W. W. Charters put it, *"curriculum content is method."*

An excellent example of how this worked out in practice was offered by two Mississippi teachers (6) in what they rather inaccurately designated as a core curriculum: "Although they vary in certain phases of their thinking about the curriculum, practically all educators agree that education for efficient and wholesome living is the most important business of our democratic society, that the American school needs a reconstructed curriculum which will train for efficient and wholesome living, and that the basis for that reconstructed curriculum should be the problems of life." These two teachers, after completing an activity analysis, came up with nine focuses to replace such traditional subject-divisions as English, history, geography, arithmetic, writing, art, nature study, and the like. The new equivalents were Protecting Life and Health, Home-Making and Raising the Standard of Material Living (major themes);

Civic Cooperation, Job Training, Getting Education, Religious Expression, Aesthetic Expression, and Recreations (secondary themes). Here was curriculum change with a vengeance!

. . . Variations of the activity school have had different names within the past quarter century. Sometimes it has been known as the "project method" school, "the life experience school," the "child-centered school." But, whatever the names given to it, the activity school cannot be limited to the confines of a name or a partial, localized definition. Whatever its name, the activity principle identifies a school which clearly is responsive to the way of life of a free democratic people. Its concepts are those which will most effectively help our young people enter into the way of life of our society because its major and original purpose and function are to help create thinking, responsible, creative personalities who will find their places in the constantly changing flow of living which is both the normal state and the heritage of living in a democracy.

Within the activity principle of education there is the full-grown awareness that the secondary school is a social institution with its roots in the customs, traditions, and aspirations of a free people, but it is also aware that its branches grow free, creating new and vital and functional ways of learning and living. It is aware of the changing needs and social climates of the people and is willing to perpetuate those traditions and folkways in our society which have virility and functional value to our changing way of life and to discard those concepts which no longer have reason to exist and through their existence create obstacles which hinder our educational development. This means, in the final sense, that outlived traditions are obstructions to the growth of our children toward greater self and social fulfillment, because of perpetuated prejudices, ignorances, fears, and reactionary attitudes in our school practices. Because so many of these attitudes persist in many high schools, it becomes imperative that they be constantly aware of the need to help our adolescents develop living processes by which they can find their greatest satisfactions, and fulfillment of their most immediate and foreseeable future needs. They must help our youth understand and accept its responsibilities in the life areas of citizenship, job getting and holding, consumer buying and selling, crea-

tive leisure time, energy expending, healthful living, and developing moral and ethical values as a basis for a good life. . . .

How can we account for the fact that our schools are still mental-discipline subject matter centered? Why are our curriculums still geared to the level of the academically capable who can benefit by an abstract and theoretical curriculum? Why are memorization-type subject matter achievement tests still used as the single most important basis for promotion or failure? Why do single grade standards still exist? Why are certain college entrance required courses like Latin, algebra, physics, required for all?

The typical academic, mental discipline, faculty psychology based curriculum is still adjusted to the student with an I.Q. of 105 and above. Individuals with I.Q.'s of 95-90 have difficulty finding school success and happiness within such curriculums. Traditional in such schools are required courses in algebra or foreign languages as courses exercising the greatest mental discipline "values," and students, on the average, must have I.Q.'s of 100 as a minimum to be successful in these areas. Approximately 35 per cent of all children have I.Q.'s of 105 or more, yet all children are expected to go to our academically selective high schools. What of the rest of the students, who have neither the capacity nor the need for algebra or foreign language? The high school as it is organized in too many of our communities is neither feasible nor functional for the larger number of students now attending it.

There is little excuse for an unrealistic, faculty psychology dominated curriculum. On the basis of the record which high schools have made there is little evidence which would lead us to believe that these schools have been successful even in teaching students to master what the schools have set out to teach. . . .

If any change is to be made in our high schools, there must be a change in our goals and purposes. There must be a change from stress on mental development, the accumulation of static and memorized information with its emphasis upon abstract learning, to an understanding that the goals and purpose of our high schools today are to help the student live at peace and in security within his own generation and within his own time.

In order to do this, our high schools must help the individual to grow as a unique personality. He must gain tolerant understandings and human

From *The Activity High School: The Principles of Its Operation* by Laurence S. Flaum, pp. 2-4, 10-19, 22-24. Copyright 1953 by Harper & Row, Publishers, Inc. Reprinted by permission of the publishers.

values through socially guided activities. He must develop skill and behavior learnings which have use value to him as an independent thinking person in a democratic society. The high school must recognize that learning is not a mechanical procedure for memorizing information; that learning can take place only when the individual participates in realistic activity which results in new personal experience. These behavior experiences are then utilized in everyday living rather than in the solving of academic problems alone.

The high school must modify its program so that students can develop self-expression and social understanding which is creative and necessary to their living. Students must develop independence in action and thought as they gain greater insight into the nature of responsibility. They must be allowed to function and participate wholesomely and constructively in cooperatively planned or self-initiated activities.

The conventional high school stresses pupil dependence upon the teacher and the textbook. It emphasizes an unquestioning obedience to the teacher and unquestioning acceptance of facts. This type of unquestioning obedience does not make for either live teaching or self-thinking learners, and certainly it does not prepare students for carrying out democratic responsibilities. The creative high school, in recognizing the limitations of the traditional practices, furthers the development of social-mindedness in the student through his participation in effective citizenship situations which exist in the school and in which he can democratically and freely participate. Citizenship is best taught through student action and planning dealing with problems which exist in the school, rather than through study of abstract materials. The effective high school recognizes that education is not a preparation for future living alone but that the student lives in the present and must be helped to live constructively today so that he may be able to live well and comprehensively tomorrow.

The high school, in order to answer students' persistent needs, must recognize the immediacy of the students' living problems and develop learning associations around them. Students learn realistically from the problems which they have. They see the problem as it is, how it developed, and how it might become other problems which must be answered. Comprehensive problem-solving situations are necessary for student learning, if learning is to be lifelike.

Whereas in the traditional high school there is a tendency to separate the school from the home and community, the high school must identify itself with home and community life as the source for both the problems of its youth and a means for finding the answers to the problems of its youth. This of necessity forces the high school to provide a functional program, flexible enough to adjust itself to the changing needs of the students and realistic in that it helps them solve their own problems. In this manner education becomes a dynamic process of growth from within the individual instead of an education that is outside of the student and is imposed upon him.

The traditional high school contents itself with assuring mastery of subject matter material regardless of its value to the student and takes little responsibility for the student's problems of individual personal living. The activity high school, on the other hand, helps the student learn the use of materials and skills in living situations, but in addition guides the student through teacher-student initiated activity projects which are based on student personal living needs. This is done through student-teacher cooperative planning, the use of personal experiences and problems, the utilization of community' problems, and the recognition of individual abilities in the group.

The activity high school considers itself a major agent in the construction of society, its perpetuation, and its reconstruction. Whereas the high school and its program have been largely dictated by adult interests, prejudices, and biases, the activity high school is determined to develop a curriculum based upon the students' problems, needs, interests, and capacities. This curriculum is to be evolutionary and evolve as the demands of society change and the students mature in their needs. Through functional projects the student is helped to develop independent understandings of society and the nature of his physical as well as his moral, aesthetic, and cultural environment. He is helped to understand the need for vocational efficiency so that he can choose an occupation which suits him and for which he can prepare so that he can develop into an effective producer.

At present the high school is only beginning to be concerned about the need which adolescents have for education for the creative use of leisure time. It needs a varied and rich program of extra-class activities in which all students can participate, where the individual develops creative interests which are carried into out-of-school life. These activities should help the student discover his own capacities and increase his understanding of himself and his talents. They should be as varied as the interests of the students. The only limitation should be one of size of staff and physical facilities. Both of these elements can be supplemented by community resources if necessary.

At present the high school places its emphasis upon teacher planning with little reference to student planning or student cooperation in helping develop course projects. The high school must encourage the development of intellectual curiosity in the adolescent through allowing him to plan with the teacher regarding his work, so that he can become an experimenter instead of an accepter. This attitude of experimentation is in keeping with the democratic principle which allows each individual to find the areas of his greatest contribution to himself and to society. It helps the student learn by independent doing, seeing, observing, testing, reading, discussing, thinking, evaluating, and creating.

The activity high school recognizes that individuals develop attitudes, emotions, reactions, habits, temperaments, and capacities, and that it must teach individuals in the light of these differences rather than ignoring them as is often true in conventional schools. It recognizes that interests, needs, and the satisfaction of these needs are the great motivations in learning and growth development. It recognizes that need learning results in the integration of meanings into the personality of the student so that he can develop clear understanding and self-imposed obligations for the completion of the learning act.

The activity high school, in order to meet the diversified needs of the students, bases its teaching upon the available sources in the community as well as its libraries and school textbooks. Visual and audio aids of all kinds are used as a means by which a world beyond the immediate community can be brought to the attention of the student so that his understandings may be quickened and deepened. Wherever possible, the materials for use in learning are actually made and developed by the students themselves.

Each class in the activity high school becomes a laboratory in which each learning situation is an outgrowth of previous experiences and is demanding of new skills and more mature attitudes and behaviors, in order to develop further growth and insight into living. Thus, while no two experiences are exactly alike, each successive maturing experience finds the individual ready to cope with it. The result of this continuous experiencing is a changing, maturing, and growing individual, increasingly more capable of adjusting himself to life problems and able to achieve success in answering the demands of his personality. Through such learning and adjustment the individual develops increased awareness of himself, his society, and his purposes in living, working, sensing, re-creating, and believing.

Throughout this laboratory experience the student's intelligence manifests itself through the use of significant and purposeful meanings in self-directed, problematic activities. The individual acts on the basis of his past values and his present learnings as they apply to immediate situations and problems. But intelligent behavior does not stop there. It also involves the recognition of future events and consequences of one's behavior. Intelligent and purposeful meanings, then, are the result of experiences and their effect upon the environment and himself. . . .

The activity principle, with its experimental, life-centered, pragmatic philosophy of education, presents to [secondary education] a constructive, democratic way for the organization of a curriculum which is sufficiently creative to begin to answer its problems.

What would be the basis for this curriculum?

First, the school and the mature life are one. The school is an enrichment of living experiences in that it helps crystallize the experiences for the student so that he understands his own experiences while he is in the process of having them.

Secondly, the school helps the student to become more independent of the teacher, more self-directive and self-reliant.

Third, subject matter becomes a tool to be used for the further enrichment of experience gaining and skill learning, not an end in itself. Subject matter, rather than remaining an inert mass of unrelated facts, becomes alive when utilized by the student in situations which have meaning *to him* and which he helps to plan, cooperatively, with his fellows and his teacher, with the teacher as coworker and guide.

Fourth, the individual personality, his differences and similarities, and the social society in which he lives, is of supreme importance in planning all his learning situations.

Fifth, the curriculum is not prearranged so that the individual is fitted into it, as if the individual were a mechanical substance to be adjusted to fit the shape and size of the academic blueprint which he must follow. There is little domination to ensure that the individual will be fitted into some educational and social pattern. The emphasis is on the abilities, talents, and interests which the student has and which he must learn to use in order to live satisfactorily in the world which he creates out of his own experiences.

Sixth, as life is constant change and modification of behavior, the curriculum and individual learning must adapt themselves to change and individual growth. Just as our scientific findings, our social patterns, change and must constantly grow, so must the curriculum be flexible and able to change as the needs of the people warrant and demand the change. No fixed curriculum can possibly meet the changing problems of our fluid society. If it could, all that need be done would be to set up a standard curriculum and stamp it on each school and each community until we were all alike, from the same mold, and both our society itself and our individual lives would become static, unvarying, and unchanging, all of which is obviously impossible and undesirable for a free, democratic people. . . .

Seventh, education is a process of guided growth. This involves the teacher-student planning toward desirable individual and social goals within the framework of the particular society of which the individual is a contributing person. The student has to learn to make choices, use skills, select from among possible solutions the one best suited to solve his problem, develop moral and ethical responses, social attitudes and behaviors, and concepts of good, participating citizenship.

The student must be able to evaluate his own growth so that he becomes constantly aware of his learning and the problem-solving process in which he is sharing, planning, and working.

The end of education as a process of guided growth is the individual's achievement of his potentialities according to his abilities and talents, and according to his needs and plans. Implicit in the whole principle is the concern for the development of the total personality of the individual as an integrated whole.

Eighth, just as the personality of the individual is made up of all sorts of experiences, each different in kind and degree, so must the curriculum be as broad, as vital, as challenging as life itself, and its areas should be composed of the typical problems of the student's living.

This does not mean that its structure, its content, or its meaning should be left to chance, or whim, or the preplanning of teachers, or the diffused curiosity of children. It must be based on the needs of society and its persistent problems as well as the specific and immediate needs of the individuals who give to the curriculum its direction and whose changing behaviors and growing beliefs and ideals are the end product of the curriculum.

Those needs which are universal, at the maturity level of the learner, are basic to the activity curriculum. It calls for creative behavior on the part of each individual as he progresses in experience at his own level of ability. Learning experiences then become a succession of vital problems, drawing upon all the resources of subject matter as needed, regardless of areas, until the problems are solved and the meanings are integrated into the life behaviors of the individual. . . .

The activity approach to learning becomes a way of life as well as a method by which school problems can be solved. The emphasis is on experimentation. The experimentalist seeks better answers to the problems of learning. The student learns to make sound assumptions and then test these assumptions against the life problem faced. The answer demands action or a behavior on the part of the learner. This behavior change reflects the growth of the student. . . .

The curriculum must develop experience areas which are wide enough for the individual student to find himself. It must open up new areas for individual growth so that the adolescent may make adjustments in his intellectual activities as well as in his social environment. What are the adolescent problems with which the curriculum must concern itself? The problems of our youth today are unique more in degree than in kind as compared with the problems of the youth in the preceding generations. The complexity of our society has intensified as well as multiplied these problems. Our youth are disturbed emotionally, physically, ethically, socially, and economically. They find fewer and fewer doorways leading to security and sense of stability in our society. The home is losing its place as it was once known in our society. The church, while making valiant efforts to regain its former position of authority and direction in the lives of our young people, is falling far short in its guidance programs for these adolescents. The school is the greatest single source for guidance that our youth have, and unless the school functionally answers the needs of youth, they will turn away from the school because they find it empty, inadequate and unrelated to life itself. Regardless of the particular course or series of courses found in our schools, youth asks these questions:

(1) How can I know myself as a person and as one who lives with and among others? How can I find emotional and spiritual peace? How can I learn to think about other people and not just myself?

(2) How can I understand the world about me and my place in it? How can I understand the large world of adults as well as the life in the world on my street, in my house, in my school? How can I learn to make wise decisions concerning the world as I know and learn about it? How can I learn how science, religion, art, and mechanics change this world? How can I understand how other people live in far-off places and here at home regardless of their color or religion? How can I understand the life of people who are not like me and who may

be poorer and weaker? Where do they fit into our democracy?

(3) How can I make a place for myself in the world whether it be in art, music, business, or a profession? How can I become an intelligent citizen, a follower when I need to be and a leader when I am chosen, and help make life better in the community where I live?

(4) How can I understand family living, parenthood, sex relations? How can I prepare myself to marry and have a family of my own?

(5) How can I learn to know what I can do best, what my talents are so that I can earn a good living and be happy and proud in my work? How can I help other people as a result of my work?

(6) How can I get people to like me for what I am and how can I learn to like people for what they are? How can I learn to accept responsibility when people give me responsibility? What can I believe so that I will have the courage to help people who are weaker or poorer than I am so that they won't be hurt or bullied? How can I help make a better world for myself and everyone else where everybody has an equal chance to live as he believes if it doesn't hurt anyone else?

(7) How can I develop my creative interests so that I can find recreations which will make my life richer, happier, and interesting? How can I appreciate the talents of others so that I can help them or share with them in their pleasure or success?

(8) How can I put in practice my ideas about the equality of all men before the law and their Creator?

(9) How can I understand the politics of my community so that I can become a good citizen in our society?

(10) How can I learn to understand that beauty is in living, not just in museums, music, or books? How can I find beauty in the everyday world in which I live and yet be aware of the beauty that other men know? How can I find enjoyment as well as appreciation in the beauty which other men make?

(11) How can I find a philosophy of living which helps me to understand and to do what is morally and socially good and not evil? How can I find beliefs which will eliminate fear and help me find happiness, idealism, and courage in living?

(12) How can I develop skills in reading, writing, seeing, and listening so that they become tools for self-expression?

(13) How can I develop the understanding necessary for good buying for myself and my family so that I will not be wasteful?

(14) How can I develop the skill to work, talk, and live with other people in the way democratic men deal with each other?

(15) How can I learn to understand why men fight so that I can learn to help men find the way to live in peace with each other?

(16) How can I develop the understandings necessary so that if I have to fight for what I believe as a democratic citizen I will carry my responsibility in good faith and with courage?

(17) How can I choose a career in time of peace which will help me work so that I can be independent and be able to take care of myself and my family?

These are the problems which our youth have. In order to be functional, our high schools must develop curriculums to answer their problems and provide our youth with the necessary skills and understandings which they must have in order to live successfully. . . .

120

Arvil S. Barr

THE ACTIVITIES CURRICULUM

The drift from a core of subject matter toward a core of activities was soon noted by education experts. One such was Professor Arvil Barr of the University of Wisconsin, a former history teacher now well launched upon a long career in educational journalism. In this succinct editorial in the *Journal of Educational Research*, Barr attempted, with a measure of successful insight rarely equaled by later critics, to balance the "pros" against the "cons" of the new and almost untried activities movement.

By 1941 the activities curriculum appeared to have captured the main armies of Progressive education, and cooperation with traditional schoolmen seemed very unlikely. William C. Bagley, a leader of the Essentialist movement, expressed the choice in these terms:

The New Education (Progressives)		*The Old Education (Essentialists)*
Student interest	vs.	Student effort
Student freedom	vs.	Student discipline
Respond to individual desires	vs.	Respond to social demands
Immediate goals	vs.	Long-range goals
Instruction by student initiative	vs.	Instruction by teacher initiative
Psychological organization	vs.	Logical organization
Activities	vs.	Subject matter
Relative truth	vs.	Absolute truth

There has grown up in this country and abroad also two fundamentally different notions of how best to organize subject matter for teaching purposes. According to one conception of teaching the best method of training boys and girls is to set them to the mastery of logically organized subject matter, such as is found in textbooks, reference books, and lectures. According to another notion the best method of training boys and girls is to set them to the thoughtful performance of various activities, such as the making of miscellaneous objects, participation in self-government, and the development of creative projects of various sorts. Lying between these extremes are all kinds of plans, some representing more and some less, of one or the other of these concepts of teaching. The drift seems, however, to be in the direction of the activities curriculum as a means of securing thoughtful participation by pupils to the end that usable knowledges, skills, and attitudes may be developed. The change is one of considerable importance, and needs careful consideration.

Four criticisms have been made of the traditional curriculum: (1) It fails to stimulate pupils' interest. Learning under the traditional system of instruction is dull and uninteresting. Pupils are driven and over-supervised. (2) Pupils fail to retain facts thus taught. Critics of the traditional curriculum point to the low scores on standardized tests and the rapidly falling curve of forgetting as evidence of the failure of this method of instruction. (3) The critics of the traditional curriculum assert that logically organized subject matter does not function in life. To overcome this weakness special attention has been given by the best teachers of this method to applications and the special uses to which the in-

formation taught pupils may be put. The critics, however, have not been satisfied by what they consider artificial applications. (4) They point out, also, the danger of a mere *verbal* education. Pupils understand only partially the symbols which they use. It would seem theoretically possible, at least, for pupils to build up an extensive vocabulary and a degree of verbal glibness without getting a fundamental grasp of the problems and tools of life. Because of these alleged shortcomings in logically organized subject matter, and because of the promise which is held out by the activities curriculum, many people have come to feel that the advantage lies in the direction of the activities curriculum.

There are, however, certain limitations to the activities curriculum program, especially as worked out in practice, that should not be overlooked: (1) There seems to be a tendency on the part of classroom teachers to limit the activities curriculum to learning by doing, in its more restricted sense. Learning by doing, notwithstanding its effectiveness, is a very slow method of learning, because of the natural restrictions of time, place and materials placed upon it. It would seem, after the fundamental experiences have been provided pupils through direct participation, that it would be educationally more economical to provide for directed observing, writing, reading, and thinking, to supply the additional experiences which underlie the organized curriculum. There are four ways of getting experience: (a) through direct participation, (b) observation, (c) reading and oral report, and (d) reflective thinking. There is a tendency among teachers to take a narrow view of the activities curriculum.

(2) There seems to be much misunderstanding about interest and the activities curriculum. This is not a new idea. Many teachers, however, take the demand for interest to mean that teachers

From *Journal of Educational Research,* January 1930, 21:49-51.

should be entertainers to amuse pupils. While this notion of interest is quite foreign to the one intended, there has doubtless been a general lowering of standards because of it.

(3) Many teachers fail to provide practice in analysis and generalization. To them the activities which constitute the curriculum become an end in themselves. There is plenty of activity, but to no conscious goal. It would seem from general observation that it is not the amount of experience which differentiates the training of individuals, but the amount of *analyzed* experience which counts. Should this observation be true, it would be quite possible to have activities instruction of a very low level of effectiveness.

(4) Teachers fail to provide for the progressive reconstruction of experience. The organization element which was particularly strong in the traditional curriculum is quite lacking in the average activities program. The activities stand isolated, unanalyzed, and unorganized. There is no building up from these activities of a system of knowledge—granting that such is desirable. The objection to the traditional curriculum, as I understand it, was not to its systematized knowledge but to the insistence of teachers upon teaching it directly from textbooks, references, and lectures. In practice the activities curriculum has failed to bring to pupils an organized view of life.

(5) Teachers fail to provide for the repetition of experiences where repetition is necessary. It seems to me that the objection to drill as originally made was not to drill itself but to unmotivated drill, that is, to drill disassociated from the activities of life. It does not seem economical to leave the matter of habit formation to chance associations and incidental learning as seems to be the case with so many teachers who purport to use the activities method.

I have had in mind in this editorial two thoughts. There is in progress in this country a fundamental movement for the reconstruction of the curriculum. In the first place, this movement for the reconstruction of the curriculum is important, but based for the most part upon theoretical considerations. While these considerations seem sound enough, it is only reasonable to suggest that they need careful evaluation. The history of education is replete with fallen projects, all of which appeared promising enough at one time or another. In the second place, the author is tremendously interested in the activities curriculum, and regrets very much to see the limitations placed upon it in so many of our public schools. The limitations here cited are, of course, really not limitations in the method itself, but misconceptions of the plan as observed in practice. The idea is one of too much promise not to have it live up to what is expected of it.

121

Albert W. Whitney

EDUCATION AND SATISFACTORY LIVING

The fact that the activity curriculum was something more than an ideal dream may be sensed in this selection from the official magazine of the American Federation of Labor. The author, Albert W. Whitney, was a safety engineer of wide experience for whom laboring men had deep respect. For certain subjects, such as safety education, which were knocking on the curriculum door for admission, the activity movement was ideally suited.

What should not be missed by the student is how *practical* the activity curriculum could seem to the average laboring man. Whitney is here presenting the way "education for life" appeared to a large sector of the public; he also foreshadows the germ of that post-World War II sequel of the activities movement now famous as the "life-adjustment" education curriculum.

. . . Everyone who has had any contact with the schools recognizes that there is something

wrong with our modern education. Education is supposed to prepare a child for life, but our education of today is not doing this. Parents that have children that are beyond the first few years of school find that their children lose interest in their studies, employers find that the boys and girls that apply to them for jobs are not well equipped for their work and society in general realizes that the youth of today are not getting the training that is necessary to make them good and useful members of society.

What can the matter be? It is easy to recognize that something is wrong but it is not so easy to discover what the trouble is and what ought to be done about it.

Some light will be thrown on the situation if we go back to the beginnings of our present education and see how it started. We inherited our educational system from Europe. In those earlier days, many hundred years ago, the situation was entirely different from that of today; the conditions of life were very simple. The child got his education in the fundamentals of living in the home itself through imitation of his elders and through taking his part in the life of the family; in those days when there were no factories or offices it was quite possible for a child to get in this way the experiences that would fit him for becoming a responsible member of society. Schools were necessary only to impart the knowledge that could not be had in the home. The first schools of Europe were schools of law, theology and medicine, and while reading was taught in the schools it was a technical matter and was only for the privileged classes.

The contribution that we have made to educational development in the United States has been in making education available not merely to the privileged classes but to all classes; reading for instance is something that we now not only offer but force upon everyone. This democratization of education, the making of education a fundamental and necessary part of the life of every member of society, is a wonderful contribution to civilization, but we have curiously overlooked the necessity of making the content of education fit our modern conditions. For while we have made education more generally available we have not essentially changed the nature of the instruction; we still begin with reading in the great mass of our public schools and we still act on the theory that education in the fundamentals of living will be had in the home.

But will it? Let us see! The situation today is entirely different from that upon which our system of education was founded. The life of the

world no longer goes on in the home; it goes on in factories and offices, and the child has little chance to learn either the technique of living or attitudes of mind at home. Furthermore there is not the opportunity that there used to be for the child to have his part in the work of the home. The apartment house, modern conveniences and the increased pace at which we live have had the result that most children do not have the chores to do that in the early days of our country were such an important part of the life of every child. Furthermore our modern conditions of living have become so complicated that most homes are no longer fitted to give instruction even in such elementary matters as health and safety.

The fact is then that our homes are not giving children the training in the fundamentals of living that they need and our schools are not doing it either for the reason that our educational system has come down to us from a time when this was not a necessary part of school work. But these things are not only necessary and important but in reality they are the most important part of education. There is little use in our children learning the technique of mathematics and science and getting the ability to speak foreign languages or even to be able to read unless they can at the same time be getting a training in those great underlying fundamentals of right living.

We have by no means been entirely unconscious of these deficiencies and the inclusion in the curriculum of such subjects as manual training and domestic science has been in recognition of the fact that the school must do something to meet these needs. Furthermore we have established trade schools where a boy or girl could learn a trade; these to some extent take the place of the homely old apprenticeship system. But trade schools do not meet the situation completely. The working man for instance does not want his children merely to get the technical ability to earn their living but he wants them to get an education even in the elementary schools that will develop character and insight and capacity for living a satisfactory and worth while life.

Well, what is the conclusion? Is it not this: that, probably the reason that our education is not satisfactory is that it is not definitely designed to fit a child for life; it is not brought to bear immediately and definitely enough upon the problem of living; the child does not get the instruction and training that he needs if he is to be a good citizen and member of society. Professor Judd of the University of Chicago has said, "Modern civilization in its complexity is like a high-powered automobile and yet we put it into

From *American Federationist*, July 1926, 33:798-801.

the hands of our children without teaching them how to run it."

Is there any escape from the conclusion that our educational system must be fundamentally modified and made to include those simple and homely elements of everyday life that were once had in the home but which now can no longer be had there. And if this is done will not the school in a multitude of cases be the means of bringing these things through the children back to the home; the current will be reversed and the children, through what they get in the schools, will help to raise the level of the homes.

But what connection has this with safety? Why simply this: safety is one of those subjects which the home has proved unable to handle successfully. Over 21,000 children of school age are being killed by accident each year. The work that has been already done in the schools shows that we can get at least a seventy-five per cent saving in child fatalities through our school work. The seriousness of the traffic situation has forced the problem of safety education into the foreground.

But there are other similar subjects that are equally important, for instance: health, conservation in general, thrift, humane education, home-nursing, sex education, citizenship in its broadest sense and character training, all of them subjects that are characterized by having a particularly close relationship to life. But this is too large a program to get into our schools without a thorough revision of the course of study. What is needed however is not so much the introduction of new subjects as the introduction of new points of view and new objectives; health and safety for instance can be introduced as attitudes of mind through all the subjects of the present curriculum.

Is this not the great need of our present time in education, to bring the work of our schools to bear more directly upon the problem of living a satisfactory life; and is it not significant that the approach to this undertaking should appear to be, as in the field of industrial relations, through such a simple and fundamental thing as the saving of human life? After all we do not strike bottom in any subject until we get down to a fundamental human need, and we can not get on the right basis until we have got to the bottom.

How in detail that is to be done is of course a difficult and involved educational problem. Many people and many schools are working upon the problem. One of the latest efforts, which may prove to have much of value, is through a Committee on Materials of Instruction appointed by Commissioner Tigert on which I am happy to say your Vice President, Mr. Matthew Woll, has agreed to serve in order to represent the interests of Labor. The ambitious purpose of this committee is no less than this: with a knowledge of our modern social needs and with a knowledge of the deficiencies of our present education, so to modify our curriculum and our methods of teaching as to make our education in reality a genuine preparation for life.

122

I. L. Kandel

ADJUSTMENT TO LIFE

The "life-adjustment" education movement arose between 1947 and 1949, chiefly as a reaction to the fact that less than half the high-school students went on to college or wanted vocational training of the sort currently available. Life-adjustment protagonists sought to change the curriculum in the interests of the "forgotten" 60 per cent who dropped out of or even refused to enroll in secondary schools. It used the "core" idea; in fact, it greatly increased the amount of time spent in core sessions. However, the core was changed from fusions of subject matter to "a large required core of subjects preparing for home living, citizenship, mental and physical health, enjoyment of life, and understanding of the world about us." In effect, the life-adjustment approach shifted curriculum emphasis from knowledge of the culture to personal behavior and attitudes. Elective courses were reduced to near zero, and direct experience via activities was the principal instructional method.

Professor Isaac Kandel of Teachers College, Columbia University, an expert in international education and editor of *School and Society*, was one of the first of many educators to express doubts about the possible implications of life-adjustment education. He also pointed out that it was much less original and unprecedented than most people had assumed.

About a quarter of a century ago C. W. Bardeen published an article under the title, "The Man Milliner in Education." During the war years there was a clear-cut job to be performed in education as in all the critical issues that faced the nation. Now that peace has come, the re-fashioning of the educational millinery has again begun. "Education for the Atomic Age" has taken the place of "Education for the Air Age" which was current just before the war. More likely to become popular, however, is the demand that education should be adjusted to life. Education as adjustment is not new in American educational literature, but it was discarded on the ground that it would result in a static society.

The principle of education as "adjustment to life" has, however, been revived. It implies that all the contingencies which human beings are likely to encounter in their lives must be anticipated and education must be adjusted to them. Among these contingencies are dating, marriage, mating, rearing of children, work experience, vocations, and all the social issues which make up the day's headlines in the newspapers. Not only is the new principle a revival of the old "education as adjustment" but it is the latter-day version of "specificity" and "functionalism" in education. Nothing can be left to chance on the assumption that no individual is likely, without appropriate courses of instruction, to have sufficient intelligence to meet the "life situations" which may arise. All the "life situations" are to be crowded

into the school years, even though it is generally held that education is a lifelong process. Accordingly courses are organized, whether there is "an immediate felt need" and whether there is or is not sufficient content to make a course. In order to insure academic respectability the courses are tricked out with the usual pattern of points, units, or credits. By the time the student really comes to the place where he has to meet a situation, the probability is that all he will remember about the course in which he was taught the methods of adjustment will be that he "had had" it.

The principle of education for "adjustment to life" is also a return to the idea of education for "deferred values," which was supposed to have been demolished some years ago. The root of the trouble lies, first, in the demand for instruction that brings immediate returns, and secondly, in a species of anti-intellectualism. The idea of education as discipline has been discarded through an easy misinterpretation of the results of research on the question of formal discipline. And yet there is something in the story told by George Herbert Palmer about his wife:

When at one time she was struggling with a new cook on the subject of bad bread, and after encountering the usual excuses of oven, flour, and yeast, had invaded the kitchen and herself produced an excellent loaf, astonished Bridget summed up the situation in an epigram which deserves to be recorded: "That's what education means—to be able to do what you've never done before."

From *School and Society*, May 1947, 65:372.

123

James D. Koerner

WHAT SHALL WE TEACH?

The "life-adjustment" movement stirred up a great amount of controversy, derision, and outright abuse. "Basic education" became the rebuttal to "life-adjustment" education, and it spoke for a "hard" rather than a "soft" curriculum.

By 1960 the reaction was in full swing, aided by the necessity to meet recent technological competition in an ever hotter "Cold War."

James D. Koerner of the Council for Basic Education provides a typical example of the argumentative bullets which turned life adjustment into a corpse. But the "basic educators" had no replacement program except to re-institute the practices of the nineteenth century. As a result, a curriculum vacuum exists, providing a wonderful opportunity for the educational statesmen of the future.

This article is reprinted from the *Congressional Record*, which daily publishes the proceedings of the House of Representatives and the Senate. A senator or a representative may request that a magazine article or a speech be printed in the *Record*. The comments of Senator Gordon L. Allott of Colorado, who did so in this instance, are given in italics.

Mr. Allott. Mr. President, in the last few years there has been a great deal of discussion of the basic problems of education. As a former member of the Subcommittee on Education, of the Committee on Labor and Public Welfare, I have had the real opportunity to hear most of the great educators of the country, as well as most of the great scientists of the country, talk about education.

By means of the bill of last year, we attempted to accomplish certain things which we thought would raise the caliber of education in the United States.

Mr. President, recently Mr. James D. Koerner, executive secretary of the Council for Basic Education, addressed the American Farm Bureau Federation, in Columbus, Ohio, on the subject of, "What Shall We Teach?" His remarks on the basic issue in education are stimulating and important, and I believe they warrant wide reading and discussion. Mr. Koerner did not present his points as unchallenged or incontrovertible facts, but, rather, he presented them as questions to be explored and pursued. In his address he attempted to point out the different schools of thought on the subject of curricula, as follows:

For example, there is a very large group of people who agree that what we should teach are the academic, intellectual subjects—the so-called hard or basic curriculum. . . . On the other hand . . . there is a very large group who believe the hard curriculum . . . is not all it's cracked up to be—that modern science, especially psychology, has disproved many of the old education truths.

In discussing what the council believes a community should look for in establishing priorities among the things it wants its schools to do, Mr. Koerner states that we must ask the following question, to which only affirmative answers should be the reply:

1. Is the subject in question one that only the school, the formal institution of the school, can teach? Or is it one that can be taught, that might well be taught, at home, by the church, by the town recreation center, by the police department, or by some other agency of society?
2. Does the subject represent a basic part of the student's cultural and intellectual heritage, a fundamental area of man's intellectual activity? Or does it represent a minor field of the intellect, an interesting but secondary outgrowth of some major field, or perhaps a nonintellectual activity altogether that might be nice for students to know about but hardly fundamental?
3. Is the subject one that, at least at the pre-college level, is studied mostly for itself—that is worthy of being studied of and for itself? Or is it a subject studied mostly for its vocational usefulness, a subject whose principal virtue lies in its utility for the student—which has, that is, a more or less immediate utilitarian application in the student's life?

Mr. President, I ask unanimous consent that there be printed in the Record some short excerpts from Mr. Koerner's address:
[There being no objection, the excerpts were ordered to be printed in the Record, as follows:]

It is no doubt evident by now that our three-criteria test . . . leaves us with only the traditional, academic, intellectual—the basic—curriculum: Language and literature, our own and others:

From *Congressional Record* (86th Congress, First Session, July 30, 1959), Volume 105, Part 11, pp. 14692-14693.

History, at least American and European; geography; mathematics; and the main sciences.

Having established this much, however, we are, I'm afraid, only at the beginning of your job at home. We have said nothing of three closely related problems. . . . The first one is how much of these basic subjects should be offered in public schools. . . . The second related problem is the number of students . . . that should be receiving this kind of education. . . . The third question, perhaps the most significant of all, is the question of quality. One should never forget that the mere establishment of certain subjects as basic, and even the establishment of the number of years they are to be taught and the percentage of students to whom they are to be taught, is no guarantee whatever of good education. . . . You must look to the quality of courses, of teachers, of administrators, not merely the quantity. In fact, the quality will dictate the quantity, not the other way around. . . .

At least 42 of our now 50 States require the study of American history in the schools of those States. And 33 specify study in American Government, civics, citizenship, or the Constitution.

One would therefore expect high school graduates to be in possession of certain fundamental information about their history, and about the political and economic principles upon which their society exists.

The last attempt to measure such information on a really large and representative basis across the country was done 2 years ago by Audience Research, Inc. Of the thousands of high school graduates questioned, many of whom were adults when the survey was made, 67 percent could not name the Senators from their own State, 63 percent could not name their Congressman, 57 percent could not say how often elections are held for the U.S. House of Representatives, 82 percent did not know who would succeed to the Presidency in the event of the death of both the President and Vice President, 52 percent could not identify the Bill of Rights—and 70 percent could not suggest one advantage of the economy of the United States over that of Russia.

There were many more questions, with similar results. And I would not want to press the matter too hard. But I suggest to you, when almost all our States require American history and government be taught in all schools, and with results like these, that one can put no faith in a course, any courses, merely because it is scheduled under an approved name for an approved number of years. What matters is what happens in the classroom. . . .

For many, many years our colleges have had to conduct elaborate remedial programs in such basic subjects as English, mathematics, and foreign languages.

Despite the fact that the students coming to them, representing generally the best of our high school graduates, have just finished studying, say, English for 12 years in public school, it commonly happens that as much as half the entering class must do remedial work in their native tongue; must do rudimentary work again, and again at taxpayers' expense, before they can even be admitted to the regular freshman English course—which is itself a remedial institution. . . .

To satisfy a host of so-called student needs—ephemeral, amorphous, often imagined—we now have a kind of gargantuan smorgasbord of offerings in our schools. I won't bore you with measuring such subjects against our set of criteria for establishing what is important in education. But when you inflict this kind of frivolous nonsense on students, together with some or much vocational work, the basic subjects run a tragic and poor third.

What indeed should we teach?

We should teach the hard curriculum. There is no better way, and perhaps no other way, of allowing the people of a free society to become truly free men.

Whether we look at public education from the point of view of society or of the individual, the primacy of the basic curriculum is perfectly clear. From the point of view of society, the importance, the indispensability, of a constant supply of highly trained manpower, of highly developed practitioners of the arts, or an informed and thinking citizenry, is manifest.

And from the point of view of the individual, the importance of knowing both himself and the Western heritage that is his birthright, and the abiding need of developing some inner resources with which to live in an explosive, crisis-driven world, is equally manifest.

For most people these ends are best attained, or best prepared for, through a schooling that trains and stretches their intellectual capacities, that furnishes their minds generously with substance from the principal areas of human knowledge, that awakens their moral faculty and disciplines their will. . . . And these ends are neither attained nor prepared for through vocational or life adjustment education.

A million former students will testify to the fact that they and all their friends changed jobs, changed occupations, even changed professions, a half-dozen, a dozen, two dozen times before they found what they wanted. Whatever the number of changes, students are almost sure not to know their destinies in high school. The school's best bet is to give them a foundation in basic subjects that will serve them steadily in any vocation as well as in their private lives.

Here is the way that case was put by the President's Science Advisory Committee in its well-publicized report of May 1959:

"The vocational necessities remain, but the best help our schools can now give many students is an intelligent understanding of the world in which they live—a basis on which they can begin to think and learn for themselves so that they will not be lost or supine in the changing world of tomorrow."

At the heart of my comments tonight lies, as I am sure you realize, an idea that has never really been tried in this land of universal education and individual freedom—the elementary idea that if we are going to make representative government work, not to mention providing the free individual with some of those inner resources we discussed earlier, we really have no choice but to expose all our students (excepting only those few whose intellectual equipment is clearly too

limited) to a rigorous, academic, liberalizing curriculum. Over 20 years ago, Sir Richard Livingstone, a great English scholar and a great schoolmaster, put the matter this way (the English, be it remembered, have had a very long experience with the liberal curriculum):

"Some people feel that the cultural subjects are unsuited for the masses. That is a possible view. But to hold it is to accept the most ruthless of class systems, to say that men differ not only in degree but in kind, and that the majority are incapable of studies without which there can be no intelligent idea either of the universe or of the greatness of the human spirit. If the majority of the electorate are incapable of these studies, we must either abandon democracy or resign ourselves to being governed by an electorate which can never know what a state should be."

Mr. Allott. Mr. President, I conclude my remarks upon this subject simply by saying I present my thoughts from the same viewpoint occupied by Mr. Koerner when he presented his views to the Farm Bureau. I do not believe we can ignore answering the questions he has asked. I commend them to my fellow Senators.

124

James B. Carey

HOW LABOR CAN HELP IMPROVE PUBLIC EDUCATION

One of the interesting developments in organized labor in recent years has been its greater interest in public education. Labor has always taken some part in education; but until now it has left educational leadership to others, and its efforts in behalf of the schools have been casual and sporadic. As these words of Vice-President Carey of the AFL-CIO indicate, we seem to have entered a new era in which the labor movement will be more active in school administration and even in curricular policy.

To compare Carey's viewpoint with that of Broun and Whitney (Readings 114 and 121) is to discover a startling shift in attitude. The incipient Progressivism of twenty-five years ago is nowhere in evidence. Instead, the space age has eliminated life adjustment as a curricular emphasis, as Carey indicates in this address to the National School Board Association. What next for the American curriculum?

[We] of labor, both as members of a militantly reformist organization and also as parents, are concerned about curriculum and about the quality of instruction.

We are deeply apprehensive about the appalling extent to which Soviet Russia has outstripped us —and according to Government sources is still outstripping us—in the training of highly skilled technical workers and scientists. It is tragic that we become concerned about our educational lag only when our very survival is threatened. As one writer put it recently, "Only with sputnik did our educational plant begin to be seriously looked at. We start worrying about brains only when we get ready to blow them out."

Obviously we need more vocational training, more technical training and—the experts tell us —a major revamping of science teaching in both elementary and secondary schools. These, together with a vastly expanded scholarship program, are absolute necessities if we are to meet the challenge of the space age and the atomic era. They are necessary if we are to preserve our freedoms, our way of life, our valuation of the dignity of man from the mounting menace of totalitarianism.

But at the same time we of labor are anxious that teaching of the humanities not be neglected. In the final analysis, the fine arts and the liberal arts together with the spiritual values of our Judao-Christian tradition constitute the true core of our civilization. The brave new world we seek is not just one centered on our conquest of space and the systematic achievement of new scientific marvels. It must be a world, also, in which man can enjoy a richer life of the intellect, a world of inner growth, a world of new intellectual, esthetic, and spiritual discovery.

What organized labor can do

A favorite quotation at teachers' conventions is the statement by Robert Hutchins, former president of the University of Chicago, that, "We do not know what education could do for us, because we have never tried it."

When I am asked "how organized labor can help improve public education," I am almost tempted to reply that "We do not know . . . because we have never tried it."

However, that wouldn't be wholly accurate. We have tried it and are trying it, to a limited extent. True, some communities—or rather the status quo minded leaders of some communities—have in years past deliberately blocked labor out from any participation on or with boards of education and prohibited any cooperation or joint programs by school officials and local labor bodies.

To a large extent, however, that picture has changed and is continuing to change, as part of a major transformation in the majority of progressive American communities. Not too many years back, as recently in fact as the years immediately prior to World War II, organized labor was strictly on the outside looking in with community chests, Red Cross chapters and virtually all social agencies.

Today organized labor is not just welcomed on the boards of directors of community chests, united funds, and other agencies. Labor's participation in the governing councils of these agencies is sought and solicited, and frequently considered indispensable. As a result, because labor has been accepted as a full-fledged partner, joining in the policymaking and sharing in the decisions, fund-raising campaigns have been successful as never before.

I believe the same process is currently under way in the Nation's educational systems. A generation ago, even two decades ago, a representative of organized labor on a school board was virtually unheard of. Today there are hundreds of unionists—either elected or appointed—on the school boards of big cities, small cities, and towns. And more and more union people are offering themselves as candidates for boards of education with every passing year.

School boards have benefited, even been enriched, by labor's participation, by the involvment of men and women representing the largest section of citizenry, wage earners and their families. School boards have been strengthened and revitalized by the inclusion of labor representatives with fresh vigorous viewpoints and with the militancy to set challenging new goals and achieve them.

But specifically now, what can organized labor do to help improve public education?

I am partisan, of course, but I think that organized labor, to one extent or another, can help find the solution to every problem that public education faces today. More than that, I am certain that organized labor can contribute more to the solution of some problems than any other section or group in our society.

Let me list, as concisely as I can, the things I think organized labor can do—and probably is already doing—today to help improve public education:

1. The labor movement can throw its strongest possible support behind the enactment by Congress of Federal legislation to assist new school construction, to facilitate the employment of more teachers, and to help raise teachers' pay scales.

From *Congressional Record* (86th Congress, First Session, January 29, 1959), Volume 105, Part 1, p. 1345.

2. The labor movement can push for the same objectives—new schools, more teachers and better-paid teachers—in State legislatures and city councils.

3. The labor movement can support, morally, organizationally, and financially, the election of Members of Congress, members of State legislatures, and members of city councils wholeheartedly committed to clear-cut programs for the improvement of public education.

4. The labor movement can help communities and school boards raise funds for new school construction and for current operating expenses by insisting on replacement of the present antiquated tax structure in which nearly 80 percent of all school revenue comes from property taxes with a new structure erected on a broader base in corporate and personal income taxes.

5. The labor movement can help communities and school boards raise funds for new construction by giving active support to the approval of school bond issues or equitable new local taxes.

6. The labor movement, for the purpose of launching school improvement programs, can use its influence to combine into one overall, co-ordinating group such organizations as parent-teacher associations, civic leagues, private welfare agencies, fraternal societies, religious bodies, citizens associations, and neighborhood groups.

7. The labor movement can support the efforts of school boards and educational societies to establish higher professional standards for teachers.

8. The labor movement can encourage and aid teachers in the formation of their own unions when and where they wish and to enjoy both the right and the benefits of collective bargaining.

9. The labor movement can help protect teachers against investigative hysteria and witch hunts, against unneeded and stupid loyalty oaths and against wholesale smear attacks by reactionary officials and superpatriotic outfits.

10. The labor movement can help make the teaching profession and, particularly, positions in local school systems more attractive by pushing for improved teacher-retirement programs and health insurance plans.

11. The labor movement can help local school boards combat the false "economy" programs and ruinous pennypinching fiscal policies of the U.S. Chamber of Commerce, its local affiliates and manufacturers' associations.

12. The labor movement can champion the cause of full academic freedom and democratic rights within the school system and in the community.

13. The labor movement can throw its weight behind State legislation and local laws raising the age levels for compulsory school attendance.

14. The labor movement can—both alone and in concert with other organizations—fight for the swift and complete eradication of segregation and Jim Crow in the Nation's schools.

15. The labor movement can campaign for free milk programs and free lunch programs in communities or in individual schools where they do not exist and where they are needed.

16. The labor movement can join with other organizations in demanding free immunization and other preventive medicine programs for schoolchildren plus X-rays and periodic eye, ear, throat, and dental examinations.

17. The labor movement can enlarge and diversify its own growing scholarship programs.

18. The labor movement can help lead community efforts to establish specialized educational programs for both gifted and retarded children. . . .

125

SCHOOLS FOUND WANTING

To see ourselves as others see us is usually a stimulating and enlightening experience, whether we agree with the other person's final judgment or not. In this case the "other" is the American Survey page of the London *Economist,* a conservative and highly respected journal of opinion. The views expressed in this article are confined to the secondary and elementary levels of instruction. This brief capsule of evaluation includes a surprising number of the curriculum factors already considered in this section, and it bears witness to the keen interest in American educational experiments which the rest of the world has felt. But, characteristic of the period following the war, no more than Americans do these English critics seem to know where the curriculum of the future is headed.

. . . As the President [Eisenhower] acknowledged when he charged school boards and Parent-Teachers' Associations to "scrutinise your schools' curriculum and standards to see whether they meet the stern demands of the era we are entering," the sickness which the sputnik has exposed is not to be cured by a halfpenny more spent on stinks. Many Americans have had a sinking feeling for a long time that their school system, of whose ideals they are justly proud, is not much good by any objective scholastic standards. The emphasis has been on life adjustment and the nursing of the childish psyche, rather than on the discipline of learning. The sacrifice seems hardly worth while, since Americans are not noticeably better adjusted to life—which presumably means less neurotic—than any one else.

Until relatively recently, the pressure to swing the pendulum away from permissiveness and towards the "three R's" has, most unfortunately,

been in the hands of extreme conservatives who had a mission to drive every kind of "dangerous idea" out of the schools and, indeed, out of the community. But in the last few years there has been an increasing number of broad-minded and tolerant people who have been turning a critical eye on "progressive education." They will now, it is hoped, be encouraged to take action since, in the words of the most civilised of American commentators, Mr. Eric Sevareid,

"suddenly it is being discovered, even by anti-intellectual Congressmen and state legislators, that the future of the American race also lies with the squares, grinds, eggheads and double-domes, with those queer ducks in bifocals who want to know why the grass is green or how to speak Hindustani, those weirdies who never made the team, dated the class queen, met a payroll, or played golf with a President."

. . . [It] will be a long time before one really knows quite how many miracles the Russian scientists have wrought.

From *The Economist of London*, November 3, 1957, 185:682.

126

D. W. Brogan

AMERICAN EDUCATION

Many competent authorities believe that D. W. Brogan, Professor of Political Science at Cambridge University, is one of the shrewdest critics of American civilization. This excerpt from his lecture at Rutgers University on American Education provides a more detailed glimpse into the kind of thinking which lies behind the succinct judgment rendered by the *Economist* (Reading 125). Currently, the United States has no better friend than Professor Brogan in English intellectual circles.

Since Brogan, of course, writes from the standpoint of an Englishman, the American student can profitably ask himself how many of Brogan's points also make sense to a young person born and raised in this country. Then he should attempt to discover just how Brogan would have us solve our problems.

. . . [The Greeks] not only preached and practiced what they called "gymnastic," they prac-

ticed what they called "music." They prized and rewarded intellectual achievement as they did physical achievement; they even prized it more. And it is the view of the current critics of the American school system that the American school system at all levels, from the primary school right through college, overdoes gymnastic and plays down music. I think the critics are right. I think that the social function of the school is overstressed and that the United States is now rich enough, unified enough, self-critical enough to ask more of the schools than that they should create a national ethos. It is mature enough, or ought to be mature enough, to be ready to ask the schools to lay less stress on making good, loyal Americans and more on making critical, technically competent citizens of a country that can no longer live to itself or be content with meeting its own self-created, historically justified but possibly obsolescent and dangerous standards. Again to harp on my implicit theme, the United States is living in a new, dangerous, unpleasant world and its educational system is in competition, as are all other sections of the American way of life. No one, I think, since Sputnik went into orbit doubts that.

All that I have described was useful, natural, defensible; it still is. The social functions of the school, especially of the high school, are not at an end. But one result of the concentration on that social function was not so much the lowering as the abandonment of standards. What was thought to be "education" in a European secondary school or old New England academy was too narrow for the new world. It was too narrow because it did neglect some useful and new and necessary techniques of the new world. But it was too narrow also because, if the old standards had been insisted on, many, many pupils whom it would have been necessary to exclude from the formal instruction would also have been excluded, to the national loss, from the social molding. So studies had to be found that these pupils could master and possibly use later, which was all right. But these were deemed to be equal with studies that a smaller group could master and use. Typing was as good as trig. This was a practical and tolerable solution a generation ago, a necessary acceptance of facts about American life. But the American school system is no longer concerned with American life, but just with life . . . and death.

That the shock given to American complacency by the Russian triumph was healthy I suppose no one doubts. It was not only an awakening to a serious military danger; it was a firm

suggestion to the American people to look at their educational system and to ponder both its defects and what can be done about them. It may be that by waking the American public from its undogmatic slumbers (in most cases it was plain slumber), Sputnik will rank with the shots at Lexington or Fort Sumter. It was certainly seen if not heard around the world.

What are the defects now being brought to the attention of the American parent? They are to some degree the reverse of the attractive medal to which I have called attention. If the main object of the school system is social and political, why should these aims be sacrificed to the mere pursuit of intellectual eminence? One answer is that among the urgent social and political aims of the United States at the present moment is survival in a highly competitive world, and that world cares little for the achievement of internal harmony in the United States and much for the distribution of mere material power. If the present school system is not producing an adequate supply of first-rate scientists and technicians, it is condemned for not doing a job that may be new but is one that must be tackled if the United States is to survive.

On the detailed criticisms of the curriculum, of the teachers, of the standards demanded and attained, I have nothing that is new and probably nothing that is valuable to say. Nevertheless, I shall say my piece. First of all, only a very rich country can afford a school system that takes so long to produce the finished product. In nearly all professions, possibly in all, the American finishes his professional training some years later than does his European opposite number. He may afford it in terms of money and the economy may afford it in terms of money, but can society afford it in terms of time? I wonder and I doubt. For the handful of absolutely top-flight and indispensable specialists perhaps the time is not too long. For the rest it is serious that entry into the productive field, whatever that field may be, should come so late. And it is so late because the boy and girl at the high school stage is not stretched enough.

I shall not inflict on you the current list of complaints. Why can't Johnny read? Why can't Sister count? Why can't Foreign Service officers speak foreign languages? Why do high schools aim so low in such vital fields as mathematics and physics? Why have colleges to do so much of what, in other countries, is regarded as schoolwork? I think all these questions are relevant, all contain some elements of just criticism. The justification of the social function of the common school that I have already given does not mean

From *America in the Modern World* by D. W. Brogan (New Brunswick, N.J.: Rutgers University Press, 1960), pp. 73-81.

that schools could not try harder and ask their pupils to try harder. Effort is not un-American; this is recognized in sport, and if schoolwork could be given some of the prestige of games, of the teams, even of the band, there might be less to complain about. In an account of life in a progressive college for young women, Randall Jarrell makes a German professor recall that the Emperor William II once expressed alarm that German parents were ruining their children's eyesight by encouraging them to work too hard at school. He went on to say that no educational system did more to protect the pupils' eyesight than the American—an unkind but not, I think, totally unjust remark.

James Bryant Conant has been inspecting the high schools of the country and has published his findings. I am in total agreement with everything that the report suggests in the way of improving the curriculum and of distinguishing between the pupils who are doing what I may be allowed to call "real" schoolwork and those who are being prepared for the unexamined life. The really bright boy and girl is the victim of the present school system and he or she must be delivered from the lockstep of promotion by age or the temptations of snap courses, as well as from the positive deprivation of good teaching given by teachers who are not tied by their own limitations to the textbook and can keep abreast and ahead of the class. If this means rethinking the function of schools of education, I am all for it.

But a European observer, especially an observer from England, will be struck by the fact that even after the Conant program is put into effect the pupil in the American high school is not going to be overworked or, if you like to put it that way, equipped to enter on university work as soon as he might be. Even after the Conant reforms, colleges will still be doing what is in France or England thought to be schoolwork. To avoid any imputation of displaying the condescension attributed to foreigners I may say that I am far from enamored of the results of the English system. We specialize too early and if our specialization produces some brilliant specimens who leave school fit to enter the junior class of a good American university, it also produces one-sided and intellectually crippled specimens who leave the university less fit for a higher education than when they entered it, victims of a system that encourages specialization from the age of fourteen and assumes that a bright boy will pick up all the surrounding knowledge that he needs to make him an educated man.

But if *we* assume, too easily and in face of the evidence, that plunging a boy into what may be a narrow specialization at an age when his curiosity ought to be wide and welcoming is a prudent proceeding, *you,* it seems to me, fall victims to what is, I firmly believe, the great American educational superstition. That is the belief that all that must be learned need be or, indeed, can be taught. It is my view that a great deal of what we need to learn we can learn only by doing, by *really* doing, not by simulating doing in school, that many problems can only be dealt with as they arise, that many problems cannot be reduced to terms of courses and textbooks. And my final heresy is that we must enter life with the knowledge that there are problems, as yet unknown, that we shall fail to solve, that what we are promised is the right to the pursuit of happiness, not happiness itself. (I have been told that the constitution of California promises happiness, but, then, California is outside normal human calculation.)

Behind the weakness of the high school curriculum, behind the weakness of much of the college curriculum, lies the belief that the school in its widest sense must take over all that the church, the town meeting, and the family did in the past, the belief that the good American is the successful applier of recipes for success and happiness learned at school and college or by postal refresher courses. What is the relevance of this belief to the burning question of the curriculum? First of all, it helps to account for the "democratic" character of the curriculum, for the equalization in formal merit of math and washing machine management. You will seldom have to use math—look at all the little reckoners you can buy—you will have to know how to run the washing machine or whatever other gadget is in question. To insist, nevertheless, that if a high school has got to choose it had better choose math or Latin is to be undemocratic. It is to insist that some things are superior to others and, in turn, that fewer people can master these than can master the techniques of mechanical living. I do not deny the importance of the machine aids to gracious living. But they can be bought; the art of running them can be learned easily. The boy who majors in filling station skills and even the girl who majors in cookery (a more fundamental and more serious art) are, from the school's point of view, a less important investment than the one who can handle concepts or can see why a machine works or why proteins are necessary to a good diet. It is not the main business of the school to prepare a boy or girl simply to earn his living or even to be a good American in the patriotic sense. At any rate, it is wrong to make this so much the aim of the school system that the exceptional boy or girl is never stretched and for that reason may never know or want to use the full potentialities of his or her talent.

Even for the average boy, even for the less than average boy, the attempt to substitute for the home, the church, and society in general has its dangers. The case for the religious neutrality of the American public school is overwhelmingly strong, but it is, I think, an illusion that because it would be dangerous or impossible to fill the gap made by the decline of formal belief (I do not say of formal or real religion) the gap is not there. To be silent on the greatest questions of human destiny is necessary, since we are not agreed on the answers, but it leaves the questions to be felt, even by the dull, as unanswered. It is wrong, then, to suggest that the school system can or should answer all the questions that an adolescent or even a young man or woman will put to the universe. Perhaps no school system can, but certainly an officially neutral system can't.

What can it do? First of all, I think, in the present crisis it should not educate the pupil "for the world he is going to live in." We don't know what kind of world he is going to live in; all that we can be certain of is that, during a normal lifetime, the world will change in ways we can't now foresee. What we can do is to suggest that the world will change, and give intellectual tools for understanding that truth, intellectual prophylaxis against the provincialism which suggests that only the most obviously current problems are the real problems. (Sputnik merely called attention to certain defects in American education; it did not create the defects.) Unless at least the more intelligent pupils are given some critical habits (including the habit of not believing all that their teachers tell them), we can be sure of one thing. They will not be at home in the world, the unknown world they are going to live in, and no textbooks, no courses, no Advice to the Lovelorn columns are going to help very much. Education would benefit in efficiency and prestige if it were more modest and more presumptuous, if it refused to claim to do so much and insisted on a hierarchy of values in what it can do.

There may be an apparent paradox in my now insisting on the encouragement of the critical spirit after applauding the success of the school system in breeding loyalty and in creating a common tradition. But it is an inevitable danger that the necessary solutions of one age are carried over to another. What the American school system did a generation ago was necessary (and the

United States could afford the wasteful elements in the solution), but today I doubt that it is necessary and that the United States can afford so much waste of time which is waste of brains.

In what sense and in what directions should the critical spirit be encouraged? Here I will begin by making a concession to the ideal of national unity. I do not suggest that the American school set out to disabuse its pupils of admiration for the American way of life. If the formation of a united nation is no longer the primary task of the schools, the formation of a disunited nation is certainly no legitimate object for a school system. It is possible to encourage the critical spirit and yet to be nearly sure that the end product will be a deeper and more intelligent appreciation of American life rather than a simple admiration for everything in America merely because it is "American." (After all, that involves admiring very different and often inconsistent things.) For the bright boy or girl, what the school can profitably do is to give him or her the habit of looking at contemporary social and political problems with the rule of judgment in his mind, not only that the American way can sometimes be wrong but also that the world, rightly or wrongly, is not necessarily destined to go the American way—at any rate, not if the blind force of things is simply left to take its course.

The pupil who has been forced to stretch himself, who because he is bright has been steered away from snap courses and quick and easy answers, should be given the habit of waiting before he makes up his mind, even in a patriotic and American direction. He should most certainly not be given the idea that we know already how the world must go, that we have a plan given to us that history must follow. One of the most dangerous illusions of the Communist world is that they have such a plan, and one of the dangers to world peace that most alarms me is the confidence that this belief breeds and the temptation that it offers to bend history, past and future, to fit the plan. The American high school pupil of the brighter type should leave school with certain intellectual tools that he can use and with an intellectual attitude incompatible with the easy belief that there is an answer ready for all questions, or even that we know what the questions will be to which we, individually and nationally, will want answers. The time for just making Americans is over, or, at any rate, it is not the only job of the schools; the time for the making of the critical and open-minded citizen has arrived. . . .

127

Philip H. Phenix

KEY CONCEPTS AND THE CRISIS IN LEARNING

Professor Philip Phenix, a member of the staff at Teachers College, Columbia University, here suggests a possible approach to the curriculum of the future. He starts from the now-famous "explosion of knowledge" and the crisis in learning which has resulted from the sheer impossibility of stuffing even the irreducible minimum of vital information into one protesting brain-case. His observations are similar to those of Webster and Eliot (Readings 112 and 113), but other thinkers had evaded the issue by the simple device of calling subject matter unimportant. Now the pendulum is swinging back again.

The solution which Phenix offers is a shift to conceptual learning; but this shift raises many new questions. Whether Phenix has the real answer to our question of "Whither the curriculum?" it is too early to say, but at least the process of re-thinking and new-thinking is under way once more.

We have become accustomed to a condition of perpetual crisis—in economic, political, military, social, moral, and many other domains of human life. Hence it will occasion no surprise that one should speak of a crisis in learning. The purpose of this discussion is to state the nature of this crisis, in which modern education is deeply involved, and to suggest one way of alleviating it.

The problem

Modern man possesses a vast and rapidly expanding supply of knowledge. There are many causes for this, including the persistent application of scientific procedures to the whole compass of human experience, the invention of instruments whereby the precision and range of inquiry have been greatly increased, the explosive growth in world population, with a corresponding rise in the numbers of workers in every field of inquiry, and the provision of extensive libraries and museums for preserving the accumulated treasures of the past. Furthermore, modern facilities for travel and communication have made available the major part of the whole world's store of knowledge to anyone who wishes to use it. In the many great collections of books, technical displays, and art exhibits anyone can get first-hand knowledge of the cultural achievements of mankind.

Not only is knowledge available in abundance, but the requirements of modern life place a premium on mastering it. A highly complex industrial society can endure only if it is cared for by persons of technical competence and social wisdom. The demand for technical mastery has been the basis for specialization in education, through which the requisite ability in a restricted field is developed at the expense of broader understanding. The demand for social wisdom, on the other hand, has been met, in the general education movement, by the complementary emphasis on breadth of comprehension.

Part of the dilemma of modern man—and of modern education—consists in this simultaneous demand for technical mastery and for liberal understanding. To keep the world machine going, an ever-increasing supply of highly trained experts is imperative. But it is precisely the narrowness of vision resulting from the concentration necessary to produce the experts that may cause that ignorance of the whole which can destroy the delicate balance of the civilized order.

Over against this phenomenal increase in the available knowledge and in the technical demands of modern civilization must be placed the fact that the human being's capacity to learn has not correspondingly increased. In fact, the swift pace of contemporary living and its attendant psychic strains may have actually diminished the ability

From *Teachers College Record*, December 1956, 58: 137-143.

to learn, by comparison with calmer and more stable eras.

The crisis in learning consists in this disproportion between what is available and necessary to know and the capacity of the individual to know it. This is perhaps the fundamental problem which contemporary education faces. Every person is embarrassed by the wealth of available knowledge which he cannot hope to appropriate.

The results of this situation are all too apparent, particularly to professional intellectuals. There is a frantic scramble to "keep up" in one's own specialized field, to have even a nodding acquaintance with the most important research and writing being done in it, and to read even cursorily the current journals of the profession. Coupled with this is the anxiety that one cannot keep abreast of even the most basic advances in other fields, whether it be in the archaeology of the Dead Sea Scrolls or in the physics of the pi-meson.

Students also know the crisis well, especially at the higher levels of education. Spurred on by specialists, each of whom acts as if he expected everyone to master the contents of his own discipline, the student becomes burdened and discouraged at the hopelessness of the task that lies before him. Little wonder that so many seek escape in the narrow and unimaginative security of a highly circumscribed academic discipline.

No doubt also the widespread anti-intellectualism of our day is another evidence of the crisis in learning. The manifest impossibility of knowing all that one needs to know and that is ready to be known begets an attitude of despair which may issue either in the average man's simple neglect of reason and his recourse to uninformed "common sense" or in the desperate intellectual's highbrow rationalization of anti-reason, as in certain aspects of the Existentialist movement.

The principle of economy

The crisis in learning points to what Ortega y Gasset called the basic principle of education, namely the *principle of economy*. According to this, the purpose of education is to organize the work of teaching and learning in such a way that the limited capacity to learn is most efficiently utilized. The primary aim of education is to minimize the disparity between available knowledge and ability to know. Teachers, schools, and curricula serve the basic purpose of making the best possible bargain out of the immensely over-balanced ratio of cultural capital to individual learning power. Selection and grouping of students, choice of subject matter and of teaching methods, and all other educational arrangements must in the last analysis be formulated and judged with reference to this principle of economy.

One type of approach to educational economy is *administrative*. Some of the basic functions of the administrator are to organize teachers and learners in the most efficient practicable ways, to make available suitable buildings, equipment, and materials, and to establish effective channels of communication and supply. All such objective regulation of conditions is an administrative contribution to economy.

A second type of approach is *psychological*. Testing procedures of many kinds, teaching methods based on research in learning, intelligent approaches to emotional development, and use of data on motivation are some of the fruits of psychological understanding which have been profitably applied to enlarge the human capacity to learn.

A third approach is *philosophical*. It attacks the crisis in learning by an analysis of the nature of knowledge in its several kinds. The thesis of this discussion is that by a philosophical analysis of the fields of human knowledge and by appropriate application of the results of this analysis, a spectacular economy in learning can be effected. Only this approach attacks the problem at its point of real difficulty, namely, the overwhelmingness of the knowledge-store. By administrative and psychological means the conditions and capacities for learning can at best be improved only moderately. It appears that only through the philosophic analysis of knowledge can a really drastic economy be realized.

Philosophers in recent times have been especially interested in the problems of knowledge in such fields as science, history, the arts, and religion. It seems clear that the results of these inquiries ought now to be applied to the concerns of education, particularly toward the solution of the basic problem of economy. The present discussion is an attempt to indicate one way in which this can be done.

Organization of knowledge

The aim of the proposal is to effect a radical simplification in the content of knowledge to be learned. This can be done by taking advantage of the fact that knowledge is not merely an accumulation of isolated and independent items of information. Individual items are interconnected within idea-systems. Each bit of knowledge resides within one or more characteristic frameworks. Among the many ideas which can be known certain dominant family resemblances can be discerned. These similarities of type make it possible to classify what is known into fields of knowledge or subject-matter areas, such as physics, psychology, literary criticism, and so on.

This process of classifying knowledge is not simply for convenience in apportioning the work of scholars and teachers. It also provides the clue to educational economy. It is possible to "know physics" not by becoming familiar with the many special facts and theories which are by convention included within that field but by understanding those common features which cause the individual items to be assigned to this field. In the same way, "knowing psychology" may consist in comprehending precisely what it is that makes a particular fact belong to psychology rather than to physics or history or art.

Economy and concept-formation

The economizing power of human intelligence lies in its ability to form class concepts. For example, the concept "dog" stands for a whole class of entities with specifiable common properties. To know what dogs are one does not need to become acquainted with all the members of this animal group. Thus by concept-formation an enormous simplification of experience becomes possible, the multiplicity of individual items being caught up in general ideas.

Now concept-formation applies not only to the classification of perceptual objects but to the organization of the facts and theories which make up the fabric of knowledge. Economy in learning requires that the principle of simplification by means of concept-formation be extended beyond the realm of things to the realm of ideas. We take for granted the economy afforded by using concepts like "dog" in lieu of individual enumerations. Not so clearly seen is the need for concepts that will summarize the essential characteristics of a distinctive class of ideas in a field of knowledge such as physics or psychology.

Key concepts

By a careful analysis of the structure of knowledge it is possible to discover certain *key concepts* distinguished by their power to epitomize important common features of a large number of more particular ideas. Such concepts are basic central ideas an understanding of which opens the door to an effective grasp of an entire field of knowledge. These key ideas provide as it were a map whereby the whole scheme of a subject may be grasped and characteristic features of individual items of knowledge may for the first time be rightly interpreted. It is doubtful, for example, whether individual propositions in mathematics can really be understood unless certain key ideas of mathematics as a whole are comprehended. Similarly, it is questionable whether or not one can rightly know a work of art without possessing a key to the whole artistic enterprise.

It is the present thesis that the only satisfactory answer to the crisis in learning lies in the formulation and persistent use of key concepts. Teachers ought above all to know the basic rationale of their disciplines and should conduct their instruction in the light of these essential principles. This does not mean that the key concepts should be taught explicitly and directly, at least to beginners. It does mean that particular items of knowledge should be selected and used with an eye to their exemplification of the basic concepts of the field.

Ineffective teaching and learning, according to this thesis, are due in no small degree either to the failure to understand the need for comprehensive organizing concepts and their function in the economy of learning or to using the wrong key concepts (e.g., having mistaken ideas about what science or history *really* is).

Two disclaimers

There is no intention here of claiming that each field has a *single* key concept which epitomizes it. Any number of relatively comprehensive ideas can be used to yield essential understanding of a given subject. What is claimed is that *some* concepts of high generality can be found which will provide truer insight into a field than could be gained by mere heaping up of isolated scraps of information.

Secondly, no claim is made for the special value or superior relevance of the traditional knowledge or subject-matter fields. As knowledge develops, better organizing principles appear from time to time, old disciplines decline and new fields are opened up. Actually, discovery of powerful key concepts applicable to a given group of ideas is the best way of defining a field of knowledge.

Key concepts in illustrative areas

In the following paragraphs some examples will be given to show in selected areas of knowledge what is meant by key concepts. Doubtless there would not be consensus even (or especially) among the experts on the choice of representative generalizations. These examples are merely meant to give substance to the basic thesis outlined above and not to argue the case for one set of key ideas rather than another. That is to say, the purpose of the present article is not to expound the philosophy of the several fields of knowledge but solely to suggest an approach to educational economy through the use of key ideas.

Science. What is science? What does it mean to "understand science"? What makes knowledge scientific as contrasted with non-scientific? What are the "big ideas" of science which, once grasped, make possible a penetrating insight into all of the detailed inquiries of the special branches of science?

The essence of science is not in its concern for fact, nor in the alleged truth of its claims, nor in power to control nature for human ends, nor in the possession of a special method (for example, techniques of problem-solving). One key concept in science is that of *abstraction*. Science is characterized by the search for valid generalizations, and this is accomplished by analyzing complete entities so as to reveal certain common properties. Thus science deals not with complete things but always with perspectives, aspects, or components of things, that is, not with the concrete but with abstractions.

A second key to science is the idea of *public verification*. Scientific knowledge is distinguished by the designation of tests which any person could in principle carry out to verify the propositions asserted. Where these procedures are not specified, the alleged knowledge does not fall within the province of science.

A third key concept in science is that of *fruitfulness*. The scientific enterprise is the search for fruitful hypotheses, for theories which lead to further inquiry and discovery. Hypotheses which open no new doors are scientifically useless.

"Understanding science" is not a matter of mastering large quantities of scientific fact but of discerning the fundamental intention of all scientific inquiry through such key ideas as abstraction, public verification, and fruitfulness. One who does not know these does not really understand science, regardless of how much scientific information he possesses.

Physical science. More specifically, learning physical science is not in essence a matter of accumulating information about material bodies, or force, or atoms, nor of becoming familiar with such principles as Newton's laws, Bohr's theory, and Einstein's cosmology. The distinctive character of the various special sciences is in their particular kinds of abstractions. One key to physical science is the abstracting of *mass, length,* and *time* characteristics of things, that is, the process of *physical measurement* by such instruments as the balance, the meter stick, and the clock. All physical science is the determination of the metric aspects of things and their interrelationships. To secure a thorough grasp of the process of mass, length, and time measurement is really to understand the genius of physical science in a way which illuminates all the innumerable special items of knowledge that make up the field.

Mathematics. Can one in some sense really know mathematics, without traversing the long road of technical discipline in the subject? Is there some elemental insight into the essential meaning of mathematical processes necessary to the professional mathematician and the layman alike?

Mathematics is not in essence knowledge about numbers, nor about techniques of calculation. The special skills and principles learned from arithmetic through tensor calculus are particular instances of a much more general type of activity common to all branches of the subject. One key idea in which all mathematics shares is the concept of the *axiomatic,* according to which mathematical entities are created by human decision about symbols and the rules of combination applicable to them. No one understands mathematics until he knows this most elemental truth: that symbols and their systems are for the choosing and that the game is to be faithfully played by the rules thus selected.

A second key to mathematics is the concept of *necessary inference,* according to which the conclusions implicit in the basic axioms are successively deduced from them. Mathematical competence, in whatever special department of the subject, rests upon correctness in deductive reasoning, and whoever fails to recognize this does not understand mathematics, regardless of how many skills in technical computation he may possess.

History. What is history? Is one's knowledge of the subject in proportion to the quantity of historical information he has collected? Or are there keys to history which afford insight into what any historian is engaged in doing? Is there a "big idea" in all historical knowledge?

History is not merely the sum total of events transpiring in time. It is not a collection of dates, a record of rulers and of wars, a statement of facts about the past. One key to history is the concept of *interpretation*. The historian tells a story—*his* story—and to do this he must select from the events of the past those which by some standard seem to him worth reporting. History is interpretation because it is necessarily selective. It is not bare events but meaningful happenings.

Hence the study of history can be seen as the study of meanings perceived by historians in events. In a fundamental sense one understands history when he has grasped the idea of interpretation and knows how to look in historical writings for the presuppositions and value systems implicit in the principles of selectivity used. This insight, perhaps generated by only a few perceptively taught examples, gives a more nearly adequate grasp of the whole field of history than any amount of quiz-show fact-gathering.

Art. The field of the arts also has its key concepts. To understand art is more than to be familiar with paintings, symphonies, dramas, and the like. It is more than to possess skill in producing beautiful things, or to have trained sensitivity in perceiving them.

One key to the understanding of art is the concept of the *concrete, individual whole*. In this respect artistic perception is at the opposite pole from the scientific. While science is concerned with analysis, abstraction, and generalization, art is always in the realm of the synthetic, complete, and particular. The art object is a complex unity, and aesthetic creation is always an act of individuation.

Another key to art is the idea of *significant form*, of patterned contrast, of different elements brought into an effective unity of thought and feeling. The peculiar service of the arts is to make manifest through concrete embodiment the endless variety of possible significant forms and thus to awaken and sustain a sense of the inexhaustible richness of existence.

To understand art is to hold the keys to what all aesthetic enterprise is fundamentally about. With such understanding it is not necessary to assume the overwhelming burden of systematic study of the whole range of art works.

Religion. A final illustrative example is the field of religion. How can one become religiously literate without engaging in an exhaustive study of the many conflicting creeds, the differing rites and ceremonies, and the diverse patterns of ecclesiastical organization? What is the key to understanding the essential nature of this multifarious phenomenon?

One possible unitary principle for religion is the idea of *ultimate concern* or of controlling life-orientation for a group or an individual. The various beliefs, practices, and institutions can then be regarded as so many symbolic and behavioral expressions of the basic pattern of supreme commitment. Accordingly, the well-educated person in respect to religion is one who understands the role of ultimate concern in human life and not necessarily the one who has laboriously acquainted himself with the myriad details about the religions of mankind.

Conclusion

There is a crisis in learning, due to the disproportion between man's limited capacity to learn and the extraordinary expansion in available knowledge. Neither personally nor socially is it satisfactory to meet this crisis by condemning individuals to specialization in a narrow discipline, to the exclusion of true understanding in other fields of knowledge. Such a plan both impoverishes the individual and undermines the foundations of social order.

To develop free men in a healthy society is the task of a truly liberal education dedicated to the growth of wide yet profound understanding. The required wisdom cannot be achieved by a prodigious effort to keep up with the onrolling tide of new knowledge nor yet by a frantic attempt to grasp the accumulated treasures of the past. The only sure way appears to be the one method whereby man's intellect has always brought order and simplicity out of the confusing multiplicities of experience, namely, the process of concept-formation.

Thus the theory of knowledge in its several areas provides a means for developing key concepts which by indicating the essential character of whole fields of knowledge can insure the necessary general understanding with relatively limited knowledge of specific details. The use of such key ideas in the organization and teaching of subject matter may effect important economies in learning effort, greatly increase the depth of comprehension, and facilitate further independent exploration in any discipline. These are the conditions for the making of well-educated persons and they are one answer, from the philosophy of education, to the crisis in learning.

THE ACTIVITIES AND SERVICES OF THE SCHOOL

In addition to the formal course of study and the academic phases of the school program, other activities and services have come to be considered a part of the school program, particularly in the secondary schools and the colleges. The range of activities includes class-related club activities, publications, musical organizations, student-government bodies, and intramural and interscholastic athletics. The problem of deciding which and how many of such activities are important is not an easy one. Once this decision has been made there is also the problem of scheduling, staffing, and financing.

Related to the development of the activities program is the decision as to what other services should be part of the school program. One of those most closely related to the traditional function of the school is the guidance function. Guidance and counseling services are considered essential in both large and small schools in order to adjust the program of the school to the needs of the students and to provide assistance in their educational problems. Other services which have been incorporated in the modern educational program include those which provide for student health, for food, for transportation, and for child welfare.

The activities and services of the school

THE ACTIVITIES OF THE MODERN SECONDARY SCHOOL

If the essential purpose of secondary schooling is intellectual development, then emphasis on the varied interests, avocations, and skills represented by participation in the activities program *may* have to be viewed as peripheral rather than central to the mission of the school. On the other hand, justification for the place of activities in the school may be based on the need to recognize the interests of peer groups, to help children commit themselves to some absorbing endeavor, and to take cognizance of the fact that the school has accepted (or had thrust upon it) responsibility for the personal and social development of its pupils. The teacher must determine the value of activities in terms of his overall responsibility and decide in what ways activities will better facilitate the total mission of the school.

Deciding how various activities contribute to a particular educational goal is sometimes a difficult philosophical problem for the teacher who has been trained as a subject specialist. To what extent is he to serve as an adolescent "baby-sitter" or as manager of a teen-age date club? Or, to what extent is he to commit himself to the critical interests of adolescents in order to better relate his educational purposes to the interests of students? In short, the viewpoint from which the high-school teacher sees the problem of school activities determines to a large extent his relationship with students. Readings 128 and 129 discuss aspects of the activities program in secondary schools and present ideas of both a philosophical and a practical nature.

128

Laurence S. Flaum

THE CREATIVE ACTIVITY PROGRAM FOR SECONDARY SCHOOLS

In this article Dr. Flaum describes in detail the problems in the operation of a creative-activity program in the modern secondary school. He cautions that in an up-to-date functional curriculum, "extracurricular" activities are by no means "extra."

The creative activity program is not an addition to or extra to the regular school program. The creative activity program is an integral part of the vital learning situation which makes up the whole school curriculum. The concept that activities are in any way extra or that they are in any way appended to the regular school schedule is a misunderstanding of what a functional curriculum is in our present day schools. It contradicts the fact that a functional curriculum may best be defined as the composite of vital experiences which pupils have under the direct or indirect supervision of the schools. Thus conceived, the curriculum includes all types of pupil activity, whether formally or informally organized and developed. It includes the creative activity program, directly organized by the school.

This is especially true and valuable to the school because the activity program recognizes that pupils, as individuals, are different, one from the other, but their differences are of degree, not of kind. Our students are more similar and have more like interests than they are dissimilar. Because of this, creative activity groupings are possible in terms of common interests, common needs, common enthusiasms, and common aspirations. The creative activity within the school day allows each individual to act individually and yet participate in a group, in activities where he can share his skills, ideas and learnings by working with others, gaining ideas from others, and projecting ideas and convictions of his own. It is within vital school guided activities that the differences in intelligence, temperament, racial background, religion, economic status, which make up the personality of each student, are used as an enrichment force in each activity, and makes each activity live realistically for each student. Activities which recognize these differences and

From *Educational Forum*, November 1950, 15:93-101.

backgrounds of individuals are doing practical, useful education because these differences individually are found in the average public high schools in our country. The total philosophy of a creative activity program is one of enriching the personal, social, and creative life of the students.

Unfortunately, in many schools today, especially in small schools, the activity program is the sole avenue by which actual needs of students are met. The required curriculum, narrow and academically conceived, does not answer the latent talent needs of the students. The activity program, however, as compared to the rigid program of academic required courses, directly concerns itself with the problems of our youth. When creatively conceived, the activity program is as broad and as realistic as the demands and needs and interests of our youth are broad and sincerely felt.

Specifically, the creative activity program in a school which is attempting to answer the needs of its community and its young, concerns itself by developing activities which include the physical, emotional and spiritual health of its students. It concerns itself with developing activities which encourage social understandings, with developing tolerance and understanding of other humans regardless of race, color, or creed. It concerns itself with developing good citizen behaviors as well as citizen competencies. It concerns itself with guidance seminar activities dealing with problems of mental hygiene, family relationships, and family participation in order to make for individual and group satisfactory adjustments to family living. It concerns itself with developing a greater understanding of the world through investigation. It concerns itself with guidance which will tend to eliminate fears and prejudices regarding this world and our place in it. It concerns itself with helping the student develop and utilize his creative talents and open up further worlds of appreciation in the areas of aesthetics. It concerns itself through guidance seminar activities with developing a student's understanding of the world of work and his place in it, as well as helping the student develop an abiding philosophy of life, both ethical and moral and social. Finally, through all the activities, there is an attempt at developing an understanding of the way free men live in a free society as well as the developing of techniques whereby students can learn to live and do, in this free society.

Definitely, the activity program faces real challenges and these challenges are not academic in nature. There is a definite feeling among our high school youth and our recent high school graduates that the school, as presently conceived and developed in many of our areas today, is failing them and has failed them. It is failing them in not providing facilities or activities which will give them enough advisement or guidance on personal problems; in not giving them advisement on vocational choices; in not giving them a sense that the school has value to them, culturally and economically; and in not giving them adequate understandings with which to face life successfully. The activity program attempts to answer these challenges through its in-curricular creative activity program within the school day in which all students participate, and through seminar guidance activities in which all students share their common problems. How is this done? How can such a program be developed which can answer the personal, social, vocational, and creative talent needs of our high school youth?

The functional school recognizes that student growth is a direct result of a guided activity. The functional school recognizes that activity for its own sake is evading the issue, is not constructive, and does not help the student or the teacher. The functional school recognizes that too much that is done today under the guise of an activity program is without a specific goal. These are the activities that are neither planned nor do they have social direction nor are they based upon the student's needs, interests or goals.

Today functional schools recognize that the creative activity program is an experience which a student must have in order to become a more creative and active personality in society. This program is developed in order to challenge the mental as well as the physical development of the student. It is created co-operatively by teachers and students according to the express needs of the students and the abilities of the teachers. The activity program is not sponsored by teachers; each activity is guided and taught by teachers as a regular class with definite activity or academic credit in physical surroundings suitable for each activity. Each activity meets within the school day at such a time when it is respected, both by students and teachers. It is not assigned to a last period of the day or the first period after lunch when the teachers and students look upon it as a nuisance. In many schools today the last period of the day is used as an activity program period and this placement is one of the weaknesses of the program. It occurs at a time of day when the teachers are tired and the students feel that the activity program is an appendage to the regular school day, and, as such, participate only half-heartedly. It is best that the activity period meet and is given a regular period during the school day so that all students may participate in the program. It is best that this period come at such a time early enough in the day when it can be followed by a regular class, commonly thought of as an academic class. (There need not be this distinction between periods or classes. When an activity is creatively organized, guided and taught, it has equal value with any of the so-called academic courses. When it is taught and guided by a competent teacher, student growth is evaluated and student interest is met. No class can claim more as its reason for existence in the school day.)

How extensive is the program? The activity program includes as many activities as the number of teachers on the staff. Every staff member is utilized in the planned activity program according to his abilities, interests, and inclinations and hobby experience. Teachers who possess the greatest outside school experience and who have a rich background of personal participation in activities make the best activity guides. Teachers are allowed choices as to activities in which they will guide and in which they wish to work just as students are allowed choices as to areas in which they wish to participate. Activities are on a semester basis.

The most common activities found in schools attempting to meet the activity needs of its students are art projects, photography, interpretative dancing, folk music, band, chorus, dramatics, and various aspects of physical education.

All creative activities are social as well as individual in nature. The experiences which a student acquired through the completion of an activity are social and are shared with his fellow students. The experience itself is enriching and rounding to his own personality. Each activity allows for true as well as vicarious learning, both of which are constructive in the growth of the student. Activity learning, thus, is not an isolated process, though each individual learns according to his individual interest and his own rate of speed and intensity.

Out of constructive activity programs and the development of latent talents in students, oftentimes future adult careers can be made. This is not to be overlooked by the functional school which is attempting to help the student meet the needs of his academic life as well as social and intellectual maturation.

Too often the activity program, as commonly developed in schools, is confused with an athletic or extracurricular program. The average layman as well as the average schoolman views the athletic program or dramatics as being the highlight of an activity program. These people are misinterpreting the function and nature of an activity program as well as misinterpreting their duty to the greatest number of students. Athletics, dramatics, music are only a small, though strong, outgrowth of an activity program of which they are part, but they are no more important in the growth of the many students in the school than photography, woodwork, handcrafts, or any other activities which are the outgrowth of student needs. The competitive athletic program, the competitive dramatic program, the competitive music program, which makes up the so-called activity program of all together too many schools, meets the needs of too few students and places the emphasis upon winning rather than the growth of the student. All of these have growth elements in them, but the growth elements are unfortunately too often understated while the competitive elements are equally unfortunately overstated.

There are certain cautions which should be observed in the planning of a creative activity program. They are: (1) Too many activity programs emphasize physical activities without regard for their guidance value, their aesthetic value, or their intellectual value. (2) There is too little recognition of the social value and social direction of activities. There is too little recognition of the necessity for teaching tolerance and understanding and adequate social adjustments through activities. (3) There is too great a gap between the aims of activities and the actual results of the activities because there is too little evaluation both of student growth and of the methods and procedures used in carrying on the activities. There is too much reliance upon placing an activity program on paper in a schedule and then in not following through to see how the activity is developing and growing. (4) There is too little in-service training of teachers for activity guidance and direction. In too many schools teachers lack a vital understanding of the purposes of an activity, how it is to be conducted, and how group learning takes place. Because of this, activities become haphazard, aimless, and, too often, both the students and teachers become

disillusioned with an activity program. (5) In many schools there is too much emphasis upon what will be the results of activities instead of a concern with how the activities are developed, how they are organized, how they are conducted, as well as the results of the activities. Because of this, there are no common grounds upon which administrators and teachers and students can meet and plan activities together.

Perhaps the most vicious element with which educators are to be concerned in regard to activity programs is the sense that they are extra, is the sense that they are frills in education, fads and whims in which students participate. There is too much verbalism and talk about activities and not enough useful doing about activities so that the people of our communities can become informed and aware of the vital nature of activities and their integral part in a realistic curriculum for our modern youth. Teachers and administrators should be aware that activities are to be evaluated in terms of their age to general education, vocational education, guidance and individual growth of the students. They are to be aware and are to inform their communities through parent-school visitation, home visitation by teachers, newspapers, and social organizations that activities have definite value in relation to the needs of the community. The ultimate test of the values of activities is what kind of citizens do our students become.

The activity program in action

In planning a creative activity program, the students and the staff as a whole should not lose sight of the fact that the activity program, because of its nature and structure, does not cover or attempt to cover the whole field of experience. It limits itself to the activities which meet the most urgent needs of its students and is adapted to the number of teachers and their abilities.

Creative activities are challenges to enterprising boys and girls and to ingenious teachers who are constantly alert to new and realistic activity needs in a flexible activity curriculum. Creative teachers and interested pupils plan the type and direction of the activity. In this way, it combines the teacher's experience and the pupils' interests and individual needs. Through such co-operation the pupil and teacher are conscious of the social direction of the activity program and the necessity for carrying each activity through to its logical educative end before the pupil undertakes a new activity.

The place of the teacher in the creative activity program is that of a dynamic guide. The teacher recognizes the importance of the pupil's creative impulses and utilizes them for the benefit of each individual within the group. Activities are the source of individual character development and activity expression. Thus, the creative activity program, through utilizing all of its school environmental possibilities and through encouraging pupil participation in planning, is an enriched experiential contribution to pupil growth. The creative teacher realizes that the social value of activities is based upon the concept that the human desire to share experiences is the spontaneous end of activity education.

The activity program must be based upon the clear recognition by the teacher of the value of pupil self direction in social group situations. Individual experimental activities are necessary for further realistic activity experimentation when individual pupil talents demand such adjustments. The concrete experiences obtained from activities which directly affect the needs of the pupil develop personal and social qualities in the pupil.

These qualities, when the pupil intelligently transfers his interest to similar problematic situations in other activity fields, enable him to respond accurately to the new situation. The teacher as a guide should be aware that the educative outcomes of the activity program should be natural to the pupil. Each activity should challenge his total personality. Activities should develop habits and skills which are of greater value than any specific subject matter used in the activities themselves.

Areas of activity. Activities for all areas are characterized by pupil initiative, participation, management and evaluation of progress. They provide for expansion and enrichment of interests and appreciations. The pupil and faculty direct their planning in harmonious co-operation toward basic, real life, educative ends. They should express themselves in the following areas:

1. *Self Government:* Within the liberal bounds of democratic administrative practice, pupils should be self governing in accordance with democratic principles of living.

2. *Seminar Activities:* These should be a creative part of the planning and administrating of school life. Programs for socialized living and pupil opinion can express themselves here.

3. *School Assemblies:* These should be student planned, organized and executed for the welfare and recreational education in the school.

4. *Special Area Activities:* Each activity should be faculty sponsored but pupil organized. Pupil needs qualify the existence of an activity, if it is to be part of the curriculum.

5. *School Publications:* These should be a creative outlet for pupil opinion as well as an experience in critical social living. They should be truly pupil activated, not faculty dominated.

6. *All Physical Activities:* Both recreational and corrective activities should be undertaken with a view to pupils' needs and be individualized rather than competitive.

7. *All Social Experiences:* These should be provided for as experiences in group living. They should answer the pupils' individual needs in terms of generally accepted democratic behavior in accordance with the social group of the local or community situation.

Activities are integrated into the school program as indispensable educational elements. Every pupil participates according to his talent or inclination.

Regular school time is assigned to activities on the daily schedule. All pupils register for, and have a choice of, activities. Each is a semester in duration. A pupil can carry two general activities—a different one each semester—or one for a full year. One activity period an hour long is a daily all-school activity period.

Activity rooms are adjusted to the needs of the particular activity. Teachers specially skilled in the activities offered are the guides. Activities cover the range of all the major interests of the pupils. They may vary from semester to semester as interest in one or another lags or their values are discovered to be transient. The commonest activities are music, band, newspaper, art, aeronautics, dramatics, physical education, manual arts, folk dancing, boys' cooking activities, metal and clothes design. All pupils register for one of these and receive academic credit for the work which they do.

Activities have educative value. These activities have educative value in that they are the outcome of pupils' interests. They justify their inclusion in the schedule in that they are educative and in that all pupils engaging in activities where their interests lie develop new attitudes toward their personality development.

Many pupils through group participation in activities develop poise and the ability to face groups, to talk to their equals and to plan, control and hold democratic meetings. Individual activities in which creative talents are of greatest importance help the creative personality to develop. And this justifies the time spent on them.

The seminar guidance activity program. The seminar guidance program for each student is planned on a year basis. The seminars consist of small groups meeting with their guidance advisors on problems common to a particular group, at the same scheduled hour as the activities previously mentioned, but on alternate days. The four year seminar guidance program is as follows:

Freshman seminars are orientation seminars centered around problems of personal hygiene, community relations, etiquette, and use of study and recreation time. It is also an orientation seminar working with problems of future courses, careers, vocational problems and problems of immediate interest which arise out of the needs of the students.

The second year students meet in seminars which consider problems of personality and achievement records which employers demand. Application forms of the various large industrial companies are analyzed by the students in this seminar. This seminar acquaints the student with the value of his actual school life in relationship to the worlds of school, business, and college. There is a broad but intensive study of the types and kinds of records used in the school, their purpose and the method of evaluation which is used by the administration and staffs.

After the second year, the guidance seminars are divided into special interest seminars. The home economics department conducts a seminar in family relations, home budgeting of finances, dietetics, marriage and child care. The vocational agriculture seminar bases its program on the various types of agriculture found in the different geographic areas in the United States and the vocational opportunities found through agriculture.

The commercial department conducts a seminar on general office practice in business as well as in problems of wages, unions, and wage scales. This carries over into areas of vocational training for office workers. Specialized vocational training departments, such as machine and print shops develop seminars for students according to their needs.

The athletic department conducts seminars on personal recreation, problems of personal health, community health, correctives, hygiene and social health problems.

A seminar is developed in the humanities in principles of philosophy and psychology, economic history, literature, art, and their application to modern living for senior students planning to enter college and who are interested in the liberal arts. Senior students not preparing for college participate in a seminar directly aimed at vocational information and opportunities in the business world. However, both seminars are available for the college preparatory as well as the non-college preparatory group.

As the student progresses through the four years of the high school curriculum, he participates in most of these seminars, and receives the benefits of a realistic approach to the problems of his relationship to himself, to his family, to the school, community, health problems, recreation problems, and vocational problems.

The seminar guidance programs have several features which more traditional classes and activities lack. They consist of small groups, informally discussing common problems in which personal experience and individual reaction are important contributions to the group. Discussion is free and the give and take of sharing experiences in an orderly constructive fashion is invaluable in giving the students the confidence to express themselves in groups, to their equals without hesitation and with clarity.

These seminars meet in rooms adjusted to the individual group's needs. All library facilities are in the room for immediate research and fact findings. The teacher or a student guides the discussion. A general core of books can be used by each group dealing with the major area for the group. Subsidiary readings for individual research are available; their uses are encouraged. Students and teachers plan the course of discussion, utilizing the needs of the group and being guided by the seminar leader.

Written assignments as a general rule are not the policy of the seminars. The primary purpose of the seminars is to develop through discussion groups common problem solving and to encourage research in the individual problems found in the group. The seminars are designed to find the actual immediate needs of the individual students.

The guidance seminars are closely coordinated with the visual aid program conducted in the school. Visual aids dealing with problems of specific interest are offered as parts of and as outcomes of the seminar problems.

Methods of procedures used in seminar guidance activities. Students and teachers meet in class groups and through discussion and planning decide as to activities for which a real need is felt. The teachers and superintendent or principal meet and discuss the various capabilities and talents for individual group activities which the various teachers may have with a view towards activity direction. From the administration viewpoint the activities must reflect community and student need, as well as enlargement of the curriculum through activities in the various student experience areas. From the teacher's viewpoint the activities represent a means of self expression through the arts of vocational creation in which students and teachers can work co-operatively. Activity sponsorship involves intelligent and trained guidance as well as personal interest. Above all, it involves willingness to spend time both in preparation and execution with students in activities for which no other credit is given other than desire to participate in an activity for its enjoyment's sake as well as its educational value.

After the number and type of activities have been decided upon by students and faculty, students may register for one or more activities as their interests and capabilities may indicate and their programs allow.

Conclusion. The activity program within the scheduled school day helps make the school active both in principle and in fact. It creates greater interest in the student body. The school becomes activated with a functional view towards student participation and planning. The carry-over which thus goes into the regular class is beneficial both to the student and the faculty. It helps create happier students and teachers and more satisfied parents.

The activity program when student governed is a tremendous aid to actual citizenship training in school. The constant co-operation between students is the basis for the success of the program. As such, citizen responsibility is emphasized in its best manner.

129

Galen Jones

STUDENT COUNCIL, THE CITIZENSHIP WORKSHOP

One of the most frequently debated phases of the activities program has to do with the role of the student body in its own control and government. Some of the potential aspects of the program are described in this selection, an address given to the New Jersey Association of High School Councils.

The idea of student participation in the management and control of school activities and school life is not recent. Plato and Aristotle both outline goals and procedures which formulate some of the ideas and ideals. Instances of student participation are found to extent in medieval European universities, in Eton and Rugby of the British Isles during the late 1700's, in the school built by Pestalozzi at Burgdorf in Switzerland, in Thomas Jefferson's comments on the College of William and Mary in 1779 as well as in his concepts of the program for the University of Virginia in 1819—to cite but a few of the historical references.

All these endeavors were based upon the sound principle that youth should learn to control themselves by being given ever greater responsibility as they are able to assume it. The major developments in the United States, nevertheless, of high school student councils have come since

1920. In fact, the number of schools which are deliberately fostering the student council as a central feature of their programs of citizenship education has been markedly accelerated during the past 15 years. . . .

What do we mean by citizenship in a democracy?

When our forefathers, almost two hundred years ago, were drawing the blueprints for the American experiment in democracy, three basic ideas appear as the heart of the enterprise. These are:

1. That the individual personality is of unique and surpassing worth,
2. That the interdependence of the individual and society accents justice, and
3. That through reasoning and working together men may best solve their common problems and attain their common goals.

In my judgment these convictions of the great thinkers of the Western World have withstood all the doubts which have arisen during the years

From *School Activities*, April 1954, 24:247-249.

of our historical development, and the faith of our people has never been undermined. Even so the present national concern over juvenile delinquency, the ominous condition of the family in mid-twentieth century, the apparent breakdown of ideals and values among so many adults are widely heralded as indices of the need for the re-thinking of our program for citizenship education.

It is encouraging, therefore, to witness the activities of national commissions, State departments of education, city school systems, several universities, and many individuals all working steadily to find better answers to basic questions in education for citizenship. Prominent among these is the recent Citizenship Education Study of the Detroit Public Schools and Wayne University, and the current Citizenship Education Project under the leadership of Teachers College, Columbia University.

The emphases of these studies, particularly the completed Detroit Study, seem to classify under four headings in answer to our question, "What do we mean by democratic citizenship?" Only brief references to them can be made this morning by reason of time limitations, but your study and experience will readily clothe them with meaning:

1. *The inherent dignity and worth of the individual* is central to our definition and faith. Respect for personality is the cornerstone of our American system of values. The preamble to our *Declaration of Independence* is an eloquent avowal of this as well as of our faith in Divine Providence.

2. Man can and should govern himself. The American conviction that the State is the creation of the people to serve them, rather than the people being creatures of the State, is all embodied in this statement. In a world sharply divided between totalitarian and governments of, by, and for the people this tenet is basic.

3. Every member of the Nation must understand Democracy's privileges and their attendant responsibilities. The Nation's schools have a peculiar obligation to stress responsibilities equally with the privileges. The hope is that all citizens, young and old, will cherish Antoine du Saint Exupery's noble statement, "To be a (free) man, precisely, to be responsible."

4. The use of the method of intelligence in solving problems is an indispensable tool for citizens. As a people we know that we must define a problem, secure all the facts, and present these through intelligent discussion which lead to persuasion, mutual adjustment and consensus.

Much of what we mean by the "American way of life" is embodied in the four criteria, sketched all too briefly above, in the endeavor to answer the question "What do we mean by democratic citizenship?"

As high school students, you are concerned with what you should learn, as well as how you should learn, in order to become effective citizens. It strikes me that a three-fold conviction, pointed up by the Detroit Citizenship Study, is pertinent. First of all you must develop a rather complete understanding of the meaning of democracy. Secondly, you must make some commitment to the values which are inherent to democracy, come to a belief which while placing a premium upon intellectual understanding also commands your affections. And, thirdly, you must have ample opportunities to practice the techniques and values which are involved.

The student council is the citizenship workshop

What has been said has been designed to point up the assertion that the student council is the citizenship workshop. As a means of putting some flesh on the skeleton of some generalizations which I wish to make later, may I submit several illustrations of high school councils in practice.

When I am at home I drive to the Office. Sometimes I pick up a student on his way to school. Usually I ask him about his school and whether the school has a council. Surprisingly, often the reply is "I don't know." Frequently when he does know he doesn't know the name of the president or what activities are being carried on by the council.

In a large mid-western city a high school council was encouraged by its sponsors to help solve problems and were completely at sea. After several unproductive sessions they talked about tardiness and turned to the sponsors for answers. They had been conditioned to "authority" until they expected to be told what to do.

Later the council members learned that sponsors were really sincere in their wish to have real problems brought up and began to introduce a great variety of personal gripes. After some months the members gained understanding and problems of concern to the total school were the order of the day in all council meetings.

Another school council was faced with a problem of real concern to the whole school, namely, traffic congestion in the halls, and began to move quickly to action. With but little information, with very limited discussion, without consideration of those who might be affected by their decisions, with no analysis of possible consequences, motions were passed and action proposed. Here we have an instance of little ability to think critically and lack of assistance in problem solving.

They did not define and delimit the problem; no tentative conclusions were proposed; no real information was gathered; there was no weighing of evidence; possible consequences of their actions were not considered; and there was no testing of their conclusions. Later when these conditions were met, there were positive and rewarding results.

A high school in the Southwest was harrassed with problems of vandalism both in the school and in the community. The school council began an investigation. They defined the problem clearly, suggested tentative conclusions, gathered information thoroughly, weighed the evidence carefully, considered all possible consequences of their proposals, reached and tested their conclusions. Their recommendations for action were considered forthrightly in the home rooms, by the entire faculty, by representative groups of school patrons and citizens, in several social studies classes, and by the city council.

The result was that their proposals for action were fully understood, the avenues of communication were open at every stage as they tried out and proved their undertakings, there were real changes in attitudes and behaviors, and the prestige of the student council and the school reached an all time high.

The foregoing illustrations are real and I trust carry their own significance. It is hoped that they may have some bearing upon the several criteria with which I would bring this presentation to a close. When and where the student council becomes the citizenship workshop most of the following conditions exist:

The council is so organized and operated that it affects the life of every member of the student body.

The students have and use the opportunity to do something for the school so that it runs better.

The students have the opportunity to think through the criteria for the selection of representatives to the council.

There are few, if any, restrictions on qualifications for candidacy to the council other than that of being a citizen of the school.

The faculty of the school understands and is involved in the student council's work and success.

The council is able to bring up, define, and try to solve the real problems of the school.

Every school citizen should have an opportunity to bring up problems for the consideration of the council. He must be aware that he can do this even though he may never use the prerogative.

The student council needs to work in some areas in which their decisions are final—really count.

The activities and services of the school

DEVELOPING THE WELL-ROUNDED PERSON

If the schools are to take the responsibility for more than just the intellectual development of the student, what are some of the aspects of his life to which attention must be given?

At one time, leisure was not a problem of the schools—or of society, for that matter. In a broad sense, there was no "leisure." Today, however, as society races toward a shorter work week, as entire industries are devoted to producing artifacts to be used in leisure time, increased emphasis has been given to the ways in which leisure is spent and its effects upon the individual.

At one time, physical activities in the schools were considered mainly as a form of organized play or as an extracurricular activity. Today, however, increased emphasis has been given to physical and health education at all levels. Among the reasons for this growing concern with physical fitness are the interest of students, the social impact of big-time spectator sports, findings about the physical health of inductees during World War II, and recent reports on the shortcomings of both children and adults in physical stamina and skills.

At one time, competition was accepted as the normal way of life—certainly, at least, for the adult in a free-enterprise system which is largely the result of individual and corporate striving. Today, however, psychological findings have made clear some of the penalties attached to undue competition—the anxieties, the fears which take their toll of the psyche. The question has thus been raised as to whether the schools have perhaps placed undue emphasis upon pitting one student against another. Certainly students of modern education, which recognizes the individuality of each learner, should be aware of any possible negative aspects of competition.

Readings 130 to 132 are concerned with these three problems as they relate to education. To the reader they will appear perhaps as organized analyses of experiences he has encountered in his own schooling. Thus he can feel more confident in his acceptance or rejection of the concepts set forth here.

130

E. DeAlton Partridge

ADOLESCENTS NEED EDUCATION FOR LEISURE

The author of this article points out the dimensions of education for leisure and goes on to discuss the appropriateness of such a program in the public schools.

Our grandfathers and great grandfathers would have thought it strange indeed had someone argued with them that it was necessary to teach children how to play and how to use their leisure time. Yet, it is one of the strange paradoxes of modern life that with the ability to produce great quantities of goods, including labor-saving devices, leisure itself has become a great problem. The leisure time that young people have at their disposal has become a problem partly because of the fact that as leisure has increased, it has become a profitable thing to exploit. The result has been the development of countless gadgets for use in leisure hours and many spectator activities to attract those who do not know how otherwise to use their spare moments.

Without laboring the points at great length there is ample evidence to substantiate the following observations: (1) Young people today are for the most part illiterate with regard to the opportunities available and the skills involved in a constructive use of leisure time; (2) One must *learn* to use his leisure time in a constructive

way just as he must learn to read or write or to quote the important dates of American history; and (3) The school has a definite responsibility to prepare young people for a situation where commercialized recreation in many of its forms may be curtailed.

Those who have worked with young people in leisure time activities, whether it be in after-school play groups, in summer camps, or whether it be a personal concern over one's own children, have come to realize that very few youngsters today are capable of developing leisure time activities which arise primarily out of their own personal skills or out of the cooperation of small groups working together. This is particularly true of adolescents. Modern industrial society discourages those who do have such abilities in the earlier years of their lives and surrounds them with a highly complicated and commercialized set of leisure activities so that by the time puberty is reached, the child has come to believe that there is no adequate way to use his leisure time unless he has money to spend or unless there is within his immediate environment an expensive and complicated machine which will entertain him.

From *High School Journal*, February 1951, 34:42-45.

No serious-minded person can help to recognize the insidious but widespread influence of such devices as the radio, television, and the motion picture upon the leisure time activities of growing young people. Without questioning the actual content of radio, television, and motion picture programs as such, one can see that any entertainment medium with as much surface attraction as these will develop in our young people a spectator attitude of passive entertainment instead of one where the activity engaged in results in creative experience or wholesome social interchange with one's peers.

Since television and radio are basically instruments which operate within the home atmosphere and since in many instances parents themselves do not have the creative attitude or skills to pass on to the young people, certainly some of the responsibility falls on the schools to provide recreational skills and activities which will help develop the kind of personalities which can be effective in our complicated modern life.

The next point is more difficult to establish, but in the opinion of this writer it is unquestionably true that there are tremendously wholesome personality values involved in the process of creative activity and social participation. Those who grow up without the thrill of personal creativeness or with the attitude that passive entertainment without any personal investment is sufficient, have a shallow and entirely unrealistic approach to the leisure time problem. There are few things as thrilling and inspiring as to watch a person discover the lasting satisfaction of creating something with his own hands. Youngsters who have never had an opportunity to carve, paint, or mold in clay, after an initial period of resistance, can with skillful guidance come to see these things as an entirely new world of discovery. Actually the artificial and expensive gadgets in our society are relegated to their proper place when a creative urge is really unleashed.

There is in New Jersey a State School of Conservation to which teachers in training, teachers in service, and youngsters in their early teens come. The children attend a demonstration camp which is devoted primarily to the idea that youngsters can and will enjoy learning about their relationship to other living things and to create useful and beautiful articles from the materials they have at hand. A special effort is made in this camp program to have young people learn the joy of companionship and social relationships, the art of conversation, and the utilization of native materials in a craft program. The campers are not selected with any particular purpose in mind other than their interest in a camp where there are few of the traditional camp activities. It has been interesting to note that even the most skeptical youngsters who are accustomed to highly organized and artificial recreation programs come to find satisfaction in doing folk dancing together, in hiking through the woods for the purpose of nature identification and study, and in the creation of artistic and useful objects from native materials. This camp program has demonstrated beyond a doubt that with proper leadership youngsters can find a wholesome and constructive set of skills and attitudes to enrich their leisure hours. In order to have a generation with the right kind of attitude toward leisure time, this kind of creative leadership is necessary; and unfortunately too little of it is available in the high schools of our country. Too many of the skills we teach in high school have little or no carry-over into later life in the community.

It may be well that our nation is entering a period when available resources will be diverted toward the sinews of war and many of the customary ways of using leisure time will not be available. Without commercialized sports and spectator activities, without money to spend to occupy leisure time, without unlimited gasoline and gadgets, the youngsters of today, just like many of their fathers and mothers, may not know how to use their time constructively.

Such a situation could have serious implications. Without constructive channels in which to guide their energy youngsters usually find other ways to express themselves. In times of national strain when nerves are taut and adults are worried, there is apt to be less patience and skill in dealing with young people who have their own ideas about what to do.

To meet these possibilities the schools should make a special effort to provide and teach activities that have real carry-over value into home and community life. These should include games with simple equipment, craft work with few tools utilizing materials to be found at hand. Music involving some kind of participation even though it is a ukulele or a record is needed and wholesome outdoor sports that can be carried on without elaborate equipment and highly organized teams.

The leisure hours of a nation are of great importance to its very existence. Educators and youth leaders generally must be concerned with the constructive possibilities of leisure and accept the challenge to do something about it.

131

Donald A. Dukelow

A DOCTOR LOOKS AT EXERCISE AND FITNESS

One of the questions most frequently raised by professional educators looking at the program of athletics and physical education is whether athletics really contribute to physical fitness. In this article an official of the Bureau of Health Education of the American Medical Association points out some of the limits which should be considered.

"What is the attitude of physicians toward exercise?" This easily asked question is impossible to answer without knowing *who* will be doing *how much* of *what kind* of exercise *when*, as well as *what* physician is expressing his opinion.

A review of the Cumulative Index of Medical Literature for the past decade discloses hundreds of papers on exercise in medical journals from the United States and many foreign countries. Generally, these discuss controlled observations and research studies which show that at the time exercise is performed it increases muscle volume, increases the heart rate, alters the tracings recorded by electrocardiography, and causes changes in the speed and volume of respiration. They tell about the effect of exercise on the nervous system, the digestive system, the excretory system, the circulatory system, the musculoskeletal system, and nearly everything else in the body.

However, these investigators rarely say whether the observed phenomena are beneficial, harmful, or of no consequence. The few physicians who do comment on the desirability of exercise range in opinion from the sports enthusiasts who endorse violent physical activity unequivocally to those who consider any exercise of little or no demonstrated value. As with so many controversial issues the truth probably lies somewhere between the extremes.

What is exercise? Popularly, it is synonymous with movement, particularly physical activity beyond the basal body functions necessary for living. A medical dictionary defines it as a form of physical exertion for the improvement of health or the correction of physical deformity. This gives the term a therapeutic connotation, implying that physical activity itself is not exercise unless directed toward "improvement."

Actually, every act of locomotion, manipulation, posturing, or conversation, regardless of purpose, can be called exercise. The purposeless waving of an infant's arms and legs and the skilled service and return of an experienced tennis player are both exercise.

In spite of the varied attitudes of physicians toward exercise, most of them, if pressed for an opinion, will say that some physical activity is desirable in normal well people. But they can rarely define what they mean by "physical activity" or by "normal people." They are likely to say that for all but the most sedentary people the usual day's activity is exercise enough. But again, they would have trouble telling just what they mean by "sedentary" or by "usual day's activity." Unless they had given the question careful thought, they would be unable to tell how the exercise they might prescribe for youth, maturity, and old age should differ quantitatively and qualitatively. As a result, the recommendations physicians make about exercise for "normal" people will vary from nothing, through formal calisthenics to periodic stress to the point of fatigue.

It is this wide variation of professional opinion that makes this phase of living so confusing. It, therefore, becomes necessary to discuss exercise from some moderate or conservative point of view in between the extremes set by the pro-exercise and anti-exercise enthusiasts. Of course, neither will accept this middle-of-the-road concept as having value, though it likely will result in less harm than either extreme.

Exercise, or movement, is noticeable in the fourth month of pregnancy. From the latter part of the fifth month to the end of pregnancy many

From *Journal of Health-Physical Education-Recreation*, September 1957, 28:24-26, 67.

women complain bitterly about "having their sides kicked out" by a very active youngster. At the moment of birth the shock of cool air on warm wet skin that never has been out of water reflexly starts most newborn infants on a wild waving of arms and legs and a fit of crying which exercises most muscles and joints in the body. This muscle activity brings air into the lungs, produces heat, and stimulates circulation.

From then on, through infancy and early childhood, the youngster pretty much sets his own activity pace. He kicks and waves, and later crawls, climbs, explores, and manipulates as he becomes neuromuscularly ready for each new adventure. Though this is not formal "exercise" in the common sense, it is a form of activity that moves every muscle in such a way as to stimulate its growth and develop the kinesthetic sense that leads to skill and strength.

Children seem to enjoy movement—any kind of movement. They seem to need activity to help coordinate bones and muscles and tendons and ligaments that grow at different rates. They enjoy testing strength and skill and learning the "feel" of new experiences. Children seem never to be still. Activity is so characteristic of childhood that one tends to associate inactivity with illness.

From the preschool period through the intermediate grades, roughly from 4 to 14, what seems to be violent activity is invariably within the physiological tolerances of the child when self-determination is possible. Though he may play hard, he never plays too hard if left to his own resources. When fatigued, or out of breath, or when he has a pain, he quits. And he rarely starts again till he is ready to start.

When adults enter the picture to give "leadership," this can be changed. Unless the adult leader or coach is aware of his own motivations, and understands the characteristics of growth and development of children, he may cause physiological and emotional limits to be exceeded. These physical and emotional stresses result from adult-inspired social pressures, particularly in team play where a community's reputation is at stake and winning at any cost seems worthwhile—at least to adults.

Older youth and young adults can enjoy considerable physical activity. Stressful situations are less hazardous if there has been proper training and conditioning to meet these physical and mental stresses. In senior high school and college, the maturity level is usually advanced enough to withstand the insult to body contact sports. Those in good health can often goad themselves to a supreme effort, even to exhaustion, without permanent harm.

On the other hand, most pupils in elementary and junior high schools, and a few in the first year or two of high school are not physically and emotionally stabilized. In the presence of such emotional stresses as victory or defeat or the failure to "make the team," they may develop all sorts of compensations. At this age, too, there are discrepancies in body proportion, muscles and ligaments are not adjusted to new responsibilities produced by longer bones, and injury to growth areas of bones is possible. At this age youngsters are "all arms and legs" and "stumble over their own feet."

Inactivity rather than overactivity is the problem at high school and college levels. Only a few are in varsity sports. Most men and all women have only formal physical education classes, intramural sports, and their own social activities to give them needed exercise. This is the age when future businessmen and housewives must learn the games they will play throughout life if they are to continue the regular muscular activity needed for body tone and stimulation. Few will continue to play team games, but many will indulge in ballroom and folk dancing and such individual activities as tennis, golf, bowling, and swimming.

The adult is the true exercise problem. The exuberance of childhood and youth is quieted, business and family pressures restrict the time available for physical activity, and entertainment tastes run to the more sedentary game of cards or watching others exercise. As one passes the forties, metabolic changes reduce the caloric needs so the same food intake causes increased weight which encourages less activity because the extra weight more quickly produces fatigue.

This becomes a vicious circle. When one tries to break the circle because he is somehow conscious that "exercise is good for you," the try usually consists of excessive overactivity for a short period. Of course, the resulting fatigue and sore muscles causes a "never again" reaction—that is, till the next overdose.

Every adult should know his need for physical activity and his tolerance or capacity for exercise. It is said that everyone should be physically "fit" and exercise is a way to acquire "fitness." The question of importance is "fit for what?" One engaged in strenuous physical activity as part of his occupation must of course be physically "fit" to do his job. On the other hand, a desk worker need not be in training for football or wrestling unless he plays football or wrestles as a pastime. He needs the exercise that will let him get to and from work safely, mow his lawn and safely play with his children.

Much of an adult's exercise can come from such games as golf and bowling, work in his yard or the many "do it yourself" jobs required in any home. Some get it by walking, others are fishermen, and some even watch birds. Whatever the interest, it produces exercise within limits of tolerance.

European "physical culture" has had limited popularity in the United States, but some northern European exercise patterns have been modestly accepted. Swedish gymnastics and the German *Turnverein* have influenced the use of formal "setting up exercises." Many who cannot exercise otherwise indulge in such activity in their own bedroom, an athletic club, or a private gymnasium.

Acceptable as these exercise patterns may be, adults should know their physical condition before indulging. In fact, most adults should have their level of exercise prescribed by their physician if there is any possibility of physical injury to heart or circulatory system. Odd as it may seem, those with some types of illness, diabetes for example, must have a certain amount of exercise to stabilize their metabolism. In the older ages, particularly after retirement, exercise is of great importance. Here, more than at any other age, it must be the right kind of the right amount, prescribed with the individual's personality and health problems in mind.

Recently, "fitness" has been a popular subject. It means different things to different people. For some it is total well-being—physical, mental, emotional, and social. For others it is the ability to perform certain limited physical activities or tests. The wide variations in expected activity levels at all ages from childhood to old age and the wide variations between people of different occupations makes the use of a single set of tests for the evaluation of "fitness" seem rather futile.

The "fitness" of youth—or any other group—is a complex phenomenon whose evaluation requires the judgment of many professions. Absolute standards of physical activity cannot accurately interpret physical fitness, let alone fitness of the whole person in its broadest sense.

Exercise means many things to physicians as well as to other people. There are few who really understand what its values may be and how best to take it. But it seems all will agree that moderate doses regularly are more valuable than large doses periodically. And few will agree either with the sports enthusiasts and body worshipers who have only one standard of "fitness"—the perfect man—or with the chap who said he got his exercise being pallbearer for his friends who exercised.

132

Henry A. Davidson

COMPETITION, THE CRADLE OF ANXIETY

In this article a prominent psychiatrist analyzes the problem of competitiveness, pointing out some of the dangerous effects of the current emphasis on competition in the schools.

Competition brings us better cosmetics, cars, and cabbages, but no one has yet proved that it brings us better education. Probably every one would agree that cooperation is better than competition just as teamwork is better than hostility. In practice, however, our culture is constructed on a cone of competition, with plenty of room at the bottom, but precious little at the top.

From *Education*, November 1955, 76:162-166. Reprinted by special permission of the Publishers, The Bobbs-Merrill Company, Inc.

In some areas, competition brings about wonderful things . . . and that is why we are so addicted to it. During the war, in northern Australia, we used to talk about how long it took to get from Cairns to Brisbane on the state-owned railroad. The compartments were ill-ventilated, the train made absurdly frequent stops, the drinking water was warm, and the cars seemed to have square wheels. I complained to the station-master at Mareeba. His answer was: "If you don't like our railroad, get to Brisbane some other way." But the Government had a monopoly of rail transportation and there was no other way. Compare this with the rail service between New York and Chicago. When one railroad puts a shower in the train, the competing line offers telephone service. When one cuts an hour from the running time, the other cuts off 90 minutes. The passenger is the beneficiary of all this, and the air-ways—competing with the railroads—try to woo him away by offering still more amenities. So, by reason of competition, the public gets a break, management is kept on its toes, progress is achieved and everybody is happy.

Since competition achieves all this, the same motif has been introduced into education. The problem, however, is one of motive rather than motif. The theory is that the pupil will get more right answers if he has to compete with his classmates. He will, to use the jargon, be better motivated. So we have developed a stockpile of medals, grades, scholarships, awards, degrees, testimonials, and promotions, all of which depend on the goal of competition.

And it does have a certain superficial effectiveness. Announce an art contest—a prize for the pupil who can draw the most fetching design for the cover of a plastic pickle container—and watch the entries roll in. You will unearth hidden talent. You will get some good drawings, squeezed out of pupils who would never have bothered to draw for the fun of it. If a cover design is your goal, you will have achieved it, and can ring up another score for competition.

Competition cannot exist in a vacuum. You must compete against another human being. In theory you could compete against a goal, against the forces of evil, against a "norm," or even against your own previous performance. But emotionally, these are less meaningful spurs to action than person-to-person competition. Even in preliminary practice the boxer needs a human sparring partner and the racer needs a pacemaker.

Two years ago I found myself in a P.T.A. meeting in a state which shall be nameless. It was an elementary school, and the principal was defending the practice of marking first-graders by adjectives instead of by numbers or letters. "It really isn't fair" said the principal "to hurt a 6-year old by letting him see a "C" or a "7" on his report card, while Pokey up the block has an "A" or a "9." Why should a six-year old be thrown into unhealthy competition with his playmates?"

The leader of the opposition told them. He was that figure so uncomfortably conspicuous at many P.T.A. meetings: the irate, mis-informed and self-assured parent; the man who has all the answers. "If you expect a first-grader to be reading to page 16 in his primer by December, then I want to know whether my boy has reached 90 per cent of that goal or only 60 per cent of it."

"But," said the principal, "it isn't that simple. A mark of "B" doesn't mean that the first-grader has accomplished such and such a per cent of reading expectancy." The irate parent snorted that that is what it ought to mean. The principal explained wearily: "each child has to move at his own pace, and we want you to know how he is doing on that track—never mind how the other pupil is doing. . "

"That" blazed the parent "is all-wrong. In fact, it is anti-American."

This startled us, but the I.P. explained that competition was the American Way and that destruction of a competitive economy was on the communist time-table. Hence who-ever opposed a competitive grade system was a you-know-what.

"To be specific" said the parent, "I reject your theory that every child must go at his own pace. Life is not like that. Life sets standards and you keep up that pace or you fall by the wayside and become one of life's rejects. I don't want that to happen to *my* children, and that is just what you will do to them if you measure them by their own standards instead of by what Society expects of them. Suppose a child's standard of behavior is to lie and steal . . do you measure him by that, and give him a "well-done" if he steals or lies artistically?"

The principal, by this time, must have felt he was riding backwards on a carousel. Somehow all his meaning had been perverted by the irate parent. Then the parent continued:

"I own an automobile agency. Some of my salesmen are good and get good commissions. Some are poor and scarcely make a living. If I followed your theory, I would add to the low commission for a poor salesman because I would try to understand that he was doing his little best but that he was worried about his wife's sinus trouble. Well, the guy who doesn't meet external standards loses out in my agency and in every other department of life . . . and first grade is not too early to find that out."

(If you are interested in the showdown, the parent got the applause but the principal got the vote. The P.T.A. voted two to one to retain the narrative marking system.)

So there it is: education is preparation for life; competition is part of our way of life; hence competition should be part of education. Here is the syllogism in all its naked simplicity. What's wrong with it?

Since I am not an educator, I cannot say whether the syllogism is sound in terms of educational practice. As a psychiatrist, however, I do have some thoughts on it. In the first place, it seems to my untutored eye, that there are at least two kinds of education: training for a vocation and education for living. The syllogism is probably valid for vocational (including professional) education. If I were running a school for beauty shop operators, I would include a course in window dressing, and I would bring in a successful operator to tell the neophyte beauticians how to meet the competition of other beauty shops. I would include a course on how to cut prices without going bankrupt, how to persuade people not to patronize the shop across the street without committing libel, and how to prepare an income tax return without actually cheating. I would prepare the students for the harsh fact that while life can be beautiful, competition can be ugly. This, I should think, would be my plain duty if I ever inherited the improbable role of pedagogue to beauticians.

Competition, let us face it, extends through every phase of our vocational life. In business this is openly recognized; the word "competition" is used there without apology. When a customer walks into the cigar store down the block, there is a sale lost to me. The competition hurts, so maybe I ought to keep my store open until 11 o'clock since Joe turns off his lights at 10 p.m. Of course, if I do that, Joe will stay open until midnight, and eventually we either sleep under the counter or Joe and I come to some agreement—that we close at the same time or we keep late hours on alternate nights. In other words, we substitute collaboration for competition.

In more ethereal circles we shun the word "competition." Take a college campus or a government bureau for instance. Under the elms on the cloistered campus, does anything as vulgar as competition stir the hearts of the professors? If the Professor of Petrology is about to retire, do the two Assistant Professors jockey for the chair? Or is this beneath their dignity? And do the four Instructors bring apples to school, each in the hope that he will become an Assistant Professor when the changes are announced? Or, on the contrary, is competition foreign to this cloistered climate? Never having been a professor, I don't know, but I suspect that the competitive spirit eats its way into the hearts of the professors—and their wives—even though, by some semantic magic, the dirty word itself is never uttered.

And so it is too, with bureaucracy. With the job and its many "rights" protected behind a bulwark of regulations, statutes, rules and practices,

is there any need for a competitive spirit? Promotion comes every few years anyway, and in-grade pay increments come almost annually. But the competitive motif is there anyway. Indeed the pyramidal hierarchy puts a sharp edge on the wedge. For when a GS-13 retires, a GS-12 moves up, and so do GS-11s, only one can become a 12. And this goes down the line, adding more fuel to the competitive fire. And through the powder-room door, you can hear a GS-4 plaintively asking: "What does she have that I don't have?"

Does this mean that irate parent is right—that competition is woven into woof of our life pattern and should therefore be fostered in school? I don't think so. It seems to me that, for most people, the job is something they must do to get the means to live. The exception to this is the rare person who loves his work. But the typical citizen works from 9 to 5; he does not "live" until after 5.

Can this nonvocational "living" be free of competition? It can and it should. There are, of course, some people who see competitive activity in going to the movies, in social contacts, in reading, resting, hiking, or making love. But most of us prefer in these things—"living," if you choose, to be cooperative rather than competitive. The amateur artist who just gets fun out of painting is spoiled if he learned in school that he *must* outdo the next man. Here is the evil of teaching competition in the "education for life" (rather than vocational training) aspect of education. It is evil because it teaches that all men are rivals instead of brothers. (Yes, I know about sibling rivalry).

The need for and the fear of competition corrode the personality. You do not have to be a psychiatrist to see that. There is a glow in the smile of friendship and warmth in the handclasp of a friend. But not if the smile can become a leer and the hand can plunge a knife into your back. Competition puts all men on guard. It strains relationships with your colleagues—the very people with whom you should feel most comfortable. You will recognize that this applies to competition among school pupils and also to competition among teachers. Competition between persons sets false standards, for soon the symbol of victory (the promotion, the prize, the testimonial) becomes the substance of victory. There are—or there could be—internal rewards in the feeling of having done a job well, accomplished a mission or solved a problem. These are not "competitive" in the sense here used, because they do not represent triumph over fellow human beings.

Most suicides are the fruits of failures in competition. Occasionally a suicide occurs when the person is at the brink of promotion or success. In those cases, the underlying factor is either a feeling of inability to meet the needs of the higher assignment; or a morbid sense of failure. And that failure is usually an inability (real or fancied) to meet human competition. We think of "loss of face" as a peculiarity of the orient. But "loss of face" traumatizes us just as much as it does the oriental. "Loss of face" is associated with a competitive situation.

In almost every large organization, the practice is for a nominating committee to present a panel of candidates, one for each office. In one organization with which I am affiliated, it was recently proposed that we require the committee to present at least two nominees for each office. This would be more democratic because it would offer us a real choice instead of a Hobson's choice. The change in the by-laws was made with everyone sure that a great blow had been struck for democracy.

But when the nominating committee tried to get candidates, it ran into a curious obstacle. The dignified elder statesman who was a natural for the office of president refused to run. His reason: he would not take part in a contested election because of the irreparable loss of face if he were defeated. This occurred right down the line. The potential officer who was particularly valuable simply would not subject himself to the hazards of a contested election. Defeat, he thought, would mean rejection—a definite slap in the face.

Not that there was any real shortage of candidates. Many members were quite willing to offer themselves. But these were the ones who had nothing to lose, since they had no outstanding

prestige in the first place. What it amounted to was this: the competitive climate favored the inferior and not, as you might expect, the superior member. It was congenial to the tough and calloused person, but intolerable to the more subtle and sensitive soul.

The psychiatrist sees another aspect to this matter of competition. The commonest source of anxiety today is repressed hostility or aggression. In Freud's time the suppressed sex drive seems to have been a major cause of emotional conflict. But today this does not loom as so large a problem—don't ask me why. Instead the suppression of hostilities and aggressions has become our number one outpatient psychiatric problem. And these hostilities develop out of competition. Whether he is an advertising executive, a school teacher or a pupil, he cannot remain long in a bath of competition without developing hostility to his rivals, and then some anxiety and guilt because of the hostility.

A teacher can stimulate the acquisition of knowledge, and stimulate it in a fast, cheap and easy way by offering prizes. With many pupils, this *would* work. The class would thus collect the desired facts. It must be much harder for a teacher to build into a child an internal satisfaction which would motivate him towards acquiring data or solving problems. Yet surely the mind of man, which has cracked the secrets of the atom, is capable of developing a technic for the noncompetitive motivation of pupils.

You hear it said again and again that we *do live* in a competitive world, and that today only the sucker acts like Santa Claus. The "realists" are alerted to act like Kilkenny cats. Maybe. But when the chips are down, I'd rather be laughed at as a Santa Claus than hated as a Scrooge. And that's the way I'd want it for my children too.

The activities and services of the school

THE GUIDANCE FUNCTION OF THE SCHOOL

Starting in the period before the First World War with an emphasis on vocational guidance, the guidance activities of the school program have constantly expanded. There was even a period in which guidance was almost considered synonymous with education. For some of its apologists, guidance is not simply a set of activities but also a point of view. In the modern school the counselor is concerned not only with the educational and vocational problems of students but with all areas of the student's life which relate to his success in school.

133

E. G. Williamson

THE FUSION OF DISCIPLINE AND COUNSELING IN THE EDUCATIVE PROCESS

A persistent problem for the counselor has been the conflict between some of the views of discipline in the school and the more personalized and permissive approach of counseling. The author of this article points out that if discipline is to lead to anything other than withdrawal and further rebellion on the part of the student, it must be an integral part of the school's counseling program.

Of the many opposite and contradictory concepts to be found in the literature of education, discipline and counseling are perhaps most sharply separated.

Discipline is characterized as	Counseling is described as
repressive	growth producing
regulatory	ego strengthening
forced conformity	self-regulating
law abiding	affect integration
orderliness	confidence development
imposed	self-initiated
forced control	self-centered

Discipline and counseling differ sharply in other respects:

Discipline is imposed by external restraining authority of parents, teachers, fellow pupils, community mores, law authorities, or principals. It is not requested by pupils in elementary school and least of all by high school students whose idea of a pure democracy is a society of adolescents with no adults anywhere in the vicinity.

Counseling long has been a self-initiated relationship at the adolescent age and a seemingly wanted one at the child level. It is centered not on the community, school or group but upon the individual and his own unique problems— as though he were more important than everyone else in the home, school, and community. This centering of counseling upon the isolated individual pupil has been characterized recently as an instance of individual relativism as opposed to cultural relativism.

Discipline is a "public" matter in two respects: It is imposed conformity to other persons, and there is nothing private or confidential about it. One either conforms voluntarily publicly to group requirements or else one is compelled to do so by social pressures, punishment, or some other means of regulation.

Counseling is highly personal and confidential. Except for certain persons who are motivated to be abnormal publicly most persons desire to discuss their intimate adjustments with one counselor at a time. This is the reason that the highly prized confidentiality of counseling is a necessity —the pupil desires it, profits most through it, and suffers relapses when it is dissipated. From the viewpoint of a counselor, the absence of privacy and confidentiality are among the four most devastating weaknesses in most programs of discipline. The ineffective use of punishment for rehabilitation is a third weakness, and the fourth is the inhuman, impersonal manner in which human beings often are handled and processed, sometimes even in education.

Discipline, as I am now using the term, is a discordant note in that type of education designed to stimulate growth of individuality—social, moral, and intellectually. Indeed, forcing conformity in behavior is often an indication that other educational methods have failed and that in desperation we have abandoned efforts to persuade and have turned to the use of superior authority. It needs to be re-emphasized, however, that many times we face situations in which too much damage to morale has been done to permit per-

From *Personnel and Guidance Journal,* September 1955, 34:74-79.

suasion to have any effect. In such cases, we must use compulsion, but we must not deceive ourselves that we are using an educational method. And we ought to return to persuasion as soon as we can.

Let me continue my contrast of discipline and counseling. I am leading up to a redefinition of discipline achieved by fusing the two into a new type of relationship between teacher and administrator, on the one hand, and pupils and students, on the other.

In a distant university, a teacher of counseling is said to have told his trainees: No counselor should have anything to do with registration of students in subjects or with discipline. Presumably, in such a school, unruly and destructive behavior would be handled by the principal or superintendent, and they, harassed by many other pressures and crises, quickly would be forced to dispose of disciplinary cases by assigning penalties, once guilt had been established. As one result of such "drum head" justice, resentment would be added to conflict and the pupil would make a test case to determine who was boss. Such conflict psychology of relationship would often preclude rehabilitation.

Moreover, the counselor, in such a school, would be freed from such conflict so that he could deal with the "behaving" students about their personal problems. Thus the delinquents, who most desperately need clarification of their own chaotic emotions, would often turn to stronger misbehavior as a substitute of counseling.

And counseling, by avoiding such disciplinary responsibilities, would become limited in its usefulness since it takes place only with "good" citizens in the school or home, requires voluntary seeking of counseling, and is of no help in dealing with the pupils who rebel against conformity. These consequences might not be a serious matter if we were content to dismiss delinquency and disciplinary cases by asserting that they are caused by pure cussedness, moral depravity, and other uncontrollable factors and that "nice" persons don't behave that way.

But we now know that misbehavior occurs in some pupils who are otherwise fine persons and quite capable of good citizenship. It is to discover the correctible causes of misbehavior that I believe discipline must be infused with counseling. Discipline as punishment is no corrective of misbehavior unless it is a part or a consequence of a counseling relationship. Alone, punishment is repressive and growth arresting. With counseling, it can become educative, corrective, and growth producing.

This is my thesis, and I now turn to a defense of it.

Many counselors are willing to be used as consultants in exploring the deeper motivations underlying misbehavior, but they understandably do not wish to play any role whatsoever when it comes to imposing restrictions and "punishment" upon the offending student. They wish to be completely without authority and to be perceived by the client as having no possible authority which could be a threat to him. Rather do they wish to serve as his advocate and friend even to the extent of pleading his case with the school authority.

In terms of its effectiveness in maintaining counseling relationships, such a course of action is necessary. But the principal is thus segregated and symbolized with all the trappings of "harsh" authority and is often perceived by the counselor and misbehaving student alike as being a repressive and threatening authority symbol. In my opinion, the counselor does not play his full and proper counseling role in an educational institution when he thus completely segregates and separates himself from such an authority symbol.

It seems to me that, in addition to the consultant role, there are three other functions that counselors properly have in disciplinary situations: first, counseling as active rehabilitation of misbehaving offenders; second, the prevention of misbehavior through counseling to achieve normal development in inner-control of self; and, finally, counseling as a way of aiding students to perceive and to accept that external authority which influences inner development and modifies unbridled individualism.

Counseling as rehabilitation. My point is best illustrated by quoting from the field of child psychology. In her delightful book, *New Ways in Discipline*, Baruch (1)[1] has illuminated the major revolution that has taken place in the home with respect to the parental-child relationship, now reconstructed so that counseling techniques, emphasis, and points of view are built into the changed normal relationship of parent and child. Baruch's book is replete with insightful transposing reorientation guidelines, such as: "If a child *misbehaves*, we'll recognize that he must have *unsatisfied emotional needs* . . . we'll try to *satisfy* it all we can." And again, "When unwanted *negative feelings* have been emptied out

---

[1] [Numbers in parentheses refer to the references at the end of this selection.]

sufficiently then—warm and good *positive feelings* flow in." And again, *"All children need release and acceptance of 'mean' feelings. All children have 'mean' feelings that need to be released."* The logic of therapy as rehabilitation in disciplinary cases is thus made clear. Misbehavior stems from the repression of "mean" feelings, and if the "mean" feelings are aired, brought up to the level of conscious communication, then the basic drive for misbehavior is lessened, if not eliminated. Rehabilitation consists, therefore, of straightforward therapy in which the individual finds substitute channels for his repressed feelings of aggression and disappointment.

So far so good. But it is one thing for the parent-child to restructure the relationship within the imposition of the home in which the child is scarcely willing or able to reject the parent, except symbolically; it is quite another thing for an adolescent, with some degree of possible freedom to reject a non-parental relationship, to be given that kind of release therapy which he does not want because he does not see the necessity of correcting his misbehavior or of being rehabilitated through counseling relationships. Here we run squarely into the complex problem of imposed counseling relationships. Counseling as rehabilitation in a disciplinary situation seems to work well when it is accepted by the counselee, but when it is not thus accepted, such voluntary counseling obviously will not be operative—according to the assumption of current therapists. Our experiences lead us to question the generalization that in all instances and in all respects, imposed counseling relationships are ineffective as well as "bad." I shall return to this point below.

There is a second way in which counseling can serve as the rehabilitation of offending students, and that way is through the transposition of points of view, techniques, and emphases from the customary one-to-one relationship of the counseling interview to the entire school situation. In much the same way as parent-child relationships in the home are now being restructured according to counseling generalizations and experiences, likewise the entire school atmosphere and the relationships between teachers and students, principals and students, and teachers and parents may be restructured with the counseling interview serving as a model. In many schools, such a revolution is well under way but there are many counselors who do not accept this opportunity to extend the influence of counseling far beyond the one-to-one counseling interview.

Prevention of misbehavior through counseling. I come to my second point, the use of counseling techniques and emphases to facilitate the achievement of normal development of *self*-control and *self*-discipline. Every counselor understands some phases of the process by means of which warm and positive feelings become a normal part of the child's development through the maintenance of satisfying affective relationships with others and with adults. Optimum development of the individual is indeed achievable, as far as affect is concerned, through the emotional climate of the school and home in which the child is encouraged, assisted, and permitted to grow up with a minimum of repression and negative attitudes and feelings.

Baruch (1) summarizes this generalization with respect to misbehavior and behavior when she says, "The more we accept a child's FEELINGS, the more will he accept our RULES." It is quite true that if the relationships of the home and school are satisfying, affectively, to the child, then there seems to be little motivation for misbehaving; that is, the child thus achieves satisfaction through conforming to the requirements of his social environment, and there is no desire or motivation to do otherwise. He is, in this sense, a normally developing individual, and he does not experience the necessity of conflicting or warring with his environment because his environment thwarts him. Thus developing effective school situations provides another opportunity for counselors to prevent misbehavior.

Counseling as an aid to perception and acceptance of external authority. I turn to my third point, counseling as a process of reorientation to the reality of external authority. As a facilitator of normal development, the school counselor enters the disciplinary situation, or at least can enter it, in a new and in many ways more important role, as an educator-counselor who seeks to help the misbehaving student perceive and accept the role of authority as it impinges upon his own "autonomous" inner life and behavior. Within the friendly home, the consequences of misbehavior are soon forgotten, and there is frequently no external legal authority acting for society to impose consequences, restrictions, and limitations upon the autonomy of the individual in the light of or as a result of his misbehavior. In most home-centered misbehavior, all is soon forgiven, and certainly the term "punishment" has no long-term connotation. But as a child grows into adolescence and begins to misbehave away from his home, all is not so readily forgiven and forgotten. Consequences flow from misbehavior and are sometimes legally imposed in the form of punishment as retribution following upon the heels of misbehavior. It is at this point that the counselor can play a very significant role in helping the individual to learn to live in a universe in which his autonomy is hedged about and "infringed" upon by external authority and to understand how the role of the forgiving parent, who generates positive feelings and warmth, is often set aside in many instances by a harsh, repressive, and sometimes vengeful authority symbol-role.

I am not advocating that a counselor enter into partnership with such a vengeful authority. But I feel certain that a counselor can play a significant role in helping the individual to perceive, and to accept emotionally, the inevitability of authority in some form or another acting as a restrictive agency upon the individual's free play of self-directed freedom. This learning is a profound one and most necessary in a democratic society of cooperative and inter-related individual persons. To be sure, it is not easy to teach such a generalization to an individual who has come into conflict with that society, or even in conflict with other individuals in a small, restricted club or school. Such an individual has already alienated himself from other individuals and from authority by his misbehavior. How then can he be aided to accept that which he has flaunted? As Kurt Lewin (2) so cogently states:

"We can now formulate the dilemma which re-education has to face in this way: How can free acceptance of a new system of values be brought about if the person who is to be educated is, in the nature of things, likely to be hostile to the new values and loyal to the old? . . .

"Re-education influences conduct only when the new system of values and beliefs dominates the individual's perception. The acceptance of the new system is linked with the acceptance of a specific group, a particular role, a definite source of authority as new points of reference. It is basic for re-education that this linkage between acceptance of new facts or values and acceptance of certain groups or roles is very intimate and that the second frequently is a prerequisite for the first."[2]

At this point counselors can and should, I believe, pioneer in testing Lewin's hypothesis by searching for counseling techniques that will aid a misbehaving individual to learn and to like the "imposed" role and the new values required of him as a member of a group, his home, and his school.

I have now stated what I mean by the fusion of discipline and counseling in an educative process; discipline becomes not "forced" conformity or punishment, but a type of re-education designed to aid the individual to so understand his emotions and feelings and to so redirect them into new behavior channels that he no longer wants to or is forced to misbehave as an unsuccessful attempt to rid himself of external authority. Parenthetically, it escapes the attention of some counselors that the state of individualistic autonomy that some students seek is, in its extreme form, self destructive or at least not a full measure of self fulfillment in the case of human beings.

There are, I repeat, two arguments for attempting such a fusion of discipline and counseling: Counseling is our present chief prospect for changing discipline from punishment to rehabilitation; and counseling as a form of growth-producing and morale building human relationship will aid the individual to achieve that degree of self-control and self-restraint so necessary in all members of an inter-dependent democratic society. And I borrow the words of a cultural anthropologist (3) who describes the way in which one individual can achieve his individuality through, and not in spite of, the imposed discipline of membership in a society:

". . . to belong to a society is to sacrifice some measure of individual liberty, no matter how slight the restraints which the society consciously imposes. The so-called free societies are not really free. They are merely those societies which encourage their members to express their individuality along a few minor and socially acceptable lines. At the same time they condition their members to abide by innumerable rules and regulations, doing this so subtly and completely that these members are largely unconscious that the rules exist. If a society has done its work of shaping the individual properly, he is no more conscious of most of the restrictions it has imposed than he is of the restraints which his habitual clothing imposes on his movements."

Let me quote my summary (4) of a recent conference on discipline and counseling:

[2]The above nine paragraphs are taken from my article, "Discipline and Counseling," *Education,* Vol. 74, No. 8, April 1954, pp. 513-16.

"To achieve full personal development, each pupil must learn to live mutually helpfully with others in group life.

"This means that each individual must learn self control or at least develop in the direction of that ideal of our democracy.

"It follows that the individual cannot grow toward self control in a social vacuum of rampant and selfish individualism.

"And that aspect involves the school (and counselor) in helping (and insisting) that the individual 'conform' to the requirements of group living involving the needs of other pupils. Such a concept bothers those who feel guilty about 'imposing' any restrictions from the outside upon the inner growth processes of the individual. Nevertheless it is clear that both types of discipline (self and group) must be fused in the personality of the individual if he is to avoid disintegration and self conflict.

"The crux of the matter is the methods the school and the counselor use to achieve this self control adjusted to group conformity. And rigid regimentation involving sharp punishment for deviation from official pathways of behavior is an ineffective way. Conversely, the maintenance of a friendly school atmosphere and the offering of a rich variety of growth-producing experiences in learning self control are effective ways of teaching self discipline.

"If we redefine 'discipline' as a constructive life style of living as a human being involving the maintaining of human relationships with others we then see new ways in which counseling can play a significant role in discipline.

"But, and this is a troublesome spot, many individuals deviate in their learning and some deviate destructively to self and to others. It is at this point that the legal authorities step in, both in the school and community, and force conformity as well as 'punish' deviation.

"Up to this point, counselors participate in discipline through their normal activities of helping the individual to achieve optimum growth and also by insisting upon accommodation to standards required by membership in society. In this sense, the counselor does not permit unbridled self-growth of any kind that is destructive of self or other selves.

"In the conflict state of disciplinary situations, the counselor becomes a teamwork consultant to the 'authorities,' participating within school and community in rehabilitating the 'offender.' It follows that he must make clear to the student that he, the counselor, is on the side of morality and 'law and order.' He is not neutral in such a situation. He also makes it clear that part of a student's behavior which is destructive of the 'right' kind of self control is balanced in counseling between the needs and rights of the disciplined student and the needs and rights of other individuals within the group."

I can sum up my point of view about the fusion of discipline and counseling by quoting a wise psychiatrist who played a major role in the conference referred to above. Dr. Carson of Potsdam, New York, capsuled the point in these words: "Discipline must be given in a matrix of love." All human beings, and especially children and adolescents, have great "affect hunger" and misbehaving children and adolescents have greater need. If their misbehavior erupts out of affect hunger and resentment from rejection in home or community, then the school and especially the counselors must substitute affection for that hunger. Punishment will not completely fill such a deep void, but the humanized relationship of counseling will be effective. Therefore, in the area of behavior (as contrasted with "inert" knowledge of the classroom), human relationships in the school will often prove to be effective in helping pupils to achieve maturity, social, moral, intellectual, and other kinds. It is not unreasonable to restructure schools so that human beings are related to each other in a way characterized as humane.

In this way, self-control discipline is cultivated by the very personal relationships of the persons in the school, and this is one of the most important goals of counseling. Discipline then becomes restructured through the adoption of counseling methods and points of view as substitutes for discipline by inhumane punishment.

References

1. Baruch, Dorothy Walter. *New ways in discipline.* New York: McGraw-Hill, 1949.

2. Lewin, Kurt. *Resolving social conflicts.* New York: Harper & Bros., 1948.

3. Linton, Ralph. *The cultural background of personality.* New York: Appleton-Century-Crofts, 1945.

4. Williamson, E. G. *A conference summary counseling in a disciplinary situation.* 1953 Potsdam Guidance Conference, State Univer. Teachers College, Potsdam, New York.

134

Edward H. Stullken

WHAT CAN THE SCHOOL DO ABOUT THE JUVENILE DELINQUENCY PROBLEM?

One dimension of the school's role in providing adequate guidance and counseling services is the relationship of the school program to the problem of
juvenile delinquency discussed in Readings 79 to 81. This article attempts to
indicate some of the possibilities for action within the school.

The subject assigned carries the implied assumption that, if the schools do something about
the problem, delinquent behavior can be corrected. There is no doubt some truth in this assumption, but juvenile delinquency is a complex
problem and no *one* agency working alone can
do very much. There are, however, some things
that schools can do.

In the first place teachers and administrators
can improve their knowledge and understanding
of the problem. Delinquency is not a separate
and distinct problem. It should be considered more
in the nature of a symptom of any one of several
or a combination of several underlying conditions, the roots of which may be found in the
family life, the school adjustment, the environmental background of the community, or sometimes in physiological or psychological aspects of
a child's personality.

Schools are concerned with all the problems
of life, the delinquency problem included; but
their concern should be primarily one of dealing
with all children in such a way that delinquent
behavior will not likely result on the part of
individual children.

Educators must also recognize that delinquent
behavior has many different meanings in different
social contexts. From the educator's point of view
delinquency is learned, and the teacher in looking for conditions that give rise to delinquency
will find many that are common to other kinds
of poor learning development—broken homes, poverty, emotional conflicts, retarded mental development, poor neighborhood conditions, *etc.* The
school should study these conditions; should discover how some children learn delinquency under

adverse circumstances while other children in
the same home, school, and neighborhood, often
with the same intelligence and basis for emotional
conflict, learn socially acceptable behavior; the
school should discover how children can unlearn
delinquent patterns of behavior; and most of all
the school must discover how desirable social
behavior can be learned.

Surveys in better schools of current practices
for children who are delinquent or in danger of
becoming so reveal three general levels of operation. These modes of attack on the problem from
the simplest to the most complex type include
the following personnel and services: (1) the
work and responsibility of the regular classroom
teacher in preventing and correcting social maladjustment; (2) the employment of school counselors, school psychologists, school social workers, and medical consultants, whose specialized
services aid and assist regular teachers in helping prevent and treat cases of maladjustment;
and (3) the organization of special classes and
schools where different techniques are employed
and where specialized services are concentrated
upon the more serious cases of maladjustment.

Every teacher faces the responsibility from time
to time of dealing with a maladjusted or delinquent child. Every teacher can have a part in
helping to identify those children who need special
help in learning to adjust in a socially acceptable
manner. Every teacher can help build wholesome
personalities by meeting the basic needs of all
children for affection, for a feeling of belonging,
for a sense of achievement, and for an opportunity
for creative expression. Every teacher can give
wise counsel and guidance to help children and
youth make proper choices and to develop responsibility and capacity for self-discipline.

Special school services enumerated in (2) above
supplement and facilitate the work of the regular

From *Bulletin of the National Association of Secondary School Principals,* April 1954, 38:181-183.

teacher and make an important contribution to the school's attempt to solve the delinquency problem. In this connection there is no substitute for the professionally trained school social worker in helping schools deal with problem children. All large school systems should provide means by which maladjusted children can receive the help of medical, psychological, psychiatric, and guidance workers. In some cases the school can cooperate with other community agencies who can furnish such services to pupils in the schools in need of them.

Special classes for maladjusted pupils sometimes are organized as units within regular school buildings and also as special schools. Detroit, New York, Philadelphia, and Chicago as well as other cities have such special schools. Such centers offer opportunity to deal informally with individual pupils and meet their specific needs and interests. Specially qualified teachers can be selected, special supplementary services for dealing with emotionally disturbed and socially maladjusted pupils can be concentrated, and regular classrooms can be relieved of those children whose symptoms of their disturbances are too severe or too upsetting to other children. Special schools and centers usually provide a wider variety of curriculum offerings than regular schools. They often are in reality a kind of combination of a special school and a child guidance clinic.

In developing the school's program to meet the problem of juvenile delinquency, experience has shown that certain principles should be followed. They should be considered whenever the relationship of the schools to the delinquency problem is under discussion.

1. All children must have the right to develop into self-respecting, useful citizens by the process of public education, and that right must not be abridged by a handicap of any kind which can be eliminated or mitigated through the facilities and resources of the schools.

2. No program for problem children is sound unless it recognizes the fact that the behavior of such children is symptomatic and purposive. An objective attitude on the part of school workers toward children's behavior may serve to prevent problem cases from developing.

3. Problem children differ from normal children more in degree than in kind. There is no hard and fast line between normal and abnormal adjustment.

4. School systems should provide for early identification and early diagnosis of children who are maladjusted.

5. The education of problem children requires a broader basis than that of mere intellectual development. These children often have warped personalities, and, consequently, their feelings and attitudes are the object of more concern than their academic attainments. Children who are deviates because of social maladjustment need a chance to develop emotional stability; they need personal, educational, and vocational guidance; they need to experience the sense of security that goes with a socially acceptable personality.

6. Schools must recognize the fact that a problem child is one who may be normal within himself but yet be exceptional because of antisocial home and community influences.

7. In organizing and administering a program of education for the problem child, school administrators must maintain a balance between the interests of pupils needing placement in special groups and the interests of the great majority of the school population. While these interests often conflict, the conflict must be resolved for the best interests of all concerned. In general, placement of any child in a special group should not be made if that child may receive as good or better training in a normal group, even though it may be necessary to give special help and additional services over and above those which are usually provided. The exception to this rule is found whenever the detriment to the normal pupils outweighs the benefits to the handicapped individual from his association with the regular group.

8. Any program of education for the socially maladjusted will be conditioned by the selection of properly qualified and trained personnel, both those who work in the program and those who administer and direct it.

PART FOUR

TEACHERS AND TEACHING

In primitive societies a great part of the teaching of the young is done by parents; a child's first teachers are his mother and father. If the society remains primitive, this suffices. If the society becomes complicated and more traditions, skills, and tribal secrets have to be handed on, certain persons are assigned to this task. Though a good deal of religious ceremony and symbolism usually comes to be associated with this task, such work may rightly be called teaching and those who do it, teachers.

As societies advance, the work of the teacher becomes more specialized and broader in scope, and the teacher is assigned responsibility as custodian of the cultural heritage. The Egyptians and Babylonians employed temple teachers and developed schools. Later, when the Jewish people grew as a nation and became powerful, the father's task of training his child in the Law became difficult and, under the influence of the prophets Ezra and Nehemiah, the first organized body of teachers in history was established, namely the Scribes. In the same way, the teaching of Roman youth was shifted into the hands of Greek slaves as Rome became an imperial state and the Roman fathers had little time to devote to the training of their sons.

It is interesting that, even in those remote times, there were conservatives who lamented the passing of "the good old days" when parents attended to the teaching of their children and did not entrust them to "some hireling nurse." Almost as far back as the written record goes there seem to have been those who have lamented the passing of the excellent teaching of days gone by. One hears this sort of thing even today. Whenever the schools come under discussion the excellent teaching of past years is almost sure to be mentioned, if indeed it does not become the principal theme of the conversation.

This is particularly likely to be the case when the perennial *subject matter vs. method* controversy comes up. Horace Mann would have understood these arguments; he listened to, and answered, similar ones again and again in his struggle to establish normal schools in Massachusetts in the 1830's. The art of teaching is as old as the human race, and much effective teaching was done before professors of education or psychology appeared or textbooks were developed.

As time passes and knowledge grows, there is more and more to be learned. In life on the frontier, skill at swinging an axe or firing a rifle were of first importance. A man had to understand forest lore; he had to know how to find food and how to withstand heat, cold, and floods. Books and reading definitely took second place. The first law requiring compulsory school attendance was passed in Massachusetts in 1852. It required that every child from eight to fourteen years of age should attend school for twelve weeks each year, "six weeks of which shall be consecutive." This requirement is in marked contrast with the situation one hundred years later when all states provided compulsory schooling, several of them from age six to eighteen.

Striking developments have taken place even in the twentieth century in subjects such as the natural sciences. One has only to compare a textbook in "natural philosophy" as used in high schools and even in some colleges around 1900 with a high-school text used today in physics, chemistry, or biology. The contrast is astonishing. So it is with even a modern text in general science prepared for the upper grades of the elementary school.

Progress in science teaching is particularly striking at present and has been forced on the attention of the public by recent developments in space travel, but equally important progress has been made in other areas. This is nowhere so clearly revealed as by a comparison of today's textbooks with those studied twenty-five, fifty, seventy-five, or one hundred years ago in just about any subject. Advance in breadth, scope, depth, and maturity of approach and treatment are apparent in every subject. Compare the third volume of Webster's *Grammatical Institute* (1785) with a modern text in world literature, or the endless factual lists of cities, products, coast waters, rivers of a geography book used fifty years ago with the rigorous content of a modern text treating such key concepts of geography as map representation, regions, and land and spatial relations.

The teacher's work has increased in other ways. More attention than ever before is given to the slow learner. The teaching of slow learners has become an important area in teacher education and many young people are planning to make this their life's work. The mentally disturbed child also needs special education, and providing educative and healthful surroundings for him has come to be a part of teacher education programs. Particularly since 1945, and more particularly since the spectacular accomplishments in the conquest of space have astonished the world, Americans have been asking themselves if the schools give sufficient attention to the discovery and education of the gifted child. The general impression appears to be that he has been the forgotten child. All in all, it is no longer adequate to aim our educational efforts at the middle ranges of human talent, trusting that the gifted will make his own way and that the dull can be largely passed over, since he is destined by fate to be a hewer of wood or a drawer of water, if not a burden on society.

All of this means that the teacher's task has steadily grown more heavy, more specialized, and more demanding with the passing years. At the same time, it has become much more interesting; the young person who decides to devote his life to teaching a particular subject, to teaching in the elementary school, to school administration, to work with slow learners or with disturbed and handicapped children is entering a field which calls for skill, for commitment to the mission of the school, for high ethical standards, and, above all, for continued study of the process of education.

THE RELATIONSHIP OF TEACHING TO THE SCHOOL AND TO THE COMMUNITY

With exceptions here and there, the prevailing "image" of the teacher in the western cultural tradition is by no means flattering. The teacher as he—or more often she—appears in the novel, in the motion picture, on the TV screen, or in the cartoon strip is to some extent a comic figure if not an out-and-out caricature. This attitude has prevailed for a long time and is pretty firmly established. A few epigrams in this vein can even be found in the Greek Anthology.

George Bernard Shaw's oft-quoted (and misquoted) aphorism, "He who can, does; he who can not, teaches," has been repeated time without number and it points up this prevailing attitude very aptly. At the same time, it contains just enough truth to be thoroughly irritating.

Teachers in America have been trying to raise the status of their profession for the past hundred years. At times the struggle has been discouraging. Fighting against an elusive tradition is likely to be unsatisfactory; much effort is misdirected and progress is of necessity slow.

Yet there are encouraging signs. A good index of the attitude of the public toward those who serve it in any way is the salaries offered. In 1939 the writer E. B. White wrote from his farm in Maine to *Harper's Magazine* that for the previous year the highest paid teacher in his town "was the high school principal (who is also the baseball and basketball coach) who received $1,400. The next highest were the high school and junior high teachers, who received $800. The lowest were the grade teachers in the one-room school, who got $504." These figures of only about twenty-five years ago appear frankly shocking today. Of course, one must remember that a dollar bought more in 1939 than it does today. But, even allowing for the decline in the purchasing power of the dollar, teachers' salaries have increased remarkably, particularly in the past ten years. The amount of money now paid the teacher would seem to indicate that he and his work are steadily rising in the public's esteem.

However, in spite of the increasing attractiveness of teaching, surveys show rather clearly that only a small percentage of the boys and girls now in high school plan to go into teaching. Census returns show that the school population is increasing at an enormous rate. Thousands of new classrooms are needed each year to take care of the increase in grade one alone. The number of new teachers trained each year in the United States is not keeping pace with the increasing number of pupils.

The "bargaining position" of the teacher is improving. While there are far too many unqualified teachers at present, this situation cannot continue indefinitely. Efforts must be made to attract more of the brightest young people into taking up teaching as their life's work; too many in the past have considered it only a stepping stone to something else.

Encouraging progress has been made in the area of salaries. Comparable efforts should be made in other directions. Another good measure of what a community thinks of education is the degree of estimation, freedom, and respect accorded its teachers. In time, it is to be hoped, the teacher will come to be recognized as a trained professional, attacking his problems in the light of his own trained judgment, rather than as a minor functionary acting under orders.

135

Henry C. Morrison

TEACHING

Though it was written in 1934, the following passage appears very timely; it was probably more "old-fashioned" then than it is now. The author was beginning a book on the fundamentals of education, and he saw as one of the first and most important of these the art of teaching.

It seems fitting to begin any discussion of the teacher with a definition of his work—a clear statement of what it is and what it is not. Never has there been a greater need for such definition in America than exists today. Though each student of education should try to work out his own definition, the following one by a distinguished teacher, administrator, and professor of education is offered as at least a model of how this can be done. Clarity and cogency are the hallmarks of Morrison's style.

The topic of the teacher's position is a controversial one. Should he take a leading position in directing what goes on in the schoolroom or should he try to remain passive, as much in the background as possible? Whereas most American educational writers of twenty to fifty years ago seem to have favored the second position, there has been a decided swing toward the first view, particularly within recent years.

In the broadest sense, *teaching is that intimate contact between a more mature personality and a less mature which is designed to further the education of the latter.* Nor is general maturity in the teacher necessarily implied. It is conceivable that an illiterate father who is in some respects mature might resort to his child for instruction in reading. If any results accrue, the father has been *taught* and the child has been his *teacher.* If the child were to suggest exercises through which the father might learn, instruction would be involved but no teaching. If the father were to learn by himself, without guidance or advice, no instruction would be involved nor yet teaching.

Games are sometimes carried on under guidance, with the expectation that either physical or moral advances will result. Instruction is involved, but no teaching. On the other hand, a coach may stand by and not only explain what must be done but see that it is done. The coach, for the time being, is teaching.

Some of the most vital parts of right education are achieved apart from any teaching at all. The most conspicuous illustration is found in that part of normal personality which is commonly called moral character. Here teaching is of little avail, for the chief influences that can be brought to bear are the school government and the general morale of the school. If, on the other hand, a systematic course in ethics is offered to the more advanced pupils, teaching is necessarily involved.

In short, the essence of teaching consists in the intimate personal contact to which reference has been made. Teaching imports that subject matter requires elucidation of some sort and *further that the more mature person feels a responsibility for seeing that the less mature learns.* Its chief instruments are suggestion and constraint. In the case of father and child which we have imagined, no child who undertook the instructional task would for a moment feel that he could stand by and watch his father learn. He would feel called upon to exercise ingenuity in seeing that his father did learn. Such is the teaching situation always.

As schools go, very little teaching is done, even in those situations in which teaching is required

From *Basic Principles in Education* by Henry C. Morrison (Boston: Houghton Mifflin Co., 1934), pp. 41-48.

by the nature of the instructional problem. Lessons are heard, activities are supervised, the pupils are kept in order, but none of these is teaching.

Didactics

The body of principles which describe and explain the teaching process is known as "didactics." Now, "didactic teaching" has frequently been held up to scorn. Something illiberal about it, I suppose. You might as well find fault with "teaching teaching." In truth, what was really censured, and justly, was the practice of submitting some educational objectives to the teaching process which in their nature do not admit of that kind of instructional procedure; and, further, the practice of requiring pupils to con books in fields of learning where the learning required could take place only by contact with various concrete objects and processes.

The first of the two contentions has already been illustrated by the case of instruction in moral character. In the second, laboratory teaching is involved.

Laboratory teaching. If it is found to be necessary that either pupils in school or students in the university should take on learnings such as those which are involved in the cooking of meals, the raising of crops, the manipulation of machines, the processes of chemistry, the structure of the human body; the instructional processes cannot be carried on through descriptive books, nor yet classroom teaching, however inspiring the latter may be. You have got to get down to the handling of things or at least to assured visual images of processes at work.

Thus laboratory teaching. Laboratory instruction is, however, as truly teaching as is classroom instruction. It is as truly didactic.

If the end of teaching cookery is to cook food, that is one thing; if the end is assured learning of principles which the girl would not be likely to acquire from a cook book, then that is quite another thing.

If carrying out the directions of a manual in chemistry and filling in blank spaces in a prepared notebook is what is required of the laboratory in chemistry, then neither teaching nor any other aspect of the instructional process is called for—nor will any learning result, save by chance. If, on the other hand, the objective is the insights which the science of chemistry is capable of generating, then teaching and a great deal of it is required.

And so it is with the other processes which I have drawn in illustration, and others as well.

On the other hand, if an advanced student in the university is working out a problem in a laboratory, he requires no teaching. He consults his professor and that is what the latter is for, but he does not require that the professor stand at his elbow to see that he learns the right thing. The high-school pupil does require just that, else he would no longer be in the high school.

Erroneous use. The word "laboratory" means a place where work goes on, but it has come to possess not a derived but rather a particularized meaning. It means a place in which science is pursued with the aid of apparatus designed for the purpose. A place in which an art is similarly pursued is called a "studio." There has, however, grown into scholastic use the expression "laboratory method," referring to the practice of having pupils in history, literature, or other schoolroom subjects, use several books, in substance use a library, instead of conning and reciting from a single textbook. Now this is an unjustifiable use of words, and it is a singularly confusing misapplication of terms. The practice referred to is merely the normal or natural procedure in teaching where the pupils of necessity use books.

Lecturing. Much as in the case of "didactic teaching," "lecturing" has fallen into disfavor as a "method of teaching." Again, an wholly undiscriminating use of terms.

Lecturing is no more teaching than writing a book is teaching. A lecture means literally a reading. The common meaning given by the International Dictionary is "a discourse on any subject, especially a formal or methodical discourse, intended for instruction; sometimes, a familiar discourse, or one delivered on an irregular occasion, in contrast with a sermon."

Now lecturing is an entirely inappropriate form of instruction below the university level, for the simple reason that it implies maturity and educational responsibility which the pupil does not possess. When the latter is capable of profiting from a course of lectures, he has ceased to be a pupil and has become a student.

Per contra, the lecture is the appropriate form of university instruction, save in those cases in which the laboratory or the seminar is the form indicated by the particular process being carried on.

Nor does it follow that any piece of schoolroom explanation which extends beyond a few minutes is a lecture. To call it that is to give it a name which does not belong to it.

Discipline

Discipline is sometimes teaching and sometimes not. Teaching for the most part bears no relation to discipline, but some phases of teaching are discipline.

The word itself is derived from *discipulus,* which means pupil or follower. The Latin form is still retained in "disciple." We are, however, more concerned with the derived than with the etymological meaning.

The meaning always has in its connotations the sense of constraint of some kind, but it also has the sense of willing acceptance of constraint, a feeling that this or that "is or is not done." Thus we speak of a school as being well-disciplined when the pupil body acts as a whole readily and when the public opinion of the school accepts right standards of conduct and condemns wrong standards. Similarly, a military company or ship's crew is well disciplined when it does its work with alertness, precision and satisfaction. In short, discipline amounts to restraint on the waywardness and self-will of the individual and constraint of all individuals in the way of group welfare and purpose. Thus all groups have to submit to discipline, in the interest not only of the group but of the self-respect and happiness of individuals within the group as well. The principle is as true of university faculties as of school children. About the only difference is in the fact that children cannot be supposed to have learned the value and meaning of discipline, while older people, and especially cultivated, civilized people, can be presumed to have done so. Unhappily, the presumption is often not borne out by the facts.

Now discipline is a process and the product is morale. Here as elsewhere, infinite confusion in thinking results from careless and indiscriminate use of terms, notably in confusion of process and product.

A school, for instance, is held down by mere main strength. That, no doubt, is often a necessary early step when the group has been badly demoralized (morale destroyed) by previous lax discipline; but in itself such government does not operate to restore morale, which always has in it the implication of preference and willing acceptance on the part of those governed. Shrewd observers note that not morale but subservience is characteristic of the group. They rush to the opposite extreme and conclude that all discipline is wrong in principle.

Conversely, the operators of such methods themselves often mistake process for product and conclude that when they have good order the essential result is secured.

So much for that aspect of discipline which operates on the group as a whole and properly conceived secures morale. The process is government and not teaching.

On the other hand, some of necessary teaching is in the nature of discipline.

Time was, and not so very long ago, when the school subjects themselves were referred to as "disciplines." There was a kernel of truth in the characterization, in so far as such use of terms carried with it the implication that subject matter is valuable not in itself but for the sake of its contribution to developing personality. More often, however, in all probability, was the implication that subject matter itself acts as discipline in the primary meaning of the term. In other words, certain subjects were supposed to have much the same kind of effect on mental powers as the use of apparatus in the gymnasium has on the muscles. This last view has long since been exploded.

It is none the less true that certain essential learning products can be attained only through what are in their nature disciplinary measures on the part of the teacher. Illustrations follow.

Learning the use of language, for example, is in large part a matter of learning through practice in the expression of thought. It is also in part a matter of acquiring insight in the structure of the sentence. But it is further a matter of practice under the constraint of the teacher. "Do you mean what this statement says?" "Does this pronoun agree with its antecedent?" "Is this a sentence?" "You know better than to employ that construction or this form of punctuation." These, and almost innumerable other instances which might be cited, are illustrations of disciplinary use of teaching, the essence of which is specific developments of volitional control in the use of language.

Again, we almost never offer in schools systematic courses in logic. To do so might be a poor way of securing habits of accurate thinking in pupils. At all events, we could scarcely hope that any such course unaided would secure the result desired. For one thing, instances of bad thinking are so varied in character that they refuse to conform to any particular pattern, or even series of patterns. Hence teaching logical thinking is in part much as language teaching is in part—disciplinary in character. "If this is true, does it follow, as you say here, that this is also true?" "This line of reasoning does not prove what you think it proves, but rather this."

Once more, habits of concentration or sustained application, sustained attention over an extended body of thought, devotion to tasks which are initially uninteresting, and similar forms of volitional achievement, cannot be learned out of

illuminating exposition, or inspiring exhortation, or book assignments, or from the government of the pupil body. They must be learned through practice, and, since no pupil can be presumed to have the learning objective in mind beforehand, they must be learned through practice which is under constraint. This is a disciplinary aspect of teaching.

136

Marcus Aurelius

MEDITATIONS: CONCERNING LEARNING

Of Marcus Aurelius Antoninus, "the noblest of the Caesars," the poet Matthew Arnold wrote:

> *"Even in a palace, life may be led well!"*
> So spake the imperial sage, purest of men, Marcus Aurelius . . .
>   On his truth sincere
>   Who spoke these words, no shadow ever came.

The *Meditations* of Marcus Aurelius (A.D. 121-180) are included in most lists of the "great books" of the Western cultural tradition. They form a brief and readable exposition of Roman stoicism—a philosophy destined to exercise a strong influence on Christianity and, through Calvinism, on early educational institutions in America.

In the following selection from the introduction to this noted work, Marcus Aurelius pays tribute to his teachers. Evidently he had the best available (since he was the son of an emperor) and made the most of his opportunities. The virtues lauded in these teachers of long ago are, naturally, different in some ways from those sought in teachers today. Some may appear surprisingly naïve to modern readers. Bertrand Russell, in his *History of Western Philosophy* (1), sums up the Roman virtues a bit cynically. Nevertheless, many of the things the young son of the Emperor learned from his teachers are exactly those whose lack in today's schools is eloquently deplored on every hand.

It behoves me to learn from Verus, my grandfather, his beauty of character and meekness of temper:

From my father's repute and my recollections of him, modesty and manliness:

From my mother, piety and liberality; abstention not merely from ill-doing but from the very

thought of evil; simplicity and frugality, and contempt for the luxuries of wealth.

To my great-grandfather I am debtor in that he sent me to the public courses of instruction, procured for me the wisest teachers at home, and taught me that on education we must spend with an open hand.

From the instructor of my youth I learned to care naught for the arena—its charioteers with their green and blue, or its gladiators with their targes and bucklers—but to endure hardship, to be content with little, to labour with my hands,

From *The Meditations of Marcus Aurelius Antoninus,* John Jackson, trans. (Oxford: The Clarendon Press, 1906), pp. 51-60.

to meddle not with what concerned me not, and to turn a deaf ear to scandal:

From Diognetus, to treat trivial things as trivial, to smile at the tales of miracle-mongers and sooth-sayers, with their incantations and their expulsions of evil spirits, to disdain to keep fighting quails or betray interest in such sports, and to bear with outspokenness. Through him I was wedded to philosophy and sat at the feet, first of Eutychius, then of Panyasis and Maecianus: through his influence I put my childish Platonizings on paper, and dreamed of the 'mattress and sheepskin' and all the other vagaries of Grecian thought.

From Rusticus I took to heart the great truth that character needs constant correction and cultivation, and was saved from straying into the arid pastures of a contentious sophistry, from scribbling didactic essays, and declaiming gratuitous good advice, as well as from essaying the rôle of the great athlete and man of action. Thanks to him, I learned to hold aloof from rhetoric, minor poetry, and cheap epigrams; to see the absurdity of pacing my palace in gala dress, and similar follies; to write my correspondence in plain Latin—as plain as his in the note he sent my mother from Sinuessa;—to be placable and ready to lay down arms against any one whose offences had stirred me to anger, so soon as he should make overtures for reconciliation; to read accurately, not to rest content with vague general ideas; to be slow in subscribing to a man with a great flow of words; and, finally, through him I first lit on the works of Epictetus, which he lent me out of his private library.

From Apollonius I know that I must strive after ingenuousness, unwavering constancy, and contempt for the gambler's hit or miss; learn, like him, never for an instant to look towards any other guiding star than reason; and, like him, remain unmoved in paroxysms of pain, in the loss of children, and in lingering disease. He was a living proof that the greatest energy is compatible with the most complete relaxation: his lectures were delivered with unruffled calm, and in him I beheld a man who, in simple truth, looked upon his skill and readiness of exposition as the least meritorious of his qualities. From him I learned in what spirit to receive kindnesses—or what the world deems such—from my friends, neither boorishly ignoring them nor sacrificing my independence in their acknowledgement.

To Sextus I owe the memory of his kindly nature, and the spectacle of a family dwelling in concord under his patriarchal sway; as well as my first notions of life in conformity with Nature. He was unassumingly dignified, an observant guardian of his friends' interests, tolerant of the ignorant and unreflecting, and at home with all sorts and conditions of men, the result being that, while his conversation had far more charm than the most skilfully conceived flattery, he at the same time inspired his listeners with genuine respect. Lucid and, withal, methodical in his search for the true and necessary principles of right living, and in classifying them when found he never displayed the least trace of anger or other strong emotion; and yet, for all his impassiveness, he was the most affectionate of men. He was ungrudging in his praise, though it was quietly given, and his great learning was carried without ostentation.

From Alexander, the grammarian, let me learn to be sparing of rebuke. Should any one, in my hearing, use a barbarism, or a solecism, or mispronounce a word, let me, like him, refrain from breaking in with a reproof, but, with what tact I may, say what the speaker ought to have said, under pretence of corroborating his arguments or contributing something to the question at issue, avoiding all reference to the disputed phrase,—or at least try to use some similarly inoffensive mode of correction.

From Fronto comes the reflection that jealousy, insincerity, and hypocrisy are the usual concomitants of a crown; and that, in general, our so-called nobility is deficient in the natural affections.

The example of Alexander, the Platonist, admonishes me neither in conversation nor in writing to use the excuse of 'urgent affairs,' save rarely and in cases of absolute need, lest, through thus continually pleading the stress of business, I come to shirk my relations and obligations to my fellow men.

From Catulus let me learn not to despise the complaint of a friend however irrational it may be, but strive to restore our former relationship; to be ungrudging in the praise of my teachers, bearing in mind the example of Domitius and Athenodotus; and, finally, to love my children as sincerely as he loved his.

My brother, Severus, taught me to love truth, justice, and my friends: through him I came to know the great names of Thrasea, Helvidius, Cato, Dio, and Brutus: from him I acquired the idea of a constitutional state founded on the principles of equality and free speech—a monarchy whose ideal is the freedom of the subject. From him, also, I may learn to pay unswerving and unfaltering homage to philosophy, to stint not in benevolence and charity, and to be hopeful and mistrust not the affection of my friends; and yet he took no pains to conceal his disapproval, and it needed no guesswork on the part of his friends to divine what he wished and what he did not: it was plain for all to see.

The example of Maximus may remind me to exercise self-control and not lightly to change my attitude on any point; to imitate his cheerfulness under all circumstances, especially in sickness, and his temperate, sweet, and venerable character. He did the work he was called to do without complaint, and no one could doubt but that what he said he meant, and what he did he did to good purpose. Nothing surprised or confounded him; without haste and without rest, he was never at a loss, never dejected; his countenance never wore a forced smile; he never gave way to anger and never cherished suspicion. He wearied not in well-doing, loved mercy, hated falsehood, and gave the impression of a man who needed not to correct himself, because he never went astray. No one could ever imagine either that Maximus looked down on him or that he was superior to Maximus. His wit, too, was bright, but inoffensive.

From the father that adopted me, let me learn to be gentle; to take no decision without careful investigation, but then to hold fast to the anchor of truth; not to be deluded into the pursuit of what men call honour, but to labour and faint not; to lend a ready ear to all who may propound something to the common good; and to reward every man according to his deserts without fear or favour. He knew by experience when there was need of stringency, when of relaxation; he suppressed unnatural vice with a strong hand, and was ever considerate to others. For instance, his friends were left free to accept his invitations or not; there was no constraint on them to accompany him on his visits to the provinces, and those who had stayed behind through one cause or another found, on his return, no change in his feelings towards them. In council he was accurate and persevering in deliberation, nor would he desist from the quest of truth satisfied with plausible commonplaces. To his friends he was constant, neither admitting them with unreasoning effusion nor changing them with each passing whim. Self-reliant and cheerful in all things, he was far-sighted, and nothing was too small for his unostentatious forethought. In his time public and private adulation were alike repressed. He consistently husbanded the resources of his empire and cut down expenses, heedless of disapproval in some quarters. In religion he was free from superstition, in dealing with men he was no popularity-hunter with the democracy or panderer to the mob, but steady and sober in all things, never in bad taste, and no innovator.

The conveniences of life, of which fortune had been lavish to him, he used alike without ostentation and without apology; if they were present, he enjoyed them unaffectedly; if absent, he felt no need of them. No one could possibly have described him as a sophist, a licensed jester, or a pedant; but, rather, as a man, ripe and finished, superior to the arts of flattery, and fit to manage either his own affairs or those of a people. In addition to this he held true philosophers in esteem; on the spurious sort he wasted no reproaches, but took good care they did not lead him into error. His conversation was familiar and gracious, but never to excess. He took reasonable care of his body, not that he was a great lover of life or cared much for personal adornment, though he did not go to the opposite extreme of neglect; the result being that his own attention enabled him, for the most part, to dispense with doctors and their drugs and plasters. Most worthy of imitation, also, was the unenvious manner in which he would give way to those who had any special faculty—for instance, for oratory, knowledge of law and custom, and the like—giving them his best help in securing the recognition due to their peculiar abilities. Though he observed the traditional institutions of the empire, he showed no affectation of so doing. He had a thorough dislike for chopping and changing, and preferred to stand by the old places and the old things. After suffering agonies through neuralgia, he would return fresh and vigorous to his usual employments. His secrets were few and far between, and the few he had were confined to matters of public policy. He showed prudence and moderation in the exhibition of public shows and the construction of public buildings, as well as in the distribution of state monies and the like, looking only to what ought to be done, not to the ensuing popularity. He was not one of those who are at all hours using the baths, nor was he afflicted with the mania for building. No connoisseur of the table, he cared little for the texture or colour of his dress and less for the looks of his slaves. At Lorium he usually wore a toga made at one of his villas on the coast; a tunic, mostly, at Lanuvium; in Tusculum he added an overcoat, about which he was rather apologetic, and all his habits were of the same simplicity. There was nothing harsh or intractable or violent about him; he never rushed around as if the doctor had ordered him to get up a perspiration;—all seemed to have been reasoned out in detail, deliberately, coolly, methodically, vigorously, and consistently. What was said of Socrates was equally applicable to him, that he could with like ease refrain from and enjoy those pleasures in the indulgence of which, with most men, the flesh is strong enough, in abstinence, weak indeed; whereas to have the strength to bear the latter and maintain sobriety in the former needs a soul perfect and invincible, such as he displayed in the illness of Maximus.

Lastly, it was Heaven that gave me good grandparents, good parents, a good sister, good teachers, good connexions, relatives, and friends almost without exception, and that prevented me from thoughtlessly offending any one of these, though my nature was such that I might only too easily have done so, had not the divine kindness ordained that no train of events should occur to expose me, and decreed, withal, that I should not long remain under the influence of my grandfather's mistress; that I should retain my youthful purity and chastity so long; that I should be placed under an imperial father who could purge me from all arrogance, and teach me that it is possible to live in a court and yet dispense with bodyguards, golden statues with torches in their hands, and all similar vanities; that a king may lower himself almost to the level of his subjects, and lose no whit of dignity or resolution in acting like a king when the common weal is at stake.

To Heaven it is due that I had a brother whose character could stir me to improve my own, and who comforted me with his respect and love; that the children born to me have been deformed in neither body nor mind; that I made but small progress in rhetoric, versifying and the kindred arts, in which I might perhaps have frittered away my time had I noticed that I was making rapid strides in them; that I gave my tutors the preferment I thought they desired, and did not

abandon them to hope deferred on the ground that they were too young; that I have known Apollonius, Rusticus, and Maximus; that I have been able to contemplate clearly and often the character of the natural life, and so to see that on the side of the divine will, its dispensations, assistance, and inspiration, there is nothing to hinder me from even now living in harmony with Nature, but that my failure is due to my own imperfections and to my non-observance of the intimations—nay, I might say, the direct instructions—of Heaven; that my bodily health has held out so long under such conditions; that I touched neither Benedicta nor Theodotus, but though once mastered by sensual passion was made whole again; that, often as I have been provoked by Rusticus, I have never had to repent of my treatment of him; that my mother, though fated to die young, yet spent her last years with me; that often as I have had to help the poor and otherwise needy, I have never had occasion to consider the question, 'Where is the money to come from?'; that it has never been my misfortune myself to need another's help; that I married a wife obedient, affectionate, and simple; that I have had no difficulty in procuring fitting tutors for my children; that oracular advice was given me in a dream at Caieta how to cure my giddiness and the spitting of blood; and that, when all my thoughts were beginning to run on philosophy, I fell in with no sophist, never sat down to waste my time on the analysis of syllogisms, or the pursuit of natural speculations above my head. —For none of these things could have been but for divine assistance and a kindly destiny.

137

George Herbert Palmer

THE IDEAL TEACHER

The distinguished American philosopher George Herbert Palmer (1842-1933) wrote the following classic account of teaching early in the present century. Reprinted frequently, it was circulated and quoted widely in its time. Much of it is still pertinent today.

The author was for some years chairman of the Philosophy Department at Harvard—probably the most distinguished group of philosophers ever assembled in an American university. He was himself primarily a teacher of philosophy rather than a builder of any philosophical system; teaching was the breath of life to him, and his concept of the teacher's work is that of a brilliantly successful man who knew it at first hand.

Professor Palmer's figures of school enrollments, expenses, and teaching force sound somewhat unimpressive today when compared with figures released periodically by the U.S. Office of Education, yet one can only feel that his optimism was justified. He saw that schools would increase in size and enrollment and that the duties of the teacher would expand. Yet he believed that certain qualities and characteristics were imperative for anybody who undertook the task of teaching the young and that these qualities were necessary everywhere and in all ages. There is a distinct challenge in his account of these four characteristics: (a) the aptitude for vicariousness; (b) accumulated wealth; (c) ability to invigorate life through knowledge; (d) readiness to be forgotten.

Though the selection is somewhat "dated," especially in its easy optimism (two world wars have been fought since it was written), the author's insight and his vision of the real rewards of teaching make it a classic.

In America, a land of idealism, the profession of teaching has become one of the greatest of human employments. In 1903-04 half a million teachers were in charge of sixteen million pupils. Stating the same facts differently, we may say that a fifth of our entire population is constantly at school; and that wherever one hundred and sixty men, women, and children are gathered, a teacher is sure to be among them.

But figures fail to express the importance of the work. If each year an equal number of persons should come in contact with as many lawyers, no such social consequences would follow. The touch of the teacher, like that of no other person, is formative. Our young people are for long periods associated with those who are expected to fashion them into men and women of an approved type. A charge so influential is committed to nobody else in the community, not even to the ministers; for though these have a more searching aim, they are directly occupied with it but one day instead of six, but one hour instead of five. Accordingly, as the tract of knowledge has widened, and the creative opportunities involved in conducting a young person over it have correspondingly become apparent, the profession of teaching has risen to a notable height of dignity and attractiveness. It has moved from a subordinate to a central place in social influence, and now undertakes much of the work which formerly fell to the church. Each year divinity schools attract fewer students, graduate and normal schools more. On school and college instruction the community now bestows its choicest minds, its highest hopes, and its largest sums. During the year 1903-04 the United States spent for teaching not less than $350,000,000.

Such weighty work is ill adapted for amateurs. Those who take it up for brief times and to make money usually find it unsatisfactory. Success is rare, the hours are fixed and long, there is repetition and monotony, and the teacher passes his days among inferiors. Nor are the pecuniary gains considerable. There are few prizes, and neither in school nor in college will a teacher's ordinary income carry him much above want. College teaching is falling more and more into the hands of men of independent means. The poor can hardly afford to engage in it. Private schools, it is true, often show large incomes; but they are earned by the proprietors, not the teachers. On the whole, teaching as a trade is poor and disappointing business.

When, however, it is entered as a profession, as a serious and difficult fine art, there are few employments more satisfying. All over the country thousands of men and women are following it with a passionate devotion which takes little account of the income received. A trade aims primarily at personal gain; a profession at the exercise of powers beneficial to mankind. This prime aim of the one, it is true, often properly becomes a subordinate aim of the other. Professional men may even be said to offer wares of their own—cures, conversions, court victories, learning—much as traders do, and to receive in return a kind of reward. But the business of the lawyer, doctor, preacher, and teacher never squares itself by equivalent exchange. These men do not give so much for so much. They give in lump and they get in lump, without precise balance. The whole notion of bargain is inapplicable in a sphere where the gains of him who serves and him who is served coincide; and that is largely the case with the professions. Each of them fur-

From *The Teacher: Essays and Addresses on Education* by George Herbert Palmer and Alice Freeman Palmer (Boston: Houghton Mifflin Co., 1908), pp. 3-30.

nishes its special opportunity for the use of powers which the possessor takes delight in exercising. Harvard College pays me for doing what I would gladly pay it for allowing me to do. No professional man, then, thinks of giving according to measure. Once engaged, he gives his best, gives his personal interest, himself. His heart is in his work, and for this no equivalent is possible; what is accepted is in the nature of a fee, gratuity, or consideration, which enables him who receives it to maintain a certain expected mode of life. The real payment is the work itself, this and the chance to join with other members of the profession in guiding and enlarging the sphere of its activities.

The idea, sometimes advanced, that the professions might be ennobled by paying them powerfully, is fantastic. Their great attraction is their removal from sordid aims. More money should certainly be spent on several of them. Their members should be better protected against want, anxiety, neglect, and bad conditions of labor. To do his best work one needs not merely to live, but to live well. Yet in that increase of salaries which is urgently needed, care should be used not to allow the attention of the professional man to be diverted from what is important,—the outgo of his work,—and become fixed on what is merely incidental,—his income. When a professor in one of our large universities, angered by the refusal of the president to raise his salary on his being called elsewhere, impatiently exclaimed, "Mr. President, you are banking on the devotion of us teachers, knowing that we do not willingly leave this place," the president properly replied, "Certainly, and no college can be managed on any other principle." Professional men are not so silly as to despise money; but after all, it is interest in their work, and not the thought of salary, which predominantly holds them.

Accordingly in this paper I address those only who are drawn to teaching by the love of it, who regard it as the most vital of the Fine Arts, who intend to give their lives to mastering its subtleties, and who are ready to meet some hardships and to put up with moderate fare if they may win its rich opportunities.

But supposing such a temper, what special qualifications will the work require? The question asked thus broadly admits no precise answer; for in reality there is no human excellence which is not useful for us teachers. No good quality can be thought of which we can afford to drop. Some day we shall discover a disturbing vacuum in the spot which it left. But I propose a more limited problem: what are those characteristics of the teacher without which he must fail, and what

those which, once his, will almost certainly insure him success? Are there any such essentials, and how many? On this matter I have pondered long; for, teaching thirty-nine years in Harvard College, I have each year found out a little more fully my own incompetence. I have thus been forced to ask myself the double question, through what lacks do I fail, and in what direction lie the roots of my small successes? Of late years I think I have hit on these roots of success and have come to believe that there are four of them, —four characteristics which every teacher must possess. Of course he may possess as many more as he likes,—indeed, the more the better. But these four appear fundamental. I will briefly name them.

First, a teacher must have an aptitude for vicariousness; and second, an already accumulated wealth; and third, an ability to invigorate life through knowledge; and fourth, a readiness to be forgotten. Having these, any teacher is secure. Lacking them, lacking even one, he is liable to serious failure. But as here stated they have a curiously cabalistic sound and show little relation to the needs of any profession. They have been stated with too much condensation, and have become unintelligible through being too exact. Let me repair the error by successively expanding them.

The teacher's art takes its rise in what I call an aptitude for vicariousness. As year by year my college boys prepare to go forth into life, some laggard is sure to come to me and say, "I want a little advice. Most of my classmates have their minds made up about what they are going to do. I am still uncertain. I rather incline to be a teacher, because I am fond of books and suspect that in any other profession I can give them but little time. Business men do not read. Lawyers only consult books. And I am by no means sure that ministers have read all the books they quote. On the whole it seems safest to choose a profession in which books will be my daily companions. So I turn toward teaching. But before settling the matter I thought I would ask how you regard the profession." "A noble profession," I answer, "but quite unfit for you. I would advise you to become a lawyer, a car conductor, or something equally harmless. Do not turn to anything so perilous as teaching. You would ruin both it and yourself; for you are looking in exactly the wrong direction."

Such an inquirer is under a common misconception. The teacher's task is not primarily the acquisition of knowledge, but the impartation of it,—an entirely different matter. We teachers are forever taking thoughts out of our minds and putting them elsewhere. So long as we are content to keep them in our possession, we are not teachers at all. One who is interested in laying hold on wisdom is likely to become a scholar. And while no doubt it is well for a teacher to be a fair scholar,—I have known several such,—that is not the main thing. What constitutes the teacher is the passion to make scholars; and again and again it happens that the great scholar has no such passion whatever.

But even that passion is useless without aid from imagination. At every instant of the teacher's life he must be controlled by this mighty power. Most human beings are contented with living one life and delighted if they can pass that agreeably. But this is far from enough for us teachers. We incessantly go outside ourselves and enter into the many lives about us,—lives dull, dark, and unintelligible to any but an eye like ours. And this is imagination, the sympathetic creation in ourselves of conditions which belong to others. Our profession is therefore a double-ended one. We inspect truth as it rises fresh and interesting before our eager sight. But that is only the beginning of our task. Swiftly we then seize the lines of least intellectual resistance in alien minds and, with perpetual reference to these, follow our truth till it is safely lodged beyond ourselves. Each mind has its peculiar set of frictions. Those of our pupils can never be the same as ours. We have passed far on and know all about our subject. For us it wears an altogether different look from that which it has for beginners. It is their perplexities which we must reproduce and—as if a rose should shut and be a bud again—we must reassume in our developed and accustomed souls something of the innocence of childhood. Such is the exquisite business of the teacher, to carry himself back with all his wealth of knowledge and understand how his subject should appear to the meagre mind of one glancing at it for the first time.

And what absurd blunders we make in the process! Becoming immersed in our own side of the affair, we blind ourselves and readily attribute to our pupils modes of thought which are not in the least theirs. I remember a lesson I had on this point, I who had been teaching ethics half a lifetime. My nephew, five years old, was fond of stories from the Odyssey. He would creep into bed with me in the morning and beg for them. One Sunday, after I had given him a pretty stiff bit of adventure, it occurred to me that it was an appropriate day for a moral. "Ulysses was a very brave man," I remarked. "Yes," he said, "and I am very brave." I saw my opportunity and seized it. "That is true," said I. "You have been gaining courage lately. You used to cry easily,

but you don't do that nowadays. When you want to cry now, you think how like a baby it would be to cry, or how you would disturb mother and upset the house; and so you conclude not to cry." The little fellow seemed hopelessly puzzled. He lay silent a minute or two and then said, "Well no, Uncle, I don't do that. I just go sh-sh-sh, and I don't." There the moral crisis is stated in its simplicity; and I had been putting off on that holy little nature sophistications borrowed from my own battered life.

But while I am explaining the blunders caused by self-engrossment and lack of imagination, let me show what slight adjustments will sometimes carry us past depressing difficulties. One year when I was lecturing on some intricate problems of obligation, I began to doubt whether my class was following me, and I determined that I would make them talk. So the next day I constructed an ingenious ethical case and, after stating it to the class, I said, "Supposing now the state of affairs were thus and thus, and the interests of the persons involved were such and such, how would you decide the question of right,—Mr. Jones." Poor Jones rose in confusion. "You mean," he said, "if the case were as you have stated it? Well, hm, hm, hm,—yes,—I don't think I know, sir." And he sat down. I called on one and another with the same result. A panic was upon them, and all their minds were alike empty. I went home disgusted, wondering whether they had comprehended anything I had said during the previous fortnight, and hoping I might never have such a stupid lot of students again. Suddenly it flashed upon me that it was I who was stupid. That is usually the case when a class fails; it is the teacher's fault. The next day I went back prepared to begin at the right end. I began, "Oh, Mr. Jones." He rose, and I proceeded to state the situation as before. By the time I paused he had collected his wits, had worked off his superfluous flurry, and was ready to give me an admirable answer. Indeed in a few minutes the whole class was engaged in an eager discussion. My previous error had been in not remembering that they, I, and everybody, when suddenly attacked with a big question, are not in the best condition for answering. Occupied as I was with my end of the story, the questioning end, I had not worked in that double-ended fashion which alone can bring the teacher success; in short, I was deficient in vicariousness,—in swiftly putting myself in the weak one's place and bearing his burden.

Now it is in this chief business of the artistic teacher, to labor imaginatively himself in order to diminish the labors of his slender pupil, that most of our failures occur. Instead of lamenting the imperviousness of our pupils, we had better ask ourselves more frequently whether we have neatly adjusted our teachings to the conditions of their minds. We have no right to tumble out in a mass whatever comes into our heads, leaving to that feeble folk the work of finding in it what order they may. Ours it should be to see that every beginning, middle, and end of what we say is helpfully shaped for readiest access to those less intelligent and interested than we. But this is vicariousness. *Noblesse oblige*. In this profession any one who will be great must be a nimble servant, his head full of others' needs.

Some discouraged teacher, glad to discover that his past failures have been due to the absence of sympathetic imagination, may resolve that he will not commit that blunder again. On going to his class to-morrow he will look out upon his subject with his pupils' eyes, not with his own. Let him attempt it, and his pupils will surely say to one another, "What is the matter to-day with teacher?" They will get nothing from that exercise. No, what is wanted is not a resolve, but an aptitude. The time for using vicariousness is not the time for acquiring it. Rather it is the time for dismissing all thoughts of it from the mind. On entering the classroom we should leave every consideration of method outside the door, and talk simply as interested men and women in whatever way comes most natural to us. But into that nature vicariousness should long ago have been wrought. It should be already on hand. Fortunate we if our great-grandmother supplied us with it before we were born. There are persons who, with all good will, can never be teachers. They are not made in that way. Their business it is to pry into knowledge, to engage in action, to make money, or to pursue whatever other aim their powers dictate; but they do not readily think in terms of the other person. They should not, then, be teachers.

The teacher's habit is well summed in the Apostle's rule, "Look not every man on his own things, but every man also"—it is double—"on the things of others." And this habit should become as nearly as possible an instinct. Until it is rendered instinctive and passes beyond conscious direction, it will be of little worth. Let us then, as we go into society, as we walk the streets, as we sit at table, practice altruistic limberness and learn to escape from ourselves. A true teacher is always meditating his work, disciplining himself for his profession, probing the problems of his glorious art, and seeing illustration of them everywhere. In only one place is he freed from such criticism, and that is in his classroom. Here

in the moment of action he lets himself go, unhampered by theory, using the nature acquired elsewhere, and uttering as simply as possible the fulness of his mind and heart. Direct human intercourse requires instinctive aptitudes. Till altruistic vicariousness has become our second nature, we shall not deeply influence anybody.

But sympathetic imagination is not all a teacher needs. Exclusive altruism is absurd. On this point too I once got instruction from the mouths of babes and sucklings. The children of a friend of mine, children of six and four, had just gone to bed. Their mother overheard them talking when they should have been asleep. Wondering what they might need, she stepped into the entry and listened. They were discussing what they were here in the world for. That is about the size of problems commonly found in infant minds. The little girl suggested that we are probably in the world to help others. "Why, no indeed, Mabel," said her big brother, "for then what would others be here for?" Precisely! If anything is only fit to give away, it is not fit for that. We must know and prize its goodness in ourselves before generosity is even possible.

Plainly, then, beside his aptitude for vicariousness, our ideal teacher will need the second qualification of an already accumulated wealth. These hungry pupils are drawing all their nourishment from us, and have we got it to give? They will be poor, if we are poor; rich if we are wealthy. We are their source of supply. Every time we cut ourselves off from nutrition, we enfeeble them. And how frequently devoted teachers make this mistake! dedicating themselves so to the immediate needs of those about them that they themselves grow thinner each year. We all know the "teacher's face." It is meagre, worn, sacrificial, anxious, powerless. That is exactly the opposite of what it should be. The teacher should be the big bounteous being of the community. Other people may get along tolerably by holding whatever small knowledge comes their way. A moderate stock will pretty well serve their private turn. But that is not our case. Supplying a multitude, we need wealth sufficient for a multitude. We should then be clutching at knowledge on every side. Nothing must escape us. It is a mistake to reject a bit of truth because it lies outside our province. Some day we shall need it. All knowledge is our province.

In preparing a lecture I find I always have to work hardest on the things I do not say. The things I am sure to say I can easily get up. They are obvious and generally accessible. But they, I find, are not enough. I must have a broad background of knowledge which does not appear in speech. I have to go over my entire subject and see how the things I am to say look in their various relations, tracing out connections which I shall not present to my class. One might ask what is the use of this? Why prepare more matter than can be used? Every successful teacher knows. I cannot teach right up to the edge of my knowledge without a fear of falling off. My pupils discover this fear, and my words are ineffective. They feel the influence of what I do not say. One cannot precisely explain it; but when I move freely across my subject as if it mattered little on what part of it I rest, they get a sense of assured power which is compulsive and fructifying. The subject acquires consequence, their minds swell, and they are eager to enter regions of which they had not previously thought.

Even, then, to teach a small thing well we must be large. I asked a teacher what her subject was, and she answered, "Arithmetic in the third grade." But where is the third grade found? In knowledge, or in the schools? Unhappily it is in the schools. But if one would be a teacher of arithmetic, it must be arithmetic she teaches and not third grade at all. We cannot accept these artificial bounds without damage. Instead of accumulated wealth they will bring us accumulated poverty, and increase it every day. Years ago at Harvard we began to discuss the establishment of a Graduate School; and I, a young instructor, steadily voted against it. My thought was this: Harvard College, in spite of what the public imagines, is a place of slender resources. Our means are inadequate for teaching even undergraduates. But graduate instruction is vastly more expensive; courses composed of half a dozen students take the time of the ablest professors. I thought we could not afford this. Why not leave graduate instruction to a university which gives itself entirely to that task? Would it not be wiser to spend ourselves on the lower ranges of learning, covering these adequately, than to try to spread ourselves over the entire field?

Doubting so, I for some time opposed the coming of a Graduate School. But a luminous remark of our great President showed me the error of my ways. In the course of debate he said one evening, "It is not primarily for the graduates that I care for this school; it is for the undergraduates. We shall never get good teaching here so long as our instructors set a limit to their subjects. When they are called on to follow these throughout, tracing them far off toward the unknown, they may become good teachers; but not before."

I went home meditating. I saw that the President was right, and that I was myself in danger

of the stagnation he deprecated. I changed my vote, as did others. The Graduate School was established; and of all the influences which have contributed to raise the standard of scholarship at Harvard, both for teachers and taught, that graduate work seems to me the greatest. Every professor now must be the master of a field of knowledge, and not of a few paths running through it.

But the ideal teacher will accumulate wealth, not merely for his pupils' sake, but for his own. To be a great teacher one must be a great personality, and without ardent and individual tastes the roots of our being are not fed. For developing personal power it is well, therefore, for each teacher to cultivate interests unconnected with his official work. Let the mathematician turn to the English poets, the teacher of classics to the study of birds and flowers, and each will gain a lightness, a freedom from exhaustion, a mental hospitality, which can only be acquired in some disinterested pursuit. Such a private subject becomes doubly dear because it is just our own. We pursue it as we will; we let it call out our irresponsible thoughts; and from it we ordinarily carry off a note of distinction lacking in those whose lives are too tightly organized.

To this second qualification of the teacher, however, I have been obliged to prefix a condition similar to that which was added to the first. We need not merely wealth, but an already accumulated wealth. At the moment when wealth is wanted it cannot be acquired. It should have been gathered and stored before the occasion arose. What is more pitiable than when a person who desires to be a benefactor looks in his chest and finds it empty? Special knowledge is wanted, or trained insight, or professional skill, or sound practical judgment; and the teacher who is called on has gone through no such discipline as assures these resources. I am inclined to think that women are more liable to this sort of bankruptcy than men. Their sex is more sympathetic than ours and they spend more hastily. They will drop what they are doing and run if a baby cries. Excellence requires a certain hardihood of heart, while quick responsiveness is destructive of the larger giving. He who would be greatly generous must train himself long and tenaciously, without much attention to momentary calls. The plan of the Great Teacher, by which he took thirty years for acquisition and three for bestowal, is not unwise, provided that we too can say, "For their sakes I sanctify myself."

But the two qualifications of the teacher already named will not alone suffice. I have known persons who were sympathetically imaginative, and who could not be denied to possess large intellectual wealth, who still failed as teachers. One needs a third something, the power to invigorate life through learning. We do not always notice how knowledge naturally buffets. It is offensive stuff, and makes young and wholesome minds rebel. And well it may; for when we learn anything, we are obliged to break up the world, inspect it piecemeal, and let our minds seize it bit by bit. Now about a fragment there is always something repulsive. Any one who is normally constituted must draw back in horror, feeling that what is brought him has little to do with the beautiful world he has known. Where was there ever a healthy child who did not hate the multiplication table? A boy who did not detest such abstractions as seven times eight would hardly be worth educating. By no ingenuity can we relieve knowledge of this unfortunate peculiarity. It must be taken in disjointed portions. That is the way attention is made. In consequence each of us must be to some extent a specialist, devoting himself to certain sides of the world and neglecting others quite as important. These are the conditions under which we imperfect creatures work. Our sight is not world-wide. When we give our attention to one object, by that very act we withdraw it from others. In this way our children must learn and have their expansive natures subdued to pedagogic exigencies.

Because this belittlement through the method of approach is inevitable, it is all-important that the teacher should possess a supplemental dignity, replacing the oppressive sense of pettiness with stimulating intimations of high things in store. Partly on this account a book is an imperfect instructor. Truth there, being impersonal, seems untrue, abstract, and insignificant. It needs to shine through a human being before it can exert its vital force on a young student. Quite as much for vital transmission as for intellectual elucidation, is a teacher employed. His consolidated character exhibits the gains which come from study. He need not point them out. If he is a scholar, there will appear in him an augustness, accuracy, fulness of knowledge, a buoyant enthusiasm even in drudgery, and an unshakable confidence that others must soon see and enjoy what has enriched himself; and all this will quickly convey itself to his students and create attention in his classroom. Such kindling of interest is the great function of the teacher. People sometimes say, "I should like to teach if only pupils cared to learn." But then there would be little need of teaching. Boys who have made up their minds that knowledge is worth while are pretty sure to get it, without regard to teachers. Our chief concern is with those who are unawakened. In the Sistine Chapel Michael Angelo has depicted the Almighty moving in clouds over the rugged earth where lies the newly created Adam, hardly aware of himself. The tips of the fingers touch, the Lord's and Adam's, and the huge frame loses its inertness and rears itself into action. Such may be the electrifying touch of the teacher.

But it must be confessed that not infrequently, instead of invigorating life through knowledge, we teachers reduce our classes to complete passivity. The blunder is not altogether ours, but is suggested by certain characteristics of knowledge itself: for how can a learner begin without submitting his mind, accepting facts, listening to authority, in short becoming obedient? He is called on to put aside his own notions and take what truth dictates. I have said that knowledge buffets, forcing us into an almost slavish attitude, and that this is resented by vigorous natures. In almost every school some of the most original, aggressive, and independent boys stand low in their classes, while at the top stand "grinds,"— objects of horror to all healthy souls.

Now it is the teacher's business to see that the onslaught of knowledge does not enfeeble. Between the two sides of knowledge, information and intelligence, he is to keep the balance true. While a boy is taking in facts, facts not allowed to be twisted by any fancy or carelessness, he is all the time to be made to feel that these facts offer him a field for critical and constructive action. If they leave him inactive, docile, and plodding, there is something wrong with the teaching. Facts are pernicious when they subjugate and do not quicken the mind that grasps them. Education should unfold us and truth together; and to enable it to do so the learner must never be allowed to sink into a mere recipient. He should be called on to think, to observe, to form his own judgments, even at the risk of error and crudity. Temporary one-sidedness and extravagance is not too high a price to pay for originality. And this development of personal vigor, emphasized in our day by the elective system and independent research, is the great aim of education. It should affect the lower ranges of study as truly as the higher. The mere contemplation of truth is always a deadening affair. Many a dull class in school and college would come to life if simply given something to do. Until the mind reacts for itself on what it receives, its education is hardly begun.

The teacher who leads it so to react may be truly called "productive," productive of human beings. The noble word has recently become Germanized and corrupted, and is now hardly more than a piece of educational slang. According to the judgments of to-day a teacher may be unimaginative, pedantic, dull, and may make his students no less so; he will still deserve a crown of wild olive as a "productive" man if he neglects his classroom for the printing press. But this is to put first things second and second things first. He who is original and fecund, and knows how to beget a similar spirit in his students, will naturally wish to express himself beyond his classroom. By snatching the fragments of time which his arduous work allows, he may accomplish much worthy writing and probably increase too his worth for his college, his students, and himself. But the business of book-making is, after all, collateral with us teachers. Not for this are we employed, desirable though it is for showing the kind of mind we bear. Many of my most productive colleagues have printed little or nothing, though they have left a deep mark on the life and science of our time. I would encourage publication. It keeps the solitary student healthy, enables him to find his place among his fellows, and more distinctly to estimate the contributions he is making to his subject. But let him never neglect his proper work for that which must always have in it an element of advertising.

Too long I have delayed the fourth, the disagreeable, section of my paper. Briefly it is this: a teacher must have a readiness to be forgotten. And what is harder? We may be excellent persons, may be daily doing kindnesses, and yet not be quite willing to have those kindnesses overlooked. Many a man is ready to be generous, if by it he can win praise. The love of praise,—it is almost our last infirmity; but there is no more baffling infirmity for the teacher. If praise and recognition are dear to him, he may as well stop work. Dear to him perhaps they must be, as a human being; but as a teacher, he is called on to rise above ordinary human conditions. Whoever has followed me thus far will perceive the reason. I have shown that a teacher does not live for himself, but for his pupil and for the truth which he imparts. His aim is to be a colorless medium through which that truth may shine on opening minds. How can he be this if he is continually interposing himself and saying, "Instead of looking at the truth, my children, look at me and see how skilfully I do my work. I thought I taught you admirably to-day. I hope you thought so too." No, the teacher must keep himself entirely out of the way, fixing young attention on the proffered knowledge and not on anything so small as the one who brings it. Only so can he be vicarious, whole-hearted in invigorating the lives committed to his charge.

Moreover, any other course is futile. We cannot tell whether those whom we are teaching have taken our best points or not. Those best points, what are they? We shall count them one thing, our pupils another. We gather what seems to us of consequence and pour it out upon our classes. But if their minds are not fitted to receive it, the little creatures have excellent protective arrangements which they draw down, and all we pour is simply shed as if nothing had fallen; while again we say something so slight that we hardly notice it, but, happening to be just the nutritive element which that small life then needs, it is caught up and turned into human fibre. We cannot tell. We work in the dark. Out upon the waters our bread is cast, and if we are wise we do not attempt to trace its return.

On this point I received capital instruction from one of my pupils. In teaching a course on English Empiricism I undertook a line of exposition which I knew was abstruse. Indeed, I doubted if many of the class could follow; but there on the front seat sat one whose bright eyes were ever upon me. It seemed worth while to teach my three or four best men, that man in particular. By the end of the term there were many grumblings. My class did not get much out of me that year. They graduated, and a couple of years later this young fellow appeared at my door to say that he could not pass through Cambridge without thanking me for his work on Locke, Berkeley, and Hume. Pleased to be assured that my questionable methods were justified, and unwilling to drop a subject so agreeable, I asked if he could tell precisely where the value of the course lay. "Certainly," he answered. "It all centred in a single remark of Locke's. Locke said we ought to have clear and distinct ideas. I don't think I got anything else out of the course."

Well, at first I was inclined to think the fellow foolish, so to mistake a bit of commonplace for gospel truth. Why did he not listen to some of the profound things I was saying? But on reflection I saw that he was right and I wrong. That trivial saying had come to him at a critical moment as a word of power; while the deep matters which interested me, and which I had been offering him so confidently day by day, being unsuited to him, had passed him by. He had not heard them.

To such proper unthankfulness we teachers must accustom ourselves. We cannot tell what are our good deeds, and shall only plague ourselves and hinder our classes if we try to find out. Let us display our subjects as lucidly as possible, allow our pupils considerable license in apprehension, and be content ourselves to escape observation. But though what we do remains unknown, its results often awake deep affection. Few in the community receive love more abundantly than we. Wherever we go, we meet a smiling face. Throughout the world, by some good fortune the period of learning is the period of romance. In those halcyon days of our boys and girls we have a share, and the golden lights which flood the opening years are reflected on us. Though our pupils cannot follow our efforts in their behalf, and indeed ought not,—it being our art to conceal our art,—yet they perceive that in the years when their happy expansion occurred we were their guides. To us, therefore, their blind affections cling as to few beside their parents. It is better to be loved than to be understood.

Perhaps some readers of this paper will begin to suspect that it is impossible to be a good teacher. Certainly it is. Each of the four qualifications I have named is endless. Not one of them can be fully attained. We can always be more imaginative, wealthy, stimulating, disinterested. Each year we creep a little nearer to our goal, only to find that a finished teacher is a contradiction in terms. Our reach will forever exceed our grasp. Yet what a delight in approximation! Even in our failures there is comfort, when we see that they are generally due not to technical but to personal defects. We have been putting ourselves forward, or have taught in mechanical rather than vital fashion, or have not undertaken betimes the labor of preparation, or have declined the trouble of vicariousness.

Evidently, then, as we become better teachers we also become in some sort better persons. Our beautiful art, being so largely personal, will at last be seen to connect itself with nearly all other employments. Every mother is a teacher. Every minister. The lawyer teaches the jury, the doctor his patient. The clever salesman might almost be said to use teaching in dealing with his customer, and all of us to be teachers of one another in daily intercourse. As teaching is the most universal of the professions, those are fortunate who are able to devote their lives to its enriching study.

138

William C. Bagley

THE PROFESSION OF TEACHING IN THE UNITED STATES

Throughout his long and active career in American education, William Chandler Bagley lost no opportunity to emphasize the dignity and importance of the teacher's calling. He believed that the work of the teacher with pupils in the classroom was of far greater importance than any other type of educational work. He deplored what he considered the unfair discrepancies between the salaries paid to principals, superintendents, supervisors, and those usually paid to teachers.

He was himself proud to be known as a teacher, although he was one of the best-known professors of education in America during his long tenure of office at Teachers College, Columbia University. Everyone connected in any way with American education knew about, and had probably read some of the books of, Professor Bagley. His espousal of the Essentialist cause in the spring of 1938 gave that movement all the prestige of his name. Yet during the many years that his biography was published in *Who's Who,* he was invariably listed, "Bagley, William Chandler. Teacher." He preferred this to "educator" or even "university professor." For him there could be no prouder title than "teacher"— a fact that the thousands of students who came under his influence were never allowed to forget.

The following article by Dr. Bagley is based on a lecture he gave to foreign students on December 18, 1928, under the auspices of the International Institute of Teachers College. The speaker was obviously proud of the progress already made in increasing the prestige and qualifications of classroom teachers in America, and he looked confidently ahead to even greater progress.

The development of American education has been beset from the outset by handicaps and obstacles, many of which undoubtedly confront our fellow-workers in other countries, but some of which are indigenous, so to speak, to our own soil, growing out of our own peculiar traditions and *mores:* our deep-seated and thoroughly dynamic ideals of local self-government; the diverse standards of our conglomerate population; the sharply contrasting needs and interests of our urban and rural people; our fondness for quantity-production and our delight in numerical magnitudes; our distrust of the expert; our zeal in making laws and our zest in breaking them; and a host of other factors and forces, many of which work in quite opposite directions, but all of which have cooperated to make extremely difficult the development of an educational system which would be constructively effective on a nation-wide basis.

And yet these unique factors in our problem, even though they have constituted serious handicaps to educational effort, have also been, perhaps for that very reason, a stimulating challenge, the continued response to which has resulted in progress of a most substantial sort, with promises for the future that should give hope and inspiration to those in other countries who are facing problems similar in difficulty although in many instances quite different in kind.

The advancement in the status of the teacher's calling, while the most recent of the large developments in American education, is in some respects the most significant and promises for the future the most far-reaching results. It is also, I believe, a development quite unprecedented in the history of education and, so far as I know, it is unparalleled in other countries.

In reviewing the handicaps that have beset this development, it goes without saying that many of them are not at all peculiar to our country. Something akin to contempt for the work of teaching, especially in the lower schools, has found expression, I suppose, in all ages and in all climes. It was the Englishman, Bernard Shaw, who coined the famous epigram, "Those who can, do; those who can not, teach." The immortal Boswell, in a ponderous effort to explain why Samuel Johnson was so complete and pitiable a failure as a teacher of youth, ventured the following sage reflection:

"The art of communicating instruction, of whatever kind, is much to be valued; and I have ever thought that those who devote themselves to this employment, and do their duty with diligence and success, are entitled to very high respect from the community, as Johnson himself often maintained. Yet I am of the opinion that the greatest abilities are not only not required in this office, but render a man less fit for it."

While this patronizing attitude of thinly veiled contempt for the work of teaching is no new thing and not at all confined to our own country, I believe that it has constituted a far more serious handicap to the development of our profession here than it has elsewhere.

In the first place, until recently, the teaching-personnel of our public schools has been transient and unstable. Twenty years ago, the average period of service of the public-school teacher was not more than four years, which meant that tens of thousands of teachers remained only one, two or three years in the service. The occupation was distinctly recognized in most communities as temporary, and those who from force of circumstances were compelled to make it a life work were naturally regarded with something akin to pity. For the able and ambitious, teaching was openly taken up as a stepping-stone to what both the teacher and the public thought of as worthier callings. One of the early university professors of education, in whose classes I sat thirty years ago, laughingly referred to public-school teachers as a group made up chiefly of immature women and feeble men.

Along with this condition, of course, went the parallel fact that the teachers as a whole were pitifully unprepared for their work. Twenty years ago, more than a majority of the public-school teachers had had no education beyond the high school, and more than ten thousand were limited in their education to what the elementary school provided.

Although every state maintained professional schools for teachers, not one in four of those employed in the public schools was a product of such an institution. As short a time ago as 1916, Judd and Parker asserted in an official bulletin of the Bureau of Education that the United States

From *School and Society,* January 26, 1929, 29: 101-110.

gave less attention to the training of teachers than did any other civilized nation. With brief tenure and lack of training quite naturally went meager compensation, and in a country where occupations won public regard in direct proportion to the material rewards that they provided, this condition was in itself a sufficient stigma to the teacher's calling.

Closely related to the handicaps which transiency, instability, low training standards and meager preparation placed in the way of professional development was the unequal competition with other occupations for talented recruits. This was most serious, of course, in connection with the problem of drawing able men into the profession. Not only did the vast development of business and industry multiply the opportunities for building huge individual fortunes, but the spectacular achievements of our captains of industry, finance and organization caught the public imagination, bringing to successful efforts in those fields a measure of renown and popular adulation beside which even the material rewards were of quite subordinate value.

There are one or two incidents in my own life that may give a concrete setting to the conditions to which I have referred. Some forty years ago I was a schoolboy in the city of Detroit. As cities went, even in those days, Detroit was an unpretentious, rather conservative urban center, surpassed in wealth, population and promise by nearly a score of American cities. One day in the early nineties, while walking along one of the streets of the city, I saw a little group gathered around a queer-looking conveyance drawn up alongside the curb. I joined the crowd, and found that the object of their interest was what we then called a horseless carriage. A young man was rather frantically engaged in overhauling the machinery, every now and again making a desperate effort to get the clumsy contraption to show some signs of life. As long as I watched, his efforts were rewarded only by a wheezy cough from the crude engine, echoed, of course, by the jeers of the crowd. That jeering crowd little dreamed that the scene which they were witnessing for the first time would be reenacted within the next thirty years on ten thousand city streets and country roads by hundreds of thousands of exasperated drivers of self-propelled vehicles; still less did they dream that the evolution of that clumsy, horseless carriage would cause their city to outdistance all but three of its competitors in population and wealth and make it the world center for the most highly organized branch of modern industry; least of all did they dream that the young man who was struggling so desperately to conjure a vital spark in that new-fangled internal-combustion engine was in all likelihood the man who, within three decades, would be recognized and acclaimed as the type and symbol of American genius at its own unique best.

It is not at all to be wondered at that the marvelous expansion of American industry, with its overwhelming rewards of wealth and fame for successful effort, should have cast a shadow over fields of endeavor less spectacular, less appealing to the concrete imagination of the public, less obviously creative of new values. It is small wonder that, with competition of this sort, the latter fields were unable to attract so large a share of superior talent as has been the case in many other countries. The relative paucity of our national contributions to pure science, to literature, music and the other fine arts, and to statesmanship of the first order may be explained at least in part by this factor. Obviously an occupation so modestly rewarded as teaching and one that offers so few opportunities for renown would have, under these conditions, a relatively low place in public esteem.

The effect of all this upon the morale of the teaching group may be readily inferred. Those who remained for any length of time in the profession acquired, in many cases, an inferiority complex of large dimensions. They openly regretted that they had not taken up another occupation. Just as openly, they advised young people against teaching as a career and commiserated one another over their hard lot. About eight years ago in visiting the college in Michigan where I spent my undergraduate days, I called on one of the two or three of my former instructors who still survived. He asked me what I had been doing over the years and where I was located. I told him that I had been teaching and was still engaged in that occupation. Then he asked me where I had come from when I entered college. He shook his head sadly when I told him, and then, with a sincere sigh of pity, he said, "And just think what you might have become if you had only gone back to Detroit and entered the automobile business." I left his office and my old college with a deep sense of my failure to reflect any worthy credit on my *alma mater.*

I could multiply concrete examples of this sort from my own experience and that of my friends, but enough has been said to indicate one of the most serious obstacles that the development of a real profession of teaching has confronted in our country. With what I have said regarding the instability, inadequate training and transiency of the great rank and file of teachers, this may give us a sufficient background against which to project the advances that our profession has made.

To-day, many of the conditions to which I have referred are radically different from what they were fifteen, ten, even five years ago. The period of service of the average teacher has been extended from four or five years to at least eight or nine years. The level of training has advanced to a much higher plane—where fifteen years ago the median public-school teacher had no more than a high-school education at most, to-day it is probable that 60 per cent of these teachers have had two years or more in advance of high-school graduation. In several states the proportion is nearly 100 per cent. The number of college graduates in the public-school service has also shown a remarkable increase. The enrolment in our normal schools and teachers' colleges has doubled in the past five years, and the output of these professional schools is now so large that, for the first time in our history, there is an actual surplus of trained teachers in most of the cities and in some of the states.

This condition has led to significant advances in the standards of our professional schools. Many of the former two-year normal schools have advanced the requirements for elementary-school teachers to three years and some are now on a full four-year basis. Paralleling these advances there has been a really remarkable development within the profession, some of the outstanding trends of which I shall mention a little later. In public esteem, too, the teacher's calling has made significant advances.

Like most profound changes, these developments have been brought about in part by conscious and deliberate purposing, and in part by the fortunate operation of forces and factors that are largely beyond either individual or social control. Let us consider first these latter, impersonal factors.

Primarily, of course, one must recognize the unprecedented material prosperity of our country. This has made possible both a wider extension of educational opportunity and a keener demand for better schools and better teachers. As a result, the level of teachers' salaries has advanced significantly, and is still advancing in spite of a tendency toward the stabilization of wage and salary levels in other occupations. Teaching can now compete with other callings on terms much more nearly equal than have prevailed heretofore.

This, however, does not tell the whole story, for the contrasts with the spectacular rewards of business and industry still persist. Yet for some reason the influence of this contrast is less noticeable to-day than it was only a few years ago.

This may be due to a recognition on the part of the public that these huge material rewards in the very nature of things can go to only a very few of the most capable or the most fortunate, while the rank and file must necessarily fare much more modestly.

Back of all this, however, is another set of facts, the full significance of which we are probably not yet in a position to grasp. The leaven of the Industrial Revolution, which has been responsible for so many fundamental social changes, is still working, and working in a more thoroughgoing fashion in our country than anywhere else. The report of the American Federation of Labor, recently published, reveals the astounding fact that, in spite of the vast development of American industry in the present decade, the number of persons actually engaged in manufacturing has decreased by approximately a million since 1920. In other words, the improvement of automatic machinery has not only kept pace with the expansion of industry; it has sent a million workers to seek other means of earning a living. In this country, too, much more than in other countries, the influence of the Industrial Revolution has profoundly affected agriculture. Power-driven machinery has apparently replaced no fewer than 800,000 farm workers since 1920.

As a mere layman in economics, it would be presumptuous in me to attempt an interpretation of these facts. I can not escape the conclusion, however, that they are related in a very direct way to the opportunities that our profession has recently enjoyed to augment its numbers, advance its standards and stabilize its service. If I am right in my inferences, these developments in invention and industrial organization are actually driving men and women out of industry and farming into the white-collar occupations. Not only have the traditional professions grown in numbers—there are 250,000 more professional workers now than in 1920, according to the Federation's report—but a veritable multitude of other white-collar occupations are advancing toward a professional status in the sense that specific and often prolonged courses of education are willingly undertaken by those seeking either employment or advancement. Banks, department stores, the great hotel syndicates, insurance companies and public service corporations are developing elaborate schools for the training of their personnel. In at least one of the big insurance companies the vice-president in charge of education is one of the highest paid and most highly respected of the executives. With this emphasis upon specialized training, there has naturally been a corresponding emphasis upon an extended and thoroughgoing general education which shall serve as a background for the specialized courses; hence another reason why the high-school enrolment has trebled in fifteen years and why the college enrolment has doubled in ten years.

May I say parenthetically that it is of the utmost significance to education that this recent turn of the Industrial Revolution has not only reduced the proportion of workers needed in industry and farming, but has also increased the numbers needed in the white-collar occupations? The development of type-setting machinery, for example, made it possible for one operator to do the work of four compositors, and thus reduced the demand for the old-time printer, but the economy and efficiency of the new process greatly multiplied the demand for writers, editors, illustrators and advertising specialists. In fact, every department of automatic machines for mass-production has opened new fields of useful employment almost all of which have meant a stepping-up of the intellectual level of the work involved. Within the past decade this change has been going on with unprecedented acceleration; hence the heavy demands now made upon the schools and colleges are something more than a mere reflex of our economic prosperity; in a very real sense, they are the expression of a tremendously enlarged need on the part of millions of people for a type of instruction and discipline that will mean for them a genuine intellectual advance. Hence the recent controversy in our field regarding the possibilities of raising through education the mass-levels of effective intelligence is concerned with something more than a merely academic question. Upon the issue that this controversy involves hangs the future of our industrialized civilization.

I have suggested that the recent development of our profession has been conditioned in part by impersonal forces, largely economic in character, which have operated to expand the field of our service, to increase the demands made upon us and to give us more and better recruits. The net result has been an almost complete transformation of the conditions under which we have been working. May I impress particularly the fact that, so far as its outward manifestations are concerned, this transformation has come very suddenly—almost overnight, so to speak? Many of our fellow-workers are still rubbing their eyes and wondering whether it is not all a dream. Others are still, in a manner of speaking, fast asleep—working on programs which reflect needs that seemed genuine enough a few years ago, but which can now be seen as based upon quite erroneous assumptions regarding the trends of contemporary

civilization; programs, for example, that would keep the farm boys on the farms to compete with gasoline engines and combined harvesters; and programs for premature vocational training based on the theory that the white-collar occupations are overcrowded when they are apparently the only occupations that have not been seriously overcrowded in the past few years and are to-day the occupations in which there are evidences of the greatest expansion.

It need hardly be said that the situation which confronts us is fairly unique to our own country. Other nations undoubtedly need heavier emphasis upon agricultural and trade education and less emphasis upon intellectual education. Be that as it may, it is clear enough that some of our own students of education have made some rather bad guesses during the past two decades and that some of them are still repeating their stereotyped pleas even though the need for their particular variety of reform no longer exists. On the other hand, it is equally true that the progress of our profession has been influenced in a very powerful positive fashion by the students of education. While they have undoubtedly made mistakes in some of their efforts to define social problems and to construct programs that would work toward the solution of these problems, they have played an important part in laying the foundations upon which a real and great profession of teaching is even now arising.

For upward of thirty years, a steadily increasing number of men and women have been devoting their lives to the serious study of the educational problem. The pioneers of this group were a few scattering school executives who conceived of their duties as comprehending something beyond the machinery of organization and the routine of administration, and who set a splendid example of constructive leadership and truly creative effort. One of these men was William Torrey Harris, who infused into the city school system of St. Louis a vigorous new life and who later served with distinction as the federal commissioner of education. Another was Francis W. Parker, who, as head of the schools of Quincy, Massachusetts, was the founder in America of what we now call the progressive school of educational theory; another was William H. Maxwell, the first superintendent of the schools of Greater New York. A fourth was Calvin Kendall, for many years superintendent of schools in Indianapolis and during the latter part of his life commissioner of education for the State of New Jersey.

Among the early colleagues and companions of these executives were the first professors of education in the colleges and universities. The real development of these departments of education may be dated from about 1890. Two years before, Clark University had been founded under the leadership of Stanley Hall, and during the following decade Clark was a nursery of educational ideals and enthusiasms. Then came the development of Teachers College under James E. Russell, and at the University of Chicago the pioneer work of John Dewey. From Clark and Columbia and Chicago men and women in increasing numbers went out to other colleges and universities either to establish or to remodel on a true university basis the departments of education. State universities, like those of Wisconsin, Iowa, Minnesota, California and Illinois, became in their turn centers of instruction, research and inspiration directed toward the problems of teaching and learning, of administration and supervision in the public schools. Private and endowed institutions like Peabody, Stanford, Yale and Harvard assumed their share of the great task.

The influence of this development of the university study of education upon the profession of teaching has been profound. In the first place, it has provided for the professional education of teachers a substantial body of knowledge. The recency of this development is exemplified by the fact that many of the men who have done the pioneer work are still in their prime. . . .

A second influence of the university study of education has been a new access of self-respect on the part of the teaching personnel. The inferiority complex, to which I referred as one of the handicaps to our professional development, is gradually but certainly giving place to a sense of professional pride and dignity, tempered as it should be and as I hope it always will be, by a keen sense of the complexities of our problem and of the serious responsibilities which one must assume who would do even the humblest work in the field of teaching.

A third influence is one of the most significant of all. The university study of education has played a most important part in integrating the teaching profession. As Dean Russell told you a few weeks ago, something akin to the old-world caste distinction between the education of the masses and the education of the classes has persisted even in our unit system which otherwise so closely articulates the elementary and secondary schools. With us, the distinction has been one primarily of training and material rewards. The elementary-school teacher has represented a narrower and briefer training than the high-school teacher and even now receives in most of our school systems a distinctly lower salary. It has

been a popular belief, shared by many members of the profession itself, that the work of teaching increases in difficulty, dignity and importance as one goes up the age scale. The university study of education has probably done more than anything else to reveal the fallacy of this popular belief, and to correct the injustice that has been done to the younger children in our schools by a deliberate policy which uses the lower grades as the testing ground for the immature and inexperienced teachers, the permanent abode of the weak and the indolent, and the final resting-place of the old and decrepit. To-day there is a growing conviction that no phase or field of teaching can lay valid claim to being more difficult or more important than any other phase. Discriminations and distinctions as to salaries are breaking down, as, for example, in the gradual extension of the single-salary schedule which does away with all distinctions except those that are based upon training, experience and meritorious service.

This general movement has been a powerful force in integrating our profession vertically, so to speak. Other forces have been operating to integrate the profession horizontally or geographically. Chief among these are our educational organizations. Foreign students sometimes wonder why, with our lack of any centralized educational authority in the nation as a whole, with the lack even of highly centralized state systems, our schools all over the country are in fundamental ways very much alike, dominated by the same aims and ideals, following fairly similar programs of study, governed by essentially uniform standards. The answer is simple. While our school systems are essentially local, the teaching profession is essentially national. For seventy years the educational leaders of the nation have met annually to discuss their common problems, but it has been only within the past twenty years that the state and national organizations have really represented the profession as a whole. To-day these organizations are made up of, and controlled very largely by, the rank and file of elementary and secondary teachers. The National Education Association has grown in active membership from 10,000 to 200,000 in a single decade. Its policies are now determined by a representative assembly made up largely of delegates elected by the state associations. Many of the latter, in turn, are controlled by similar representative assemblies elected by district and local associations. The total enrolment in all of these organizations aggregates nearly three quarters of a million, which means that three out of every four members of our profession can have a vote and a voice in determining where our profession will go and how it will get there—in formulating our collective ideals and devising the means of realizing them through collective action. To this end the national association employs a headquarters staff with a personnel of more than one hundred men and women, including expert research workers, editors, legislative agents, publicity agents and specialists in the major educational fields. Several of the state organizations have similar staffs, and practically all of them employ full-time secretaries and publish official journals. May I emphasize the fact that this development has taken place almost entirely within a single decade?

One of the striking characteristics of this and other phases of our professional development has been the clear-cut tendency toward a thoroughgoing democracy. Not only are the distinctions between the elementary-school service and the high-school service being obliterated, but the equally unfortunate distinctions between the classroom teacher and the executive and supervisory officials are being minimized. In our professional organizations, as in our classes in education, all the workers in our field can meet on a common footing.

This tendency, which has been abetted by many of the administrators themselves, merits an especial emphasis in a discussion of the profession of teaching in the United States. It is distinctly a conscious effort to counteract in education some of the admitted evils that elaborate organization has brought about in business and industry. In the latter fields, the magnification of the executive and supervisory officers in contrast with those who do the first-hand work has perhaps been inevitable. Quite naturally, as our school systems expanded, a similar hierarchy of administrative authority was established, and the distinctions involved in this administrative hierarchy became in effect professional distinctions. To be transferred from the first-hand work of teaching boys and girls to an executive or administrative post was generally, and still is in many places, looked upon as a professional promotion. Under these conditions a large city school system became quite analogous to a great factory with its board of directors, its superintendent, managers, foremen, bosses and "hands." In school work, the classroom teachers were the "hands."

Now whatever may be the advantages or the dangers of such a hierarchy in business and industry, it works veritable mischief when applied to education. A simple contrast will, I think, make this clear.

If I buy an automobile I am not particularly concerned, except from a humanitarian point of view, with the workmen who have actually put it together. I can be reasonably certain that a few highly competent engineers designed the car, that a few others devised elaborate machinery for making and testing the various parts, and that a competent hierarchy of executives, superintendents, managers, foremen and bosses formed a responsible overhead for supervising its construction. The factory hands who operated the automatic machinery, screwed up the nuts, clinched the cotter-pins and sprayed on the paint and varnish: these may have been morons or they may have been near-geniuses; they may have had no interest whatsoever in their work beyond their pay-checks or they may have been true craftsmen with a fine pride in good workmanship; they may have been human automata going through their motions with as little real understanding of what it all meant as the machines that they operated, or they may have been men of keen insight, seeing their work in clear relation to the completed product. To me, merely as a purchaser of an automobile, it would make little difference. I can trust the machinery of production and testing under the supervision of the overhead. In fact, I can be fairly certain that if any one of the factory-hands were a near-genius and tremendously interested in his work for its own sake and able to see his work clearly in its relation to the completed product, he would very quickly be taken from the ranks and promoted to the overhead.

So much if I should buy an automobile.

When I send my children to school, however, my attitude toward the person who does the actual, first-hand work of their education is almost completely reversed. It is true that I would wish plans and specifications of that education to be well drawn by highly competent students of the problem; I would like the text-books to be authoritative and well-written; I would like the tests to be objective and accurate; I would like an organization that would guarantee a healthful school environment. But above all I would want for my children a real teacher. No virtues of the "overhead" could compensate for a teacher who had no interest in his work, who saw nothing beyond his pay-check, who found no joy and felt no pride in doing his work as well as it could be done irrespective of the material rewards that it brought, who had no vision of what it meant and no understanding of what his efforts contributed to the completed product.

One of the prominent objectives of our profession at the present time is to give to those who do the actual first-hand work of teaching an adequate recognition. Within the past ten years there has been a distinct tendency toward the participation of classroom teachers in the construction of educational policies and programs. In some school systems, councils elected by the teachers have a recognized function in the government of the schools. Probably the most characteristic expression of this tendency, however, is found in the work that is now going on all over the country in the revision and construction of curricula by groups of classroom teachers.

While practices such as these tend to dignify the actual first-hand work of teaching, they have, I think, an even deeper significance. They represent a quite new type of control for public education—and a type of control which has vast possibilities for the future. It goes without saying that some of the results will be disappointing. There must necessarily be groping and stumbling and blundering; but in the end the progress that is made is likely to be both substantial and enduring.

And this I take it is the fundamental justification of democracy as a mode of social control. Autocratic leadership gets results more quickly; and, under extremely competent leadership, the results may mean genuine progress. But dependence upon autocratic leadership suffers under two handicaps. In the first place, a really competent leader may not appear for years or even generations; in the second place, progress which is made possible only by a dictatorship is not likely to be sustained when the strong hand loses its grip. Given a reasonably high level of trained intelligence, the democratic group will be able to carry on even if competent leadership does not appear; and although its progress may be slow, it is much more likely to be certain and sustained.

I have attempted to present in general outline the development of the profession of teaching in the United States. I have called attention to some of the typical handicaps that this development has encountered; to the economic forces which have transformed in a striking fashion some of these handicaps; to the contributions that the students of education have made to our professional development; and to some of the factors that have worked toward professional solidarity and integration. I have probably set forth certain of the characteristics of our profession as though they were full-fledged achievements rather than ideals and aspirations many of which are still far from realization. My aim has been, however, to portray substantial trends, in the future fruition of which some of our dreams may come true. Certain it is that the present situation is full of promise. Whether this great army of teachers, now numbering in all branches of education upward of a million men and women, can think together and work together toward the fulfilment of this promise is another question. There are, of course, social forces and economic factors that will constitute handicaps in the future as similar forces and factors have been handicaps in the past. But personally I am optimistic; the transformation that I have myself witnessed in thirty years is so thoroughgoing that I can not but believe that another generation will carry us much further on the road to better things. It is literally true that through our profession every significant unit in our vast population can be touched and quickened. It is within our power as an organized and responsible group to make the American school the greatest single constructive force in American life. I have every faith that our profession will prove neither recreant nor inadequate to its great trust and its great opportunity.

139

Jacques Barzun

PROFESSION: TEACHER

The following selection is the first chapter of a significant and challenging book that appeared toward the end of World War II. Jacques Barzun was born in France and attended school there; his university training was received in America. He is thus able to view education against the background of two cultures. Though it was published in 1945, the book continues to be read and discussed by people of widely divergent interests.

Whenever the topic of education comes up, there are almost certain to be those who try to dispose of it by repeating some of the standard clichés—vague and abstract though they are. Each decade seems to produce its characteristic crop of educational epigrams. Professor Barzun makes bold to examine a number of these and tries to find out just what they mean, whether or not and to what extent they are pertinent. He is not at all convinced that "pertinent" and "contemporary" are synonymous terms. He believes that people who discuss education should know what they are talking about and should understand the terms they use.

In addition, the prospective teacher needs to consider the duties actually connected with his profession. Does the present-day American tendency to lay the blame for youthful ignorance, near-illiteracy, or delinquency on the schools represent a widespread misconception of their function? Are teachers being impelled by a number of forces largely outside their control to attempt too many things under the name of education? Should the teacher's main task vary in content and purpose from age to age, or does it in its essentials remain much the same?

The bore of all bores was the third. His subject had no beginning, middle, nor end. It was education. Never was such a journey through the desert of the mind, the Great Sahara of intellect. The very recollection makes me thirsty.

—T. L. Peacock

Education is indeed the dullest of subjects and I intend to say as little about it as I can. For three years past, now, the people of this country have knitted their brows over the shortcomings of the schools; at least that is the impression one gets from newspapers and periodicals. And by a strange necessity, talk about education never varies. It always seems to resolve itself into undeniable truths about "the well-rounded man" and "our precious heritage." Once in a while, in a fit of daring, the man who lectures you about education points out that the phrase "liberal arts" means "liberating." Then he is off on a fine canter about freedom of the mind and democracy. Or again, hypnotized by your glazed eyeballs, he slips into the old trap of proclaiming that "education" comes from the Latin word meaning to "lead out." Alas! the Latin root has nothing to do with "leading out"; it means simply—to educate. But no matter, it is all in a good cause: "Education should be broadening." Of course! "It should train a man for practical life." Of course again! "Education should be democratic—but nothing radical, nat-

urally. Education must be thorough, but rapid too. No waste of precious time conning over our precious heritage." Those for whom these fundamental principles are rehearsed never argue: they are too drowsy.

This narcotic state is not due merely to the fact that we have latterly had too much educational discussion. After all, we have also been chewing the cud of peace plans, labor problems, and expert strategy. No. I am convinced that at any time brooding and wrangling about education is bad. It is as bad as it would be to perpetually dig around the roots of government by talking political theory. Both political and educational theory are for the rare genius to grapple with, once in a century. The business of the citizen and the statesman is not political theory but politics. The business of the parent and the teacher is not education but Teaching. Teaching is something that can be provided for, changed, or stopped. It is good or bad, brilliant or stupid, plentiful or scarce. Beset as it is with difficulties and armed with devices, teaching has a theory too, but it is one that can be talked about simply and directly, for it concerns the many matters of human knowledge which affect our lives, from the three R's to electronics. To deal with it in that fashion is in fact what I am going to do . . . .

Education is obviously something else, something intangible, unpredictable. Education comes from within; it is a man's own doing, or rather it happens to him—sometimes because of the teaching he has had, sometimes in spite of it. When Henry Adams wrote *The Education of*

From *Teacher in America* by Jacques Barzun. Copyright 1944, 1945 by Jacques Barzun, pp. 3-12. Reprinted by permission of Little, Brown and Company-Atlantic Monthly Press.

Henry Adams, he gave thirty pages out of five hundred to his schooling. Common usage records the same distinction. No man says of another: "I educated him." It would be offensive and would suggest that the victim was only a puppy when first taken in hand. But it is a proud thing to say "I taught him"—and a wise one not to specify what.

To be sure, there is an age-old prejudice against teaching. Teachers must share with doctors the world's most celebrated sneers, and with them also the world's unbounded hero-worship. Always and everywhere, "He is a schoolteacher" has meant "He is an underpaid pitiable drudge." Even a politician stands higher, because power in the street seems less of a mockery than power in the classroom. But when we speak of Socrates, Jesus, Buddha, and "other great teachers of humanity," the atmosphere somehow changes and the politician's power begins to look shrunken and mean. August examples show that no limit can be set to the power of a teacher, but this is equally true in the other direction: no career can so nearly approach zero in its effects.

The odd thing is that almost everybody is a teacher at some time or other during his life. Besides Socrates and Jesus, the great teachers of mankind are mankind itself—your parents and mine. First and last, parents do a good deal more teaching than doctoring, yet so natural and necessary is this duty that they never seem aware of performing it. It is only when they are beyond it, when they have thoroughly ground irremediable habits of speech, thought, and behavior into their offspring that they discover the teacher as an institution and hire him to carry on the work.

Then begins the fierce, secret struggle out of which education may come—the struggle between home and school, parent and child, child and teacher; the struggle also that lies deep within the parent and within society concerning the teacher's worth: Is this man of knowledge to be looked up to as wise and helpful, or to be looked down on as at once servile and dangerous, capable and inglorious, higher than the parent yet lower than the brat?

Most people meet this difficulty by alternately looking up and looking down. At best the title of teacher is suspect. I notice that on their passports and elsewhere, many of my academic colleagues put down their occupation as Professor. Anything to raise the tone: a professor is to a teacher what a cesspool technician is to a plumber. Anything to enlarge the scope: not long ago, I joined a club which described its membership as made up of Authors, Artists, and Amateurs—an excellent reason for joining. Conceive my dis-

appointment when I found that the classifications had broken down and I was now entered as an Educator. Doubtless we shall have to keep the old pugilistic title of Professor, though I cannot think of Dante in Hell coming upon Brunetto Latini, and exclaiming "Why, Professor!" But we can and must get rid of "Educator." Imagine the daily predicament: someone asks, "What do you do?"—"I profess and I educate." It is unspeakable and absurd.

Don't think this frivolous, but regard it as a symbol. Consider the American state of mind about Education at the present time. An unknown correspondent writes to me: "Everybody seems to be dissatisfied with education except those in charge of it." This is a little less than fair, for a great deal of criticism has come from within the profession. But let it stand. Dissatisfaction is the keynote. Why dissatisfaction? Because Americans believe in Education, because they pay large sums for Education, and because Education does not seem to yield results. At this point one is bound to ask: "What results do you expect?"

The replies are staggering. Apparently Education is to do everything that the rest of the world leaves undone. Recall the furore over American History. Under new and better management that subject was to produce patriots—nothing less. An influential critic, head of a large university, wants education to generate a classless society; another asks that education root out racial intolerance (in the third or the ninth grade, I wonder?); still another requires that college courses be designed to improve labor relations. One man, otherwise sane, thinks the solution of the housing problem has bogged down—in the schools; and another proposes to make the future householders happy married couples—through the schools. Off to one side, a well-known company of scholars have got hold of the method of truth and wish to dispense it as a crisis reducer. "Adopt our nationally advertised brand and avert chaos."

Then there are the hundreds of specialists in endless "vocations" who want Education to turn out practised engineers, affable hotelkeepers, and finished literary artists. There are educational shops for repairing every deficiency in man or nature: battalions of instructors are impressed to teach Civilian Defense; the FBI holds public ceremonies for its graduates; dogs receive short courses in good manners, and are emulated at once by girls from the age of seven who learn Poise and Personality. Above and beyond all these stand the unabashed peacemakers who want Kitty Smith from Indiana to be sent to Germany, armed with Muzzey's *American History,* to undo Hitler's work.

These are not nightmarish caricatures I have dreamed but things I have recently seen done or heard proposed by representative and even distinguished minds: they are so many acts of faith in the prevailing dogma that Education is the hope of the world.

Well, this is precisely where the use of the right word comes in. You may teach spot-welding in wartime and indeed you must. But Education is the hope of the world only in the sense that there is something better than bribery, lies, and violence for righting the world's wrongs. If this better thing is education, then education is not merely schooling. It is a lifelong discipline of the individual by himself, encouraged by a reasonable opportunity to lead a good life. Education here is synonymous with civilization. A civilized community is better than the jungle, but civilization is a long slow process which cannot be "given" in a short course.

No one in his senses would affirm that Schooling is the hope of the world. But to say this is to show up the folly of perpetually confusing Education with the work of the schools; the folly of believing against all evidence that by taking boys and girls for a few hours each day between the ages of seven and twenty-one, our teachers can "turn out" all the human products that we like to fancy when we are disgusted with ourselves and our neighbors. It is like believing that brushing the teeth is the key to health. No ritual by itself will guarantee anything. Brushing won't even keep your teeth clean, by itself. There is no key to health and there is none to education. Do you think because you have an expensive school system there shall be no more spelling mistakes? Then why suppose that you can eradicate intolerance more easily? Free compulsory "education" is a great thing, an indispensable thing, but it will not make the City of God out of Public School No. 26.

The whole mass of recrimination, disappointment, and dissatisfaction which this country is now suffering about its schools comes from using the ritual word "Education" so loosely and so frequently. It covers abysses of emptiness. Everybody cheats by using it, cheats others and cheats himself. The idea abets false ambitions. The educator wants to do a big job in the world, so he takes on the task of reorienting Germany and improving human relations. The public at large, bedeviled as it is with these "problems," is only too glad to farm them out, reserving the right of indignant complaint when the educator breaks down or the Institute for Human Relations fails to reduce appreciably the amount of wife beating.

Dissatisfaction remains, and not unmixed with ill will. For in this vast sideshow of illusions and misplaced effort, educators find an opportunity to belabor one another in clans: College teachers cry out, "Why can't high school boys write decent English?" The Deans exclaim, "Why can't our college graduates speak foreign languages and be ready to serve in wartime? Look at what the Army is doing!" Up and down the line others say, "Discipline is the thing—the Navy knows more about training boys than we do." And the rhetorical questions continue, answered by the askers themselves: "Why is there so much juvenile delinquency?"—"It's the schools." "Why did army doctors find so many neurotics?"—"It's the colleges." "Educators are Confused," read one front-page headline a couple of years ago, and down below the explanation was: "It's the fault of our Higher Education."

This is certainly looping the loop. Like the jurymen in *Alice in Wonderland,* the parents, the children in high schools, the men and women in colleges, are bewildered by claims and counter-claims. They are stunned by solicitations to follow this or that course, for this or that imperative reason. And like the jurymen, they repeat "Important," "Unimportant," while making futile motions with their forefingers. Inside the academic precincts, plans, curriculums, and methods whirl by with newsreel speed. Labels change; the Progressives become Conservative, the Conservatives Progressive, while the Classicals form a Third Party with adherents and attackers in every camp. From a distance the academic grove looks remarkably like Chaos and Old Night.

Happily there is something stable and clear and useful behind this phantasmagoria of Education—the nature of subject matter and the practice of teaching.

The word helps us again to the idea. The advantage of "teaching" is that in using it you must recognize—if you are in your sober senses—that practical limits exist. You know by instinct that it is impossible to "teach" democracy, or citizenship or a happy married life. I do not say that these virtues and benefits are not somehow connected with good teaching. They are, but they occur as by-products. They come, not from a course, but from a teacher; not from a curriculum, but from a human soul.

It is indeed possible so to arrange school and college work that more play is given to good human influences than in other conceivable arrangements. But it is not possible by fiddling with vague topics to insure or even to increase the dissemination of virtue. I should think it very likely that a course in Democracy would make most healthy students loathe the word and all its associations. And meanwhile the setup (no other word will better express my contempt) takes the room and time and energy which should legitimately be used to teach somebody something teachable—English or History, Greek or Chemistry. . . .

Meanwhile I dwell on the necessity of teaching, that is to say on the need for teachers. There are never enough. Statistics tell us that at this moment we are one hundred thousand short—one in ten. This does not include men fighting or putting their special skill at the war plant's disposal. One hundred thousand have simply jumped at the chance for higher pay. That is their right and in a competitive system they must be free from blame. Nevertheless we have here an estimate of the number who are normally in teaching for want of better jobs. The "call" cannot be strong if a teacher will leave the classroom to floor-walk in a department store. Doctors are poor too, but they stick to their rounds and their patients.

But in truth, American schoolteachers as such may well be forgiven their recent desertion—or what looks like it—when we remember how so many college and university administrators acted under the emergency of war. In a twinkling, all that they had professed to believe in for thirty years was discarded as useless. Subjects, schedules, principles, were renounced, with tossing of caps in the air and whoops of joy. Naturally and fortunately, there were notable exceptions to this stampede and much indignation within the ranks. But the bandwagon pressure was great

and solid institutions found it hard to resist. One wonders what would have happened if we had been blitzed like England—where no such academic jamboree ensued—or economically hampered like Canada—where academic calm has continued to reign.

I am inclined to think . . . that this excitement signalized a release from long pretense. With us many people who pass as professional teachers are merely "connected with education." They live on the fringes of the academic army—campus followers, as it were—though too often it is they who have the honors and emoluments while the main body lives on short rations. Dislocation by war naturally mixes up the doers with the drones and produces the academic riot that our newspapers depict. To judge fairly, it would be well to draw a veil over the scene since Pearl Harbor and say that on that day the United States suspended all serious educational projects—excepting of course the people's wise award of a traveling fellowship to Mr. Wendell Willkie. Looking at the situation in this way would give us perspective, and something like a fresh start—again from the base of Teaching as against Education. For if anything is more alarming than the demand for education as a cure-all, it is the chuckle-headed notion that many educators have of teaching. . . .

Teaching is not a lost art but the regard for it is a lost tradition. Hence tomorrow's problem will not be to get teachers, but to recognize the good ones and not discourage them before they have done their stint. In an age of big words and little work, any liberal profession takes some sticking to, not only in order to succeed, but in order to keep faith with oneself. Teaching is such a profession. . . .

140

Aubrey de Selincourt

TEACHING AS A PERSONAL RELATIONSHIP

Though much is made—and rightly—in educational literature of the teacher's need to understand and sympathize with children, not enough is said of those matters in which he should keep his distance from them. But the stubborn fact remains that the teacher is an adult, while the pupil is still, to a greater or lesser extent, immature. This distinction should never be lost sight of, though it too often tends to be.

In numerous communities teachers are often pressured into accepting the direction of Boy Scouts and Girl Scouts, Sunday School classes, and the like. While all these organizations are excellent and require on the part of those in charge a good deal of knowledge of children, such work is not for the young teacher. Though he could probably do it effectively, his out-of-school hours should be spent associating with adults. One can become so absorbed in work with children that one becomes too much like them! At best, the teacher spends the greater part of his time working among children and adolescents, thinking and planning near their level; he needs all the adult association possible to restore his adult perspective.

The author of the passage that follows points up this aspect of teaching very clearly. A teacher of long experience and a writer on education, he also is known for his writings on nature study and on boating.

[The danger of the teaching profession is that the] necessary absorption of the teacher in the community of school, and the peculiar nature of that community, produce . . . distortions . . . . They are very difficult to avoid. Every teacher must be aware of the kind of thing I mean: the exaggeration of trivial matters, the magnifying of misdemeanours into moral offences, the glooms, triumphs and despairs over things in their essence trifling. I have been present at a staff meeting at which some thirty adult men and women argued with passion for an hour about whether the first lesson in the morning should begin at nine or at eight-fifty-five, while the headmaster, presiding, did his best to control the mutual anger, malice and contempt of the two diverse factions. My own opinion I did not dare to express: it was merely that it made little difference—at any rate only *five minutes'* difference. And every schoolmaster will remember the atmosphere in Common Room after the discovery of some offence: the peculiar tension, the whispering groups, the quick glance at the door when it opens to admit a newcomer, the half-shocked, half-delighted speculation, the weight of care on those specially concerned—the offender's tutor, maybe, or housemaster, or form-master—the breezy and malicious nonchalance of those untouched by the dark stain; tempers on edge; the heightened emotional atmosphere, the brooding sense of a calamity which is yet not wholly without its charm. . . .

Ah well, such things are serious in the life of a school; and no doubt it is important too that the time-table should be nicely adjusted. No work can be too well done, and it would ill become one who was once a schoolmaster to mock those who have a sharper eye for perfection than he had himself. But—and this is the point I would urge—there is always the danger that the pressing and immediate affairs of school should so wholly absorb a man that they become for him the one reality. He surrenders unconditionally, and is thereby, as a person, diminished. I suppose it is possible in all walks of life to become co-extensive with one's job; and to do so is a mark of failure as a human being. For a sailor, say, or a civil servant to become co-extensive with his job, does not, I think, make him a worse civil servant or a worse sailor; but for a schoolmaster to become co-extensive with his job, does make him a worse schoolmaster. The reason is plain: teaching . . . is a personal relationship; and the quality of a personal relationship depends upon the quality of the persons who enter into it. The complete surrender, the total absorption in the life of the school, may give a man a certain mechanical efficiency which is valuable in any trade, and certainly valuable in teaching; but it will diminish him as a person; it will block up the sources of life which should come to him 'from afar,' and he will have, in consequence, less to give.

I have dwelt on this subject, because it seems to me vitally important that the true centre of a teacher's life should be not in the school, but outside it. Even the most elementary teaching— and even in its mechanical aspect of the mere imparting of fact—is, as it were, the overflow from a well of knowledge, the deeper the better; and the subtler essence of teaching, which proceeds from the relationship of a person who knows more with a person who knows less, is also, and in a much profounder sense, an overflow— not from a well of knowledge, but from a well of being. A teacher, that is, must be a person in his own right; to teach efficiently, he must be

From *The School Master* by Aubrey de Selincourt (London: John Lehmann, 1951), pp. 112-119.

more than a mere teacher. Real teaching is the sharing of a man's self, and that carries with it the need of having a self to share.

All this is so obvious that it would not be worth mentioning, if it were not so fatally easy even for the most promising teachers after a year or two of work to abandon their independence, to contract their vision, to get bogged and sunk in the life of the school, happily (and that is the worst of it) taking that life for their own. That is the Gorgon threat I spoke of, a threat of petrifaction almost more insidious than that other which comes from mere boredom and weariness —more insidious because it has an appearance of life and vigour. The teacher who has dwindled, so to speak, into his job may often appear more successful by external standards than the teacher who brings to it a life perpetually refreshed from without; but in the end he will fail. He will fail because his work will be all form and no matter —and form without substance soon shrinks into mere formula.

The surrender is at its worst and most dangerous when it involves the emotions: when a teacher comes to find not only all his interests and intellectual satisfaction in the work of school, but his emotional satisfaction in the companionship of the children. I believe that this happens more often than is usually supposed. It won't do. Teaching is a personal relationship: it is a relationship between an adult and a child. But an adult who can be emotionally involved with other people's children, is not really adult at all: he has got stuck somewhere, and his relationship with the children is thereby falsified. Good will and benevolence a teacher must indeed have; through all his angers and irritations and intolerances, he must wish the children well—all of them, all the time. But he must not *need* them. A teacher who needs them has already abandoned his adult prerogative, and with it the essential element in his relationship with the young. Many schoolmasters take parties of boys on holiday jaunts abroad, or wherever it may be, and such trips are often of great educational value. I used to admire the men who undertook this work; for a schoolmaster has a hard life and deserves his rest. Now, however, I admire only those who do not enjoy it over-much. It is an odd thing when a man, or a woman either, after thirteen weeks of exhausting companionship with other people's young, should not wish to be utterly and gloriously free of them until next term begins.

I once heard of a schoolmaster who invited six boys to accompany him and his wife on their honeymoon.

A taste for learning—and with it the capacity to learn—is caught as much as taught. A boy or girl is not likely to catch it if the things he is set to study appear to him as school subjects only. Teachers are overworked, and this is a pity; for to teach well they need more leisure than school holidays can give. They should be students, and their pupils should know them as such. Any subject which is taught in school becomes at once more alive to those who are learning it, when they see that it is important in its own right to the teacher. A good teacher, therefore, ought to have not only the time but also the desire to pursue his studies actively and continuously. The overflow from them should be the matter of his teaching. What is the use of a teacher of painting, if his pupils never see him engaged upon a picture of his own; or of music, if he never touches his instrument for his own pleasure? How can children be expected to be wakened to languages or literature or history, unless they know that those things are living interests to the people they are supposed to respect? I have said already that children learn only what they want to learn; only what answers to a deep and unconscious need; it is no less true that a man can teach only what he has thus come to possess—only the knowledge in which he is still actively adventuring, and which remains for him a still living experience. Without that he is not a teacher but an instructor—as we used to call the sergeants in the army who instructed us in the mechanism of the Lewis gun. We are all tired and bored sometimes, and goodness knows there is a deal of instruction we all have to hand out during the long hours of a school term. But it must not be all instruction; there must be some teaching now and then—but there won't be any unless the teacher is a learner too, and ready to admit it.

Some teachers are like cisterns: they run the water off through pipes for their pupils' use. I think an image for a good teacher is a stream rather than a cistern: or, rather, a good teacher is a person through whom the stream flows, always new, and the pupils can drink the water if they want to. The most inward quality of good teaching is a sharing of experience; and experience is always a matter of the moment, actual and alive, not something acquired or remembered. Being so, it has power in it. Who said, "I prefer love poems to poems about love"? Experience is unpredictable and immediate. If a man is alive, he communicates life. A small spark of life, of almost any colour or quality, caught direct from a living person, is of deeper educational significance than the best ideal system built up from the works of Plato and the Christians.

It is difficult for a schoolmaster not to be a hypocrite: I don't mean all the time, but for some of the time. This is unfortunate, because children know hypocrisy at first glance, and hate it. For instance, it is difficult for a teacher always to say "I don't know," when such happens to be the case—as it does fifty times a day. It is difficult not to work up a factitious indignation at small offences which, dispassionately considered, matter little, if at all. It is difficult in, say, an English lesson for a teacher to let it appear that he, too, is bored stiff with the book under discussion. Nevertheless, in all such cases it is better that the fact should not be concealed: or rather that no attempt should be made to conceal it; for it will appear anyway. Of course—to consider my last instance—it would be unfortunate if the teacher were always bored with the book under discussion. Sometimes this happens: but then the teacher should have chosen a different subject to teach at the outset of his career: say cookery. For it is only when he is not bored that he can teach at all.

When I say that teaching is a sharing of experience, I do not mean those accumulated experiences which are said to constitute the superior wisdom of age. I mean experience actual and immediate: the thing felt, the thing perceived, in the present—now. Like revelation, to repeat Buber's phrase, teaching tolerates no perfect tense. A teacher may have admirable 'ideas' about this, that and the other; but he cannot teach those ideas. Or, rather, he can; but if he does, they remain ideas, and that's no good. It is like saying to a class: "Milton is a good poet," and the class replies in chorus: "Yes, Milton is a good poet." But nothing has happened: both Milton and the class remain precisely as they were before.

I do not wish to be unpractical on this subject; and I do indeed know that nine-tenths of a man's work in school is necessarily what I have called 'instruction.' Nevertheless, the distinction between instruction and what I believe to be 'teaching' is important, and a teacher who is willing to recognise it is the more likely to succeed. What I have suggested applies to all teaching, except of subjects—if there are any—which consist only of facts; but I have of course had particularly in mind what are called 'arts' subjects. In literature, for instance, there is a great deal to be learnt *about* it, which is necessary to know and interesting in itself. This anyone can teach, either from his own knowledge or from a text book. But it is only a frame, without the picture. Can the picture be 'taught' too? It cannot; but certain obstacles which make it more difficult for others to see it, can be removed. That process is the teacher's work: the rest belongs to the instructor.

I have said nothing about scholarship, except that it is not enough. In the old days the great Public Schools were better staffed *for their purpose* than most schools are to-day, with certain distinguished exceptions where the tradition of scholarship is unchanged. I suppose, when I was a boy, there was not a man on the school staff who was not a 'First' in something or other. First-class men to-day, especially scientists, rarely go into schools. The inducements are not strong enough. This is in many ways a pity. If teaching is, as I have suggested, the overflow of a man's knowledge, the well from which it comes can hardly be too deep. But we cannot have everything, and it is better by far that our schools nowadays, with the changes of emphasis and outlook which have taken place, should be staffed by men and women of sound and average scholarship together with the other qualities which I have tried to outline, than by the most brilliant who may nevertheless lack them.

141

Henry W. Simon

HOW NOT TO BE A SCHOOLMARM

The notion of the teacher as a somewhat contemptible figure, personifying most of the negative virtues, never dies. Ichabod Crane and the lovable but ineffective Mr. Chips are still with us, as are a host of others more or less like them.

Benjamin Franklin's statement that of the pupils attending his Academy, those "of the poorer sort" might become teachers finds its echo even today; though the words are usually less frank, the insinuation is clear.

The National Education Association has for more than one hundred years been trying to raise the professional status of teachers and most, if not all, of the lesser educational organizations have followed suit. But is teaching even yet regarded as a real profession comparable to law or medicine? Every young person who contemplates spending his life in the classroom should ponder this question long and earnestly. What proportion of American parents really hope that their children will go into teaching?

Perhaps some of the energy heretofore expended in group efforts to raise the status of teaching has been misdirected. It may be that the issue is rather one of changing individual teachers—that each teacher has an obligation to avoid the stereotype of the schoolmarm. Henry Simon thinks so. He was associated in the 1930's with a rather short-lived venture to discover and train master teachers in what was known as New College of Teachers College, Columbia University. An entertaining writer, he has obviously observed teachers at all levels and is keenly alive to their strengths and to their weaknesses.

The sallow, virgin-minded, studious
Martyr to mild enthusiasm.
                              —Browning

The wretched souls of those who lived
Without or praise or blame, with that ill band
Of angels mix'd, who nor rebellious proved
Nor yet were true to God.
                              —Dante

Much have I seen and known,—cities of men,
And manners, climates, councils, governments,
Myself not least, but honoured of them all,—
And drunk delight of battle with my peers,
Far on the ringing plains of windy Troy.
I am a part of all that I have met . . .
                              —Tennyson

The 'typical' representative of a profession is seldom a distinguished member of it. There is the type of man you would classify on sight as 'lawyer'—but not Abraham Lincoln, Francis Bacon, or Franklin Roosevelt. Such men are too broad in outlook and in background to fit readily into any type. So is John Dewey. So was Socrates.

The typical school-teacher—the schoolmarm of either sex—is something no one wants to be. His characteristics . . . are timidity, a peculiar refinement or super-gentility, and an over-conscientiousness about trivialities. Such a man or woman cannot be a good teacher because he cannot be a

leader. Yet it is difficult to avoid acquiring these characteristics: they are thrust upon one partly by the nature of school life but even more by public opinion.

A teacher's life is, in a small town, practically public property: almost everyone regards himself as a duly constituted censor of a teacher's behavior—not to mention his professional skill, though that does not concern us here. Your physician may play cards if he wants to and your chauffeur get drunk on his nights off; but in many places the teacher dare not do the first and almost nowhere dare he do the second. He is expected to live up to the standards that parents and school boards preach, let them practise what they will. The board is usually composed of a community's most respected citizens, and it sees to it that the teachers exhibit the virtues for which the board is respected.

The underlying principle is sound enough. If the school is an agent of the state and if a teacher's whole life affects his teaching, then it is up to the school board to see to it that the teacher leads a desirable life. The difficulty and the injustice comes in the narrow interpretation given by most school boards to the phrase 'desirable life.' It is too likely to be based on superficial convention and desk-motto philosophy.

In small towns particularly the teacher thus becomes not a courageous, independent thinker and an adventuresome person, as the leader of children ought to be, but a timid soul censored by a board and spied upon by everyone. Consideration of his every action is prefaced by those two ham-stringing words, '*Dare I?*' 'Dare I wear these

From *Preface to Teaching* by Henry W. Simon (New York: Oxford University Press, 1938), pp. 48-57. Copyright 1938 by Henry W. Simon.

clothes?' 'Dare I go to this restaurant?' 'Dare I be seen soon again with this young man or woman?' 'Dare I vote thus?' 'Dare I say this?' And finally, 'Dare I think so-and-so?' He must attend certain functions and not others, live in a certain district, and maintain a certain standard of living even though his salary may not justify it. The result is almost inevitably a timidity and conservatism dictated not by conviction but by social pressure. So long as he does and says only what the most staid, respectable, and conservative members of the community do and say, he is safe; so long as he thinks no thoughts that cannot be uttered in the presence of the tenderest girl in school, his job is secure. Beyond this there may lie danger—a danger he should be ready to welcome.

This picture is extreme but not exaggerated. Some places permit more growth and freedom than others, but the principle is the same. In Russia the teacher must believe in Communism, at Munich in Nazism, throughout Tennessee in fundamentalism. He is permitted far more latitude in a New York high school than in a Kentucky mountain district, but so is everyone else. Where everyone has great latitude, he is given some; where everyone has some, he has little; where everyone has little, he has none.

It would be almost as foolish to argue with this state of affairs as to argue with a law of nature. With possibly the single exception of Mexico, where economic and political control are not closely identified with each other, a people gets the sort of education its controlling group wants it to have. In the United States, where there is more local option in education than in any other great western country, local prejudices are sure to affect the teacher intimately. And local prejudices will as a rule tend to make a schoolmarm of a teacher. You cannot, as I said, argue with the general principle; but you can, if you are courageous, do something about the force of local prejudices. You can make a community let you think and act as a self-respecting man or woman should. You must bow to the law of society that a people gets the sort of education its controlling group wants, but you can also do something toward making it want a better sort—the sort that is given by one who is not only a leader of children but a leader of men as well. Only when the teacher himself becomes a force in the community, only when he has earned the respect of the adults among whom he lives, can he become a genuine force in education. From Socrates and Jesus down, occasional teachers have earned the serious consideration of their communities in varying degrees. So far as I know, no American teachers have ever achieved a cup of hemlock or a cross while fighting for consideration, nor have they encountered shotguns or concentration camps as some Mexican and German teachers have. Our opponents have been only Mrs. Grundys and narrow-minded legislators, our punishments gossip or, at worst, dismissal.

But one must not underestimate the difficulties that can be put in the way of a teacher who wishes to become a leader in the community. The first and most obvious one I have already mentioned—the strait-laced ideas and conduct that are sometimes demanded. The easy course is to knuckle under, get used to it, and lead a dull, respectable life forever after. There is nothing inherently wrong about respectability so long as one does not assume that cloistered virtue for fear of developing more vigorous ones. But unquestioning acceptance of *any* set of values is deadening and makes bad teachers. The opposite course is to kick over the traces, to flaunt an independence of gossip, or, to call it by a more polite name, public opinion. This is equally unwise because it readily leads to quixoticism. If local prejudice demands that you give up cards or smoking or certain restaurants, you had better not make an issue of the matter before you are firmly established. Such deprivations are superficial and essentially unimportant even though they may be highly annoying. There is no sense in rubbing a community of Mrs. Grundys the wrong way on precisely those matters which appear the most important to them but which are in reality only symbols. Give them victory with symbols every time: that will only strengthen your position when it comes to something important. The issue worth fighting for will come soon enough, and you can recognize it by knowing that it involves principles much more far-reaching than your personal convenience. Such an issue may be professional and involve the question of whether or not you give true historical interpretations or only sugar-coated half-truths. It may, on the other hand, be personal, and involve the question of whom you marry or even, if you are a girl, whether you may marry at all. The teacher who has not flaunted his disrespect for the conventions of his community in regard to symbols is in a far better position to fight his real battles. 'We might have known—' will be the attitude of the school board whose new appointee wore a low-cut dress one week and mentioned Karl Marx the next. If she could have earned the reaction expressed in the words 'Such a fine person—maybe there's something in it,' she might have taken a first step toward academic freedom. Give in on little issues with grace if you cannot do it with conviction. Then you may be able to win the big ones. This is not hypocrisy; it is tact. It clears the decks for a clean fight when the big issue does come up. Then, if you lose, you can do it with self-respect; and if you win you will be on the road to forcing respect from a community that wanted to withhold it. It is one thing to risk your post for a breach of local etiquette; it is quite another to risk it for what you regard as truth.

A second difficulty the teacher faces lies in his social position. This varies inversely with the prosperity of the place in which he teaches: in a really impoverished village he is likely to be on top of the heap, while in a wealthy suburb he may be regarded as a superior nurse-maid. In the average American town, however, his position tends to be anomalous. His superior education and traditional gentility prevent his association on equal terms with those in whose proximate income class he falls—that is, according to a recent statistical study, slightly above routine clerical workers and slightly below workers in manufacturing industries. On the other hand, his low income prevents his association with men and women of analogous education who have gone into business or taken up one of the better paid professions. The result is that he tends to associate too much with his own kind. He eats his lunches at the school cafeteria with his fellows; he invites and is invited by them to dinner parties; he even takes his vacations with them. There is nothing wrong with the society of teachers; the difficulty arises when it is made an exclusive diet. Plumbers associate with butchers and lawyers with physicians, but teachers largely only with each other. The result is an over-preponderance of shop-talk with its emphasis on detail. One way to lessen this danger is occasionally to risk your lunch money away from the school cafeteria. Another way to lessen it is to face squarely the fact that your income is smaller than that of other similarly educated groups and that everyone knows it is. No man you might really want to associate with would let this difference in income stand in both your ways unless a false pride prompted you to embarrass him with hospitalities he knows you cannot afford.

The ultimate way to avoid the danger of getting narrow is to leave teaching. I do not mean this as a counsel of despair or as a joke. To develop as a broad, well-informed teacher, I can think of no better prescription than to leave the profession for a year or two early in your career and earn your living in some totally different way—as a secretary, a store clerk, a farmhand. This is especially valid advice for those who have gone directly into teaching after four years of college and with virtually no experience of life outside of academic places. It is almost the only valid way to achieve a realistic perspective on your job and its social significance. It may also show you—by contrast—how extraordinarily pleasant the life of a teacher can be.

But not only can the life of a teacher be pleasant; it can present opportunities for development of the individual that no other profession has. Any professional may become so wrapped up in his work that he sees the world only from his own corner. The teacher has least excuse for such narrowness, for he has more time away from his job than any other professional has. Most schools are closed twenty of the year's fifty-two weeks. The vacations should be used to face outward from the job, to experience something new. And by 'something new' I do not mean listening to a series of lectures or visiting five countries in a six-weeks' tour of Europe. While study and travel are the two obvious ways for a teacher to spend a summer vacation, if he can afford them, they must be made to mean more than an extended travelogue or a series of lyceum lectures. Here are some do's and don't's about summer travel:

1. Don't go on a conducted tour unless it is for some specific purpose like a study of housing conditions or of the drama and is led by a reputable authority in that field.

2. Travel alone or with only one or two companions. Larger groups often do more things for less money, but you spend too much time with your kind and it is all too safe and comfortable to be much more than a prolonged picnic.

3. Don't visit more than one or two countries and don't move about constantly within those two. Railroad stations, tourist hotels, and monuments are the accidents of a civilization. A month as a house-holder in a Dorset village will give you a better understanding of English life and psychology than two months of buses and bargains.

4. Visit no large countries whose language and civilization you have not studied. Know just why you are going and what you expect to find. Your experience will still be unexpected enough.

And here are some do's and don't's about summer study—particularly at university summer sessions:

1. Consider the summer an opportunity for travel and life in different surroundings almost as much as a strictly academic experience. Choose your institution not merely for the courses it has to offer, but also because it is in New York or Berkeley or Grenoble. Then register for a course

light enough to let you explore ways of living in new surroundings.

2. Summer sessions are usually too short and the classes too large to train experts. Their academic function is introduction to new ideas and review. In England they are called 'refresher courses.' Therefore you should plan to do your really serious advanced study either by yourself or during a year's leave of absence if you can afford it.

3. Do not confine your courses to lectures on education. Not only should you broaden your interests, but you should avoid, for reasons mentioned earlier in this chapter, a companionship made up exclusively of teachers.

Both study and travel take money, and you may not be able to save enough out of the small salary most beginners receive. You may, particularly the first few years, find it absolutely necessary to support yourself by earning money during the summer. Many young teachers meet such an emergency by securing a position in a summer camp—a good idea if you do not do it too often. The routine, the confinement, and the relationship with children at a summer camp is not so different from that at school as to develop new facets of your personality. Others, failing to qualify for camp posts, earn a less agreeable living in a shop, office, farm, or factory. Such jobs, while they may not be so healthy as camp, can still turn out disguised blessings.

The modern teacher, the one who is alert, courageous, and capable of understanding the life around him with other than academic insight—in other words, the teacher who will never be called schoolmarm—must have first-hand experience of the non-academic life. I have suggested above that it is wise to leave the profession for at least one year during your early career. If circumstances make this impossible, then the least you can do is to step into other shoes for a summer. I have tried office, farm, and factory myself and know that the fresh types of contact, the new understanding of 'routine,' the totally different ways of looking at life such experiences afford, are each worth several summer sessions of lectures.

Whatever activities you engage in outside of school work, whether during summer holidays or not, play their part in keeping the hallmark of the profession off you and therefore in making you a better teacher. Whether it is political work, string quartets, or even selling magazine subscriptions, there is the chance to develop those sides of you which are not professionally 'teacher.' All such activities are obviously not equally valuable. Gardening is probably a better hobby to have than bridge. What is most necessary, however, is to have *some* outside interests. For teaching, while it can be the best way in the world to earn a living, can also be social, intellectual, and emotional stagnation. . . .

142

Marten ten Hoor

IN PRAISE OF TEACHING

The teacher's proper equipment for his job has long been a matter of concern to educators. W. E. Hocking's trenchant statement is particularly appropriate in the connection: ". . . Education has two functions and not one only. It must communicate the type, and it must provide for growth beyond the type" (2). To fulfil the first of these functions the teacher must have a firm grasp of that part of the cultural heritage which it is his duty to pass on—he must, in other words, know a lot about his subject. Is this knowledge enough? The educator would reply that he needs teaching skill as well and, to a certain extent, he would be right. But the teacher needs still more; he needs a keen sense of his responsibility as one to whom this knowledge and the task of transmitting it have been entrusted.

Here we approach Hocking's second function of education. We do not educate the young to maintain a static and unchanging society. We hope that the children now in the schools will, when they grow up, make a somewhat better world than the present generation has made. Teaching with this aim calls for a degree of dedication on the part of the teacher, for his having certain ideals. He must believe in his task, not only in vaguely idealistic terms but in a sincere, well-thought-out *credo,* consonant with and applicable to teaching. This will, of course, be revised as the knowledge of teaching grows, but it is nevertheless a necessary part of the teacher's equipment for his task.

There is much to be said "in praise of teaching," as the author of the following selection states.

I would like to begin by asking and answering the question, "Why do schools and teachers exist?" In general, they exist because society perpetually feels itself in need of improvement. Specifically, schools and teachers are concrete evidence of a conviction held by parents that children are not born perfect and that children can be educated to be better than their parents. Of course, there are some parents who desire merely accurate copies of themselves and who are satisfied with a second edition without improvements. However, as the philosopher Plato said, this type of education is flattery and not education at all. Schools and teachers are not agencies whose function it is merely to reproduce the same model. Nature produces a constant stream of little savages. Education must not only bring them up to the contemporary standard but must improve on the parent generation.

The existence of schools and teachers is also evidence of the persistent hope of mankind for social progress, of the hope that education will produce better citizens for a better state. The existence of the teaching profession indicates the hope that poverty, disease, ignorance, economic injustice, personal and public immorality can be reduced if not abolished.

It appears from this that schools and teachers are custodians of civilization. Education reveals the mistakes of the past; it conserves and passes on the accumulated experience of mankind. Science, technology, art, religion, these are in the permanent custody of the teacher. Schools and teachers are therefore the enduring repository of human hopes and ideals. By means of teaching, man hopes to redeem himself and his fellows. All the varied forms of educational practice and experiment are symptoms of repentance.

It is obvious from the above what the essential qualities of the good teacher are. *The teacher must first of all have knowledge.* Lack of knowledge or pretense of knowledge is quickly sensed

by children. What I mean by knowledge here is saturation with the subjectmatter. The teacher must know immeasurably more than he needs for the teaching of a class or course. This does not mean a teacher is merely a repository of facts. For this textbooks are quite as serviceable. Nor is the teacher a mere purveyor of information. Mechanical instruments, such as the victrola, are quite as useful for this purpose. I mean that the teacher should be the *living subject which he teaches.*

A *second essential quality is technical skill.* Here again I do not mean that the teacher should have a standardized technic. The teacher is not a machine; professional skill should be his servant, not his master.

Third, a good teacher must have a deepgoing understanding of children. The basic virtue here is sympathy. The teacher must have a genuine and sincere liking for children; for many hours a day he stands *in loco parentis.* The teacher must remember that he deals with the most impressionable and sensitive of raw materials—the young personality. The teacher must be guided not only by knowledge and skill but by affection. Remember Cudworth's famous lines, "Truth and love are two of the most powerful things in the world and when they go together they cannot easily be withstood." The teacher must therefore not quarrel with human nature but understand it and use such knowledge in his teaching.

In the fourth place, the teacher must have moral ideals. In the field of moral education we have been least successful. For centuries teachers have taught facts and what to do with, or about them, but they have to a dangerous extent forgotten to teach what *ought* to be done with, or about them. Education in moral ideals is much more difficult than education in facts, for ideals cannot easily be taught formally. Example, and the revelation of personal conviction and belief, and faith in moral ideas are the real educative influences here.

In the fifth place, the teacher must have the true experimental spirit. Like the physician, he

NEA Personal Growth Leaflet No. 145 (Washington: National Education Association, 1942), pp. 3-16.

must be constantly on the lookout for better ways of accomplishing his aims. He must not be a pure experimentalist, but must find a happy medium between the worship of tradition and the naive acceptance of the latest fads and fancies.

Sixth, the teacher must have a stout heart. Teaching is often discouraging business. In a teacher's lifetime, literally thousands of pupils stream thru his classes. Every year there is a new batch and he must start all over again. Then his charges disappear and he sees little of the fruits of his labor. Thus he must have a stout heart. He must believe in himself and in his work. It is fatal for him to be dissatisfied with his work. He must constantly recall Hardy's lines:

He who is with himself dissatisfied,
Tho all the world finds satisfaction in him,
Is like a rainbow-colored bird gone blind,
That gives the light it shares not.

Finally, the teacher must have deep and abiding faith. Teaching is the only profession outside of the ministry which makes the teaching of ideals its life work. The task is difficult, often discouraging, frequently criticized; its effects are often neutralized; its job is never finished. The teacher must constantly be revitalized by faith in the ultimate success of education.

It seems logical to consider next the rewards of the teacher, for certainly a profession which plays such an important part in civilization and which requires such fine qualities of its members should be well-rewarded. There are two types of rewards which men can enjoy—material and spiritual. What are the material rewards of the teacher?

It is astounding that many people actually think this question should not be raised. The attitude of the public toward the question of the material rewards of the teacher is somewhat of a mystery. However, some clue is to be found in history, for the unsympathetic attitude of the general public to the material rewards of the teacher is an historical and traditional one. The Greek aristocrat thought it was shameful to teach for pay and looked with disdain on the Sophist teacher. The classical attitude was strengthened rather than weakened during medieval times. For some fifteen or sixteen centuries A.D., education was almost entirely in the hands of the clergy. The members of this profession naturally expected to get their reward in heaven. Honor as we must the devotion, selfsacrifice, and almost ascetic attitude of medieval teachers, none of us today would answer Charlemagne as did the Irish teachers when he asked them what they required:

"Only proper places and noble souls, and such things as we cannot live without, food and wherewith to clothe ourselves." No teacher today would consider the bare necessities of life as sufficient reward for his work.

In spite of history and tradition, the attitude of contemporary society toward material rewards for the teacher remains inexplicable; for it requires no great acumen to realize that it is a grave mistake to pay poor salaries to teachers. Only the best intelligences should be permitted to practice this profession. Such intelligences are not to be had for the asking. In a competitive and materialistic civilization, material rewards are an important and justifiable attraction. It should be obvious to all that a teacher should be paid enough so that he can devote his whole life, all his energy, and all his powers to teaching. Teaching requires a reasonable security of mind. The notion of the noble poverty of the teacher is a romantic delusion, like the notion of love in a garret. Furthermore, teachers require and are entitled to some of the fine things of life: music, books, fine art, and travel. They need these things to be good teachers.

Finally, the lack of deserved material reward distracts the teacher from his great mission. It may develop in him a sense of injustice, with the result that his mind is too much occupied with thoughts of protest and plans of action to obtain justice. He cannot well be blamed, altho there may occasionally be good reason to criticize some of the methods he uses to call the attention of society to his predicament. What must be impressed upon society is that the teacher is more important than any building, than textbooks, than boards of education, or than any of the machinery necessary for the conduct of the enterprise of education. It is to be hoped that in the future society will more willingly and concretely recognize this.

Fortunately for the teacher—and for society— there are also spiritual rewards for teaching. There is the pleasure which comes from imparting knowledge, from being, so to speak, an instrument of revelation. There is the pleasure which comes from winning the trust, affection, and gratitude of young children. To win these is one of the greatest goods in this world. There is the pleasure which comes from watching the child grow and develop as a personality. All men know the pleasures of watching flowers grow in response to care and the pleasure of the artist in modeling his work of art. The true teacher experiences a pleasure akin to these. There is also the satisfaction which comes from the consciousness of being a part of the greatest single agency for social progress, from knowing that one is a part of the institution which is the custodian of truth and ideals. These rewards are after all the most important rewards. The teacher who teaches for material rewards alone is out of place in the profession. In fact, such a person would be out of place almost anywhere.

We are living in an age of confusion, an age in which civilization seems to be more seriously threatened than at any period in modern times. We are daily witnessing the enslavement of education in countries in which we would not have thought this to be possible. More and more, propaganda is taking the place of true education. Never was it more important to hold fast to our professional ideals and to our faith as teachers. Never was it more important to reexamine and to restate our professional faith. For this reason, I am going to be so bold as to suggest some articles for the credo of the teacher:

I believe that children are the most important things on earth.

I believe that our schools are the enduring repositories of human experience.

I believe that teaching is the blood-stream of intellectual and moral progress and that teaching is therefore the noblest of all professions.

I believe that the teacher is the guardian of truth, of goodness, and of beauty, and therefore the custodian of civilization.

I will not be discouraged by the absence of adequate and just material rewards.

I will not be discouraged by misguided parents, by selfseeking and insincere politicians, and by false leaders in education.

I will not be discouraged by the collapse of ideals in the world about us and by the prostitution of education in some foreign countries.

I will not be discouraged by the failure of our product to be perfect or by our inability to measure fully the results of our labors.

I will not be disheartened by the occasional failures of educational theories and practices.

I will not be discouraged by the fact that the family and society are placing increasing responsibilities on my shoulders and expecting more and more of me as a teacher.

I will constantly remember that the child entrusted to me is the most helpless, delicate, and sensitive being on earth, and I will never forget that my strength as a teacher lies in my devotion to the welfare of this child.

In teaching this child I will have constantly before me the words of Carlyle: "The wealth of a man is the number of things which he loves and blesses and which he is blessed by."

143

Robert H. Anderson

TEAM TEACHING

The present scarcity of good teachers, the wide variety of teaching ability, the increasing numbers of pupils to be taught, and numerous other reasons have led educators in recent years to question the long-established one-teacher-one-class arrangement in schools. Granted that a teacher is conspicuously able in presenting some particular topic (and much teaching is of necessity expository), why should his lecture and/or demonstration be presented to successive groups of twenty to thirty? Why not save time by teaching one hundred or one hundred and fifty simultaneously?—or even thousands by closed-circuit TV if the numbers are that large? A great amount of time could thus be saved and many teachers released for other types of tasks, such as checking written work or preparing other lessons.

Such considerations have led to schemes by which three or four teachers pool their resources, each one doing that for which his abilities and training best fit him. Many of these attempts are interesting and seem to promise economy of time and increased effectiveness of teaching. Naturally they are still in the experimental stage and should not be set forth as finished products. In addition they call for much cooperation on the part of participating teachers and for skillful coordination by the persons in charge. Some educators see these experiments as heralding a bright new day in teaching, while others see them as just another fad destined to pass as so many have already done in the past fifty years. Some of the problems and possibilities of team teaching are discussed in the following article.

Teaching teams and similar forms of staff organization are currently attracting widespread attention. What is team teaching? Where may examples be found? How did it come about, and what are its strengths and weaknesses? Is team teaching just another bandwagon for the unwary educator?

Team teaching is both old and new. In team teaching, many teachers will recognize certain processes of co-operative endeavor which are frequently found in good schools. Varieties of informal, co-operative teaching have probably existed for some time.

Nonetheless, in the present decade we are witnessing the first significant development of the team-teaching idea and its translation into personnel policy, program arrangements, and architecture. This has in turn stimulated much fresh thinking about class size and organization, grouping practices, basic curriculum decisions, division of the work load among the teaching staff, and the bases of pupil welfare.

Specifically, a teaching team is a group of several teachers (usually between three and six) jointly responsible for planning, carrying out, and evaluating an educational program for a group of children. For example, a team may consist of four elementary teachers, sharing about 3500-4000 square feet of classroom space and working with about 115 children. These children could be all at the same grade level, say fourth grade, or from adjoining grade levels.

One of the teachers might be a specialist in science and arithmetic, another in language arts, a third in social studies, and a fourth in the creative arts. While each specialist might take leadership for planning and perhaps for a major share of the teaching in his area of special competence, all four teachers would be involved in the total instructional program, and there would not be departmentalization in the usual sense.

One of the four, on the strength of special qualifications and training, would be designated as team leader with responsibility for overall program co-ordination.

In most secondary schools where there are teams and in a few elementary schools, the teams are organized vertically within a subject area or group of subjects. For example, a three-teacher team in a small junior high school might handle all English instruction for the pupils in grades seven, eight, and nine.

At present there are about 100 communities throughout the United States engaged in one form or another of team teaching; hundreds of other communities are known to be planning toward it.

Research in the status of team teaching is complicated by the fact that the term "team teaching" is being used very broadly: Many of the arrangements now labeled as "team teaching," some believe, should be given a name such as "co-operative teaching," "collaborative teaching," or the like. A number of arrangements are merely old-fashioned departmentalization under a new flag.

The essential ingredients of team teaching are not only co-operation and collaboration in the planning and presentation of the program, but also the assignment of specific leadership and responsibility (with the accompanying prestige and recognition) to career-oriented teachers of superior training and competence. Communication among the staff is also required by the definition of each person's role. In many so-called "team" enterprises, what actually exists is merely a voluntary federation of sovereign teachers enjoying a co-operative-collaborative relationship, but within which no one can be held specifically accountable for failures of communication, of program integration, or of performance.

Forerunners

Though team teaching is new in a certain sense, it is actually an outgrowth of other trends and movements in this and other centuries, rooted particularly in previous systems of deploying personnel and arranging the pupils' daily programs.

One important and recent forerunner of team teaching was the Bay City (Michigan) Study, involving the use of teacher aides. Although the team idea does not necessarily involve the use

From *NEA Journal*, March 1961, 50:52-54.

of nonprofessional assistants, Bay City opened the way to a fresh understanding of the multitude of routine but time-consuming tasks for which teachers are held responsible, and to new insights into ways pupils can be grouped and taught.

As a result, many other school systems have made great strides toward re-appraising teacher work loads and redistributing certain repetitive, nontechnical functions among subprofessional assistants. Often this happens within the framework of teaching teams.

Examples

The Lexington plan. A pioneer project in team teaching at the elementary school level was begun in 1957 in the Franklin School in Lexington, Massachusetts, as part of Harvard University's School and University Program for Research and Development (SUPRAD). At present there are three teams in Franklin School, each having a team leader.

Each team teaches two grades. In each team, characteristically, the pupils spend the day in a succession of varying-sized groups, and all six of the teachers have at least some responsibility for each child.

The school principal and the three team leaders constitute an administrative cabinet for the school, and the senior teachers join the group in an instructional cabinet responsible for school-wide curriculum planning. Each team also has the services of part-time clerical aides and teacher aides. Of the SUPRAD funds supporting the project, about two-thirds goes into activities of research and development by the Harvard staff.

The Norwalk plan. A somewhat similar set-up is found in Norwalk, Connecticut. It began in 1958-59 with four elementary school teams of three members: team leader, co-operating teacher, and teacher aide. Each of the original teams worked with about seventy-five to eighty pupils at a single grade level and in spaces equal to three standard classrooms.

In 1960-61, expanded operations include fourteen elementary school teams, one team teaching language arts and social studies in grades seven and eight, and a special team (team leader and two teachers) working with mentally handicapped children in a junior-senior high school.

Most of the elementary teams now include two grades, say grades three and four. Seven of these teams are five-member teams (team leader, three co-operating teachers, and a teacher aide, working with approximately 135 children), and several

are four-member teams (leader, two co-operating teachers, and aide) with about 105-110 pupils. Two schools are organized entirely on a team-teaching basis.

The Norwalk Plan has made extensive use of audio-visual materials, including overhead projectors and tape-recorded lessons. Aides relieve teachers of numerous non-instructional functions.

University of Wisconsin plan. Several projects are based upon the premise that the teaching team offers an especially appropriate framework for the training and induction of beginning teachers. The University of Wisconsin has recently launched such a program, placing five teams in the co-operating cities of West Bend (kindergarten level), Janesville (primary and intermediate levels), and Madison (also primary and intermediate).

Each team serves about ninety pupils, and each team consists of two experienced teachers and two teacher-interns (each semester), plus some clerical assistance. Thus, four interns—each partly on salary and partly in a training status—are inducted into teaching over the year. A many-faceted research study is a part of the Wisconsin project.

The Jefferson County plan. Perhaps the largest team-teaching project in existence may be found in Jefferson County, Colorado, School District R-1. It involves seven high schools, approximately 3000 students, fifty teachers, and nine clerks. It has included a wide variety of experiments touching every curriculum area during its three years of existence as one of the staff utilization studies of NEA's National Association of Secondary-School Principals.

Basically, a Jefferson County teaching team consists of four persons: a team leader, two qualified teachers, and one clerk. There have been experimental teams which have included specialists (such as a librarian or guidance consultant), students, and community consultants. Most teams concentrate upon one subject area, but interdisciplinary teams have been tried.

Grouping procedures and schedule modifications take many different forms, and teachers are encouraged to develop new teaching materials and techniques to fit the new methods of organization.

Evanston plan. Evanston (Illinois) Township High School, another of the staff utilization studies supported by NASSP, was one of the first high schools to work with teacher teams.

Fourteen different courses involve fifty-five teachers and fourteen instructional aides in teaching teams which provide instruction for 2600 students. The teams are as small as three and as large as nine; students assemble for large group presentations in groups ranging from sixty-eight to 130. Such large group instruction embraces about half of the regular class time and may often include use of closed-circuit television or a presentation by a talented member of the community.

These and dozens of other team-teaching projects have published reports now available in the growing literature.

Results

Since team teaching is still in its infancy, many questions as to its ultimate form and its merit must necessarily be postponed. An immediate need, however, is to make certain that team teaching is not disadvantageous to children. This applies especially to the elementary school, where the so-called self-contained classroom has long been considered to be the cause of certain benefits to children (both academically and emotionally).

Data thus far are incomplete and tentative, but there is at least sufficient evidence to justify further exploration and development of team-teaching organization.

Measures of personality growth and of pupil adjustment have been the chief yardstick used in gauging the effect of team teaching on the emotional personal-social welfare of children. Psychologists and trained observers have gathered case studies, recorded individual and group behavior, and interviewed children and adults in both team situations and control schools. Standardized test results have been the chief yardstick in determining pupil achievement.

Data reported to date show that team-teaching results are no less satisfactory than those from typical conventional teaching in elementary and secondary schools. There are some slight indications that team teaching is particularly beneficial to markedly advanced and retarded pupils, and also signs that certain children find greater stimulation and security within team-teaching situations.

No data have as yet appeared in support of the fear (expressed by critics) that some children will suffer emotionally or academically from team teaching.

Reports indicate that teachers on the whole have responded favorably to participation in hierarchically organized teams, although much remains to be done in training personnel for leadership roles and in devising efficient procedures for team operation. Reports indicate that a number of other problems or questions also arise.

Problems

A major problem reported by teams (and, we would add, by thousands of other teachers) is finding adequate time for planning and evaluation. Most teams have found themselves quite overwhelmed by the curriculum problems that come to light as they work together. Adequate guidelines to daily operations and scheduling, to techniques of instructing groups of various sizes, and to role performance are not yet available.

Communication within teams and between teams has yet to be perfected, and because of the frequency and intensity of contact, there are many complex problems of human relations.

Especially in elementary school teams, it has proved difficult to find and to train persons for the specialist roles in subject areas. Persons with the training, experience, and temperament for leader roles are also scarce. Persons in these roles encounter many difficult and unfamiliar problems. Sometimes, for example, leaders are confused as to when consensus is needed on a given policy or practice and when it is not. At times, team members confuse structure with process, and vice versa.

There is also the question of cost. Although new buildings designed for team teaching probably cost no more per pupil served than conventional buildings, the use of existing facilities generally requires at least minor changes in structure and physical arrangement. Teams usually require greater quantities and varieties of teaching materials, library resources, and equipment than are found in most schools. Some projects (for example, the Norwalk and the Wisconsin teams) do not cost more for total personnel budget, but others involve salary supplements and/or teacher aides. Perhaps most of these extra costs ought to be incurred by all schools irrespective of team teaching, but nonetheless it remains to be seen whether the expenditures pay adequate academic dividends.

Theoretical advantages

Among the arguments supporting team teaching is that the superior teacher can be of much greater influence in the school while still remaining within classroom teaching. Heretofore, the unusually gifted teacher has influenced the lives of only a relatively few children, and opportunity for exemplary or semisupervisory influence over fellow teachers has been virtually nonexistent.

Another argument is that while the traditions of self-containment and of the independent departmentalized teacher have tended to insulate teachers from each other, team teaching provides for frequent interchange at the same time that it extends the influence of the career teacher with special competence.

In the long run, it is also argued, the team-leader role will attract greater numbers of superior persons into the teaching profession. Reports from pilot projects call attention to the high caliber of recent applications for team positions, lending support to this expectation.

Team teaching theoretically provides a great deal of flexibility and efficiency in the use of time, space, materials, and teaching talents. Team members, not administrators, make decisions concerning the program on the basis of their joint observations and evaluations. Communication is not left to chance, but is required by both process and structure. Specialization is both possible and necessary. Instructional groupings of almost any desired size and composition can be arranged.

Perhaps the greatest potential advantage of team teaching is that it furnishes an impetus to significant curriculum improvement. Only the most naïve person would expect major gains in curriculum and instruction to result automatically from a change in school organization.

Whatever pattern of organization we choose to adopt or continue, we must realize that the basic problems of instruction will remain to be solved, as will many problems of teacher preparation and competency, adequacy of budgets, and the like. Team teaching does not solve these problems, but it does invigorate teacher concern for them and offer an alternative approach to them.

The full merit of team teaching remains to be measured.[1] It is now clear that several varieties of team teaching are feasible and that advantages once ascribed exclusively to the self-contained arrangement and departmental organization are enjoyed at least equally by these patterns. All the evidence necessary to a final judgment may require many years of further research. Our obligation in the meanwhile is to maintain an open mind.

---

[1] For a more scholarly analysis, see *Team Teaching,* Judson T. Shaplin and Henry F. Olds, Jr., eds. (New York: Harper & Row, 1963).

144

Anne Hoppock

TEAM TEACHING: FORM WITHOUT SUBSTANCE?

Team teaching—like teaching machines, educational TV, and other new techniques and devices for improving the instruction of the young—needs to be criticized searchingly and dispassionately. There is every indication that it will be. The day of the stifling or ignoring of honest criticism, such as went on in the twenties, is past.

Educators need to recall, now and again, some of the exaggerated claims made for the role of radio in education in the years following World War I and how few of these were realized. Is team teaching a fad for which great things will also be claimed for a few years but which will then cease to attract much attention?

Not many years ago the acquisition of "mere facts" and "skills" tended to be played down in educational literature. The primary purpose of the schools was the development of character, the integration of personality, and the socialization of the emotions. Today most of the new devices seem to be aimed squarely at imparting the heretofore undervalued facts and skills. This would seem to indicate a shift in educational philosophy that calls for long and careful consideration. It is definitely not the type of change the schools should drift into while following a new fad. The author of the following brief article, writing in response to the article by Robert Anderson (Reading 143), raises some pertinent questions about team teaching which its advocates will need to answer carefully in the near future.

"Team Teaching" by Robert Anderson . . . presents a concise description of the locale and organization of team teaching. It seems, however, that the description raises more questions than it answers.

What is team teaching for?

In Dr. Anderson's article, as in various other reports, considerable space is given to describing how team teaching is organized, scheduled, and housed. Its proponents claim that the plan is promising, that it provides flexibility and efficiency in the use of time, space, materials, and teaching talent. In short, the major intent of this scheme is to improve teaching.

Practically everyone, including most teachers, agrees that teaching can and should be improved. But what kinds of improvements is team teaching intended to produce? In what observable ways will the quality of team teaching differ from the teaching it replaces?

What kind of teaching does it foster?

In the absence of a clear statement of principles of teaching and learning which team teaching seeks experimentally to develop and demonstrate, one can only turn to the literature for clues. These may be found in abundance in a presumably authoritative publication by the Ford Foundation dated June 1960 and called *Time, Talent and Teachers.* This is one of a series of brochures describing activities supported by the Ford Foundation, the agency which provides financial support and publicity for most, if not all, of the projects described by Dr. Anderson.

Teaching, as envisaged in this publication, is largely a process of "imparting information," providing whatever repetition or practice the learner needs to take it in, and checking by test or review to assure that he can give the information back again. According to the foundation brochure:

"Teachers involved in school experiments have found that the large class is appropriate and educationally sound for imparting the basic infor- mation all students must have in a course. No longer, for example, need five biology teachers repeat essentially the same thing about the classi- fication of living things into class, order, family, genus, and species five times a day for a total of twenty-five presentations."

Instead, one teacher (the one with most com- petence in this segment of subject matter) "im- parts the basic information" by lecturing to all five sections in one fell swoop.

How the lecture method of imparting informa- tion sets the limits of the teaching-learning activi- ties is vividly pictured in the pamphlet's account of a week in the life of a biology teacher:

On Monday, he lectures fifty-five minutes to 170 students. (The remainder of the day he reads professional materials, sets up difficult experi- ments in the lab, tutors a boy who failed to grasp a difficult point in the lecture, gives advance as- signments to a bright girl who has read the text- book through and needs more challenging ma- terial, and grades papers.)

On Tuesday, he meets smaller groups sep- arately for a discussion lesson. ("Monday's lecture was not interrupted by questions.") On Wednes- day and Thursday, he meets groups in the lab, for two consecutive lab periods each, to work on experiments and see demonstrations. On Friday, he meets 170 pupils in a group for a test or review and is then free from classroom teaching for the day.

As a supplementary means of imparting in- formation, Dr. Anderson and the Ford Founda- tion report cite the use by teacher teams of audio-visual techniques such as tape-recorded lessons and overhead projection.

The Ford Foundation report observes that one reason for the projector's appeal is that the teach- er can "readily project information to the class without having to turn around!" Further, the tape recorder enhances the efficiency of the teacher by enabling students to receive instruction from him while he performs other teaching roles.

In essence, according to such descriptions of practice, it is the teacher, not the pupils, who does the questioning, the researching, the or-

From *NEA Journal*, April 1961, 50:47-48.

ganizing, the interpreting and generalizing, the using. According to *Time, Talent and Teachers:*

"In the large class the teacher is primarily a giver and interpreter of information; in the small class, where presumably he confronts factually informed students, he acts both as a consultant who raises questions and counselor who guides students in their search for answers."

What creative ideas about teaching are emerging?

It seems reasonable to expect that the resources of time, money, and intelligence used in carrying on a series of research projects such as team teaching purports to' be should produce some fresh, creative ideas about effective ways of stimulating and guiding learning. The kind of "tell and test" teaching based on the imparting-information concept has been too prevalent too long; its ineffectiveness has been demonstrated long since.

Rather than giving aid and comfort to the *status quo* in teaching, experimentation should develop new and improved ways to put into practice the knowledge about human growth and learning which is now available. These findings show that we need to know better how to utilize and nurture the curiosity of pupils; how to encourage them to be questioners, to learn the techniques of finding answers to their questions, to relate what is to be learned to their present concerns so they can use it to improve their living; how to provide the personal support and understanding which releases their power to learn.

Adults must realize that they cannot impart their skill and wisdom to the young; they can only arrange those conditions which make it possible for each young learner to find his own. It is not enough for a teacher to know his subject; he must know how to help a child know.

How are the outcomes of team teaching evaluated?

One could be accused, perhaps with some justification, of reading the wrong reports of team teaching or of drawing too sweeping conclusions from them. For this reason, it is important to turn to the proof of the pudding—Dr. Anderson's summary of the outcomes of team teaching.

Dr. Anderson writes, "An immediate need . . . is to make certain that team teaching is not disadvantageous to children," and reports that "no data have as yet appeared in support of the fear

(expressed by critics) that some children will suffer emotionally or academically from team teaching."

If it turns out that the children aren't hurt, this is encouraging, but is it too much to expect that the results in learning will be markedly superior? And should we not ask that there be some valid evidence that it is beneficial to *most* children rather than be satisfied with some "slight indications" that it may be markedly beneficial to *some* children?

Many problems seem to be created by team teaching. Dr. Anderson reports: finding adequate time for planning and evaluation, communication, difficulties in and between teams, complex problems of human relations (could the establishment of two different levels of teaching status have anything to do with this?), difficulty in finding and training elementary school "subject area specialists," confusion in assuming leadership roles and in group process, the need for new buildings designed for team teaching or the remodeling of existing structures.

Should not the creation of problems so costly in human resources and perhaps in money be offset by quite superior learning outcomes?

It is disappointing to read in Dr. Anderson's summary that "standardized test results have been the chief yardstick in determining pupil achievement." The makers of achievement tests would be the first to say that standardized tests measure only a limited area of desired learning and this only to a limited degree.

What does this "new" organization produce in the way of power to do more and better thinking, to behave more creatively, to apply democratic values in problem situations, to become increasingly self-directing? How is evidence to be gathered regarding progress toward such goals of education as these?

The case studies by psychologists and trained observers of personality growth and pupil adjustment have indicated that results are no less satisfactory than in "typical conventional teaching in elementary and secondary schools." What data are there to show that the unmet emotional needs of children and youth are *better* met?

We have much to do in our schools to help the unmotivated children, those with ability they are unable to use, those who drop out as soon as the law permits, those for whom school is a meaningless and frequently damaging experience because they are culturally deprived and come from a cultural background so unlike that of their teachers. Again, one might ask, why create a new form (if it can be said to be new) unless it will serve a new or better function and make an impact on problems which have haunted humane teachers for many years?

Is it research in the area of organization we need?

Dr. Anderson states that "whatever pattern of organization we choose to adopt or continue, we must realize that the basic problems of instruction will remain to be solved. . . ."

It may be that the worst feature of our current preoccupation with organization, with moving children and teachers and subjects about, is that it diverts us from facing up to the hard task of improving teaching. Dr. Anderson writes that "all the evidence necessary to a final judgment (about the merits of team teaching) may require many years of further research."

Our obligation, he believes, is to keep an open mind, to see if this focus on organization will improve teaching. With all due respect to Dr. Anderson's superior experience in this matter, one must venture to question his advice regarding the open mind while further years of research in this area go on.

It might be more profitable, in the long run, to risk the danger of acquiring a reputation for having a closed mind and turn instead to areas of research more devoted to substance, less to form.

THE EDUCATION OF TEACHERS

Many an excellent teacher has learned his job by doing it. And some of those persons whose training has been more or less incidental have attained a high degree of skill, whether their instructional methods were arrived at by long and serious thought or by the avenue of trial, error, and accidental success.

Men have become skilled carpenters simply by sawing, planing, and driving nails into wood; they have learned their trade on the job. Similarly, many people have become first-rate teachers by trying to teach and by learning from their mistakes. There is this difference, however: Whereas wood is patient and does not protest, human nature isn't and does. The would-be carpenter merely spoils a lot of lumber, but the material spoiled by the self-taught teacher is not so expendable; the errors from which the latter apprentice learns can lead to serious complications—even to disaster.

The teacher's task becomes harder and calls for more education year by year. He must not only possess a mastery of his subject and modern methods of teaching it, he must also be a part-time psychologist; he must be able to adapt the work of the classroom to the pupil who does not like to study and to the pupil who is a slow learner—both of whom, fifty years ago, would have been out of school and at work as soon as they had completed the elementary grades, if not sooner. The teacher must also avoid the "colorless mean, too fast for the slow, too slow for the fast," and he must provide tasks that will call forth the best efforts of the brightest pupil in his class.

The principal or superintendent is now expected to be less a scholar than a skilled administrator, one who can interpret the functions and needs of the school to those in charge of municipal or state finances as well as to the parents of the pupils in his schools. The head of a school or college tends to be no longer like Paul Ansel Chadbourne, president of Williams College from 1872 to 1881, who, according to Bliss Perry, "once boasted to President Eliot that he could go into any classroom at Williams and conduct the recitation." (Perry adds, "Eliot was shocked.") Those principals and supervisors who still do classroom teaching, as they occasionally do in small centers, usually admit it with an apology which, if it does not actually imply that they feel demeaned by the task, usually contains some reference to teacher scarcity and overwork.

The teacher's work is steadily narrowing in scope with regard to subject matter taught and widening with regard to expertness in one particular subject. His responsibilities have also been immeasurably increased in recent years, since many matters heretofore considered the responsibility of the home and the church have tended to be shifted to the school, which is expected to give some attention to the pupil's physical and mental health and social adjustment as well as to furnish some vocational guidance and also to set up and supervise programs of extracurricular activities.

145

LEARNING THE TRADE OF A SCHOOLMASTER

It has for a long time been believed that teachers have a profound influence on the characters and personalities of their pupils. Even today this is likely to be readily assumed, on the basis of little or no considered evidence. If a survey were conducted to find out what proportion of pupils now in school wished to resemble their teachers in any way, the results might be surprising. One may even hazard the guess that a significant number would prefer to be as unlike their teachers as possible.

Yet the public, by and large, expects the teacher to be a personification of all the negative virtues to which it gives lip service even though it may not practice them. A parent who swears like the proverbial pirate, at home and elsewhere, will complain to the school board or superintendent if his son's teacher has somewhere been heard to utter even a mild expletive. This attitude has a long history. A good many documents exist attesting to the degree and type of religious orthodoxy expected of teachers, the moral code they have been expected to follow, even the dress and manners prescribed for them. These matters seem to have been insisted on in great detail long before intellectual and scholarly attainments were even mentioned. As for knowledge of *how* to teach a subject, that has only recently been regarded as a qualification as essential as beliefs and behavior.

For centuries one who could read, write, and cipher a little was presumed to be able to teach children to do the same. He might safely be hired to do so, if there were no more lucrative or important jobs available for him. Hence the apprenticing of a boy for ten years to a practicing teacher in the eighteenth century represents an early attempt at teacher training.

Registered for Mr. George Brownell Schoolmaster ye 18th day of July 1722.

This Indenture Wittnesseth that John Campbel Son of Robert Campbell of the City of New York with the Consent of his father and mother hath put himself and by these presents doth Voluntarily put and bind himself Apprentice to George Brownell of the Same City Schoolmaster to learn the Art Trade or Mystery and with the Said George Brownell to Serve from the twenty ninth day of May one thousand seven hundred and twenty one for and during the Term of ten years and three Months to be Compleat and Ended During all which term the said Apprentice his said Master and Mistress faithfully Shall Serve their Secrets keep and Lawfull Commands gladly everywhere obey he Shall do no damage to his said Master or Mistress nor suffer it to be done by others without Letting or Giving Notice thereof to his

From *Citty of N. Yorke Indentures*, 1694-1727, pp. 145-147.

said Master or Mistress he shall not Waste his said Master or Mistress Goods or Lend them Unlawfully to any he shall not Committ fornication nor Contract Matrimony within the Said Term at Cards Dice or any other unlawfull Game he shall not Play: he Shall not absent himself by Day or by Night from his Said Master or Mistress Service without their Leave; nor haunt Alehouses Taverns or Playhouses but in all things behave himself as a faithfull Apprentice ought to Do towards his said Master or Mistress during the Said Term. And the said George Brownell Doth hereby Covenant and Promise to teach and Instruct or Cause the said Apprentice to be taught and Instructed in the Art Trade or Calling of a Schoolmaster by the best way or means he or his wife may or can if the Said Apprentice be Capable to Learn and to find and Provide unto the Said Apprentice sufficient meat Drink Apparel Lodging and washing fitting for an Apprentice during the Said

Term: and at the Expiration thereof to give unto the Said Apprentice one Suit of Cloth new Consisting of a coatvest coat and Breeches also one New hatt Six New Shirts Three pair of Stockings one pair of New Shoes Suitable for his said Apprentice. In Testimony Whereof the Parties to these Presents have hereunto Interchangeably Sett their hands and Seals the third day of August in the Eighth year of the Reign of our Sovereign Lord George King of Great Brittain &c. Anno Domini One thousand seven hundred and Twenty-One. John Campbel. Signed Sealed and Delivered in the presence of Mary Smith Cornelius Kiersted Memorandum Appeared before me John Cruger Esq. Alderman and One of his Majesties Justices of the Peace for this City and County. John Campbell and Acknowledged the within Indenture to be his Voluntary Act and Deed New York the 9th Aprill 1722.

John Cruger.

146

TEACHING HOW TO TEACH

The need for courses in the art and science of teaching was recognized by the German universities in the first part of the nineteenth century. The first professorships of education in America, however, were established considerably later. Though claims of "firsts" in American education have many times been advanced to be upset later, it is currently believed that the first professor of education in an American university was William H. Payne, who was appointed at the University of Michigan in 1879. The editorial which follows appeared in *Harper's Weekly* at that time.

State normal schools for the training of elementary teachers had already been established in many states, beginning with Massachusetts in 1839. But the growth of secondary education, both in interest and depth, had called for teachers with more information than they could acquire in two years at a normal school. The educational casualties resulting from the employment of young bachelors of arts fresh out of college, who were forced to learn their job while doing it, caused a good deal of heart-searching among the universities. Thus the first professors of education were appointed to the faculties of some American and Scottish universities at about the same time. Their appearance aroused mixed feeling at the time, traces of which are not difficult to detect even now.

The University of Michigan is one of the most progressive as well as efficient of our great schools of learning, and adapts itself with singular facility

From *Harper's Weekly*, July 26, 1879, p. 583.

to the situation in a rapidly developing country. It was, we believe, the first of our larger universities to adopt the elective system of study, and its spirit has been always hospitable and generous. The most striking fact in its recent annals is the establishment of a chair of the history, theory, and art of education. The value of such a chair is seen at once from the fact that the public schools of Michigan generally fall under the control of the graduates of the university. The State Normal School is engaged in the same general work, but upon another plane. In a society like ours, whose security depends upon educated intelligence, there is no more important function and service than that of teaching the teachers. The art of the teacher is that of effectively communicating knowledge. But this can be taught, like every art and science, only by those who are especially fitted for the work; and the University of Michigan is fortunate in finding for its new chair apparently the very man to fill it.

The authorities of the university have invited to the new professorship the late Superintendent of the Public Schools of Adrian, Professor Payne. He has been twenty-one years continuously in the public school service of the State, and his admirable influence has been gladly and generally acknowledged. But his efficient administration has only deepened his interest in the philosophic principles of his profession, and his views were fully set forth in a course of lectures delivered last year in the Normal Department of Adrian College, which have commanded the interested attention of "educators" as an admirable exposition of the subject. He is now called to the first chair of the kind established in this country, and the University of Michigan again justifies its position as the head of the educational system of the State.

This action will promote the highest interests of education, not only by tempting future teachers to the training of the university, but by apprising the public that teaching is itself an art, and that the knowledge how to teach may make all the difference between school money well or uselessly spent in the community. Both the educational and charitable systems of Michigan have an enviable reputation, and the good example again set by its university will be doubtless heeded and followed elsewhere.

147

Samuel Read Hall

QUALIFICATIONS OF AN INSTRUCTOR

The first institution in America for the preparation of teachers was a private normal school established in 1823 in Concord, a small village in upstate Vermont. The founder and director of this school was the Reverend Samuel Read Hall, a Congregational minister. Hall's students evidently became successful teachers: they were in demand throughout New England and the neighboring states.

Hall's lectures delivered in his normal school were published in 1829 in a book known as *Hall's Lectures on School-keeping*. Though other books on education had already been published in America, this appears to have been the first to gain a really wide circulation. Because it endeavored to answer the questions that inexperienced teachers were eager to ask, it rapidly became popular. It might almost be called the first educational "best seller."

Though the author's style may seem a trifle formal and stilted today, the book contains a great deal of practical advice, particularly valuable for the young teacher. The selection reprinted here, listing the qualities desirable in a teacher, reflects Hall's native shrewdness, his knowledge of teaching, his common sense, and a remarkable degree of psychological insight.

. . . I shall, in this, call your attention to *the requisite qualifications of an instructer*. The subject is one of high importance. It is not every one of those, even, who possesses the requisite literary attainments, who is qualified to assume the direction of a school. Many entirely fail of usefulness, though possessed of highly culti-vated minds. Other ingredients enter into the composition of a good schoolmaster. Among these *common sense* is the first. This is a qualification exceedingly important, as in teaching school one has constant occasion for its exercise. Many, by no means deficient in intellect, are not persons of common sense. I mean by the term, that faculty by which things are seen as they are. It implies judgment and discrimination, and a proper sense of propriety in regard to the common affairs of life. It leads us to form judicious plans of action, and to be governed by our circumstances, in such a way as men in general will approve. It is the exercise of reason, uninfluenced by passion or prejudice. It is in man nearly what instinct is in brutes. It is very different from genius or talent, as they are commonly defined, but is better than either. It never blazes forth with the splen-dour of noon, but shines with a constant and useful light.

2. *Uniformity of temper* is another important trait in the character of an instructer. Where this is wanting, it is hardly possible to govern or teach with success. He, whose temper is constantly varying, can never be uniform in his estimation of things around him. Objects change in their appearance as passions change. What appears right in any given hour may seem wrong in the next. What appears desirable to-day, may be held with aversion to-morrow. An uneven temper, in any situation of life, subjects one to many incon-veniences. But when placed in a situation where his every action is observed, and where his author-ity must be in constant exercise, the man who labours under this malady is especially unfortu-nate. It is impossible for him to gain and preserve respect among his pupils. No one who comes under the rule of a person of uneven temper, can know what to expect or how to act.

3. A capacity to *understand and discriminate character,* is highly important in him who engages in school-keeping. The dispositions of children are so various, the treatment and government of parents so dissimilar, that the most diversified modes of governing and teaching need to be em-ployed. The instructer who is not able to dis-criminate, but considers all alike, and treats all alike, does injury to many. The least expression of disapprobation to one, is often more than the severest reproof to another; a word of encourage-ment will be sufficient to excite attention in some, while another will require to be urged, by every motive that can be placed before him. All the

From *Hall's Lectures on School-keeping*, Arthur D. Wright and George E. Gardner, eds. (Hanover, N.H.: The Dartmouth Press, 1929), pp. 65-68.

varying shades of disposition and capacity should be quickly learned by the instructer, that he may benefit all and do injustice to none. Without this, well meant efforts may prove hurtful, be-cause ill-directed, and the desired object may be defeated, by the very means used to obtain it.

4. It is desirable that teachers should possess much *decision of character*. In every situation of life this trait is important, but in none more so than in that of which I am treating. The little world, by which he is surrounded, is the minia-ture of the older community. Children have their aversions and partialities, their hopes and fears, their plans, schemes, propensities and desires. These are often in collision with each other, and not unfrequently in collision with the laws of the school, and in opposition to their own best interest. Amidst all these, the instructer should be able to pursue a uniform course. He ought not to be easily swayed from what he considers right. If he be easily led from his purpose, or in-duced to vary from established rules, his school must become a scene of disorder. Without de-cision, the teacher loses the confidence and re-spect of his pupils. I would not say, that, if convinced of having committed an error, or of having given a wrong judgment, you should persist in the wrong. But I would say, that it should be known as one of your first principles in school-keeping, that what is required must be complied with in every case, unless cause can be shown why the rule ought, in a given instance, to be dispensed with. There should *then* be a frank confession of error. In a word, without decision of purpose in a teacher, his scholars can never be brought under that discipline, which is requi-site for his own ease and convenience, or for their improvement in knowledge.

5. A schoolmaster ought to be *affectionate*. The human heart is so constituted, that it cannot resist the influence of kindness. When affectionate intercourse is the offspring of those kind feelings which arise from true benevolence, it will have an influence on all around. It leads to ease in behaviour, and genuine politeness of manners. It is especially desirable in those who are sur-rounded by the young. Affectionate parents usu-ally see their children exhibit similar feelings. Instructers, who cultivate this state of temper, will generally excite the same in their scholars. No object is more important than to gain the love and good will of those who are to teach. In no way is this more easily accomplished than by a kind interest manifested in their welfare; an interest which is exhibited by actions as well as words. This cannot fail of being attended with desirable results.

6. A just *moral discernment,* is of pre-eminent importance in the character of an instructer. Unless governed by a consideration of his moral obligation, he is but poorly qualified to discharge the duties which devolve upon him, when placed at the head of a school. He is himself a moral agent, and accountable to himself, to his employers, to his country and to his God, for the faithful discharge of duty. If he have no moral sensibility, no fear of disobeying the laws of God, no regard for the institutions of our holy religion, how can he be expected to lead his pupils in the way that they should go? The cultivation of virtuous propensities is more important to children than even their intellectual culture. The *virtuous* man, though illiterate, will be happy, while the learned, if *vicious,* must be miserable in proportion to his attainments. The remark of the ancient philosopher, that "boys ought to be taught that which they will most need to practise when they come to be men," is most true. To cultivate virtuous habits, and awaken virtuous principles; —to excite a sense of duty to God, and of dependence on Him, should be the first objects of the teacher. If he permits his scholars to indulge in vicious habits—if he regard nothing as sin, but that which is a transgression of the laws of the school, if he suffer lying, profaneness, or other crimes, to pass unnoticed and unpunished, he is doing an injury for which he can in no way make amends. An instructer without moral feeling, not only brings ruin to the children placed under his care, but does injury to their parents, to the neighbourhood, to the town, and, doubtless, to other generations. The moral character of instructers should be considered a subject of very high importance; and let every one, who knows himself to be immoral, renounce at once the thought of such an employment, while he continues to disregard the laws of God, and the happiness of his fellow men. Genuine piety is highly desirable in every one entrusted with the care and instruction of the young; but morality, at least, should be *required,* in every candidate for that important trust. . . .

148

Calvin E. Stowe

OBSERVATIONS ON WOMEN AS ELEMENTARY TEACHERS

Around the middle of the nineteenth century a number of influential reports on European education were published in the United States. Individual states were beginning to establish their systems of public education, and educational leaders looked to Europe for ideas. Probably the most influential report was that of the Frenchman, Victor Cousin, on German—more particularly Prussian— education which appeared in 1831. This was soon translated and published in both England and America. Much in the reports of such Americans as John Griscom, Calvin E. Stowe, Alexander Dallas Bache, and even Horace Mann appears to have been to some degree inspired by, if not actually based on, Cousin's report.

The following brief passage on women as elementary teachers was undoubtedly significant in its day. It is easy to forget at present, when a sizable majority of the elementary teachers in America are women, that teaching was for a long time regarded as essentially a task for men. Some even regarded Paul's admonition to Timothy about "permitting a woman to teach" as a prohibition that allowed no question of its rightness.

Though the "Dame School" with its elderly teacher could be found early in Colonial America, most of the teachers of boys and girls approaching (or in) their teens were men. It is of interest that Stowe, in his report to the Ohio Legislature in 1837, found it necessary to justify the employment of women as teachers in the elementary schools.

. . . Indeed, such is the state of things in this country, that we cannot expect to find male teachers for all our schools. The business of educating, especially young children, must fall, to a great extent, on female teachers. There is not the same variety of tempting employment for females as for men, they can be supported cheaper, and the Creator has given them peculiar qualifications for the education of the young. Females, then, ought to be employed extensively in all our elementary schools, and they should be encouraged

and aided in obtaining the qualifications necessary for this work. There is no country in the world where woman holds so high a rank, or exerts so great an influence, as here; wherefore, her responsibilities are the greater, and she is under obligations to render herself the more actively useful. I think our fair countrywomen, notwithstanding the exhortations of Harriet Martineau, Fanny Wright, and some other *ladies* and *gentlemen*, will never seek distinction in our public assemblies for public discussion, or in our halls of legislation; but in their appropriate work of educating the young, of forming the opening mind to all that is good and great, the more they distinguish themselves the better.

From *Reports on European Education,* Edgar W. Knight, ed. (New York: McGraw-Hill Book Co., Inc., 1930), p. 311.

149

Paul Woodring

THE TEACHERS COLLEGE IN AMERICA

American teachers have been trained in normal schools, state teachers colleges, and state colleges as well as in other colleges and universities. The majority of them are today trained in state colleges, most of which were a few years ago known as state teachers colleges. These institutions have, particularly in the past two decades, come under a great deal of criticism, much of which is ill-founded and even grossly unfair.

Young people who consider going into teaching need to have a clear idea of the training offered; it is important for them to be able to distinguish fact from fiction both in educational publications and in the articles on the schools that appear frequently in magazines of general circulation. Some of the latter may be rightly described as sensational.

Mr. Paul Woodring is a teacher of teachers who writes from long experience. His volume *Let's Talk Sense About Our Schools* lives up to its title. He knows American teacher-training institutions; he recognizes their faults as well as their strong points. His chapter on the teachers college in America was written in 1953; consequently the salaries he quotes would need to be increased somewhat to bring his discussion into line with present-day conditions. Otherwise, the chapter gives a fair and informative account of teacher education in the United States today.

If all institutions of higher learning were ranked in terms of prestige, it seems likely that the teachers college would find itself low man

on the educational totem pole. Yet this much-maligned and frequently ridiculed institution probably exerts more influence upon the American scene than does any other type of college; for if the graduate of the teachers college is badly educated, the children in the public schools, and eventually the American people, will be badly educated. And there is reason to question whether

From *Let's Talk Sense About Our Schools* by Paul Woodring, pp. 70-87. Copyright 1953 by the McGraw-Hill Book Co., Inc. and reprinted by their permission.

a nation of badly educated men and women can permanently maintain its free institutions.

If liberally educated and thoughtful Americans are dubious about the way in which the teachers college is doing its work, it is not enough that they regard it with scorn. They must examine it carefully; they must become familiar with the facts—not with the facts of 1920 but with the facts of 1953—and with the direction being taken, which will tell something of the teachers college of the future.

The facts are somewhat obscured by the substantial differences which exist among the teachers colleges in the various states and the equally great differences which exist among liberal arts colleges. The observer or the critic is likely to form his generalizations on the basis of the teachers colleges as he sees them in his own section of the country. A conspicuous example of this fallacy was found in the widely read article "Who Teaches the Teachers" under the pseudonym of John William Sperry, which appeared in *Life's* famous education issue of October 16, 1950.

Mr. Sperry says, "Teachers' Colleges usually do not have equipment, buildings, or campuses comparable to those of liberal arts colleges or universities. Several teachers' colleges I saw looked more like grammar schools than colleges . . . a great many of the teachers' colleges bring an inferior faculty and an inferior student body together in an inferior physical plant." And farther on in the article Mr. Sperry makes the flat statement, "All were distinctly inferior to *every* liberal arts college or university I have ever seen." (The italics are mine.)

Now this covers a lot of ground—or perhaps it suggests that Mr. Sperry had *not* covered much ground. It appears that he formed his judgments on the basis of a few colleges on the East Coast. He does say that he had visited some teachers colleges in the Middle West and the South, but one is forced to conclude that he thinks of western Pennsylvania as the Middle West, for surely he did not get as far as Ohio where he would have found that the state teachers colleges—now called universities—at Bowling Green and Kent have physical plants far superior to those of most of the numerous private liberal arts colleges in that state.

The American teachers college is, in its most important development, a phenomenon of the Middle West and the Far West. Along the Eastern seaboard, where the liberal arts college was well entrenched before the teachers college got its start, the newer institution has in many states remained a neglected school with inadequate facilities, downtrodden faculties, a student body consisting all too often of those who could not gain admittance to the more selective colleges of liberal arts.

But west of the Alleghenies the teachers college is frequently a very different type of institution, and so, in many cases, is the college of liberal arts.

What is a teachers college? At first glance it might seem obvious that a teachers college is any college which prepares teachers. But what are we to say when we find that there are a great many so-called "liberal arts" colleges half or more of whose graduates enter the teaching profession and when we find many institutions called teachers colleges, fewer than half of whose students have any intention of entering that profession? Many of our state teachers colleges offer a liberal arts course or a general education course for those who prefer not to become teachers and the number is increasing yearly.

The student who does plan to teach finds that the course of study laid out for him is very much the same whether he enrolls in an institution calling itself a liberal arts college or one which is called a teachers college. In either case about three-fourths of his work will be in academic areas, including English, social studies, natural sciences, and fine arts. The other one-fourth will consist of courses in the philosophy and the methodology of education and in practice teaching. If he plans to become a high-school teacher, the proportion of his time devoted to academic work will be somewhat higher regardless of the type of institution in which he enrolls, and if he plans to teach in the lower grades a larger part of his time will be devoted to methods and to practice teaching. If he happens to study in one of the few states which have the General Certificate—the certificate which purports to represent preparation for teaching at all levels—there will be no such distinction.

The fact is that in those states west of Pennsylvania the difference between the teachers college and the college of liberal arts has all but disappeared. The proof of this statement does not require an elaborate survey. It is true that an accurate evaluation of the true merits of any college is difficult if not impossible, but the kind of superficial facts about physical plants mentioned in Mr. Sperry's article can be gathered for all colleges without moving out of one's library. An excellent source is the volume *American Colleges and Universities*, published by the American Council on Education. Let us take a look at some of the measurable facts as given in the latest edition published in 1952.

I begin by looking up the facts of my own college, Western Washington College of Education in Bellingham, Washington. I find that the plant and equipment are valued at eight million dollars. This figure exceeds that given for such well-known liberal arts colleges as Amherst, Colgate, Hamilton, Barnard, Swarthmore, Antioch, and Santa Clara, each of which is comparable to the Bellingham institution in enrollment.

And Western Washington's facilities are not greatly different from those found at many other colleges of education throughout the states from Ohio westward. The State Teachers College at Terre Haute, Indiana, has a plant valued at ten million dollars. There are dozens of liberal arts colleges with equipment valued at less than one-tenth that amount. Iowa State Teachers College at Cedar Falls has a plant valued at six million, Michigan State Normal College at Ypsilanti over eleven million, and there are comparable plants in teachers colleges from Michigan to California. But these figures should be adequate to establish the fact that the inferiority of the teachers college, if such inferiority exists, cannot be attributed to poor buildings and facilities.

Faculties are another matter—and obviously the most important matter in judging the quality of a college. Unfortunately there is no satisfactory measure of the quality of a faculty. We can count doctoral degrees, academic honors, and publications, but no one believes that these are a completely valid index of quality of teaching.

Mr. Sperry, in his effort to evaluate the teaching in teachers colleges, rather naïvely resorted to the technique of asking the opinion of professors at liberal arts colleges. This is naïve because it overlooks the unhappy fact that the two types of institutions are currently engaged in a bitter competition for public support and for the more able students. Asking an Amherst professor for his opinion of a teachers college professor is roughly comparable to asking a Marine Corps colonel for his opinion of the faculty at West Point.

It seems reasonable to assume that in the long run the most able college teachers will find their way to those colleges which offer the greatest rewards. The rewards sought by American college professors are of many kinds; they include such things as prestige, the opportunity to live in a community of scholars where the interchange of ideas and the battle of wits will stimulate continued intellectual growth, the opportunity to work with able students, intellectual freedom, and, by no means least, the opportunity to enjoy the advantages of living in the world's wealthiest nation. These advantages are not fully available to one living on a minimum income, and so the professor, for all his interest in ideas, is con-

cerned just as is the engineer, the physician, the clerk, or the shoemaker with increasing his income. Other things being equal he will, in time, find his way to the college which pays the best salary for his services.

The colleges which compete most vigorously for the professors who are teachers rather than research experts are the small liberal arts colleges and the teachers colleges. How well able are the teachers colleges to meet the competition?

It is not true that the average salaries paid to faculty members of teachers colleges throughout the United States are lower than the average paid by liberal arts colleges if we exclude a dozen private liberal arts colleges having exceptional endowments. A college, whether it be a teachers college or a college of liberal arts, can, in 1953, secure the services of a reasonably competent young teacher for four or five thousand dollars. For ten thousand a year it can get the very best professor available, not a nonteaching celebrity such as is sometimes used as window dressing by the private college but a real teacher, broad in outlook, brilliant, scholarly, skillful at making difficult ideas understandable, and capable of providing the human environment in which a confused adolescent can grow into an intellectually and emotionally mature adult.

A ten-thousand-dollar salary may not seem excessive to the businessman or to the man who has succeeded in another profession, but there is not a single teachers college in the United States, other than the graduate schools attached to universities, which offers such a salary to even its greatest teacher. The reason is not hard to find. A college will receive only minor criticism and much admiration for spending an extra hundred thousand dollars for nonfunctional Gothic decorations for the library, while it will receive far more criticism than approval if it spends one-tenth that amount for a professor's salary. A good building is impressive. A good professor usually looks pretty unimpressive to the average citizen.

The remarkable fact is that some superb teachers remain on the faculties of the teachers colleges despite the salaries. Thousands of teachers in Ohio will agree that the late Clayton C. Kohl of Bowling Green State Normal (now Bowling Green State University) was such a man. Only students have any real basis for judging a teacher, and I speak as one of Dr. Kohl's students. Though I have since attended some famous universities, I have known no one who could compare with Kohl as a teacher. So far as I know he never wrote a book. His skills were those of imparting great ideas orally, and he devoted all his time to teaching and to preparing himself to teach. His influence, through the thousands of teachers whom he taught, has left its mark on more than a full generation of Ohio school children and adolescents. Certainly his influence in northern Ohio was far greater than that of any physician, lawyer, or engineer in that area. I doubt if his salary ever exceeded six or seven thousand dollars a year. It is no exaggeration to say that he was worth a million.

But for every Kohl there are dozens of potential Kohls who are more ambitious for the things money can buy. They teach briefly in a small college and then move on to more remunerative work. Within recent years many of them have gone into the various types of government work available to academic people. If they join a university staff, they quickly find that it is writing and not teaching that pays. In an effort to gain promotion they neglect their teaching and become second-rate writers of semischolarly tomes and unread journal articles.

So it may well be true, as Mr. Sperry suggests, that the poor faculties which he reports finding in many of the teachers colleges are in part the result of inadequate salaries. But when a teachers college professor leaves his position for one which is better paid, he moves, in most cases, not to a liberal arts college but to a state college or state university. In many a western state the teachers colleges can successfully compete with salaries paid by private colleges, but their salaries are still distinctly lower than those paid to professors of engineering, law, agriculture, and dentistry at the state university. The citizen who wishes to improve the teachers colleges and who pays all the salaries through taxation may reasonably ask why.

If your state legislature provides, as it almost certainly does, higher salaries for the professor of animal husbandry at the state agricultural college than for the professor in the teachers college, it appears that the pedigreed bull is held in higher regard than is the human child. Such a contemptuous attitude toward children and toward their teachers may reasonably make the teacher cynical about the citizens' groups which profess to have as their aim the advancement of the schools, for I have yet to hear of any such group which has called the attention of the legislatures to this discrepancy.

Even if we are to conclude that the physical plants of our teachers colleges are already good in many sections of the country and are rapidly improving elsewhere, and if we are to conclude that the salaries are at least as good as those paid by many small private colleges, it by no mean follows that all is well with the colleges of education. They have some very serious deficiencies, weaknesses which are all the more serious because they are not apparent to the casual observer and cannot be detected through the reading of catalogues or the blue book of colleges.

The teachers college—and this is true whether it exists as a separate institution or as part of a university—is in all too many cases a house divided against itself. On the one hand is the teacher-training division which supervises the practice teaching and which may or may not include the department of education—usually it does. On the other hand is the group of departments which is primarily concerned with what the first division scornfully refers to as "subject matter."

An outsider might reasonably expect to find these two groups working in harmony. He might expect that those who deal with the skills, the techniques, and the procedures of teaching would feel great need for subject-matter departments and that the academic departments would understand the need for and recognize the importance of the aspects of teacher education with which the other group is most concerned. But anyone who has taught in a college of education or has been a student in such a college can report that such an expectation is naïve, to say the least.

Almost any academic professor will tell you, if you promise not to quote him, that those in the teacher training division are trying to run the school, that they demand far too large a portion of the curriculum for themselves, that they waste too much time in needless repetition of educational clichés; if he gets really warmed up—as he probably will—he will add that the "educators" are intellectually inferior anyway.

The director of teacher training, or any member of his staff, is likely to say, again with assurance that he will not be quoted, that his biggest problem is the "subject-matter mindedness" of the academic professors. He will assure you that they know nothing of the realities of dealing with children and with practical school problems, that they consider facts more important than children, that they allow far too little room in the curriculum for practice teaching and for the learning of educational procedures; if he gets really warmed up—as he undoubtedly will—he will state that the "academicians" are a lot of vague theorists and stuffed shirts.

Viewed at a distance this schism is so fantastic as to be humorous, but from the standpoint of the student learning to become a teacher it is tragic. It leaves the student torn, confused, and troubled. It very seriously interferes with the proper functioning of the college. And this schism is even worse in the university or the liberal arts college which has a department of education than it is in the separate teachers college.

In fairness it should be said that there are a few teachers colleges in which this problem has been reduced somewhat in recent years, largely by the selection, over a period of time, of faculty members from both sides of the barrier who are sufficiently broad in their understandings to avoid such pettiness and who are sufficiently self-confident to avoid the defensiveness which has led to the schism. But for each such institution there are a dozen in which the two groups are almost incapable of talking the same language professionally.

The schism which we have been discussing is based, in part, upon a fundamental conflict of philosophies. Many of our professors in the academic departments have come through liberal arts colleges and graduate schools of the large universities. The large university, and this is particularly true of the state university, usually holds to no consistent philosophy; often different philosophical assumptions are made by each department. The small liberal arts college frequently bases its teaching upon a firmer and more consistent philosophic foundation. In some schools this foundation is frankly theological, the theology being that of the church which supports the college. In many other private colleges, less closely associated with a specific religious denomination, the philosophical basis is some variety of idealism, often with a humanistic bent.

In sharp contrast, the philosophy of the teachers colleges has come almost exclusively to be the type of pragmatism which Dewey calls instrumentalism or experimentalism. These schools base their procedures upon the assumptions that pragmatism has replaced other philosophies, that all other philosophies are outmoded. Yet such assumptions are totally unacceptable to the graduates of most liberal arts colleges and to a very considerable proportion of informed people everywhere.

Liberal arts graduates usually hold that education is a means to an end, though they may not entirely agree among themselves as to just what the ends are. But at least they will agree that mastery of subject matter is important.

Educators, on the contrary, agree with Dewey that "the educational process has no end beyond itself; it is its own end." "There is nothing to which growth is relative save more growth, there is nothing to which education is subordinate save more education," and further "education is all one with growing; it has no end beyond itself"

(*Democracy and Education,* The Macmillan Company, New York, 1916, pp. 59-62).

Moreover the philosophy of the teachers college as represented by the educators is that education is a total process and that the schools must accept the major responsibility for this process. The school must concern itself with the child's health, his recreation, his character, his citizenship, his emotional development, his social adjustment, his vocational training, and his intellectual development. The teachers college is unwilling to concede that any one of these concerns is more important than the others because it considers any separation to be impossible. This point of view is consistent with and an outgrowth of the philosophy of pragmatism.

The attitude toward teaching which is held by the liberal arts college, on the other hand, was well stated by Charles A. Beard (writing in *School and Society,* Vol. 43, pp. 278-279, Feb. 29, 1936):

"The teacher is not a physician, a nurse, a soldier, a policeman, a politician, a businessman, a farmer, or an industrial worker. . . . The teacher's principle business is the training of minds and the dissemination of knowledge . . . the teacher is another kind of person with other duties and other responsibilities—the duty and responsibilities of the scholar."

It is obvious that these two conceptions of the role of the teachers are totally at variance, and there appears to be no real compromise or midpoint between them. Yet in most of the schools which prepare teachers half the faculty holds firmly to one point of view while the other half holds with equal firmness to the other. It is small wonder that the teacher graduating from such a college is confused.

Though no immediate solution to this conflict is apparent the explanation for the schism may be found in the history of teacher education.

Prior to about 1920, high-school teachers and teachers for the elementary school were rarely educated in the same institutions. Most high schools recruited their teachers from universities or liberal arts colleges while the elementary teachers came from the normal schools.

The normal schools had their origin in New England. A private normal was opened at Concord, Vermont, in 1823, but it was Massachusetts which in 1839 established the first state-supported normal school at Lexington. Similar institutions were established in Connecticut in 1850 and in Rhode Island in 1852. Several Middle Western states followed suit prior to the Civil War, and after the war the movement spread rapidly until 1900 when all but a very few of the states in the Union were maintaining state normal schools. But these early normal schools bore little resemblance to anything which can properly be called higher education. Most of them accepted students directly from the elementary schools, and they were essentially high schools with some added work of a more or less professional nature.

After 1900, normal schools gradually increased their entrance requirements, for with the growth of public high schools it was no longer necessary for the normal school to provide secondary instruction. But as recently as 1920—and in many states much more recently—the commonly accepted standard for elementary teachers was one or two years of normal school beyond high school, and a great many rural and village teachers entered the profession with one summer term of normal-school preparation.

It is obvious that even during the early years of the present century these normal schools were not colleges. Most of them offered little or no subject matter at a college level. Their courses were of a so-called "practical" nature. Catalogues listed such subjects as School Management and Discipline, School Hygiene, Child Study, and Practical Pedagogy. Such academic work as was included was designed to reinforce the prospective teachers' knowledge of elementary-school subjects. Consequently the normal schools were in no way qualified to prepare teachers for the high schools or academies.

The development of the normal school into a teachers college or a college of education occurred during the period from about 1925 to 1940, and it was not until that period that the state normal began seriously to compete with the private liberal arts college in the preparation of teachers for secondary schools.

When the state normal schools were first established they gave no thought to the training of teachers for the high schools for the obvious reason that there were almost no high schools. There were, to be sure, academies or prep schools but these were preoccupied with the preparation of students for the colleges, usually one specific college, and it seemed natural that a school which prepared for, let us say, Princeton should get its faculty from among the graduates of that college.

But with the development of the public high school which followed the Civil War and continued at a much faster pace after the turn of the century, the preparation of high-school teachers became of paramount importance. Though a liberal arts degree was considered the proper preparation for teachers in secondary schools, many high-school

administrators felt that their teachers could profit from some courses in pedagogy, and a few colleges and universities gave thought to the problem.

A chair in the philosophy of education had been established at the University of the City of New York (now New York University) in 1832. In 1853 the subject of pedagogy was introduced at Antioch College by Horace Mann, and by 1880 several other colleges and universities had followed suit. The movement spread rapidly, and by 1900 some 200 colleges and universities included education among their offerings.

But it would be erroneous to assume that pedagogy, or education as it came to be called, was accepted as a legitimate subject of study at the college level. The prevailing opinion was that teaching called for no special preparation, that the teacher needed only to know his subject thoroughly and to have a modicum of common sense. The professor of pedagogy was looked upon by his academic peers as an excrescence on the face of the community of scholars. He was scorned, humiliated, and ridiculed. In some institutions only a few daring students risked taking his elective courses, and the makers of collegiate curriculums rarely required such courses even of those who were planning to teach. In many colleges and universities more than a trace of this attitude persists to the present day. If those professional educators who have recently come to positions of great power occasionally show a touch of arrogance toward their academic associates, their attitude may be only a very natural compensation for their earlier humiliations.

The position of the professional educator in the normal school was very different from that of his brother in the college or university; in the normal school his field was considered to be one of prime importance. It was natural that many of the most competent teachers of education courses found their way to the normal schools rather than to the universities.

Though a few teachers colleges came into existence prior to World War I, the development of the normal school into the teachers college has, in most states, been a phenomenon of the past thirty years. During the 1920s normal schools in several states changed their names to teachers colleges or colleges of education, extended their courses to four years, and began granting college degrees. The movement spread during the succeeding two decades until by 1950 the state normal school had all but become a thing of the past. It is a curious commentary that in many a community this change seems to have come about without much public awareness; one frequently hears these schools referred to as "the normal" even in cities in which there has been no normal school for twenty years.

The change has by no means been in name only because the teachers college of 1953 bears little resemblance to the normal school of 1920. The faculty of the normal school of thirty years ago consisted largely of the more successful teachers and county superintendents of the region who had been called in to instruct prospective teachers. Some of the faculty members were college graduates, but many were graduates of other normal schools and held no college degrees. Only a very few had completed any graduate work in a university, and a doctoral degree was so rare as to be a subject for comment. Today the picture is very different. All, or very nearly all, of the present-day faculty members hold masters' degrees, and from one-fourth to one-third, in a few cases as many as one-half, hold doctoral degrees.

The subject matter taught consisted largely of educational methods, educational philosophy and history, a few lower-level college courses, and a review of the elementary subjects. Handwriting and spelling were commonly included among the offerings.

The teachers college of today offers a full four-year sequence of collegiate courses. Strictly professional courses usually account for about one-fourth of the curriculum, but all the other offerings are so nearly identical with those found in liberal arts colleges and universities that a student usually experiences no difficulty in transferring to such a school without loss of credit.

In a great many cases the teachers college of 1953 offers a general or liberal arts degree, and many offer the master's degree in education as well.

This extraordinarily rapid development of the normal school into the teachers college has not been accomplished without difficulty, confusion, and turmoil. If the teachers college has become a house divided against itself, as has been suggested, the division has been a consequence of rapid expansion and the resultant appointment of faculty members who propounded conflicting educational philosophies. For as the normal school became a college it became necessary for it to add to its academic staff. The county superintendents and experienced elementary teachers who made up its faculty in 1920 were not prepared to teach collegiate courses at the upper-division level, nor in many cases were they interested in doing so. A few of them hied themselves to the universities for additional graduate work. Those who did went most often to Columbia's Teachers College, for it was this institution which was most sympathetic with their problems.

It was this institution also which offered masters' degrees without the formal requirement of oral examinations or a thesis, and it was these hurdles which were most awesome or which seemed most unreasonable to the older normal-school instructors, who after years of teaching elementary subjects found it necessary to compete with younger graduate students. Moreover Columbia's Teachers College had a way of convincing you that you really learned more about teaching within its halls than you would have learned in a graduate school with the customary graduate degree requirements. Here the student could sit at the feet of Dewey, Kilpatrick, and a host of lesser celebrities. Perhaps not quite at their feet because the class might number four or five hundred and you might find yourself in the back row where you could see little and hear less, but at least you could say you had had a course from the great men while others had only read their books.

So teachers from the normal schools came to Columbia by the thousands. Even so there were not enough to fill the swelling faculties of the new teachers colleges, particularly in the academic fields.

These teachers had to be recruited from other graduate schools. Many of these newcomers had not taught in the elementary and high schools nor were they particularly interested in public school teaching. They were interested primarily in their specialties, in history, physics, literature, or mathematics. They accepted positions in the teachers colleges because collegiate teaching positions were not plentiful and the teachers colleges, though their salaries were not spectacular, frequently offered more than that paid to the lowest ranks at the universities. Even today many a teachers college can, and must, offer the new doctor of philosophy four thousand dollars a year or more with an assistant professorship when the best the same candidate is offered at the largest universities is an instructorship at perhaps thirty-six hundred dollars.

These new recruits from the graduate schools brought to the teachers colleges a new level of scholarship. They brought also many of the prejudices of their university professors regarding educators and education. In the university it had been the custom to speak scornfully of education and to think of education as something with which the college professor has nothing to do. But in the teachers college such scorn was a different matter, for here the educator was not to be so easily pushed around. The president of the college and the dean were educators and proud of it. The newly arrived doctor of philosophy in physics or history found that his scorn of things educational made him *persona non grata*. Often he became embittered and in his bitterness increased his scorn for professional educators, but he learned to be careful where he made his remarks.

Well-concealed scorn is not a stable basis for a harmonious working relationship, however, and the battle between the subject-matter specialists and the educators continues unabated in many a teachers college.

150

Milton S. Eisenhower

POINTS OF EMPHASIS FOR TEACHER EDUCATION

The teacher's task in fitting young people to take their place as intelligent voting citizens of a democracy has grown enormously in extent and complexity, particularly in the past hundred years. The basic skills of reading, writing, and computation, although as important as they ever were, are no longer the sole end of teaching.

Economic, political, and ethical questions will soon face the boys and girls who are today in school. The ability and skill necessary to face a problem, to see its real issues, to analyze and appraise relevant evidence, and to think through to a rational solution are today regarded as part of the equipment of the intelligent adult, and a majority of American educators feel that one of the teacher's most important duties revolves around developing such behaviors. The discussion of controversial questions is a part of democratic living, and the school is the place where the young should early learn that logic is to be preferred to unreasoning thought.

There are those even today who contend that knowledge of the subject taught is all that is necessary for a teacher—that if he knows a lot about mathematics, for example, he can stride boldly into the classroom and proceed to teach it. Yet students need to know something about the *human* uses of the subject. What are their obligations as people to whom this knowledge has been entrusted? A more than superficial consideration of other subjects reveals that they too bristle with questions of this tenor.

What, then, are the necessary qualifications for a teacher who is to approach his task in a manner adequate to the demands and challenges of the twentieth century? Milton Eisenhower, now president of the Johns Hopkins University, presents a list which aspirants to teaching can profitably read and discuss.

The novelist James Hilton, who created that winsome portrayal of an English schoolmaster, *Goodbye, Mr. Chips,* once said that if a son of his were entering upon a career as a teacher, he would say farewell to him as though he were departing for war.

By this, Mr. Hilton certainly meant to stress the spirit of dedication which motivates the true teacher and the vital importance of his function in society. The soldier-like aspects of the profession of teaching are all too apparent in these times, to teachers and to those engaged in educating teachers, at any rate. As one crisis is piled on another—social, economic, and political—*education* is continually being called from the barracks to man the ramparts and save our way of life, even to preserve civilization itself.

The fact is that education must do these very things, if they are to be done at all, for in our day there is no other single agency that can do them. The danger is that those who work in

From *Journal of Teacher Education,* June 1951, 2: 88-89.

education, like the villagers in the story of the boy who cried, "Wolf!" will become satiated with alarms and will relax their vigilance, or become perfunctory in their responses to the challenges of the times.

It requires no argument to demonstrate that most Americans live today under pressures which less than a generation ago were exerted on the comparatively few.

Today, not only is the world council table in the family living room, but so are the witness stand, the political forum, and the battlefield itself. The sights and sounds of human affairs, at all levels from the personal and local to the international and global, are interwoven with the fabric of family daily living, and their impact is supplemented by numberless ubiquitous spoken and written opinions, commentaries, and exhortations.

There was a time not so long ago, when the progress of a war, for instance, could be judged by the considered reports of the movements of entire armies, by the comparatively slow daily progress of a black line on a newspaper map. The grist of a thousand-and-one front-line and headquarters reports had been ground, and the man or woman at home received a condensed, largely predigested body of information on which to form his judgments, usually some time after the event.

Today, John and Mary Doe *and their children* are, in effect, omnipresent in the whole area of intellectual, political, and physical conflict. Out of a welter of the personal, eye-witness accounts of the experiences of individual soldiers, the press releases of commanding generals, the arguments of congressmen, the debates of national representatives, and the impressions and opinions of reporters and commentators—presented with little, if any, delay as they are expressed—out of this continuous bombardment of ideas by the press, radio, television, and motion pictures, the ordinary American must attempt to form his own comprehensive evaluation of the world in which he lives.

On the domestic scene the same conditions prevail; judgments on moral, intellectual, social, economic issues of great import must be made on evidence conglomerate enough to bewilder a Solomon.

One of two eventualities will occur: either the American people will develop and strengthen their individual abilities to discriminate between truth and falsehood, between the trivial and the important, and between right and wrong, or they will erect a psychological barrier of idea-deafness and become apathetic to the significance of fac-

tors that affect the integrity of our civilization. Education must bear the greater share of the responsibility for bringing about the former result and preventing the latter.

A truly perceptive college president recently stated that the real purpose of the liberal-arts college is to educate people to grasp the "main idea." Is not this the essential of *all* educational effort, not only the liberal-arts college but of all teaching from the level of the nursery school through the graduate university: to help boys and girls, and men and women, to discern shades of difference, to weigh values, to judge critically, and to form valid conclusions—in other words, to grasp the main idea?

Grasping the main idea is certainly the heart of the solution of any physical or biological problem, whether it involves the simplest carpentry or the most complex medical diagnosis. Discernment and judgment are no less vital factors in the solution of the less tangible problems which make up our individual and common lives, the problems involving economic forces, social relationships, and moral values.

By force of circumstances, the individual American must form judgments, if only subconsciously, on such complicated and varied issues as price and wage control versus uncontrolled economy, character assassination versus legitimate investigation of subversion, and underworld influence versus good government and clean sports. The quality of the judgments arrived at by the ordinary, everyday American is a vital factor in the shaping of our future.

The task of educating people to think critically and judge intelligently requires teachers who themselves have developed their critical faculties, who themselves have been trained to discern, to analyze, to weigh, and to evaluate through rational processes. This is the challenge for all those who educate teachers. It is a challenge that must be met.

There is no pat formula by which young men and women can be made into teachers adequate for the task which faces them. But in view of the importance in modern life of the ability to make value-judgments, added emphasis might well be placed on the following elements in the education of teachers:

(1) The acquisition of a broad background in history, economics, sociology, psychology, and philosophy, for knowledge of social man precedes the understanding of human affairs and relationships. Considerable depth as well as breadth in this intellectual background also contributes to the teacher's own ability to grasp the "main idea."

(2) Practice in critical thinking. Precision in the analysis and evaluation of ideas can best be achieved through active, disciplined exercise of the critical faculties.

(3) Intensified training and practice in communication—in reading, listening, writing, and speaking. The teacher, now as never before, must himself be able to read and listen accurately and with comprehension, and to express himself with clarity and precision on paper and in speech.

(4) The development through contemplation and association of a *personal philosophy of living equal to the teacher's vocation*—a philosophy which, as Sir Richard Livingstone put it, will serve "for shaping conduct, for reference in doubt, for challenge, stimulus, and driving power." This is perhaps the essential factor in the transformation of an individual into an effective teacher.

(5) The achievement by every teacher of a genuine and abiding commitment to the democratic way—a commitment based upon a thorough understanding of the sources and cardinal principles of democracy and of the principles underlying other forms of social endeavor, ancient and modern. This commitment must be the framework within which all other critical thinking proceeds and value-judgments develop.

151

Roger P. McCutcheon

THE MASTER'S DEGREE AND THE TEACHER REQUIREMENTS

Within the past fifty years graduate degrees, especially the M.A., have come to have a distinct cash value for teachers. Not so very long before the beginning of the present century, the M.A. appears to have been all but automatic in most institutions. In the words of the late Justice Oliver Wendell Holmes, one got it "by living 3 years and paying $5." With the coming of the graduate school and the (German) Ph.D., certain academic requirements were prescribed for the M.A.—course work, comprehensive examination, one foreign language, and a thesis—so that the lesser degree might not suffer too much by comparison with the Ph.D.

As schools able to pay higher salaries began to look for the best-qualified teachers, academic degrees formed the most obvious criterion of selection. The M.A. had a market value. So numerous was the crowd of teachers soon thronging the graduate schools of universities and teachers colleges that the M.A. requirements were in many places simplified and streamlined. By 1930 the majority of M.A. degrees were awarded practically on the basis of one year of course work above the B.A. or B.S. Much of this work was, in many cases, in education.

Hence the present highly controversial situation has developed. On the one hand, the academic folk maintain that the M.A. as it is usually awarded to teachers today has been hopelessly diluted. On the other hand, the educators hold that an M.A. in education is a greater asset to a teacher than additional courses in the subject he teaches. In the meantime, more state institutions are awarding the M.A. in education, and tens of thousands of teachers receive it and a consequent salary increase each year.

Within recent months several searching criticisms of our public schools have appeared. Our schools are always subject to attacks, of course, but the latest seem to indicate that the American taxpayer is becoming interested in getting some-

From *School and Society*, September 22, 1951, 74: 177-181.

thing for his money. In particular, considerable hostility has been shown to the present certification requirements for teachers. It is charged that these requirements actually deter the more able young men and women from entering the teaching profession.

Now the requirements for teacher certification and the requirements of our graduate schools have long been in sharp conflict. The purpose of this paper is to examine briefly both sets of requirements in the hope of finding some workable solution for this serious problem.

The requirements for teacher certification present one very important method of selection of teachers. These requirements usually have their origin in schools of education and are set by the state boards of education. The requirements become law by action of the state legislatures. They are, in brief, the product of human beings and are not revelations from the All-highest. They may therefore be discussed and criticized, and perhaps occasionally improved, even though there is a tendency in some places to regard them as closely akin to the Decalogue.

The second most influential body concerned with the selection and education of teachers is a composite, made up of undergraduate colleges and graduate schools. In particular, graduate-school regulations and procedures will concern us here. These, too, are the result of tradition and compromise, and there is no evidence that any graduate-school regulation is now or ever was a direct revelation from on high. They can be examined by us, just as the certification regulations can be examined, without our incurring the charge of blasphemy or of profanation of the mysteries.

The graduate schools, the best and most famous of which have developed from our strongest colleges of liberal arts, have stressed scholarship and research. They have undertaken as their especial province the increase of our knowledge. They have succeeded notably in this endeavor. Their methods have been rigorous and have included a rigid selection of high-quality students with a strong undergraduate major field, a stiff discipline in scholarly method, and an insistence upon a thesis as a demonstration of the quality of the products. Most graduate schools have believed that their type of scholarly activity requires a knowledge of other languages besides English. Most graduate teachers believe that training in research and some achievement in research are also among the best bases for training teachers.

The eminent success of the graduate-school training was, perhaps unfortunately, noted by the people in charge of teacher certification. In many states, the possession of a master's degree has become a requirement for advance in a teacher's salary. The source of the degree is not a matter of great concern, nor is the content of the degree; the mere possession of the degree is sufficient to warrant a substantial salary increment. After such inducements were established, there came knocking at the doors of our graduate schools many worthy people in quest of the master's degree. There was nothing wrong with their motives, to be sure; for that matter, probably none of us is completely disinterested in this business of higher learning. Their attainments, however, were sometimes slender. They had been out of college for some years; their college records had often been undistinguished. They found it well-nigh impossible to write a thesis or to pass a reading examination in a foreign language. Yet in their school systems they held positions of importance and responsibility. Frequently, they sacrificed their summer vacations in the effort to achieve the degree. One had to respect their industry and sympathize with their struggles.

The pressures mounted; the "social responsibility" of the graduate schools was challenged, and some schools made a few modifications in their regulations. Instead of requiring for admission a B grade in the undergraduate college, some graduate schools abandoned this entrance barrier. After all, a high-school diploma, which nowadays can be attained by everybody who stays on a high-school campus four years or four years and a summer term, is a passport into the state university, even if it is no longer a guarantee of anything except attendance. So, why should not an undergraduate degree automatically entitle the holder to entrance into the graduate school? Isn't this a democracy? Don't you know that the imparting of knowledge is no longer a major function of the public schools? And why insist, in the graduate school, that a student be able to use a foreign language, when colleges graduate so many students who have never had any foreign language? And why bother about a thesis? Most of the good subjects have already been worked over; it is a vestigial remnant without any validity today, of no more use than the vermiform appendix. And why expect a teacher to be able to write? Haven't you heard of multiple-choice examinations? This familiar line of reasoning has in many places resulted in the abandonment of the master's degree as a mark either of research ability or of cultural achievement. The establishment of the Master of Education degree, a professional degree usually without the thesis or the foreign-language requirement, has certainly made it possible for more teachers to qualify for the higher salary brackets. Whether this degree has improved the quality of the teachers who take it is not yet clearly determined.

The subject-matter departments, to the best of my knowledge, have not often made any serious attempts to meet the very real needs of teachers who wish advanced work. Most departments, such as English, mathematics, and political science, to name one from each of the three broad fields, draw up their graduate programs on the assumption that the graduate student is to be trained in research and, therefore, should have had an undergraduate major on which to base the graduate training. This usually amounts to at least 24 semester hours of undergraduate-course work in the subject. Sometimes this basic requirement is increased by the need of tools for research, such as training in statistical methods or in the mathematics nowadays required for any real comprehension of most of the natural sciences. But the cold facts of school life will show many a teacher in the elementary and secondary schools without an undergraduate major in the subject field that he is teaching. My first teaching was done in a small Virginia high school. My college major had been English. But I taught, in addition to four English classes, civil government, Caesar, German, physics, and chemistry. My college work in these last two fields had amounted to one year in each. Nowadays they do it better down our way, and the science courses are likely to be taught by people trained in home economics or in physical education.

Since the point can be most clearly made in connection with the teaching of science courses, let us follow this a bit farther. Science teachers in high schools are likely to be teaching two or three sciences, not one only. Or, and this is more frequently the pattern, they teach general science. In college, if they took a major in chemistry, they had to have mathematics at least through calculus, and their only other science was perhaps two years of physics. Yet they may also be teaching biology, and certainly in general science they are supposed to know something of geology and astronomy.

When a high-school science teacher comes to the typical graduate school and wants to get a Master of Science degree, he gets a series of shocks. For admission to graduate work in chemistry, for instance, he must be able to use calculus and to read German. Also, thanks to the undergraduate requirements, set not by educators but by the American Chemical Society, he must present undergraduate courses which include organic, inorganic, analytical, and physical chemistry. His own college work in chemistry, however, may

very well have included only one or two of these divisions. If he is persistent, he may choose to spend from one to two years making up his undergraduate deficiencies, after which he has the privilege of spending nearly two more years getting his master's with a chemistry major. But life is short and all too busy. He needs more training in chemistry, to be sure, but the price of getting it is too high. So he takes the Master of Education degree, and goes back to his job richer in salary but no richer in knowledge of his subject-matter field.

When I have presented such a case to our department of chemistry and suggested that this student be given some chance to get what he wants and needs, instead of being forced into more work in education courses, the department is mildly concerned but not very helpful. Our job, they tell me, is to train chemists; our students must have the mathematics and the full range of undergraduate courses in order to profit by our training. If we chemists accept into graduate courses students who have not had these prerequisites, such students will almost certainly fail. In our efforts to hold the class level up to the graduate plane, we have no time to review the elementary courses which most high-school teachers need. Then, still an incurable optimist, I suggest: How about setting up some graduate courses designed especially for the improvement of high-school teachers in chemistry? But so far the suggestion has borne no fruit. Indeed, it has been met with a mixture of polite contempt at my own ignorance and effrontery and genuine shock at the idea of any novelty being instituted without the sanction of the American Chemical Society. It is as if they were saying, your idea may seem plausible, but, had there been any merit in it, the American Chemical Society would have ordained such courses long ago. Yet even our chemists say they wish it were possible to improve the teaching of chemistry in the high schools.

The graduate-school regulations, then, present some important obstacles to the high-school teacher who wishes to take major work in the subject he is teaching. If chemistry and the other physical sciences represent the extreme, similar difficulties are found in other subjects as well. To what degree do the requirements for teacher certification also contribute to the difficulties of providing suitable programs for teachers who wish a graduate degree?

These requirements are not without both merit and danger. Most states nowadays require that an applicant must have had both a general education and special courses in teaching methods.

In these latter courses practice teaching is usually, and properly, emphasized. We should all prefer to have our children taught by those whose own range of intellectual interests and information is broad and by those who had had some classroom experience under observation prior to their appointment to our schools.

The emphasis upon general education, however, is not without some potential dangers. Our increase in academic knowledge has led to the multiplication of subjects and courses. The typical arts college, for the degree of Bachelor of Arts, has set up a program which requires broad basic training in the first two years, followed by more specialized training in a major and perhaps one or two minor subjects in the junior and senior years. It is well that every college graduate knows something of the humanities, something of the social studies, and something of the physical and biological sciences, no matter what his major subject be. The present vogue for "area majors" has a strong reason for its appeal, since in an area major a student may be introduced to many different fields of knowledge. All too often, however, the acquaintance stops with the introduction.

Most of the certification plans I know require from 12 to 18 hours of college work in a subject-matter field; in English, for instance, this means that a teacher may be certified for high-school English with freshman and sophomore English only. Not many of us in English believe that this is a sufficient emphasis upon the subject-matter fields.

And what of the requirements in professional education? Courses in education have proliferated more than in any other department. Fifty years ago most colleges offered only one course in education and that was usually, with becoming modesty, called pedagogy. Whether the subject matter has expanded or is now being spread much thinner is a question which it is difficult to get clearly answered.

Certainly it is true that at present, in the region I know best, there is a movement to increase the hours in professional education required for teacher certification. The Southern Association has indicated that 18 semester hours seem desirable. But in Louisiana the requirement varies from 24 to 36 and in some fields to almost half of the hours required for the undergraduate degree. An elementary-school teacher in Texas, according to proposals now being considered, will have to present from 48 to 56 hours in professional education. Such a requirement means that a person wishing to qualify as an elementary-school teacher will of necessity take an undergraduate major in education. It will be difficult for such a person to take anything except education in the junior and senior years. Not even the American Chemical Society has as yet gone quite this far. If we really want those who teach our children to have stopped their subject-matter education at the sophomore level, well and good, but we should realize it. We are now face to face with a plan that will require prospective teachers to abandon the Bachelor of Arts degree for an undergraduate degree in education. Furthermore, there is as yet no convincing proof that these education requirements make better teachers.

In Louisiana teachers who wish to improve their salary by taking a master's degree are virtually forced into a major in education by the state requirements. Even if the subject-matter departments could make better provision for teachers wishing graduate work, the teachers are required to take so many hours of professional education that they can only minor in a subject-matter field.

Now, I think that a high-school teacher of history should know some history, a good deal of history, in fact; I have a similar conviction about the other departments also. I do not know the real merits or demerits of courses in education. Many graduate students tell me there is considerable repetition in them and that after 12 or 18 hours you get the same old thing under new names. The education people tell me that this is not correct and justify the heavy concentration in professional education by reminding me that, after all, teachers have to teach; then they insist that departments of education are the only ones capable of imparting that art. Student opinion does not always bear this out. Also, I have permitted myself to wonder why the education departments need so many hours to impart this skill. A concentration of 30 to 40 hours in professional education is by no means unusual. When I ask whether these prospective teachers will teach "education" to the students in elementary and high school, I get a sharp, "No, of course not; our teachers nowadays teach the students; that is what the schools exist for." All right, agreed; but can you teach a student without teaching him something? And is it really true that the colleges of education have a corner on all information as well as on methods?

Even though the thesis for the master's degree is now gone beyond recall, along with the dear dead days, I venture the suggestion that it possibly had some merit. It made plain to the writer that the establishment of any truth was a difficult process. It also showed the writer some of the ways in which a portion of truth might be established. This, I firmly believe, is a value of some magnitude for a teacher to possess. I do not believe that course work alone creates this value so surely.

Somewhere along the line, too, our prospective teacher should be getting an introduction into at least one of the great arts. In the leisure spaces of the 40-hour week, what shall a teacher do with his time? Thanks to radio and television he can now remain passive and soak himself in the eloquence of soap operas and commercials. If he is an administrator, he can be dreaming up a new type of questionnaire. But if he is a warmly human being, with a spirit which craves the release that great art gives, he will be a much better human being if he has learned to appreciate one of the arts. He will also be a much better teacher. To escape from the elementary or high-school classroom into the movie or the radio is not always likely to improve one's cultural level. The wisdom of the ages, or at least some small part of it, should be made available to our teacher through his college work. I suggest that the over-crowded curriculum now necessary to meet the technical requirements does not always result in the best use of the priceless college years.

Can we reconcile these differences? We cannot, unless both the graduate schools and the departments of education modify their present requirements. In my opinion, this could be done without too serious a lowering of the standards of either,

and the seriousness of the situation calls for some relief.

I suggest that every prospective teacher should have had an undergraduate major in a subject-matter field instead of in professional education. The certification requirements in professional education should be reduced in order to make room for this subject-matter major. On the graduate-school level, the professional education should be a minor, not a major, requirement.

The graduate schools, for their part, should institute courses in subject-matter fields designed not to create research scholars, but to broaden the knowledge and the culture of prospective teachers. The subject-matter fields, in my opinion, should also organize courses in the teaching of their subjects. There should be enough training in research to give the prospective teacher an idea of how truth may be established. The admission requirements should be more realistic.

That these suggestions will be immediately welcomed and adopted is beyond my wildest dreams. I close, therefore, with a sentence from Daniel Defoe's "Essay upon Projects." Defoe had just been proposing that there should be much greater opportunity for women to get an education, an opinion quite advanced for 1696. So he ends with these words: "This chapter is but an essay at the thing, and I refer the practice to those happy days, if ever they shall be, when men shall be wise enough to mend it."

152

Michael Belok & Fred Dowling

THE TEACHER IMAGE AND THE TEACHER SHORTAGE

It is most unlikely that the prospect of following a despised calling attracts very many young people. This may have something to do with teacher shortages. While most statesmen, military leaders, scientists, businessmen, and industrialists can usually be counted on for a mention of teaching as a noble profession—with perhaps a grateful tribute to the influence of some teacher in their own lives—the disturbing question nevertheless persists. What does the public really think of teachers? Is the teacher not, more than anything else, an object of contempt?

Attempts to answer this question with sociological studies have brought forth some interesting results. By and large, the prevailing "teacher image" is not flattering. This hard truth needs to be faced by young people who propose to make teaching their life's work. It is not something to shrink from; teachers are generally too prone to shrink from things—from difficult disciplinary problems, from controversial questions, from the risk of holding unpopular opinions, even from wearing a striking hairdo!

As portrayed in literature, the teacher is rarely an engaging figure. Perhaps this should present a challenge to young people with courage and with firm personal convictions to dare to teach and yet to live their own lives.

Teaching is in the strange position of being a highly honored occupation and yet one constantly ridiculed. Not an insignificant source of the ridicule is popular fiction. Among our favorite fictional images are the gentle, competent Mr. Chips and the pioneering schoolmarm; but at least as well known are the figures of Ichabod Crane and the bumbling taskmaster. There is good reason to believe that the latter figures more closely resemble the stereotype pre-eminent in the public mind. Numerous studies of teachers portrayed in fiction in recent years provide evidence that more often than not the teacher is pictured in an unfavorable light.

The present shortage of teachers on all levels poses an intriguing question. Has the unfavorable image of teachers as depicted in comic strips, motion pictures, television, plays, and novels contributed in any way to this shortage? This is a question which is extremely difficult to answer, and perhaps we won't know what to do with the answer if we get it; nevertheless, it is a query which deserves examination. Our chief purpose here is to summarize significant studies of the teacher image in these media.

Erskine[1] investigated the characterization of teachers in forty-six Broadway plays presented between 1920 and 1950. Teachers were characterized as maladjusted in 68 per cent of the cases, as having economic troubles in 37 per cent, as experiencing sexual tension in 33 per cent, and as being poorly clothed in 19 per cent. Erskine states that teachers for the most part were treated seriously but with what amounts to pity, and concluded that the characterization of teachers as neurotic does damage to the status of the profession. (Unfortunately, Erskine does not tell us what per cent of the representatives of other professions are similarly characterized by dramatists.)

Foff[2] examined the teacher stereotype in American novels. He selected sixty-two novels published since 1900, twenty-two of them since 1945. He found that novelists insist that the male teacher is solitary, effeminate, and impractical. The same attitude prevails toward women. They were characterized as either young and unmarried or as old maids, sexless creatures devoid or depleted of femininity. Foff concludes that the stereotype of the school teacher harms the profession. He maintains that an effect is to attract this type to the profession and produce more of the type within it.

Deegan,[3] studying the stereotype of single women in novels, found that teachers were often depicted as very unfeminine women. In several cases they are shown as wielding a destructive influence in the community. Gurko,[4] writing about the treatment of teachers in both fiction and motion pictures, makes the point that the teacher fares no better in films than he does in fiction, and that the characterizations are almost always very unfavorable.

Several studies have also been made of college teachers as depicted in fiction and popular magazines. Boys,[5] in a study of college life as portrayed in fiction between 1900 and 1943, concluded that fiction writers show the college professor as a "queer person" and one who should not be judged by our usual standards of human conduct.

Belok[6] also examined the characterizations of professors in novels. After studying fifty novels published since 1940, he concluded that the treatment of the male professor was not stereotyped but that there were a disproportionate number of odd, vicious, or disagreeable professors in the novels. The women professors were also characterized in an unfavorable manner. They were often shown as hostile and aggressive women, filled with hate, and physically unattractive.

Interestingly enough, some uncomplimentary characterizations can be traced to teachers them-

From *Phi Delta Kappan,* March 1961, 43:255-256.
[1]Andrew H. Erskine. *An Analysis and Evaluation of the Characterization of American Teachers in Broadway Productions,* 1920-1950, unpublished doctor's dissertation, New York University, 1951.
[2]Arthur Foff, *Teacher Stereotypes in the American Novel,* unpublished doctor's dissertation, Stanford University, 1953.
[3]Dorothy Yost Deegan. *The Stereotype of the Single Women in American Novels.* New York: King's Crown Press, 1951.
[4]Leo Gurko. *Heroes, Highbrows, and the Popular Mind.* New York: The Bobbs-Merrill Company, Inc., 1953.
[5]Richard C. Boys, "The American College in Fiction," *College English,* April, 1946.
[6]Michael V. Belok, *The College Professor in the Novel, 1940-1957,* unpublished doctor's dissertation, University of Southern California, Los Angeles, 1958.

selves. Bowman[7] analyzed 375 articles in general magazines to determine what attitudes toward professors are most common. About one-third of the articles were written by professors. These professor-authors were more critical toward their colleagues than non-academic writers, although both groups were critical. The unfavorable characterizations pictured professors as dull, dry, unsocial, unmanly, impractical, and lazy. Bowman drew attention to what he considers unfair characterizations, pointing out that the professor is never pictured as handsome, gay, or brilliant.

Thus researchers agree that there is much in various communications media that is extremely unfavorable in the depiction of teachers. If they are correct, and we see no reason to doubt it, is not the cumulative effect likely to be a significant one? As individuals read novels and magazines and view movies, aren't they likely to develop an unfavorable image of the teacher? And may not this unfavorable image tend to have a stronger effect on the young reader or viewer? Many young people lack the sophistication or acumen to assess this fictional image properly. It seems likely that they will have grave reservations about entering

an occupation which is largely an object of ridicule or disdain.

Certainly it is unlikely that the public image of a profession does not have some effect upon both the people in the profession and those contemplating entering it. Foff thinks that it does, and most other researchers concur. During the past decade a substantial number of teachers have left teaching for other work. Economic factors and poor working conditions have been advanced as chief causes. But the prevailing image of the teacher, as part of that complex we call "teacher status in the community," may be equally important. Is there not a possibility that many left teaching because they felt oppressed in the teaching role, believing the public considered them, among other unattractive things, as some sort of third-sexed creature? We know that individuals are not always aware of their own motivations, and teachers who leave the profession may not really know why they do so. They simply choose the most comfortable rationalization. Perhaps they prefer to ignore the unconscious distaste they feel for the role society has set for them. And perhaps, as Foff suggests, the image draws a certain type of individual into teaching, just as it drives out others. Art imitates nature—and nature imitates art.

[7]Claude Bowman, *The College Professor in America.* Philadelphia: University of Pennsylvania, 1938.

TEACHING AS A PROFESSION

No people are more given to forming organizations than are Americans, and American teachers are as fond of organizing themselves as any other group. There are national, state, city, and county teachers' associations, as well as those made up of administrators, teachers of particular subjects, and advocates of particular educational theories. And this list is by no means complete.

In view of the large number of teachers' organizations that appear to be flourishing in America, one might hastily conclude that there is a high degree of professional spirit and solidarity among teachers. But the mere existence of organizations does not tell the whole story. People talk easily about "the teaching profession," but there is no general agreement in the public mind as to whether teaching can be rightly called a profession—that is, in the sense that law and medicine are professions.

Membership in organizations is not enough. Even if it were, there are thousands of teachers in America who do not belong to any professional organization. Some are excluded because they are not qualified to teach; they have simply been hired because qualified teachers are not available. Others refuse to join because they are not interested. Many others have paid their membership fee in one or more professional associations because principals or superintendents have told them they "are expected to do so." Evidence of this sort of thing can be found by anyone who takes the trouble to inquire, particularly among young teachers. When membership is virtually coerced, not much real group solidarity or loyalty is likely to result.

True professional spirit is hard to define, though its presence is easily felt, as is its lack. Ever since the guilds of the Middle Ages, groups of people have organized themselves to protect their jobs, to regulate unfair competition, and to maintain the quality of their service. The last of these three purposes is the most important. This fact should be borne in mind whenever teaching is compared as a profession to medicine or law. It has been pointed out, though not often, that whereas the bar examinations that allow one to practice law and the board examinations that allow one to practice medicine are of long standing, there is no comparable examination system to allow one to teach. It has been maintained that until teaching wins the right to grant or withhold permission to teach, it cannot rightly be termed a profession.

There also exists a wide divergence of opinion as to the composition and program of teachers' associations. Some people feel that such organizations should be open to anyone who is in any way associated with education, and that they should strive to bring about desirable change by persuasion and by educating the public. Others feel that an organization so constituted is apt to be dominated by administrators and that its methods are apt to be slow and ineffective. They would therefore exclude administrators and supervisors from membership and resort to strikes to obtain what they demand. Both types of organization are effectively represented in the United States.

In the meantime, standards of teacher certification are slowly—often *too* slowly—rising in most states. Teachers are working to bring about these improvements, but they can do so only indirectly; regulations governing certification in any state are actually made by state authority, not by the vote of any teachers' organization.

153

William Russell

NATIONAL ORGANIZATION OF TEACHERS

The first organization of teachers on a national scale was the National Teachers Association, founded on August 27, 1857, at Philadelphia. The name was changed some years later to the National Education Association—today most often referred to as the NEA. Some attempts had previously been made (as in the American Institute of Instruction), but these were usually more or less regional and did not continue into the twentieth century. The NEA has caught the imagination and called forth the loyalty of the teachers of America.

The following address—the only one delivered at the founding of the NEA —is a notable one. It presents a challenge to the teachers of America to make of teaching a genuine profession, similar to law, medicine, or theology. The speaker feels that this is possible, granted sufficient knowledge, determination, and *esprit de corps* on the part of teachers.

To what extent has teaching become a profession? Teachers should ask themselves this question from time to time. So also should young people who talk glibly about entering "the teaching profession."

Fellow teachers: We are met on a great occasion. For the first time in the history of our country, the teachers of youth have assembled as a distinct professional body, representing its peculiar relations to all parts of our great national union of states. The event is a most auspicious one, as regards the intellectual and moral interests of the whole community of which, as citizens, we are members; and, to ourselves, professionally and individually, it opens a view of extended usefulness, in efficient action, such as never yet has been disclosed to us.

We meet not as merely a company of friends and wellwishers to education, one of the great common interests of humanity, in which we are happy to cooperate with philanthropic minds and hearts of every class and calling; but we have at length recognized our peculiar duty to come forward and take our own appropriate place as the immediate agents and appointed organs of whatever measures are best adapted to promote the highest interests of society, by the wider diffusion of whatever benefits are included in the whole range of human culture. In stepping forward to take the professional position now universally accorded to us, we do so in no exclusive or selfish spirit. We are, in fact, only complying with the virtual invitation given us, by all who feel an interest in the advancement of education, to assume, in regular form, the acknowledged responsibilities of our office, as guardians of the mental welfare of the youth of our country, responsible to the whole community for the fidelity and efficiency with which we discharge our trust. The liberal measures recently adopted in so many of our states for the establishment of permanent systems of public education; the generous recognition, now so general, of the value of the teacher's office and his daily labors; the warm reception offered to every form of teachers associations—from those which represent whole states down to the local gatherings in our towns and villages —all intimate the universal readiness of society to welcome the formation of a yet more extensive professional union of teachers—of one coextensive with our national interests and relations.

We meet the invitation, not as a mere professional recognition, entitling us to withdraw from the ground which we have hitherto occupied, in common with the friends of education, whether of the learned professions or of other occupations, in the promotion of its interests, and, by an exclusive organization, to cut ourselves off from all communication beyond the limited sphere of a

close corporation. It is in no such spirit that we would act. But we do feel that there is a duty devolving on us, as teachers, which we desire to fulfill. We feel that, as a professional body, we are distinctly called on to form a national organization, that we may be the better enabled to meet the continually enlarging demands of our vocation for higher personal attainments in the individual and for more ample qualifications adequately to fill the daily widening sphere of professional action.

We wish, as teachers, to reap whatever benefits our medical brethren derive from their national association, in opportunities of communication for mutual aid and counsel. We desire to see annually a professional gathering, such as may fairly represent the instructors of every grade of schools and higher institutions, thruout the United States. We hope to see a numerous delegation, at such meetings, from every educating state in the Union, of the men who, in their respective state associations of teachers, are already responding to the manifest demand for distinct appropriate professional action, on the part of those on whom devolves the immediate practical business of instruction.

Teaching is, in our day, an occupation lacking neither honor or emolument. Those who pursue this employment are in duty bound to recognize the position which is so liberally assigned them. The vocation is well entitled to all the aid and support which an acknowledged professional rank can confer upon it. The personal interest of every individual who pursues the calling, or who means to adopt it, is concerned in every measure which tends to elevate its character or extend its usefulness. Every teacher who respects himself, and whose heart is in his work, will respond, we think, with alacrity to the call which the establishment of such an association as we propose makes upon him for his best efforts in its aid.

From the formation of a *national* association of teachers, we expect great *national* benefits:

1. As regards *wider* and *juster views of education*, and *corresponding methods of instruction.*

In a progressive community like ours, amid the vast and rapid developments of science by which our times are characterized, and the universal craving for yet better modes of human culture, to imagine that we have already attained to perfection in our modes of education, would be absurd. The statistics of society proclaim the falsity of such an opinion. The daily records of our race tell too plainly the sad story of our deficiencies and our failures, in the prevalent feeble organizations of body, and the imperfect

From *NEA Addresses and Proceedings*, 1952, pp. 435-443.

health, which we still owe to our culpable neglect of proper educational training, by which physical vigor and efficiency might be, in great measure, secured to every human being. The teacher, in our large cities, at least, daily finds himself compelled to limit his intellectual requirements to the condition of many minds incapable of sustaining lengthened or vigorous application, or of retaining the rudimental germs which it is his desire to implant. Of our acknowledged defective moral education, it is unnecessary to speak. Thruout our country, the parent is appealing to the teacher, and the teacher to the parent, for efficient efforts which may bring about a better state of things. Who will venture, in such circumstances, the assertion that we are already perfect?

The whole ground of education needs a thoro survey and revision, with a view to much more extensive changes and reforms than have yet been attempted. The cry for more healthful, more invigorating, more inspiring, more effective modes of culture, comes up from all classes of society, on behalf of the young who are its treasured hope. A truer and deeper investigation is everywhere needed in regard to the constitution, the capabilities, and the wants of man, equally in his temporal and his eternal relations.

Adverting thus to the acknowledged need of a renovation in the form and character of education, we would not be understood as desiring the indiscriminate subversion of existing modes of culture, or of the institutions to which we have been so largely indebted for whatever degree of mental attainment has characterized the past, or benefits the present. It belongs to others than teachers to propose those rash and headlong changes, unsanctioned by true philosophy or stable theory, which have demolished without reconstructing, and whose toppling fabrics have served the sole purpose of forming the sepulchral monuments of "zeal without knowledge."

No: one of the surest and best results of a great national association of teachers, will be the careful retention of all unquestionable good residuum gained by the sure filtration of experience; another will be the building up, to yet nobler heights of beneficial influence, the high places of all true learning. Room can be made for the cultivation of all invigorating and purifying influences in human development, without the sacrifice of one valuable acquisition; or, rather, with the addition of many, which a more genial nurture will certainly introduce. But it is high time that the broad experience and observation of teachers, the tried servants of humanity, in all the relations of culture, should unite to claim a hearing

on the great subject of their daily duties and endeavors; and that their voice should have its weight in the adoption of the successive steps which the ceaseless advances of knowledge will always require at the hands of education. A harmonious cooperation of educational skill with scientific progress and parental interests, may thus be fully secured for the enlargement and fertilizing of the whole field of mental and moral culture.

A professional association, founded on the broad basis which we now contemplate, will necessarily give unity and effect to communications expressing the views and bearing the sanction of such a body; and instructors thruout our country will thus have an opportunity of contributing more widely, and more effectively, to the furtherance of whatever good is embraced in the whole range of education, whether in its immediate or its remotest results.

2. From the establishment of a national society of teachers, we may justly expect a large amount of *professional benefit to its members.* Fellow teachers! we are not assembled to boast of the dignity of our vocation, or of the intellectual eminence of those who pursue it; but rather, in the spirit of faithful and earnest endeavor, to do what we can to render ourselves, individually and collectively, more worthy of its honors, by becoming more capable of fulfilling its duties.

Contemplating then, in this sober light, the aggregate of such learning and skill as the annual communications of a national reunion of teachers must contribute to our advancement individually, in professional qualifications, we may well congratulate one another on the advantages anticipated as accruing from such occasions. Nor need these advantages be temporary or evanescent. A national association of teachers will necessarily give rise to an appropriate organ of communication between its members themselves, and the community in general. By this means, the fruits of the maturest minds in the ranks of our profession, in the ample discussion of the great primary questions of education, may be daily reaped by the youngest of our corps, while the zeal and enthusiasm, and the ardent aspirations of the youngest, may communicate life and fire to all.

But it is not merely in our professional relations that a national association will benefit us. It will be an invaluable aid to us, as students of the sciences which we teach. We arrogate nothing for our profession, when we say that it includes among its members men of the highest attainments—not to say eminence—in the various departments of science and literature. Their communications with us will be instruction of the highest order, to which it will be a peculiar privilege to listen. If there be any doubt on this point, in any mind, we will verify our assertion by pointing to such men as Agassiz and Guyot, who, in the true spirit of the teacher's vocation, have, for years, so generously dispensed the rich fruits of their own surpassing attainments for the benefit of their fellow teachers, thruout their adopted country. Passing by, however, those luminaries of the upper sphere of science, have we not many in all parts of the Union, who, in comparison of such names, would not be unwilling to be ranked but as among the "lesser lights," and who have no ambition beyond that of contributing their silent personal endeavor to the advancement of knowledge and to the instruction of youth, yet have minds fraught with untold wealth of acquirement, which they would readily lend for the profit and pleasure of others less amply furnished?

But to return to our strictly professional relations. Education is now studied both as a science and as an art. We have among us already, not only those who, by extensive acquirements, and professional skill, and special study, are amply competent to guide the minds of others in the path of philosophical investigation of the principles of education, and to exhibit, in actual application, the methods of instruction which spring from such principles: we have, already, the products of such minds, nurtured and matured in wellendowed and wellconducted professional seminaries, established by enlightened legislation, for the express purpose of furnishing such products in the persons of welltrained, capable, enlightened and successful teachers, of both sexes. With the aid of such minds, in addition to that of the many widely known individuals who have made a lifetime's business of education, and daily live amid an atmosphere of grateful feeling, emanating from the surrounding hearts of more than one generation which their labors have enlightened and elevated—with such aid to rely on, can we be accounted rash if we say we feel that we are ready to meet the exigency of our time which calls us to unite, under the sanction of our free political institutions, for the establishment of a professional society dedicated to the effective advancement of education by its own executive agents.

Other associations of a more general character, which are nobly engaged in promoting the interests of education, we recognize with respect and gratitude. Many of us have helped to found and to maintain these; and the thought of superceding

or impairing them is the last that would enter our minds. But in our individual capacity as teachers, and in our relations as—many, perhaps most of us—members of state associations of teachers, we feel that the time is fully come when our own professional interests, and the educational progress of our country, demand the institution of a strictly professional association of teachers, embracing in its scope and design all who are engaged in our occupation thruout the United States, and having for its aim a faithful and persevering endeavor to enlarge the views, unite the hearts, strengthen the hands, and promote the interests of all its members.

The annual meetings of such an association as we contemplate, would form a most attractive scene, not only as one of extensive fellowship and sympathy in common labors and common interests, but one of peculiar and elevated intellectual advancement and gratification. At one hour we might enjoy an enlightened exposition or discussion of a great principle of education, in which we might be benefitted by all the lights of philosophic theory, verified and attested by practical experience. At another, we might experience similar benefit from the statement and illustration of methods and subjects of instruction. Again, we might have opportunity of listening to vital suggestions on moral culture, on appropriate physical exercise and training, on the control and direction of schools, on the classification of pupils, on motives to application, on cooperation with parental influence, on the teacher's position in society, and in short, on every topic of importance usually advanced at our teachers meetings —but with this superior advantage, that we should hear the results of experience and observation from a much wider circle than in the case of associations of more limited range of action.

All the subjects which have been mentioned, and many others, might be intrusted to committees appointed to exhibit or discuss them in regular forms, by which we might avoid, when we thought proper, the formality of set lectures, and avoid, also, the comparative loss of time in mere formalities of debate, which often consume the precious hours of anniversary meetings designed for the despatch of actual business, or the investigation of important subjects. Our scientific associations, with their strict classification of subjects, their brief practical papers, and special committees, set an instructive example in these respects which a body so large as our National Association of Teachers would find it advantageous to follow. The papers presented at our annual meetings, by the committees respectively appointed, together with the reports of discussions and other proceedings, would easily furnish sufficient matter for a regular issue in the periodical form, so as to provide a useful manual for the teacher's table, and enable absent members to receive thus the benefit of our annual meetings.

One important advantage to be derived from such an association as we propose, may I be permitted to dwell upon more fully? I refer to the distinct recognition of teaching as a profession. This is a result, on the desirableness of which all teachers, I believe, are agreed. On the question of how it is to be brought about, there is not a similar unanimity; and this diversity of opinion is, in part, owing to current mistakes regarding the proper distinction between a profession and any ordinary vocation.

In the liberal courtesy of popular usage among us, we are too apt to extend the designation of "profession" to any regular pursuit or calling whatever. The term "profession," being one of university origin and application, is not duly appreciated, or properly discriminated, when adopted in current phraseology. The word recalls the ancient practice in colleges of examining a student when he "professed" to be prepared for advancement from one stage or form of study to another, or to have finished the requisite studies of a given course. The individual thus professing himself qualified to enter on new relations, was subjected to rigorous examination, and approved or rejected, according to his attainments.

A student, who judged himself competent, after the completion of the regular course of study in law, medicine, or theology, to stand an examination in any of these subjects, with a view to receiving a certificate of qualifications, in the form of license, degree, or diploma, "professed" himself ready for such examination. The three pursuits above named, being the only ones for which, in former times, a course of preparatory study in the *"literae humaniores"* (*liberal* arts), was deemed indispensable, came to be figuratively designated as the "liberal professions." On other vocations persons of any class might enter at will, but for admission to the ranks of the liberal callings a previous profession of qualifications, and correspondent examination and license, were indispensable.

Before entering on the practice of any of the professions mentioned, the candidate had still another process of examination to undergo, at the hands of the actual members of the profession, as is virtually the case at the present day when a lawyer is admitted to the bar, a physician to the membership of a state or national medical association, or a licentiate is ordained for the ministry.

Whenever it shall please the members of any of our state professional associations of teachers to adopt a similar practice, and subject all candidates for membership to examination as a condition of receiving a certificate of membership, the vocation of teaching will be legally entitled, under such circumstances, to become and to be recognized as a "profession," in virtue of the candidate being found, on examination, qualified to discharge its duties as he *professed* to be.

The supposition that a state association of teachers, when once formed and recognized as such by the legislature of the state, needs any further legislative sanction to enable it to confer a certificate of membership, is a mistake which has unduly delayed the proper action of such associations in more than one instance. It is for such an association itself, not the state, to say whether it shall become a "close corporation," an exclusive, examining, and selflicensing body or not. No act of legislation can constitute teaching a profession. The thing depends on the will and action of the association itself. The processes of examining candidates and of conferring a certificate of membership, on satisfactory examination, are the only prerequisites after the legislature of a given state has conferred a charter of incorporation on a teachers association. The case has its perfect analogy in that of a state medical association, or in that of admission to practice at the bar.

The action of state associations of teachers, wherever these are formed, might speedily effect the issue so desirable for all who follow the vocation of teaching as the intended business of their lives. To such persons it would seem but an act of simple justice, that a distinction should be made between them and those who take up the employment in a transient way, and for temporary convenience only. To young men of liberal education and of corresponding acquirements, who voluntarily forego the advantage of adopting more lucrative occupations, and follow, for life, the exhausting labor of teaching, the regular recognition of instruction as a liberal profession, is due as an equivalent for opportunities relinquished, and as an expression of general sentiment on the value of the benefits conferred on the community, by the services of those whose own education has opened to them the way to the highest positions in society.

The professional examination and recognition of candidates for the teacher's office, seem equally due, as a matter of justice, to instructors as a body confessedly competent to the task of judging of the fitness of individuals for the office which they themselves sustain; and in all matters pertaining to which, they ought to be better qualified to judge than the members of any other profession can be. A certificate of competency to teach, warranted by a teachers association, ought, moreover, to be a far more satisfactory passport to employment, than a similar document from any other source, even when that source is official, and sanctioned by law. Were teachers to come forward and claim their proper position in this respect, persons engaged in other pursuits would, in all probability, gladly resign the onerous task which is now so commonly imposed on them, and free themselves from a responsibility always irksome, partly from the apprehension of doing injustice, perhaps, to a diffident candidate, and partly, in not a few cases, from the consciousness of incompetency to judge with exactness of details of knowledge which do not come within the sphere of the examiner's personal information.

A national association of teachers, when duly organized and incorporated, might perform a valuable service to the interests of education, both for teachers and the community in general, by assuming the responsibility of admitting or rejecting candidates for membership, and for our various grades of schools, by some fixed and universal standard. Certificates founded on such a principle would possess a high value as professional documents, whose currency would properly be coextensive with the Union, and would insure to their possessors immediate acceptance in their profession, wherever they might establish themselves, while the security in such cases would be equally valuable to the community, as the assurance of obtaining a competent teacher in whatever grade of schools the applicant might be employed.

The question, How would the proposed examination of teachers be conducted? has been started as an obstacle to such a course of procedure as is now proposed. The answer to this question, whether put with reference to a state or national association, is, we admit, that, *at first*, in the actual condition of things among us, as regards the whole matter of education, it cannot be expected that admission to membership can take place in virtue of the process of examination, in the absence of a preexisting recognized authority; and not till such authority exists, by act of the association, can any regular examination be conducted. As a selfconstituted and selfperpetuating body—so far as examination and certificates are concerned—it must commence its operations on the basis of such members as it consists of, previous to instituting examinations. This would render it necessary to make a beginning by constituting every individual whose membership dated from the commencement of the association, a "passed" member, at the end of three years, or any other definite period of satisfactory length. All subsequent admissions to membership, in the capacity of passed members, might be regularly conducted by committees appointed by the association, for the various grades of schools. Certified members of state associations would of course, be entitled, on joining the national association, to certificates of membership in the latter, by personal introduction from their state association.

The duty of conducting professional examinations has, by some, been supposed a thing impracticable, from its onerous demands of time and care. But the value necessarily attached to a state or a national certificate of examination and qualifications, would make it worth a reasonable sum as compensation for time and trouble on the part of the examiner; and a fixed rate could easily be assigned as the proper limit of expense incurred in such cases.

All precautions and securities usually adopted on behalf of other associations, as regards admission or exclusion, on proper moral grounds, must be presupposed as applied with reference to membership in a society of teachers. A right professional spirit would doubtless be an adequate protection in this respect.

In the way now proposed, or in any equivalent to it, the end desired might, without insuperable difficulty, be attained, and the best interests of our calling and of the community be effectually promoted. A powerful incitement to professional study and to professional diligence would thus be held up. A definite and an honorable rank would thus also be assigned to every worthy member of the profession.

But whatever disposal may be made of the subject of professional rank and recognition for teachers, the great considerations of personal duty in regard to associated and united effort for the advancement of education, are the subjects that lie immediately before us. Fellow teachers, we are happy, we are honored, in being called to become the first movers in the contemplated national association. Let the record of this day tell, by the unanimity and efficiency of our procedure, and by the beneficent spirit of our endeavors, how faithfully we have labored in our part of the wide field of human welfare. May the Wisdom which cometh from above guide all our measures to the happiest results!

154

R. Freeman Butts & Lawrence A. Cremin

FINANCIAL AND SOCIAL STATUS OF TEACHERS

The amount of money the public is willing to pay a public servant is one index of the degree of respect and professional status in which he is held. Much has recently been said and written about the need for increasing teachers' salaries and in many states the actual increases have been considerable. However, as it has in many other occupations, the decline in purchasing power of the dollar has often resulted in a decrease in salary, in spite of the increase in actual dollars. There are also wide variations in salaries over the country, resulting in much migration of able and ambitious teachers to the places where the pay is good.

Another aspect of the teacher-salary discussion is that of salary scales as contrasted with merit pay. The first system is said to reward age and decrepitude and the second to result in widespread favoritism. Which system is better seems to be one of those perennial questions in education which will never be conclusively answered but for which a tentative solution must continually be sought.

Another perennial question is that of professional ethics—of standards of personal conduct for the teacher. Has the community a right to expect of the teacher standards of personal behavior that few if any of its other members actually live up to? Can the teacher be regarded as a true professional if his way of life is to be prescribed by the public and his ethical code is to consist mainly of prohibitions?

One measure of the social status of a professional group, though not the only one, is the financial return for its members. Teachers' salaries rose during the 1920's until they stood at a high point around 1930 after which they dropped to their lowest levels by 1935. By 1940 they had regained the losses and were almost back up to the 1930 levels. At the close of World War II they jumped upward sharply until they had reached their all-time high levels in 1951-1952, when average annual salaries for teachers amounted to something like $3,300 for the whole country. Even this figure was low enough, but when these gains in actual dollars are compared with the gains in other occupations and with the increased cost of living, the teachers' plight was even more clear. While teachers' salaries rose on the average some 84 percent between 1925 and 1949, the earnings of production workers in industry were rising 125 percent. Up to 1940 teachers remained ahead

of the average wage and salary workers in the country, but they dropped significantly behind during the 1940's. War work brought rapid gains to employed persons between 1940 and 1945, and the teachers never caught up. From 1940 to 1949 teachers' salaries increased about 100 percent, but average wages of other employed persons increased 120 percent. In 1951 the average salary for physicians was $12,518, for lawyers $9,375, and for dentists $7,743.

The comparison of teachers' salaries with the rise in cost of living, however, made teachers' salaries seem still worse. If the average price level between 1935 and 1939 is figured as a base of 100, the price index in 1951 came to about 180. This meant that the purchasing power of the average teachers' salaries of $3,300 in 1951 was equivalent to only about $1,833 in prewar dollars. Thus, the increases in actual dollar salaries for teachers in the last twenty years have virtually been wiped out by the rise in cost of living and the increase in taxes.

Up to this point all the figures have been given in averages which do not indicate the range of

From *A History of Education in American Culture* by R. Freeman Butts and Lawrence A. Cremin, pp. 601-603. Copyright 1953 by Holt, Rinehart and Winston, Inc. and reprinted by their permission.

salaries or the extremely low salaries paid in some sections of the country. In the fall of 1951 New York State paid its teachers an average annual salary of about $4,500, the highest of any state. At the other extreme, Arkansas paid an average annual salary of $1,700 and Mississippi paid only $1,475. Sixteen states paid some of their teachers as little as $25 a week or less. In general, the lowest salaries went to Negro teachers in the South and to rural teachers everywhere. The larger the community the more likely were teachers' salaries to be higher. In view of the fact that almost any occupation above unskilled labor paid more than teaching, it is not surprising that teachers deserted the schools by the thousands during World War II and that the growing shortage of teachers in the postwar years gave evidence of the difficulty in luring them back to the schools. When members of the other professions, such as physicians, dentists, lawyers, engineers, and architects, averaged from two to four times as much as teachers, it is no wonder that teaching had difficulty in making good its claim to the status of a profession.

Within the teaching profession itself, however, considerable gains were made in overcoming some of the discrepancies among the various kinds of jobs. In the last twenty years the wide gap in salaries between elementary school teachers and secondary school teachers has been narrowed, as has the gap between classroom teachers and administrators. The improvement in elementary school teachers' salaries has resulted from the need to keep teachers in the schools in competition with other occupations and in competition with the rising cost of living. Also, the salaries of beginning and inexperienced teachers have had to be raised in order to attract enough new teachers into the schools to keep them going. Even so, the estimate was made in 1951 that anywhere from one sixth to one half of the elementary school teachers of the nation fell below minimum standards of acceptability.

Great gains have been made in establishing standard salary schedules in most of the cities and states of the country. Virtually 90 percent of the cities have established some kind of definite salary schedule, and since 1940 there has been a rapid gain in the number of salary schedules based upon qualifications of training, experience, and preparation of teachers rather than simply upon the position, the grade level, or subject taught. Tenure, sick leave, and retirement provisions have all been strengthened for most teachers. Improvement has also come in many sections where married women have been permitted to continue teaching and where the pro-

portion of men teachers has increased. In 1947-1948 some states had as few as 10 percent of men teachers in the classrooms; other states ranged as high as 30 percent, for an average of about 19 percent in the country as a whole. If elementary school salaries could be raised significantly close to high school salaries, more men might be attracted to the elementary schools of the nation. Despite the gains made, one great problem that remained before teaching could achieve full status as a profession was the perennial problem of raising salaries sufficiently to attract the most able persons and hold them.

Another measure of the social status of teachers was the pressure put upon teachers to conform to the mores of the community which supported them. . . . [Much] of this concern by the public is legitimate. But many communities go much beyond these professional matters in insisting upon conformity in the private affairs as well as the public life of teachers. This has been a long tradition in American education going back to colonial times . . . . Taboos against smoking, dancing, dating, drinking, card playing, and many forms of amusement and recreation are levied upon teachers long after they have been relaxed for adults in general or for parents themselves. Similarly, pressures are exerted upon teachers to teach Sunday school, remain in the community over weekends, and to shape their personal behavior in other ways in communities where no one would think of requiring similar conduct of its lawyers, physicians, engineers, or other professional personnel. Clergymen and librarians, however, were likely to be subjected to somewhat the same pressures that were felt by teachers.

Teachers as a whole have been subjected to these kinds of pressures for a number of reasons. Most teachers have been women; and until recent years they were either too timid or not accustomed to asserting equal rights of personal freedom and of full citizenship. Teachers are public employees and dependent for their salaries and appointment upon representatives of the community. They have therefore felt that they could not afford to risk offense by expecting the freedoms that others enjoyed. Teachers have come from the middle or lower middle classes in the population where there has been little tradition of organized effort to improve salaries or status by group action. And many teachers have had such meager preparation for their jobs that they were not able to command the respect or exert the leadership expected of competent professional personnel. These were some of the problems that required attention from the profession and the public at mid-century.

155

Charles A. Beard

THE SCHOLAR IN AN AGE OF CONFLICTS

Probably no other nation has expected as much of its schools as has America. An unexampled prosperity, a highly mobile population, the appearance of women in business and the professions, and many other causes have made very difficult, if not impossible, many of the duties formerly entrusted to the home. Hence, for the past hundred years at least, one burden after another has been shifted to the schools.

Much of this shift has been half unconscious. Many of the Founding Fathers were, in the early years of this country, eloquent in their declarations of what education was to do in building citizens fit for a free nation. Educational pioneers in the nineteenth century predicted great things as a certain consequence of universal free public education. It is probably no exaggeration to say that the American people have been brought up to have a firm trust in what the schools can accomplish. The country needs honest, industrious, law-abiding citizens, and it is the school's function to develop them.

But the schools do not operate twenty-four hours a day; in some overcrowded areas, a pupil attends for five hours or even less. And the school year is not twelve months long. Obviously, a child is exposed to the influence of school for only a fraction of his time. Other institutions which have been discussed in detail earlier are designed to contribute their share to the proper upbringing of the rising generation of Americans.

There exists a great deal of confusion in the mind of the public as to exactly what is the function of the school and what is not. The late Charles Beard, a distinguished social historian, brings ripe scholarship and a keen analytical mind to the examination of this problem.

All about us are signs of stresses and strains. Optimism can not overlook them. Nor can indifference deny their exigency. East and west, war looms on the horizon, while the President and Congress of the United States seek ways and means of keeping the nation out of impending conflicts. At home ten million men and women search hopelessly for a chance to make a decent livelihood, and millions of young people hunt vainly for opportunities in which to try their talents. With staggering burdens forced upon government and society by an economic crisis, there can be no doubt about the gravity of the issues before us.

In such a time it is above all things fitting for us, on this occasion, to inquire, with the powers of mind we can command, into the present duties and responsibilities of the teacher and the school in America. Taking account of these stresses and strains, and painfully aware of the perplexities involved, I venture to lay before you my opinions on the subject for your consideration, and at the conclusion to suggest a program of action appropriate to the challenge of the hour.

At the very outset we face this pertinent question: What is the primary function of the public school system in American democracy? It is, as I see things, the training of minds and the dissemination of knowledge—knowledge useful in the good life, in the conduct of the practical arts and in the maintenance and improvement of American society. The teacher is not a physician, a nurse, a soldier, a policeman, a politician, a businessman, a farmer or an industrial worker. These officers have their rights and duties, but

From School and Society, February 29, 1936, 43: 278-283.

the rights and duties of the teacher's office are marked by special features. To be sure, all citizens of the United States have many common responsibilities, but we are concerned here with the immediate interests of the profession. The teacher's principal business is the training of minds and the dissemination of knowledge.

For the training of minds, a trained mind is required. For the dissemination of knowledge, a mastery of knowledge is required. The union of the trained mind and knowledge makes scholarship. So the teacher is under obligation to be a scholar—not a pedant, but a scholar dedicated to the cultivation of the mind and the transmission of knowledge useful in the good life, the arts and the management of social affairs.

There are many, no doubt, who deny this conception of public education. They look to the schools to correct all the ills of humanity. Society creates conditions that foster crime; the schools must serve as crime prevention agencies. Society sends undernourished, ill-clad and sick children to school; teachers must feed and nurse the unfortunate. Parents quarrel and fight at home; teachers must make saints of children so trained at the fireside. Parents refuse to read good literature and insist on maintaining an intellectual and moral vacuum at home; teachers must turn the victims of the vacuum into wise and good men and women. Parents surround children with trashy newspapers, flashy movies and radio nonsense; teachers must overcome the distempers and follies of such a life. Special interests in society demand this or oppose that; teachers must bow to the winds of these passions and pressures. Self-constituted professors of all righteousness think they have the way of universal salvation; teachers must force the creed upon the rising generation. These views of education run counter to my notion of its duties in American society.

If the primary function of the public schools is the training of minds and the dissemination of knowledge that is useful to individuals and society, then the teacher can not be a fire warden, policeman, soldier and politician combined. On the contrary, the teacher is another kind of person, with other duties and responsibilities—the duties and responsibilities of the scholar. It is right and proper, of course, that any individual teacher may feel bound to assume the obligations of the soldier, propagandist or politician. In this case let the teacher take up the profession with which such obligations are properly associated.

Accepting this conception of the public schools, what then are the qualities of the scholar—of the trained and well-equipped mind? It would be absurd to assume that the question can be answered with a light heart and once for all. Of the qualities required in the field of the physical sciences, I certainly should not venture to speak. But out of some experience as a student and teacher in the sphere of the humanities, I hazard an opinion and submit it to your judgment.

The first quality of mind required of the scholar in the humanities may be described as judicial. Some prefer the term scientific. Over that I do not wish to quarrel, but it has always seemed to me that the materials with which the humanities deal are not identical with the materials that fall within the domain of natural science. There is a border line, to be sure, but the distinction should be maintained, for convenience, and with a strict regard for the nature of things. The scientist may be entirely neutral in respect of performances in the physical world. The student of the humanities can not be cold, detached and Olympian. His nearest approach to the scientific spirit is represented by the judicial temper.

The spirit of the judicial mind is the spirit of the quest for truth in cases particular and general. It is not given to mortals, apparently, to know the whole truth about anything; but humanity has found by long experience that it can not live well without truth, without the knowledge that can only be attained by patient inquiry in the equitable temper. If the mind is closed and made up at the outset, if blinders are deliberately put on, if there is a resolve to hear and see only one part of each case, particular and general, then accurate knowledge and the utmost truth can not be attained. Surely there can be a consensus of opinion on this proposition.

The judicial mind tries to look deeply into every subject in hand and all around it. It tries to grasp the uttermost ramifications. The good judge, as Justice Oliver Wendell Holmes once said, must listen to things that are shocking and hateful to him, as well as to the pleasing and gratifying. He must confess that he is not God, endowed from the beginning with omniscience. He gives all parties their day in court. He hears what they have to say for themselves. He knows the fragile character of direct and circumstantial evidence. He allows for extenuating circumstances. He seeks to enter into the minds of witnesses and counsel through the channel of sympathetic understanding.

Unless mankind is to surrender to utter irrationality and blind partisanship, unless the achievements of the scientific and judicial method are to be discarded as worthless, unless our very eyes deceive us, we must concede that the quest for truth in this spirit is indispensable to the conduct of private and public affairs, to the advancement of learning and to the improvement of life and society. Having taken this position, it is incumbent upon us to preserve and defend it as one of the obligations imposed upon the scholar as teacher. Others may enjoy the luxury of imagining themselves omniscient and omnipotent; others may claim by partisan revelation the one and only truth, and assert the right to impose their will upon their neighbors and countrymen by terror, fire and sword. To the scholar as teacher this luxury is denied. With the office of teacher go obligations not imposed on physicians, nurses, policemen, soldiers, propagandists and promoters of special interests.

The judicial mind is only attained by study and practise. Before it must be kept the examples of the world's thinkers who have represented it at the best, who have advanced knowledge and served mankind by the patient quest for truth. The galleries of history are crowded with such figures, and in its better hours mankind pays tribute to them. If in moments of rage and distemper, it defies and spurns them, in all hours of constructive effort it must seek wisdom in their achievements and resort to their methods in dealing with life's exigent problems. Otherwise it must surrender to passion and brute force.

The bitter fruits garnered by those who surrender to brute force, to unreason and to untruth are immortalized by Shelley in fourteen lines on the fate of Ozymandias, the supreme master of tyranny:

I met a traveler from an antique land
Who said: Two vast and trunkless legs of stone
Stand in the desert. Near them, on the sand,
Half sunk, a shattered visage lies, whose frown,
And wrinkled lip, and sneer of cold command,
Tell that its sculptor well those passions read
Which yet survive, stamped on these lifeless things,
The hand that mocked them and the heart that fed:
And on the pedestal these words appear:
"My name is Ozymandias, king of kings:
Look on my works, ye Mighty, and despair!"
Nothing beside remains. Round the decay
Of that colossal wreck, boundless and bare
The lone and level sands stretch far away.

If the public schools are to aid in preserving American society against the fruits of unreason and the sneer of cold command, then they are compelled by the very nature of their function to assert and defend the judicial spirit, the scientific temper, against passion and tyranny.

But the judicial mind, the mind of the scholar, does not operate in a vacuum. It functions in American society. The knowledge which it discovers, accumulates and disseminates is bound to have influence upon the prevailing conceptions of the good life, the conduct of the practical arts and the governance of society. Here the teacher of the humanities departs from the absolute neutrality of science. The chemist as chemist may be neutral; he may not care whether the chemical he compounds is used to heal the sick or poison a personal enemy. The teacher of finance and banking, doubtless, may say that he does not care whether the knowledge he disseminates is employed in useful banking practises or in wrecking banks and robbing the public; but he can not, in fact, in his selection and presentation of materials, give effect to any such sublime indifference.

So we seem driven to the conclusion that the knowledge disseminated in the schools should be knowledge useful in the good life, the conduct of the practical arts and the maintenance and improvement of American society. Then, what kind of knowledge can be deemed to possess such utilities?

Surely it must be accurate, realistic and relevant, not false and fantastic. It can only be gained by patient study and by the exercise of the judicial or scientific temper. It must be comprehensive knowledge—knowledge that takes into consideration the known facts and factors that are relevant to any subject, topic or theme in hand. At once elements condemned as "controversial" by the thoughtless are introduced into instruction. How could it be otherwise? Does any one really believe that there can be a true history of the United States, for example, that does not deal with the great issues of banking, tariff, taxes, budgets, agriculture, industry and labor that have formed, and still form, so much of the substance of American history and practise? Surely no intelligent American believes that European history should be deliberately falsified by omitting all references to communism, and by teaching, as one school persecutor has urged, "only the geographical facts of Russia."

Such perversion of instruction in the schools is more than a betrayal of knowledge and truth. It assumes that knowledge and truth are of no importance, that a nation can live by lies and deception. It is not an outgrowth of patriotism, as alleged. It represents an effort of partisan and narrow interest to intimidate and conquer the schools for their own purposes and ends. It is not only a false philosophy. It is an attempt to impose on the schools a species of tyranny foreign

542 Teaching As a Profession

to American traditions, to the principles of American constitutional law and to everything that scholarship must regard as its obligation. The judicial spirit and loyalty to realistic knowledge forbid scholars to surrender to this yoke of perversion and falsehood. If the schools must surrender to it, then let the schools renounce scholarship and accept the sneer of cold command.

Yet it would be idle to suppose that the path of scholarship is smooth and easy. Teachers are mortals and find the way hard. And all around them are individuals, societies, organizations and associations, well-financed, strong in lungs, powerful in publicity. All around them are violent conflicts of ideas and interests. A prominent business leader calls on businessmen to "gang up" against the New Deal. Labor leaders call strikes. Governors mobilize the militia and declare martial law. Everywhere, in the press and the forum, controversial issues of American life are discussed, sometimes reasonably, often bitterly. The tariff, foreign policy, war and armaments, agriculture, industry, labor, feminism, socialism, communism, civil liberties, are examined, debated and agitated. Propagandists of every variety, many well supplied with funds, direct their fire upon teachers and the schools. Individuals and cliques wrap the American flag around their shoulders; they vociferously proclaim themselves to be the only wise, true and honest patriots; and then they demand that the schools accept their versions and commands. Whole volumes have been written to describe the nature, methods and purposes of these pressures on the schools and scholarship.

So fierce is the fire that the timid are likely to seek escape in evasion, by surrendering the obligation and mission of the public schools, by bowing to the whim or pressure dominant for the moment. Sometimes even this evasion is called impartiality, but in truth it means capitulation to special interests. It means, in effect, if not purpose, a partisanship for worse, intellectually and morally, than open partisanship; for it lends the sanction of learning to the sneer of command. It is not by surrender that scholarship wins victories. Only by the vigorous and unremitting assertion of its values against sheer pressure and force can scholarship discharge an obligation to American society that transcends all partial and special interests—the obligation of training minds and disseminating knowledge—knowledge useful in the good life, the conduct of the practical arts and the maintenance and improvement of American society.

If the above conception of the schools and scholarship be accepted, if the doctrine of servile obedience to the sneer of cold command be rejected, then what is the next important step to be taken in the field of public education? It is, in my opinion, the clarification of the obligations of education, a definition of the relation of the schools to a society ever marked by conflicts of ideas and interests, a statement of the teachers' responsibilities and rights and the establishment of open procedures that will protect the schools against raids and enable them to fulfil honestly their transcendent duties.

It seems that we have reached a point in American life where the maintenance of educational liberty can no longer be taken for granted. All over the country, schools are attacked by highly organized and well-financed minorities that seek to browbeat legislatures, the Congress of the United States, school boards and teachers. The precious values of liberty and scientific inquiry are threatened with extinction and with them the principles upon which democratic government rests.

If we are to uphold and defend the liberties and responsibilities of education, we must take a leaf from the book of the patriots who founded the American Republic. They wrote the principles of liberty in fundamental laws and they provided agencies, tribunals and procedures for their enforcement. From the field of constitutional law, organized education in America must borrow its guiding rules. In the light of constitutional experience, its immediate obligations are clear. They are:

(1) To draft a national code of good practise for the teaching of subjects which in their nature involve or touch upon controversial questions —a code incorporating the fundamental liberties of press, speech and religious worship guaranteed by our constitutions.

(2) To define the rights and duties of teachers and pupils in conducting classroom exercises.

(3) To secure the cooperation of parents and school boards.

(4) To provide rules of procedure for the examination and adjudication of specific cases of controversy.

(5) To publish a constitution for the teaching profession, setting forth the principles, rules and procedure of good practise.

(6) To educate teachers and the public in the liberties, responsibilities and duties of inquiry, research and scholarship in American society.

(7) To establish a national body, perhaps connected with the National Education Association, provided with funds and competent legal talent and charged with the duty of promoting and defending the rights of free scientific inquiry be-

fore the public in general and in particular communities beset by witchburners and fanatics.

With Europe turning to a tyranny more frightful than that against which the founders of the American Republic waged war in the eighteenth century, with voices crying that liberty is a delusion and that brute force is a virtue, a crisis is upon us. Recognition of this fact lies in suggestions already at hand, actions already taken and projects for the future. The Commission on the Social Studies, sponsored by the American Historical Association, saw the challenge and made proposals for coping with it. Other materials, supplementing the commission's findings, have been published in separate volumes, thus adding concrete illustrations to general principles. In July, 1935, there was held at the summer school of Harvard University a conference on "Academic Freedom in the Public Schools," at which the subject was thoughtfully explored by some of the most competent minds in America. The discussion was summarized in the *Harvard Teachers Record* for October, 1935—a prime document in the development of knowledge respecting the issue. The theme is also treated in the current Yearbook published by the Department of Superintendence, especially in the chapter by Dr. Leslie Butler. There the question is examined from various angles, and positive procedures respecting academic freedom are presented for consideration. The many-sided nature of the problem is recognized by Dr. Butler. Reciprocal rights and duties are accepted as fundamental, and parents, school boards, administrators, teachers and

pupils are called upon to explore and assume their appropriate responsibilities.

The task before us is to carry forward the work thus far competently advanced. Drifting is perilous. Already in large sections of Europe teachers belie known truths, and prostrate themselves before the possessors of sheer power won by assassination and intimidation. Already the drill sergeant, aided by the yellow press, is abroad in many parts of our own country, seeking to terrify, malign and dominate school boards, superintendents and teachers.

Divided and trusting to luck, we may be overcome by belligerent minorities; united we can defy powers that seem omnipotent. Let us study the problem. Let us clarify our minds. Let us set up a constitution of safeguards for scholarship, and devise processes for enforcing it. Let us rededicate ourselves to the American tradition of liberty and to the faith that error need not be feared where reason is free to combat it. Let us assert anew against brute force the values of independent scientific inquiry, of the unhampered search for truth, of the fair hearing and the fair play, and uphold them by fearless and united effort. Not for the gratification of pride, nor with any gesture of false superiority. Not out of any academic pique. But because in this spirit and by this procedure alone can American democracy cope with its gravest problems under the forms of law, thus maintaining amid the wreck and ruin of parliamentary institutions, East and West, the example of a nation that has not lost its head or its heart.

156

I. L. Kandel

THE ACADEMIC CIVIL WAR

Just about every college or university in the United States that undertakes the training of teachers for the public schools has felt some of the effects of the dispute between the professors of education and those of the liberal arts. On some campuses this has become almost an open war. Numerous apostles of peace, brotherhood, and cooperation have suggested means of rapprochement, but despite their efforts the war goes on. Though some have professed to see signs of its abatement they are indulging, for the most part, in wishful thinking. The conflict is still with us and its resolution will not be accomplished by mere discourses on the virtues of togetherness or by similar homilies.

This conflict touches some of the fundamentals of the educative process. To understand it one must know something of the real nature of education and what educators are trying to accomplish. One must also be well acquainted with the various subject-matter fields, particularly the liberal arts. The author of the following article has had long experience in the training of teachers. His knowledge and appreciation of the liberal arts are both broad and profound. Consequently he is in a position to discuss the "academic civil war" with complete understanding of all the issues involved.

Considerable progress has obviously been made in the past thirty years since normal schools became teachers colleges. The development has not, however, escaped the traditional criticism that they lack the standards of a liberal education and devote too much time to professional studies. Undoubtedly, the expansion in number and scope of these studies as a major activity in the advanced study of education and the wave of experimentation both in research and in practice have had a strong influence on teachers colleges intended for the preservice training of teachers. Another cause for this emphasis is a certain desire to professionalize teaching by basing it on a foundation of somewhat esoteric subjects, a cause which may also explain the cult of a special jargon which has been termed "pedagese." This raised the old question, already propounded by Josiah Royce more than half a century earlier, whether teaching is an art or a science. There is no doubt that what has been contributed to a better knowledge of the psychological and physiological growth and development of the child and the adolescent, of individual differences of ability, of interests, and of the learning process has been of pre-eminent value for the improvement of the art of education. Equally important has been the inclusion in a philosophical consideration of the interrelation of education with society and the culture patterns of the environment. But how much of such material the cadet-teacher should study and how much a clear interpretation would contribute more effectively to better teaching has not been considered. This question does not exclude the desirability of expanding the bounds of our knowledge of education in its many facets. But to attempt to impart such knowledge to those about to enter the teaching career would be like including the latest and still unverified contributions of an advanced medical research institute in a medical school course.

Nevertheless, much of the criticism of teacher education from the outside is due to ignorance of the actual distribution of time between general and professional studies as well as of the inherent problems of teaching. Those who claim that he who knows his subject can teach are apt to forget that even in such a case the master of

a subject acquires his skill as a teacher through experience with pupils or students and often at their expense. On the other hand, those who emphasize professional preparation forget that those are three data in the educative process. Sir John Adams, a professor of education with experience in teaching Scottish, English, and American students, once summarized that process in the simple statement that it was directed "to teaching John X," that is, that it involves a knowledge of subject matter (X), of the pupil (John), and of the art of instruction. The critics of systems of teacher education stress the subject matter; those who emphasize professional studies today stress the child on the principle, to use a phrase which first appeared in English educational literature, that there has been a shift of emphasis from the subject to the child. At the same time, in America there has been a shift in the emphasis of the art of teaching from imparting knowledge and information to pupils to putting them in "a learning situation" where they learn by their own "experiencing."

Another broadside attack on educators is to the effect that their theories have produced the anti-intellectualism that now prevails. The emphasis on learning by experience, on doing rather than on thinking, on the "how" rather than the "what," on emotional rather than intellectual development, and on life-adjustment education—the slogans of the period since World War I—have produced a great deal of busy-ness in education but in the long run few results intellectually. The stress on the contemporaneous, current social problems has failed to develop an understanding of the past that has produced them and have not succeeded in developing any better understanding or appreciation of the meaning of democracy, which their proponents profess to be their goal.

Whether the charge that anti-intellectualism is a product of the schools or whether the practical

From *American Education in the Twentieth Century* by Isaac Leon Kandel (Cambridge, Mass.: Harvard University Press), pp. 208-213. Copyright 1957 by The President and Fellows of Harvard College. Reprinted by permission of the publishers.

has not always been more appreciated than the intellectual in American culture need not be discussed here. The scholars who are the chief among the critics have themselves been the products of American educational institutions. There is a tendency to forget, in the flush of pride over the nation's achievement in providing equality of educational opportunities, that schools previously attended by a select minority have been thrown open to pupils whose I.Q. ranges from that of a moron to the highest possible figure. The academically able students are less numerous than the less able who lack the intellectual ability needed to pursue a traditional academic course and who come from a less favorable background, social and cultural. It is in the interests of the average and particularly of those who are not likely to proceed to college that many of the changes went on in the curriculum reconstruction of the past generation. It is only since the end of World War II that serious attention has been devoted to the education of the able and gifted student. In the current situation the major attention is being devoted to the search for promising students in the sciences; the need of gifted students in the humanities and social sciences is equally urgent in the interests of the nation. Given a choice between Jeffersonian and Jacksonian principles, educators in the main have chosen the latter. The unfortunate part of the proceeding is that they have sought to rationalize on the value of the latest as the best not only for the majority but also for the minority. And to that end they have tended to adjust their definition of democracy.

The objecting scholars cannot be blamed for criticism of the exaggerated claims put forward on "scientific" and "social" grounds for the unacademic and anti-intellectualistic trend. On the other hand, these scholars have not made any effort to recognize the problem or to suggest methods of putting the Jeffersonian principle into operation. They have on the whole remained aloof without even coming to the protection and preservation, until very recently, of the subjects that they themselves profess.

Referring to this "academic civil war" between scholars and educators, President James Bryant Conant in a lecture delivered at Teachers College, Columbia University, in 1944 suggested a truce between the combatants on the two sides of the academic fence. While he deplored the lack of knowledge, understanding and sympathy on the part of scholars, he might also have viewed with regret a certain prejudice among educators against scholars not unlike that which Emerson discussed more than a century ago. . . . Scholars are be-

ginning to see the need of showing an interest in public education . . . . Any understanding or *rapprochement* that may result from the report, prepared by Professors Howard Mumford Jones, Francis Keppel, and Robert Ulich for the Committee on the Teaching Profession of the American Academy of Arts and Sciences and submitted to the Committee on the Relation of Learned Societies to American Education, will redound to the advantage of teacher education practices and the public schools of the nation. The promotion of a better understanding between the academic and pedagogical or professional faculties was recommended by the President's Committee on Higher Education in vol. III, p. 61, of its report published in 1947.

The "academic civil war" also arises out of the shift of the educational pendulum to an extreme that is not realized by the scholars, nor endorsed by all educators. The public and the scholars tend to be misled by the vociferous claims made for the latest innovation. Nevertheless, if changes in the work of the classroom teacher are limited to the contributions that have come from educational psychologists and a realistic study of the movements in American culture, it is clear that the responsibilities of the teacher have changed considerably. He is no longer responsible for imparting lessons with the aid of a textbook to pupils regarded as an undifferentiated mass. To teach successfully he must be familiar with each pupil as an individual and with a cultural background which has to be supplemented or enriched. He must find out what a pupil can do and help him do it in accordance with his ability. He is expected to put his pupils in the way of learning by their own efforts rather than memorizing what they are told in class or learn from a textbook. He must be able to relate what the pupils learn to their environment and to the society in which they live in order to ascertain whether they are able to understand the meanings of what they learn. Whether the teacher shall also be a social engineer to help the pupils to reform society, or a mental and physical hygienist, counselor and adviser, functions which are sometimes suggested as the teacher's responsibilities, is a question open to debate. If the major aim of helping pupils to understand the world in which they live and which is constantly expanding in range and scope of meaning as they grow and develop—intellectually, emotionally, morally and aesthetically—is accepted, common ground can be discovered to restore the unity of the teaching profession at all levels.

157

Edgar W. Knight

INCREASE IN DIGNITY OF TEACHING

The author of the following passage, reflecting on a lifetime devoted to the education of teachers, comes to the conclusion that the status and intellectual accomplishments of the American teacher have grown steadily since this nation was established. There is, of course, room for more growth, as has been pointed out in preceding readings, but there is no real cause for discouragement or despair.

Whatever added status teachers gain in the years ahead will be the result of their own efforts toward self-improvement. Not much will be gained by bitter lamentations about neglect or lack of public recognition. Nor will agitation, political or otherwise, bring much reward if teachers do not first make the effort to deserve what they seek.

Teaching calls for people of the best type—people with a degree of dedication to their work. Its monetary rewards may never be comparable to those of some other occupations (although gratifying increases have recently been noted) but the richest rewards of anyone really devoted to his work are in the feeling of accomplishment that comes to any artist-performer. Teaching draws much upon scientific investigation for techniques and skills but, at its best, it is more an art than a science. Like any other art it calls for the complete devotion of those who would practice it successfully.

Although teaching has probably not yet reached the professional level that is demanded in medicine or perhaps even in law in most American states, the tendency is ever toward a higher and more dignified professional status. Teaching now ranks favorably in professional requirements with the ministry, and it does not always suffer by comparison with engineering and other specialized professions. The increased and increasing public confidence in the power of the school and other means of instruction, and the recognized dependence of civilization upon education, give to the teacher a more important position than he has ever known in this country. His social position is higher today than it has ever been, and in general he is better trained, is more nearly adequately rewarded, and occupies a larger place in public confidence. "Let the soldier be abroad if he will, he can do nothing in this age. There is another personage,—a personage less imposing in the eyes of some, perhaps insignificant. The

schoolmaster is abroad, and I trust him, armed with his primer, against the soldier in full military array." For many years before it was expressed by Lord Brougham more than a century ago, few leaders even shared this view of the teacher. Too long had he been an object of contempt and often even reproach, but he is now increasing in dignity and enlarging his sphere of influence. More adequately equipped than ever before, he is now trusted more confidently as a light to guide, although not every American community has gained Brougham's perspective.

But the people are slowly getting this view and demand better teachers than formerly. The public is coming to ask that those to whom children are intrusted for instruction shall be men and women of stalwart moral constitution, that they shall possess the thing called character. It is coming to know that teachers are not teachers merely of subject matter, but of youth and of men and women, and that personal and business integrity should be to them matters of inner principles rather than of legalistic requirements externally imposed—that they should be men and women of conscience as well as of science. The

From *Education in the United States* by Edgar W. Knight (New York: Ginn and Company, 1951), pp. 365-367.

public knows that no teacher can climb beyond the limitations of his own character. It asks that the teacher possess not only good educational and professional training, but also those qualities which make him a person and not a thing; that he be human, with initiative and resourcefulness, industry, tact, intellectual and moral honesty, and perhaps some sense of humor—a great help to the teacher in time of trouble. But although the public applauds a sane sense of humor, history is full of warning to the teacher who becomes a buffoon through the indulgence of levity. The history of American education reveals that few humorists have been elevated to superintendencies, college presidencies, deanships, headships of departments, or similar posts of educational responsibility. These places are usually filled by solemn men, some of whom, however, have been known to become comical afterwards.

158

Melvin W. Barnes

MORE TIME TO TEACH

Tasks other than teaching have been taking up more and more of the teacher's time. Schools are becoming progressively larger. More and more subjects are being taught. The range of activities is being widened enormously. More and more elaborate and detailed records have to be kept. For these and other reasons, the teacher's available time for teaching subject matter to boys and girls becomes less and less.

Teachers have complained bitterly about this state of affairs—usually among themselves, although now and again one has broken into print on the theme. The well-trained chemistry teacher, devoted to his subject and anxious to pass his knowledge on to someone else, does not enjoy filling out forms or policing playgrounds. Nor does the teacher of any other subject.

In recent years, school boards and superintendents have begun to consider this situation with a view to protecting the teacher's actual teaching time. Many schemes have been advanced; some are obviously impossible but several contain much promise. These are being tried out and studied, and it now appears likely that some of the "busy work" of the schools will in time be taken out of the hands of teachers and given to someone else.

Many of these tasks will also be "streamlined" and unnecessary duplication will be avoided. Instead of being performed in bits by a number of teachers, the tasks will be consolidated and put into the hands of capable persons whose sole responsibility they are. This article summarizes some of the more promising and recent developments in this area.

No school can be better than its teachers. In the last analysis, the quality of instruction a student gets depends on how he is taught. If teaching is the primary concern of our school systems, efforts toward improvement call for several courses of action: helping teachers to improve themselves, reorganizing subject matter, and experimenting with new methods that may produce better results.

A teacher cannot live long on hoarded intellectual capital. He must have the incentive to keep mentally in tune with what is new and changing. As long as he teaches, he needs the stimulation of other scholars in his subject field. Every school system should provide for the constant cultivation of intellect on the staff, and one means of doing so is the use of consultants.

From *Atlantic Monthly,* November 1960, pp. 128-131.

During the last three years, the board of education in Oklahoma City has brought to its teachers some one hundred outstanding specialists from universities and public school systems throughout the country. This has been made possible through increasingly large appropriations for the program. Last June when school closed, more than five hundred teachers, counselors, and principals assembled for a two-week workshop under the leadership of twenty-five consultants. This hand-picked faculty worked with our staff on fifteen sets of problems that are faced in schools.

One consultant, for example, discussed with principals ways to change a high school's teaching program. The study considered means of faculty self-training, the role of the principal in producing effective guidance, and the evaluation of teaching results. The problem of a group across the hall was the teaching of written expression.

Such work has to be done in the summer. The school year is too busy for this kind of planning and curriculum building. The number attending these summer workshops is remarkable, inasmuch as enrollment is voluntary and no credit is given. The main inducements are the prestige of the faculty and the desire for self-improvement.

No teacher, however competent, can be effective unless he has time to teach. Teaching requires time for preparation, time for classes, time for evaluation and for consultation. When asked, our staff said one of the major hindrances to better instruction was the load of clerical work. They saw fund drives, unnecessary bookkeeping, ticket sales, and minor interferences in classroom activity as hostile to significant learning. In attempting to protect time for classwork, we are trying assistant teachers to do noninstructional tasks, teachers' secretaries to keep records, post test scores, and mimeograph materials, and extensive use of IBM equipment to handle student enrollments, class rosters, attendance records, and certain kinds of report cards. Through a recent appropriation, the board of education considerably increased the capacity of our data-processing equipment in order to relieve teachers of non-teaching duties.

One way to save the time of teachers and students is to furnish the instructional supplies and equipment that lend efficiency to teaching. Anyone can see that a school building needs repairs. But the need for teaching materials, books, films, and instructional aids is less easily detected. Some people think that all a classroom should have is one book for each child. But we know, for example, that a science teacher who wants to teach a lesson on seed dispersal can do more in ten minutes with a good film than he could in an hour by lecturing on the subject.

We have been making large increases in the budget for textbooks, library books, magazines, projectors, television receivers, films, and recordings. Such aids are the teacher's best friends. In television (we have two educational channels) we use a video tape recorder and a Kinescope. Both these instruments record television broadcasts electronically, the former on magnetic tape, the latter on movie film. Thus, good teaching can be saved for re-use. Our teachers are beginning to use many film clips.

In 1955, the board of education bought a Spitz planetarium as a teaching aid in astronomy. The astronomy teacher tailors his lecture to the needs of each individual class. More than five thousand students last semester went to the planetarium for lessons on subjects under study in their science courses.

Laymen can help with teaching. A group of our students strongly devoted to science hold a weekly evening seminar with research scientists as their guests. These students have come to have access to most of the laboratories, research instruments, and other resources in the community.

The improvement of teachers also depends on the principal's leadership. His personal value system is perhaps the most potent influence on the character of the instructional program. A good principal can work wonders with a mediocre staff, while laissez-faire leadership will soon spoil the best. In the selection and preparation of principals, we use a program of tests, observation, and experience. We give promising young people the experience to prepare them for leadership roles. For example, a young man who has recently come to us from a university staff is taking a year to prepare for a principalship. He was first assigned as assistant to the superintendent, and in this position he has had an opportunity to see the school system as a whole. Later he will transfer to the instructional department to assist in planning the program of the school, now under construction. When he joins the ranks of the principals, he will be expected to have an understanding of system-wide philosophy and organization.

The Oklahoma City schools are engaged in several research ventures concerned with the principalship. In one study, directed by Columbia University, twenty of our principals spent a week taking tests, solving on-the-job problems, and meeting the varied requirements of their jobs. The principals, while performing leadership tasks under the eye of a research team, were being evaluated. In a second investigation we are co-operating with Harvard University in a study of the role of the principal.

Next in importance to teachers is subject matter. What we teach is always becoming outmoded. Thus, we must be continually rearranging subject matter and supplanting worn topics with fresh content. In mathematics, science, and English we are writing our own texts, student study guides, and teachers' manuals, giving us a reconstructed program in each subject from the seventh to the twelfth grade. By developing our own basic materials, we are able to adapt forward-looking ideas to the varying levels of difficulty, interest, and ability of particular groups of students. The preparation of instructional books and guides is in the hands of selected teachers who, with consultant leadership, are employed during the summer months.

Perhaps the teaching of mathematics best illustrates the current reorientation in subject matter and its presentation. The chief aim of this reform is a concern for unifying the concepts of the discipline. The beginning algebra student typically learned many techniques, often on the level of tricks. For this reason, geometry was strange, because he was suddenly asked to prove everything. Algebra is now playing a large part in the development of geometry. If geometry is associated in a definite way with the algebra the student already knows, his understanding of geometry should come more quickly and be more deeply rooted than if the geometry were presented as an isolated body of knowledge.

Three-dimensional, or solid, geometry is considered along with two-dimensional geometry. The Commission on Mathematics of the College Entrance Examination Board is interested in the integration of geometry, algebra, and trigonometry, and has even recommended that these terms be dropped and that our high school courses be known as Elementary Mathematics, Intermediate Mathematics, and Advanced Mathematics.

While this idea of unification is supported today by both mathematicians and mathematics educators, one still has the right to raise the question as to whether unification will improve learning. There is substantial reason for believing that it will. Those things are best remembered which are associated with other things. More importantly, unification and association also help in understanding.

In harmony with this philosophy, we have modified our mathematics program, offering new courses and providing for the acceleration of abler students. Our senior course, Mathematical Analysis, parallels a university course and thus permits a student to enter college with advanced standing.

To improve method, the rewritten courses have built-in techniques to promote discovery and inquiry in learners and to require self-dependent study. We agree with the committee reporting to President Eisenhower that one way to improve education is to provide "more student responsibility for self-education."

In science, as in mathematics, the revision of our program provides for new topics, new courses, and saves time for the student who can learn faster. We are completing a two-year tryout of a junior high school course called Scientific Geography which integrates world geography and earth science and which builds on the elementary school background. This course is taught by a daily thirty-minute lesson on television, followed by supplementary teaching. Especially for this course, two school auditoriums have been equipped with theater-type projecting devices that amplify a television picture on an eight by twelve foot screen. One advantage is that this teaching guarantees a systematic coverage of subject matter. Our evaluative studies show good results.

For several years we have used in experimental classes chemistry and physics courses recorded on film. Each course contains 160 thirty-minute lessons produced by university professors. Classroom follow-up and laboratory work are added to extend and reinforce teaching. Not only are the filmed courses used by students in Oklahoma City high schools, but they are also broadcast over the state to several hundred rural high school students. Since most of these students are in small schools lacking qualified science teachers, they mail their lessons and tests to the studio staff. We are not ready to say that these films are the best courses or the best way to teach, but we find that able students learn successfully from them and that the films also aid inexperienced teachers.

No account of curriculum revision in high schools these days can ignore foreign language. Because of the importance of beginning early, our teaching of French and Spanish starts in the third grade. For elementary schools we use television because of the shortage of qualified teachers. Having the use of two television channels, we are able to repeat the morning lessons in the afternoon, so that a class has a choice of listening time. Various aids, including tapes, drill exercises, and helps from the studio, are supplied to the teacher.

In high schools, foreign language enrollments are steadily increasing. And students are taking language for a longer period of years. Much of their motivation comes from five language laboratories and the appeal of the conversational method now used in the introductory courses.

In teaching mathematics, science, and foreign language, we are aware that English plays an important part. We are seeking more effective written expression and a deeper understanding of literature. In the summer of 1958, three consultants assisted our English teachers with such teaching tasks as spelling, reading, and mechanics for all students. One of the consultants, a university professor of English, discussed the teaching of language skills recommended by the National Council of Teachers of English. For the next two weeks, a leader in the field of linguistics presented English from his point of view. These experiences and considerable additional study are resulting in a new, tentative teaching program for all high school grades.

Since it proves wise to encourage teachers to explore various techniques, we foster thoughtful suggestions for innovation. As teachers showed interest, we established several courses in Great Books. The use of the Socratic method, which limits leader participation to a certain mode of questioning, is an excellent hedge against the tendency of teachers to overtalk in class.

These varied efforts are working no miracles, but they are unquestionably strengthening the teaching in our schools.

Participation in research almost automatically enlivens instruction and leads to more effective techniques. We noticed that a high school staff, when it became engaged in a regional study of guidance for specially talented students, showed an increased awareness of individual variation in learners. In another high school, a team teaching project has aroused general interest.

This team technique combines an experienced teacher, a new teacher, a student teacher, and a secretary in the instruction of a student group of approximately seventy. Team classes allow many techniques. For purposes of discussion, the group may be divided into small units. When a panel is reporting, all students may be together. For large group activities, a room with special equipment may be used. In their planning periods, the teachers consider their own skills and divide the classroom tasks accordingly.

Some purposes of the team idea are to find better ways to use the skills that teachers possess, to orient new teachers, and to spread good practices. No teacher is excellent in all phases of the teaching role. One may be good at presenting ideas, while another is best at reteaching the slower learners who missed some of the ideas in the first presentation. One is able to diagnose a learner's needs. Another does well in correcting written expression. Through observing one another and planning together, team teachers deepen their sensitivity to the complexities of teaching and learning.

When a school system engages in research, teaching comes out of its rut. Heightened morale and better instruction result.

Several of our fairly ambitious experiments, supported by grants from the Fund for the Advancement of Education, have used television. These have yielded an unexpected bonus in staff growth. Good teaching in a classroom is known to only a few, but good teaching on television is visible to everybody. Teachers who observe skillful performance learn from it.

In the summer of 1957, the Oklahoma City board of education sent a teacher to work with a University of Illinois group on curriculum revision in mathematics. Upon his return he taught a new course on television for a few restricted classes. Fellow teachers, recognizing his superior competence, wrote a memo to the superintendent asking for an opportunity to work with the staff at the University of Illinois. The arrangements were made, and it was announced that the staff would be in town one Saturday a month to work with interested teachers. Without any effort to recruit for the program, on the first Saturday morning eighty-four teachers appeared. All followed the year's work through to completion. This gained them no college credit and no reward except the satisfaction of becoming better teachers.

We believe that television may be the best means of quickly showing a whole staff new ways to teach. While the nature of the medium imposes certain limitations, it is possible for an imaginative instructor to teach inductively by using illustrations, problems, and case studies.

Somebody may ask, "How do you reconcile the use of television with your concern for teaching each student as an individual?" If we use television where it is appropriate, in large groups, for example, and in ways that provide a variety of experiences for those students who can learn from it, we can free a good many teachers to work with individuals. Of course, we must recognize also that some students learn better by television than others. If a student is not learning efficiently, he can be moved to classes where the usual classroom practices are employed. This is not difficult to do through the ordinary guidance procedures. Unless we differentiate teaching tasks and use wise guidance, television can result in mass depersonalized education. But any tool or technique used in teaching is subject to abuse unless the user is careful to keep in mind both his goals and the nature of the teaching-learning process.

Changing schools is slow, hard work, since changes that make a real difference must occur in people. To date no one has found any technique that produces very rapid results. However, in Oklahoma City, as in hundreds of cities and towns, efforts to reform the American high school are making progress. Daily reports that tell of increased student performance, more serious purpose in learning, and better high school preparation indicate that both students and teachers are responding to the demands of the times.

159

Carl Becker

IN SUPPORT OF THE CONSTITUTION

Interest in loyalty oaths seems to follow periods of national or international stress and conflict. After the Jacobite uprising in Britain in 1715, after the American Revolution, after World Wars I and II came loyalty oath laws and resulting objections from those who disapproved.

Particularly in the 1920's and the 1950's, some of these controversies aroused national interest, even indignation. Oaths as proposed or legislated in various states were discussed pro and con in the press and on public platforms, more often passionately than dispassionately. Loyalty oaths passed by the legislatures of their states were promptly vetoed by Governor Smith of New York in 1920 and by Governor Dixon of Montana in 1921.

The question as to whether formally taking an oath to support the state and federal constitutions and to perform faithfully one's prescribed task will or will not make one more loyal and efficient has been often debated. The eminent historian Professor Carl Becker of Cornell questioned the efficacy of loyalty oaths. Here he discusses the structure, the purpose, and the possible result of one law requiring such an oath—without rancor or excitement, but with keen insight and the wonderful subtle humor for which he was known to a whole generation of students at Cornell.

In compliance with the Ives law, an official of Cornell University recently requested me to sign the following statement: "I do solemnly swear (or affirm) that I will support the Constitution of the United States of America and the Constitution of the State of New York, and that I will faithfully discharge, according to the best of my ability, the duties of the position to which I am now assigned."

After reading this statement carefully, I signed it, willingly and without resentment. I always wish to conform to the laws, and in this instance there was no difficulty in doing so, since this law, so far as I could see, neither deprived me of any rights that I formerly had nor imposed upon me any duties not already imposed. There was even a certain advantage in having the statement presented for my signature: it made me think about the obligation of citizens to support the constitution and the laws. I asked this question: are citizens not obliged to support the Constitution and the laws unless they take an oath to do so? Applying a well-known rule for interpreting legal documents, one might infer that formerly no citizens of New York, except public officials taking such an oath, were so obliged, and that now no citizens except public officials and teachers are so obliged. That was a new and intriguing idea. I had taken it for granted that all citizens are obligated to support the laws; and with the best will in the world I still fail to see what meaning any law can have if it has not the one meaning

From *The Nation*, January 2, 1935, 140:13-14.

without which it would not be a law—namely, that all citizens are obligated to conform to its provisions. What, then, does the Ives law mean? So far as I can see, nothing except this: that teachers in New York State are obliged to acknowledge in writing that they are obligated by the obligations imposed upon them by the duties they have assumed, and by the obligations imposed upon all citizens by the Constitution of the United States and the Constitution of the State of New York.

Having reached this conclusion, I asked another question: Does the New York Legislature think that a subordinate authority can make an obligation imposed by a superior authority any more obligatory than it already is? The Constitution of the United States, so I have at least been told, is the supreme law of the land. The Constitution of the State of New York is, within limits defined by the Constitution of the United States, the supreme law of New York State. The New York Legislature is a subordinate authority, its jurisdiction being defined by provisions in both constitutions. It has no authority to modify either constitution, nor can it create any rights or duties not explicitly or implicitly authorized by one or the other of the two constitutions. I can make nothing of the Ives law as a legal document except that it is a redundancy, unless it be also an impertinence: by enacting it, the New York Legislature presumes to reimpose obligations already imposed by the supreme law of the land.

All this laborious thinking led me to ask a third question: Have I up to now "supported" the Constitution of the United States and the Constitution of the State of New York, and have I faithfully "discharged" the duties of "the position to which I am assigned"? Taking the first point first (in literary discourse it is well to be systematic), I feel sure that I have always supported the Constitution of the United States, and that I have supported the Constitution of the State of New York during the seventeen years that I have resided in that State. I intend to go on supporting both constitutions, and as a down payment on that promised intention I hereby declare that the Ives law, in my opinion, was unnecessary and unwise: unnecessary, because it imposes on teachers no obligations that did not already exist, except the formal one of signing the statement quoted above; unwise, because the obligation to sign the statement will irritate many teachers all of the time, without making any of them at any time support the constitution more loyally, or discharge their duties more faithfully, than they did before.

In making this explicit statement about the Ives law, I am clearly "discharging" the duties "of the position to which I am now assigned," and I am "supporting" both the Constitution of the United States and the Constitution of the State of New York. To take the second point first (in literary discourse one should aim at variety), both constitutions rest upon the principle that laws should be enacted by representatives freely chosen by the citizens, and that it is not only the right but the duty of citizens to express, either orally or in print, their approval or disapproval of the conduct of their representatives, and of the laws enacted by them. Both constitutions, unless I am mistaken, contain provisions which guarantee citizens against any infringement, by statute or otherwise, of that right. Happily (returning now to the first point), the "duties of the position to which I am now assigned" do not, so far as I can learn, conflict in any way with my obligation to support the Constitution of the United States and the Constitution of the State of New York. I am a teacher of history. The duty of a teacher of history, as I understand it, is to learn, and encourage his pupils to learn, what has actually happened in some period of human history, and to discuss with the utmost freedom before his pupils any opinion, judgment, or theory that may be formed about the cause or the effect or the importance of what has happened. The Ives law is something that has happened, and so far as that law is concerned I can "discharge the duties of the position to which I am assigned" only by declaring that it would have been better, in my opinion, if the Governor and Assembly of New York had prevented it from happening. I have now discharged that duty in writing, and I intend, whenever occasion seems fitting, to discharge it orally.

In closing I wish it clearly understood that this expression of an adverse opinion on the Ives law does not exhaust my capacity to support the Constitution of the United States and the Constitution of the State of New York. I reserve the right, for the future, to support these admirable high authorities by freely expressing my opinion about any social or political question that may arise. If at any time it should seem to me highly desirable to amend or to abolish the Constitution of the United States or the Constitution of New York State, I shall, availing myself of the principle that "all just governments rest upon the consent of the governed," support both constitutions, and at the same time "faithfully discharge the duties of the position to which I am now assigned," saying so. At present I am not in favor of abolishing either constitution, nor have

I any amendments to propose to either. In times past there have been people who believed that men could be made wise and good by proper laws and constitutions. I have never been convinced of this, but I am open to conviction. When anyone devises a constitution that will make legislators wise enough to know that people cannot be made loyal to the constitution, or faithful in the discharge of their duties, by passing laws requiring them to be so, I will support that constitution as faithfully and loyally as I am now supporting the Constitution of the United States and the Constitution of the State of New York.

160

Sterling M. McMurrin

THE PRESENT CONDITION OF AMERICAN EDUCATION

A number of men with differing degrees of ability have filled the office of United States Commissioner of Education since its establishment in 1867. Surely one of the most scholarly is Sterling McMurrin, who was appointed on January 1, 1961, and held office until July 1962.

Commissioner McMurrin's address before the Appropriations Subcommittee of the House of Representatives on May 8, 1961, is notable for throwing new light on a number of long-standing questions. It presents an overview of the duties and responsibilities of teaching, admirably reflecting the best educational thought of the times.

The speaker sees the teacher neither as simply a taskmaster, assigning and hearing lessons, nor as a mere custodian, mainly occupied with keeping children amused. He would put training and furnishing the mind of the pupil in first place. To this end he calls for teachers who know thoroughly the subjects they try to teach and are skilled in imparting knowledge. He is keenly alive to the excesses of the extreme wing of the Progressives of some years ago and he is also aware of the amount of wasted intellectual effort that characterized many schools in the pre-Progressive period. His address is thoughtful and timely, a valuable analysis for those who select and educate teachers. It is offered here as a temperate yet forward-looking estimate of teaching that is appropriate to the present time.

Mr. Chairman, I appreciate your gracious invitation to present for your committee's record a statement on the present condition and prospects of American education. This is a most appropriate time for such a statement, as there is now a growing recognition of the crucial importance of education to the Nation and a realization that the character and quality of our educational institutions are quite properly the urgent concern of the Congress.

Without question, one of our greatest assets in the effort to improve our educational establishment is the intense interest in education that presently pervades the Nation, an interest that is involving countless persons from every vocation and profession in a general discussion of the ends of education and the ways of achieving them. Fortunately there is developing among us that spirit of genuine criticism that is always an essential ingredient of institutional and civic improvement.

The character of this discussion and criticism indicates that in the matter of education we are now facing a crisis of conscience and that collectively we are experiencing a sense of national guilt. This consciousness of guilt grows out of the realization that in general we have failed to establish and maintain an educational program

From *Higher Education,* July 1961, 17:3-9.

of the quality of which we are capable and which is now essential to the well-being of all our people taken individually and to the achievement of the full enrichment of our culture and the strength of our Nation. There is an increasing concern for our failure to fully cultivate the talents and capacities of our people and a realization that we are not adequately satisfying the demands that our national life now properly and necessarily places upon the educational process. We cannot deny that today we would command far more knowledge and have far more creativity, civic character, and national strength if our schools generally had been more rigorous in their intellectual discipline and had been more adequately structured to the needs of our society. We have with lavish prodigality wasted the talent and energy of countless persons who should have been educated at higher levels of skills and knowledge, and whose education would have been a substantial asset to a nation that makes an ever-increasing demand for high competence in its people.

In referring to the demands placed upon education by our national life, I do not mean to recommend that we educate toward narrow nationalistic political ends or for the achievement of cultural parochialism and isolation. Far from it. One of our great needs as a nation is the cultivation of a genuine cosmopolitanism, a world-mindedness that will assure us not only an understanding and appreciation of other cultures, but even an actual participation in them. Without the perspective that such a sophistication would afford, we cannot hope to satisfy the obligation of world leadership that history has conferred upon us.

Nor is this a proposal that we emulate the totalitarian states in regimenting and manipulating the potential manpower of our Nation. Nothing could compensate for the loss of freedom that such a procedure would entail, and perhaps nothing could fill the breach that would thereby be made in the foundations of our democracy. The strength of a democratic society can be guaranteed only by a genuine individualism that encourages and protects independence in thought and action. Too often we have been so anxious to accommodate the individual painlessly to his social environment that we have seriously endangered this individualism. But if we are to build full strength into our Nation we must invest the individual with a sense of civic purpose and dedication and cultivate in him the internal intellectual and moral discipline requisite to the role of an intelligent citizen in a free society.

Certainly now in the presence of great peril, not only to our own Nation but to the entire free world, we must avoid confusion in our educational program as in the administration of public affairs generally. There must be in education as elsewhere a supreme effort through information, counsel, encouragement, thoughtful planning, and material assistance to direct the Nation's energies and abilities in the common interest.

Under the stress of adverse world conditions our people are seeking a clear definition of what we have come to call the national goals. For a society that has traditionally concerned itself primarily with the individual and his interests, this is not an easy task. But we can be very sure that unless our educational program at all levels takes careful cognizance of these goals they will not be realized. As our society becomes more complex, with increasing intercommunication, urbanization, and industrialization, and as the Nation assumes a larger role of leadership in the free world, and as the body of available knowledge in all fields continues to expand, the task of education will become immeasurably greater and our schools, colleges, and universities will assume a new importance in both domestic and international affairs.

It is clear that we must achieve broad national perspectives on educational purposes to insure that our educational program develops in a direction commensurate with this increased responsibility. It is here that the Federal Government must play an important role in providing sound leadership as well as material support. But this does not mean that we should in any way depart from the principle and practice of local and State determination and control of our educational institutions, for much of the strength of American education, and indeed of American society generally, is the product of that tradition.

In urging that our education more adequately satisfy our changing social needs, I do not mean to propose that every specific task in our complex social order be allowed to dictate the curriculum of our schools, whether public or private, academic or vocational, elementary or advanced. Already we are in some difficulty at every level, because in our effort to relate education effectively to the lives of the students we have too often divided and splintered until far too much of our energy is dissipated on unrewarding peripheral detail or trivial matters that deserve no place in the economy of a serious formal education. An intensive mastery of fundamental principles and techniques that will have general theoretical application or practical usefulness should replace the not infrequent expansiveness that has made the curriculum attractive and interesting, but sometimes somewhat superficial. It is education in the most basic sense, whether it be in the humanities, the social or natural sciences, in technology or the professions, that will be most rewarding to the individual and at the same time will best satisfy the needs of our society in providing adequate manpower for our trades and professions and in guaranteeing the expansion of knowledge and the disciplined habits of mind that are so crucial to the well-being of our people.

There is a sense in which American education seems destined to become a major testing ground for democracy, for it is a basic assumption of the democratic political ideal that there is a coincidence of what is good for the individual with what is good for society as a whole. It is the faith of a free democratic society that when the good of the individual is intelligently pursued, the well-being of the total social order is in some way enhanced. The task facing the leaders of American education is to so organize and administer our educational institutions that the best interest of every individual will be served and that this process will at the same time contribute to the fundamental quality of our culture and add genuine strength to our national character. We must make sure that the maximum cultivation of the individual's intellectual, moral, artistic, and spiritual capacities that makes of him a genuinely free person yields also the protection and perpetuation of those institutions that are essential to a free society.

Here two things should be kept foremost in our thinking. First, that the total education of an individual is a task in which all of our social institutions participate. The schools should not be expected to do everything. Their primary task is the achievement and dissemination of knowledge and the cultivation of the intellect. It is only when this task is firmly established as the central purpose of a school that it will produce effectively those results in personal and civic character that we rightly expect of it.

Secondly, we must guard against the tendency to suppose that our national well-being is served primarily by advances in technology, however important and timely these may be. Knowledge is of value for its own sake as well as for its uses, and unless the sciences are supported in their own right the capital of knowledge on which our technology is nourished will surely diminish. And the social sciences and the humanities and fine arts are as important to the quality of our culture and eventually to the strength of our Nation as are engineering and the physical sciences, upon which now so much obviously depends. The study of politics, history, and philosophy is fundamental to our cultural life, and no nation can achieve a lasting strength unless its character is expressed in great literature, art, and music.

We should not fear that a more effective accommodation of education to social needs and national goals must destroy the freedom and individual initiative and creativity of our people. On the contrary, countless persons would thereby find a new freedom, for they would be brought into the educational process on a higher level, and through institutions designed for their peculiar abilities on the one hand and the needs of our social and economic order on the other.

It is entirely obvious, of course, that we cannot now be satisfied with any educational endeavor that is not genuinely committed to the highest standards of which we are capable. Whatever may be the disposition of some individuals, the Nation cannot afford anything less than is now so commonly called the pursuit of excellence. At every step of the educational ladder we must make those demands for achievement that will call forth the full capabilities of every student.

I believe that we are guilty, and that we know that we are guilty, of often following a path of inordinate ease and comfort in our educational policy and practice. And we are suddenly aware that all too often we have sacrificed excellence to a large measure of mediocrity, because we have been unwilling to pay the price that excellence demands—rigor, discipline, and genuinely hard work.

Like so many other departments of our society and culture, our educational establishment at many points is comfortable and soft. At times we have been far too willing to entertain and to tolerate when we should have disciplined, directed and inspired—inspired by great teaching, of the type that moves the mind to a genuine love of knowledge and to an insatiable demand to possess and to create it; directed by wisdom that grasps the proper ends of learning, profound wisdom that is sensitive to whatever is most precious to the human soul, whatever is most worthy of human endeavor; and disciplined by that internal discipline whereby a genuinely moral person orders his life, determines the means appropriate to his ends, and achieves a proper integration of his intellect and affections.

To the extent that we have failed to challenge the full capabilities of our students, from kindergarten through graduate school, we have betrayed the democratic ideal that is so precious to us. The meaning of democracy in education is not found in a dead-leveling process that attempts to conform all men to a simple equality. We believe not that all men are of equal capacity but that all are entitled to the opportunity to develop fully such capacities as they have. We combine this with a belief in the inherent dignity of the individual person. These are powerful ideas with tremendous implications. They mean, certainly, that the creative artist, the professional person, and the artisan alike deserve the full esteem of their fellow men and that every man is entitled to his measure of self-respect who is doing his best in a vocation that contributes to the total life of our society.

When we demand in our schools and elsewhere something less than the individual is capable of doing, we rob him of his self-respect and we corrupt our most basic ideals. We have been too often guilty on this count, and our schools must bear a large measure of responsibility for that guilt.

It is not a proper reply to say that our children learn more now than they did 50 years ago. No doubt this is true, for more knowledge is now available. But measurable increases in the amount of knowledge gained in the course of a year, while important, are beside the point. Educational excellence, as a goal, is never realized. It is neither visible nor tangible. Perhaps it is not, strictly speaking, a goal at all, but an attitude that informs the total process of education. In any event, we can approach excellence in education only by demanding of all—administrators, teachers, students, and the general public—all that they are capable of achieving. If ever in the past there were reason for asking less, there is none now, for our times are perilous and will accept no less.

We have not lacked great teaching, and we may be grateful for the innumerable highly qualified and dedicated teachers who have provided it. Their contribution to our society is immeasurable. But the quality of teaching, generally, is lower by far than it should be, and lower, too, than it need be. It is here that we confront our greatest failure in matters pertaining to education. That failure consists of a stubborn refusal by our society to commit to the teaching profession a large enough measure of the best that we have in human resources. The quality of teaching is our basic educational problem. It will not be solved until all of our teachers have the competence that is now enjoyed by those whom we all recognize for their great and inspiring work in our classrooms, seminars, and laboratories.

The identification and education of teachers for our schools is now a matter of major concern for the Nation. It is a national tragedy that the generality of our teachers are not fully qualified to assume the burden of responsibility that we must place upon them in the future. Many are lacking the native talent demanded by the art of teaching. Others in large numbers are inadequately prepared by general education or education in their teaching specialties. The responsibility for this rests partially upon our society as a whole, for it has failed to raise the teaching profession to that level of stature and esteem that would make it attractive to highly talented people in numbers adequate to fully satisfy the demand for qualified teaching personnel, and our public leaders have not insisted that our colleges and universities devote their best efforts to the education of teachers.

It would be unwise to suppose that this predicament of the teaching profession is due simply to inadequate salaries for teachers, even though the problem will never be solved until the average salary level of the profession is made competitive with that of other employed professions. It is due in part at least to the fact that the education of prospective teachers in our society has quite commonly failed to fully challenge the intellectual abilities and creative talents of the more capable segment of our students. Persons of high ability look to a profession that demands rigorous preparation and high competence. The range of students entering our professional education schools is far too wide for the good of our Nation. It encompasses many who enjoy the highest capabilities, but also many who are near failures in any scholastic endeavor.

In the future every effort must be made to identify persons of high intellectual competence and talent in the art of teaching and to attract them to the teaching profession. And the standards of our colleges of education must be raised to exclude those who do not have real promise. The finest education must be made available to those who qualify: first, a genuine and rigorous liberal education in the full sense of that word, an education in the arts and the sciences of the kind that frees the mind, that acquaints it with at least the rudiments of the world's basic knowledge, and cultivates critical and creative intelligence. To insure this kind of education, the education school must become a part of the mainstream of the intellectual life of our universities. The education of teachers is properly the task of the entire faculty, not simply of those who specialize in the teaching art and its related sciences.

It is a national scandal that large numbers of our teachers are inadequately prepared in the subject matter that they teach. We should not be satisfied until this situation is entirely corrected, as its perpetuation is the surest guarantee of mediocrity in the classroom. There will never be a substitute for a teacher's full mastery of his subject.

Finally, education in the art of teaching has too commonly been narrowly conceived in terms of psychological studies descriptive of the learning process. Teaching is an art that must be rooted in the entire gamut of the behavioral sciences as well as in psychology, involving such disciplines as sociology, descriptive ethics, and cultural anthropology. But far more than this, even a simple comprehension of the proper aims of education involves necessarily an intimate knowledge of the value structure of the culture and entails some acquaintance with the essentials of its intellectual and moral tradition. For the meaning of education is found in part in the great task of understanding, appreciating, criticizing, and perpetuating the culture of which we are a part and in which are lodged our value traditions and commitments. To put it briefly, there is no easy road in the preparation of teachers of the kind that we must now guarantee our schools. Our society will make heavy demands upon them in the future.

Mr. Chairman, we may take much satisfaction in the fact that American education has firm foundations and has cultivated numerous precious virtues and has made solid and notable gains. That many of our schools at all levels are institutions of outstanding quality is entirely obvious. And there are instances among them of surpassing excellence. Our primary asset is the firm tradition of freedom that is the foundation of our intellectual life and that unfailingly supports the open and uninhibited quest for knowledge that generally characterizes our schools and colleges. And our most important advance, of course, has been the achievement and implementation of a democratic ideal in education. We have virtually affected a general literacy and have created abundant opportunities for advanced education on many levels and in a variety of directions. In the matter of quantity we have done well. And although our quality often leaves much to be desired, we must turn a deaf ear to those reactionaries among us who are forever insisting that we abandon our democratic ideal and model our education on the aristocratic patterns of some European nations. There can be no turning back from what has been a high and sacred purpose. We must dedicate ourselves to the improvement of our intellectual life within the context of an educational philosophy that is native to our culture and appropriate to the ends that have been defined by our democratic commitment.

The real values of the modern American curriculum are another notable instance of our educational achievement. But it is not necessary to devote precious time and energy to trivial studies and activities to demonstrate our concern for the student as well as for the subject or to prove our emancipation from the classical European education. It is not necessary to abandon genuine learning just because we have discovered that schools should be congenial to students as well as to books, information, and ideas. We have done well to encourage broad general education. But it is wise to remember that one cannot know anything in general without knowing something in particular. Nor, as I have already urged, is it a demand of our democratic ideal that we direct our educational effort so commonly toward average talent and intellectual capacity and thereby involve our Nation in mediocrity while betraying countless numbers of persons of high intelligence and creative ability.

We are progressing well on many fronts, in educational research and experimentation, for instance, where notable achievements are becoming common, and in the upgrading and updating of the basic courses of our secondary schools, where important work is being done in the sciences and must be done in the social and humanistic studies. And in our graduate work and research seminars and laboratories great advances are being made in the extension of knowledge on all fronts. Moreover, progress is being made in adult and vocational education, areas of immense importance to a democratic society. The increased involvement of the Federal Government in educational matters, as evidenced, for instance, by the National Defense Education Act of 1958, has given to American education a new strength and a new promise of future accomplishments. The President's legislative proposals now before the Congress would add immeasurably to that strength and promise.

We have made real gains—great gains, of which we can be justly proud. It is a pride in which all our people may share, just as they must all share the responsibilities for our educational failures. But now the hour is late and we must move ahead with an even more firm resolve and dedication.

There is a sense in which our crisis in education may be said to have a spiritual dimension in that it relates to the uncertainties and anxieties that now so frequently characterize our people in their quest for meaningful and purposeful endeavor. Education is an important bearer of the spiritual life as this is broadly conceived as a life of purpose and value. It is a creator, protector, critic, and continuator of those values that mark our culture in its higher reaches, that impart to it its distinguishing character and determine in large measure what will be precious to the individual and worth the price of his commitment and pursuit. It is inevitable, therefore, that any radical disturbance or confusion in our educational life reflects the condition of our society and culture at their very center and that the resolution of major educational difficulties will affect with utmost importance the spiritual foundations of our Nation.

There are perhaps two things more, Mr. Chairman, to which I would like to draw your attention. First is the genuineness of our commitment to education. It would seem initially that there is no justification for questioning that commitment. The achievement of a general literacy would alone testify to the seriousness of our educational enterprise, to say nothing of our obvious accomplishments in many directions and at every level of the educational process. Nevertheless it should be equally obvious that our commitment is not what we would like to believe it to be, that it has proved inadequate to guarantee our full success in the tasks that are upon us, and that we are not yet willing to invest in education that measure of our resources that will give us such a guarantee.

By resources, of course, I do not mean simply financial resources. It is too characteristic of us to assume that money will solve all of our problems—money for more buildings, more research equipment, more scholarships and fellowships, more teachers, and higher salaries. Money will solve no problems whatsoever without talent, energy, creative initiative, inspiration, and plain hard work. But our problems will not be solved without more money, and far more, than is now being invested in our educational establishment. They will not be solved without those student loans, fellowships, and higher salaries. If we continue to pay only the price of second- and third-class education we will deserve to suffer the comparative decline of our intellectual life that will inevitably be upon us. If we intend to remain in the first rank of intellectual achievement, of scholarly and scientific and technological advancement, we must accept the fact that a much larger share of our national income than the allowance now made must be invested in education.

But by resources I refer also and especially to those human resources already named, resources that are so commonly misdirected or left unidentified or uncultivated and therefore wasted

—wasted both for society and the individuals who possess them. What achievements would not be possible to us, and to what heights could we not aspire if we were to fit our educational patterns to the real abilities of our people, from the preschool age through secondary schools, vocational and technological institutes, colleges and universities, and graduate schools.

If our commitment to education were what we like to think it is, we would move rapidly and more directly toward the expenditure of our resources on it for the high rewards that this would bring. The Soviet Union has here set for us an important example, the example of a generous investment in education. I do not suppose for a moment that the generality of Russian people are more genuinely devoted to education than we are. But those few who determine Soviet public policy have invested a remarkably large proportion of their nation's resources in education and they are reaping a high return on their investment. Let us not make such decisions in terms of the affairs of other nations; but also let us not live indefinitely in ease and luxury while convincing ourselves that we cannot afford to pay the price in human energy and talent to achieve the best education of which we are intellectually and spiritually capable.

There is a second aspect of our educational predicament that deserves notice. I refer to our growing sense of failure, of having been wrong in something of utter importance where we should have been right. No doubt it is healthy to recognize and frankly admit our errors. But for a nation to accuse itself, as ours is now doing, of having erred fundamentally in a matter central not only to its well-being but to its very security, and erred where error was by no means inevitable and might well have been avoided—this is a matter of the greatest moment. We in America are accustomed to assume that whatever temporary ups and downs of our fortunes and whatever occasional criticisms from our conscience may be our lot, our collective fate is secure in the hands of a benevolent God or at least under the dominion of an encompassing providence, and that with us or without us our Nation and our culture will be preserved and will move forward inevitably. We are accustomed to the belief that we are on the side of righteousness and whatever our individual wisdom and effort, righteousness will prevail.

But it is evident to us now, and our national spirit is affected by this evidence, that if it is true that we are on the side of righteousness it is yet not inconceivable that we may fail and fail profoundly and that righteousness may fail with us.

A generation ago the eminent philosopher, Alfred North Whitehead, dramatically and with great prescience insisted on the profound danger of failure in education. His words have been quoted often in recent years, but they are no less important for that:

"When one considers in its length and in its breadth the importance of this question of the education of a nation's young, the broken lives, the defeated hopes, the national failures, which result from the frivolous inertia with which it is treated, it is difficult to restrain within oneself a savage rage. In the conditions of modern life the rule is absolute, the race which does not value trained intelligence is doomed. Not all your heroism, not all your social charm, not all your wit, not all your victories on land or at sea, can move back the finger of fate.

Today we maintain ourselves. Tomorrow science will have moved forward yet one more step, and there will be no appeal from the judgment which will then be pronounced on the uneducated."

The facts become increasingly plain. The handwriting on the wall is there for all to read. If the United States is to continue to move forward and to make its proper contribution to its children and to the world, its people must be willing to dedicate a much larger share than ever before of their human and material resources to the support of education. There is no point in searching for an alternative. There is none if we are serious in our determination to educate our people in such a way that through their collective assertion of the autonomy of human freedom over the otherwise meaningless drift of history they will secure the future life and enrichment of our culture.

161

William C. Rock

AUTOMATION CHALLENGES EDUCATION

Automation, which seems to be affecting most phases of life, is beginning to affect education. The much-discussed automated teaching devices of various types are but a promise of bigger and more startling things to come. Educators should realize that these devices are still in the experimental stage and should not allow themselves to be carried away by enthusiasm for a development which has still to prove itself. Any experiment which appears to promise well is worth consideration—as an *experiment*.

It is of interest that the various mechanical teaching devices already invented are designed to teach the basic subjects, such as the three R's, geography, history, science, etc. The machine to "teach children, not subjects" seems not yet to have been invented. This should be reassuring to the Essentialists and advocates of "basic education," provided the automated teaching devices prove effective after sufficient trial.

If teaching machines come into general use in the schools at some time in the near future, what will be the place and function of the teacher? This is a question that all educators must begin to ask themselves. Could machines perhaps relieve the teacher shortage by taking over many of the duties at present performed by teachers? Or will machines ultimately create a demand for more and better-trained teachers? Mr. Rock's article deals with fundamental matters underlying these and many similar questions—questions that call for thought and discussion, although definite answers can be provided only by much trial and experimentation.

If this were the year 1975, you might, after reading this article, call your home, give the machine answering the telephone a number indicating the menu you wish prepared for this evening's dinner, tell the machine what time dinner should be served, and find dinner on the table upon arriving home. Your call would have set machinery into operation which would have taken the needed materials out of the refrigerator, cooked them, and set the table for dinner.

On your way home from work you might stop at a supermarket to do your weekly shopping. Instead of pushing a cart, you would simply walk through the store marking the goods with a stamp you had picked up at the entrance. As you stamped the goods, you would deposit them in nearby receptacles. After completing your selections, you would find your goods neatly packed and waiting for you at a check-out counter. After you had paid for them, a machine would load them into your car. The entire process of sorting, packaging, and billing would have been done without the benefit of human energy.

Although the foregoing may seem like science fiction, they are examples of automaticity which are being used today and which should become common within a short span of years along with other improvements in our way of living. The world is now entering the age of automation.

Dr. L. T. Rader of General Electric has defined automation as follows: Automation is the progressive, step-by-step improvement of manufacturing operations until continuous automatic production results: this means that products would be made, inspected, assembled, tested, and packaged in one continuous flow.

Automatic machinery can learn from past experience, can make choices, can draw logical conclusions from data, and can duplicate the human senses. Automatic machinery can tend machines, can repair them, can order materials, and can keep records of production and distribution.

In many industries it is possible today to run entire plants with only a handful of production workers or none at all. For instance, many oil refineries are run without any production employees but only special duty employees who supervise the work of the oil refining machines.

In the business world the use of computers is becoming widespread. All have heard of the wonders of these machines in forecasting the weather and the results of elections. On a smaller scale, computers are being made today which will sell

for under a thousand dollars and which will be available to small as well as large businesses. These computers will be able to handle many of the mechanical chores now being performed by office workers.

The introduction of automatic machinery into all phases of man's life will have many important effects. It will particularly affect the rate of productivity, the vocational life of the individual, and the amount of leisure available to the worker.

The most encouraging effect of automation will be an increase in the number of goods produced with an accompanying rise in the standard of living. It is quite possible that in the future the average man will enjoy a standard of living comparable or superior to that of the wealthy today. Under a system of automation there is no practical ceiling on the amount of goods which can be produced. Part of the reason for this is the fuller utilization of plant which can be made with automatic machinery and the reduction of human error. More important is the increased speed with which automatic machinery can produce goods. The primary importance of automatic machinery is not that it can do jobs now done by man, but that it can accomplish tasks beyond the capabilities of man.

Another obvious result of automation will be the displacement of many workers. As automatic machinery takes over much of the drudgery that now characterizes man's work, man will be forced to upgrade his skills and to perform tasks that are more stimulating and interesting.

Many feel that automation will result in widespread unemployment, but in actuality automation may create more jobs than it destroys. This has been the case to date. This is explained by the increased productivity which results from automation and the need for more people in such areas as engineering and distribution.

Much of the harmful effect of displacement can be avoided by close co-operation between labor and management. However, the harmful effect of displacement cannot be avoided without a more adaptable worker, who will have not only the skills necessary to operate in the age of automation, but also the broad general understandings necessary for maintaining a positive attitude toward a constantly changing world.

Another way in which widespread unemployment will be avoided is through the shortening of the work week. This, in turn, will create more leisure time. The taking over of many tasks by automatic machinery will allow the work week to be cut drastically. Today many industries are moving toward the 35 hour week, and eventually

From *American School Board Journal*, April 1961, pp. 18-20.

workers may be on their jobs for three days a week or less. Obviously, much more provision must be made by society for leisure time, and adults will face the problem of learning how to make the best possible use of this leisure.

The effect of automation which overshadows all others is the creation of a constantly changing world. No matter how certain trends may appear at the moment, the rapid change that is taking place in technological development may alter the pattern. The present generation of adults is bewildered and confused by the many changes taking place. Many seem unable to cope with the changes that are affecting our basic institutions and values, and some try to resist these changes to no avail.

The primary educational task, then, is to prepare students for life in a changing world in which it is impossible to predict with any great degree of accuracy what the world will be like when they are adults. To do this requires that attention be given to the skills of problem-solving, research, leadership, self-discipline, self-direction, and decision-making. Modern society demands that students be encouraged to think creatively.

These skills cannot be taught in a situation where the teacher is always in front of the class filling the children with "pearls of wisdom." To gain these skills, children must have the opportunity to work in small groups, to plan some of their own activities, and to pursue topics in which they are interested. It is further essential that students have some opportunity to work in groups where there is an absence of teacher control at some point during their schooling.

In terms of general education, the curriculum should be based upon areas of living with an eye to the future rather than broken down into less comprehensive subjects. As long as these subjects exist as separate entities, students will continue to find it difficult to see society as a whole and to integrate their thoughts concerning it. For example, a course might be built around the problem of leisure. Science and mathematics would play an important part in the reasons why leisure time is increasing. The arts of government, music, painting, literature, and handicraft skills would portray important outlets for this leisure. History would provide the vehicle to show the increasing growth in leisure time. In other words the problem of leisure, when viewed historically and in the present and future, presents a problem of living on which all areas of the traditional curriculum come to bear.

This does not mean that there should be no technical courses. There is a stronger need than ever before for students to be aware of the technical processes of modern society. Throughout their schooling, students should be constantly made aware of the vast technological world through field trips, research, and films. As students begin to reach a point where vocational preparation is important, these students should be provided opportunities to actually work under supervision in factories and offices. To do this will require close co-operation with the business and industrial community. Moreover, it will become increasingly important to emphasize broad understandings in the vocational subjects rather than to drill students on practices that may well be outmoded by the time they are ready to enter the occupation. It will also be necessary to attract better students into the areas of business and industrial arts.

Since much of the curriculum will be devoted to the guidance of students in helping them to understand a changing society, the guidance specialist will have more time to act as a resource person in supplying teachers with needed information to carry out their task. The guidance office must pay more attention to follow-up work if it is to provide meaningful information.

It will be necessary for schools to expand their programs of adult education to help retrain displaced workers. It is essential that these programs be developed in close co-operation with industrial and business leaders. Another major part of the adult education program will need to be devoted to the improved use of leisure time. It is surprising to note that some educators today are criticizing existing programs of adult education for devoting too much attention to leisure time activities when leisure is in the process of replacing work as one of the main focuses of man's life.

The basic task of keeping abreast of new developments in society and of keeping the schools as far up-to-date as possible will be a major responsibility of the school administrator in the local situation. The process of rapid change will force the administrator to make wide use of lay and staff committees in formulating basic school policies, especially in the area of curriculum. The administrator who plans from the front office will not possibly be able to keep up with the rapid changes that society is undergoing, and his students will be the victims of his conceit or insecurity.

What administrator knows but a few of the developments in all of the broad areas of society? What science teacher knows more than several of the many discoveries made in science last year? What social studies teacher is aware of the many complex issues that are arising due to new inventions? To build the curriculum of the future, the talents and knowledge of the whole school and community will have to be utilized. The need for democracy in education has never been more clear than it is today.

It is also clear that local communities may not have all of the intellectual resources available which are necessary for planning. It is essential that school boards begin to give consideration to the possibility of calling in consultants more often to aid the local community in planning changes. It will also be necessary to give more consideration to changes taking place in the national community as well as to those changes taking place in the local situation.

Communities will also have to give much more attention to the possibilities of new types of automatic equipment that are becoming available to the schools. Too high a proportion of money is being spent at present on the building rather than the equipment. Schools of the future must become more efficient if students are to receive enough education to cope with society. This may require the spending of a proportion as high as 75 per cent on school equipment as against the cost of the entire building. Although this proportion might seem high to some educators, it would seem quite natural to industrial leaders who are already doing this to increase the efficiency of their plants.

Machines can and will be built that can take over many of the routine tasks performed by teachers, thereby permitting the teacher to spend more time on planning and working with individual students. Machines could keep attendance, drill students, grade papers, and supply routine information to the students. One need only consider the advantages of a machine which would supply the students with detailed information concerning an occupation at the flick of a switch. The material in the machine would be the result of the extensive research of many experts in the field of vocational information. It would obviously be impossible for a single guidance counselor to be aware of all the many occupations which exist whereas a machine can store this much information and supply it on demand. At the same time, the counselor would have more time to help the student understand himself since he would not also have to explain the merits and requirements of various occupations.

Automation is one of the most vital challenges that education has faced. It will take the combined efforts of all citizens to meet this challenge by providing adequate education to meet the needs of the coming age. Failure to accomplish this task will be costly to the total well-being of the nation.

bibliographical notes

Bibliographical references for the introductory headnotes are given below. These references are keyed to the numbers given in parentheses in the text.

PART I: THE PROCESS OF EDUCATION

1. Theodore Roosevelt, Foreword to *Democracy's High School* by William D. Lewis (Boston: Houghton Mifflin, 1914), p. vi.
2. *Independent*, December 17, 1903, 55:2959-2962.
3. *New Englander*, October 1887, 47:267.
4. *A Mencken Chrestomathy* (New York: Knopf, 1953), pp. 315-316.
5. "A Business Point of View on Education," *Education*, June 1942, 62:592-595.
6. *Self-Culture* (Boston: Houghton Mifflin, 1908), p. 36.
7. *Creed of a Schoolmaster* (Boston: Little, Brown, 1939).
8. *Prejudices, Third Series* (New York: Knopf, 1922), p. 260.
9. See, for example, Ernest R. Hilgard, *Theories of Learning*, Second Edition (New York: Appleton-Century-Crofts, 1956).
10. "A New Kind of School Examination," *Journal of Educational Research*, January 1920, 1:33-46.
11. Samuel Tenenbaum, "Project Method: A Criticism of Its Operation in the School System," *School and Society*, June 17, 1939, 49:770-772.
12. *Study of History*, Vol. 12 *Reconsiderations* (New York: Oxford University Press, 1961), pp. 103-104.

PART II: THE ROLE AND STATUS OF AMERICAN EDUCATION

1. Newton Edwards and Herman G. Richey, *The School in the American Social Order* (Boston: Houghton Mifflin, 1947), p. 3.
2. Sources of information on comparative education include:
   Comparative Education Review (3 issues a year), Comparative Education Society, Kent State University, Kent, Ohio.
   Encyclopedia of Educational Research, Third Edition, Chester W. Harris, Ed. (New York: Macmillan, 1960). See sections on elementary, secondary, and higher education and descriptions of education abroad.
   International Yearbook of Education, UNESCO (Paris: UNESCO, 1955-   ).

World Survey of Education, UNESCO (Geneva: International Bureau of Education).

3. A detailed examination of the factors influencing the development and present status of education in the United States is presented in *Social Forces Influencing American Education,* Part 2 of the 60th Yearbook of the National Society for the Study of Education, 1961.

4. William H. Lucio and John D. McNeil, *Supervision: A Synthesis of Thought and Action* (New York: McGraw-Hill, 1962), p. 249.

5. See, for example, *The Dynamics of Instructional Groups,* Part 2 of the 59th Yearbook of the National Society for the Study of Education, 1959, and James S. Coleman, *Social Climates in High Schools,* Cooperative Research Monograph No. 4, U.S. Department of Health, Education, and Welfare, Office of Education OE-33016, 1961.

6. The findings of the Project are published in two volumes—*Delinquent Behavior: Culture and the Individual,* William C. Kvaraceus and Walter B. Miller (from which Reading 80 was taken) and *Delinquent Behavior: Principles and Practices,* William C. Kvaraceus and William E. Ulrich (Washington, D.C., National Education Association, 1959).

7. For further information on the vocation of educational administration see:
   Roald F. Campbell, John E. Corbally, Jr., and John A. Ramseyer, *Introduction to Educational Administration* (Boston: Allyn and Bacon, 1962).
   Laurence D. Haskew, *This Is Teaching,* pp. 456-492 (Chicago: Scott, Foresman, 1962).
   Stephen J. Knezevich, *Administration of Public Education* (New York: Harper & Row, 1962).

8. *Cooper et al., Members of the Board of Directors of the Little Rock, Arkansas Independent School District, et al.,* v. *Aaron et al.*

PART III: THE STRUCTURE OF THE AMERICAN SCHOOL SYSTEM

1. References helpful in studying current views of school organization and curriculum include:
   American Educational Research Association, "Curriculum Planning and Development," *Review of Educational Research,* Vol. XXX, No. 3, June 1960.
   Association for Supervision and Curriculum Development, *New Insights and the Curriculum,* 1963 Yearbook, Alexander Frazier, Ed. (Washington, D.C.: N.E.A., 1963).
   John I. Goodlad and Robert H. Anderson, *The Nongraded Elementary School* (New York: Harcourt, Brace, 1959).

2. In *Frontiers of Secondary Education V* (Syracuse, N.Y.: Syracuse University Press, 1961), pp. 1-15.

3. James B. Conant, *The American High School Today: A First Report to Interested Citizens* (New York: McGraw-Hill, 1959); Committee for the White House Conference on Education, *A Report to the President:* Full Report (Washington, D.C.: U.S. Government Printing Office, 1956).

4. Ralph R. Fields, "Community Colleges in the U.S.A.—A Link Between School and University," *Higher Education*, The Yearbook of Education, 1959, George Z. F. Bereday and Joseph A. Lauwerys, Eds. (Yonkers-on-Hudson, N.Y.: World Book, 1959), pp. 507-513.
5. Harold Benjamin, *The Saber-Tooth Curriculum* (New York: McGraw-Hill, 1939).
6. O. I. Frederick and Lucile J. Farquear, "Problems of Life," *School Review*, May and June 1938 (46:337-345, 415-422).

PART IV: TEACHERS AND TEACHING

1. Bertrand Russell, *History of Western Philosophy* (New York: Simon and Schuster, 1945).
2. William Ernest Hocking, *Human Nature and Its Remaking*, New Edition (New Haven: Yale University Press, 1929).

2 3 4 5 6 7 8 9 10 11 12 13 14 15 16 17 18 19 20 21 22 23 24 25   B   75 74 73 72 71 70 69 68 67 66 65 64